Best Wishes

# LUTON TOWN

## THE MODERN ERA

### – *A Complete Record* –

(Second edition)

## DESERT ISLAND FOOTBALL HISTORIES

| CLUB HISTORIES | ISBN |
|---|---|
| Aberdeen: A Centenary History 1903-2003 | 1-874287-57-0 |
| Aberdeen: Champions of Scotland 1954-55 | 1-874287-65-1 |
| Aberdeen: The European Era – A Complete Record | 1-874287-11-2 |
| Bristol City: The Modern Era – A Complete Record | 1-874287-28-7 |
| Bristol City: The Early Years 1894-1915 | 1-874287-74-0 |
| Cambridge United: The League Era – A Complete Record | 1-874287-32-5 |
| Cambridge United: 101 Golden Greats | 1-874287-58-9 |
| The Story of the Celtic 1888-1938 | 1-874287-15-5 |
| Chelsea: Champions of England 1954-55 | 1-874287-77-5 |
| Colchester United: Graham to Whitton – A Complete Record | 1-874287-27-9 |
| Coventry City: The Elite Era – A Complete Record | 1-874287-83-X |
| Coventry City: An Illustrated History | 1-874287-59-7 |
| Dundee: Champions of Scotland 1961-62 | 1-874287-86-4 |
| Dundee United: Champions of Scotland 1982-83 | 1-874287-71-6 |
| History of the Everton Football Club 1878-1928 | 1-874287-14-7 |
| Halifax Town: From Ball to Lillis – A Complete Record | 1-874287-26-0 |
| Hereford United: The League Era – A Complete Record | 1-874287-18-X |
| Huddersfield Town: Champions of England 1923-1926 | 1-874287-88-0 |
| Ipswich Town: The Modern Era – A Complete Record | 1-874287-43-0 |
| Ipswich Town: Champions of England 1961-62 | 1-874287-63-5 |
| Kilmarnock: Champions of Scotland 1964-65 | 1-874287-87-2 |
| Luton Town: The Modern Era – A Complete Record | 1-874287-90-2 |
| Luton Town: An Illustrated History | 1-874287-79-1 |
| Manchester United's Golden Age 1903-1914: Dick Duckworth | 1-874287-80-5 |
| The Matt Busby Chronicles: Manchester United 1946-69 | 1-874287-53-8 |
| Motherwell: Champions of Scotland 1931-32 | 1-874287-73-2 |
| Norwich City: The Modern Era – A Complete Record | 1-874287-67-8 |
| Peterborough United: The Modern Era – A Complete Record | 1-874287-33-3 |
| Peterborough United: Who's Who? | 1-874287-48-1 |
| Plymouth Argyle: The Modern Era – A Complete Record | 1-874287-54-6 |
| Plymouth Argyle: 101 Golden Greats | 1-874287-64-3 |
| Plymouth Argyle: Snakes & Ladders – Promotions and Relegations | 1-874287-82-1 |
| Portsmouth: From Tindall to Ball – A Complete Record | 1-874287-25-2 |
| Portsmouth: Champions of England – 1948-49 & 1949-50 | 1-874287-50-3 |
| The Story of the Rangers 1873-1923 | 1-874287-16-3 |
| The Romance of the Wednesday 1867-1926 | 1-874287-17-1 |
| Seventeen Miles from Paradise – Saints v Pompey | 1-874287-89-9 |
| Stoke City: The Modern Era – A Complete Record | 1-874287-76-7 |
| Stoke City: 101 Golden Greats | 1-874287-55-4 |
| Potters at War: Stoke City 1939-47 | 1-874287-78-3 |
| Tottenham Hotspur: Champions of England 1950-51, 1960-61 | 1-874287-84-8 |
| West Ham: From Greenwood to Redknapp | 1-874287-19-8 |
| West Ham: The Elite Era – A Complete Record | 1-874287-31-7 |
| Wimbledon: From Southern League to Premiership | 1-874287-09-0 |
| Wimbledon: From Wembley to Selhurst | 1-874287-20-1 |
| Wimbledon: The Premiership Years | 1-874287-40-6 |
| Wrexham: The European Era – A Complete Record | 1-874287-52-X |
| WORLD CUP HISTORIES | |
| England's Quest for the World Cup – A Complete Record | 1-874287-61-9 |
| Scotland: The Quest for the World Cup – A Complete Record | 1-897850-50-6 |
| Ireland: The Quest for the World Cup – A Complete Record | 1-897850-80-8 |
| MISCELLANEOUS | |
| Red Dragons in Europe – A Complete Record | 1-874287-01-5 |
| The Book of Football: A History to 1905-06 | 1-874287-13-9 |
| Football's War & Peace: The Tumultuous Season of 1946-47 | 1-874287-70-8 |

# LUTON TOWN

## THE MODERN ERA

## – A Complete Record –

(Second Edition)

Series Editor: Clive Leatherdale
Series Consultant: Leigh Edwards

ROGER WASH

with

MICHAEL GROOM

DESERT ISLAND BOOKS

Second Edition published 2004
First Edition published 1998

DESERT ISLAND BOOKS
89 Park Street, Westcliff-on-Sea, Essex SS0 7PD
United Kingdom
www.desertislandbooks.com



British Library Cataloguing-in-Publication Data
A catalogue record for this book is available from the British Library

ISBN 1-874287-90-2



Printed in Great Britain
by
Biddles Ltd, King's Lynn

The publishers acknowledge with thanks Gareth Owen, Bedfordshire Newspapers, and *Herald & Post* for the provision of photographs for this book.

# CONTENTS

# Preface

This book is about the events and the people who make up the recent history of Luton Town Football Club. The players, supporters, managers, directors and staff, who have shared our dreams, hopes, desires, ambitions, triumphs, successes and disappointments.

I class myself as a supporter and we all agree that the club is all about players, with three immediately springing to mind – Terry Branston, Brian Horton and Steve Foster, captains supreme, leaders of men in our three major trophy winning years.

The teams that achieved those goals deserve special mention, and I was proud to be part of one of them, as do the managers who guided them – Allan Brown who started us back up the ladder from the depths of the Fourth Division, and David Pleat, who built a Second Division championship team and recruited the majority of the players whom Ray Harford led to our Littlewoods Cup win.

There is no doubt in my mind that the players we were privileged to watch during the ten years 1982-1992 – performing in the highest level of English football – were a delight to the supporters and a credit to Luton Town Football Club.

Other highlights in our roller coaster ride up and down the leagues include promotion in the 1970 and 1974 seasons under the guidance of Alec Stock and Harry Haslam – and not forgetting Jim Ryan for his endeavours and service to the club.

There are far too many people to mention individually on this page. It is my pleasure to be able to pay tribute to each and every one of you, whom I have known and worked with. Your contribution has been immense and I hope some of the people who follow can match up to the standards you have set.

Our hope for the future is in being able to still provide and produce our own young players.

JOHN MOORE

# Author's Note

When I was originally commissioned by Clive Leatherdale to write the first edition of this book (1998), I firstly needed to decide when 'The Modern Era' started. I plumped for 1967, the start of the Division Four championship season, thinking that, during the 31 seasons covered, around 80 per cent of Luton Town supporters would have watched the team in action for the first time. That figure is now, no doubt, much higher.

Since that first edition, only six years ago, much has happened on and off the pitch at Kenilworth Road. The club has suffered the turmoil of administration not once but twice, endured a relegation, won promotion and undergone the farce of the summer of 2003. As such, this new updated edition should make interesting reading.

This book would not have been possible without the invaluable help of Michael Groom, who completed the statistical grids from my dictation, Michael's then partner, now his wife, Iris for teaching him the rudiments of computer programmes, and my own long-suffering wife Mary, who verbally checked the statistical section. Her original problems with pronouncing the name 'Peschisolido' have now been replaced by 'Jaszczun'!

I am indebted to Brian Swain, the ex-Sports Editor of the *Luton News*, now retired to Falmouth, who unknowingly provided most of the excellent raw material for the match summaries. Also, grateful thanks are due to long-standing supporters Les Miller and Mick McConkey, for digging out additional information, John Oliver, Dave Flett and Andy McKenzie, Sports Editor and reporters past and present on the *Luton News* for their assistance, and all at Luton Town Football Club for their encouragement.

Gareth Owen and Bedfordshire Newspapers kindly provided, or gave permission for the use of most of the photographs in the book.

ROGER WASH

# Introduction

It is generally regarded and accepted that Luton Town Football Club was formed from the merger of two teams, Luton Wanderers and Luton Excelsior, in April 1885. To confuse matters, however, Wanderers had in January of that year already assumed the name 'Luton Town' and went on to compete in the FA Cup in 1885-86 with the remnants of their old side, but this time under the name of 'Luton Wanderers'. This little cameo illustrates that, even from the club's earliest days, there has never been a dull moment. Apart from becoming the first club in southern England, as we shall see, to pay their players, they also fought first to join, and then to leave, the Football League. Through their subsequent promotions and relegations, triumphs and tragedies, the history of the club has it all.

Following their formation, the club embarked on a string of friendly matches and interspersed these with the annual foray into the FA Cup. As the sport grew in popularity, the Town decided to follow the practice of their northern counterparts and pay their players. In December 1890, an initial three players were paid five shillings (25p) per match but, by the following summer, everyone was on the payroll.

Needing more than friendly matches to keep them going, the Town were happy to be asked in 1894 to become founder members of the Southern League and, in the first two years of the competition they finished as runners-up to Millwall. Perhaps harbouring ideas above their station, they decided in 1896 to apply for membership of the Football League but the votes went against them. Having burnt their boats, they had to make do with a season in the newly formed United League, where they were again runners-up to Millwall, before successfully applying to join the big boys.

Luton Town's entry to the Football League in 1897 coincided with a move from Dallow Lane to Dunstable Road, but the crowds did not appreciably increase and, with the majority of league opponents being northern based, travelling costs became a considerable burden.

A bold decision was eventually taken three years later to resign from the Football League and apply to re-join a now much stronger Southern League. The application was successful and the Town were back amongst their old friends but were no longer a big fish in a small pond. They were unable to revisit their glory days of ten years previously, nor make a challenge for the title. In fact, they suffered relegation to Division 2, where for two seasons they had to ply their trade against a string of Welsh sides before fighting their way back just before World War I.

After hostilities ceased, the Southern League, en bloc, was asked to constitute a new Division 3 of the Football League, at which level Luton then enjoyed seventeen seasons, mostly as a 'middle of the road' side. In the mid-1930's, with the growth in the population of the town and surrounding area, the board decided to make a concerted bid to achieve a higher status.

Players were bought in to help them achieve this objective and their highest ever position was achieved in 1936 when they finished runners-up to Coventry. Those were the days when only one club was promoted. During that campaign, wing-half Joe Payne was given his debut at centre-forward and he rewrote the record books at a stroke when scoring ten goals in a 12-0 victory over Bristol Rovers.

Payne continued into the next season as he left off, and his remarkable feat of scoring 55 goals – more than half the team's total of 103 – helped secure promotion to Division 2 on the back of a tremendous home record.

It was decided at once to extend the Kenilworth Road ground, where the Town had moved in 1905, increasing the capacity to a theoretical 34,000. Even though the Town held their own in the higher sphere, that capacity was never seriously tested. In their second season in Division 2, however, a strong and settled squad, ably led from the front by local boy Hugh Billington, came close to achieving promotion to the top flight.

Over Easter 1939 a sequence of good results had forced the team into contention for promotion, but a draw and two defeats from the final three games meant that they missed out. Unfortunately, no one will ever know how far this squad could have progressed as, in September 1939, and with the Town sitting proudly at the top of the table, war broke out.

Upon the resumption seven years later, Luton registered a few seasons of mid-table mediocrity until, in 1950-51, they came perilously close to relegation back to Division 3. They only survived through a three-game winning run as the season drew to a close.

Luckily this scare was not repeated as the Town's youth policy, nurtured by manager Dally Duncan, began to bear fruit. Future all-time Hatters' leading scorer, Gordon Turner, learnt the ropes under the expert guidance of ex-England international Jesse Pye and, with a settled side, the Town just missed out on promotion in both 1953 and 1954.

The final, decisive push for a place in Division 1 came in 1954-55, when the Town eventually succeeded, following a titanic struggle

**DID YOU KNOW?**

**In view of the local hat-trade, Luton Town's first nickname was 'the Straw Plaiters'. By the 1930's they had become popularly known as 'the Hatters'.**

with Birmingham and Rotherham. The Hatters finally clinched the runners-up spot on goal-average, with the Millers the unlucky side to lose out.

Sweeping all before them, early the following season, the Town were the talk of the football world, handsomely beating Newcastle, Blackpool, Wolves and league leaders Sunderland in quick succession. The winning ways did not last, though a final mid-table position was probably better more than most supporters had bargained for the previous August.

In 1957-58 the Town finished in eighth position, their highest ever, and early in the following campaign actually hit top spot before dropping back to mid-table. If Luton's failure to sustain their league challenge was a disappointment, then the supporters were in for a treat in another way.

The Hatters had never previously progressed beyond the quarter-finals in the FA Cup but in 1958-59 their Wembley journey slowly gathered momentum as they disposed of Leeds, Leicester, Ipswich and Blackpool, before seeing off Norwich in the semi-final. The whole of Luton was in the grip of Cup euphoria, with a record Kenilworth Road crowd of 30,069 turning out for the quarter-final replay against Blackpool, and seemingly just as many travelling to White Hart Lane for the first semi-final, which was drawn, with the Town winning through in the replay.

The final itself was a huge disappointment. The Hatters failed to perform on the day, leaving Nottingham Forest to win comfortably, 2-1. The defeat was worse than it sounds, for Forest had to play most of the match a man short after Roy Dwight broke his leg. No substitutes were permitted in those days.

From that moment the Hatters' fortunes went into terminal decline. Manager Dally Duncan had left the previous October, and it was not until after the final that recently retired captain and centre-half Syd Owen was appointed into the hot seat. Owen took charge of an ageing side. Nor did he find it easy to overcome the difficulties encountered in moving from the changing room to the manager's chair. The upshot was that in 1959-60 the Town finished bottom of Division 1 and were relegated after five years at the top.

Although Syd Owen was replaced by ex-Charlton goalkeeper Sam Bartram, the rot had set in. A total of 33 players were used in the 1960-61 season, but they could not keep the Town in the top half of the table. Supporters blamed the board for allowing the money earned from the 1959 Cup run to be handed over to the tax-man, rather than invested on players, but it was now academic.

Having finished the 1961-62 campaign in mid-table in Division 2, there was a general consensus that Bartram was slowly turning the ship around, but he was given no chance to regain past glories, being relieved of his duties 'by mutual consent'. His replacement was to have been the ex-Town coach, Jack Crompton, but after a week in the job Crompton left the club on medical grounds.

Bristol City coach Bill Harvey then took over, presiding over another relegation campaign when, in 1962-63, the Town sunk dismally into Division 3. Once there, instead of being allowed to consolidate, the team plunged headlong towards Division 4, saving themselves only by virtue of a nine-game unbeaten run as the season reached its climax. The stay of execution proved to be short-lived, as the Town, just six years after participating in an FA Cup final, slumped to the football basement amidst apathetic crowds of less than 3,000. Harvey had resigned mid-season, to be replaced by ex-Town player and manager George Martin. Although Martin brought an iron fist to bear, he was, frankly, too old for the job.

Having said that, the Hatters tried hard to climb out of Division 4 at the first attempt, and were frustrated chiefly by rows over player bonuses as the season entered its climax. Lack of money, crowds at an all-time low, and all the club's experienced players released as a legacy of the row over bonuses, combined to force George Martin to resign. He was replaced in November 1966 by Allan Brown, one of the Town's stars in the 1959 Cup run.

Brown had much work to do, with the team one off the bottom in the league. Soon after he rejoined the club, they crashed 1-8 to bottom-placed Lincoln, arguably the Hatters' lowest spot in their history.

Gradually things improved with Brown's enthusiasm and astute sorties in the transfer market ensuring a final position of seventeenth. Twelve months later all would be rosy in the Luton garden.

1

# BROWN & STOCK 1967-1972

## LEAGUE DIVISION 4 1967-68

| | |
|---|---|
| Division 4 | 1st (Champions) |
| League Cup | 2nd Round |
| FA Cup | 2nd Round |

After the disaster of the 1966-67 season, when the Town finished only four points off the re-election places, supporters were obviously hoping for happier times and a wave of optimism surged through the club as a result of several new signings. Former inside-forward at Kenilworth Road, Allan Brown, had taken over the manager's position the previous November when the situation was at its blackest, and had gradually pulled the club up by its bootstraps. He had made valuable signings in Max Dougan from Leicester and Keith Allen from Stockport.

These two were joined at Kenilworth Road in the close season by the veteran of several promotions at Northampton, Terry Branston, as well as Billy McDerment, a £12,000 buy from Leicester and lofty centre-forward Rodney Green from Charlton. Much was also expected of local youngsters Bruce Rioch and Alan Slough, who both now had a couple of seasons of Fourth Division football under their belts, not to mention the 'poor man's George Best', mercurial winger Graham French.

Each of these new signings lined up on the opening day at Wrexham, where in a nasty game with two players sent off, the Town equalised in the final minute. Nothing special in this, one might say but, as the team had only gathered six points on its travels the previous campaign, and had rolled over and died more often than not, this result was looked upon to signal a change for the better.

**DID YOU KNOW?**

**At Doncaster in October 1967, the Town had to borrow Watford's yellow strip, as their first strip of white and second strip of red clashed with Rovers'.**

Despite all this, early results were nothing to shout about. Unspectacular home wins were interspersed with away draws, apart from a 0-3 thumping at Southend, albeit with an injury-hit Luton side. When Rodney Green tore a cartilage, manager Brown stepped straight into the transfer market and paid £11,000 to Derby for Ian Buxton, an all-round sportsman who combined clever inside-forward play on the football pitch with county cricket for Derbyshire.

Buxton made his debut in late September in a 3-1 revenge win over Southend, and from that point the season took off. The first away victory soon followed, at Chester, and was then topped by a remarkable 5-0 victory at Exeter, the Town's biggest win on their travels for twelve years. That game was a personal triumph for John Ryan, making his debut following a move from Brown's old club, Wigan Athletic, as he inflicted mayhem on the right wing. Unfortunately, Ryan's good days were not as frequent as his bad.

By now the team had settled into place, with centre-half Terry Branston, installed as skipper, leading by example, shouting at and cajoling his fellow defenders. These included Dougan and Slough, as well as long-serving Fred Jardine, ex-Motherwell left-half John Moore, and popular goalkeeper Tony Read who, when signed from Peterborough two years previously, was found to have a broken foot. Mercifully the break mended completely but his misfortune was a further example of the depths plumbed by the club in the mid-1960's.

A phenomenal run of eight straight victories was halted at Bradford City in early December and the Hatters then entered an uncertain spell which endured to February. Luton's nadir during this grey period was probably the defeat at bottom-placed Bradford Park Avenue, but Allan Brown stuck to his guns and refused to tinker with the side, holding to the belief that a good team does not become a bad one overnight.

After a dismal display at York the forwards clicked once again the following week, with poor Rochdale on the receiving end of a four-goal first-half salvo. By close of play on 17 February, a 2-0 victory at Brentford saw the Hatters sitting proudly on top of Division 4 for the first time.

The next two games were also won, consolidating the position at the top, whereupon Brown whipped the players away to Blackpool for a mid-season break. This was intended to prepare for the away fixture at Chesterfield, which was looked upon as the toughest test of the season so far. As it turned out, the suitably refreshed Hatters were rarely extended and returned with a point from a 0-0 draw.

Since the beginning of the season, Bruce Rioch had been attracting scouts from near and far, who were enticed by his explosive pace and searing shot. Typical of these qualities was his goal against Port Vale on the Saturday following the Chesterfield stalemate, when he turned on a sixpence outside the area and volleyed into the top corner of the net. 'Rioch for England', chanted the crowd, little realising that he would in time turn out for Scotland, his father's birthplace.

Three straight away wins arrived in the weeks prior to Easter, including a valuable victory at Aldershot, who were coming up on the rails. This victory was particularly sweet as twice previously the fixture had been postponed, on both occasions the news being broken too late to prevent Luton supporters travelling.

A stutter over Easter, with points dropped at home to Chester and away at Notts County, was followed by a solitary Bruce Rioch strike at Halifax, which was enough to win the points. That goal confirmed the inevitable; promotion to Division 3. The Hatters were on their way back! A huge crowd – by contemporary Division 4 standards – of 18,904 turned out the following Wednesday evening to greet the team and see if the championship could be confirmed. Few sides would have lived with the Hatters that night as they steamed into promotion-chasing Crewe and were 4-0 up at the interval. At the final whistle skipper Branston was carried around the pitch by the rest of the players to ecstatic applause.

The Town could perhaps be forgiven for losing their next two games to teams which needed the points more than they, but on the closing day a 2-1 home win over Brentford, in a match which graced the nation's TV screens, sealed a remarkable season which equalled Peterborough's record points-haul of 66 for Division 4.

The cups both terminated in glorious early failure. In the League Cup the Town saw off Second Division Charlton in a replay, after extra-time, only to fall at the next stage to all-conquering Leeds, or more particularly Peter Lorimer, who bagged a hat-trick at Elland Road. In the FA Cup, the Town were drawn away to Isthmian League side Oxford City but the game was postponed due to snow. The Town protested about playing a midweek evening tie under the Oxford's floodlights, which meant a switch to Kenilworth Road on the following Thursday. A less than easy 2-1 win ensued, but a famous exit in the next round to powerful Swindon at least meant that minds could be focused on the pressing business of promotion.

**DID YOU KNOW?**

**Luton's 27 league wins in their Division 4 championship season 1967-68 equalled the club record set in 1936-37.**

## Match of the Season 1967-68

### Luton Town 4 Crewe Alexandra 0

Division 4, 24 April 1968

The jubilant roar from the Luton faithful that greeted the final whistle at Halifax the previous Saturday signalled the end of the slide that had seen the Town plummet from Division 1 in 1960 to Division 4 in the space of five short years. Only one point was now needed to secure the championship, and it fell upon Ernie Tagg's Crewe to attempt to deny the Hatters that point.

A crowd of 18,904, the best at Kenilworth Road for four years, turned out on a warm evening to greet the would-be champions, who took to the field in a carnival atmosphere. A Luton win appeared to be a foregone conclusion, but Crewe, who started the game in second place, albeit an uncatchable seven points behind the Hatters, had not yet secured their own promotion. The previous season they had finished fifth, missing promotion by one place, and their players and supporters were as tense as could be imagined. Crewe caused an early scare when Gordon Wallace netted, but the effort was disallowed for offside.

Stung by this let-off, the Town embarked on an all-out assault, and Crewe keeper Willie Mailey trudged off at the interval shell-shocked, having picked the ball out of the net four times. John Moore, with a rare effort, opened the scoring, with 'golden boy' Bruce Rioch, with two, and Alan Slough completing the rout. The second half compensated in sheer endeavour for what it lacked in goals. In fact, all the forwards went close to scoring, with Rioch particularly unlucky not to secure his hat-trick. The players undertook a lap of honour at the end but it took several minutes for the fans to coax manager Allan Brown onto the pitch. His eventual appearance was greeted by the biggest cheer of the evening.

It was not all doom and gloom for Crewe. They sealed their promotion in their final game – by beating Luton at Gresty Road.

# LEAGUE DIVISION 3 1968-69

| | |
|---|---|
| Division 3 | 3rd (only two clubs promoted) |
| League Cup | 3rd Round |
| FA Cup | 3rd Round |

The summer of 1968 was a good time to be a Luton supporter. Buoyed by the success of the previous campaign and backed by the wealth of club directors Tony Hunt and Reggie Burr, the club was in no mood to stagnate and considerable amounts of money were spent improving the facilities at Kenilworth Road.

Manager Allan Brown was instructed to scour the country for new recruits, with money no object to strengthen the side to push for further promotion. In Luton Town terms, the £7,000 paid to Blackburn for former England Under-23 international winger Mike Harrison, and £18,000 to Coventry for inside-forward Brian Lewis was 'big money'. When Rodney Green expressed a desire to go part-time he was shown the door and a further £10,000 was found to prise centre-forward Laurie Sheffield from Oldham.

The local press speculated that the club had spent £90,000 that summer. The fans responded to this positive approach by snapping up season tickets in unprecedented numbers.

The summer of 1968 was also a good time on the football field, with the Town reacting to the starting gun by thrashing Oldham 4-0 in the Kenilworth Road sunshine and then embarking on an eight-game unbeaten run which brought top spot in the division. The run peaked with a 4-2 home win over Mansfield in a match talked about to this day due to controversial dismissals and a wonder goal from winger Graham French.

As summer turned to autumn, the wheels gradually started to drop off the promotion train. The team was still invincible at home but a string of away defeats looked ominous and Brown started to play about with his starting line-up in an attempt to arrest the slide. Even the supporters accepted that to play with six men in attack was wonderful at home but not so clever away, where sides of a higher quality than found in Division 4 packed their midfield.

Full-back Jack Bannister, from Crystal Palace, and goalkeeper Sandy Davie, from Dundee United, were signed to bolster the defence and both made their debuts in the 2-1 home win against Northampton, the seventh straight victory at Kenilworth Road, but the following week it was back to the now-customary away defeat.

But before the two new boys had a chance to settle in, the news broke that manager Allan Brown had been sacked. He had applied for, but failed to land, the manager's job at Leicester. Brown was clearly ambitious, but found himself unceremoniously dumped by an equally ambitious Luton board for 'disloyalty'.

Within hours of Brown's departure Alec Stock was installed in the hot seat at Kenilworth Road. The vastly experienced Stock had himself been shown the door in controversial fashion by QPR the previous summer, just after taking Rangers into Division 1 for the first time. 'I specialise in this sort of situation,' said Stock on his appointment, a mite ambiguously.

Once he had gathered his bearings Stock sprung a radical tactical change, dispensing with wingers for away fixtures. The win at Northampton shortly after Christmas was Luton's first on 'foreign' soil since August. Stock swooped on Loftus Road to land Mike Keen, his former skipper, for £18,500 to strengthen the midfield, but Keen's arrival was offset by Bruce Rioch – who continued to attract the scouts like bees round a honey pot – having to miss two months of the season with a knee injury.

Having lost to Crewe at the end of January, the Town embarked upon an unbeaten run of thirteen games which saw them haul in the leading pair, Watford and Swindon. During this spell the team were indebted to Brian Lewis for banging in the goals, but his ability to raise the hackles of opposing defenders to the extent that they were frequently booked and occasionally sent off seemed to endear him to the Luton fans even more! Unfortunately, the bubble burst over Easter with a fumbling 0-1 defeat at lowly Mansfield, followed by a frustrating 0-0 home draw with Southport the next day. In the latter game, keeper Sandy Davie took a heavy kick from ex-Luton forward George Andrews and could take no further part. Town resorted to using Brian Lewis between the sticks, wearing a shirt two sizes too big. Mercifully, Lewis was up to the task, but for Davie the season was over.

With the team enjoying another winning spurt, the local press peddled thoughts of promotion, even though most supporters knew better and had resigned themselves to another season in Division 3. The final game saw champions Watford descend on Kenilworth Road. To clinch promotion the Town needed to win and hope that Swindon lost their two outstanding games. The biggest league crowd since 1959 – and one that has not been bettered since – packed the stadium to see the Town win 2-1 in a ill-tempered clash that sparked trouble in the crowd as well as on the pitch, with Barry Endean and Tom Walley of Watford sent packing along with Luton's Alan Slough.

Swindon, sadly, did not slip up, leaving the Town to rue their wretched pre-Christmas record, when the points lost in seven straight away defeats had proved irredeemable. A final position of third with 61 points (equivalent to 86 in the days of three points for a win) would have ensured promotion in most years.

In the League Cup, the Town had cantered past both Watford and Brighton during that early season show of power but came unstuck at Everton in Round 3, where the Toffees, who would win the League championship the following season, put on an unstoppable display to win 5-1.

The Town also reached Round 3 of the FA Cup for the first time since 1965, but after disposing, first, of Athenian League side Ware, and then Gillingham, they found themselves paired with League champions Manchester City at Maine Road, where a Francis Lee penalty settled the issue. At least the Town made money from their share of the gate.

## Match of the Season 1968-69

### Luton Town 4 Mansfield Town 2

Division 3, 18 September 1968

Following their promotion to Division 3 the Town had started off in August as they had left off in May. By the time of the visit by Mansfield they were unbeaten in seven games and sitting proudly at the top of the table. Tommy Eggleston's Mansfield were just two places behind, though their early season bubble would burst and they would slither down to fifteenth by April. A crowd of 19,315, the biggest since 1964, turned out to see if the Town could extend that record against a Stags outfit which had clocked up four wins already and who were expected to test Luton to the limit.

After only three minutes a frantic melee in the Mansfield goalmouth, when at least five shots were blocked, turned ugly with players swinging at each other. In the bedlam Town's Alan Slough lay pole-axed in the back of the net. Referee Malcolm Sinclair, however, ordered off local favourite, Bruce Rioch, for allegedly striking an opponent. The crowd reacted furiously, adding to the volatile atmosphere.

Flushed by the injustice of it all, the ten men of Luton, ably marshalled from the back by skipper Terry Branston, knuckled down, and when a penalty came Luton's way the crowd almost sucked Mike Harrison's spot-kick into the net.

The Stags equalised shortly into the second half. By this time the Town were reduced to eight fit men – John Moore and Branston were visibly limping – though the referee tried to even things up by sending-off Mansfield's Phil Waller for up-ending Brian Lewis.

**DID BRUCE RIOCH STRIKE A MANSFIELD PLAYER IN SEPTEMBER 1968?**

**For the first time, photographs from a local paper were used as evidence for an FA tribunal. Rioch's dismissal and suspension were quashed.**

The Town players now found their second wind, and goals from Laurie Sheffield and Lewis put them firmly in command. Then came the most fantastic goal of a fantastic evening. Winger Graham French, collecting the ball in his own area, loped the length of the field, skipping past player after player before driving the ball past Dave Hollins in the Mansfield goal.

The Stags scored a second goal just before the end, but the night belonged to the Luton players, the fans and in particular Graham French.

# LEAGUE DIVISION 3 1969-70

| | |
|---|---|
| Division 3 | 2nd (promoted) |
| League Cup | 3rd Round |
| FA Cup | 2nd Round |

After the high expectations of the previous campaign, when the Town narrowly failed to win promotion, the fans were brought sharply back down to earth when it was revealed that golden boy Bruce Rioch would be leaving. Whether he would have stayed had the Town gone up is conjecture, but the fee of £100,000 received from Aston Villa – a then record sale for a Division 3 club – could not be lightly ignored, and Rioch was understandably anxious to better himself.

Manager Alec Stock immediately pledged the whole of the fee for team building, returning to Fulham to snap up 19-year-old Malcolm MacDonald for £17,500. MacDonald joined forces with free-transfer signing John Ryan, who had also arrived from Craven Cottage. On the eve of the new season Stock acquired the signature of forward John Collins – who had played for him at QPR – from Reading for £10,000.

The Hatters started off the new campaign as they had finished the last, comfortably winning their first two fixtures. A pre-season injury crisis, however, meant that new signing MacDonald, bought as a full-back, was invited to try his luck in the forward line, where his dashing, cavalier play raised eyebrows.

In the home draw with Halifax, however, MacDonald was well-shackled by the visitors' commanding centre-half, Chris Nicholl, who impressed Stock to such an extent that he promptly bought him for £35,000. The manager also signed striker Matt Tees from Charlton for £25,000. Stock obviously wanted his own men, but had been prepared to bide his time before dipping into the Rioch pot.

The signings seemed well-judged as the Town extended their undefeated run for the season to thirteen games. They were top of the league, and MacDonald, still playing in attack, was proving to be an inspired purchase. The venom of his shooting took the breath away. Under the watchful eye of Tees, his new tutor, MacDonald was slowly having the rough edges knocked off his forward play.

Luton's first defeat came at Doncaster against a resurgent Rovers, but this proved an isolated setback as the Hatters set off on another seven-game unbeaten run. This culminated in a 5-0 home thrashing of Bradford City, and is remembered fondly as the occasion when MacDonald bagged his first hat-trick for the club.

**DID YOU KNOW?**

**Tony Read, signed as a goalkeeper in 1965, played 27 times as a forward and scored 12 goals, including a hat-trick against Notts County.**

All seemed set fair for promotion but a run of four straight defeats, starting with a 0-1 reversal in the Orient mud on Boxing Day, took the wind out of Luton's sails and saw them deposed from the top by the 'O's. A powerful win at Bury appeared to have stopped the rot, but losses at Bristol Rovers and Barrow saw the Town slipping back to fourth.

Alec Stock pulled the side apart following the Barrow defeat, irked by what he saw as a lack of passion from the best paid players in the division. His changed team showed no shortage of spirit at Torquay, where they did enough to have returned with both points. The following week leaders Brighton were fortunate to draw at Kenilworth Road, but lowly Tranmere were turned over and Luton then triumphed at Reading – who had been coming up on the blind side. The promotion bandwagon seemed to be on the march once more.

Or so it seemed. The Town started losing again and by Easter thoughts of promotion appeared to have vanished into thin air. Stock stirred the pot yet again, the new recipe yielding back-to-back home wins, including another MacDonald hat-trick in a 5-0 humiliation of Reading.

Defeat at Barnsley and a dull 0-0 draw at Halifax dampened spirits, but then, just as everyone was writing them off, Luton responded with a valiant win at Fulham, with MacDonald scoring the only goal, just as he had done in the home fixture the previous November. On the evening of the FA Cup final, Walsall visited Kenilworth Road, a big crowd urging the home team to one last effort. Promotion back to Division 2 was tantalisingly within reach for the first time since 1963.

The players did not disappoint, destroying the Saddlers with three goals in the first half, including one from Viv Busby, a young forward signed from Wycombe Wanderers, and who had won the hearts of supporters ever since his debut on Good Friday. Southport were the next visitors, and another large, tense crowd assembled, mindful of the spoiling tactics employed by the Sandgrounders in the same fixture the previous season, which had virtually dashed the Town's promotion hopes. Busby eased the tension with a rocket shot into the roof of the net, and that proved to be the winner against stubborn opponents. News came through that Gillingham had won at promotion rivals Bristol Rovers, leaving the Town just one point short of their target, and with two games left in which to secure it.

That point was duly extracted from Mansfield in a cheerless game at Field Mill, and the season was rounded off by a 2-1 win at Rochdale on a bog of a pitch. The Town had achieved their dream but had made hard work of it, with a talented, expensively assembled squad which die-hard Luton fans believed had the requisite talent to stroll away with the divisional title. In the end, the Town were left to thank Gillingham – with their improbable victory at Eastville – for saving their bacon.

The cup competitions understandably took a back seat this season. Peterborough were overcome in the League Cup, after which Millwall were seen off in a replay at the Den in controversial fashion. An indirect free-kick to Millwall was hammered directly into the net, but despite vigorous protests that the ball had touched a player en route the referee refused a goal. Keith Allen settled the tie soon afterwards with a speculative shot from near the halfway line which left the locals in a sour mood. A superior Sheffield United ended the Town's dreams in the next round.

The FA Cup road started at Bournemouth, with the Town lucky to earn a second chance, but the replay went to form. The reward was a trip to Southern League leaders Hillingdon Borough, where an over-confident Town took an early lead and then sat back thinking they had done the job. They hadn't, with the result that Jim Langley's Hillingdon earned that season's giant-killer tag.

## *Match of the Season 1969-70*

**Reading 0 Luton Town 1**

Division 3, 11 March 1970

After topping Division 3 for most of the autumn, the Town's promotion form nose-dived over Christmas with four games lost in a row, including the first home defeats since April 1968. Nor had form noticeably picked up by mid-March, by which time the Town's chances of securing promotion were receding with every match.

Reading, on the other hand, were enjoying a purple patch. Their unbeaten run of fifteen games dated back to November and they had even overtaken Luton in the league table. Interest in the game, especially from a Reading point of view, was such that it attracted a gate of 18,929, which was never to be exceeded in a league fixture at Elm Park. The attendance might have been yet higher but for inclement weather which reduced the pitch to a quagmire and deterred fair-weather fans from venturing out.

The game kicked-off one man short. Reading keeper Steve Death had been delayed by traffic, but stand-in Dennis Butler was not properly tested by the Luton front line before the breathless latecomer dashed on two minutes after the start.

Most of the early play favoured the Town, whose bigger and stronger players seemed better suited to the conditions. Malcolm MacDonald was unlucky with a header that cannoned off the bar. Gradually, however, the tide turned and Reading began to impress with their close-passing style. Luton full-back Fred Jardine needed to head off the line from Dick Habbin with keeper Sandy Davie out of position.

The second half continued to reflect an absorbing contrast of styles, with Reading winning the corner count but the Town looking more dangerous on the break with their powerful front runners, MacDonald and Matt Tees.

Only twenty seconds remained when this duo finally decided the outcome. Tees drove a long ball down the middle to MacDonald, who ploughed through the mud, fending off his marker and skipping past Death to score into an empty net. Promotion was on the cards once again.

Jack Mansell's Reading failed to go up, finishing eighth.

# LEAGUE DIVISION 2 1970-71

| | |
|---|---|
| Division 2 | 6th |
| League Cup | 3rd Round |
| FA Cup | 3rd Round |

After the ecstasy of promotion, hard reality set in. Manager Alec Stock had even more reason to strengthen the squad, and, in a summer of intense activity, decided to do most of his shopping at Old Trafford. His four summer buys from Manchester United totalled £35,000, with Don Givens and Jim Ryan the best known of the imports. David Court, whose progress Stock had followed for several months, was enticed from Arsenal for a further £35,000, and indestructible midfielder Roger Hoy from Crystal Palace for £20,000. One absentee, however, was winger Graham French, talented but wayward, who had been arrested and subsequently jailed following a firearms incident.

For the fourth close-season running, Kenilworth Road was a hive of activity with season tickets selling as quickly as they could be printed. Supporters viewed the coming season in Division 2 as a novelty, and were anxious to absorb anything coming out of the club, whether the written or spoken word.

On the pitch the season started inauspiciously, with the Town comprehensively beaten by Bolton on the opening day and following up with draws against Norwich and Birmingham. The first win was delayed until game four, when Oxford were thrashed 4-0. That win prefaced a gradual climb up the table with the summit being reached, albeit briefly, after beating Blackburn 2-0 at home on 20 October.

That win, putting Luton on top of the division, reverberated around the football world. But so did the 5-1 mauling of relegated Sheffield Wednesday at Hillsborough. The TV cameras were on hand to record a cavalier hat-trick from Malcolm MacDonald and, if people had not heard of him before, they could not help but take notice now. The English game was agog at his exploits. It was now no longer a case of 'if' he would leave, but 'when', and 'where to'.

Success on the pitch raised average attendances to their highest since 1958. Even away from Kenilworth Road football-goers turned out in their thousands to see the Hatters, who invariably turned on the style, attacking whenever the opportunity presented itself and exploiting to the full the talents of MacDonald and his foil, the unsung Don Givens. It was also around this period that director Eric Morecambe found a means of dropping in the words 'Luton

Town' at every opportunity on the 'Morecambe and Wise Show', which was amongst the most popular television programmes of the time.

Top of the table in early January, the Town appeared to suffer from altitude sickness. Defeats at lowly Blackburn and high-flying Sheffield United contributed to their slide towards less exalted heights. MacDonald lost his goalscoring touch for a while, going five weeks without scoring. It took the appearance of the TV cameras to re-ignite his fuse.

The occasion was the visit of fellow promotion chasers Hull in mid-March. The Match of the Day cameras were present to see the Town put the Tigers to the sword and shake off their previous two months' lethargy. MacDonald was back to his best, the football was exciting, but still the club could not shake off its 'little Luton' tag, with BBC commentator David Coleman expressing astonishment at the crowd of 'only' 19,566.

It was at this point in Luton's fortunes that events behind the scenes took on deeper significance. The Town's elevation from the football basement had been underpinned by the money of chairman Tony Hunt and director Reg Burr, who owned the Vehicle and General insurance company. Rumours had been rife that the company was struggling financially, but in early March came the bombshell that it had entered into a voluntary arrangement with its creditors. This meant that the V&G shares which guaranteed the club's overdraft became worthless overnight, leaving the bank with no security.

Tony Hunt resigned the chairmanship immediately, leaving the club's accountant, Robert Keens, to take over and steady the ship. It was reluctantly agreed that the club would go into unofficial receivership, but it was obvious that money had to be found from somewhere. The chief saleable assets were the players, foremost amongst them Malcolm MacDonald.

Whether these financial headaches were responsible for the Hatters' disastrous Easter is difficult to know, but the very future of the club had now been put in jeopardy, notwithstanding the excitement generated on the field. Nor is it easy to explain how a winning team could become a losing one over the course of four short days.

Those four days, starting at Bristol City on Good Friday, still haunt supporters who attended the matches. At Ashton Gate the Town were 2-0 up at half-time and cruising, yet their second-half disintegration was agonising to behold. Even harder to fathom was the capitulation to Millwall at the Den the following day, when the Lions ran the Town ragged, running in four goals. The Easter

Monday home defeat by Leicester, albeit to a strong Foxes side, was accomplished despite the gift to the Hatters of a John Sjoberg own-goal in the opening minutes.

The rest of the season was a complete anti-climax, with the support dropping away like a stone. MacDonald saved his swan-song performance for the final game, when the Town needed to score two goals against Cardiff to qualify for the long-forgotten Watney Cup competition, which was open to the highest scoring teams in each division who had not claimed a trophy of any description. Mac duly obliged with a hat-trick, the third goal delayed until the final minute.

Alec Stock always maintained that the Town could have won promotion that season but for the V&G collapse, in which case he might have been able to keep hold of MacDonald a while longer. But the harsh reality was that an era had ended at Kenilworth Road.

The early-season league surge overshadowed performances in the cups, but they were not without their thrills and spills. Gillingham and Workington were comfortably accounted for in the League Cup before the Town were given a home tie with Arsenal. The Gunners, on their way to the league and FA Cup double, drew a crowd of 27,023 to Kenilworth Road, a figure never subsequently overtaken. They lived up to their 'lucky Arsenal' tag by somehow keeping the Town at bay during a frantic opening half-hour before sneaking out to scramble the only goal.

The FA Cup produced a classic contest against Nottingham Forest in a Third Round replay at Kenilworth Road. The Town had earned a hard-fought draw at the City Ground in a game interrupted by the oddity of a snapped goal-post, but the replay had everything – ranging from a MacDonald hat-trick to a Forest winner scored moments from time to clinch the tie 4-3. The coaching staffs of both sides probably winced at the antics of their defenders; not so the 23,483 paying customers, who certainly got their money's worth.

## Match of the Season 1970-71

### Sheffield Wednesday 1 Luton Town 5

Division 2, 10 October 1970

After a sluggish start the Town slowly found their feet in the new division and by the time of their trip to Hillsborough were up among the leading pack. The only defeats to date were an opening day baptism at Bolton and a narrow reversal at Leicester.

**DID YOU KNOW?**

**Luton have yet to visit Scarborough in the Football League, yet ironically their visit in 1938 in the FA Cup still stands as Seamer Road's biggest attendance.**

Wednesday on the other hand, having suffered relegation in May, had found life no easier in the lower division, though recent results suggested they were on the mend. They had won their last home game 3-0 against Carlisle and had gone down narrowly at neighbours Sheffield United on the succeeding Saturday.

The visit to Hillsborough was seen in the minds of most Luton supporters as an excursion to the big time, and no doubt by the players too, considering that the Town had visited outposts like Barrow less than twelve months previously.

The Hatters were far from overawed by the occasion and pressed forward from the start, MacDonald scoring after fourteen minutes with what was becoming his trademark, a thumping left-foot drive. Two more goals arrived in the minutes prior to half-time, with MacDonald setting up Don Givens and then helping himself to number three with another left-foot special.

The second half saw more of the same, Givens and MacDonald scoring one apiece, the Owls managing no more than a late consolation through Jackie Sinclair. Luton's travelling supporters looked on in exhilaration at the verve shown by their team and the brute power of MacDonald's shooting. With the TV cameras also in attendance, the fans' excitement was no doubt shared by millions from the comfort of their armchairs.

Although this game proved to be the making of MacDonald, his secret was now out. He did much to try to deflect the praise heaped upon him by emphasising the unselfish play of Givens, who pulled the Wednesday defenders all over the place to create space.

As a Luton newspaper scribe reported afterwards: 'If the Town maintain this form, they will win not only the League and the Cup but the Grand National as well!'

# LEAGUE DIVISION 2 1971-72

| | |
|---|---|
| Division 2 | 13th |
| League Cup | 2nd Round |
| FA Cup | 3rd Round |

After all the traumas of the previous season, it was back to normal for the Hatters. No money!

The Vehicle & General crash precipitated the sale of Malcolm MacDonald but the proceeds had been swept up by the club's bankers. This left manager Alec Stock with little more than a piggy bank to delve into, as opposed to the blank chequebook he had enjoyed in previous years.

Newcastle United had always been favourites to sign MacDonald and it is said that Stock raised the asking price by £30,000 on account of the hat-trick Mac scored at Kenilworth Road on the closing day of the previous season. The eventual fee of £180,000 was a then Division 2 record. MacDonald, fittingly, made a grand entrance at his new club by turning up in a chauffeur driven white Rolls-Royce.

The loss of this extrovert terrace favourite was obviously going to take some getting used to. As Stock himself put it, when the ink on Mac's signature was dry: 'How will I replace a 30-goal-a-season man with no money? For the time being, Stock would have to make do with the current squad and hope that he could uncover another diamond from the lower divisions.

Oh, how the Town missed Mac, who quickly became as popular on Tyneside as he had been in Bedfordshire. Luton could do no better than draw six out of their first seven games, losing the other. The defence, with Chris Nicholl the anchor, stood firm but the new attacking partnership of Don Givens and Viv Busby found goals hard to come by.

In mid-September, Stock phoned Craven Cottage to conclude a deal which brought back forward Vic Halom for £35,000. Halom's first match was at home to Birmingham, which finished goalless. But his introduction soon paid dividends, with back-to-back home wins over Middlesbrough and Fulham, which earned the players their first win bonuses of the campaign. Halom and local youngster Robin Wainwright both scored in each game, but the wins proved illusory, two bright spots in a season of mediocrity.

The forward line was further depleted when winger Jim Ryan dislocated a shoulder at Hull in early October, which effectively ended his season. Draws now started turning into defeats and, by the time of the local derby at fellow strugglers Watford on 13 November, the Town had suffered four defeats from the previous five games – the other game, predictably, being drawn.

What stuck in the gullet following the 1-2 reverse at Vicarage Road was not so much the defeat as the lack of spark or passion in Luton's performance. This invited much soul-searching behind the scenes, with next opponents Blackpool earmarked to feel the backlash. In the event, that match nearly became the match that wasn't. Players and supporters alike journeyed north on a special chartered train, only to find themselves at the mercy of a derailment at Warrington. Hatters coach Jimmy Andrews had to phone through the team line-up to Chris Nicholl, who happened to be up in the north-west visiting relatives. Nicholl was instructed to pass the team-sheet to the referee, thereby preventing a fine. The rest of the team, already kitted out, arrived at Bloomfield Road with barely twenty minutes to kick-off, having been whizzed through the streets – where a local carnival was in full-flow – escorted by a fleet of police cars. The supporters were not so lucky. They had to get to the ground on Shanks' Pony.

To top all this, a blizzard swept across the stadium at the start of play. But unlike at Watford, the Town had fire in their bellies, winning 1-0 with a goal from Don Givens.

When Luton then overturned a 0-2 half-time deficit to beat Portsmouth at home, supporters would have been forgiven for supposing the corner had been turned. But it was soon back to the dull diet of draws, with the fifth goalless game of the campaign coming at Bristol City in early December.

Fortunes picked up over Christmas and New Year, with Orient defeated at Kenilworth Road and Sheffield Wednesday held to a 2-2 draw at Hillsborough. On New Year's Day, promotion hunting Millwall were overcome 2-1 in a thriller, and the Town returned from Preston with both points following a 1-0 victory. The home side had had to endure the sight of a penalty saved by Hatters' keeper Tony Read.

Hovering over Luton Town like the sword of Damocles were the club's bankers, who were again starting to make threatening noises, and, in light of the marked drop in attendances, hard decisions had to be taken. Viv Busby was farmed out to Newcastle on loan to see if his previous partnership with Malcolm MacDonald would prosper in the top flight, but after two months he returned, disillusioned, although probably a better player for the experience.

Luton, by this time, had gone into free-fall, so that by the time of the return fixture against doomed Watford in early March, alarm bells were ringing loudly. In the circumstances, a tedious 0-0 draw with the Hornets was a point gained, not a point dropped. The club decided, reluctantly, to cash in on Chris Nicholl. Although the fee of £90,000 kept creditors temporarily at bay, Nicholl moved in the direction opposite to that which had been predicted – his new club, Aston Villa, were in Division 3.

Stripped of the team's star forward and star defender, there were many who expected Luton to collapse. Perversely, the Town won their next game, 1-0 at home to Burnley, in a fixture which saw the belated debut of Alan Garner, a close-season free-transfer from Millwall.

Inconsistency coloured the dying weeks of this miserable season. Vic Halom netted three times in the 3-1 home win over Sheffield Wednesday, but then masqueraded as the Invisible Man in two subsequent away defeats. Defender John Ryan was asked to play in attack at Portsmouth, and scored twice in a 3-0 win, but the experiment was not repeated. Ryan was withdrawn to midfield for the rest of the campaign.

Not surprisingly, supporters greeted the curtain-fall at Cardiff – which ended 1-1 – with a huge sigh of relief. Perhaps they had been spoiled by four seasons of unremitting success but, if so, 1971-72 certainly made them pay for the pleasure.

In such a season, progress in the cups would have been a godsend. Unfortunately the Town fell at the first hurdle in both competitions, unluckily at Crystal Palace in the League Cup and, bravely, at West Ham in the FA Cup.

## *Match of the Season 1971-72*

### West Ham 2 Luton Town 1

FA Cup, 3rd Round, 15 January 1972

This was the second successive season in which Luton had been drawn away to Division 1 opposition in Round 3. The Town had a simple game-plan – to keep it tight for the first twenty minutes in order to draw the sting from their illustrious hosts.

Unfortunately, the Hammers had other ideas. It took them just 91 seconds before England centre-forward Geoff Hurst powered an unstoppable header in off the underside of the bar, following a pinpoint cross from Trevor Brooking.

The loss of skipper Bobby Moore after nine minutes with a trapped nerve in his leg did not seem to disturb West Ham, who doubled their lead when their muscular Bermudan, Clyde Best, hammered in the rebound after Luton goalkeeper Tony Read could only parry Brooking's header.

**WHAT DO MANSFIELD, EVERTON AND NEWCASTLE HAVE IN COMMON?**

**Over the years, each of these clubs has arrived at Kenilworth Road with strips that clashed with Luton's, having to take the field in the Hatters' second strip.**

The half-time advice from the Hatters' ex-Hammer coach, Jimmy Andrews, was to keep it simple, and gradually the Town clawed their way back into the game, pulling a goal back after 54 minutes. A short-corner routine saw Gordon Hindson send over the ball where it was met by Don Givens, who raced in to connect with a spectacular header.

The goal injected the first sign of uncertainty in the Hammers defence and both David Court and Mike Keen went close with fierce shots. The outcome, however, seemed to have been settled when John Moore was penalised for a challenge on Brooking in the area, but Tony Read blocked Hurst's full-blooded penalty, with Bryan 'Pop' Robson blazing the rebound over the bar.

There were more thrills yet to come in this pulsating tie, with Hindson's header striking the bar near the end. The final whistle blew with the Town camped in West Ham's half, Chris Nicholl forcing a brilliant save from goalkeeper Bobby Ferguson in the dying seconds.

'This was a day of pride,' said manager Alec Stock afterwards. 'Unfortunately, bad luck does not count.' Ron Greenwood's Hammers went out of the competition to Division 1 Huddersfield in Round 5.

2

# HARRY HASLAM 1972-1978

## LEAGUE DIVISION 2 1972-73

| | |
|---|---|
| Division 2 | 12th |
| League Cup | 2nd Round |
| FA Cup | Quarter-Finals |

It was all-change behind locked doors at Kenilworth Road during the summer of 1972. Alec Stock resigned immediately the curtain fell on 1971-72, citing constant travelling to and from his home in Epsom, which was affecting his health. Privately, he was probably sick and tired of the constant financial restraints imposed upon him, and disillusioned at the consequences for team-building.

Coach Jimmy Andrews also left, in his case to take up the reins at Cardiff City. The vacant managerial job at Luton was offered to Harry Haslam, who had come to Kenilworth Road as promotions manager three years earlier. Haslam's first appointment was Roy McCrohan – whom he knew from his Fulham days – as chief coach. Equally significant was the arrival of two new directors – local businessman Denis Mortimer and Tricentrol director Roger Smith.

Haslam commenced wheeling and dealing straight away, with David Court, Mike Keen, Don Givens, Robin Wainwright and Tony Read all heading for pastures new, and Rodney Fern (bought from Leicester), John Aston (Manchester United) and Bobby Thomson (Birmingham) coming the other way. The intake joined forces with John Faulkner, signed by Alec Stock from Leeds in the wake of the Nicholl transfer, but who, due to injury, had yet to play a game.

Haslam adhered to a different philosophical school to his predecessor. He aspired to make the Town more adventurous and devised a system which involved just one player up front, supported by a 'floating' five in midfield. This was a novel idea at the time but it turned out to be flawed in its use at home, though away it enabled the team to counter-attack with relish.

After all the pre-season hype, the Town lost on the opening day at Cardiff, despite a debut goal from John Aston. In the early games Luton created plenty of chances but their conversion rate was poor. Gradually, however, the ratio of goals scored to chances created improved, so that by mid-October the Hatters had climbed to third. They might have been yet higher but for occasional lapses at home.

John Aston, in particular, proved to be a revelation on the wing, exhibiting all his experience gained from playing at Old Trafford and in European competition. The good form of ex-England international full-back Bobby Thomson suggested that Birmingham were short-sighted to grant him a free transfer. John Faulkner and Alan Garner had formed a reliable double act in central defence. The one newcomer to struggle in his new environment was record signing Rodney Fern, who looked a shadow of the player who in Leicester's shirt had destroyed Luton two years previously.

The League Cup paired the Hatters with Birmingham and – proving they could live with the best – the Town took their top-flight opponents to three games before bowing out. On their league travels, the chemistry of the team up to Christmas enabled the Town to boast the best away record in the Football League. A 2-0 win at fellow promotion chasers Aston Villa, who fielded ex-Hatters Bruce Rioch and Chris Nicholl, was probably the best result of all. Home fixtures against the likes of Hull, Swindon and Carlisle proved more problematic: in the weeks leading up to Christmas all three teams snatched wins at Kenilworth Road.

So frustrated was Haslam by his players' phobia about playing at home that he splashed out £50,000 to buy Derby's reserve striker, Barry Butlin. Nearer to home, another forward was straining at the leash in order to play. The now slimmer former favourite Graham French had paid his debt to society and was keen to make his comeback.

French made his first-team return at home to Millwall on 16 December. In Roy of the Rovers style he scored to the noisy appreciation of the crowd. Sadly, his time out of the game had taken its toll, and French never recaptured his former heights. He was more often out of Haslam's team than in.

Haslam had no magic wand to restore home confidence. From mid-September to the end of January, Luton failed to win at all at Kenilworth Road. This, coupled with a downturn in away results, meant the Town were unable to make a sustained challenge on leaders Burnley and QPR, who appeared to have sewn up the two promotion places. All that was left for Luton was the FA Cup.

Ever since 1961, Round 4 had marked the summit of Luton's achievement. Nor did the team give supporters any reason to think that this season would be any different when lowly Crewe put up stern resistance in Round 3. A pairing with Newcastle at St James' Park at the next stage certainly set the press talking, mainly, of course, because of Luton's imminent reacquaintance with Malcolm MacDonald.

A full house in a three-sided St James' Park – the stadium was undergoing restructuring – coupled with MacDonald's Muhammed Ali-style boast that he would score six, ensured that Luton came out with their dander up. Unlike Muhammed Ali, whose predictions often came true, MacDonald was left with egg all over his face. His words ruffled the feathers of the Town players who, in a classic display of counter-attacking, won the tie through two first-half goals from Aston.

An away trip to Division 3 leaders Bolton Wanderers was the Town's 'reward' in Round 5. Alan Garner's header, in front of another big crowd, broke the Trotters' twelve-month unbeaten home record and earned Luton a quarter-final place for the first time since 1959.

Two days later Barry Butlin was badly hurt in a game at Millwall. As his striking understudy, Vic Halom, had recently been sold – ironically, to quarter-final opponents Sunderland – Luton's biggest day for years was in danger of turning sour.

A patched up Luton side – minus Butlin, Alan Slough and John Faulkner, and whose semi-fit goalkeeper, Keith Barber, was pushed back into the team prematurely – took the field at Sunderland before a crowd of 53,151, a massive attendance never subsequently exceeded at Roker Park.

Back in October, Luton had won 2-0 at Roker in the league, but that seemed light years away as, this time, the Town folded, going out 0-2 with hardly a whimper. Luton's season died there and then. The rest of the campaign was a non-event. Haslam rejuggled his team-sheet seemingly week to week, but two wins from the last ten games told its own story as his team slid gently downhill to finish in the bottom half.

## Match of the Season 1972-73

### Newcastle United 0 Luton Town 2

FA Cup, 4th Round, 3 February 1973

The pairing of the Town with mighty Newcastle was a match made in heaven, so far as the nation's sports hacks were concerned.

**DID YOU KNOW?**

**The Hatters' first sponsored match was against Swindon in October 1973. Local Vauxhall dealers Shaw and Kilburn paid £1,000 for the privilege.**

Malcolm MacDonald, who had left the Hatters to the accompany ment of fanfares and blazing headlines two years previously, could still be relied upon to come up with a punchy quote or two. Indeed, in the week leading up to the game the brash MacDonald was rarely off the back pages, feeding outrageous stories to the press as to what lessons he was about to hand out to his old chums.

Harry Haslam and the rest of the Luton staff maintained a dignified silence, knowing full well that they were unlikely to win any war of words with the darling of Tyneside. The Town would hope to let their football do the talking.

The game kicked off amid a cauldron of noise. Newcastle started brightly and MacDonald fashioned an early chance but fluffed his kick – perhaps being over-anxious to execute his pre-match threats. The Town delegated Alan Garner to trail MacDonald wherever he went, and asked full-back Bobby Thomson to keep a tight grip on Magpies' winger Stewart Barraclough, thus severing the supply to Mac and his striking partner, John Tudor.

Attacking on the break whenever they could, the Hatters then executed two simple goals. Both were created by the wing play of Jim Ryan, who tormented the Newcastle defence throughout, and both chances were put away by the clinical left foot of John Aston, who demonstrated all his experience by refusing to snatch at the opportunities.

Stung by manager Joe Harvey's half-time pep-talk, Newcastle came out for the second half like a wounded tiger. The total corner count of 26-5 in their favour gives some idea of the overall balance of play and the intense pressure applied to the Town defence. John Moore was inspirational, throwing his body into the line of fire at every opportunity and demonstrating in Moore's own words 'how true defenders do their job'.

Gradually Newcastle ran out of steam and their supporters ran out of patience, heading for the exits long before the final whistle. MacDonald had the last word, graciously admitting that the Town had deserved their win.

## LEAGUE DIVISION 1 1973-74

| | |
|---|---|
| Division 2 | 2nd (promoted) |
| League Cup | 4th Round |
| FA Cup | 5th Round |

Having survived his first season in charge, manager Harry Haslam appeared reasonably satisfied with the overall strength of his squad. He permitted Alan Slough and Viv Busby to depart to Fulham, secure in the knowledge that several promising youngsters were clamouring to replace them. The only pre-season purchase of any significance was the nominal sum paid to the Northern Ireland club Crusaders for a certain Tom Finney, whose name obviously lent itself to several cheeky newspaper articles. The young Tom Finney would need a thick skin to avoid unkind comparisons with the old.

After the financial traumas of the past couple of seasons the board convened during the summer to devise a five-year plan, at the end of which they hoped Luton would be back in Division 1. Little did they know that promotion would be achieved four years ahead of schedule, and the directors would probably be the first to admit that the club's finances were not yet secure enough to cater for this dramatic elevation in status.

Luton received a quick kick up the pants with a 0-4 thrashing at Nottingham Forest, where the 'lucky to get nil' joke sprang to mind. In the wake of that result bookies would have offered long odds against Luton, not Forest, gaining promotion. Effectively, after much soul searching and post-match inquests, Luton's season had to start all over again.

That opening-day result shook the Town to the core. The shake-up did everyone the power of good, as was demonstrated in the second game, when Carlisle were stung by a six-goal avalanche in the first half, with Finney, on his full debut, netting twice. The eventual score was 6-1 but Carlisle boss Alan Ashman was no less shell-shocked than Haslam had been the week before.

The Town embarked on an eight-game unbeaten run, winning at Bristol City, Crystal Palace and FA Cup holders Sunderland along the way. Finney proved to be living up to his namesake in these early games, netting five times, but as opposing defences learned how to counter him his confidence faded, his goals dried up, and he drifted first into the reserves, then, a year later, to Sunderland. There was, after all, 'only one Tom Finney'.

Luton's first defeat since Forest was delayed until 20 October, at Orient. Ironically the Town had recently signed ex-England Under-

23 international Alan West from Burnley. It was West's misfortune to make his debut in the team's shoddy display at Brisbane Road. The Hatters took time to readjust after that defeat, and the points they did gather were too often attributable to luck rather than judgment.

Typical of their good fortune was the home game against Bolton when, after the Trotters had taken the lead, John Aston saw his penalty saved. Luton were later awarded another penalty. Jim Ryan assumed responsibility instead of the shame-faced Aston, but managed to score only at the second attempt. If that was not enough, Bolton conceded an own-goal in the final minutes to gift the two points to the Town.

An objective view at this time was that Luton were no more than an average side competing in a poor division. This was evidenced by Jack Charlton's Middlesbrough, who had opened up a huge lead over everyone else, grinding out narrow wins through negative, graceless football. Trailing in Boro's wake, a cluster of hopefuls battled with each other for the second promotion spot, each raising everyone else's hopes by virtue of their own inconsistency.

The Town made hard work of advancing in the League Cup, squeezing past Grimsby and Bury only after replays, and then losing at Millwall, which begged the question, 'Was it all worth it?'

Haslam's next foray into the transfer market was to bring Everton forward Jim Husband to Kenilworth Road. Husband made his debut in a 0-2 defeat by West Brom at an icy Kenilworth Road. Coming in the wake of Alan West's losing baptism, supporters drew their own conclusions, demanding that Haslam now stay clear of the transfer market, as defeat was sure to follow!

Barry Butlin returned to the side the following week, having recovered from a broken jaw suffered a month earlier. His arrival signalled better fortunes, as Luton did a Boro and chiselled out three straight 1-0 victories. Subsequent defeat, 0-3 at Blackpool, in a crazy game, was matched by the helter-skelter form of everyone else. By the turn of the year, the Town found themselves still occupying third place, but with a modest points tally that in most other seasons would have seen then slip back to sixth or seventh.

Attention now switched to the FA Cup. A spirited Port Vale gave the Hatters a scare or two in Round 3, though Bradford City were seen off rather more easily at the next stage. Leicester City at home was the reward in Round 5 and if further evidence was required of Luton's inflated league position, First Division Leicester provided it. Goals flew in from all angles, four in total, and all credited to the Foxes. If that was symptomatic of life in Division 1 next season, did Luton want any part of it?

The Town banished such thoughts to the backs of their minds by beating relegation-haunted Crystal Palace, a win which lifted them to second, and there they stayed for the rest of the season, no matter how well or badly they played. Creditable wins at Swindon and Hull, and at home over fellow challengers Orient (with Husband scoring a hat-trick) were offset by defeats at Fulham and Bolton and at home to champions-in-waiting Middlesbrough – by the margin of 0-1, naturally.

Come Easter, the Town could do no better than draw at the Manor Ground with struggling Oxford. If that was disappointing, losing 0-1 at home in the return fixture would surely prove costly. That it did not was due once again to the nerves or sheer inability of everyone else. Hopes solidified in the next match, a 3-0 home triumph over Millwall, on a day when promotion rivals all dropped points. Now only a draw was needed, either at West Brom or at home to Sunderland, to claim a place in the top flight for the first time since 1960.

Barry Butlin headed the Town into the lead at the Hawthorns, to steady the nerves, but a late and questionable penalty awarded to the Baggies kept the Town on tenterhooks until the final whistle, at which point players and supporters alike erupted in celebration.

The final game, against Sunderland, was played in a carnival atmosphere. The Wearsiders could not go up, though their 4-3 win denied them promotion by a mere two points. Carlisle claimed the third promotion slot with a meagre tally of 49, the lowest ever to secure a place in the top division of the Football League. Luton had managed just one point more. The supporters did not care a fig, but the directors now had some serious thinking to do.

## *Match of the Season 1973-74*

### Luton Town 3 Millwall 0

Division 2, 20 April 1974

Following the wretched Easter, in which Luton somehow dropped three precious points to lowly Oxford, the Town management team could see promotion ebbing away. Drastic measures were called for.

Having invested £1,000 on videotape equipment, which in those days was a considerable outlay on a newfangled gadget, Harry Haslam and the team spent hours mulling over the Oxford home defeat. Several players felt they had been victims of bad luck, pure and simple, but viewing the game again, they appreciated that their attacks carried little variety, and that the high balls played into the opposing penalty box were meat and drink to Oxford's big defenders.

**DID YOU KNOW?**

**In November 1973 Luton played Sheffield Wednesday at Hillsborough, but the coach driver took the players to Bramall Lane, home of Sheffield United.**

Luton's next opponents were Ben Fenton's Millwall, who were unbeaten in seven games, but – determined to put their own house in order – the Town attacked from the start and, by switching the means of attack, tore great holes in the Lions' defence. John Faulkner headed a goal from a Jim Ryan corner after only eight minutes, and from then on it was one-way traffic. Millwall were brushed aside like confetti.

Peter Anderson lobbed a second goal ten minutes later, and such was the fluency the Town exhibited for the rest of the 90 minutes that supporters did not know whether to laugh or cry. Why hadn't the team played like that all season? Millwall did not muster a shot on target during the whole match, with danger-man, 24-goal Alf Wood, well shackled by Faulkner. When Alan Garner hoisted a ball forward for substitute Gordon Hindson to run through to score the third, the scoreline was given a more realistic look.

A perfect afternoon was made even better when news came through of rivals stumbling elsewhere. Luton now needed only one more point to realise their dream.

# LEAGUE DIVISION 1 1974-75

| | |
|---|---|
| Division 1 | 20th (relegated) |
| League Cup | 3rd Round |
| FA Cup | 3rd Round |

As the Town rejoined Division 1 for the first time since 1960, the enthusiasm of the fans had to be tempered by the fact that the financial vultures were hovering overhead, leaving manager Harry Haslam precious little money to spend on team-building. Chairman Robert Keens, an accountant by profession, was hospitalised with double pneumonia, otherwise it was likely he would have vetoed the £125,000 spent on the Futcher twins from Chester, a record for the purchase of teenagers at that time.

The remaining board members were no less reluctant to spend, but had to weigh financial stringency against the paramount need to insure against an instant return to Division 2. The supporters, having short memories of the Vehicle & General crash only three years previously, saw things differently. Blind to financial realities, as is the way with supporters at most clubs, they demanded that the board spend, come what may. In short, the transfer fees paid out in 1974-75 looked likely to have repercussions for years to come.

Of more immediate significance were the appointments of ex-player David Pleat and Uruguayan Danny Bergara. They joined the coaching staff with the instruction to bring on and develop the crop of promising youngsters coming up through the ranks.

The season opened to blue skies, the green grass of a newly drained pitch, and the white shirts of Liverpool, who were the first visitors to Kenilworth Road. Liverpool were still recovering from the shock retirement of Bill Shankly. Barry Butlin set pulses racing by scoring first, but Liverpool, playing their first league game under Bob Paisley, simply did what they nearly always did when falling behind. They stepped up a gear and cruised to victory.

Points and goals were hard to come by for Luton early on in the season. It was not until game ten, with Carlisle the visitors, that the Town recorded their first win. Ironically, the victory was achieved without top scorer Barry Butlin, whose transfer to Nottingham Forest had been finalised on the morning of the match. It appeared that ex-Luton manager Allan Brown, now at Forest, had money to burn following the sale of Duncan McKenzie, and the £120,000 he offered for Butlin was too good for Luton to refuse.

Without a recognised goalscorer, the Town went into free-fall, picking up only two points from the next eleven games. It was during this depressing period that Peter Spiring was purchased from Liverpool for £90,000. He was on target just once that season, but on a more positive note young full-back Steve Buckley, signed from non-League Burton Albion, was thrown straight into the deep end, and, credit to him, he held his head up well.

Haslam had to pull rabbits from hats if the Town were not to register the lowest number of points Division 1 had ever seen. He sensed he had nothing to lose by throwing in more youngsters. For the fixture at Chelsea on 7 December, he axed skipper Bobby Thomson, replacing him with Steve Buckley, and called up 18-year-old Paul Futcher in place of Alan Garner.

Luton lost that game 0-2, but Futcher was a revelation, stroking the ball around like a veteran and giving the air of someone who had graced the big stage for years. Haslam fielded the same side at Anfield. The result was the same. But on the Saturday before Christmas, with the home fixture against Derby drifting towards a 0-0 draw, Spiring was up-ended in the box. Jim Ryan stepped up to score, sealing the first win bonus since September.

Spiring broke his toe in the foul that brought about the penalty, and his place at league leaders Ipswich on Boxing Day was taken by Ron Futcher, Paul's twin brother. Luton survived an almost uninterrupted bombardment until, in the dying seconds, Ron Futcher broke away to score to present the Town with another two points, albeit fortuitously. Two days later Futcher scored a hat-trick in the 3-2 win against Wolves and the Town's season was picking up quickly.

The climb away from the bottom was not without its setbacks. Luton had plenty of catching up to do, but the youngsters coming through brought with them an infectious enthusiasm that rubbed off on the senior players. All of a sudden, supporters started to believe the impossible, that there was substance behind Harry Haslam's insistence that the team could defy relegation.

Operation A, to climb off the bottom rung, was achieved by mid-March. Operation B, to overhaul the next two clubs, would take Luton and their angst-ridden supporters right to the wire.

Three wins in the space of ten days, away at Carlisle and at home to Leeds United and Arsenal, injected realistic hope and served warning to the other clubs in the nether reaches that Luton's demise was no longer stamped and sealed. Those supporters old enough to recall will testify that the atmosphere at Kenilworth Road games in this period has seldom been equalled and never been bettered. Capacity crowds revelled in the sheer bravado of Luton's play, with the whole team racing into attack, then all racing back to defend.

**DID YOU KNOW?**

**In January 1961, Manchester City led Luton 6-2 in the FA Cup when the tie was abandoned. Luton won the re-match 3-1. Denis Law scored all seven City goals.**

The Easter games pitched the Town against Derby and Wolves, both away, and in a collapse of epic proportions Luton found themselves caned on both occasions. Future champions Derby won 5-0, with Roger Davies scoring all five and missing as many again, while at Molineux, Luton went from 2-1 up to 2-5 down. Worse was to come when, on the following Saturday, the Hatters lost to fellow strugglers Tottenham at White Hart Lane, with the winner coming from Alfie Conn, who was blatantly offside. Paul Futcher was sent off for what is officially termed 'dissent' but which covers a multitude of verbal sins – most of which Futcher committed.

These cumulative setbacks meant that relegation was now all but inevitable. It says much for the spirit of the players that negative thoughts never appeared to enter their heads. The next three games brought three handsome wins. The Town needed to extend that sequence to four, by winning their final game of the season at home to Manchester City. But even that might not be enough, for rivals Tottenham still had one outstanding fixture to be played after Luton had wound up their programme.

Luton's 1-1 draw with Manchester City threw the advantage to Tottenham, who still had to entertain Leeds. Tottenham needed to lose to save Luton, but they won 4-2. The Hatters were back to Division 2.

The disparity between the two halves of Luton's season was such that had they gleaned the same number of points in the first half as they did in the second, they would have qualified for Europe!

In the context of Luton's valley of tears, the cups were almost an irrelevance that season, with early exits in both competitions.

## Match of the Season 1974-75

### Luton Town 2 Leeds United 1

Division 1, 22 March 1975

In March 1975 Luton were still trying to claw their way up the league table after an appalling start. Three recent defeats had been followed by victory at bottom-placed Carlisle, which put smiles on the faces of supporters as they looked forward to the visit of mighty Leeds United.

Leeds were the team everyone liked to beat but few did. League champions at the end of the previous campaign, they had fought their way through to the European Cup final where they were due to play Bayern Munich.

Architect of their success was manager Don Revie, who had left the previous summer to take the England job, to be replaced by Brian Clough for his infamous 44 days. Clough, in turn, had been succeeded by a safer pair of hands in ex-England full-back Jimmy Armfield, and although their mid-table position showed this was not the Leeds of old, they still represented formidable opposition.

The Hatters took the bit between their teeth, attacking Leeds from the start and going ahead after only three minutes, when the wily John Aston, ignoring the obvious pass into a crowded goal-mouth, side-stepped a defender and shot inside the unguarded near post. The crowd went wild, and went even wilder nine minutes later when Peter Anderson collected a pass from John Ryan and blasted a second goal.

Luton continued to attack with gay abandon until half-time, and might have been rewarded with more goals. After the break it was a different story. They had little option but to try to contain a bullish Leeds, and with Johnny Giles suddenly patrolling midfield as if it were his personal fiefdom, the Luton rearguard survived several scares. Leeds' solitary goal, from Joe Jordan, came courtesy of a mix-up between Paul Futcher and goalkeeper Keith Barber, but it thankfully arrived too late to prevent the Town from claiming a famous scalp.

# LEAGUE DIVISION 2 1975-76

| | |
|---|---|
| Division 2 | 7th |
| League Cup | 2nd Round |
| FA Cup | 4th Round |

Yo-yo teams are customarily ridiculed. But having gone up, then down, Luton would have welcomed the yo-yo tag if they could bounce straight back up again. Harry Haslam, for one, was confidently predicting a quick return and, based on the Hatters' form since Christmas, his hopes did not seem unrealistic. The youngsters he had blooded had acquitted themselves well and, with a further crop waiting in the wings, the future looked bright.

Off the field, however, the spectre of financial disaster loomed darker than ever. For one thing, most of the players were still on lucrative Division 1 contracts. For another, attendances were bound to drop in Division 2, affecting revenue. And this is to ignore the shock waves still reverberating around Kenilworth Road following the Vehicle & General collapse.

None of this outwardly seemed to bother the players. Hull were comfortably beaten on the opening day, with local boy Andy King scoring on his full debut and reinforcing the manager's pride in the quality of the young talent at his disposal. But the good start proved to be a false dawn. From a position of sixth, following a 2-0 win at Portsmouth, a dispiriting run of one win in the next ten games – not to mention a red-faced defeat at Darlington in the League Cup – saw the Hatters dip into the bottom half of the table and set the alarm bells ringing.

Injuries to the influential John Aston and Alan West did not help the Town's cause, but rumours of severe financial problems behind the scenes evidently began to prey on players' minds. There is no smoke without fire, it is said, and certainly there was plenty of smoke billowing about, as tongues wagged about the cash crisis at Kenilworth Road.

Evidence was not hard to find. Haslam, for example, was refused permission to sign the ex-Celtic and Scotland winger Jimmy Johnstone. He would have come on a free transfer, but the directors balked at the signing-on fee demanded by the player. Eric Morecambe resigned from the board, citing 'pressure of work', though everyone knew that he did not see eye to eye with the new breed of director at the club. Nor was his the only departure from the boardroom. Three other directors also walked out, leaving Denis Mortimer to assume the role of chief executive.

Talk of the electricity being cut off, and other veiled threats by creditors, spread like wildfire. All this innuendo did no one any good, so it was with a sense of relief when everything finally came out into the open. The press confirmed that a large injection of cash had to be raised within 28 days or the club would go into liquidation. Behind the scenes a deal had been arranged to sell prize asset Peter Anderson to Antwerp, using a Belgium-based Luton fan as a go-between. But the press bombshell about possible liquidation scuppered the deal. Haslam's bargaining powers were slashed at a stroke. A fee of £105,000 had been agreed for Anderson; that figure was halved by the time the deal was done. To add salt to the wound, it was not many months since Aston Villa had bid £150,000 for the player, but Luton had turned it down. As a codicil to the Anderson saga, his final game for the Town was at Charlton, in front of a delegation of Antwerp officials sitting up in the stand. Luton won 5-1 and Anderson scored two goals.

No one was now in any doubt that the Luton Town patient was very sick indeed. Fans rallied round with messages of support coming from far and near. A fighting fund was set up, with promises of financial help even coming from the likes of Malcolm MacDonald, but the biggest beneficiary of Luton's plight was Alan Slough. By chance, his testimonial had been arranged for a date when the club's problems were hot news. In a show of defiant solidarity, almost 10,000 turned up for the game, but of course the proceeds rightly went to Alan Slough, not to Luton Town FC.

With everything out in the open, and any immediate threat to the club now temporarily lifted, the players extended their winning sequence to seven games, eight if one includes the FA Cup. These victories spanned Christmas and New Year, which was in consequence a more joyous time than most supporters had bargained for. The team shot up from seventeenth to sixth, and the loss of Anderson was barely noticed.

The team seemed to be firing on all cylinders. Attacking full-backs John Ryan and Steve Buckley were well supported in midfield by Alan West and Brian Chambers, while the central defensive partnership of the no-nonsense John Faulkner and the smooth Paul Futcher proved largely impregnable. Up front, Andy King and Ron Futcher banged in the goals, assisted by the experience of Jim Husband and John Aston.

Defeat in the FA Cup at Norwich, in front of over 3,000 Luton supporters, seemed to take the wind out of the players' sails and try as they might they failed to capitalise upon the good work of mid-season. The Hatters won their home games more or less as they pleased, but away from home they embarked on a series of 0-3 defeats, five of them in all, which would have produced good odds for any far-seeing pundit who cottoned onto that score quickly enough.

Haslam's solution was to dip into the reserves and pluck out a youngster or two. Paul Price and Lil Fuccillo made their full debuts in the 3-2 win at strugglers York, and both repaid their selection. Price had, in fact, come on as substitute on the closing day of the 1972-73 season, but had since been sorely incapacitated by injury, not least two broken legs, which had deprived him of nearly three seasons of his playing career. Fuccillo, despite his Italian-sounding name, was born in Bedford. He scored one of the goals at York and, like Price, was by the end of the season a first-team regular. Another youngster making a name for himself, Andy King, had to be sold when Everton put in a bid which, in Luton's straitened circumstances, could not be refused. The fee, a paltry £40,000, said more about Luton's parlous finances than it did about Andy King's true worth.

Considering the turmoil that had enveloped the club off the field, the team did well to finish seventh, just five points adrift from a promotion spot. The season ended on the high of three straight wins, the victims being doomed Oxford, along with Bristol Rovers – in what was Ricky Hill's memorable debut – and Blackpool. When the final whistle went in the final match, supporters invaded the pitch to demand that Harry Haslam take a bow.

It would take time before the new board could sort out the money worries but, player-wise, the youth policy masterminded by David Pleat and Danny Bergara pointed the way ahead.

## Match of the Season 1975-76

### Luton Town 3 Bristol Rovers 1

Division 2, 19 April 1976

Having averted the threat of bailiffs, the Town's season was winding down with little to get excited about. Easter Monday's visitors, Bristol Rovers, had not enjoyed the best of seasons, but they had fended off the threat of relegation and were buoyed by a recent draw with promotion chasing neighbours Bristol City, followed by a win over FA Cup finalists Southampton.

Luton winger John Aston was absent with flu, but centre-half John Faulkner returned after a month's absence with a knee injury. Keeping the subs' bench warm for the first time was 17-year-old Ricky Hill, yet another in the procession of young talents being slowly groomed for stardom.

**DID YOU KNOW?**

**Since World War II, only three league games at Kenilworth Road have had to be abandoned: Darlington (1967-68), Watford (1968-69) and Blackburn (1976-77).**

The game had 'end of season' written all over it, but it is nevertheless worthy of revisiting. Luton were guilty of several missed chances in the first half, with the shooting of Jim Husband, Ron Futcher and John Ryan posing considerable danger to spectators standing behind the goal. Rovers carved out just two chances in the same period, but Martyn Britten accepted one of them from close range, capitalising on lax marking at a long throw-in.

In the second half the Town soon drew level, with Paul Price scoring his first senior goal, heading in Alan West's corner, but despite enjoying the bulk of possession Luton could not force a second goal.

A recurrence of John Faulkner's knee injury presented the opportunity for young Ricky Hill to strip off and make his debut. It was late in the game, but Hill, whom most supporters had never seen in action, immediately had them roaring his name. With what was almost his first touch he threaded an inch-perfect pass through to Brian Chambers, who lobbed Jim Eadie in the Rovers goal.

The cheering had hardly subsided when Hill, accepting a short pass from Jim Husband, lashed a low twenty-yarder past Eadie. The scorer's reaction said much about the boy: he turned nonchalantly to trudge back to the centre-circle, only to be engulfed by his team mates, including goalkeeper Keith Barber.

Never had Town fans seen such a virtuoso performance on a debut. Perhaps more would be heard of this lad!

# LEAGUE DIVISION 2 1976-77

| | |
|---|---|
| Division 2 | 6th |
| League Cup | 2nd Round |
| FA Cup | 4th Round |

Harry Haslam was up-beat. Having come reasonably close last time, he saw no reason why Luton should not have a further tilt at promotion. The time was right, he felt, to pack off some of the older, fringe players, especially with so many youngsters pushing their way through and intensifying competition for first-team places.

Out went Adrian Alston, Peter Spiring, John Seasman and Matt Pollock, players who had never claimed a regular spot in the side. The same could not be said of ex-England and Wolves defender Bobby Thomson, who had given sterling service to the Town as a reliable full-back and skipper, and who was now allowed to leave on a free-transfer. Another departure was full-back cum midfielder, ex-skipper John Ryan, who was given the opportunity to chance his luck in Division 1 again, this time with Norwich, who paid £46,000 for his services.

The only new signing of note was that of ex-Scotland and Celtic striker Dixie Deans, who cost £20,000. Deans made his debut on the opening day against relegated Sheffield United and scored both goals in a 2-0 win. Short and squat, Deans did not look like an international striker but he made his presence felt and scored his share of goals. Of uneven temperament, he fell out with Haslam after becoming involved in petty vendettas on the pitch at Bolton, just before Christmas, which had him sent off.

The first weeks of the new season were exasperating for supporters, who never knew whether their team was on the up or the down. Defeats at Hull and Charlton were followed by a thrilling win at previously unbeaten Wolves. A 1-4 home defeat by Southampton left supporters holding their heads in their hands, yet not many weeks later they were celebrating a 4-0 thumping of table-toppers Chelsea.

One especially memorable game was the 4-0 triumph at Notts County, in the course of which goalkeeper Keith Barber was rushed to hospital with broken ribs. His place between the sticks was taken by tiny Dixie Deans, who seemed to relish the task, prompting Haslam to remark that he had been trying to get Barber to punch like that all season. The Town even had the temerity to break away and score two goals while Deans was performing his pugilistic heroics at the other end.

**DID YOU KNOW?**

**Although Luton went 36 home league games without defeat between May 1968 and December 1969, it did not beat their record – 39 games – between 1925-27.**

Haslam tried out 17-year-old Tony Knight in goal for the next game. Knight's rawness showed, so Haslam recruited the experienced Milija Aleksic from Plymouth. Aleksic, the English-born son of Yugoslav parents, was an instant success and the confidence that his presence instilled helped spark another winning sequence.

On New Year's Day the Town lay twelfth, following a 0-1 defeat at Bristol Rovers. The next game, at Sheffield United, was televised on Match of the Day. Millions of armchair spectators witnessed the Town take the blade to the Blades. At the time, most supporters attributed Luton's 3-0 win to a flash in the pan, fully expecting the team to crumble in their next two games – Hull and Burnley at home. To general astonishment both games were won. The Hatters had won three games out of three. Surely they couldn't make it four out of four at promotion-chasing Nottingham Forest. But they did, 2-1. Winger John Aston showed all his class and experience to run at the Forest defence and shoot an unforgettable goal.

Home attendances began to rise as word spread that Luton were taking wing. Blackburn were the next in line at Kenilworth Road, for a rearranged fixture, the original having been abandoned when the Town were 2-0 ahead. Rovers' defenders had been slithering all over the place on the bone-hard surface and their repeated appeals to the referee to abandon the contest eventually found favour, much to the disgust of the Luton players and spectators. Murphy's Law usually dictates that in such circumstances the side ahead in the first match loses the second. But not this time. Justice was now seen to be done when the Town won by the same score, 2-0.

Highly fancied Charlton were next up at Kenilworth Road. The match was fiercely contested but Ron Futcher's two goals determined the outcome. When Fulham were beaten with the minimum of fuss at Craven Cottage – thus exacting revenge for Luton's inept defeat earlier in the campaign – the Hatters' winning run had extended to seven, and suddenly the air was thick with talk of promotion.

Win number eight came at the expense of third-placed Wolves, who arrived at Kenilworth Road boasting a long unbeaten record. They went home with their tails between their legs, beaten by two goals in two minutes.

Luton's settled side was now playing with supreme confidence, stemming in no small part from an impregnable defence. New keeper Aleksic had already earned the nickname 'Elastic', as a result of his acrobatics that thwarted many an opposing forward. In front of Aleksic, the adventurous young full-backs, Steve Buckley and Paul Price, flanked the solid central pairing of John Faulkner and Paul Futcher. Seemingly able to pin-point his twin telepathically, Paul set up Ron with any number of goalscoring chances. Ron responded by enjoying his most productive scoring spell since joining the Hatters.

Luton's winning run was already the longest since 1967. It was to get even longer, though the Town left it late before accounting for Oldham in win number nine. Substitute David Geddis, on loan from Ipswich, netted the all-important goal four minutes from time. Few teams have ever recorded ten wins in a row, and that historic achievement was denied Luton when Plymouth, more by luck than judgment, escaped with a 1-1 draw at Kenilworth Road.

The winning sequence may have come to an end, but not the undefeated run. Luton's next two opponents were the two bottom teams in the division. The Town climbed to third after an unconvincing victory at Hereford, but were wholly convincing when thrashing Carlisle 5-0. At this point, having generated a seemingly unstoppable momentum, promotion for the Hatters seemed probable rather than possible. But the bubble burst suddenly and painfully. Alan Ball's quick goal at Southampton ended the glory and set in train a grotesque sequence of results. One point from three games over Easter put paid to the promotion dream. Luton never recovered, though it would haunt them throughout the summer to know that they finished just four points adrift of the third promotion team.

## *Match of the Season 1976-77*

### **Luton Town 2 Wolves 0**

Division 2, 5 March 1977

Wolves' visit for this much-hyped promotion showdown was billed as a clash between an irresistible force and an immovable object. The Town had won seven games in a row, while Wolves' unbeaten run of sixteen matches extended back to November. The Wolves also had a score to settle, as Luton had been the first side to lower their colours when winning 2-1 at Molineux in September.

The early play favoured Wolves. As befitted the leading scorers in the Football League, they carved out five clear chances in the first six minutes, and only a combination of lax finishing and bold goalkeeping prevented an early breakthrough for the visitors.

Gradually, the Town's defensive duo of Faulkner and Paul Futcher gained the ascendancy over Wolves' danger-men, John Richards and Alan Sunderland. And with Luton winning on points in midfield, it was the Wanderers' back line that was increasingly asked the most demanding questions.

Luton's wingers, for once, struggled to break free, and it was left to Ron Futcher and Jim Husband to make nuisances of themselves. This they did by constantly switching positions to confuse their markers.

The first goal arrived when Ron Futcher headed down Steve Buckley's free-kick for Jim Husband to lash the ball home. Straight from the kick-off, with the Wolves defenders still arguing amongst themselves, Lil Fuccillo made ground on the left and – with players on both sides expecting a cross – lobbed Gary Pierce in the Wolves goal from the narrowest of angles.

That double-strike knocked the stuffing out of Wolves, who seldom threatened thereafter. The margin of victory could have been greater, as Wolves defender Geoff Palmer confessed after the game that, unseen by the officials, he had punched away a goal-bound shot from Futcher.

It was a good day all round for Harry Haslam, who before the match had been named Division 2's Manager of the Month.

Sammy Chung's Wolves went up as champions.

# LEAGUE DIVISION 2 1977-78

| | |
|---|---|
| Division 2 | 13th |
| League Cup | 3rd Round |
| FA Cup | 4th Round |

Although finances meant belts still needed tightening, the Town's ambition to return to the top flight was undiminished. Haslam forked out for Phil Boersma from Middlesbrough to add fire-power to the front line. To balance the wage bill, however, Brian Chambers was allowed to move to Millwall and, early in the new campaign, John Aston, who had been a magnificent servant to the club, transferred to newly promoted Mansfield. The only other change of note was the appointment to the board of David Evans, an ex-professional footballer with Aston Villa and now a successful businessman.

Although Ron Futcher, Paul Price and Alan West were missing for the opening game, having been delayed whilst travelling back from their summer season in the USA, Luton carried enough guns to shoot down Orient at Kenilworth Road. The second home game, with the wanderers having returned, heralded the Town's biggest win for twenty years. Poor Charlton were on the receiving end of the 7-1 score, with Jim Husband netting four, the first Luton player to achieve this feat since John O'Rourke in the 6-2 win at Brentford in 1964.

Home-grown talents such as Lil Fuccillo, Ricky Hill and Paul Price were all now fully established, blending well with the more wizened professionals. Autumn was kind to Luton, whose winning ways lifted them to second place by mid-October. The only losses in this period were at Tottenham and Brighton, who lay first and second respectively, the games being only four days apart and watched by an aggregate attendance of over 58,000. Luton showed sufficient appetite in these fixtures to feel themselves hard done by to lose both.

The Hatters also dallied in the League Cup longer than usual. Having beaten Wolves, the Division 1 new boys, at the first stage, they were paired with mighty Manchester City at Kenilworth Road in the next. After two titanic struggles the Hatters finally succumbed only after extra-time in the second replay. But by this time, however, a season that promised cheers was rapidly turning into one of jeers.

The Manchester City defeat proved to be a turning point in more ways than one. Phil Boersma was lost to the side through injury for several crucial matches, while Paul Futcher, now on the verge of great things, was badly hurt in a road accident shortly before the third game with the Manchester giants. It would be over three months before he returned, and in the eyes of some fans he was never to be the same player again. Minus Boersma and Paul Futcher, the Town slumped badly, from second in mid-October to eleventh in early December.

Every cloud has a silver lining, and in Luton's case it was provided by a young South African, Brian Stein, who made his debut at neutral Old Trafford in that epic second replay with Manchester City. Though he still had plenty of rough edges, having only recently started his full-time football career after signing from Edgware Town, before the season was out discerning judges were taking Stein very seriously.

Matters on the pitch were not helped by unsettling rumours off it. For once, these rumours had nothing to do with money or how to pacify Luton's creditors. They concerned the manager, and the question of his long-term commitment to the Hatters. It was widely reported that Harry Haslam had been tapped by several clubs, Millwall among them, who wanted him as manager, and Manchester United, who wanted him as chief scout. It was no secret at Kenilworth Road that Haslam had sought the security of a longer contract and that his views on the way the club should be run were not always in tune with those of new board members. Newspaper speculation that ex-Chelsea and Scotland player Eddie McCreadie was waiting to step into Haslam's shoes only poured oil onto troubled waters.

Tensions worsened just before Christmas when chief coach Roy McCrohan left abruptly to become assistant manager of Detroit Express, joining a procession of British coaches and players who, at that time, felt the USA represented the 'land of milk and honey'.

Before long the exodus had extended to players. Left-back Steve Buckley was sold to Derby, the intention being, in the words of Rams' boss Tommy Docherty, to create with David Langan 'the best young full-back partnership in the country'. Although fans were sad to see him go, the fee of £160,000 represented a massive profit on the former Burton Albion defender. 'Balancing the books' was now the maxim of Luton directors and supporters alike.

Haslam himself was the third rapid departure. Sheffield United offered him the long-term contract that Luton had denied him. The Town board wasted no time in offering the vacant position to David Pleat who – as Haslam had invited him to be his number two at Bramall Lane – requested 24 hours to think about it. Pleat weighed the options and plumped for Luton.

**DID YOU KNOW?**

**The Hatters' record for successive home wins is 15 – established between 12 April 1967 and 26 December 1967.**

Pleat, who had risen in the space of a few months from reserve team coach to chief coach, and now to manager, faced the task of stemming the exodus by persuading Danny Bergara to stay, rather than hitch his wagon to Haslam's. Failing to do so, he filled the breach by approaching a former Southern League colleague, Ken Gutteridge, then at Brighton. Responsibility for tutoring the youngsters was offered to old Town favourite, John Moore, who happily accepted.

The new management team was installed in time for the FA Cup-tie at Millwall. It was an inauspicious baptism, for the Town collapsed 0-4. Not until his fifth game in charge did David Pleat taste victory.

Pleat needed to establish himself as his own man and, while he encountered few problems dealing with the younger players, most of whom he had discovered, signed and coached, it was a different story with some of the senior pros. John Faulkner and Jim Husband were the first to fall foul of the new regime. Both had hankered to play in the United States, and Pleat had no intention of standing in their way. It soon became clear that Faulker and Husband were just the beginning, and that Pleat's broom would sweep through Kenilworth Road in the close season.

But that is to peer into the future. The immediate need was to guard against relegation, the threat of which receded with three home wins in the space of ten days in March. The last of these was a thrilling victory over high-flying Bolton, which meant that the Hatters need no longer look anxiously over their shoulders. Skipper Alan West was particularly prominent at this time, leading by example and encouraging the kids around him. Those 'kids' would develop into the backbone of Pleat's team of the future.

This was to be an extraordinary season, not just for the Hatters, but for other teams caught up in the lower reaches of Division 2. Luton failed to win any of their last six games and ended up with 38 points, the same number as six other clubs, all of whom had an inferior goal-difference, and all of whom escaped the drop by just one point. The victims of this relegation bottleneck were Blackpool, who in March had been chasing promotion and who as late as 14 April were still ninth. Two weeks later they had plummeted to twentieth and were down. The margin between success and failure had never been so thin.

# *Match of the Season 1977-78*

## **Luton Town 7 Charlton Athletic 1**

Division 2, 3 September 1977

The Town had opened the new season fitfully, winning and losing their first two matches by the only goal of the game. Such results were not guaranteed to set the heart thumping. The third game was at home to Charlton. The Town were virtually back to full strength, the only absentee being the injured Phil Boersma. In his place, making his first team debut, was 19-year-old Gary Heale.

Charlton had ended the previous campaign among the promotion also-rans, and with a win and a draw already under their belts they were threatening to make a fist of it this time too.

On a hot, cloudless day the Town started off as if they meant business, taking the lead from a free-kick routine perfected on the training ground. Alan West flicked the kick over the Charlton wall to Husband, who timed his run to smash the ball past Jeff Wood. Full-back Steve Buckley hammered a second goal after the Luton midfield had sliced through the Charlton rearguard. When the whistle blew for half-time no one could have predicted the fun and games about to be unveiled in the second period.

Hill began the rout, firing a 25-yard dipper underneath the crossbar. With the destination of the points no longer in doubt, Jim Husband took centre-stage to put on a virtuoso performance. In a thirteen-minute spell, starting in the 65th minute, Husband struck three times, including a penalty. Sandwiched in between his strikes was a debut goal from Heale, who headed in at the far post from a cross by John Faulkner.

Surprisingly, last season's top scorer, Ron Futcher, back from America for his first outing of the season, missed out on the goals, but was praised afterwards by four-goal Husband for his unselfish contribution.

Charlton manager Andy Nelson had only two words to say, the second of which was '... ashamed'.

3

# DAVID PLEAT: PART 1 1978-1986

## LEAGUE DIVISION 2 1978-79

| | |
|---|---|
| Division 2 | 18th |
| League Cup | 5th Round |
| FA Cup | 3rd Round |

As promised at the end of the last campaign, the new manager, David Pleat, spent the summer of 1978 showing that he was a man of his word, carrying out possibly the biggest change of personnel in the history of the club.

In order to raise funds to bring in his own players, Pleat extracted £350,000 from Manchester City for Paul Futcher. Although sad to see the talented defender leave, most Luton supporters felt that he was a shadow of his former self following the long lay-off caused by his serious car crash. Brother Ron followed soon afterwards for £80,000, though his loss to the side was immediately nullified when that well-travelled striker, Bob Hatton, was signed from relegated Blackpool for £50,000.

Pleat was aware of the sort of players he wanted. Supporters were left hoping that he knew what he was doing when he dipped deep to pay £110,000 for Swindon winger, David Moss, £40,000 on Mark Aizlewood from Newport and – after protracted negotiations – signed centre-half Chris Turner from Peterborough United via New England Tea Men of the USA.

In fact, barely a day seemed to pass without supporters reading about new comings and goings. Defender Mal Donaghy, for example, was 'stolen' from Larne in Northern Ireland while Larne's manager was on holiday. Kirk Stephens arrived from one of Pleat's former clubs, Nuneaton Borough, and Steve Sherlock signed on a free transfer from Manchester City.

Pleat seemed quite satisfied with his signings but fired a verbal salvo at the start of the season with a call for patience. It might take time for his wholesale changes to pay off. At half-time on the opening day, with Luton 0-1 down at home to Oldham, supporters shared his misgivings, but, by the end of the game, with the Hatters scoring six without reply in an extraordinary turnaround, the mood on the terraces had sweetened.

That autumn the Hatters racked up some memorable home performances. Charlton were beaten 3-0 in a display no less comprehensive than the previous season's 7-1 thrashing; Cardiff – with ex-Luton favourite Keith Barber making his final Football League appearance in goal for the Bluebirds – were hammered 7-1 and, best of all, Notts County were turned over 6-0.

Away from Kenilworth Road results were not so clever. The draws were turning into defeats and when the home bubble burst in early November, with Leicester winning 1-0, the warning signs were there for all to see. Pleat's pre-season words were coming home to roost.

Despite this stumble in league form, the team advanced further in the Football League Cup than ever before. After Wigan and Crewe had been sent packing in the early rounds, the Town were drawn to play First Division Aston Villa at Villa Park. Putting on a superb performance to earn a 2-0 victory, the Hatters became the darlings of the media. Unfortunately, Wembley dreams vanished at the next stage with Leeds holding too many aces at Elland Road.

Following a behind-the-scenes row, goalkeeper Milija Aleksic was off-loaded to Tottenham, to be replaced shortly afterwards by Aston Villa reserve, Jake Findlay. Another enforced change was brought about when midfield general Lil Fuccillo broke his leg following a frightful tackle by Brighton's Paul Clark at the Goldstone Ground. The Town were at one stage determined to sue the Brighton player, though that threat came to nothing. Fuccillo's loss deprived the engine room of much-needed thrust, another reason for the team's uncertain form.

David Moss was proving to be an astute buy, though his presence lent the team a certain air of unpredictability. He was, to be sure, capable of turning a game on his own with his pace, powershooting with both feet, and competence with the dead-ball. But Moss's niggling groin strain became aggravated as the season wore on, with a commensurate loss of effectiveness that led to his prolonged absence from the side.

When young forward Brian Stein went off the boil – going over four months without scoring a goal – Pleat delved into the transfer market again, signing Steve Taylor from Oldham Athletic for

£50,000. Unfortunately, Taylor was not the answer, scoring only once in a brief stay at Kenilworth Road.

Further problems for Pleat arose with centre-half Chris Turner's hankering to return to the USA. In March he was allowed to leave, to be replaced by the unlikely named Forbes Philipson-Masters, who arrived on loan from Southampton. By this time, the balmy days of the previous autumn seemed a lifetime away.

But not everything was gloom and doom. Positive contributions were made by all-action terrace favourite Kirk Stephens, the ever-improving Ricky Hill, wily Bob Hatton and skipper Alan West, together with brief, but timely, virtuoso performances from loan signings Barry Silkman and Alan Birchenall.

After Christmas, however, the team's travel sickness got worse, and unacceptable slip-ups at home meant the Town were spiralling downwards. A string of four straight defeats, with only one goal scored, pushed the team down to sixteenth, a position aggravated by the fact that most fellow strugglers had games in hand.

Luton's 4-1 thumping of a poor Burnley side provided temporary respite, and with the semi-fit Moss intermittently returning to the side to lend his match-winning powers, welcome draws were scraped at home to Millwall and Brighton, and away at Stoke and – most significantly – at Preston. The Town were struggling, 0-2 down at Deepdale, when Moss came on as sub and turned the game, forcing an own-goal from Preston's Haslegrave and then equalising with a sublime chip.

Haslegrave's blunder, oddly, was one of four own-goals that came Luton's way in four consecutive games. With Fulham's John Beck netting for the Hatters in the 2-0 win over the Cottagers in the penultimate game, thereby confirming Luton's safety for another season, supporters would be eternally grateful for their opponents' vital contribution.

It had been a traumatic first full season for David Pleat but he would not be swayed from his beliefs in the type of football that his team should play, and with a bit of fine tuning, better luck with injuries and strengthening in a couple of positions, the foundations were in place for a tilt at promotion.

## *Match of the Season 1978-79*

### Aston Villa 0 Luton Town 2

League Cup, 4th Round, 8 November 1978

The Town had never previously survived beyond Round 4 of the League Cup, and after they were drawn away to mighty Aston Villa most pundits felt that modest record was likely to stay intact. Having limped past Wigan and Crewe in the previous rounds, and having little in the way of pedigree in the competition, the Hatters had few grounds for confidence. Fearing the worst, hoping for the best, supporters travelled to Villa Park with their fingers firmly crossed.

Villa had disposed of Sheffield Wednesday and Crystal Palace in earlier rounds and had won the competition three times already in its short existence. Manager Ron Saunders hoped to win the pre-match psychological war by announcing that he would be fielding his strongest side for the first time that season.

Once play commenced Luton survived an early scare when danger-man Andy Gray forced Hatters' goalkeeper Milija Aleksic into action in the opening minutes. But Villa's much-vaunted full-strength side was disrupted in the twelfth minute when Gray hobbled off with damaged ankle ligaments following a hard but fair tackle from Hatter's Mal Donaghy. Villa reshuffled, but it soon became apparent that the Town had gained the upper hand.

Villa, in fact, had not won at home for ten weeks, the anxiety of which began to spread through their side the longer the game went on. Saunders was a disciple of the long-ball game, which was meat and drink to Chris Turner and Mal Donaghy at the heart of the Luton defence. The Town became ever more dominant and Villa goalkeeper Jimmy Rimmer had to save smartly from Turner. David Moss won an indirect free-kick in the area when fouled by Ken McNaught, and Hatton shortly had the ball in the net but was flagged for offside.

The goal that Luton were increasingly threatening to score came on 66 minutes, when Lil Fuccillo threaded a delightful ball through to Hatton, who took it in his stride and fired a fierce shot into the top corner of the net. Brian Stein added a second in the final minute when he found himself unmarked in front of goal, tapping in a cross from David Moss to seal a famous victory.

Pragmatist that he was, David Pleat was more concerned by the lack of league points than fleeting glories in the cup, and threatened to make changes in the side for the forthcoming trip to Oldham, inferring that too many minds had been distracted by the cup-tie at the expense of the bread-and-butter league.

He did remark, cryptically, that Chris Turner was the 'best centre-half in America', which gave clues that his new defender already had his mind drifting across the Atlantic.

# LEAGUE DIVISION 2 1979-80

| | |
|---|---|
| Division 2 | 6th |
| League Cup | 1st Round |
| FA Cup | 3rd Round |

David Pleat had insisted, when appointed to the manager's chair at Kenilworth Road, that stabilising the club was a three-year exercise. After the traumas of 1978-79, he was determined to prove he was on the right lines in his attempts to bring Division 1 football to Luton. By his own criteria, he had two years left to achieve that objective.

Off the pitch, the Town embarked on a series of marketing ideas, inspired by Chief Executive John Smith, aimed at raising funds as well as the profile of the club. A new strip was introduced, one that placed less emphasis on the orange of the past six years, and for the first time a sponsor's name, 'Tricentrol', was emblazoned across the players' shirts.

Pleat activated another merry-go-round of transfers, with centre-half Mike Saxby arriving from Mansfield for £200,000 and Republic of Ireland international midfielder Tony Grealish coming from Orient for £150,000. Orient had originally demanded £350,000, but in one of the earliest transfer tribunals Pleat exploited the system cleverly to his advantage, as he was to do time and time again in the future.

On the departing side, Steve Taylor, who had failed to live up to expectations, left for Mansfield in exchange for £75,000, and fringe players Gary Heale, Alan Birchenall and David Carr were transferred to Reading, Hereford and Lincoln respectively.

The season had an inauspicious start. Gillingham of Division 3 were well worth their League Cup victory over two legs. Nor did a home draw with Cambridge and a defeat at Bristol Rovers in the opening two league games set pulses racing, but by the end of the fifth game, following three straight wins, the Town stood top of the table for the first time since 1970-71. Orient had been beaten only with difficulty, but a 3-1 victory at Leicester made even sceptical supporters sit up and take notice, and when Division 2 newcomers Swansea were hammered 5-0 in the Kenilworth Road sunshine the season took off.

Saxby and Grealish took no time to settle in. For the first time since taking charge, Pleat was able to pick his strongest side, unhindered by queues of injured players clogging the physio's room. A stable line-up was a prerequisite for better results.

**DID YOU KNOW?**

**In the 37 years covered by this book, no fewer than 26 Luton players have gone on to manage a Football League club.**

Though the Town were soon deposed from the top, wins at Fulham and at home to Bristol Rovers and Sunderland kept up the pressure on rival aspirants. A crunch match against highly fancied West Ham at Upton Park ended 2-1 to the visitors, although the Hatters won few friends with their negative play and excessive back-passing. The players turned deaf ears, as the win put them back on top.

Spirited away wins at places like Cambridge and Shrewsbury were offset by a tendency to drop points at home, particularly in the shape of draws against lesser lights. This was particularly galling to supporters, as the Town invariably seemed in control at Kenilworth Road but were unable to press home the advantage. Too often pressure was not translated into goals, especially against the division's strugglers.

Notwithstanding, home crowds were on average up by over 2,000 from the previous campaign and scouts from big clubs were usually encamped at Kenilworth Road to run their eyes over young Brian Stein, Ricky Hill and Paul Price. International recognition was also coming Luton's way in increasing numbers. Along with Tony Grealish, a regular for the Republic of Ireland, Mal Donaghy was earning his first caps for Northern Ireland and Paul Price was selected for Wales – Price opting for the country that was the birthplace of his father.

The darling of the Kenilworth Road crowd, however, was a fit again and seemingly reborn David Moss. Having recovered from the groin and pelvic problems that had so hampered him in his first season with the club, he was now demonstrating why David Pleat had paid so highly, in Luton terms, for his services. Able to play on either wing, and beat opposing full-backs both inside and outside, Moss also possessed a hard shot and an enviable ability to cross the ball at speed. His dead-ball kicking was normally so accurate that he was the natural choice for taking penalties.

In an attempt to inject competition for the front places, Pleat did a deal with Bristol Rovers to procure the services of Steve White, whose performance against Luton earlier in the season at Eastville had deeply impressed him. Though White cost £175,000, his appearances were mainly restricted to that of substitute, Pleat clinging to the hope that his established front runners would suddenly convert chances into goals.

Not since 1972 had the Town found themselves in the same division as arch-rivals Watford, and the renewal of these keenly awaited local derbies brought added joy to Luton, who beat the Hornets twice. The Boxing Day fixture at Vicarage Road was particularly sweet, with victory secured in the closing seconds through full-back Kirk Stephens' first goal for the club.

Life is tough at the top, and it was not long before the Hatters were eating humble pie. At one stage they went seven games without a victory, tumbling as a result down to sixth. The nadir of this terrible spell was the home defeat by Cardiff and, seen with hindsight, this was the match that spelt the end of the promotion dream. Hampered by injuries to Moss and Stephens, and playing on thick mud against ruthless opposition, the Hatters lost a miserable game 1-2.

Pleat was not yet ready to throw in the towel, insisting, at least publicly, that the Town could still muster a final push. Results over Easter, so often a burial ground for Luton's hopes, for once supported his words. Wins at Charlton and at home to Watford were followed by a trip to high-flying Chelsea. Despite dominating throughout,, the Town conceded the cruellest of late goals which enabled Chelsea to salvage an undeserved point.

The final throw of the dice came in a classic confrontation with Birmingham at St Andrews. The Town thought they had played too well to lose, but two more points had been tossed away and from that moment there could be no reprieve. Luton's season slumbered to a close, leaving them to occupy a final position of sixth.

Pleat was outwardly upbeat, and pointed out with some justification that sixth was an improvement on the previous year. Nor was it hard to pin-point the source of Luton's failings. Ten home draws was hardly promotion form.

## *Match of the Season 1979-80*

### Luton Town 3 Chelsea 3

Division 2, 1 January 1980

The 1980's were ushered in by this tumultuous clash between two of the top sides in the division, a thrill-a-minute contest enlivened by a pitch that was barely playable. Pleat had misgivings playing on the rock-hard icy surface, but once referee David Letts had given the go-ahead the Luton boss had no alternative but to be positive. The crowd of 19,717, the largest of the season at Kenilworth Road, turned up fully expecting an error-strewn game, but perhaps not anticipating such colossal commitment shown from both sides.

Chelsea's Mike Fillery began the goal bonanza early on with a twenty-yard drive. Mal Donaghy, playing in midfield in place of the injured Tony Grealish, hammered in a shot off the underside of the bar to level. It was Donaghy's first league goal for the Hatters.

A minute before the interval, Mike Saxby headed the Town ahead and 35 seconds later Ricky Hill unleashed a bullet shot that flew into the net from outside the area. Infuriatingly, the linesman flagged to indicate that Bob Hatton had strayed offside.

Ian Britton levelled for Chelsea shortly after the resumption. The visitors were then granted a penalty when Kirk Stephens handled an effort by Clive Walker. It took ferocious protests from Luton players to encourage the referee to go over to speak to his linesman, who confirmed that the ball had gone out of play and that he had signalled a throw-in before the penalty incident took place. So the score remained for the moment 2-2.

Moss headed home a long throw from Paul Price to put Luton's noses in front once more, only for Chelsea to level again in this topsy-turvy game when Clive Walker skipped through the Luton defence.

But Luton had one final arrow to fire, Donaghy heading against the bar in the closing seconds. The ball stayed out.

# LEAGUE DIVISION 2 1980-81

| | |
|---|---|
| Division 2 | 5th |
| League Cup | 3rd Round |
| FA Cup | 4th Round |

For the first time since David Pleat took over the hot seat at Kenilworth Road, the close season was relatively quiet on the transfer front. Veteran striker Bob Hatton, staying true to his 'much-travelled' tag, moved on to Sheffield United for £50,000, the same sum that he had cost the Town two years earlier. 'I only stay a couple of years at any club; otherwise I feel part of the furniture,' were Hatton's parting words.

Arriving in the opposite direction was the first of many players Pleat would eventually sign from abroad. Radomir Antic, a Yugoslav, was picked up from the Spanish side Real Zaragoza for £50,000. Pleat was impressed both by Antic's attitude and his ability, not to mention the wealth of experience he brought with him, having played club football in Yugoslavia, Turkey and Spain, not to mention having been capped by his country five times.

Off the pitch, and of greater importance to the club in the long term, was the decision by the local authority to proceed with the proposed Luton-Dunstable relief road. If completed, this highway would necessitate slicing through the rear of the stadium's main stand and lay waste to various function rooms, as well as disrupt access points and the already restricted parking available at the ground. Chief executive John Smith warned that if the scheme went ahead as planned, Luton Town FC would be in danger of folding, given the consequential loss of vital revenue-producing facilities.

Most fans, as they made their way to West Ham for the opening game of the season, were probably unaware of the potential severity of these problems and how they would intensify over the coming years. The Hammers paraded the FA Cup around Upton Park before the game to ecstatic applause and, fired by their raucous backing they ripped into the Luton rearguard from the start. They broke through via the penalty spot but the Hatters were made of stern stuff and fought back to take both points, with two penalties of their own, in what was one of the shock results of the day.

Teams do not always get their just desserts. This was evidenced in Luton's next two matches. The run of the ball certainly favoured the Hatters when defeating arch-enemies Watford, but the boot was on the other foot four days later when Derby stole the points, again at Kenilworth Road. This spread of uneven results would typify the unfolding season, as the players tried to rid themselves of the injustice of being denied promotion the previous spring.

Indeed, such lingering frustrations were the only logical explanation as to why the team should plummet to nineteenth by the middle of October. Luton won only one of ten games, and in a particularly traumatic spell lost three matches in the space of seven days.

Emergency measures were called for. Pleat rushed to buy Andy Harrow from Raith Rovers for £50,000 in an attempt to boost the forward line. But Harrow did not fit the bill and was soon on his way back to Scotland. Alex Ferguson wanted him for Aberdeen and paid enough to recoup Luton's outlay, though Harrow was no more of a hit with the Dons than with the Hatters. With everyone at Kenilworth Road at their wits' end, the patient suddenly cured itself, as often happens in the bewildering sport of football. The same players who could not stop losing, suddenly and with no obvious cause, could not stop winning.

The turnaround in fortunes can be traced to a win at Cambridge at the end of October, where the players had to dig in and find extra supplies of courage after goalkeeper Jake Findlay was carried off with broken ribs. Although the Town were 2-1 ahead at the time of the incident, they had already employed their substitute and in a backs-to-the-wall display managed to protect makeshift goalkeeper Mal Donaghy, even finding time to break out to score a third goal.

That victory seemed to galvanise the players and the following week they trounced Sheffield Wednesday 3-0 in a performance that had the supporters wondering what all the fuss had been about. A gradual push up the table followed, with wins over West Ham – who had remained unbeaten since the Town's victory at Upton Park on the opening day – Watford at Vicarage Road, followed by four victories in a row during December. New Year dawned to find Luton in sixth position.

Ricky Hill was buzzing, showing silky-smooth midfield skills that were bringing calls for international recognition. Brian Stein – after a sluggish start to the campaign following the departure of his mentor, Hatton – was now banging in the goals. Defensively the team had more backbone, and though Mike Saxby had yet to show the consistency of the previous season, his defensive partner, Paul Price, was quietly sweeping up alongside full-backs Kirk Stephens and Mal Donaghy.

Defeat at home to Grimsby in late-February dashed the promotion aspirations, at least according to those supporters of pessimistic disposition. An unexpected win at second-placed Notts County, where Pleat played Antic as a sweeper, raised hopes once more, only for them to be dashed again following a 1-3 reversal at Sheffield Wednesday. Easter then produced three straight wins to shoot the team up to third place, the highest of the campaign. This mini-run commenced with a 3-0 home win over QPR, when Ricky Hill played like the England international he was destined to become, and was followed by a tight 1-0 victory over relegation-threatened Bristol Rovers and a comfortable 2-0 win at Chelsea.

The bubble burst in the next game, at home to Oldham, just as the fans had been lulled into thoughts of happy expectancy. In a bad-tempered affair, the Latics won 2-1, with the scorer of both Oldham goals, Rodger Wylde, lucky not to have been expelled following an elbowing offence in front of the referee.

The last two games saw the Town gain a hard-earned point at Swansea and then finish off the season in style, winning 3-0 at Bolton and giving supporters a taste of things to come as Pleat made plans to ensure it would be third-time-lucky for promotion.

The cups were again a source of disenchantment, with Manchester City displaying their superiority in the League Cup and Newcastle, backed by a passionate crowd, making sure that the Town would advance no further than Round 4 in the FA Cup.

## Match of the Season 1980-81

### Luton Town 3 West Ham 2

Division 2, 15 November 1980

The Town had kicked off the campaign by winning at promotion favourites and FA Cup holders West Ham, but, in the wake of that shock result Luton's form had turned sour and by the middle of October they were hovering above the relegation places.

West Ham had no such worries and quickly put that early defeat behind them. By the time of the return fixture they had gone fifteen games without defeat, winning eleven, and in their most recent match had thumped Bristol City 5-0.

The scent of revenge therefore dominated West Ham's team-talks. The biggest crowd of Luton's season, including a large influx from East London, packed Kenilworth Road to see whether the opening-day win was a fluke or if the Town could maintain their recent revival and inflict upon the Hammers' their second defeat of the campaign.

On a chill, damp day the Town amazed their followers by taking a two-goal lead while late-comers were still queuing outside. Brian Stein smacked in a low shot after Steve White had played the ball into his path, and followed up by taking advantage of Billy Bonds'

**DID YOU KNOW?**

**Former Luton favourite Graham French turned out twice for Southport in 1975. He used the assumed name of 'Lafite'.**

slackness to score a second from a narrow angle. The little men on Kenilworth Road's new £100,000 electronic scoreboard danced with delight.

To their credit, the Hammers fought back from these early shocks, gaining the ascendancy and pulling a goal back just before half-time, when Trevor Brooking scored with a close-range header.

It was level pegging early in the second period when Brooking, taking advantage of several rebounds, scuffed the ball into the net. Luton supporters feared the worst, but surprisingly the Hatters found their second wind. The remainder of the game was an end-to-end struggle on a pitch that deteriorated more and more into a swamp.

The final twist came with five minutes remaining. David Moss, who until then had been well manacled, took advantage of a misdirected Ricky Hill header to slam the ball into the net and send the home supporters wild.

West Ham were destined to lose only two more fixtures that season, on their way to the championship, which made the Hatters' double all the more impressive.

# LEAGUE DIVISION 2 1981-82

| | |
|---|---|
| Division 2 | 1st (champions) |
| League Cup | 2nd Round |
| FA Cup | 4th Round |

After the narrow misses of the two previous seasons, David Pleat was hoping for third time lucky. In view of what lay in store, it must be said his summer transfer dealings baffled many supporters and appeared to make a mockery of the manager's aspirations. Local boy Paul Price, for example, who had been at Kenilworth Road since leaving school, was allowed to go, signing for Tottenham for £250,000, while former skipper Alan West moved to Millwall for £45,000.

By far the most inexplicable transfer – as it seemed at the time – involved a swap, plus cash adjustment, with Brighton. Republic of Ireland international Tony Grealish moved to the Goldstone Ground with veteran Brian Horton coming the other way. As it turned out, the supporters were wrong to doubt Pleat's judgment. Horton proved to be the final piece in the jigsaw, whilst Price and West were rarely missed.

The season opened with a home game against newly promoted Charlton and, in a one-sided affair, the Town won 3-0 at a canter. QPR in midweek proved to be a much tougher proposition, largely because it was the first Football League game to be played on an artificial surface. At half-time the Hatters trudged off one goal in arrears, with the players probably cursing the pitch, but in the second period, when they had acclimatised and realised there was nothing to fear, their superior technique turned the game around. Goals from Mark Aizlewood and a screamer from Ricky Hill secured a famous victory.

After winning at Bolton in game three, the Town were sitting proudly at the top of the table. In this they were aided by a change in the rules, which now awarded three points for a win instead of two. Alas, much of the good work was undone when Sheffield Wednesday visited Kenilworth Road. They hammered the Hatters 3-0, reminding the players to keep their feet on the ground.

The unpredictable early season form continued with a 2-1 win at Leicester followed by a 2-3 home defeat by a resolute Cardiff City side. Following this latest setback David Pleat exhibited no outward sign of nerves. In fact, he persevered with the same squad of twelve players four days later when the Town tackled Watford at Kenilworth Road.

**DID YOU KNOW?**

**When Luton beat Shrewsbury at home in April 1982, it was the first time they had clinched promotion at Kenilworth Road since 1937.**

In a sparkling performance, the Hatters ripped into the Hornets, finding themselves 3-0 up at half-time and going on to record a 4-1 victory, the biggest margin between the two rivals since 1936. A weight seemed to be lifted from the players' minds, with the home hangover seemingly cured. Luton were destined to stay undefeated at Kenilworth Road in the league for the rest of the campaign.

The 100% away record continued with a 3-0 win at Orient, only to be surrendered in a 1-1 draw at Oldham. Grimsby were battered 6-0 at Kenilworth Road, with Steve White scoring four and silencing the barrackers who had questioned his ability, before the Town won at Wrexham for the first time ever, avenging a home defeat at the hands of the Welshmen in the League Cup.

Sailing away clear at the top of the table, the Hatters seemed without a care in the world, but an injury to defensive rock Mike Saxby in the home fixture with Crystal Palace threatened to undermine all Pleat's plans. Twisting sharply in the penalty area, Saxby slumped in a heap and the later diagnosis of cruciate ligament damage meant that his playing days at Kenilworth Road were over.

Luckily, Pleat had a ready made replacement in Clive Goodyear who, after a shaky start, settled comfortably into the slot alongside Northern Ireland international Mal Donaghy. Goodyear was blameless when the Town finally surrendered their unbeaten away record at Newcastle at the end of November.

By Christmas, following a 3-1 win at Norwich when the Town scored three times in the opening fifteen minutes, they had opened up a gap of eleven points over the fourth-placed side. With a game in hand, too, Luton seemed to be romping towards the title. The settled side was playing smooth, free-flowing football and it was difficult to see which of their rivals might be able to sustain a challenge to their dominance.

Brian Horton was nothing less than a revelation, using his vast experience to bind the midfield together. Leading by example, as well as playing a holding role, he allowed Ricky Hill to venture forward, safe in the knowledge that no holes would open behind him. On the left, the swift interplay between Lil Fuccillo and David Moss set up goals a-plenty for Steve White, whilst on the right, Hill and Brian Stein enjoyed a similar telepathic understanding.

Defensively, Kirk Stephens and Mal Donaghy provided cover for the emerging Goodyear, and keeper Jake Findlay offered a stout defence of his goal to anyone who broke through. The only doubts in Pleat's mind appeared to concern the left-back position: the supporters sensed that the manager was not entirely reassured by the defensive qualities of Mark Aizlewood.

After the Norwich win, inclement weather curtailed all but two league games until the end of January. The FA Cup began with a fortuitous win over Swindon, followed by a home thumping by Division 1 table-toppers Ipswich, who emphasised the gulf that divided the top two divisions.

The Town then hit another rocky patch, but such was the inherent quality in the side that only one loss was suffered in this period, 3-4 at Barnsley. To the supporters, who had become a touch blasé perhaps, a run of five games without a win seemed little short of calamitous.

Fortunately the indifferent run ended with a string of home wins. Top sides Blackburn, Norwich and Newcastle were all sent packing in quick succession. The run coincided with the purchase of Richard Money from Liverpool, to replace Mark Aizlewood at left-back.

Seen in retrospect, those three home wins were decisive in clinching promotion. A tough Blackburn side who took no prisoners, a Norwich outfit coming up fast on the rails, and a Newcastle team that sat back to try to protect a two-goal lead, each came unstuck at Kenilworth Road as the Hatters turned on the heat.

A 2-2 draw at Rotherham, where stand-in goalkeeper Alan Judge saved a last-minute penalty, meant that a win at home to struggling Shrewsbury the following Friday night would guarantee promotion. In a tense game the floodgates opened and the fans surged onto the pitch to signal a 4-1 victory and promotion back to the top flight.

The championship itself was secured two weeks later with a 3-2 home win over FA Cup finalists QPR. At the conclusion of a long but enjoyable campaign, David Pleat had stuck to his guns and won promotion with style, the way he had always advocated.

## *Match of the Season 1981-82*

### Luton Town 4 Shrewsbury Town 1

Division 2, 30 April 1982

All the trials and tribulations of the past three seasons were about to be distilled into 90 minutes of football. One more win and Luton were up. Following near misses in 1979-80 and 1980-81, the Town had swept to the top of the table in early October and, apart from a three-day spell in late March, had remained there ever since.

Luton's form before Christmas had opened up clear sky at the top. The second half of the season had witnessed too many draws, but taking the wider picture, the team was merely following the proven route to success – winning at home and drawing away.

Graham Turner's Shrewsbury, the visitors to Kenilworth Road on a warm Friday evening, were battling at the wrong end of the table and needed points for a different reason. They were quickest to settle against a nervous Town side, but lacked the thrust necessary to worry the home crowd and players.

The first goal came after fourteen minutes when Brian Stein, seizing upon a poor back-pass from Shrews' Colin Griffin, lobbed the ball over keeper Bob Wardle. Frustration then set in as the Town were unable to grab a second goal. A mixture of poor finishing and sound goalkeeping thwarted the Luton forwards, and the equaliser thrashed home by Ian Atkins on the hour had an air of inevitability about it.

Home supporters had become resigned to the fact that it was going to be 'one of those nights' when Player of the Year Ricky Hill volleyed in a headed pass from Mal Donaghy. The goal stemmed from a corner with just twelve minutes remaining, and now the sluice-gates opened. With the tension visibly lifted, individual efforts from Steve White and David Moss gave the final scoreline a look that seemed impossible a few minutes earlier. It was probably undeserved by battling Shrewsbury. The supporters cared little – the Hatters were up!

Shrewsbury finished eighteenth, escaping relegation by two points.

# LEAGUE DIVISION 1 1982-83

| | |
|---|---|
| Division 1 | 18th |
| Milk Cup | 4th Round |
| FA Cup | 4th Round |

Managers of promoted sides invariably say that they will give the existing players a chance to prove themselves in the higher sphere, and David Pleat was no exception to this rule. Only one significant purchase was made during the close season, when highly rated youngster Paul Walsh was enticed from Charlton.

Unfortunately, Walsh's transfer came with a high price-tag, as Charlton demanded Steve White as part of the deal. White, who had commanded eighteen league goals as the Town raced to the title, was naturally crestfallen, having yearned to have a crack at playing at the highest level. David Pleat, however, was determined not to lose Walsh, so White was sacrificed.

Walsh's arrival meant that the Hatters now boasted two nimble, ball-playing forwards, and Walsh's proposed partnership with Brian Stein meant dispensing with the services of a big target man. This raised a few eyebrows amongst supporters, even though they appreciated it was in keeping with the vision of football that Pleat had always preached.

The Town's first game back amongst the elite of football was at White Hart Lane against FA Cup holders Tottenham. In baking hot conditions Spurs ripped through the Luton defence to take an early two-goal lead. Refusing to accept the inevitable, the Hatters fought back to earn a creditable 2-2 draw, but this achievement was undone when West Ham visited Kenilworth Road three days later and handed out a lesson in how to take chances in the big league.

After a tentative start, Paul Walsh soon showed the Luton supporters why David Pleat had gambled so much money on him. He netted a stunning hat-trick in a 5-3 home victory over Notts County, one of his efforts being an early contender for goal of the season.

Following a 1-4 setback at European Cup holders Aston Villa, the Hatters drew 3-3 at Liverpool – in a remarkable game that saw the Reds score against three different goalkeepers – before thumping a poor Brighton side at home 5-0.

The pattern was now set for the season, with the Town infuriatingly unpredictable, likely to score goals in abundance but just as likely to concede even more. This was typified by the clash at Stoke, where the final whistle sounded to a 4-4 draw, the Hatters even contriving to miss a late penalty.

The media was now beginning to sit up and take notice of Luton's goal frenzy, and television companies started to follow the Hatters' matches with unprecedented enthusiasm – the obvious reason being that games involving Luton were packed with incident and, more often than not, awash with goals.

By the middle of October, following a 3-2 win at Birmingham, the Town had climbed up to eighth position, but a subsequent run of eight games without a win sent them tumbling back again. Hopes of an extended run in the League Cup ended in a narrow defeat at Tottenham in Round 4.

The dismal league spell ended with a 3-1 home victory over Manchester City, then in tenth position, but was achieved at a heavy cost. Leading scorer Brian Stein broke a bone in his foot, which virtually finished his season. Stein had forged an effective strike partnership with Walsh, and Luton were now to discover that they had little strength in depth in this department. The lack of alternative options placed a huge burden on the shoulders of young Walsh, and more was also expected from veteran David Moss, as well as from Ricky Hill – who had finally earned his first England cap.

Inconsistent results over the Christmas period did little to help the Town's cause, with a 0-5 capitulation at Everton followed by a merited 1-0 home win over high-flying Watford. Defeats at Norwich and at home to Coventry were succeeded by a thrilling 3-2 victory at West Ham, when Paul Walsh scored a hat-trick with the winner coming in the last minute.

FA Cup ambitions foundered early, with Manchester United too professional and powerful at Kenilworth Road, whilst in the league, away wins at Brighton and Nottingham Forest seemed to arrest the slide. In an effort to bolster the forward line, Pleat introduced David Geddis, on loan from Aston Villa, and then turned to Steve White – sold to Charlton pre-season – to permit him a belated stab at Division 1 football. Sadly, neither loan solved the problem.

Pleat had no choice but to buy. Paul Elliott came from Charlton for £100,000 to replace the unfortunate Clive Goodyear – who seemed to be singled out for blame for the team's defensive lapses – and £50,000 was paid for big centre-forward Trevor Aylott from Millwall. Aylott's signing signalled a shift, temporarily perhaps, in Pleat's philosophy – tall, strong strikers seemed anathema to his preferred style. But at least it presented him with a variety of attacking options.

Unfortunately, these signings coincided with a string of four defeats, culminating in a 2-5 reversal at Watford that gave the Hornets their first win over the old enemy in nine attempts. Luton's needle had now dipped into the red zone: they were bottom of the table and could go no lower.

Despite the result at Vicarage Road, astute supporters detected the germ of a revival in the performance. Their optimism was borne out in the next game when a last-minute winner from David Moss accounted for Aston Villa at Kenilworth Road. This was the start of a run of six games without defeat, which gradually hoisted the team back up the table. Following a home draw with Stoke at the beginning of May, the Town occupied the heady heights of sixteenth.

Three points from the final home fixture, against Everton, would virtually guarantee safety after an arduous campaign. But, after scoring first through Ricky Hill, the Town disintegrated and conceded five goals. Matters were exacerbated when other results came through: each of Luton's fellow strugglers had won, dumping the Hatters back into the drop zone.

The Town had just two games left, both away. In the first, their injury-weakened side was rolled over by Manchester United, leaving a do-or-die battle against Manchester City to determine the final relegation place. That game would write a page in the annals of Luton history and provide TV viewers across the land with the glorious sight of one of soccer's great impromptu dances.

## *Match of the Season 1982-83*

### Manchester City 0 Luton Town 1

Division 1, 14 May 1983

Bottom of the table at Easter, the Town showed commendable resolve in clawing their way back up with a six-match unbeaten run. The final home game against Everton was meant to be a carnival affair, as three points would more or less ensure safety. As already noted, the fates conspired otherwise. Now, only a win at Maine Road on the final Saturday would save the Town from relegation. Spice was added to the fixture because of Manchester City's own plight. These perennial giants were in the mire themselves, one place above the Hatters and needing to draw to stay there. In short, City needed to draw; Luton to win. At the final whistle, one team would rejoice, the other would weep. Not surprisingly, the eyes of the footballing world descended on Maine Road, expecting – and receiving – gladiatorial drama.

Luton's players were surprisingly upbeat, rather more so than the supporters and the manager, it would appear. More than 5,000 Luton fans descended on Manchester, boosting the attendance to a massive 42,843.

**DID YOU KNOW?**

**In the opening fixture of three consecutive seasons – 1981-82, 1982-83 and 1983-84 – opponents gifted Luton with an own-goal.**

The fact that John Benson's City needed only a point probably acted in the Town's favour, as the home side instinctively sat back throughout a sterile first-half. In the second period the Town had no option but to push forward but, with the minutes ticking away, they had still failed to create a golden opportunity to score. Pleat sent on Raddy Antic to replace the tiring Wayne Turner and, with just five minutes to go, the Yugoslav scored one of the most precious goals in the Town's history.

Brian Stein, playing his first game for three months, squeezed in a cross at the second attempt. The ball was punched out by City goalkeeper Alex Williams straight to Antic. The Yugoslav hit it first-time into the net via Williams' cruel deflection, which carried the ball wide of defenders deployed on the goal-line, and who otherwise would have cleared.

The remaining minutes seemed like an eternity to both sides, but when the moment came, and the referee blew, David Pleat danced his now-famous jig across the pitch in celebration. He commented later: 'I'm not a religious man but perhaps someone up there decided that justice should be done.'

Raddy Antic became an instant folk-hero in Luton, whose better players – Ricky Hill, Brian Stein and Mal Donaghy – certainly did not deserve to suffer relegation. The Hatters lived to fight another day, albeit a little wiser.

# CANON DIVISION 1 1983-84

| | |
|---|---|
| Canon League Division 1 | 16th |
| Milk Cup | 2nd Round |
| FA Cup | 3rd Round |

After the hair-raising escape from relegation, David Pleat would have been forgiven spending the summer trying to get his breath back. Though determined to avoid a repetition, for health reasons as much as anything, he decided his existing squad was well enough equipped not to need reinforcements. Its blend of youth and experience, buttressed by the best of John Moore's promising youth team, which had reached the semi-final of the FA Youth Cup, ought to be able to withstand further attacks of relegation jitters.

The local press, meanwhile, carried stories regarding the club's proposed move to Milton Keynes, following the failure of the board and the local authority to find a suitable alternative site within the Luton boundaries. Various factions were determined to block the move and were busy mobilising for action. Threats of a boycott of home games were being aired even before a ball was kicked in anger.

The playing season opened at Arsenal and on a hot summer's day and in front of a shirt-sleeved crowd the Town did as well as could be expected but lost 1-2. Big wins over Leicester, Sunderland and Wolves followed and by the end of October the Hatters had moved up to fourth place in the table.

Forwards Brian Stein and Paul Walsh had started the season in fine fettle, Ricky Hill was showing international class in midfield, with Mal Donaghy and Paul Elliott forming a solid bond in central defence.

This early season promise was typified by a sparkling 3-1 home win over a powerful Southampton side with everyone in the team turning on the style. Brian Stein's scoring volley would have been a contender for Goal of the Season had it been televised nationally. Not surprisingly, the Hatters were in confident mood when they travelled to Anfield to take on a Liverpool side en route to another championship. Liverpool were not inclined to take it easy and their 6-0 win hurt badly, not least because Ian Rush was allowed to create his own personal landmark, scoring five goals. It is testimony to Liverpool's omnipotence at that time, as well as Luton's powers of recovery, that the Hatters overcame QPR 1-0 at Loftus Road the following week.

David Moss's pelvic injury would keep him out until the end of March. His absence certainly affected the team, though they performed well enough until the end of the year, fortified by away wins at Watford, Stoke and Notts County. Heavy home defeats by Tottenham and Coventry, however, left Pleat tearing his hair out, as the old defensive frailty raised its ugly head again.

The 3-0 win at Notts County on Boxing Day hoisted the Town into third place, but that would mark their zenith this season. The fall from bronze medal position was rapid and spectacular. Next day West Ham departed from Kenilworth Road clutching all three points, and a run of a further three defeats triggered the Hatters' slide down the table.

Emeka Nwajiobi, a 24-year-old pharmacist playing non-league football only a couple of months earlier, made his debut in the 2-3 home defeat by Nottingham Forest but had the consolation of scoring. He retained his place for two epic struggles with Watford in the FA Cup, which saw the Hornets triumph 4-3 – after extra-time in a replay. With that, Luton's season effectively died.

The loss of form can be attributed to several causes. The anti-Milton Keynes lobby was beginning to exert itself during home games and no doubt even the most thick-skinned player was distracted by the demonstrations. A long-term injury to Ricky Hill deprived the midfield of much-needed creativity. David Moss's injury also closed down an attacking option, which meant that Brian Stein often had to forsake his central role in order to forage down the wing. Paul Walsh was the subject of press gossip about a move to Liverpool, Manchester United or even a top Italian club, which reached such a crescendo that his head started to spin. Finally, England international call-ups for Walsh and Stein came at an inopportune time from Luton's point of view. Nor did the duo do themselves justice wearing the Three Lions, as the England team came badly unstuck against France in Paris. Post-match inquests were particularly harsh on Stein, in particular, which did little to reinvigorate his club form.

Between Boxing Day and the end of the season Luton played 23 games, won just three, drew seven, and lost thirteen – relegation form in anyone's language. A humiliating 0-5 home defeat by Manchester United, in the first live televised league game to involve Luton Town, vividly illustrated the depths to which the Hatters had sunk.

During these dark days the only bright spots were the debuts of youngsters such as Rob Johnson, Tim Breacker, Stacey North and Mark Stein, all of whom were catapulted into the first team earlier than Pleat would ideally have preferred. Those young players who were barely a rung or two further up the ladder – Gary Parker and Mitchell Thomas – were now looked upon as seasoned campaigners. Pleat was not happy, having to play so many youngsters match after match, and doubtless would have avoided doing so, given a full squad from which to choose.

With five games to go the Town were too close to the relegation zone for comfort, especially as, given their current form, it was difficult to see where the next win would come from. Notts County, no less desperate for points themselves, journeyed to Luton in late April. The Hatters were overdue some luck, and it duly arrived in the dying seconds when Frank Bunn's goal brought a 3-2 victory. Those three points were enough to ensure First Division football for another season.

The close season saw the granting of free transfers to Brian Horton and Raddy Antic, together with the inevitable transfer of Paul Walsh, which meant that another era had closed at Kenilworth Road, with a new one about to dawn.

## Match of the Season 1983-84

### Watford 4 Luton Town 3

FA Cup, 3rd Round replay, 10 January 1984

After three straight league defeats the Town looked forward to an FA Cup Third Round pairing with Watford as a way of getting back to winning ways. At the time, the Hatters held an 'Indian sign' over the Hornets.

The original tie at Kenilworth Road could have gone either way, with Watford having the better of the first half and Luton the second. Perversely, four goals were scored in the first period with both of Luton's coming via deflections to frustrate Watford. By full-time, both sides felt that they had deserved to win, the replay being scheduled for Vicarage Road on the following Tuesday. The Town would be without Ricky Hill, who was suffering from what was later diagnosed as a calcified hamstring, and his place went to Gary Parker.

If the supporters thought the first game was a thriller, then the replay was a classic, fought between two sides adhering to contrasting philosophies. Nigel Callaghan gave the Hornets an early lead, which was increased against the run of play when George Reilly scored with a soft header. Just before the interval Mal Donaghy's shot deceived Hornets goalkeeper Steve Sherwood to reduce the deficit. With the Town chasing the game, Watford increased their lead with a cracker from John Barnes.

**DID YOU KNOW?**

**Between 26 February 2002 and 20 April 2002, Luton won SIX away league games in succession. This is an all-time record for the club.**

The Town had no option but to throw caution to the wind, and with Brian Stein dragging the Watford defence all over the place, Paul Walsh scored two goals to level the scores.

Extra-time saw the initiative swing back towards the hosts, thanks largely to injuries that left Brian Horton limping with a bruised shin and Trevor Aylott reduced to a passenger on the flank. The winning goal had an air of inevitability about it and was scored by Mo Johnson. Watford finished the game physically stronger, but grateful that Luton had not been able to put away late chances that came their way.

England manager Bobby Robson, who had come along to watch Stein, Walsh and John Barnes said afterwards: 'A marvellous match and a marvellous occasion.'

Graham Taylor's Watford reached Wembley that season, where they lost to Everton.

# CANON DIVISION 1 1984-85

| | |
|---|---|
| Canon League Division 1 | 13th |
| Milk Cup | 4th Round |
| FA Cup | Semi-final |

The summer transfer sagas took a new twist in 1984 with both Aston Villa and QPR approaching the Luton board to try to entice away the manager. David Pleat was sufficiently ambitious to have meetings with both clubs but sufficiently wise to reject them. He agreed for the moment to stay at Kenilworth Road, much to the relief of chairman Denis Mortimer.

Pleat, though, would have to do without Paul Walsh, who was sold to Liverpool for £750,000, the biggest fee Luton had ever received for one player. The club's bankers demanded the whole amount to reduce the overdraft, and were displeased to learn that Pleat had already gone on a spending spree, signing Vince Hilaire from Crystal Palace, Andy Dibble from Cardiff, Ashley Grimes from Coventry and Steve Elliott from Preston. In mitigation, the club pointed out that Kirk Stephens had departed to Coventry as part of the Grimes deal, and that the overall wage bill had been reduced when Raddy Antic and Brian Horton left at the end of the previous season on free transfers.

The mood among supporters regarding the club moving to Milton Keynes was no sweeter. Their boycott of home matches continued to bite, and the lowest opening-day crowd for five years saw the Town easily brush aside dreadful Stoke. The result flattered no one, nor did a subsequent draw at Ipswich, for Luton's frailties were there for all to see. Too many boys were being asked to do men's work, they had insufficient experience around them on the pitch, and the team had no recognised target man.

The sceptics were proved right when the Town laboured through September without a win. A third straight victory on QPR's Omniturf in early October, together with a 3-2 home win over Watford, did little to alleviate Luton's precarious league position.

Steve Elliott, a summer signing from Preston, looked out of his depth in the top division, which meant that goals were always liable to be at a premium this season. When namesake Paul, who had been one of the Town's few early season successes, broke a leg in a Milk Cup-tie against Leicester, the spine of Luton's team finally shattered.

In desperation, Pleat swooped to bring in giant centre-half Micky Droy, on loan from Chelsea, plus the experienced Colin Todd on a short-term contract. But Pleat was clutching at straws: his team went another six matches without a win. Only Stoke were now keeping the Town off the bottom of the league.

Kenilworth Road was not a happy place in the last months of 1984, and the directors bunkered in the boardroom even quarrelled among themselves. Chairman Denis Mortimer resigned, sick to the teeth with the personal abuse heaped on his shoulders in the wake of the Milton Keynes saga. He was replaced by entrepreneur David Evans, who immediately set about reorganising the club's finances to make money available to David Pleat.

Evans declared boldly that, come what may, the Town would not be relegated and Pleat, who needed no second invitation, dashed out to buy ex-England international centre-half Steve Foster. The head-banded Foster had been dropped to the reserves at Aston Villa and made his Luton debut in a 1-3 defeat at Arsenal.

The following week, Pleat introduced David Preece, signed from Walsall for £150,000 with Steve Elliott going to Fellows Park in part-exchange, and the tiny left-sided midfielder scored the only goal as the Town beat Aston Villa to clock up only the fourth victory of the season. A massive £250,000 was then spent on centre-forward Mick Harford from Birmingham, and Harford wasted no time repaying a slice of his fee when scoring an injury-time equaliser at Leicester on his debut.

Pleat had stiffened the team's spine, his first priority, and now needed a midfield anchorman to complete his immediate rebuilding programme. He got his man when Peter Nicholas was prised away from Second Division Crystal Palace.

The four newcomers played together for the first time in the home game against Tottenham in early February. They clicked at once, making the Town overnight a much tougher proposition. Encouraged by joyful supporters – celebrating the New Towns Commission's rejection of the club's plans to re-locate to Milton Keynes – the Hatters held title-chasing Spurs to a 2-2 draw. One swallow does not make a summer, however, and relegation still hovered ominously. But gradually the points started to come, enabling Luton to gain ground on the teams above them.

Just when David Pleat could have done without it, the FA Cup intervened. It is a moot point whether in the circumstances Pleat would have welcomed an early exit. But Luton kept up their new-found winning ways, bundling out Stoke and Huddersfield before finding themselves paired with Watford in Round 5. The tie required three games to separate the sides, this time with the Town triumphant, exacting revenge on the Hornets for the previous season's cup defeat. Luton's reward was a quarter-final home tie against Millwall from Division 3 and, on a night remembered for all the wrong reasons, with images of lunatic pitch invasions transmitted around the world, it appeared almost incidental that the Town squeezed through to the semi-finals.

Cup runs, even long ones, are worthless if the end product is relegation, and Pleat made no secret of his anxieties in this regard. Fortunately for the divided loyalties of manager and players, Luton won three vital relegation matches – against QPR, struggling Ipswich and doomed Stoke – before the semi-final at Villa Park against treble-chasing Everton.

The mid-season signings of so many important players, most of whom were cup-tied, meant that Pleat's 'cup team' was significantly different from his league side. The cup eleven included Gary Parker and local boy Wayne Turner, both of whom had been dropped from the league team to make way for Preece and Nicholas. In the semi-final the Hatters came within an ace of beating the Toffees. Only a late, disputed free-kick enabled the favourites to draw level before going on to win in extra-time.

Allowed to concentrate on the league, the Town bounced back to defeat Norwich and Manchester United at home, the latter result bringing belated revenge for the previous season's thrashing. Wins at home to Arsenal and away at Aston Villa in early May virtually ensured safety, and by the end of the campaign the supporters were left wondering what all the worry had been about.

The mid-season signings were obviously vital, as it was difficult to envisage how the pre-Christmas squad would have picked up the necessary points to guarantee survival. The new boys had fitted in superbly; in central defence Foster and Donaghy formed as good a partnership as any in the country, whilst up front Harford and Stein did likewise. David Preece laid claim to the problematic left side midfield position, leaving Peter Nicholas to hold everything in place around him.

## Match of the Season 1984-85

### Everton 2 Luton Town 1

FA Cup, Semi-final, 13 April 1985

Luton's FA Cup run of 1984-85 was almost a non-starter when lowly Stoke scored at Kenilworth Road with only a few minutes left to play, leaving Steve Foster to rescue the Hatters at the death. This set the Town up for a sprint through to the quarter-finals, where they were paired at home with Millwall of Division 3 in a game marred by so-called supporters of the Lions. The record books show

**DID YOU KNOW?**

**Mal Donaghy won 58 caps for Northern Ireland while a Luton Town player. This is by far and away a club record for caps earned for any country.**

that the Town won the tie, courtesy of a slickly taken Brian Stein goal. The Hatters were now in the semi-final for the first time since 1959.

Opponents Everton were well clear in the race for the league championship. They had also fought their way through to the Cup Winners' Cup semi-final and had every intention of retaining the FA Cup which they had won the previous May at the expense of Watford.

If league form was any guide, the outcome was a foregone conclusion, though Luton had stabilised of late, largely thanks to four recent signings. Two of these were cup-tied, leaving places available to Gary Parker and Wayne Turner as the Town reverted to their 'cup team'.

The 18,000 Luton supporters at Villa Park watched with bated breath as their cobbled-together side took the game to the Toffees. Luton might have been three goals ahead at the interval, with Emeka Nwajiobi the player guilty of the worst misses. The Hatters did, however, score a cracker through Ricky Hill, which flew in off a post after good work from Mick Harford.

Everton came into it a shade more in the second period but the Town defence appeared to be holding firm. When a rainbow appeared in the Birmingham sky with ten minutes remaining, Luton supporters felt this to be an omen. Unfortunately, the rainbow was meant for Everton. With five minutes to play Mick Harford gave away a disputed free-kick, which was powered in by Kevin Sheedy to bring about extra-time.

The Toffees imposed themselves in the extra half-hour and scored the winner with a header from Derek Mountfield. The Town could claim to be moral victors, as confirmed by the press and television afterwards. Whether the price of reaching Wembley would have been relegation was a question that would never be answered.

## CANON DIVISION 1 1985-86

| | |
|---|---|
| Canon League Division 1 | 9th |
| Milk Cup | 3rd Round |
| FA Cup | Quarter-finals |

David Pleat breathed a deep sigh of relief, not needing to be told that his mid-season signings had saved his bacon. But those players were vital not just in the short term but also in the long. His toughest task now was to warn off predatory clubs, and to keep his battle-hardened team together as long as he could. He had, for example, to withstand intense press speculation about the futures of Ricky Hill and Brian Stein, who were both out of contract, but the pair eventually decided that their best interests were served by staying put. Pleat also made overtures to sign Frank McAvennie from St Mirren, as a contingency plan, should his persuasive powers fail with Hill and Stein, but the Scot opted for West Ham, whom he joined for £340,000.

In the wake of the Millwall fiasco the football authorities acted in haste, demanding that Luton erect fences around the pitch. Given the layout of the stadium, this would have ruined the view of patrons in the low-slung Bobbers Stand, and representations from the board obliged the authorities to repent at leisure. The stadium was already undergoing major changes, installing for example a new artificial surface, only the second in the country. Luton hoped manufacturing advances could counter the exaggerated bounce experienced on the Omniturf at QPR. However, the bedding-in process took time. When the Town entertained Nottingham Forest on the opening day of the new season, spurts of sand shot into the air every time the ball was kicked.

Brian Stein had the honour of being the first player to score on the new surface, but Forest also seemed to relish the truer bounce, which encouraged precision passing, spoiling Luton's big day by equalising near the end.

Having to become acquainted with a new pitch to some extent nullified the advantage of playing at home. Luton found wins hard to come by, and by the time of Ipswich's visit in early October some supporters were voicing disquiet, predicting another relegation dogfight. Luton defeated Ipswich 1-0, but the turning point of the whole season came the following Saturday with the visit of Manchester United.

Ron Atkinson's United had won their first ten games and were attempting to equal the eleven-match winning run set by Tottenham at the start of the 1960-61 season. In front of the biggest crowd of the season, the Town never looked inferior, and if anything the draw flattered the visitors. But for an open goal, squandered by substitute Paul Elliott in the closing minutes, Luton might have secured a famous victory.

The season seemed to take off at this point and the next visitors, Southampton, were thrashed 7-0, with Brian Stein netting a hat-trick and England goalkeeper Peter Shilton being inconsolable at the end. The Town duly recorded their first win at Tottenham since 1948, and polished off Watford, Manchester City and Newcastle in quick succession.

Around this time a problem arose with the centre-half position. The problem was unusual in that it concerned not a shortage of top quality candidates, but an excess. Paul Elliott was now fully fit following the break to his leg twelve months previously. Naturally enough, he considered the number five shirt belonged to him and wanted it back. Unfortunately for Elliott, his replacement, Steve Foster, had recaptured the form that brought him international recognition by Ron Greenwood and a place in England's World Cup squad in 1982. A club of Luton's modest proportions could hardly hope to cling on to two star players vying for the same position, so when Aston Villa put in a handsome bid of £400,000 for Elliott, it was accepted.

By Christmas the upturn in Luton's fortunes meant that they were in the top ten, and this time looked likely to stay there. An easy win at struggling West Brom on Boxing Day was eclipsed by a 3-1 victory over Leicester on 1 January, with Mick Harford netting a hat-trick and demonstrating that in the long term he might be the ideal international striking partner for Gary Lineker.

But that was to be Harford's last game for some time, as cartilage problems soon necessitated an appointment with a surgeon's knife. Pleat's short-term solution was to sign Mike Newell from Wigan for £85,000. Newell would be justified in being miffed when Harford made a rapid recovery, reclaiming his place within a month.

Unlike the previous season, when the FA Cup was an irritation they could have done without, this time Luton looked upon it with relish. A potential upset was avoided when Crystal Palace were overcome at Selhurst Park, and in Round 4 Bristol Rovers were no match for the precision football played by the Town on their artificial surface. The pairing of the Hatters with Arsenal in Round 5 set the pulses racing, no more so than for Peter Nicholas, who had been discarded by the Gunners a couple of seasons previously.

The Town had recently lost at Highbury in a bruising league encounter, and the bad blood was evident in the cup-tie, which finished 2-2, with all the goals coming in the first half. Brian Stein suffered a knee injury in the game that would keep him sidelined for two months, but David Pleat now had a ready-made replacement waiting in the wings, in the shape of Stein's younger brother, Mark.

The replay, on an ice-rink of a pitch, finished goal-less after extra-time, requiring a second replay 48 hours later at Kenilworth Road. This time the Town triumphed 3-0 in what many supporters argue was probably David Pleat's finest moment at the club.

Cup-ties were coming thick and fast, with Everton the quarter-final visitors to Kenilworth Road just three days later. The Town looked to be on their way to avenging the previous season's semi-final defeat when taking a two-goal lead. But Everton were no pushovers. This, allied to the fact that the Town were playing their fourth game in a week, helped turn the tide in Everton's favour and the Toffees fought back to level at 2-2. In the replay the Hatters lost to a solitary Lineker goal, but not before they had caused a few scares amongst the Goodison faithful. Thoughts of Wembley were banished for another year.

Everton were punished in the most painful manner, for their league defeat at Kenilworth Road two weeks later ultimately cost them the championship. Luton's league season wound down to a gentle close, Harford netting his second hat-trick of the year in the 3-2 home win over Watford. It helped the Hatters to finish ninth, their highest position since 1958.

## Match of the Season 1985-86

**Luton Town 3 Arsenal 0**

FA Cup, 5th Round second replay, 5 March 1986

After two titanic cup struggles with the Gunners, the Town won the toss to decide the venue for the third game, which was to be played on Luton's artificial surface.

The first clash had ended 2-2 but the Hatters could justifiably claim that they were deserving winners with Arsenal on the rack for much of the second half. The first replay, delayed because of the weather, took place on a dangerous, icy Highbury pitch and this time it was Luton's turn to be hanging on by the end.

With the quarter-final ties scheduled for the following Saturday, the FA decreed that the second replay take place just two days after the first. With little time for proper preparations, the two teams squared up to one another for the fourth time in league or cup in little more than a month.

**DID YOU KNOW?**

**By 2004, Luton had sold 7 players for £1 million upwards – Gary Doherty, Matthew Upson, John Hartson, Paul Telfer, Mark Pembridge, Kingsley Black, and Roy Wegerle.**

Mark Stein was recalled from a loan spell at Aldershot, as replacement for the injured Marc North, in what would be his first game of the season, whilst the Gunners brought in Martin Hayes for Graham Rix.

First blood was drawn by the Town, thanks to a raging shot from skipper Steve Foster, following Andy King's corner. But it was in the second period that the Hatters really turned on the style. Mark Stein, out to prove a point, turned David O'Leary inside out and fired a shot that rebounded first off keeper Lukic, then the unfortunate O'Leary, and into the net. With their tails up, Luton were unstoppable, and it was no surprise when they added a third goal. Stein and Preece saw shots hit Lukic, with Stein finally scoring at the third attempt. David Pleat was to be seen jumping off the bench in delight, with goalkeeper Les Sealey careering around his penalty area, arms wide, making a passable impression of an aeroplane in flight.

Arsenal manager Don Howe offered no excuses and accepted that the Town were deserved winners. He resigned shortly afterwards, to usher in the George Graham era. For Luton supporters, their win was certainly the most invigorating of recent memory, and perhaps even the best recorded under David Pleat's eight-year reign.

# 4

# MOORE, HARFORD & RYAN – 1986-1991

## TODAY DIVISION 1 1986-87

| | |
|---|---|
| Today League Division 1 | 7th |
| Littlewoods Cup | Did not compete |
| FA Cup | 4th Round |

As the Town celebrated their highest league position since 1958, all seemed set fair for even greater triumphs, but then came the bombshell. Chairmen of successful smaller clubs live in dread of tremors at big ones. One labouring giant was Tottenham Hotspur, who took out their frustration on manager Peter Shreeve, sacked him, and promptly swooped for David Pleat.

Chairman David Evans did what he could to make Pleat stay, pointing out the obvious, that it is better to be a big fish in a small pond than a small fish in a lake, and that with Pleat at the helm Luton could blossom into a more powerful club than ailing Tottenham. Pleat did not need telling. Nor, after eight years in the job, did he need lessons in loyalty. Pleat weighed his options, and plumped for Spurs, taking assistant Trevor Hartley with him.

Coach John Moore was also invited to decamp to north London, but he declined, preferring to put his name forward for the vacant managership. Given Luton's recent policy of promoting from within, this seemed a shrewd decision. The board agreed and Moore, who had originally arrived at Luton as a player in 1965, was installed as the club's twelfth manager since World War II.

Moore lost no time appointing Fulham manager Ray Harford as his assistant, along with ex-Town winger Jim Ryan as coach. As is inevitable in these situations, the new boss faced an uncertain dressing room, the better players casting their eyes on the big lights and contemplating fatter pay-cheques that might be earned elsewhere. The first Luton player to be tempted was Mal Donaghy, for whom Chelsea were apparently willing to pay big money. Moore's persuasion paid off, and Donaghy agreed to stay, but the new manager was less successful with full-back Mitchell Thomas, partly because it was Spurs – and Pleat – who wanted him. For Thomas it was not so much a case of changing clubs as staying with the same manager. The transfer caused friction between Luton and their former boss, not for the act of taking Thomas but for the tribunal figure of a paltry £250,000. Everyone in football knew Thomas to be worth more than that. Luton had benefited many times in the past from Pleat's mastery of the intricacies of the tribunal system, and it hurt to find themselves on the receiving end for once.

In a summer of change, a roof was erected over the Kenilworth Road terrace, executive boxes were installed in the Bobbers Stand and membership cards issued to supporters. Of more pressing significance, however, was the decision to ban all away supporters, the first blanket ban ever imposed by a Football League club. The curse of Millwall's thugs made such a decision inevitable, or so the club argued, though its implementation was to cause Luton much grief as the season unfolded.

On the playing side, the Hatters had to kick off the campaign without the services of David Preece and Mick Harford, who was recovering from his second knee operation in six months, but they achieved a comfortable 1-1 draw at Leicester and a home win over Southampton. The forwards never looked like packing a punch, but compensation was found in the defence, which looked meaner than ever – a testament to John Moore's influence.

The first repercussions over the ban on away fans came when Luton were drawn to play Cardiff over two legs in the Littlewoods Cup. Luton's decision effectively prohibited a supposed 5,000 Welsh folk from seeing their little club compete against First Division opponents, albeit in a midweek Second Round cup-tie. Cardiff protested to the Football League, Luton refused to budge, whereupon they found themselves expelled from the competition.

In the league, fate conspired to ask Luton to tackle Manchester United and Liverpool back to back. Losing 0-1 at United was hard to take, especially as Brian Stein's penalty miss helped maintain Luton's Old Trafford hoodoo. Far from being downcast for the visit of Liverpool, the Town suddenly went goal crazy. Mike Newell, so often the butt of the crowd, who were quick to remind him that he was not Mick Harford, bagged a hat-trick as the Town won 4-1.

That result set up a run of four straight victories, culminating in a 4-2 home win over Nottingham Forest, with three Luton goals coming in the opening quarter.

With the two Stein brothers flanking Mike Newell up front, Harford was not missed as badly as was feared. In midfield, Ashley Grimes and new signing from Oldham, Darron McDonough, filled in well for the injured Preece and Ricky Hill. The backbone of the side, in more senses than one, was the defensive partnership between Steve Foster and Mal Donaghy, with Peter Nicholas playing just ahead of them. With Les Sealey performing as well in goal as he had ever done, it always looked as though it would take something special to break through Luton's rearguard.

After two further operations on his knee, Mick Harford finally returned, just before the year's end. The player dropped to make way was the unfortunate Mark Stein. Harford presided over three straight wins during January as well as three classic ties against Liverpool in the FA Cup. Under intense pressure from Liverpool, never mind the FA, Luton reluctantly agreed to permit some away supporters for the televised home clash with the Reds in Round 3, which ended goal-less. On the day of the replay, severe weather in the south threatened to close motorways leading north. Anticipating this, the club opted to fly the players up instead. But once they arrived at Heathrow they found that flights were grounded too. In short, there was no way to get to Liverpool in the time available.

The upshot was that the tie had to be called off at the eleventh hour, much to the irritation of Liverpool FC. Catering provisions were already in place, so countless thousand hot pies went to waste. Manager Kenny Dalglish publicly lambasted Luton, insisting that even amateur sides would have taken better precautions. With hindsight, the Town would have been wiser to travel up the day before. They had no one to blame but themselves, and such was the public scorn heaped upon them that the distressed John Moore contemplated resigning.

When the game was eventually played, the Hatters had to contend not merely with the best team in the land, but also with the derision of the Anfield crowd. It was therefore a fine achievement to keep the Liverpool forwards at bay for two hours, including extra-time. The second replay – the venue decided by the toss of a coin – was back at Kenilworth Road two days later. Luton trounced the Reds 3-0, the same margin as the league game back in October.

This time Dalglish was even more scathing in his condemnation. Unable to blame the weather, he turned his ire on Luton's pitch, which he held wholly accountable for Liverpool's exit from the competition. In the wake of Heysel, Dalglish was a much revered figure and his words won sympathy far and wide. Luton, for their part, were widely vilified, and the stigma of being among the most disliked clubs in the land would take years to shake off.

That unpopularity had multiple causes, notably the decision to install an artificial surface and, one year later, to ban away supporters from Kenilworth Road. The first decision, taken in 1985, was taken on purely financial grounds. QPR had pioneered the process in 1981 and it had proved a commercial success, for Loftus Road could be hired out at any time without fear of wear and tear on the pitch. Although the QPR surface was castigated for its high and uneven bounce, technological advances had addressed the problem.

Luton's new surface received little adverse comment until a year later, when the board took the decision to ban away supporters, or, more exactly, to introduce a 'home only' membership scheme. The club had suffered terribly at the hands of Millwall yobs two years previously, when seats had been ripped out and the area around the ground was left looking like a war zone. English football in general was in the dock. The horrors of Heysel and elsewhere were uppermost in the minds of the Conservative Government, and Prime Minister Margaret Thatcher in particular.

Membership cards were mooted as a nationwide deterrent, and up stepped Luton chairman David Evans, himself a Conservative MP, to present a scheme that would, in effect, test the water. Evans was accused of using the scheme to further his own political ambitions. Not so, he retorted, pointing out that the stadium and its environs would be a more pleasant place to visit on a Saturday afternoon without the hordes of marauding hooligans.

At first the scheme was strictly enforced, but was then gradually relaxed, notably for cup-ties. For the most part, the sporting press was sympathetic to Luton's predicament. It was only when the likes of Everton and Liverpool were beaten at Kenilworth Road and their respective managers, Kendall and Dalglish, grumbled about the pitch and the absence of their own fans that the tide of popular opinion began to turn. All of a sudden the rumblings turned into a roar and the Hatters were being pilloried from all quarters.

It took the Taylor Report, which implemented all-seater stadia, to transform the unsavoury image of the game at large. No longer was there any need for membership restrictions. When the Football League came down against artificial pitches Luton fell in with the new mood and returned to grass. Numbed by the backlash against the ban on away supporters, the club decided to invite them back. Grass and visiting fans returned to Kenilworth Road in the summer of 1991 as football entered a new era.

Seen in retrospect, the artificial pitch had its positive factors. No matches were postponed during the six years it was in situ. The true surface was consistent in winter mud and summer drought and encouraged ball skills and passing ability.

As for the membership scheme, the small increase in local supporters did not compensate for the absence of away fans and, in truth, the exercise was probably a financial disaster. Although the supposed lack of atmosphere was presumably no different to the pre-motorway days, when mass travel by car was impossible, the benefits of lifting of the ban were more psychological than financial. Luton supporters were happy to know that their club was no longer regarded as a social pariah.

Let us now return to the euphoria at beating Liverpool in the FA Cup. It was short-lived, for three days later a tired Luton put up little opposition to a QPR side that cruised through after a replay. Foster was lost to the side for the rest for the season with knee ligament damage. The team won only two of their final eight games and drifted down to seventh, still the highest position in the club's 102 year history. Not a bad start for John Moore in his first season.

## Match of the Season 1986-87

### Luton Town 4 Liverpool 1

Division 1, 25 October 1986

Liverpool arrived at Kenilworth Road as winners of the league and cup double. They were missing player-manager Kenny Dalglish through injury, but lined up as expected with Jan Molby as sweeper. Exploiting the Dane's lack of pace, nimble forwards Mark Stein and Mike Newell soon had the Liverpool defence at sixes and sevens, and it came as no surprise when Newell outpaced Molby to blaze a low shot past Bruce Grobbelaar in the Liverpool goal.

Liverpool pushed up their full-backs in an attempt to squeeze Stein and Newell, which had the effect of opening spaces down the wings. Donaghy took full advantage, charging through before crossing the ball to Newell, who scored with a shot that flew in off the keeper's body. The third goal came soon afterwards. Grobbelaar flapped at a cross, leaving Preece to square the ball to Ricky Hill.

The Reds regrouped after half-time but were unable to prevent a fourth Luton goal – Newell notched his hat-trick when reacting quickest to Hill's header which came back off the bar. Molby replied from the spot after he had been felled by Steve Foster in the area.

Newell, proudly clutching the match ball afterwards, reluctantly told the waiting press that as a lad he had been a Liverpool fan, and had even been on the Reds' books at one time. Skipper Foster revealed that Luton had anticipated that Liverpool would employ a sweeper and had arranged a full-scale rehearsal against the youth team, who used the sweeper system. 'And we only beat them 3-1!'

# BARCLAYS DIVISION 1 1987-88

| | |
|---|---|
| Barclays League Division 1 | 9th |
| Littlewoods Cup | Winners |
| FA Cup | Semi-finals |

In the mid-1980's there never seemed to be a dull moment at Kenilworth Road. The latest earthquake to convulse the club was John Moore's summer resignation. Whereas David Pleat's departure had been on the cards for some time, Moore's decision was a bolt from the blue. His explanation was that he felt personally uncomfortable with such a high-profile job. He was also irritated by carping about his preferred style of play, and by constantly having to fend off criticisms of the club that had nothing to do with him. Luton Town at that time were synonymous with plastic pitches and banning away supporters. Moore, of course, had no say in either matter.

The board turned to his assistant, Ray Harford, who accepted the post of manager with alacrity. Harford, in turn, appointed club skipper Steve Foster as player-coach.

Harford's first venture into the murky world of transfer dealing earned him the prize signing of Brighton's Danny Wilson for £150,000. But no sooner had one midfielder arrived than another left. Luton did not relish losing Peter Nicholas to Aberdeen, but the £350,000 fee was substantial, added to which the Welsh international yearned for the European football that could be guaranteed at Pittodrie season after season.

The new campaign was barely four minutes old when Mick Harford was sent off at Derby, and bereft of their robust striker the Town tumbled to defeat. They lost their second match too, 0-1 at home to Coventry, and it was clear that Ray Harford's ways of thinking had yet to take root.

They never did. The new system was discarded after five winless games, and freed from its pressures the players responded in style, thrashing Oxford 5-2 at the Manor Ground and enjoying a 2-1 home win over champions Everton. Harford's next venture into the transfer market brought in winger Micky Weir from Hibernian – the £200,000 fee being determined by a tribunal. To balance the books the unfairly maligned Mike Newell went to Leicester for £350,000.

Gradually, the Hatters worked their way up the table. A push became a shove in November, when they notched up three straight wins – over Newcastle, Sheffield Wednesday and Tottenham.

Injuries seriously hampered the Town in their bid to climb even higher. David Preece's damaged ankle would keep him out for seven months. Emeka Nwajiobi also broke an ankle and Ricky Hill a leg. Ironically, these setbacks came at a time when Luton were embarking on a Wembley run that would see them win a major trophy for the first time in the club's 103-year history.

That unforgettable Littlewoods Cup campaign started off with a comfortable two-leg win over Wigan. The next round was made extra difficult as a result of the club's refusal – segregation of rival supporters not being possible – to grant Coventry City a full allocation of 3,500 terrace and stand tickets. This time, rather than finding themselves expelled, Luton agreed to forfeit home advantage and to play instead at neutral Leicester.

On a wet night, the Town won through 3-1. Round 4 saw them victorious at Ipswich, courtesy of an early Brian Stein strike which was then defended at all costs. The quarter-final pitched the Hatters at home to Bradford City. On this occasion, segregation plans were drawn up and the game went ahead. A mistake by the City keeper helped propel the Town into the semi-finals.

By this time the FA Cup was also well under way. Goals from Weir and McDonough at Hartlepool, where the Hatters had never previously won, eased the team through to a Fourth Round home tie against Southampton. The dream of two Wembley appearances seemed shattered when the Saints led with just seven minutes to play. But in a pulsating climax Ian Allinson – a mid-season £10,000 buy from Stoke – and Brian Stein turned the tables to set up an away tie with QPR. Luton put paid to the Hoops, too, after a replay, thanks to Rangers' Warren Neill putting through his own goal for the second season running at Kenilworth Road.

The Hatters were now truly reaching for the stars. They had reached the semi-finals of one cup and the quarter-finals of another. Attention now switched to the Littlewoods Cup two-leg semi against Oxford. In the first leg, away, Brian Stein gave the Town a half-time lead. After the turnaround, United's Dean Saunders tried to turn the tables on his own, with the assistance of gymnastics and an obliging referee, Keith Hackett. The first penalty decision to go Saunders' way, within seconds of the re-start, looked dubious. The kick was converted to make it 1-1. But it was shortly followed by a second penalty award that in the eyes of most neutrals was preposterous. Mercifully, Sealey was able to save, which had the added bonus of defusing a situation that might have turned ugly.

But Saunders was not done, and nor was the referee. The Oxford striker tumbled a third time, this time legitimately. Hackett, however, could not bring himself to award the home team three penalties in one match and turned his back, even though on this occasion it would have provoked no argument.

**DID YOU KNOW?**

**QPR's Warren Neill scored own-goals for Luton at Kenilworth Road in both the league (1986-87) and the FA Cup (1987-88). The Hatters won both matches 1-0.**

Luton did the business in the second leg. Once they had gone in front there was no way back for Oxford, and long before the end both sides knew their fate. Kenilworth Road was awash with song, ecstatic in the knowledge that Wembley – and Arsenal – awaited.

Cup-ties were now coming thick and fast. Portsmouth, in the FA Cup, were next up, but they were no match for the Town on the day, although their cause was not helped by the dismissal of Mick Quinn. Luton were now one match away from two major cup finals in one season. Actually, they were on course for *four* visits to Wembley, having eased their way through to the final of the Full Members (Simod) Cup – a competition introduced to compensate clubs for the post-Heysal European ban – not to mention a date with the twin towers in the Mercantile Credit Centenary competition.

The league, understandably, had taken a back seat amidst all this cup euphoria. In fact, during the first three months of 1988 Luton had played only eight league fixtures. It was as well that the Hatters had banked plenty of points pre-Christmas, as insurance against loss of form or injuries caused by their congested fixture list.

It was now finals or semi-finals for the rest of the season. The first of these titanic clashes was the FA Cup semi-final with Wimbledon at White Hart Lane. The gate, just 25,963, was the lowest of any semi-final since the War. First blood was drawn by the Hatters, Mick Harford scoring, but the Crazy Gang pulled the game around.

Two weeks later 35,000 Luton fans helped to turn Wembley stadium into a sea of noise and colour. A last-minute goal against Arsenal by Brian Stein produced a fairy-tale end to a brilliant day. As Steve Foster lifted the Littlewoods Cup, many Luton supporters were no doubt thinking back to the wet evenings at Barrow and Southport and pinching themselves to see if it was all a dream.

Having enjoyed the open-top bus ride and celebration dinners, Luton had to fit in seven league games in sixteen days. It was a perfect opportunity for Ray Harford to throw one or two youngsters in at the deep end. David Oldfield, in particular, made the most of the chance to unleash his speed and enthusiasm. Luton lost just one of those seven games, and their final position of ninth was a tribute to the club, especially given their limited resources. The magnificent season ended on a sad note, however, with the granting of a free transfer to Brian Stein, whose very last kick of a ball for the Hatters had won them the Littlewoods Cup.

# Match of the Season 1987-88

## Arsenal 2 Luton Town 3

Littlewoods Cup final, 24 April 1988

As the big day approached, Ray Harford faced selection headaches. Goalkeeper Les Sealey, who had enjoyed a terrific season, was still incapacitated by a shoulder injury that had kept him out for three weeks. Darron McDonough had injured himself in training two days before the final, and fitness questions hung over Ricky Hill, David Preece and Mal Donaghy. Donaghy's injury had occurred at Wembley a week earlier, in the Mercantile Credit Centenary competition, when he had been carried off. Hill had not played since breaking a leg at Everton on Boxing Day, and Preece had played only one game since suffering ankle ligament damage in September.

Harford was reassured by the fitness of Hill and Preece and pencilled them in. Donaghy declared himself fit, leaving Harford to agonise about Mark Stein. Harford finally came down against him, preferring 19-year-old local boy Kingsley Black. Mark Stein was substitute. Andy Dibble replaced Sealey in goal.

On paper, Luton's line-up carried more experience than George Graham's Arsenal, but lack of match practice was an unknown quantity. As it turned out, the Hatters enjoyed the better possession in the first half and claimed a deserved interval lead when Brian Stein capitalised on skipper Steve Foster's delicate forward pass.

A critical moment arrived soon after the break. Brian Stein had a chance to double Luton's advantage, but was frustrated by John Lukic's splendid save. Reprieved, Arsenal stormed back to score twice in three minutes through Martin Hayes and Alan Smith.

Few would have given favourable odds on Luton turning the game around, least of all against the likes of Arsenal, and for a while the Town were indebted to Dibble for making the saves that kept the contest alive. All seemed lost, however, when David Rocastle, challenged by Donaghy, tumbled in the box. The penalty, if converted, would have given the Gunners a practically unassailable 3-1 lead, but Dibble dived the right way to pull off a breathtaking save from Nigel Winterburn.

Encouraged, Luton raced to the other end. Gunners defender Gus Caesar made the initial error and the ball cannoned around the box before Danny Wilson stooped to head past John Lukic.

Then came the best moment of all. With only seconds remaining, substitute Ashley Grimes, out on the right, swept over a cross with the outside of his left foot for Brian Stein to crash home the winning goal. Luton had won the Cup!

# BARCLAYS DIVISION 1 1988-89

| | |
|---|---|
| Barclays League Division 1 | 16th |
| Littlewoods Cup | Losing finalists |
| FA Cup | 3rd Round |

It took time for the euphoria to subside, but when it did Ray Harford had to look to the future and take stock. Yesterday's glories quickly fade. The Hatters had finished in the top ten for three years running, the downside of which meant that the mainstays of the team were now three years older. Many of the better players were pushing thirty, and some were almost over the hill.

Harford had already allowed Brian Stein to move to French club Caen, and throughout the summer the air was thick with rumours about other imminent departures. The names most frequently to catch the wind were Mick Harford, Ricky Hill and Steve Foster, though in the event none of the three was to leave just yet.

Attempting to reduce the average age of the squad, without unduly destabilising the team, requires a difficult balancing act. Too often in these circumstances acting in haste is to repent at leisure, but Harford snapped up Chelsea's Roy Wegerle, Alec Chamberlain from Everton, John Dreyer from Oxford and, in a major coup, Steve Williams from Arsenal for a Luton record pay-out of £300,000. As for the departures, goalkeeper Andy Dibble – to whom so much was owed for that Wembley penalty save – would be less than human if he was content to play second fiddle to the fit Les Sealey. Dibble preferred to drop down a division and join Manchester City, for which Luton received £240,000. Another malcontent to leave was Mark Stein, who joined QPR for £300,000. The coaching staff also saw a new face. Steve Foster decided to concentrate on playing to the exclusion of his coaching duties, so to fill the void Harford recruited a long-standing friend, Richie Barker.

When the dust had settled, those closest to the club reckoned they had the biggest and best squad in Luton's history, and the mood was bullish about the prospects for the coming season. Not that the first game did much to justify such confidence. For the second season running the Town succumbed by the only goal to a team that was there for the taking. Sheffield Wednesday were no great shakes, but at the end of ninety minutes Luton's strengths and weaknesses were there for all to see. The defence was as gritty and sure-footed as ever, but in attack too much rested on the shoulders of Mick Harford, who was expected to plough a lone furrow. It was not until the fifth game that the Hatters secured their first win, in a surprising 2-0 success at Everton, though this was followed up with a merited 1-0 home victory over Liverpool.

The jungle telegraph had been reverberating for some time with rumours that Alex Ferguson's Manchester United were chasing Mal Donaghy. Donaghy, it appears, was not desperate to move. After all, in 1988 Old Trafford was hardly the theatre of dreams that it would become in the 1990's. But after much soul-searching Luton agreed to sell the player – who boasted the highest number of international caps at Kenilworth Road – the fee being £650,000. Luton had received sterling service from Donaghy and few supporters begrudged him the rewards of signing for the sleeping giants, even though his departure marked another step in the break-up of Luton's cup-winning side.

With league points still hard to come by, Ray Harford finally ditched his preferred 4-4-2 playing system in favour of 4-3-3. The players had complained loudly about the earlier formation, which they felt was costing them more points than was necessary. The switch to 4-3-3, however, meant jettisoning a midfield player. That player was record signing Steve Williams. The team as a whole reacted positively to the change. Luton beat West Ham 4-1 at Kenilworth Road and, with newcomer Roy Wegerle finding his feet, drew 2-2 at Carrow Road against league leaders Norwich.

By this time the Littlewoods Cup was in full swing again. The Town had shrugged off a determined Burnley side in the opening round and achieved a creditable 2-0 victory at Leeds at the next stage. Division 2 title challengers Manchester City were the visitors to Kenilworth Road in Round 4, where Roy Wegerle had one of those games he is unlikely ever to forget. Wegerle was blessed with remarkable close control and ball skills, and for a period of perhaps three months he was the talk of English football, especially for his performances on Luton's artificial surface. Manchester City were on the receiving end of one of those displays and the Town swept through to the quarter-finals on the back of a 3-1 win.

In the league – inspired by Wegerle, a fully fit Mick Harford and local boy Kingsley Black tormenting defenders down the left flank – Luton's results picked up. Southampton were overturned 6-1 at Kenilworth Road and by mid-February the Town appeared safe in mid-table.

Southampton were also the visitors in the quarter-finals of the Littlewoods Cup. In their case, forewarned was to be forearmed and they never looked like being sunk by another six goals. The Saints reinforced their defence and held out for a 1-1 draw. In a rip-roaring replay, the Town triumphed 2-1 after extra-time, courtesy of goals from old stagers Hill and Harford.

**DID YOU KNOW?**

**In 1988, after six months out with injury, Darron McDonagh – on the eve of his return to the side – ricked his back tying up a shoelace.**

Awaiting the Hatters in the semi-finals were fellow Division 1 dawdlers West Ham. In the first leg at Upton Park Luton introduced Donaghy's replacement, Dave Beaumont from Dundee United, but he had little to do as the Hammers pressed the self-destruct button, leaving the Town to romp to an easy 3-0 victory. West Ham did not have the firepower to make inroads into such a deficit in the second leg, allowing Luton and their supporters to dust down the boaters and head off for another trip to Wembley.

This year's opponents in the final were not Arsenal but Brian Clough's Nottingham Forest, who had looked the most talented team to have crossed the Hatters' path that season, when winning 3-2 at Kenilworth Road in February.

The final itself was anti-climactic. Though Mick Harford powered the Town into an interval lead, an unforced error by goalkeeper Les Sealey gifted Forest a penalty and from then on the game seemed to drift away from the Hatters. Forest proved to be a bridge too far, inflicting on the cup-holders their first defeat in the competition for two seasons, a run that spanned seventeen cup-ties.

Another factor behind Luton's subdued performance was that this time the Damocles sword of relegation hung over their heads. Cup-ties notwithstanding, the Hatters were wretchedly out of form. From mid-February they had gone ten league games without a win and once Wembley was out of the way they found themselves in the relegation mire with just four matches left in which to pull clear.

Nor were the staff all pulling in the same direction. Shortly before the Wembley final, chief coach Richie Barker left the club to join Sheffield Wednesday. He was replaced by Terry Mancini, who arrived just in time to supervise the Town's run-in. Luton aimed to win their three outstanding home games and hope that none of the other strugglers could mount a winning run.

Against the odds, the Town managed to conjure the results they needed to stay up. They beat Derby and fellow laggards Charlton at Kenilworth Road, with Mick Harford an irresistible presence, and although losing at West Ham, the Hatters knew that victory over Norwich in their final game would probably see them safe.

In a nail-biting match Danny Wilson missed an early penalty but bravely stepped up to take another in the second half which he converted. There was no change to the scoring, and when results elsewhere came in they confirmed that relegation had been averted.

# Match of the Season 1988-89

**West Ham 0 Luton Town 3**

Littlewoods Cup, Semi-final, 1st leg, 12 February 1989

For the second season running Luton were through to the Littlewoods Cup semi-final, where their opponents this time were to be West Ham. Both sides had reserved their best performances that season for the cups, with the Town winning difficult ties at Burnley, Leeds and Southampton. The Hammers had, in turn, overcome Derby, Liverpool and Aston Villa at Upton Park, scoring eleven goals in the process.

The Hatters gave a cup debut to new signing Dave Beaumont, who was to partner Steve Foster in central defence as a replacement for Mal Donaghy. This was the first live televised game Luton had been involved in since the previous year's final.

The Hammers had to be taken as serious opponents, especially as they had taken delight in thrashing other Division 1 sides in the competition. Luton, however, enjoyed so much early possession that it was some surprise that the game remained scoreless until added time at the end of the first half. Mick Harford, on his thirtieth birthday, leapt into Danny Wilson's cross and powered in a header past West Ham's stranded keeper Allen McKnight.

Luton expected the home team to hit them hard at the start of the second period, so it was doubly sweet when Roy Wegerle fastened on to Harford's flicked header, waltzed round Julian Dicks and Tony Gale and slammed the ball in at the near post from an acute angle. Upton Park was hushed.

It was soon like a morgue, but this time West Ham's wounds were self-inflicted. In a rush of blood, Dicks wrestled Wegerle to the ground in the penalty area and Danny Wilson's aim was true from the spot.

Upton Park was now emptying fast, those supporters who stayed berating McKnight, whom they blamed for the first two goals. The difference in the two keepers was amply demonstrated in the closing minutes when Les Sealey, a virtual spectator for most of the match, acrobatically tipped over a Leroy Rosenior header.

Although Ray Harford afterwards played down the score, and in time-honoured fashion spoke about it being 'only half-time', the Luton supporters knew that Wembley Stadium, 9 April, was a date stamped in the diary.

# BARCLAYS DIVISION 1 1989-90

| | |
|---|---|
| Barclays League Division 1 | 17th |
| Littlewoods Cup | 3rd Round |
| FA Cup | 3rd Round |

The process of dismantlement continued apace, so that soon little would remain of the 1988 Littlewoods Cup winning side. Ricky Hill was the latest to depart, joining French club Le Havre in May in slightly acrimonious circumstances. Ray Harford had told Hill that he could leave on a free transfer, even though he still had a year left to run on his contract. Chairman David Evans vetoed this, and demanded a fee of £50,000, which Hill allegedly paid out of his signing-on fee. Skipper Steve Foster was next to go, teaming up with his former Brighton team-mate Brian Horton, now manager at Oxford, for a fee of £175,000.

Ray Harford considered his squad to be three players short of what was required, in order that the Hatters could contest a place in the top half of the table. He filled two of those slots by signing Graham Rodger from Coventry and bringing in Mick Kennedy from Leicester in a swap deal that took another Wembley hero, Rob Johnson, to Filbert Street.

David Evans had threatened many times to stand down as chairman, and this time he carried out his threat, to be replaced by long-time Hatters supporter Brian Cole. Also joining the board around this time were Ray Pinney and – following in the footsteps of his father and grandfather – Henry Richardson.

The opening day brought a 1-2 defeat at Tottenham, where stadium reconstruction restricted the capacity all-ticket crowd. In the eyes of the few Luton supporters present, there was no shame attached to defeat. With Mick Harford under the surgeon's knife yet again, this time for repairs to a damaged ankle, the team's main problem would be no different from former years. It could keep goals out, but would have difficulty knocking them in.

Luton sought to nip the problem in the bud by smashing their transfer record. The target was Danish international forward Lars Elstrup, who signed from Odense for a reported £650,000. Elstrup made his debut as a substitute in the goal-less home draw against Liverpool the following week, and it would take a month before he finally broke his duck, netting five goals in an 11-5 aggregate win over Mansfield in the Littlewoods Cup.

Elstrup's slowness out of the traps did not seem to bother the Town unduly. The team were handily placed in mid-table after five games, but it was then that injury struck down Ray Harford's squad like the plague. In quick succession Luton were deprived of three central defenders – Graham Rodger, Dave Beaumont and Darron McDonough. Each was lost to the side for months and with no adequate replacements Luton plunged towards the abyss.

In a particularly dark period at the end of 1989 they slumped from the Littlewoods Cup at Everton and in the league went nine games without a win, a sequence that saw them plummeting down the table. By now the crowd was getting on the back of Ray Harford who, in an attempt to shore up the defence, took Mal Donaghy back from Manchester United on loan.

Although publicly denied at the time, money problems lay at the root of the £1 million sale of Roy Wegerle to QPR. It was, after all, a matter of public record that the ban on away supporters and the 'membership scheme' had been costly to implement and had brought in few if any extra paying customers. From published accounts, the club's outgoings on wages and bonuses still doubled revenue coming in through the turnstiles.

Chairman Brian Cole tried to rationalise the decision to sell Wegerle, pointing out that Mick Harford was almost fit again. With Elstrup and Iain Dowie contesting places in attack, it also made good business sense for Luton to secure £1 million for a player who cost only £75,000. Circumstances soon conspired to cast doubt on that decision. No sooner was Mick Harford ensconced back in the side, on Boxing Day, than Elstrup tore a cartilage, so that he too was destined for surgery, followed by lengthy recuperation.

A national newspaper ran a muck-raking story in which Brian Cole was allegedly critical of Ray Harford's lack of charisma and his inability to relate to supporters. More often than not there is little substance to such tabloid 'exclusives', and Cole was quick to insist that he had been misquoted. But the timing of the outburst – with Luton without a win in nine, and with a squad ravaged by injury – suggested that in this instance there was no smoke without fire. Manager and chairman thrashed out their differences behind closed doors, whereupon it was announced to the press that Harford had left the club 'by mutual consent'.

Assistant manager Terry Mancini briefly found himself at the helm, but a 1-4 FA Cup defeat at Second Division Brighton meant that his first match in charge was also his last. Coach Jim Ryan was next in line, as the club adhered to its policy of trying where possible to promote from within. All this disruption inevitably took its toll on the chairman, who resigned to be replaced by Roger Smith. The supporters were by this time tuning in hourly to local radio stations in an attempt to keep pace with the comings and goings.

**DID YOU KNOW?**

**Luton's 7-4 victory over Oxford in 1988 was not a record. Three Luton games have seen 12 goals – the most recent being 12-0 versus Bristol Rovers in 1936.**

Ryan was given the toughest possible baptism, away to league leaders Liverpool. Despite all the upheavals, the players knuckled down to secure a gritty 2-2 draw, with teenager Kurt Nogan silencing the Kop with a goal he will never forget.

One of Ryan's first tasks was to sell terrace hero Mick Harford. Derby's £480,000 bid for a 30-year-old forward who was increasingly prone to injury was simply too good to turn down, as director David Evans explained to irate supporters.

As often happens with a change of manager, with players trying extra hard to impress, early results picked up. In mid-February the Town finally broke their away duck by winning at Wimbledon, their first away win since December 1988. Home victories over Coventry and Millwall followed but, with the Town still in the danger zone someone had to be found quickly to fill Harford's boots.

Israeli international Ronnie Rosenthal was the player earmarked. The fee of £500,000 would be funded by a refinancing operation that would introduce new men to the board. But no sooner was the deal done than it was undone. Rosenthal did not hang around for a second invitation and signed instead for Liverpool. Such was the furore in the Luton boardroom that Ray Pinney resigned.

Ryan therefore had no choice but to make do with the existing squad, and was left with little option but to pitch in youngsters before their time. Results stayed gloomy, the worst of them being a 0-3 hiding at Nottingham Forest. With just three fixtures left to complete, the Hatters' eight-year spell in Division 1 seemed about to end.

The following week a never-say-die performance accounted for defending champions Arsenal at Kenilworth Road. This threw the Hatters a lifeline. A last-gasp goal from Iain Dowie on the penultimate Saturday then earned a 1-0 home victory over Crystal Palace. This meant that, yet again, Luton's survival would go to the wire. They needed to win at Derby, but – crucially – that might not be enough. Results elsewhere could still conspire to send them down.

Blotting out news of what was happening on other grounds, Luton did what was demanded of them. Goals from leading scorer Kingsley Black earned them their second away win of the season. After an agonising wait it was learned that Sheffield Wednesday had lost 0-3 at home to Forest, which meant that in the closest of finishes the Town had survived on goal-difference.

# Match of the Season 1989-90

## Derby County 2 Luton Town 3

Division 1, 5 May 1990

Home wins over Arsenal and Crystal Palace had given a chink of light to Luton supporters, 5,000 of whom journeyed up the M1 on a warm spring day. The Hatters knew what had to be done to stay up. The job in hand was to beat Derby at the Baseball Ground. But Ron Atkinson's ailing Sheffield Wednesday also had to lose at home to Nottingham Forest. Form and motivation were the jokers in the pack. Luton had won only once away all season, while Clough's Forest had no stimulus other than to cause havoc at one club and celebration at another.

Derby boasted big-money signings Peter Shilton in goal, centre-half Mark Wright, and Welsh international striker Dean Saunders. They also included a certain Mick Harford who had moved from Kenilworth Road only four months previously. The thought of him scoring the goal that would send Luton down was too painful to contemplate.

The game got off to a sensational start as, after only 66 seconds, the Town were awarded a free-kick thirty yards out. Ignoring all the set piece routines drummed into him, full-back Tim Breacker ran up and cracked the ball into the top corner of the net. The celebrating Luton fans were in seventh heaven after eighteen minutes when Kingsley Black coolly slotted home Danny Wilson's cross, by which time news had filtered through from Hillsborough that the Owls were trailing to Forest.

Seventh heaven quickly transformed into seventh hell. Mark Wright halved Derby's deficit. Alec Chamberlain then performed heroics to keep County at bay, but was beaten for a second time on the stroke of half-time, when Paul Williams thundered the ball past him following a free-kick. Luton had to start all over again.

Supporters might have expected their team to be jittery in the second half. But far from it – the players tore into the Rams' defence with an irresistible display of attacking football. On the balance of play Luton ought to have been rewarded with a goal, but the minutes were ticking rapidly away by the time they scored it. Black drove a shot into a wall of defenders which rebounded back to him. Granted a second attempt, Black placed the ball right-footed past Shilton.

Understandably, the Hatters shut up shop, but Derby were a beaten side and when the final whistle blew and radios confirmed Wednesday's defeat, the celebrations went on long into the night.

# BARCLAYS DIVISION 1 1990-91

| | |
|---|---|
| Barclays League Division 1 | 18th |
| Rumbelows Cup | 2nd Round |
| FA Cup | 4th Round |

The top stories to break during the close season of 1990 were all connected with off-field activities, chiefly concerning the take-over of the club by two London property developers, Peter Nelkin and David Kohler.

Talks of a take-over bid had been rumoured for several months, but when the new owners were announced in May it came as a shock, mainly due to the speed with which the operation had been conducted. David Evans, whose tenure as chairman and, latterly, as director had been controversial, to say the least, quit the board immediately to concentrate on furthering his political career.

The new men at the helm soon realised that they had inherited a beast with a gargantuan appetite. Money was pouring out of the club at double the rate at which it was coming in through match receipts. Their understandable policy of 'good husbandry' – which translated into less money to spend – were the last words manager Jim Ryan wanted to hear. Without money he could not buy, and if he could not buy, Luton would probably go down.

Kohler and Nelkin caused further ructions in some quarters by announcing that the artificial pitch would be taken up at the end of the coming campaign. The decision displeased many in the local community who enjoyed its use as an all-purpose facility. The ban on away supporters was also scheduled to be lifted, as Luton strove to get back in step with other clubs. This time it was the police and local residents who objected, fearing that opposing fans meant more policing and more vandalism. In short, Messrs Nelkin and Kohler, whatever the good sense behind their decisions, ruffled feathers from the outset.

One consequence of this belt-tightening was that Luton bought no one over the summer. Some players departed, however, notably Danny Wilson, who threw in his lot with relegated Sheffield Wednesday in return for £200,000. Wilson was said to have been disillusioned by Luton's lack of ambition, citing the absence of new signings as evidence. Also on the way out was Mick Kennedy who, when told of Stoke's interest, had signed on the dotted line within 24 hours.

On the positive side, John Moore returned as reserve team coach after an absence of three years, following his resignation as team manager. His work was going to be cut out, as much would rest on the shoulders of the youngsters placed under his tutelage.

As it turned out, the Town, in their ninth season in the top division, started off gallantly, assisted no doubt by staying clear of injuries in those early weeks. Wins at Southampton and at home to Leeds United and Coventry were eclipsed by a superb 3-1 victory at Norwich. Recalled to the side for the first time since December, Steve Williams engineered the win at Carrow Road, setting up fit-again Lars Elstrup with two of the goals in the Dane's hat-trick.

Everything in the Luton garden appeared to be rosy. Then, out of the blue, it was announced that right-back Tim Breacker was to be sold to Second Division West Ham for £600,000. Breacker, it appears, was not over keen on dropping down a division, but in the face of a £1 million Luton overdraft, saleable assets had to be cashed in.

The Hatters limped through until Christmas. Too often they flattered to deceive, playing pretty football but failing to convert enough of the chances that came their way. This was to prove costly in the long term as too many games in this period were lost by the odd goal.

On Boxing Day Luton lost the services of one of their brighter prospects when Ceri Hughes' knee injury curtailed his season. All of a sudden all was doom and gloom. Wimbledon beat the Hatters on New Year's Day, Southampton won a fluctuating game at Kenilworth Road 4-3, and Leeds held too many trump cards at Elland Road, where the home crowd pressured the referee into awarding a phantom penalty. Worse was to follow when West Ham trounced Luton 5-0 at Upton Park in the FA Cup, and QPR's Les Ferdinand broke clear to score a last-minute winner at Kenilworth Road.

All things considered it was a good time to face Liverpool, in the wake of Kenny Dalglish's traumatic resignation, and Luton took full advantage, winning 3-1 at Kenilworth Road with two goals from the recalled Iain Dowie. The Northern Ireland international scored the following week, too, in a 1-0 victory over a strangely defensive Nottingham Forest. And when this was topped by a 2-1 win at Aston Villa, helped by a breathtaking volley from youth product Mark Pembridge, fans began to think of putting away their relegation tranquillisers for another year. Plans to increase the size of the top division from twenty to 22 clubs meant that only two clubs instead of the usual three would face the chop. That was good news for Luton and for everybody else down in the mire. This, and the Hatters' fleeting upturn in fortunes, meant the spectre of relegation receded into the distance.

**DID YOU KNOW?**

**At the end of the 1978-79 season Luton benefited from four own-goals in four consecutive matches. They earned four vital points and fended off relegation.**

The supporters relaxed a little too soon, for the team suddenly went into free-fall. First they lost by the odd goal at Coventry, having led for half the game. Then they did everything but score at home to Norwich, only to lose to another goal snatched on the break.

By and large, supporters had reacted with commendable stoicism to the slings and arrows of outrageous fortune. But when West Ham's bid of £480,000 for Iain Dowie was accepted the natives became restless, firing off numerous letters to the local press and voicing their disapproval at home matches in no uncertain terms. Like Breacker earlier in the season, Dowie did not want to drop down a division, but the dire finances at Kenilworth Road followed their own inescapable logic. Dowie went. Many supporters with a nose for the way the wind was blowing sniffed relegation in the air with the irresistibility of a coming typhoon.

Results seemed to underline their fears. Defeats at Manchester United and Sheffield United were followed by a 0-0 home draw with Tottenham and a 3-3 draw at Chelsea. That last result hammered in a further nail, as the Hatters led 3-0 at one stage, but were left hanging on desperately against ten-man opponents. Wimbledon shaded another victory at Kenilworth Road, and then, in a relegation 'six-pointer', Sunderland displayed greater appetite for the scrap and returned to Wearside with three precious points under their belts.

Thankfully, Sunderland failed to capitalise on their 2-1 victory, so that by the time of the final fixture they were level on points with the Town. The Hatters had to play doomed Derby County at home, while Sunderland travelled to play Manchester City at Maine Road.

Although on paper the Town's looked the easier task, they had not tasted victory in any of their last nine games. For the third year running they somehow escaped at the death, this time when ex-Hatter Mick Harford obligingly put through his own goal. Lars Elstrup added a second, clinching goal, so that Sunderland's 2-3 defeat became immaterial.

Manager Jim Ryan and his players celebrated in front of jubilant supporters, who massed for the last time on the soon-to-be torn up artificial pitch. Manager, players and fans had no inkling of the storms that lay ahead.

# *Match of the Season 1990-91*

**Luton Town 2 Derby County 0**

Division 1, 11 May 1991

For the third season running Luton's survival was down to the final game. Although this time the Hatters did not have to rely on others stumbling, the situation at the bottom was still extremely tight.

The last relegation spot was between the Town and Sunderland. The two teams were locked together on points and had an identical goal-difference, though the Hatters had a slight advantage by virtue of having scored four more goals. In short, Luton had to equal whatever score Sunderland achieved at Maine Road. Tactically, Jim Ryan dispensed with the sweeper system that had come unstuck at Everton the previous week, knowing that it was imperative to win.

Derby, the Town's final opponents at the end of the previous season, were already down, but possessed a formidable threesome in the shape of Peter Shilton, Mark Wright, and Dean Saunders. As was the case the previous year, Luton were also up against Mick Harford who, whatever his outward protestations, would surely have preferred not to be placed in such an invidious position.

The Hatters had not won for nine games and had only scored once at home in that time. These were bad omens, but they were offset by playing the worst team in the division, and one that was unlikely to raise their game – even if that was possible. Luton's valedictory match on their artificial pitch saw them attack their opponents from the start. Skipper John Dreyer headed over the bar after two minutes. Harford replied with a header that passed too close for comfort, but that was the last seen of Derby during a first half which saw both Kingsley Black and Sean Farrell squander reasonable opportunities.

Just when supporters were fearing the worst, a Jason Rees free-kick skidded off Harford's head for an unfortunate, but gratefully received, own-goal. Coming at the death of the first half the timing could not have been bettered. Luton added a second goal shortly after the restart, when Lars Elstrup headed in a corner that had been helped on by Dreyer and Black. Coming with the news that Sunderland were trailing at Manchester City, supporters commenced a premature survival party on the terraces.

The Town survived a late scare when Wright headed against the bar, but the defence held out until the end, which signalled another pitch invasion. Luton's 2-0 win would have counted for nothing had Sunderland won by three clear goals, but such a score belonged to the realms of fantasy.

5

# DAVID PLEAT: PART 2 1991-1995

## BARCLAYS DIVISION 1 1991-92

| | |
|---|---|
| Barclays League Division 1 | 20th (relegated) |
| Rumbelows Cup | 2nd Round |
| FA Cup | 3rd Round |

No sooner had the dust settled on Luton's latest escape from the jaws of relegation, which ushered in a tenth season's football in the top flight, than rumours circulated thick and fast that manager Jim Ryan was to lose his job.

That these rumours had substance was apparent when chairman Peter Nelkin announced that Ryan would be leaving due to a 'clash of personalities' and admitted that the decision had been taken several weeks previously. The outcome had not been made public at the time so as to avoid undermining the fight against relegation.

The obvious candidate to replace Ryan was David Pleat, currently out of a job after being shown the door at Leicester. After prolonged negotiations, Pleat eventually agreed to return, having been away from Kenilworth Road for five years.

Most supporters were furious at Ryan's departure. He had, after all, performed minor miracles on a shoestring budget, staving off relegation two seasons running. Such was the fans' strength of feeling on the matter that Peter Nelkin saw fit to resign, with Roger Smith once again taking over the role of chairman.

Pleat, in other words, stepped into a vessel rocking crazily in a storm. If Ryan's task was hard, Pleat's was rendered even harder when last season's leading scorer, Lars Elstrup, decided to return to Odense. The Danish club could not afford the agreed transfer fee, at which point Elstrup threatened to quit the professional game altogether and revert to being a bank cashier. In the end a compromise had to be thrashed out, the final fee of £250,000 representing a huge loss on Luton's original outlay.

Brian Stein rejoined the club after three years in France. Phil Gray also arrived for £275,000 from Tottenham, Pleat having had the player under his wing at White Hart Lane, and before the season was many weeks old veteran centre-half Trevor Peake signed from Coventry for £100,000. Only a few days previously Peake had helped the Sky Blues embarrass Luton 5-0.

The new season saw great changes at Kenilworth Road on and off the field. A new grass pitch had been laid to replace the artificial surface. A new stand had been erected adjacent to the main stand, and away supporters were to be allowed back for the first time since 1986. One thing that did not change, however, was the club's basic insolvency. More money was going out than was coming in.

With this in mind, the board sold Kingsley Black to Nottingham Forest for £1.5 million. Luton took Forest's Lee Glover on loan, with a view to a permanent transfer, but Glover was badly injured in his first outing.

Poor Pleat was hardly viewed as the returning hero. It took the Town 407 minutes to score their first goal and six games to secure their first win. Knowing that an injection of fire-power was needed, regardless of cost, Pleat persuaded the board to bring back terrace icon Mick Harford for £325,000, quite a sum for a 30-something, injury-prone striker.

Harford made his second Hatters debut in mid-September at home to Oldham, and in true Roy of the Rovers fashion scored twice in the closing minutes to clinch a valuable victory. The idea had been for Harford to forge a striking partnership with Phil Gray, but events were to take a different turn. Gray, a Northern Ireland international, injured a knee in October which, with later added complications, effectively kept him out for the season.

Pleat has few peers when it comes to wheeling and dealing in the transfer market. In came Steve Thompson from Bolton for £180,000, only to be discarded after five games due to his lack of pace at the top level. Thompson was exchanged for the Leicester pair Des Linton and Scott Oakes, with the former injuring himself after only three games.

Out too, after just nine league games, went young Matt Jackson, who was snapped up by Everton for an initial £600,000, with more cash to follow, depending on how may times he played for his new club. Meanwhile, in came another veteran, Chris Kamara, from Leeds for £150,000.

Pleat was evidently attempting to rebuild the spine of the side, as he had done back in 1984-85. This time, however, he was not quite so sure-footed. The new intake of players were solid enough, but they were a little long in the tooth and lacked that little bit extra that could transform a struggling side into one that might challenge for honours.

Luton were down among the dead-men of the division virtually all season, so that apart from three straight home wins over Christmas, which raised false hopes, they never looked to have what it takes to stay up. Luton's home record was good enough to have warranted mid-table respectability, if only their away form had kept pace. But it on was their travels that the Hatters touched new depths. They did not win away all season, and their ability to snatch defeat from the jaws of victory on opposing grounds, particularly by conceding late goals, left supporters with plenty of miserable journeys home.

Continuing financial pressures inevitably tied one hand behind Pleat's back. Cash had been raised totalling £400,000 from the sale of Dave Beaumont to Hibs, Sean Farrell to Fulham, Graham Rodger to Grimsby and Darron McDonough to Newcastle. Pleat hoped to spend some of that money on goalkeeper Steve Sutton from Forest, who arrived on loan following Alec Chamberlain's lapse in form, and who had quickly endeared himself to the home crowd. The £300,000 deal was, however, blocked on financial grounds. Sutton went back to Forest and with him, in the eyes of many supporters, went Luton's last chance of staying up.

Loan signings came and went, youngsters were blooded and players returned from injury only to be injured again. That was the sad story of Luton's final months in the top division. In the circumstances it was remarkable that they were not dead and buried long before the season's end. With one game to go, Luton still had an outside chance of staying up.

The Hatters had to win at already relegated Notts County and trust that Coventry lost at Aston Villa. 5,000 Luton supporters travelled to Nottingham, fully expecting the Town to pull off yet another great escape, but this time it was a bridge too far. Julian James' early goal was cancelled out by two efforts from Rob Matthews who, incidentally, was later to move to Kenilworth Road.

Luton's decade at the top came to an end just as the old Division 1 was transformed into the Premier League with all its riches. Whether or not the club slipped deeper into the red in a bid to stay up did not matter greatly to the average supporter. It had been a struggle at times but it was great fun rubbing shoulders with and beating the top sides in the country. But now it was back to Luton's spiritual home, the old Division 2, which was now perversely renamed Division 1.

# Match of the Season 1991-92

**Luton Town 1 Manchester United 1**

Division 1, 18 April 1992

For the fourth successive season Luton found themselves embroiled in last-day dramas. This time the fates had other teams to smile upon, casting Luton back into the doldrums whence they had risen ten years earlier. Let us not dwell on the sad tidings at Notts County, but turn the clock back to the Easter clash with Manchester United, the one team fighting for their First Division survival, the other striving to shake off the cobwebs of glories past.

Luton Town and Manchester United were perfect examples of how, year upon year, the rich got richer and the poor got poorer. In many ways the two clubs no longer inhabited the same planet, never mind the same league. In such circumstances, for Luton to fend off relegation to book another league visit to Old Trafford would have been a triumph in itself.

United at one stage had looked odds on to win that elusive first championship since 1967 and lay the ghost of Sir Matt Busby. But Howard Wilkinson's Leeds had refused to be shrugged off, so that by the time of Manchester United's visit to Kenilworth Road the pressure on Alex Ferguson's men was colossal.

What the Hatters lacked in pace and power they made up for in experience. Pleat's game plan was to hassle United for every ball and refuse to let them get into their elegant stride. The plan worked well for the first twenty minutes and the Town put the United defence under considerable pressure. Oakes, Varadi and Pembridge all went close to giving Luton the lead.

It was then that the Hatters were undone by a route one United goal. Peter Schmeichel unleashed a punt downfield to Lee Sharpe, whose speed carried him past Trevor Peake and enabled him to nutmeg Alec Chamberlain. The goal had come against the run of play and Alex Ferguson knew it, switching his formation after the interval to attempt to combat the aerial power of Mick Harford.

Luton's equaliser came in the 50th minute, when a long free-kick to the far post was met by Harford, who first headed against the bar, and then reacted quickest to nod the ball in. This was exactly the sort of goal that Ferguson had tried to combat.

United nervously clung on to the draw, but survived a scare in the closing minutes when substitute Brian Stein forced a brilliant save from Schmeichel.

It would be the last time Luton entertained Manchester United in a league fixture for who knows how many years.

# BARCLAYS DIVISION 1 1992-93

| | |
|---|---|
| Division 1 (New style) | 20th |
| Coca-Cola Cup | 2nd Round |
| FA Cup | 4th Round |

After ten years at the top, but missing out on the dawn of the new Premier League, Luton had to become reacquainted with life in Barclays League Division 1, or the old Division 2 as die-hard supporters preferred to call it. Those same supporters tried to comfort themselves by pointing out that the Hatters had spent most of their history in this division, so things would not be that bad. Or would they? The division had changed since Luton last competed in it. Then, Division 2 comprised just 22 teams. Now, swollen as a result of the trimmed size of the top league, it contained 24.

David Pleat was ideally qualified to get the best out of Luton, not least for his ability to turn the transfer market to advantage. How ironic, then, that his first job was to sell Mark Pembridge to Derby for £1.25 million. Pembridge, who had come up through the ranks, had turned down a move to Derby on transfer deadline day the previous season, but the Rams, though also in the new Division 1, were persistent.

With the bank off the club's back for the time being, Pleat trawled the market for bargain replacements. There was talk of Thomas Ravelli, the veteran eccentric Swedish international keeper, coming to Kenilworth Road, but that failed to materialise. In fact the only signing of note was Steve Claridge from Cambridge United, whose fee was fixed by a tribunal at £160,000.

With supporters keeping their fingers crossed that the existing squad was strong enough to mount a promotion challenge, Mick Harford was sold for a second time. This time Chelsea valued his services at £300,000, creaking joints and all. Harford's departure split the fans into two camps, those who felt that such a stalwart deserved one more signing-on fee from a big club, and those who thought the Town had sold the family silver. Pleat was thought to have misgivings, both about the transfer and its timing, and leaked veiled quotes to the press to that effect.

Club owner and managing director David Kohler was the chief target of supporters' disaffection. His tight control of the purse strings ran counter to the desperate need of the club to buy its way out of trouble. Unwilling to outstay his welcome, he was happy in principle to sell out. But whenever potential purchasers made themselves known the deal seemed to fall through, either because their pockets were not deep enough or too many strings were attached, depending on which side of the fence you sat.

At the height of the protest, fans paraded 'Kohler Out' placards, and though the immediate crisis subsided, discontent with the board simmered throughout the season. The bottom line, however, was that there was no magic wand, and supporters had to accept that there was no bottomless well of money. Luton Town FC had to live or die with the current squad of players and the current boardroom.

Those players familiar with the rarefied heights of top flight football were also in for a shock. If they expected life in the lower division to be easier they had another think coming. The Town got off to a dreadful start and were down amongst the strugglers from day one.

The opening day defeat at Leicester set the tone. Pretty football – as football-goers over the years have come to expect from David Pleat – but no punch. The Hatters looked to be on their way to a point when in the last minute their beleaguered defence finally caved in. It was at home that Luton's shortcomings were rudely exposed. Opposing teams came to attack on the break, exploiting defenders who were short of pace, so that Bristol City, Portsmouth and Grimsby all headed home with three points in the kitty. It was not until late November that victory was tasted at Kenilworth Road. But for the occasional win away from home, the Town would have been cast adrift at the bottom.

The next financial crisis was not long in coming. In October, in order to meet VAT demands, Steve Claridge was sold back to Cambridge. He was replaced by Ian Benjamin from Southend, who thereby added Luton Town to his extraordinarily long list of clubs. Benjamin brought a bit of height to the Town's forward line. His first appearance was at home to high-flying Millwall. First impressions were favourable, with the Lions lucky to escape with a draw. Maybe Luton were turning the corner.

If only. The next blow to strike the club had nothing to do with football and happened far from Kenilworth Road. Paul Telfer and Darren Salton were involved in a fatal car crash. Although Telfer escaped relatively unscathed, Salton was badly hurt and his promising career was cut short. Not surprisingly, the mood among the players was subdued the following Sunday when they trotted out for the televised home game with Watford. It was all the more creditable, then, that Luton should record their first home win of the campaign. 'We did it for Darren,' said David Preece.

Although the team touched bottom early in the New Year, form gradually improved and seven games without conceding a goal

**DID YOU KNOW?**

**In season 1992-93, ten Luton league games finished 0-0. The record number of goal-less league draws in one season is 13, set by Blackpool in 1974-75.**

elevated them – momentarily – out of danger. With the sporting press preoccupied by this sequence of shut-outs, which equalled the Town record set in 1923, the eighth game produced a 2-2 draw, which was probably greeted with relief by the nervy defence. Records of that nature may be fun for supporters and grist to sports writers, but they invariably act as millstones around players' necks.

With Ian Benjamin flattering to deceive, Pleat swooped for Kerry Dixon. Dixon had been capped for England and had been prolific in his Chelsea heyday, but a transfer to Southampton had not worked out and the Saints were happy to off-load him on loan. Ironically, Dixon was born in Luton and had been part of the club's youth team. It was Pleat, of all people, who saw no future for the boy and showed him the door. Fifteen years later, Pleat knew the player's worth and brought him back.

Dixon worked well in tandem with Phil Gray, who benefited to the extent of scoring in six consecutive games, a sequence not bettered since the days of the great Joe Payne in 1936. The run came to an end when Gray's exploits began to alert the high and mighty, Chelsea putting in a bid which was rejected.

Four games without a win meant that once again Luton were staring relegation in the face. Tension eased following home wins over fellow strugglers Cambridge – with Dixon at his most majestic – and promotion chasing West Ham. Draws were earned at Sunderland and Derby, where last-minute goals earned Luton a point at Roker but denied them two at the Baseball Ground.

A home win in the penultimate game, against Peterborough, would ensure survival, but as the Posh funnelled back into defence to force a goal-less draw, Luton's celebration party had to be postponed. In the event, the party fizzled out into a non-event. By the time of the final match, at Roots Hall, midweek defeats by other strugglers meant Luton were all but safe. Southend too, were above the drop zone, and they banished any lingering doubts by winning 2-1, Stan Collymore playing his last match for the Shrimpers. The result hoisted Southend above the Hatters, and the final whistle greeted scenes of mutual affability as both sets of supporters applauded one another.

For Luton, thirteen home draws over the season told its own story. No matter what division the team were in, supporters needed long memories to remember anything other than relegation battles.

# Match of the Season 1992-93

**Luton Town 2 West Ham 0**

Division 1, 13 April 1993

In the spring of 1993 the Town could never string together enough points to haul themselves clear of the dreaded trap-door. Two consecutive relegations would have spelled curtains to a club with Luton's limited resources. Losing 0-1 at Swindon to a late Paul Bodin strike, when the Hatters felt they had done enough to win, shunted them towards the red zone. Other results had done Luton no favours, and their next match, at home to promotion chasing West Ham, if it went to form, could end up pointless too.

In fact, the Hammers were feeling the heat. At one stage a promotion place had seemed theirs for the taking. But three defeats in their last four away games had coincided with a powerful surge from Portsmouth, who had leap-frogged into second place behind runaway leaders Newcastle. West Ham needed to stop the rot: Luton wanted it to continue.

Both clubs, of course, had shared the pain of relegation twelve months previously, and both seemed to be making frantic efforts to escape Division 1 at the first attempt, albeit in different directions. Kenilworth Road's biggest crowd of the season witnessed an enthralling end-to-end contest that produced 33 goal attempts and nineteen corner-kicks.

The two goalkeepers, Alec Chamberlain and Ludek Miklosko, were the men of the match, pulling off save after save as both sides threw caution to the wind. Phil Gray missed a couple of sitters for the Town, and they looked likely to be costly as the game, still goal-less, entered its final decisive stage. There were just six minutes left when Kerry Dixon's goal-bound shot was handled on the line by Julian Dicks. Referee Gurnam Singh awarded a penalty, but did not add to Dicks' unenviable tally of red cards, presumably because other defenders were covering on the line. Phil Gray atoned for his earlier misses by coolly shooting into the top corner.

The Hammers' fire had been extinguished, and two minutes from time Hatters' substitute Martin Williams exchanged passes with Gray, cut inside Dicks, and fired in the first league goal of his career. The win pushed the Town three places up the table. West Ham still secured promotion.

# ENDSLEIGH DIVISION 1 1993-94

| | |
|---|---|
| Endsleigh Division 1 | 20th |
| Coca-Cola Cup | 1st Round |
| FA Cup | Semi-finals |

After the trials and tribulations of recent seasons the summer of 1993 was relatively uneventful. As expected, Phil Gray got his move to the north-east, where his family was living, with Sunderland paying £800,000 for his services. Not all of that sum was pocketed by Luton Town FC. A percentage had to be diverted to Tottenham, a consequence of the complicated deal agreed when Luton bought him.

Also headed to Roker Park was goalkeeper Alec Chamberlain, in his case as a result of a 'technicality' in his contract. Football League regulations dictated that new contracts could not offer lesser terms than the old, otherwise the player was entitled to a free transfer. This was the case with Chamberlain. Pleat would not budge, on principle, the outcome of which was that Luton received nothing at all for the departing goalkeeper.

The only notable import was Scott Houghton on a free from Tottenham. Hitchin born, Houghton had been on Spurs' books since he was thirteen. His appearances for them had been few and far between, and he appeared to have saved his best performance for the time when he came on as a Spurs sub against Luton during the relegation season.

The new campaign brought a quick win, but little cause for optimism. The victims were Watford, but the Town made hard work of beating the Hornets, who were disgraced by a couple of dismissals. It was only when Kerry Dixon, still on loan from Southampton, fired a tremendous second goal that the Hatters could breathe easily.

Points were not so easy to come by over the next few weeks. The Town lost four games on the trot, with supporters not knowing who to blame, chairman David Kohler or manager David Pleat. Attempts were made to bolster the side with the loan signings of Everton's Alan Harper and Paul Dickov from Arsenal, but they made little immediate difference as the team sank to the bottom of the table.

An injury to Kerry Dixon did not help, but results improved after his return to the side in October. Dixon had become, if not a one-man team, at least an essential component of it. Luton were therefore delighted to hear that Southampton were prepared to write off the £575,000 they had paid Chelsea only one year earlier, and allow him to sign permanently for the Hatters.

Also arriving at the club, initially on loan, was old boy Mitchell Thomas from West Ham, and he played his part in steadying the ship as the New Year dawned. The side at this time more or less picked itself, with Dixon, Peake, Dreyer, Preece and Harper the elder statesmen, and youngsters Hughes, Telfer, Hartson and Oakes learning quickly alongside them

But if the team appeared to have stabilised, the same could not be said of the boardroom. The 'Kohler out' faction appeared to have got their wish when John Mitchell, the ex-Fulham and Millwall player, together with his business partner David Ellingham, offered to buy the chairman out.

The bid was apparently accepted, but two months later the deal was still unsigned as both sides indulged in claim and counter claim. By this time, local businessman and long-time Luton fan Chris Green, together with Cliff Bassett, boss of Universal Salvage Auctions – the Hatters' sponsors – stepped in to bail out the club's immediate financial worries and join the board.

This season would be marked by an extraordinary run in the FA Cup. In truth, the cup run almost never got started, and had Southend not squandered several gilt-edged chances in the first half at Kenilworth Road, Luton would never have lived to fight another day. Paul Telfer taught the Shrimpers a lesson in finishing when he blasted the only goal after the interval to set up a headline-making tie at Premier League Newcastle.

At St James' Park, Tony Thorpe, on his full debut, made an instant name for himself when he uncorked a 25-yard rocket to silence the vociferous home crowd. A questionable penalty, won and taken by Peter Beardsley, spared the home side's blushes and set up a replay that would test Kevin Keegan's crew to the utmost. On the tight Kenilworth Road enclosure, the multi-million pound Magpies were harried and hassled from the start and another youngster, John Hartson, deputising for the injured Dixon, showed coolness and maturity beyond his years when he took the ball around Newcastle goalkeeper Mike Hooper to score. Scott Oakes sealed a famous victory with Keegan offering no excuses.

Cardiff of Division 2 were the next opponents. Although struggling in the league, they had put out Manchester City in Round 4. Ninian Park's reputation for crowd trouble was not ill-deserved. Trouble may have been confined to a minority, but that minority did their best to sully the name of their club. In an intimidating atmosphere, whose recriminations lingered for weeks afterwards, Luton's players did well to keep their cool. Goals from Oakes and a disputed effort from Preece, with the crowd baying for offside, settled the outcome.

Another Premier League side, West Ham, awaited the Town in the quarter-finals. By playing five across the middle, Pleat got his tactics exactly right, and the scoreless game brought the Hammers back to Kenilworth Road for another famous night of cup football. That midweek replay saw Scott Oakes play probably his finest game in a Luton shirt, claiming a hat-trick with his pace and accurate shooting.

The FA's ill-advised and short-lived experiment of staging Cup semi-finals at Wembley meant that Luton were now back at the Twin Towers one round before they should have been. They were denied a chance to appear a second time, in the final, by turning in a limp performance against Chelsea in the semi-final, despite the vociferous backing of 25,700 Luton supporters. Chelsea won more or less at a stroll, and Luton's players trudged off at the end knowing that instead of a return date at Wembley to look forward to they had another relegation battle on their hands.

Indeed, the weight of the Chelsea defeat hung heavily over Luton's heads for weeks to come. The Hatters went into the semi-final on the back of a win over Peterborough; they emerged from it to be beaten five times on the trot, failing to score a goal in seven and a half hours of league football. If Luton could not arrest the slide, they would go down the plug hole.

Home draws with Millwall and Southend helped a little, but the crunch match was the third from last, when fellow strugglers West Brom were the visitors to Kenilworth Road. On a night of high drama, on a heavily watered pitch – too heavily watered, complained the Albion chairman – the Town's neat passing game was rewarded with a 3-2 win. But the score tells only half the story. Both keepers had to go off injured and both sides had a man sent off. The win secured Luton's safety, which set a small record of its own. For the first time since 1988 nothing hinged on the Hatters' last match of the season.

## *Match of the Season 1993-94*

### **Luton Town 2 Newcastle United 0**

FA Cup, 4th Round replay, 9 February 1994

Newcastle United were taking the football world by storm. Winning the new Division 1 by a mile they continued where they had left off, and Kevin Keegan's vibrant brand of attacking football meant that the Magpies were the team everyone wanted to see.

**DID YOU KNOW?**

**In 1969-70, Luton kept 20 clean sheets in the league, equalling the figure set in 1921-22. The record is held by Liverpool, with 28 shut-outs in 1978-79.**

No one had given the Town a prayer when the draw for Round 4 had been made. A team that cost £7.5 million to assemble should steamroller the paupers of Luton, whose combined cost was just £500,000. It seemed a mis-match of epic proportions but, after 19-year-old Tony Thorpe fired the Hatters into the lead, the Magpies were saved from defeat only by a dubious penalty.

For the replay the Town were missing striker Kerry Dixon, who gashed a shin in the first game. His replacement was named as 18-year-old John Hartson, whose reputation – hitherto confined to darkest Bedfordshire – was magnified a thousand-fold by the cool, controlled way he shot the Town into the lead in the sixteenth minute. Accepting Trevor Peake's long pass in his stride, Hartson clipped the ball past the advancing Magpies goalkeeper, Mike Hooper, before calmly slotting it into the net.

Newcastle fought back, Peter Beardsley hitting a post with a fierce shot, but the Town were equally out of luck when Hartson's header beat Hooper but was acrobatically cleared by Barry Venison.

The Magpies squeezed the Luton defence hard after the change of ends but the central partnership of Trevor Peake and John Dreyer was equal to everything hurled at them. The tie was finally settled ten minutes from time, when Scott Oakes's shot was blocked by Hooper. The loose ball ran to Des Linton, who drove it back into the box for Oakes to side-foot home.

Kevin Keegan was gracious in defeat, praising the Town and adding: 'Luton deserved to win, fair and square, and good luck to them. I hope they go all the way to the final at Wembley.'

# ENDSLEIGH DIVISION 1 1994-95

| | |
|---|---|
| Barclays Division 1 | 16th |
| Coca-Cola Cup | 1st Round |
| FA Cup | 4th Round |

Following the excitement of the FA Cup run, the summer was very quiet. In view of the crop of bright, young players who were forcing their way into contention, it was only the forward line which needed strengthening. David Pleat's target was Crewe striker Tony Naylor. After a fee of £200,000 had been agreed, the player appeared to consult the Professional Footballers Association before coming back to demand better terms. Pleat was unhappy with the PFA for interfering, but as they were in effect acting as Naylor's agent, there was little he could do but cast his net elsewhere. Naylor eventually moved to a club closer to home, Port Vale.

Pleat's search for replacements eventually alighted on speedy Dwight Marshall from Plymouth for £150,000 and veteran Tony Adcock from Peterborough for £10,000. Leaving the Hatters was Alan Harper, keen to return to the north-west, who signed for Burnley on a free transfer.

Of greater significance was the free transfer of reliable defender John Dreyer to Stoke City. As had happened with the loss of Alec Chamberlain the previous summer, Luton had offered Dreyer reduced terms under a new contract. As such, this entitled the player to a technical free transfer. This, it should be recalled, was the pre-Bosman era, when a club retained a player's registration irrespective of whether his contract had expired.

It was easy to put the finger on why Luton did not start the new season firing on all cylinders. They couldn't score goals. All the pretty football in the world was not enough to satisfy the fans. It was goals and victories that counted!

Luton's style was more suited to away games, where nippy forwards Scott Oakes and Dwight Marshall could catch teams on the break. This style was less effective at home, where the Hatters found it difficult to break down massed defences and, as play became more frantic, Luton's rearguard too often left itself open to a sucker punch.

The Hatters' away form up to Christmas was the best in the Football League, with eye-catching victories being recorded at Port Vale, Watford, Stoke, Sheffield United, Wolves and Swindon. Home results were as disappointing as the away ones were brilliant, and a string of defeats sent home gates tumbling.

**DID YOU KNOW?**

**In season 1994-95, Sheffield United's Brian Gayle gifted Luton with an own-goal both at home and away.**

Pleat recruited veteran Gary Waddock from Bristol Rovers, initially on loan, in a bid to strengthen the backbone of the side. But this was tempered by Welsh international Ceri Hughes seeking a transfer. No sooner had his request been withdrawn, than the midfielder badly injured a knee, his season over.

The next problem concerned the manager. There were persistent rumours that Tottenham wanted David Pleat to return to White Hart Lane. Having quit Spurs in October 1987, following newspaper allegations regarding his private life, Pleat's managerial record was there for all to see. He had built one of the more successful and entertaining Tottenham sides of recent times. Having been informed by David Kohler of Spurs' interest, Pleat weighed up the pros and cons. At one time the pros seemed to outweigh the cons and Pleat seemed on the point of leaving. But the post of general manager at White Hart Lane would have meant little contact with the players and Pleat was not yet ready to hang up his tracksuit. He decided to stay.

As if to celebrate, the Hatters shot up to fifth place, and instead of talk of relegation the hushed words 'play-off' could be heard in some quarters. The players, however, were flattering to deceive.

Young striker John Hartson was beginning to make a name for himself with his uncompromising physical presence and no mean ability on the floor. Out of the blue, Premier League Southampton tabled a £1 million bid for the Welshman, with Iain Dowie thrown in as a make-weight. Saints' bid was peremptorily rejected, but supporters now knew it was only a matter of time before the right offer would take Hartson away. In January, Arsenal's bid of £2.5 million astonished the football world, who thought it silly money to pay for such a rough diamond. Luton would have been crazy to turn down such a sum and they grasped the money with both hands. The fee constituted a Luton record and Hartson became the most expensive teenager in the history of the British game. A proportion of the money received was set aside for team-building.

The loss of Hartson was quickly followed by a humiliating FA Cup exit at the hands of Southampton. The Saints drew the original Fourth Round tie at Kenilworth Road, with the Hatters' Marvin Johnson missing a penalty, but in the replay a virtuoso performance from Matt Le Tissier orchestrated a 0-6 defeat for the Hatters and with it their season went into terminal decline.

**DID YOU KNOW?**

**In September 1982 Liverpool scored against 3 different Luton keepers. Injured Jake Findlay was replaced first by Kirk Stephens, then by Mal Donaghy.**

Pleat had difficulty spending his hard-earned money. The asking price was instantly inflated whenever it was known that Luton Town were on the prowl. Rob Matthews, whose two goals for Notts County had consigned the Town to relegation from the old Division 1 in 1992, was picked up for £80,000 and John Taylor, a long time target, was signed from Bradford City for £200,000.

The newcomers provided the Hatters with the know-how to start winning at home, but at a cost to their remarkable away record. The Town won at Notts County on New Year's Eve but did not taste victory on their travels again before the end of the campaign.

As the team bedded into mid-table obscurity, events off the pitch whetted the appetite for a more secure future when plans were unveiled for a new stadium, to be called the Kohlerdome, which was to be situated close to the slip road off junction 10 of the M1 motorway. This roofed-in arena would have a removable grass pitch and seating for 20,000, but almost before the plans were dry various protest groups were mobilising in what was to become a long running saga.

With all this distracting attention from what was happening on the pitch, it was hardly noticed that the playing season ended ominously with four straight defeats, pushing the Hatters down to sixteenth. That was not much higher than the previous campaign.

## Match of the Season 1994-95

### Luton Town 5 Middlesbrough 1

Division 1, 15 October 1994

The Town's home form during the early part of the 1994-95 season was little short of disastrous. Three defeats and two draws from the first five games played at Kenilworth Road stood in complete contrast to the away record, where three out of four games had been won.

David Pleat was sure that the home jinx was about to end and that Middlesbrough would end it. He felt confident that Bryan Robson – in his first season as manager – would come to Kenilworth Road and play for a win, rather than soak up pressure and hit on the break like other sides. Pleat's players also had a habit of raising their game against the better sides and needed little motivation against a team that had spent vast sums of money to try to 'buy' promotion. In John Hendrie and Paul Wilkinson, Boro had arguably the best striking spearhead in the division, though they had just been knocked off the top, following a one-goal home defeat by Tranmere.

The Town were boosted by an early goal when a long cross from Ceri Hughes was inadvertently headed into his own net by Paul Wilkinson, under pressure from Hartson. The lead was doubled when Marshall slammed in a Hartson lay-off and the contest was effectively settled before the interval, with Preece's volley beating keeper Stephen Pears all ends up.

Playing for pride after the break, Middlesbrough were repeatedly repulsed on the edge of the Luton penalty area. The Town, with their intricate passing moves slicing holes in the Boro rearguard, added goal number four when Marshall followed up Pears' save, and number five when Hartson hit a scorcher into the top corner.

Derek Whyte grabbed a late consolation for Boro, but afterwards manager Robson had to concede: 'Luton outran, outfought and outpassed us. We have no excuses, we just did not perform. We were well beaten by the better team on the day.'

Middlesbrough went up as champions that season, and this was their heaviest defeat.

# 6

# WESTLEY & LAWRENCE 1995-2000

## ENDSLEIGH DIVISION 1 1995-96

| | |
|---|---|
| Endlseigh League Division 1 | 24th (bottom) |
| Coca-Cola Cup | 1st Round |
| FA Cup | 3rd Round |

No sooner was the 1994-95 season concluded than Sheffield Wednesday came knocking for manager David Pleat. This time he seemed happy to go. The trouble was, Pleat was under contract, and chairman David Kohler had Luton Town FC's interests uppermost when demanding hefty compensation from Wednesday. After a war of words that spanned several weeks, an agreeable figure was eventually settled upon.

The likely identity of Pleat's successor was a subject that filled many a column inch in the local press, with the club receiving more than forty enquiries for the job and with the air humming with big and yet bigger names. But, keeping faith with previous managerial appointments at Kenilworth Road, the board again promoted from within. Youth coach Terry Westley took up the position and recruited ex-Ipswich boss Mick McGiven as his number two. Wayne Turner and John Moore were retained on the coaching staff.

Weeks of feverish transfer activity then ensued. Veteran David Preece exercised his options and moved to Derby, though not before another battle of words over whether he was, or was not eligible to go under freedom of contract. Scottish midfielder Paul Telfer transferred to Coventry for a fee fixed by tribunal at £1.15 million.

On the incoming side, Gavin Johnson, Graham Alexander, Steve Davis, David Oldfield, Bontcho Guentchev and Darren Patterson all signed up to strengthen the squad. Each of them caught the eye at one time or another, as Terry Westley experimented with a 'three at the back' system during a pre-season tour of the west country.

Unfortunately, the system was terribly exposed when the season opened, and relegated Norwich were easy winners at Kenilworth Road against a Luton side that looked nervous and disjointed. A win against the odds at Southend the following week, despite Ceri Hughes' early dismissal, only flattered to deceive as the team went another seven games without the scent of victory.

Injuries to key players Scott Oakes and John Taylor hardly improved the situation; nor did the fact that new signing Darren Patterson was laid up on the treatment table almost as soon as he joined the club. Depending on which group of supporters were canvassed, or which game was referred to, the team was shot-shy, shaky in defence, lacking an influential midfielder, tactically naive or all four! A recipe for disaster.

But whichever view they took, they blamed Westley. It was not long before supporters began calling for the head of the manager, who responded by diving into the transfer market to buy two Danes – Johnny Vilstrup from Lyngby and Vidar Riseth from Kongsvinger. Their combined fee of over £300,000 meant a small fortune had been spent in an effort to produce attacking thrust in midfield and added punch up front.

The bewildered Danes joined a team that was weaving pretty patterns up to the edge of the opponents' penalty area, but seemed unequal to the next task of belting the ball into the net. The consequence of this failing was that the Hatters were always looking up at all the other clubs in the division. A shock win at Ipswich, from which club Westley had been discarded as a youngster, offered a glimmer of light in an ocean of gloom. But overall, with total confusion reigning on the field, the directors took the bit between the teeth in an attempt to halt the inevitable slide to Division 2.

Following the team's 0-4 capitulation at Portsmouth, just before Christmas, the decision was taken to relieve Westley of his duties 'by mutual consent'. The supporters voiced some sympathy for Westley but accepted that a change at the top was in everyone's interests. David Kohler took full responsibility for the team's predicament, knowing that a safe pair of hands was needed for the manager's position, and appointing ex-Charlton, Middlesbrough and Bradford City boss Lennie Lawrence to restore an element of calm to the club. Lawrence, of course, had no previous connections with the Hatters, so Kohler was aware that he was bucking recent trends by not appointing from within.

The players greeted their new boss with a fighting performance to draw 2-2 at home to Huddersfield, having been reduced to ten men following the dismissal of Steve Davis. If that result papered over the cracks, the next exposed them in full. Luton were crushed 1-7 at Grimsby in the FA Cup, and Lawrence knew he had a crisis on his hands.

Having taken stock, Lawrence waved his magic wand and somehow injected sufficient self-belief in the players that they stayed unbeaten for the next seven games, climbing from 24th to the heady heights of nineteenth. The team owed a debt to one of Westley's final signings, giant American goalkeeper Ian Feuer, who arrived – following a productive loan period – from West Ham for £580,000. Feuer and Dwight Marshall, whose pace injected life into the side, helped transform the players into something resembling a team.

The run came to an abrupt end in late February at Sunderland, when a spectacular own-goal by Julian James was not nearly so hurtful to the team as Marshall's broken ankle. Bad news comes in threes, they say, and three days later Reading came to Kenilworth Road for a relegation 'six pointer' and stole a win after the Town had taken a quick lead. These back-to-back defeats seemed to knock the stuffing out of the side and it was to be another four games before the next victory was claimed, by which time the Hatters had slipped back into the relegation positions.

Knowing that a strong target-man was imperative, Lawrence trawled the market and eventually settled upon a player he knew from his Charlton days, Kim Grant signing for £250,000. Grant's arrival was backed up by Middlesbrough's Paul Wilkinson on loan, but Wilkinson lasted only three games before breaking a toe, typifying the bad luck that hovered over Kenilworth Road.

A mini-run, to give the supporters heart, lasted all of two games before Stoke scored twice at the death at Kenilworth Road to win a match that the Hatters should have sewn up long before. The fans now accepted that relegation was inescapable. The next four games garnered just one point. Another loan player, Graeme Tomlinson from Manchester United, broke a leg on his full debut during the 0-1 reverse at Port Vale. Relegation was confirmed after a 1-3 home defeat by Barnsley, when the crowd understandably gave vent to their disapproval, the more so as some of the players seemed to throw in the towel.

The season concluded with a performance at Oldham that summed up the season. The Town enjoyed most of the possession, played plenty of controlled football but failed to trouble the home goalkeeper all afternoon and ended up losing 0-1. The 'goals for' column said it all, with only forty scored, of which a paltry ten were away from home.

**DID YOU KNOW?**

**Of current Premiership clubs, only Blackburn have never won at Kenilworth Road (after 18 attempts). Luton have lost all 16 matches at Old Trafford.**

## *Match of the Season 1995-96*

### Luton Town 3 Grimsby Town 2

Division 1, 10 February 1996

The 1-7 debacle at Grimsby in the FA Cup, marking Lawrence's second game in charge, seemed a distant memory as Luton pulled themselves together for a four-game unbeaten run. Such was the extent of the turnaround that Lawrence was named Manager of the Month for January. The award was announced before the league fixture with Grimsby, who – for their part – had not won at all since the last occasion the sides met.

The Hatters got off to the best possible start when Graham Alexander, collecting the ball in his own half, ran unchallenged before hammering a shot past Paul Crichton, the Mariners' keeper. It was Alexander's first goal for Luton. Grimsby, however, were made of stern stuff and, on seventeen minutes a free-kick taken by Ivano Bonetti was only partially cleared, leaving Jamie Forrester with a simple chance to equalise.

When Forrester took advantage of slack marking to put Grimsby in front, just before the hour, it seemed the Hatters' bubble had burst, and all their old faults – nervousness and incoherence – resurfaced.

An inspired double substitution by Lawrence soon changed all that, with David Oldfield and Dwight Marshall immediately upping the tempo. A pass from Ceri Hughes was handled by Grimsby's Vance Warner on the edge of the box, but the referee played the advantage, leaving Bontcho Guentchev to carefully curl the ball past Crichton. The winner came with sixteen minutes left, when substitute Oldfield threaded a shrewd pass to Marshall, who outpaced the defence before firing home.

It was alleged that Grimsby player-manager Brian Laws was so irate after the defeat, especially by a team his side had thrashed only a few weeks previously in the FA Cup, that he flung a plate of food at Bonetti in the changing room. The plate inflicted serious damage to Bonetti's face, leading to court cases and much mileage for the tabloids.

# NATIONWIDE DIVISION 2 1996-97

| | |
|---|---|
| Nationwide Division 2 | 3rd |
| Coca-Cola Cup | 3rd Round |
| FA Cup | 3rd Round |

The Town were now to be reacquainted with a division they last left in 1970. Manager Lennie Lawrence had inherited a sizeable squad and he now set himself the task of pruning the wage bill. Out went Vidar Riseth and Johnny Vilstrup to Linz and Aarhus respectively, and Sheffield Wednesday's David Pleat poached Scott Oakes, who had lost his way at Kenilworth Road.

Crystal Palace enquired about Welsh midfielder Ceri Hughes and took him on loan to Selhurst Park. Hughes, however, though talented, had spent much of his Luton career either injured or suspended. This made him a dubious investment for any interested buyer. Lawrence felt that a change of scenery might benefit the player, but Hughes eventually returned to fight for his place with the Hatters.

The only incoming player was £35,000 Paul Showler from Lawrence's old club Bradford City. Despite the size of the existing squad, only a few players were genuinely left sided and Showler, a purpose-built left-winger, fitted the bill.

The season opened dreadfully with three quick defeats, the most painful of which was at Brentford – where the Town led with only ten minutes left to play, yet contrived to lose 2-3 – and the most embarrassing at Bristol City, where the Hatters were overturned 0-5. During that match Tony Thorpe was sent off for retaliation, and Lawrence made a public apology to supporters for the team's abject performance.

In this division Lawrence felt that more teams employed spoiling tactics, especially away from home. Tactically, he felt Luton's defence was sitting too deep, and that offensively the team needed greater variety, interspersing a patient build-up with a more direct assault on the opponents' goal.

A 1-0 home win over an equally poor Rotherham stopped the rot, but it was soon back to square one when the Town took a three-goal first-leg lead to Bristol Rovers in the Coca-Cola Cup and found themselves 0-2 down at half-time. A change of tactics in the second period was needed to snatch a killer goal, and from then on the season seemed to take off.

Luton's first ever visit to Wycombe Wanderers ended with a valuable win and Gillingham were seen off at home. Chesterfield halted the climb with a dour, defensive performance at Kenilworth Road but five wins and two draws out of the next seven games sent the Hatters hurtling up the table. A prosperous run in the Coca-Cola Cup was valuable for morale, with Premiership Derby beaten over two legs and Wimbledon only bettering the Hatters in extra-time in a replay.

More than 5,000 Luton supporters travelled to Watford for a midweek game in late October to see if the Hatters could climb into the promotion places. All seemed set fair when a rocket shot from Paul Showler earned a 1-0 lead. Unfortunately, a Hornets equaliser deep in stoppage time meant that a top slot would have to wait a while.

David Oldfield was injured in that game, and was sidelined for six weeks. His absence did not seem to disturb the team's equilibrium, though it placed a greater goalscoring burden on the shoulders of Tony Thorpe. Oldfield and Thorpe were first and foremost midfield players, but Lawrence pushed them forward as often as possible, where they proved extremely effective, Oldfield for his hard running, and Thorpe for his quick feet and eye for a goal. Thorpe continued to bang them in, netting hat-tricks against Plymouth and fellow promotion hopefuls Crewe. As Christmas approached, the Hatters were playing with a confidence not seen for several seasons.

The week before Christmas the Town travelled to Millwall, where a 1-0 victory, courtesy of Hughes' last-minute strike, lifted the Hatters to top spot. The team then won 2-1 at Gillingham on Boxing Day, with Feuer saving a late penalty, and all seemed set fair for the New Year.

For once, the local newspapers were full of positive reportage. The switch from Kenilworth Road to the Kohlerdome was still on ice, pending the outcome of the public enquiry. The board were quietly funding the club's promotion challenge, and there were no cries for the manager's head. What could go wrong?

The answer? Plenty! First the weather. After Boxing Day frozen pitches prevented the Town playing for over three weeks. When the players returned to action they seemed rusty, managing a couple of scoreless home draws during the rest of January, and tumbling badly from the FA Cup at Bolton.

Injuries to Showler, Hughes and Waddock further incapacitated the Hatters, who were by now clinging on desperately to the coat-tails of the leaders. The return of the injured players for the visit of Preston at the end of February helped inspire a hat-trick by Oldfield in a 5-1 win, just the tonic, surely, for a headlong assault on the divisional championship.

**DID YOU KNOW?**

**In season 1996-97, Luton conceded only two league goals at the Kenilworth Road end of the ground. Both were scored by Plymouth.**

All eyes were now focused on the coming home clash with long-time leaders Brentford. A live TV audience witnessed a single Thorpe strike divide the teams and send the Town leapfrogging over the Bees to the top. The picture looked better in theory than in practice, for the head of the division was extremely congested. In addition to Brentford, Bury, Stockport and Crewe were all breathing down the Hatters' necks, with Bristol City coming up fast on the rails.

In a bid to insure the squad against injuries or loss of form Lawrence brought in two more players on loan – Gavin McGowan from Arsenal and Andy Kiwomya from Bradford City. Both made their debuts in a demanding Easter fixture at Burnley. The gloss of the Town's 2-0 win was somewhat taken off by a subsequent home draw with Bristol City. Likewise, a 3-0 win at doomed Rotherham was followed by a 0-0 stalemate at home to Wycombe and a critical 2-3 reverse at Walsall. With the other top sides picking up points the Hatters slid out of the two automatic promotion places, further draws against Blackpool and Bury widening the gap still further.

With two games left, Luton had to rely on others slipping up. No one obliged, and Stockport's win at Chesterfield condemned the Hatters to the play-offs for the first time in their history.

For some teams, of course, those putting together a late run, the play-offs are a godsend. For others, like Luton, whose goal not so long ago had been the championship, they represented a last resort, a shot of the dice where form played second fiddle to fortune.

Crewe were the Hatters' semi-final opponents. Despite Crewe's 6-0 thrashing by Luton in December, the Railwaymen were well worth their overall 4-3 aggregate victory over two legs. The Hatters scored first in both matches but, quite simply, Crewe were the better side on each occasion, fully deserving their eventual promotion after beating Brentford in the Wembley final.

## Match of the Season 1996-97

### Luton Town 6 Crewe Alexandra 0

Division 2, 14 December 1996

After being left behind in the starting traps, effectively giving all the other sides a three-game start, Luton gradually pulled themselves up by their bootstraps. Now, as Christmas approached, they were within touching distance of leaders Brentford. Luton's morale was not helped by being taken the distance by little Borehamwood in the FA Cup, and they expected to be given a stern test by the team regarded as the best footballing side in the division. Under the tutelage of Dario Gradi, the present Crewe team appeared impregnable at home but did not travel too well, as evidenced by seven away defeats in ten games. There, perhaps, lay Luton's best chance of winning.

They enjoyed the perfect start. Alexander fired the Hatters ahead after only two minutes, when Thorpe's shot was parried by Jason Kearton, the Crewe keeper. Thorpe volleyed Luton's second goal after twenty minutes, and nine minutes later Shaun Smith felled Marshall in the area and was sent off. Thorpe converted the spot kick.

But for Kearton's heroics, the Town could have doubled their lead by the interval, but even he was powerless to prevent Thorpe completing his hat-trick when the ball deflected in off his knee. Showler added to the fun with a far-post header from a cross by Alexander, before Crewe defender Ashley Westwood felled Thorpe and was dismissed for a second bookable offence. The rout of nine-man Crewe was completed when Oldfield seized upon Showler's pass to net number six in the final minute.

Lawrence was quite rightly euphoric, while his counterpart Dario Gradi admitted, 'Luton were too good for us and are better than any side we have played this season. We couldn't pass the ball because their midfield pressurised us so well and Luton always looked comfortable on the ball. With ten men we were struggling and with nine we had no chance. Having said that, the result might not have been much different if there had been no dismissals.'

The score represented Luton's biggest win since Southampton were crushed 7-0 in 1985. The Hatters were now up to third, they were the highest goalscorers in the division, and had just completed eight straight home victories. Who would have guessed that, come May, Crewe would end their season in tears.

# NATIONWIDE DIVISION 2 1997-98

| | |
|---|---|
| Nationwide Division 2 | 17th |
| Coca-Cola Cup | 2nd Round |
| FA Cup | 1st Round |

The line between success and failure can be narrow, as Lennie Lawrence already knew from his years in the game. He now had to galvanise the squad and engineer a positive bid for promotion back to Division 1.

His first task was to oversee the departure of teenager Matthew Upson to Arsenal. There were echoes of John Hartson in the deal, for Arsene Wenger was prepared to pay £1 million for a lad who had made just one league appearance for the Hatters, and that as substitute. The Gunners evidently saw him as one for the future, and when add-ons were taken into account the total fee would rise to around £2 million.

The money from Upson's sale meant that Lawrence was under no pressure to sell again that summer. To that extent it was a surprise that Wimbledon's bid for Welsh international Ceri Hughes was also accepted. Also on his way out was Kim Grant, who had never settled at Kenilworth Road. Millwall paid £200,000 to take him to the New Den.

A large Luton following travelled to Blackpool on the opening day, but in a lacklustre display in the sun the Hatters went down 0-1, and that defeat rather set the tone for the season. A 1-0 home victory over Southend in a turgid affair followed, but goalkeeper Ian Feuer tore a shoulder muscle and was sidelined for three months.

Injuries laid low several Hatters in those early weeks, to such an extent that Lawrence's team sheet was different week by week. Loan signings Gavin McGowan from Arsenal and Bryan Small from Bolton tried to shore up the side, but more often than not it seemed to be a case of one step forward, two steps back, as no sooner did one player return from injury than two others got crocked. The physio had to deal with back strains, hamstring tears, torn ankle ligaments, knee ligaments, three hernias and an infected toenail, not to mention Feuer's shoulder problem and everyday dead-legs and thigh strains

This injury epidemic peaked in late September in an away game at Bristol City, when four youngsters had to be called upon to make their debuts. By this time it was virtually a case of picking anyone who was fit. In the circumstances, the 0-3 defeat was almost acceptable. It could have been so much worse.

**DID YOU KNOW?**

**At Bristol City in season 1997-98, Luton's three substitutes had not mustered a single league appearance between them.**

Worse was to follow when table-topping Watford descended on Kenilworth Road and scored four goals in the first half hour. Lennie Lawrence was berated ferociously by the home crowd, and at one stage the match threatened to boil over. Had Watford banged in another four goals, it might have done. Thankfully, no further damage was inflicted, but the knives were out for Luton's embattled manager.

With the injury crisis subsiding, the team harvested enough points in the coming weeks to ease out of the relegation positions. Phil Gray returned from Fortuna Sittard for a substantial £400,000 and Alan White signed from Middlesbrough for a more modest £40,000. Gray did not last long before he too joined the sick-list, and as for White, he was thrown in at the deep end with little previous league experience. A 2-2 draw at Wycombe in early November, in which gaping holes opened up in the Hatters' defence, was the harbinger of yet more misery. Luton lost four home games in a row, including a sad defeat to Torquay in the FA Cup. It was the first occasion the Town had gone out in Round 1 since 1929. The vitriol from the terraces spilled over once again.

The weeks before Christmas were the worst of Lawrence's managerial career, as he later admitted. He could never seem to get the jigsaw right. If the defence looked strong, he could bank on the forward line firing blanks. If the goals went in at one end, the defence was sure to let in even more at the other. The one indisputable fact was that the team played with greater confidence away from Kenilworth Road. Lawrence put this down to their inability to stretch teams at home and probe behind them, especially when opponents sat deep. Lack of pace and height in attack was also a worry.

A mini cabinet reshuffle took place, with assistant manager Wayne Turner demoted and coach Trevor Peake taking his place. Turner, Luton born and bred, was not happy with the new deal on offer and turned his back on the club. He eventually accepted a coaching post at Wycombe Wanderers, but by the summer had left them as well.

A gritty 2-2 draw at home to Northampton on Boxing Day prefaced three straight wins. Keeper Ian Feuer's crisis of confidence then handed wins on a plate to Oldham and Fulham. Feuer made way for Kelvin Davis, but on Davis's first league game back, at home to Bournemouth, uncertainly spread like the plague around the whole defence, leading to yet another defeat.

The turning point, with hindsight, can be pinpointed to the return game at Watford in mid-February. The Town fought back from a goal down to level with minutes to go, showing a spirit that many thought lacking in recent months.

As with all cures, the patient had to get worse before he could get better, and home draws with Bristol City and Wigan provoked abuse for Lawrence that verged on the malicious. Chairman David Kohler was castigated for selling Tony Thorpe to Fulham for £800,000. Supporters pondered the wisdom of selling the team's top scorer when it was desperately trying to fend off relegation.

With transfer deadline day looming, the Town languished one place off the bottom. Lawrence searched hither and thither to bring in a striker on loan. Thwarted at every turn, a lifeline was thrown by ex-Town boss David Pleat, now Director of Football at Tottenham, who recommended that he borrow Rory Allen from White Hart Lane.

Allen had been highly regarded as a teenager but had suffered a serious ankle injury and was only now coming back to full fitness. Lawrence had struggled with enough injured players in one season to take serious risks with another, but not wishing to look a gift horse in the mouth he accepted. It was a good job he did!

With eight games remaining, Allen made his debut at Walsall and showed a refreshing willingness to enter the fray that was not always the case with other loan players. He also scored a critical goal as the Town won 3-2.

A 3-0 home win over York was followed by a vital 1-0 victory at high-flying Grimsby, Allen again on target. And by the time Chesterfield were tamed at Kenilworth Road relegation fears were all but extinguished. Safety was assured in a bruising encounter at Brentford, with Allen netting the Hatters' second goal in a 2-2 draw, and he signed off in style, volleying the winner at home to Carlisle in the last minute of the final match.

## *Match of the Season 1997-98*

**Walsall 2 Luton Town 3**

Division 2, 28 March 1998

Transfer deadline day had come and gone. Despite manager Lennie Lawrence's best endeavours to land a proven goal-machine, the best he had come up with was Tottenham's Rory Allen, out of the game for many months through injury.

**DID YOU KNOW?**

**Luton used a total of 33 players in 1997-98, equalling the record number used in 1960-61.**

Allen would play at Jan Sorenson's Walsall, who could themselves still be sucked into the relegation dog-fight. Although Luton had stacked up a few draws of late, they needed wins if they were to climb out of the bottom four.

The Town opened strongly, but were thankful to the referee who waved play on when Saddlers' Didier Tholot tumbled convincingly in the area. The ref turned his back. The opening goal came when Allen retrieved a ball that seemed to be going for a goal-kick and floated over a cross that Oldfield toe-ended over James Walker in the Walsall goal.

Walsall rolled up their sleeves in the second period, exerting considerable pressure on the Hatters defence and equalising when Adrian Viveash headed in Dean Keates' corner from close range.

Just as the Town seemed about to fold, two breakaway goals effectively saved the day. Firstly Oldfield, seizing on a Waddock clearance, bore down on the Saddlers goal and smacked a shot against a post. Allen was quickest to respond to poke the ball home. Then Marshall played a perfect wall pass with Oldfield and dribbled around Walker before slotting the ball in from a narrow angle.

Walsall replied within seconds through Tholot, but the Town closed ranks and held out for a valuable victory. The three points hoisted them up two places, leaving them just two points behind the Saddlers.

Walsall finished that season nineteenth, avoiding relegation.

# NATIONWIDE DIVISION 2 1998-99

| | |
|---|---|
| Nationwide Division 2 | 12th |
| Worthington Cup | 5th Round |
| FA Cup | 2nd Round |

After the narrow escape from relegation at the end of the previous campaign, manager Lennie Lawrence knew that he was likely to endure another season of problems, given the parlous financial state at Kenilworth Road. He was resigned to losing the experienced David Oldfield and Darren Patterson, who moved on to bigger clubs to earn bigger pay-packets, as well as the veteran Garry Waddock, who had proved so influential in the twilight of his career. Waddock was set to move back to his first love, QPR, where he had been offered a coaching post.

Lawrence was heartened by the clutch of good quality youngsters coming through the system, but Division 2 was not forgiving for youngsters, and without a dash of experience in the squad another relegation battle was on the cards. He was, therefore, grateful to be able to call on the likes of Mitchell Thomas, Marvin Johnson, Phil Gray and Steve Davis in the months ahead.

Pre-season went particularly well and a new star was unearthed in the shape of ex-Monaco striker Herve Bacque, who shone in friendly games against Arsenal and Coventry. Fan-power possibly forced Lawrence's hand to sign the Frenchman, but Bacque was unable to withstand the 'muck and bullets' of Division Two football and his star was soon on the wane.

With the sun on their backs the Town players opened the league season well and by September were in second place. A month later they were still a top-three side when they inflicted the only home defeat of the season on moneybags Fulham, in a display that caught the eye and showed what this Luton Town team could achieve on its day.

While prospering in the league, the Hatters were also advancing forward in the Worthington Cup. Their run would take them through to the quarter-finals, the furthest they had reached since contesting the final in 1989. Division One sides Oxford and Ipswich were seen off in the opening rounds, with the latter dispatched on a memorable, breathless evening where the game ebbed and flowed. The winner came in the last minute of extra-time from the head of unlikely goalscorer Marvin Johnson.

The reward was a home tie with Premiership Coventry, but on the night the Sky Blues failed to perform, much to the anger and embarrassment of manager Gordon Strachan. The Town strolled through 2-0 before overcoming another higher division opponent, Barnsley, in the next round.

Injuries, suspensions and loss of form, particularly with some of the youngsters, meant that the wheels were beginning to come off before Lawrence announced that the last week of November was to be 'the club's biggest of the 90's'. Manchester City were due at Kenilworth Road for a league fixture, after which the Hatters faced a trip to the Stadium of Light for a Worthington Cup clash with Sunderland. If that wasn't enough to whet the appetite, the Town could then relish a home FA Cup-tie with lowly Hull.

As it turned out, the Town managed to scrape a draw with Manchester City, but were then cruelly deprived of a Worthington Cup semi-final place by referee Eddie Lomas, who decided to take centre stage at Sunderland and send off Mitchell Thomas. It was an extraordinary decision that puzzled everyone in the ground and effectively killed the tie. Luton's 'biggest' week ended with FA Cup humiliation by a Hull side who were rock bottom of Division 3 and also without ten first-team regulars.

Chairman David Kohler then confirmed what supporters had for weeks suspected was about to happen, when he announced that players had to be sold to raise money. The talismanic Steve Davis departed to Burnley in exchange for £750,000 just after Christmas, and even Lawrence had to admit that the Town's play-off chances had effectively bitten the dust for another year.

In fact, the Town went into free-fall, despite sterling efforts from loanees Sean Dyche and Gerry Harrison. By mid-March, culminating in a 1-3 defeat at Chesterfield, supporters were worried that another relegation battle was on the cards.

It is said that out of darkness comes light, and this is certainly true as far as the Town were concerned that season. Chairman Kohler decided to resign his position after an alleged petrol bomb incident at his home. His departure was quickly followed by the dismissal of his High Court appeal against the Government's decision to turn down planning permission for a new ground for the club on land adjacent to Junction 10 of the M1.

Director and chief creditor Cliff Bassett then put the Hatters into receivership after failing to force Kohler's hand over his financial interests in the club. This particular bombshell broke just as the Town were due to play an important league game with Reading at Kenilworth Road.

Perversely, all these off-field problems galvanised the players, the staff and supporters as one. After a fighting 1-1 draw with Reading, matters improved. Although Graham Alexander and Sean

Evers needed to be sold on transfer deadline day, the receiver permitted Dyche to return to Kenilworth Road on loan. With Dyche came his Bristol City colleague Tony Thorpe on a short-term loan deal. It was only a year earlier that Thorpe had been sold for £1 million. Although Thorpe was hardly match fit, once he had shaken off the rustiness with a couple of games under his belt he scored four goals in three games. Those goals earned nine points and pushed the Town up to a respectable twelfth position by the season's end.

For the second season in a row, the Town had used 33 players on a roller-coaster ride that saw only four of the team that took part in the opening-day fixture at Wycombe in August included in the final fixture.

## Match of the Season 1998-99

### Fulham 1 Luton Town 3

Division 2, 3 October 1998

After a promising start to the season, when the young Hatters side had moved as high as second in the table by early September, the exertions of performing to the highest levels in the league each week, interspersed with a fine run in the Worthington Cup, meant that individual performances were beginning to falter. Following a narrow defeat at Blackpool, the Town entertained Ipswich in a rip-roaring Worthington Cup-tie. After straining every sinew Luton managed to win through by the odd goal on aggregate after extra-time.

A tired performance against Walsall at Kenilworth Road followed, together with another narrow defeat, so a trip to moneybags Fulham in the next game was seen as a keen test of the mental strength of the Hatters.

The millions poured into the Fulham playing squad by Mohammed Al Fayed were just beginning to take effect, and the Cottagers looked set fair to walk away with the divisional championship at the season's end. Household names such as Chris Coleman and Peter Beardsley had been tempted to Craven Cottage to make it a star-studded squad, the likes of which had rarely before been seen in this modest division.

Over 2,000 Luton supporters made the trip to London and most could sense a spring in the step of the players during the warm-up and a show of bubbly enthusiasm, which had been conspicuously absent the previous week. The players were up for the occasion – let battle commence!

**DID YOU KNOW?**

**The only current club Luton Town have played in the Football League but never yet beaten is Macclesfield Town.**

Manager Lennie Lawrence had done his homework and deployed Gavin McGowan and Sean Evers to shackle the dangerous Fulham wing-backs, Gus Uhlenbeek and Rufus Brevett. Evers would not only be able to carry out his task to perfection, but also found time to use his indefatigable energy to control the midfield and set up opportunities for his colleagues.

The first evidence of this master class from Evers came in the third minute when, after taking a clever through-pass from skipper Steve Davis, he skipped down the wing and put over an inch-perfect cross onto the head of Phil Gray, who made no mistake when heading past a hopelessly exposed Maik Taylor in the Fulham goal.

Fulham huffed and puffed for the remainder of the half without troubling the Luton defence, while at the other end Taylor needed to be at his most alert to keep out efforts from Gray and his striking partner Stuart Douglas. It was Douglas who doubled the Town's lead, shortly after the interval, when he arced a header past Taylor following a cross from McGowan. The third goal came soon afterwards, with the unmarked Davis making it a hat-trick of headers when he nodded in Ray McKinnon's free-kick.

Naturally, the Hatters' tails were up now and McKinnon, Gray and Douglas all went close to making it a totally embarrassing afternoon for the home side. The scoring was completed by Fulham, however, when future Hatter Alan Neilson headed in Peter Beardsley's corner in the 86th minute. That was Fulham's only effort on target the whole afternoon.

Afterwards, Fulham manager Kevin Keegan heaped praise on the Luton side and confirmed that it had been the best display anyone had put up against the Cottagers since his arrival in charge of the west London club.

Lawrence confirmed what all the supporters present knew: it had been the best league performance in his three years at the club.

# NATIONWIDE DIVISION 2 1999-2000

| | |
|---|---|
| Nationwide Division 2 | 13th |
| Worthington Cup | 1st Round |
| FA Cup | 3rd Round |

With the Hatters finishing 1998-99 in receivership, manager Lennie Lawrence had his hands tied as he prepared for the new campaign. With no money to spend, vultures circling overhead ready to pounce on some of his younger players, not to mention the real threat to league football at Kenilworth Road, no wonder he looked on the summer of 1999 as the most disturbing in his long career.

Lawrence was forced to sell Chris Willmott and Kelvin Davis to Premiership Wimbledon in quick succession, as the receiver sought to balance the books. Behind the scenes, majority shareholder Cliff Bassett was involved in protracted discussions with ex-chairman David Kohler in a bid to purchase Kohler's shareholding.

Until Bassett had wrested control, the club could not move out of receivership. As the sorry saga dragged on, the Football League were getting tired and agitated, and finally set a time limit of midnight on Friday, 6 August for the two protagonists to come to an agreement. Otherwise the plug would have been pulled and 114 years of history would have been just that ... history.

Many supporters travelled up to Notts County on the opening day unsure as to whether they would have a team to support. But word soon spread that Bassett and Kohler had signed the necessary documents, which were faxed to Lytham St Annes just as the clock struck midnight the previous day.

Although the game at Meadow Lane was a drab affair, the many Luton supporters present did not give a jot, although they realised that the club was not yet out of the woods and that it would be some time before the spectre of receivership could be banished and some semblance of normality could return. It had all been a little too close for comfort.

Despite the loss of Willmott and Davis, along with the experienced Mitchell Thomas, the Town started off the season rather well, to most people's surprise. 17-year-old Matthew Taylor, who made his debut on the opening day after jumping straight from youth team to first team football, was a revelation. Also taking the eye were other teenagers off the Kenilworth Road conveyor belt – Gary Doherty, Matthew Spring and Liam George.

The quote by football pundit Alan Hansen – 'You don't win anything with kids' – was to prove true as far as the Hatters were concerned. The team's form began to falter as autumn turned to winter. The experienced Phil Gray received a serious injury which would keep him out for two months. That left only three players in the side – Marvin Johnson, Adam Locke and Julian Watts – with any real experience.

The Hatters' home form stood up well, but from a high spot of second in late August the team had dropped to twelfth by Christmas, mainly due to a poor away record and patchy form from the younger element in the side.

The new millennium dawned with a 4-1 home thumping of Scunthorpe, but performances remained inconsistent. By March the Hatters looked more likely to be dragged into the relegation dogfight than looking for a play-off place.

Due to the lack of money, Lennie Lawrence had persevered with rookie goalkeeper Tanny Abbey, but Abbey's confidence was shattered once too often following a 1-4 home defeat at the hands of Bristol Rovers and the experienced Ben Roberts was brought into the side on loan. Roberts looked shaky in his first few outings – attributed to lack of match practice – but once he had got his eye in he steadied the defence. On the back of four games without defeat the Hatters had the unusual experience of having nothing to play for with several matches left to contest.

As the season drew to a close, Gary Doherty was sold to Tottenham for an initial £1 million, with the sale paving the way for reluctant Luton Town owner, chairman and saviour Cliff Bassett to sell his majority shareholding. The buyer was Mike Watson-Challis, who had been on the Luton board ten years before. He now became the new chairman and immediately invited some of his own men to join him. Lennie Lawrence, meanwhile, began the summer sifting through the lists of released players looking for the three experienced players he reckoned he needed to add to the squad to push the Hatters into the play-off positions next season.

Whether he would be allowed to continue chasing the dream remained to be seen.

## *Match of the Season 1999-2000*

### Fulham 2 Luton Town 2

FA Cup, 3rd Round, 11 December 1999

With the cash-strapped Hatters drifting down the league table after a promising start to the season, a good run in the FA Cup was vital, especially as the team had suffered defeat at the first stage of both the Worthington and AWS cups.

**DID YOU KNOW?**

**On 28 December 1999, Bristol City's match programme listed Tony Thorpe as playing for both sides! He had been on loan at Luton, but went back just before Christmas.**

Kingstonian, with ex-Hatter Dwight Marshall making a welcome return to Kenilworth Road, proved more difficult opposition than the difference in standing would suggest, and it took a wonder strike from Matthew Spring to finally see off the skilful non-leaguers. A home game with Lincoln of Division Three was the reward in the next round. It was covered by Sky, whose choice was clearly governed by hopes of an upset. They nearly got their wish as the Town struggled to make any impact on the game. It was only after the versatile Gary Doherty was sent up into attack in the second half that a goal looked likely. Doherty scored twice, levelling the score on each occasion, with his second coming only six minutes from time. Lucky Luton lived to fight another day.

In the replay at Sincil Bank the game was ruined as a spectacle by a strong wind that played tricks with the ball. Despite this, a professional performance from the Town limited Lincoln to only a few opportunities and it was left to Stuart Douglas to net the only goal near the end. This time the Hatters deserved the result.

The reward for the win over the Red Imps was a trip to Division One Fulham. The Cottagers had run away with Division Two the previous season, with the Town inflicting their only home defeat along the way, but they were now even stronger and had just knocked Premiership side Tottenham out of the Worthington Cup.

The sixteen-man squad that the Hatters took to west London cost nothing in transfer fees, whereas the home side boasted £14 million worth of talent. On the bench Fulham could call upon substitutes costing a combined total of £2.5 million, while Luton manager Lennie Lawrence named three substitutes without a Football League appearance between them.

Despite the mis-match, 2,346 Luton fans travelled to Craven Cottage hoping for some sort of upset and they were duly rewarded when Liam George opened the scoring after only six minutes. George was on hand to tap the ball home after Fulham goalkeeper Maik Taylor could only parry a fierce drive from Matthew Taylor.

Stung by this reversal, Fulham's response was swift. Slack defending allowed Chris Coleman space to cross to the far post, where Kit Symons headed down for Geoff Horsfield to mis-hit a shot past the exposed Nathan Abbey in the Luton goal. Soon afterwards Sean Davis added a second for the home side, sliding in unchallenged to convert Barry Hayles' cross from close range.

Following their spell of madness, Luton defended for the rest of the game with great determination and after the interval started to push forward in search of an equaliser. Doherty hit the inside of the post and then fired the rebound into the side-netting before George dragged a shot wide after Efetobore Sodje had sprinted 60 yards out of defence with the ball.

Stuart Douglas and Taylor wasted good opportunities and Sodje headed wide before Spring equalised on 83 minutes with a goal that was well worth the wait. Demonstrating textbook technique, Spring slammed a 30-yard half-volley into a helpless Taylor's bottom corner after George's lay-off. The ferocity and quality of the strike heralded a second's silence before the Luton supporters applauded a goal that was every bit as good as the one that sank Kingstonian.

The Town hung on with ease until the final whistle to earn a result that felt just like a victory.

7

# FALL AND RISE 2000-2004

## NATIONWIDE DIVISION 1 2000-01

| | |
|---|---|
| Nationwide Division 2 | 22nd (relegated) |
| Worthington Cup | 2nd Round |
| FA Cup | 3rd Round |

Lennie Lawrence did not have much time to prepare for the forthcoming season as, out of the blue, he was dismissed from his post, with the untried and untested Ricky Hill taking his place in the hot seat.

Hill had some coaching experience behind him, but had not been exposed at managerial level in this country – although he did carry a huge amount of goodwill on his shoulders based on his sublime displays as a player at Kenilworth Road over many years.

Chris Ramsey was immediately appointed as Hill's assistant and the pair made up for lost time by bringing in several – mostly unheard of – players on free transfers. Eyebrows were then raised when £425,000, a massive amount by Luton standards, was spent on goalkeeper Mark Ovendale from Bournemouth. Supporters felt that, although Ovendale came with a high reputation, the fee seemed excessive and it was hoped that Hill's inexperience in the transfer market had not been instrumental in the transaction.

Despite any misgivings, the fans gave Hill a hero's reception on the opening day of the season, but Notts County completely ruined the party when winning 1-0 in a tedious and frustrating game. The Notts County game set the tone for the season and although the Luton players flattered to deceive with several early season draws, those draws soon turned into defeats. The Town were soon in the relegation positions where they would remain throughout the whole sorry campaign.

Youngsters were thrown into a struggling side before they were ready, panic buys were made – with the £100,000 paid to Dutch club NAC Breda for Peter Thomson being a notable waste of money. There were undercurrents of unrest amongst some of the players, particularly concerning Ramsey's training methods, and Kenilworth Road was not a happy place.

Ramsey was dismissed after only three months at the club, whereupon Hill appointed ex-Luton favourites Lil Fuccillo and Brian Stein to his coaching staff. Unfortunately, results did not improve and after an awful 0-3 home reversal at the hands of Bristol City in November the inevitable happened and Hill was sacked.

Lil Fuccillo, who had enjoyed previous managerial experience at Peterborough, took charge and presided over a rare victory – 1-0 against Rushden in the FA Cup – in his first game in charge. But once the initial euphoria had died down it was back to losing ways as the Hatters plunged headlong towards the football basement.

Fuccillo sought to bring in experienced players on loan to help reverse Hill's policy of taking on youngsters, only to be thwarted at just about every turn. After all, what sensible, ambitious player wanted to join a struggling club nose-diving towards Division 3?

Another bombshell exploded in early February, with strong rumours circulating that Joe Kinnear was taking over at Kenilworth Road. Supporters could not believe that a manager who had made his mark in the Premiership, performing wonders at down-at-heel Wimbledon year after year, would want to resurrect his career at Luton, of all places. But the rumours turned out to be true and Kinnear became the fourth manager at Kenilworth Road in a little over six months.

In March 1999, when Kinnear suffered his heart-attack, the Dons were sixth and chasing a UEFA Cup place. He departed from the club that summer but was now ready for a return to the stresses of football management. He immediately set about trying to shake up the Hatters from top to bottom. Bizarrely, Lil Fuccillo, who had apparently never signed a managerial contract, was kept on as a coach.

The euphoria that had greeted Ricky Hill in August reappeared in February, with Kinnear's first game in charge – at Northampton – a sell-out. The 1-0 win at Sixfields was a glorious start and prefaced a run of five wins from the new man's first seven games in charge. With sixteen points quickly rattled up, the club entertained real hopes of clambering out of the drop zone.

Unfortunately, following a 1-0 home victory over Cambridge in early March, the Town failed to win another game and sank back to a division that they had last left in 1968.

Despite various prophesies from Kinnear about how relegation could be avoided, anyone with any knowledge of football could see that the squad he had inherited was poor and a major overhaul was required. Getting rid of the deadwood, some players being on long contracts, was not likely to be easy however.

Steve Howard had been signed from Northampton on transfer deadline day to provide Luton with the big target man they strived for, but it was too little too late. Howard's day would no doubt come in the future. Of the 33 players used during this fateful campaign, only five would still be at Kenilworth Road three years later.

## Match of the Season 2000-01

### Swindon Town 1 Luton Town 3

Division 2, 24 February 2001

Joe Kinnear's appointment to the managerial hot-seat at Kenilworth Road had brought with it a new surge of enthusiasm amongst the supporters, who turned out in their droves to witness a 1-0 win at Northampton in his first game in charge. A midweek win at Notts County followed, and when Swansea were seen off 5-3 at Kenilworth Road in a pulsating game, some supporters genuinely felt that what had recently been a threadbare, lopsided squad, completely lacking in any quality, could pull off an amazing escape from relegation.

The supporters were quickly brought back down to earth when the team lost 1-3 to a strong Walsall outfit, but were still prepared to travel in their thousands to Swindon for the next episode of the 'Great Escape'. Swindon were also struggling at the wrong end of the division but were still five points ahead of the Town. This was seen to be a true test, as the Robins would be one of the teams that would need to be overtaken if relegation were to be avoided.

The Hatters started the game confidently but Swindon's policy of pumping high balls into the box caused concern, most notably for Mark Ovendale in the Luton goal, who fumbled one such cross and was relieved to see Michael Reddy turn and fire the loose ball past an unguarded net. Ovendale was punished for his second blunder, however, when he dropped a cross right onto the head of a surprised Gary Alexander, who gratefully accepted the invitation to open the scoring in the 39th minute.

Swindon's joy was short-lived, though. The Hatters equalised three minutes later when Keith Rowland, on loan from QPR, ghosted into the box and headed Emmerson Boyce's cross firmly into the net.

**DID YOU KNOW?**

**The Hatters used 33 players in 1997-98, equalling the number used back in 1960-61. That record was broken in 2002-03 and 2003-04, when 34 players were used.**

Kinnear's men grew in confidence as the second half unfolded and Mark Stein forced a brilliant save out of Steve Mildenhall in the Swindon goal with a close-range header.

It was not long before the Town took the lead. Rowland returned his first-half favour by firing in a left-wing free-kick which was met by the unmarked Boyce, who planted his header past Mildenhall.

Although the Hatters were never in any real danger after this, it took super-sub Lee Mansell to make the game safe when he netted in the final minute. Peter Thomson was set free by a clever through ball from Liam George, but although he lost control trying to round the goalkeeper, Mansell was on hand to steer the loose ball into the empty net.

Even the most cynical of Luton supporters felt that perhaps the drop could be avoided as they drove happily back to Bedfordshire, but with only one further win being enjoyed over the next fifteen games until the season's end, their confidence was unfortunately severely misplaced. The victory at Swindon would be the only time during the whole campaign that the Town fought back to win after going behind.

# NATIONWIDE DIVISION 3 2001-02

| | |
|---|---|
| Nationwide Division 3 | 2nd (promoted) |
| Worthington Cup | 1st Round |
| FA Cup | 1st Round |

With the Hatters back in the basement division for the first time since 1968, following the bleakest run of results and with the poorest team in living memory, it was always going to be a summer of frantic activity as far as manager Joe Kinnear was concerned. Arguably his best signing was Mick Harford as his number two. Harford still enjoyed legendary status at Kenilworth Road, as was proved by subscribers to the first edition of this book, who voted him their most popular Hatter ever.

Several players who were deemed surplus to requirements were granted free transfers or had their contracts paid up as Kinnear set about building a squad that would stand the rigours of Division 3 and beyond. Seven new players were signed during the summer, with five making their debuts on the opening day of the new season at Carlisle, and with two more the following week. Understandably, it took a while for the new intake to gel. The early-season results were patchy, although the much-travelled Carl Griffiths was looking a bargain due to his experience and predatory instincts in front of goal.

The season really took off towards the end of September, with the introduction of Jean-Louis Valois to the Kenilworth Road faithful for the home game against Torquay. Valois immediately had the supporters on the edge of their seats in anticipation. His ball control, skill and vision were something to behold, and he capped a virtuoso performance with a stunning long-range effort which brought the house down in the 5-1 victory.

That win gave the team the impetus to climb the table. Valois often looked bewildered as the ball was hacked back and forth. With Division Three defenders having scant regard for his silky skills, he was often on the periphery of the action. Having said that, whenever he had the ball and was allowed to unfurl his repertoire of tricks, he was a cut above anything else in the division.

After netting seven goals in only ten starts, Griffiths suffered a hairline fracture of the shin, perversely against his old employers Leyton Orient. Complications set in and Griffiths missed the rest of the campaign. Dean Crowe was signed from Stoke, initially on loan, and immediately picked up the mantle of the little player alongside the big Steve Howard.

A mini-run of defeats in November culminated with 24 players being unavailable before the away fixture at Kidderminster. A flu epidemic, injuries and suspensions left the club unable to send a team to Aggborough. Kinnear, armed with medical sick-notes, pulled out of the fixture the day before. As expected, Kidderminster and the Football League were not pleased and there was talk of a points deduction as well as a fine, but in the end a hefty £30,000 was levied which included compensation to the home club. The Hatters took immense delight in winning 4-1 when the game was eventually played.

Once Kinnear was able to call upon a virtual full squad, it was back to winning ways. It was a long haul to try to claw back points on runaway leaders Plymouth, who were remarkably consistent. The big clash between the top two at Kenilworth Road took place in early February and the biggest crowd since the visit of Southampton in the FA Cup in 1995 saw the Hatters win a titanic struggle 2-0, through late goals from Kevin Nicholls and Steve Howard.

Strangely, rather than instil the team with confidence, victory over Plymouth had the opposite effect. The next two games were lost, but another harsh lecture by Kinnear galvanised the side once more as they embarked on a fourteen-game unbeaten run which carried them through to the end of the season. The run began with a 3-0 home win over Bristol Rovers on a wet and windy night and gradually built up a head of steam as York, Lincoln, Torquay and Leyton Orient went the same way. These wins enabled the Town to consolidate their second spot in the table.

The trip to fellow promotion challengers Rushden and Diamonds was seen as the toughest game since the meeting with Plymouth but, with Matt Taylor imperious on the wing, the Hatters won through 2-1 in hurricane conditions and with it came the virtual certainty of promotion. The next three games, all at home, yielded a maximum nine points, and promotion was confirmed after a 3-1 victory at Swansea on Easter Saturday. There were still four matches remaining in which to try to overtake Plymouth.

Easter Monday saw fourth-placed Mansfield come to Kenilworth Road. In a carnival atmosphere the Town put on a carnival display, winning 5-3 and avenging the hammering they suffered at Field Mill the previous November. A 4-0 win at Hull the following week extended Luton's winning sequence to twelve and also enabled them to claim top spot. Plymouth, however, had a game in hand which they won. With the Town drawing their penultimate game, the championship went to Devon.

In any normal season the Town would have romped away with the divisional title, but the sheer consistency of the Pilgrims meant that not only the champions, but also the runners-up, broke many club records. As far as Luton Town were concerned, the most wins, the most away wins, the most away goals, the most points and the most consecutive wins was just reward for a brilliant season. Many supporters wondered, though, about how the team would have fared had Carl Griffiths not been injured!

## Match of the Season 2001-02

### Luton Town 5 Torquay United 1

Division 3, 22 September 2001

The Town started their first season back in the football basement tentatively. By the end of September, although a position in the top six had been maintained, the performances had been nothing to brag about and were certainly not those of a team that hoped to bounce straight back to Division 2.

On top of this, big striker Steve Howard had infuriated manager Joe Kinnear by defying his instructions during the game at York. Kinnear had told him not to take any penalties that might be awarded, but Howard went ahead, took one, and missed. Howard's punishment was to be dropped for the visit of Lincoln to Kenilworth Road, which ended in a dismal 1-1 draw, with his future at the club shrouded in doubt.

Torquay were next up at Kenilworth Road and the talk in the stands before kick-off was of the recall of Howard after patching up his differences with Kinnear. Little notice was taken of the inclusion of a French left-sided player. After all, Luton Town had not seen a decent foreign player since the days of Lars Elstrup and the more cynical supporters were not expecting much from Jean-Louis Valois, or whatever his name was.

Those cynics were soon made to eat their words, however. From his first touch of the ball it could be seen that Valois possessed skills that were completely out of keeping with Division 3.

Before Valois could unleash his bag of tricks, though, Steve Howard was quickest to react to a Carl Griffiths shot that had come back off the post. Howard was mobbed by his team-mates – he had been forgiven. Valois then set up Matthew Taylor for a cross to the head of Griffiths, before Town midfielder Kevin Nicholls gave Torquay a lifeline when heading past Ovendale in the Luton goal. Griffiths headed his second on the stroke of half-time from a pin-point Valois cross, and from that moment it became a personal contest between the Hatters attack and Luton-born Kevin Dearden in the Torquay goal.

**DID YOU KNOW?**

**Luton Town's artificial surface was laid in 1985 and rolled up in 1991. Coincidentally, the club's ban on away fans was officially in operation from 1986 to 1991.**

The ex-Challney schoolboy defied Howard and Griffiths before Valois brought the house down with a shot from 35 yards that arrowed into the top corner of the net. Taylor then crossed for Griffiths to complete his hat-trick with a diving header, before Valois left the field to a standing ovation after being substituted by Stuart Douglas.

Torquay boss Roy McFarland said of Valois: 'I was glad to see the back of him when he came off towards the end. He tore us apart and teased us all afternoon. He will be revelation in this league if he stays.' Kinnear purred: 'I do not like to make comparisons but he is like David Ginola. He's got two wonderful feet and can turn up anywhere on the pitch. He puts bums on seats!'

# NATIONWIDE DIVISION 2 2002-03

| | |
|---|---|
| Nationwide Division 2 | 9th |
| Worthington Cup | 2nd Round |
| FA Cup | 2nd Round |

Luton manager Joe Kinnear refused to rest on his laurels after masterminding the club's immediate promotion from the bowels of Division Three after only one season. He knew that certain of the players who had performed so admirably during the previous campaign might not be up to scratch at a higher level and, for the second summer running, the rumours of players coming in and going out were circulating the town on a daily basis.

When the dust eventually settled the main signings were old favourite Tony Thorpe, who returned from Bristol City, and Northern Ireland international midfielder Steve Robinson, who had endured a torrid time at Preston. Prior to going to Deepdale, Robinson had starred for Bournemouth in Division 2 and was therefore fully aware of the challenge ahead.

On the debit side, most fans sadly accepted that the brilliant Matthew Taylor deserved to be playing at a higher level than Division 2. After much speculation that he was about to sign for Tottenham, it came as a surprise when Taylor joined Division 1 Portsmouth for what seemed a ridiculously small fee. Unfortunately, lower league players, no matter how good, nowadays rarely commanded premium prices. The big clubs preferred to look abroad where fees were lower. Financial prudence was the new commandment. The days of millions paid for the likes of John Hartson and Matthew Upson were consigned to history.

On the eve of the season, forward Adrian Forbes tore cruciate knee ligaments. The injury would keep him out for most of the campaign, and that in itself meant that the Town were always likely to be light up front, should further injuries strike.

The new season opened with Peterborough the visitors to Kenilworth Road. Posh tore the Town apart during the first half and although the Hatters staged a fight-back in the second period the match was still lost 2-3. Everyone left the ground at the end wondering whether Division 2 had improved greatly in the one year the Town had been away, or whether the team were not as good as they thought they were.

It was a mixture of both. The Hatters lost their first four games and seemed set for relegation before Christmas. Kinnear kept the players locked in the changing room for two hours following the 2-3 defeat at home to Barnsley in game four, and his reading of the Riot Act seemed to work as the team drew 0-0 at promotion favourites Cardiff two days later.

The first league win came at Kenilworth Road the following Saturday. The season was now up and running, as further confirmed with a 2-1 win at Watford in the Worthington Cup. Unfortunately, the cup run came to an end in the next round when Premiership Aston Villa made light work of a ponderous Hatters and ran out 3-0 winners.

In the league, a run of six wins and a draw from seven games in late September and October hoisted the Hatters into the top ten and banished the disappointments of the early-season form. Another good run over Christmas moved the club into the play-off positions but inconsistency, especially at Kenilworth Road, meant that the Town were always hovering on the periphery of the action at the top of the table, which was frustrating for everyone.

In defence, Chris Coyne and Emmerson Boyce, together with Taylor's replacement Sol Davis, were solid enough, but there were constant problems in the goalkeeping department, with six different occupants of the position. The experimentation culminated with teenager Rob Beckwith, showing maturity beyond his years, handed the jersey as the season drew to a close. Up front, Steve Howard and Tony Thorpe, whenever they were fit enough to play together, showed a good understanding and scored 35 goals between them. Injuries took their toll and once again a ridiculously high number of 34 players were used over the course of the campaign.

Only two wins from the last thirteen games meant a disappointing end to the season. As if to highlight the inconsistency of the side, the run included a 0-4 hammering at the hands of Crewe at Kenilworth Road and a 5-0 victory at Colchester, the biggest away win since 1967. The season ended with a limp 1-2 defeat at Swindon. Afterwards, Joe Kinnear said: 'Thank God it's over.' Would those words come back to haunt him?

## Match of the Season 2002-03

**Watford 1 Luton Town 2**

Worthington Cup, 1st, 10 September 2002

Before the season started, when the draw was made for the first round of the Worthington Cup, it was immediately decided to make the trip to bitter rivals Watford all-ticket. This seemed a trifle over the top to all those football supporters who lived far from the environs of Beds and Herts.

**DID YOU KNOW?**

**Luton broke many club records during 2002-03 – points, total wins, away wins, away goals scored, consecutive away wins, consecutive wins. But the Town finished second!**

This would be the first meeting of the sides since 1998. Previous clashes had been a tad tribal. The Hatters were fresh from a record-breaking promotion season, while Watford were anxious to beat their neighbours at Vicarage Road for the first time in fifteen years. In these circumstances, the all-ticket billing seemed eminently sensible.

Neither side had started the league season well, but all this was forgotten as 4,500 Luton supporters swelled the Vicarage Road attendance to over 14,000. Crowd problems before the start delayed the kick-off by fifteen minutes but by then the atmosphere had been whipped up and once the game was under way the Hatters clattered into tackles to let the opposition know they were there.

The first chance of the game fell to Steve Howard, who had been neatly set up by Kevin Nicholls, but the big forward dragged his shot wide. Watford then came more into it and Carl Emberson in the Luton goal had to be alert to a long shot from Jamie Hand. Emberson was deputising for loanee Ben Roberts, who Charlton had refused permission to play to prevent him being cup-tied.

The breakthrough came on 31 minutes, and what a goal it was. Taking a Howard pass in his stride, Matthew Spring strode forward and unleashed a rocket from 35 yards which flew past ex-Hatter Alec Chamberlain in the Watford goal into the top corner. Buoyed by this strike, the Town pressed and doubled their lead ten minutes later. Spring threaded through a pass to Howard who, taking advantage of a moment's hesitancy by central defender and another ex-Hatter Sean Dyche, shot low and hard past Chamberlain.

Watford gambled after the interval by bringing on young winger Anthony McNamee. This meant they were effectively playing with four up front. McNamee saw plenty of the ball but seemed unable to propel his crosses any further than the near post, leaving the Watford forwards increasingly frustrated. The Hornets eventually pulled a goal back when Dominic Foley headed in a Micah Hyde cross with fifteen minutes left. That set up a frantic finale but the Luton defence held firm and the last chance of the game fell to Howard who saw his shot well saved by Chamberlain.

Afterwards Joe Kinnear said: 'I was brought up in Watford, played for Watford boys and my mother and sister still live here. I am going round to see my mother now and she will probably give me a clip around the ear and not talk to me for a week!'

# NATIONWIDE DIVISION 2 2003-04

| | |
|---|---|
| Nationwide Division 1 | 10th |
| Carling Cup | 2nd Round |
| FA Cup | 4th Round |

The old season had just ended and as players, staff and supporters were preparing for their summer holidays the first of several disasters struck the club, making Luton Town FC the talking point of the whole of the football world for weeks on end. The story as it unfolded over that long, hot summer could not have been made up and will, no doubt, be turned into a book one day entitled 'How not to run a football club!'

It all started on 20 May when the club's owner, Mike Watson-Challis, announced that he was to sell it to an, as yet un-named, consortium. It had been rumoured that Watson-Challis had invested £20 million in the club that he loved but felt that the time was right to move on, leaving the Hatters in the hands of those who could take it on one stage further.

Supporters were concerned by the fact that the prospective new owners would not reveal themselves. They were then mortified to hear that Joe Kinnear and his number two, Mick Harford, had been sacked, and had learned of their dismissals through the post. When Roger Terrell and Lee Power were introduced to oversee the football side of the club, angry supporters were waiting for them *en masse* outside the main gates. An unruly demonstration ensued, the effect of which was to warn all newcomers that they had a fight on their hands. Terrell and Power soon departed, having realised the depth of feeling that they had unleashed among supporters.

The front man for the supposed consortium was then revealed as John Gurney, who had been involved in several other ventures – among them football and rugby clubs – most of which had ended in tears. When he announced his bizarre plans for Luton Town, they included changing the name to London-Luton and building a 70,000-capacity stadium adjacent to Junction 10 of the M1. The complex would embrace a Grand Prix racing circuit and a 20,000-space underground car park to service the airport. Never bashful about his ambitions, Gurney predicted that before long Luton Town would rank alongside Manchester United and Real Madrid, and would boast its own American Football, Baseball and Ice Hockey team under the title of Team Europe.

Quite naturally, the Hatters became a laughing stock in the national press but behind the scenes supporters were rallying.

Within days 'Trust in Luton' (TiL) was formed with 3,000 pledging their support. The first objective was to refuse to renew season tickets, thus depriving the club of cash. Seemingly oblivious to all that was going on around him, Gurney then announced that the next Luton manager would be selected after a ludicrous phone vote. Naturally, no Luton supporters were prepared to demean themselves by entering into this charade. Surprise, surprise, Gurney's preferred candidate, ex-Hatter Mike Newell, was installed having narrowly beaten ex-manager Joe Kinnear in the poll for the job in the hot seat.

TiL was, in the meantime, beavering away behind the scenes and brokered a deal which sought to place the club into administrative receivership, thereby bringing to an end the short career of John Gurney. Another well-attended TiL meeting was held at Kenilworth Road, during which it was warned that this was only the start of the battle, as administrative receivership meant tightening belts and unpopular decisions being made whilst seeking out new owners for the club. Warm applause was given to Chief Executive Cherry Newbery, who had battled behind the scenes to keep the ship floating whilst being placed in an intolerable situation.

Administrative Receiver Barry Ward immediately announced that the club would not be running a reserve side over the next season. There would also be a complete embargo on player signings, but on the bright side Mick Harford would return to Kenilworth Road as first-team coach and Director of Football.

New manager Mike Newell had both hands tied behind his back. He had to win over the fans as well as put together a winning team within the straightjacket imposed on him of no player signings. That he achieved both over the course of the season is to his great credit, as the Hatters were on the fringes of the play-off positions throughout the campaign. They did so without necessarily looking real promotion candidates, due to an understandable lack of depth in the playing squad.

Newell managed to keep the squad together, with the only notable departure that of Tony Thorpe who, days before, had begged everyone to rally around the club. Thorpe's transfer to QPR certainly added spice to the coming games against the team from west London.

The goalkeeping position was once again causing problems, with Newell only having teenagers Dean Brill and Rob Beckwith to choose from initially. Dispensation was granted to sign Marlon Beresford on a short-term contract and his introduction brought about arguably the best spell of the campaign. Due to the financial constraints he could not be offered a longer deal and he reluctantly left. Too many games were lost after conceding late goals which in normal circumstances would have been extremely frustrating but, given the club's position, was now the least of anyone's worries. Supporters were simply glad to have a team to watch, win or lose, when they had faced the very real prospect of complete liquidation the previous summer.

For once the Hatters enjoyed a good run in the FA Cup, but injuries and suspensions hit their peak around the time of the fourth-round tie against Tranmere Rovers. The Hatters team was severely depleted and money-spinning further progress slipped away.

Yet another consortium, this one headed by ex-Town General Manager Bill Tomlins, was identified as the best way forward for the club. But the red tape imposed by the Football League meant that numerous hurdles had to be overcome before the administrative receiver could pack his bags and allow the new men to take charge.

No one believes it will be easy in the future for a club like Luton Town, but with new men at the helm, a strong management team, promising youngsters coming through on the playing side and a hoped-for new ground, the way ahead looks brighter than for most other clubs of similar size.

## *Match of the Season 2003-04*

### Charlton Athletic 4 Luton Town 4

Carling Cup, 2nd Round, 23 September 2003

What with all the problems surrounding the club over the summer, Luton Town supporters were glad to merely have a football team to support. A trip to a Premiership club in the Carling Cup was therefore seen as more of a bonus than normal, and a good many Hatters supporters made their way to the Valley hoping for a better display than their team had put up against Aston Villa twelve months earlier.

In a pre-match boost it was learned that Gary McSheffrey, the Town's on-loan signing from Coventry, had been given permission to play and, after the opening exchanges which saw both sides go close, the little forward weaved his way past Charlton defender Mark Fish before slotting a ball through to the overlapping Kevin Foley who netted with ease. Two minutes later David Bayliss was on hand at the far post to head in a Matthew Spring corner and suddenly the ecstatic Luton supporters could see a major upset on the cards.

**DID YOU KNOW?**

**When Luton fought their way through to the fourth round of the FA Cup in 2003-04, it was the first time since 1933 they had gone so far after entering in the first round.**

On 40 minutes, however, a momentary lapse of concentration in the Luton defence gave Paulo Di Canio and Kevin Lisbie the chance to set up Scott Parker to bring Charlton back into the game. The leveller came soon after the interval when Lisbie headed home a Claus Jensen cross, but the Hatters refused to lie down and when McSheffrey curled home a wonder goal with twelve minutes remaining it looked like it was going to be the Town's night after all. With the game deep in stoppage time and the referee looking at his watch, Di Canio headed in a cruel equaliser that was timed at 93 minutes.

The breathless game now went into extra-time and when Jensen fired in to put Charlton ahead for the first time it seemed that the brave fight was over. But after finding extra stores of resolve, skipper Chris Coyne levelled the tie once again five minutes later. At last the referee blew the final whistle leaving the score at an incredible 4-4 with the lottery of a penalty shoot-out now reality.

In common with everything that had gone before, neither side would give way, and the first fifteen penalties all found the back of the net after Charlton had won the toss to take the first kick. It was left to Coyne to take number sixteen and he was left holding his head in his hands after seeing Charlton goalkeeper Dean Kiely block his effort.

Afterwards, Charlton manager Alan Curbishley was full of praise for the Luton side, while his counterpart, Mike Newell, although immensely proud of his charges, was disappointed at yet another goal conceded in injury-time.

Ian Buxton and Keith Allen pester the Aldershot defence at Kenilworth Road. (March 1968)

Terry Branston shows off the Division Four championship trophy. (May 1968)

Laurie Sheffield heads the winner against Orient. (March 1969)

John Collins tries to lob the Rochdale keeper, watched by Malcolm MacDonald and Keith Allen. (November 1969)

Manager Alec Stock shows off Don Givens and Jimmy Ryan, his new signings from Manchester United. (May 1970)

Skipper Mike Keen rises to head the only goal of the game at Watford. (December 1970)

Birmingham's Trevor Francis closely patrolled by John Moore. (April 1971)

Vic Halom in an aerial duel with the Swindon defenders. (October 1971)

The ball is in the back of the net as Vic Halom wheels away after scoring against Huddersfield. (September 1972)

John Aston gets a cross in during the FA Cup quarter-final clash at Roker Park, Sunderland. (March 1973)

New signings on the road to promotion, Alan West and Jim Husband. (December 1973)

Hatters director, Eric Morecambe, joins in the promotion celebrations at West Bromwich. (April 1974)

Luton players infiltrate the Liverpool wall at Kenilworth Road. (August 1974)

Ron Futcher and Peter Anderson appeal for a goal at Portsmouth. (September 1975)

Goalmouth action at West Bromwich. (August 1975)

Jim Husband lets loose at Bristol City. (March 1976)

Ron Futcher attempts to beat the Tottenham defence. (September 1977)

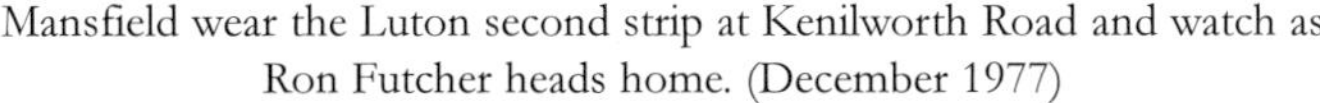
Mansfield wear the Luton second strip at Kenilworth Road and watch as Ron Futcher heads home. (December 1977)

'Look what I have done!' Lil Fuccillo scores against Oldham in the FA Cup. (January 1978)

David Pleat introduces his new signing, Chris Turner. (August 1978)

Alan West fires in during the 6-0 thrashing of Notts County at Kenilworth Road. (October 1978)

Bob Hatton forces his way through the Swansea defence. (September 1979)

Staff Christmas Fancy Dress party. (December 1980)

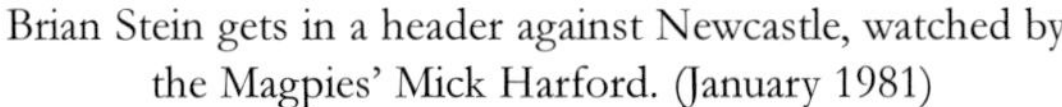

Brian Stein gets in a header against Newcastle, watched by the Magpies' Mick Harford. (January 1981)

Brian Stein lobs the only goal at Notts County. (March 1981)

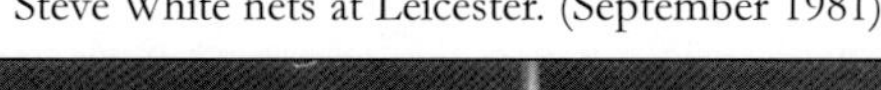
Steve White nets at Leicester. (September 1981)

Ricky Hill chips the goalkeeper during the championship-clinching home win over QPR. (May 1982)

Graeme Souness and Mark Lawrenson are spellbound by Ricky Hill's skills at Anfield. (September 1982)

Manchester United players crowd the penalty area at a wet Kenilworth Road, while Brian Stein and Paul Walsh wait for a corner to come over. (October 1982).

Tottenham's Gary O'Reilly (left) heads into his own goal at Kenilworth Road. (January 1983)

You would never guess that Brian Stein and Paul Walsh have been picked to play for England against France. (February 1984)

Mick Harford rises highest to head in at Everton. (January 1985)

David Preece rushes to congratulate Mick Harford after he scores against Manchester United. (April 1985)

Mike Newell and Mick Harford celebrate Brian Stein's goal at Southampton. (February 1986)

Brian Stein stabs home at Leicester. (August 1986)

The Luton and Arsenal teams are led out before the 1988 Littlewoods Cup final. (April 1988)

The last-gasp Wembley winner scored by Brian Stein. (April 1988)

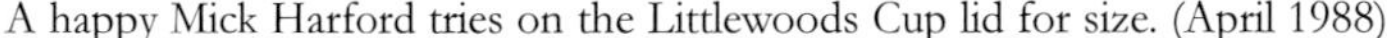

A happy Mick Harford tries on the Littlewoods Cup lid for size. (April 1988)

Ricky Hill tries to dribble around Steve Sutton in the Forest goal at Wembley. (April 1989)

David Preece manages to cut the ball back at Southampton. (November 1989)

Tim Breacker has just scored during the 3-2 win at Derby, which helped avoid relegation. (May 1990)

Record signing Lars Elstrup tangles with Leeds' Gordon Strachan at Kenilworth Road. (September 1990)

Liverpool's Nicky Tanner has just put through his own goal at Anfield, much to the delight of Mark Pembridge. (January 1992)

Phil Gray falls on the Watford goalkeeper at Vicarage Road. (April 1993)

Kerry Dixon fights his way through the Peterborough defence. (May 1993)

Julian James in full flight at Portsmouth. (August 1993)

John Hartson closes in on the Newcastle defence during the FA Cup thriller at Kenilworth Road. (February 1994)

David Preece on the ball at Leicester. (February 1994)

Des Linton and Paul Telfer converge on Chelsea's Gavin Peacock at Wembley. (April 1994)

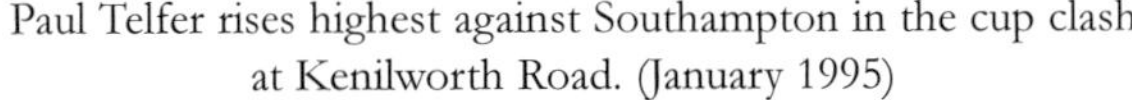
Paul Telfer rises highest against Southampton in the cup clash at Kenilworth Road. (January 1995)

Gary Waddock tangles with Crewe's Danny Murphy. (December 1996)

On loan Rory Allen just fails to connect at Grimsby. (April 1998)

Matthew Spring slaloms through the Manchester City defence. (November 1998)

Gary Doherty is first to the ball at Scunthorpe. (April 2000)

Andrew Fotiadis heads in during the 3-3 FA Cup draw with QPR. (January 2001)

Another goal on the road to promotion. Ian Hillier nets a scorcher at York. (September 2001)

Dean Crowe scores on his debut at Plymouth. (September 2001)

Kevin Foley opens his Luton account against Yeovil in the Carling Cup. (August 2003)

Gary McSheffrey is mobbed after scoring during the 4-4 thriller at Charlton in the Carling Cup. (September 2003)

Big Steve Howard puts himself about at Wycombe. (February 2004)

Kevin Nicholls hits the bar at Barnsley. (March 2004)

Chris Coyne (on floor) nets against Plymouth at Kenilworth Road. (March 2004)

Enoch Showunmi forces his way through at QPR. (March 2004)

Chris Coyne in a determined mood at Tranmere. (April 2004)

# GUIDE TO SEASONAL SUMMARIES

Col 1: Match number (for league fixtures); Round (for cup-ties).
e.g. 4R means 'Fourth round replay.'

Col 2: Date of the fixture and whether Home (H), Away (A), or Neutral (N).

Col 3: Opposition.

Col 4: Attendances. Home gates appear in roman; Away gates in *italics*.
Figures in bold indicate the largest and smallest gates, at home and away.
Average home and away attendances appear after the final league match.

Col 5: Respective league positions of Luton and opponents after the game.
Luton's position appears on the top line in roman.
Their opponents' position appears on the second line in *italics*.
For cup-ties, the division and position of opponents is provided.
e.g. 2:12 means the opposition are twelfth in Division 2.

Col 6: The top line shows the result: W(in), D(raw), or L(ose).
The second line shows Luton's cumulative points total.

Col 7: The match score, Luton's given first.
Scores in bold show Luton's biggest league win and heaviest defeat.

Col 8: The half-time score, Luton's given first.

Col 9: The top line shows Luton's scorers and times of goals in roman.
The second line shows opponents' scorers and times of goals in *italics*.
A 'p' after the time of a goal denotes a penalty; 'og' an own-goal.
The third line gives the name of the match referee.

Team line-ups: Luton line-ups appear on top line, irrespective of whether they are home or away. Opposition teams are on the second line in *italics*.
Players of either side who are sent off are marked !
Luton players making their league debuts are displayed in bold.

Substitutes: Names of substitutes appear only if they actually took the field.
A player substituted is marked *
A second player substituted is marked ^
A third player substituted is marked "
These marks do not indicate the sequence of substitutions.

N.B. For clarity, all information appearing in *italics* relates to opposing teams.

| No | Date | | Att | Pos | Pt | F-A | H-T | Scorers, Times, and Referees | 1 | 2 | 3 | 4 | 5 | 6 | 7 | 8 | 9 | 10 | 11 | 12 sub used |
|---|---|---|---|---|---|---|---|---|---|---|---|---|---|---|---|---|---|---|---|---|
| 1 | A | WREXHAM | | | D | 1-1 | 0-0 | Green 88 | Read | **Hare** | Jardine | Slough* | **Branston** | Moore | French ! | Allen | **Green** | Rioch | Whittaker | Johnson |
| | 19/8 | | 9,514 | | 1 | | | Smith 46 | Schofield | Ingle | Stacey | Showell | Mielczarek | Bradbury ! | Beanland | Griffiths | Smith | McMillan | McLoughlin | |
| | | | | | | | | Ref: C Robinson | In a bad-tempered clash, Luton's Graham French and Wrexham's Terry Bradbury are given their marching orders for fighting in the 66th minute. Town are then reduced to nine men following an injury to substitute Brian Johnson but debutant Rodney Green scores a late equaliser. | | | | | | | | | | | |
| 2 | H | BARNSLEY | | | W | 2-0 | 0-0 | Rioch 75, Allen 84 | Read | Hare | Jardine* | **McDerment** | Branston | Slough | French | Allen | **Brown** | Rioch | Whittaker | **Walker** |
| | 26/8 | | **7,887** | | 3 | | | | Wood | Murphy | Brookes | Bettany | Winstanley | Howard | Earnshaw | Evans | Thomas | Barton* | Taylor | Raggett |
| | | | | | | | | Ref: D Nippard | Due to the newly-introduced 'four-step' law, ex-England and Manchester United goalkeeper Ray Wood is pressurised into making a poor clearance, which Rioch seizes on to break the stalemate. Dennis Walker comes on for the last twelve minutes for his only Luton appearance. | | | | | | | | | | | |
| 3 | A | SWANSEA | | | D | 2-2 | 2-1 | Brown 25, Rioch 40 | Read | McDerment | Slough | Moore | Branston | Rioch | French | Brown | Green | Allen | Whittaker* | Dougan |
| | 2/9 | | 6,674 | | 4 | | | Williams 14, Todd 89 | John | Evans R | Gomersall* | Coughlin | Purcell | Jones | Humphries | Williams | Todd | Allchurch | Evans B | Thomas |
| | | | | | | | | Ref: J Taylor | Town look to have gained their first away win of the season until skipper Branston makes a fatal slip in the dying seconds to let in Swansea's Keith Todd for a close-range header. Town keeper and former inside-forward, Tony Read, keeps the Hatters in the game with many fine saves. | | | | | | | | | | | |
| 4 | A | SOUTHEND | | | L | **0-3** | 0-1 | | Tinsley | Hare | Jardine | McDerment | Branston | Moore | **Beaven** | Allen | Green* | Rioch | Brown | Slough |
| | 4/9 | | 11,355 | | 4 | | | Smillie 20, 75, Baber 56 | Roberts | Bentley | Birks | Ashworth | May | Stevenson | Ferguson | Chisnall | Smillie | Baber | McKinven | |
| | | | | | | | | Ref: E Wallace | Playing slick, powerful football worthy of a higher grade, Southend cut through the Luton defence at will to maintain their unbeaten record. On a miserable night, Brown blasts a penalty five yards wide for injury-hit Luton and new signing, Rodney Green, goes off with a cartilage injury. | | | | | | | | | | | |
| 5 | H | HARTLEPOOLS | | 12 | W | 1-0 | 0-0 | Rioch 56 | Read | Hare | Jardine | McDerment | Branston | Moore | French | Brown | Allen | Rioch | Whittaker | |
| | 9/9 | | 8,347 | 5 | 6 | | | | Smith | Goad | Drysdale | Sheridan | Gill | Hepplewhite | McGovern | Broadbent | Phythian | Mulvaney | Somers | |
| | | | | | | | | Ref: K Burns | Hartlepools throw up a ten-man defence in their attempt to thwart Luton. Bruce Rioch collects the ball on the halfway line and runs through, evading three tackles, before rounding the goalkeeper to score the only goal of the game. Jim Mulvaney squanders two late chances for Pools. | | | | | | | | | | | |
| 6 | A | NEWPORT | | 10 | D | 1-1 | 0-1 | Slough 60 | Read | Hare | Jardine | McDerment | Branston | Moore | Brown* | Allen | Dougan | Rioch | Whittaker | Slough |
| | 16/9 | | 4,625 | 8 | 7 | | | King 44 | Timson | Williams D | Wilson | Wood ! | Williams A | Rowland | Thomas* | Melling | Jones | Hill | King | Wookey |
| | | | | | | | | Ref: R Barker | Substitute Slough scores with his first kick of the game to equalise for the Hatters, although a handball is claimed. This comes after a strike just before half-time from ex-Luton forward, Gerry King. County's Alan Wood is sent off in the final minute after an innocuous clash with Rioch. | | | | | | | | | | | |
| 7 | H | YORK | | 6 | W | 3-1 | 1-1 | Rioch 36, 84, Whittaker 55p | Read | Hare | Jardine | Dougan | Branston | Moore | French | Allen | McDerment | Rioch | Whittaker | |
| | 23/9 | | 7,977 | 23 | 9 | | | McDougall 22 | Fallon | Baker | Turner | Walker | Jackson | Burrows | Alderson | McDougall | Spencer | Hawksby | Horrey | |
| | | | | | | | | Ref: R Tinkler | Bruce Rioch is watched by scouts from three Division 1 clubs and does not disappoint. York's Ted McDougall, later to score against better defences than Luton's, gives the Minstermen a shock lead. Paul Aimson of Bury is the latest centre-forward target for manager Allan Brown. | | | | | | | | | | | |
| 8 | H | SOUTHEND | | 4 | W | 3-1 | 1-0 | Moore 23, Branston 71, French 78 | Read | Hare | Jardine | Dougan | Branston | Moore | French | **Buxton** | Allen | Rioch | Whittaker | |
| | 27/9 | | 13,332 | 2 | 11 | | | Ferguson 69 | Roberts | Bentley | Birks | Ashworth | May | Stevenson | Ferguson | Chisnall* | Smillie | McMillan | McKinven | Beasley |
| | | | | | | | | Ref: N Burtenshaw | New signing from Derby, Ian Buxton, looks bemused as the ball is continually thumped over his head. In a tough game, played at breakneck speed, a knife is flung on to the pitch after Town's second goal. Southend lose their unbeaten record but Luton keep their home record intact. | | | | | | | | | | | |
| 9 | A | ROCHDALE | | 5 | D | 2-2 | 2-1 | Buxton 26, Rioch 32 | Read | Hare | Jardine | Dougan | Branston | Moore | French | Buxton | Allen | Rioch | Whittaker | |
| | 30/9 | | **1,884** | 17 | 12 | | | Winspear 38, Jenkins 65 | Green | Cockcroft | Calloway | Taylor | Smith | Eastham | Winspear | Jenkins* | Fletcher | Reid | Riley | Melledew |
| | | | | | | | | Ref: R Payne | A two-goal lead is thrown away in front of the lowest crowd to watch the Hatters since before the War. Ian Buxton opens his Luton account with a clever overhead kick but is foiled late on by good saves from future Derby goalkeeper Les Green. Dale have not won in seven games. | | | | | | | | | | | |
| 10 | A | DONCASTER | | 8 | L | 0-2 | 0-0 | | Read | Hare* | Jardine | Dougan | Branston | Moore | McDerment | Buxton | Allen | Rioch | Whittaker | Slough |
| | 3/10 | | 5,529 | 12 | 12 | | | Gilfillan 70, Watson 86 | Morritt | Kelly | Shaw | Ricketts | Robertson | Leigh | Watson | Kettlebor'ugh | Warboys | Jeffrey | Gilfillan | |
| | | | | | | | | Ref: J Finney | Rovers chalk up their second successive 2-0 home win in a match played in heavy rain. Golden boys Rioch and Alick Jeffrey are well held by the respective defences and Ian Buxton hits the bar in the 16th minute. Full-back Tommy Hare's gashed shin will keep him out for six weeks. | | | | | | | | | | | |
| 11 | A | CHESTER | | 6 | W | 3-1 | 1-1 | Buxton 39, Allen 66, 86 | Read | Dougan | Jardine | Slough | Branston | Moore | McDerment | Buxton* | Allen | Rioch | Whittaker | Brown |
| | 7/10 | | 3,967 | 22 | 14 | | | Jones 44 | Carling | Ashworth | Bennett | Metcalf | Evans | Sutton | Moir | Jones | Loyden | Ryden | Morris | |
| | | | | | | | | Ref: H Williams | Town have now won as many points away from home as they gained in the whole of last season. Chester, currently with only one home win to their credit, are brushed aside as Keith Allen finally gets back on the goal trail, but both sides are severely troubled by the swirling cross-wind. | | | | | | | | | | | |

| No | Date | Venue | Opposition | Att | Pos | Res / Pts | F-A | H-T | Scorers, Times, and Referees | 1 | 2 | 3 | 4 | 5 | 6 | 7 | 8 | 9 | 10 | 11 | 12 |
|---|---|---|---|---|---|---|---|---|---|---|---|---|---|---|---|---|---|---|---|---|---|
| 12 | | H | CHESTERFIELD | | 5 | W | 1-0 | 0-0 | Buxton 63 | Read | Dougan | Jardine | Slough | Branston | Moore | French | Buxton | Allen | Rioch | Whittaker | |
| | 14/10 | | | 10,441 | *3* | 16 | | | | *Roberts* | *Holmes* | *Sears* | *Hughes* | *Neale* | *Phelan* | *Reid** | *Lord* | *Randall* | *Hollett* | *Wilson* | *Moore* |
| | | | | | | | | | Ref: H New | Newly-wed Bruce Rioch joins the rest of the forward line in squandering many chances on a skating-rink of a pitch. Graham French hits the post as Town run riot in the second half to close the gap on the Spireites at the top of the table. The final score bears no relation to the play. | | | | | | | | | | | |
| 13 | | A | EXETER | | 5 | W | **5-0** | 1-0 | Whittaker 15, Slough 55, Allen 63, 77, | Read | Dougan | Jardine | Slough | Branston | Moore | **Ryan** | Buxton | Allen | Rioch | Whittaker | |
| | 21/10 | | | *3,434* | *24* | 18 | | | [Buxton 80] | *Smout* | *Smyth* | *Crawford* | *Wilkinson* | *Harvey* | *Huxford* | *Hart* | *Fudge* | *Blain* | *Hamilton* | *Watling* | |
| | | | | | | | | | Ref: W Gow | A devastating debut from John Ryan secures the Town's biggest away win for twelve years. Ryan, signed from Cheshire League side Wigan Athletic, Allan Brown's former club, sets up the first three Luton goals. Exeter play into the Hatter's hands by using the new 4-2-4 formation. | | | | | | | | | | | |
| 14 | | H | DONCASTER | | 4 | W | 5-3 | 5-1 | Buxton 5,13, Slough 6, Allen 17, Rioch 33 | Read | Dougan | Jardine | Slough | Branston | Moore | Ryan | Buxton | Allen | Rioch | Whittaker | |
| | 25/10 | | | 13,925 | *18* | 20 | | | *Watson 28, Warboys 80, Kelly 83* | *Morritt* | *Kelly* | *Shaw* | *Kettleboro'gh* | *Robertson* | *Leigh* | *Warboys* | *Jeffrey* | *Webber* | *Watson* | *Gilfillan* | |
| | | | | | | | | | Ref: R Spittle | The Town thrill their biggest crowd of the season with a superb display in the first half, despite continuous rain. Complacency and over-elaboration set in during the second period and the game is almost thrown away. Luton are now only two points away from the top of the table. | | | | | | | | | | | |
| 15 | | H | WORKINGTON | | 5 | W | 4-0 | 1-0 | Slough 1, Whittaker 52, 65, Rioch 86 | Read | Dougan | Jardine | Slough | Branston | Moore | Ryan | Buxton | Allen | Rioch | Whittaker | |
| | 11/11 | | | 10,935 | *22* | 22 | | | | *Ower* | *Ogilvie* | *Butler* | *Kirkman* | *Tugman* | *Middlemass* | *Geidmintis* | *Brayton* | *Tinnion* | *Spratt* | *Trail* | |
| | | | | | | | | | Ref: W Castle | After a blank week caused by the weather, the Town eased their way to a comfortable win over a neat but always ineffectual Workington, who have only one away point to their name. 'We were bad, very bad in the first half' said manager Allan Brown 'but a half-time team talk helped'. | | | | | | | | | | | |
| 16 | | H | SWANSEA | | 4 | W | 4-0 | 0-0 | French 76, Buxton 78, 82, Rioch 79 | Read | Dougan | Jardine | Slough | Branston | Moore | French | Buxton | Allen | Rioch | Whittaker | |
| | 15/11 | | | 14,981 | *17* | 24 | | | | *John* | *Evans R* | *Gomersall* | *Jones* | *Purcell* | *Davis* | *Humphries* | *Williams* | *Todd* | *Screen* | *Evans B* | |
| | | | | | | | | | Ref: C Nicholls | Swansea, by far the quicker and more imaginative side, left the pitch protesting to the referee. Graham French looked suspiciously offside for the first goal while Swansea expected goals two and three to be disallowed for fouls. Manager Allan Brown celebrates his first year in charge. | | | | | | | | | | | |
| 17 | | A | LINCOLN | | 4 | W | 3-2 | 2-1 | Whittaker 19p, Allen 44, French 73 | Read | Dougan | Hare | Slough | Branston | Moore | French | Buxton | Allen | Rioch | Whittaker* | McDerment |
| | 18/11 | | | *6,052* | *15* | 26 | | | *Pilgrim 35, Corner 78* | *Kennedy* | *Brooks* | *Peden* | *Grummett* | *Harford* | *Pilgrim* | *Gregson* | *Holmes* | *Corner* | *Samuels** | *Ford* | *Thom* |
| | | | | | | | | | Ref: W Handley | The Town gain revenge for their 1-8 thrashing at Sincil Bank the previous season although the players are unsure as to why the referee awarded a penalty. Future Luton boss, Ray Harford, was unable to contain the talents of Graham French, whose winning goal seemed to be going wide. | | | | | | | | | | | |
| 18 | | H | HALIFAX | | 3 | W | 2-0 | 1-0 | Buxton 26, Moore 54 | Read | Dougan | Jardine | Slough | Branston | Moore | Ryan | Buxton | Allen | Rioch | French | |
| | 25/11 | | | 11,572 | *11* | 28 | | | | *White* | *Hampton* | *Snedden* | *Smith* | *Ryden* | *Russell* | *McCarthy* | *Flower* | *Massie* | *Parks** | *Taylor* | *Pickering* |
| | | | | | | | | | Ref: I Jones | It is now eight straight wins as Ian Buxton squeezes the ball home from a narrow angle and John Moore scores from close range. The new Halifax manager, Alan Ball, admits afterwards he had planned to come for a point but only succeeded in shackling £40,000 rated Bruce Rioch. | | | | | | | | | | | |
| 19 | | A | BRADFORD CITY | | 4 | L | 0-2 | 0-1 | | Read | Dougan | Jardine | Slough | Branston | Moore | French | Buxton | **McLeish** | Rioch | Whittaker | |
| | 2/12 | | | *7,957* | *2* | 28 | | | *Aimson 9, Rackstraw 46* | *Liney* | *Smith* | *Hallett* | *Swallow* | *Cooper* | *Stowell* | *Leek* | *Hall* | *Bannister* | *Aimson* | *Rackstraw* | |
| | | | | | | | | | Ref: R Barker | Debutant Hugh McLeish is desperately unlucky with a shot that hits the post ten minutes from the end. By then, the damage had been done and slick City end Hatters unbeaten run. Early season Luton target, Paul Aimson, takes advantage of a defensive mix-up to give City a swift lead. | | | | | | | | | | | |
| 20 | | H | WREXHAM | | 2 | W | 2-1 | 0-0 | Rioch 62, Branston 87 | Read | Dougan | Jardine | Slough | Branston | Moore | Ryan | Buxton | Allen | Rioch | Whittaker | |
| | 16/12 | | | 9,598 | *8* | 30 | | | *Ingle 85* | *Livesey* | *Bermingham* | *Turner* | *Bradbury* | *Stacey* | *Beanland* | *Powell* | *Griffiths* | *Weston* | *Smith** | *Kinsey* | *Ingle* |
| | | | | | | | | | Ref: H Williams | Skipper Terry Branston is the Luton rock, setting up Rioch's goal and scoring the winner with a superb header. The closing minutes would not have been so tense had Keith Allen not fluffed several first-half chances. Liverpool winger, David Wilson, is Allan Brown's £11,000 target. | | | | | | | | | | | |
| 21 | | A | BARNSLEY | | 2 | D | 2-2 | 1-1 | Rioch 44, Ryan 46 | Read | Dougan | Jardine | Slough* | Branston | Moore | Ryan | Buxton | Allen | Rioch | Whittaker | McDerment |
| | 23/12 | | | *8,704* | *7* | 31 | | | *Hamstead 19, Bettany 48* | *Ironside* | *Murphy* | *Howard* | *Winstanley* | *Brookes* | *Bettany* | *Taylor* | *Earnshaw* | *Hobson* | *Graham* | *Hamstead* | |
| | | | | | | | | | Ref: R Tinkler | In a cracking end-to-end game Bruce Rioch scores with a 40-yard volley to spark off three goals in a four-minute spell bridging the interval. Barnsley, boasting the best home defensive record in the Football League, never give up and the result remains in doubt until the final whistle. | | | | | | | | | | | |
| 22 | | H | BRADFORD PA | | 2 | W | 2-0 | 0-0 | Branston 52, Whittaker 65p | **Taylor** | Dougan | Jardine | Slough | Branston | Moore | Ryan | Buxton | Allen | McDerment* | Whittaker | Read |
| | 26/12 | | | 16,599 | *24* | 33 | | | | *Hardie* | *Andrews* | *Rowley* | *Lightowler* | *Dinsdale* | *Tanner* | *Clancy* | *Ham* | *Down* | *Draper* | *Robinson* | |
| | | | | | | | | | Ref: B Daniels | For the second consecutive home game, Branston is the Luton hero, heading home from a corner. Winger Whittaker shoots wide from the spot after David Down handles but makes amends when getting another chance after Buxton is fouled. Trialist goalkeeper Taylor is not troubled. | | | | | | | | | | | |
| 23 | | A | BRADFORD PA | | 3 | L | 1-2 | 1-1 | Green 29 | Taylor | Dougan | Jardine* | Slough | Branston | Moore | Ryan | Buxton | Green | Allen | Johnson | McLeish |
| | 30/12 | | | *3,674* | *24* | 33 | | | *Lloyd 41, Down 61* | *Hardie* | *Barnes* | *Dinsdale* | *Lightowler* | *Tanner* | *Robinson* | *Draper* | *Clancy* | *Lloyd* | *Down* | *Ham* | |
| | | | | | | | | | Ref: N Callender | Bottom club Bradford never let listless Town gain their stride. It is a sad return for long-term injury victim Green, replacing Rioch, but he scores with an overhead shot, his back to the goal. This is Bradford's first league win in nine games and is Town's final visit to Park Avenue. | | | | | | | | | | | |

| No | Date | Att | Pos | Pt | F-A | H-T | Scorers, Times, and Referees | 1 | 2 | 3 | 4 | 5 | 6 | 7 | 8 | 9 | 10 | 11 | 12 sub used |
|---|---|---|---|---|---|---|---|---|---|---|---|---|---|---|---|---|---|---|---|
| 24 | A | HARTLEPOOLS | 4 | L | 1-2 | 0-0 | Branston 58 | Taylor | Hare | Jardine | Dougan | Branston | Moore | Ryan | Buxton | Allen | Rioch | Whittaker | |
| | 13/1 | *4,766* | *7* | 33 | | | *Phythian 55, Bell 71* | *Smith* | *Bircumshaw* | *Drysdale* | *Parry* | *Gill* | *Hepplewhite* | *McGovern* | *Blowman* | *Phythian* | *Bell* | *Somers* | |
| | | | | | | | Ref: D Payne | Hard-fighting Hartlepools lift themselves into the promotion struggle on a treacherous snowy surface which was barely playable. Ex-Notts County goalkeeper, George Smith, saves well from Buxton and Branston while John McGovern and Pete Blowman play havoc at the other end. | | | | | | | | | | | |
| 25 | H | NEWPORT | 3 | D | 1-1 | 0-1 | Allen 59 | Read | Hare | Jardine | Dougan | Branston | Moore | **Denton** | Buxton | Allen | Rioch | French | |
| | 20/1 | 10,992 | *18* | 34 | | | *Hill 44* | *Weare* | *Wilson* | *Deacy* | *Woods* | *Williams* | *Rowland* | *Robinson* | *Jones* | *Hill* | *Buck* | *King* | |
| | | | | | | | Ref: G Cooper | Hatters lose their 100% home record due to an inspired display by County's veteran goalkeeper, Len Weare. Town's defence lacks its usual authority and the visitors have chances to score the winner, one notable effort from Gerry King going wide. Debutant, Peter Denton, is lively. | | | | | | | | | | | |
| 26 | A | PORT VALE | 4 | D | 0-0 | 0-0 | | Read | Dougan | Jardine | Slough | Branston | Moore | Denton | Buxton | Allen | Rioch* | Whittaker | Brown |
| | 26/1 | *5,970* | *17* | 35 | | | | *Sharratt* | *James* | *Sproson* | *Steele* | *Asprey* | *Wilson* | *Mahon** | *Goodfellow* | *Morris* | *Chapman* | *Cullerton* | *Gibbon* |
| | | | | | | | Ref: J Lewis | A drab game is enlivened by a diving save by Luton goalkeeper, Read, from Vale's Mick Cullerton and a shot from Denton which hits the bar with seven minutes left. The managers and scouts present to watch Rioch are disappointed as he limps off with a knee injury after 76 minutes. | | | | | | | | | | | |
| 27 | A | YORK | 6 | D | 1-1 | 0-0 | Allen 73 | Read | Dougan | Jardine | Slough | Branston | Moore | Denton | Allen | Green | Rioch | Whittaker | |
| | 3/2 | *2,747* | *22* | 36 | | | *Ross 48* | *Walker* | *Baker* | *Jackson* | *Turner* | *Burrows* | *Collinson* | *Hodgson* | *Horrey* | *Ross* | *Spencer* | *Provan* | |
| | | | | | | | Ref: J Warburton | The Town do not produce anything like their real ability in a muddled display and goalkeeper, Tony Read, once again saves the day whilst Keith Allen scrambles home an ill-deserved equaliser. Doug Davidson will be replacing Dennis Evans as trainer at Kenilworth Road shortly. | | | | | | | | | | | |
| 28 | H | ROCHDALE | 2 | W | 4-1 | 4-1 | Rioch 15, Allen 24, Buxton 39, Branston 43 | Read | Dougan | Jardine | Slough | Branston | Moore | French | Buxton* | Allen | Rioch | Whittaker | Green |
| | 10/2 | 10,040 | *10* | 38 | | | *Fletcher 22* | *Green* | *Cockcroft* | *Reid* | *Taylor* | *Jenkins* | *Smith* | *Harley* | *Russell* | *Fletcher* | *Melledew** | *Hutchinson* | *Calloway* |
| | | | | | | | Ref: D Nippard | Hatters recall French to mastermind a magical display by the forward line to earn their first win since Boxing Day. Barry Hutchinson misses an open goal in the second minute but the Town then go goal-crazy and former Luton skipper, John Reid, is unable to contain the wave of attacks. | | | | | | | | | | | |
| 29 | A | BRENTFORD | 1 | W | 2-0 | 0-0 | Slough 56, Rioch 60 | Read | Dougan | Jardine | Slough | Branston | Moore | French | Buxton | Allen | Rioch | Whittaker | |
| | 17/2 | *7,726* | *12* | 40 | | | | *Phillips* | *Hawley* | *Jones* | *Hooker* | *Gelson* | *Richardson* | *Dobson* | *Fenton* | *Ross* | *Thomson* | *Mansley* | |
| | | | | | | | Ref: C Thomas | The Bees start their 'I'm backing Brentford' campaign and, for the first half, it looks as if Luton are going along with the idea. Link-men Alan Slough and Rioch score almost identical goals as Town change up a gear after the break and go top of the league for the first time this season. | | | | | | | | | | | |
| 30 | H | LINCOLN | 1 | W | 4-2 | 4-1 | Whittaker 7, 30p, Rioch 10, Allen 44 | Read | Dougan | Jardine | Slough* | Branston | Moore | French | Buxton | Allen | Rioch | Whittaker | Brown |
| | 24/2 | 11,159 | *16* | 42 | | | *Grummett 25, Thom 89* | *Kennedy* | *Brown* | *Corner* | *Harford* | *Peden* | *Gregson* | *Pilgrim* | *Cobb** | *Holmes* | *Grummett* | *Thom* | *Ford* |
| | | | | | | | Ref: J Osborne | In another devastating display from the Hatters, the game is all but over by the interval. Buxton is unlucky not to get on the scoresheet as he leads Ray Harford a merry dance. The second half is practically a non-event as players try to conserve energy for their next game in two days. | | | | | | | | | | | |
| 31 | H | DARLINGTON | 1 | W | 3-1 | 2-0 | Rioch 6, Allen 39, Moore 86 | Read | Dougan | Jardine* | Slough | Branston | Moore | French | Buxton | Allen | Rioch | Whittaker | McDerment |
| | 26/2 | 13,948 | *22* | 44 | | | *Moore 89 (og)* | *Moor* | *Chapman* | *Keeble* | *Davidson* | *Thompson* | *Jacques* | *O'Neill J* | *O'Neill L* | *Peverell* | *Sproates* | *Kirk* | |
| | | | | | | | Ref: R Johnson | The Town surge to a three-point lead at the top of the division after beating defence-minded Darlington. Rioch, in front of the Arsenal scouts, opens the scoring after waltzing past four defenders in his 60-yard dash. Hatter's defender, Moore, scores at either end in the closing minutes! | | | | | | | | | | | |
| 32 | A | CHESTERFIELD | 1 | D | 0-0 | 0-0 | | Read | Dougan | McDerment | Slough | Branston | Moore | French | Buxton | Allen | Rioch | Whittaker | |
| | 2/3 | ***14,075*** | *5* | 45 | | | | *Roberts* | *Holmes* | *Lumsden* | *Pugh* | *Neale* | *Phelan* | *Moore* | *Randall* | *Hollett* | *Kettleboro'gh* | *Wilson* | |
| | | | | | | | Ref: N Burtenshaw | After a break in Blackpool, the Town squad comes back to face what is looked upon as their toughest test on the road to promotion. In a game dominated by the defences, Allen comes the nearest to getting on to the scoresheet when his header bounces against the bar in the second half. | | | | | | | | | | | |
| 33 | H | PORT VALE | 1 | W | 2-0 | 1-0 | Buxton 24, Rioch 64 | Read | Dougan | Jardine | Slough | Branston | Moore | French* | Buxton | Allen | Rioch | Whittaker | McDerment |
| | 9/3 | 12,749 | *16* | 47 | | | | *Sharratt* | *James* | *Asprey* | *Sproson* | *Wilson* | *Poole* | *Boulton* | *Cullerton* | *Mahon* | *Chapman* | *Goodfellow* | |
| | | | | | | | Ref: J Clarke | Bruce Rioch is again the star of the show with a 25-yard left-foot half-volley taken on the turn. Apart from scoring twice, the Town also hit the bar on two occasions. Stanley Matthews says after the match 'Luton are sure to go up'. Town are still three points clear at the top of the table. | | | | | | | | | | | |
| 34 | H | EXETER | 1 | D | 0-0 | 0-0 | | Read | Dougan | Jardine | McDerment | Branston | Moore | French | Buxton | Allen | Rioch | Whittaker* | **Potter** |
| | 16/3 | 12,409 | *20* | 48 | | | | *Smout* | *Smyth* | *Harvey* | *Newman* | *Huxford* | *Balson* | *Curtis* | *Blain* | *Fudge* | *Coughlin* | *Banks* | |
| | | | | | | | Ref: M Sinclair | Hatters fail to score at home for the first time this season as Exeter form a red barrier in front of their goalkeeper. Injuries to left-back, Jardine, and winger, Whittaker, give the home attack a lop-sided look. Exeter, mindful of their hammering earlier in the campaign, deserve their point. | | | | | | | | | | | |

| No | Venue | Opponent | Att | Pos | Res | F-A | H-T | Scorers, Times, and Referees | 1 | 2 | 3 | 4 | 5 | 6 | 7 | 8 | 9 | 10 | 11 | 12 |
|---|---|---|---|---|---|---|---|---|---|---|---|---|---|---|---|---|---|---|---|---|
| 35 | A | ALDERSHOT | | 1 | W | 1-0 | 0-0 | Buxton 70 | Read | Dougan | McDerment | Potter | Branston | Moore | Ryan* | Buxton | Allen | Rioch | French | Brown |
| | 20/3 | | *9,724* | *7* | 50 | | | | *Godfrey* | *Dawes* | *Renwick* | *McAnearney** | *Madden* | *Walker* | *Walton* | *Edwards* | *Howarth* | *Priscott* | *Burton* | *Gowans* |
| | | | | | | | | Ref: T Dawes | In a twice postponed game, due to bad weather, a headed goal from Ian Buxton is enough to inflict the Shots first home defeat for over a year. Hatters have two 'goals' disallowed by referee Tommy Dawes. Eleven games unbeaten and the Town are starting to walk away with the title. | | | | | | | | | | | |
| 36 | A | DARLINGTON | | 1 | W | 2-1 | 1-0 | Rioch 11, Green 63 | Read | Dougan | McDerment | Potter* | Branston | Moore | Brown | Buxton | Green | Allen | Rioch | Denton |
| | 23/3 | | *4,336* | *18* | 52 | | | *O'Neill J 53* | *Moor* | *Peverell* | *Albeson* | *Atkinson* | *Keeble* | *Sproates* | *Hunter* | *O'Neill L* | *Lawton* | *O'Neill J* | *Kirk* | |
| | | | | | | | | Ref: G Singleton | Proving that the real strength of teams seeking promotion lie in their reserves, the 'wingless wonders' earn another two points to tighten their grip on the title. Rioch again plays a major role, scoring from a free-kick; another is converted by Green and Buxton hits the post near the end. | | | | | | | | | | | |
| 37 | H | ALDERSHOT | | 1 | W | 3-1 | 2-1 | Rioch 1, 19, Brown 64 | Read | Dougan | Jardine | Potter | Branston | Moore | Brown | Buxton | Allen | Rioch | French | |
| | 30/3 | | 10,618 | *7* | 54 | | | *Gowans 28* | *Godfrey* | *Dawes* | *Madden* | *Walker* | *Renwick* | *McAnearney* | *Priscott* | *Walton** | *Edwards* | *Howarth* | *Gowans* | *O'Brien* |
| | | | | | | | | Ref: R Kirkpatrick | Luton are completely dominant but then let the visitors into the game with some slip-shod defensive work. The game is decided by reserve forward, Brown, who sees his shot go through the hands of goalkeeper, Tony Godfrey. This defeat sees the end of Shots' promotion challenge. | | | | | | | | | | | |
| 38 | A | WORKINGTON | | 1 | W | 1-0 | 0-0 | French 68 | Read | Dougan | Jardine | Allen | Branston | Moore | Buxton | French | Green | Whittaker | Rioch | |
| | 6/4 | | *2,195* | *23* | 56 | | | | *Rogan* | *Tugman* | *Upton* | *Butler* | *Geidmintis* | *Kirkman** | *Griffin* | *Greig* | *McLean* | *Spencer* | *Middlemass* | *Tinnion* |
| | | | | | | | | Ref: G Jones | The pre-match talk is of Rangers' interest in Rioch, who has a quiet game. Workington player-manager, Frank Upton, on his team debut, is fortunate not to be dismissed after several dubious tackles; his team are unlucky not to get a penalty when Tom Spencer is fouled by Dougan. | | | | | | | | | | | |
| 39 | H | NOTTS CO | | 1 | W | 2-0 | 1-0 | Allen 5, French 82 | Read | Dougan | Jardine | Slough | Branston | Moore | French | Buxton | Allen | Rioch | Whittaker | |
| | 12/4 | | 16,631 | *19* | 58 | | | | *Rose* | *Cartwright* | *Smith K* | *Ball* | *Gibson* | *Murphy Jim* | *Bates* | *Oakes* | *Smith J* | *Murphy John* | *Elliott** | *Marshall* |
| | | | | | | | | Ref: K Markham | An early goal by Keith Allen settles the nerves but the Town are unconvincing in front of a big Easter holiday crowd. Four balls are kicked out of the ground before a superb shot from French, totally out of place with all that had gone before, seals both points. County pose little threat. | | | | | | | | | | | |
| 40 | H | CHESTER | | 1 | D | 0-0 | 0-0 | | Read | Dougan | Jardine | Slough | Branston | Moore | French | Buxton | Allen* | Rioch | Whittaker | Green |
| | 13/4 | | 13,266 | *22* | 59 | | | | *Carling* | *Jones R* | *Singleton* | *Ashworth* | *Turner* | *Evans* | *Haddock** | *Sutton* | *Loyden* | *Jones L* | *Metcalf* | *Bennett* |
| | | | | | | | | Ref: J Taylor | A hard ground and a swirling wind combine to make a scrappy game against a Chester side who are desperately fighting to avoid a re-election application. Chester deserve their point for their dogged determination; however, the Hatters' unbeaten run is now extended to sixteen matches. | | | | | | | | | | | |
| 41 | A | NOTTS CO | | 1 | D | 2-2 | 1-0 | Allen 15, Buxton 58 | Read | Dougan | Jardine | Slough | Branston | Moore | French | Buxton | Allen | Rioch | Whittaker | |
| | 15/4 | | *7,920* | *19* | 60 | | | *Bates 64, Murphy Jim, 70p* | *Rose* | *Cartwright* | *Ball* | *Oakes* | *Gibson* | *Smith K* | *Bates* | *Murphy Jim* | *Smith J* | *Murphy John* | *Elliott* | |
| | | | | | | | | Ref: K Walker | A defensive nightmare as Hatters throw away a two-goal lead. County, playing with more purpose than at Kenilworth Road on Good Friday, almost snatch both points in the closing minutes in an end-to-end tussle. Bruce Rioch has an off-night, missing several good opportunities. | | | | | | | | | | | |
| 42 | A | HALIFAX | | 1 | W | 1-0 | 0-0 | Rioch 82 | Read | Dougan | Jardine | Slough* | Branston | Moore | Brown | Buxton | Allen | Rioch | French | McDerment |
| | 20/4 | | *5,091* | *11* | 62 | | | | *Smith* | *Russell* | *Pickering* | *Holt* | *Hampton* | *Wallace* | *Massie* | *Ryden* | *Flower* | *Morris* | *McCarthy* | |
| | | | | | | | | Ref: R Capey | A thundering free-kick from Bruce Rioch clinches both points which secures promotion to Division 3. Halifax rock the Town in the second half and the goal is against the run of play. Manager Allan Brown has the foresight to have the champagne on order before coming to the game. | | | | | | | | | | | |
| 43 | H | CREWE | | 1 | W | 4-0 | 4-0 | Moore 8, Rioch 20, 36, Slough 28 | Read | Dougan | Jardine | Slough* | Branston | Moore | French | Buxton | Allen | Rioch | Whittaker | McDerment |
| | 24/4 | | **18,904** | *3* | 64 | | | | *Mailey* | *Lowry* | *Ratcliffe* | *Stott* | *Barnes* | *Gannon* | *McHale* | *Curley* | *Regan* | *Wallace* | *Dearden* | |
| | | | | | | | | Ref: B Daniels | In front of the biggest crowd at Kenilworth Road for four years, the players do a lap of honour after a champagne performance in clinching the title. Promotion-seeking Crewe are swept aside in a game, fitting of the occasion. After slipping to Division 4, Town are on the way up again. | | | | | | | | | | | |
| 44 | H | BRADFORD CITY | | 1 | L | 1-3 | 0-1 | Whittaker 60p | Read | Dougan | Jardine | Slough | Branston | Moore | French | Buxton | Allen | Rioch | Whittaker | |
| | 27/4 | | 14,147 | *4* | 64 | | | *Ham 12, Swallow 73, Rackstraw 87p* | *Liney* | *Atkins* | *Hallett* | *Swallow* | *Cooper** | *Stowell* | *Rackstraw* | *Hall* | *Ham* | *Leighton* | *Walker* | *Bannister* |
| | | | | | | | | Ref: E Wallace | Promotion-seeking City take full advantage of lethargic Luton and inflict the Town's first home defeat for over a year. Whittaker scores from the spot to equalise, after Swallow handles, but the points are secured by Rackstraw's twice-taken penalty at the death, his 39th without a miss. | | | | | | | | | | | |
| 45 | A | CREWE | | 1 | L | 1-2 | 1-1 | Rioch 42 | Read | Dougan | Jardine | Slough | Branston* | Moore | French | Allen | Green | Rioch | Whittaker | Potter |
| | 4/5 | | *8,634* | *4* | 64 | | | *Talbot 40, McHale 74* | *Mailey* | *Lowry* | *Leigh* | *Stott* | *Barnes* | *Gannon* | *McHale* | *Bradshaw* | *Talbot* | *Wallace* | *Ratcliffe* | |
| | | | | | | | | Ref: G Kew | Crewe clinch promotion, and a £300 per man bonus, in a display of all-out attacking football. Rioch threatens to spoil the party with a left-footed hammer drive for the equaliser but the game belongs to the home side and their supporters who chair their team off the pitch at the end. | | | | | | | | | | | |
| 46 | H | BRENTFORD | | 1 | W | 2-1 | 0-0 | Rioch 55, Whittaker 60 | Read | Dougan | Jardine | Slough | Branston | Moore | French | Allen | Green | Rioch | Whittaker | |
| | 11/5 | | 14,643 | *14* | 66 | | | *Moore 75 (og)* | *Phillips* | *Hawley* | *Richardson* | *Gelson* | *Jones* | *Higginson* | *Lawther* | *Dobson* | *Fenton** | *Ross* | *Mansley* | *Hooker* |
| | Home | | Away | | | | | Ref: R Pritchard | Mr Len Shipman presents the Championship trophy and medals before the game and, in front of the ATV cameras, the Town equal the 66 points record set by Peterborough. Ray Whittaker misses from the spot after Green is pulled down and suffer the jitters as Bees threaten to equalise. | | | | | | | | | | | |
| Average | 12,400 | | 6,371 | | | | | | | | | | | | | | | | | |

# LEAGUE DIVISION 4 (CUP-TIES) Manager: Allan Brown SEASON 1967-68

| League Cup | | | F-A | H-T | Scorers, Times, and Referees | 1 | 2 | 3 | 4 | 5 | 6 | 7 | 8 | 9 | 10 | 11 | 12 sub used |
|---|---|---|---|---|---|---|---|---|---|---|---|---|---|---|---|---|---|
| 1 H CHARLTON | | D | 1-1 | 0-0 | Allen 70 | Read | Hare | Jardine | McDerment | Branston | Moore | French | Allen | Green | Rioch | Whittaker | |
| 23/8 | 9,001 *D2* | | | | *Campbell 49* | *Wright* | *Curtis* | *Kinsey* | *Reeves* | *King* | *Halom* | *Peacock* | *Campbell* | *Went* | *Moore* | *Glover* | |
| | | | | | Ref: K Wynn | Charlton goalkeeper, Charlie Wright, keeps the away side in the tie with a series of thrilling saves which earn a replay chance at The Valley. Campbell's diving header in off the post is against the run of play but Allen swoops on to a defensive error by Brian Kinsey to level the score. | | | | | | | | | | | |
| 1R A CHARLTON | | W | 2-1 | 1-1 | Rioch 37, 107 | Read | McDerment | Slough | Allen | Branston | Moore | French | Brown | Green | Rioch | Whittaker | |
| 30/8 | *7,659* *D2* | | | | *Tees 1* | *Wright* | *Curtis* | *Kinsey* | *Went* | *King S* | *Keirs** | *Woodley* | *Campbell* | *Tees* | *Moore* | *Glover* | *Peacock* |
| | | | | | Ref: R Kirkpatrick | A goal after 55 seconds from future Hatter, Matt Tees, does not upset the Town who equalise through a Rioch tap-in. In extra time, Rioch nods a Whittaker cross home but Charlton almost take the game to a second replay when Tees's header is pushed onto a post in the dying seconds. | | | | | | | | | | | |
| 2 A LEEDS | 12 | L | 1-3 | 0-0 | Whittaker 62p | Read | Hare | Jardine | McDerment | Branston | Moore | Brown | Allen | Dougan | Rioch | Whittaker | |
| 13/9 | *11,473* *1:20* | | | | *Lorimer 58, 67p, 88* | *Sprake* | *Reaney* | *Bell* | *Bremner* | *Charlton* | *Hunter* | *Lorimer* | *Belfitt** | *Greenhoff* | *Gray* | *Cooper* | *Johnson* |
| | | | | | Ref: H Richards | A powerful Leeds side finally win through after suffering a few scares, especially when Ray Whittaker equalises from the spot after Gary Sprake pulls down Micky Brown. The Leeds manager Don Revie and coach, former Town skipper Syd Owen, are away scouting for a forward. | | | | | | | | | | | |

| FA Cup | | | | | | | | | | | | | | | | | |
|---|---|---|---|---|---|---|---|---|---|---|---|---|---|---|---|---|---|
| 1 A OXFORD CITY | 4 | W | 2-1 | 0-0 | Rioch 60, Buxton 65 | Read | Dougan | Jardine | Slough* | McDerment | Moore | French | Buxton | Allen | Rioch | Whittaker | Hare |
| 14/12 | *13,394* *Isth* | | | | *Woodley 48* | *Shippey* | *Jackson* | *Lamb* | *Goodison* | *Shufflebot'm* | *Bradbury* | *Hellyer* | *Cassel* | *Woodley* | *Metcalf* | *Morton* | |
| (at Luton) | | | | | Ref: M Sinclair | Postponed the previous Saturday, the match is now switched to Luton as the Town refuse to play under City's floodlights. The visitors put up a brave performance with goalkeeper John Shippey outstanding; his only error is dropping the ball at the feet of Buxton for the Town's winner. | | | | | | | | | | | |
| 2 A SWINDON | 4 | L | 2-3 | 0-2 | Allen 60, Whittaker 63p | Taylor | Hare | Jardine | Slough* | Branston | Moore | Dougan | Ryan | Allen | Buxton | Whittaker | Brown |
| 6/1 | *18,203* *3:3* | | | | *Rogers 17p, 40, Heath 85* | *Downsborough* | *Dawson* | *Nurse* | *Harland* | *Trollope* | *Butler* | *Smart* | *Heath* | *Penman** | *Terry* | *Rogers* | *Giles* |
| | | | | | Ref: T Hill | Third Division promotion-chasers Swindon look as though they will race away with the game at the start with Don Rogers' twice-taken penalty a killer blow. The Town level the tie, only for Swindon to score a late and undeserved winner. They go out to Sheffield Wednesday in Round 4. | | | | | | | | | | | |

| | | Home | | | | | Away | | | | | |
|---|---|---|---|---|---|---|---|---|---|---|---|---|
| | P | W | D | L | F | A | W | D | L | F | A | Pts |
| 1 LUTON TOWN | 46 | 19 | 3 | 1 | 55 | 16 | 8 | 9 | 6 | 32 | 28 | 66 |
| 2 Barnsley | 46 | 17 | 6 | 0 | 43 | 14 | 7 | 7 | 9 | 25 | 32 | 61 |
| 3 Hartlepools | 46 | 15 | 7 | 1 | 34 | 12 | 10 | 3 | 10 | 26 | 34 | 60 |
| 4 Crewe | 46 | 13 | 10 | 0 | 44 | 18 | 7 | 8 | 8 | 30 | 31 | 58 |
| 5 Bradford City | 46 | 14 | 5 | 4 | 41 | 22 | 9 | 6 | 8 | 31 | 29 | 57 |
| 6 Southend | 46 | 12 | 8 | 3 | 45 | 21 | 8 | 6 | 9 | 32 | 37 | 54 |
| 7 Chesterfield | 46 | 15 | 4 | 4 | 47 | 20 | 6 | 7 | 10 | 24 | 30 | 53 |
| 8 Wrexham | 46 | 17 | 3 | 3 | 47 | 12 | 3 | 10 | 10 | 25 | 41 | 53 |
| 9 Aldershot | 46 | 10 | 11 | 2 | 36 | 19 | 8 | 6 | 9 | 34 | 36 | 53 |
| 10 Doncaster | 46 | 12 | 8 | 3 | 36 | 16 | 6 | 7 | 10 | 30 | 40 | 51 |
| 11 Halifax | 46 | 10 | 6 | 7 | 34 | 24 | 5 | 10 | 8 | 18 | 25 | 46 |
| 12 Newport | 46 | 11 | 7 | 5 | 32 | 22 | 5 | 6 | 12 | 26 | 41 | 45 |
| 13 Lincoln | 46 | 11 | 3 | 9 | 41 | 31 | 6 | 6 | 11 | 30 | 37 | 43 |
| 14 Brentford | 46 | 13 | 4 | 6 | 41 | 24 | 5 | 3 | 15 | 20 | 40 | 43 |
| 15 Swansea | 46 | 11 | 8 | 4 | 38 | 25 | 5 | 2 | 16 | 25 | 52 | 42 |
| 16 Darlington | 46 | 6 | 11 | 6 | 31 | 27 | 6 | 6 | 11 | 16 | 26 | 41 |
| 17 Notts Co | 46 | 10 | 7 | 6 | 27 | 27 | 5 | 4 | 14 | 26 | 52 | 41 |
| 18 Port Vale | 46 | 10 | 5 | 8 | 41 | 31 | 2 | 10 | 11 | 20 | 41 | 39 |
| 19 Rochdale | 46 | 9 | 8 | 6 | 35 | 32 | 3 | 6 | 14 | 16 | 40 | 38 |
| 20 Exeter | 46 | 9 | 7 | 7 | 30 | 30 | 2 | 9 | 12 | 15 | 35 | 38 |
| 21 York | 46 | 9 | 6 | 8 | 44 | 30 | 2 | 8 | 13 | 21 | 38 | 36 |
| 22 Chester | 46 | 6 | 6 | 11 | 35 | 38 | 3 | 8 | 12 | 22 | 40 | 32 |
| 23 Workington | 46 | 8 | 8 | 7 | 35 | 29 | 2 | 3 | 18 | 19 | 58 | 31 |
| 24 Bradford PA | 46 | 3 | 7 | 13 | 18 | 35 | 1 | 8 | 14 | 12 | 47 | 23 |
| | 1104 | 270 | 158 | 124 | 910 | 575 | 124 | 158 | 270 | 575 | 910 | 1104 |

Odds & ends

Double wins: (6) Aldershot, Brentford, Darlington, Halifax, Lincoln, Workington.
Double losses: (1) Bradford City.

Won from behind: (3) York (h), Charlton (LC), Oxford City (FAC).
Lost from in front: (1) Bradford PA (a).

High spots: Champions of Division 4.
Eight consecutive wins, scoring 27 goals and conceding just 6 during the first half of the season, followed by 19 games unbeaten during the second half of the season.
Winning at Second Division Charlton in League Cup.
The goalscoring form of Bruce Rioch.

Low spots: Losing to bottom-placed Bradford Park Avenue.
Failing to break the Division 4 points record.
Losing narrowly at Swindon in FA Cup.

Player of the Year: Terry Branston.
Ever-presents: (1) Terry Branston (League only).
Hat-tricks: (0).
Leading scorer: Bruce Rioch (27).

| | Appearances | | | | | | Goals | | | |
|---|---|---|---|---|---|---|---|---|---|---|
| | Lge | *Sub* | LC | *Sub* | FAC | *Sub* | Lge | LC | FAC | Tot |
| Allen, Keith | **45** | | 3 | | 2 | | **14** | 1 | 1 | **16** |
| Beaven, Ken | **1** | | | | | | | | | |
| Branston, Terry | **46** | | 3 | | 1 | | **5** | | | **5** |
| Brown, Mick | **8** | *4* | 2 | | | *1* | **2** | | | **2** |
| Buxton, Ian | **36** | | | | 2 | | **13** | | 1 | **14** |
| Denton, Peter | **3** | *1* | | | | | | | | |
| Dougan, Max | **41** | *1* | 1 | | 2 | | | | | |
| French, Graham | **31** | | 2 | | 1 | | **5** | | | **5** |
| Green, Rodney | **9** | *2* | 2 | | | | **3** | | | **3** |
| Hare, Tommy | **12** | | 2 | | 1 | *1* | | | | |
| Jardine, Fred | **41** | | 2 | | 2 | | | | | |
| Johnson, Brian | **1** | *1* | | | | | | | | |
| McDerment, Billy | **13** | *6* | 3 | | 1 | | | | | |
| McLeish, Hugh | **1** | *1* | | | | | | | | |
| Moore, John | **45** | | 3 | | 2 | | **4** | | | **4** |
| Potter, George | **3** | *2* | | | | | | | | |
| Read, Tony | **42** | *1* | 3 | | 1 | | | | | |
| Rioch, Bruce | **44** | | 3 | | 1 | | **24** | 2 | 1 | **27** |
| Ryan, John | **10** | | | | 1 | | **1** | | | **1** |
| Slough, Alan | **32** | *3* | 1 | | 2 | | **6** | | | **6** |
| Taylor, Bill | **3** | | | | 1 | | | | | |
| Tinsley, Colin | **1** | | | | | | | | | |
| Walker, Dennis | | *1* | | | | | | | | |
| Whittaker, Ray | **38** | | 3 | | 2 | | **10** | 1 | 1 | **12** |
| **24 players used** | **506** | *23* | **33** | | **22** | *2* | **87** | **4** | **4** | **95** |

| No | Date | | Att | Pos | Pt | F-A | H-T | Scorers, Times, and Referees | 1 | 2 | 3 | 4 | 5 | 6 | 7 | 8 | 9 | 10 | 11 | 12 sub used |
|---|---|---|---|---|---|---|---|---|---|---|---|---|---|---|---|---|---|---|---|---|
| 1 | H | OLDHAM | | | W | 4-0 | 2-0 | Harrison 17p, Allen 43, Jardine 61, | Read | Dougan | Jardine | Allen | Branston | Slough | French* | **Lewis** | **Sheffield** | Rioch | **Harrison** | Moore |
| | 10/8 | | 14,747 | | 2 | | | [Lewis 89] | *Best* | *Doyle* | *Hunter* | *Joyce** | *Wood* | *Blair* | *Philpott* | *Magee* | *Chapman* | *Johnston* | *Aitken* | *Bowie* |
| | | | | | | | | Ref: J Osborne | The Hatters laugh at the antics of their new supporter, Eric Morecambe, and go on a four-goal romp against the Latics in brilliant sunshine. Mike Harrison opens his account from the penalty spot after Walter Joyce pulls down debutant, Brian Lewis, who scores in the dying minutes. | | | | | | | | | | | |
| 2 | A | BARROW | | | D | 0-0 | 0-0 | | Read | Dougan | Jardine | Allen | Branston | Slough | Brown | Lewis | Sheffield | Rioch | Whittaker | |
| | 17/8 | | *6,628* | | 3 | | | | *Else* | *Mallon* | *Edwards* | *Arrowsmith* | *Harrison* | *Bebbington* | *Ellison* | *Riley* | *McLean* | *Mulholland* | *McCarthy* | |
| | | | | | | | | Ref: H Williams | The Town earn a point in an efficient, rather than brilliant, performance, punctuated by many stoppages for fouls. Luton skipper, Branston, and Barrow striker, George McLean, are pole-axed by each other at different times during the game and out of the sight of the referee and linesmen. | | | | | | | | | | | |
| 3 | H | ROTHERHAM | | 1 | W | 3-1 | 3-1 | Rioch 9, 15, Lewis 42 | Read | Dougan | Jardine | Allen | Branston | Slough | French | Lewis | Sheffield* | Rioch | Harrison | Moore |
| | 24/8 | | 14,163 | *13* | 5 | | | *Storrie 24* | *Hill* | *Swift* | *Hague* | *Quinn* | *Watson** | *Tiler* | *Leggat* | *Storrie* | *Downes* | *Bentley* | *Todd* | *Harrity* |
| | | | | | | | | Ref: G Hill | Two long-range early efforts from the golden boots of £80,000-rated Bruce Rioch ends this game as a contest with bargain buy Brian Lewis pinching another before the break. Millers' manager, Tommy Docherty, later to take charge at Aston Villa, watches Rioch with keen interest. | | | | | | | | | | | |
| 4 | H | BARNSLEY | | 1 | W | **5-1** | 3-0 | Rioch 19, Branston 29, Lewis 34, 54, | Read | Dougan | Jardine* | Allen | Branston | Slough | French | Lewis | Sheffield | Rioch | Harrison | Moore |
| | 28/8 | | 15,899 | *21* | 7 | | | *Earnshaw 51* [Allen 64] | *Arblaster* | *Murphy* | *Booth* | *Bettany* | *Howard* | *Brookes* | *Earnshaw* | *Evans* | *Robson* | *Bradbury* | *Hamstead* | |
| | | | | | | | | Ref: P Walters | Rioch beats four men in an 80-yard run to grab the first goal and set the Town up as early league leaders of Division 3. Everything goes right for the Hatters, apart from Laurie Sheffield, who misses several good chances against a fast and skilful Barnsley side who never give up trying. | | | | | | | | | | | |
| 5 | A | GILLINGHAM | | 1 | W | 3-1 | 2-1 | Lewis 5, 70, Sheffield 40 | Read | Dougan | McDerment | Allen | Branston* | Slough | Ryan | Lewis | Sheffield | Rioch | French | Moore |
| | 31/8 | | *8,227* | *19* | 9 | | | *Williams 42* | *Bellotti* | *Simpson* | *Green* | *Williams* | *Bailey* | *Machin* | *Meredith* | *Woodley* | *Gibbs* | *Riddick* | *Yeo* | |
| | | | | | | | | Ref: R Johnson | The Gills' Mel Machin sees his penalty kick saved by Tony Read thus failing to equalise at 2-1. Brian Lewis repays a large slice of his transfer fee by scoring twice, including the clincher, when he beats two men in a solo dash for goal. An injury to skipper, Branston, unsettles the Town. | | | | | | | | | | | |
| 6 | A | ORIENT | | 1 | D | 0-0 | 0-0 | | Read | Dougan | Jardine | Allen | Slough | Moore | Ryan | Lewis | Sheffield | Rioch | French* | McDerment |
| | 7/9 | | *13,719* | *11* | 10 | | | | *Goddard* | *Jones* | *Mancini* | *Taylor* | *Howe* | *Harper* | *Allen* | *Slater* | *Massey** | *Halom* | *Brabrook* | *Bloomfield* |
| | | | | | | | | Ref: G McCabe | Orient's best home league crowd for over two years sees the Town successfully play for a point. 'I can't remember a team play the offside game so much,' says O's player-manager, Jimmy Bloomfield. The scouts watch Rioch, despite him having just signed a new two-year contract. | | | | | | | | | | | |
| 7 | H | TRANMERE | | 1 | W | 3-1 | 1-1 | Sheffield 22, Lewis 60, Branston 65 | Read | Dougan | Jardine | Slough | Branston | Moore | French | Lewis | Sheffield | Rioch | Harrison | |
| | 14/9 | | 12,965 | *8* | 12 | | | *McNamee 42* | *Cumbes* | *Pointon* | *Robertson* | *Casey* | *Smith* | *King* | *Rowlands* | *Pritchard* | *Yardley* | *Sinclair* | *McNamee* | |
| | | | | | | | | Ref: H New | Surrey fast-bowler and Tranmere goalkeeper, Jimmy Cumbes, saves his side from a heavy defeat in the pouring rain. The visitors manage to equalise, against the run of play, but Terry Branston, returning to the side after injury, smashes home the winning goal and secures both points. | | | | | | | | | | | |
| 8 | H | MANSFIELD | | 1 | W | 4-2 | 1-0 | Harrison 21p, Sheffield 69, Lewis 73, | Read | Dougan | Jardine | Slough | Branston* | Moore | French | Lewis | Sheffield | Rioch ! | Harrison | McDerment |
| | 18/9 | | 19,315 | *5* | 14 | | | *Jones 48, Partridge 82* [French 77] | *Hollins* | *Roberts* | *Hopkinson* | *Quigley* | *Boam* | *Waller !* | *Frude* | *Partridge* | *Ledger* | *Goodfellow* | *Jones* | |
| | | | | | | | | Ref: M Sinclair | Bruce Rioch is sent off after three minutes for supposedly striking an opponent. Mansfield's Phil Waller is dismissed in the second-half and the Town go on to win a sensational game. French's goal, when he runs the length of the pitch with the ball, will be talked about for years to come. | | | | | | | | | | | |
| 9 | A | BRIGHTON | | 1 | L | 0-1 | 0-1 | | Read | McDerment | Jardine | Allen | Branston | Slough* | Ryan | Lewis | Sheffield | Rioch | Harrison | French |
| | 21/9 | | *11,930* | *10* | 14 | | | *Wilkinson 44* | *Burns* | *Henderson* | *Gall* | *Turner* | *Napier J* | *Smith* | *Wilkinson* | *Lawton* | *Napier K* | *Livesey* | *Armstrong* | |
| | | | | | | | | Ref: K Walker | The Hatters lose their unbeaten record when Brighton, in their third game against the Town this season, beat an injury-weakened side. The only goal of the game is scored by future Leeds manager, Howard Wilkinson. However, the Hatters are still two points clear at the top of the table. | | | | | | | | | | | |
| 10 | H | TORQUAY | | 1 | W | 1-0 | 0-0 | Lewis 48 | Read | Dougan | Jardine | Slough* | Branston | McDerment | French | Lewis | Sheffield | Rioch | Harrison | Allen |
| | 28/9 | | 14,936 | *8* | 16 | | | | *Donnelly* | *Smith* | *Bond* | *Brown* | *Dunne* | *Kitchener* | *Benson* | *Scott* | *Barnes** | *Stubbs* | *Rowlands* | *Matthews* |
| | | | | | | | | Ref: R Johnson | The ex-West Ham duo of John Bond and Ken Brown marshal the Torquay defence admirably, but Brian Lewis scores his ninth goal of the season to end the stalemate. The Hatters are down to ten men during part of the second half whilst Terry Branston has a head wound stitched. | | | | | | | | | | | |
| 11 | A | WATFORD | | 1 | L | 0-1 | 0-1 | | Read | Dougan | Jardine | Slough* | Branston | McDerment | Ryan | Lewis | Sheffield | Rioch | Harrison | Allen |
| | 5/10 | | ***22,133*** | *8* | 16 | | | *Low 2* | *Walker* | *Welbourne* | *Williams* | *Eddy* | *Garvey* | *Walley* | *Scullion* | *Hale* | *Garbett* | *Dyson* | *Low* | |
| | | | | | | | | Ref: N Burtenshaw | The biggest Division 3 crowd of the season sees the game over almost as soon as it has started when a defensive error lets in Roy Low. Alan Slough storms off angrily and goes straight home after being substituted for tactical reasons. The Hornets rely mainly on using the offside trap. | | | | | | | | | | | |

| No | H/A | Date / Opponent | Att | Pos | Res / Pts | F-A | H-T | Scorers, Times, and Referees | 1 | 2 | 3 | 4 | 5 | 6 | 7 | 8 | 9 | 10 | 11 | 12 |
|---|---|---|---|---|---|---|---|---|---|---|---|---|---|---|---|---|---|---|---|---|
| 12 | A | BARNSLEY | | 2 | L | **1-3** | 0-2 | Sheffield 48 | Taylor | Dougan | Jardine | Allen | Branston | Slough | Ryan | Buxton | Sheffield | Rioch | Harrison* | McDerment |
| | | 8/10 | *13,019* | *15* | 16 | | | *Evans 15, Earnshaw 38, Hamstead 76* | *Ironside* | *Murphy* | *Brookes* | *Bettany* | *Winstanley* | *Howard* | *Earnshaw* | *Evans* | *Robson* | *Bradbury* | *Hamstead* | |
| | | | | | | | | Ref: P Baldwin | Town's leading scorer, Brian Lewis, misses the match through injury as Barnsley gain vengeance for the hammering they received at Luton earlier in the season. Tyke's John Bettany runs the show as the Town lose their third successive away game and are deposed from the top spot. | | | | | | | | | | | |
| 13 | H | HARTLEPOOL | | 1 | W | 3-0 | 1-0 | Sheffield 27, Rioch 49, Lewis 79 | Taylor | McDerment | Jardine | Allen | Branston | Slough | French | Lewis | Sheffield | Rioch | Whittaker | |
| | | 12/10 | 13,415 | *22* | 18 | | | | *Smith* | *Bircumshaw* | *Gill* | *Goad* | *Drysdale* | *Sheridan* | *Wright* | *Young* | *Cummings* | *Bell* | *Hepplewhite* | |
| | | | | | | | | Ref: R Kirkpatrick | After much deliberation the referee, Roger Kirkpatrick, allows the game to proceed but, on a treacherous, rain-sodden surface, good football is virtually impossible. Bruce Rioch, celebrating his escape from suspension after his dismissal against Mansfield, scores with a rocket of a shot. | | | | | | | | | | | |
| 14 | A | PLYMOUTH | | 4 | L | 0-2 | 0-2 | | Taylor | McDerment | Jardine* | Allen | Branston | Slough | Buxton | Lewis | Sheffield | Rioch | Whittaker | Brown |
| | | 19/10 | *12,659* | *8* | 18 | | | *Burnside 12, Piper 25* | *Dunne* | *Reeves* | *Neale* | *Saxton* | *Molyneux* | *Piper* | *Davey* | *Bickle* | *Trainor* | *Burnside* | *Maher* | |
| | | | | | | | | Ref: I Jones | Managers Allan Brown and Billy Bingham, team-mates in Luton's 1959 Cup Final team, meet up again with Bingham winning the day due to the devastating wing display by new signing from Everton, Aiden Maher. Brown steps up his search for new players in order to halt the slide. | | | | | | | | | | | |
| 15 | H | NORTHAMPTON | | 3 | W | 2-1 | 2-0 | Allen 25, Sheffield 27 | **Davie** | Slough | Dougan | Allen | McDerment | **Bannister** | French | Lewis | Sheffield | Rioch | Whittaker | |
| | | 26/10 | 17,818 | *12* | 20 | | | *Fairbrother 63* | *Morritt* | *Faulkes* | *Rankmore* | *Roberts* | *Fairfax* | *Mackin* | *Byrne* | *Flowers* | *Weaver* | *Hatton* | *Fairbrother* | |
| | | | | | | | | Ref: K Markham | New signings, Sandy Davie from Dundee United and Jack Bannister from Crystal Palace, assist the Town in beating Northampton in a tense affair. Two goals in a minute help to settle the nerves but the Cobblers, inspired by ex-England and Wolves player, Ron Flowers, fight back. | | | | | | | | | | | |
| 16 | A | WALSALL | | 6 | L | 0-2 | 0-1 | | Davie | Dougan | McDerment | Allen | Slough | Bannister | Denton | Lewis | Sheffield | Rioch | Whittaker* | Potter |
| | | 5/11 | *5,381* | *14* | 20 | | | *Murray 35, Morris 70* | *Wesson* | *Harrison* | *Harris* | *Trevis* | *Jones* | *Atthey* | *Murray* | *Baker* | *Wilson* | *Bennett* | *Morris* | |
| | | | | | | | | Ref: R Darlington | The Town start brightly enough, with Peter Denton making his first appearance of the season, but are gradually overrun in the midfield with Saddler's Alan Baker behind every move. Hatters suffer their fifth consecutive away defeat, although they do still have a 100% home record. | | | | | | | | | | | |
| 17 | H | SWINDON | | 6 | W | 2-0 | 0-0 | Sheffield 57, Lewis 77 | Davie | Dougan | McDerment | Slough | Branston | Bannister | French | Lewis | Sheffield | Rioch | Harrison | |
| | | 9/11 | 17,250 | *3* | 22 | | | | *Downsborough* | *Dawson* | *Thomas* | *Butler* | *Burrows* | *Harland* | *Heath* | *Smart* | *Smith* | *Noble* | *Rogers* | |
| | | | | | | | | Ref: J Hunting | The Town preserve their perfect home record but receive criticism for muscling their way to victory. Peter Downsborough, in the Swindon goal, is clattered by Sheffield who scores against the still-groggy keeper shortly afterwards. Referee Jim Hunting awards 29 free-kicks for fouls. | | | | | | | | | | | |
| 18 | H | BOURNEMOUTH | | 5 | D | 1-1 | 1-1 | Branston 17 | Davie | Dougan | McDerment | Slough | Branston | Bannister | French | Lewis | Allen | Rioch | Whittaker* | Sheffield |
| | | 23/11 | 14,150 | *1* | 23 | | | *Bumstead 39* | *Jones* | *White* | *Miller* | *Naylor** | *Stocks* | *Gater* | *Bumstead* | *Pound* | *East* | *Hold* | *Bolton* | *Peters* |
| | | | | | | | | Ref: N Burtenshaw | The Hatters lose their 100% home record to top-of-the-table Cherries. Referee Norman Burtenshaw allows the game to degenerate in the thick Kenilworth Road mud and, for once, Brian Lewis is on the receiving end of several bad tackles, which leave him limping long before the end. | | | | | | | | | | | |
| 19 | A | STOCKPORT | | 8 | L | 0-2 | 0-0 | | Davie | McDerment | Bannister | Slough | Branston | Dougan | French | Lewis | Sheffield | Allen | Rioch | |
| | | 29/11 | *13,246* | *3* | 23 | | | *Goodwin 54, Atkins 78* | *Ogley* | *Haydock* | *Hartle* | *Goodwin* | *Milner* | *Low* | *Allchurch* | *Atkins* | *Mulholland* | *Harley* | *Young* | |
| | | | | | | | | Ref: A Bone | The biggest crowd for years is at Edgeley Park to welcome Jimmy Meadow's new signing from Everton, Alex Young, the 'Golden Vision'. Town's hopes of winning a point are ended by a 25-yard thunderbolt shot from wing-half Fred Goodwin and a bullet-header from Bill Atkins. | | | | | | | | | | | |
| 20 | A | HARTLEPOOL | | 8 | L | 0-1 | 0-1 | | Davie | Dougan | Bannister | Allen | Branston | Slough | French | Lewis | Buxton | **Stevenson** | Harrison | |
| | | 14/12 | *3,887* | *16* | 23 | | | *Blowman 11* | *Smith* | *Bircumshaw* | *Goad* | *Sheriden* | *Gill* | *Parry* | *Blowman* | *Cummings* | *Thompson* | *Wright* | *Young* | |
| | | | | | | | | Ref: D Fieldsend | A blunder by the normally-reliable Sandy Davie gifts both the points to Hartlepool. The Hatters batter away at the Pool rearguard but all to no avail and new signing from Morton, Morris Stevenson, has only a gashed head to show for his troubles. Pool's George Smith is in great form. | | | | | | | | | | | |
| 21 | H | PLYMOUTH | | 6 | W | 2-0 | 2-0 | Lewis 32, Allen 39 | Davie | Dougan | Bannister | Slough | Branston | Moore | French | Lewis | Allen | Rioch | Harrison | |
| | | 21/12 | **10,971** | *11* | 25 | | | | *Dunne* | *Reeves* | *Neale* | *Hore* | *Molyneux* | *Piper* | *Davey* | *Bickle* | *Tedesco** | *Burnside* | *Maher* | *Reynolds* |
| | | | | | | | | Ref: D Smith | Alec Stock takes over at Kenilworth Road and sees his new boys put up a spirited performance. Ex-Manchester United goalkeeper, Pat Dunne, performs heroics for the visitors and receives a standing ovation at the end. 'What a lot of honesty there is in this side,' says Stock afterwards. | | | | | | | | | | | |
| 22 | A | NORTHAMPTON | | 6 | W | 2-0 | 2-0 | Rioch 7, 21 | Davie | Dougan | Bannister | Slough | Branston | Moore | French | Lewis | Allen | Rioch | Harrison | |
| | | 28/12 | *15,161* | *11* | 27 | | | | *Morritt* | *Fairfax* | *Walker* | *Townsend* | *Rankmore* | *Kiernan* | *Roberts* | *Felton* | *Fairbrother* | *Hatton* | *Hawkins* | |
| | | | | | | | | Ref: R Capey | The Town end their run of seven successive away defeats in their first league encounter with Northampton for 32 years. The Hatters settle more quickly on the icy pitch and Bruce Rioch accepts a gift opportunity from Cobblers' goalkeeper Gordon Morritt when scoring the second goal. | | | | | | | | | | | |
| 23 | A | SHREWSBURY | | 6 | L | **1-3** | 1-2 | Slough 32 | Davie | Dougan | Bannister | Slough | Branston | Moore | French | Lewis* | Allen | Rioch | Harrison | McDerment |
| | | 8/1 | *4,729* | *23* | 27 | | | *Douglas 43, Meredith 44p, Wood 77* | *Phillips* | *Gregory* | *Fellows* | *Pountney* | *Wood* | *Dolby* | *Meredith* | *Boardman* | *Hawkins* | *Douglas* | *McLaughlin** | *Clapham* |
| | | | | | | | | Ref: C Robinson | Alec Stock tastes defeat for the first time as a disputed penalty swings the game in favour of the home side. Dennis Hawkins is seemingly brought down outside the area but the referee sees it differently and awards a spot-kick. French squanders several good second-half chances. | | | | | | | | | | | |

| No | Date | Att | Pos | Pt | F-A | H-T | Scorers, Times, and Referees | 1 | 2 | 3 | 4 | 5 | 6 | 7 | 8 | 9 | 10 | 11 | 12 sub used |
|---|---|---|---|---|---|---|---|---|---|---|---|---|---|---|---|---|---|---|---|
| 24 | A SWINDON | | 8 | D | 0-0 | 0-0 | | Davie | Dougan | Bannister | Slough | Branston | Moore | Ryan | Lewis | Allen | Rioch | Harrison | |
| | 18/1 | *19,105* | *4* | 28 | | | | *Downsborough* | *Dawson* | *Burrows* | *Harland* | *Thomas* | *Heath* | *Smart* | *Penman** | *Noble* | *Jones* | *Rogers* | *Trollope* |
| | | | | | | | Ref: R Kirkpatrick | Swindon, on their way to a Wembley League Cup triumph, batter the Hatters rearguard. The defence stands firm with goalkeeper Sandy Davie enjoying the muddy surface. One of his saves is witnessed by millions of viewers as the Town appear on 'Match of the Day' for the first time. | | | | | | | | | | | |
| 25 | H WALSALL | | 5 | W | 1-0 | 1-0 | Rioch 4 | Davie | Dougan | Bannister | Slough | Branston | Moore | French* | Keen | Lewis | Rioch | Whittaker | Allen |
| | 25/1 | *15,205* | *17* | 30 | | | | *Wesson* | *Gregg* | *Jones* | *Bennett* | *Evans* | *Atthey* | *Trevis* | *Stephens* | *Wilson* | *McMorran** | *Morris* | *Baker* |
| | | | | | | | Ref: J Lewis | Alec Stock goes back to QPR to sign Mike Keen, who steps straight into the Luton side in a disappointing game. Golden boy Bruce Rioch scores an early goal but is then carried off on a stretcher, after sustaining a knee injury, which will keep him out of the game for two months. | | | | | | | | | | | |
| 26 | A CREWE | | 5 | L | 0-2 | 0-0 | | Davie | Dougan | Bannister | Slough | Branston | Moore | Lewis | Keen | Buxton | Allen | Harrison | |
| | 29/1 | *5,053* | *18* | 30 | | | *Stott 51, Tarbuck 65* | *Mailey* | *Lowry* | *Leigh* | *Stott* | *Barnes* | *Gannon* | *Curley* | *McHale* | *Hollett* | *Tarbuck* | *Bradshaw* | |
| | | | | | | | Ref: J Yates | The away jinx strikes again as lowly Crewe show far more enterprise and effort. Stock berates the Town's £60,000 forward line for throwing in the towel. The Luton defenders complain to referee John Yates that goalkeeper Sandy Davie is fouled before Keith Stott scores the first goal. | | | | | | | | | | | |
| 27 | H READING | | 5 | W | 2-1 | 2-0 | Slough 3, Lewis 41p | Davie | Dougan | Bannister | Slough | Branston | Moore | French | Buxton | Allen | Lewis | Harrison* | McDerment |
| | 1/2 | 11,871 | *9* | 32 | | | *Yard 78* | *Brown* | *Bacuzzi* | *Spiers !* | *Thornhill* | *Hitchcock* | *Yard* | *Allen* | *Collins* | *Sainty* | *Silvester* | *Harris* | |
| | | | | | | | Ref: C Thomas | Veteran Reading defender, Dick Spiers, is sent off for the first time in a long career after he brings down Brian Lewis from behind. The Town appear to be cruising before this incident but the visitors now start to make a proper game of it and cause several jitters in the Hatter's defence. | | | | | | | | | | | |
| 28 | A BOURNEMOUTH | | 4 | W | 2-0 | 0-0 | Sheffield 57, Jardine 68 | Davie | Dougan | Bannister | Slough | Branston | Moore | French | Lewis | Sheffield | Allen | Jardine | |
| | 8/2 | *9,253* | *3* | 34 | | | | *Jones* | *Gulliver* | *Miller* | *White* | *Stocks* | *Longhorn* | *Bumstead* | *Pound* | *East* | *Bolton* | *Peters** | *Burns* |
| | | | | | | | Ref: J Osborne | With the rest of the country snowbound, the game against the high-flying Cherries goes ahead, the Town adapting better to the icy conditions. Jardine scores a rare goal but Keith Allen is the star of the show. Goalkeeper Sandy Davie complains that he has nothing to do to keep warm! | | | | | | | | | | | |
| 29 | H CREWE | | 5 | W | 2-0 | 1-0 | Slough 43, Allen 81 | Davie | Dougan | Bannister | Slough | Branston | Moore | French | Keen | Allen | Lewis | Jardine | |
| | 26/2 | 13,384 | *20* | 36 | | | | *Mailey* | *Lowry* | *Leigh* | *Stott* | *Barnes* | *Gater* | *Ratcliffe* | *McHale* | *Hollett* | *Tarbuck* | *Gannon* | |
| | | | | | | | Ref: T Locket | Crewe pull everyone back behind the ball in an attempt to win a point. However, they are undone by Slough, who cracks the ball into the top corner of the net, just before half-time. 'Crewe made it very difficult for us by pulling both wingers back, but we lacked rhythm,' moans Stock. | | | | | | | | | | | |
| 30 | A OLDHAM | | 4 | W | 1-0 | 1-0 | Lawson 1 (og) | Davie | Dougan | Bannister | Slough | Branston | Moore | French* | Keen | Sheffield | Allen | Jardine | Lewis |
| | 1/3 | *3,946* | *24* | 38 | | | | *Gordine* | *Blair* | *Wood* | *Hunter* | *Lawson* | *Joyce* | *Colquhoun* | *Spence* | *Blore* | *Bebbington* | *Chapman* | |
| | | | | | | | Ref: D Turner | Town take a sensational lead after only 30 seconds, when a Sandy Davie punt down-field is headed by Latics centre-half Alan Lawson back to his keeper, who had advanced too far! Oldham spend the rest of the game battering the Town's defence, but spoil chances by being too eager. | | | | | | | | | | | |
| 31 | H SHREWSBURY | | 3 | W | 2-1 | 1-0 | Allen 12, Keen 46 | Davie | Dougan | Bannister | Slough* | Branston | Moore | French | Keen | Sheffield | Allen | Jardine | Lewis |
| | 5/3 | 14,733 | *24* | 40 | | | *Harkin 68* | *Phillips* | *Mathias* | *Fellows* | *Moore* | *Wood* | *Dolby* | *Bridgwood* | *Boardman** | *Harkin* | *Douglas* | *Hawkins* | *Pountney* |
| | | | | | | | Ref: R Kirkpatrick | The Hatters struggle against lowly opposition and the visitors fight back to nearly claim a point at the death. Slough is fouled in the area with five minutes to go but Allen blasts the penalty-kick over the bar. 17-year-old John Phillips shows bravery and anticipation far beyond his years. | | | | | | | | | | | |
| 32 | A READING | | 3 | D | 1-1 | 0-0 | Sheffield 64 | Davie | Dougan | Bannister | McDerment | Slough | Moore | French | Lewis | Sheffield | Allen | Jardine | |
| | 12/3 | *6,146* | *13* | 41 | | | *Sainty 63* | *Brown* | *Bacuzzi* | *Meldrum* | *Yard* | *Spiers* | *Thornhill* | *Docherty* | *Sainty* | *Silvester* | *Collins* | *Harris* | |
| | | | | | | | Ref: H New | The players have to contend with fog, rain, sleet and mud but they provide a fast-moving and exciting tussle which is deserving of better conditions and a larger audience. Max Dougan, skipper for the night in the absence of Terry Branston, shackles nippy wingman, George Harris. | | | | | | | | | | | |
| 33 | A ROTHERHAM | | 3 | D | 2-2 | 0-1 | French 48, Lewis 65 | Davie | Dougan | Bannister | McDerment | Slough | Moore | French | Allen | Sheffield | Lewis* | Jardine | Ryan |
| | 15/3 | *9,873* | *12* | 42 | | | *Quinn 36, Storrie 73* | *Furnell* | *Mealand* | *Watson* | *Swift* | *Leigh* | *Quinn* | *Bentley* | *Brogden* | *Storrie* | *Downes* | *Mullen* | |
| | | | | | | | Ref: C Robinson | The Hatters hold out against a Millers team which has taken seven points out of the last eight. French and Lewis score goals from almost the same spot on a quagmire of a pitch but it is Sandy Davie who wins the day with a great save in the last minute from ex-Leeds man, Jim Storrie. | | | | | | | | | | | |
| 34 | H BRISTOL ROV | | 3 | W | 3-0 | 1-0 | Sheffield 2, Lewis 62, Allen 85 | Davie | Dougan | Bannister | Slough | Branston | Moore | French | Allen | Sheffield | Lewis | Rioch | |
| | 19/3 | 14,506 | *16* | 44 | | | | *Taylor L* | *Jones B* | *Parsons* | *Taylor S* | *Lloyd* | *Williams* | *Ronaldson* | *Barney* | *Jones W* | *Brown* | *Jarman* | |
| | | | | | | | Ref: G Gill | Town have now gone eight games without defeat as they put pressure on the leading pair, Watford and Swindon. An early goal from Sheffield knocks the stuffing out of Rovers, who are beaten well before the end. Spurs manager, Bill Nicholson, watches Rioch on his return from injury. | | | | | | | | | | | |

| No/Date | Venue | Opponent | Att | Pos | Res/Pts | Score | HT | Scorers | 1 | 2 | 3 | 4 | 5 | 6 | 7 | 8 | 9 | 10 | 11 | 12 |
|---|---|---|---|---|---|---|---|---|---|---|---|---|---|---|---|---|---|---|---|---|
| 35 | H | GILLINGHAM | | 3 | D | 1-1 | 0-1 | Sheffield 84 | Davie | Dougan | Bannister | Slough | Branston | Moore | French | Allen | Sheffield | Lewis | Rioch | |
| 22/3 | | | 14,562 | *19* | 45 | | | *Yeo 44* | *Simpson J* | *Weston* | *Williams* | *Quirke* | *Green* | *Simpson T* | *Bailey* | *Riddick* | *Yeo* | *Smillie* | *Meredith* | |
| | | | | | | | | Ref: D Counsell | Tense and over-anxious, the Town struggle against a Gillingham side that takes an interval lead. A loud-speaker message, announcing that Swindon are losing at Plymouth, acts like magic. Sheffield equalises but John Moore blasts over the bar when well placed in the final minute. | | | | | | | | | | | |
| 36 | H | BARROW | | 3 | W | **5-1** | 3-1 | Slough 20, Rioch 42, Lewis 44, 77, Allen 72 | Davie | Dougan | Bannister | Slough | Branston | Moore | French* | Allen | Sheffield | Lewis | Rioch | Jardine |
| 26/3 | | | 14,244 | *18* | 47 | | | *Knox 30* | *Else* | *McDonald* | *Davis* | *Harrison* | *Arrowsmith* | *Hartland* | *McCarthy* | *Morris* | *Hopkinson* | *Knox* | *Storf** | *Riley* |
| | | | | | | | | Ref: R Spittle | The Hatters are now only two points behind the leaders following this emphatic win. Barrow have little to offer and only ex-Blackburn goalkeeper, Fred Else, keeps the score down. The solitary Barrow goal is scored by part-timer, Bobby Knox, who is also a shipyard worker! | | | | | | | | | | | |
| 37 | H | ORIENT | | 3 | W | 2-1 | 1-1 | Branston 35, Sheffield 62 | Davie | Dougan | Bannister | Slough | Branston* | Moore | Ryan | Allen | Sheffield | Lewis | Rioch | Potter |
| 29/3 | | | 13,915 | *14* | 49 | | | *Rofe 38* | *Goddard* | *Howe* | *Mancini* | *Taylor* | *Rofe* | *Harper* | *Allen* | *Slater** | *Bullock* | *Dyson* | *Parmenter* | *Massey* |
| | | | | | | | | Ref: W Castle | Branston is accidentally kicked by team-mate, Sheffield, when scoring Town's first goal and has to go off. Hatters storm forward in the second half but a late Terry Mancini header hits the bar and nearly earns a point for the O's. The match proves to be poor fare for the TV cameras. | | | | | | | | | | | |
| 38 | A | BRISTOL ROV | | 3 | D | 0-0 | 0-0 | | Davie | Dougan | Bannister | Keen | Slough | Moore | Rioch | Allen | Sheffield* | Lewis | Jardine | McDerment |
| 31/3 | | | *8,112* | *16* | 50 | | | | *Taylor L* | *Jones B* | *Stanton* | *Taylor S* | *Lloyd* | *Petts* | *Ronaldson* | *Barney* | *Jones W* | *Brown* | *Jarman* | |
| | | | | | | | | Ref: K Markham | 'Never has the ball been kicked so far, so high and so blatantly into the terraces,' reports the *Daily Mirror* as Town deliberately play for a point and stretch the unbeaten run to twelve games. Only twice did the Hatters break out of defence and on each occasion, Bruce Rioch shoots wide. | | | | | | | | | | | |
| 39 | A | TORQUAY | | 2 | D | 1-1 | 1-0 | McDerment 9 | Davie | Dougan | Bannister* | Keen | Slough | Moore | McDerment | Lewis | Allen | Rioch | Jardine | Potter |
| 4/4 | | | *11,427* | *6* | 51 | | | *Cave 59* | *Donnelly* | *Benson** | *Baxter* | *Dunne* | *Young* | *Morgan* | *Cave* | *Stubbs* | *Kitchener* | *Rudge* | *Barnes* | *Scott* |
| | | | | | | | | Ref: E Wallace | Hatters move into second place following a hard-fought draw against ex-manager Allan Brown's new team. Billy McDerment, heads home his first goal for the club and Micky Cave hits a volley to level the scores. Torquay's promised magnum of champagne for winning stays on ice! | | | | | | | | | | | |
| 40 | A | MANSFIELD | | 3 | L | 0-1 | 0-0 | | Davie | Dougan | Jardine | Keen | Slough | Moore | French | Lewis | Allen | Rioch | McDerment* | Harrison |
| 7/4 | | | *8,681* | 22 | 51 | | | *Sharkey 51p* | *Hollins* | *Pate* | *Hopkinson* | *Quigley* | *Boam* | *Waller* | *Keeley* | *Jones* | *Sharkey* | *Roberts* | *Goodfellow* | |
| | | | | | | | | Ref: K Styles | The unbeaten run comes to an end in front of 3,500 Town supporters at Field Mill. In a disappointing display, Fred Jardine fouls ex-Sunderland striker, Nick Sharkey, who scores from the spot. Stags kick the ball out of the ground at every possible opportunity during the last ten minutes. | | | | | | | | | | | |
| 41 | H | SOUTHPORT | | 3 | D | 0-0 | 0-0 | | Davie | Dougan | Jardine* | Slough | Branston | Moore | French | Lewis | Rioch | Keen | Harrison | Buxton |
| 8/4 | | | 15,963 | *16* | 52 | | | | *Reeves* | *Alty* | *Curwen* | *Peat* | *Aindow* | *Clarke* | *Russell M* | *Field* | *Andrews* | *Russell A* | *Redrobe* | |
| | | | | | | | | Ref: P Walters | On a frustrating evening, Southport pack their defence and fight like their nearest and dearest live in Watford! Brian Lewis has to drop back in to defence when Jardine is injured and then takes over in goal to replace Sandy Davie. The promotion dream is all but over for another year. | | | | | | | | | | | |
| 42 | H | BRIGHTON | | 3 | W | 3-0 | 1-0 | French 23, Lewis 52, Slough 85 | Read | Dougan | Bannister | Slough | Branston* | Moore | French | Lewis | Buxton | Keen | Rioch | Whittaker |
| 12/4 | | | 11,695 | 7 | 54 | | | | *Powney* | *Henderson* | *Templeman* | *Turner* | *Napier J* | *Gall* | *Wilkinson* | *Napier K* | *Dawson* | *Spearritt* | *Armstrong* | |
| | | | | | | | | Ref: M Sinclair | A weakened Hatters side turns on the style against the team with the best scoring record in the Football League. French has a hand in all of the goals on a hard, dust-blown surface and Rioch quietly keeps out of the way of referee Malcolm Sinclair, who sent him off earlier in the season. | | | | | | | | | | | |
| 43 | A | SOUTHPORT | | 3 | D | 1-1 | 0-0 | Lewis 55 | Read | Dougan | Bannister | Slough | Branston | Moore | French | Lewis | Buxton | Keen | Rioch | |
| 14/4 | | | ***3,392*** | *10* | 55 | | | *Russell A 60* | *Reeves* | *Curwen* | *Clarke* | *Peat* | *Russell M* | *Aindow* | *Alty* | *Field* | *Andrews* | *Russell A* | *Redrobe* | |
| | | | | | | | | Ref: R Barker | On a wet and blustery evening, the Town keep out Southport for the first half and then, with the wind at their backs, go all out for a win in the second period. Lewis gets his head to a perfect cross from French but Alex Russell scores direct from a corner five minutes later to equalise. | | | | | | | | | | | |
| 44 | A | TRANMERE | | 3 | W | 2-0 | 0-0 | Moore 47, Rioch 54 | Read | Dougan | Bannister | Allen | Slough | Moore | French | Lewis | Buxton | Keen | Rioch | |
| 18/4 | | | *6,723* | *6* | 57 | | | | *Cumbes* | *Storton S* | *Dempsey* | *Moorcroft* | *Storton T* | *King* | *Rowland* | *Scott* | *Smith* | *Beamish* | *McNamee* | |
| | | | | | | | | Ref: G Singleton | Tranmere have a terrible home record for a top side, with seven home defeats recorded so far. The Town stroll to victory after John Moore thunders home the first goal. Swindon need five points from four games to be sure of promotion. 'It makes life interesting,' muses Alec Stock. | | | | | | | | | | | |
| 45 | H | STOCKPORT | | 3 | W | 4-1 | 2-0 | Lewis 6, 61, 80, Rioch 7 | Read | Dougan | Bannister | Keen | Slough | Moore | French | Lewis | Buxton | Allen | Rioch | |
| 25/4 | | | 12,055 | 7 | 59 | | | *Young 59p* | *Ogley* | *Griffiths* | *Hartle* | *Kinsella** | *Milner* | *Campbell* | *Price* | *Goodwin* | *Young* | *Harley* | *Mulholland* | *Ledgard* |
| | | | | | | | | Ref: J Yates | A hat-trick from Brian Lewis brings his goal tally to 23 for the season as the Town keep alive their slim promotion hopes. John Moore catches the ball in the area after reacting to a whistle from the crowd and Alex Young slams home the resultant penalty amidst a crescendo of boos. | | | | | | | | | | | |
| 46 | H | WATFORD | | 3 | W | 2-1 | 1-0 | Buxton 29, Allen 70 | Read | Dougan | Bannister | Keen | Slough ! | Moore | French | Lewis | Buxton | Allen | Rioch | |
| 30/4 | | | **25,253** | *1* | 61 | | | *Scullion 87* | *Walker* | *Welbourne* | *Williams* | *Eddy* | *Lees* | *Walley !* | *Scullion* | *Hale* | *Sinclair* | *Endean !* | *Owen** | *Garbett* |
| Average | | Home 14,896 | Away 9,670 | | | | | Ref: K Burns | 'A brutal, bloody and belligerent night,' says manager Stock after a game which sees three players sent off and 100 spectators injured after fighting amongst the largest Kenilworth Road crowd since 1961. Buxton scores in his final appearance for the Town on a night best forgotten. | | | | | | | | | | | |

| League Cup | | | | | F-A | H-T | Scorers, Times, and Referees | 1 | 2 | 3 | 4 | 5 | 6 | 7 | 8 | 9 | 10 | 11 | 12 sub used |
|---|---|---|---|---|---|---|---|---|---|---|---|---|---|---|---|---|---|---|---|
| 1 | H | WATFORD | | W | 3-0 | 1-0 | Harrison 8p, 48, Lewis 71 | Read | Dougan | Jardine | Allen | Branston | Slough | Ryan | Lewis | Sheffield | Rioch | Harrison* | McDerment |
| | 14/8 | 20,167 | *D3* | | | | | *Slater* | *Welbourne* | *Williams* | *Hale* | *Garvey* | *Eddy* | *Scullion* | *Dyson* | *Garbett* | *Walley* | *Lewis** | *Owen* |
| | | | | | | | Ref: B Daniels | Mike Harrison, the Hatters' new signing from Plymouth, scores twice and makes the third in a tough game which includes 45 fouls. 'Watford made no attempt to play football,' says Allan Brown. 'You cannot play football on a ground this small,' replies Watford manager, Ken Furphy. | | | | | | | | | | | |
| 2 | A | BRIGHTON | 1 | D | 1-1 | 1-0 | Sheffield 38 | Read | Dougan | McDerment | Allen | Slough | Moore | Ryan | Lewis | Sheffield | Rioch | French | |
| | 4/9 | *15,200* | *3:5* | | | | *Lawton 62* | *Burns* | *Henderson* | *Gall* | *Templeman* | *Napier J* | *Turner* | *Wilkinson* | *Lawton* | *Napier K* | *Livesey* | *Flood* | |
| | | | | | | | Ref: R Challis | After Howard Wilkinson misses a sitter for Albion, the Town settle down and take the lead through a Sheffield left-foot drive into the top corner. Brighton are the stronger team in the second period and Nobby Lawton hits a deserved equaliser. Town manage to hang on for a replay. | | | | | | | | | | | |
| 2R | H | BRIGHTON | 1 | W | 4-2 | 0-0 | Slough 49, 55, Sheffield 52, Rioch 70 | Read | Dougan | Jardine | Slough | Branston | Moore | French | Lewis | Sheffield | Rioch | Harrison | |
| | 11/9 | 18,679 | *3:6* | | | | *Livesey 51, Napier K 87* | *Burns* | *Henderson* | *Gall* | *Templeman* | *Napier J* | *Turner* | *Wilkinson* | *Lawton* | *Napier K* | *Livesey* | *Flood* | |
| | | | | | | | Ref: R Spittle | The match erupts after the interval with four goals in six minutes, including a well-worked free-kick routine from man-of-the-match, Slough. French and Albion's Norman Gall are lucky not to be sent off after a bad-tempered scuffle. Town's reward is a money-spinning trip to Everton. | | | | | | | | | | | |
| 3 | A | EVERTON | 1 | L | 1-5 | 0-3 | Sheffield 72 *[Morrissey 89]* | Read | Dougan | Jardine | Slough* | Branston | McDerment | French | Lewis | Sheffield | Buxton | Harrison | Ryan |
| | 24/9 | *30,405* | *1:6* | | | | *Husband 2, Royle 7, 83p, Ball 44,* | *West* | *Wright* | *Brown* | *Kendall** | *Labone* | *Harvey* | *Husband* | *Ball* | *Royle* | *Hurst* | *Morrissey* | *Kenyon* |
| | | | | | | | Ref: J Taylor | The Toffees are awesome as they crush a Luton side who, to their credit, never give up. Town are two goals down before they have settled and Read appears overwhelmed by the occasion. Sheffield receives generous applause from the Goodison crowd after he scores a consolation goal. | | | | | | | | | | | |

| FA Cup | | | | | | | | | | | | | | | | | | | |
|---|---|---|---|---|---|---|---|---|---|---|---|---|---|---|---|---|---|---|---|
| 1 | H | WARE | 6 | W | 6-1 | 0-0 | Potter 58, Slough 63, 89, Allen 71, 74, 82p | Davie | Dougan | McDerment | Slough | Branston | Bannister | French | Lewis | Sheffield* | Potter | Rioch | Allen |
| | 16/11 | 10,952 | *Ath* | | | | *Francis 87* | *Abrey* | *Stevens* | *Messer* | *Johnson* | *Webb* | *Garrod* | *Francis* | *Stockwell* | *Sherriff* | *Williams* | *Ward* | |
| | | | | | | | Ref: R Challis | The Hatters are frustrated by the Athenian League amateurs but the game livens up in the second period when Keith Allen becomes the first substitute to score a hat-trick in top-class football. George Potter, making his seasonal debut, opens the scoring with his first goal for the club. | | | | | | | | | | | |
| 2 | H | GILLINGHAM | 8 | W | 3-1 | 2-0 | French 16, Harrison 24, 72p | Davie | Dougan | McDerment | Bannister | Branston | Slough | French | Lewis | Buxton | Rioch | Harrison | |
| | 7/12 | 12,035 | *3:17* | | | | *Yeo 80p* | *Bellotti* | *Weston* | *Williams* | *Quirke* | *Green* | *Bailey* | *Simpson* | *Meredith* | *Woodley* | *Yeo* | *Riddick* | |
| | | | | | | | Ref: T Reynolds | The Town ease into the Third Round in an uncompromising game which is not helped by a lenient referee. Harrison scores from the spot after a handling offence by Gill's Brian Yeo, who scores his side's only goal with a penalty after Branston fouls ex-Luton forward, Gordon Riddick. | | | | | | | | | | | |
| 3 | A | MANCHESTER C | 6 | L | 0-1 | 0-1 | | Davie | Dougan | Bannister | Slough | Branston | Moore | French | Lewis* | Allen | Rioch | Harrison | McDerment |
| | 4/1 | *37,120* | *1:14* | | | | *Lee 26p* | *Dowd* | *Pardoe* | *Booth* | *Oakes* | *Mann* | *Doyle* | *Bell* | *Lee* | *Owen* | *Young* | *Coleman* | |
| | | | | | | | Ref: K Burns | City's Francis Lee collapses spectacularly in the area to win a penalty which he converts himself. The Hatters have their chances against the lacklustre League Champions, with Rioch twice going close in the second half. 'Luton scared me to death,' quotes City manager, Joe Mercer. | | | | | | | | | | | |

| | | Home | | | | | Away | | | | | |
|---|---|---|---|---|---|---|---|---|---|---|---|---|
| | P | W | D | L | F | A | W | D | L | F | A | Pts |
| 1 Watford | 46 | 16 | 5 | 2 | 35 | 7 | 11 | 5 | 7 | 39 | 27 | 64 |
| 2 Swindon | 46 | 18 | 4 | 1 | 38 | 7 | 9 | 6 | 8 | 33 | 28 | 64 |
| 3 LUTON TOWN | 46 | 20 | 3 | 0 | 57 | 14 | 5 | 8 | 10 | 17 | 24 | 61 |
| 4 Bournemouth | 46 | 16 | 2 | 5 | 41 | 17 | 5 | 7 | 11 | 19 | 28 | 51 |
| 5 Plymouth | 46 | 10 | 8 | 5 | 34 | 25 | 7 | 7 | 9 | 19 | 24 | 49 |
| 6 Torquay | 46 | 13 | 4 | 6 | 35 | 18 | 5 | 8 | 10 | 19 | 28 | 48 |
| 7 Tranmere | 46 | 12 | 3 | 8 | 36 | 31 | 7 | 7 | 9 | 34 | 37 | 48 |
| 8 Southport | 46 | 14 | 8 | 1 | 52 | 20 | 3 | 5 | 15 | 19 | 44 | 47 |
| 9 Stockport | 46 | 14 | 5 | 4 | 49 | 25 | 2 | 9 | 12 | 18 | 43 | 46 |
| 10 Barnsley | 46 | 13 | 6 | 4 | 37 | 21 | 3 | 8 | 12 | 21 | 42 | 46 |
| 11 Rotherham | 46 | 12 | 6 | 5 | 40 | 21 | 4 | 7 | 12 | 16 | 29 | 45 |
| 12 Brighton | 46 | 12 | 7 | 4 | 49 | 21 | 4 | 6 | 13 | 23 | 44 | 45 |
| 13 Walsall | 46 | 10 | 9 | 4 | 34 | 18 | 4 | 7 | 12 | 16 | 31 | 44 |
| 14 Reading | 46 | 13 | 3 | 7 | 41 | 25 | 2 | 10 | 11 | 26 | 41 | 43 |
| 15 Mansfield | 46 | 14 | 5 | 4 | 37 | 18 | 2 | 6 | 15 | 21 | 44 | 43 |
| 16 Bristol Rov | 46 | 12 | 6 | 5 | 41 | 27 | 4 | 5 | 14 | 22 | 44 | 43 |
| 17 Shrewsbury | 46 | 11 | 8 | 4 | 28 | 17 | 5 | 3 | 15 | 23 | 50 | 43 |
| 18 Orient | 46 | 10 | 8 | 5 | 31 | 19 | 4 | 6 | 13 | 20 | 39 | 42 |
| 19 Barrow | 46 | 11 | 6 | 6 | 30 | 23 | 6 | 2 | 15 | 26 | 52 | 42 |
| 20 Gillingham | 46 | 10 | 10 | 3 | 35 | 20 | 3 | 5 | 15 | 19 | 43 | 41 |
| 21 Northampton | 46 | 9 | 8 | 6 | 37 | 30 | 5 | 4 | 14 | 17 | 31 | 40 |
| 22 Hartlepool | 46 | 6 | 12 | 5 | 25 | 29 | 4 | 7 | 12 | 15 | 41 | 39 |
| 23 Crewe | 46 | 11 | 4 | 8 | 40 | 31 | 2 | 5 | 16 | 12 | 45 | 35 |
| 24 Oldham | 46 | 9 | 6 | 8 | 33 | 27 | 4 | 3 | 16 | 17 | 56 | 35 |
| | 1104 | 296 | 146 | 110 | 915 | 511 | 110 | 146 | 296 | 511 | 915 | 1104 |

Odds & ends

Double wins: (3) Northampton, Oldham, Tranmere.
Double losses: (0).

Won from behind: (0).
Lost from in front: (1) Shrewsbury (a).

High spots: Unbeaten in first eight games.
No home defeats during the season.
13-game unbeaten run after Christmas.
The sharp-shooting of Brian Lewis.
Graham French's goal against Mansfield at Kenilworth Road.

Low spots: The death of coach Doug Davidson just before the start of the season.
Seven consecutive away defeats before Christmas.
Defeat at Mansfield on Easter Monday, which virtually spelled the end of the promotion bid.
Losing at Manchester City to a dubious Francis Lee penalty.

Player of the Year: Alan Slough.
Ever-presents: (1) Alan Slough.
Hat-tricks: Brian Lewis (1), Keith Allen (1).
Leading scorer: Brian Lewis (23).

| | Appearances | | | | | | Goals | | | |
|---|---|---|---|---|---|---|---|---|---|---|
| | Lge | *Sub* | LC | *Sub* | FAC | *Sub* | Lge | LC | FAC | Tot |
| Allen, Keith | **37** | *3* | 2 | | 1 | *1* | **9** | | 3 | **12** |
| Bannister, Jack | **30** | | | | 3 | | | | | |
| Branston, Terry | **35** | | 3 | | 3 | | **4** | | | **4** |
| Brown, Mick | **1** | *1* | | | | | | | | |
| Buxton, Ian | **10** | *1* | 1 | | 1 | | **1** | | | **1** |
| Davie, Sandy | **27** | | | | 3 | | | | | |
| Denton, Peter | **1** | | | | | | | | | |
| Dougan, Max | **43** | | 4 | | 3 | | | | | |
| French, Graham | **35** | *1* | 3 | | 3 | | **3** | | 1 | **4** |
| Harrison, Mike | **18** | *1* | 3 | | 2 | | **2** | 2 | 2 | **6** |
| Jardine, Fred | **23** | *1* | 3 | | | | **2** | | | **2** |
| Keen, Mike | **14** | | | | | | **1** | | | **1** |
| Lewis, Brian | **43** | *2* | 4 | | 3 | | **22** | 1 | | **23** |
| McDerment, Billy | **15** | *6* | 2 | *1* | 2 | *1* | **1** | | | **1** |
| Moore, John | **29** | *4* | 2 | | 1 | | **1** | | | **1** |
| Potter, George | | *3* | | | 1 | | | | 1 | **1** |
| Read, Tony | **16** | | 4 | | | | | | | |
| Rioch, Bruce | **37** | | 3 | | 3 | | **10** | 1 | | **11** |
| Ryan, John | **7** | *1* | 2 | *1* | | | | | | |
| Sheffield, Laurie | **28** | *1* | 4 | | 1 | | **12** | 3 | | **15** |
| Slough, Alan | **46** | | 4 | | 3 | | **5** | 2 | 2 | **9** |
| Stevenson, Morris | **1** | | | | | | | | | |
| Taylor, Bill | **3** | | | | | | | | | |
| Whittaker, Ray | **7** | *1* | | | | | | | | |
| (own-goals) | | | | | | | **1** | | | **1** |
| **24 players used** | **506** | ***26*** | **44** | ***2*** | **33** | ***2*** | **74** | **9** | **9** | **92** |

| No | Date | | Att | Pos | Pt | F-A | H-T | Scorers, Times, and Referees | 1 | 2 | 3 | 4 | 5 | 6 | 7 | 8 | 9 | 10 | 11 | 12 sub used |
|---|---|---|---|---|---|---|---|---|---|---|---|---|---|---|---|---|---|---|---|---|
| 1 | H | BARROW | | | W | 3-0 | 2-0 | Allen 27, Collins 37, Keen 89 | Read | **Ryan** | Bannister | Keen | Branston | Moore | **Collins** | Lewis* | Sheffield | Allen | **MacDonald** | French |
| | 9/8 | | 12,080 | | 2 | | | | *Heyes* | *Cooper* | *Davis* | *Street* | *Arrowsmith* | *Hollis* | *Garbett* | *Morris* | *McArthur* | *Mulvaney** | *Storf* | *Ellison* |
| | | | | | | | | Ref: R Challis | New-look Luton gently breeze past a poor Barrow side in humid conditions. Debutant John Collins is impressive and opens his goal account when reacting to a rebound from a Lewis penalty. French shows some exciting wing play when coming on as a substitute for last 25 minutes. | | | | | | | | | | | |
| 2 | A | BOURNEMOUTH | | | W | 1-0 | 1-0 | MacDonald 28 | Read | Ryan | Bannister | Keen | Branston | Slough | Collins | MacDonald | Sheffield | Allen | French | |
| | 16/8 | | *9,578* | | 4 | | | | *Jones* | *Gulliver* | *Foote* | *White* | *Stocks* | *Bumstead* | *Hartley* | *Meredith* | *East** | *MacDougall* | *Hold* | *Powell* |
| | | | | | | | | Ref: D Laing | Malcolm MacDonald, a £17,500 transfer from Fulham in the close season, scores his first goal for the Club to earn a narrow victory over one of the bookmakers' favourites for promotion. Latching on to a through-ball from Keen, he side-steps Roger Jones and strokes the ball home. | | | | | | | | | | | |
| 3 | H | ORIENT | | | W | 3-2 | 0-1 | Collins 74, French 80, MacDonald 86 | Read | Ryan | Bannister | Keen | Branston | Slough | Collins | MacDonald | Sheffield* | Allen | French | Lewis |
| | 23/8 | | 13,761 | | 6 | | | *Jones 14, Bullock 60* | *Goddard* | *Jones* | *Rofe* | *Taylor* | *Mancini* | *Harper* | *Slater* | *Bullock* | *Allen* | *Dyson* | *Brabrook* | |
| | | | | | | | | Ref: F Nicholson | The Hatters' proud 30-game unbeaten home record looks to be at risk after Orient take a two-goal lead inside the hour. The Anglia TV cameras witness a thrilling finale after winger Collins moves inside. 19-year-old MacDonald hits a spectacular winner but Orient throw the game away. | | | | | | | | | | | |
| 4 | H | HALIFAX | | 1 | D | 1-1 | 1-1 | MacDonald 5 | Read | Ryan | Bannister | Keen | Slough | Moore | Collins | MacDonald | Lewis* | Allen | French | Sheffield |
| | 26/8 | | 13,759 | *13* | 7 | | | *Hill 27* | *Smith* | *Wallace* | *Burgin* | *Pickering* | *Nicholl* | *Robertson* | *Ryden** | *Lennard* | *Lawther* | *Hill* | *McCarthy* | *Shawcross* |
| | | | | | | | | Ref: R Spittle | On a wet and miserable evening, impressive Halifax look good for their point, with ex-England inside-forward, Freddie Hill, showing his class. MacDonald scores an early goal but is then stifled by tall Halifax centre-half Chris Nicholl, who signs for Luton for £35,000 after the game. | | | | | | | | | | | |
| 5 | A | GILLINGHAM | | 1 | W | 2-0 | 1-0 | MacDonald 13p, Green 76 (og) | Read | Ryan | Bannister | Keen | **Nicholl** | Slough | Collins | MacDonald | **Tees** | Allen | French | |
| | 30/8 | | *7,792* | *24* | 9 | | | | *Simpson* | *Weston* | *Green* | *Machin* | *Williams* | *Quirke* | *Woodley* | *Yeo* | *Riddick* | *Smillie* | *Pound* | |
| | | | | | | | | Ref: D Fieldsend | Pointless Gillingham dish out the rough stuff after Andy Smillie needlessly handles the ball for the Luton opener from the spot. Matt Tees, a new signing from Charlton, is singled out by Gills' defender, Mike Green, but he has the last laugh as Green deflects a centre into his own net. | | | | | | | | | | | |
| 6 | H | BRISTOL ROV | | 1 | W | 4-0 | 1-0 | Collins 12, Tees 55, MacDonald 56, [Allen 88] | Read | Dougan | Bannister | Keen | Nicholl | Slough | Collins | MacDonald | Tees | Allen | French | |
| | 6/9 | | 15,198 | *7* | 11 | | | | *Sheppard* | *Roberts* | *Parsons* | *Marsland* | *Taylor* | *Munro* | *Graydon* | *Jones W* | *Stubbs* | *Jones R* | *Jarman* | |
| | | | | | | | | Ref: D Pugh | 'If there is a better 19-year-old striker around at the moment, then I have still to see him' enthuses Hatter's manager, Alec Stock after Malcolm MacDonald runs riot with the Rovers defence. Chris Nicholl blots out new Pirates' signing, Robin Stubbs, and Tees scores on his home debut. | | | | | | | | | | | |
| 7 | A | BRADFORD CITY | | 1 | D | 1-1 | 0-0 | Allen 53 | Davie | Dougan | Bannister | Keen | Nicholl | Slough | Collins | MacDonald | Tees | Allen | French | |
| | 13/9 | | *10,851* | *6* | 12 | | | *Ham 77* | *Liney* | *Bayliss* | *Cooper* | *Stowell* | *Hallett* | *Leighton* | *Hall* | *Ham* | *Corner* | *McConnell* | *Bannister* | |
| | | | | | | | | Ref: C Thomas | Graham French runs the City defence ragged but the Hatters' forwards are unable to make full use of his succession of crosses. Hard-working Bradford probably just deserved a draw. Their goal is the first conceded by the Town in 257 minutes of football away from Kenilworth Road. | | | | | | | | | | | |
| 8 | A | SOUTHPORT | | 1 | W | 3-0 | 0-0 | MacDonald 57, French 71, Nicholl 86 | Davie | Dougan | Bannister | Keen | Nicholl | Slough | Collins | MacDonald | Tees | Allen | French | |
| | 16/9 | | *4,003* | *18* | 14 | | | | *Wraith* | *Pearson* | *Alty* | *Peat* | *Harrison* | *Clarke* | *McCarthy* | *Field* | *Andrews* | *Russell* | *Pring* | |
| | | | | | | | | Ref: A Green | The Hatters' end Southport's record of 23 home league games without defeat to consolidate their position at the top of the table. The first half was lifeless but Town apply pressure after the break and score their second goal when a soft shot from French eludes a diving Bobby Wraith. | | | | | | | | | | | |
| 9 | H | SHREWSBURY | | 1 | D | 2-2 | 0-0 | Collins 54, Slough 88 | Davie | Dougan | Bannister | Keen | Nicholl | Slough | Collins | MacDonald | Tees | Allen | French | |
| | 20/9 | | 15,396 | *21* | 15 | | | *Slough 53 (og), Roberts 79* | *Phillips* | *Gregory* | *Fellows* | *Moore* | *Wood* | *Pountney* | *Roberts* | *Bridgwood* | *Harkin** | *Hawkins* | *Meredith* | *Moir* |
| | | | | | | | | Ref: R Paine | The Shrews adopt spoiling tactics in order to preserve a point and visitors' centre-half, Alf Wood is fortunate not to be sent off after conceding the majority of the 22 fouls awarded against his side. Alan Slough makes up for his earlier headed own-goal by equalising towards the end. | | | | | | | | | | | |
| 10 | A | PLYMOUTH | | 1 | W | 3-1 | 1-0 | Tees 44, 79, French 81 | Davie | Dougan | Bannister | Keen | Nicholl | Slough | Collins | MacDonald | Tees | Allen | French | |
| | 27/9 | | *14,111* | *14* | 17 | | | *Nicholl 50 (og)* | *Dunne* | *Reeves* | *Sullivan* | *Hore* | *Molyneux* | *Reynolds* | *Tedesco* | *Piper* | *Burnside* | *Bickle** | *Hutchins* | *Lean* |
| | | | | | | | | Ref: T Reynolds | Two train-loads of Hatters' supporters accept the club's offer to travel for 25 shillings. They are not disappointed as Tees leads the Home Park defence a merry dance. Pat Dunne in the Pilgrims' goal, lets a speculative 25-yard shot from Tees slip through his hands for the second goal. | | | | | | | | | | | |
| 11 | A | WALSALL | | 1 | W | 3-1 | 1-1 | Tees 1, 58, Collins 68 | Davie | Dougan* | Bannister | Keen | Nicholl | Slough | Collins | MacDonald | Tees | Allen | French | Jardine |
| | 30/9 | | *7,557* | *18* | 19 | | | *Taylor 2* | *Parkes* | *Gregg* | *Harrison* | *Atthey* | *Jones* | *Trevis* | *Morris* | *Crowe* | *Woodward* | *Train* | *Taylor* | |
| | | | | | | | | Ref: M Kerkhof | After just 35 seconds, Walsall keeper Phil Parkes is penalised for taking too many steps with the ball, and Tees heads home Collins' free-kick. The Saddlers level a minute later with a Colin Taylor spot-kick after John Woodward is impeded in the area. Town dominate in the second half. | | | | | | | | | | | |

| No | Venue | Opponent | Pos | Res | FT | HT | Scorers, Times, Referees | 1 | 2 | 3 | 4 | 5 | 6 | 7 | 8 | 9 | 10 | 11 | 12 |
|---|---|---|---|---|---|---|---|---|---|---|---|---|---|---|---|---|---|---|---|
| 12 | H | STOCKPORT | 1 | W | 2-0 | 1-0 | Nicholl 16, MacDonald 61p | Davie | Jardine | Bannister | Keen | Nicholl | Slough | Collins | MacDonald | Tees | Allen | French | |
| 4/10 | | 15,944 | *23* | 21 | | | | *Ogley* | *Haydock* | *Hartle* | *Goodwin* | *Campbell* | *Low* | *Price* | *Chapman* | *Rowlands* | *Beddington* | *Morton* | |
| | | | | | | | Ref: T Reynolds | Stockport show their hand early by passing the ball back to their goalkeeper straight from the kick-off. The Town win through, despite the visitors' negative play, when Nicholl scores his first goal and MacDonald converts a penalty after Tees is tripped in the box by Fred Goodwin. | | | | | | | | | | | |
| 13 | H | BOURNEMOUTH | 1 | D | 0-0 | 0-0 | | Davie | Jardine | Bannister | Keen | Nicholl | Slough* | Collins | MacDonald | Tees | Allen | French | Sheffield |
| 7/10 | | **18,065** | *21* | 22 | | | | *Jones* | *White* | *Miller* | *Naylor* | *Stocks* | *Foote* | *Hartley* | *Rowles* | *MacDougall* | *Hold* | *Meredith* | |
| | | | | | | | Ref: J Hunting | 'The tension is terrific and everyone is frightened to death of losing,' says Alec Stock after the Hatters fail to score in a League match for the first time this season and in front of the biggest crowd of the campaign. Barnsley close to within two points after their win over Bristol Rovers. | | | | | | | | | | | |
| 14 | A | DONCASTER | 1 | L | 0-2 | 0-1 | | Davie | Jardine | Bannister* | Keen | Nicholl | Slough | Collins | MacDonald | Tees | Allen | French | Sheffield |
| 11/10 | | *17,380* | *4* | 22 | | | *Slough 33 (og), Briggs 48* | *Ogston* | *Wilcockson* | *Gray* | *Flowers* | *Robertson* | *Haselden* | *Watson* | *Regan* | *Briggs* | *Johnson* | *Usher* | |
| | | | | | | | Ref: S Kayley | The Hatters finally fail at the 20th hurdle. Slough is unfortunate to head into his own net for the Rovers opener and Briggs hammers home the second. MacDonald moves to defence after an injury to full-back Bannister. Sheffield goes close late on but Doncaster are the worthy winners. | | | | | | | | | | | |
| 15 | A | BRIGHTON | 1 | W | 2-1 | 1-0 | Collins 27, 46 | Davie | Jardine* | Bannister | Keen | Nicholl | Slough | Collins | MacDonald | Tees | Allen | French | **Phillips** |
| 18/10 | | ***20,016*** | *10* | 24 | | | *Bell 68* | *Powney* | *Henderson* | *Bell* | *Everitt* | *Napier J* | *Turner* | *Spearritt* | *Lawton* | *Napier K* | *Dawson** | *Armstrong* | *Gall* |
| | | | | | | | Ref: D Nippard | The Town bounce back in front of a big crowd at a sun-soaked Goldstone Ground. Two accurate crosses from French are converted by Collins. Willie Bell reduces the deficit but Town keeper, Davie, saves the day. MacDonald again moves back to defence after an injury to Fred Jardine. | | | | | | | | | | | |
| 16 | H | TORQUAY | 1 | D | 1-1 | 0-1 | Tees 57 | Davie | Ryan | Bannister | Keen | Nicholl | Slough | Collins* | MacDonald | Tees | Allen | French | Lewis |
| 25/10 | | 16,087 | *5* | 25 | | | *Ryan 20 (og)* | *Donnelly* | *Sandercock* | *Glozier* | *Dunne* | *Young* | *Kitchener* | *Benson* | *Cave* | *Rudge** | *Mitchinson* | *Scott* | *Welsh* |
| | | | | | | | Ref: N Graham | The Hatters' full-back, John Ryan, scores a spectacular own-goal with his head in front of the television cameras. Brian Lewis goes close twice after the break before Tees gets a deserved equaliser. The referee turns down a penalty appeal when Alan Young appears to handle in the area. | | | | | | | | | | | |
| 17 | A | ROTHERHAM | 2 | D | 1-1 | 0-1 | Allen 54 | Davie | Ryan | Bannister | Keen | Nicholl | Slough | Collins | MacDonald | Tees | Allen | French | |
| 1/11 | | *8,911* | *20* | 26 | | | *Leigh 42p* | *Furnell* | *Mealand** | *Leigh* | *Hague* | *Watson* | *Hudson* | *Lill* | *Fantham* | *Downes* | *Bentley* | *Warnock* | *Womble* |
| | | | | | | | Ref: A Bone | In a hard-fought display, Town keep up their amazing away record. Allen is penalised for punching the ball in the area, Dennis Leigh scoring from the spot. Allen atones for his error when heading home the equaliser and the Hatters have a shot cleared off the line in the dying minutes. | | | | | | | | | | | |
| 18 | H | BARNSLEY | 1 | D | 1-1 | 1-0 | MacDonald 6 | Davie | Ryan | Bannister | Keen | Branston | Slough | French | MacDonald | Tees | Allen | Harrison | |
| 8/11 | | 17,422 | *3* | 27 | | | *Howard 49* | *Arblaster* | *Murphy* | *Robson* | *Howard* | *Booth* | *Bettany* | *Boardman* | *Earnshaw* | *Loyden* | *Evans* | *Hamstead* | |
| | | | | | | | Ref: J Taylor | Barnsley are swept aside at Kenilworth Road but MacDonald misses lots of chances after scoring an early opener. Barnsley's goal is subject to controversy as an indirect free-kick is hammered straight into the net by Pat Howard. Experienced referee, Jack Taylor, allows the goal to stand. | | | | | | | | | | | |
| 19 | H | ROCHDALE | 1 | W | 2-0 | 0-0 | Collins 76, Allen 86 | Davie | Ryan | Bannister | Keen | Branston | Slough | Collins | MacDonald* | Tees | Allen | French | Harrison |
| 22/11 | | 15,876 | *2* | 29 | | | | *Harker* | *Smith* | *Ryder* | *Leech* | *Parry* | *Ashworth* | *Whitehead* | *Rudd* | *Buck* | *Jenkins* | *Butler* | |
| | | | | | | | Ref: C Thomas | BBC Match of the Day cameras are present to record this top-of-the-table clash. The game then turns on a substitution, when Harrison replaces MacDonald, although the final scoreline flatters the Town. Rochdale were unlucky when a 25-yard pile-driver from Dennis Butler hits the bar. | | | | | | | | | | | |
| 20 | H | FULHAM | 1 | W | 1-0 | 0-0 | MacDonald 47 | Davie | Ryan | Bannister | Keen | Nicholl | Slough | French | MacDonald | Tees | Allen | Harrison | |
| 25/11 | | 16,485 | *12* | 31 | | | | *Seymour* | *Tranter* | *Brown* | *Horne* | *Matthewson* | *Callaghan* | *Conway* | *Richardson* | *Earle* | *Haynes* | *Barrett* | |
| | | | | | | | Ref: H Ellis | Four floodlight failures, combined with a blinding snowstorm make conditions difficult. MacDonald, in his first appearance against his former club, latches onto a pass from French to score his 12th goal of the season. Johnny Haynes brings out a diving save from Luton keeper, Davie. | | | | | | | | | | | |
| 21 | H | BRADFORD CITY | 1 | W | **5-0** | 3-0 | Tees 10, MacDonald 14, 84, 89p, [Collins 44] | Davie | Ryan | Bannister | Keen | Nicholl | Slough | MacDonald | Collins | Tees* | Allen | French | Phillips |
| 13/12 | | 11,857 | *4* | 33 | | | | *Liney* | *Atkins* | *Cooper* | *Stowell* | *Hallett* | *Leighton* | *Hall* | *Ham* | *Corner* | *Bannister* | *Middleton** | *McConnell* |
| | | | | | | | Ref: D Lyden | Following their FA Cup beating by non-League Hillingdon, Town bounce back with a crushing defeat of City, who were the last side to win at Kenilworth Road, 20 months ago. MacDonald scores his first hat-trick, the third from the spot after Dennis Atkins hacks him down in the area. | | | | | | | | | | | |
| 22 | A | ORIENT | 1 | L | 0-1 | 0-1 | | Davie | Ryan | Bannister | Keen | Nicholl | Slough | Collins | MacDonald | Phillips* | Allen | French | Lewis |
| 26/12 | | *17,619* | *3* | 33 | | | *Allen 7* | *Goddard* | *Jones* | *Rofe* | *Taylor* | *Mancini* | *Harper** | *Lazarus* | *Bullock* | *Allen* | *Dyson* | *Brabrook* | *Fairbrother* |
| | | | | | | | Ref: G Hill | Both teams receive a standing ovation after a titanic tussle in the thick mud of Brisbane Road. The O's show superiority in the first half but Town are stronger after the break and do everything but score. 'What a pity one side had to lose,' says Town Chairman, Tony Hunt afterwards. | | | | | | | | | | | |
| 23 | H | GILLINGHAM | 1 | L | 1-2 | 0-0 | Keen 52 | Davie | Ryan | Bannister | Keen | Nicholl | Slough | MacDonald | Collins | Phillips | Allen | French | |
| 27/12 | | 17,402 | *22* | 33 | | | *Green 73, 78* | *Simpson* | *Machin* | *Peach* | *Bailey* | *Galvin* | *Quirke* | *Woodley* | *Tydeman* | *Green* | *Smillie* | *Pound* | |
| | | | | | | | Ref: T Dawes | Luton see their unbeaten home record of 36 league matches shattered by relegation-haunted Gillingham. The game against Orient the previous day is given as the prime reason for this defeat. The Town take the lead but two headed goals from Mike Green win the points for the visitors. | | | | | | | | | | | |

| No | Date | | Att | Pos | Pt | F-A | H-T | Scorers, Times, and Referees | 1 | 2 | 3 | 4 | 5 | 6 | 7 | 8 | 9 | 10 | 11 | 12 sub used |
|---|---|---|---|---|---|---|---|---|---|---|---|---|---|---|---|---|---|---|---|---|
| 24 | A | SHREWSBURY | | 1 | L | **1-5** | 0-4 | Harrison 59 *[Harkin 75]* | Davie | Ryan | Bannister | Keen* | Nicholl | Slough | MacDonald | Collins | Tees | Allen | Harrison | Moore |
| | 10/1 | | *4,406* | *12* | 33 | | | *Andrews 11, Moir 24, 43, McLaughlin 28,* | *Tooze* | *Gregory* | *Fellows* | *Moore* | *Wood* | *Moir** | *Roberts* | *Bridgwood* | *Harkin* | *Andrews* | *McLaughlin* | *Hawkins* |
| | | | | | | | | Ref: J Thacker | After missing two chances in the first ten minutes, Town go to pieces and concede four goals by some atrocious defending in the first half. As a damage-limitation exercise, Moore is brought on to bolster the defence after the interval and Mike Harrison reduces the deficit with a low shot. | | | | | | | | | | | |
| 25 | H | PLYMOUTH | | 3 | L | 0-2 | 0-1 | | Davie | Ryan | Bannister | Slough | Nicholl | Moore | Collins | MacDonald | Tees* | Allen | French | Keen |
| | 17/1 | | 12,358 | *17* | 33 | | | *Rickard 45, Bickle 72* | *Clamp* | *Piper* | *Sullivan* | *Lean* | *Foster* | *Hore* | *Davey* | *Reynolds* | *Rickard* | *Bickle* | *Maher* | |
| | | | | | | | | Ref: H Davey | The Town slump deeper into their losing rut against struggling Plymouth. Several first-half chances go begging and Argyle score against the run of play in first-half injury-time. The crowd give vent to their anger when Moore mis-kicks the ball across his own goal to gift a second. | | | | | | | | | | | |
| 26 | A | BURY | | 2 | W | 3-1 | 2-0 | MacDonald 5, Tees 29, 72 | Davie | Ryan | Bannister | Moore | Nicholl | Slough | Collins | MacDonald | Tees* | Keen | French | Allen |
| | 24/1 | | *6,813* | *15* | 35 | | | *Anderson 68* | *Forrest* | *Parnell* | *Tinney* | *Turner* | *Lyon* | *Anderson* | *Hince* | *Arrowsmith* | *Jones* | *Kerr* | *Grundy* | |
| | | | | | | | | Ref: E Jennings | The Hatters rediscover their old sparkle as French gives Bury full-back Roy Parnell a torrid afternoon. Moore man-marks Shakers' dangerman, Jimmy Kerr, out of the game and Matt Tees gets back on the goal trail. The killer third goal is 'route one' from goalkeeper Davie's clearance. | | | | | | | | | | | |
| 27 | A | STOCKPORT | | 2 | D | 1-1 | 0-0 | Tees 46 | Davie | Ryan | Bannister | Moore | Nicholl | Slough | Collins | Tees | MacDonald | Keen | French | |
| | 31/1 | | *3,922* | *22* | 36 | | | *Goodwin 85* | *Ogley* | *Haydock* | *Hartle* | *Goodwin* | *Coddington* | *Smith* | *Price* | *Broadbent* | *Rowlands** | *Ryden* | *Collier* | *Elgin* |
| | | | | | | | | Ref: K Styles | Town were expected to win against lowly Stockport but have to make do with a point. This is the first time they have returned from Edgeley Park with any reward. Tees takes advantage of a cross from French straight after the interval but Stockport deserve to equalise towards the end. | | | | | | | | | | | |
| 28 | H | DONCASTER | | 1 | W | 4-0 | 1-0 | Slough 40, MacDonald 51, 81p, Tees 83 | Davie | Ryan | Bannister | Keen | Nicholl | Slough | Collins | Tees | Allen | MacDonald | French | |
| | 7/2 | | 12,828 | *13* | 38 | | | | *Wesson* | *Branfoot* | *Gray* | *Flowers* | *Robertson* | *Hasleden* | *Irvine* | *Gilfillan* | *Johnson* | *Usher* | *Regan* | |
| | | | | | | | | Ref: D Laing | Due to a strange combination of results, Town find themselves back on top of the League after their goalscoring touch was rediscovered in the second half. MacDonald is back to his best and his second goal is from the penalty spot after on-loan goalkeeper Bob Wesson pulls down Tees. | | | | | | | | | | | |
| 29 | A | BRISTOL ROV | | 2 | L | 0-3 | 0-1 | | Davie | Ryan | Bannister | Keen | Nicholl | Slough | Moore | MacDonald | Tees | Allen* | French | Collins |
| | 10/2 | | *13,304* | *8* | 38 | | | *Graydon 19, Munro 53p, Ford 78p* | *Sheppard* | *Ford* | *Munro !* | *Roberts* | *Taylor* | *Jones B* | *Graydon* | *Jones W* | *Jones R* | *Gilbert* | *Higgins* | |
| | | | | | | | | Ref: A Jones | Ray Graydon scored Rovers first goal but appeared to be six yards offside which caused an angry reaction by Alec Stock. Two fouls from John Ryan result in penalty decisions and Bristol full-back Alex Munro is sent off in the final minute for kicking Collins in a dropped-ball incident. | | | | | | | | | | | |
| 30 | A | BARROW | | 3 | L | 1-2 | 0-0 | French 54 | Davie | Ryan | Bannister | Keen | Nicholl | Slough | MacDonald | Collins | Tees | Allen* | French | Branston |
| | 14/2 | | *3,843* | *23* | 38 | | | *Mulvaney 68, Morrin 71* | *Heyes* | *Dean* | *Cooper* | *Noble* | *Arrowsmith* | *Hartland* | *Garbett* | *Morrin* | *Ledger* | *Mulvaney* | *Ellison* | |
| | | | | | | | | Ref: V James | Seven of Town's players are turned out for a midweek reserve team game against Chelsea after allowing bottom-placed Barrow to win both points. 'The days of pleasant treatment are now positively over,' storms manager Alec Stock, who saw the home side play with more passion. | | | | | | | | | | | |
| 31 | A | TORQUAY | | 4 | D | 2-2 | 0-0 | Harrison 71, MacDonald 72 | Davie | Ryan | Jardine | Slough | Nicholl | Moore | French | MacDonald | Tees | Keen | Harrison | |
| | 21/2 | | *6,964* | *10* | 39 | | | *Mitchinson 63, Rudge 86* | *Donnelly* | *Joy* | *Benson* | *Dunne** | *Young* | *Kitchener* | *Welsh E* | *Cave* | *Rudge* | *Mitchinson* | *Welsh A* | *Potter* |
| | | | | | | | | Ref: R Paine | Several changes are made to the team that lost to Barrow last week and, in a much-improved display, Town are only four minutes away from capturing both points. Hatters score two goals inside a minute with Mike Harrison's shot from outside the area probably the goal of the season. | | | | | | | | | | | |
| 32 | H | BRIGHTON | | 4 | D | 1-1 | 0-1 | MacDonald 54p | Davie | Ryan | Jardine | Slough | Nicholl | Moore | French | Collins | MacDonald | Keen | Harrison* | Tees |
| | 28/2 | | 17,584 | *1* | 40 | | | *Ryan 43 (og)* | *Sidebottom* | *Henderson* | *Bell* | *Spearritt* | *Napier J* | *Gall* | *Smith* | *Duffy* | *Gilliver* | *Turner* | *Napier K* | |
| | | | | | | | | Ref: A Morrissey | Brighton gain a hard-earned point to remain top of the table after John Ryan panics and concedes an own goal. Hatters are the stronger side in the second half but MacDonald, who wins his penalty after being upended by Bobby Smith, misses a chance to seal victory in the final minute. | | | | | | | | | | | |
| 33 | H | TRANMERE | | 4 | W | 2-0 | 1-0 | MacDonald 42, Ryan 60 | Davie | Ryan | Jardine | Slough | Branston | Moore | MacDonald | Collins | Tees | Keen | French | |
| | 3/3 | | **11,368** | *22* | 42 | | | | *Lane* | *Griffiths* | *Gill* | *Moorcroft* | *Knapp* | *King* | *Kennedy* | *Mathias* | *Beamish* | *Pritchard* | *Crossley* | |
| | | | | | | | | Ref: D Smith | Town return to winning ways against a struggling Tranmere, who have little to offer apart from some acrobatics by goalkeeper Frankie Lane. MacDonald breaks the deadlock with his 21st goal of the season and then Ryan abandons his defensive role to score his first goal since 1967. | | | | | | | | | | | |
| 34 | A | READING | | 4 | W | 1-0 | 0-0 | MacDonald 89 | Davie | Ryan | Jardine | Slough | Branston | Moore | Collins | MacDonald | Tees | Keen | French* | Allen |
| | 11/3 | | *18,929* | *5* | 44 | | | | *Death* | *Dixon* | *Butler* | *Wagstaff B* | *Allen* | *Sharpe* | *Cumming* | *Chappell* | *Habbin* | *Wagstaff T* | *Williams* | |
| | | | | | | | | Ref: D Turner | Before this match, Reading were unbeaten in 15 games; however, they have not beaten the Hatters since 1935. In heavy rain and on a muddy pitch, their biggest league crowd for many years saw the Town as the stronger side, even though Reading's pretty football was always a threat. | | | | | | | | | | | |

| No | Venue | Opponent / Date | Att | Pos | Res / Pts | F-A | H-T | Scorers, Times, Referees | 1 | 2 | 3 | 4 | 5 | 6 | 7 | 8 | 9 | 10 | 11 | 12 |
|---|---|---|---|---|---|---|---|---|---|---|---|---|---|---|---|---|---|---|---|---|
| 35 | H | MANSFIELD | | 4 | D | 2-2 | 1-0 | Ryan 23, Harrison 53 | Davie | Ryan | Jardine | Slough | Nicholl | Moore | MacDonald | Collins | Tees* | Keen | Harrison | Allen |
| | | 14/3 | 12,690 | *13* | 45 | | | *Roberts 51, Partridge 58* | *Brown* | *Pate** | *Walker* | *Quigley* | *Boam* | *Waller* | *Partridge* | *Stenson* | *Jones* | *Roberts* | *Goodfellow* | *McKenzie* |
| | | | | | | | | Ref: J Jones | Another point thrown away and many of home crowd are sentencing the Town to another season in Division 3. By half-time, Luton could have scored six but instead led by just the one goal which is thumped in by full-back, Ryan. Graham Brown pulls off some fine saves after the break. | | | | | | | | | | | |
| 36 | H | BURY | | 4 | D | 0-0 | 0-0 | | Davie | Ryan | Bannister | Slough | Branston | Moore | MacDonald | Collins* | Tees | Keen | Harrison | Allen |
| | | 17/3 | 12,751 | *17* | 46 | | | | *Ramsbottom* | *Tinney* | *Saile* | *Hughes* | *Lyon* | *Holt* | *McDermott* | *Arrowsmith** | *Jones* | *Kerr* | *Hince* | *Towers* |
| | | | | | | | | Ref: B Daniels | Against the side with the worst defensive record in the Division, the Hatters squander many opportunities, including when Harrison and Ryan mess up a free-kick, and the players are heckled for the first time this season. Luckily, the other promotion chasers also struggle to gain points. | | | | | | | | | | | |
| 37 | A | TRANMERE | | 4 | L | 2-3 | 1-2 | Allen 19, Slough 82 | Davie | Ryan | Bannister | Slough | Branston | Moore | Collins* | Allen | MacDonald | Keen | French | Tees |
| | | 21/3 | *4,035* | *21* | 46 | | | *Yardley 3, Pritchard 44, Beamish 73* | *Lane* | *Storton* | *Mathias* | *Moorcroft* | *Knapp* | *Pritchard* | *Beamish* | *King* | *Yardley* | *Hinch* | *Gill* | |
| | | | | | | | | Ref: P Partridge | Luton's promotion hopes take a nose-dive into the Merseyside mud in a performance that is skeletal compared with the rip-roaring days of the previous autumn. Lowly Tranmere show more heart and after ex-Town striker, George Yardley, gives them the lead, there is only one winner. | | | | | | | | | | | |
| 38 | H | ROTHERHAM | | 4 | W | 2-1 | 2-1 | Allen 9, Slough 32 | **Starling** | Ryan | Bannister | Slough | Branston | Moore | **Busby** | Allen | MacDonald | Keen | French* | Harrison |
| | | 27/3 | 14,315 | *11* | 48 | | | *Swift 14* | *Tunks* | *Houghton* | *Leigh* | *Hague* | *Watson* | *Swift* | *Warnock** | *Lill* | *Phillips* | *Bentley* | *Mullen* | *Fantham* |
| | | | | | | | | Ref: R Darlington | Local youngster, Alan Starling, makes his debut in the Luton goal, replacing Sandy Davie, but is a bag of nerves in the first half and gifts an equaliser to the visitors after juggling with the ball. The Hatters' goals both come from accurate crosses by Bannister and debutant, Viv Busby. | | | | | | | | | | | |
| 39 | H | READING | | 3 | W | **5-0** | 1-0 | MacDonald 11, 46, 51, Busby 58, [Harrison 85] | Starling | Ryan | Bannister | Slough | Branston | Moore | Collins | Busby | MacDonald | Keen | Harrison | |
| | | 28/3 | 14,401 | *5* | 50 | | | | *Death* | *Morgan* | *Butler* | *Wagstaff B* | *Allen* | *Sharpe* | *Harley* | *Bell* | *Habbin* | *Wagstaff T* | *Williams* | |
| | | | | | | | | Ref: K Howley | After making a meal over mopping up Rotherham on Good Friday, the Town bounce back to top form and finish off the promotion challenge of Reading. Viv Busby scores his first goal for the club, after a MacDonald hat-trick, and Alan Starling has a quiet afternoon in the Luton goal. | | | | | | | | | | | |
| 40 | A | BARNSLEY | | 4 | L | 1-2 | 0-1 | Keen 59 | Starling | Ryan | Bannister | Slough | Branston | Moore | Collins | Busby | MacDonald | Keen | Harrison | |
| | | 31/3 | *9,988* | *5* | 50 | | | *Dean 36, Hamstead 89* | *Sherratt* | *Murphy* | *Raggett* | *Bettany* | *Winstanley* | *Howard* | *Dean* | *Hamstead* | *Loyden* | *Boardman* | *Barrowclo'gh* | |
| | | | | | | | | Ref: D Corbett | The Town fight back well to equalise in atrocious conditions, only to concede both a last-minute goal and both points. In a goalmouth mix-up, Starling lets the greasy ball squirt out of his arms and into the path of George Hamstead. 'Lack of concentration,' reasoned manager Stock. | | | | | | | | | | | |
| 41 | A | HALIFAX | | 4 | D | 0-0 | 0-0 | | Starling | Ryan | Bannister | Slough | Branston | Moore | Collins | Busby | MacDonald | Keen | Harrison* | Phillips |
| | | 4/4 | ***3,482*** | *13* | 51 | | | | *Smith* | *Burgin* | *Lee* | *Shawcross* | *Pickering* | *Wallace* | *Chadwick* | *Robertson* | *Brierley* | *Atkins* | *McCarthy* | |
| | | | | | | | | Ref: W Castle | Lacklustre Luton fail to maximise their opportunities against a weakened Halifax team, who have most of their better players missing through injury. The game is immediately forgettable with the final whistle bringing a sense of relief to those who turned up at The Shay to watch. | | | | | | | | | | | |
| 42 | A | FULHAM | | 4 | W | 1-0 | 1-0 | MacDonald 10 | Starling | Ryan | Bannister | Keen | Branston | Moore | Slough | Busby | MacDonald | Allen | French | |
| | | 8/4 | *18,987* | *7* | 53 | | | | *Webster* | *Pentecost* | *Moreline* | *Brown* | *Matthewson* | *Callaghan* | *Conway* | *Halom* | *Earle* | *Lloyd* | *Barrett* | |
| | | | | | | | | Ref: C Thomas | The Town turn their recent form upside down with a magnificent win at Craven Cottage to end another team's promotion hopes. Slough plays as a sweeper and Fulham rarely threaten to score. The goal comes from MacDonald, who sweeps onto a weak back-pass from David Moreline . | | | | | | | | | | | |
| 43 | H | WALSALL | | 3 | W | 3-0 | 3-0 | Busby 8, Collins 25, MacDonald 43 | Starling* | Ryan | Bannister | Slough | Branston | Moore | Collins | Busby | MacDonald | Keen | French | Allen |
| | | 11/4 | 17,173 | *18* | 55 | | | | *Parkes* | *Gregg* | *Evans* | *Harrison* | *Jones* | *Atthey* | *Taylor* | *Seal** | *Woodward* | *Trevis* | *Morris* | *Baker* |
| | | | | | | | | Ref: C Nicholls | On FA Cup final evening, the Town destroy the Saddlers with a first-half surge of power football that leads to three magnificent goals. Starling is injured in the 55th minute and replaced by an unwilling Keith Allen, who is kept well-protected as Walsall pepper the goal from all angles. | | | | | | | | | | | |
| 44 | H | SOUTHPORT | | 2 | W | 1-0 | 0-0 | Busby 48 | Read | Dougan | Ryan | Slough | Branston | Moore | Collins | Busby | MacDonald | Keen | French | |
| | | 14/4 | 16,756 | *21* | 57 | | | | *Wraith* | *Pearson* | *Alty* | *Peat* | *Dunleavy* | *Russell M* | *Russell A* | *Aindow* | *Redrobe* | *Cheetham* | *Pring* | |
| | | | | | | | | Ref: P Walters | A promotion position is achieved after a frenzied game at Kenilworth Road. Busby, who was playing in the Isthmian League for Wycombe Wanderers only three months ago, squeezes the tension out of the evening when he drives the ball into the roof of the net just after half-time. | | | | | | | | | | | |
| 45 | A | MANSFIELD | | 2 | D | 0-0 | 0-0 | | Read | Ryan | Bannister | Keen | Branston | Moore | Slough | Busby | MacDonald | Allen | French | |
| | | 20/4 | *10,301* | *8* | 58 | | | | *Brown* | *Pate* | *Walker* | *Quigley* | *Boam* | *Waller* | *McKenzie* | *Stenson* | *Jones* | *Roberts* | *Goodfellow* | |
| | | | | | | | | Ref: A Oliver | A point is all that is required to gain promotion and it is duly obtained in a dour game where only the final result matters. The Town pack their defence and have only one worthwhile attack during the whole game. The final whistle heralds a pitch invasion by the joyful Luton supporters. | | | | | | | | | | | |
| 46 | A | ROCHDALE | | 2 | W | 2-1 | 1-0 | Busby 15, MacDonald 54 | Read | Ryan | Bannister | Slough | Branston | Moore | Collins | Busby | MacDonald | Tees* | Keen | Allen |
| | | 25/4 | *5,886* | *9* | 60 | | | *Jenkins 62* | *Harker* | *Smith* | *Ryder* | *Riley* | *Parry* | *Ashworth* | *Butler* | *Rudd* | *Cross* | *Jenkins* | *Downes* | |
| | | Home Average 14,808 | Away 9,942 | | | | | Ref: K Burns | 2,000 Luton supporters trek to Lancashire to see a game that would surely have been postponed had anything been hinging on the result. After 18 hours of continual rain, the pitch is water-logged. Town players wade through the thick mud to record their tenth away win of the campaign. | | | | | | | | | | | |

| League Cup | | | | | F-A | H-T | Scorers, Times, and Referees | 1 | 2 | 3 | 4 | 5 | 6 | 7 | 8 | 9 | 10 | 11 | 12 sub used |
|---|---|---|---|---|---|---|---|---|---|---|---|---|---|---|---|---|---|---|---|
| 1 | A | PETERBOROUGH | | D | 1-1 | 1-1 | Sheffield 22 | Read | Ryan | Bannister | Keen | Branston | Moore | Slough | MacDonald | Sheffield | Allen | French | |
| | 13/8 | *10,249* | *D4* | | | | *Price 11* | *Drewery* | *Potts* | *Noble* | *Hampton* | *Wile* | *Wright* | *Moss* | *Price* | *Hall* | *Iley* | *Robson* | |
| | | | | | | | Ref: H Ellis | MacDonald hits the post in the first 20 seconds but it is Posh who score first when Bobby Moss speeds through the square Hatters' defence to set up Peter Price for a neat header. After Sheffield levels the score, the Town sit back and contain Peterborough, who resort to long-ball tactics. | | | | | | | | | | | |
| 1R | H | PETERBOROUGH | | W | 5-2 | 3-1 | MacDonald 20, Branston 31, Lewis 40, 55p, [Allen 85] | Read | Ryan | Bannister | Keen | Branston | Slough | Lewis | MacDonald | Sheffield | Allen | French | |
| | 19/8 | 13,105 | *D4* | | | | *Iley 8, Robson 52* | *Drewery* | *Potts* | *Noble* | *Hampton* | *Wile* | *Wright* | *Moss* | *Holliday* | *Hall* | *Iley* | *Robson* | |
| | | | | | | | Ref: M Fussey | In a seven-goal thriller, Town find themselves a goal down early on but the game hinges on two penalties. Lewis runs straight at a defender and falls over. Justice is done when Drewery saves the spot-kick but Lewis scores from the rebound. He then nets the second after a Noble handball. | | | | | | | | | | | |
| 2 | H | MILLWALL | 1 | D | 2-2 | 2-1 | MacDonald 8, Sheffield 30 | Read | Dougan | Bannister | Keen | Branston | Slough* | Collins | MacDonald | Sheffield | Allen | French | Lewis |
| | 2/9 | 17,372 | *2:18* | | | | *Possee 5, Weller 62* | *King* | *Brown* | *Nichols* | *Jacks* | *Kitchener* | *Burnett* | *Possee* | *Neil* | *Weller* | *Bolland* | *Dunphy** | *Dear* |
| | | | | | | | Ref: E Wallace | Although the Town did not win, they did show that they could play in Division 2 without too much trouble. In an end-to-end contest, it is the Lions who hold on and waste time at the end, presumably confident of getting the right result for a replay as they bring the tickets with them. | | | | | | | | | | | |
| 2R | A | MILLWALL | 1 | W | 1-0 | 0-0 | Allen 117 | Davie | Dougan | Bannister | Keen | Branston | Slough | Collins | MacDonald | Sheffield | Allen | French | |
| | 8/9 | *14,125* | *2:19* | | *aet* | | | *King* | *Brown* | *Nichols* | *Jacks* | *Kitchener* | *Burnett* | *Possee* | *Bolland* | *Weller* | *Dear* | *Neil* | |
| | | | | | | | Ref: G Hill | Both sides go close in normal time but in extra-time, controversy strikes when Millwall are awarded an indirect free-kick just outside the area. Keith Weller smacks the ball through the wall and directly into the net but the referee disallows the 'goal'. Allen scores with a 50-yard winner. | | | | | | | | | | | |
| 3 | A | SHEFFIELD UTD | 1 | L | 0-3 | 0-1 | | Davie | Dougan | Bannister | Keen | Branston | Slough | Collins | MacDonald | Tees* | Allen | French | Sheffield |
| | 23/9 | *16,884* | *2:2* | | | | *Woodward 28, 54, Tudor 76* | *Hodgkinson* | *Badger* | *Heaton* | *Barlow* | *Colquhoun* | *Powell** | *Woodward* | *Addison* | *Tudor* | *Staniforth* | *Reece* | *Salmons* |
| | | | | | | | Ref: R Kirkpatrick | The club run a charter train to an away game for the first time but the supporters see the Town's players run off their feet by a sizzling second-half display from United. The Hatters give as good as they get for 30 minutes but then crumble as Alan Woodward proves to be unstoppable. | | | | | | | | | | | |

| FA Cup | | | | | | | | | | | | | | | | | | | |
|---|---|---|---|---|---|---|---|---|---|---|---|---|---|---|---|---|---|---|---|
| 1 | A | BOURNEMOUTH | 1 | D | 1-1 | 1-1 | Collins 45 | Davie | Ryan | Bannister | Keen | Branston | Slough | Collins | MacDonald | Tees | Allen | French* | Jardine |
| | 15/11 | *7,352* | *3:21* | | | | *Hartley 10* | *Baker* | *Gulliver* | *Foote* | *Summerhill* | *Stocks* | *Powell* | *Hartley* | *MacDougall* | *White* | *Hold* | *Meredith* | |
| | | | | | | | Ref: M Kerkhof | Trevor Hartley sees his initial shot blocked by goalkeeper Davie but reacts quickly to score from the rebound. French, who was concussed after one minute, crosses for Collins to score on the stroke of half-time but then takes no further part in the game. Luton are flattered by the draw. | | | | | | | | | | | |
| 1R | H | BOURNEMOUTH | 1 | W | 3-1 | 2-1 | Collins 32, Tees 38, MacDonald 47 | Davie | Ryan | Bannister | Keen | Branston | Slough | Collins | MacDonald | Tees | Allen | French | |
| | 18/11 | 13,384 | *3:21* | | | | *White 3* | *Baker* | *Gulliver* | *Foote* | *Summerhill* | *Stocks* | *Powell* | *Hartley* | *MacDougall* | *White* | *Hold** | *Meredith* | *Rowles* |
| | | | | | | | Ref: M Kerkhof | 5,000 'stay-away' Luton fans miss a treat as the Town shrug off the Cup blues and hammer the Reds. Despite taking an early lead, the Cherries are soon rocking, the corner count of 11-1 reflecting the Hatters' superiority. MacDonald scores with a classic header from a cross by French. | | | | | | | | | | | |
| 2 | A | HILLINGDON | 1 | L | 1-2 | 1-1 | Tees 7 | Davie | Ryan | Bannister | Keen | Nicholl | Slough | Collins | MacDonald* | Tees | Allen | French | Harrison |
| | 6/12 | *9,330* | *SL* | | | | *Reeve 42, Townend 54* | *Lowe* | *Batt* | *Langley* | *Reeve* | *Newcombe* | *Moore* | *Fairchild* | *Cozens* | *Terry* | *Carter** | *Vafiadis* | *Townend* |
| | | | | | | | Ref: P Byford | Division 3 table-toppers Luton go out to Southern League Hillingdon in a major upset. A record crowd at the Leas Stadium sees the Hatters take an early lead but then sit back, believing the job to be done. Gary Townend scores the winner to create a 50-match unbeaten home run. | | | | | | | | | | | |

| | Home | | | | | | Away | | | | | |
|---|---|---|---|---|---|---|---|---|---|---|---|---|
| | P | W | D | L | F | A | W | D | L | F | A | Pts |
| 1 Orient | 46 | 16 | 5 | 2 | 43 | 15 | 9 | 7 | 7 | 24 | 21 | 62 |
| 2 LUTON TOWN | 46 | 13 | 8 | 2 | 46 | 15 | 10 | 6 | 7 | 31 | 28 | 60 |
| 3 Bristol Rov | 46 | 15 | 5 | 3 | 51 | 26 | 5 | 11 | 7 | 29 | 33 | 56 |
| 4 Fulham | 46 | 12 | 9 | 2 | 43 | 26 | 8 | 6 | 9 | 38 | 29 | 55 |
| 5 Brighton | 46 | 16 | 4 | 3 | 37 | 16 | 7 | 5 | 11 | 20 | 27 | 55 |
| 6 Mansfield | 46 | 14 | 4 | 5 | 46 | 22 | 7 | 7 | 9 | 24 | 27 | 53 |
| 7 Barnsley | 46 | 14 | 6 | 3 | 43 | 24 | 5 | 9 | 9 | 25 | 35 | 53 |
| 8 Reading | 46 | 16 | 3 | 4 | 52 | 29 | 5 | 8 | 10 | 35 | 48 | 53 |
| 9 Rochdale | 46 | 11 | 6 | 6 | 39 | 24 | 7 | 4 | 12 | 30 | 36 | 46 |
| 10 Bradford City | 46 | 11 | 6 | 6 | 37 | 22 | 6 | 6 | 11 | 20 | 28 | 46 |
| 11 Doncaster | 46 | 13 | 4 | 6 | 31 | 19 | 4 | 8 | 11 | 21 | 35 | 46 |
| 12 Walsall | 46 | 11 | 4 | 8 | 33 | 31 | 6 | 8 | 9 | 21 | 36 | 46 |
| 13 Torquay | 46 | 9 | 9 | 5 | 36 | 22 | 5 | 8 | 10 | 26 | 37 | 45 |
| 14 Rotherham | 46 | 10 | 8 | 5 | 36 | 19 | 5 | 6 | 12 | 26 | 35 | 44 |
| 15 Shrewsbury | 46 | 10 | 12 | 1 | 35 | 17 | 3 | 6 | 14 | 27 | 46 | 44 |
| 16 Tranmere | 46 | 10 | 8 | 5 | 38 | 29 | 4 | 8 | 11 | 18 | 43 | 44 |
| 17 Plymouth | 46 | 10 | 7 | 6 | 32 | 23 | 6 | 4 | 13 | 24 | 41 | 43 |
| 18 Halifax | 46 | 10 | 9 | 4 | 31 | 25 | 4 | 6 | 13 | 16 | 38 | 43 |
| 19 Bury | 46 | 13 | 4 | 6 | 47 | 29 | 2 | 7 | 14 | 28 | 51 | 41 |
| 20 Gillingham | 46 | 7 | 6 | 10 | 28 | 33 | 6 | 7 | 10 | 24 | 31 | 39 |
| 21 Bournemouth | 46 | 8 | 9 | 6 | 28 | 27 | 4 | 6 | 13 | 20 | 44 | 39 |
| 22 Southport | 46 | 11 | 5 | 7 | 31 | 22 | 3 | 5 | 15 | 17 | 44 | 38 |
| 23 Barrow | 46 | 7 | 9 | 7 | 28 | 27 | 1 | 5 | 17 | 18 | 54 | 30 |
| 24 Stockport | 46 | 4 | 7 | 12 | 17 | 30 | 2 | 4 | 17 | 10 | 41 | 23 |
| | 1104 | 271 | 157 | 124 | 888 | 572 | 124 | 157 | 271 | 572 | 888 | 1104 |

Odds & ends

Double wins: (5) Fulham, Reading, Rochdale, Southport, Walsall.
Double losses: (0).

Won from behind: (2) Orient (h), Bournemouth (FAC).
Lost from in front: (3) Barrow (a), Gillingham (h), Hillingdon (FAC).

High spots: Promotion back to Division 2.
13 game unbeaten run at the start of the season.
Gillingham's win at Bristol Rovers on 14 April virtually seals promotion.
The goals of Malcolm MacDonald.
Winning at Millwall in the League Cup.
Valuable double victories over promotion rivals Reading and Fulham.
Recovering from two goals down to beat Orient at Kenilworth Road.

Low spots: Beaten by non-League Hillingdon Borough in the FA Cup.
The run of four straight defeats at Christmas and into the New Year.
The 2-3 defeat at Tranmere, which seemed to end hopes of promotion.
The terrible 1-5 thrashing at Shrewsbury.

Player of the Year: Malcolm MacDonald.
Ever-presents: (1) Malcolm MacDonald.
Hat-tricks: Malcolm MacDonald (2).
Leading scorer: Malcolm MacDonald (28).

| | Appearances | | | | | | Goals | | | |
|---|---|---|---|---|---|---|---|---|---|---|
| | Lge | *Sub* | LC | *Sub* | FAC | *Sub* | Lge | LC | FAC | Tot |
| Allen, Keith | **32** | *6* | 5 | | 3 | | **7** | 2 | | **9** |
| Bannister, Jack | **40** | | 5 | | 3 | | | | | |
| Branston, Terry | **18** | *1* | 5 | | 2 | | | 1 | | **1** |
| Busby, Viv | **9** | | | | | | **4** | | | **4** |
| Collins, John | **39** | *1* | 3 | | 3 | | **10** | | 2 | **12** |
| Davie, Sandy | **31** | | 2 | | 3 | | | | | |
| Dougan, Max | **7** | | 3 | | | | | | | |
| French, Graham | **38** | *1* | 5 | | 3 | | **4** | | | **4** |
| Harrison, Mike | **10** | *2* | | | | *1* | **4** | | | **4** |
| Jardine, Fred | **9** | *1* | | | | *1* | | | | |
| Keen, Mike | **45** | *1* | 5 | | 3 | | **3** | | | **3** |
| Lewis, Brian | **2** | *3* | 1 | *1* | | | | 2 | | **2** |
| MacDonald, Malcolm | **46** | | 5 | | 3 | | **25** | 2 | 1 | **28** |
| Moore, John | **22** | *1* | 1 | | | | | | | |
| Nicholl, Chris | **27** | | | | 1 | | **2** | | | **2** |
| Phillips, Peter | **2** | *3* | | | | | | | | |
| Read, Tony | **9** | | 3 | | | | | | | |
| Ryan, John | **36** | | 2 | | 3 | | **2** | | | **2** |
| Sheffield, Laurie | **3** | *3* | 4 | *1* | | | | 2 | | **2** |
| Slough, Alan | **45** | | 5 | | 3 | | **4** | | | **4** |
| Starling, Alan | **6** | | | | | | | | | |
| Tees, Matt | **30** | *2* | 1 | | 3 | | **11** | | 2 | **13** |
| (own-goals) | | | | | | | **1** | | | **1** |
| **22 players used** | **506** | ***25*** | **55** | ***2*** | **33** | ***2*** | **77** | **9** | **5** | **91** |

| No | Date | | Att | Pos | Pt | F-A | H-T | Scorers, Times, and Referees | 1 | 2 | 3 | 4 | 5 | 6 | 7 | 8 | 9 | 10 | 11 | 12 sub used |
|---|---|---|---|---|---|---|---|---|---|---|---|---|---|---|---|---|---|---|---|---|
| 1 | A | BOLTON | | | L | 2-4 | 1-2 | Keen 25, MacDonald 89p | Starling | Slough | Ryan John | **Hoy** | Branston | Moore | **Ryan Jim** | **Givens** | MacDonald | Keen | Busby | |
| | 15/8 | | *11,350* | | - | | | *Wharton 18p, 62, 76p, Greaves 37* | *Clarke* | *Ritson* | *Farrimond* | *Williams* | *Hulme* | *Rimmer* | *Wharton* | *Byrom* | *Hunt* | *Greaves* | *Taylor* | |
| | | | | | | | | Ref: C Thomas | Alec Stock is unhappy with Town's poor performance in their first game back in Division 2 for seven years. Terry Wharton and Gordon Taylor rip the Hatters' defence to shreds, although Slough inadvertently handles - unable to get out of the way of the ball - for Bolton's first penalty. | | | | | | | | | | | |
| 2 | H | NORWICH | | | D | 0-0 | 0-0 | | Read | Ryan John | Slough | Hoy | Nicholl | Moore | Ryan Jim* | **Court** | MacDonald | Keen | Givens | Busby |
| | 22/8 | | 16,110 | | 1 | | | | *Keelan* | *Butler* | *Black* | *Stringer* | *Forbes* | *Howard* | *Briggs* | *Bennett* | *Silvester* | *Paddon* | *Foggo* | |
| | | | | | | | | Ref: H New | Three changes are made to the side and MacDonald is unlucky with three first-half efforts. The Canaries then 'shut up shop' and, although substitute, Busby, sees a late effort well saved, the visitors return to Norfolk with the point their manager, Ron Saunders, admits they came for. | | | | | | | | | | | |
| 3 | A | BIRMINGHAM | | | D | 1-1 | 0-1 | MacDonald 83p | Read | Ryan John | Slough | Hoy | Nicholl | Moore | MacDonald | Court | Tees* | Keen | Givens | Bannister |
| | 29/8 | | *30,141* | | 2 | | | *Vowden 24* | *Kelly* | *Thomson* | *Pendrey* | *Hockey* | *Hynd* | *Robinson* | *Murray* | *Vowden* | *Latchford* | *Vincent* | *Summerill* | |
| | | | | | | | | Ref: R Challis | Geoff Vowden gives Birmingham the lead with a superb 25-yard shot and the home side then try to coast through on a hot day. The dull second half is petering out when MacDonald escapes his marker and is brought down in the area. He converts the penalty-kick himself to earn a draw. | | | | | | | | | | | |
| 4 | H | OXFORD | | 10 | W | 4-0 | 3-0 | Tees 11, 39, MacDonald 24, 57 | Read | Ryan John | Slough | Hoy* | Nicholl | Moore | MacDonald | Court | Tees | Keen | Givens | Ryan Jim |
| | 1/9 | | 16,173 | *6* | 4 | | | | *Kearns* | *Lucas* | *Shuker* | *Smithson* | *Clarke* | *Thompson* | *Sloan* | *Atkinson G* | *Skeen* | *Clayton* | *Atkinson R* | |
| | | | | | | | | Ref: B Daniels | Previously unbeaten Oxford show amazing generosity by gifting Luton three goals in the first half. Their defence is static as Tees helps himself to two free headers and MacDonald, stealing the ball from Rodney Smithson, scores with ease. Court is now living up to his £35,000 price tag. | | | | | | | | | | | |
| 5 | H | MIDDLESBROUGH | | 5 | W | 1-0 | 1-0 | Givens 16 | Read | Ryan John | Slough | **Guild** | Nicholl | Moore | MacDonald | Court* | Tees | Keen | Givens | Ryan Jim |
| | 5/9 | | 16,018 | *21* | 6 | | | | *Whigham* | *Allen* | *Jones* | *Moody* | *Maddren* | *Spraggon* | *Laidlaw* | *Webb* | *McIlmoyle** | *Hickton* | *Myton* | *Gates* |
| | | | | | | | | Ref: A Morrissey | A furious spell of pressure in the second half sees MacDonald almost score a hat-trick to add to Givens' early headed goal. Firstly, he is through on goal but then hauled down by Bill Gates, sees another shot tipped round the post; his third effort hits an upright and rolls along the goal-line. | | | | | | | | | | | |
| 6 | A | LEICESTER | | 10 | L | 0-1 | 0-0 | | Read | Ryan John | Slough | Hoy | Nicholl | Moore | Ryan Jim | Court | MacDonald | Keen | Givens* | Bannister |
| | 12/9 | | *23,397* | *6* | 6 | | | *Brown 79* | *Shilton* | *Whitworth* | *Nish* | *Kellard* | *Sjoberg* | *Cross* | *Farrington* | *Fern* | *Brown* | *Matthews* | *Glover* | |
| | | | | | | | | Ref: V James | Leicester gain an undeserved victory with a deflected goal towards the end of the game. David Nish hacks a MacDonald shot off the line and Givens' header hits the bar with Peter Shilton beaten. 'This match shows there is not much to fear in this Division,' summarises skipper Keen. | | | | | | | | | | | |
| 7 | H | ORIENT | | 7 | W | 4-0 | 2-0 | Slough 36, 38, MacDonald 48, 70 | Read | Ryan John | Slough | Hoy | Nicholl | Moore | Ryan Jim | Court | MacDonald | Keen | Busby | |
| | 19/9 | | 16,711 | *14* | 8 | | | | *Goddard* | *Jones* | *Rofe* | *Taylor* | *Mancini* | *Allen* | *Lazarus* | *Bullock* | *Fairbrother* | *Dyson* | *Parmenter** | *Plume* |
| | | | | | | | | Ref: E Wallace | Town move further up the league table following another four-goal home victory. Orient have no answer to Town's power play; Slough moves up to score twice in a minute and MacDonald completes the job. Terry Mancini is booked for disputing the fourth goal, claiming it was offside. | | | | | | | | | | | |
| 8 | A | SWINDON | | 5 | D | 0-0 | 0-0 | | Read | Ryan John | Slough | Hoy | Nicholl | Moore | Ryan Jim | Court | MacDonald | Keen | Busby* | Givens |
| | 26/9 | | *18,698* | *17* | 9 | | | | *Downsboro'* | *Thomas* | *Trollope* | *Butler* | *Burrows* | *Harland* | *Smith* | *Gough* | *Horsfield* | *Noble* | *Rogers* | |
| | | | | | | | | Ref: R Darlington | Town go into the game hoping for a point and very nearly get both. Three minutes from time, Jim Ryan cleverly heads the ball over the keeper but the goal is disallowed for a shouting offence. Ex-Town manager, Bill Harvey, rates Don Rogers and Nicholl, saying 'you can have the rest'. | | | | | | | | | | | |
| 9 | A | QP RANGERS | | 5 | W | 1-0 | 1-0 | Keen 1 | Read | Ryan John | Slough | Hoy | Nicholl | Moore | Ryan Jim | Court | MacDonald* | Keen | Givens | Busby |
| | 29/9 | | *19,268* | *21* | 11 | | | | *Parkes* | *Watson* | *Clement* | *Busby* | *Mobley* | *Sibley* | *Francis* | *Venables* | *Saul* | *Marsh* | *Morgan* | |
| | | | | | | | | Ref: R Tinkler | It is a night to remember for manager, Alec Stock, and skipper, Mike Keen, as they return to Loftus Road for the first time. Stock is still being cheered to his seat as Keen runs on to a 35-yard free-kick and hammers the ball into the top corner of the net. The home side go close late on. | | | | | | | | | | | |
| 10 | H | BRISTOL CITY | | 3 | W | 3-0 | 2-0 | MacDonald 18, 34, Slough 55 | Read | Ryan John | Slough | Hoy | Nicholl | Moore | Ryan Jim | Court | MacDonald | Keen | Givens* | Busby |
| | 3/10 | | 15,992 | *12* | 13 | | | | *Gibson* | *Stacey* | *Drysdale* | *Wimshurst** | *Rooks* | *Parr* | *Skirton* | *Garland* | *Galley* | *Gow* | *Sharpe* | *Tainton* |
| | | | | | | | | Ref: A Jones | Bristol City are unimpressive as they concede two first-half efforts from MacDonald. His first is an opportunist strike and his second a header into the top corner from a fierce cross from Hoy. Goalkeeper Mike Gibson makes several brave saves and keeps the final goal tally at three. | | | | | | | | | | | |

| No | Date | Opponent | Att | Pos | Pt | F-A | H-T | Scorers, Times, and Referees | 1 | 2 | 3 | 4 | 5 | 6 | 7 | 8 | 9 | 10 | 11 | 12 sub used |
|---|---|---|---|---|---|---|---|---|---|---|---|---|---|---|---|---|---|---|---|---|
| 11 | A | SHEFFIELD WED | | 4 | W | **5-1** | 3-0 | MacDonald 14, 45, 82, Givens 44, 64 | Read | Ryan John | Slough | Hoy | Nicholl | Moore | Ryan Jim | Court | MacDonald | Keen | Givens | |
| | 10/10 | | *15,189* | **17** | 15 | | | *Sinclair 68* | *Grummitt* | *Wilcockson* | *Burton* | *Thompson* | *Ellis* | *Craig* | *Sinclair* | *Prendergast* | *Downes* | *Warboys* | *Sissons* | |
| | | | | | | | | Ref: J Finney | MacDonald scores a classic hat-trick, in front of the TV cameras, with Givens playing his part in making decoy runs. Town have now scored more goals and conceded fewer than any other side in the Division. Eustace is heard to say 'The Owls should not be losing to teams like Luton!' | | | | | | | | | | | |
| 12 | H | BOLTON | | 2 | W | 2-0 | 2-0 | Nicholl 9, Givens 22 | Read | Ryan John | Slough | Hoy | Nicholl | Moore | Ryan Jim | Court | MacDonald | Keen | Givens | |
| | 17/10 | | 19,055 | *16* | 17 | | | | *Boswell* | *Ritson* | *Farrimond* | *Williams* | *Hurley* | *Hulme* | *Fletcher* | *Byrom* | *Manning* | *Phillips* | *Taylor* | |
| | | | | | | | | Ref: W Gow | Two goals ahead after a glorious 20 minutes, the Hatters cannot keep up the pace and Bolton have several chances to change the score, despite the solid play of Nicholl at the centre of the Luton defence. Hoy and MacDonald both hit the woodwork before Givens heads the second goal. | | | | | | | | | | | |
| 13 | H | BLACKBURN | | 1 | W | 2-0 | 1-0 | Givens 1, MacDonald 72 | Read | Ryan John | Slough | Hoy | Nicholl | Moore | Ryan Jim | Court* | MacDonald | Keen | Givens | Busby |
| | 20/10 | | 16,372 | *21* | 19 | | | | *Jones* | *Wilson* | *Wood* | *Hunter* | *Mulvaney* | *Eccles* | *Goodwin* | *Knighton* | *Conlon* | *Rogers* | *Kerr* | |
| | | | | | | | | Ref: W Castle | Town go to the top of the Division, albeit for only 24 hours, after a low-key performance against a team who had the greater number of chances against a defence that has yet to concede a goal at home this season. Jim Ryan sets up the first goal, a header from MacDonald secures both points. | | | | | | | | | | | |
| 14 | A | CHARLTON | | 2 | D | 1-1 | 1-0 | Givens 6 | Read | Ryan John | Slough | Hoy | Nicholl | Moore | Ryan Jim | Court | MacDonald | Keen | Givens* | Busby |
| | 24/10 | | *12,928* | *22* | 20 | | | *Treacy 86* | *Wright* | *Curtis* | *Bruck* | *Moore* | *Went* | *Reeves* | *Ellis** | *Treacy* | *Plumb* | *Davies* | *Peacock* | *Kinsey* |
| | | | | | | | | Ref: E Jolly | When Givens converts a Keen pass it seems easy for the Town, who rely on hefty clearances as their main tactic. Ray Treacy nets the equaliser after the furious scramble which results from a tame back-pass from Slough. Two strong penalty appeals by the Hatters are both turned down. | | | | | | | | | | | |
| 15 | H | SUNDERLAND | | 3 | L | 1-2 | 0-1 | MacDonald 78 | Read | Ryan John | Slough | Hoy | Nicholl | Moore | Ryan Jim | Court* | MacDonald | Keen | Givens | Busby |
| | 31/10 | | 19,202 | *9* | 20 | | | *Baker 40, Kerr 83* | *Montgomery* | *Irwin* | *Harvey* | *Todd* | *Pitt* | *McGiven** | *Park* | *Porterfield* | *Baker* | *Kerr* | *Hughes* | *Chambers* |
| | | | | | | | | Ref: D Pugh | The manager is remarkably upbeat after a somewhat ragged second-half performance against a strong Sunderland side, who gained the win with a diving header from Bobby Kerr. After several lacklustre performances, this defeat was on the cards and the long unbeaten home run is ended. | | | | | | | | | | | |
| 16 | A | HULL | | 2 | W | 2-0 | 2-0 | Givens 11, MacDonald 28 | Read | Ryan John | Slough | Hoy | Nicholl | Moore | Ryan Jim | Court | MacDonald | Keen | Givens | |
| | 7/11 | | *18,343* | *5* | 22 | | | | *McKechnie* | *Beardsley** | *Devries* | *Wilkinson* | *Neill* | *Simpkin* | *Holbrook* | *Houghton* | *Chilton* | *Wagstaff* | *Butler* | *Banks* |
| | | | | | | | | Ref: D Laing | Jimmy Andrews, returning as coach after an operation, masterminds a superb victory. The BBC cameras witness the Town players working for each other far more than of late and the game is all but over before half-time. Yorkshire appears to be a happy hunting ground for the Hatters! | | | | | | | | | | | |
| 17 | H | CARLISLE | | 3 | D | 3-3 | 0-2 | Ryan Jim 73, Slough 75, MacDonald 89 | Read | Ryan John | Slough | Hoy | Nicholl* | Moore | Ryan Jim | Court | MacDonald | Keen | Givens | Busby |
| | 14/11 | | 14,837 | *7* | 23 | | | *Hemstead 12, Bald'stone 17, Martin 55* | *Ross* | *Hemstead* | *Davis* | *Ternent* | *Winstanley* | *Sutton* | *Martin* | *Barton* | *Hatton* | *Owen* | *Balderstone* | |
| | | | | | | | | Ref: H Williams | In an amazing game played in torrential rain Town fight back from a three-goal deficit to level the scores and almost win the game in the dying seconds when ex-Hatter Alan Ross saves. Carlisle take a shock lead when Derek Hemstead lofts the ball over the heads to score from 25 yards. | | | | | | | | | | | |
| 18 | H | PORTSMOUTH | | 2 | W | 2-1 | 1-1 | Ryan John 8, Givens 52 | Read | Ryan John | Slough | Hoy | Nicholl | Moore* | Ryan Jim | Givens | MacDonald | Keen | Busby | Bannister |
| | 21/11 | | 16,876 | *13* | 25 | | | *McCann 9* | *Milkins* | *Hand* | *Ley** | *Piper* | *Blant* | *Munks* | *McCann* | *Trebilcock* | *Hiron* | *Bromley* | *Jennings* | *Travers* |
| | | | | | | | | Ref: J Thacker | Albert McCann, who began his professional career at Luton, equalises for Pompey with a solo effort after Ryan gives the Hatters an early lead. The Town apply the pressure in the second period and win the game when a MacDonald shot deflects to beat courageous keeper John Milkins. | | | | | | | | | | | |
| 19 | A | CARDIFF | | 2 | D | 0-0 | 0-0 | | Read | Ryan John | Bannister | Hoy | Nicholl | Slough | Ryan Jim | Court | MacDonald | Keen | Givens | |
| | 28/11 | | *26,689* | *3* | 26 | | | | *Eadie* | *Carver* | *Bell* | *Sutton* | *Murray* | *Harris* | *Gibson* | *Clark* | *Phillips* | *Woodruff* | *King* | |
| | | | | | | | | Ref: I Smith | The opportunity to secure a ticket to see the Bluebirds' game against Real Madrid in the European CWC swells the home crowd to a record for the season. Cardiff are dominant for most of the game but the Town manage to thwart the twin strike-force of Brian Clark and Bobby Woodruff. | | | | | | | | | | | |
| 20 | H | SHEFFIELD UTD | | 2 | W | 2-1 | 1-0 | MacDonald 28, Ryan Jim 47 | Read | Ryan John | Bannister | Hoy | Nicholl | Slough | Ryan Jim | Court | MacDonald | Keen | Givens | |
| | 5/12 | | 19,665 | *5* | 28 | | | *Currie 78p* | *Hodgkinson* | *Badger* | *Hemsley* | *Powell* | *Colquhoun* | *Addison** | *Woodward* | *Tudor* | *Dearden* | *Currie* | *Salmons* | *Reece* |
| | | | | | | | | Ref: D Turner | A top-of-the-table 'four-pointer' sees the Town hold on to beat a Sheffield United side, unbeaten in their last 16 league matches. Tony Currie reduces the Hatters' two-goal advantage from the spot after Jack Bannister trips Billy Dearden and the Blades pressurise until the final whistle. | | | | | | | | | | | |
| 21 | A | WATFORD | | 2 | W | 1-0 | 1-0 | Keen 28 | Read | Ryan John | Bannister | Hoy* | Nicholl | Slough | Ryan Jim | Court | MacDonald | Keen | Givens | Collins |
| | 12/12 | | *24,456* | *17* | 30 | | | | *Walker* | *Butler* | *Packer* | *Garbett* | *Lees* | *Eddy* | *Scullion* | *Wigg* | *Lugg** | *Walley* | *Woods* | *Welbourne* |
| | | | | | | | | Ref: D Lyden | This local derby never lives up to the pre-match hype and is settled by the single goal, a towering header from Town skipper Mike Keen. In an instantly forgettable game, both Don Givens and Roger Hoy pick up injuries which are likely to keep them out of action for a couple of weeks. | | | | | | | | | | | |

| No | Date | | Att | Pos | Pt | F-A | H-T | Scorers, Times, and Referees | 1 | 2 | 3 | 4 | 5 | 6 | 7 | 8 | 9 | 10 | 11 | 12 sub used |
|---|---|---|---|---|---|---|---|---|---|---|---|---|---|---|---|---|---|---|---|---|
| 22 | A | NORWICH | | 2 | D | 1-1 | 1-0 | MacDonald 13 | Read | Ryan John | Bannister | Collins | Nicholl | Slough | Ryan Jim | Court | MacDonald | Keen | Givens | |
| | 19/12 | | *17,438* | *6* | 31 | | | *Foggo 89p* | *Keelan* | *Payne* | *Black* | *Stringer* | *Forbes* | *Briggs** | *Livermore* | *Silvester* | *Howard* | *Paddon* | *Foggo* | *Anderson* |
| | | | | | | | | Ref: R Crabb | MacDonald is watched by England manager Alf Ramsey, who sees him score his 19th goal of the season when seizing on to a slip by Dave Stringer. Ken Foggo equalises from the penalty spot in the final minute after a header from Terry Anderson is punched away by Jack Bannister. | | | | | | | | | | | |
| 23 | H | QP RANGERS | | 1 | D | 0-0 | 0-0 | | Read | Ryan John | Bannister | Hoy | Nicholl | Slough | Ryan Jim | Court | MacDonald | Keen | Givens* | Busby |
| | 9/1 | | 22,024 | *16* | 32 | | | | *Parkes* | *Watson* | *Clement* | *Venables* | *Hunt* | *Sibley* | *Morgan* | *Francis* | *Leach** | *Marsh* | *Ferguson* | *McCulloch* |
| | | | | | | | | Ref: R Challis | The biggest crowd of the season sees manager Alec Stock receive a gallon of whisky before the game, his reward as 'Manager of the Month' for December. A fast and furious game follows and Town are frustrated by a Rangers side who try to impress their new manager, Gordon Jago. | | | | | | | | | | | |
| 24 | A | BLACKBURN | | 2 | L | 0-1 | 0-0 | | Read | Ryan John | Bannister | Hoy* | Nicholl | Slough | Ryan Jim | Court | MacDonald | Keen | Givens | Busby |
| | 16/1 | | *8,385* | *21* | 32 | | | *Russell 70* | *Jones* | *Goodwin* | *Wilson* | *Hunter* | *Mulvaney* | *Knighton* | *Metcalfe* | *Russell* | *Eccles* | *Rogers* | *Hill* | |
| | | | | | | | | Ref: W Johnson | Town appear to have settled for a point until Malcolm Russell fires a goal for lowly Blackburn with 20 minutes to go. The Hatters now start to belatedly apply some pressure in order to equalise but only manage to force a number of quality saves from Rovers' goalkeeper Roger Jones. | | | | | | | | | | | |
| 25 | A | SHEFFIELD UTD | | 5 | L | 1-2 | 0-0 | Ryan Jim 68 | Read | Ryan John | Slough | Hoy | Nicholl | Moore | Ryan Jim | Court | MacDonald | Keen | Givens | |
| | 6/2 | | ***30,386*** | *2* | 32 | | | *Woodward 47, 65* | *Hope* | *Badger* | *Hemsley* | *Powell* | *Colquhoun* | *Hockey* | *Woodward* | *Ford* | *Dearden* | *Currie* | *Reece* | |
| | | | | | | | | Ref: K Burns | The Town are totally outplayed by the home side, who have three new signings in Trevor Hockey, John Hope and David Ford on parade. Jim Ryan accepts a gift of a goal when Hope drops the ball, a scoreline which flatters, and Tony Currie misses a penalty after Woodward is fouled. | | | | | | | | | | | |
| 26 | H | WATFORD | | 4 | W | 1-0 | 1-0 | MacDonald 10 | Read | Ryan John | Slough | Hoy | Nicholl | Moore | Ryan Jim | Givens | MacDonald | Keen | **Anderson** | |
| | 13/2 | | 20,099 | *18* | 34 | | | | *Edmonds* | *Butler* | *Williams* | *Garbett* | *Lees* | *Walley* | *Welbourne* | *Wigg* | *Jennings* | *Sinclair* | *Farley** | *Scullion* |
| | | | | | | | | Ref: K Howley | Peter Anderson makes his debut in an untidy game which is settled when Malcolm MacDonald shoots past Derek Edmonds in the Hornets goal following an astute pass from Don Givens. Lowly Watford have little to offer, although Billy Jennings, who later becomes a Hatter, is lively. | | | | | | | | | | | |
| 27 | A | PORTSMOUTH | | 3 | W | 1-0 | 1-0 | Givens 44 | Read | Ryan John | Slough | Hoy | Nicholl | Moore | Ryan Jim | Givens | MacDonald | Keen | Anderson | |
| | 20/2 | | *13,661* | *17* | 36 | | | | *Milkins* | *Smith* | *Ley* | *Hand* | *Blant* | *Munks* | *Piper* | *Pointer** | *Hiron* | *Travers* | *Jennings* | *Youlden* |
| | | | | | | | | Ref: A Oliver | Luton rarely show the talents that have made them promotion challengers, but inflict Pompey's third consecutive league defeat. Givens scores the only goal of the game when heading home a long cross from Jim Ryan, after an error from John Milkins who had come to collect but failed. | | | | | | | | | | | |
| 28 | A | SUNDERLAND | | 6 | D | 0-0 | 0-0 | | Read | Ryan John | Slough | Hoy | Nicholl | Moore | Ryan Jim | Givens | MacDonald | Keen | Anderson | |
| | 27/2 | | *12,471* | *12* | 37 | | | | *Montgomery* | *Malone* | *Harvey* | *McGiven* | *Pitt* | *Porterfield* | *Park* | *Kerr* | *Watson* | *Harris* | *Tueart* | |
| | | | | | | | | Ref: M Fussey | An end-to-end game sees the sides finishing with the point they started with. Malcolm MacDonald goes close twice and Chris Nicholl, at the other end, has to be at his best to keep out Sunderland danger-man Dave Watson. Roker Park has a capacity of 60,000 but is only 20% full. | | | | | | | | | | | |
| 29 | H | CHARLTON | | 5 | D | 1-1 | 0-0 | Busby 75 | Read | Ryan John | Slough | Hoy* | Nicholl | Moore | Ryan Jim | Givens | MacDonald | Keen | Anderson | Busby |
| | 6/3 | | 15,262 | *22* | 38 | | | *Went 69p* | *Wright* | *Curtis* | *Bruck* | *Reeves* | *Went* | *Shipperley* | *Bond* | *Treacy* | *Plumb* | *Endean* | *Peacock* | |
| | | | | | | | | Ref: C Thomas | The Town struggle against a Charlton side who are fighting desperately to avoid relegation. All seems to be going wrong for the Hatters when John Ryan is penalised for a seemingly fair tackle on Peacock and Went scores with the penalty. Busby levels with a header six minutes later. | | | | | | | | | | | |
| 30 | A | CARLISLE | | 6 | L | 0-1 | 0-1 | | Read | Ryan John | Slough | Givens | Nicholl | Moore | Ryan Jim | Busby* | MacDonald | Keen | Anderson | **Goodeve** |
| | 13/3 | | *13,681* | *5* | 38 | | | *Owen 40* | *Ross* | *Davis* | *Gorman* | *Ternent* | *Winstanley* | *Sutton* | *Barton* | *Martin** | *Owen* | *Hatton* | *Balderstone* | *Webb* |
| | | | | | | | | Ref: R Judson | The Town are awarded a penalty after ten minutes when Mike Sutton handles on the line but MacDonald sees his spot-kick saved by ex-Hatter Alan Ross. He later sees a shot hit the bar and also misses three other good opportunities, making this a game he will wish to hurriedly forget. | | | | | | | | | | | |
| 31 | H | HULL | | 5 | W | 3-1 | 1-0 | Moore 44, Busby 74, MacDonald 80 | Read | Ryan John | Slough | Givens | Nicholl | Moore | Ryan Jim | Busby | MacDonald | Keen | Anderson | |
| | 20/3 | | 19,566 | *6* | 40 | | | *Houghton 57* | *McKechnie* | *Baxter* | *Beardsley* | *Wilkinson* | *Neill* | *Simpkin* | *Houghton* | *Knighton* | *Lord* | *Wagstaff* | *Butler* | |
| | | | | | | | | Ref: D Smith | MacDonald misses a penalty for the second week running as the Town beat fellow promotion-challengers, Hull City, in a TV game. Moore opens the scoring with a tremendous strike and MacDonald scores the winner after a thunderous shot from Busby is parried by Ian McKechnie. | | | | | | | | | | | |

| No | Date | Opponent / Att | Pos | Res / Pts | F-A | H-T | Scorers, Times, and Referees | 1 | 2 | 3 | 4 | 5 | 6 | 7 | 8 | 9 | 10 | 11 | 12 sub used |
|---|---|---|---|---|---|---|---|---|---|---|---|---|---|---|---|---|---|---|---|
| 32 | A | MIDDLESBROUGH | 6 | L | 1-2 | 1-0 | MacDonald 13 | Read | Ryan John | Slough | Givens | Nicholl | Moore | Ryan Jim | Busby | MacDonald | Keen | Anderson | |
| | 27/3 | *19,579* | *7* | 40 | | | *McIlmoyle 70, 80* | *Whigham* | *Smith* | *Jones* | *Laidlaw* | *Gates* | *Maddren* | *Downing** | *McMordie* | *Hickton* | *Vincent* | *Burluraux* | *McIlmoyle* |
| | | | | | | | Ref: J Finney | Town appear to have another away victory when one up at half-time due to a remarkable goal from MacDonald, who spots Willy Whigham off his line and coolly hits a 30-yard lob over his head. McIlmoyle, a substitute after half-time, scores both goals to turn the game in Boro's favour. | | | | | | | | | | | |
| 33 | H | MILLWALL | 5 | D | 1-1 | 1-0 | Keen 30 | Read | Ryan John | Bannister | Hoy | Slough | Moore | Ryan Jim | Busby | MacDonald | Keen | Givens | |
| | 30/3 | 17,578 | *10* | 41 | | | *Brown 87* | *King* | *Brown* | *Cripps* | *Dorney* | *Kitchener* | *Burnett* | *Possee* | *Bolland* | *Bridges* | *Dunphy* | *Allder* | |
| | | | | | | | Ref: T Dawes | Keen opens the scoring when powering home a header from a Jim Ryan corner after half an hour. The visitors soak up the pressure, attacking on the break after the interval. They fully deserve their late equaliser, a scrambled shot by Brian Brown. Stock moans at the slack defending. | | | | | | | | | | | |
| 34 | H | BIRMINGHAM | 4 | W | 3-2 | 2-2 | Busby 36, 43, Slough 48 | Read | Ryan John | Slough | Givens | Nicholl | Moore | Ryan Jim | Busby | MacDonald | Keen | Anderson | |
| | 3/4 | **25,172** | *9* | 43 | | | *Latchford 5, Summerill 22* | *Kelly* | *Martin* | *Page* | *Smith* | *Hynd* | *Robinson* | *Campbell* | *Francis** | *Latchford* | *Summerill* | *Taylor* | *Pendrey* |
| | | | | | | | Ref: F Nicholson | Birmingham have established a 14-game unbeaten run, inspired by 16-year-old wonder boy Trevor Francis. Their 10,000 following see them take an early two-goal lead but Town fight back to level the scores by the interval. Slough secures both points for the Hatters after the break. | | | | | | | | | | | |
| 35 | A | BRISTOL CITY | 5 | L | 2-3 | 2-0 | Busby 23, MacDonald 43 | Read | Ryan John | Slough | Givens | Nicholl | Moore | Ryan Jim | Busby | MacDonald | Keen | Anderson* | Goodeve |
| | 9/4 | *18,846* | *18* | 43 | | | *Rooks 59, Garland 66, 67* | *Cashley* | *Jacobs* | *Drysdale* | *Wilson* | *Rooks* | *Hill** | *Tainton* | *Garland* | *Galley* | *Wimshurst* | *Gow* | *Merrick* |
| | | | | | | | Ref: D Nippard | Bristol City hit the woodwork twice and miss several other good chances as the Hatters take a two-goal half-time lead at Ashton Gate. Chris Garland inspires the home side's forward line in the second period as they tear the Luton defence to shreds and the scoreline flatters the Town. | | | | | | | | | | | |
| 36 | A | MILLWALL | 6 | L | **0-4** | 0-3 | | Read | Ryan John | Bannister | Hoy | Slough | Moore | Ryan Jim* | Busby | MacDonald | Keen | Court | Givens |
| | 10/4 | *13,864* | *10* | 43 | | | *Possee 18, 32, Bridges 24, Brown 82* | *King* | *Brown* | *Cripps* | *Dorney* | *Kitchener* | *Burnett* | *Possee* | *Bolland* | *Bridges* | *Dunphy* | *Allder* | |
| | | | | | | | Ref: V James | Twenty-four hours later and the Town find themselves being mauled once more, this time in the Lions' Den. Doug Allder orchestrates the first three goals and is part of the five-man move that earns the fourth. It is difficult to understand why the Hatters have collapsed in such a manner. | | | | | | | | | | | |
| 37 | H | LEICESTER | 8 | L | 1-3 | 1-1 | Sjoberg 2 (og) | Read | Ryan John | Slough | Givens | Nicholl | Moore | Ryan Jim* | Busby | MacDonald | Keen | Anderson | Bannister |
| | 12/4 | 24,405 | *1* | 43 | | | *Manley 37, Farrington 63, Brown 65* | *Shilton* | *Whitworth* | *Nish* | *Manley* | *Sjoberg* | *Cross* | *Farrington* | *Fern* | *Brown* | *Carlin* | *Partridge* | |
| | | | | | | | Ref: M Sinclair | Promotion hopes finally disappear when top-of -the-table Leicester hand out a lesson in both football control and finishing. An early setback, when John Sjoberg deflects a fierce John Ryan centre in to his own net, is soon countered with future Hatter, Rodney Fern, the main architect. | | | | | | | | | | | |
| 38 | H | SHEFFIELD WED | 7 | D | 2-2 | 1-1 | Anderson 2, Givens 52 | **Barber** | Ryan John | Bannister | Court | Slough | Moore | Anderson | Busby | MacDonald | Keen | Givens | |
| | 17/4 | 12,308 | *15* | 44 | | | *Sinclair 32, Sunley 55* | *Grummitt* | *Rodrigues* | *Burton* | *Thompson* | *Prophett* | *Pugh* | *Sinclair* | *Craig* | *Sunley* | *Prendergast* | *Sissons* | |
| | | | | | | | Ref: L Callaghan | With nothing left to play for this season, Alec Stock decides to make several team changes. Peter Anderson scores his first goal for the club in the opening minutes but Wednesday, showing a fighting spirit not often seen away from Hillsborough this season, come back twice to equalise. | | | | | | | | | | | |
| 39 | A | ORIENT | 6 | W | 2-1 | 1-0 | Busby 33, 88 | Barber | Ryan John | Slough | Hoy | Nicholl | Moore | Busby | Court | MacDonald | Keen | Givens* | Anderson |
| | 24/4 | ***6,339*** | *18* | 46 | | | *Brabrook 89* | *Goddard* | *Jones* | *Rofe* | *Bennett* | *Mancini* | *Allen* | *Lazarus* | *Brisley** | *Bullock* | *Dyson* | *Brabrook* | *Riddick* |
| | | | | | | | Ref: K Walker | Two goals in the final minute liven up an otherwise dull encounter which is not helped by the blustery wind. The Town start as though they mean business as Givens goes close and Court hits the bar. Busby rounds the keeper to score the winner, Brabrook replying from the kick-off. | | | | | | | | | | | |
| 40 | A | OXFORD | 7 | L | 1-2 | 1-2 | Busby 43 | Barber | Ryan John | Slough | Hoy | Nicholl | Moore | Busby | Court* | MacDonald | Keen | Givens | Ryan Jim |
| | 28/4 | *9,531* | *14* | 46 | | | *Clarke D 5, Cassidy 25* | *Kearns* | *Lucas* | *Shuker* | *Roberts* | *Clarke C* | *Evanson* | *Clarke D* | *Atkinson G* | *Skeen* | *Cassidy* | *Atkinson R* | |
| | | | | | | | Ref: W Castle | Oxford prove to be the more inventive side and deserve both points after a lacklustre Luton display. Confirmation that MacDonald is to leave Kenilworth Road at the end of the season brings the scouts to see him. Keith Barber, playing his third game, is to blame for both Oxford goals. | | | | | | | | | | | |
| 41 | H | SWINDON | 8 | D | 1-1 | 1-0 | Givens 44p | Read | Ryan John | Goodeve | Hoy | Nicholl | Slough | Anderson* | Busby | MacDonald | Keen | Givens | Ryan Jim |
| | 1/5 | **10,205** | *12* | 47 | | | *Jones 59* | *Downsboro'* | *Thomas* | *Trollope* | *Butler* | *Potter* | *Harland* | *Peplow* | *Smart* | *Horsfield* | *Jones* | *Rogers* | |
| | | | | | | | Ref: B Homewood | MacDonald, who has not scored since Good Friday, and Busby are marked out of the game, which results in a boring draw. Givens scores from the penalty spot after MacDonald is pulled down in the area. Chris Jones equalises for Swindon following a mix-up between Nicholl and Slough. | | | | | | | | | | | |
| 42 | H | CARDIFF | 6 | W | 3-0 | 1-0 | MacDonald 20, 85, 89 | Read | Ryan John | Goodeve | Slough | Nicholl | Moore | Anderson | Busby | MacDonald | Keen | Givens | |
| | 4/5 | 10,784 | *3* | 49 | | | | *Eadie* | *Carver* | *Bell* | *Sutton* | *Murray* | *Derrett* | *Gibson* | *Clark* | *Phillips* | *Warboys* | *King* | |
| | Home | Away | | | | | Ref: P Partridge | A place in the Watney Cup, a competition for the team in each division which scores the most goals but wins nothing else, is open to Luton if they can score two goals. MacDonald bows out in style, his second goal five minutes from time, greeted as if the Town had won the Cup Final. | | | | | | | | | | | |
| Average | 17,353 | 17,363 | | | | | | | | | | | | | | | | | |

| League Cup | | | | | F-A | H-T | Scorers, Times, and Referees | 1 | 2 | 3 | 4 | 5 | 6 | 7 | 8 | 9 | 10 | 11 | 12 sub used |
|---|---|---|---|---|---|---|---|---|---|---|---|---|---|---|---|---|---|---|---|
| 1 | A | GILLINGHAM | | W | 1-0 | 1-0 | MacDonald 32 | Read | Slough | Ryan John | Hoy | Nicholl | Moore | Ryan Jim | Court | MacDonald | Keen | Givens | |
| | 19/8 | *7,328* | *D3* | | | | | *Simpson* | *Bailey* | *Peach* | *Yeo* | *Williams* | *Quirke* | *Woodley* | *Tydeman* | *Green* | *Ronaldson* | *Pound** | *Watson* |
| | | | | | | | Ref: H Sinclair | Luton do just enough to win their way through to the second round in a scrappy match at Priestfield. Although the opposition is enthusiastic, there is an obvious division of difference between the two sides. Court, Town's expensive signing from Arsenal, makes his debut in midfield. | | | | | | | | | | | |
| 2 | H | WORKINGTON | 5 | W | 3-0 | 1-0 | Givens 9, 77, MacDonald 50 | Read | Ryan John | Slough | Guild | Nicholl | Moore | MacDonald | Court | Tees* | Keen | Givens | Ryan Jim |
| | 8/9 | 11,072 | *4:12* | | | | | *Burridge* | *Wilson* | *Butler* | *Geidmintis* | *Spencer* | *Wood* | *Tyrer* | *Spratt* | *Massie** | *Goodfellow* | *Martin* | *Wookey* |
| | | | | | | | Ref: M Washer | Another scrappy game that improves when Jimmy Ryan comes on as a substitute in the second half. The flying winger sets up MacDonald for the important second goal and causes problems for the visitors. Massie poses a threat but is well held by his former Halifax colleague, Nicholl. | | | | | | | | | | | |
| 3 | H | ARSENAL | 3 | L | 0-1 | 0-1 | | Read | Ryan John | Slough | Hoy | Nicholl | Moore | Ryan Jim | Court | MacDonald | Keen | Givens* | Busby |
| | 6/10 | 27,023 | *1:4* | | | | *Graham 27* | *Wilson* | *Rice* | *McNab* | *Kelly* | *McLintock* | *Roberts* | *Armstrong* | *Storey* | *Radford* | *Kennedy* | *Graham* | |
| | | | | | | | Ref: K Burns | With more than 5,000 locked out at Kenilworth Road, the biggest crowd since 1959 see the Town take on the 'double-chasing' Gunners. Bob Wilson makes several astonishing saves during the first 30 minutes but, after Arsenal take the lead, the Hatters run out of both steam and ideas. | | | | | | | | | | | |

| FA Cup | | | | | | | | | | | | | | | | | | | |
|---|---|---|---|---|---|---|---|---|---|---|---|---|---|---|---|---|---|---|---|
| 3 | A | NOTT'M FOREST | 2 | D | 1-1 | 0-1 | MacDonald 70 | Read | Ryan John | Bannister | Hoy | Nicholl | Slough | Ryan Jim | Court | MacDonald | Keen | Givens | |
| | 2/1 | 23,230 | *1:20* | | | | *McIntosh 18* | *Barron* | *Hindley* | *Winfield* | *Chapman* | *O'Kane* | *Jackson* | *McIntosh* | *Lyons* | *Cormack* | *Richardson** | *Storey-Moore* | *Rees* |
| | | | | | | | Ref: H New | The Hatters are on the wrong end of a pounding when a broken goal-post, after 33 minutes, saves the day. The delay gives a chance for coach Jimmy Andrews to reorganise the side. Read flaps at the ball for the opening goal whilst MacDonald needs two attempts to score the equaliser. | | | | | | | | | | | |
| 3R | H | NOTT'M FOREST | 2 | L | 3-4 | 1-1 | MacDonald 20, 67p, 84 *[Rees 87]* | Read | Ryan John | Bannister | Hoy | Nicholl | Slough | Ryan Jim | Court | MacDonald | Keen | Givens | |
| | 11/1 | 23,483 | *1:20* | | | | *Cormack 17, Collier 65, Richards'n 66,* | *Barron* | *Hindley* | *Winfield* | *Chapman* | *O'Kane* | *Jackson* | *McIntosh** | *Lyons* | *Cormack* | *Richardson* | *Rees* | *Collier* |
| | | | | | | | Ref: H New | In a topsy-turvy game, both sides opt for all-out attack. Forest score the winning goal near the end, just as the game appears to be destined for extra-time. MacDonald scores a hat-trick but ends up on the losing side. Forest substitute, Alan Collier, scores with his first touch of the ball. | | | | | | | | | | | |

| | | Home | | | | | Away | | | | | |
|---|---|---|---|---|---|---|---|---|---|---|---|---|
| | P | W | D | L | F | A | W | D | L | F | A | Pts |
| 1 Leicester | 42 | 12 | 7 | 2 | 30 | 14 | 11 | 6 | 4 | 27 | 16 | 59 |
| 2 Sheffield Utd | 42 | 14 | 6 | 1 | 49 | 18 | 7 | 8 | 6 | 24 | 21 | 56 |
| 3 Cardiff | 42 | 12 | 7 | 2 | 39 | 16 | 8 | 6 | 7 | 25 | 25 | 53 |
| 4 Carlisle | 42 | 16 | 3 | 2 | 39 | 13 | 4 | 10 | 7 | 26 | 30 | 53 |
| 5 Hull | 42 | 11 | 5 | 5 | 31 | 16 | 8 | 8 | 5 | 23 | 25 | 51 |
| 6 LUTON TOWN | 42 | 12 | 7 | 2 | 40 | 18 | 6 | 6 | 9 | 22 | 25 | 49 |
| 7 Middlesbro | 42 | 13 | 6 | 2 | 37 | 16 | 4 | 8 | 9 | 23 | 27 | 48 |
| 8 Millwall | 42 | 13 | 5 | 3 | 36 | 12 | 6 | 4 | 11 | 23 | 30 | 47 |
| 9 Birmingham | 42 | 12 | 7 | 2 | 30 | 12 | 5 | 5 | 11 | 28 | 36 | 46 |
| 10 Norwich | 42 | 11 | 8 | 2 | 34 | 20 | 4 | 6 | 11 | 20 | 32 | 44 |
| 11 QP Rangers | 42 | 11 | 5 | 5 | 39 | 22 | 5 | 6 | 10 | 19 | 31 | 43 |
| 12 Swindon | 42 | 12 | 7 | 2 | 38 | 14 | 3 | 5 | 13 | 23 | 37 | 42 |
| 13 Sunderland | 42 | 11 | 6 | 4 | 34 | 21 | 4 | 6 | 11 | 18 | 33 | 42 |
| 14 Oxford | 42 | 8 | 8 | 5 | 23 | 23 | 6 | 6 | 9 | 18 | 25 | 42 |
| 15 Sheffield Wed | 42 | 10 | 7 | 4 | 32 | 27 | 2 | 5 | 14 | 19 | 42 | 36 |
| 16 Portsmouth | 42 | 9 | 4 | 8 | 32 | 28 | 1 | 10 | 10 | 14 | 33 | 34 |
| 17 Orient | 42 | 5 | 11 | 5 | 16 | 15 | 4 | 5 | 12 | 13 | 36 | 34 |
| 18 Watford | 42 | 6 | 7 | 8 | 18 | 22 | 4 | 6 | 11 | 20 | 38 | 33 |
| 19 Bristol City | 42 | 9 | 6 | 6 | 30 | 28 | 1 | 5 | 15 | 16 | 36 | 31 |
| 20 Charlton | 42 | 7 | 6 | 8 | 28 | 30 | 1 | 8 | 12 | 13 | 35 | 30 |
| 21 Blackburn | 42 | 5 | 8 | 8 | 20 | 28 | 1 | 7 | 13 | 17 | 41 | 27 |
| 22 Bolton | 42 | 6 | 5 | 10 | 22 | 31 | 1 | 5 | 15 | 13 | 43 | 24 |
| | 924 | 225 | 141 | 96 | 697 | 444 | 96 | 141 | 225 | 444 | 697 | 924 |

Odds & ends

Double wins: (4) Hull, Orient, Portsmouth, Watford.
Double losses: (1) Leicester.

Won from behind: (1) Birmingham (h).
Lost from in front: (3) Bristol City (a), Leicester (h), Middlesbrough (a).

High spots: Not conceding a goal during a run of seven home games at the start of the season.
Topping the Division for a while, after being in Division 4 in 1967-68.
The brilliant 5-1 win at Sheffield Wednesday.
The goal-scoring form of Malcolm MacDonald.
Coming back to draw with Carlisle after trailing 0-3.

Low spots: Failing to win promotion for the third time in four seasons.
The disastrous Easter with three straight defeats.
The loss of Malcolm MacDonald at the end of the season.
0-1 defeats by Arsenal in the League Cup and Blackburn in the league.

Player of the Year: Chris Nicholl.
Ever-presents: (4) Mike Keen, Malcolm MacDonald, John Ryan, Alan Slough.
Hat-tricks: Malcolm MacDonald (3).
Leading scorer: Malcolm MacDonald (30).

| | Appearances | | | | | | Goals | | | |
|---|---|---|---|---|---|---|---|---|---|---|
| | Lge | *Sub* | LC | *Sub* | FAC | *Sub* | Lge | LC | FAC | Tot |
| Anderson, Peter | **13** | *1* | | | | | **1** | | | **1** |
| Bannister, Jack | **9** | *4* | | | 2 | | | | | |
| Barber, Keith | **3** | | | | | | | | | |
| Branston, Terry | **1** | | | | | | | | | |
| Busby, Viv | **17** | *10* | | *1* | | | **8** | | | **8** |
| Collins, John | **1** | *1* | | | | | | | | |
| Court, David | **27** | | 3 | | 2 | | | | | |
| Givens, Don | **39** | *2* | 3 | | 2 | | **11** | 2 | | **13** |
| Goodeve, Ken | **2** | *2* | | | | | | | | |
| Guild, Alan | **1** | | 1 | | | | | | | |
| Hoy, Roger | **32** | | 2 | | 2 | | | | | |
| Keen, Mike | **42** | | 3 | | 2 | | **4** | | | **4** |
| MacDonald, Malcolm | **42** | | 3 | | 2 | | **24** | 2 | 4 | **30** |
| Moore, John | **35** | | 3 | | | | **1** | | | **1** |
| Nicholl, Chris | **38** | | 3 | | 2 | | **1** | | | **1** |
| Read, Tony | **38** | | 3 | | 2 | | | | | |
| Ryan, Jim | **34** | *4* | 2 | *1* | 2 | | **1** | | | **1** |
| Ryan, John | **42** | | 3 | | 2 | | **3** | | | **3** |
| Slough, Alan | **42** | | 3 | | 2 | | **5** | | | **5** |
| Starling, Alan | **1** | | | | | | | | | |
| Tees, Matt | **3** | | 1 | | | | **2** | | | **2** |
| (own-goals) | | | | | | | **1** | | | **1** |
| **21 players used** | **462** | *24* | **33** | *2* | **22** | | **62** | **4** | **4** | **70** |

| No | Date | | Att | Pos | Pt | F-A | H-T | Scorers, Times, and Referees | 1 | 2 | 3 | 4 | 5 | 6 | 7 | 8 | 9 | 10 | 11 | 12 sub used |
|---|---|---|---|---|---|---|---|---|---|---|---|---|---|---|---|---|---|---|---|---|
| 1 | H | NORWICH | | | D | 1-1 | 0-0 | Givens 70p | Read | Ryan John | Slough | Keen | Nicholl | Moore | Ryan Jim | Busby | Givens | Court | Anderson | |
| | 14/8 | | 12,428 | | 1 | | | *Paddon 89p* | *Keelan* | *Payne* | *Butler* | *Stringer* | *Forbes* | *Anderson* | *Livermore* | *Silvester* | *Howard* | *Paddon* | *Foggo* | |
| | | | | | | | | Ref:H Hackney | Norwich come to Kenilworth Road in the hope of obtaining a point. Neither side appears likely to break the deadlock until Anderson is floored in the area by his namesake and Givens makes no mistake from the spot. Graham Paddon scores from a twice-taken penalty in the final minute. | | | | | | | | | | | |
| 2 | A | BURNLEY | | | L | 1-2 | 0-0 | Busby 65 | Read | Ryan John | Slough | Keen | Nicholl | Moore | Ryan Jim | Busby | Givens | Court | Anderson | |
| | 21/8 | | *13,333* | | 1 | | | *Casper 58, Kindon 60* | *Waiters* | *Angus* | *Wilson* | *Bellamy* | *Waldron* | *Dobson* | *Thomas* | *West* | *Fletcher* | *Casper* | *Kindon* | |
| | | | | | | | | Ref: W Gow | Newly-relegated Burnley give the Town the run-around at Turf Moor, in front of the BBC 'Match of the Day' cameras. Busby stabs home from close range for a consolation goal but it is the Clarets who look the more likely to score again, showing why they are favourites for promotion. | | | | | | | | | | | |
| 3 | H | PRESTON | | | D | 1-1 | 0-1 | Anderson 82 | Read | Ryan John | **Shanks** | Keen | Nicholl | Moore | Busby* | Slough | **Wainwright** | Givens | Anderson | Ryan Jim |
| | 28/8 | | 11,772 | | 2 | | | *Heppolette 29* | *Kelly* | *McMahon* | *McNab* | *Bird* | *Hawkins* | *Lyall* | *Heppolette* | *Ham* | *McIlmoyle* | *Spark* | *Clark** | *Wilson* |
| | | | | | | | | Ref: F Bassett | Don Shanks and local boy Robin Wainwright make their debuts and acquit themselves well. They are unable to prevent Bombay-born Ricky Heppolette from giving Preston the lead and a number of bored supporters are already making their way to the exits when Anderson equalises. | | | | | | | | | | | |
| 4 | A | OXFORD | | | D | 1-1 | 1-1 | Givens 9 | Read | Ryan John | Shanks | Keen | Nicholl | Moore | Busby | Slough | Wainwright | Givens | Anderson | |
| | 1/9 | | *10,490* | | 3 | | | *Clarke D 12* | *Kearns* | *Lucas* | *Shuker* | *Roberts* | *Clarke C* | *Evanson* | *Sloan* | *Atkinson G* | *Clarke D* | *Atkinson R* | *Cassidy** | *Skeen* |
| | | | | | | | | Ref: J Taylor | There are only three minutes of positive action in this match. Givens takes advantage of some defensive hesitation, following a corner, to smash the ball home from close range and then Derek Clarke equalises for United. The Town are starting to earn a reputation as the 'draw' specialists. | | | | | | | | | | | |
| 5 | A | ORIENT | | 16 | D | 0-0 | 0-0 | | Read | Ryan John | Shanks | Keen | Nicholl | Moore | Busby | Slough | Wainwright | Givens | Anderson | |
| | 4/9 | | *8,703* | *11* | 4 | | | | *Goddard* | *Jones* | *Rofe* | *Sewell* | *Mancini* | *Harris* | *Lazarus* | *Brisley* | *Bullock* | *Dyson** | *Bowyer* | *Fairbrother* |
| | | | | | | | | Ref: D Nippard | Busby and Anderson interchange their wing positions in an attempt to worry the O's at Brisbane Road. Despite this activity, the Town never look like scoring. The same can be said for the home side, in spite of the overlapping support play by Dennis Rofe, and the points are shared. | | | | | | | | | | | |
| 6 | H | BIRMINGHAM | | 15 | D | 0-0 | 0-0 | | Read | Ryan John | Shanks | Keen | Nicholl | Moore | Busby | Slough | **Halom** | Givens | Anderson | |
| | 11/9 | | 14,678 | *12* | 5 | | | | *Latchford D* | *Martin* | *Hynd* | *Robinson* | *Pendrey* | *Smith* | *Page* | *Campbell* | *Francis* | *Latchford B* | *Phillips* | |
| | | | | | | | | Ref: V James | Centre-forward Vic Halom, a £35,000 signing from Fulham, makes his debut for the Town and is unfortunate not to score when his goal-bound shot is deflected over the bar by team-mate Anderson. The away contingent watch as Bob Latchford lobs the ball over the bar from five yards. | | | | | | | | | | | |
| 7 | A | MILLWALL | | 16 | D | 2-2 | 1-2 | Anderson 9, 70 | Read | Ryan John | Shanks | Slough | Nicholl | Moore | Busby* | Keen | Halom | Givens | Anderson | Wainwright |
| | 18/9 | | *12,433* | *5* | 6 | | | *Possee 2, Cripps 29p* | *King* | *Brown B* | *Cripps* | *Dorney* | *Kitchener* | *Burnett* | *Possee* | *Bolland* | *Bridges* | *Dunphy** | *Allder* | *Brown S* |
| | | | | | | | | Ref: I Smith | Derek Possee scores early on and Anderson replies with a header from a Givens cross. Huge Millwall full-back, Harry Cripps, crumples in the area following a tackle by John Ryan, but jumps up immediately to score from the penalty spot. Anderson scores from a narrow angle to level. | | | | | | | | | | | |
| 8 | H | MIDDLESBROUGH | | 14 | W | 3-2 | 1-1 | Halom 17, Wainwright 54, Anderson 84 | Read | Ryan John | Shanks | Slough | Nicholl | Moore | Wainwright | Keen | Halom | Givens | Anderson | |
| | 25/9 | | 13,001 | *8* | 8 | | | *Hickton 11, Maddren 88* | *Whigham* | *Craggs* | *Jones* | *Stiles** | *Boam* | *Gates* | *Downing* | *McMordie* | *Maddren* | *Hickton* | *Vincent* | *Laidlaw* |
| | | | | | | | | Ref: M Washer | Vic Halom and Robin Wainwright open their accounts for the Town in an end-to-end tussle. Boro are unfortunate not to gain a point, but their second goal, through Willie Maddren, comes too late. 1966 World Cup star, Nobby Stiles, looks a sorry sight as he limps off with a leg injury. | | | | | | | | | | | |
| 9 | H | FULHAM | | 10 | W | 2-0 | 1-0 | Wainwright 13, Halom 68 | Barber | Ryan John | Shanks | Slough | Nicholl | Moore | Wainwright | Keen | Halom | Givens | Anderson* | Ryan Jim |
| | 28/9 | | 14,017 | *20* | 10 | | | | *Webster* | *Brown* | *Callaghan* | *Richardson* | *Matthewson* | *Dunne** | *Conway* | *Cross* | *Earle* | *Lloyd* | *Barrett* | *Moreline* |
| | | | | | | | | Ref: K Walker | Fulham, without an away goal to their credit this season, never look likely to score. Ex-Fulham players, John Ryan, Shanks and Halom are determined to secure the win and Halom scores the second goal to kill off the game. Barber has only one significant save to make all evening. | | | | | | | | | | | |
| 10 | A | HULL | | 9 | D | 0-0 | 0-0 | | Barber | Ryan John | Shanks | Slough | Nicholl | Moore | Wainwright | Keen | Halom | Givens | Ryan Jim* | Court |
| | 2/10 | | *13,904* | *12* | 11 | | | | *McKechnie* | *Banks* | *Beardsley* | *Greenwood P* | *Neill* | *Knighton** | *Lord* | *Simpkin* | *O'Riley* | *Houghton* | *Butler* | *Greenwo'd R* |
| | | | | | | | | Ref: A Morrissey | Luton are now proving to be a difficult side to beat and they underline this with another good show, partly due to the acrobatic goalkeeping of Barber. Hull are unable to break through a well-organised back-five. Jimmy Ryan dislocates a shoulder and will now miss most of this season. | | | | | | | | | | | |

| No | Venue | Date | Opponent | Att | Pos | Res | F-A | H-T | Scorers, Times, and Referees | 1 | 2 | 3 | 4 | 5 | 6 | 7 | 8 | 9 | 10 | 11 | 12 |
|---|---|---|---|---|---|---|---|---|---|---|---|---|---|---|---|---|---|---|---|---|---|
| 11 | H | | SWINDON | | 9 | D | 0-0 | 0-0 | | Barber | Ryan John | Shanks | Slough | Nicholl | Moore | Wainwright | Keen | Halom* | Givens | Anderson | Busby |
| | | 9/10 | | 13,423 | 14 | 12 | | | | *Downsboro'* | *Thomas* | *Trollope* | *Butler* | *Burrows** | *Mackay* | *Bunkell* | *Harland* | *Horsfield* | *Noble* | *Rogers* | *Jones* |
| | | | | | | | | | Ref: R Perkin | A slow handclap is heard to echo around Kenilworth Road as the Town are unable to break down a stubborn Swindon defence, ably marshalled by veteran, Dave Mackay. Anderson, back after injury, has a good penalty appeal turned down when he finds himself upended by Rod Thomas. | | | | | | | | | | | |
| 12 | A | | NORWICH | | 9 | L | 1-3 | 1-0 | Slough 28 | Barber | Ryan John | Shanks | Slough | Nicholl | Moore | Anderson | Keen | Halom | Givens | **Hindson** | |
| | | 16/10 | | *22,558* | *1* | 12 | | | *Foggo 56, 76, Howard 89* | *Keelan* | *Payne* | *Butler* | *Stringer* | *Forbes* | *Anderson* | *Livermore** | *Silvester* | *Cross* | *Paddon* | *Foggo* | *Howard* |
| | | | | | | | | | Ref: J Hunting | On a rain-soaked pitch, the Hatters give the league leaders an early scare when Slough scores with a 25-yard shot before the break. A spirited fight-back by the Canaries earns the points, the third goal coming as the Town are chasing the game. New signing Hindson has a quiet start. | | | | | | | | | | | |
| 13 | A | | QP RANGERS | | 11 | L | 0-1 | 0-1 | | Barber | Ryan John | Shanks | Slough | Nicholl | Moore | Anderson | Keen | Halom | Givens | Hindson | |
| | | 19/10 | | *15,858* | *6* | 12 | | | *Leach 44* | *Parkes* | *Clement* | *Gillard* | *Venables* | *Mancini* | *Hazell* | *Busby* | *Leach* | *O'Rourke** | *Marsh* | *Saul* | *Hunt* |
| | | | | | | | | | Ref: R Challis | A goal just on half-time from Ranger's first real shot settles the game. Vic Halom has a late chance to equalise but he hooks the ball over the bar when faced with an empty net. Rodney Marsh is well-shackled by Don Shanks and ex-Town forward, John O'Rourke, has to go to hospital. | | | | | | | | | | | |
| 14 | H | | CARLISLE | | 12 | L | 0-2 | 0-1 | | Barber | Ryan John | Shanks | Slough | Nicholl | Moore | Anderson* | Keen | Halom | Givens | Hindson | Busby |
| | | 23/10 | | 11,963 | *14* | 12 | | | *Hatton 22, Balderstone 80* | *Ross* | *Hemstead* | *Gorman* | *Ternent** | *Winstanley* | *Sutton* | *Barton* | *Martin* | *Owen* | *Hatton* | *Balderstone* | *Webb* |
| | | | | | | | | | Ref: R Armstrong | The first home defeat comes amidst a crescendo of boos due to the poor performance and the seeming inability to put the ball in to the net. Bob Hatton snatches the opening goal when Barber drops the ball at his feet and Balderstone gets the second shortly after Anderson is substituted. | | | | | | | | | | | |
| 15 | A | | SUNDERLAND | | 15 | D | 2-2 | 0-1 | Nicholl 57, Anderson 76 | Read | Ryan John | Slough | Shanks | Nicholl | Moore | Anderson | Keen | Halom | Givens | Hindson | |
| | | 30/10 | | *17,979* | *7* | 13 | | | *Watson 18, McGiven 78* | *Montgomery* | *Malone* | *Coleman* | *Harvey* | *Pitt* | *Porterfield** | *McGiven* | *Kerr* | *Watson* | *Hughes* | *Tueart* | *Hamilton* |
| | | | | | | | | | Ref: F Nicholson | Promotion-seeking Sunderland power their way to an early lead and gain a penalty when Nicholl deliberately handles a goalbound header from Dennis Tueart; Billy Hughes sees his spot kick hit a post. A header from Nicholl and a tap-in from Anderson nearly earn both points for Town. | | | | | | | | | | | |
| 16 | H | | CHARLTON | | 18 | L | 1-2 | 1-0 | Keen 13 | Read | Ryan John | Slough | Shanks | Nicholl | Moore | Anderson | Keen | Halom | Givens | Hindson | |
| | | 6/11 | | 11,011 | *16* | 13 | | | *Peacock 62, 69* | *Dunn* | *Reeves* | *Warman* | *Bond* | *Went* | *Shipperley* | *Davies* | *Hunt* | *Treacy* | *Rogers* | *Peacock* | |
| | | | | | | | | | Ref: W Castle | Keen scores after 13 minutes to give a casual-looking Luton a slender one-goal lead, which should have been five by the interval. Town let the points slip away when giving acres of space to Keith Peacock, who scores twice in seven minutes, to record an unlikely victory for the Valiants. | | | | | | | | | | | |
| 17 | A | | WATFORD | | 19 | L | 1-2 | 1-1 | Halom 12 | Read | Ryan John | Slough | Anderson | Nicholl | Moore | Busby* | Keen | Halom | Givens | Hindson | Court |
| | | 13/11 | | *14,000* | *21* | 13 | | | *Eddy 34, Franks 68* | *Walker* | *Butler* | *Williams* | *Eddy* | *Baxter* | *Walley* | *Lees* | *Wigg* | *Franks* | *Lindsey* | *Farley* | |
| | | | | | | | | | Ref: P Partridge | Watford centre-half Bill Baxter gets the ball caught under his feet and Halom accepts the easiest of chances. Baxter clears off the line before Keith Eddy scores when racing on to a long free-kick from Tom Walley. Colin Franks appears to be ten yards offside when scoring the winner. | | | | | | | | | | | |
| 18 | A | | BLACKPOOL | | 16 | W | 1-0 | 1-0 | Givens 35 | Read | Ryan John | Slough | Court | Nicholl | Moore | Anderson | Busby | Givens | Keen | Hindson | |
| | | 20/11 | | *8,432* | *15* | 15 | | | | *Burridge* | *Hatton* | *Mann* | *Suddaby* | *Alcock* | *Simpkin* | *Hutchison* | *Suddick* | *Dyson* | *Lennard** | *Burns* | *Kemp* |
| | | | | | | | | | Ref: P Baldwin | The charter train is delayed, due to a derailment and, on arrival at Blackpool station, a carnival procession is cleared by the police to enable the Luton coach to get to the ground in time. Givens scores the only goal during a blizzard in the first half after some clever play from Anderson. | | | | | | | | | | | |
| 19 | H | | PORTSMOUTH | | 15 | W | 3-2 | 0-2 | Keen 52, Hindson 58, Anderson 87 | Read | Ryan John | Slough | Court | Nicholl | Moore | Anderson | Busby* | Givens | Keen | Hindson | Halom |
| | | 27/11 | | 9,910 | *12* | 17 | | | *Reynolds 2, 39* | *Standen* | *Smith* | *Ley* | *Hand* | *Youlden* | *Munks* | *Piper* | *Reynolds* | *Trebilcock* | *McCann* | *Jennings* | |
| | | | | | | | | | Ref: C Nicholls | The home attendance drops below 10,000 for the first time since 1967. Town make a fighting comeback after trailing by two first-half goals and being reduced to ten men when Givens limped off the pitch soon after the interval. Anderson steals the winner with just three minutes left. | | | | | | | | | | | |
| 20 | A | | BRISTOL CITY | | 14 | D | 0-0 | 0-0 | | Read | Ryan John | Slough | Court | Nicholl | Moore | Anderson | Keen | Halom | Givens | Hindson | |
| | | 4/12 | | *12,921* | *10* | 18 | | | | *Gibson* | *Wimshurst* | *Drysdale* | *Wilson* | *Rooks* | *Merrick* | *Tainton* | *Spiring* | *Broomfield* | *Sweeney* | *Gow** | *Bruton* |
| | | | | | | | | | Ref: C Robinson | The fifth goal-less draw of the season and the tenth draw in 21 matches, comes on a miserable day at Ashton Gate. Mike Gibson shows great anticipation to keep out a shot from Keen and a Nicholl header. Read has little to do against the team who topped the League three months ago. | | | | | | | | | | | |
| 21 | H | | CARDIFF | | 13 | D | 2-2 | 1-1 | Anderson 24, Givens 76p | Read | Ryan John | Slough | Court | Nicholl | Moore | Anderson | Keen | Halom | Givens | Hindson | |
| | | 11/12 | | 10,606 | *21* | 19 | | | *Phillips 34, Clark 80* | *Irwin* | *Carver* | *Bell* | *Phillips* | *Morgan* | *Derrett* | *Villars** | *Clark* | *Couch* | *Warboys* | *Gibson* | *Woodruff* |
| | | | | | | | | | Ref: K Burns | Twice the Hatters take the lead, only for the Bluebirds to equalise on each occasion. The Town carve out a number of opportunities but pepper the advertising hoardings rather than the Cardiff goal. Givens falls spectacularly in the box to win a penalty-kick which he converts himself. | | | | | | | | | | | |

| No Date | Att | Pos | Pt | F-A | H-T | Scorers, Times, and Referees | 1 | 2 | 3 | 4 | 5 | 6 | 7 | 8 | 9 | 10 | 11 | 12 sub used |
|---|---|---|---|---|---|---|---|---|---|---|---|---|---|---|---|---|---|---|
| 22 H ORIENT | | 12 | W | 2-0 | 0-0 | Slough 62, Givens 81 | Read | Ryan John | Slough | Court | Nicholl | Moore | Anderson* | Keen | Halom | Givens | Hindson | Ryan Jim |
| 18/12 | 9,193 | *19* | 21 | | | | *Goddard* | *Jones* | *Rofe* | *Bennett* | *Hoadley* | *Harris* | *Fairbrother* | *Allen* | *Bullock* | *Walley* | *Bowyer* | |
| | | | | | | Ref: R Crabb | Stock joins an ever-increasing number of club officials who are against the hard-line refereeing policy issued by the Football League after Don Givens is booked for the third time this season. The turning point in this keenly-fought match comes when Alan Slough bursts through to score. | | | | | | | | | | | |
| 23 A SHEFFIELD WED | | 13 | D | 2-2 | 1-0 | Givens 35, Anderson 86 | Read | Ryan John | Slough | Keen | Nicholl | Moore | Anderson | Court | Halom | Givens | Hindson | |
| 27/12 | *31,391* | *10* | 22 | | | *Craig 48p, Holsgrove 66* | *Grummitt* | *Rodrigues* | *Clements* | *Prophett* | *Holsgrove* | *Pugh* | *Sinclair* | *Craig* | *Joicey* | *Prendergast** | *Sissons* | *Thompson* |
| | | | | | | Ref: R Matthewson | A big Christmas crowd sees the Town escape with a share of the spoils in a 'cracker' of an encounter. Givens fires the first with a stunning shot and Tommy Craig levels from the penalty spot after Nicholl handles. Holsgrove heads the Owls' second and Anderson scores to gain the draw. | | | | | | | | | | | |
| 24 H MILLWALL | | 12 | W | 2-1 | 2-0 | Nicholl 19, Anderson 34 | Read | Ryan John | Slough | Keen | Nicholl | Moore | Anderson | Court | Halom | Givens | Hindson | |
| 1/1 | 15,113 | *2* | 24 | | | *Possee 53* | *King* | *Brown* | *Cripps* | *Dorney* | *Kitchener* | *Burnett* | *Bridges* | *Bolland* | *Possee* | *Smethurst* | *Dunphy** | *Allder* |
| | | | | | | Ref: F Bassett | High-riding Millwall suffer their third defeat of the season as Luton put on one of their best performances. Town take a two-goal lead through headers from Nicholl and Anderson but then endure a second-half fight-back by the Lions. Bryan King injures his leg but bravely continues. | | | | | | | | | | | |
| 25 A PRESTON | | 10 | W | 1-0 | 1-0 | Slough 12 | Read | Ryan John | Slough | Keen | Nicholl | Moore | Anderson | Court | Halom | Givens | Hindson | |
| 8/1 | *12,844* | *9* | 26 | | | | *Kelly* | *McMahon* | *McNab* | *Bird* | *Hawkins* | *Lamb* | *Heppolette* | *Clark* | *McIlmoyle* | *Lyall* | *Tarbuck** | *Wilson* |
| | | | | | | Ref: J Williams | Luton gain the lead when Keen strokes a free-kick sideways and Slough blasts the ball past Alan Kelly. Preston then batter the Luton defences and look to be back in the contest when Read brings down Clive Clark in the area. Alan Tarbuck mis-hits his penalty and Read saves easily. | | | | | | | | | | | |
| 26 A FULHAM | | 10 | L | 1-3 | 0-2 | Anderson 59 | Read | Ryan John | Slough | Keen | Nicholl | Moore | Anderson | Court | Halom | Givens | Hindson | |
| 22/1 | *11,328* | *19* | 26 | | | *Johnston 30, 38 Barrett 89* | *Webster* | *Moreline* | *Callaghan* | *Dunne* | *Matthewson* | *Richardson* | *Johnston* | *Cross* | *Earle* | *Lloyd* | *Barrett* | |
| | | | | | | Ref: R Kirkpatrick | The Town suffer a disappointing defeat at Craven Cottage after the good result of last week. George Johnston scores with two headers, after an evenly matched opening period. Anderson reduces the deficit after a good spell of pressure but Les Barrett scores Fulham's third on the break. | | | | | | | | | | | |
| 27 H QP RANGERS | | 11 | D | 1-1 | 1-1 | Ryan John 20 | Read | Ryan John | Slough | Keen | Nicholl | Moore | Anderson | Court | Halom | Givens | Hindson | |
| 29/1 | **17,280** | *3* | 27 | | | *Francis 4* | *Parkes* | *Clement* | *Hazell* | *Venables* | *Hunt* | *Mancini* | *Saul* | *Francis* | *Leach* | *Marsh* | *Ferguson* | |
| | | | | | | Ref: K Wynn | Rodney Marsh puts on a virtuoso performance although it is the Town who play better as a team. Gerry Francis catches the Hatters out with an early goal but John Ryan equalises with a tremendous shot for his first goal of the season in front of the biggest League crowd of the campaign. | | | | | | | | | | | |
| 28 H OXFORD | | 12 | L | 1-2 | 0-1 | Halom 52 | Read | Ryan John | Slough | Keen | Nicholl | Moore | Anderson* | Court | Halom | Givens | Hindson | Ryan Jim |
| 5/2 | 9,892 | *11* | 27 | | | *Skeen 45, Atkinson 54* | *Burton* | *Way* | *Shuker* | *Smithson* | *Clarke* | *Evanson* | *Skeen* | *Atkinson* | *Clayton* | *Cassidy* | *Aylott* | |
| | | | | | | Ref: N Burtenshaw | The attendance again drops below 10,000 and Oxford give the Hatters a lesson in both attacking and defending as a team. After Atkinson scores United's second goal, the Town desperately struggle in vain for a point. Jim Ryan returns from injury, having dislocated a shoulder in October. | | | | | | | | | | | |
| 29 A CARLISLE | | 11 | D | 0-0 | 0-0 | | Read | Ryan John | Slough | Keen | Nicholl | Moore | Busby | Court | Wainwright | Halom | Givens* | Hindson |
| 12/2 | *8,731* | *7* | 28 | | | | *Ross* | *Hemstead* | *Gorman* | *Ternent* | *Winstanley* | *Bowles* | *Barton* | *Martin* | *Owen* | *Train* | *Balderstone* | |
| | | | | | | Ref: J Wrennall | Carlisle is a long way to go for a goal-less draw but the Town are thankful for the point after their recent run of poor results. Busby makes his reappearance after a two-month loan spell at Newcastle and has a goal ruled out for offside. Ross saves from Court with a superb mid-air catch. | | | | | | | | | | | |
| 30 H SUNDERLAND | | 13 | L | 1-2 | 0-1 | Nicholl 85 | Read | Ryan John | Slough | Keen | Nicholl | Moore | Busby | Wainwright | Halom* | Court | Givens | Anderson |
| 19/2 | 10,994 | *4* | 28 | | | *Pitt 6, Tueart 75* | *Forster* | *Malone* | *Coleman* | *Harvey* | *Pitt* | *Porterfield* | *McGiven* | *Kerr* | *Watson* | *Lathan* | *Tueart* | |
| | | | | | | Ref: F Nicholson | A number of chances are squandered as the Hatters gift the points to Sunderland. The Wearsiders, playing their fifth game in eleven days, see Richie Pitt score with a brave, diving header followed by a fine individual effort from Dennis Tueart. Forster is equal to anything thrown at him. | | | | | | | | | | | |
| 31 A CHARLTON | | 15 | L | 0-2 | 0-1 | | Barber | Ryan John | Slough | Keen | Nicholl | Moore | Anderson | Busby* | Wainwright | Court | Givens | Halom |
| 26/2 | ***7,941*** | *16* | 28 | | | *Rogers 40, Went 61p* | *Dunn* | *Jones* | *Went* | *Shipperley* | *Warman* | *Davies* | *Rogers* | *Peacock** | *Treacy* | *Hunt* | *Flanagan* | *Plumb* |
| | | | | | | Ref: E Jolly | Charlton score two controversial goals in a mediocre match, the first when Ray Treacy appears guilty of holding Barber as a corner-kick from Eamonn Rogers goes directly in to the goal and then from a penalty-kick, given when Court is adjudged to have body-checked Keith Peacock. | | | | | | | | | | | |

| No | Venue / Date | Opponent | Att | Pos | Pt | Res | F-A | H-T | Scorers, Times, and Referees | 1 | 2 | 3 | 4 | 5 | 6 | 7 | 8 | 9 | 10 | 11 | 12 |
|---|---|---|---|---|---|---|---|---|---|---|---|---|---|---|---|---|---|---|---|---|---|
| 32 | H | WATFORD | | 16 | | D | 0-0 | 0-0 | | Barber | Ryan John | Shanks | Keen | Nicholl | Slough | Ryan Jim | Court | Halom | Givens* | Hindson | Anderson |
| | 4/3 | | 10,816 | *22* | 29 | | | | | *Walker* | *Butler* | *Williams* | *Lugg* | *Franks* | *Eddy* | *McGettigan** | *Wigg* | *Morrissey* | *Lindsay* | *Welbourne* | *Farley* |
| | | | | | | | | | Ref: J Taylor | Struggling Watford pick up their first point in ten matches. Barber fumbles a 30-yard shot from Jimmy Lindsay in to the path of Pat Morrissey but he spurns the chance. The Town dominate but fail to score, the best chance falls to Anderson who treads on the ball in front of an open goal. | | | | | | | | | | | |
| 33 | H | BURNLEY | | 15 | | W | 1-0 | 1-0 | Busby 35 | Barber | Ryan John | Shanks | Keen | **Garner** | Slough | Ryan Jim | Court | Anderson | Givens | Busby | |
| | 18/3 | | 8,490 | *9* | 31 | | | | | *Stevenson* | *Docherty* | *Wilson* | *Bellamy* | *Waldron* | *Dobson* | *Thomas** | *Casper* | *Fletcher* | *Probert* | *James* | *Collins* |
| | | | | | | | | | Ref: C Thomas | Nicholl is transferred to Aston Villa and Alan Garner takes over at centre-half. The Town are fortunate to take both points in an ill-tempered match, the only goal coming when Keen lashes in a free-kick which Alan Stevenson cannot hold and Busby accepts the simplest of chances. | | | | | | | | | | | |
| 34 | A | BIRMINGHAM | | 17 | | L | 0-1 | 0-0 | | Barber | Ryan John | Shanks | Keen | Garner | Slough | Ryan Jim | Court | Anderson | Busby | Givens | |
| | 25/3 | | ***34,395*** | *3* | 31 | | | | *Hatton 89* | *Latchford D* | *Page* | *Pendrey* | *Smith* | *Hynd* | *Harland* | *Campbell* | *Francis* | *Latchford B* | *Hatton* | *Taylor* | |
| | | | | | | | | | Ref: H Williams | The Town are unlucky to lose to the Blues in front of a partisan crowd. The home side enjoy most of the play but the Hatters defend well and chances are kept down to a minimum. A hit-and-hope ball into the wind by Gary Pendrey in the dying seconds is latched on to by Bob Hatton. | | | | | | | | | | | |
| 35 | A | MIDDLESBROUGH | | 17 | | D | 0-0 | 0-0 | | Barber | Ryan John | Shanks | Keen | Garner | Slough | Halom | Court | Anderson | Busby | Givens* | Moore |
| | 31/3 | | *11,720* | *6* | 32 | | | | | *Platt* | *Craggs* | *Jones* | *Maddren* | *Boam* | *Spraggon* | *Stiles** | *McMordie* | *Laidlaw* | *Hickton* | *Vincent* | *Downing* |
| | | | | | | | | | Ref: F Nicholson | A single point takes the Hatters out of immediate relegation trouble but the players have goalkeeper Barber to thank for yet another outstanding performance. The defence deals with all that is thrown at it but slow handclapping erupts when it is obvious that Town are playing for a draw. | | | | | | | | | | | |
| 36 | H | SHEFFIELD WED | | 13 | | W | 3-1 | 0-1 | Halom 76, 85, 87 | Barber | Ryan John | Shanks | Moore | Garner | Slough* | Halom | Court | Anderson | Keen | Busby | Givens |
| | 1/4 | | 9,121 | *18* | 34 | | | | *Joicey 11* | *Pearson* | *Rodrigues* | *Thompson* | *Todd* | *Clements* | *Pugh* | *Craig* | *Sissons* | *Sinclair* | *Joicey* | *Sunley* | |
| | | | | | | | | | Ref: K Sweet | Brian Joicey opens the scoring for the Owls in the first half. Alec Stock brings on Don Givens to add extra weight to the forward line and, in the space of eleven minutes, Vic Halom silences the 'boo-boys' by cracking home a superb hat-trick which brings the game to an unreal end. | | | | | | | | | | | |
| 37 | H | HULL | | 14 | | L | 0-1 | 0-0 | | Barber | Ryan John | Shanks | Keen | Garner | Slough | Ryan Jim* | Court | Givens | Halom | Anderson | Moore |
| | 4/4 | | 9,763 | *12* | 34 | | | | *Knighton 57* | *McKechnie* | *Banks* | *Devries* | *Wilkinson* | *Neill* | *Baxter* | *Knighton* | *Lord* | *O'Riley* | *Wagstaff* | *Butler* | |
| | | | | | | | | | Ref: A Hart | The Town appear to have weathered the Easter period well but, with Northern Ireland captain Terry Neill commanding the Hull side in the first half, the Hatters are unable to break through the barrier. Ken Knighton, the former Preston midfielder, bangs in a good goal to gain the victory. | | | | | | | | | | | |
| 38 | H | BLACKPOOL | | 16 | | L | **1-4** | 0-3 | Keen 55 *[Slough 61 (og)]* | Barber | Ryan John | Shanks | Keen | Garner | Slough | Wainwright | Court* | Halom | Busby | Givens | Moore |
| | 8/4 | | **7,270** | *6* | 34 | | | | *Dyson 14, Simpkin 20, Burns 40,* | *Burridge* | *Hatton* | *Bentley* | *Suddaby* | *James* | *Simpkin* | *Hutchison* | *Suddick* | *Dyson* | *Hardcastle* | *Burns* | |
| | | | | | | | | | Ref: D Biddle | Blackpool take command and score three goals in the first half to secure the points. The Hatters showed great spirit and fight back in the second period. Keen reduces the deficit but hopes of a revival are dashed when Slough slices the ball into his own net. Halom hits the inside of a post. | | | | | | | | | | | |
| 39 | A | PORTSMOUTH | | 12 | | W | **3-0** | 2-0 | Givens 15p, Ryan John 31, 66 | Barber | Slough | Shanks | Keen | Garner | Moore | Wainwright | Halom | Givens | Ryan John | Hindson | |
| | 15/4 | | *8,552* | *17* | 36 | | | | | *Milkins* | *Smith* | *Collins* | *Blant* | *Youlden* | *Munks* | *Piper* | *Reynolds* | *Wilson* | *Ley* | *Hiron* | |
| | | | | | | | | | Ref N Pagett: | John Ryan plays as a striker in an attempt to resolve the goalscoring problems and he relishes the opportunity. His first goal is as a result of a flying header and the second is driven home with great confidence. 'I loved it up front and I would like another crack at it,' he said afterwards. | | | | | | | | | | | |
| 40 | A | SWINDON | | 13 | | L | 1-2 | 1-0 | Givens 28 | Barber | Slough | Shanks | Keen | Garner | Moore | Wainwright | Halom | Givens | Ryan John | Hindson | |
| | 18/4 | | *8,960* | *11* | 36 | | | | *Rogers 60, Horsfield 82* | *Downsboro'* | *Thomas* | *Trollope* | *Bunkell* | *Burrows* | *Butler* | *Hubbard* | *Smart* | *Horsfield* | *Noble* | *Rogers* | |
| | | | | | | | | | Ref: A Jones | Relegation fears are now forgotten as Givens opens the scoring with a scorching shot in this end-of-season game. Don Rogers equalises with a splendid solo effort after 30 minutes and Barber, hampered by an earlier injury, drops a cross for Arthur Horsfield to scramble home the winner. | | | | | | | | | | | |
| 41 | H | BRISTOL CITY | | 15 | | D | 0-0 | 0-0 | | Barber | Slough | Shanks | Keen | Garner | Moore | Wainwright | Halom | Givens | Ryan John | Hindson | |
| | 22/4 | | 8,329 | *9* | 37 | | | | | *Cashley* | *Sweeney* | *Drysdale* | *Emanuel* | *Bruton* | *Merrick* | *Tainton* | *Spiring* | *Galley* | *Gow* | *Bartley* | |
| | | | | | | | | | Ref: R Challis | On a cold afternoon, a small crowd is bored stiff with another goal-less draw. Defence-minded Town dominate as midfielder John Ryan tries to get the forwards working without success. Keen, playing his last home game for the Hatters, blocks a Bartley effort three minutes from time. | | | | | | | | | | | |
| 42 | A | CARDIFF | | 13 | | D | 1-1 | 1-1 | Wainwright 43 | Barber | Slough | Shanks | Keen | Garner | Moore | Wainwright | Halom | Givens | Ryan John | Hindson | |
| | 29/4 | | *12,587* | *19* | 38 | | | | *Warboys 41* | *Irwin* | *Carver* | *Pethard* | *Sutton* | *Murray* | *Phillips* | *Gibson* | *Clark* | *Woodruff* | *Warboys* | *King* | |
| | | Home | Away | | | | | | Ref: V Batty | Cardiff need a point to ensure staying up and, for the majority of the game, they control the midfield. Ian Gibson is the instigator of most of their moves but, despite this dominance, have only one goal from Warboys to show for their efforts. Wainwright equalises two minutes later. | | | | | | | | | | | |
| | Average | 11,384 | 14,240 | | | | | | | | | | | | | | | | | | |

| League Cup | | | | | | F-A | H-T | Scorers, Times, and Referees | 1 | 2 | 3 | 4 | 5 | 6 | 7 | 8 | 9 | 10 | 11 | 12 sub used |
|---|---|---|---|---|---|---|---|---|---|---|---|---|---|---|---|---|---|---|---|---|
| 2 | A | CRYSTAL PALACE | 16 | L | | 0-2 | 0-0 | | Read | Ryan John | Shanks | Keen | Nicholl | Moore | Busby | Slough | Wainwright | Givens | Anderson | |
| | 7/9 | *13,838* | *1:21* | | | | | *Taylor 80, Queen 89* | *Jackson* | *Hoadley* | *Wall* | *Payne* | *McCormick* | *Blyth* | *Scott* | *Kember* | *Queen* | *Tambling* | *Taylor* | |
| | | | | | | | | Ref: M Sinclair | The Town are eliminated from the competition but the score flatters the Division 1 side. In the 77th minute, Anderson smashes in a shot which beats Jackson, but the ball hits the bar. Three minutes later, Taylor scores a lucky goal and Queen adds a second with Town chasing the game. | | | | | | | | | | | |

| FA Cup | | | | | | F-A | H-T | Scorers, Times, and Referees | 1 | 2 | 3 | 4 | 5 | 6 | 7 | 8 | 9 | 10 | 11 | 12 sub used |
|---|---|---|---|---|---|---|---|---|---|---|---|---|---|---|---|---|---|---|---|---|
| 3 | A | WEST HAM | 10 | L | | 1-2 | 0-2 | Givens 52 | Read | Ryan John | Slough | Keen | Nicholl | Moore | Anderson | Court | Halom | Givens | Hindson | |
| | 15/1 | *32,099* | *1:12* | | | | | *Hurst 1, Best 25* | *Ferguson* | *McDowell* | *Lampard* | *Bonds* | *Taylor* | *Moore** | *Redknapp* | *Best* | *Hurst* | *Brooking* | *Robson* | *Eustace* |
| | | | | | | | | Ref: K Burns | A magnificent second-half display by the Hatters, which includes a headed goal by Givens from an Anderson cross, transforms the game in to a classic FA Cup battle. The Hammers win the game in the first period, despite the injury to Bobby Moore. Read saves a penalty from Hurst. | | | | | | | | | | | |

| | | Home | | | | | Away | | | | | |
|---|---|---|---|---|---|---|---|---|---|---|---|---|
| | P | W | D | L | F | A | W | D | L | F | A | Pts |
| 1 Norwich | 42 | 13 | 8 | 0 | 40 | 16 | 8 | 7 | 6 | 20 | 20 | 57 |
| 2 Birmingham | 42 | 15 | 6 | 0 | 46 | 14 | 4 | 12 | 5 | 14 | 17 | 56 |
| 3 Millwall | 42 | 14 | 7 | 0 | 38 | 17 | 5 | 10 | 6 | 26 | 29 | 55 |
| 4 QP Rangers | 42 | 16 | 4 | 1 | 39 | 9 | 4 | 10 | 7 | 18 | 19 | 54 |
| 5 Sunderland | 42 | 11 | 7 | 3 | 42 | 24 | 6 | 9 | 6 | 25 | 33 | 50 |
| 6 Blackpool | 42 | 12 | 6 | 3 | 43 | 16 | 8 | 1 | 12 | 27 | 34 | 47 |
| 7 Burnley | 42 | 13 | 4 | 4 | 43 | 22 | 7 | 2 | 12 | 27 | 33 | 46 |
| 8 Bristol City | 42 | 14 | 3 | 4 | 43 | 22 | 4 | 7 | 10 | 18 | 27 | 46 |
| 9 Middlesbro | 42 | 16 | 4 | 1 | 31 | 11 | 3 | 4 | 14 | 19 | 37 | 46 |
| 10 Carlisle | 42 | 12 | 6 | 3 | 38 | 22 | 5 | 3 | 13 | 23 | 35 | 43 |
| 11 Swindon | 42 | 10 | 6 | 5 | 29 | 16 | 5 | 6 | 10 | 18 | 31 | 42 |
| 12 Hull | 42 | 10 | 6 | 5 | 33 | 21 | 4 | 4 | 13 | 16 | 32 | 38 |
| 13 LUTON TOWN | 42 | 7 | 8 | 6 | 25 | 24 | 3 | 10 | 8 | 18 | 24 | 38 |
| 14 Sheffield Wed | 42 | 11 | 7 | 3 | 33 | 22 | 2 | 5 | 14 | 18 | 36 | 38 |
| 15 Oxford | 42 | 10 | 8 | 3 | 28 | 17 | 2 | 6 | 13 | 15 | 38 | 38 |
| 16 Portsmouth | 42 | 9 | 7 | 5 | 31 | 26 | 3 | 6 | 12 | 28 | 42 | 37 |
| 17 Orient | 42 | 12 | 4 | 5 | 32 | 19 | 2 | 5 | 14 | 18 | 42 | 37 |
| 18 Preston | 42 | 11 | 4 | 6 | 32 | 21 | 1 | 8 | 12 | 20 | 37 | 36 |
| 19 Cardiff | 42 | 9 | 7 | 5 | 37 | 25 | 1 | 7 | 13 | 19 | 44 | 34 |
| 20 Fulham | 42 | 10 | 7 | 4 | 29 | 20 | 2 | 3 | 16 | 16 | 48 | 34 |
| 21 Charlton | 42 | 9 | 7 | 5 | 33 | 25 | 3 | 2 | 16 | 22 | 52 | 33 |
| 22 Watford | 42 | 5 | 5 | 11 | 15 | 25 | 0 | 4 | 17 | 9 | 50 | 19 |
| | 924 | 249 | 131 | 82 | 760 | 434 | 82 | 131 | 249 | 434 | 760 | 924 |

Odds & ends

Double wins: (1) Portsmouth.
Double losses: (1) Charlton.

Won from behind: (3) Middlesbrough (h), Portsmouth (h), Sheffield Wednesday (h).
Lost from in front: (4) Charlton (h), Norwich (a), Swindon (a), Watford (a).

High spots: A nine-game unbeaten run at the start of the season.
The performance at West Ham in the FA Cup.
The two goals scored by defender John Ryan in the 3-0 win at Pompey.

Low spots: The lack of goals, with nine 0-0 draws.
Losing to a last-minute goal at Birmingham.
Defeat at Watford.
Crowds dipping below 10,000 for the first time in four years.

Player of the Year: John Ryan.
Ever-presents: (4) Don Givens, Mike Keen, John Ryan, Alan Slough.
Hat-tricks: Vic Halom (1).
Leading scorer: Peter Anderson (10).

| | Appearances | | | | | | Goals | | | |
|---|---|---|---|---|---|---|---|---|---|---|
| | Lge | *Sub* | LC | *Sub* | FAC | *Sub* | Lge | LC | FAC | Tot |
| Anderson, Peter | **33** | *2* | 1 | | 1 | | **10** | | | **10** |
| Barber, Keith | **18** | | | | | | | | | |
| Busby, Viv | **18** | *2* | 1 | | | | **2** | | | **2** |
| Court, David | **23** | *2* | | | 1 | | | | | |
| Garner, Alan | **10** | | | | | | | | | |
| Givens, Don | **41** | *1* | 1 | | 1 | | **8** | | 1 | **9** |
| Halom, Vic | **32** | *2* | | | 1 | | **7** | | | **7** |
| Hindson, Gordon | **22** | *1* | | | 1 | | **1** | | | **1** |
| Keen, Mike | **42** | | 1 | | 1 | | **3** | | | **3** |
| Moore, John | **36** | *3* | 1 | | 1 | | | | | |
| Nicholl, Chris | **32** | | 1 | | 1 | | **3** | | | **3** |
| Read, Tony | **24** | | 1 | | 1 | | | | | |
| Ryan, Jim | **7** | *4* | | | | | | | | |
| Ryan, John | **42** | | 1 | | 1 | | **3** | | | **3** |
| Shanks, Don | **25** | | 1 | | | | | | | |
| Slough, Alan | **42** | | 1 | | 1 | | **3** | | | **3** |
| Wainwright, Robin | **15** | *1* | 1 | | | | **3** | | | **3** |
| **17 players used** | **462** | ***18*** | **11** | | **11** | | **43** | | **1** | **44** |

| No | Date | Att | Pos | Pt | F-A | H-T | Scorers, Times, and Referees | 1 | 2 | 3 | 4 | 5 | 6 | 7 | 8 | 9 | 10 | 11 | 12 sub used |
|---|---|---|---|---|---|---|---|---|---|---|---|---|---|---|---|---|---|---|---|
| 1 | A CARDIFF | | | L | 1-2 | 1-1 | Aston 39p | Barber | Ryan John | **Thomson** | Anderson | **Faulkner** | Garner | Ryan Jim | **Fern** | Busby | Halom | **Aston** | |
| | 12/8 | *16,364* | | - | | | *Bell 44p, Warboys 61* | *Irwin* | *Carver* | *Bell* | *Foggon** | *Murray* | *Larmour* | *Gibson* | *Clark* | *Phillips* | *Warboys* | *Showers* | *Villars* |
| | | | | | | | Ref: I Smith | Foggon sees his shot crash against the bar and the counter-attack, launched from the rebound, ends when Larmour fouls Jim Ryan in the area. Aston scores from the spot but Cardiff level, also with a penalty, after Anderson handles. The Hatters then fade and Warboys hits the winner. | | | | | | | | | | | |
| 2 | H PRESTON | | 11 | W | 1-0 | 1-0 | Anderson 36 | Barber | Ryan John | Thomson | Anderson | Faulkner | Garner | Ryan Jim | Fern | Busby* | Halom | Aston | Slough |
| | 19/8 | 11,507 | *22* | 2 | | | | *Kelly* | *McMahon* | *McNab* | *Bird* | *Hawkins* | *Connor** | *Heppolette* | *Wilson* | *Tarbuck* | *Young* | *Clark* | *Spark* |
| | | | | | | | Ref: T Spencer | Harry Haslam is disappointed that the Town do not have five goals to show for their afternoon's work, but knows that signing a striker is now a priority. Injury-hit Preston try hard but are limited in attack, concentrating instead on keeping the Hatters at bay. Anderson heads the only goal. | | | | | | | | | | | |
| 3 | A ORIENT | | 7 | W | 1-0 | 0-0 | Busby 56 | Barber | Ryan John | Thomson | Anderson | Faulkner | Garner | Ryan Jim | Fern | Busby | Halom | Aston | |
| | 26/8 | *6,494* | *21* | 4 | | | | *Goddard* | *Arber* | *Hoadley* | *Bennett* | *Harris* | *Allen* | *Downing* | *Brisley* | *Bullock* | *Dyson* | *Bowyer* | |
| | | | | | | | Ref: H Hackney | Busby latches on to a weak back-pass by Peter Allen and swerves the ball into the net. Orient, who are missing recently departed Dennis Rofe, are apprehensive and do not look likely to trouble the Town back four. Aston and Fern go close with three good chances in a five minute spell. | | | | | | | | | | | |
| 4 | H OXFORD | | 9 | L | 0-1 | 0-0 | | Barber | Ryan John | Thomson | Anderson | Faulkner | Garner | Ryan Jim | Fern | Busby* | Halom | Aston | Slough |
| | 30/8 | 10,891 | *12* | 4 | | | *Cassidy 82* | *Burton* | *Lucas* | *Shuker* | *Roberts* | *Clarke C* | *Evanson* | *Sloan* | *Atkinson** | *Clarke D* | *Cassidy* | *Aylott* | *Fleming* |
| | | | | | | | Ref: A Oliver | Nigel Cassidy snatches the points for Oxford, eight minutes from time, when United suddenly break away after being pinned down by a barrage of Luton attacks. The game is played at a fast pace but is never dirty although there are three bookings during a six-minute spell in the first half. | | | | | | | | | | | |
| 5 | H HUDDERSFIELD | | 7 | W | **4-1** | 2-0 | Halom 2, 25, Ryan Jim 57, Aston 73p | Barber | Ryan John | Thomson | Slough | Faulkner | Garner | Ryan Jim | Fern | Busby | Halom | Aston | |
| | 2/9 | 8,495 | *13* | 6 | | | *Gowling 49* | *Wood* | *Jones* | *Smith** | *Pugh* | *Dolan* | *Nicholson* | *Fairclough* | *Lawson* | *Gowling* | *Smith* | *Chapman* | *McGifford* |
| | | | | | | | Ref: R Crabb | The bonus of a goal in the first 90 seconds gives the Town the confidence to sweep on to a convincing victory over a brave, but limited, newly-relegated Huddersfield side, who have lost defenders Trevor Cherry and Roy Ellam. Aston scores from the spot after a Jones handling offence. | | | | | | | | | | | |
| 6 | A NOTT'M FOREST | | 9 | W | 1-0 | 1-0 | Aston 26 | Barber | Shanks | Thomson | Anderson | Faulkner | Garner | Ryan Jim | Fern | Busby | Halom | Aston | |
| | 9/9 | *9,133* | *6* | 8 | | | | *Barron* | *Hindley* | *Gemmell* | *Serella* | *Cottam* | *Fraser* | *McIntosh* | *Lyall* | *McKenzie* | *Robertson* | *O'Neill* | |
| | | | | | | | Ref: R Johnson | The Hatters end the unbeaten league run of Forest, who appear to have completely lost their form, with only the minimum amount of effort. Jim Ryan sets up John Aston, who picks his spot and scores from twelve yards. The Town are then able to coast through the remainder of the game. | | | | | | | | | | | |
| 7 | H BRIGHTON | | 4 | W | 2-1 | 1-1 | Fern 34, Halom 55 | Barber | Ryan John | Thomson | Anderson | Faulkner | Garner | Ryan Jim | Fern | Busby* | Halom | Aston | Slough |
| | 16/9 | 11,627 | *18* | 10 | | | *Templeman 29* | *Powney* | *Howell* | *Spearritt* | *Templeman* | *Napier* | *Gall* | *Murray* | *Bridges* | *Beamish* | *Bromley* | *O'Sullivan** | *Lutton* |
| | | | | | | | Ref: R Armstrong | Brighton take a shock lead with a 20-yard shot from John Templeman, but the Hatters equalise with a similar long-range effort from Rodney Fern. Vic Halom nods the winner after capitalising on a wild back-header by the Brighton goalscorer, following a long throw by Alan Garner. | | | | | | | | | | | |
| 8 | A SHEFFIELD WED | | 9 | L | **0-4** | 0-2 | *[Prendergast 60, Eustace 77]* | Barber | Ryan John | Thomson | Anderson | Faulkner | Slough | Ryan Jim | Fern* | Busby | Halom | Aston | Moore |
| | 23/9 | *18,913* | *2* | 10 | | | *Holsgrove 26, Rodrigues 30* | *Grummitt* | *Rodrigues* | *Clements* | *Mullen* | *Holsgrove* | *Craig** | *Henderson* | *Eustace* | *Sunley* | *Prendergast* | *Sissons* | *Swan* |
| | | | | | | | Ref: K Burns | A nightmare performance by Barber gifts two goals to the home side in the first half. The final scoreline exaggerates the merit of the win and takes no account of the number of times the Hatters come close to scoring themselves. Peter Eustace scores the final goal with a cheeky lob. | | | | | | | | | | | |
| 9 | A SWINDON | | 5 | W | 2-0 | 0-0 | Halom 57,62 | **Carrick** | Ryan John | Thomson | Anderson | Faulkner | Slough | Ryan Jim | Fern | Busby | Halom | Aston | |
| | 26/9 | *8,469* | *16* | 12 | | | | *Downsboro'* | *Thomas* | *Trollope* | *Howell* | *Potter* | *Butler* | *Peplow** | *Hubbard* | *Treacy* | *Noble* | *Rogers* | *Moss* |
| | | | | | | | Ref: W Castle | Swindon make a bright start but soon get demoralised when goals are not forthcoming and the Town are then able to dominate. A header from Halom slips through the hands of Peter Downsborough and he doubles the lead five minutes later. Anderson is booked after just ten seconds. | | | | | | | | | | | |
| 10 | H BURNLEY | | 5 | D | 2-2 | 1-1 | Aston 16p, Halom 54 | Carrick | Ryan John | Thomson | Anderson | Faulkner | Slough | Ryan Jim | Fern | Busby | Halom | Aston | |
| | 30/9 | 12,197 | *3* | 13 | | | *James 3, 88* | *Stevenson* | *Docherty* | *Newton* | *Dobson* | *Waldron* | *Thomson* | *Thomas** | *Casper* | *Fletcher* | *Collins* | *James* | *Nulty* |
| | | | | | | | Ref: K Walker | Young keeper Willie Carrick is left helpless when Leighton James scores with a tremendous shot early on. Aston scores from the spot and then a poor back-pass from Colin Waldron is intercepted by Halom to take the lead. The deserved equaliser comes from James towards the end. | | | | | | | | | | | |

| No | Venue / Date | Opponent | Att | Pos | Res / Pts | F-A | H-T | Scorers, Times, and Referees | 1 | 2 | 3 | 4 | 5 | 6 | 7 | 8 | 9 | 10 | 11 | 12 |
|---|---|---|---|---|---|---|---|---|---|---|---|---|---|---|---|---|---|---|---|---|
| 11 | H | BLACKPOOL | | 7 | D | 2-2 | 2-2 | Slough 3, Aston 43 | Barber | Ryan John | Thomson | Anderson | Faulkner | Slough | Ryan Jim | Fern | Busby | Halom | Aston | |
| | 7/10 | | 12,073 | *9* | 14 | | | *Hutchinson 20, Ainscow 25* | *Burridge* | *Hatton* | *Bentley* | *James* | *Suddaby* | *Barton* | *Hutchinson** | *Suddick* | *Parker* | *Ainscow* | *Burns* | *Fuschillo* |
| | | | | | | | | Ref: W Gow | Slough is the first to react when a header from Fern rebounds off the bar but the Seasiders score two quick goals, against the run of play, to take the lead. Aston levels and then 19-year-old keeper, John Burridge, pulls off a tremendous save in injury-time to rob Luton of a deserving win. | | | | | | | | | | | |
| 12 | A | SUNDERLAND | | 5 | W | 2-0 | 2-0 | Halom 25, Ryan Jim 34 | Barber | Ryan John | Thomson | Anderson | Faulkner | Slough | Ryan Jim | Fern | Busby | Halom | Aston* | Hindson |
| | 14/10 | | *13,394* | *14* | 16 | | | | *Montgomery* | *Malone* | *Coleman* | *Horswill* | *Ashurst* | *Porterfield* | *Hughes* | *Kerr* | *Watson* | *Lathan* | *Tueart* | |
| | | | | | | | | Ref: G Hill | The Hatters survive a torrid opening spell at Roker Park with the ball coming back off the woodwork three times. The Town steal the lead on the break when Halom directs a header past Jim Montgomery. Jim Ryan, in acres of space, latches on to a route-one ball to secure the victory. | | | | | | | | | | | |
| 13 | H | PORTSMOUTH | | 3 | D | 2-2 | 2-2 | Halom 30, Busby 44 | Barber | Ryan John | Thomson | Anderson | Faulkner | Slough | Ryan Jim | Fern | Busby | Halom | Aston | |
| | 18/10 | | 9,813 | *16* | 17 | | | *Thomson 3 (og), Price 20* | *Horn* | *Smith* | *Collins* | *Wilson* | *Stephenson* | *Munks* | *Piper* | *Reynolds* | *Price* | *McCann* | *Lewis** | *Hiron* |
| | | | | | | | | Ref: B Daniels | Busby, under pressure from the supporters since losing his goalscoring touch for two months, scores a gem of an equaliser to record the third consecutive home 2-2 draw. Busby nearly seals a victory when, after a brilliant dash down the middle, his drive flashes inches over the bar. | | | | | | | | | | | |
| 14 | H | HULL | | 5 | L | 1-2 | 1-0 | Halom 10 | Barber | Ryan John | Thomson | Anderson | Garner | Slough | Ryan Jim | Fern | Hindson* | Halom | Aston | **Harfield** |
| | 21/10 | | 11,560 | *8* | 17 | | | *Houghton 58, 70* | *Wealands* | *Banks* | *Beardsley* | *Kaye** | *Neill* | *Knighton* | *McGill* | *Houghton* | *Pearson* | *Holme* | *Butler* | *Wilkinson* |
| | | | | | | | | Ref: S Kayley | Defensive errors are blamed for both of the Hull goals, resulting in an hour-long inquest being held after the game in the Town dressing-room. 'Luton were playing it straight up and down the pitch and we could see everything coming,' ventures the Hull skipper, John Kaye, at the end. | | | | | | | | | | | |
| 15 | A | BRISTOL CITY | | 4 | W | 1-0 | 1-0 | Faulkner 12 | Barber | Ryan John | Thomson | Anderson | Faulkner | Garner | Ryan Jim | Slough | Halom | Hindson | Aston | |
| | 28/10 | | *13,562* | *11* | 19 | | | | *Cashley* | *Wilson* | *Sweeney* | *Emanuel** | *Bruton* | *Merrick* | *Ritchie* | *Spiring* | *Galley* | *Gow* | *Bartley* | *Fear* |
| | | | | | | | | Ref: R Lee | Faulkner scores his first goal for the Hatters to record their fifth away win of the season. He goes up for Jim Ryan's curling corner and heads in unchallenged. City, without a home win this season, stage a late rally but the Town defence stands firm, Barber making two tremendous saves. | | | | | | | | | | | |
| 16 | H | SWINDON | | 4 | L | 0-1 | 0-0 | | Barber | Ryan John | Thomson | Anderson* | Faulkner | Garner | Ryan Jim | Slough | Hindson | Halom | Aston | Fern |
| | 4/11 | | 10,596 | *16* | 19 | | | *Treacy 55* | *Downsboro'* | *Thomas* | *Trollope* | *Smart* | *Burrows* | *Potter* | *Peplow* | *Howell* | *Treacy* | *Noble* | *Butler* | |
| | | | | | | | | Ref: B Homewood | Swindon star player Don Rogers is transferred before the game and manager Dave Mackay also leaves the club. The Town control most of the first half with Jim Ryan, Aston and Slough all going close. As the game wears on, Luton run out of ideas and Ray Treacy scores the only goal | | | | | | | | | | | |
| 17 | A | PORTSMOUTH | | 4 | D | 2-2 | 0-2 | Stephenson 63 (og), Fern 66 | Barber | Ryan John | Thomson | Slough | Faulkner | Garner | Ryan Jim* | Fern | Hindson | Halom | Aston | Goodeve |
| | 11/11 | | *7,601* | *18* | 20 | | | *Piper 10, Jennings 13* | *Horn* | *Hand* | *Wilson* | *Piper* | *Stephenson* | *Munks* | *McCann* | *Reynolds* | *Price* | *Hiron* | *Jennings* | |
| | | | | | | | | Ref: T Reynolds | After taking an early two-goal lead, Pompey take their foot off the pedal and the Town, who are without Anderson because he missed the train, are galvanised with the introduction of John Ryan in midfield. The two goals could have been more, but for Graham Horn saving from Slough. | | | | | | | | | | | |
| 18 | A | ASTON VILLA | | 3 | W | 2-0 | 1-0 | Fern 22, Aston 70 | Barber | Ryan John | Thomson | Anderson | Faulkner | Garner | Ryan Jim | Slough | Halom | Fern | Aston | |
| | 18/11 | | ***29,144*** | *4* | 22 | | | | *Cumbes* | *Ross* | *Aitken* | *Rioch* | *Nicholl* | *Turnbull* | *Graydon* | *Evans* | *Lochhead* | *Vowden* | *Anderson** | *McMahon* |
| | | | | | | | | Ref: D Smith | Playing against old colleagues Bruce Rioch and Chris Nicholl, the Hatters enjoy the open spaces of Villa Park and turn in a classic display of counter-attacking in this top-of-the-table clash. Fierce shooting from Rioch threatens to unlock the Town defence but slick passes fuel the win. | | | | | | | | | | | |
| 19 | H | CARLISLE | | 5 | L | 0-1 | 0-1 | | Barber | Ryan John | Thomson | Anderson | Faulkner | Garner | Ryan Jim | Fern | Halom* | Slough | Aston | Goodeve |
| | 25/11 | | 10,091 | *14* | 22 | | | *Owen 23* | *Ross* | *Derrett* | *Gorman* | *O'Neill* | *Winstanley* | *Tiler* | *Train* | *Martin* | *Owen* | *Balderstone* | *Laidlaw* | |
| | | | | | | | | Ref: H Davey | Carlisle take full advantage of the poor home form shown by the Hatters and attack from the start. They look the more dangerous, by far, when in possession and after a superb drive from Bobby Owen opens the scoring, Carlisle frustrate the Town attack with a well-disciplined rearguard. | | | | | | | | | | | |
| 20 | H | QP RANGERS | | 5 | D | 2-2 | 1-2 | Butlin 9, Halom 51 | Barber | Ryan John | Thomson | Slough* | Faulkner | Garner | Ryan Jim | Anderson | **Butlin** | Halom | Aston | Fern |
| | 9/12 | | 13,670 | *3* | 23 | | | *Givens 19, Clement 29* | *Parkes* | *Clement* | *Gillard* | *Venables* | *Mancini* | *Hazell* | *Thomas* | *Francis* | *Delve* | *Bowles* | *Givens* | |
| | | | | | | | | Ref: E Wallace | Barry Butlin scores on his debut for the Town when heading home a corner from Aston in the tenth minute. The Hoops dominate thereafter and 'old-boy' Don Givens gets on the scoresheet. The floodlights go out with the score at 2-2 but, after a 15-minute delay, the early sparkle is lost. | | | | | | | | | | | |
| 21 | H | MILLWALL | | 8 | D | 2-2 | 1-0 | Butlin 6, French 50 | Barber | Shanks | Thomson | Anderson | Garner | Ryan John | Ryan Jim | French | Butlin | Halom | Aston | |
| | 16/12 | | 11,550 | *16* | 24 | | | *Possee 52, Bolland 70p* | *King* | *Bolland* | *Cripps* | *Dorney* | *Kitchener* | *Burnett* | *Brown* | *Possee* | *Wood* | *Dunphy* | *Allder* | |
| | | | | | | | | Ref: R Kirkpatrick | French returns to the side, after a spell behind bars, for his first game in almost three years. He latches onto a long clearance from Barber and steals through the Millwall defence to hit a superb shot past Bryan King. Barber brings down Doug Allder and Bolland equalises from the spot. | | | | | | | | | | | |

| No | Date | Opponent | Att | Pos | Pt | F-A | H-T | Scorers, Times, and Referees | 1 | 2 | 3 | 4 | 5 | 6 | 7 | 8 | 9 | 10 | 11 | 12 sub used |
|---|---|---|---|---|---|---|---|---|---|---|---|---|---|---|---|---|---|---|---|---|
| 22 | A | MIDDLESBROUGH | | 5 | W | 1-0 | 0-0 | Butlin 72 | Barber | Shanks | Thomson | Ryan John | Garner | Moore | Anderson | Fern | Butlin | Halom | Aston | |
| | 23/12 | | *10,122* | *9* | 26 | | | | *Platt* | *Craggs* | *Jones* | *Stiles* | *Maddren* | *Taylor* | *McMordie* | *Gates** | *Mills* | *Hickton* | *Armstrong* | *Smith* |
| | | | | | | | | Ref: R Matthewson | A workmanlike Hatters side grab both points when former Derby striker, Butlin, keeps up his sequence of scoring in every match with his third goal. Barber is called on to make a couple of saves from an attack that appears to have lost its way and wastes most of the chances created. | | | | | | | | | | | |
| 23 | H | SHEFFIELD WED | | 6 | D | 0-0 | 0-0 | | Barber | Shanks | Thomson | Anderson | Garner | Moore | Ryan Jim | Fern | Butlin | Halom | Aston | |
| | 26/12 | | **15,799** | *8* | 27 | | | | *Grummitt* | *Rodrigues* | *Clements* | *Thompson* | *Holsgrove* | *Craig* | *Sunley* | *Eustace* | *Joicey* | *Prendergast* | *Coyle** | *Sissons* |
| | | | | | | | | Ref: N Paget | Town's poor home record is extended against a defence-minded Wednesday. Jim Ryan nearly succeeds in breaking the deadlock when his shot, in the 80th minute, rises just over the bar. The game is held up for two minutes during the second half due to a pitch invasion by warring fans. | | | | | | | | | | | |
| 24 | A | PRESTON | | 6 | L | 0-2 | 0-1 | | Barber | Shanks | Thomson | Anderson | Garner | Moore | Ryan Jim | Ryan John | Butlin | Halom | Aston* | Slough |
| | 30/12 | | *9,638* | *8* | 27 | | | *Wilson 36, Bruce 90* | *Kelly* | *McMahon* | *McNab* | *Bird* | *Hawkins* | *Connor* | *Wilson* | *Spark* | *McIlmoyle* | *Tarbuck* | *Bruce* | |
| | | | | | | | | Ref: V James | The Preston defence, which has conceded twelve goals in the last four games, remains unbeaten against a Luton side which relies on shooting from long range, Anderson going close on five occasions. Alex Bruce secures the win with a late strike, adding to a first-half goal by Wilson. | | | | | | | | | | | |
| 25 | H | ORIENT | | 7 | D | 1-1 | 1-1 | Aston 21 | Barber | Shanks | Thomson | Ryan John | Garner | Moore | Ryan Jim | Anderson* | Butlin | Halom | Aston | Slough |
| | 6/1 | | 8,344 | *20* | 28 | | | *Brisley 24* | *Goddard* | *Arber* | *Wall* | *Hoadley* | *Harris* | *Allen* | *Heppolette* | *Downing* | *Brisley* | *Queen* | *Bowyer* | |
| | | | | | | | | Ref: J Yates | Thomson takes a throw-in which the linesman seems to be signalling the other way and, with the Orient defence standing still, Aston thumps the ball into the net. Brisley scores off the underside of the bar shortly after to earn the O's a well-deserved point in their battle against relegation. | | | | | | | | | | | |
| 26 | A | HUDDERSFIELD | | 6 | W | 2-1 | 1-1 | Butlin 25, Lyon 68 (og) | Barber | Shanks | Thomson | Slough | Garner | Moore | Ryan Jim | Ryan John | Butlin | Hindson | Aston | |
| | 20/1 | | ***3,871*** | *19* | 30 | | | *Hutt 22* | *Poole* | *Clarke* | *Hutt* | *Smith* | *Lyon* | *Nicholson* | *Pugh* | *Fairclough* | *Gowling** | *Lawson* | *Barry* | *Krzywicki* |
| | | | | | | | | Ref: P Reeves | The snow-covered pitch makes the playing conditions treacherous and all three goals are a farce. Hutt swings in a cross which hits the post and goes in, a back-pass from Clarke sticks in the snow with Butlin racing in to score and then Lyon slips, diverting the winner past his own keeper. | | | | | | | | | | | |
| 27 | H | NOTT'M FOREST | | 6 | W | 1-0 | 0-0 | Slough 66 | Barber | Shanks | Thomson | Ryan John | Garner | Moore | Ryan Jim | Hindson | Butlin | Slough | Aston | |
| | 27/1 | | 10,083 | *13* | 32 | | | | *Barron* | *Hindley* | *Winfield* | *Chapman* | *Serella** | *Fraser* | *McIntosh* | *Robertson* | *Martin* | *Galley* | *O'Neill* | *Lyall* |
| | | | | | | | | Ref: D Nippard | Barron blocks a close-range shot from John Ryan but the ball rebounds kindly to Slough, who jabs it home to earn the Hatters their first home win in ten matches. 'Now we have got rid of this hoodoo, we must be in with a good promotion chance,' quips jubilant manager, Harry Haslam. | | | | | | | | | | | |
| 28 | A | BRIGHTON | | 5 | L | 0-2 | 0-0 | | Barber | Shanks* | Thomson | Slough | Garner | Moore | Ryan Jim | Ryan John | Butlin | Hindson | Aston | **Hales** |
| | 10/2 | | *11,404* | *22* | 32 | | | *Beamish 52, 85* | *Hughes* | *Templeman* | *Spearritt* | *Bromley* | *Piper* | *Goodwin* | *Hilton* | *Murray* | *Beamish* | *O'Sullivan* | *Towner** | *Howell* |
| | | | | | | | | Ref: W Gow | The team with the best away record in the Football League lose to a side with a run of 13 consecutive defeats to their name to create the 'shock of the day'. Albion have two youngsters, Tony Towner and Pat Hilton, making their debuts and their zest and enthusiasm seems to lift the side. | | | | | | | | | | | |
| 29 | H | CARDIFF | | 7 | D | 1-1 | 1-0 | Hales 12 | Carrick | Ryan John | Thomson | Slough | Garner | Moore | Ryan Jim | Hales | Butlin | Hindson | Aston | |
| | 17/2 | | 10,422 | *19* | 33 | | | *Woodruff 50* | *Irwin* | *Dwyer* | *Pethard* | *Phillips* | *Murray* | *Morgan* | *Kellock* | *McCullough* | *Woodruff* | *Showers* | *Vincent* | |
| | | | | | | | | Ref: M Lowe | 19-year-old debutant Derek Hales heads an Aston corner against the post and then brilliantly maintains his balance to drive home the rebound. The Luton team appear to be more interested in the upcoming cup-tie against Bolton, and Cardiff level after having the better of the second half. | | | | | | | | | | | |
| 30 | A | MILLWALL | | 8 | L | 2-3 | 0-1 | Aston 65, 70 | **Horn** | Shanks | Thomson | Slough | Garner | Moore | French | Ryan John | Butlin* | Busby | Aston | Goodeve |
| | 26/2 | | *10,504* | *11* | 33 | | | *Bolland 30, 76, Smethurst 46* | *King* | *Brown B* | *Cripps* | *Dorney* | *Kitchener* | *Burnett* | *Brown S* | *Smethurst* | *Wood* | *Bolland* | *Dunphy* | |
| | | | | | | | | Ref: R Perkin | All thoughts of promotion disappear at the Den as the Lions take a two-goal lead. Cup-weary Luton stage a fight-back with two opportunist goals from Aston but Millwall gain the win with a diving header from Bolland. Harry Cripps goes feet first in to Horn and starts a 15-man melee. | | | | | | | | | | | |
| 31 | A | BLACKPOOL | | 8 | D | 1-1 | 0-1 | Ryan Jim 71 | Carrick | Ryan John | Thomson | Shanks | Garner | Moore | Ryan Jim | Anderson* | Hindson | Busby | Aston | Fern |
| | 3/3 | | *6,947* | *7* | 34 | | | *Suddick 10* | *Wood* | *Hatton* | *Bentley* | *Alcock* | *James* | *Suddaby* | *Burns* | *Suddick** | *Rafferty* | *O'Neill* | *Ainscow* | *Tulley* |
| | | | | | | | | Ref: H Williams | In front of the lowest attendance at Bloomfield Road since the War, the home side hang on to a precarious lead. Alan Suddick opens the scoring with a 25-yard free-kick but Jim Ryan levels with a rising drive midway through the second-half. Aston nearly succeeds in inspiring the win. | | | | | | | | | | | |

| No | Date | Opponent / Att | Pos | Res / Pts | F-A | H-T | Scorers, Times, and Referees | 1 | 2 | 3 | 4 | 5 | 6 | 7 | 8 | 9 | 10 | 11 | 12 |
|---|---|---|---|---|---|---|---|---|---|---|---|---|---|---|---|---|---|---|---|
| 32 | H | SUNDERLAND | 6 | W | 1-0 | 1-0 | Shanks 42 | Horn | Ryan John | Thomson | Shanks | Faulkner | Goodeve | Ryan Jim | Anderson | Hales* | Hindson | Fern | Busby |
| | 10/3 | 12,458 | *16* | 36 | | | | *Montgomery* | *Ellison** | *Guthrie* | *Ashurst* | *Watson* | *Young* | *Latham* | *Chambers* | *Halom* | *Porterfield* | *Hamilton* | *Bolton* |
| | | | | | | | Ref: K Styles | This FA Cup quarter-final preview, to be played at Roker Park on Saturday, is a complete nonsense with Luton fielding four reserves and the visitors, six. Jim Montgomery equals the Sunderland appearance record but is beaten when Don Shanks runs onto a through-ball from Hales. | | | | | | | | | | | |
| 33 | H | BRISTOL CITY | 9 | L | 1-3 | 1-0 | Garner 34 | Horn | Shanks | Thomson | Ryan John | Garner | Moore | Fern* | Anderson | Busby | Hindson | Aston | Hales |
| | 24/3 | 7,102 | *11* | 36 | | | *Gow 47, Gillies 55, Fear 68* | *Cashley* | *Sweeney* | *Drysdale* | *Emanuel* | *Rodgers* | *Collier* | *Fear* | *Ritchie* | *Gillies* | *Gow* | *Gould* | |
| | | | | | | | Ref: J Wrennall | The Hatters put up a spirited display in the first half and could have scored three times. City then rip the home defence to shreds after the break and the third, the killer strike, comes when Keith Fear races half the length of the pitch with the ball before beating Town keeper, Graham Horn. | | | | | | | | | | | |
| 34 | A | FULHAM | 9 | W | 1-0 | 1-0 | Fern 16 | Barber | Shanks | Thomson | Ryan John | Faulkner | Goodeve | Ryan Jim | French | Hales | Hindson | Fern | |
| | 27/3 | *7,442* | *7* | 38 | | | | *Mellor* | *Cutbush* | *Callaghan* | *Mullery* | *Went* | *Shrubb* | *Strong* | *Earle* | *Mitchell* | *Pinkney** | *Barratt* | *Lloyd* |
| | | | | | | | Ref: N Burtenshaw | Referee Norman Burtenshaw turns down two Fulham penalty appeals in the space of a minute, the first for a handling offence by Faulkner and then John Mitchell being felled with an elbow by Shanks. Town win with their only attack of the match when Fern heads home from Shanks. | | | | | | | | | | | |
| 35 | A | CARLISLE | 9 | L | 0-2 | 0-2 | | Barber | Shanks | Thomson | Anderson | Faulkner | Goodeve | Ryan Jim | Slough | Hales* | Hindson | Fern | **O'Connor** |
| | 31/3 | *5,517* | *15* | 38 | | | *Gorman 26, Owen 45* | *Ross* | *Carr* | *Gorman* | *O'Neill* | *Winstanley* | *Tiler* | *Train* | *Martin* | *Owen* | *Balderstone* | *Laidlaw* | |
| | | | | | | | Ref: J Goggins | The Brunton Park crowd are entertained to the best Carlisle display since the 6-1 hammering of Preston on Boxing Day. John Gorman swings in a speculative centre which is caught on the wind and drifts in to the net, over the head of Hatters' goalkeeper, Keith Barber, for a freak goal. | | | | | | | | | | | |
| 36 | H | FULHAM | 8 | W | 1-0 | 1-0 | Ryan 22 | Horn | Shanks | Thomson | Anderson | Faulkner | Goodeve | Ryan Jim | French | Hindson | Fern | Aston | |
| | 7/4 | 8,430 | *9* | 40 | | | | *Mellor* | *Cutbush* | *Callaghan* | *Mullery* | *Went* | *Horne* | *Pinkney** | *Earle* | *Mitchell* | *Lloyd* | *Strong* | *Conway* |
| | | | | | | | Ref: H New | The Hatters show more poise and the better ball control against a disjointed defence. Peter Anderson puts Aston away on the left and, from his cross, Jim Ryan hooks in a left-foot volley from the edge of the box. In a final flurry, French lobs over the bar when it appears easier to score. | | | | | | | | | | | |
| 37 | A | HULL | 8 | L | **0-4** | 0-2 | *[Knighton 81]* | Barber | Shanks | Thomson | Anderson | Faulkner | Garner | Ryan Jim | French | Fern | Hindson | Aston | |
| | 10/4 | *5,278* | *14* | 40 | | | *Houghton 35, Kaye 39, Holme 58,* | *McKechnie* | *Banks* | *Lord* | *Kaye* | *Neill* | *Knighton* | *McGill* | *Houghton* | *Pearson* | *Holme** | *Greenwood* | *Butler* |
| | | | | | | | Ref: E Jolly | In the Hatters' worst performance of the season, the Tigers maul the Luton defence and make a mockery of their impressive away record. Alan Garner, deputising for the injured Ken Goodeve, shackles Hull's leading scorer, Stuart Pearson, but is powerless to stop the other forwards. | | | | | | | | | | | |
| 38 | A | QP RANGERS | 10 | L | 0-2 | 0-2 | | Barber | Shanks | Thomson | Anderson | Faulkner | Ryan John | Ryan Jim | French | Busby | Hindson ! | Aston | |
| | 14/4 | *16,471* | *2* | 40 | | | *Mancini 25, Givens 38* | *Parkes* | *Clement** | *Hazell* | *Mancini* | *Watson* | *Venables* | *Francis* | *Leach* | *Thomas* | *Bowles* | *Givens* | *Delve* |
| | | | | | | | Ref: I Jones | The Hatters have three goals disallowed and Aston has a header kicked off the line by Terry Venables; however, the home side are too skilful and, with the win, move to within two points of Division 1 football. In a fit of frustration, Gordon Hindson is sent off for kicking Gerry Francis. | | | | | | | | | | | |
| 39 | H | ASTON VILLA | 10 | D | 0-0 | 0-0 | | Barber | Shanks | Thomson | Anderson | Faulkner | Ryan John | Ryan Jim | French | Busby | Hindson | Aston* | Goodeve |
| | 21/4 | 10,981 | *3* | 41 | | | | *Cumbes* | *Ross* | *Robson* | *Rioch N* | *Nicholl* | *McMahon* | *Little* | *Vowden* | *Lochhead* | *Brown* | *Hamilton* | |
| | | | | | | | Ref: M Sinclair | Neither goalkeeper has much to do in this typical 'end-of-season' game. John Robson nearly scores an own-goal when, under pressure from Busby, he plays a hasty back-pass which Jim Cumbes has to dive full length to save. French crashes a drive against the post in the second half. | | | | | | | | | | | |
| 40 | H | MIDDLESBROUGH | 11 | L | 0-1 | 0-1 | | Barber | Shanks | Thomson | Anderson | Faulkner | Goodeve | Ryan Jim | Ryan John | Busby* | Hindson | French | Fern |
| | 23/4 | **6,177** | *5* | 41 | | | *Maddren 7* | *Platt* | *Creamer* | *Spraggon* | *Craggs* | *Boam* | *Maddren* | *Gates* | *Mills* | *Hickton* | *Armstrong* | *Foggon* | |
| | | | | | | | Ref: T Spencer | On a miserable afternoon, the last home game of the season is played in front of the lowest league attendance at Kenilworth Road since 1967. Luton keeper, Barber, is at fault for a soft goal from Willie Maddren, whilst his opposite number, Jim Platt, performs heroics in the second half. | | | | | | | | | | | |
| 41 | A | BURNLEY | 12 | L | 0-3 | 0-0 | | Barber | Shanks | Thomson | Anderson | Faulkner | Goodeve | Ryan Jim | Ryan John | Fern | Hindson | Hales | |
| | 24/4 | *17,689* | *1* | 41 | | | *James 62, Thomson 67, Collins 73* | *Stevenson* | *Ingham* | *Newton* | *Dobson* | *Waldron* | *Thomson* | *Nulty* | *Casper** | *Fletcher* | *Collins* | *James* | *Hankin* |
| | | | | | | | Ref: J Williams | The Town attempt to frustrate their rivals but do not have a worthwhile shot on target all evening. Once Burnley score, the floodgates open and Doug Collins is their midfield general behind every move, although his off-the-ball foul on Anderson in the third minute is a dismissal offence. | | | | | | | | | | | |
| 42 | A | OXFORD | 12 | L | 1-2 | 1-1 | Slough 30 | Horn | Shanks | Thomson | Slough | Faulkner | Goodeve | Ryan Jim | Anderson | Busby | Hindson* | O'Connor | **Price** |
| | 28/4 | *6,318* | *7* | 41 | | | *Cassidy 32, Roberts 74* | *Burton* | *Light* | *Roberts* | *Clarke C* | *Shuker* | *Atkinson* | *Aylott* | *Clarke D* | *Cassidy* | *Curran* | *Gough** | *Skeen* |
| | Home | Away | | | | | Ref: R Raby | Anderson twice goes close before the Town take the lead through a 25-yard strike from Slough. On a bone-hard pitch, both sides struggle in an untidy match. Oxford finally grind out a result when Welsh international, Dave Roberts, hits a simple goal and clinches both points for his side. | | | | | | | | | | | |
| Average | 10,643 | 11,156 | | | | | | | | | | | | | | | | | |

# LEAGUE DIVISION 2 (CUP-TIES) Manager: Harry Haslam SEASON 1972-73

| League Cup | | | F-A | H-T | Scorers, Times, and Referees | 1 | 2 | 3 | 4 | 5 | 6 | 7 | 8 | 9 | 10 | 11 | 12 sub used |
|---|---|---|---|---|---|---|---|---|---|---|---|---|---|---|---|---|---|
| 2 A | BIRMINGHAM | 7 D | 1-1 | 1-0 | Anderson 8 | Barber | Ryan John | Thomson | Anderson | Faulkner | Garner | Ryan Jim | Fern | Busby | Halom | Aston | |
| 5/9 | *20,962* | *1:19* | | | *Latchford 54* | *Cooper* | *Howitt* | *Want* | *Campbell* | *Hynd* | *Harland* | *Pendrey* | *Francis* | *Latchford* | *Hope* | *Taylor** | *Burns* |
| | | | | | Ref: C Fallon | The Town take a shock lead when Anderson heads an indirect free-kick from Aston past Cooper. Birmingham equalise when Fern inadvertently kicks the ball against Jim Ryan and Gary Pendrey picks up the rebound. He passes to Latchford, who hammers the ball into the roof of the net. | | | | | | | | | | | |
| 2R H | BIRMINGHAM | 9 D | 1-1 | 0-0 | Aston 65 | Barber | Ryan John | Thomson | Anderson | Faulkner | Garner | Ryan Jim | Fern | Busby | Halom | Aston | |
| 13/9 | 13,806 | *1:15* | *aet* | | *Campbell 88* | *Latchford D* | *Carroll* | *Pendrey* | *Campbell* | *Hynd* | *Harland* | *Burns* | *Francis* | *Latchford R* | *Hope** | *Hatton* | *Taylor* |
| | | | | | Ref: C Thomas | The Hatters take the lead after Birmingham goalkeeper, Dave Latchford, parries a shot from Halom and John Aston pounces to slam the ball into the net. A late goal from Alan Campbell dashes the hopes of a Town victory, sending the match into an inconclusive period of extra-time. | | | | | | | | | | | |
| 2 A | BIRMINGHAM | 4 L | 0-1 | 0-0 | | Barber | Ryan John | Thomson | Anderson | Faulkner | Garner* | Ryan Jim | Fern | Busby | Halom | Aston | Slough |
| RR 19/9 | *11,451* | *1:18* | | | *Francis 77* | *Latchford D* | *Carroll* | *Pendrey* | *Campbell* | *Hynd* | *Page* | *Burns* | *Francis* | *Latchford R* | *Hope* | *Hatton* | |
| | (at Northampton) | | | | Ref: E Jolly | Three Birmingham players are booked as they try to stifle the supremacy of the Luton forwards, who give them the run-around in a game where the Town should have scored a hatful of goals. Trevor Francis nets to make the final scoreline a mockery of all that has gone before. | | | | | | | | | | | |

| FA Cup | | | F-A | H-T | Scorers, Times, and Referees | 1 | 2 | 3 | 4 | 5 | 6 | 7 | 8 | 9 | 10 | 11 | 12 sub used |
|---|---|---|---|---|---|---|---|---|---|---|---|---|---|---|---|---|---|
| 3 H | CREWE | 7 W | 2-0 | 0-0 | Ryan Jim 71, Butlin 77 | Barber | Shanks | Thomson | Ryan John | Garner | Moore | Ryan Jim | Litt* | Butlin | Slough | Aston | Hindson |
| 13/1 | 9,411 | *4:16* | | | | *Crudgington* | *Lowry* | *Kelley* | *Bradshaw* | *Nicholls* | *Peat* | *Tewley** | *Nicholl* | *Riley* | *Humphreys* | *Gillett* | *Fairhurst* |
| | | | | | Ref: W Castle | All-out attack is the order of the day from manager Harry Haslam, but it is the visitors who are unlucky not to be two goals up at the break. The deadlock is broken when Don Shanks provides a through-ball for Jim Ryan to head home, much to the relief of players and supporters alike. | | | | | | | | | | | |
| 4 A | NEWCASTLE | 6 W | 2-0 | 2-0 | Aston 28,44 | Barber | Shanks | Thomson | Slough | Garner | Moore | Ryan Jim | Ryan John | Butlin | Hindson | Aston | |
| 3/2 | 42,170 | *1:6* | | | | *McFaul* | *Craig* | *Clark* | *Nattrass* | *Howard* | *Moncur* | *Barrowclough* | *Smith* | *MacDonald* | *Tudor* | *Hodgson** | *Reid* |
| | | | | | Ref: J Williams | Aston scores twice before the interval to set up a shock result. Newcastle huff and puff in the second period but find John Moore, in particular, impassable. After the game, manager Harry Haslam says: 'I always thought we'd win - we had more trouble beating Crewe in the last round.' | | | | | | | | | | | |
| 5 A | BOLTON | 7 W | 1-0 | 1-0 | Garner 42 | Carrick | Shanks | Thomson | Slough | Garner | Moore | Ryan Jim | Ryan John | Butlin | Hindson | Aston | |
| 24/2 | 39,556 | *3:1* | | | | *Wright* | *Ritson* | *McAllister* | *Rimmer* | *Jones P* | *Waldron* | *Nicholson* | *Jones G* | *Greaves* | *Lee* | *Phillips* | |
| | | | | | Ref: D Smith | Bolton enter this match with an unbeaten run of 26 home games behind them but it is the Hatters, the 'away team' specialists, who earn the narrow victory. A perfectly timed goal comes when Trotters' keeper, Charlie Wright, is unable to reach an Aston corner and Garner heads in. | | | | | | | | | | | |
| QF A | SUNDERLAND | 6 L | 0-2 | 0-0 | | Barber | Ryan John | Thomson | Shanks | Garner | Moore | Ryan Jim | Anderson | Busby | Hindson | Aston* | Hales |
| 17/3 | 53,151 | *2:16* | | | *Watson 55, Guthrie 78* | *Montgomery* | *Malone* | *Guthrie* | *Horswill* | *Watson* | *Pitt* | *Kerr* | *Hughes* | *Halom* | *Porterfield* | *Tueart* | |
| | | | | | Ref: J Taylor | An anti-climax for the Town who, on the day, are second best in every department to a side they have beaten twice already this season. In a dangerously full Roker Park, the tide of expectation threatens to overwhelm the injury-hit Hatters team, who put in a lacklustre performance. | | | | | | | | | | | |

| | Home | | | | | | Away | | | | | |
|---|---|---|---|---|---|---|---|---|---|---|---|---|
| | P | W | D | L | F | A | W | D | L | F | A | Pts |
| 1 Burnley | 42 | 13 | 6 | 2 | 44 | 18 | 11 | 8 | 2 | 28 | 17 | 62 |
| 2 QP Rangers | 42 | 16 | 4 | 1 | 54 | 13 | 8 | 9 | 4 | 27 | 24 | 61 |
| 3 Aston Villa | 42 | 12 | 5 | 4 | 27 | 17 | 6 | 9 | 6 | 24 | 30 | 50 |
| 4 Middlesbro | 42 | 12 | 6 | 3 | 29 | 15 | 5 | 7 | 9 | 17 | 28 | 47 |
| 5 Bristol City | 42 | 10 | 7 | 4 | 34 | 18 | 7 | 5 | 9 | 29 | 33 | 46 |
| 6 Sunderland | 42 | 12 | 6 | 3 | 35 | 17 | 5 | 6 | 10 | 24 | 32 | 46 |
| 7 Blackpool | 42 | 12 | 6 | 3 | 37 | 17 | 6 | 4 | 11 | 19 | 34 | 46 |
| 8 Oxford | 42 | 14 | 2 | 5 | 36 | 18 | 5 | 5 | 11 | 16 | 25 | 45 |
| 9 Fulham | 42 | 11 | 6 | 4 | 32 | 16 | 5 | 6 | 10 | 26 | 33 | 44 |
| 10 Sheffield Wed | 42 | 14 | 4 | 3 | 40 | 20 | 3 | 6 | 12 | 19 | 35 | 44 |
| 11 Millwall | 42 | 12 | 5 | 4 | 33 | 18 | 4 | 5 | 12 | 22 | 29 | 42 |
| 12 LUTON TOWN | 42 | 6 | 9 | 6 | 24 | 23 | 9 | 2 | 10 | 20 | 30 | 41 |
| 13 Hull | 42 | 9 | 7 | 5 | 39 | 22 | 5 | 5 | 11 | 25 | 37 | 40 |
| 14 Nott'm Forest | 42 | 12 | 5 | 4 | 32 | 18 | 2 | 7 | 12 | 15 | 34 | 40 |
| 15 Orient | 42 | 11 | 6 | 4 | 33 | 18 | 1 | 6 | 14 | 16 | 35 | 36 |
| 16 Swindon | 42 | 8 | 9 | 4 | 28 | 23 | 2 | 7 | 12 | 18 | 37 | 36 |
| 17 Portsmouth | 42 | 7 | 6 | 8 | 21 | 22 | 5 | 5 | 11 | 21 | 37 | 35 |
| 18 Carlisle | 42 | 10 | 5 | 6 | 40 | 24 | 1 | 7 | 13 | 10 | 28 | 34 |
| 19 Preston | 42 | 6 | 8 | 7 | 19 | 25 | 5 | 4 | 12 | 18 | 39 | 34 |
| 20 Cardiff | 42 | 11 | 4 | 6 | 32 | 21 | 0 | 7 | 14 | 11 | 37 | 33 |
| 21 Huddersfield | 42 | 7 | 9 | 5 | 21 | 20 | 1 | 8 | 12 | 15 | 36 | 33 |
| 22 Brighton | 42 | 7 | 8 | 6 | 32 | 31 | 1 | 5 | 15 | 14 | 52 | 29 |
| | 924 | 232 | 133 | 97 | 722 | 434 | 97 | 133 | 232 | 434 | 722 | 924 |

Odds & ends

Double wins: (4) Fulham, Huddersfield, Nott'm Forest, Sunderland.
Double losses: (3) Carlisle, Hull, Oxford.

Won from behind: (2) Brighton (h), Huddersfield (a).
Lost from in front: (4) Bristol City (h), Cardiff (a), Hull (h), Oxford (a).

High spots: Reaching the FA Cup quarter-finals for the first time since 1959.
Second only to champions Burnley in the total number of away wins.
The return of Graham French.

Low spots: Only six home wins.
Losing to Birmingham City in the League Cup.
Going out to Sunderland in the FA Cup, having beaten them twice in the league.
Losing the last five away games.
Losing new signing Barry Butlin through injury after just a few games.

Player of the Year: Bobby Thomson.
Ever-presents: Bobby Thomson.
Hat-tricks: (0).
Leading Scorer: John Aston (12).

| | Appearances | | | | | | Goals | | | |
|---|---|---|---|---|---|---|---|---|---|---|
| | Lge | *Sub* | LC | *Sub* | FAC | *Sub* | Lge | LC | FAC | Tot |
| Anderson, Peter | **34** | | 3 | | 1 | | **1** | 1 | | **2** |
| Aston, John | **36** | | 3 | | 4 | | **9** | 1 | 2 | **12** |
| Barber, Keith | **33** | | 3 | | 3 | | | | | |
| Busby, Viv | **20** | *1* | 3 | | 1 | | **2** | | | **2** |
| Butlin, Barry | **11** | | | | 3 | | **4** | | 1 | **5** |
| Carrick, Willie | **4** | | | | 1 | | | | | |
| Faulkner, John | **29** | | 3 | | | | **1** | | | **1** |
| Fern, Rodney | **26** | *4* | 3 | | | | **4** | | | **4** |
| French, Graham | **8** | | | | | | **1** | | | **1** |
| Garner, Alan | **27** | | 3 | | 4 | | **1** | | 1 | **2** |
| Goodeve, Ken | **7** | *4* | | | | | | | | |
| Hales, Derek | **5** | *2* | | | | *1* | **1** | | | **1** |
| Halom, Vic | **25** | | 3 | | | | **10** | | | **10** |
| Harfield, Les | | *1* | | | | | | | | |
| Hindson, Gordon | **20** | *1* | | | 3 | *1* | | | | |
| Horn, Graham | **5** | | | | | | | | | |
| Litt, Steve | | | | | 1 | | | | | |
| Moore, John | **11** | *1* | | | 4 | | | | | |
| O'Connor, Phil | **1** | *1* | | | | | | | | |
| Price, Paul | | *1* | | | | | | | | |
| Ryan, Jim | **39** | | 3 | | 4 | | **4** | | 1 | **5** |
| Ryan, John | **36** | | 3 | | 4 | | | | | |
| Shanks, Don | **22** | | | | 4 | | **1** | | | **1** |
| Slough, Alan | **21** | *5* | | *1* | 3 | | **3** | | | **3** |
| Thomson, Bobby | **42** | | 3 | | 4 | | | | | |
| (own-goals) | | | | | | | **2** | | | **2** |
| **25 players used** | **462** | ***21*** | **33** | ***1*** | **44** | ***2*** | **44** | **2** | **5** | **51** |

# LEAGUE DIVISION 2 — Manager: Harry Haslam — SEASON 1973-74

| No | Date | | Att | Pos | Pt | F-A | H-T | Scorers, Times, and Referees | 1 | 2 | 3 | 4 | 5 | 6 | 7 | 8 | 9 | 10 | 11 | 12 sub used |
|---|---|---|---|---|---|---|---|---|---|---|---|---|---|---|---|---|---|---|---|---|
| 1 | A | NOTT'M FOREST | | | L | **0-4** | 0-2 | *[McKenzie 89]* | Barber | Shanks | Thomson | Garner | Faulkner | Anderson | Ryan, Jim | Ryan, John | Butlin | **Cruse*** | Aston | **Finney** |
| | 25/8 | | *10,792* | | 0 | | | *Jackson 12, 37p, Martin 48,* | *Barron* | *O'Kane* | *Winfield* | *Serella* | *Cottam* | *Jackson* | *McKenzie* | *Dennehy* | *O'Neill* | *Martin* | *Lyall* | |
| | | | | | | | | Ref: R Raby | The Hatters get off to a disastrous start to the new season and Forest are made to look like world-beaters by a lethargic-looking Luton. Tommy Jackson scores with a free-kick from the edge of the area and the remainder of the game is used as a shooting practice session by the home side. | | | | | | | | | | | |
| 2 | H | CARLISLE | | | W | **6-1** | 6-0 | Finney 13, 20, Anderson 15, 25, | Horn | Shanks | Thomson | Anderson | Faulkner | Garner | Ryan, Jim | Ryan, John | Butlin | Finney | Aston | |
| | 1/9 | | 7,231 | | 2 | | | *Owen 64* [Aston 22, Butlin 36] | *Ross* | *Carr* | *Gorman* | *Ternent* | *Green* | *Winstanley* | *Train** | *Owen* | *Clarke* | *Laidlaw* | *Martin* | *Delgado* |
| | | | | | | | | Ref: D Nippard | What a difference a week makes in football. The Hatters score at will, led by new signing from Crusaders, Tom Finney. Luton are 6-0 in front at the interval with Aston's volley the pick of the bunch. Understandably, the Town are unable to continue the onslaught in the second period. | | | | | | | | | | | |
| 3 | A | BRISTOL CITY | | | W | 3-1 | 2-1 | Aston 2, Ryan John 3, Finney 47 | Horn | Shanks | Thomson | Anderson | Faulkner | Garner | Ryan, Jim | Ryan, John | Butlin | Finney | Aston | |
| | 8/9 | | *12,208* | | 4 | | | *Gould 38p* | *Cashley* | *Sweeney* | *Merrick* | *Emanuel* | *Rodgers** | *Collier* | *Tainton* | *Ritchie* | *Gould* | *Gow* | *Fear* | *Drysdale* |
| | | | | | | | | Ref: R Perkin | It seems like Carlisle all over again as the Town take a two-goal lead in the opening three minutes. City eventually settle down, Bobby Gould scoring from the spot before half-time after Trevor Tainton is fouled in the area. Tom Finney secures the win when latching on to a Butlin pass. | | | | | | | | | | | |
| 4 | A | NOTTS CO | | 9 | D | 1-1 | 1-0 | Finney 23 | Horn | Shanks | Thomson | Anderson | Faulkner | Garner | Ryan, Jim | Ryan, John | Butlin | Finney | Aston | |
| | 11/9 | | *8,509* | *17* | 5 | | | *Bradd 54* | *McManus* | *Brindley* | *Worthington* | *Masson* | *Needham* | *Stubbs* | *Nixon* | *Randall* | *Bradd* | *Probert* | *Mann* | |
| | | | | | | | | Ref: J Wrennall | Finney heads Luton into the lead when getting on the end of a Jim Ryan free-kick and the Meadow Lane crowd show their displeasure when the teams leave the pitch at half-time. County step up the pace after the interval and equalise when Les Bradd holds off Faulkner to fire home. | | | | | | | | | | | |
| 5 | H | PORTSMOUTH | | 9 | D | 3-3 | 2-1 | Thomson 33, Garner 35, Finney 75 | Horn | Shanks | Thomson | Anderson | Faulkner | Garner | Ryan, Jim | Ryan, John | Butlin | Finney | Aston | |
| | 15/9 | | 11,552 | *19* | 6 | | | *Kellard 17, Lewis 56p, Davies 63* | *Tilsed* | *Roberts* | *Wilson* | *Piper* | *Stephenson* | *Hand* | *Marinello* | *Kellard* | *Davies* | *Lewis* | *Hiron* | |
| | | | | | | | | Ref: W Hall | Pompey claim that their reward of a point did not match their effort. Finney is about to be substituted when he squares the game at 3-3. It was later discovered that Ron Tilsed, in the Portsmouth goal, had broken his arm just before this final goal but had bravely completed the match. | | | | | | | | | | | |
| 6 | A | SUNDERLAND | | 7 | W | 1-0 | 1-0 | Butlin 35 | Horn | Shanks | Thomson | Anderson | Faulkner | Garner | Ryan, Jim | Ryan, John | Butlin | Finney | Aston | |
| | 22/9 | | ***27,334*** | *16* | 8 | | | | *Montgomery* | *Malone* | *Bolton* | *Horswill** | *Watson* | *Pitt* | *Kerr* | *Hughes* | *Halom* | *Porterfield* | *Tueart* | *Young* |
| | | | | | | | | Ref: R Porterhouse | FA Cup holders, Sunderland, are still seeking their first home win of the season and, although they enjoy more of the game, Horn is only called upon to deal with the occasional cross. Thomson fires in a fierce shot which Jim Montgomery is unable to hold and Butlin forces the ball home. | | | | | | | | | | | |
| 7 | H | BLACKPOOL | | 3 | W | 3-0 | 2-0 | Butlin 13, 23, Anderson 47 | Horn | Shanks | Thomson | Anderson | Faulkner | Garner | Ryan, Jim | Ryan, John | Butlin* | Finney | Aston | **Holmes** |
| | 29/9 | | 10,365 | *17* | 10 | | | | *Wood* | *Hatton* | *Bentley* | *Alcock* | *James* | *Suddaby* | *Burns* | *Suddick* | *Davies* | *Rafferty* | *Walsh** | *Curtis* |
| | | | | | | | | Ref: I Jones | In addition to the three goals scored, the Hatters have a further two efforts disallowed for offside. Blackpool defender, Bill Bentley is carried off with concussion and, with the substitute already on the pitch, the visitors are forced to play the remainder of the match with only ten men. | | | | | | | | | | | |
| 8 | A | CRYS PALACE | | 4 | W | 2-1 | 0-0 | Anderson 51, Butlin 61 | Horn | Shanks | Thomson | Anderson | Faulkner | Garner | Hindson | Ryan, John | Butlin | Finney | Aston | |
| | 6/10 | | *20,322* | *21* | 12 | | | *Rogers 58* | *Hammond* | *Mulligan* | *Taylor* | *Cannon* | *Barry* | *Jeffries* | *Cooke** | *Possee* | *Whittle* | *Tambling* | *Rogers* | *Swindlehurst* |
| | | | | | | | | Ref: K Styles | The Hatters do not have to over-exert themselves against a Palace side who have yet to win a game this season. Anderson hits the opening goal from an Aston free-kick but Don Rogers levels soon after. Butlin heads the winning goal minutes later, the Town defence holding on for the win. | | | | | | | | | | | |
| 9 | H | SWINDON | | 2 | W | 2-1 | 2-1 | Aston 20p, Anderson 44 | Horn | Shanks | Thomson | Anderson | Faulkner | Garner | Ryan, Jim* | Ryan, John | Butlin | Cruse | Aston | Hindson |
| | 13/10 | | 10,732 | *22* | 14 | | | *Jenkins 22* | *Allan* | *Thomas* | *Trollope* | *Butler* | *Burrows* | *Stroud* | *Moss* | *McGovern* | *Treacy* | *Legge* | *Jenkins* | |
| | | | | | | | | Ref: A Grey | In a game packed with skill, the Hatters force four corners in the first two minutes of the match. The deadlock is broken when Kenny Stroud handles a long throw from Garner and Aston converts from the spot. Tom Jenkins equalises and Anderson heads home a Jim Ryan free-kick. | | | | | | | | | | | |
| 10 | A | ORIENT | | 5 | L | 0-2 | 0-0 | | Barber | Shanks | Thomson | Anderson | Faulkner | Garner | Ryan, Jim | Ryan, John | Butlin | **West** | Aston | |
| | 20/10 | | *11,135* | *6* | 14 | | | *Queen 67, Fairbrother 82* | *Jackson* | *Payne* | *Downing* | *Allen* | *Hoadley* | *Walley* | *Fairbrother* | *Brisley* | *Bullock* | *Queen* | *Heppolette* | |
| | | | | | | | | Ref: R Challis | The biggest crowd at Brisbane Road for two years enjoys 90 minutes of sustained aggression from the O's. The Town are, for once, second best in all areas and new signing from Burnley, Alan West, has little chance to shine. Barber is kept busy all afternoon, making several daring saves. | | | | | | | | | | | |

| | | | | | | | | | | | | | | | | | | | | |
|---|---|---|---|---|---|---|---|---|---|---|---|---|---|---|---|---|---|---|---|---|
| 11 | H | HULL | | 6 | D | 2-2 | 2-2 | Anderson 28, Butlin 35 | Barber | Shanks | Thomson | Anderson | Faulkner | Garner | Ryan, Jim | Finney | Butlin | West | Aston | |
| 27/10 | | | 11,408 | *10* | 15 | | | *Greenwood 42, Lord 44* | *Wealands* | *Banks* | *Devries* | *Blampey* | *Deere* | *Galvin* | *Hawley* | *Lord* | *Pearson* | *Wagstaff* | *Greenwood* | |
| | | | | | | | | Ref: R Lee | Hull fight back to level after the Town have taken a two-goal lead and are fast becoming a bogey side. Anderson converts from a West cross, followed shortly afterwards by a Butlin header from an Aston corner. Concerns are expressed by the way in which the two goals are conceded. | | | | | | | | | | | |
| 12 | A | MIDDLESBROUGH | | 11 | L | 1-2 | 1-0 | Butlin 32 | Barber | Shanks | Thomson | Anderson | Faulkner | Garner | Ryan, Jim | Finney | Butlin | West | Aston | |
| 3/11 | | | *22,590* | *1* | 15 | | | *Foggon 51, Armstrong 55* | *Platt* | *Craggs* | *Spraggon* | *McAndrew* | *Boam** | *Maddren* | *Murdoch* | *Foggon* | *Smith* | *Hickton* | *Armstrong* | *Mills* |
| | | | | | | | | Ref: M Lowe | Butlin gives the Hatters a deserved lead against the team currently in top spot in the division. A half-time salvo by Boro manager, Jack Charlton, does the trick for the home side and they quickly score two goals although Finney nearly gains a point when hitting the post in the final minute. | | | | | | | | | | | |
| 13 | H | BOLTON | | 8 | W | 2-1 | 0-1 | Ryan Jim 55, McAllister 87 (og) | Horn | Shanks | Thomson | Anderson | Faulkner | Garner | Ryan, Jim | Finney | Butlin* | West | Aston | Cruse |
| 10/11 | | | 9,528 | *17* | 17 | | | *Whatmore 37* | *Siddall* | *Ritson* | *McAllister* | *Rimmer* | *Jones P* | *Waldron* | *Nicholson* | *Jones G* | *Greaves* | *Whatmore** | *Darling* | *Lee* |
| | | | | | | | | Ref: W Castle | Butlin suffers a fractured jaw in the 32nd minute which is to keep him out for several weeks. Aston has a spot-kick saved by Barry Siddall, who repeats the feat five minutes later from Jim Ryan, but is unable to prevent him from scoring from the rebound. An own-goal settles the game. | | | | | | | | | | | |
| 14 | A | CARDIFF | | 7 | D | 0-0 | 0-0 | | Horn | Shanks | Thomson | Anderson | Faulkner | Garner | Ryan, Jim | Cruse* | **Sims** | West | Aston | Fern |
| 14/11 | | | *5,999* | *20* | 18 | | | | *Irwin* | *Dwyer* | *Bell* | *Impey* | *Murray* | *Phillips* | *Villars* | *McInch* | *Showers* | *Woodruff* | *Reece** | *Vincent* |
| | | | | | | | | Ref: J Williams | Lowly Cardiff, trying to impress their new manager, Frank O'Farrell, deserve both points but have to settle for just the one after a splendid display from Luton goalkeeper, Horn, in keeping out shots from McInch, Reece and Woodruff. The Town do not have one worthwhile attack. | | | | | | | | | | | |
| 15 | H | SHEFFIELD WED | | 6 | W | 2-1 | 2-1 | Aston 14, Sims 40 | Horn | Shanks | Thomson | Anderson | Faulkner | Garner | Ryan, Jim | Fern | Sims | West | Aston | |
| 17/11 | | | 9,543 | *17* | 20 | | | *Joicey 43* | *Springett* | *Rodrigues* | *Shaw* | *Thompson* | *Kent* | *Craig* | *Henderson* | *Knighton* | *Joicey* | *Prendergast* | *Potts* | |
| | | | | | | | | Ref: R Crabb | The Town maintain their unbeaten home record with a workmanlike performance. Sims, a loan signing from Derby, makes his home debut and, after weathering some vigorous tackles, scores the second goal with a left-foot drive. Brian Joicey has the chance to win a point but hits the bar. | | | | | | | | | | | |
| 16 | A | PRESTON | | 5 | D | 2-2 | 1-2 | Aston 29, Fern 51 | Horn | Shanks | Thomson | Anderson | Faulkner | Garner | Ryan, Jim | Fern | Sims* | West | Aston | Ryan, John |
| 24/11 | | | *10,279* | *13* | 21 | | | *Young 23, 38* | *Brown* | *McMahon* | *Snookes* | *Sadler* | *Bird* | *Stiles** | *Lamb* | *Spark* | *Bruce* | *Burns* | *Young* | *Carrick* |
| | | | | | | | | Ref: P Baldwin | The Hatters dominate but find themselves twice in arrears. Alex Bruce is brought down in the area and Neil Young scores from the rebound after his penalty is blocked. Aston levels but Preston, attacking on the break, get a second when Young is again on target. Fern earns the draw. | | | | | | | | | | | |
| 17 | H | WEST BROM | | 6 | L | 0-2 | 0-0 | | Horn | Shanks | Thomson | Ryan, John | Faulkner | Garner | Ryan, Jim | **Husband** | Fern | West | Aston | |
| 1/12 | | | 10,192 | *7* | 21 | | | *Shaw 66, Hartford 84* | *Latchford* | *Nisbet* | *Wilson* | *Cantello* | *Wile* | *Robertson* | *Johnston* | *Brown* | *Mayo** | *Hartford* | *Glover* | *Shaw* |
| | | | | | | | | Ref: E Jolly | Jim Husband, a new £70,000 signing from Everton, makes his debut on the frozen Kenilworth Road pitch, but it is substitute David Shaw who opens the scoring after Horn fails to hold an Alan Glover shot. Asa Hartford gets the second, inflicting Town's first home defeat of the season. | | | | | | | | | | | |
| 18 | A | MILLWALL | | 3 | W | 1-0 | 0-0 | Butlin 50 | Horn | Shanks | Thomson | Anderson | Faulkner | Garner | Ryan, Jim | Husband | Butlin | West | Aston | |
| 8/12 | | | *6,976* | *17* | 23 | | | | *King* | *Donaldson* | *Jones* | *Dorney* | *Kitchener* | *Allder* | *Brown** | *Clark* | *Wood* | *Kelly* | *Hill* | *Bolland* |
| | | | | | | | | Ref: J Hunting | Butlin returns to the side after a one-month absence and scores the only goal of the game when neatly heading a cross by Shanks past Bryan King. Millwall teenager, Gordon Hill, misses two late chances and Brian Clark hits the post late on but the Hatters survive for a deserved win. | | | | | | | | | | | |
| 19 | H | CARDIFF | | 3 | W | 1-0 | 0-0 | Ryan Jim 47 | Horn | Shanks | Thomson | Anderson | Faulkner | Garner | Ryan, Jim | Husband | Butlin | West | Aston | |
| 12/12 | | | 7,139 | *16* | 25 | | | | *Irwin* | *Dwyer* | *Bell* | *Powell* | *Murray* | *Woodruff* | *Farrington* | *McCulloch* | *Reece* | *Carlin** | *Phillips* | *Smith* |
| | | | | | | | | Ref: P Reeves | The 'three-day week' and regular power cuts combine to persuade the club to hire a generator in order that this game may go ahead. After 16 minutes play, the generator fails and a 40-minute delay ensues whilst the faulty temperature gauge is repaired. Ryan's goal earns the two points. | | | | | | | | | | | |
| 20 | H | ASTON VILLA | | 2 | W | 1-0 | 0-0 | Anderson 53 | Horn | Shanks | Thomson | Anderson | Faulkner | Garner | Ryan, Jim | Fern | Butlin | West | Aston | |
| 15/12 | | | 10,020 | *12* | 27 | | | | *Cumbes* | *Gidman* | *Aitken* | *Hockey* | *Nicholl* | *Ross* | *McMahon* | *Brown* | *Rioch* | *Hamilton* | *Little* | |
| | | | | | | | | Ref: M Sinclair | The Hatters move up to second place in the table after securing the win. Peter Anderson heads home a corner from Aston for the only goal but Villa make a game of it with veteran full-back, Charlie Aitken, equalling the appearance record of Billy Walker, creating three good chances. | | | | | | | | | | | |
| 21 | A | BLACKPOOL | | 3 | L | 0-3 | 0-0 | | Horn | Shanks | Thomson | Anderson | Faulkner | Garner | Ryan, Jim | Husband | Butlin | West | Aston | |
| 22/12 | | | *7,796* | *4* | 27 | | | *Burns 46, 56, 71* | *Burridge* | *Curtis* | *James* | *Suddaby* | *Hatton* | *Alcock* | *Suddick* | *Bentley* | *Burns* | *Ainscow** | *Dyson* | *Walsh* |
| | | | | | | | | Ref: P Willis | The Town find ex-Skelmersdale forward, Micky Burns, in top form as he scores a hat-trick. The Hatters have much the better of the first half but face an uphill struggle after Burns scores straight from the kick-off after the break. Harry Haslam puts it down to 'just one of those days'. | | | | | | | | | | | |

| No | Date | Att | Pos | Pt | F-A | H-T | Scorers, Times, and Referees | 1 | 2 | 3 | 4 | 5 | 6 | 7 | 8 | 9 | 10 | 11 | 12 sub used |
|---|---|---|---|---|---|---|---|---|---|---|---|---|---|---|---|---|---|---|---|
| 22 | H FULHAM | | 3 | D | 1-1 | 1-0 | Fraser 8 (og) | Horn | Shanks | Thomson | Anderson | Faulkner | Garner | Ryan, Jim | Husband | Butlin | West | Aston | |
| | 26/12 | 15,259 | *10* | 28 | | | *Conway John 79* | *Mellor* | *Cutbush* | *Fraser* | *Mullery* | *Lacy* | *Dunne* | *Conway J'n* | *Conway Jim* | *Busby* | *Slough* | *Barrett* | |
| | | | | | | | Ref: K Baker | A valuable home point is lost when an early lead is surrendered to a persistent Fulham side. The Cottagers' unbeaten six match run appears to be over when John Fraser turns a centre from Aston past his own keeper. Ex-Hatter, Viv Busby crosses for John Conway to force the equaliser. | | | | | | | | | | | |
| 23 | H BRISTOL CITY | | 3 | W | 1-0 | 1-0 | Anderson 37 | Horn | Shanks | Thomson | Anderson | Faulkner | Garner | Ryan, Jim | Husband | Butlin | West | Aston | |
| | 29/12 | *11,398* | *12* | 30 | | | | *Bond* | *Tainton* | *Drysdale* | *Sweeney* | *Collier* | *Merrick* | *Durrell* | *Ritchie** | *Gillies* | *Gow* | *Fear* | *Griffin* |
| | | | | | | | Ref: K Burns | Hatters make hard work of beating a City side which has won only once in the last seven games. Anderson scores when looping a header past Len Bond from a Thomson free-kick. Butlin narrowly misses on two occasions in the second half but good saves from Horn earn both points. | | | | | | | | | | | |
| 24 | A CARLISLE | | 3 | L | 0-2 | 0-0 | | Horn | Shanks | Thomson | Anderson | Faulkner | Garner | Ryan, Jim | Husband | Butlin | West | Aston* | Ryan, John |
| | 1/1 | *9,245* | *4* | 30 | | | *Green 54, Martin 70* | *Ross* | *Winstanley* | *Gorman* | *O'Neill** | *Green* | *Tiler* | *Martin* | *Train* | *Owen* | *Clarke* | *Laidlaw* | *Balderstone* |
| | | | | | | | Ref: J Goggins | Carlisle centre-half Bill Green climbs highest to the ball to head home a corner from Dennis Martin, who then scores the second after his initial shot rebounds off a post. The Hatters promotion aspirations are now rapidly fading due to inconsistency, whilst Carlisle make a bid for the top. | | | | | | | | | | | |
| 25 | A PORTSMOUTH | | 3 | D | 0-0 | 0-0 | | Horn | Ryan, John | Thomson | Shanks | Faulkner | Garner | Ryan, Jim | Finney | Anderson | West | Aston | |
| | 12/1 | *18,476* | *10* | 31 | | | | *Milkins* | *Roberts* | *Collins* | *Piper* | *Went* | *Manley* | *Marinello* | *Kellard* | *Davies* | *Reynolds* | *Mellows* | |
| | | | | | | | Ref: R Kirkpatrick | When the generator breaks down in the 71st minute, Pompey chairman, John Deacon, orders that the floodlights are switched over to the mains electricity. He nearly regrets his decision when, with just three minutes left, defender Malcolm Manley slices the ball against his own crossbar. | | | | | | | | | | | |
| 26 | H NOTT'M FOREST | | 3 | D | 2-2 | 1-1 | Ryan Jim 13, 89p | Horn | Ryan, John | Thomson | Shanks | Litt | Garner | Ryan, Jim | Finney* | Anderson | West | Aston | Butlin |
| | 19/1 | 11,888 | *7* | 32 | | | *McKenzie 12, Richardson 71* | *Barron* | *O'Kane* | *Winfield* | *Chapman* | *Cottam* | *Richardson** | *Lyall* | *McKenzie* | *Martin* | *Jackson* | *Bowyer* | *Serella* |
| | | | | | | | Ref J Taylor: | Jim Ryan scores with an injury-time penalty to snatch an unlikely draw for the Hatters at the end of a scrappy game. The Forest manager, Allan Brown, instructs his men to cut out the midfield and the plan would have worked but for centre-half John Cottam needlessly handling the ball. | | | | | | | | | | | |
| 27 | A ASTON VILLA | | 3 | W | 1-0 | 0-0 | Ryan Jim 89p | Horn | Ryan, John | Thomson | Shanks | Faulkner | Garner | Ryan, Jim | Finney | Anderson | West | Butlin | |
| | 2/2 | *26,180* | *16* | 34 | | | | *Cumbes* | *Gidman* | *Aitken* | *Rioch* | *Nicholl* | *Ross* | *Graydon** | *Brown* | *Morgan* | *Hamilton* | *Evans* | *Little* |
| | | | | | | | Ref: H Davey | Ryan scores with a last-gasp penalty after Villa full-back, Charlie Aitken, fouls Anderson in the area. The Luton defence is under a fair amount of pressure but Villa, who have not won a league game in twelve matches, lack confidence in front of goal. Rioch just misses with a fierce shot. | | | | | | | | | | | |
| 28 | H NOTTS CO | | 3 | D | 1-1 | 0-0 | Anderson 65 | Horn | Ryan, John | Thomson | Anderson | Faulkner | Garner | Ryan, Jim | Husband | Fern | West | Butlin | |
| | 5/2 | **4,908** | *8* | 35 | | | *Probert 80* | *McManus* | *Brindley* | *Cliff** | *McVay* | *Bolton* | *Mann* | *Randall* | *Masson* | *Bradd* | *Probert* | *Carter* | *Nixon* |
| | | | | | | | Ref: J Yates | A Tuesday afternoon kick-off is arranged in order to comply with the power rotation system. A small crowd see a poor game, the only bright spots being a 30-yard drive from Anderson, which is deflected past Eric McManus for the opener, and an equaliser driven in by Eric Probert. | | | | | | | | | | | |
| 29 | H CRYS PALACE | | 2 | W | 2-1 | 1-0 | Ryan Jim 33p, Butlin 71 | Horn | Ryan, John | Thomson | Anderson | Litt | Garner | Ryan, Jim | Husband | Butlin | West | Aston | |
| | 23/2 | 14,287 | *21* | 37 | | | *Possee 80* | *Hammond* | *Jump* | *Wall* | *Johnson* | *Anderson* | *Blyth* | *Jeffries* | *Possee* | *Hill* | *Rogers* | *Taylor* | |
| | | | | | | | Ref: P Walters | Ben Anderson handles the ball in the area and Jim Ryan makes no mistake from the spot. Palace are in the middle of a belated, unbeaten run and, after Peter Anderson hits the bar, they take control until Butlin heads home a corner from Aston. Possee heads a consolation goal late on. | | | | | | | | | | | |
| 30 | A SWINDON | | 2 | W | 2-0 | 2-0 | Butlin 23, 43 | Horn | Ryan, John | Thomson | Anderson | Faulkner | Garner | Ryan, Jim | Husband | Butlin | West | Aston | |
| | 26/2 | ***2,791*** | *22* | 39 | | | | *Spratley* | *McLaughlin* | *Trollope* | *Butler* | *Burrows* | *Munks* | *Moss* | *Dixon* | *Compton* | *Clarke* | *Jenkins* | |
| | | | | | | | Ref: D Nippard | Another midweek afternoon game, this time watched by what turns out to be the lowest attendance of the season. The Robins face a stiff uphill task after Butlin heads the Town into a two-goal half-time lead. Poor finishing by Hatters' forwards after the break prevents a 'cricket score'. | | | | | | | | | | | |
| 31 | A FULHAM | | 2 | L | 1-2 | 0-0 | Husband 57 | Horn | Ryan, John | Thomson | Anderson | Faulkner | Garner | Ryan, Jim | Husband | Butlin | West | Aston | |
| | 5/3 | *10,071* | *11* | 39 | | | *Lloyd 58, 80* | *Mellor* | *Fraser* | *Strong* | *Mullery* | *Lacy* | *Dunne* | *Friend* | *Slough* | *Busby* | *Lloyd* | *Barrett* | |
| | | | | | | | Ref: T Dawes | The Town take the lead when Husband heads home a corner from Aston but the visitors level from the kick-off when Barry Lloyd drives a low shot past Horn. Lloyd's winner, from a Les Barrett cross, gives Fulham their fourth consecutive victory, a just reward for their determination. | | | | | | | | | | | |

| No | H/A | Opponent | Att | | | F-A | H-T | Scorers, Times, and Referees | 1 | 2 | 3 | 4 | 5 | 6 | 7 | 8 | 9 | 10 | 11 | 12 sub used |
|---|---|---|---|---|---|---|---|---|---|---|---|---|---|---|---|---|---|---|---|---|
| 32 | A | HULL | | 2 | W | 3-1 | 1-0 | West 19, Anderson 57, Aston 63 | Horn | Ryan, John | Thomson | Anderson | Faulkner | Garner | Ryan, Jim | Husband | Butlin | West | Aston | |
| | 9/3 | | *7,027* | *8* | 41 | | | *O'Riley 72* | *Wealands* | *McGill* | *Devries* | *Burnett* | *Deere* | *Blampey* | *Hawley* | *Lord* | *Pearson* | *Hemmerman* | *Greenwood** | *O'Riley* |
| | | | | | | | | Ref: T Bosi | Luton record an easy victory over a Hull side that has been beaten only once at Boothferry Park this season. Alan West scores the 'goal of the game' when he lobs a stranded Jeff Wealands from 25 yards. Better sides than this Hull team would have punished the slack, Hatters' defence. | | | | | | | | | | | |
| 33 | H | ORIENT | | 2 | W | 3-1 | 1-1 | Husband 6, 75, 80 | Horn | Ryan, John | Thomson | Anderson | Faulkner | Garner | Ryan, Jim | Husband | Butlin | West | Aston | |
| | 16/3 | | 17,045 | *3* | 43 | | | *Hoadley 10* | *Jackson* | *Payne* | *Roffey* | *Boyle* | *Hoadley* | *Walley* | *Fairbrother* | *Brisley* | *Queen* | *Allen* | *Downing* | |
| | | | | | | | | Ref: V James | Since signing for the Hatters, Husband has been struggling to get down to his optimum weight but he makes 'light' of the Orient defence by cracking a brilliant hat-trick in this promotion 'four-pointer'. West and Butlin are instrumental in providing the support to bring down the O's. | | | | | | | | | | | |
| 34 | A | BOLTON | | 2 | L | 0-1 | 0-0 | | Horn | Ryan, John | Thomson | Anderson | Faulkner | Garner | Ryan, Jim | Husband | Butlin | West | Aston | |
| | 23/3 | | *15,903* | *12* | 43 | | | *Greaves 82* | *Siddall* | *Ritson* | *Nicholson* | *McAllister* | *Jones P* | *Waldron* | *Byrom* | *Jones G* | *Greaves* | *Whatmore* | *Thompson* | |
| | | | | | | | | Ref: D Turner | The Trotters put the Town defence under severe pressure from the start and have a dozen chances to take the lead. Ex-England and Liverpool winger, Peter Thompson, is unstoppable and he is the provider of the cross which enables Roy Greaves to head home the only goal of the game. | | | | | | | | | | | |
| 35 | H | MIDDLESBROUGH | | 2 | L | 0-1 | 0-0 | | Horn | Ryan, John | Thomson | Anderson | Faulkner | Garner | Ryan, Jim | Husband | Butlin | West | Aston | |
| | 30/3 | | 19,812 | *1* | 43 | | | *Mills 76* | *Platt* | *Craggs* | *Cochrane* | *Souness* | *Boam* | *Maddren* | *Murdoch* | *Mills* | *Hickton* | *Foggon* | *Armstrong* | |
| | | | | | | | | Ref: T Spencer | Middlesbrough clinch the Division 2 title with their eighth successive win, courtesy of a mis-hit shot from David Mills that trickles over the line and a mean defence which takes no prisoners. After the game, boss Jack Charlton forecasts 'I still fancy Luton to go up; they are a good team.' | | | | | | | | | | | |
| 36 | H | PRESTON | | 2 | W | 4-2 | 2-2 | Husband 3, Butlin 30, 52, 66 | Horn | Ryan, John | Thomson | Anderson | Faulkner | Garner | Ryan, Jim | Husband | Butlin | West | Aston | |
| | 6/4 | | 11,806 | *21* | 45 | | | *Burns 13, Sadler 41* | *Brown* | *McMahon* | *Spark* | *Stiles* | *Baxter* | *Hawkins* | *Lamb* | *Burns* | *Elwiss* | *Smith** | *Sadler* | *Treacy* |
| | | | | | | | | Ref: W Johnson | It is Butlin's turn to score a hat-trick, all with his head, to inflict a fifth successive defeat on Preston. The game is lacking in thrills and most of the scoring efforts are as a result of goalkeeping errors. The two points are most welcome following the disappointments of the last two games. | | | | | | | | | | | |
| 37 | A | OXFORD | | 2 | D | 1-1 | 1-1 | Ryan Jim 19 | Horn | Ryan, John | Thomson | Anderson | Faulkner | Garner | Ryan, Jim* | Husband | Butlin | West | Aston | Hindson |
| | 12/4 | | *13,714* | *19* | 46 | | | *Curran 2* | *Burton* | *Light* | *Shuker* | *Roberts* | *Clarke C* | *Briggs* | *Gough* | *Fleming* | *Clarke D** | *Curran* | *Atkinson* | *Bray* |
| | | | | | | | | Ref: A Hart | A large influx of Luton supporters swells the Manor Ground crowd to make it the highest of the season. A headed opening goal by Hugh Curran is cancelled out when a 40-yard free-kick by Jim Ryan is completely misjudged by Roy Burton. The stalemate is reached long before the end. | | | | | | | | | | | |
| 38 | A | SHEFFIELD WED | | 2 | D | 2-2 | 0-1 | Husband 55, Butlin 77 | Horn | Ryan, John | Thomson | Anderson | Faulkner | Garner | Hindson | Husband | Butlin | West | Aston | |
| | 13/4 | | *16,685* | *18* | 47 | | | *Joicey 10, Potts 46* | *Springett* | *Rodrigues* | *Shaw* | *Mullen* | *Holsgrove* | *Coyle* | *Henderson* | *Sunley** | *Joicey* | *Craig* | *Potts* | *Prudham* |
| | | | | | | | | Ref: G Hill | Relegation-threatened Wednesday take a two-goal lead when Willie Henderson first sets up Brian Joicey, and then Eric Potts to score. Poor finishing from the home side allows the Town back into the game and they are unlucky not to take both points having got back on level terms. | | | | | | | | | | | |
| 39 | H | OXFORD | | 2 | L | 0-1 | 0-1 | | Horn | Ryan, John | Thomson | Anderson | Faulkner | Garner | Ryan, Jim | Husband | Butlin | West | Aston | |
| | 16/4 | | 16,357 | *18* | 47 | | | *Skeen 15* | *Burton* | *Light* | *Shuker* | *Roberts* | *Clarke C* | *Briggs* | *Skeen* | *Fleming* | *Curran* | *Bray* | *Aylott* | |
| | | | | | | | | Ref: A Oliver | In this Easter return game, the Hatters stumble badly in a frustrating match. Oxford score an early goal with a fierce volley from veteran Ken Skeen and then defend with the ferocity expected from relegation strugglers. Roy Burton is in inspired form and Dave Roberts is outstanding. | | | | | | | | | | | |
| 40 | H | MILLWALL | | 2 | W | 3-0 | 2-0 | Faulkner 8, Anderson 18, Hindson 69 | Horn | Ryan, John | Thomson | Anderson | Faulkner | Garner | Ryan, Jim | Husband | Butlin | West | Aston* | Hindson |
| | 20/4 | | 15,740 | *11* | 49 | | | | *King* | *Jones* | *Cripps* | *Dorney* | *Kitchener* | *Allder* | *Saul* | *Clark* | *Wood* | *Smethurst* | *Hill* | |
| | | | | | | | | Ref: T Reynolds | The Lions catch the full backlash as the Town turn on a display of forceful football, worthy of Division 1. In a game marred by crowd violence, the Town's sweeping attacks, orchestrated by Anderson, leave the Londoners looking second-rate. Just one point is now needed for promotion. | | | | | | | | | | | |
| 41 | A | WEST BROM | | 2 | D | 1-1 | 1-0 | Butlin 5 | Horn | Ryan, John | Thomson | Anderson | Faulkner | Garner | Ryan, Jim | Husband | Butlin | West | Aston* | Hindson |
| | 27/4 | | *13,164* | *8* | 50 | | | *Brown Tony 72p* | *Latchford* | *Thompson* | *Wilson* | *Hughes* | *Wile* | *Robertson* | *Johnston* | *Brown Tony* | *Mayo* | *Brown Ally* | *Glover* | |
| | | | | | | | | Ref: K McNally | The promotion point is achieved, despite some anxious moments late on in the game. Butlin heads home a Faulkner free-kick early on which helps to settle the nerves but a dubious penalty decision is given against Faulkner for a tackle on Willie Johnston, which Tony Brown converts. | | | | | | | | | | | |
| 42 | H | SUNDERLAND | | 2 | L | 3-4 | 3-3 | Husband 17, 30, Butlin 41 *[Halom 77]* | Horn | Ryan, John | Thomson | Anderson | Faulkner | Garner | Ryan, Jim | Husband | Butlin | West | Hindson | |
| | 1/5 | | **20,285** | *6* | 50 | | | *Hughes 2, Towers 26, Ashurst 35,* | *Montgomery* | *Malone* | *Guthrie* | *Longhorn* | *Watson* | *Belfitt* | *Kerr* | *Hughes* | *Halom* | *Ashurst* | *Towers* | |
| | | Home | Away | | | | | Ref: R Matthewson | The biggest crowd of the season is entertained by a light-hearted seven-goal thriller. Both defences are in a generous mood and the goals seem to rain in from all angles. Ex-Hatters' forward, Vic Halom, spoils the promotion party by scoring the winner with the softest goal of the evening. | | | | | | | | | | | |
| Average | | 12,214 | 13,199 | | | | | | | | | | | | | | | | | |

| League Cup | | | | | | F-A | H-T | Scorers, Times, and Referees | 1 | 2 | 3 | 4 | 5 | 6 | 7 | 8 | 9 | 10 | 11 | 12 sub used |
|---|---|---|---|---|---|---|---|---|---|---|---|---|---|---|---|---|---|---|---|---|
| 2 | H | GRIMSBY | | 2 | D | 1-1 | 1-0 | Hindson 22 | Horn | Shanks | Thomson | Anderson | Faulkner | Garner | Hindson | Ryan, John | Butlin | Finney | Aston | |
| | 10/10 | | 9,656 | *3:14* | | | | *Chatterley 86* | *Wainman* | *Beardsley* | *Booth* | *Chatterley* | *Wiggington* | *Gray* | *Barton* | *Hickman* | *Hubbard* | *Czuczman* | *Sharp* | |
| | | | | | | | | Ref: H Powell | Free-scoring Luton can have little complaint about the final score as a tenacious Grimsby side take control of the midfield. In the driving rain, Gordon Hindson powers home a left-foot drive, against the run of play, and the equalising volley from Lew Chatterley comes as no surprise. | | | | | | | | | | | |
| 2R | A | GRIMSBY | | 2 | D | 0-0 | 0-0 | | Horn | Shanks | Thomson | Anderson | Faulkner | Garner | Hindson | Ryan, John | Butlin | Cruse | Aston | |
| | 16/10 | | *13,643* | *3:12* | | *aet* | | | *Wainman* | *Beardsley* | *Booth* | *Chatterley* | *Wiggington* | *Gray* | *Barton* | *Hickman* | *Hubbard* | *Czuczman* | *Sharp** | *Lewis* |
| | | | | | | | | Ref: H Powell | The Town start off as the better side but are gradually pushed back and it is only poor finishing by the Mariners that stops them from winning in normal time. Butlin then hits the bar and Garner has a header cleared off the line. Hatters lose the toss for the choice of venue for the replay. | | | | | | | | | | | |
| 2R | A | GRIMSBY | | 5 | W | 2-0 | 2-0 | Finney 17, Faulkner 39 | Barber | Shanks | Thomson | Anderson | Faulkner | Garner | Ryan, Jim | West | Butlin | Finney | Aston | |
| R | 23/10 | | *15,365* | *3:12* | | | | | *Wainman* | *Beardsley* | *Booth* | *Chatterley* | *Wiggington* | *Gray* | *Barton* | *Hickman* | *Hubbard* | *Czuczman* | *Sharp** | *Lewis* |
| | | | | | | | | Ref: J Hunting | Grimsby give the Town defence several uneasy moments but the Hatters prove to be the superior team with new signing, Alan West, linking well with the forwards. Harry Wainman fails to collect a corner from Aston, leaving Faulkner to head in the second goal, which kills the game. | | | | | | | | | | | |
| 3 | H | BURY | | 6 | D | 0-0 | 0-0 | | Barber | Shanks | Thomson | Anderson | Faulkner | Garner | Ryan, Jim | Finney* | Butlin | West | Aston | Cruse |
| | 31/10 | | 8,191 | *4:4* | | | | | *Forrest* | *Hoolickin* | *Kennedy* | *Tinsley* | *Swan* | *Howitt* | *Hughes* | *Williams* | *Murray* | *Rudd* | *Hamstead* | |
| | | | | | | | | Ref: H New | The Town again make hard work of playing against lower opposition with Allan Brown's Division 4 side surviving a battering in the second half. Ex-Sheffield Wednesday centre-half, Peter Swan, back playing football after his long ban from the game, survives two penalty appeals. | | | | | | | | | | | |
| 3R | A | BURY | | 11 | W | 3-2 | 1-2 | Anderson 23, Shanks 46, West 74 | Barber | Shanks | Thomson | Anderson | Faulkner | Garner | Ryan, Jim | Finney | Butlin | West | Aston | |
| | 6/11 | | *7,827* | *4:7* | | | | *Rudd 17p, Hamstead 25* | *Forrest* | *Hoolickin* | *Kennedy* | *Tinsley* | *Swan* | *Holt* | *Hughes* | *Murray* | *Spence* | *Rudd* | *Hamstead* | |
| | | | | | | | | Ref: H New | A last-minute penalty from Billy Rudd, awarded after Aston fouls Hamstead a yard outside the box, is saved when Barber guesses correctly. Earlier, Rudd had scored from the spot when Derek Spence was pulled down. Aston is booked for whispering 'poetic justice!' to the referee. | | | | | | | | | | | |
| 4 | A | MILLWALL | | 6 | L | 1-3 | 0-1 | Jones 65 (og) | Horn | Shanks | Thomson | Anderson | Faulkner | Garner | Ryan, Jim | Fern | Sims | West | Aston | |
| | 21/11 | | *8,777* | *2:15* | | | | *Allder 37, Kelly 47, Clark 70* | *King* | *Donaldson* | *Jones* | *Dorney* | *Kitchener* | *Allder* | *Bolland* | *Kelly* | *Wood* | *Clark* | *Hill** | *Brown* |
| | | | | | | | | Ref: J Taylor | Giving a tepid performance, the Hatters are harassed out of their stride by a determined Millwall, for whom winger Gordon Hill sets up two goals with accurate crosses. A penalty is conceded when Don Shanks brings down Hill but Gordon Bolland sees his spot-kick saved by Horn. | | | | | | | | | | | |

| FA Cup | | | | | | | | | | | | | | | | | | | | |
|---|---|---|---|---|---|---|---|---|---|---|---|---|---|---|---|---|---|---|---|---|
| 3 | A | PORT VALE | | 3 | D | 1-1 | 0-0 | Ryan Jim 84 | Horn | Ryan, John | Thomson | Anderson | Faulkner | Garner | Ryan, Jim | Husband | Butlin | West | Aston* | Finney |
| | 5/1 | | *8,127* | *3:16* | | | | *Harris 59* | *Boswell* | *Brodie** | *Griffiths* | *Harris* | *Sum'rscales* | *Horton* | *Lacey* | *Woodward* | *Williams* | *Mountford* | *McLaren* | *Tartt* |
| | | | | | | | | Ref: K Burns | John Ryan returns to the side after Don Shanks is dropped, having failed to turn up for the team talk on Friday. After going a goal down through a Dave Harris header, Hatters fight back against an enthusiastic side. Ryan feeds his namesake with the opportunity to fire home the equaliser. | | | | | | | | | | | |
| 3R | H | PORT VALE | | 3 | W | 4-2 | 0-1 | Aston 59, Anderson 73, 89, Ryan Jim 86 | Horn | Ryan, John | Thomson | Shanks | Faulkner | Garner | Ryan, Jim | Finney | Anderson | West | Aston | |
| | 9/1 | | 5,833 | *3:16* | | | | *Mountford 13, Woodward 66* | *Boswell* | *Carr* | *Griffiths* | *Sum'rscales* | *Harris* | *Horton* | *McLaren* | *Woodward* | *Williams* | *Lacey* | *Mountford* | |
| | | | | | | | | Ref K Burns: | The match is more closely contested than the final score-line suggests and is a splendid advertisement for cup football. Vale lead twice in a game which is played on a Wednesday afternoon in order to avoid wasting electricity, due to the effects of the oil crisis and the three-day week. | | | | | | | | | | | |
| 4 | H | BRADFORD CITY | | 3 | W | 3-0 | 2-0 | Fretwell 1 (og), Butlin 39, Ryan Jim 89 | Horn | Ryan, John | Thomson | Shanks | Faulkner | Garner | Ryan, Jim | Finney | Anderson | West | Butlin | |
| | 26/1 | | 12,470 | *4:10* | | | | | *Downsboro'* | *Fretwell* | *Cooper* | *Oates* | *Napier* | *Cooke* | *Baker* | *Ham* | *Ingram* | *Johnson* | *Brown* | |
| | | | | | | | | Ref: J Kew | The Town take the lead after just 20 seconds, when Finney charges down the wing straight from the kick-off and plays in a cross which City right-back, Dave Fretwell, turns past his own goalkeeper. Butlin scores to seal the win and earn a home tie against either Leicester or Fulham. | | | | | | | | | | | |
| 5 | H | LEICESTER | | 3 | L | 0-4 | 0-1 | | Horn | Ryan, John | Thomson | Anderson | Faulkner | Garner | Ryan, Jim | Husband | Fern* | West | Butlin | Aston |
| | 16/2 | | 25,712 | *1:7* | | | | *Earle 18, 50, Worthington 60, Weller 85* | *Shilton* | *Whitworth* | *Rofe* | *Earle* | *Munro* | *Cross* | *Weller* | *Sammels* | *Worthington* | *Birchenall* | *Glover* | |
| | | | | | | | | Ref: D Smith | The Town are well beaten by a rampant Leicester side who succeed, in spectacular fashion, with everything they try. After an opening flurry, the Town are forced back and the faster, more skilful visitors are worthy winners. Keith Weller scores the best goal after beating five players. | | | | | | | | | | | |

| | | Home | | | | | Away | | | | | |
|---|---|---|---|---|---|---|---|---|---|---|---|---|
| | P | W | D | L | F | A | W | D | L | F | A | Pts |
| 1 Middlesbro | 42 | 16 | 4 | 1 | 40 | 8 | 11 | 7 | 3 | 37 | 22 | 65 |
| 2 LUTON TOWN | 42 | 12 | 5 | 4 | 42 | 25 | 7 | 7 | 7 | 22 | 26 | 50 |
| 3 Carlisle | 42 | 13 | 5 | 3 | 40 | 17 | 7 | 4 | 10 | 21 | 31 | 49 |
| 4 Orient | 42 | 9 | 8 | 4 | 28 | 17 | 6 | 10 | 5 | 27 | 25 | 48 |
| 5 Blackpool | 42 | 11 | 5 | 5 | 35 | 17 | 6 | 8 | 7 | 22 | 23 | 47 |
| 6 Sunderland | 42 | 11 | 6 | 4 | 32 | 15 | 8 | 3 | 10 | 26 | 29 | 47 |
| 7 Nott'm Forest | 42 | 12 | 6 | 3 | 40 | 19 | 3 | 9 | 9 | 17 | 24 | 45 |
| 8 West Brom | 42 | 8 | 9 | 4 | 28 | 24 | 6 | 7 | 8 | 20 | 21 | 44 |
| 9 Hull | 42 | 9 | 9 | 3 | 25 | 15 | 4 | 8 | 9 | 21 | 32 | 43 |
| 10 Notts Co | 42 | 8 | 6 | 7 | 30 | 35 | 7 | 7 | 7 | 25 | 25 | 43 |
| 11 Bolton | 42 | 12 | 5 | 4 | 30 | 17 | 3 | 7 | 11 | 14 | 23 | 42 |
| 12 Millwall | 42 | 10 | 6 | 5 | 28 | 16 | 4 | 8 | 9 | 23 | 35 | 42 |
| 13 Fulham | 42 | 11 | 4 | 6 | 26 | 20 | 5 | 6 | 10 | 13 | 23 | 42 |
| 14 Aston Villa | 42 | 8 | 9 | 4 | 33 | 21 | 5 | 6 | 10 | 15 | 24 | 41 |
| 15 Portsmouth | 42 | 9 | 8 | 4 | 26 | 16 | 5 | 4 | 12 | 19 | 46 | 40 |
| 16 Bristol City | 42 | 9 | 5 | 7 | 25 | 20 | 5 | 5 | 11 | 22 | 34 | 38 |
| 17 Cardiff | 42 | 8 | 7 | 6 | 27 | 20 | 2 | 9 | 10 | 22 | 42 | 36 |
| 18 Oxford | 42 | 8 | 8 | 5 | 27 | 21 | 2 | 8 | 11 | 8 | 25 | 36 |
| 19 Sheffield Wed | 42 | 9 | 6 | 6 | 33 | 24 | 3 | 5 | 13 | 18 | 39 | 35 |
| 20 Crys Palace | 42 | 6 | 7 | 8 | 24 | 24 | 5 | 5 | 11 | 19 | 32 | 34 |
| 21 Preston* | 42 | 7 | 8 | 6 | 24 | 23 | 2 | 6 | 13 | 16 | 39 | 31 |
| 22 Swindon | 42 | 6 | 7 | 8 | 22 | 27 | 1 | 4 | 16 | 14 | 45 | 25 |
| | 924 | 212 | 143 | 107 | 665 | 441 | 107 | 143 | 212 | 441 | 665 | 923 |

* 1 pt deducted

Odds & ends

Double wins: (5) Aston Villa, Bristol City, Crystal Palace, Millwall, Swindon.
Double losses: (1) Middlesbrough.

Won from behind: (3) Bolton (h), Bury (LC), Port Vale (FAC).
Lost from in front: (2) Fulham (a), Middlesbrough (a).

High spots: Promotion back to Division 1 for the first time since 1960.
Jim Husband's hat-trick against Orient.
The end-of-season carnival performance against Sunderland.
Jim Ryan's last-minute penalty winner at Aston Villa.

Low spots: The FA Cup thrashing by Leicester City.
The opening day defeat at Nottingham Forest.
Winning only once in the last six games.
Exiting the League Cup at Millwall after taking five games to get to Round 4.

Player of the Year: Peter Anderson.
Ever-presents: (2) Alan Garner, Bobby Thomson.
Hat-tricks: Jim Husband (1), Barry Butlin (1).
Leading scorer: Barry Butlin (18).

| | Appearances | | | | | | Goals | | | |
|---|---|---|---|---|---|---|---|---|---|---|
| | Lge | *Sub* | LC | *Sub* | FAC | *Sub* | Lge | LC | FAC | Tot |
| Anderson, Peter | **41** | | 6 | | 4 | | **11** | 1 | 2 | **14** |
| Aston, John | **39** | | 6 | | 2 | *1* | **6** | | 1 | **7** |
| Barber, Keith | **5** | | 3 | | | | | | | |
| Butlin, Barry | **36** | *1* | 5 | | 3 | | **17** | | 1 | **18** |
| Cruse, Peter | **3** | *1* | 1 | *1* | | | | | | |
| Faulkner, John | **40** | | 6 | | 4 | | **1** | 1 | | **2** |
| Fern, Rodney | **5** | *1* | 1 | | 1 | | **1** | | | **1** |
| Finney, Tom | **13** | *1* | 4 | | 2 | *1* | **5** | 1 | | **6** |
| Garner, Alan | **42** | | 6 | | 4 | | **1** | | | **1** |
| Hindson, Gordon | **3** | *4* | 2 | | | | **1** | 1 | | **2** |
| Holmes, Billy | | *1* | | | | | | | | |
| Horn, Graham | **37** | | 3 | | 4 | | | | | |
| Husband, Jim | **22** | | | | 2 | | **8** | | | **8** |
| Litt, Steve | **2** | | | | | | | | | |
| Ryan, Jim | **40** | | 4 | | 4 | | **7** | | 3 | **10** |
| Ryan, John | **29** | *2* | 2 | | 4 | | **1** | | | **1** |
| Shanks, Don | **27** | | 6 | | 2 | | | 1 | | **1** |
| Sims, John | **3** | | 1 | | | | **1** | | | **1** |
| Thomson, Bobby | **42** | | 6 | | 4 | | **1** | | | **1** |
| West, Alan | **33** | | 4 | | 4 | | **1** | 1 | | **2** |
| (own-goals) | | | | | | | **2** | 1 | 1 | **4** |
| **20 players used** | **462** | *11* | **66** | *1* | **44** | *2* | **64** | **7** | **8** | **79** |

# LEAGUE DIVISION 1 | Manager: Harry Haslam | SEASON 1974-75

| No | Date | | Att | Pos | Pt | F-A | H-T | Scorers, Times, and Referees | 1 | 2 | 3 | 4 | 5 | 6 | 7 | 8 | 9 | 10 | 11 | 12 sub used |
|---|---|---|---|---|---|---|---|---|---|---|---|---|---|---|---|---|---|---|---|---|
| 1 | H | LIVERPOOL | | | L | 1-2 | 1-1 | Butlin 27 | Horn | Ryan John | Thomson | Anderson | Litt | Garner | Hindson | Husband | Butlin | West | Aston | |
| | 17/8 | | 21,216 | | | | | *Smith 32, Heighway 74* | *Clemence* | *Smith* | *Lindsay* | *Thompson* | *Cormack* | *Hughes* | *Keegan* | *Hall* | *Heighway* | *Boersma* | *Callaghan* | |
| | | | | | | | | Ref: H Davey | The Town are back in the top flight for the first time since 1960 and have the better of the first half, taking a deserved lead when Butlin back-heads a long throw past Ray Clemence. New manager, Bob Paisley, sees his team level soon after, then hit Luton on the break for the winner. | | | | | | | | | | | |
| 2 | A | WEST HAM | | | L | 0-2 | 0-2 | | Horn | Ryan John | Thomson | Anderson | Litt | Garner* | Aston | Husband | Butlin | West | Hindson | Shanks |
| | 19/8 | | *23,182* | | | | | *Lampard 5, Bonds 18* | *Day* | *McDowell* | *Lampard* | *Bonds* | *Taylor* | *Lock* | *Holland* | *Paddon* | *Ayris* | *Brooking* | *Best* | |
| | | | | | | | | Ref: R Kirkpatrick | Luton soon learn that even small errors are punished at this level. Horn punches a centre, rather than catching it, which presents Frank Lampard with an easy chance. The near post is left unguarded and Billy Bonds steals in to head home a corner. Town apply pressure but without success. | | | | | | | | | | | |
| 3 | A | MIDDLESBROUGH | | 20 | D | 1-1 | 0-1 | Butlin 89 | Horn | Shanks | Thomson | Anderson | Faulkner | Ryan John | Hindson | Husband | Butlin | West | Aston | |
| | 24/8 | | *21,478* | *10* | 1 | | | *Mills 18* | *Platt* | *Craggs* | *Spraggon* | *Souness* | *Boam* | *Maddren* | *Murdoch* | *Mills* | *Hickton* | *Foggon* | *Armstrong* | |
| | | | | | | | | Ref: W Johnson | The visitors make several good chances in the first half but Boro lead by a single goal at the break, scored by David Mills after a weak clearance from Horn. Town apply pressure after the break and Butlin fires home with just seven seconds remaining, leaving Boro kicking themselves. | | | | | | | | | | | |
| 4 | H | WEST HAM | | 20 | D | 0-0 | 0-0 | | Barber | Shanks | Thomson | Anderson | Faulkner | Ryan John | Hindson | Husband | Butlin | West | Aston* | **Alston** |
| | 28/8 | | 16,931 | *16* | 2 | | | | *Day* | *Coleman* | *Lampard* | *Bonds* | *Taylor* | *Lock* | *Holland* | *Paddon* | *Gould* | *McDowell* | *Best* | |
| | | | | | | | | Ref: C Thomas | The Hatters are deprived of their first victory in Division 1 by the skills of teenage goalkeeper, Mervyn Day, and his solid defence, who easily deal with hopeful long balls. Hammers nearly steal the game when a shot from Kevin Lock is tipped onto the bar by recalled keeper, Barber. | | | | | | | | | | | |
| 5 | H | QP RANGERS | | 17 | D | 1-1 | 1-1 | Ryan John 7 | Barber | Shanks | Thomson | Anderson | Faulkner | Ryan John | Hindson | Husband | Butlin | West | Alston | |
| | 31/8 | | 18,535 | *12* | 3 | | | *Bowles 34p* | *Parkes* | *Busby* | *Gillard* | *Venables* | *Mancini* | *Webb* | *Thomas* | *Francis* | *Beck* | *Bowles* | *Givens* | |
| | | | | | | | | Ref: L Hayes | For the first 20 minutes, the Town threaten to run away with the game, with Australian World Cup striker, Alston, seemingly everywhere. Ryan scores with a low drive and then Faulkner concedes a penalty, taken twice as a second ball is thrown onto the pitch as the kick is being taken. | | | | | | | | | | | |
| 6 | A | LEEDS | | 18 | D | 1-1 | 1-1 | Butlin 32 | Barber | Shanks | Thomson | Anderson | Faulkner | Ryan John | Hindson | Husband | Butlin | West | Alston* | Ryan, Jim |
| | 7/9 | | *26,516* | *19* | 4 | | | *Clarke 26* | *Harvey* | *Reaney* | *Cherry* | *McGovern* | *McQueen* | *Hunter* | *Lorimer* | *Clarke* | *O'Hare* | *Giles* | *Madeley* | |
| | | | | | | | | Ref: J Hunting | Brian Clough and his stuttering champions are jeered off the pitch by the Elland Road crowd. Former Leeds centre-half, Faulkner, organises the defence well and the Hatters are worthy of their point. Allan Clarke scores with an instinctive finish and Butlin heads the deserved equaliser. | | | | | | | | | | | |
| 7 | H | IPSWICH | | 20 | L | 1-4 | 0-2 | Alston 65 *[Whymark 87]* | Barber | Shanks | Thomson | Anderson | Faulkner | Ryan John | Hindson | Husband | Butlin | West | Alston | |
| | 14/9 | | 17,577 | *1* | 4 | | | *Talbot 10, 60p, Hamilton 25,* | *Sivell* | *Burley* | *Mills* | *Talbot* | *Hunter* | *Beattie* | *Hamilton* | *Viljoen* | *Woods* | *Whymark* | *Lambert** | *Gates* |
| | | | | | | | | Ref: T Reynolds | Top-of-the-table Ipswich hand out a lesson in football with winger Clive Woods cutting through the Luton defence at will. Apart from a short revival in the second-half, when Alston thunders in a header from a cross by Shanks, the Blues' quick approach work enthrals the home crowd. | | | | | | | | | | | |
| 8 | A | ARSENAL | | 21 | D | 2-2 | 0-1 | Alston 52, Shanks 80 | Barber | Shanks | Thomson | Anderson | Faulkner | Ryan John | Hindson | Ryan, Jim | Butlin | West | Alston | |
| | 21/9 | | *21,649* | *16* | 5 | | | *Kidd 43, 61* | *Rimmer* | *Simpson* | *Nelson* | *Storey* | *Blockley* | *Matthews* | *Armstrong* | *Kelly* | *Radford* | *Kidd* | *Brady* | |
| | | | | | | | | Ref: R Challis | Brian Kidd opens the scoring with a 20-yard free-kick, just before the interval, for a poor Gunners side lacking penetration up front. Alston hits the woodwork before scoring and full-back Shanks scores with a tremendous volley to equalise after Kidd had prodded home his second goal. | | | | | | | | | | | |
| 9 | A | COVENTRY | | 21 | L | 1-2 | 0-2 | Ryan Jim 84p | Barber | Shanks | Thomson | Anderson | Faulkner | Ryan John | Hindson | Ryan, Jim | Butlin | West | Alston | |
| | 24/9 | | *15,643* | *19* | 5 | | | *Stein 9, Cross 40* | *Ramsbottom* | *Oakey* | *Cattlin* | *Mortimer* | *Lloyd* | *Hindley* | *Holmes* | *Alderson* | *Stein* | *Cross* | *Hutchison* | |
| | | | | | | | | Ref: E Jolly | Playing for the future of their manager, the Sky Blues turn in a fighting performance and completely overwhelm the Hatters. Jim Ryan converts a penalty, after being fouled by Larry Lloyd, to make a mockery of the final score. Luton are now the only team in the division without a win. | | | | | | | | | | | |
| 10 | H | CARLISLE | | 17 | W | 3-1 | 1-1 | Anderson 13, Alston 54, Ryan Jim 77p | Barber | Shanks | Thomson | Anderson | Faulkner | Ryan John | Hindson | Ryan, Jim | Husband | West | Alston | |
| | 28/9 | | 12,987 | *11* | 7 | | | *Laidlaw 37* | *Ross* | *Carr* | *Gorman* | *O'Neill* | *Green* | *Parker* | *Martin* | *Train* | *McIlmoyle* | *Balderstone* | *Laidlaw* | |
| | | | | | | | | Ref: J Homewood | Top-scorer and crowd favourite, Barry Butlin is sold to Nott'm Forest on the morning of the game and then Town go out and record their first win of the season. In response to Haslam's call for more effort, Carlisle are swept aside. A solo effort from Alston is the pick of Luton's goals. | | | | | | | | | | | |

| No | H/A | Opponent | Pos | Res | F-A | H-T | Scorers, Times, Referees | 1 | 2 | 3 | 4 | 5 | 6 | 7 | 8 | 9 | 10 | 11 | 12 |
|---|---|---|---|---|---|---|---|---|---|---|---|---|---|---|---|---|---|---|---|
| 11 | A | LEICESTER | 18 | D | 0-0 | 0-0 | | Barber | Shanks | **Buckley** | Anderson | Litt | Ryan John | Hindson | Ryan, Jim | Husband | West | Alston | |
| 5/10 | | *19,024* | **16** | 8 | | | | *Shilton* | *Whitworth* | *Rofe* | *Sammels* | *Munro* | *Woollett** | *Weller* | *Earle* | *Worthington* | *Waters* | *Glover* | *Cross* |
| | | | | | | | Ref: P Partridge | The Hatters are imaginative, inventive and totally in control throughout the game, but are repeatedly foiled by a man dressed all in white, Peter Shilton, in the Foxs' goal. 18-year-old Steve Buckley makes his debut for Luton and controls the experienced Leicester winger, Keith Weller. | | | | | | | | | | | |
| 12 | H | BIRMINGHAM | 20 | L | 1-3 | 1-2 | Hindson 30 | Barber | Shanks | Thomson | **Chambers** | Litt | Ryan John | Hindson | Ryan, Jim | Husband | West | Alston | |
| 12/10 | | 15,097 | *14* | 8 | | | *Francis 4, 5, 70* | *Latchford* | *Martin* | *Bryant* | *Kendall* | *Gallagher* | *Pendrey* | *Campbell* | *Francis* | *Burns* | *Hatton* | *Calderwood* | |
| | | | | | | | Ref: W Gow | Trevor Francis hits a hat-trick for the visitors, the first two goals coming within five minutes of the start. The Town pull a goal back before the break but, rather than continue with the attacking policy, surrender the midfield, which allows the Blues to come back and secure the victory. | | | | | | | | | | | |
| 13 | H | MIDDLESBROUGH | 21 | L | 0-1 | 0-1 | | Barber | Shanks | Ryan John | Anderson | Litt | Garner | Hindson | Chambers | Alston | West | Husband | |
| 16/10 | | **10,464** | *6* | 8 | | | *Foggon 15* | *Platt* | *Craggs* | *Spraggon* | *Souness* | *Boam* | *Maddren* | *Murdoch* | *Mills* | *Hickton** | *Foggon* | *Armstrong* | *Willey* |
| | | | | | | | Ref: G Hill | Alan Foggon creates problems for the home defence throughout the match and is rewarded for his efforts when scoring with a solo effort. After the interval, Town force Boro back and Chambers is unlucky not to score when his volley hits a post and rebounds to goalkeeper Jim Platt. | | | | | | | | | | | |
| 14 | A | MANCHESTER C | 21 | L | 0-1 | 0-0 | | Barber | Shanks | Thomson | Chambers | Litt | Garner | Hindson | Husband | Alston | West | Aston | |
| 19/10 | | *30,649* | *2* | 8 | | | *Summerbee 67* | *MacRae* | *Hammond* | *Donachie* | *Doyle* | *Clarke* | *Oakes* | *Summerbee* | *Bell* | *Marsh* | *Henson* | *Barnes* | |
| | | | | | | | Ref: M Lowe | Hard work and energetic running are not enough to save the Town from a third successive defeat, this time against championship-chasing City. Mike Summerbee scores the only goal of the game from close range. Litt is unlucky not to score when his header hits the bar towards the end. | | | | | | | | | | | |
| 15 | H | TOTTENHAM | 22 | D | 1-1 | 0-0 | Aston 87 | Barber | Shanks | Thomson | Chambers | Litt | Garner | Hindson | Fern | Anderson | West | Aston | |
| 26/10 | | 22,420 | *20* | 9 | | | *Chivers 67* | *Jennings* | *Evans* | *Knowles* | *Pratt* | *England* | *Naylor* | *Neighbour** | *Perryman* | *Chivers* | *Peters* | *Duncan* | *Coates* |
| | | | | | | | Ref: P Reeves | Aston is rebuked by the Club during the week after failing to report for several training sessions. However, he turns in a gutsy performance and scores a last-gasp equaliser, which earns a much-needed point, after Northern Ireland keeper, Pat Jennings, is impeded by his own defenders. | | | | | | | | | | | |
| 16 | A | NEWCASTLE | 22 | L | 0-1 | 0-0 | | Barber | Shanks | Thomson | Chambers | Litt | Garner | Hindson | Fern | Anderson | West | Aston | |
| 2/11 | | *30,141* | *9* | 9 | | | *Tudor 77* | *McFaul* | *Nattrass* | *Clark* | *Cassidy* | *Keeley* | *Howard* | *Barrowclough* | *Kennedy* | *MacDonald* | *Tudor* | *Hibbitt* | |
| | | | | | | | Ref: R Tinkler | A scrambled effort by John Tudor earns both points for the home side and keeps Luton firmly anchored at the foot of the division. Hindson and Chambers both try to lift the Town but Iam McFaul in the Newcastle goal has little to do. Ex-Hatter MacDonald hits the bar in the first minute. | | | | | | | | | | | |
| 17 | H | SHEFFIELD UTD | 22 | L | 0-1 | 0-0 | | Barber | Shanks | Thomson | Chambers | Faulkner | Garner | Hindson | Fern* | Anderson | West | Aston | **Futcher R** |
| 9/11 | | 12,670 | *6* | 9 | | | *Currie 58* | *Brown* | *Badger* | *Hemsley* | *Garbett* | *Colquhoun* | *Eddy* | *Woodward* | *Speight* | *Dearden* | *Currie* | *Field* | |
| | | | | | | | Ref: M Sinclair | Tony Currie continually spread-eagles the Luton defence with his intelligent ball distribution and scores the only goal of the game when running through the defence to shoot past Barber. The Town deserve to take the share the points as a reward for their dogged enthusiasm and endeavour. | | | | | | | | | | | |
| 18 | A | STOKE | 22 | L | 2-4 | 1-1 | Anderson 29, Garner 73 | Barber | Ryan John | Thomson | Anderson | Faulkner | Garner | Ryan, Jim | Husband | Alston | West | **Spiring** | |
| 16/11 | | *20,646* | *6* | 9 | | | *Hudson 2, Robertson 60, G'hoff 62, 67* | *Farmer* | *Marsh* | *Pejic* | *Mahoney* | *Smith* | *Dodd* | *Robertson* | *Greenhoff* | *Hurst** | *Hudson* | *Salmons* | *Moores* |
| | | | | | | | Ref: H New | Man-of-the-match, Peter Anderson, leaves the pitch shaking his head in disbelief as the bold attacking play from the Town produces two goals but ends in a 2-4 defeat. After equalising, he then hits the crossbar with a header but high-flying Stoke reply with three goals in seven minutes. | | | | | | | | | | | |
| 19 | H | BURNLEY | 22 | L | 2-3 | 1-1 | Faulkner 40, Spiring 51 | Barber | Ryan John | Thomson | Anderson | Faulkner | Garner | Ryan, Jim | Husband* | Spiring | West | Aston | Alston |
| 30/11 | | 11,816 | *9* | 9 | | | *Hankin 35, 53, James 49* | *Stevenson* | *Newton* | *Brennan* | *Ingham* | *Waldron* | *Rodaway* | *Noble* | *Hankin* | *Fletcher* | *Collins* | *James* | |
| | | | | | | | Ref: J Taylor | Burnley always have the edge in class as they gain the win by the odd goal, with striker Ray Hankin winning most things in the air. 'Luton are the worst team I have ever seen at this level of football,' states Welsh international Leighton James. Peter Spiring is enthusiastic but little else. | | | | | | | | | | | |
| 20 | A | CHELSEA | 22 | L | 0-2 | 0-0 | | Horn | Ryan John | Buckley | Anderson | Faulkner | **Futcher P** | Ryan, Jim | Alston | Spiring | West | Aston | |
| 7/12 | | *19,009* | *19* | 9 | | | *Hutchinson 49, Kember 75* | *Phillips* | *Locke* | *Wilkins G* | *Hay* | *Harris* | *Wilkins R* | *Cooke* | *Kember* | *Garland* | *Hutchinson* | *Sissons* | |
| | | | | | | | Ref: P Walters | A header from Ian Hutchinson and a tap-in from Steve Kember earn the points for the visitors in this bottom-of-the-table clash. The Town rue their missed chances; Alston misses the ball in front of an open goal, Spiring slices an Alston through-ball wide when it seems easier to score. | | | | | | | | | | | |
| 21 | A | LIVERPOOL | 22 | L | 0-2 | 0-0 | | Horn | Ryan John | Buckley | Anderson | Faulkner | Futcher P | Ryan, Jim | Husband | Spiring | West | Aston | |
| 14/12 | | *35,151* | *2* | 9 | | | *Toshack 47, Heighway 84* | *Clemence* | *Smith* | *Neal* | *Thompson* | *Cormack* | *Hughes* | *Keegan* | *McDermott* | *Heighway* | *Toshack* | *Callaghan* | |
| | | | | | | | Ref: K Burns | Liverpool are made to work hard for their first win in nine games and leave Luton with six defeats in a row. John Toshack, recalled to the side, misses three good chances in the first half before opening the scoring after the interval. Paul Futcher is a tower of strength in the Town defence. | | | | | | | | | | | |

| No | Date | | Att | Pos | Pt | F-A | H-T | Scorers, Times, and Referees | 1 | 2 | 3 | 4 | 5 | 6 | 7 | 8 | 9 | 10 | 11 | 12 sub used |
|---|---|---|---|---|---|---|---|---|---|---|---|---|---|---|---|---|---|---|---|---|
| 22 | H | DERBY | | 22 | W | 1-0 | 0-0 | Ryan Jim 81p | Horn | Ryan John | Buckley | Anderson | Faulkner | Futcher P | Ryan, Jim | Husband | Spiring* | West | Aston | **Fuccillo** |
| | 21/12 | | 12,862 | *10* | 11 | | | | *Boulton* | *Webster* | *Thomas* | *Rioch* | *Daniel* | *Todd* | *Newton* | *Gemmill* | *Davies** | *Bourne* | *Lee* | *Hinton* |
| | | | | | | | | Ref: A Lees | The first victory in three months comes from the penalty spot after Derby defender Colin Todd and Spiring, later discovered to have broken a toe, go down in a heap in the penalty area as they chase a through-ball. The referee awards the spot-kick after taking the advice of his linesman. | | | | | | | | | | | |
| 23 | A | IPSWICH | | 22 | W | 1-0 | 0-0 | Futcher R 89 | Horn | Ryan John | Buckley | Anderson | Faulkner | Futcher P | Ryan, Jim | Husband | Futcher R | West | Aston | |
| | 26/12 | | *23,406* | *3* | 13 | | | | *Sivell* | *Burley* | *Mills* | *Talbot* | *Peddelty* | *Beattie* | *Osborne* | *Hamilton* | *Johnson* | *Whymark* | *Lambert* | |
| | | | | | | | | Ref: D Nippard | Aston crosses the ball from the right to give Ron Futcher, on his full league debut, the opportunity to score with a brilliant header in the dying seconds of the game. Ipswich do not create a single scoring chance against a defence which plays the ball back to Horn whenever possible. | | | | | | | | | | | |
| 24 | H | WOLVES | | 22 | W | 3-2 | 2-1 | Futcher R 38, 44, 85 | Horn | Ryan John | Buckley | Anderson | Faulkner | Futcher P | Ryan, Jim | Husband | Futcher R | West | Aston | |
| | 28/12 | | 19,642 | *12* | 15 | | | *Munro 23, Powell 68* | *Parkes* | *Williams* | *Parkin* | *Bailey* | *Munro* | *McAlle* | *Hibbitt** | *Powell* | *Richards* | *Kindon* | *Farley* | *Daley* |
| | | | | | | | | Ref: J Goggins | The Luton faithful applaud their new hero, Ron Futcher, as he scores three magnificent goals on his home league debut. After the game, Luton Director and comedian Eric Morecambe quips 'I am not going to shave until we lose and on this form, I will have whiskers down to my knees.' | | | | | | | | | | | |
| 25 | H | CHELSEA | | 21 | D | 1-1 | 0-0 | Husband 63 | Horn | Ryan John | Buckley | Anderson | Faulkner | Futcher P | Ryan, Jim | Husband | Futcher R | West | Aston | |
| | 11/1 | | **23,096** | *19* | 16 | | | *Kember 82* | *Phillips* | *Locke* | *Harris* | *Hollins* | *Dempsey** | *Hay* | *Kember* | *Wilkins* | *Garland* | *Hutchinson* | *Cooke* | *Houseman* |
| | | | | | | | | Ref: J Hunting | A serious error by Horn in failing to collect a corner from Charlie Cooke gives Steve Kember the chance to score and earn a point for his side, which they scarcely deserve, in this crucial relegation struggle. The Hatters maintain their recent improved form, except with their finishing. | | | | | | | | | | | |
| 26 | A | BURNLEY | | 22 | L | 0-1 | 0-1 | | Horn | Ryan John | Buckley | Anderson | Faulkner | Futcher P | Ryan, Jim | Husband | Futcher R | West | Aston | |
| | 18/1 | | *17,237* | *3* | 16 | | | *Ingham 33* | *Stevenson* | *Ingham* | *Newton* | *Noble* | *Thomson* | *Rodaway* | *Brennan* | *Hankin* | *Fletcher* | *Collins* | *James* | |
| | | | | | | | | Ref: K McNally | A brilliant performance by Burnley keeper, Alan Stevenson prevents the Hatters from gaining at least a point. The only time he is beaten is when John Faulkner rattles his crossbar from 25 yards. Billy Ingham scores after an exchange of passes with Ray Hankin, firing in a low drive. | | | | | | | | | | | |
| 27 | A | SHEFFIELD UTD | | 22 | D | 1-1 | 0-1 | Anderson 81 | Horn | Ryan John | Buckley | Anderson | Faulkner | Futcher P | Ryan, Jim | Husband | Futcher R | West | Aston | |
| | 1/2 | | *17,270* | *12* | 17 | | | *Woodward 30* | *Brown* | *Goulding* | *Hemsley* | *Speight* | *Colquhoun* | *Franks* | *Woodward* | *Bradford* | *Dearden* | *Currie* | *Field* | |
| | | | | | | | | Ref: G Hill | Paul Futcher, called up by manager Don Revie for an England get-together, plays a short pass to Faulkner but the ball jumps over his foot and Alan Woodward runs through to score for the Blades. The Town storm forward and Anderson scores from close range, causing much jubilation. | | | | | | | | | | | |
| 28 | H | NEWCASTLE | | 21 | W | 1-0 | 0-0 | Futcher R 56 | Horn | Ryan John | Buckley | Anderson | Faulkner | Futcher P | Ryan, Jim | Husband | Futcher R | West | Aston | |
| | 8/2 | | 18,019 | *13* | 19 | | | | *McFaul* | *Craig D* | *Kennedy* | *Smith* | *Keeley* | *Clark* | *Barrowclough* | *Nulty* | *MacDonald* | *Burns* | *Craig T* | |
| | | | | | | | | Ref: R Perkin | MacDonald returns to Kenilworth Road for the first time following his transfer of four years ago and is captain for the day. He tries his hardest to upset his old club but the Town defence holds firm. Ron Futcher scores the winning goal with a 15-yard drive following a Buckley free-kick. | | | | | | | | | | | |
| 29 | H | STOKE | | 20 | D | 0-0 | 0-0 | | Horn | Ryan John | Buckley | Anderson | Faulkner | Futcher P | Ryan, Jim | Husband | Futcher R | West | Aston | |
| | 22/2 | | 19,894 | *1* | 20 | | | | *Shilton* | *Marsh* | *Lewis* | *Mahoney* | *Dodd* | *Skeels* | *Moores** | *Greenhoff* | *Conroy* | *Hudson* | *Salmons* | *Hurst* |
| | | | | | | | | Ref: A Lees | Geoff Salmons squanders the opportunity to secure both points for the visitors when shooting wide from the penalty spot after Faulkner brings down Terry Conroy. A shot from Jimmy Greenhoff clearly crosses the goal-line but the referee inexplicably decides to award a corner-kick. | | | | | | | | | | | |
| 30 | A | EVERTON | | 20 | L | 1-3 | 0-2 | Aston 68 | Horn | Ryan John | Buckley | Anderson | Faulkner | Futcher P | Ryan, Jim | Husband | Futcher R | West | Aston | |
| | 25/2 | | ***35,714*** | *1* | 20 | | | *Telfer 15, Dobson 26, Latchford 51* | *Davies* | *Bernard* | *Seargeant* | *Clements* | *Kenyon* | *Hurst* | *Jones* | *Dobson* | *Lyons* | *Latchford* | *Telfer** | *Buckley* |
| | | | | | | | | Ref: A Morrissey | Everton return to the number one spot in the division after capitalising on the early breaks and securing a three-goal lead. Aston pulls a goal back and Town continue to apply pressure without further success in the last 20 minutes, most chances falling to Husband who is disappointing. | | | | | | | | | | | |
| 31 | A | QP RANGERS | | 21 | L | 1-2 | 1-1 | Alston 40 | Horn | Ryan John | Buckley | Anderson | Faulkner | Futcher P | Ryan, Jim | Alston | Futcher R | West | Aston | |
| | 1/3 | | *19,583* | *10* | 20 | | | *Givens 38, Rogers 83* | *Parkes* | *Clement* | *Gillard* | *Masson* | *McLintock* | *Webb* | *Thomas** | *Busby* | *Beck* | *Bowles* | *Givens* | *Rogers* |
| | | | | | | | | Ref: A Jones | 'Luton deserved a point and are too good to go down if they play like this,' states QPR manager and ex-Luton player, Dave Sexton, after the game. The result is settled when Don Rogers realises that Horn has come off his line and cleverly chips the ball over his head from 25 yards. | | | | | | | | | | | |

| No | Date | Opponent | Att | Pos | Pt | F-A | H-T | Scorers, Times, and Referees | 1 | 2 | 3 | 4 | 5 | 6 | 7 | 8 | 9 | 10 | 11 | subs used |
|---|---|---|---|---|---|---|---|---|---|---|---|---|---|---|---|---|---|---|---|---|
| 32 | H | COVENTRY |  | 21 | L | 1-3 | 0-2 | Aston 56 | Horn | Ryan John | Buckley | Anderson | Faulkner | Futcher P | Ryan, Jim | Alston | Futcher R | West | Aston |  |
|  | 8/3 |  | 14,423 | *14* | 20 |  |  | *Alderson 25,35, Green 79* | *Ramsbottom* | *Oakey* | *Cattlin* | *Cartwright* | *Craven* | *Dugdale** | *Carr* | *Alderson* | *Ferguson* | *Green* | *Hutchison* | *Holmes* |
|  |  |  |  |  |  |  |  | Ref: H Davey | Luton take a step nearer to relegation when a Coventry side adapt better to the thick mud of Kenilworth Road, using the short-ball game to gain a two-goal lead. Aston pulls a goal back but Alan Green takes a pass in his stride from Willie Carr and rounds two defenders to score the third. |  |  |  |  |  |  |  |  |  |  |  |
| 33 | A | CARLISLE |  | 21 | W | 2-1 | 0-0 | Aston 61, Futcher R 88 | Barber | Ryan John | Buckley | Anderson | Faulkner | Futcher P | Ryan, Jim | Husband | Futcher R | West | Aston* | Alston |
|  | 15/3 |  | ***8,339*** | *22* | 22 |  |  | *Laidlaw 56* | *Ross* | *Carr* | *Gorman* | *O'Neill* | *Green* | *Parker* | *Martin* | *Train* | *Owen* | *Laidlaw* | *McIlmoyle* |  |
|  |  |  |  |  |  |  |  | Ref: J Rice | Only two minutes remain in this relegation tussle when Ron Futcher, on the touchline, swings in a centre in the general direction of Carlisle goalkeeper, Alan Ross. He is deceived by the flight of the ball in the wind and is powerless to prevent it from entering the net off the far post. |  |  |  |  |  |  |  |  |  |  |  |
| 34 | H | LEEDS |  | 21 | W | 2-1 | 2-0 | Aston 3, Anderson 12 | Barber | Ryan John | Buckley | Anderson | Faulkner | Futcher P | Ryan, Jim | Husband | Futcher R | West | Aston |  |
|  | 22/3 |  | 23,048 | *11* | 24 |  |  | *Jordan 88* | *Stewart* | *Reaney* | *Gray F* | *Madeley* | *McQueen** | *Hunter* | *McKenzie* | *Yorath* | *Jordan* | *Giles* | *Gray E* | *Cherry* |
|  |  |  |  |  |  |  |  | Ref: B Daniels | Luton dispel any hopes the visitors have in completing the treble by settling the game in the first 12 minutes. Aston has time to control a centre from Husband before scoring and then gives Anderson the chance to extend the lead with a rasping shot. Jordan pulls one back near the end. |  |  |  |  |  |  |  |  |  |  |  |
| 35 | H | ARSENAL |  | 20 | W | 2-0 | 0-0 | Ryan Jim 48p, Futcher R 55 | Barber | Ryan John | Buckley | Anderson | Faulkner | Futcher P | Ryan, Jim | Husband | Futcher R | West | Aston |  |
|  | 25/3 |  | 22,120 | *17* | 26 |  |  |  | *Rimmer* | *Rice* | *Nelson* | *Storey* | *Mancini* | *Simpson* | *Rostron* | *Ball* | *Radford* | *Hornsby* | *Brady* |  |
|  |  |  |  |  |  |  |  | Ref: R Capey | Sammy Nelson concedes a penalty when he handles a shot from Husband and Jim Ryan makes no mistake from the spot. Ron Futcher squeezes a header between Rimmer and the post for a deserved winner to record the third win in eleven days and throw the relegation issue wide open. |  |  |  |  |  |  |  |  |  |  |  |
| 36 | A | DERBY |  | 21 | L | **0-5** | 0-3 |  | Barber | Ryan John | Buckley | Anderson | Faulkner | Futcher P | Ryan, Jim | Husband* | Futcher R | West | Aston | **Seasman** |
|  | 29/3 |  | *24,619* | *6* | 26 |  |  | *Davies 8, 12, 33, 80, 87* | *Boulton* | *Thomas* | *Nish* | *Rioch* | *Daniel* | *Todd* | *Powell* | *Gemmill* | *Davies* | *Hector* | *Hinton* |  |
|  |  |  |  |  |  |  |  | Ref: R Tinkler | Roger Davies becomes the first Derby player since the days of Hughie Gallacher to score five goals in a match. He also has two other efforts disallowed, hits the post and has a shot cleared off the line in a game in which the Rams are totally dominant and the Town will wish to forget. |  |  |  |  |  |  |  |  |  |  |  |
| 37 | A | WOLVES |  | 21 | L | 2-5 | 2-3 | Seasman 15, Ryan Jim 29 | Barber | Ryan John | Buckley | Anderson | Faulkner | Futcher P | Ryan, Jim | Seasman | Futcher R* | West | Aston | Spiring |
|  | 31/3 |  | *22,689* | *12* | 26 |  |  | *Carr 7, Hibbitt 33p, 42, 57, Withe 60* | *Pierce* | *Williams* | *Parkin* | *Jefferson* | *Munro* | *McAlle* | *Hibbitt* | *Carr* | *Withe* | *Kindon** | *Daly* | *Gardner* |
|  |  |  |  |  |  |  |  | Ref: P Partridge | An in-swinging corner from Willie Carr eludes Barber for the first goal but Seasman, a recent signing from Tranmere, equalises with a diving header. Ryan gives Town the lead with a 30-yard shot before Wolves take over, Kenny Hibbitt scoring a hat-trick, Withe completing the rout. |  |  |  |  |  |  |  |  |  |  |  |
| 38 | A | TOTTENHAM |  | 21 | L | 1-2 | 1-1 | West 35 | Barber | Ryan John | Buckley | Anderson | Faulkner | Futcher P ! | Ryan, Jim | Husband | Futcher R* | West | Aston | Spiring |
|  | 5/4 |  | *25,796* | *20* | 26 |  |  | *Duncan 25, Conn 86* | *Jennings* | *Kinnear* | *Knowles* | *Beal* | *Osgood* | *Pratt* | *Conn* | *Perryman* | *Jones* | *Duncan* | *Neighbour** | *Chivers* |
|  |  |  |  |  |  |  |  | Ref: P Willis | Spurs are fortunate to win this relegation 'four-pointer' and make it a miserable Easter period for the Town. Alfie Conn receives the ball in a seemingly offside position and dribbles around Barber for the late winner. An incensed Paul Futcher is sent off for arguing with the linesman. |  |  |  |  |  |  |  |  |  |  |  |
| 39 | H | EVERTON |  | 21 | W | 2-1 | 2-1 | Anderson 40, 43 | Barber | Ryan John | Buckley | Anderson | Faulkner | Litt | Ryan, Jim | Husband | Alston | West | Aston |  |
|  | 9/4 |  | 13,437 | *2* | 28 |  |  | *Latchford 20* | *Davies* | *Bernard* | *Clements* | *Buckley* | *Kenyon* | *Hurst* | *Jones* | *Dobson* | *Latchford* | *Smallman* | *Pearson* |  |
|  |  |  |  |  |  |  |  | Ref: A Grey | Everton come to Kenilworth Road in second place and bombard the Town for the opening 30 minutes, during which time Bob Latchford opens the scoring with a soft goal. Aston and Alston both set up goals for Anderson before the interval, a shock from which the visitors never recover. |  |  |  |  |  |  |  |  |  |  |  |
| 40 | H | LEICESTER |  | 21 | W | 3-0 | 2-0 | Alston 22, Weller 36 (og), Husband 78 | Barber | Ryan John | Buckley | Anderson | Faulkner | Litt | Ryan, Jim | Husband | Alston | West | Aston |  |
|  | 12/4 |  | 18,298 | *16* | 30 |  |  |  | *Wallington* | *Whitworth* | *Rofe* | *Lee* | *Blockley* | *Cross** | *Weller* | *Sammels* | *Worthington* | *Birchenall* | *Garland* | *Earle* |
|  |  |  |  |  |  |  |  | Ref: J Williams | Cavalier, attacking play wins the day for the Hatters as they continue their fight against relegation. In a fitting revenge for last season's FA Cup beating, the best goal comes from City's Keith Weller who, from the touchline, hits a 25-yard back-pass to beat his keeper, Mark Wallington. |  |  |  |  |  |  |  |  |  |  |  |
| 41 | A | BIRMINGHAM |  | 20 | W | **4-1** | 2-0 | Ryan Jim 14, Alston 43, 48, Husband 80 | Barber | Ryan John | Buckley | Anderson | Faulkner | Litt | Ryan, Jim ! | Husband | Alston | West | Aston |  |
|  | 19/4 |  | *28,755* | *18* | 32 |  |  | *Francis 78* | *Latchford* | *Page* | *Bryant* | *Kendall* | *Gallagher* | *Pendrey* | *Calderwood** | *Francis* | *Burns* | *Hatton* | *Taylor* | *Smith* |
|  |  |  |  |  |  |  |  | Ref: D Richardson | Jim Ryan scores the opening goal with a 25-yard free-kick, Alston scores with a shot and then a header either side of half-time and Husband gets the fourth, chipping the goalkeeper. The win is soured by the dismissal of Jim Ryan in the closing minutes after a clash with Kenny Burns. |  |  |  |  |  |  |  |  |  |  |  |
| 42 | H | MANCHESTER C |  | 19 | D | 1-1 | 0-1 | Ryan Jim 72 | Barber | Ryan John | Buckley | Anderson | Faulkner | Litt* | Ryan, Jim | Husband | Alston | West | Aston | **King** |
|  | 26/4 |  | 20,768 | *8* | 33 |  |  | *Tueart 14* | *Corrigan* | *Hammond* | *Donachie* | *Doyle* | *Booth* | *Oakes* | *Hartford* | *Bell* | *Marsh** | *Daniels* | *Tueart* | *Keegan* |
|  |  | Home | Away |  |  |  |  | Ref: D Wallace | Jim Ryan lobs City goalkeeper Joe Corrigan from 30 yards to make up for his earlier slip, which allowed Dennis Tueart to open the scoring, and gain a point for Luton. If Totenham win one point from their last game against Leeds, then Town are back to Division 2 after just one season. |  |  |  |  |  |  |  |  |  |  |  |
| Average | | 17,396 | 23,166 |  |  |  |  |  |  |  |  |  |  |  |  |  |  |  |  |  |

| League Cup | | | | | F-A | H-T | Scorers, Times, and Referees | 1 | 2 | 3 | 4 | 5 | 6 | 7 | 8 | 9 | 10 | 11 | 12 sub used |
|---|---|---|---|---|---|---|---|---|---|---|---|---|---|---|---|---|---|---|---|
| 2 | H | BRISTOL ROV | 18 | W | 1-0 | 1-0 | Alston 36 | Barber | Shanks | Thomson | Anderson | Garner | Ryan John | Hindson | Husband | Butlin | West | Alston | |
| | 11/9 | *10,073 2:15* | | | | | | *Eadie* | *Jacobs* | *Parsons** | *Aitken* | *Taylor* | *Prince* | *Stephens* | *Stanton* | *Warboys* | *Bannister* | *Fearnley* | *Rudge* |
| | | | | | | | Ref: T Spencer | The first win of the season, albeit against a Division 2 side, is welcome. The only goal of the match is scored by Adrian Alston, his first for the club, when timing his leap perfectly to head a cross from Hindson past Jim Eadie in the Pirates' goal. Rovers rally in the final 20 minutes. | | | | | | | | | | | |
| 3 | A | SHEFFIELD UTD | 18 | L | 0-2 | 0-1 | | Barber | Shanks | Buckley | Litt | Ryan John | Ryan, Jim | Anderson* | West | Husband | Alston | Hindson | Garner |
| | 8/10 | 14,150 *1:8* | | | | | *Eddy 22, Bradford 59* | *Brown* | *Badger** | *Hemsley* | *Eddy* | *Colquhoun* | *Franks* | *Woodward* | *Bradford* | *Dearden* | *Currie* | *Field* | *Garbett* |
| | | | | | | | Ref: G Hill | The Blades canter into the last 16 of the competition against a Luton side who seem unable to offer a competitive edge to the match. Ex-Hornet Keith Eddy fires a tremendous 25-yard shot past Barber for the first goal and Dave Bradford, in his second game for the club, hits the winner. | | | | | | | | | | | |

| FA Cup | | | | | | | | | | | | | | | | | | | |
|---|---|---|---|---|---|---|---|---|---|---|---|---|---|---|---|---|---|---|---|
| 3 | H | BIRMINGHAM | 22 | L | 0-1 | 0-0 | | Horn | Ryan John | Buckley | Anderson | Faulkner | Futcher P | Ryan, Jim | Husband* | Futcher R | West | Aston | Pollock |
| | 4/1 | 17,543 *1:16* | | | | | *Kendall 46* | *Latchford* | *Page* | *Styles* | *Kendall* | *Gallagher* | *Pendrey* | *Emmanuel* | *Taylor* | *Burns* | *Hatton* | *Calderwood* | |
| | | | | | | | Ref: P Reeves | A speculative 40-yard strike from wily cup veteran, Howard Kendall, puts the visitors through to the next round after a shaky performance. John Ryan hits the post with a 25-yard shot in the first half and Husband has the chance to level the scores in the final minute but misses the ball. | | | | | | | | | | | |

| | | Home | | | | | Away | | | | | |
|---|---|---|---|---|---|---|---|---|---|---|---|---|
| | P | W | D | L | F | A | W | D | L | F | A | Pts |
| 1 Derby | 42 | 14 | 4 | 3 | 41 | 18 | 7 | 7 | 7 | 26 | 31 | 53 |
| 2 Liverpool | 42 | 14 | 5 | 2 | 44 | 17 | 6 | 6 | 9 | 16 | 22 | 51 |
| 3 Ipswich | 42 | 17 | 2 | 2 | 47 | 14 | 6 | 3 | 12 | 19 | 30 | 51 |
| 4 Everton | 42 | 10 | 9 | 2 | 33 | 19 | 6 | 9 | 6 | 23 | 23 | 50 |
| 5 Stoke | 42 | 12 | 7 | 2 | 40 | 18 | 5 | 8 | 8 | 24 | 30 | 49 |
| 6 Sheffield Utd | 42 | 12 | 7 | 2 | 35 | 20 | 6 | 6 | 9 | 23 | 31 | 49 |
| 7 Middlesbro | 42 | 11 | 7 | 3 | 33 | 14 | 7 | 5 | 9 | 21 | 26 | 48 |
| 8 Manchester C | 42 | 16 | 3 | 2 | 40 | 15 | 2 | 7 | 12 | 14 | 39 | 46 |
| 9 Leeds | 42 | 10 | 8 | 3 | 34 | 20 | 6 | 5 | 10 | 23 | 29 | 45 |
| 10 Burnley | 42 | 11 | 6 | 4 | 40 | 29 | 6 | 5 | 10 | 28 | 38 | 45 |
| 11 QP Rangers | 42 | 10 | 4 | 7 | 25 | 17 | 6 | 6 | 9 | 29 | 37 | 42 |
| 12 Wolves | 42 | 12 | 5 | 4 | 43 | 21 | 2 | 6 | 13 | 14 | 33 | 39 |
| 13 West Ham | 42 | 10 | 6 | 5 | 38 | 22 | 3 | 7 | 11 | 20 | 37 | 39 |
| 14 Coventry | 42 | 8 | 9 | 4 | 31 | 27 | 4 | 6 | 11 | 20 | 35 | 39 |
| 15 Newcastle | 42 | 12 | 4 | 5 | 39 | 23 | 3 | 5 | 13 | 20 | 49 | 39 |
| 16 Arsenal | 42 | 10 | 6 | 5 | 31 | 16 | 3 | 5 | 13 | 16 | 33 | 37 |
| 17 Birmingham | 42 | 10 | 4 | 7 | 34 | 28 | 4 | 5 | 12 | 19 | 33 | 37 |
| 18 Leicester | 42 | 8 | 7 | 6 | 25 | 17 | 4 | 5 | 12 | 21 | 43 | 36 |
| 19 Tottenham | 42 | 8 | 4 | 9 | 29 | 27 | 5 | 4 | 12 | 23 | 36 | 34 |
| 20 LUTON TOWN | 42 | 8 | 6 | 7 | 27 | 26 | 3 | 5 | 13 | 20 | 39 | 33 |
| 21 Chelsea | 42 | 4 | 9 | 8 | 22 | 31 | 5 | 6 | 10 | 20 | 41 | 33 |
| 22 Carlisle | 42 | 8 | 2 | 11 | 22 | 21 | 4 | 3 | 14 | 21 | 38 | 29 |
| | 924 | 235 | 124 | 103 | 753 | 460 | 103 | 124 | 235 | 460 | 753 | 924 |

Odds & ends

Double wins: (1) Carlisle.
Double losses: (3) Burnley, Coventry, Liverpool.

Won from behind: (3) Carlisle (a), Everton (h), Wolves (h).
Lost from in front: (2) Liverpool (h), Wolves (a).

High spots: The form after Christmas.
The introduction of the Futcher twins and Steve Buckley.
The home wins over Leeds and Arsenal within three days in March.
The top versus bottom Boxing Day clash when Luton beat Ipswich 1-0.

Low spots: The form before Christmas.
The terrible Easter, with all three games lost, including a 0-5 collapse at champions-to-be Derby.
Spurs' unlikely 4-2 win over Leeds, which ended the Town's tenure in the top division.

Player of the Year: Alan West.
Ever-presents: (1) Alan West.
Hat-tricks: Ron Futcher (1).
Leading scorer: Adrian Alston (8).

| | Appearances | | | | | | Goals | | | |
|---|---|---|---|---|---|---|---|---|---|---|
| | Lge | *Sub* | LC | *Sub* | FAC | *Sub* | Lge | LC | FAC | Tot |
| Alston, Adrian | **18** | *3* | 2 | | | | **7** | 1 | | **8** |
| Anderson, Peter | **40** | | 2 | | 1 | | **6** | | | **6** |
| Aston, John | **32** | | | | 1 | | **5** | | | **5** |
| Barber, Keith | **26** | | 2 | | | | | | | |
| Buckley, Steve | **24** | | 1 | | 1 | | | | | |
| Butlin, Barry | **9** | | 1 | | | | **3** | | | **3** |
| Chambers, Brian | **6** | | | | | | | | | |
| Faulkner, John | **34** | | | | 1 | | **1** | | | **1** |
| Fern, Rodney | **3** | | | | | | | | | |
| Fuccillo, Lil | | *1* | | | | | | | | |
| Futcher, Paul | **19** | | | | 1 | | | | | |
| Futcher, Ron | **16** | *1* | | | 1 | | **7** | | | **7** |
| Garner, Alan | **9** | | 1 | *1* | | | **1** | | | **1** |
| Hindson, Gordon | **17** | | 2 | | | | **1** | | | **1** |
| Horn, Graham | **16** | | | | 1 | | | | | |
| Husband, Jim | **33** | | 2 | | 1 | | **3** | | | **3** |
| King, Andy | | *1* | | | | | | | | |
| Litt, Steve | **12** | | 1 | | | | | | | |
| Pollock, Matt | | | | | | *1* | | | | |
| Ryan, Jim | **30** | *1* | 1 | | 1 | | **7** | | | **7** |
| Ryan, John | **38** | | 2 | | 1 | | **1** | | | **1** |
| Seasman, John | **1** | *1* | | | | | **1** | | | **1** |
| Shanks, Don | **15** | *1* | 2 | | | | **1** | | | **1** |
| Spiring, Peter | **5** | *2* | | | | | **1** | | | **1** |
| Thomson, Bobby | **17** | | 1 | | | | | | | |
| West, Alan | **42** | | 2 | | 1 | | **1** | | | **1** |
| (own-goals) | | | | | | | **1** | | | **1** |
| **26 players used** | **462** | *11* | **22** | *1* | **11** | *1* | **47** | **1** | | **48** |

| No | Date | Att | Pos | Pt | F-A | H-T | Scorers, Times, and Referees | 1 | 2 | 3 | 4 | 5 | 6 | 7 | 8 | 9 | 10 | 11 | 12 sub used |
|---|---|---|---|---|---|---|---|---|---|---|---|---|---|---|---|---|---|---|---|
| 1 | H HULL | | | W | 2-0 | 2-0 | Futcher R 21, King 30 | Barber | Ryan, John | Buckley | Faulkner | Litt | Anderson | King | West | Alston | Futcher R | Aston | |
| | 16/8 | 10,389 | | 2 | | | | *Wealands* | *Banks* | *Devries* | *Grimes* | *Croft* | *Roberts* | *Galvin* | *Lord* | *Wood* | *Wagstaff* | *Greenwood* | |
| | | | | | | | Ref: R Challis | Playing in brilliant sunshine, Aston's ball control is too much for Hull full-back Frank Banks, and he is able to cross for Futcher to hit the first. King, making his full league debut, scores after a shot from Futcher rebounds off the bar. The Hull forwards are unable to trouble Keith Barber. | | | | | | | | | | | |
| 2 | A WEST BROM | 18 | | L | 0-1 | 0-0 | | Barber | Ryan, John | Buckley | Anderson | Faulkner | Futcher P | King | Alston | Futcher R | West | Aston | |
| | 23/8 | *14,062* | *12* | 2 | | | *Trewick 76* | *Osborne* | *Nisbet* | *Wilson* | *Robson* | *Wile* | *Robertson* | *Trewick* | *Brown* | *Hurst* | *Giles* | *Johnston* | |
| | | | | | | | Ref: H Hackney | The only goal of the game comes when, following a scramble in the penalty area, the ball is beaten out to John Trewick whose speculative shot goes in off a post. 'I thought we took the first half from them easily, and we should have taken at least a point,' moans Luton manager Haslam. | | | | | | | | | | | |
| 3 | H CHELSEA | 8 | | W | 3-0 | 1-0 | Anderson 25, Buckley 46p, Futcher R 60 | Barber | Ryan, John | Buckley | Anderson | Faulkner | Futcher P | King | Alston | Futcher R | West* | Aston ! | Chambers |
| | 30/8 | **18,565** | *7* | 4 | | | | *Sherwood* | *Wilkins G** | *Sparrow* | *Bason* | *Droy* | *Dempsey* | *Britton* | *Wilkins R* | *Maybank* | *Swain* | *Cooke* | *Harris* |
| | | | | | | | Ref: E Read | Anderson scores the first goal against a young Chelsea side after a header from Faulkner rebounds off the post. Buckley converts from the spot after Futcher, who later scores the third goal, is fouled by Brian Bason. Aston is dismissed with 17 minutes left after a tangle with Ian Britton. | | | | | | | | | | | |
| 4 | A PORTSMOUTH | 6 | | W | 2-0 | 1-0 | King 39, Alston 50 | Barber | Ryan, John | Buckley | Anderson | Faulkner | Futcher P | King | Alston | Futcher R | Chambers | Spiring | |
| | 6/9 | *9,835* | *20* | 6 | | | | *Lloyd* | *Roberts* | *Piper* | *Reynolds* | *Went* | *Hand* | *Kamara* | *Kane* | *Graham* | *Foster* | *Marinello* | |
| | | | | | | | Ref: C White | Although key players Alan West and John Aston are both absent for this match, the Town are able to dispose of Portsmouth without too much ado. The Town open up the Pompey defence at will, but the only strikes that count come from soft efforts from Andy King and Adrian Alston. | | | | | | | | | | | |
| 5 | H BOLTON | 9 | | L | 0-2 | 0-1 | | Barber | Ryan, John | Buckley | Anderson | Faulkner | Futcher P | King | Alston | Futcher R | Ryan, Jim | Aston | |
| | 13/9 | 11,217 | *7* | 6 | | | *Futcher P 37 (og), Curran 71* | *Siddall* | *Ritson* | *Nicholson* | *Greaves* | *Jones P* | *Allardyce* | *Byrom* | *Curran* | *Jones G* | *Reid* | *Thompson* | |
| | | | | | | | Ref: K Burns | Paul Futcher is unfortunate to score with a back-headed own-goal. Ex-England international Peter Thompson attacks down the left before crossing to Hugh Curran, who has time and space to choose his spot for the second goal and extend the Trotters' unbeaten run to three games. | | | | | | | | | | | |
| 6 | A NOTTS CO | 11 | | L | 0-1 | 0-0 | | Barber | Ryan, John | Buckley | Anderson | Faulkner | Futcher P | King | Alston | Futcher R | Ryan, Jim | Aston* | Husband |
| | 20/9 | *11,173* | *1* | 6 | | | *Scanlon 66* | *McManus* | *Richards* | *O'Brien* | *Bolton* | *Needham* | *Stubbs* | *Carter* | *Probert* | *Bradd* | *McVay* | *Scanlon* | |
| | | | | | | | Ref: B Newsome | County, early leaders of the Division, hit the Hatters with a hotly disputed goal when Ian Scanlon fires home from a seemingly offside position, much to the disgust of the Hatters' manager, Harry Haslam, and centre-half, Faulkner, who is lucky to stay on the field following his protests. | | | | | | | | | | | |
| 7 | H PLYMOUTH | 12 | | D | 1-1 | 1-0 | Husband 19 | Barber | Ryan, John | Buckley | Anderson | Faulkner | Futcher P | King | Husband | Futcher R | Ryan, Jim | Seasman | |
| | 24/9 | 9,226 | *15* | 7 | | | *Johnson 62* | *Aleksic* | *Hore* | *Burrows* | *Horswill* | *Green* | *Delve* | *Randell* | *Johnson* | *Mariner** | *Rafferty* | *McAuley* | *Foster* |
| | | | | | | | Ref: C Thomas | Smarting from two recent defeats, the Town tear holes in the Plymouth defence in a lively first half and score once, through a Husband tap-in, and miss six more chances. Victory is thrown away after the interval when an error by Faulkner provides Brian Johnson with an easy chance. | | | | | | | | | | | |
| 8 | H BLACKBURN | 10 | | D | 1-1 | 0-0 | Husband 55 | Barber | Ryan, John | Buckley | Anderson | Faulkner | Futcher P | Ryan, Jim | Husband | Futcher R | West | Seasman | |
| | 27/9 | 8,458 | *16* | 8 | | | *Kenyon 66* | *Jones* | *Wilkinson* | *Hutt* | *Hawkins* | *Fazackerley* | *Metcalfe* | *Oates* | *Beamish* | *Martin* | *Kenyon** | *Parkes* | *Hickman* |
| | | | | | | | Ref: R Perkins | West returns to the side after missing four games through a shoulder injury to give the midfield more flair and bite. With a strong gale behind them in the second half, the Town become more menacing and Husband scores after West curls in a pass. A Futcher error lets in John Kenyon. | | | | | | | | | | | |
| 9 | A BLACKPOOL | 13 | | L | 2-3 | 1-1 | Anderson 5, Spiring 52 | Barber | Ryan, John | Buckley | Anderson | Faulkner | Futcher P | Ryan, Jim | Alston | Spiring | West | Seasman* | Chambers |
| | 4/10 | *7,864* | *8* | 8 | | | *Suddaby 40, 72, Walsh 84* | *Wood* | *Curtis* | *Bentley* | *Hart* | *Suddaby* | *Hatton* | *Ronson* | *Suddick* | *Walsh* | *Ainscow* | *Harrison* | |
| | | | | | | | Ref: G Nolan | Injury-hit Luton nearly pull off a shock win. Anderson puts the Town in front after a slip by Peter Suddaby, who makes amends by heading an equaliser, albeit against the run of play. Spiring restores the lead but the Hatters defence crumbles in the last 20 minutes under intense pressure. | | | | | | | | | | | |
| 10 | A CARLISLE | 11 | | D | 1-1 | 1-1 | Seasman 11 | Barber | Ryan, John | Thomson | Anderson | Faulkner | Futcher P | Ryan, Jim | Alston | Spiring* | Chambers | Seasman | King |
| | 11/10 | *6,621* | *21* | 9 | | | *Clarke 18* | *Burleigh* | *Spearritt* | *Gorman* | *Barry* | *Green* | *Carr* | *Owen* | *Prudham* | *Clarke* | *O'Neill* | *Laidlaw* | |
| | | | | | | | Ref: M Lowe | With two minutes left and a 1-1 draw looking the inevitable result, the Hatters are awarded a penalty when the Carlisle goalkeeper brings down Seasman. Jim Ryan sends Martin Burleigh the wrong way but sees his spot-kick hit the post before being cleared to safety by a grateful defence. | | | | | | | | | | | |

| No | Venue | Opponent | Pos | Res | F-A | H-T | Scorers, Times, and Referees | 1 | 2 | 3 | 4 | 5 | 6 | 7 | 8 | 9 | 10 | 11 | 12 |
|---|---|---|---|---|---|---|---|---|---|---|---|---|---|---|---|---|---|---|---|
| 11 | H | FULHAM | 10 | W | 1-0 | 1-0 | Chambers 27 | Barber | Ryan, John | Thomson | Anderson | Faulkner | Futcher P | Ryan, Jim | Spiring | Futcher R | Chambers | Seasman* | West |
| | 18/10 | 14,086 | *4* | 11 | | | | *Mellor* | *James* | *Slough* | *Mullery* | *Howe* | *Moore* | *Mitchell** | *Conway* | *Busby* | *Lloyd* | *Barrett* | *Dowie* |
| | | | | | | | Ref: G Flint | The Hatters welcome former players Slough and Busby, together with ex-manager Alec Stock, to Kenilworth Road, but spoil their day when Chambers hits a terrific shot over the head of Fulham keeper Peter Mellor, who had advanced off his line, and into the top corner of the net. | | | | | | | | | | | |
| 12 | A | NOTT'M FOREST | 10 | D | 0-0 | 0-0 | | Barber | Ryan, John | Thomson | Anderson | Faulkner | Futcher P | Ryan, Jim | Spiring | Futcher R | Chambers | West | |
| | 21/10 | *12,290* | *14* | 12 | | | | *Middleton* | *Anderson* | *Clark* | *McGovern* | *Cottam* | *Richardson* | *Curran* | *O'Neill* | *O'Hare* | *Butlin* | *Robertson* | |
| | | | | | | | Ref: N Ashley | The midfield players cancel each other out in a game devoid of incident. Ex-Town striker, Barry Butlin, playing after a long absence, is well guarded by defenders Faulkner and Paul Futcher, and Haslam is more pleased with the single point than is his opposite number, Brian Clough. | | | | | | | | | | | |
| 13 | A | SUNDERLAND | 10 | L | 0-2 | 0-0 | | Barber | Ryan, John | Thomson | Anderson | Faulkner | Futcher P | Ryan, Jim | Chambers | Seasman | West | Aston* | King |
| | 25/10 | ***28,338*** | *1* | 12 | | | *Kerr 55, Robson 56* | *Montgomery* | *Malone* | *Ashurst* | *Towers** | *Clarke* | *Moncur* | *Kerr* | *Hughes* | *Halom* | *Robson* | *Porterfield* | *Holden* |
| | | | | | | | Ref: C Seel | Sunderland maintain their 100% home league record for the season when shackling the gritty resilience of the Hatters, albeit a changed team up front due to injury problems. Both goals come about from the skills of the small inside-forwards who play the ball intelligently along the floor. | | | | | | | | | | | |
| 14 | H | BRISTOL CITY | 12 | D | 0-0 | 0-0 | | Barber | Ryan, John | Thomson | Chambers | Faulkner | Futcher P | Ryan, Jim* | King | Anderson | West | Aston | Husband |
| | 1/11 | 11,446 | *2* | 13 | | | | *Cashley* | *Gillies* | *Drysdale* | *Gow* | *Collier* | *Merrick* | *Tainton* | *Ritchie* | *Mann* | *Cheesley* | *Whitehead* | |
| | | | | | | | Ref: H Davey | Anderson plays in the forward line as an experiment, but it is Aston, returning to the side from his early-season injury, who causes the greatest problems for the high-flying City defence. The game is watched by prospective new Hatters' signing, Jimmy Johnstone, the ex-Celtic winger. | | | | | | | | | | | |
| 15 | H | YORK | 10 | W | 4-0 | 1-0 | Husband 35, West 56, King 58, | Barber | Ryan, John | Thomson | Chambers | Faulkner | Futcher P | Husband | King | Anderson | West | Aston | |
| | 4/11 | 7,982 | *22* | 15 | | | [Anderson 74] | *Crawford* | *Oliver* | *Downing* | *Cave* | *Swallow* | *Topping* | *Pollard* | *Holmes* | *Seal* | *Jones* | *Wann* | |
| | | | | | | | Ref: A Lees | After just one win in ten weeks and two goals in five games, the Town put their indifferent form behind them by hitting bottom-placed York for four goals. York show plenty of fight but are decidedly short on class and pose no real threat to the Hatters, who press home their advantage. | | | | | | | | | | | |
| 16 | A | SOUTHAMPTON | 11 | L | 1-3 | 0-2 | Ryan John 78 | Barber | Ryan, John | Thomson | Chambers | Faulkner | Futcher P | Husband* | King | Anderson | West | Aston | Ryan, Jim |
| | 8/11 | *13,885* | *7* | 15 | | | *McCalliog 15, Stokes 20, Channon 75* | *Middleton* | *Rodrigues** | *Steele* | *Holmes* | *Andruszewski* | *Blyth* | *Stokes* | *Channon* | *Osgood* | *McCalliog* | *Peach* | *O'Brien* |
| | | | | | | | Ref: J Homewood | In an open game, the Saints are flattered by an early two-goal lead but, by the time of the third goal when Mick Channon drives a free-kick past Barber, the Hatters realise that they are to become the eighth successive team to suffer defeat at the Dell. John Ryan scores a late consolation. | | | | | | | | | | | |
| 17 | H | OLDHAM | 15 | L | 2-3 | 1-2 | Husband 3, Chambers 72 | Barber | Ryan, John | Thomson | Chambers | Faulkner | Futcher P | Husband | King | Futcher R* | West | Aston | Ryan, Jim |
| | 15/11 | 8,237 | *8* | 15 | | | *Chapman 25, McVitie 26, Shaw 89* | *Platt* | *Wood* | *Whittle* | *Bell* | *Hicks !* | *Holt* | *McVitie* | *Shaw* | *Blair* | *Chapman* | *Groves* | |
| | | | | | | | Ref: A Turvey | David Shaw earns Oldham their first away win for 32 games when scoring in the last minute. Husband scores the opening goal but Oldham get two in a minute to lead at the interval. Chambers equalises before Oldham defender Keith Hicks is dismissed after 78 minutes for retaliation. | | | | | | | | | | | |
| 18 | A | FULHAM | 17 | L | 0-2 | 0-1 | | Barber | Ryan, John | Thomson | Chambers | Faulkner | Futcher P | Husband | King | Spiring | West | Aston | |
| | 22/11 | *9,626* | *6* | 15 | | | *Conway 21, 83* | *Mellor* | *Fraser* | *Strong* | *Mullery* | *Howe* | *Moore* | *Dowie* | *Conway* | *Busby* | *Slough* | *Barrett* | |
| | | | | | | | Ref: D Nippard | The problems emanating from the Boardroom are affecting the players performances on the pitch, admits Town manager, Harry Haslam. Busby, against his old club, sets up both goals for Jimmy Conway, making this the first time that Fulham have scored twice in a game since September. | | | | | | | | | | | |
| 19 | H | ORIENT | 15 | W | 1-0 | 1-0 | Husband 10 | Barber | Ryan, John | Buckley | Chambers | Faulkner | Futcher P | Husband | King* | **Pollock** | West | Aston | Spiring |
| | 29/11 | 7,897 | *14* | 17 | | | | *Jackson* | *Fisher* | *Grealish* | *Bennett* | *Hoadley* | *Walley* | *Cunningham* | *Roeder* | *Queen* | *Mooney** | *Heppolette* | *Allder* |
| | | | | | | | Ref: A Robinson | Town end the O's run of six unbeaten games in a busy match. After three successive defeats, the Hatters have to win this game if they are to avoid a relegation struggle. Nerves are settled early on when Aston beats Bobby Fisher and puts a perfect cross onto the head of Jim Husband. | | | | | | | | | | | |
| 20 | A | CHARLTON | 13 | W | **5-1** | 1-1 | Anderson 38, 72, Husband 57, 59, | Barber | Ryan, John | Buckley | Chambers | Faulkner | Futcher P | King | Anderson | Husband | West | Aston | |
| | 3/12 | *8,703* | *18* | 19 | | | *Flanagan 8* [Chambers 60] | *Tutt* | *Penfold* | *Warman* | *Bowman* | *Giles* | *Young* | *Powell* | *Hales* | *Flanagan* | *Hunt* | *Peacock* | |
| | | | | | | | Ref: D Lloyd | The Town launch a four-goal second-half blitz to sink a Charlton team who, when Mike Flanagan headed them into the lead, had looked the more likely winners. Peter Anderson, playing his last game for the Hatters, equalises and is then instrumental in setting up the other four goals. | | | | | | | | | | | |
| 21 | H | WEST BROM | 10 | W | 2-1 | 1-0 | King 44, Aston 79 | Barber | Ryan, John | Buckley | Chambers* | Faulkner | Futcher P | Husband | King | Futcher R | West | Aston | Ryan, Jim |
| | 13/12 | 10,203 | *6* | 21 | | | *Martin 46* | *Osborne* | *Mulligan* | *Wilson* | *Brown Tony* | *Robson* | *Robertson* | *Martin* | *Brown Ally* | *Mayo* | *Giles !* | *Johnston* | |
| | | | | | | | Ref: E Read | The home gate is swelled by 2,000 extra supporters, who are anxious to help the Club and contribute to the 'Save the Town' fund. Promotion-chasing West Brom are reduced to ten men when their player-manager, Johnny Giles, is dismissed after 20 minutes for a foul on Ron Futcher. | | | | | | | | | | | |

| No | | Date | Att | Pos | Pt | F-A | H-T | Scorers, Times, and Referees | 1 | 2 | 3 | 4 | 5 | 6 | 7 | 8 | 9 | 10 | 11 | 12 sub used |
|---|---|---|---|---|---|---|---|---|---|---|---|---|---|---|---|---|---|---|---|---|
| 22 | A | HULL | | 10 | W | 2-1 | 1-0 | Husband 24, King 56 | Barber | Ryan, John | Buckley | Chambers | Faulkner | Futcher P | Husband | King | Futcher R | West | Aston | |
| | | 20/12 | *5,449* | *16* | 23 | | | *Wood 49* | *Wealands* | *Daniel* | *Croft* | *Haigh* | *Devries** | *Hawley* | *Grimes* | *Lyall* | *Fletcher* | *Wood* | *Greenwood* | *Gibson* |
| | | | | | | | | Ref: T Farley | A fighting victory at Hull gives the Town a flying Christmas holiday start. Buckley crosses from the left wing and Husband hits a first timer to score. Alf Wood equalises for the home side before Aston sets up a picture goal for King, which leaves the Hatters with 35 minutes to hold out. | | | | | | | | | | | |
| 23 | H | OXFORD | | 9 | W | 3-2 | 2-0 | Futcher R 34, 41, King 60 | Barber | Ryan, John | Buckley | Chambers | Faulkner | Futcher P | Husband | King | Futcher R | West | Aston | |
| | | 26/12 | *13,101* | *20* | 25 | | | *Shuker 87, Jeffrey 89* | *Burton* | *Taylor* | *Shuker* | *Lowe* | *Clarke* | *Jeffrey* | *Houseman* | *Aylott* | *Foley* | *McCulloch* | *Tait* | |
| | | | | | | | | Ref: J Bent | Hatters spoil a five-star show by conceding two goals in the last three minutes to give the scoreline an unrealistic look. Playing brilliantly in the opening period, Town take the lead when West and Aston combine down the left to set up Ron Futcher, who scores again seven minutes later. | | | | | | | | | | | |
| 24 | A | BRISTOL ROV | | 6 | W | 1-0 | 0-0 | King 88 | Barber | Ryan, John | Buckley | Chambers | Faulkner | Futcher P | Husband | King | Futcher R | West | Aston | |
| | | 27/12 | *11,042* | *10* | 27 | | | | *Eadie* | *Jacobs* | *Parsons* | *Bater* | *Day* | *Smith* | *Stephens* | *Williams* | *Warboys* | *Bannister* | *Evans* | |
| | | | | | | | | Ref: E Wallace | The Town leave it late to record their sixth successive win when, with 90 seconds to go, King produces the only shot to beat Rovers' inspired goalkeeper, Jim Eadie. At least six good chances are wasted and Rovers' manager, Don Megson, admits that the Town are the worthy winners. | | | | | | | | | | | |
| 25 | H | PORTSMOUTH | | 8 | W | 3-1 | 2-0 | Faulkner 8, King 37, Futcher R 58 | Barber | Ryan, John | Buckley | Chambers | Faulkner | Futcher P | Husband | King | Futcher R | West | Aston | |
| | | 17/1 | 10,464 | *22* | 29 | | | *Piper 71* | *Lloyd* | *Lawler** | *Mellows* | *Roberts* | *Went* | *Cahill* | *McGuinness* | *Piper* | *Graham* | *Reynolds* | *Eames* | *Wilson* |
| | | | | | | | | Ref: D Richardson | Pompey attempt to play a defensive game, but fail to stop Faulkner scoring the first goal when he meets an in-swinging corner from West. King adds a second to give a comfortable half-time lead. Portsmouth improve after the break but are unable to prevent Ron Futcher scoring the third. | | | | | | | | | | | |
| 26 | A | BOLTON | | 8 | L | **0-3** | 0-3 | | Barber | Ryan, John | Buckley | Chambers | Faulkner | Futcher P | Ryan, Jim | King | Futcher R | West | Aston | |
| | | 27/1 | *22,037* | *2* | 29 | | | *Jones G 3, Byrom 23, Allardyce 36* | *Siddall* | *Ritson* | *Dunne* | *Greaves* | *Jones P* | *Allardyce* | *Byrom** | *Whatmore* | *Jones G* | *Reid* | *Thompson* | *Nicholson* |
| | | | | | | | | Ref: J Taylor | Bolton miss out on going top of the table on goal-difference, but they put on a first-half display of vintage, free-flowing football. The Hatters' winning run is abruptly ended by Bolton's quick movement and precision passing, Allardyce scoring the pick of the goals with a diving header. | | | | | | | | | | | |
| 27 | H | NOTT'M FOREST | | 7 | D | 1-1 | 0-0 | Futcher R 71 | Barber | Ryan, John | Buckley | Chambers | Faulkner | Futcher P | Husband | King | Futcher R | West | Aston | |
| | | 31/1 | 8,503 | *16* | 30 | | | *Curran 67* | *Wells* | *O'Kane* | *Clark* | *McGovern* | *Chapman* | *Bowyer* | *Curran* | *O'Neill* | *O'Hare* | *Butlin* | *Robertson* | |
| | | | | | | | | Ref: T Bune | Referee Tom Bune makes a mistake in passing the pitch fit, the frozen surface turning the game into a lottery. The players are unable to turn or change direction, relying on a long-ball game which invites plenty of errors. Surprisingly, only two goals are scored and a draw is the fair result. | | | | | | | | | | | |
| 28 | A | YORK | | 7 | W | 3-2 | 2-1 | Chambers 5, Futcher R 26, Fuccillo 54 | Barber | Ryan, John | Buckley | Chambers | Price | Futcher P | Fuccillo | King | Futcher R | West | Ryan, Jim | |
| | | 7/2 | ***3,507*** | *21* | 32 | | | *Holmes 35p, Pollard 75* | *Crawford* | *Stone* | *Woodward* | *James* | *Swallow* | *Topping* | *Pollard* | *Holmes** | *Seal* | *Cave* | *McMordie* | *Hosker* |
| | | | | | | | | Ref: K Walmsley | Chambers opens the scoring after playing a 'one-two' with King. Then Futcher adds the second from a Fuccillo cross. Holmes scores from the spot after the ball hits John Ryan on the shoulder, but Fuccillo, making his full league debut, restores the two-goal advantage with a solo effort. | | | | | | | | | | | |
| 29 | A | OLDHAM | | 7 | D | 1-1 | 0-1 | Husband 86 | Barber | Ryan, John | Buckley | Chambers | Faulkner | Futcher P | Husband | King | Pollock* | West | Fuccillo | Aston |
| | | 21/2 | *8,796* | *8* | 33 | | | *Shaw 33* | *Platt* | *Wood* | *Whittle* | *Bell* | *Edwards* | *Holt* | *Blair* | *Chapman* | *Young** | *Shaw* | *Groves* | *Robins* |
| | | | | | | | | Ref: K Burns | David Shaw hits home a short-range effort, against the run of play, to give Oldham the lead but, with just four minutes left, Husband swoops to hit a Faulkner centre past John Platt. The Hatters gain a richly deserved share of the spoils and end the promotion aspirations of the visitors. | | | | | | | | | | | |
| 30 | A | PLYMOUTH | | 7 | L | **0-3** | 0-1 | | Barber | Ryan, John | Buckley | Chambers | Faulkner* | Futcher P | Husband | King | Fuccillo | West | Aston | Pollock |
| | | 24/2 | *13,927* | *13* | 33 | | | *Randell 14, Rafferty 57,58* | *Furnell* | *Horswill* | *Burrows* | *Sutton* | *Green* | *Delve* | *Randell* | *Johnson* | *Mariner* | *Rafferty** | *McAuley* | *Foster* |
| | | | | | | | | Ref: P Walters | A new cash crisis hits the Club with £40,000 being needed immediately. On the field, wholesale changes are threatened by the manager, Harry Haslam, after Plymouth sink the Hatters without trace with a two-goal burst in the second-half. The Town squander many good opportunities. | | | | | | | | | | | |
| 31 | H | SUNDERLAND | | 7 | W | 2-0 | 0-0 | Moncur 65 (og), Futcher R 85 | Barber | Ryan, John | Buckley | Chambers | Faulkner | Futcher P | Husband | King | Futcher R | West | Fuccillo | |
| | | 28/2 | 15,338 | *3* | 35 | | | | *Montgomery* | *Malone* | *Bolton* | *Towers* | *Clarke* | *Moncur* | *Kerr* | *Ashurst* | *Holden* | *Robson* | *Finney** | *Greenwood* |
| | | | | | | | | Ref: L Haynes | Ron Futcher misses three clear-cut chances to score in the first half. The first goal eventually comes when Husband forces Bobby Moncur into conceding an own-goal. He then beats Jim Montgomery for speed and tees up Ron Futcher, who blasts the ball into an empty net for the second. | | | | | | | | | | | |

| No | Date | Opponents | Att | Pos | Res | F-A | H-T | Scorers, Times, and Referees | 1 | 2 | 3 | 4 | 5 | 6 | 7 | 8 | 9 | 10 | 11 | 12 |
|---|---|---|---|---|---|---|---|---|---|---|---|---|---|---|---|---|---|---|---|---|
| 32 | H | SOUTHAMPTON | | 6 | W | 1-0 | 0-0 | Husband 72 | Barber | Ryan, John | Buckley | Chambers | Faulkner | Futcher P | Husband | King | Futcher R | West | Fuccillo | |
| | 2/3 | | 13,737 | *5* | 37 | | | | *Turner* | *Rodrigues* | *Peach* | *Blyth* | *Bennett* | *Holmes* | *Fisher* | *Osgood* | *McCalliog* | *Channon* | *Stokes* | |
| | | | | | | | | Ref: J Hunting | A headed goal from Husband, following a left-wing corner from Chambers, gives the Hatters their second victory in four days. In a frenzied and untidy match, the Saints' goalkeeper, Ian Turner, is required to make excellent saves from both King and Buckley during the first period. | | | | | | | | | | | |
| 33 | A | BRISTOL CITY | | 7 | L | **0-3** | 0-0 | | Barber | Ryan, John | Buckley | Chambers | Faulkner | Futcher P | Husband | King | Futcher R | West | Fuccillo* | Aston |
| | 6/3 | | *15,872* | *1* | 37 | | | *Ritchie 54, 57, Cheesley 72* | *Cashley* | *Gillies* | *Drysdale* | *Collier* | *Merrick* | *Sweeney* | *Gow* | *Tainton* | *Whitehead* | *Ritchie* | *Cheesley* | |
| | | | | | | | | Ref: J Hough | After a bad-tempered first half, the Town are given a lesson in attacking football which finally overwhelms them. The Robins score three times after the interval and also miss a penalty, which is awarded when John Ryan is penalised for pushing, Gerry Gow grazing the bar with his kick. | | | | | | | | | | | |
| 34 | H | CARLISLE | | 6 | W | 3-0 | 1-0 | Husband 12, 83, King 60 | Barber | Ryan, John | Buckley | Fuccillo | Faulkner | Futcher P | Husband | King | Futcher R | West | Aston | |
| | 13/3 | | 8,856 | *17* | 39 | | | | *Ross* | *Spearritt** | *Gorman* | *Bonnyman* | *Owen* | *Barry* | *Latham* | *O'Neill* | *Martin* | *Clarke* | *Laidlaw* | *McVitie* |
| | | | | | | | | Ref: W Gow | Promotion hopes are kept flickering as the Town dispose of the Cumbrian challenge in a game that could have gone either way. The visitors hit the woodwork twice and have another effort headed off the line. Husband heads two goals from crosses by Aston with King adding the third. | | | | | | | | | | | |
| 35 | A | ORIENT | | 7 | L | **0-3** | 0-2 | | Barber | Ryan, John | Buckley | Fuccillo | Faulkner* | Futcher P | Husband | King | Futcher R | West | Aston | Pollock |
| | 20/3 | | *5,544* | *16* | 39 | | | *Bennett 31, 37, Heppolette 56* | *Jackson* | *Payne* | *Grealish* | *Hoadley* | *Walley* | *Allen* | *Heppolette* | *Allder* | *Cunningham** | *Bennett* | *Queen* | *Cotton* |
| | | | | | | | | Ref: G Trevett | Faulkner limps off the Brisbane Road pitch after 18 minutes with an ankle injury. The Hatters' defence disintegrates and Orient have a field-day. Peter Bennett heads home a cross from Laurie Cunningham and then scores with a 40-yard free-kick; Ricky Heppolette heads the third. | | | | | | | | | | | |
| 36 | H | CHARLTON | | 5 | D | 1-1 | 1-0 | Ryan John 39 | Barber | Ryan, John | Buckley | Fuccillo | Price | Futcher P | Husband | King | Futcher R | West | Aston | |
| | 27/3 | | 9,947 | *9* | 40 | | | *Hales 78* | *Wood* | *Berry* | *Young D* | *Giles* | *Curtis** | *Young A* | *Powell* | *Peacock* | *Hales* | *Flanagan* | *Hunt* | *Bowman* |
| | | | | | | | | Ref: R Lee | Teenage goalkeeper Jeff Wood is penalised under the four-steps rule, and captain Alan West touches the resultant free-kick to John Ryan, who hammers it into the net. Ex-Hatters striker, Derek Hales, scores his 25th goal of the season and earns a point for his team in a scrappy game. | | | | | | | | | | | |
| 37 | A | BLACKBURN | | 6 | L | **0-3** | 0-1 | | Barber | Ryan, John | Buckley | Pollock | Price | Futcher P | Husband | Spiring* | Futcher R | West | Aston | Chambers |
| | 3/4 | | *7,911* | *18* | 40 | | | *Parkes 24, Waddington 47, Beamish 75* | *Bradshaw* | *Waddington* | *Wood* | *Hawkins* | *Fazackerley* | *Metcalfe* | *Taylor* | *Parkes* | *Downes* | *Beamish* | *Hird* | |
| | | | | | | | | Ref: P Richardson | Aston takes advantage of a bad back-pass by Parkes and then has his feet whipped away by Bradshaw. The referee waves play on and Parkes goes on to score at the other end. Aston and Ron Futcher each hit the woodwork prior to Blackburn scoring. It is just not the Hatters' day! | | | | | | | | | | | |
| 38 | H | NOTTS CO | | 8 | D | 1-1 | 1-0 | West 43 | Barber | Ryan, John | Buckley | Fuccillo | Price | Futcher P | Husband | Chambers | Futcher R | West | Aston | |
| | 10/4 | | 8,277 | *7* | 41 | | | *Sims 77* | *McManus* | *Richards* | *O'Brien* | *Needham* | *Stubbs* | *Smith* | *Birchenall* | *Mann** | *Carter* | *Sims* | *Bradd* | *Scanlon* |
| | | | | | | | | Ref: L Burden | Buckley wins the ball in his own half and passes to West, who hits his first-time shot past Eric McManus. County deservedly equalise after a long clearance is helped on by Brian Stubbs to ex-Luton loan player John Sims, who wrong-foots Paul Futcher and slips the ball into the net. | | | | | | | | | | | |
| 39 | A | CHELSEA | | 8 | D | 2-2 | 1-1 | Husband 12, Chambers 63 | Barber | Ryan, John | Buckley | Chambers | Price | Futcher P | Husband | Fuccillo | Futcher R | West | Aston | |
| | 16/4 | | *19,873* | *11* | 42 | | | *Finnieston 33, Hay 53* | *Bonetti** | *Harris* | *Wilkins G* | *Wicks* | *Hay* | *Stanley* | *Britton* | *Wilkins R* | *Lewington* | *Finnieston* | *Swain* | *Garner* |
| | | | | | | | | Ref: L Shapter | Town take the lead in an entertaining game when Husband lobs Peter Bonetti and Steve Finnieston levels after a good spell of pressure. Bonetti leaves the field with a dislocated finger and is replaced by Bill Garner. David Hay chips a second before Chambers equalises with a half-volley. | | | | | | | | | | | |
| 40 | A | OXFORD | | 7 | W | 3-1 | 1-1 | Buckley 23, Fuccillo 78, Husband 89 | Barber | Ryan, John | Buckley | Fuccillo | Price | Futcher P | Husband | Chambers | Futcher R | West | Aston* | Pollock |
| | 17/4 | | *7,881* | *20* | 44 | | | *Clarke D 43* | *Burton* | *Taylor* | *Shuker* | *Lowe* | *Clarke C* | *Briggs* | *Houseman* | *Foley* | *Tait* | *Clarke D* | *Gibbins** | *Aylott* |
| | | | | | | | | Ref: B James | Luton control the game against a weary-looking Oxford side. A spectacular 25-yard shot from Buckley opens the scoring, but Derek Clarke heads the equaliser before the break. Fuccillo's centre creeps into the net and Husband gets a late goal after Ron Futcher's shot strikes a post. | | | | | | | | | | | |
| 41 | H | BRISTOL ROV | | 6 | W | 3-1 | 0-1 | Price 58, Chambers 86, Hill 87 | Barber | Price | Buckley | Chambers | Faulkner* | Futcher P | Husband | Fuccillo | Futcher R | West | Ryan, John | **Hill** |
| | 19/4 | | **7,646** | *16* | 46 | | | *Britten 42* | *Eadie* | *Parsons* | *Day* | *Taylor* | *Pulis* | *Williams* | *Britten* | *Smith** | *Evans* | *Staniforth* | *Fearnley* | *Stephens* |
| | | | | | | | | Ref: D Turner | Ricky Hill makes his league debut as a late substitute and, with his first touch of the ball, sets up Chambers to score and break the deadlock of a 1-1 draw. His next touch, a minute later, is a terrific shot which skims into the net past a shocked Rovers' keeper Jim Eadie. A star is born! | | | | | | | | | | | |
| 42 | H | BLACKPOOL | | 7 | W | 3-0 | 2-0 | Futcher R 20, 42, Fuccillo 71 | Barber | Price | Buckley | Chambers | **Jones** | Futcher P | Husband | Fuccillo | Futcher R | West | Hill | |
| | 24/4 | | 8,757 | *10* | 48 | | | | *Wood* | *Hatton* | *Hart* | *Suddaby* | *Harrison* | *Bentley* | *Evanson** | *Suddick* | *Ronson* | *Walsh* | *Ainscow* | *McEwan* |
| | Home | Away | | | | | | Ref: C Thomas | The end of one of the most traumatic seasons in the club's history is climaxed by a victory provided by some youthful enthusiasm. Teenager Graham Jones makes his debut and Ricky Hill plays from the start. Ron Futcher sets up a two-goal interval lead and Fuccillo bends in the third. | | | | | | | | | | | |
| Average | 10,587 | 11,630 | | | | | | | | | | | | | | | | | | |

| League Cup | | | | | | | F-A | H-T | Scorers, Times, and Referees | 1 | 2 | 3 | 4 | 5 | 6 | 7 | 8 | 9 | 10 | 11 | 12 sub used |
|---|---|---|---|---|---|---|---|---|---|---|---|---|---|---|---|---|---|---|---|---|---|
| 2 | A | DARLINGTON | | 6 | L | | 1-2 | 1-0 | Futcher R 37 | Barber | Ryan, John | Buckley | Anderson | Faulkner | Futcher P | King* | Spiring | Futcher R | Chambers | Aston | Ryan, Jim |
| | 9/9 | | 6,601 | 3:3 | | | | | *Webb 68, 76* | *Ogley* | *Nattress* | *Cochrane* | *Cattrell* | *Smith* | *Blant* | *Holbrook* | *Sinclair* | *Webb* | *Crosson* | *Young* | |
| | | | | | | | | | Ref: J Rice | The Hatters are hustled and harried at every opportunity in front of the capacity crowd and the storm appears to have been weathered when Ron Futcher scores with a great individual effort. Webb levels with an unstoppable shot and then heads home the winner from a left-wing free-kick. | | | | | | | | | | | |

| FA Cup | | | | | | | F-A | H-T | Scorers, Times, and Referees | 1 | 2 | 3 | 4 | 5 | 6 | 7 | 8 | 9 | 10 | 11 | 12 sub used |
|---|---|---|---|---|---|---|---|---|---|---|---|---|---|---|---|---|---|---|---|---|---|
| 3 | H | BLACKBURN | | 6 | W | | 2-0 | 0-0 | Futcher R 70, Chambers 76 | Barber | Ryan, John | Buckley | Chambers | Faulkner | Futcher P | Husband | King | Futcher R | West | Aston | |
| | 3/1 | | 11,195 | *2:19* | | | | | | *Jones* | *Heaton* | *Wood* | *Waddington* | *Fazackerley* | *Metcalfe* | *Oates* | *Parkes* | *Hoy* | *Mullen* | *Svarc* | |
| | | | | | | | | | Ref: B Daniels | Andy King lays on a chance for Chambers, who sees his shot parried by Roger Jones and Ron Futcher is quickly on hand to score from close range. King beats three men in a run down the wing and crosses for Chambers to hit a first-time shot into the corner of the net and seal the win. | | | | | | | | | | | |
| 4 | A | NORWICH | | 8 | L | | 0-2 | 0-1 | | Barber | Ryan, John | Buckley | Chambers | Faulkner | Futcher P | Husband | King | Futcher R | West | Aston | |
| | 24/1 | | *24,328* | *1:17* | | | | | *Peters 24, Jones 53* | *Keelan* | *Jones* | *Sullivan* | *McGuire* | *Forbes* | *Stringer* | *Howell* | *MacDougall* | *Boyer* | *Suggett* | *Peters* | |
| | | | | | | | | | Ref: J Yates | Norwich avenge their 1959 FA Cup semi-final defeat as they ease through to a fifth round tie against Bradford City. Colin Sullivan appears to run the ball out of play before crossing for Martin Peters to head home the opening goal. David Jones heads the second goal from a corner-kick. | | | | | | | | | | | |

| | | P | W | D | L | F | A | W | D | L | F | A | Pts |
|---|---|---|---|---|---|---|---|---|---|---|---|---|---|
| | | | Home | | | | | Away | | | | | |
| 1 | Sunderland | 42 | 19 | 2 | 0 | 48 | 10 | 5 | 6 | 10 | 19 | 26 | 56 |
| 2 | Bristol City | 42 | 11 | 7 | 3 | 34 | 14 | 8 | 8 | 5 | 25 | 21 | 53 |
| 3 | West Brom | 42 | 10 | 9 | 2 | 29 | 12 | 10 | 4 | 7 | 21 | 21 | 53 |
| 4 | Bolton | 42 | 12 | 5 | 4 | 36 | 14 | 8 | 7 | 6 | 28 | 24 | 52 |
| 5 | Notts Co | 42 | 11 | 6 | 4 | 33 | 13 | 8 | 5 | 8 | 27 | 28 | 49 |
| 6 | Southampton | 42 | 18 | 2 | 1 | 49 | 16 | 3 | 5 | 13 | 17 | 34 | 49 |
| 7 | LUTON TOWN | 42 | 13 | 6 | 2 | 38 | 15 | 6 | 4 | 11 | 23 | 36 | 48 |
| 8 | Nott'm Forest | 42 | 13 | 1 | 7 | 34 | 18 | 4 | 11 | 6 | 21 | 22 | 46 |
| 9 | Charlton | 42 | 11 | 5 | 5 | 40 | 34 | 4 | 7 | 10 | 21 | 38 | 42 |
| 10 | Blackpool | 42 | 9 | 9 | 3 | 26 | 22 | 5 | 5 | 11 | 14 | 27 | 42 |
| 11 | Chelsea | 42 | 7 | 9 | 5 | 25 | 20 | 5 | 7 | 9 | 28 | 34 | 40 |
| 12 | Fulham | 42 | 9 | 8 | 4 | 27 | 14 | 4 | 6 | 11 | 18 | 33 | 40 |
| 13 | Orient | 42 | 10 | 6 | 5 | 21 | 12 | 3 | 8 | 10 | 16 | 27 | 40 |
| 14 | Hull | 42 | 9 | 5 | 7 | 29 | 23 | 5 | 6 | 10 | 16 | 26 | 39 |
| 15 | Blackburn | 42 | 8 | 6 | 7 | 27 | 22 | 4 | 8 | 9 | 18 | 28 | 38 |
| 16 | Plymouth | 42 | 13 | 4 | 4 | 36 | 20 | 0 | 8 | 13 | 12 | 34 | 38 |
| 17 | Oldham | 42 | 11 | 8 | 2 | 37 | 24 | 2 | 4 | 15 | 20 | 44 | 38 |
| 18 | Bristol Rov | 42 | 7 | 9 | 5 | 20 | 15 | 4 | 7 | 10 | 18 | 35 | 38 |
| 19 | Carlisle | 42 | 9 | 8 | 4 | 29 | 22 | 3 | 5 | 13 | 16 | 37 | 37 |
| 20 | Oxford | 42 | 7 | 7 | 7 | 23 | 25 | 4 | 4 | 13 | 16 | 34 | 33 |
| 21 | York | 42 | 8 | 3 | 10 | 28 | 34 | 2 | 5 | 14 | 11 | 37 | 28 |
| 22 | Portsmouth | 42 | 4 | 6 | 11 | 15 | 23 | 5 | 1 | 15 | 17 | 38 | 25 |
| | | 924 | 229 | 131 | 102 | 684 | 422 | 102 | 131 | 229 | 422 | 684 | 924 |

Odds & ends

Double wins: (5) Bristol Rovers, Hull, Oxford, Portsmouth, York.
Double losses: (1) Bolton.

Won from behind: (2) Bristol Rovers (h), Charlton (a).
Lost from in front: (3) Blackpool (a), Oldham (h), Darlington (LC).

High spots: Seven straight wins between 29 November and 17 January.
The introduction of Ricky Hill.
The five-game unbeaten run at the end of the campaign.
Winning at Oxford for the first time.

Low spots: The severe financial difficulties.
The necessary sale of Peter Anderson and Andy King.
Losing at Darlington in the League Cup.
The string of five 0-3 away defeats after Christmas.

Player of the Year: Keith Barber.
Ever-presents: Keith Barber.
Hat-tricks: (0).
Leading scorer: Jim Husband (14).

| | Appearances Lge | *Sub* | LC | *Sub* | FAC | *Sub* | Goals Lge | LC | FAC | Tot |
|---|---|---|---|---|---|---|---|---|---|---|
| Alston, Adrian | **8** | | | | | | **1** | | | **1** |
| Anderson, Peter | **17** | | 1 | | | | **5** | | | **5** |
| Aston, John | **28** | *2* | 1 | | 2 | | **1** | | | **1** |
| Barber, Keith | **42** | | 1 | | 2 | | | | | |
| Buckley, Steve | **33** | | 1 | | 2 | | **2** | | | **2** |
| Chambers, Brian | **30** | *3* | 1 | | 2 | | **6** | | 1 | **7** |
| Faulkner, John | **35** | | 1 | | 2 | | **1** | | | **1** |
| Fuccillo, Lil | **14** | | | | | | **3** | | | **3** |
| Futcher, Paul | **41** | | 1 | | 2 | | | | | |
| Futcher, Ron | **31** | | 1 | | 2 | | **10** | 1 | 1 | **12** |
| Hill, Ricky | **1** | *1* | | | | | **1** | | | **1** |
| Husband, Jim | **28** | *2* | | | 2 | | **14** | | | **14** |
| Jones, Graham | **1** | | | | | | | | | |
| King, Andy | **30** | *2* | 1 | | 2 | | **9** | | | **9** |
| Litt, Steve | **1** | | | | | | | | | |
| Pollock, Matt | **3** | *3* | | | | | | | | |
| Price, Paul | **8** | | | | | | **1** | | | **1** |
| Ryan, Jim | **12** | *3* | | *1* | | | | | | |
| Ryan, John | **41** | | 1 | | 2 | | **2** | | | **2** |
| Seasman, John | **6** | | | | | | **1** | | | **1** |
| Spiring, Peter | **7** | *1* | 1 | | | | **1** | | | **1** |
| Thomson, Bobby | **9** | | | | | | | | | |
| West, Alan | **36** | *1* | | | 2 | | **2** | | | **2** |
| (own-goals) | | | | | | | **1** | | | **1** |
| **23 players used** | **462** | ***18*** | **11** | ***1*** | **22** | | **61** | **1** | **2** | **64** |

| No | Date | Att | Pos | Pt | F-A | H-T | Scorers, Times, and Referees | 1 | 2 | 3 | 4 | 5 | 6 | 7 | 8 | 9 | 10 | 11 | 12 sub used |
|---|---|---|---|---|---|---|---|---|---|---|---|---|---|---|---|---|---|---|---|
| 1 | H SHEFFIELD UTD | | | W | 2-0 | 0-0 | Deans 53, 62 | Barber | Price | Buckley | Chambers | Faulkner | Futcher P | Husband | Hill | **Deans** | Fuccillo | Aston | |
| | 21/8 | 10,687 | | 2 | | | | *Brown* | *Franks* | *Garner* | *Flynn* | *Colquhoun* | *Ludlam* | *McGeady* | *Woodward* | *Guthrie* | *Stainrod* | *Hamilton* | |
| | | | | | | | Ref: J Hunting | After weathering 30 minutes of pressure from one of last season's relegated teams, new signing Dixie Deans makes it a dream debut, converting two John Aston centres. Town are without Alan West, Ron Futcher and Jim Ryan, who are still playing summer football in the United States. | | | | | | | | | | | |
| 2 | A HULL | | | L | 1-3 | 1-1 | Hill 4 | Barber | Price | Buckley | Chambers | Faulkner | Futcher P | Husband | Hill* | Deans | Fuccillo | Aston | **Smith** |
| | 24/8 | ***5,499*** | | 2 | | | *Sunley 1, Daniel 52p, Hemmerman 58* | *Wealands* | *Daniel* | *Devries* | *Haigh* | *Croft* | *Hawley* | *Lyall* | *Gibson* | *Sunley* | *Hemmerman* | *Stewart* | |
| | | | | | | | Ref: M Lowe | The Town defence is asleep as Dave Sunley scores from close range after a first-minute corner. Hill equalises with a well-placed shot but it is then downhill all the way. 'Some of them showed more fire playing cards on the bus than they did out there,' fumes Harry Haslam afterwards. | | | | | | | | | | | |
| 3 | A BURNLEY | | 8 | W | 2-1 | 1-1 | Deans 42, Hill 79 | Barber | Price | Buckley | Chambers | Faulkner | Futcher P | Husband | Hill | Deans | Fuccillo | Aston | |
| | 28/8 | *12,262* | *10* | 4 | | | *Bradshaw 36* | *Peyton* | *Scott* | *Pashley* | *Ingham* | *Thomson* | *Rodaway* | *Summerbee* | *Noble* | *Hankin* | *Flynn* | *Bradshaw* | |
| | | | | | | | Ref: P Willis | John Aston has the beating of the Burnley full-back, Derek Scott, but his centres all come to nothing as the Clarets take a shock lead with a soft goal. Stepping up a gear, Deans and Hill do eventually score, both with headers coming from Aston centres, to earn two well-deserved points. | | | | | | | | | | | |
| 4 | H NOTT'M FOREST | | 8 | D | 1-1 | 0-1 | Barrett 88(og) | Barber | Price | Buckley | West | Faulkner | Futcher P | Husband* | Hill | Deans | Fuccillo | Aston | Futcher R |
| | 4/9 | 11,231 | *15* | 5 | | | *Curran 12p* | *Middleton* | *Barrett* | *Clark* | *McGovern** | *Chapman* | *Bowyer* | *Curran* | *O'Neill* | *O'Hare* | *Butlin* | *Robertson* | *Anderson* |
| | | | | | | | Ref: J Yates | Forest take an early lead when Hill handles a Barry Butlin shot on the line and Terry Curran scores from the spot. The Town score a fortunate goal when Colin Barrett deflects a Fuccillo header past his own goalkeeper to save the day. Ron Futcher and Alan West are back from the USA. | | | | | | | | | | | |
| 5 | A CHARLTON | | 9 | L | 3-4 | 1-2 | Deans 22, Aston 62, Hill 86 | Barber | Price | Buckley | Ryan | Faulkner | Futcher P | Husband* | Hill | Deans | Fuccillo | Aston | Futcher R |
| | 10/9 | *9,191* | *18* | 5 | | | *Hales 26, 37, 60, Curtis 71p* | *Wood* | *Hammond* | *Warman* | *Hunt* | *Giles* | *Curtis* | *Powell* | *Hales* | *Flanagan* | *Young* | *Peacock* | |
| | | | | | | | Ref: M Taylor | Derek Hales, sold by the Town two years previously for £10,000, destroys his old colleagues with a hat-trick to give Charlton their first win of the season. Bob Curtis scores the fourth from the spot after a shot from Hales hits Paul Futcher on the arm. The Hatters are always second best. | | | | | | | | | | | |
| 6 | H FULHAM | | 17 | L | 0-2 | 0-1 | | Barber | Price | Buckley | Ryan | Faulkner | Futcher P | Husband | West | Deans | Fuccillo* | Aston | Hill |
| | 18/9 | **19,929** | *8* | 5 | | | *Barrett 33, Marsh 64* | *Mellor* | *Cutbush* | *Howe* | *Moore* | *Strong* | *Slough* | *Evanson* | *Barrett* | *Best* | *Marsh* | *Mitchell* | |
| | | | | | | | Ref: K Baker | An additional 10,000 supporters turn up to see the extrovert pair of George Best and Rodney Marsh play at Kenilworth Road. Marsh scores after skipping past four defenders and the Town forwards are rarely in the game, with ex-England skipper, Bobby Moore, in commanding form. | | | | | | | | | | | |
| 7 | A WOLVES | | 13 | W | 2-1 | 1-0 | Husband 29, Deans 67 | Barber | Price | Buckley | Ryan | Faulkner | Futcher P | Husband | West | Deans | Fuccillo | Futcher R | |
| | 25/9 | *19,826* | *2* | 7 | | | *Hibbitt 61* | *Pierce* | *Palmer* | *Bailey* | *McAlle* | *Parkin* | *Hibbitt* | *Daley* | *Carr* | *Sunderland* | *Kindon** | *Gould* | *Patching* |
| | | | | | | | Ref: A Porter | Apart from a brief period at either end of the game, the Town outplay the home side and thoroughly merit their victory. Wolves concede their first home goal of the season when Husband scores and, after the equaliser, Dixie Deans hits his fifth goal of the season into the roof of the net. | | | | | | | | | | | |
| 8 | A PLYMOUTH | | 16 | L | 0-1 | 0-0 | | Barber | Price | Buckley | Ryan | Faulkner | Futcher P | Husband | West | Deans* | Fuccillo | Futcher R | Hill |
| | 2/10 | *12,187* | *15* | 7 | | | *Johnson 48p* | *Ramsbottom* | *Randell* | *Horswill* | *Delve* | *Sutton* | *Green* | *Johnson* | *Harrison* | *Mariner* | *Collins* | *Hall* | |
| | | | | | | | Ref: D Nippard | Barber has to be at his best to keep out a ferocious shot from Brian Johnson but can do nothing about the penalty after West is adjudged to have fouled ex-Liverpool winger, Brian Hall, in the area. Dixie Deans has a goal disallowed for offside and Futcher sees his shot cleared off the line. | | | | | | | | | | | |
| 9 | H HEREFORD | | 12 | W | 2-0 | 0-0 | Husband 55, Futcher P 89 | Barber | Price | Buckley | Ryan | Faulkner | Futcher P | Husband | West | Futcher R | Fuccillo | Chambers | |
| | 9/10 | 9,395 | *21* | 9 | | | | *Charlton* | *Byrne* | *Burrows* | *Layton* | *Turner* | *Lindsay* | *Carter* | *Tyler* | *Sinclair** | *Galley* | *Briley* | *Preece* |
| | | | | | | | Ref: D Smith | Don Revie and his England squad leave five minutes before the end and unfortunately miss the only bright spot of a game, marred by 52 fouls, when Paul Futcher picks up a loose ball in midfield, runs 20 yards and hits a perfect right-foot shot for his first, and only, goal for the Town. | | | | | | | | | | | |
| 10 | A CARLISLE | | 13 | D | 1-1 | 1-1 | Husband 20 | Barber | Price | Buckley | West | Faulkner | Futcher P | Ryan* | Husband | Futcher R | Fuccillo | Chambers | Aston |
| | 16/10 | *6,972* | *16* | 10 | | | *Rafferty 37* | *Ross* | *Bonnyman* | *Gorman* | *Smith* | *MacDonald* | *Parker* | *Martin* | *Barry* | *Lathan* | *Rafferty* | *Owen* | |
| | | | | | | | Ref: D Shaw | Husband opens the scoring from close range and Billy Rafferty heads the equaliser. Carlisle had the chance to win both points when, in the last minute, Bobby Owen hoists the ball over the bar when faced with an open goal. A draw was probably the fairest result in this physical game. | | | | | | | | | | | |

| No | Venue | Opponent | Pos | Res | F-A | H-T | Scorers, Times, and Referees | 1 | 2 | 3 | 4 | 5 | 6 | 7 | 8 | 9 | 10 | 11 | 12 sub used |
|---|---|---|---|---|---|---|---|---|---|---|---|---|---|---|---|---|---|---|---|
| 11 | H | SOUTHAMPTON | 16 | L | **1-4** | 0-2 | Chambers 69 *[Holmes 78]* | Barber | Price | Buckley | Chambers | Faulkner | Futcher P | Husband | West | Deans | Fuccillo | Aston | |
| 23/10 | | 12,123 | 11 | 10 | | | *Peach 11p, 43, MacDougall 73,* | *Montgomery* | *Rodrigues* | *Peach* | *Holmes* | *Waldron* | *Blyth* | *Williams* | *Channon* | *MacDougall* | *McCalliog* | *Fisher* | |
| | | | | | | | Ref: B James | The Hatters are expecting an indirect free-kick to be awarded after Buckley blocks Mick Channon in the area; however, a penalty is given and David Peach makes no mistake with his kick. Chambers reduces the deficit after the break but Saints wrap up the points with two late efforts. | | | | | | | | | | | |
| 12 | A | BLACKBURN | 18 | L | 0-1 | 0-1 | | Barber | Price | Buckley | Chambers | Faulkner | Futcher P | Husband | West | Futcher R | Fuccillo | Aston | |
| 30/10 | | *8,674* | *11* | 10 | | | *Silvester 12* | *Bradshaw* | *Fazackerley* | *Bailey* | *Metcalfe* | *Keeley* | *Hawkins* | *Hird* | *Silvester* | *Wagstaffe* | *Parkes* | *Svarc* | |
| | | | | | | | Ref: E Garner | In a bad-tempered clash, the Town are marginally the better of two poor sides but the defeat could have been worse. Rovers miss a penalty, on the hour, after Bobby Svarc is fouled by Paul Futcher. Peter Silvester beats John Faulkner to a cross to score the winner, against the run of play. | | | | | | | | | | | |
| 13 | H | BRISTOL ROV | 13 | W | 4-2 | 2-1 | Futcher R 9, 50, Aston 40, Husband 67 | **Knight** | Price | Buckley | Chambers | Faulkner | Futcher P | Husband | West | Futcher R | Fuccillo | Aston | |
| 6/11 | | **7,066** | *14* | 12 | | | *Bannister 33, Warboys 58* | *Eadie* | *Day* | *Williams* | *Aitken* | *Taylor* | *Prince* | *Stephens* | *Fearnley* | *Warboys* | *Bannister* | *Powell* | |
| | | | | | | | Ref: R Lewis | After a string of poor results, the Hatters bounce back with a superb display of attacking football, during which Ron Futcher scores two goals. 17-year-old Tony Knight makes his debut in Luton's goal and has to make smart saves in the last five minutes as Rovers go all out for a point. | | | | | | | | | | | |
| 14 | A | MILLWALL | 18 | L | 2-4 | 1-2 | West 2, Buckley 52p *[Seasman 89]* | Barber | Price | Buckley | Chambers | Jones | Futcher P | Husband* | West | Futcher R | Fuccillo | Aston | Deans |
| 13/11 | | *10,380* | *8* | 12 | | | *Kitchener 3, Brisley 4, Walker 62,* | *Goddard* | *Evans* | *Donaldson* | *Brisley* | *Kitchener* | *Hazell* | *Lee* | *Seasman* | *Harris* | *Walker* | *Shanahan* | |
| | | | | | | | Ref: A Glasson | West hits his first goal of the season with a 35-yard shot but within two minutes Millwall score twice to take the lead. Buckley nets from the spot and then Phil Walker touches in a long free-kick from Kitchener to keep the Lions ahead. John Seasman scores against his old club late on. | | | | | | | | | | | |
| 15 | H | CARDIFF | 13 | W | 2-1 | 2-0 | Deans 16, Futcher R 31 | Barber | Price | Buckley | Chambers | Jones | Futcher P | Deans | West | Futcher R | Fuccillo | Aston | |
| 20/11 | | 8,845 | *16* | 14 | | | *Evans 74* | *Healey* | *Dwyer* | *Pethard** | *Buchanan* | *Went* | *Larmour* | *Sayer* | *Livermore* | *Evans* | *Showers* | *Anderson* | *Alston* |
| | | | | | | | Ref: B Homewood | Deans, after missing five games with a broken nose, returns to goalscoring form when tapping in a cross from Price, and Ron Futcher adds the second from an awkward angle. Ex-Hatter, Adrian Alston, comes on as a substitute and lays on a goal for Tony Evans to keep the game alive. | | | | | | | | | | | |
| 16 | A | NOTTS CO | 11 | W | 4-0 | 1-0 | West 41, Aston 52, Husband 81, [Buckley 84] | Barber* | Price | Buckley | Chambers | Faulkner | Futcher P | Deans | West | Futcher R | Fuccillo | Aston | Husband |
| 27/11 | | *10,009* | *12* | 16 | | | | *McManus* | *Richards* | *Mann* | *Probert* | *Needham** | *Stubbs* | *Carter* | *Vinter* | *Bradd* | *Busby* | *Scanlon* | *Sims* |
| | | | | | | | Ref: H Hackney | Diminutive Dixie Deans takes over in the Luton goal after Keith Barber breaks ribs in a clash with Mick Vinter after 70 minutes. By this time, the Town are two goals up against a team which won 5-1 the previous week. Two goals late on reflect the overall superiority of the Hatters. | | | | | | | | | | | |
| 17 | H | BLACKPOOL | 10 | D | 0-0 | 0-0 | | Knight | Price | Buckley | Chambers | Faulkner | Futcher P | Deans | West | Futcher R | Fuccillo | Aston | |
| 4/12 | | 9,183 | *2* | 17 | | | | *Wood* | *Gardner* | *Harrison* | *Ronson* | *Hart* | *Suddaby* | *Weston* | *Spence* | *Walsh* | *Hatton* | *Bentley* | |
| | | | | | | | Ref: L Burden | Knight returns to the Luton goal as a replacement for the injured Keith Barber and is the star of the show in an exciting game played on an icy pitch. He is beaten once but, fortunately, the 25-yard shot from Derek Spence hits the bar. Aston is well marked by the Seasiders' Paul Gardner. | | | | | | | | | | | |
| 18 | A | BOLTON | 12 | L | 1-2 | 1-0 | Fuccillo 33 | **Aleksic** | Price | Buckley | Chambers | Faulkner | Futcher P | Deans ! | West | Futcher R | Fuccillo | Ryan | |
| 21/12 | | *18,463* | *2* | 17 | | | *Whatmore 60, Greaves 75* | *McDonagh* | *Nicholson* | *Dunne* | *Greaves* | *Jones* | *Allardyce* | *Morgan* | *Whatmore* | *Taylor* | *Reid* | *Smith** | *Thompson* |
| | | | | | | | Ref: B Newsome | Town are holding their own against high-flying Bolton when Deans is booked for jostling big Sam Allardyce and is sent off a minute later after chopping down Roy Greaves. Any chance the Hatters had of salvaging a point went with this dismissal. Deans will not play again for Luton. | | | | | | | | | | | |
| 19 | A | ORIENT | 14 | L | 0-1 | 0-0 | | Aleksic | Price | Buckley | Chambers | Faulkner | Futcher P | Husband | West | Futcher R | Fuccillo | Ryan | |
| 27/12 | | *8,354* | *21* | 17 | | | *Bennett 80* | *Jackson* | *Payne* | *Fisher* | *Allen* | *Hoadley* | *Roeder* | *Cunningham* | *Bennett* | *Possee* | *Whittle* | *Queen* | |
| | | | | | | | Ref: T Bune | Lowly Orient are put on the rack for long periods of the game but secure both points through the pace of Laurie Cunningham, who provides the only scoring opportunity. Harry Haslam is not amused as the Town lose another game in which a point should have been won, at the very least. | | | | | | | | | | | |
| 20 | H | CHELSEA | 11 | W | 4-0 | 2-0 | Fuccillo 1, Chambers 12, Husband 58, [Buckley 88p] | Aleksic | Price | Buckley | Chambers | Faulkner | Futcher P | Husband | West | Futcher R | Fuccillo | Ryan | |
| 29/12 | | 17,107 | *1* | 19 | | | | *Phillips* | *Locke* | *Wilkins G* | *Stanley* | *Wicks* | *Hay* | *Britton* | *Wilkins R* | *Finnieston* | *Lewington* | *Swain* | |
| | | | | | | | Ref: C White | The snow-covered surface is passed fit for play just before the scheduled kick-off time. The Hatters adapt quickly to the tricky conditions and score twice in the first twelve minutes. Chelsea, currently top of the table, skid and blunder around as the Town make the most of their chances. | | | | | | | | | | | |
| 21 | A | BRISTOL ROV | 12 | L | 0-1 | 0-0 | | Aleksic | Price | Buckley | Chambers | Faulkner | Futcher P | Husband | West | Futcher R | Fuccillo | Ryan | |
| 1/1 | | *7,185* | *9* | 19 | | | *Aitken 53* | *Eadie* | *Bater* | *Parsons* | *Aitken* | *Taylor* | *Williams* | *Stephens* | *Fearnley* | *Warboys* | *Staniforth* | *Hamilton* | |
| | | | | | | | Ref: D Lloyd | An efficient and industrious Luton side return from Eastville with nothing after Husband misses a gilt-edged opportunity in the last minute. The Rovers goal comes from a breakaway after a Faulkner shot rebounds off the bar. A foul in the area by Phil Bater on Jim Ryan goes unpunished. | | | | | | | | | | | |

| No | Date | | Att | Pos | Pt | F-A | H-T | Scorers, Times, and Referees | 1 | 2 | 3 | 4 | 5 | 6 | 7 | 8 | 9 | 10 | 11 | 12 sub used |
|---|---|---|---|---|---|---|---|---|---|---|---|---|---|---|---|---|---|---|---|---|
| 22 | A | SHEFFIELD UTD | | 11 | W | 3-0 | 1-0 | Futcher R 11, Husband 60, 72 | Aleksic | Price | Buckley | Chambers | Faulkner | Futcher P | Husband | West | Futcher R | Fuccillo | Aston | |
| | 22/1 | | *16,257* | *9* | 21 | | | | *Brown* | *Franks* | *Garner* | *Longhorn* | *Colquhoun* | *Faulkner* | *Woodward* | *Hamilton* | *Guthrie* | *Hamson* | *McKee* | |
| | | | | | | | | Ref: R Perkin | In front of the BBC Match of the Day cameras, United, who have now conceded nine goals in their last three home games, always look second-best. Jim Husband scores the second goal with a spectacular 25-yard shot, the Blades' only real scoring chances coming in the first ten minutes. | | | | | | | | | | | |
| 23 | H | HULL | | 9 | W | 2-1 | 0-1 | Aston 84, Husband 89 | Aleksic | Price | Buckley | Chambers | Faulkner | Futcher P | Husband | West | Futcher R | Fuccillo | Aston | |
| | 24/1 | | *8,455* | *15* | 23 | | | *Lyall 3* | *Wealands* | *Daniel* | *Devries* | *Croft* | *Haigh* | *Bremner* | *Nisbet* | *Lyall* | *McIntosh* | *Sunley* | *Hickton* | |
| | | | | | | | | Ref: J Hunting | George Lyall gives Hull an early lead. They then opt to defend in depth and attempt to frustrate the Town. Aston gets on the end of a long pass from West to slam the ball into the roof of the net and, with ten seconds left, Husband is the first to react to a ball fumbled by Jeff Wealands. | | | | | | | | | | | |
| 24 | H | BURNLEY | | 9 | W | 2-0 | 1-0 | Price 11, Aston 85 | Aleksic | Price | Buckley | Chambers | Faulkner | Futcher P | Husband | West | Futcher R | Fuccillo | Aston | |
| | 5/2 | | 8,638 | *19* | 25 | | | | *Stevenson* | *Newton* | *Brennan* | *Robinson* | *Thomson* | *Rodaway* | *Cochrane* | *Noble* | *Fletcher* | *Flynn* | *Smith* | |
| | | | | | | | | Ref: T Bosi | Superb goalkeeping from Alan Stevenson keeps the Clarets in the game in the first half after Price smashes home the opener. Town fall away after the break and Peter Noble misses the chance to level from close range before Aston rounds the keeper and places the ball in the empty net. | | | | | | | | | | | |
| 25 | A | NOTT'M FOREST | | 6 | W | 2-1 | 0-0 | Futcher R 54, Aston 75 | Aleksic | Price | Buckley | Chambers | Faulkner | Futcher P | Husband | West | Futcher R | Fuccillo | Aston* | **Geddis** |
| | 12/2 | | *18,225* | *5* | 27 | | | *Lloyd 86* | *Middleton* | *Anderson* | *Clark* | *McGovern* | *Lloyd* | *Bowyer* | *Haslegrave* | *O'Hare* | *Chapman* | *Woodcock* | *Robertson* | |
| | | | | | | | | Ref: A Hamil | Promotion-chasing Forest return from a mid-season break in Spain and slump to their third successive defeat. Aston seals the win after Futcher opens the scoring, when he holds off the full-back in a 20-yard run and fires the ball into the corner of the net. Lloyd gains a late consolation. | | | | | | | | | | | |
| 26 | H | BLACKBURN | | 6 | W | 2-0 | 1-0 | Geddis 35, Futcher R 65 | Aleksic | Price | Buckley | Chambers | Faulkner | Futcher P | Geddis | West | Futcher R | Fuccillo | Aston | |
| | 15/2 | | 9,044 | *16* | 29 | | | | *Bradshaw* | *Hird* | *Wood* | *Metcalfe* | *Fazackerley* | *Keeley* | *Taylor* | *Svarc* | *Byrom** | *Parkes* | *Waddington* | *Mitchell* |
| | | | | | | | | Ref: B Martin | David Geddis, on loan from Ipswich, celebrates his full debut for the Town when hitting a cross from Aston past Paul Bradshaw. The linesman flags for offside but, after strong protests from the Hatters, the referee overrules his official. Blackburn are demoralised when Futcher scores. | | | | | | | | | | | |
| 27 | H | CHARLTON | | 5 | W | 2-0 | 0-0 | Futcher R 57, 77 | Aleksic | Price | Buckley | Chambers | Faulkner | Futcher P | Husband | West | Futcher R | Fuccillo | Aston | |
| | 19/2 | | 11,625 | *8* | 31 | | | | *Wood* | *Curtis* | *Woodman* | *Tydeman* | *Giles* | *Berry* | *Powell* | *Hunt* | *Flanagan* | *Peacock* | *McAuley* | |
| | | | | | | | | Ref: W Gow | Ron Futcher settles the issue with two superb strikes, after the visitors have the better of the period before the interval, to put the Town into the promotion race. 'We threw away four good chances in the first half and then conceded two bad goals,' moans Charlton manager Andy Nelson. | | | | | | | | | | | |
| 28 | A | FULHAM | | 5 | W | 2-1 | 2-1 | Aston 21, Husband 35 | Aleksic | Price | Buckley | Chambers | Faulkner | Futcher P | Husband | West | Futcher R | Fuccillo | Aston | |
| | 26/2 | | *11,071* | *19* | 33 | | | *Warboys 30* | *Peyton* | *Strong* | *Slough* | *Bullivant* | *Lacy* | *Moore* | *Barrett* | *Mitchell** | *Warboys* | *Marsh* | *Evanson* | *Margerrison* |
| | | | | | | | | Ref: R Crabbe | The Cottagers are not a patch on the side that beat the Town earlier in the season and they are now struggling to avoid relegation. The Hatters appear to be half a yard quicker and should have scored more than twice in the first half. Luton then set out to contain Fulham after the break. | | | | | | | | | | | |
| 29 | H | WOLVES | | 4 | W | 2-0 | 2-0 | Husband 36, Fuccillo 37 | Aleksic | Price | Buckley | Chambers | Faulkner | Futcher P | Husband | West | Futcher R* | Fuccillo | Aston | Geddis |
| | 5/3 | | 19,200 | *3* | 35 | | | | *Pierce* | *Palmer* | *Parkin* | *Daley* | *Munro* | *McAlle* | *Hibbitt* | *Richards* | *Sunderland* | *Patching** | *Carr* | *Gould* |
| | | | | | | | | Ref: R Lewis | The promotion race is thrown wide open after the visitors' 16-game unbeaten run is ended and Luton extend their unbeaten run to eight games. Wolves go close on five occasions in the first six minutes but the Hatters settle down and then breach the suspect back four twice in a minute. | | | | | | | | | | | |
| 30 | H | OLDHAM | | 4 | W | 1-0 | 0-0 | Geddis 86 | Aleksic | Price | Buckley | Chambers | Faulkner | Futcher P | Husband | West* | Futcher R | Fuccillo | Aston | Geddis |
| | 8/3 | | 12,301 | *10* | 37 | | | | *Platt* | *Wood* | *Blair* | *Bell* | *Hicks* | *Hurst* | *Robins* | *Shaw* | *Halom* | *Chapman* | *Groves** | *Valentine* |
| | | | | | | | | Ref: M Baker | The Town are refused a penalty when Husband is hacked down by the Oldham centre-half. The game is drifting towards a goal-less draw when Geddis, on as a substitute for West, runs on to a through-ball by Paul Futcher and shoots past John Platt to notch up a ninth consecutive win. | | | | | | | | | | | |
| 31 | H | PLYMOUTH | | 4 | D | 1-1 | 0-1 | Aston 50 | Aleksic | Price | Buckley | Chambers | Faulkner | Futcher P | Husband | West | Geddis | Fuccillo | Aston | |
| | 12/3 | | 12,793 | *17* | 38 | | | *Foster 13* | *Ramsbottom* | *Smart* | *Darke* | *Peddelty* | *Sutton* | *Horswill* | *Foster* | *Randell* | *Austin* | *Bannister* | *Rogers* | |
| | | | | | | | | Ref: R Robinson | The winning run is ended as lowly Plymouth pack their defence against a below-par Luton side. George Foster steals in for a 13th-minute header and Aston equalises with a similar effort. Former Ipswich defender, John Peddelty, keeps a tight hold on his old team-mate, David Geddis. | | | | | | | | | | | |

| No | Date | Opponent | Att | Pos | Res | F-A | H-T | Scorers, Times, and Referees | 1 | 2 | 3 | 4 | 5 | 6 | 7 | 8 | 9 | 10 | 11 | 12 |
|---|---|---|---|---|---|---|---|---|---|---|---|---|---|---|---|---|---|---|---|---|
| 32 | A | HEREFORD | | 3 | W | 1-0 | 0-0 | Futcher R 89 | Aleksic | Price | Buckley | Chambers* | Faulkner | Futcher P | Husband | West | Futcher R | Fuccillo | Aston | Jones |
| | 19/3 | | *6,737* | *22* | 40 | | | | *Hughes* | *Emery* | *Ritchie* | *Marshall* | *Jefferson* | *Lindsay* | *Carter* | *Spiring** | *Davey* | *McNeil* | *Briley* | *Paine* |
| | | | | | | | | Ref: D Turner | Ron Futcher adds the finishing touch, heading home a cross from Aston in the final minute which moves the Hatters up to third place in the League. Hereford have their chances to win the game and complain, long and hard, about a Steve Davey effort which is ruled out for offside. | | | | | | | | | | | |
| 33 | H | CARLISLE | | 3 | W | **5-0** | 2-0 | Fuccillo 20, Futcher R 35, Husband 52, [West 76, Aston 89] | Aleksic | Price | Buckley | Chambers | Faulkner | Futcher P | Husband | West | Futcher R | Fuccillo | Aston | |
| | 26/3 | | 11,735 | *21* | 42 | | | | *Ross* | *Carr* | *Bailey* | *Martin* | *MacDonald* | *Parker* | *McVitie* | *Bonnyman** | *Tait* | *Rafferty* | *McCartney* | *O'Neill* |
| | | | | | | | | Ref: R Kirkpatrick | Relegation-threatened Carlisle are totally overwhelmed as five different Luton players get on the scoresheet with a potential sixth one, Paul Futcher, missing a penalty. Cumbrians' ex-Luton keeper, Alan Ross, is frequently called upon to race from his area and clear the ball into touch. | | | | | | | | | | | |
| 34 | A | SOUTHAMPTON | | 4 | L | 0-1 | 0-1 | | Aleksic | Price | Buckley | Chambers | Faulkner | Futcher P | Husband* | Jones | Futcher R | Fuccillo | Aston | Geddis |
| | 2/4 | | *19,923* | *14* | 42 | | | *Ball 2* | *Wells* | *Rodrigues* | *Peach* | *Holmes* | *Blyth* | *Waldron* | *Ball* | *Channon* | *Osgood* | *Williams* | *MacDougall* | |
| | | | | | | | | Ref: B Stevens | Alan Ball runs through, unchallenged, after two minutes to score the only goal of the game and end the Town's 12-match unbeaten run. Ron Futcher rounds Saints keeper, Wells, but fires his shot over the bar. 'They didn't win - we lost it,' moaned manager Haslam after the game. | | | | | | | | | | | |
| 35 | A | CHELSEA | | 5 | L | 0-2 | 0-2 | | Aleksic | Price* | Buckley | Chambers | Faulkner | Futcher P | Husband | West | Geddis | Fuccillo | Aston | Jones |
| | 9/4 | | ***32,911*** | *1* | 42 | | | *Finnieston 14, Sparrow 38* | *Bonetti* | *Locke* | *Sparrow* | *Stanley* | *Wicks* | *Harris* | *Britton* | *Wilkins R* | *Finnieston* | *Lewington* | *Swain* | |
| | | | | | | | | Ref: J Taylor | Top-of-the-table Chelsea gain ample revenge for their 0-4 humiliation at Kenilworth Road earlier in the season. John Sparrow hits the second for the home side with a superb 20-yard volley and, with neither side looking likely candidates for promotion, the game degenerates rapidly. | | | | | | | | | | | |
| 36 | H | ORIENT | | 5 | D | 0-0 | 0-0 | | Aleksic | Jones | Buckley | Chambers | Faulkner | Futcher P | Husband | West | Geddis | Fuccillo* | Aston | Futcher R |
| | 11/4 | | 11,066 | *16* | 43 | | | | *Jackson* | *Fisher* | *Roffey* | *Payne* | *Gray* | *Roeder* | *Possee* | *Glover* | *Bennett* | *Grealish** | *Whittle* | *Chiedozie* |
| | | | | | | | | Ref: A Robinson | The visitors succeed in securing the point they came for after battling for the full ninety minutes, with eight men back in their own penalty area, to thwart wave after wave of naïve Luton attacks. After the game, Orient's manager, George Petchey, apologises for his team's negative play. | | | | | | | | | | | |
| 37 | H | MILLWALL | | 5 | L | 1-2 | 0-2 | Fuccillo 49 | Aleksic | Price | Buckley | Chambers | Faulkner | Futcher P | Geddis | West | Futcher R | Fuccillo | Aston | |
| | 12/4 | | 10,459 | *9* | 43 | | | *Buckley 41 (og), Alexander 44* | *Johns* | *Donaldson* | *Moore* | *Brisley* | *Kitchener* | *Hazell* | *Alexander* | *Seasman* | *Harris** | *Walker* | *Jeffries* | *Summerill* |
| | | | | | | | | Ref: T Reynolds | Another Easter period to forget as the Hatters fail against a third London side in four days and lose at home for the first time since October. The Town have the better of the first half but are hit by two goals just before the interval, one an over-hit back-pass from Buckley into his own net. | | | | | | | | | | | |
| 38 | A | CARDIFF | | 6 | L | 2-4 | 1-3 | Futcher R 20, Chambers 75 | Aleksic | Price | Buckley | Chambers | Faulkner | Futcher P | Geddis | West* | Futcher R | Fuccillo | Aston | Husband |
| | 16/4 | | *10,438* | *19* | 43 | | | *Sayer 10, Friday 23, 39, Dwyer 80* | *Healey* | *Attley* | *Pethard* | *Campbell* | *Went* | *Larmour* | *Grapes* | *Dwyer* | *Sayer* | *Friday** | *Giles* | *Livermore* |
| | | | | | | | | Ref: A Lees | The Town defence suffers a torrid time with Cardiff's enigmatic Robin Friday playing a blinder to steer his side away from the relegation zone. Harry Haslam is furious with his senior professionals and threatens to bring in the young players for the remaining four games of the season. | | | | | | | | | | | |
| 39 | H | NOTTS CO | | 6 | W | 4-2 | 3-1 | Futcher R 23, 43, Hill 44, Geddis 70 | Aleksic | Price | Buckley | Chambers | Faulkner | Futcher P | Geddis | Hill | Futcher R | Fuccillo | Aston | |
| | 23/4 | | 9,585 | *3* | 45 | | | *Bradd 30, Mann 88* | *McManus* | *Richards* | *O'Brien* | *Busby* | *Needham* | *Stubbs* | *Carter* | *Vinter* | *Bradd* | *Mann* | *Smith** | *Scanlon* |
| | | | | | | | | Ref: B Daniels | What a difference a week makes, as the Town turn on a performance which is as good as any seen this season. The Hatters end County's six-match unbeaten run in emphatic style and could easily have scored ten. Ricky Hill scores the best goal of the game with a 20-yard net buster. | | | | | | | | | | | |
| 40 | A | BLACKPOOL | | 7 | L | 0-1 | 0-0 | | Aleksic | Price | Buckley | Chambers | Faulkner | Futcher P* | Geddis | Hill | Futcher R | Fuccillo | Aston | Husband |
| | 30/4 | | *9,257* | *6* | 45 | | | *Hatton 85* | *Wood* | *Gardner* | *Harrison* | *Ronson* | *Hart* | *Suddaby* | *Spence** | *McEwan* | *Walsh* | *Hatton* | *Bentley* | *Finnigan* |
| | | | | | | | | Ref: P Partridge | Any lingering hopes of promotion finally disappear when Bob Hatton takes advantage of some hesitancy in the Town defence to score a late winner. Hill is surprisingly guilty of missing two good chances in a game which the Hatters should have had sewn up long before the end. | | | | | | | | | | | |
| 41 | H | BOLTON | | 7 | D | 1-1 | 0-1 | Geddis 48 | Aleksic | Price | Buckley | Chambers | Faulkner | **McNichol** | Husband | Hill | Geddis | Fuccillo | Aston | |
| | 7/5 | | 11,164 | *4* | 46 | | | *Reid 8* | *McDonagh* | *Ritson* | *Nicholson* | *Greaves* | *Jones P* | *Allardyce* | *Morgan* | *Whatmore* | *Taylor* | *Reid* | *Train* | |
| | | | | | | | | Ref: A Grey | Alan West and Ron Futcher have now left to play a summer season of football in the States. The Hatters find themselves a goal behind early on to a Bolton side who are chasing the third promotion place. Geddis heads home a corner from John Aston, needlessly conceded, to earn a point. | | | | | | | | | | | |
| 42 | A | OLDHAM | | 6 | W | 2-1 | 1-0 | Fuccillo 13, Aston 65 | Aleksic | Price | Buckley | Chambers | Faulkner | McNichol | Husband | Hill* | **Carr** | Fuccillo | Aston | Jones |
| | 14/5 | | *7,231* | *13* | 48 | | | *Halom 60* | *Ogden* | *Wood* | *Hoolickin* | *Holt* | *Hurst* | *Bell* | *Valentine* | *Chapman* | *Shaw* | *Halom* | *Groves* | |
| | Average | Home 11,387 | Away 12,431 | | | | | Ref: T Farley | In a lively end-of-season game, Aston sets up Fuccillo for a rocket shot which beats Chris Ogden all ends up. Ex-Hatter, Vic Halom, heads in a corner-kick from Carl Valentine before Aston, standing on the penalty spot, thrashes home the rebound after a shot from Fuccillo hits the post. | | | | | | | | | | | |

| League Cup | | | | | Scorers, Times, and Referees | 1 | 2 | 3 | 4 | 5 | 6 | 7 | 8 | 9 | 10 | 11 | 12 sub used |
|---|---|---|---|---|---|---|---|---|---|---|---|---|---|---|---|---|---|
| | | | F-A | H-T | | | | | | | | | | | | | |
| 2 A SUNDERLAND | 8 | L | 1-3 | 1-3 | Husband 25 | Barber | Price | Buckley | Chambers | Faulkner* | Futcher P | Hill | Husband | Deans | Fuccillo | Aston | Ryan |
| 31/8 | 22,390 1:16 | | | | *Hughes 23, 38 Robson 41* | *Montgomery* | *Malone* | *Bolton* | *Towers* | *Clarke* | *Moncur* | *Kerr* | *Holden* | *Hughes* | *Robson* | *Train* | |
| | | | | | Ref: P Partridge | Two goals in three minutes, just before the interval, sets the Town a mountain to climb. Sunderland are forced back after the break with Deans, Husband and Hill all going close amidst a chorus of slow handclapping from the Roker crowd as the home side rarely breaks out from defence. | | | | | | | | | | | |

| FA Cup | | | | | | | | | | | | | | | | | |
|---|---|---|---|---|---|---|---|---|---|---|---|---|---|---|---|---|---|
| 3 A HALIFAX | 12 | W | 1-0 | 1-0 | Aston 22 | Aleksic | Price | Buckley | Chambers | Faulkner | Futcher P | Husband | West | Futcher R | Fuccillo | Aston | |
| 8/1 | 5,519 4:20 | | | | | *Gennoe* | *Trainer* | *Loska* | *Bradley* | *Dunleavy* | *Phelan* | *Hoy* | *Carroll* | *Bullock** | *Lawson* | *Johnstone* | *Jones* |
| | | | | | Ref: J Yates | England manager, Don Revie, is at The Shay to watch Luton's International Under-21 defender, Paul Futcher. Hard-battling Halifax give their all, but find the gulf in class too much. A long shot from Chambers is fumbled by keeper, Terry Gennoe and Aston is left with a simple tap-in. | | | | | | | | | | | |
| 4 A CHESTER | 9 | L | 0-1 | 0-0 | | Aleksic | Price | Buckley | Chambers | Faulkner | Futcher P | Husband | West | Futcher R | Fuccillo | Aston | |
| 29/1 | 10,608 3:14 | | | | *Edwards I 88* | *Millington* | *Edwards N* | *Walker* | *Storton* | *Delgado* | *Oakes* | *Deardon* | *Richardson* | *Edwards I* | *Howat* | *Crossley* | |
| | | | | | Ref: P Willis | Chester reach Round 5 for the first time in their history with a goal in the closing seconds of a rousing tie. The Town have the better of the first half, with Jim Husband hitting a post, but are pushed back after the break. The game is held up for several minutes after a barrier wall collapses. | | | | | | | | | | | |

| | P | W | D | L | F | A | W | D | L | F | A | Pts |
|---|---|---|---|---|---|---|---|---|---|---|---|---|
| | | Home | | | | | Away | | | | | |
| 1 Wolves | 42 | 15 | 3 | 3 | 48 | 21 | 7 | 10 | 4 | 36 | 24 | 57 |
| 2 Chelsea | 42 | 15 | 6 | 0 | 51 | 22 | 6 | 7 | 8 | 22 | 31 | 55 |
| 3 Nott'm Forest | 42 | 14 | 3 | 4 | 53 | 22 | 7 | 7 | 7 | 24 | 21 | 52 |
| 4 Bolton | 42 | 15 | 2 | 4 | 46 | 21 | 5 | 9 | 7 | 29 | 33 | 51 |
| 5 Blackpool | 42 | 11 | 7 | 3 | 29 | 17 | 6 | 10 | 5 | 29 | 25 | 51 |
| 6 LUTON TOWN | 42 | 13 | 5 | 3 | 39 | 17 | 8 | 1 | 12 | 28 | 31 | 48 |
| 7 Charlton | 42 | 14 | 5 | 2 | 52 | 27 | 2 | 11 | 8 | 19 | 31 | 48 |
| 8 Notts Co | 42 | 11 | 5 | 5 | 29 | 20 | 8 | 5 | 8 | 36 | 40 | 48 |
| 9 Southampton | 42 | 12 | 6 | 3 | 40 | 24 | 5 | 4 | 12 | 32 | 43 | 44 |
| 10 Millwall | 42 | 9 | 6 | 6 | 31 | 22 | 6 | 7 | 8 | 26 | 31 | 43 |
| 11 Sheffield Utd | 42 | 9 | 8 | 4 | 32 | 25 | 5 | 4 | 12 | 22 | 38 | 40 |
| 12 Blackburn | 42 | 12 | 4 | 5 | 31 | 18 | 3 | 5 | 13 | 11 | 36 | 39 |
| 13 Oldham | 42 | 11 | 6 | 4 | 37 | 23 | 3 | 4 | 14 | 15 | 41 | 38 |
| 14 Hull | 42 | 9 | 8 | 4 | 31 | 17 | 1 | 9 | 11 | 14 | 36 | 37 |
| 15 Bristol Rov | 42 | 8 | 9 | 4 | 32 | 27 | 4 | 4 | 13 | 21 | 41 | 37 |
| 16 Burnley | 42 | 8 | 9 | 4 | 27 | 20 | 3 | 5 | 13 | 19 | 44 | 36 |
| 17 Fulham | 42 | 9 | 7 | 5 | 39 | 25 | 2 | 6 | 13 | 15 | 36 | 35 |
| 18 Cardiff | 42 | 7 | 6 | 8 | 30 | 30 | 5 | 4 | 12 | 26 | 37 | 34 |
| 19 Orient | 42 | 4 | 8 | 9 | 18 | 23 | 5 | 8 | 8 | 19 | 32 | 34 |
| 20 Carlisle | 42 | 7 | 7 | 7 | 31 | 33 | 4 | 5 | 12 | 18 | 42 | 34 |
| 21 Plymouth | 42 | 5 | 9 | 7 | 27 | 25 | 3 | 7 | 11 | 19 | 40 | 32 |
| 22 Hereford | 42 | 6 | 9 | 6 | 28 | 30 | 2 | 6 | 13 | 29 | 48 | 31 |
| | 924 | 224 | 138 | 100 | 781 | 509 | 100 | 138 | 224 | 509 | 781 | 924 |

Odds & ends

Double wins: (6) Burnley, Hereford, Notts County, Oldham, Sheffield United, Wolves.
Double losses: (2) Millwall, Southampton.

Won from behind: (2) Burnley (a), Hull (h).
Lost from in front: (3) Bolton (a), Charlton (a), Millwall (a).

High spots: Nine-game winning run which sends the team shooting up the table.
Winning 4-0 at Notts County with a stand-in goalkeeper – Dixie Deans.
Completing the double over champions Wolves.

Low spots: A disastrous Easter to end the promotion hopes.
The defeat at Chester in the FA Cup.
Losing to an early Alan Ball goal at Southampton.

Player of the Year: Paul Futcher.
Ever-presents: (2) Steve Buckley, Lil Fuccillo.
Hat-tricks: (0).
Leading scorer: Ron Futcher and Jim Husband (13).

| | Appearances | | | | | | Goals | | | |
|---|---|---|---|---|---|---|---|---|---|---|
| | **Lge** | *Sub* | LC | *Sub* | FAC | *Sub* | **Lge** | LC | FAC | **Tot** |
| Aleksic, Milija | **25** | | | | 2 | | | | | |
| Aston, John | **34** | *1* | 1 | | 2 | | **10** | | 1 | **11** |
| Barber, Keith | **15** | | 1 | | | | | | | |
| Buckley, Steve | **42** | | 1 | | 2 | | **3** | | | **3** |
| Carr, David | **1** | | | | | | | | | |
| Chambers, Brian | **37** | | 1 | | 2 | | **3** | | | **3** |
| Deans, Dixie | **13** | *1* | 1 | | | | **6** | | | **6** |
| Faulkner, John | **40** | | 1 | | 2 | | | | | |
| Fuccillo, Lil | **42** | | 1 | | 2 | | **6** | | | **6** |
| Futcher, Paul | **40** | | 1 | | 2 | | **1** | | | **1** |
| Futcher, Ron | **30** | *3* | | | 2 | | **13** | | | **13** |
| Geddis, David | **9** | *4* | | | | | **4** | | | **4** |
| Hill, Ricky | **9** | *2* | 1 | | | | **4** | | | **4** |
| Husband, Jim | **33** | *3* | 1 | | 2 | | **12** | 1 | | **13** |
| Jones, Graham | **4** | *3* | | | | | | | | |
| Knight, Tony | **2** | | | | | | | | | |
| McNichol, Jim | **2** | | | | | | | | | |
| Price, Paul | **41** | | 1 | | 2 | | **1** | | | **1** |
| Ryan, John | **10** | | | *1* | | | | | | |
| Smith, Tim | | *1* | | | | | | | | |
| West, Alan | **33** | | | | 2 | | **3** | | | **3** |
| (own-goals) | | | | | | | **1** | | | **1** |
| **21 players used** | **462** | ***18*** | **11** | ***1*** | **22** | | **67** | **1** | **1** | **69** |

# LEAGUE DIVISION 2

## Manager: Harry Haslam ⇨ David Pleat

## SEASON 1977-78

| No | Date | | Att | Pos | Pt | F-A | H-T | Scorers, Times, and Referees | 1 | 2 | 3 | 4 | 5 | 6 | 7 | 8 | 9 | 10 | 11 | 12 sub used |
|---|---|---|---|---|---|---|---|---|---|---|---|---|---|---|---|---|---|---|---|---|
| 1 | H | ORIENT | | | W | 1-0 | 0-0 | Buckley 52 | Aleksic | Jones | Buckley | Carr | Faulkner | Futcher P | Husband | Smith | **Boersma*** | Fuccillo | Aston | Hill |
| | 20/8 | | 8,061 | | 2 | | | | *Jackson* | *Fisher* | *Roffey* | *Hoadley* | *Roeder* | *Allen* | *Glover* | *Payne** | *Chiedozie* | *Mayo* | *Kitchen* | *Grealish* |
| | | | | | | | | Ref: R Toseland | A well-balanced Orient defence collectively polices the young Luton side until left-back Buckley puts the Town ahead. The visitors then snap out of their defensive frame of mind and reflex saves by Aleksic from both Peter Kitchen and Phil Hoadley averts the points from being shared. | | | | | | | | | | | |
| 2 | A | OLDHAM | | 14 | L | 0-1 | 0-0 | | Aleksic | Price | Buckley | Carr | Faulkner | Futcher P ! | Husband | Hill | West | Fuccillo | Aston | |
| | 27/8 | | *7,553* | *2* | 2 | | | *Chapman 57* | *Ogden* | *Hoolickin* | *Holt* | *Edwards* | *Hurst* | *Bell* | *Blair* | *Chapman* | *Valentine* | *Halom* | *Groves* | |
| | | | | | | | | Ref: K McNally | In a game of few clear-cut chances, the best coming in the final ten minutes, Paul Futcher is first booked for dissent and then, within a minute, is sent off for a late tackle on Alan Groves. Ex-Luton striker, Vic Halom, is fortunate to stay on the field after a bad foul on keeper Aleksic. | | | | | | | | | | | |
| 3 | H | CHARLTON | | 11 | W | **7-1** | 2-0 | Husband 19, 65, 75p, 78, Buckley 30, | Aleksic | Price | Buckley | Fuccillo | Faulkner | Futcher P | Husband | Hill | Futcher R | West | **Heale** | |
| | 3/9 | | 9,061 | *17* | 4 | | | *Flanagan 82p* [Hill 59, Heale 72] | *Wood* | *Curtis** | *Warman* | *Campbell* | *Berry* | *Tydeman* | *Burman* | *Peacock* | *Powell* | *Flanagan* | *McAuley* | *Gritt* |
| | | | | | | | | Ref: R Kirkpatrick | The Town score seven goals in a game for the first time since 1958 and Jim Husband is the first Luton player to score four times in a match since 1964. 'It will never happen again,' vows Charlton coach, Harry Cripps. The 25-yard dipping shot from Ricky Hill is the goal of the match. | | | | | | | | | | | |
| 4 | A | BRISTOL ROV | | 7 | W | 2-1 | 1-1 | Boersma 21, Buckley 63 | Aleksic | Price | Buckley | Fuccillo | Faulkner | Futcher P | Husband | Hill | Futcher R | West | Boersma* | Carr |
| | 10/9 | | *5,836* | *16* | 6 | | | *Randall 25* | *Thomas* | *Bater* | *Taylor T* | *Day* | *Taylor S* | *Prince* | *Barry** | *Evans* | *Williams* | *Randall* | *Staniforth* | *Hendrie* |
| | | | | | | | | Ref: D Nippard | Rovers create more scoring chances than Luton but are unable to finish. Ron Futcher centres accurately for Phil Boersma to head his first league goal for the Town and, after a mix-up allows an equaliser, Lil Fuccillo sets Buckley up for a fierce shot from outside the box which is decisive. | | | | | | | | | | | |
| 5 | H | BLACKBURN | | 6 | D | 0-0 | 0-0 | | Aleksic | Price | Buckley | Fuccillo | Faulkner | Futcher P | Husband | Hill | Futcher R | Boersma | Carr | |
| | 17/9 | | 9,149 | *9* | 7 | | | | *Bradshaw* | *Fazackerley* | *Bailey* | *Keeley* | *Hawkins** | *Metcalfe* | *Brotherston* | *Hird* | *Lewis* | *Parkes* | *Wagstaffe* | *Mitchell* |
| | | | | | | | | Ref: R Challis | Blackburn's unbeaten away record is under threat when the Town force three corners in the first two minutes and Boersma scoops the ball over the bar from close range, when it appeared easier to score. Aleksic keeps the visitors at bay in the dying minutes, making several fine saves. | | | | | | | | | | | |
| 6 | A | TOTTENHAM | | 9 | L | 0-2 | 0-1 | | Aleksic | Price | Buckley | Fuccillo | Faulkner | Futcher P | Husband | Hill | Futcher R | Boersma | Carr | |
| | 24/9 | | ***32,814*** | *1* | 7 | | | *Osgood 44p, Jones 51* | *Daines* | *Naylor* | *Holmes* | *Osgood* | *Perryman* | *Hoddle* | *Pratt* | *McNab* | *Duncan** | *Jones* | *Taylor* | *Armstrong* |
| | | | | | | | | Ref: R Lewis | West misses this game through injury but the Town are still able to create more scoring chances than the current league leaders. John Duncan appears to fall over, unchallenged, in the area and Keith Osgood scores from the spot. Chris Jones stabs in a rebound from a Neil McNab shot. | | | | | | | | | | | |
| 7 | A | BRIGHTON | | 9 | L | 2-3 | 0-0 | Futcher R 72, Husband 88 | Aleksic | Price | Buckley | Carr | Faulkner | Futcher P | Husband | Hill | Futcher R | Fuccillo | Boersma | |
| | 27/9 | | *25,199* | *2* | 7 | | | *Ward 59, Fell 84, 87* | *Steele* | *Tiler* | *Cattlin* | *Winstanley* | *Lawrenson* | *Horton* | *Piper** | *O'Sullivan* | *Potts* | *Ward* | *Mellor* | *Fell* |
| | | | | | | | | Ref: B Homewood | Peter Ward wins a penalty after he is fouled in the area by John Faulkner but sends his kick high over the bar. In an incident packed, end-to-end tussle, all the goals come in the final half hour and the Hatters are unlucky not to earn a point when Husband has a shot deflected onto the bar. | | | | | | | | | | | |
| 8 | H | NOTTS CO | | 8 | W | 2-0 | 0-0 | Fuccillo 52, Boersma 54 | Aleksic | Price | Buckley | West | Faulkner | Futcher P | Husband | Hill | Futcher R | Fuccillo | Boersma | |
| | 1/10 | | 7,593 | *21* | 9 | | | | *McManus* | *Benjamin* | *O'Brien* | *Ladd** | *Stubbs* | *Chapman* | *Richards* | *Birchenall* | *Mann* | *Bradd* | *Hooks* | *Sims* |
| | | | | | | | | Ref: D Smith | The Town thump long balls at a five-man defensive wall during the first period but, with a change of tactics after the break, score twice in two minutes. Fuccillo takes advantage of an astute pass from West, whilst Boersma is quickest to react after Brian Stubbs loses the ball in the box. | | | | | | | | | | | |
| 9 | H | MILLWALL | | 6 | W | 1-0 | 0-0 | Price 86 | Aleksic | Price | Buckley | West | Faulkner | Futcher P | Husband* | Hill | Futcher R | Fuccillo | Boersma | Carr |
| | 4/10 | | 9,119 | *13* | 11 | | | | *Johns* | *Donaldson* | *Walker* | *Kitchener* | *Hazell* | *Adams* | *Hamilton* | *Pearson* | *Chambers* | *Seasman* | *Lee** | *Smith* |
| | | | | | | | | Ref: J Hunting | Attractive build-up work by the Town is not matched by finishing power in the box. The Hatters are awarded a penalty but the referee then changes his decision and gives a free-kick on the edge of the area; Alan West plays it short for Paul Price to hammer home and justice is done. | | | | | | | | | | | |
| 10 | A | CARDIFF | | 4 | W | 4-1 | 1-1 | Byrne 25 (og), Fuccillo 55, Futcher R 83, | Aleksic | Price | Buckley | West | Faulkner | Futcher P | Heale | Hill | Futcher R | Fuccillo | Boersma | |
| | 8/10 | | *8,726* | *19* | 13 | | | *Dwyer 43* [Hill 89] | *Irwin* | *Dwyer* | *Attley* | *Went* | *Pontin* | *Byrne* | *Campbell* | *Buchanan* | *Sayer* | *Evans* | *Robson* | |
| | | | | | | | | Ref: T Spencer | A fortunate own-goal from Gerry Byrne sets the Town up for a win which leaves the Cardiff manager, Jimmy Andrews, fuming. The Bluebirds equalise as they pile on the pressure in the second half but the Hatters, who are forced to attack on the break, make the most of their chances. | | | | | | | | | | | |

| No | Venue | Opponent / Date | Att | Pos | Res / Pts | F-A | H-T | Scorers, Times, and Referees | 1 | 2 | 3 | 4 | 5 | 6 | 7 | 8 | 9 | 10 | 11 | 12 |
|---|---|---|---|---|---|---|---|---|---|---|---|---|---|---|---|---|---|---|---|---|
| 11 | H | FULHAM | | 2 | W | 1-0 | 1-0 | Faulkner 36 | Aleksic | Price | Buckley | West | Faulkner | Futcher P | Husband | Hill | Futcher R | Fuccillo | Boersma | |
| | | 15/10 | 12,736 | *12* | 15 | | | | *Peyton* | *Evans* | *Strong* | *Howe* | *Lacy* | *Gale* | *Margerrison* | *Evanson* | *Best* | *Mitchell* | *Mahoney* | |
| | | | | | | | | Ref: B Martin | Fulham goalkeeper Gerry Peyton makes a superb reflex save from a Fuccillo header before Faulkner ends the deadlock, running on to a corner from West with the visitors defence guilty of ball-watching. 17-year-old defender Tony Gale nearly salvages a point, but his header hits the bar. | | | | | | | | | | | |
| 12 | A | BLACKPOOL | | 4 | L | 1-2 | 1-1 | Husband 7 | Aleksic | Price | Buckley | West | Faulkner | Futcher P | Husband | Hill | Futcher R | Fuccillo | Boersma | |
| | | 22/10 | *12,167* | *5* | 15 | | | *Ronson 26, Ainscow 73* | *Ward* | *Gardner* | *Milligan** | *McEwan* | *Suddaby* | *Hart* | *Ronson* | *Ainscow* | *Weston* | *Walsh* | *Hatton* | *Finnigan* |
| | | | | | | | | Ref: T Mills | The Town have the better of the opening exchanges and Boersma crosses accurately to Husband, who heads in at the far post. Billy Ronson hits the equaliser and then sets up Alan Ainscow for the winner. 'We will play much worse than this and win,' moans a disappointed Harry Haslam. | | | | | | | | | | | |
| 13 | A | BOLTON | | 7 | L | 1-2 | 1-0 | Futcher R 7 | Aleksic | Price | Buckley | West | Faulkner | Futcher P | Husband | Hill | Futcher R | Fuccillo | Heale | |
| | | 29/10 | *21,973* | *1* | 15 | | | *Morgan 52, Worthington 82* | *McDonagh* | *Nicholson* | *Dunne* | *Walsh* | *Allardyce* | *Greaves* | *Train* | *Reid* | *Morgan* | *Whatmore* | *Worthington* | |
| | | | | | | | | Ref: G Courtney | This is another game where the Town lose out after scoring an early goal. Ron Futcher puts in a soft shot which is fumbled by Jim McDonagh but then Willie Morgan takes over, firing in a volley to level the scores and then setting up bargain buy Frank Worthington for the late winner. | | | | | | | | | | | |
| 14 | H | HULL | | 7 | D | 1-1 | 1-0 | Husband 34 | Aleksic | Price | Buckley | West | Faulkner | Futcher P | Husband | Hill | Futcher R | Fuccillo | Heale | |
| | | 5/11 | 8,936 | *12* | 16 | | | *Bannister 68* | *Wealands* | *Daniel* | *Devries* | *Dobson* | *Haigh* | *Bremner* | *Galvin* | *Grimes* | *Stewart* | *Warboys* | *Bannister* | |
| | | | | | | | | Ref: T Bune | After the League Cup marathon against Manchester City, the Town are jaded and drop a valuable home point. The Hatters only have a stooping header from Husband to show for their superiority, with hesitation in defence allowing Vince Grimes to set up Bruce Bannister for the equaliser. | | | | | | | | | | | |
| 15 | A | MANSFIELD | | 7 | L | 1-3 | 0-2 | Hill 89 | Aleksic | Price | Buckley | West | Faulkner | McNichol | Husband | Hill | Futcher R | Fuccillo | Heale* | **Stein** |
| | | 12/11 | *7,519* | *15* | 16 | | | *Sharkey 10, Syrett 31, Miller 69* | *Arnold* | *Bird* | *Phillips* | *Saxby* | *Wood* | *Morris* | *Sharkey* | *Hodgson* | *Moss* | *Syrett* | *Miller* | |
| | | | | | | | | Ref: G Nolan | The Stags end a run of six games without a win by taking full advantage of some sloppy Luton defending, despite often pulling ten men back in to defence. Hill scores with a 20-yard cross shot but it is too late. Brian Stein starts his long career when coming on as a substitute for Heale. | | | | | | | | | | | |
| 16 | H | STOKE | | 10 | L | 1-2 | 0-2 | Buckley 73 | Aleksic | Price | Buckley | West | Faulkner | McNichol | Husband | Hill | Futcher R | Fuccillo | Heale* | Stein |
| | | 19/11 | 9,384 | *9* | 16 | | | *Kendall 26, Crooks 37* | *Jones* | *Marsh* | *Lindsay* | *Smith* | *Dodd* | *Kendall* | *Waddington* | *Bowers** | *Gregory* | *Busby* | *Crooks* | *Richardson* |
| | | | | | | | | Ref: J Sewell | The Town are missing Paul Futcher, who was recently injured in car crash, as they gift the visitors two first-half goals. In a barn-storming display after the break, Steve Buckley thunders in a terrific shot to reduce the deficit but the experienced Potters defensive back-four holds firm. | | | | | | | | | | | |
| 17 | A | SUNDERLAND | | 11 | D | 1-1 | 1-0 | Futcher R 43 | Aleksic | Price | Buckley | West | Faulkner | McNichol | Husband | Hill | Futcher R | Fuccillo | Carr | |
| | | 26/11 | *26,915* | *9* | 17 | | | *Bolton 54* | *Siddall* | *Henderson* | *Bolton* | *Elliott* | *Ashurst* | *Kerr* | *Arnott* | *Rowell* | *Rostron* | *Greenwood* | *Holden* | |
| | | | | | | | | Ref: J Wrennall | In a delicately poised game, the Town play with a new-found confidence which belies their recent poor run. Jim Husband hits the bar before a shot from Price is turned in by Futcher. Sunderland mount an assault after the break and a 25-yard volley from Joe Bolton breaches the defence. | | | | | | | | | | | |
| 18 | H | BURNLEY | | 11 | L | 1-2 | 0-1 | Hill 79 | Aleksic | Price | Buckley | West | Faulkner | McNichol | Husband | Hill | Futcher R | Fuccillo | Boersma | |
| | | 3/12 | 6,921 | *22* | 17 | | | *Hall 29, Kindon 50* | *Stevenson* | *Newton* | *Brennan* | *Thomson* | *Rodaway* | *Noble* | *Ingham* | *Hall* | *Morley* | *Fletcher* | *Kindon* | |
| | | | | | | | | Ref: D Biddle | Burnley travel to Kenilworth Road as the bottom club in the League and without a point away from home. Yet they sink an abysmal Town side with goals from recent signing, Brian Hall, and Steve Kindon. Ex-Chelsea boss, Eddie McCreadie, is rumoured to be taking over from Haslam. | | | | | | | | | | | |
| 19 | A | SOUTHAMPTON | | 10 | W | 1-0 | 0-0 | Futcher R 72 | Aleksic | Price | Buckley | West | Faulkner | Jones | Husband | Hill | Futcher R | Fuccillo | Boersma | |
| | | 10/12 | *19,907* | *6* | 19 | | | | *Wells* | *Waldron* | *Andruszewski* | *Nicholl* | *Pickering* | *Williams* | *Ball* | *Holmes* | *Boyer* | *MacDougall* | *Neville** | *Hebberd* |
| | | | | | | | | Ref: W Gow | The Town succeed in winning for the first time in eight matches to end the Saints' impressive home record of 22 unbeaten games. Lil Fuccillo, who squanders two good chances early on, hits a free-kick which is deflected past the wrong-footed goalkeeper, Peter Wells, by Ron Futcher. | | | | | | | | | | | |
| 20 | H | MANSFIELD | | 10 | D | 1-1 | 0-1 | Futcher R 85 | Aleksic | Price | Buckley | West | Faulkner | Jones | Husband* | Hill | Futcher R | Fuccillo | Boersma | Stein |
| | | 17/12 | 6,401 | *21* | 20 | | | *Syrett 28* | *Arnold* | *Bird* | *Foster B* | *Wood* | *Foster C* | *Sharkey* | *Miller* | *Goodwin** | *Miller* | *Syrett* | *Aston* | *Saxby* |
| | | | | | | | | Ref: B Daniels | It is now two months since the Town last won at home and they never look capable of changing matters against a lowly Mansfield side. John Aston has a quiet game on his return to Kenilworth Road but the Stags take a first-half lead with Luton leaving it late to level through Futcher. | | | | | | | | | | | |
| 21 | A | CRYS PALACE | | 9 | D | 3-3 | 3-1 | Price 18, Boersma 28, Futcher R 37 | Aleksic | Price | Buckley | West | Faulkner | Jones | Stein | Hill | Futcher R | Fuccillo | Boersma | |
| | | 26/12 | *22,405* | *10* | 21 | | | *Silkman 23, 59, Sansom 89* | *Burns* | *Hinshelwood* | *Sansom* | *Cannon* | *Nicholas* | *Holder** | *Chatterton* | *Fenwick* | *Swindlehurst* | *Harkouk* | *Silkman* | *Walsh* |
| | | | | | | | | Ref: H Robinson | A Christmas cracker of a game at Selhurst Park sees the Hatters catch Palace on the break and race in to a 3-1 half-time lead. The Eagles fight back, however, and a tremendous 30-yard shot from full-back Kenny Sansom earns them a share of the points in the final seconds of the game. | | | | | | | | | | | |

| No | Date | | Att | Pos | Pt | F-A | H-T | Scorers, Times, and Referees | 1 | 2 | 3 | 4 | 5 | 6 | 7 | 8 | 9 | 10 | 11 | 12 sub used |
|---|---|---|---|---|---|---|---|---|---|---|---|---|---|---|---|---|---|---|---|---|
| 22 | H | SHEFFIELD UTD | | 6 | W | 4-0 | 1-0 | Futcher R 7, Fuccillo 55p, Stein 57, 88 | Aleksic | Price | Buckley | West | Carr | Jones | Stein | Hill | Futcher R | Fuccillo | Boersma | |
| | 27/12 | | 10,885 | *9* | 23 | | | | *Brown* | *Cutbush* | *Franks* | *Colquhoun* | *Flynn** | *Calvert* | *Speight* | *Kenworthy* | *Woodward* | *Campbell* | *Hamilton* | *Stainrod* |
| | | | | | | | | Ref: K Salmon | The home fans see Luton score more than one goal for the first time in three months when, in a powerful performance, Futcher starts the rout with a far-post header and Fuccillo nets from the spot after Tony Kenworthy palms Futcher's shot over the bar. Stein scores his first Town goals. | | | | | | | | | | | |
| 23 | H | BRIGHTON | | 6 | W | 1-0 | 1-0 | Boersma 32 | Aleksic | Price | Buckley | West | Carr | Jones | Stein | Hill | Futcher R | Fuccillo | Boersma | |
| | 31/12 | | *13,200* | *5* | 25 | | | | *Steele* | *Cattlin** | *Williams* | *Rollings* | *Lawrenson* | *Horton* | *Towner* | *Clark* | *Ward* | *Maybank* | *O'Sullivan* | *Potts* |
| | | | | | | | | Ref: A Hamil | Stein puts on another superb performance, narrowly missing on two occasions and then providing the centre for Boersma to dive in and head the only goal. Teddy Maybank claims that he should have been awarded two penalties, a view confirmed by the Match of the Day cameras. | | | | | | | | | | | |
| 24 | A | ORIENT | | 6 | D | 0-0 | 0-0 | | Aleksic | Price | Buckley | West | Carr | Jones | Stein | Hill | Futcher R | Fuccillo | Boersma | |
| | 2/1 | | *9,270* | *15* | 26 | | | | *Jackson* | *Fisher* | *Hoadley* | *Roeder* | *Gray* | *Roffey* | *Grealish* | *Bennett* | *Chiedozie* | *Mayo* | *Kitchen* | |
| | | | | | | | | Ref: D Reeves | Steve Buckley plays his last game for the Hatters before a big money move to Derby County but the game will not live long in his memory with the defences dominating. Rumours of the imminent departure of Luton manager, Harry Haslam, have been circulating for the past week. | | | | | | | | | | | |
| 25 | H | OLDHAM | | 7 | L | 0-1 | 0-1 | | Aleksic | Price | Carr* | Hill | Faulkner | Jones | Husband | Stein | Futcher R | Fuccillo | Boersma | **Ingram** |
| | 14/1 | | 7,792 | *6* | 26 | | | *Taylor 29* | *Platt* | *Hoolickin* | *Blair* | *Edwards* | *Holt* | *Bell* | *Wood* | *Chapman* | *Young* | *Taylor* | *Gardner* | |
| | | | | | | | | Ref: M Sinclair | The Town meet Oldham for the third time in a week but, with West missing, the Hatters have no one to control the midfield. Steve Taylor nets a soft goal and Futcher misses an easy chance late on. John Faulkner is presented with a silver tray to mark his 200th league game for the Town. | | | | | | | | | | | |
| 26 | A | CHARLTON | | 7 | D | 0-0 | 0-0 | | Aleksic | Price | Carr | Hill | Faulkner | Futcher P | Husband | Jones | Futcher R | Fuccillo | Boersma | |
| | 21/1 | | *8,267* | *13* | 27 | | | | *Wood* | *Curtis* | *Warman* | *Berry* | *Dugdale* | *Tydeman* | *Brisley* | *Peacock* | *McAuley* | *Gritt* | *Flanagan* | |
| | | | | | | | | Ref: A McDonald | Paul Futcher returns to the team after his car crash in early November in what turns out to be the last game in charge for Luton manager, Harry Haslam. The Valiants' negative formation makes it a dull encounter which the Charlton manager, Andy Nelson, justifies as 'a necessary evil'. | | | | | | | | | | | |
| 27 | H | BRISTOL ROV | | 7 | D | 1-1 | 0-0 | Futcher R 87 | Aleksic | Price | Carr | West | Faulkner | Futcher P | Stein | Jones* | Futcher R | Fuccillo | Boersma | Hill |
| | 8/2 | | **5,913** | *14* | 28 | | | *Harding 89* | *Thomas* | *Aitken* | *Bater* | *Harding* | *Taylor* | *Prince* | *Williams* | *Pulis* | *Gould* | *Staniforth* | *Randall* | |
| | | | | | | | | Ref: B Newsome | David Pleat watches his Luton side put the Rovers' goal under seemingly constant pressure in the second half, with Ron Futcher hitting a post and turning another chance just wide before hitting a late goal which appears to have won the game. Steve Harding equalises in the last minute. | | | | | | | | | | | |
| 28 | A | BLACKBURN | | 9 | L | 0-2 | 0-0 | | Aleksic | Price | Carr | West | Faulkner | Futcher P | Husband | Hill | Futcher R | Fuccillo* | Boersma | Stein |
| | 11/2 | | *11,511* | *5* | 28 | | | *Round 69, Brotherston 83* | *Butcher* | *Hird* | *Bailey* | *Keeley* | *Fazackerley* | *Metcalfe* | *Waddington* | *Taylor** | *Brotherston* | *Hargreaves* | *Wagstaffe* | *Round* |
| | | | | | | | | Ref: B Newsome | On a dangerous, rock-hard, frosty pitch, Blackburn defender Glen Keeley up-ends Fuccillo, who lands on his head and is taken to hospital. The game is a farce with Aleksic adding to it by throwing the ball to Rovers' Noel Brotherston, who chips it back over his head for the second goal. | | | | | | | | | | | |
| 29 | H | TOTTENHAM | | 9 | L | **1-4** | 0-1 | West 78 | Aleksic | Price | Carr | Hill | Faulkner | Futcher P | Fuccillo | West | Futcher R | Jones* | Boersma | Stein |
| | 22/2 | | **17,024** | *1* | 28 | | | *Hoddle 32, 58, McAllister 74, Duncan 86* | *Daines* | *Naylor* | *Holmes* | *Hoddle* | *McAllister** | *Perryman* | *Pratt* | *McNab* | *Duncan* | *Lee* | *Taylor* | *Moores* |
| | | | | | | | | Ref: A Gunn | In a frenzied game played in front of the biggest crowd of the season, Tottenham deserve their win, but not by the 4-1 margin. Glenn Hoddle controls the midfield but Boersma goes close in each half with long shots which just clear the bar. The Town are still without a win this year. | | | | | | | | | | | |
| 30 | A | NOTTS CO | | 9 | L | 0-2 | 0-1 | | Aleksic | Price | Carr | Hill | Faulkner | Futcher P | Fuccillo | West | Futcher R | Jones* | Boersma | Stein |
| | 25/2 | | *8,558* | *16* | 28 | | | *Bradd 13, Mann 72* | *McManus* | *Richards* | *O'Brien* | *Chapman* | *Stubbs* | *Birchenall* | *McVay* | *Mann* | *Carter** | *Bradd* | *Vinter* | *Hooks* |
| | | | | | | | | Ref: D Civil | The Hatters dig their own grave with some sloppy finishing on David Pleat's return to his home city. Ron Futcher blasts the ball into the side-netting with only the keeper, Eric McManus to beat, whilst his twin brother, Paul, hits the crossbar when it appears simpler for him to score. | | | | | | | | | | | |
| 31 | H | CARDIFF | | 7 | W | 3-1 | 2-1 | Boersma 11, 80, Faulkner 34 | Aleksic | Price | Carr | Jones | Faulkner | Futcher P | Stein | West | Futcher R | Fuccillo | Boersma | |
| | 4/3 | | 6,029 | *18* | 30 | | | *Buchanan 27* | *Healey* | *Dwyer* | *Pethard* | *Pontin* | *Larmour* | *Campbell* | *Grapes* | *Giles* | *Buchanan* | *Went* | *Bishop* | |
| | | | | | | | | Ref: B Martin | David Pleat is away on a scouting trip and misses the first victory since taking charge of the team. On a muddy pitch, the Hatters use the wings to good effect and they are also helped by Bluebirds' goalkeeper, Ron Healey, who fumbles a free-kick from Phil Boersma for the opening goal. | | | | | | | | | | | |

| No Date | H/A | Opponent Att | Pos | Res Pts | F-A | H-T | Scorers, Times, and Referees | 1 | 2 | 3 | 4 | 5 | 6 | 7 | 8 | 9 | 10 | 11 | 12 sub used |
|---|---|---|---|---|---|---|---|---|---|---|---|---|---|---|---|---|---|---|---|
| 32 | A | FULHAM | 9 | L | 0-1 | 0-1 | | Aleksic | Price | Carr | Jones | Faulkner | Futcher P | Stein* | West | Futcher R | Fuccillo | Boersma | Hill |
| 10/3 | | 7,796 | 8 | 30 | | | Mahoney 14 | Peyton | Evans | Strong | Lacy | Gale | Money | Evanson | Margerrison | Mahoney | Greenaway | Mitchell | |
| | | | | | | | Ref: A Grey | Tony Mahoney heads home a deep centre to give Fulham an early lead which is the flash-point for some previously unseen rough play from Luton. The lenient referee allows some bad tackles by the Town to go unpunished, with both Jones and Ron Futcher lucky to stay on the pitch. | | | | | | | | | | | |
| 33 | H | BLACKPOOL | 7 | W | 4-0 | 1-0 | West 39, Futcher R 77, Boersma 79, | Aleksic | Price | Carr | Hill | Faulkner | Futcher P | Stein | West | Futcher R | Fuccillo | Boersma | |
| 18/3 | | 6,041 | 8 | 32 | | | [Fuccillo 88] | Ward | Gardner | Milligan | McEwan | Suddaby | Ronson | Tong* | Chandler | Waldron | Walsh | Ainscow | Wilson |
| | | | | | | | Ref: R Challis | Shaken by the bad press received following their defeat last week, the Town tear into their weakened opposition. After missing several first-half chances, fortune turns in their favour and David Pleat, seeing his side win for the first time, beams 'there was more application and spirit'. | | | | | | | | | | | |
| 34 | H | BOLTON | 7 | W | 2-1 | 1-0 | West 19, Boersma 87 | Aleksic | Price | Carr | Hill | Faulkner | Futcher P | Stein | West | Futcher R | Fuccillo | Boersma | |
| 21/3 | | 8,306 | 2 | 34 | | | Jones 88 | McDonagh | Dunne | Walsh | Jones | Allardyce | Greaves | Train | Reid | Morgan | Whatmore | Worthingt'n* | Gowling |
| | | | | | | | Ref: G Flint | Ambitious Bolton are brought back to earth when their offside trap fails, which enables the Town to surge into the lead after Hill chests down a cross from Price into the path of West, who fires home. The Trotters have their chances, but Boersma catches them on the break near the end. | | | | | | | | | | | |
| 35 | A | SHEFFIELD UTD | 7 | L | 1-4 | 0-3 | Calvert 75 (og) [Woodward 65] | Knight | Price | Carr | Hill* | Jones | Futcher P | Stein | West | Futcher R | Fuccillo | Boersma | McNichol |
| 25/3 | | 12,587 | 14 | 34 | | | Stainrod 22, 42, Speight 38, | Brown | Cutbush | Calvert | Franks | Flynn | Speight | Keeley | Hamson | Woodward | Campbell | Stainrod | |
| | | | | | | | Ref: P Richardson | Harry Haslam masterminds a convincing win for his new side in a game which should not have started, owing to the incessant rain resulting in a water-logged pitch. Good football is impossible and the Hatters' goal is a farce with Cliff Calvert lobbing his own goalkeeper from 20 yards. | | | | | | | | | | | |
| 36 | H | CRYS PALACE | 7 | W | 1-0 | 0-0 | Fuccillo 58p | Knight | Price | Carr | McNichol | Jones | Futcher P | Stein | West | Futcher R | Fuccillo | Boersma | |
| 27/3 | | 9,816 | 9 | 36 | | | | Burridge | Hinshelwood | Sansom | Cannon | Boyle | Chatterton | Hilaire | Holder ! | Swindlehurst | Walsh | Silkman* | Murphy |
| | | | | | | | Ref: A Robinson | The defences dominate in this Easter bore with the only goal coming after Fuccillo is hacked down in the area by Nicky Chatterton, the injured party picking himself up and scoring from the spot. Phil Holder is sent off after measuring the required distance for a free-kick for the referee! | | | | | | | | | | | |
| 37 | A | HULL | 7 | D | 1-1 | 0-0 | West 53 | Knight | Jones | Carr | Hill | McNichol | Futcher P | Stein | West | Futcher R | Fuccillo | Boersma | |
| 1/4 | | 4,054 | 20 | 37 | | | Roberts 73 | Blackburn | Nisbet | Daniel | Croft | Roberts | Bremner | Haigh | Lord | Stewart | Warboys | Hawley | |
| | | | | | | | Ref: J Sewell | The Hatters play some neat and effective football in front of the lowest gate of the season at Boothferry Park but only have an Alan West strike to show for it. Dave Roberts heads an undeserved equaliser for the relegation favourites after Knight fails to cut out a cross from Peter Daniel. | | | | | | | | | | | |
| 38 | H | SUNDERLAND | 8 | L | 1-3 | 0-2 | Stein 67 | Knight | Price | Carr | Hill | McNichol | Futcher P | Stein | West* | Futcher R | Fuccillo | Boersma | **Sperrin** |
| 8/4 | | 7,616 | 7 | 37 | | | Lee 18, Rowell 21, Gregoire 79 | Siddall | Gilbert | Bolton | Clarke | Ashurst | Kerr | Docherty | Rowell | Armstrong* | Rostron | Lee | Gregoire |
| | | | | | | | Ref: E Hughes | Sunderland adapt better to the bumpy pitch and shock the Town by scoring twice in a minute, halfway through the first half. Brian Stein evades three tackles to score a lifeline goal, but substitute Roly Gregoire taps in a third to give the Rokermen only their second away win of the season. | | | | | | | | | | | |
| 39 | A | STOKE | 9 | D | 0-0 | 0-0 | | Aleksic | Price | Carr | Hill | McNichol | Futcher P | Stein | West | Futcher R | Fuccillo | Boersma | |
| 15/4 | | 15,546 | 8 | 38 | | | | Jones | Marsh | Scott | Smith | Dodd | Kendall | Waddington | Richardson | Busby* | O'Callaghan | Crooks | Cook |
| | | | | | | | Ref: N Midgley | After five successive home wins, Stoke come down to earth with a bump in a match crammed with errors and end-of-season apathy. The Town defence restricts the Potters to just a few chances, most of which seem to fall to luckless ex-Hatter Viv Busby, who has a nightmare of a game. | | | | | | | | | | | |
| 40 | H | SOUTHAMPTON | 10 | L | 1-2 | 0-0 | Hill 63 | Aleksic | Price | Carr* | Hill | McNichol | Futcher P | Stein | West | Futcher R | Fuccillo | Boersma | Jones |
| 22/4 | | 14,302 | 1 | 38 | | | MacDougall 52, Peach 88p | Wells | Adruszewski | Peach | Nicholl | Pickering | Williams | Ball | Holmes | Boyer | MacDougall | Funnell | |
| | | | | | | | Ref: B Homewood | Saints' early fire is snuffed out by the Luton defence. A free-kick from Alan Ball allows Ted MacDougall to steal a goal but Hill levels soon after. The match ends in controversy when Paul Futcher fouls Ball outside the area but the referee awards a penalty which David Peach converts. | | | | | | | | | | | |
| 41 | A | MILLWALL | 12 | L | 0-1 | 0-0 | | Aleksic | Price | Jones | Hill | McNichol | Futcher P | Stein | West | Futcher R | Fuccillo* | Boersma | Ingram |
| 25/4 | | 7,593 | 19 | 38 | | | Price 63 (og) | Johns | Donaldson | Moore | Kitchener | Hazell | Allen | Walker | Mehmet | Lee | Seasman* | Hamilton | Pearson |
| | | | | | | | Ref: A Glasson | The Hatters create most of the chances against relegation-threatened Millwall but show little punch in front of goal. The game is settled when a long free-kick from Tony Hazell is deflected into his own net by Paul Price. The referee angers the crowd by failing to play the advantage rule. | | | | | | | | | | | |
| 42 | A | BURNLEY | 13 | L | 1-2 | 1-1 | Ingram 35 | Aleksic | Price | Jones | Hill | McNichol | Futcher P | Stein | West | Ingram | Fuccillo* | Heale | Boersma |
| 29/4 | | 11,648 | 11 | 38 | | | Futcher P 36 (og), Smith 54 | Stevenson | Scott | Brennan | Thomson | Robinson | Noble | Ingham | Cochrane | Smith | Fletcher | Kindon | |
| Average | Home 9,252 | Away 13,706 | | | | | Ref: N Ashley | Luton take the lead when Ingram hits his first league goal with a 25-yard rocket shot but, one minute later, Futcher heads a cross from Malcolm Smith into his own net. Burnley take the lead but the Hatters are denied a penalty in the last minute, when a handball is missed by the referee. | | | | | | | | | | | |

## LEAGUE DIVISION 2 (CUP-TIES) Manager: Harry Haslam ⇨ David Pleat SEASON 1977-78



| League Cup | | | | | F-A | H-T | Scorers, Times, and Referees | 1 | 2 | 3 | 4 | 5 | 6 | 7 | 8 | 9 | 10 | 11 | 12 sub used |
|---|---|---|---|---|---|---|---|---|---|---|---|---|---|---|---|---|---|---|---|
| 2 | A | WOLVES | 14 | W | 3-1 | 1-1 | Husband 29, Boersma 54, Carr 83 | Aleksic | Price | Buckley | Fuccillo | Faulkner | McNichol | Husband | Hill | Boersma* | West | Futcher R | Carr |
| | 30/8 | | *14,682 1:5* | | | | *Richards 26* | *Parkes* | *Palmer* | *Daly* | *Parkin* | *McAlle* | *Daley* | *Patching* | *Carr* | *Richards* | *Kindon* | *Sunderland* | |
| | | | | | | | Ref: D Lloyd | The home side take the lead with a John Richards header but Husband takes advantage of some brilliant play from West to equalise soon after. Another slick passing movement allows Boersma to open his Luton account before substitute David Carr wraps up victory with a late tap in. | | | | | | | | | | | |
| 3 | H | MANCHESTER C | 4 | D | 1-1 | 0-0 | Futcher R 50 | Aleksic | Price | Buckley | West | Faulkner | Futcher P | Husband | Hill | Futcher R | Fuccillo | Heale | |
| | 25/10 | | 16,443 *1:5* | | | | *Barnes 53* | *Corrigan* | *Clements* | *Donachie* | *Watson* | *Booth* | *Owen* | *Keegan* | *Power* | *Barnes* | *Channon* | *Kidd* | |
| | | | | | | | Ref: A Robinson | Dave Watson blocks a Fuccillo shot on the line and Mick Channon hits the post for City. After the break, Futcher curls a shot past Joe Corrigan but Peter Barnes levels when his shot hits the underside of the bar before bouncing down just behind the line. City are relieved to earn a replay. | | | | | | | | | | | |
| 3R | A | MANCHESTER C | 7 | D | 0-0 | 0-0 | | Aleksic | Price | Buckley | West | Faulkner | Futcher P | Husband | Hill | Futcher R | Fuccillo | Heale | |
| | 1/11 | | *28,254 1:4* | | *aet* | | | *Corrigan* | *Clements* | *Donachie* | *Doyle* | *Booth* | *Kidd* | *Hartford* | *Power* | *Barnes* | *Channon* | *Royle* | |
| | | | | | | | Ref: R Kirkpatrick/F Phipps | The referee is looking at his watch before blowing for the end of normal time when 17-year-old Gary Heale is presented with an open goal after Joe Corrigan diverts a Ron Futcher drive. Somehow the chance is missed and Aleksic is called upon to keep the Town in the game in extra-time. | | | | | | | | | | | |
| 3R | A | MANCHESTER C | 7 | L | 2-3 | 2-1 | Heale 11, 25 | Aleksic | Price | Buckley | West | Faulkner | McNichol | Stein* | Hill | Futcher R | Fuccillo | Heale | Sperrin |
| R | 9/11 | | *13,043 1:6* | | *aet* | | *Tueart 34p, Channon 58, Kidd 115* | *Corrigan* | *Clements* | *Donachie* | *Doyle* | *Watson* | *Power* | *Barnes* | *Channon* | *Kidd* | *Hartford* | *Tueart* | |
| | (at Old Trafford) | | | | | | Ref: K Burns | Injury-hit Luton take a two-goal lead through Heale but end up losing the tie. Hill clips the heels of Paul Power in the area and Dennis Tueart scores from the spot. Channon equalises and Milija Aleksic saves a Tueart spot-kick in extra-time but is unable to stop a shot from Brian Kidd. | | | | | | | | | | | |

| FA Cup | | | | | | | | | | | | | | | | | | | |
|---|---|---|---|---|---|---|---|---|---|---|---|---|---|---|---|---|---|---|---|
| 3 | H | OLDHAM | 6 | D | 1-1 | 1-0 | Fuccillo 28 | Aleksic | Price | Carr | West* | Faulkner | Jones | Husband | Hill | Futcher R | Fuccillo | Boersma | Ingram |
| | 7/1 | | 9,851 *2:8* | | | | *Taylor 74* | *Platt* | *Wood* | *Holt* | *Hicks* | *Hurst* | *Bell* | *Valentine* | *Halom* | *Chapman* | *Taylor* | *Young* | |
| | | | | | | | Ref: R Challis | Fuccillo scores a brilliant solo goal after going past four defenders. In a hard-fought match, West is carried off with a damaged ankle after a bad tackle by Ian Wood. This unbalances the Luton side and they concede an equaliser when Steve Taylor fires in a headed pass from Keith Hicks. | | | | | | | | | | | |
| 3R | A | OLDHAM | 6 | W | 2-1 | 1-1 | Boersma 13, 48 | Aleksic | Price | Carr | Hill | Faulkner | Jones | Husband | Ingram | Futcher R | Fuccillo | Boersma | |
| | 10/1 | | *13,802 2:8* | | | | *Young 28* | *Platt* | *Wood* | *Holt* | *Edwards* | *Hurst* | *Gardiner* | *Valentine* | *Chapman* | *Taylor* | *Halom* | *Young** | *Hoolickin* |
| | | | | | | | Ref: R Challis | A weak shot from Boersma squeezes through the hands of Platt, who points out that the ball has punctured, but the referee refuses to disallow the goal. The Latics equalise when Aleksic drops the ball, leaving Alan Young with a simple chance. Ingram sets up the winner for Boersma. | | | | | | | | | | | |
| 4 | A | MILLWALL | 7 | L | 0-4 | 0-2 | | Knight | Price | Carr | Hill | Faulkner | Futcher P | Husband | Jones | Futcher R | Fuccillo | Boersma | |
| | 31/1 | | *8,763 2:22* | | | | *Pearson 37, 70, 86, Seasman 45* | *Johns* | *Donaldson* | *Moore* | *Kitchener* | *Hazell* | *Walker* | *Hamilton* | *Chambers* | *Pearson* | *Seasman* | *Lee* | |
| | | | | | | | Ref: R Toseland | Pleat makes a disastrous start to his managerial career with Luton as Ian Pearson notches a hat-trick for the Lions. The Hatters make a spirited fight-back in the second half but are caught on the break by two superb Pearson strikes, one from a header, the other after he robs Paul Futcher. | | | | | | | | | | | |

| | | Home | | | | | Away | | | | | |
|---|---|---|---|---|---|---|---|---|---|---|---|---|
| | P | W | D | L | F | A | W | D | L | F | A | Pts |
| 1 Bolton | 42 | 16 | 4 | 1 | 39 | 14 | 8 | 6 | 7 | 24 | 19 | 58 |
| 2 Southampton | 42 | 15 | 4 | 2 | 44 | 16 | 7 | 9 | 5 | 26 | 23 | 57 |
| 3 Tottenham | 42 | 13 | 7 | 1 | 50 | 19 | 7 | 9 | 5 | 33 | 30 | 56 |
| 4 Brighton | 42 | 15 | 5 | 1 | 43 | 21 | 7 | 7 | 7 | 20 | 17 | 56 |
| 5 Blackburn | 42 | 12 | 4 | 5 | 33 | 16 | 4 | 9 | 8 | 23 | 44 | 45 |
| 6 Sunderland | 42 | 11 | 6 | 4 | 36 | 17 | 3 | 10 | 8 | 31 | 42 | 44 |
| 7 Stoke | 42 | 13 | 5 | 3 | 38 | 16 | 3 | 5 | 13 | 15 | 33 | 42 |
| 8 Oldham | 42 | 9 | 10 | 2 | 32 | 20 | 4 | 6 | 11 | 22 | 38 | 42 |
| 9 Crys Palace | 42 | 9 | 7 | 5 | 31 | 20 | 4 | 8 | 9 | 19 | 27 | 41 |
| 10 Fulham | 42 | 9 | 8 | 4 | 32 | 19 | 5 | 5 | 11 | 17 | 30 | 41 |
| 11 Burnley | 42 | 11 | 6 | 4 | 35 | 20 | 4 | 4 | 13 | 21 | 44 | 40 |
| 12 Sheffield Ud | 42 | 13 | 4 | 4 | 38 | 22 | 3 | 4 | 14 | 24 | 51 | 40 |
| 13 LUTON TOWN | 42 | 11 | 4 | 6 | 35 | 20 | 3 | 6 | 12 | 19 | 32 | 38 |
| 14 Orient | 42 | 8 | 11 | 2 | 30 | 20 | 2 | 7 | 12 | 13 | 29 | 38 |
| 15 Notts Co | 42 | 10 | 9 | 2 | 36 | 22 | 1 | 7 | 13 | 18 | 40 | 38 |
| 16 Millwall | 42 | 8 | 8 | 5 | 23 | 20 | 4 | 6 | 11 | 26 | 37 | 38 |
| 17 Charlton | 42 | 11 | 6 | 4 | 38 | 27 | 2 | 6 | 13 | 17 | 41 | 38 |
| 18 Bristol Rov | 42 | 10 | 7 | 4 | 40 | 26 | 3 | 5 | 13 | 21 | 51 | 38 |
| 19 Cardiff | 42 | 12 | 6 | 3 | 32 | 23 | 1 | 6 | 14 | 19 | 48 | 38 |
| 20 Blackpool | 42 | 7 | 8 | 6 | 35 | 25 | 5 | 5 | 11 | 24 | 35 | 37 |
| 21 Mansfield | 42 | 6 | 6 | 9 | 30 | 34 | 4 | 5 | 12 | 19 | 35 | 31 |
| 22 Hull | 42 | 6 | 6 | 9 | 23 | 25 | 2 | 6 | 13 | 11 | 27 | 28 |
| | 924 | 235 | 141 | 86 | 773 | 462 | 86 | 141 | 235 | 462 | 773 | 924 |

Odds & ends

Double wins: (1) Cardiff.
Double losses: (3) Burnley, Oldham, Tottenham.

Won from behind: (1) Wolves (LC).
Lost from in front: (4) Blackpool (a), Bolton (a), Burnley (a), Man C (LC).

High spots: The introduction of Brian Stein.
The continuing good form of the youngsters Steve Buckley, Lil Fuccillo, Paul Futcher, Ricky Hill and Paul Price.
The 7-1 home win over Charlton.
The win at Wolves in the League Cup.
The surprise victory at Southampton, after seven games without a win.

Low spots: The sale of Steve Buckley.
The defeat by Manchester City in the League Cup.
Failing to win any of the final six games of the campaign.
Losing at Millwall in the FA Cup in David Pleat's first game in charge.

Player of the Year: Paul Futcher.
Ever-presents: (1) Lil Fuccillo.
Hat-tricks: Jim Husband (1).
Leading scorer: Phil Boersma and Ron Futcher (11).

| | Appearances | | | | | | Goals | | | |
|---|---|---|---|---|---|---|---|---|---|---|
| | Lge | *Sub* | LC | *Sub* | FAC | *Sub* | Lge | LC | FAC | Tot |
| Aleksic, Milija | **38** | | 4 | | 2 | | | | | |
| Aston, John | **2** | | | | | | | | | |
| Boersma, Phil | **34** | *1* | 1 | | 3 | | **8** | 1 | 2 | **11** |
| Buckley, Steve | **24** | | 4 | | | | **4** | | | **4** |
| Carr, David | **25** | *2* | | *1* | 3 | | | 1 | | **1** |
| Faulkner, John | **31** | | 4 | | 3 | | **2** | | | **2** |
| Fuccillo, Lil | **42** | | 4 | | 3 | | **5** | | 1 | **6** |
| Futcher, Paul | **31** | | 2 | | 1 | | | | | |
| Futcher, Ron | **39** | | 4 | | 3 | | **10** | 1 | | **11** |
| Heale, Gary | **7** | | 3 | | | | **1** | 2 | | **3** |
| Hill, Ricky | **37** | *3* | 4 | | 3 | | **5** | | | **5** |
| Husband, Jim | **22** | | 3 | | 3 | | **7** | 1 | | **8** |
| Ingram, Godfrey | **1** | *2* | | | 1 | *1* | **1** | | | **1** |
| Jones, Graham | **19** | *1* | | | 3 | | | | | |
| Knight, Tony | **4** | | | | 1 | | | | | |
| McNichol, Jim | **11** | *1* | 2 | | | | | | | |
| Price, Paul | **40** | | 4 | | 3 | | **2** | | | **2** |
| Smith, Tim | **1** | | | | | | | | | |
| Sperrin, Martin | | *1* | | *1* | | | | | | |
| Stein, Brian | **18** | *6* | 1 | | | | **3** | | | **3** |
| West, Alan | **36** | | 4 | | 1 | | **4** | | | **4** |
| (own-goals) | | | | | | | **2** | | | **2** |
| **21 players used** | **462** | *17* | **44** | *2* | **33** | *1* | **54** | **6** | **3** | **63** |

| No | Date | Att | Pos | Pt | F-A | H-T | Scorers, Times, and Referees | 1 | 2 | 3 | 4 | 5 | 6 | 7 | 8 | 9 | 10 | 11 | 12 sub used |
|---|---|---|---|---|---|---|---|---|---|---|---|---|---|---|---|---|---|---|---|
| 1 | H OLDHAM | | | W | 6-1 | 0-1 | Hatton 46, 89, Moss 47, 76, Stein 71, | Aleksic | **Stephens** | **Sherlock** | Hill | **Turner** | **Aizlewood** | Stein | Fuccillo | **Donaghy** | **Hatton** | **Moss** | |
| | 19/8 | 8,043 | | 2 | | | *Wood 8* [Fuccillo 73p] | *McDonnell* | *Wood* | *Holt* | *Hurst* | *Edwards* | *Blair* | *Halom* | *Chapman* | *Gardner* | *Young* | *Taylor* | |
| | | | | | | | Ref: K Baker | Seven players make their league debuts for the Hatters, who find themselves 0-1 down at the break. In an amazing second-half, Bob Hatton latches onto a through ball from Chris Turner to fire home,15 seconds after the restart, as the Town smash in six goals to overwhelm the Latics. | | | | | | | | | | | |
| 2 | A CRYS PALACE | | | L | 1-3 | 1-1 | Fuccillo 9p | Aleksic | Stephens | Sherlock | Donaghy | Turner | Aizlewood | Hill | Fuccillo* | Stein | Hatton | Moss | Ingram |
| | 22/8 | *17,880* | | 2 | | | *Swindlehurst 3, Hilaire 51, Murphy 89* | *Burridge* | *Hinshelwood* | *Sansom* | *Cannon* | *Gilbert* | *Chatterton* | *Nicholas* | *Murphy* | *Swindlehurst* | *Elwiss* | *Hilaire* | |
| | | | | | | | Ref: P Reeves | Dave Swindlehurst heads the Eagles into an early lead, which is wiped out six minutes later when Lil Fuccillo converts with a spot-kick after Peter Nicholas brings down Stein. Luton, a shadow of the team which beat Oldham, are eventually worn down by the superior Palace side. | | | | | | | | | | | |
| 3 | A NEWCASTLE | | 15 | L | 0-1 | 0-1 | | Aleksic | Stephens* | Aizlewood | Donaghy | Turner | Price | Hill | West | Stein | Hatton | Moss | McNichol |
| | 26/8 | *24,112* | *18* | 2 | | | *Pearson 23* | *Mahoney* | *Kelly* | *Barker* | *Bird* | *Blackley* | *Cassidy* | *Suggett* | *Hibbitt* | *Pearson* | *Withe* | *Connolly* | |
| | | | | | | | Ref: M Lowe | The Town hit rock bottom with this defeat, and the score flatters them. Magpies' new signing from Everton, Jim Pearson, heads the only goal and then watches as the team waste many good chances. The Newcastle victory brings to an end their eight-month spell without a home win. | | | | | | | | | | | |
| 4 | H CHARLTON | | 8 | W | 3-0 | 1-0 | Hatton 25, Stein 71, Hill 80 | Aleksic | Jones | Aizlewood | Hill | Turner* | Price | Donaghy | Fuccillo | Stein | Hatton | Boersma | West |
| | 2/9 | 8,509 | *15* | 4 | | | | *Wood* | *Berry* | *Campbell* | *Shipperley* | *Dugdale* | *Tydeman* | *Brisley* | *Peacock* | *Gritt* | *Hales* | *Flanagan* | |
| | | | | | | | Ref: D Hutchinson | Inconsistent Luton steamroller Charlton with as competent a demolition job as the 7-1 victory over the Valiants last season. Hatton has a part in all three goals and Donaghy shows his versatility by deputising at centre-half for the injured Turner. Aleksic plays with six stitches in his hand. | | | | | | | | | | | |
| 5 | A BRISTOL ROV | | 14 | L | 0-2 | 0-0 | | Aleksic | Jones | Aizlewood | Hill | Turner | Price | Donaghy* | Fuccillo | Stein | Ingram | Moss | West |
| | 9/9 | *6,505* | *6* | 4 | | | *Staniforth 47, Randall 74* | *Thomas* | *Pulis* | *Bater* | *Day* | *Taylor* | *Prince* | *Williams* | *Barry* | *Dennehy* | *Staniforth* | *Randall* | |
| | | | | | | | Ref: T Reynolds | The Town keep Rovers at bay with ease in the first half but then concede two sloppy goals after the break. A Frankie Prince free-kick rebounds off the bar with Dave Staniforth reacting the quickest. Rovers attack on the break and bag the second, killer goal through a Paul Randall tap-in. | | | | | | | | | | | |
| 6 | H CARDIFF | | 9 | W | **7-1** | 2-0 | Moss 12, 81, Hatton 18, Stein 51, 55, | Aleksic | Jones | Aizlewood | Hill | Turner | Price | Donaghy* | West | Stein | Hatton | Moss | Fuccillo |
| | 16/9 | 7,752 | *22* | 6 | | | *Bishop 79* [Fuccillo 77p, Dwyer 87(og)] | *Barber* | *Thomas* | *Pethard* | *Pontin** | *Roberts* | *Campbell* | *Grapes* | *Burns* | *Buchanan* | *Dwyer* | *Stevens* | *Bishop* |
| | | | | | | | Ref: M Taylor | Ex-Luton keeper Keith Barber returns to Kenilworth Road for his final league appearance but, with hindsight, probably wishes he had retired a week earlier. The Hatters go goal-crazy as efforts fly in from all angles, a 30-yard curling shot from David Moss being the pick of the bunch. | | | | | | | | | | | |
| 7 | H CAMBRIDGE | | 9 | D | 1-1 | 1-0 | Stein 2 | Aleksic | Jones | Aizlewood | Hill | Turner | Price | Donaghy* | West | Stein | Hatton | Moss | Fuccillo |
| | 23/9 | 10,801 | *15* | 7 | | | *Biley 54p* | *Webster* | *Howard* | *Smith* | *Stringer* | *Fallon* | *Leach* | *Cozens** | *Spriggs* | *Buckley* | *Finney* | *Biley* | *Watson* |
| | | | | | | | Ref: T Bune | The first meeting between the two teams. The Town score after just 90 seconds, when Stein heads in from close range. The players and crowd anticipate another goal avalanche but Cambridge stifle the efforts and ex-Hatter, Alan Biley, scores from the spot after Jones fouls Steve Spriggs. | | | | | | | | | | | |
| 8 | A SHEFFIELD UTD | | 10 | D | 1-1 | 0-1 | Hatton 61 | Aleksic | Price | Aizlewood | Hill | Turner | Donaghy | Fuccillo | West | Stein | Hatton | Moss | |
| | 30/9 | *15,295* | *18* | 8 | | | *Anderson 44* | *Conroy* | *Cutbush* | *Calvert* | *Kenworthy* | *Matthews* | *Keeley* | *Speight* | *Hamson* | *Anderson* | *Franks* | *Stainrod* | |
| | | | | | | | Ref: J Worrall | Ex-Hatter Peter Anderson, making his debut for the Blades after signing from Tampa Bay Rowdies, fires the opener from 15 yards. Free-scoring Town pick up their first away point of the season when goalkeeper, Steve Conroy, misjudges a cross, allowing Hatton to steal in and head home. | | | | | | | | | | | |
| 9 | H WREXHAM | | 8 | W | 2-1 | 2-1 | Stein 9, Fuccillo 13 | Aleksic | Price | Aizlewood* | Hill | Turner | Donaghy | West | Fuccillo | Stein | Hatton | Moss | Jones |
| | 7/10 | 8,683 | *15* | 10 | | | *Thomas 43* | *Niedzwiecki* | *Hill* | *Whittle* | *Davies* | *Roberts* | *Thomas* | *Sutton* | *Griffiths** | *Cartwright* | *Shinton* | *McNeil* | *Lyons* |
| | | | | | | | Ref: B Daniels | The Town fail to make the most of their chances and end up hanging on at the close of the game as lively Wrexham fight back. The Hatters go two goals up through a Stein header and a 20-yard shot from Fuccillo but Mike Thomas scores for the Welshmen with a swirling, angled drive. | | | | | | | | | | | |
| 10 | A BLACKBURN | | 8 | D | 0-0 | 0-0 | | Aleksic | Price | Aizlewood | Hill | Turner | Donaghy | West | Fuccillo | Stein | Hatton | Moss | |
| | 14/10 | *7,450* | *21* | 11 | | | | *Butcher* | *Hird* | *Bailey* | *Keeley** | *Fazackerley* | *Metcalfe* | *Fowler* | *Birchenall* | *Brotherston* | *Craig* | *Radford* | *Waddington* |
| | | | | | | | Ref: R Bridges | The Hatters are happy to leave Blackburn with a goal-less draw, even though they might have scored half a dozen times. The Towns' midfield of Fuccillo, Hill and West dominates the game, but hasty shooting and some fine goalkeeping by Rovers' John Butcher keeps the game level. | | | | | | | | | | | |

| | | | | | | | | | | | | | | | | | | | | |
|---|---|---|---|---|---|---|---|---|---|---|---|---|---|---|---|---|---|---|---|---|
| 11 | H | NOTTS CO | | 4 | W | 6-0 | 2-0 | Hatton 22, Stein 44, 86 , West 48, [Moss 57, Fuccillo 79p] | Aleksic | Price | Aizlewood | Hill | Turner | Donaghy | West | Fuccillo | Stein | Hatton* | Moss | Jones |
| 21/10 | | | 8,561 | 11 | 13 | | | | *McManus* | *Richards* | *O'Brien* | *Stubbs* | *Mann* | *Benjamin* | *Masson* | *Hunt** | *McCulloch* | *Hooks* | *Vinter* | *McVay* |
| | | | | | | | | Ref: C Downey | Majestic Luton completely overwhelm Notts County with a truly magnificent second-half performance which even overshadows the victories over Oldham and Cardiff. The Magpies do not give up, even though they are completely outplayed, and McManus keeps the scoreline down. | | | | | | | | | | | |
| 12 | A | ORIENT | | 10 | L | 2-3 | 1-1 | Fuccillo 13, 89 | Aleksic | Donaghy | Aizlewood | Hill | Turner | Price | West | Fuccillo | Stein | Hatton | Moss | |
| 28/10 | | | *7,035* | *15* | 13 | | | *Coates 17, Kitchen 66, 75* | *Jackson* | *Fisher* | *Roffey* | *Gray* | *Went* | *Grealish* | *Hughton* | *Coates* | *Moores* | *Mayo* | *Kitchen* | |
| | | | | | | | | Ref: D Reeves | Orient end their League and Cup goal-less run of ten games, aided by their new signing from Tottenham, Ralph Coates. The Town take the lead through a well-worked Fuccillo free-kick routine, but then let the O's equalise with a soft goal . Suitably boosted, they go on to win the game. | | | | | | | | | | | |
| 13 | H | LEICESTER | | 12 | L | 0-1 | 0-0 | | Aleksic | Donaghy | Aizlewood | Hill | Turner | Price* | West | Fuccillo | Stein | Hatton | Moss | Carr |
| 4/11 | | | 10,608 | *16* | 13 | | | *Christie 86* | *Wallington* | *Whitworth* | *Rofe* | *Williams* | *May* | *Kelly* | *Weller* | *Ridley* | *Henderson** | *Christie* | *Hughes* | *White* |
| | | | | | | | | Ref: B Homewood | A defensive Leicester team prevent the Hatters from scoring at home for the first time this season although they are helped by the referee, who only awards an indirect free-kick for a foul on Moss in the area. The Foxes break out to score with a header from Trevor Christie near the end. | | | | | | | | | | | |
| 14 | A | OLDHAM | | 14 | L | 0-2 | 0-1 | | Aleksic | Price | Aizlewood | Hill* | Turner | Donaghy | West | Fuccillo | Stein | Hatton | Moss | Stephens |
| 11/11 | | | *6,876* | *16* | 13 | | | *Halom 27, Taylor 79* | *McDonnell* | *Wood* | *Blair* | *Hicks* | *Hurst* | *Bell* | *Chapman* | *Gardner* | *Halom* | *Taylor* | *Young* | |
| | | | | | | | | Ref: M Scott | The Town never look capable of ending their dismal away record, and keeper Milija Aleksic prevents an even bigger defeat. He is powerless to prevent ex-Luton forward Vic Halom firing home from close range or to stop a Steve Taylor header from flying into the top corner of the net. | | | | | | | | | | | |
| 15 | H | NEWCASTLE | | 13 | W | 2-0 | 1-0 | Stein 23, Turner 84 | **Lawson** | Price | Aizlewood | Carr | Turner | Donaghy | West | Fuccillo | Stein | Hatton | Moss | |
| 18/11 | | | 10,434 | *12* | 15 | | | | *Hardwick* | *Kelly** | *Barton* | *Blackley* | *Brownlie* | *Walker* | *Mitchell* | *Hibbitt* | *Suggett* | *Withe* | *Connolly* | *McGee* |
| | | | | | | | | Ref: M Sinclair | David Pleat drops goalkeeper Aleksic after a row and brings in ex-Everton player, David Lawson. The replacement is rarely tested as the Town make hard work of winning the two points: the game was not made safe until centre-half Turner heads his first goal for the club near the end. | | | | | | | | | | | |
| 16 | A | CHARLTON | | 11 | W | 2-1 | 0-1 | Moss 55, Hatton 70 | Lawson | Price | Aizlewood | Carr | Turner | Donaghy | West | Fuccillo | Stein | Hatton | Moss | |
| 21/11 | | | *10,191* | *8* | 17 | | | *Robinson 33* | *Wood* | *Campbell* | *Madden* | *Shaw* | *Berry* | *Gritt* | *Brisley* | *Peacock* | *Powell* | *Robinson* | *Flanagan* | |
| | | | | | | | | Ref: W Bombroff | The Town win their first away game since last December with a fighting performance after Charlton take the lead through a Martin Robinson near-post header. Moss equalises with a low drive and then leaves Hatton to score the winner, having run from inside his own half with the ball. | | | | | | | | | | | |
| 17 | H | SUNDERLAND | | 13 | L | 0-3 | 0-2 | | Lawson | Price | Aizlewood | Hill | Jones | Donaghy | West | Fuccillo | Stein | Hatton | Moss | |
| 25/11 | | | 10,249 | *6* | 17 | | | *Rowell 20, 65, Entwistle 38* | *Siddall* | *Henderson* | *Bolton* | *Clarke* | *Elliott* | *Chisholm* | *Buckley* | *Rostron* | *Lee* | *Entwistle* | *Rowell* | |
| | | | | | | | | Ref: A Seville | Sunderland sweep the Hatters aside with all three goals coming from headers, courtesy of long balls crossed in from the wings. Luton have now slipped from fourth, one month ago, to below mid-table in the League. Aston Villa keeper Jake Findlay is signed for £100,000 after the game. | | | | | | | | | | | |
| 18 | H | PRESTON | | 13 | L | 1-2 | 1-1 | Price 16 | **Findlay** | Price | Aizlewood | Hill | Turner | Donaghy | West | Fuccillo | Stein | Hatton | Moss | |
| 9/12 | | | 7,036 | *18* | 17 | | | *Robinson 30p, Baxter 53* | *Tunks* | *Taylor* | *Baxter* | *O'Riordan* | *Cameron* | *Burns* | *Coleman* | *Haslegrave* | *Potts* | *Robinson* | *Bruce* | |
| | | | | | | | | Ref: R Lewis | The Hatters start brightly with Price heading home a Fuccillo free-kick. Jake Findlay makes his debut but is unable to prevent Mick Robinson converting a penalty after a handball by Aizlewood. Eric Potts centres for Mick Baxter to head home the second as Preston bypass the midfield. | | | | | | | | | | | |
| 19 | A | BRIGHTON | | 16 | L | 1-3 | 1-2 | Moss 29 | Findlay | Price | Aizlewood | Carr | Turner | Donaghy | West | Fuccillo | Ingram* | Hatton | Moss | Stein |
| 16/12 | | | *16,216* | *4* | 17 | | | *Horton 15p, Rollings 41, Sayer 89* | *Moseley* | *Cattlin* | *Williams* | *Rollings* | *Lawrenson* | *Horton* | *Sayer* | *O'Sullivan* | *Ryan* | *Ward* | *Poskett** | *Clark* |
| | | | | | | | | Ref: J Martin | The game is marred by a terrible tackle by Brighton substitute Paul Clark on Fuccillo ten minutes from the end which leaves the Luton mid-fielder with a compound fracture of the left leg. As a result of this injury, the Town are reduced to ten men and Brighton score a late clincher. | | | | | | | | | | | |
| 20 | A | MILLWALL | | 14 | W | 2-0 | 2-0 | Moss 22, 36 | Findlay | Price | Aizlewood | Carr* | Turner | Donaghy | West | Hill | Stein | Hatton | Moss | Jones |
| 26/12 | | | ***6,041*** | *22* | 19 | | | | *Cuff* | *Donaldson* | *Gregory* | *Kitchener* | *Blyth* | *Chambers** | *Towner* | *Walker* | *Chatterton* | *Seasman* | *Mitchell* | *Mehmet* |
| | | | | | | | | Ref: C Thomas | Playing delightful, flowing football, the Town are the easy winners against a poor Millwall side who are languishing at the wrong end of the table. The two goals from David Moss, a header from Bob Hatton's cross and a 25-yard chip, are both worthy of a 'goal-of-the-season' award. | | | | | | | | | | | |
| 21 | A | FULHAM | | 16 | L | 0-1 | 0-1 | | Findlay | Price | Aizlewood | Carr | Turner* | Donaghy | West | Hill | Stein | Hatton | Moss | Jones |
| 30/12 | | | *8,984* | *5* | 19 | | | *Aizlewood 7 (og)* | *Peyton* | *Evans* | *Strong* | *Lock** | *Money* | *Evanson* | *Bullivant* | *Margerrison* | *Davies* | *Guthrie* | *Marinello* | *Greenaway* |
| | | | | | | | | Ref: M Taylor | In a drab game, both sides find the swirling wind difficult to contend with. Luton goalkeeper Jake Findlay drops a Chris Guthrie shot and Mark Aizlewood turns the ball into his own net as Gordon Davies challenges. The Town rally after the break but cannot find a way past Gerry Peyton. | | | | | | | | | | | |

| No | Date | | Att | Pos | Pt | F-A | H-T | Scorers, Times, and Referees | 1 | 2 | 3 | 4 | 5 | 6 | 7 | 8 | 9 | 10 | 11 | 12 sub used |
|---|---|---|---|---|---|---|---|---|---|---|---|---|---|---|---|---|---|---|---|---|
| 22 | H | BRISTOL ROV | | 14 | W | 3-2 | 0-2 | Moss 58, Price 85, Hill 89 | Findlay | Stephens | Aizlewood | Jones* | Price | Donaghy | West | Hill | **Taylor** | Hatton | Moss | Stein |
| | 16/1 | | **6,002** | *13* | 21 | | | *White 5, 16* | *Thomas* | *Bater* | *Harding* | *Taylor* | *Emmanuel* | *Day** | *Hendrie* | *Williams* | *Aitken* | *White* | *Staniforth* | *Dennehy* |
| | | | | | | | | Ref: R Kirkpatrick | Due to the bad weather, this is the only league game to be played during January. Luton trail 0-2 with future Hatter, Steve White, scoring both goals but the fight-back in the second half is memorable and, with Rovers on the back foot throughout, the winner is struck with a minute left. | | | | | | | | | | | |
| 23 | A | CAMBRIDGE | | 14 | D | 0-0 | 0-0 | | Lawson | Stephens | Aizlewood | Donaghy | Turner | Price | West | Hill | Taylor | Hatton | Moss | |
| | 3/2 | | *8,125* | *12* | 22 | | | | *Webster* | *Smith* | *Stringer* | *Fallon* | *Spriggs* | *Leach* | *Cozens* | *Christie* | *Finney* | *Garner* | *Biley* | |
| | | | | | | | | Ref: P Richardson | In the Hatters' first ever league game at the Abbey Stadium, both sides appear rusty after their three week lay-off. In a grim struggle, chances are at a premium. Bob Hatton sees a brilliant header kicked off the line whilst, at the other end, Price heads away a certain Cambridge goal. | | | | | | | | | | | |
| 24 | H | STOKE | | 13 | D | 0-0 | 0-0 | | Lawson | Stephens | Carr | Donaghy | Turner | Price | West | Hill | Taylor | Hatton | Moss | |
| | 6/2 | | 6,462 | *8* | 23 | | | | *Jones* | *Dodd* | *Scott** | *Smith* | *Doyle* | *Kendall* | *Irvine* | *Richardson* | *Randall* | *O'Callaghan* | *Crooks* | *Busby* |
| | | | | | | | | Ref: R Challis | On a rock-hard, icy surface, the ball is difficult to control and Stoke are the better side in the opening period. Town control the game after the break and run almost non-stop at the Potters' defence. Donaghy nets near the end but the goal is disallowed for a handling offence by Taylor. | | | | | | | | | | | |
| 25 | H | SHEFFIELD UTD | | 13 | D | 1-1 | 1-0 | Turner 44 | Findlay | Stephens | Aizlewood | Donaghy | Turner | Price | West | Hill | Stein | Hatton | Moss* | Taylor |
| | 10/2 | | 7,025 | *18* | 24 | | | *Hamson 76p* | *Conroy* | *Calvert* | *Kenworthy** | *McPhail* | *Speight* | *Matthews* | *Anderson* | *Sabella* | *Franks* | *Stainrod* | *Hamson* | *Smith* |
| | | | | | | | | Ref: T Spencer | Harry Haslam and Danny Bergara return to Kenilworth Road for the first time and see their new side under the cosh. Town hit the woodwork twice before Turner heads home. The Blades steal a point with a twice-taken penalty after Donaghy fouls Argentinian Alex Sabella in the area. | | | | | | | | | | | |
| 26 | H | BLACKBURN | | 10 | W | 2-1 | 0-1 | West 64, Turner 87 | Findlay | Stephens | Aizlewood | West | Turner | Price | Hill | Carr | Stein* | Hatton | **Silkman** | Taylor |
| | 24/2 | | 6,247 | *22* | 26 | | | *Garner 18* | *Butcher* | *Fowler* | *Bailey* | *Round* | *Fazackerley* | *Metcalfe* | *Hird* | *Birchenall* | *Parkes* | *Garner* | *Craig* | |
| | | | | | | | | Ref: G Napthine | Simon Garner opens the scoring with a diving header and Alan West equalises in the second half. Loan signing from Plymouth, Barry Silkman, makes a sparkling debut and runs at the Blackburn defence at every opportunity. He provides the corner for Chris Turner to head the winner. | | | | | | | | | | | |
| 27 | H | WEST HAM | | 11 | L | **1-4** | 0-0 | Turner 70 | Findlay | Stephens | Aizlewood | West | Turner | Price | Silkman | Carr | Taylor | Hatton | Hill | |
| | 26/2 | | **14,205** | *4* | 26 | | | *Devonshire 59, Cross 60, 88, Robson 89* | *Parkes* | *McDowell* | *Brush* | *Martin* | *Bonds* | *Curbishley* | *Holland* | *Devonshire* | *Brooking* | *Cross* | *Robson* | |
| | | | | | | | | Ref: D Civil | The Hammers are on the rack for an hour before getting the breakthrough with two quick goals. Turner heads in for the Town, the goal being the first to be conceded by expensive signing Phil Parkes. Hatton heads against the bar before two late goals give an unrealistic final scoreline. | | | | | | | | | | | |
| 28 | A | NOTTS CO | | 12 | L | 1-3 | 0-0 | Hatton 75 | Findlay | Stephens | Aizlewood | Donaghy | Turner | Price | West | Carr | Taylor | Hatton | Silkman | |
| | 3/3 | | *7,624* | *7* | 26 | | | *Mann 52, Hunt 83, Hooks 86* | *McManus* | *Richards* | *O'Brien* | *Blockley* | *Stubbs* | *Mann* | *Masson* | *Hunt* | *McCulloch* | *Hooks* | *Vinter* | |
| | | | | | | | | Ref: R Chadwick | Two late goals spoil the day for the Hatters after Bob Hatton heads an equaliser from a Price centre and Alan West misses a golden opportunity from three yards out. Notts seal their first win in ten games with a David Hunt volley and a Paul Hooks free header as the Town chase the game. | | | | | | | | | | | |
| 29 | H | ORIENT | | 8 | W | 2-1 | 1-1 | Turner 27, Hill 88 | Findlay | Stephens | Aizlewood | Donaghy | Turner | Hill | West | Carr | Taylor | Hatton | Stein | |
| | 10/3 | | 6,003 | *9* | 28 | | | *Moores 2* | *Jackson* | *Fisher* | *Roffey* | *Gray* | *West* | *Grealish* | *Hughton* | *Coates* | *Chiedozie* | *Moores* | *Mayo* | |
| | | | | | | | | Ref: J Sewell | A brilliant goal from Hill, two minutes from time, robs Orient of a point which veteran goalkeeper, John Jackson, almost earns on his own. 'We would have won 6-1 but for him' says David Pleat. Findlay saves a penalty from Ian Moores, awarded after Kirk Stephens fouls Ralph Coates. | | | | | | | | | | | |
| 30 | A | BURNLEY | | 11 | L | 1-2 | 0-1 | Hatton 59 | Findlay | Stephens | Aizlewood | Donaghy | Turner | Hill | West | Carr | Taylor | Hatton | Stein | |
| | 13/3 | | *7,691* | *10* | 28 | | | *Noble 42p, 53* | *Stevenson* | *Scott* | *Brennan* | *Thomson* | *Rodaway* | *Noble* | *Jakub* | *Robinson** | *Fletcher* | *Kindon* | *James* | *Hall* |
| | | | | | | | | Ref: T Mills | Findlay dives at the feet of Steve Kindon and gathers the ball but a penalty is awarded. The first attempt is saved but the referee orders it to be retaken and this time Peter Noble makes no mistake. He adds a second after the break before Hatton scores with a shot from the edge of the box. | | | | | | | | | | | |
| 31 | H | CRYS PALACE | | 14 | L | 0-1 | 0-1 | | Findlay | Stephens | Price | Donaghy | Turner | Carr* | Hill | Aizlewood | Taylor | Hatton | Stein | West |
| | 24/3 | | 11,008 | *3* | 28 | | | *Nicholas 18* | *Burridge* | *Hinshelwood* | *Sansom* | *Cannon* | *Gilbert* | *Kember* | *Nicholas* | *Murphy* | *Swindlehurst* | *Hilaire* | *Walsh* | |
| | | | | | | | | Ref: M Baker | Peter Nicholas hits a tremendous left-foot drive to score the only goal in a one-sided game. Paul Hinshelwood hits a shot from 40 yards which crashes against the post and Hatton misses the only Luton chance when he intercepts a poor throw-out, his shot going the wrong side of the post. | | | | | | | | | | | |

| No | H/A | Opponent | Att | Pos | Res | F-A | H-T | Scorers, Times, and Referees | 1 | 2 | 3 | 4 | 5 | 6 | 7 | 8 | 9 | 10 | 11 | 12 sub used |
|---|---|---|---|---|---|---|---|---|---|---|---|---|---|---|---|---|---|---|---|---|
| 32 | A | LEICESTER | | 15 | L | 0-3 | 0-2 | | Findlay | Stephens | Price | Donaghy | Turner | Hill | West | **Birchenall** | Taylor | Hatton | Stein | |
| | 28/3 | | *10,464* | *14* | 28 | | | *May 30, Smith 43, Williams 62* | *Wallington* | *Goodwin* | *Rofe* | *O'Neill* | *May* | *Kelly* | *Peake* | *Williams* | *Smith* | *Henderson* | *Buchanan* | |
| | | | | | | | | Ref: N Glover | Playing in torrential rain, the Hatters slither to yet another away defeat with defensive errors leading to the demise. Foxes' winger Bobby Smith taunts the Town defence throughout the game with some tricky runs and has a hand in all three goals. Chris Turner decides to return to the USA. | | | | | | | | | | | |
| 33 | A | SUNDERLAND | | 16 | L | 0-1 | 0-0 | | Findlay | Stephens | Price | Donaghy | **P-Masters** | Birchenall | Hill | West | Taylor | Hatton* | Stein | Carr |
| | 31/3 | | *23,358* | *3* | 28 | | | *Rostron 70* | *Siddall* | *Whitworth* | *Bolton** | *Clarke* | *Elliott* | *Docherty* | *Chisholm* | *Rostron* | *Buckley* | *Entwistle* | *Lee* | *Brown* |
| | | | | | | | | Ref:J Worrall | Forbes Phillipson-Masters, on loan from Southampton, helps to frustrate a promotion-chasing Sunderland, who are reduced to some desperate play before Wilf Rostron scores from 12 yards to ease the tension. Luton keeper Findlay takes four minutes to recover from a kick on the head. | | | | | | | | | | | |
| 34 | H | BURNLEY | | 16 | W | 4-1 | 2-0 | Hatton 1, 66, Stein 7, Taylor 87 | Findlay | Stephens | Aizlewood | Donaghy | P-Masters | Birchenall* | Hill | West | Stein | Hatton | Moss | Taylor |
| | 7/4 | | 6,466 | *9* | 30 | | | *Noble 59p* | *Stevenson* | *Scott* | *Brennan* | *Thomson* | *Robinson* | *Noble* | *Jakub** | *Ingham* | *Morley* | *Fletcher* | *James* | *Kindon* |
| | | | | | | | | Ref: A McDonald | Moss returns after a two-month injury absence and, with loan signing Alan Birchenall, helps the Town to an emphatic win. The Town sweep to victory with early goals from Hatton and Stein with only a Peter Noble penalty, awarded after Birchenall fouls Paul Fletcher, spoiling the day. | | | | | | | | | | | |
| 35 | A | WEST HAM | | 16 | L | 0-1 | 0-0 | | Findlay | Stephens | Aizlewood | Donaghy | P-Masters | Carr | Hill | West | Stein | Hatton | Moss* | Taylor |
| | 9/4 | | ***25,398*** | *5* | 30 | | | *Carr 65 (og)* | *Parkes* | *McDowell* | *Brush* | *Martin* | *Taylor* | *Bonds* | *Holland* | *Devonshire* | *Morgan* | *Pike* | *Robson* | |
| | | | | | | | | Ref: D Reeves | A centre by Hammers' Geoff Pike is deflected into his own net by the luckless Town defender David Carr to give West Ham a narrow victory. The Town have only stout defending to offer as they rarely look like scoring against a side which has five senior players absent through injury. | | | | | | | | | | | |
| 36 | H | MILLWALL | | 17 | D | 2-2 | 2-2 | Moss 38p, 43 | Findlay | Stephens | Aizlewood | Donaghy | P-Masters | Hill | Moss | West | Stein* | Hatton | Birchenall | Taylor |
| | 14/4 | | 8,292 | *21* | 31 | | | *Chambers 22, Seasman 32* | *Cuff* | *Donaldson* | *Sparrow* | *Kitchener* | *Tagg* | *Chatterton* | *Walker* | *Chambers* | *O'Callaghan** | *Seasman* | *Mitchell* | *Mehmet* |
| | | | | | | | | Ref: J Bray | Ex-Hatters Brian Chambers and John Seasman are given too much time and space and put the Lions ahead. Moss converts a disputed penalty, when Chambers brings down Stephens and then equalises just before the break. The Town then have 15 corners but fail to capitalise on them. | | | | | | | | | | | |
| 37 | A | STOKE | | 14 | D | 0-0 | 0-0 | | Findlay | Stephens | Aizlewood | Donaghy | P-Masters | Price | Hill | West | Taylor | Hatton | Birchenall | |
| | 16/4 | | *19,214* | *2* | 32 | | | | *Jones* | *Dodd* | *Scott* | *Smith* | *Doyle* | *Kendall** | *Irvine* | *Crooks* | *Richardson* | *Randall* | *O'Callaghan* | *Conroy* |
| | | | | | | | | Ref: A Challinor | The Town manage to frustrate the opposition with a battling defensive display. The Potters are far too predictable in their approach play and the crowd streams away long before the end. Garth Crooks is booked for a foul on Taylor, who was through on goal in a rare Hatters' attack. | | | | | | | | | | | |
| 38 | H | BRIGHTON | | 15 | D | 1-1 | 1-0 | Williams 32 (og) | Findlay | Stephens | Aizlewood | Donaghy | P-Masters | Birchenall | Hill | West | Taylor | Hatton | Moss | |
| | 21/4 | | 13,132 | *2* | 33 | | | *Maybank 83* | *Steele* | *Cattlin* | *Williams** | *Horton* | *Winstanley* | *Clark* | *Ryan* | *Sayer* | *Ward* | *Maybank* | *O'Sullivan* | *Poskett* |
| | | | | | | | | Ref: C Thomas | The Hatters take the lead when a shot from West is deflected by Gary Williams past his own goalkeeper. The Hatters fail to take their chances in the second half and allow the Seagulls to equalise from a short free-kick routine with Teddy Maybank slamming a 20-yard shot past Findlay. | | | | | | | | | | | |
| 39 | A | CARDIFF | | 19 | L | 1-2 | 0-1 | Roberts 80 (og) | Findlay | Stephens | Aizlewood | Donaghy | P-Masters | Price | Hill | West | Taylor | Hatton | Birchenall | |
| | 25/4 | | *10,522* | *18* | 33 | | | *Moore 11, Stevens 85* | *Healey* | *Jones* | *Sullivan* | *Campbell** | *Roberts* | *Thomas* | *Bishop* | *Evans* | *Moore* | *Stevens* | *Buchanan* | *Grapes* |
| | | | | | | | | Ref: E Read | The Hatters are in deep trouble at the foot of the table following this defeat at Ninian Park. Ronnie Moore scores the opener but the Town fight back and Dave Roberts heads an own-goal to level the scores. A lapse in concentration allows Gary Stevens to net the winner five minutes later. | | | | | | | | | | | |
| 40 | A | PRESTON | | 18 | D | 2-2 | 0-1 | Haslegrave 62 (og), Moss 80 | Findlay | Stephens | Aizlewood | Donaghy | P-Masters | Price | Hill | West | Taylor | Hatton | Birchenall* | Moss |
| | 28/4 | | *8,946* | *10* | 34 | | | *Doyle 37, Coleman 55* | *Tunks* | *Taylor* | *Cameron* | *Uzelac* | *O'Riordan* | *Doyle* | *Haslegrave* | *Bell* | *Coleman* | *Robinson* | *Bruce* | |
| | | | | | | | | Ref: M Lowe | The Town are two goals down and struggling with only 30 minutes left to play when substitute Moss crosses a high ball which Preston skipper Sean Hazlegrave heads in to his own net. All-out attack is then rewarded when Moss spots Roy Tunks off his line and chips in from 25-yards. | | | | | | | | | | | |
| 41 | H | FULHAM | | 14 | W | 2-0 | 1-0 | Beck 22 (og), West 65 | Findlay | Stephens | Aizlewood | Donaghy | P-Masters | Price | Hill | West | Stein | Hatton | Moss | |
| | 5/5 | | 9,122 | *7* | 36 | | | | *Digweed* | *Evans* | *Strong* | *Money* | *Hatter* | *Lock* | *Gale* | *Beck* | *Davies* | *Guthrie* | *Kitchen* | |
| | | | | | | | | Ref: D Richardson | For the fourth consecutive game, the Town are gifted with an own goal when John Beck, under pressure from West, turns a Stein cross past his own goalkeeper. With the pressure lifted, a second goal is added when West hits in a low drive and relegation is avoided for another season. | | | | | | | | | | | |
| 42 | A | WREXHAM | | 18 | L | 0-2 | 0-1 | | Findlay | Stephens | Aizlewood ! | Donaghy | P-Masters | Price | Hill | West | Taylor | Hatton | **Turner W*** | Stein |
| | 7/5 | | *7,842* | *15* | 36 | | | *Buxton 30, Williams 82* | *Davies* | *Cegielski* | *Dwyer* | *Jones J* | *Jones F* | *Giles* | *Sutton** | *Fox* | *Williams* | *McNeil* | *Buxton* | *Roberts* |
| | Home | | Away | | | | | Ref: C Seel | Four minutes before the second goal is scored, a header from Hill is clearly handled by Welsh defender Joey Jones. The referee waves play on but then dismisses Aizlewood for persistent dissent. Wrexham gain their first win in eight games but the final result is meaningless to both sides. | | | | | | | | | | | |
| Average | 8,792 | | 12,179 | | | | | | | | | | | | | | | | | |

# LEAGUE DIVISION 2 (CUP-TIES)

## Manager: David Pleat

## SEASON 1978-79

| League Cup | | | | | F-A | H-T | Scorers, Times, and Referees | 1 | 2 | 3 | 4 | 5 | 6 | 7 | 8 | 9 | 10 | 11 | 12 sub used |
|---|---|---|---|---|---|---|---|---|---|---|---|---|---|---|---|---|---|---|---|
| 2 | H | WIGAN | 15 | W | 2-0 | 0-0 | Stein 63, 86 | Aleksic | Stephens | Aizlewood | Donaghy | Turner | Price | West | Fuccillo | Stein | Hatton | Moss | |
| | 29/8 | | *6,618 4:22* | | | | | *Brown* | *Gore* | *Smart* | *Ward* | *Gillibrand* | *Seddon* | *Corrigan* | *Wright* | *Purdie* | *Houghton* | *Wilkie** | *Davids* |
| | | | | | | | Ref: J Hunting | Wigan, Football League new boys, meet Luton for the first time and try to stifle the game in the hope of gaining a draw. Town are frantic and anxious but Stein hits home a low drive following a long throw-in by Price and then heads home a Moss corner to break the strong resistance. | | | | | | | | | | | |
| 3 | H | CREWE | 10 | W | 2-1 | 0-0 | Hill 46, Hatton 49 | Aleksic | Price | Aizlewood | Hill | Turner | Donaghy | West | Fuccillo | Stein | Hatton | Moss | |
| | 3/10 | | 6,602 *4:20* | | | | *Bowles 71p* | *Caswell* | *Rimmer* | *Bowles* | *Purdie* | *Roberts* | *Robertson* | *Wilshaw* | *Bevan* | *Tully** | *Davies* | *Nelson* | *Coyne* |
| | | | | | | | Ref: A Grey | Crewe endure some anxious moments before Ricky Hill manages to prise open their defence with a 25-yard dipping shot. Hatton adds another soon afterwards with a far-post header. Donaghy brings down Steven Wilshaw and Paul Bowles converts from the spot, against the run of play. | | | | | | | | | | | |
| 4 | A | ASTON VILLA | 12 | W | 2-0 | 0-0 | Hatton 66, Stein 89 | Aleksic | Price | Aizlewood | Hill | Turner | Donaghy | West | Fuccillo | Stein | Hatton | Moss | |
| | 8/11 | | *32,737 1:10* | | | | | *Rimmer* | *Gidman* | *Williams* | *Evans* | *McNaught* | *Mortimer* | *Craig* | *Little* | *Gray** | *Deehan* | *Gregory* | *Cowans* |
| | | | | | | | Ref: D Richardson | Luton are always in control, following an early injury to Villa danger-man Andy Gray, and it comes as no surprise when Bob Hatton steams through the middle to blast the opener. The icing on the cake is added to a famous victory when Brian Stein taps in a second in the final minute. | | | | | | | | | | | |
| QF | A | LEEDS | 13 | L | 1-4 | 0-1 | Stein 88 *[Gray F 71]* | Findlay | Price | Aizlewood | Hill | Turner | Donaghy | West | Fuccillo | Stein | Hatton | Moss | |
| | 13/12 | | *28,177 1:9* | | | | *Cherry 43, Currie 46, Gray E 57,* | *Harvey* | *Cherry* | *Gray F* | *Hart* | *Madeley* | *Flynn* | *Gray E* | *Currie* | *Hankin* | *Hawley* | *Harris* | |
| | | | | | | | Ref: K McNally | Playing in the quarter-finals for the first time, Luton are eventually well beaten by a strong Leeds side, with Trevor Cherry opening the scoring from close range just before the interval. Tony Currie runs the show in the second period and his 25-yard curling shot is the 'goal of the game'. | | | | | | | | | | | |

| FA Cup | | | | | | | | | | | | | | | | | | | |
|---|---|---|---|---|---|---|---|---|---|---|---|---|---|---|---|---|---|---|---|
| 3 | A | YORK | 16 | L | 0-2 | 0-1 | | Findlay | Jones | Aizlewood | Carr | Price | Donaghy | West | Hill | Stein | Hatton | Sherlock* | Heale |
| | 9/1 | | *6,700 4:16* | | | | *Staniforth 3, Randall 83* | *Brown* | *Kay* | *Walsh* | *Faulkner* | *Clements* | *Pugh* | *Ford* | *McDonald* | *Randall* | *Loggie* | *Staniforth* | |
| | | | | | | | Ref: P Willis | After conceding an early goal, the Town go all out for the equaliser but a combination of bad luck and poor finishing lets them down. Stein hits the post, Hatton blasts wide of an empty goal and Heale shoots straight at the keeper when it appears easier to score - the Town's tale of woe. | | | | | | | | | | | |

|  | Home |  |  |  |  |  | Away |  |  |  |  |  |
|---|---|---|---|---|---|---|---|---|---|---|---|---|
|  | P | W | D | L | F | A | W | D | L | F | A | Pts |
| 1 Crys Palace | 42 | 12 | 7 | 2 | 30 | 11 | 7 | 12 | 2 | 21 | 13 | 57 |
| 2 Brighton | 42 | 16 | 3 | 2 | 44 | 11 | 7 | 7 | 7 | 28 | 28 | 56 |
| 3 Stoke | 42 | 11 | 7 | 3 | 35 | 15 | 9 | 9 | 3 | 23 | 16 | 56 |
| 4 Sunderland | 42 | 13 | 3 | 5 | 39 | 19 | 9 | 8 | 4 | 31 | 25 | 55 |
| 5 West Ham | 42 | 12 | 7 | 2 | 46 | 15 | 6 | 7 | 8 | 24 | 24 | 50 |
| 6 Notts Co | 42 | 8 | 10 | 3 | 23 | 15 | 6 | 6 | 9 | 25 | 45 | 44 |
| 7 Preston | 42 | 7 | 11 | 3 | 36 | 23 | 5 | 7 | 9 | 23 | 34 | 42 |
| 8 Newcastle | 42 | 13 | 3 | 5 | 35 | 24 | 4 | 5 | 12 | 16 | 31 | 42 |
| 9 Cardiff | 42 | 12 | 5 | 4 | 34 | 23 | 4 | 5 | 12 | 22 | 47 | 42 |
| 10 Fulham | 42 | 10 | 7 | 4 | 35 | 19 | 3 | 8 | 10 | 15 | 28 | 41 |
| 11 Orient | 42 | 11 | 5 | 5 | 32 | 18 | 4 | 5 | 12 | 19 | 33 | 40 |
| 12 Cambridge | 42 | 7 | 10 | 4 | 22 | 15 | 5 | 6 | 10 | 22 | 37 | 40 |
| 13 Burnley | 42 | 11 | 6 | 4 | 31 | 22 | 3 | 6 | 12 | 20 | 40 | 40 |
| 14 Oldham | 42 | 10 | 7 | 4 | 36 | 23 | 3 | 6 | 12 | 16 | 38 | 39 |
| 15 Wrexham | 42 | 10 | 6 | 5 | 31 | 16 | 2 | 8 | 11 | 14 | 26 | 38 |
| 16 Bristol Rov | 42 | 10 | 6 | 5 | 34 | 23 | 4 | 4 | 13 | 14 | 37 | 38 |
| 17 Leicester | 42 | 7 | 8 | 6 | 28 | 23 | 3 | 9 | 9 | 15 | 29 | 37 |
| 18 LUTON TOWN | 42 | 11 | 5 | 5 | 46 | 24 | 2 | 5 | 14 | 14 | 33 | 36 |
| 19 Charlton | 42 | 6 | 8 | 7 | 28 | 28 | 5 | 5 | 11 | 32 | 41 | 35 |
| 20 Sheffield Utd | 42 | 9 | 6 | 6 | 34 | 24 | 2 | 6 | 13 | 18 | 45 | 34 |
| 21 Millwall | 42 | 7 | 4 | 10 | 22 | 29 | 4 | 6 | 11 | 20 | 32 | 32 |
| 22 Blackburn | 42 | 5 | 8 | 8 | 24 | 29 | 5 | 2 | 14 | 17 | 43 | 30 |
|  | 924 | 218 | 142 | 102 | 725 | 449 | 102 | 142 | 218 | 449 | 725 | 924 |

Odds & ends

Double wins: (1) Charlton.
Double losses: (4) Crystal Palace, Leicester, Sunderland, West Ham.

Won from behind: (5) Blackburn (h), Bristol Rovers (h), Charlton (a), Oldham (h), Orient (h).
Lost from in front: (2) Orient (a), Preston (h).

High spots: The early season home form.
The tremendous win at Aston Villa in the League Cup.
The own-goals scored by the opposition in four successive games at the end of the season.
Battling through to Round 5 of the League Cup for the first time.

Low spots: The poor away form.
The permanent fears of relegation, only erased in the last home game.
Losing winger David Moss through injury for much of the season.
Defeat at York in the FA Cup.

Player of the Year: Kirk Stephens.
Ever-presents: (0).
Hat-tricks: (0).
Leading scorer: (14) Brian Stein.

|  | Appearances |  |  |  |  |  | Goals |  |  |  |
|---|---|---|---|---|---|---|---|---|---|---|
|  | Lge | *Sub* | LC | *Sub* | FAC | *Sub* | Lge | LC | FAC | Tot |
| Aizlewood, Mark | **39** |  | 4 |  | 1 |  |  |  |  |  |
| Aleksic, Milija | **14** |  | 3 |  |  |  |  |  |  |  |
| Birchenall, Alan | **8** |  |  |  |  |  |  |  |  |  |
| Boersma, Phil | **1** |  |  |  |  |  |  |  |  |  |
| Carr, David | **13** | *2* |  |  | 1 |  |  |  |  |  |
| Donaghy, Mal | **40** |  | 4 |  | 1 |  |  |  |  |  |
| Findlay, Jake | **23** |  | 1 |  | 1 |  |  |  |  |  |
| Fuccillo, Lil | **16** | *2* | 4 |  |  |  | **7** |  |  | **7** |
| Hatton, Bob | **41** |  | 4 |  | 1 |  | **11** | 2 |  | **13** |
| Heale, Gary |  |  |  |  |  | *1* |  |  |  |  |
| Hill, Ricky | **38** |  | 3 |  | 1 |  | **3** | 1 |  | **4** |
| Ingram, Godfrey | **2** | *1* |  |  |  |  |  |  |  |  |
| Jones, Graham | **6** | *4* |  |  | 1 |  |  |  |  |  |
| Lawson, David | **5** |  |  |  |  |  |  |  |  |  |
| McNichol, Jim |  | *1* |  |  |  |  |  |  |  |  |
| Moss, David | **29** | *1* | 4 |  |  |  | **13** |  |  | **13** |
| P-Masters, Forbes | **10** |  |  |  |  |  |  |  |  |  |
| Price, Paul | **34** |  | 4 |  | 1 |  | **2** |  |  | **2** |
| Sherlock, Steve | **2** |  |  |  | 1 |  |  |  |  |  |
| Silkman, Barry | **3** |  |  |  |  |  |  |  |  |  |
| Stein, Brian | **31** | *3* | 4 |  | 1 |  | **10** | 4 |  | **14** |
| Stephens, Kirk | **24** | *1* | 1 |  |  |  |  |  |  |  |
| Taylor, Steve | **15** | *5* |  |  |  |  | **1** |  |  | **1** |
| Turner, Chris | **30** |  | 4 |  |  |  | **5** |  |  | **5** |
| Turner, Wayne | **1** |  |  |  |  |  |  |  |  |  |
| West, Alan | **37** | *3* | 4 |  | 1 |  | **3** |  |  | **3** |
| (own-goals) |  |  |  |  |  |  | **5** |  |  | **5** |
| **26 players used** | **462** | *23* | **44** |  | **11** | *1* | **60** | **7** |  | **67** |

# LEAGUE DIVISION 2

## Manager: David Pleat

## SEASON 1979-80

| No | Date | | Att | Pos | Pt | F-A | H-T | Scorers, Times, and Referees | 1 | 2 | 3 | 4 | 5 | 6 | 7 | 8 | 9 | 10 | 11 | 12 sub used |
|---|---|---|---|---|---|---|---|---|---|---|---|---|---|---|---|---|---|---|---|---|
| 1 | H | CAMBRIDGE | | | D | 1-1 | 0-0 | Moss 88 | Findlay | Stephens | Turner | **Grealish** | Birchenall | Price | Hill | Donaghy | Stein | Hatton | Moss | |
| | 18/8 | | 8,202 | | 1 | | | *Biley 80* | *Webster* | *Graham* | *Stringer* | *Fallon* | *Smith* | *Spriggs* | *Cozens* | *Buckley* | *Christie** | *Biley* | *Finney* | *Murray* |
| | | | | | | | | Ref: B Newsome | Ex-Hatter Alan Biley strikes a 25-yard shot which hits the bar and bounces down. The referee and linesman, both of whom are behind play, award a goal and Cambridge, who appeared to have settled for a point, nearly succeed in getting two. A late free-kick from Moss saves the day. | | | | | | | | | | | |
| 2 | A | BRISTOL ROV | | | L | 2-3 | 0-0 | Moss 84, 88p | Findlay | Stephens | Turner | Grealish | **Saxby** | Price | Hill | Donaghy | Stein* | Hatton | Moss | Birchenall |
| | 21/8 | | ***5,621*** | | 1 | | | *Dennehy 57, White 64, 68* | *Thomas* | *Pulis* | *Bater* | *Aitken* | *Harding* | *Emmanuel* | *Williams* | *Clarke* | *Barrowclough* | *White* | *Dennehy* | |
| | | | | | | | | Ref: L Shapter | Rovers score three times in 11 minutes to take a commanding lead but the Hatters give the Pirates a late fright when Moss firstly curls a clever 20-yard free-kick in to the net and then rams home a penalty after Williams fouls Grealish. Unfortunately for the Town, it all comes too late. | | | | | | | | | | | |
| 3 | H | ORIENT | | 11 | W | 2-1 | 2-0 | Hatton 20, Hill 27 | Findlay | Stephens | Donaghy | Grealish | Saxby | Price | Hill | West | Stein | Hatton | Moss | |
| | 25/8 | | **6,705** | *14* | 3 | | | *Margerrison 55* | *Day* | *Fisher* | *Roffey* | *Mayo* | *Taylor* | *Margerrison* | *Hughton* | *Coates* | *Chiedozie* | *Whittle* | *Jennings* | |
| | | | | | | | | Ref: K Baker | West returns to the Luton midfield after a summer spell in the USA and, with ex-Orient player, Grealish, drives the Hatters to their first win. The O's come too close for comfort in the second half. The search for another striker is intensified as the scoring chances not being converted. | | | | | | | | | | | |
| 4 | A | LEICESTER | | 5 | W | 3-1 | 2-0 | Moss 12p, 89, Hill 30 | Findlay | Stephens | Donaghy | Grealish | Saxby | Price | Hill | West | Stein | Hatton | Moss | |
| | 1/9 | | *16,241* | *4* | 5 | | | *May 77* | *Wallington* | *Williams* | *Rofe* | *May* | *Stevens* | *Kelly* | *Byrne* | *Peake* | *Lee** | *Henderson* | *Young* | *Goodwin* |
| | | | | | | | | Ref: D Civil | Gregor Stevens handles the ball in the area, when under pressure, and David Moss drives home the resultant spot-kick. The Hatters never look back against a below-par Leicester side and Moss hits a cracker of a shot into the top corner of the net in the final minute to secure the win. | | | | | | | | | | | |
| 5 | H | SWANSEA | | 1 | W | **5-0** | 2-0 | Moss 10p, 89, Hatton 17, West 58, [Hill 60] | Findlay | Stephens | Donaghy | Grealish | Saxby | Price | Hill | West | Stein | Hatton | Moss | |
| | 8/9 | | 10,004 | *10* | 7 | | | | *Crudgington* | *Attley* | *Marustik* | *Charles* | *Phillips* | *Rushbury* | *Craig* | *Mahoney* | *Callaghan* | *Waddle** | *Baker* | *Stevenson* |
| | | | | | | | | Ref: J Bray | The Town move to the top of the table after beating one of the Divisions' new boys, Swansea, with a breathtaking display of attacking football. Luton are awarded an early penalty-kick after Dave Rushbury fouls Stein and dead-ball expert David Moss makes no mistake from the spot. | | | | | | | | | | | |
| 6 | A | NOTTS CO | | 2 | D | 0-0 | 0-0 | | Findlay | Stephens | Donaghy | Grealish | Saxby | Price | Hill | West | Stein | Hatton | Moss | |
| | 15/9 | | *9,582* | *3* | 8 | | | | *Leonard* | *Richards* | *O'Brien* | *Stubbs* | *Blockley* | *Hunt** | *McCulloch* | *Masson* | *Mair* | *Christie* | *Hooks* | *Benjamin* |
| | | | | | | | | Ref: A Challinor | Stand-in Notts County goalkeeper Mike Leonard is the difference between the two sides and makes two tremendous saves from Bob Hatton. Brian Stein misses the best chance of the game when he weaves his way through the home defence, only to direct his shot into the side-netting. | | | | | | | | | | | |
| 7 | H | OLDHAM | | 2 | D | 0-0 | 0-0 | | Findlay | Stephens | Donaghy | Grealish | Saxby | Price | Hill* | West | Stein | Hatton | Moss | Aizlewood |
| | 22/9 | | 8,711 | *15* | 9 | | | | *McDonnell* | *Wood* | *Edwards* | *Clements* | *Hurst* | *Hilton* | *Keegan* | *Halom* | *Steele* | *Stainrod* | *Heaton* | |
| | | | | | | | | Ref: P Reeves | David Pleat is pleased that his team have not conceded a goal for three games but is still on the look-out for a new striker. The Town resort to a long-ball game in order to break down a stubborn Oldham defence. Brian Stein is denied a penalty when John Hurst fouls him in the area. | | | | | | | | | | | |
| 8 | A | FULHAM | | 2 | W | 3-1 | 1-0 | Moss 5p, Hill 56, Hatton 80 | Findlay | Stephens | Donaghy | Grealish | Saxby | Price | Hill | West | Stein | Hatton | Moss | |
| | 29/9 | | *9,944* | *14* | 11 | | | *Lock 65p* | *Peyton* | *Peters* | *Strong** | *Money* | *Gale* | *Bullivant* | *Beck* | *Lock* | *Marinello* | *Mahoney* | *Davies* | *Kitchen* |
| | | | | | | | | Ref: A Gunn | Fulham have a lot of the play but the Town counter-attack effectively and Moss scores with another penalty after being up-ended by Gary Peters. Findlay is penalised for pushing Gordon Davies and Kevin Lock reduces the arrears from the spot. Bob Hatton clinches the points near the end. | | | | | | | | | | | |
| 9 | A | CARDIFF | | 3 | L | 1-2 | 1-1 | Hatton 23 | Findlay | Stephens | Donaghy | Grealish | Saxby | Price | Hill | West | Stein | Hatton | Moss | |
| | 6/10 | | *9,402* | *9* | 11 | | | *Bishop 31, 82* | *Healey* | *Jones* | *Sullivan* | *Pontin* | *Dwyer* | *Campbell* | *Ronson* | *Hughes** | *Bishop* | *Stevens* | *Moore* | *Buchanan* |
| | | | | | | | | Ref: A Seville | Mike Saxby has a header cleared off the line before the Bluebirds steal the winning goal in a game which the Hatters' slick passing movements were sweet to watch but lacked the finishing touch. 'David Moss should have had four goals - three of them from the penalty spot' fumes Pleat. | | | | | | | | | | | |
| 10 | H | BRISTOL ROV | | 2 | W | 3-1 | 3-0 | Hatton 19, 25, 40 | Findlay | Stephens | Donaghy | Grealish | Saxby | Price | Hill | West* | Stein | Hatton | Moss | Aizlewood |
| | 9/10 | | 8,507 | *18* | 13 | | | *Emmanuel 75* | *Thomas* | *Mabbutt* | *Bater* | *Aitken* | *Harding* | *Emmanuel* | *Barrowclough* | *Prince* | *Cooper* | *Dennehy* | *Penny* | |
| | | | | | | | | Ref: B Daniels | The Town put on a magnificent display of attacking football in the first period, with Hatton hitting a hat-trick. His first goal comes from a move started by Findlay and he scores without a Rovers' player touching the ball. Bristol change to 4-3-3 after the break, preventing further scoring. | | | | | | | | | | | |

| No | Venue / Date | Opponent / Att | Pos | Res | FT | HT | Scorers, Times, and Referees | 1 | 2 | 3 | 4 | 5 | 6 | 7 | 8 | 9 | 10 | 11 | 12 sub used |
|---|---|---|---|---|---|---|---|---|---|---|---|---|---|---|---|---|---|---|---|
| 11 | H | SUNDERLAND | 2 | W | 2-0 | 1-0 | Moss 41, 60 | Findlay | Stephens | Donaghy | Grealish | Saxby | Price | Hill | West | Stein | Hatton | Moss | |
| | 13/10 | 13,504 | 13 | 15 | | | | *Turner* | *Whitworth* | *Gilbert* | *Clarke* | *Hindmarch* | *Arnott* | *Elliott* | *Lee* | *Robson* | *Hawley* | *Dunn** | *Brown* |
| | | | | | | | Ref: C Maskell | Moss is now back to his best, after his injury problems of last season and, although Sunderland have more of the play in the first half, hitting the bar twice, he masterminds the win with a cool chip and a tap-in, either side of the break. Stein sees a shot rebound off the bar near the end. | | | | | | | | | | | |
| 12 | A | WEST HAM | 1 | W | 2-1 | 2-0 | Stein 16, Saxby 35 | Findlay | Stephens | Donaghy | Grealish | Saxby | Price | Hill | West | Stein | Ingram | Moss | |
| | 20/10 | *25,049* | *16* | 17 | | | *Allen 64* | *Parkes* | *Stewart* | *Lampard* | *Martin* | *Bonds* | *Holland* | *Allen* | *Pike* | *Neighbour* | *Lansdowne* | *Cross* | |
| | | | | | | | Ref: B Bombroff | The Hatters take a two-goal lead against an injury-hit Hammers side and then, in the second period, resort to an efficient combination of back-passing and an offside trap which does not win many admirers amongst the home supporters. This win puts the Town back on top of the table. | | | | | | | | | | | |
| 13 | H | PRESTON | 1 | D | 1-1 | 0-0 | Moss 76p | Findlay | Stephens | Donaghy | Grealish | Saxby | Price | Hill | West | Stein | Hatton | Moss | |
| | 27/10 | 11,648 | *8* | 18 | | | *Elliott 61* | *Tunks* | *Taylor* | *Cameron** | *Baxter* | *Blackley* | *Burns* | *Bell* | *Haslegrave* | *Elliott* | *Thomson* | *Bruce* | *McGee* |
| | | | | | | | Ref: A Robinson | Preston create more chances and their opening goal, a Steve Elliott far-post header, is thoroughly deserved. Lilywhites goalkeeper, Roy Tunks, hauls down Grealish in the area and Moss gratefully crashes home the point-saving kick from the spot which keeps the Hatters top of the table. | | | | | | | | | | | |
| 14 | A | CAMBRIDGE | 1 | W | 2-1 | 0-0 | Hatton 58, Moss 61p | Findlay | Stephens | Donaghy | Grealish | Saxby | Price | Hill | West | Stein | Hatton | Moss | |
| | 3/11 | *8,104* | *16* | 20 | | | *Biley 87* | *Webster* | *Turner* | *Smith* | *Stringer* | *Fallon* | *O'Neill* | *Spriggs* | *Murray** | *Biley* | *Christie* | *Gibbins* | *Finney* |
| | | | | | | | Ref: A Grey | Luton always look good in the midfield but their finishing is woeful. Hatton gets onto the end of a through-ball from West to open the scoring and Moss converts his sixth penalty of the season after Malcolm Webster pulls down Stein. Alan Biley's consolation comes too late to matter. | | | | | | | | | | | |
| 15 | H | QP RANGERS | 1 | D | 1-1 | 1-0 | Saxby 44 | Findlay | Stephens | Donaghy | Grealish | Saxby | Price | Hill | West | Stein | Hatton | Moss | |
| | 10/11 | 19,619 | *4* | 21 | | | *Allen 64* | *Woods* | *Shanks* | *Gillard* | *Hazell* | *Wicks* | *McCreery* | *Roeder* | *Currie** | *Bowles* | *Allen* | *Goddard* | *Burke* |
| | | | | | | | Ref: B Martin | The Town pass up a great opportunity to consolidate their position at the top of the league by outplaying Rangers but failing to accept their chances. England manager Ron Greenwood is on hand to check the form of Tony Currie but ends up by being more impressed with Stephens. | | | | | | | | | | | |
| 16 | A | BURNLEY | 1 | D | 0-0 | 0-0 | | Findlay | Stephens | Donaghy | Grealish | Saxby | Price | Hill | West | Stein | Hatton | Moss | |
| | 17/11 | *7,119* | *22* | 22 | | | | *Stevenson* | *Arins* | *Brennan* | *Overson V* | *Dixon* | *Overson R** | *Dobson* | *Young* | *Tate* | *James* | *Fletcher* | *Burke* |
| | | | | | | | Ref: M Heath | Top versus bottom, but the Town are surprisingly negative against a team who have not won for 29 games. Brian Stein is hauled down in the area but the referee turns a blind eye. Jake Findlay finger-tips a Martin Dobson 30-yard drive around his post in the final seconds of the game. | | | | | | | | | | | |
| 17 | H | BIRMINGHAM | 4 | L | 2-3 | 1-1 | Moss 41p, Stein 70 | Findlay | Stephens | Donaghy | Grealish | Saxby | Price | Hill | West | Stein | Hatton | Moss | |
| | 24/11 | 13,720 | *6* | 22 | | | *Bertschin 6, 71, 89* | *Wealands* | *Lees* | *Dennis* | *Gallagher* | *Todd* | *Curbishley* | *Towers* | *Dillon* | *Lynex* | *Bertschin* | *Johnston* | |
| | | | | | | | Ref: J Sewell | The Hatters have no answer to Birmingham winger Willie Johnston, who has a hand in all three of the goals scored by Keith Bertschin. Moss levels from the spot after Terry Lees handles and then Luton take the lead when Stein scores; however, the visitors always look the more fluent. | | | | | | | | | | | |
| 18 | A | SHREWSBURY | 3 | W | 2-1 | 2-1 | Stein 33, Hatton 38 | Findlay | Stephens | Donaghy | Grealish | Saxby | Price | Hill | West | Stein | Hatton | Moss | |
| | 1/12 | *8,565* | *19* | 24 | | | *Keay 31* | *Mulhearn* | *King* | *Larkin* | *Griffin* | *Keay* | *Lindsay* | *Tong* | *Atkins* | *Biggins* | *Dungworth* | *Maguire* | |
| | | | | | | | Ref: R Banks | The home side dominates the opening minutes with Ian Atkins particularly dangerous but the Hatters' defence holds firm. Jack Keay gives the Shrews the lead but they throw it away with two mistakes. The Town take full advantage of them and then hold on, under pressure, for the win. | | | | | | | | | | | |
| 19 | H | NEWCASTLE | 2 | D | 1-1 | 1-0 | Moss 44 | Findlay | Stephens | Donaghy | Grealish | Saxby | Price | Hill | West | Stein | Hatton | Moss | |
| | 8/12 | 14,845 | *1* | 25 | | | *Rafferty 65* | *Hardwick* | *Brownlie* | *Carney* | *Barton* | *Boam* | *Martin** | *Cartwright* | *Hibbitt* | *Shoulder* | *Withe* | *Rafferty* | *Connolly* |
| | | | | | | | Ref: D Vickers | In an end-to-end game, neither side puts on a performance to convince that they are Division 1 class in this top-of-the-table clash. David Moss hits the back of the net with a fierce drive on the stroke of half-time but Peter Withe heads down for Billy Rafferty to equalise after the break. | | | | | | | | | | | |
| 20 | A | WREXHAM | 3 | L | 1-3 | 0-1 | Hatton 83 | Findlay | Stephens | Donaghy | Grealish | Saxby* | Price | Hill | West | Stein | Hatton | Moss | Aizlewood |
| | 15/12 | 9,145 | *8* | 25 | | | *McNeil 15, Fox 61, Edwards 75* | *Davies* | *Darracott* | *Dwyer* | *Davis** | *Jones* | *Fox* | *Carrodus* | *McNeil* | *Vinter* | *Edwards* | *Cartwright* | *Sutton* |
| | | | | | | | Ref: V Callow | Findlay can only parry a fierce shot from Alan Dwyer and Dixie McNeil stabs the ball home for the opening goal. A weak punch from the Luton goalkeeper goes to the feet of Steve Fox who blasts the second goal. Ian Edwards nets the third before Bob Hatton taps in for a late consolation. | | | | | | | | | | | |
| 21 | H | CHARLTON | 3 | W | 3-0 | 2-0 | Stein 5, 37, Hatton 50 | Findlay | Stephens | Donaghy | Grealish | Saxby | Price | Hill | West | Stein | Hatton | Moss | |
| | 21/12 | 7,277 | *19* | 27 | | | | *Wood* | *Hazell* | *Shaw* | *Berry* | *Madden* | *Tydeman* | *Jacobson** | *Walker* | *Powell* | *Hales* | *Gritt* | *Robinson* |
| | | | | | | | Ref: B Stevens | The Town record an easy win against a struggling Charlton side who are unable to master the difficult playing conditions. On a snow-covered Kenilworth Road pitch, the Hatters and Brian Stein in particular, are far sharper and the Valiants do not have a single shot on target all evening. | | | | | | | | | | | |

| No | Date | Att | Pos | Pt | F-A | H-T | Scorers, Times, and Referees | 1 | 2 | 3 | 4 | 5 | 6 | 7 | 8 | 9 | 10 | 11 | 12 sub used |
|---|---|---|---|---|---|---|---|---|---|---|---|---|---|---|---|---|---|---|---|
| 22 | A WATFORD | | 2 | W | 1-0 | 0-0 | Stephens 89 | Findlay | Stephens | Donaghy | Grealish | Saxby | Price | Hill | West | Stein | Hatton | Moss | |
| | 26/12 | *20,187* | *17* | 29 | | | | *Steele* | *Henderson* | *Harrison* | *Sims* | *Bolton* | *Patching* | *Downes* | *Train* | *Rostron* | *Mercer* | *Blissett* | |
| | | | | | | | Ref: M Scott | The first derby game between the clubs since 1972 appears to be heading for a boring 0-0 draw when Hatters' full-back, Kirk Stephens, drifts upfield and, at the far post, heads home a long cross from Hatton for his first goal for the Town. Earlier, Stein saw his shot rebound off the bar. | | | | | | | | | | | |
| 23 | A ORIENT | | 2 | D | 2-2 | 2-0 | Moss 29, 38p | Findlay | Stephens | Donaghy | Grealish | Saxby | Price | Hill | West | Stein | Hatton | Moss* | **White** |
| | 29/12 | *9,292* | *11* | 30 | | | *Jennings 57, Godfrey 87* | *Day* | *Fisher* | *Smith* | *Gray* | *Taylor* | *Moores* | *Hughton* | *Coates* | *Chiedozie** | *Mayo* | *Jennings* | *Godfrey* |
| | | | | | | | Ref: D Reeves | Hatters cruise to a comfortable half-time lead with two goals from Moss, a curling cross which is misjudged by Day and a penalty after Fisher trips Stein. An outrageous back-pass allows Jennings to reduce the arrears and the O's steal a point when Godfrey seizes onto a Stephens' error. | | | | | | | | | | | |
| 24 | H CHELSEA | | 2 | D | 3-3 | 2-1 | Donaghy 35, Saxby 44, Moss 75 | Findlay | Stephens | Donaghy | Aizlewood | Saxby | Price | Hill | West | Stein | Hatton | Moss | |
| | 1/1 | 19,717 | *3* | 31 | | | *Fillery 8, Britton 47, Walker 76* | *Borota* | *Locke* | *Sparrow* | *Pates* | *Chivers* | *Bumstead* | *Britton* | *Fillery* | *Harris* | *Langley* | *Walker* | |
| | | | | | | | Ref: D Letts | In a free-scoring clash played on a treacherous, rock-hard surface, Luton have two efforts disallowed for offside and the referee awards Chelsea a penalty kick but then decides to change his mind. 'It was one of the most exciting games I have ever seen,' says Blues manager Geoff Hurst. | | | | | | | | | | | |
| 25 | H LEICESTER | | 3 | D | 0-0 | 0-0 | | Findlay | Stephens | Donaghy | Grealish | Saxby | Price | Hill | West | Stein | Hatton | Moss | |
| | 12/1 | 14,141 | *4* | 32 | | | | *Wallington* | *Williams* | *Welsh* | *May* | *O'Neill* | *Goodwin* | *Wilson* | *Kelly** | *Henderson* | *Young* | *Smith* | *Strickland* |
| | | | | | | | Ref: R Robinson | This scrappy and frantic affair has little to offer in the way of constructive football. Both teams are anxious to redeem themselves after their respective embarrassing Cup defeats, Leicester having been humiliated by non-League Harlow and the Hatters losing to 3rd Division Swindon. | | | | | | | | | | | |
| 26 | H NOTTS CO | | 3 | W | 2-1 | 0-1 | Saxby 78, Hatton 80 | Findlay | Stephens | Donaghy | Grealish* | Saxby | Price | Hill | West | Stein | Hatton | Moss | White |
| | 2/2 | 9,007 | *14* | 34 | | | *Donaghy 3 (og)* | *Avramovic* | *Benjamin* | *O'Brien* | *Stubbs* | *Blockley* | *Hunt* | *McCulloch** | *Masson* | *Mair* | *Christie* | *Hooks* | *Doherty* |
| | | | | | | | Ref: M Taylor | The Town dominate the game territorially, but have difficulty in unlocking a stubborn defence. The Magpies steal an early lead when Donaghy turns a Masson free-kick past Findlay. A Saxby header, from a Moss free-kick, and a low drive from Hatton earns the first win bonus of 1980. | | | | | | | | | | | |
| 27 | A OLDHAM | | 4 | L | 1-2 | 1-0 | Moss 43 | Findlay | Stephens ! | Donaghy | Grealish | Saxby | Price | Hill* | West | Stein | Hatton | Moss | White |
| | 9/2 | *7,555* | *17* | 34 | | | *Halom 57, 62* | *Platt* | *Wood* | *Holt* | *Clements* | *Blair* | *Kowenicki* | *Halom* | *Atkinson* | *Valentine* | *Steel* | *Stainrod* | |
| | | | | | | | Ref: K Hackett | A goal from Moss is all the Town have to show for their first half supremacy. Oldham attack down the Boundary Park slope after the break and put the Hatters under pressure with Vic Halom scoring two quality goals. Stephens is sent off near the end for unwise words said to a linesman. | | | | | | | | | | | |
| 28 | H FULHAM | | 1 | W | 4-0 | 3-0 | Moss 3, 29, 33, Stein 71 | Findlay | Aizlewood | Donaghy | Grealish | Saxby | Price | Hill | West | Stein | Hatton | Moss | |
| | 16/2 | 9,179 | *22* | 36 | | | | *Peyton* | *Peters* | *Strong* | *Banton* | *Money* | *Gale* | *Beck** | *Lock* | *Gayle* | *Maybank* | *Kitchen* | *Marinello* |
| | | | | | | | Ref: G Flint | Leading scorer Moss bags a hat-trick before half-time in a ruthless display of attacking football to put the Hatters back on top of the league on goal-difference. 'We were outplayed by a Luton side who are difficult to beat on their own pitch,' moans Fulham manager Bobby Campbell. | | | | | | | | | | | |
| 29 | A SUNDERLAND | | 2 | L | 0-1 | 0-0 | | Findlay | Stephens | Donaghy | Grealish | Saxby | Price | Hill | West | Stein | Hatton | Moss | |
| | 23/2 | *25,387* | *8* | 36 | | | *Cooke 61* | *Turner* | *Whitworth* | *Hinnigan* | *Clarke* | *Hindmarch* | *Elliott** | *Arnott* | *Marangoni* | *Cooke* | *Robson* | *Cummins* | *Dunn* |
| | | | | | | | Ref: R Chadwick | A tense game fails to produce flowing football in the first period. Chris Turner bravely blocks an effort from Hatton and, seconds later, sees a shot from Stein curl wide. 17-year-old John Cooke scores his first league goal when he is left unmarked to meet a deep cross from Kevin Arnott. | | | | | | | | | | | |
| 30 | H WEST HAM | | 3 | D | 1-1 | 1-0 | Hill 3 | Findlay | Stephens | Donaghy | Grealish | Saxby | Price | Hill | West | Stein* | Hatton | Moss | White |
| | 1/3 | **20,040** | *5* | 37 | | | *Stewart 74* | *Parkes* | *Lampard* | *Brush* | *Stewart* | *Martin* | *Devonshire* | *Allen* | *Brooking* | *Holland** | *Cross* | *Pike* | *Pearson* |
| | | | | | | | Ref: S Bates | In front of the biggest crowd seen at Kenilworth Road for five years, Ricky Hill volleys home a Moss free-kick after three minutes. West Ham fight back and Brooking, after a 40-yard run, is clumsily pulled down by Grealish. Stewart scores from the rebound after his spot-kick is parried. | | | | | | | | | | | |
| 31 | A SWANSEA | | 3 | L | 0-2 | 0-0 | | Findlay | Stephens | Donaghy | Grealish | Saxby | Price | Hill | West | Stein | Hatton | Moss | |
| | 4/3 | *12,775* | *12* | 37 | | | *Giles 70, 78* | *Stewart* | *Robinson* | *Rushbury* | *Phillips* | *Charles* | *Marustik* | *Craig* | *Callaghan* | *Giles* | *James* | *Toshack* | |
| | | | | | | | Ref: A Glasson | Luton lose the chance to go back to the top when Kevin Keegan look-alike, David Giles, latches onto a knock-down from John Toshack to open the scoring midway through the second-half. Eight minutes later he takes advantage of a cross from Robbie James to score the winning goal. | | | | | | | | | | | |

| No Date | | | Att | Pos | Res | Pts | F-A | H-T | Scorers, Times, and Referees | 1 | 2 | 3 | 4 | 5 | 6 | 7 | 8 | 9 | 10 | 11 | 12 sub used |
|---|---|---|---|---|---|---|---|---|---|---|---|---|---|---|---|---|---|---|---|---|---|
| 32 | A | PRESTON | | 2 | D | | 1-1 | 0-1 | Hatton 65 | Findlay | Stephens | Donaghy | Grealish | Saxby | Price | Aizlewood* | West | Stein | White | Moss | Hatton |
| 8/3 | | | *8,203* | *16* | | 38 | | | *McGee 18* | *Tunks* | *Cameron* | *McAteer* | *Baxter* | *Blackley* | *Doyle** | *Bell* | *Coleman* | *Elliott* | *Potts* | *McGee* | *Taylor* |
| | | | | | | | | | Ref: D Owen | Hatton scores within two minutes of coming on as a substitute, having been left out of the starting line-up for the first time since joining Luton. 'I will always defend a manager's right to make any decision he wants, but I like to put my point of view if I am involved,' he says afterwards. | | | | | | | | | | | |
| 33 | H | CARDIFF | | 5 | L | | 1-2 | 1-1 | Moss 24 | Findlay | Stephens | Donaghy | Grealish | Saxby | Price | Hill | West | Stein | Hatton | Moss* | White |
| 14/3 | | | 9,246 | *12* | | 38 | | | *Buchanan 44, Stevens 49* | *Healey* | *Dwyer* | *Lewis* | *Pontin* | *Thomas* | *Campbell* | *Ronson* | *Grapes* | *Buchanan* | *Stevens* | *Moore* | |
| | | | | | | | | | Ref: M Bidmead | On a pitch made virtually unplayable by two days of heavy rain, Moss scores with a brilliant solo effort but is then carried off after injuring his ankle in the process. John Buchanan scores direct from a free-kick and, with Stephens off the pitch with a hand injury, Stevens hits the winner. | | | | | | | | | | | |
| 34 | A | QP RANGERS | | 5 | D | | 2-2 | 0-2 | Stein 73, Hill 81 | Findlay | Jones | Donaghy | Grealish | Aizlewood | Price | Hill | West | Stein | Hatton | White* | **Pearson** |
| 22/3 | | | *15,054* | *4* | | 39 | | | *Goddard 2, 31* | *Woods* | *Shanks* | *Gillard* | *Hazell* | *Wicks* | *McCreery* | *Roeder** | *Currie* | *Goddard* | *Allen* | *Burke* | *Harkouk* |
| | | | | | | | | | Ref: A Hamil | Missing the suspended Mike Saxby and injury victims Moss and Stephens, the Town trail by two goals at the interval. Two headed goals, from Stein and Hill, see a second-half revival and Rangers' manager Tommy Docherty admits afterwards that Luton were the better footballing side. | | | | | | | | | | | |
| 35 | H | BURNLEY | | 6 | D | | 1-1 | 0-0 | Hatton 68 | Findlay | Stephens | Donaghy | Grealish | Saxby | Price | Hill | West | Stein | Hatton | Pearson | |
| 29/3 | | | 8,507 | *20* | | 40 | | | *Hamilton 60* | *Stevenson* | *Arins* | *Brennan* | *Overson* | *Dixon* | *Scott* | *Robertson* | *Jakub* | *James* | *Hamilton* | *Smith* | |
| | | | | | | | | | Ref: R Lewis | On a quagmire of a pitch, the Towns' close-passing football is ineffective. The Clarets, fighting against relegation, take the lead through Billy Hamilton but Hatton levels when converting a Stein cross. This is the eighth game without a win and the Hatters are sliding down the League. | | | | | | | | | | | |
| 36 | A | CHARLTON | | 5 | W | | 4-1 | 2-0 | Moss 8p, Grealish 12, West 48, [Hatton 84] | Findlay | Stephens | Donaghy | Grealish | Saxby | Price | Hill | West | Stein | Hatton | Moss | |
| 4/4 | | | *8,971* | *22* | | 42 | | | *Hales 85* | *Johns* | *Shaw* | *Madden* | *Hazell* | *Berry* | *Tydeman* | *Powell* | *Gritt* | *Walker* | *Hales* | *Robinson* | |
| | | | | | | | | | Ref: C Downey | Charlton look relegation 'certainties' as the Town stroll to an easy victory. Moss scores his 23rd goal of the season when he bangs home a spot-kick, after Stein is fouled by Lawrie Madden, to start the rout. If the Hatters had taken all of their chances, the scoreline would have doubled. | | | | | | | | | | | |
| 37 | H | WATFORD | | 5 | W | | 1-0 | 1-0 | Hatton 15 | Findlay | Stephens | Donaghy | Grealish | Saxby | Price | Hill | West | Stein | Hatton | Moss* | Aizlewood |
| 5/4 | | | 12,783 | *19* | | 44 | | | | *Steele* | *Henderson* | *Harrison** | *Sims* | *Bolton* | *Patching* | *Booth* | *Train* | *Poskett* | *Blissett* | *Rostron* | *Jenkins* |
| | | | | | | | | | Ref: J Martin | After Bob Hatton converts a cross by Alan West, Watford rarely look like adding to their paltry tally of 28 goals for the season in this Easter fixture. In a bruising and untidy local derby game, the number of fouls pile up, with the referee, John Martin, awarding a total of 62 free kicks. | | | | | | | | | | | |
| 38 | A | CHELSEA | | 5 | D | | 1-1 | 1-0 | Grealish 20 | Findlay | Stephens | Donaghy | Grealish | Saxby | Price | Hill | West | Stein | Hatton | Moss* | Aizlewood |
| 7/4 | | | ***28,460*** | *3* | | 45 | | | *Lee 89* | *Borota* | *Chivers* | *Rofe** | *Pates* | *Nutton* | *Viljoen* | *Britton* | *Harris* | *Lee* | *Langley* | *Walker* | *Fillery* |
| | | | | | | | | | Ref: T Bune | The Town take the lead at Stamford Bridge midway through the first half, when Tony Grealish scores from 30 yards. The Blues fail to take advantage of a limping Jake Findlay in the Luton goal until 20 seconds from the final whistle when Colin Lee scores his first goal for Chelsea. | | | | | | | | | | | |
| 39 | H | SHREWSBURY | | 5 | D | | 0-0 | 0-0 | | Findlay | Stephens | Donaghy | Grealish | Saxby | Price | Hill* | West | Stein | Hatton | Moss | White |
| 12/4 | | | 10,793 | *15* | | 46 | | | | *Wardle* | *King* | *Leonard* | *Larkin* | *Keay* | *Turner* | *Tong* | *Atkins* | *Cross* | *Biggins* | *Dungworth* | |
| | | | | | | | | | Ref: A Grey | The tenth home draw of the season seems to signal the end of the Hatters' promotion drive, thanks to superb saves from Bob Hatton, Brian Stein and Alan West by the Shrewsbury keeper, Bob Wardle. 'I still believe that we can do it,' says Luton manager David Pleat defiantly. | | | | | | | | | | | |
| 40 | A | BIRMINGHAM | | 5 | L | | 0-1 | 0-1 | | Findlay | Stephens | Donaghy | Grealish | Saxby | Price | Hill | West* | Stein | Hatton | Moss | White |
| 19/4 | | | *23,662* | *4* | | 46 | | | *Bertschin 25* | *Wealands* | *Broadhurst* | *Dennis* | *Gallagher* | *Todd* | *Curbishley* | *Gemmill* | *Ainscow* | *Worthingt'n** | *Bertschin* | *Dillon* | *Lynex* |
| | | | | | | | | | Ref: J Worrall | In an amazing game, just one goal separates the two teams at the end although quite how the Birmingham goal survived the battering it received in the final 15 minutes remains a mystery. Archie Gemmill blasts a penalty-kick, given after Mike Saxby fouls Dillon, straight at Jake Findlay. | | | | | | | | | | | |
| 41 | H | WREXHAM | | 5 | W | | 2-0 | 0-0 | Moss 65, Stein 89 | Findlay | Stephens | Donaghy | Grealish | **Goodyear** | Price | Hill | **Madden** | Stein | Hatton | Moss | |
| 26/4 | | | 9,049 | *16* | | 48 | | | | *Niedzwiecki* | *Jones* | *Whittle* | *Roberts* | *Davis* | *Hill* | *Arkwright* | *Fox** | *Carrodus* | *Vinter* | *McNeil* | *Buxton* |
| | | | | | | | | | Ref: R Challis | Clive Goodyear makes his debut for the Hatters and has an impressive game against 19-goal Wrexham striker Dixie McNeil. In the last home game of the season, David Moss and Brian Stein leave the fans with a taste of what might have been as Luton narrowly miss out on promotion. | | | | | | | | | | | |
| 42 | A | NEWCASTLE | | 6 | D | | 2-2 | 2-1 | Hatton 15, 24 | **Judge** | Stephens | Donaghy | Grealish | Saxby | Price | Aizlewood | West | Stein | Hatton | Moss | |
| 3/5 | | | *13,765* | *9* | | 49 | | | *Shoulder 3, Rafferty 62* | *Carr* | *Brownlie* | *Davies* | *Cartwright* | *Boam* | *Barton* | *Rafferty* | *Ferguson* | *With* | *Hibbitt* | *Shoulder* | |
| | Home | | Away | | | | | | Ref: A Porter | Bob Hatton, making his last appearance for the Town, scores two brilliant first-half goals which enable the Hatters to end the season on a high note. After taking an early lead, the Magpies are gifted an equaliser, following some sloppy play, to give them an undeserved share of the points. | | | | | | | | | | | |
| Average | 11,676 | | 13,432 | | | | | | | | | | | | | | | | | | |

| League Cup | | | | F-A | H-T | Scorers, Times, and Referees | 1 | 2 | 3 | 4 | 5 | 6 | 7 | 8 | 9 | 10 | 11 | 12 sub used |
|---|---|---|---|---|---|---|---|---|---|---|---|---|---|---|---|---|---|---|
| 1:1 A | GILLINGHAM | | L | 0-3 | 0-2 | | Findlay | Stephens | Aizlewood | Grealish | Saxby | Price | Hill | Donaghy | Stein | Hatton | Moss | |
| 11/8 | 6,222 | | | | | *Price 7, 88, Barker 24p* | *Hillyard* | *Sharpe* | *Barker* | *Overton* | *Weatherley* | *Crabbe* | *Nicholl* | *Bruce* | *Westwood** | *Price* | *Richardson* | *Funnell* |
| | | | | | | Ref: G Napthine | Third division Gillingham dominate the first leg of this League Cup game. Price is first to a corner from Richardson and then Barker converts a penalty, awarded after Aizlewood brings down Richardson. Price adds the third before Steve Bruce, making his debut, and Moss are booked. | | | | | | | | | | | |
| 1:2 H | GILLINGHAM | | D | 1-1 | 0-0 | Aizlewood 87 | Findlay | Stephens | Aizlewood | Grealish | Saxby | Price | Hill | Donaghy | Stein | Hatton | Moss | |
| 14/8 | 5,509 | | | | | *Crabbe 55* | *Hillyard* | *Young* | *Barker* | *Overton* | *Weatherley* | *Crabbe* | *Nicholl* | *Bruce* | *Price* | *Westwood* | *Richardson* | |
| | | | | | | Ref: C Downey<br>(Hatters lose 1-4 on aggregate) | The Gills make the game safe on aggregate when John Crabbe scores from just inside the box following a breakaway move. Although Mark Aizlewood equalises, following a Ricky Hill and David Moss free-kick routine, the supporters are streaming for the exits long before the end. | | | | | | | | | | | |

| FA Cup | | | | | | | | | | | | | | | | | | |
|---|---|---|---|---|---|---|---|---|---|---|---|---|---|---|---|---|---|---|
| 3 H | SWINDON | 2 | L | 0-2 | 0-1 | | Findlay | Stephens | Donaghy | Grealish | Saxby | Price | Hill | West | Stein* | Hatton | Moss | White |
| 5/1 | 12,458 | *3:4* | | | | *Rowland 28, Williams 82* | *Allan* | *Lewis* | *Stroud* | *Tucker* | *Carter* | *McHale* | *Kamara* | *Miller* | *Williams* | *Rowland* | *Mayes* | |
| | | | | | | Ref: C Downey | Keith Rowland stabs home the first goal for the Third Division giant-killers after Findlay drops the ball under pressure. Ian Miller, who has a sparkling game on the wing, back-heels to Brian Williams and his speculative shot takes a vicious deflection past the helpless Luton keeper. | | | | | | | | | | | |

| | | Home | | | | | Away | | | | | |
|---|---|---|---|---|---|---|---|---|---|---|---|---|
| | P | W | D | L | F | A | W | D | L | F | A | Pts |
| 1 Leicester | 42 | 12 | 5 | 4 | 32 | 19 | 9 | 8 | 4 | 26 | 19 | 55 |
| 2 Sunderland | 42 | 16 | 5 | 0 | 47 | 13 | 5 | 7 | 9 | 22 | 29 | 54 |
| 3 Birmingham | 42 | 14 | 5 | 2 | 37 | 16 | 7 | 6 | 8 | 21 | 22 | 53 |
| 4 Chelsea | 42 | 14 | 3 | 4 | 34 | 16 | 9 | 4 | 8 | 32 | 36 | 53 |
| 5 QP Rangers | 42 | 10 | 9 | 2 | 46 | 25 | 8 | 4 | 9 | 29 | 28 | 49 |
| 6 LUTON TOWN | 42 | 9 | 10 | 2 | 36 | 17 | 7 | 7 | 7 | 30 | 28 | 49 |
| 7 West Ham | 42 | 13 | 2 | 6 | 37 | 21 | 7 | 5 | 9 | 17 | 22 | 47 |
| 8 Cambridge | 42 | 11 | 6 | 4 | 40 | 23 | 3 | 10 | 8 | 21 | 30 | 44 |
| 9 Newcastle | 42 | 13 | 6 | 2 | 35 | 19 | 2 | 8 | 11 | 18 | 30 | 44 |
| 10 Preston | 42 | 8 | 10 | 3 | 30 | 23 | 4 | 9 | 8 | 26 | 29 | 43 |
| 11 Oldham | 42 | 12 | 5 | 4 | 30 | 21 | 4 | 6 | 11 | 19 | 32 | 43 |
| 12 Swansea | 42 | 13 | 1 | 7 | 31 | 20 | 4 | 8 | 9 | 17 | 33 | 43 |
| 13 Shrewsbury | 42 | 12 | 3 | 6 | 41 | 23 | 6 | 2 | 13 | 19 | 30 | 41 |
| 14 Orient | 42 | 7 | 9 | 5 | 29 | 31 | 5 | 8 | 8 | 19 | 23 | 41 |
| 15 Cardiff | 42 | 11 | 4 | 6 | 21 | 16 | 5 | 4 | 12 | 20 | 32 | 40 |
| 16 Wrexham | 42 | 13 | 2 | 6 | 26 | 15 | 3 | 4 | 14 | 14 | 34 | 38 |
| 17 Notts Co | 42 | 4 | 11 | 6 | 24 | 22 | 7 | 4 | 10 | 27 | 30 | 37 |
| 18 Watford | 42 | 9 | 6 | 6 | 27 | 18 | 3 | 7 | 11 | 12 | 28 | 37 |
| 19 Bristol Rov | 42 | 9 | 8 | 4 | 33 | 23 | 2 | 5 | 14 | 17 | 41 | 35 |
| 20 Fulham | 42 | 6 | 4 | 11 | 19 | 28 | 5 | 3 | 13 | 23 | 46 | 29 |
| 21 Burnley | 42 | 5 | 9 | 7 | 19 | 23 | 1 | 6 | 14 | 20 | 50 | 27 |
| 22 Charlton | 42 | 6 | 6 | 9 | 25 | 31 | 0 | 4 | 17 | 14 | 47 | 22 |
| | 924 | 227 | 129 | 106 | 699 | 463 | 106 | 129 | 227 | 463 | 699 | 924 |

Odds & ends

Double wins: (3) Charlton, Fulham, Watford.
Double losses: (2) Birmingham, Cardiff.

Won from behind: (2) Notts County (h), Shrewsbury (a).
Lost from in front: (4) Birmingham (h), Cardiff (a), Cardiff (h), Oldham (a).

High spots: Table-toppers for part of the campaign.
The goal-scoring form of David Moss.
The unbeaten Easter programme, resurrecting hopes for promotion.
The 1-0 win at Watford on Boxing Day, secured in the final seconds.
Beating Watford twice in one season!
A relatively injury-free campaign.

Low spots: Early exits from both of the major Cup competitions.
The home defeat by Cardiff in March which all but ended any hopes of promotion.
Chelsea's last-gasp equaliser at Stamford Bridge, to earn them an undeserved point.

Player of the Year: Jake Findlay.
Ever-presents: (3) Mal Donaghy, Paul Price, Brian Stein.
Hat-tricks: Bob Hatton (1), David Moss (1).
Leading scorer: David Moss (24).

| | Appearances | | | | | | Goals | | | |
|---|---|---|---|---|---|---|---|---|---|---|
| | **Lge** | *Sub* | LC | *Sub* | FAC | *Sub* | **Lge** | LC | FAC | **Tot** |
| Aizlewood, Mark | **5** | *5* | 2 | | | | | 1 | | **1** |
| Birchenall, Alan | **1** | *1* | | | | | | | | |
| Donaghy, Mal | **42** | | 2 | | 1 | | **1** | | | **1** |
| Findlay, Jake | **41** | | 2 | | 1 | | | | | |
| Goodyear, Clive | **1** | | | | | | | | | |
| Grealish, Tony | **41** | | 2 | | 1 | | **2** | | | **2** |
| Hatton, Bob | **40** | *1* | 2 | | 1 | | **18** | | | **18** |
| Hill, Ricky | **40** | | 2 | | 1 | | **6** | | | **6** |
| Ingram, Godfrey | **1** | | | | | | | | | |
| Jones, Graham | **1** | | | | | | | | | |
| Judge, Alan | **1** | | | | | | | | | |
| Madden, Neil | **1** | | | | | | | | | |
| Moss, David | **40** | | 2 | | 1 | | **24** | | | **24** |
| Pearson, Andy | **1** | *1* | | | | | | | | |
| Price, Paul | **42** | | 2 | | 1 | | | | | |
| Saxby, Mike | **39** | | 2 | | 1 | | **4** | | | **4** |
| Stein, Brian | **42** | | 2 | | 1 | | **8** | | | **8** |
| Stephens, Kirk | **40** | | 2 | | 1 | | **1** | | | **1** |
| Turner, Wayne | **2** | | | | | | | | | |
| West, Alan | **39** | | | | 1 | | **2** | | | **2** |
| White, Steve | **2** | *7* | | | | *1* | | | | |
| **21 players used** | **462** | *15* | **22** | | **11** | *1* | **66** | **1** | | **67** |

| No | Date | | Att | Pos | Pt | F-A | H-T | Scorers, Times, and Referees | 1 | 2 | 3 | 4 | 5 | 6 | 7 | 8 | 9 | 10 | 11 | 12 sub used |
|---|---|---|---|---|---|---|---|---|---|---|---|---|---|---|---|---|---|---|---|---|
| 1 | A | WEST HAM | | | W | 2-1 | 0-0 | Moss 75p, 88p | Findlay | Stephens | Donaghy | Grealish | Saxby | Price | Hill | Stein | White* | **Antic** | Moss | West |
| | 16/8 | | *28,033* | | 2 | | | *Stewart 57p* | *Parkes* | *Stewart* | *Brush* | *Martin* | *Bonds* | *Devonshire* | *Brooking* | *Pike* | *Holland* | *Goddard** | *Cross* | *Lampard* |
| | | | | | | | | Ref: D Reeves | The Hammers parade the FA Cup before the game and then tear into the Hatters with the woodwork and saves from Findlay denying them the half-time lead. Stewart scores from the spot after Grealish fouls Holland, but Luton fight back with two penalties from Moss to gain the points. | | | | | | | | | | | |
| 2 | H | WATFORD | | | W | 1-0 | 1-0 | White 25 | Findlay | Stephens | Donaghy | Grealish | Saxby | Price | Hill | Stein | White | Antic* | Moss | West |
| | 19/8 | | 13,887 | | 4 | | | | *Steele* | *Henderson* | *Jackett* | *Sims* | *Bolton* | *Patching* | *Train* | *Rostron* | *Blissett* | *Poskett* | *Jenkins* | |
| | | | | | | | | Ref: A Seville | The Hatters grab the lead when Steve White hits home a cross from Moss to record his first goal for the club. The remainder of the game sees the Town under pressure and Malcolm Poskett nets in the second half but the effort is disallowed by the referee who fails to play the advantage. | | | | | | | | | | | |
| 3 | H | DERBY | | | L | 1-2 | 1-1 | Stein 42 | Findlay | Stephens | Donaghy | Grealish | Saxby | Price | Hill | Stein | **Bunn*** | Antic | Moss | Aizlewood |
| | 23/8 | | 11,025 | | 4 | | | *Osgood 44, Swindlehurst 73* | *Jones* | *Emery* | *Buckley* | *Osgood* | *Ramage* | *Powell S* | *Powell B* | *Clark* | *Biley* | *Swindlehurst* | *Emson** | *Richards* |
| | | | | | | | | Ref: R Lewis | Outplayed in both of their previous games, the roles are now reversed and it is the Rams who undeservedly win both points. Stein scores with a neat back-header following a Moss corner but Keith Osgood levels with a 20-yard free-kick. Swindlehurst hits the winner after an error by Saxby. | | | | | | | | | | | |
| 4 | A | NEWCASTLE | | 12 | L | 1-2 | 1-0 | Stein 8 | Findlay | Stephens | Donaghy | Grealish | Saxby* | Price | Hill | Stein | Bunn | Antic | Moss | Aizlewood |
| | 30/8 | | *13,175* | *21* | 4 | | | *Hibbitt 60, Koenen 72* | *Hardwick* | *Carney* | *Davies* | *Boam* | *Barton** | *Shoulder* | *Walker* | *Hibbitt* | *Koenen* | *Rafferty* | *Nicholson* | *Wharton* |
| | | | | | | | | Ref: T Morris | For an hour, the Hatters look capable of burying Newcastle but have only the one goal, which is scored from close range by Stein, to show for their superiority. Hibbitt's equaliser is a surprise and Saxby is off the pitch having treatment for an injury, when the Magpies snatch the winner. | | | | | | | | | | | |
| 5 | H | WREXHAM | | 11 | D | 1-1 | 0-0 | Bunn 89 | Findlay | Stephens | Donaghy | Grealish | Saxby | Price | Hill | Stein | Bunn | Antic* | Moss | West |
| | 6/9 | | 8,244 | *17* | 5 | | | *Edwards 60* | *Davies* | *Jones* | *Dwyer* | *Davis* | *Cegielski* | *Carrodus* | *Sutton* | *Cartwright* | *McNeil* | *Vinter* | *Edwards* | |
| | | | | | | | | Ref: A Challinor | Ian Edwards scores after a quick break to give a deserved lead to a Wrexham side that dominates the match and frustrates the Luton forwards with their resolute defence for 89 minutes. In the final minute, Bunn cracks the Hatters' equaliser to record his first League goal for the club. | | | | | | | | | | | |
| 6 | A | BLACKBURN | | 18 | L | **0-3** | 0-0 | | Findlay | Stephens | Donaghy | Grealish | Saxby | Price | Hill | Stein | Ingram | West | Moss* | White |
| | 13/9 | | *9,076* | *1* | 5 | | | *Garner 60, 63, Stonehouse 89* | *Arnold* | *Branagan* | *Devries* | *Keeley* | *Fazackerley* | *Kendall* | *McKenzie* | *Speight* | *Brotherston* | *Stonehouse* | *Garner* | |
| | | | | | | | | Ref: G Flint | Unbeaten Blackburn look an ordinary side but, after Findlay drops the ball leaving Simon Garner with a tap in on the hour, they are made to look world-beaters. Garner heads a second and then sets up Stonehouse in the final minute. Town have not scored at Ewood Park for 20 years. | | | | | | | | | | | |
| 7 | H | ORIENT | | 11 | W | 2-1 | 0-0 | Stein 55, Hill 89 | Findlay | Stephens | Donaghy | Grealish | Saxby | Price | Hill | Stein | West | Antic | Moss | |
| | 20/9 | | 8,506 | *13* | 7 | | | *Moores 56* | *Day* | *Fisher* | *Roffey* | *Taylor* | *Gray* | *Bowles* | *Margerrison* | *Parsons* | *Chiedozie* | *Moores* | *Mayo* | |
| | | | | | | | | Ref: B Stevens | Stein opens the scoring but Orient deservedly equalise through Ian Moores a minute later. The O's press forward for the winner and miss many good chances. Ricky Hill steals the points for the Hatters when he hits an injury-time winner, following up on his header which had hit the bar. | | | | | | | | | | | |
| 8 | A | GRIMSBY | | 12 | D | 0-0 | 0-0 | | Findlay | Aizlewood | Donaghy | Grealish | Saxby | Price | Hill | Stein | West | Antic* | Moss | **Harrow** |
| | 27/9 | | *9,044* | *19* | 8 | | | | *Batch* | *Czuczman* | *Crosby* | *Wigginton* | *Moore* | *Waters* | *Cumming* | *Mitchell* | *Ford* | *Liddell* | *Drinkell* | |
| | | | | | | | | Ref: P Willis | Gary Liddell and Bob Cumming are both lucky to stay on the pitch after over-the-top tackles. The Hatters are forced to defend in depth against sustained aerial assaults. David Moss misses his first penalty for the club, when shooting wide after being fouled in the area by Kevin Moore. | | | | | | | | | | | |
| 9 | H | NOTTS CO | | 13 | L | 0-1 | 0-1 | | Findlay | Stephens | Donaghy | Grealish | Saxby | Price | Hill | Stein | Harrow | West* | Moss | Antic |
| | 4/10 | | 8,786 | *2* | 8 | | | *Hunt 17* | *Avramovic* | *Benjamin* | *O'Brien* | *Kilcline* | *Richards* | *Kelly* | *Masson* | *Hunt* | *McCulloch* | *Christie* | *Hooks* | |
| | | | | | | | | Ref: D Letts | A well-drilled County side are fully deserving of both points as they restrict the Hatters to just a few half-chances. David Hunt scores the only goal after Ian McCulloch and Ian Hooks had created the opening. 'County played well and will surprise a few teams this season,' admits Pleat. | | | | | | | | | | | |
| 10 | A | BRISTOL CITY | | 16 | L | 1-2 | 1-0 | Saxby 38 | Findlay | Stephens | Donaghy | Grealish | Saxby | Price | Hill | Stein | Harrow | West | Moss | |
| | 7/10 | | *7,571* | *21* | 8 | | | *Ritchie 58p, Mabbutt 64* | *Cashley* | *Sweeney* | *Hay* | *Whitehead* | *Merrick* | *Gow* | *Fitzpatrick* | *Ritchie* | *Tainton* | *Mabbutt* | *Smith* | |
| | | | | | | | | Ref: B Newsome | Saxby follows up on a partially-cleared corner and scores from close range against a poor City side. A shot from three yards by Trevor Tainton hits Mal Donaghy on the hand and the harshly-awarded spot-kick is converted by John Ritchie. Kevin Mabbutt hits the winner six minutes later. | | | | | | | | | | | |

| | | | | | | | | | | | | | | | | | | | | |
|---|---|---|---|---|---|---|---|---|---|---|---|---|---|---|---|---|---|---|---|---|
| 11 | A | PRESTON | | 19 | L | 0-1 | 0-1 | | Findlay | Stephens | Donaghy | Grealish | Saxby | Price | Hill | Stein | Harrow* | West | White | Aizlewood |
| | 11/10 | | *5,637* | *17* | 8 | | | *Elliott 44* | *Tunks* | *Taylor* | *Blackley* | *Baxter* | *O'Riordan* | *Burns* | *Doyle* | *Coleman* | *Elliott* | *Bruce* | *McGee* | |
| | | | | | | | | Ref: P Partridge | David Moss is dropped for the first time since joining the Club but the new attacking formation fails to make one meaningful shot. Steve Elliott is surrounded by Town defenders but manages a shot which is deflected past Findlay, leaving the Hatters to record their third successive defeat. | | | | | | | | | | | |
| 12 | H | SHREWSBURY | | 19 | D | 1-1 | 0-1 | White 75 | Findlay | Stephens | Donaghy | Grealish | Goodyear | Price | Hill | Stein | White | Aizlewood | Moss | |
| | 18/10 | | 8,014 | *20* | 9 | | | *Turner 44* | *Wardle* | *King* | *Leonard* | *Griffin* | *Larkin** | *Turner* | *Tong* | *Atkins* | *Biggins* | *Dungworth* | *Cross* | *Lindsay* |
| | | | | | | | | Ref: D Vickers | Player-manager, Graham Turner, hits the opening goal for the visitors when swooping on to a fierce cross by Ian Atkins. The Town fight back in the second half and White forces the ball home from close range, following a corner kick from Moss, for a much-needed share of the spoils. | | | | | | | | | | | |
| 13 | H | SWANSEA | | 17 | D | 2-2 | 1-1 | Stein 40, Moss 58 | Findlay | Stephens | Donaghy | Grealish | Goodyear | Price | Hill | Stein | White | Aizlewood | Moss | |
| | 21/10 | | 8,402 | *4* | 10 | | | *Waddle 20, 53* | *Stewart* | *Attley* | *Hadziabdic* | *Stevenson* | *Phillips* | *Mahoney* | *Charles* | *James L* | *Robinson* | *Giles** | *Waddle* | *James R* |
| | | | | | | | | Ref: B Daniels | Town show a good fighting spirit to equalise on two occasions against John Toshack's Swansea, one of the best sides to visit Kenilworth Road this season. The Swans' defence is kept under pressure with a display of attacking football from the Hatters that could have yielded more goals. | | | | | | | | | | | |
| 14 | A | CAMBRIDGE | | 14 | W | 3-1 | 1-1 | Moss 20p, Goodyear 53, Stein 89 | Findlay | Stephens | Donaghy | Grealish | Goodyear | Price | Hill | Stein | White | Aizlewood | Moss* | Antic |
| | 25/10 | | *7,218* | *11* | 12 | | | *Reilly 32* | *Key* | *Donaldson* | *Murray* | *Fallon* | *Smith* | *Gibbins* | *O'Neill* | *Spriggs* | *Finney* | *Reilly* | *Christie* | |
| | | | | | | | | Ref: T Mills | Goodyear nets his first goal for the club with a header before the Hatters are reduced to ten men. Antic is already on for Moss when Findlay is carried off with broken ribs. Makeshift goalkeeper Donaghy keeps a clean sheet and a late strike from Stein secures the first win for a month. | | | | | | | | | | | |
| 15 | H | SHEFFIELD WED | | 11 | W | **3-0** | 0-0 | Moss 51p, 68, White 80 | Judge | Stephens | Donaghy | Grealish | Goodyear | Price | Hill | Stein | White | Aizlewood | Moss | |
| | 1/11 | | 12,092 | *6* | 14 | | | | *Bolder* | *Blackhall* | *Grant* | *Smith* | *Pickering* | *Hornsby* | *Taylor** | *Johnson* | *Sterland* | *McCulloch* | *Curran* | *Mirocevic* |
| | | | | | | | | Ref: T Bune | The visitors dogged determination to keep the point they started with is finally broken down and they are then swept aside as the Hatters regain their lost form in front of the Match of the Day cameras. Moss opens the floodgates from the penalty spot after Hill is fouled by Mark Smith. | | | | | | | | | | | |
| 16 | A | QP RANGERS | | 13 | L | 2-3 | 2-2 | Stein 27, Moss 38 | Judge | Stephens | Donaghy | Grealish | Goodyear | Price | Hill | Stein | White | Aizlewood | Moss | |
| | 8/11 | | *10,082* | *17* | 14 | | | *Neal 36, 88, King 41* | *Woods* | *Shanks* | *Gillard* | *Wicks* | *Howe* | *Waddock* | *Roeder* | *King** | *Langley* | *Neal* | *Silkman* | *McCreery* |
| | | | | | | | | Ref: A Gunn | Terry Venables enjoys his first victory as QPR manager. His team comes back from being behind twice in the first half and then, with the Town adopting a negative attitude, sees Gary Waddock dispossess Donaghy to set up Dean Neal for the winning goal, just before the end of the game. | | | | | | | | | | | |
| 17 | A | WATFORD | | 10 | W | 1-0 | 1-0 | White 11 | Findlay | Stephens | Donaghy | Grealish | Saxby | Price | Hill | Stein | White | Aizlewood* | Moss | West |
| | 11/11 | | *16,993* | *17* | 16 | | | | *Steele* | *Henderson* | *Harrison* | *Sims* | *Jackett* | *Blissett* | *Train* | *Callaghan** | *Rostron* | *Poskett* | *Jenkins* | *Taylor* |
| | | | | | | | | Ref: A Hamil | The Town record their fourth consecutive 1-0 win against their near neighbours with Steve White scoring the only goal following some superb play by Brian Stein. David Pleat is attacked after the game for his excessive use of the offside-trap, a view not shared by the Hatters' supporters! | | | | | | | | | | | |
| 18 | H | WEST HAM | | 10 | W | 3-2 | 2-1 | Stein 13, 18, Moss 85 | Findlay | Stephens | Donaghy | Grealish | Saxby | Price | Hill | Stein | White | Aizlewood* | Moss | West |
| | 15/11 | | **17,031** | *1* | 18 | | | *Brooking 44, 49* | *Parkes* | *Stewart* | *Lampard* | *Martin* | *Bonds* | *Holland* | *Devonshire* | *Brooking* | *Pike* | *Goddard* | *Cross* | |
| | | | | | | | | Ref: C White | Luton are the only team to have beaten top-of-the-table, West Ham, this season and duly win again in difficult, muddy conditions. Stein scores twice before the Hammers settle down with Trevor Brooking levelling the score with two goals before Moss hits a merited winner near the end. | | | | | | | | | | | |
| 19 | A | CARDIFF | | 11 | L | 0-1 | 0-0 | | Findlay | Stephens | Donaghy* | Grealish | Saxby | Price | Hill | Stein | White | Aizlewood | Moss | West |
| | 22/11 | | *6,041* | *14* | 18 | | | *Buchanan 53* | *Healey* | *Jones* | *Thomas* | *Pontin* | *Dwyer* | *Hughes* | *Ronson* | *Giles* | *Buchanan** | *Kitchen* | *Stevens* | *Lewis* |
| | | | | | | | | Ref: M Robinson | After the superb performance of last week, this match at Ninian Park develops into an anti-climax for the Luton supporters. There is very little ambition shown by the Hatters in the first half but, after gifting the Bluebirds a goal, they then bombard the Welsh side when it is all far too late. | | | | | | | | | | | |
| 20 | H | BOLTON | | 11 | D | 2-2 | 1-0 | Hill 19, Stein 81 | Findlay | Stephens | Donaghy | Grealish* | Saxby | Price | Hill | Stein | White | Aizlewood | Moss | West |
| | 29/11 | | 8,302 | *13* | 19 | | | *Whatmore 53, 67* | *Poole* | *Graham* | *McElhinney* | *Jones* | *Walsh* | *Wilson* | *Nicholson* | *Gowling* | *Whatmore* | *Hoggan* | *Kidd* | |
| | | | | | | | | Ref: V Callow | On a bitterly cold day, the driving snow makes the Kenilworth Road pitch slippery. Both teams turn on a glittering display of football and the equalising goal from Brian Stein is worthy of a much higher standard, beating five defenders in an individual run down the middle of the field. | | | | | | | | | | | |
| 21 | A | OLDHAM | | 11 | D | 0-0 | 0-0 | | Findlay | Stephens* | Donaghy | Grealish | Saxby | Price | Hill | Stein | White | Aizlewood | Moss | West |
| | 6/12 | | *4,854* | *20* | 20 | | | | *Platt* | *Sinclair* | *Blair* | *Clements* | *Hurst* | *Keegan* | *Futcher* | *Hilton** | *Heaton* | *Steel* | *Palmer* | *Kowenicki* |
| | | | | | | | | Ref: D Richardson | Only 12 goals have been scored at Boundary Park this campaign and neither side looks like adding to that tally in a poor game of little incident. The Hatters opt to defend for the whole of the 90 minutes rather than attempt to gain the extra point which appeared to be there for the taking. | | | | | | | | | | | |

# LEAGUE DIVISION 2    Manager: David Pleat    SEASON 1980-81



| No | Date | | Att | Pos | Pt | F-A | H-T | Scorers, Times, and Referees | 1 | 2 | 3 | 4 | 5 | 6 | 7 | 8 | 9 | 10 | 11 | 12 sub used |
|---|---|---|---|---|---|---|---|---|---|---|---|---|---|---|---|---|---|---|---|---|
| 22 | H | PRESTON | | 10 | W | 4-2 | 1-0 | Moss 42p, 48, Fuccillo 69, Ingram 81 | Findlay | Stephens | Donaghy | Fuccillo | Saxby* | Price | Hill | Stein | Ingram | Aizlewood | Moss | Antic |
| | 13/12 | | **7,874** | *20* | 22 | | | *Elliott 52, Bruce 85* | *Tunks* | *Taylor* | *Westwell* | *Anderson* | *Baxter* | *Burns* | *Bell* | *Doyle* | *Elliott* | *Bruce* | *McGee** | *Sayer* |
| | | | | | | | | Ref: M Bidmead | Fuccillo returns to the side for the first time in two years, having suffered two broken legs, to score the all-important third goal in an open game of end-to-end football. Transfer-listed Ingram tries to prove his critics wrong when beating two players for speed and hammering the fourth goal. | | | | | | | | | | | |
| 23 | A | SHREWSBURY | | 10 | W | 1-0 | 0-0 | Ingram 65 | Findlay | Stephens | Donaghy | Grealish | Saxby | West | Hill | Stein | Ingram* | Aizlewood | Moss | Antic |
| | 19/12 | | *4,521* | *17* | 24 | | | | *Wardle* | *King* | *Larkin* | *Griffin** | *Keay* | *Petts* | *Tong* | *Atkins* | *Cross* | *Bates* | *Dungworth* | *Biggins* |
| | | | | | | | | Ref: N Ashley | Ingram, replacing Steve White who is injured, scores for the second time in a week when reacting quickly after Shrews' keeper, Bob Wardle, can only parry a shot from Stein. The home side have no answer to the midfield thrusts of Hill, and Findlay has little to do in the Luton goal. | | | | | | | | | | | |
| 24 | H | CHELSEA | | 8 | W | 2-0 | 0-0 | Stein 66, 73 | Findlay | Stephens | Donaghy | Grealish | West | Price | Hill | Stein | Ingram | Aizlewood | Moss | |
| | 26/12 | | 16,006 | *3* | 26 | | | | *Borota* | *Locke* | *Rofe* | *Pates* | *Nutton** | *Bumstead* | *Fillery* | *Hutchins* | *Driver* | *Lee* | *Mayes* | *Elmes* |
| | | | | | | | | Ref: A Grey | The promotion favourites are made to look second-best as two headed goals from Brian Stein in a seven-minute spell, each from a perfect cross provided by David Moss, ease the Town to a comfortable win. The pair also hit the woodwork and a further two shots are hacked off the line. | | | | | | | | | | | |
| 25 | A | BRISTOL ROV | | 6 | W | 4-2 | 3-2 | Stein 12, 35, 81, Hill 37 | Findlay | Stephens* | Donaghy | Grealish | West | Price | Hill | Stein | Ingram | Aizlewood | Moss | Antic |
| | 27/12 | | *7,010* | *22* | 28 | | | *Barrowclough 8, Mabbutt 17* | *Thomas* | *Jones* | *Bater* | *Hughes** | *Williams D* | *Emmanuel* | *Cooper* | *Mabbutt* | *Williams S* | *Barrowclough* | *Barrett* | *Gillies* |
| | | | | | | | | Ref: A Glasson | Stephens is forced to go off when he suffers an early injury which then leaves the Hatters without a recognised right-back. Rovers take full advantage and twice take the lead but Brian Stein hits the first hat-trick of his career to help the Town record their fifth away win of the season. | | | | | | | | | | | |
| 26 | H | CARDIFF | | 6 | D | 2-2 | 1-1 | Moss 25, Price 62 | Findlay | West | Donaghy | Grealish | Saxby | Price | Hill | Stein | Ingram | Aizlewood | Moss | |
| | 10/1 | | 9,013 | *17* | 29 | | | *Kitchen 10, Giles 46* | *Healey* | *Roberts* | *Pontin* | *Dwyer* | *Thomas* | *Hughes* | *Ronson* | *Buchanan** | *Giles* | *Kitchen* | *Stevens* | *Micallef* |
| | | | | | | | | Ref: D Hutchinson | On a slippery Kenilworth Road surface, this match is good entertainment for the neutrals as the Hatters battle out a draw against a Cardiff side who twice take the lead in the blizzard conditions. The Bluebirds are now unbeaten in eight games and are becoming a jinx team for the Town. | | | | | | | | | | | |
| 27 | H | NEWCASTLE | | 7 | L | 0-1 | 0-1 | | Findlay | Stephens | Donaghy | Grealish | West | Price | Hill | Stein | Ingram* | Aizlewood | Moss | Fuccillo |
| | 17/1 | | 10,774 | *13* | 29 | | | *Harford 9* | *Carr* | *Carney* | *Halliday* | *Boam* | *Johnson* | *Martin* | *Trewick* | *Wharton* | *Shinton* | *Harford* | *Waddle* | |
| | | | | | | | | Ref: H Taylor | Two pitch inspections are required before the game is allowed to proceed and Mick Harford scores for the Magpies with a deflected shot. Luton have a gilt-edged chance to level, when Peter Johnson fouls Hill in the box, but Kevin Carr stretches to make a simple save from David Moss. | | | | | | | | | | | |
| 28 | A | DERBY | | 8 | D | 2-2 | 0-1 | Moss 49, Ingram 56 | Findlay | Stephens | Donaghy | Turner | West | Price | Hill | Stein | Ingram | Fuccillo | Moss | |
| | 31/1 | | *16,479* | *6* | 30 | | | *Wilson 8, Hector 57* | *Jones* | *Emery* | *McFarland* | *Osgood* | *Buckley* | *Powell S* | *Powell B* | *Hector* | *Biley* | *Wilson* | *Emson* | |
| | | | | | | | | Ref: D Allison | The Rams open the scoring when Kevin Wilson succeeds with a bicycle kick but the Town fight back to take the lead after the interval. Kevin Hector scores his 150th League goal for Derby when he gets on to the end of a cross from ex-Hatter, Alan Biley, to head home at the far post. | | | | | | | | | | | |
| 29 | H | BLACKBURN | | 6 | W | 3-1 | 0-1 | Price 53, Hill 61, Moss 81 | Findlay | Stephens | Donaghy | Grealish | West | Price | Hill | Stein | Ingram | Aizlewood | Moss | |
| | 7/2 | | 9,350 | *7* | 32 | | | *Burke 9* | *Arnold* | *Branagan* | *Keeley* | *Fazackerley** | *Rathbone* | *Kendall* | *Burke* | *Speight* | *Brotherston* | *Garner* | *Lowey* | *Stonehouse* |
| | | | | | | | | Ref: J Bray | After a sloppy first-half performance, the Town get their act together to destroy the visitors in the second period. 'It wasn't a case of us playing badly or making a lot of silly mistakes - Luton just played very well in the second-half,' reflects Blackburn player-manager, Howard Kendall. | | | | | | | | | | | |
| 30 | H | GRIMSBY | | 10 | L | 0-2 | 0-1 | | Findlay | Stephens | Donaghy | Grealish | West | Price* | Hill | Stein | Ingram | Aizlewood | Moss | White |
| | 21/2 | | 9,217 | *4* | 32 | | | *Cumming 24, Waters 51* | *Batch* | *Stone* | *Wigginton* | *Moore* | *Crombie* | *Waters* | *Brolly* | *Mitchell* | *Whymark* | *Drinkell** | *Cumming* | *Kilmore* |
| | | | | | | | | Ref: R Challis | Bob Cumming misses an open goal for the Mariners before scoring with a low shot which is deflected past a helpless Jake Findlay in the Luton goal. Joe Waters seals the win in the second half with a tremendous 25-yard drive to give one of the promotion dark-horses two valuable points. | | | | | | | | | | | |
| 31 | A | ORIENT | | 11 | D | 0-0 | 0-0 | | Findlay | Stephens | Donaghy | Grealish | Saxby* | Price | Hill | Stein | Ingram | Fuccillo | Moss | Antic |
| | 1/3 | | *7,974* | *12* | 33 | | | | *Day* | *Fisher* | *Taylor T* | *Gray* | *Roffey* | *Bowles* | *Margerrison* | *Taylor P* | *Chiedozie* | *Jennings* | *Moores* | |
| | | | | | | | | Ref: L Shapter | A reshuffled Town side plays its first ever fixture on a Sunday. The morning kick-off does not help the players, who take some time to adjust, with the result that the match is no classic. Orient goalkeeper Mervyn Day has an inspired game, saving well from both Fuccillo and Stein. | | | | | | | | | | | |

| No | Ven | Opponent | Att | Pos | Res | F-A | H-T | Scorers, Times, Referees | 1 | 2 | 3 | 4 | 5 | 6 | 7 | 8 | 9 | 10 | 11 | 12 |
|---|---|---|---|---|---|---|---|---|---|---|---|---|---|---|---|---|---|---|---|---|
| 32 | A | NOTTS CO | | 9 | W | 1-0 | 1-0 | Stein 37 | Findlay | Stephens | Donaghy | Grealish | Saxby | Price | Hill | Stein | White | Antic | Moss | |
| | 7/3 | | *8,075* | *2* | 35 | | | | *Avramovic* | *Benjamin* | *Kilcline* | *Richards* | *O'Brien* | *Kelly* | *Masson* | *Hunt* | *Hooks* | *McCulloch* | *Christie** | *Harkouk* |
| | | | | | | | | Ref: J Hough | Raddy Antic is recalled to the team to play as a sweeper, which completely foxes the Magpies in the first half. The Hatters catch County on the break and Stein volleys a picture goal. After the break Luton revert to a more conventional formation and leave Meadow Lane with both points. | | | | | | | | | | | |
| 33 | H | BRISTOL CITY | | 7 | W | 3-1 | 2-1 | White 24, 35, Moss 75p | Findlay | Stephens | Donaghy | Grealish | Saxby | Price | Hill | Stein | White | Antic | Moss | |
| | 14/3 | | 8,745 | *21* | 37 | | | *Pritchard 8* | *Moller* | *Stevens* | *Marshall* | *Whitehead* | *Hay* | *Aitken* | *Tainton** | *Fitzpatrick* | *Pritchard* | *Mabbutt* | *Smith* | *Mann* |
| | | | | | | | | Ref: L Burden | A controversial decision kills the game as a contest when Moss is body-checked by Peter Aitken on the angle of the penalty area. City consider it to be obstruction, outside the box, but the referee awards a penalty-kick which Moss gratefully strokes home for his 17th goal of the season. | | | | | | | | | | | |
| 34 | H | CAMBRIDGE | | 8 | D | 0-0 | 0-0 | | Findlay | Stephens | Donaghy | West | Saxby | Price | Hill | Stein | White | Antic | Moss | |
| | 28/3 | | 9,412 | *10* | 38 | | | | *Key* | *Evans* | *Smith* | *Fallon* | *Murray* | *Finney* | *Streete* | *Spriggs* | *Christie* | *Reilly* | *Lyons* | |
| | | | | | | | | Ref: J Hunting | The U's pull everyone back behind the ball to frustrate the Hatters and then miss the best chance to win with two minutes remaining. United manager John Docherty storms out of the post-match press conference when asked to comment on the defensive tactics used by his team. | | | | | | | | | | | |
| 35 | A | WREXHAM | | 7 | D | 0-0 | 0-0 | | Findlay | Stephens | Donaghy | Grealish | Saxby | Price | Hill | Stein | White* | Antic | Moss | Ingram |
| | 31/3 | | ***4,157*** | *16* | 39 | | | | *Davies* | *Hill* | *Jones J* | *Cegielski* | *Dwyer* | *Carrodus* | *Fox* | *Arkwright* | *Vinter* | *Buxton* | *Jones S** | *Williams* |
| | | | | | | | | Ref: R Chadwick | Wrexham have now gone nine home games without a win and pose little threat to the Luton defence. The Hatters also lack punch and only two efforts from midfielder Raddy Antic, which hit the bar look likely to break the deadlock. Amazingly, the Town move up one place in the table. | | | | | | | | | | | |
| 36 | A | SHEFFIELD WED | | 8 | L | 1-3 | 0-1 | Ingram 75 | Findlay | Stephens | Aizlewood | Grealish | Saxby | Price | Hill* | Stein | Donaghy | Antic | Moss | Ingram |
| | 4/4 | | *17,196* | *6* | 39 | | | *Mirocevic 26, Curran 50, 51* | *Bolder* | *Blackhall* | *Smith* | *Shirtliff* | *Grant* | *Mirocevic* | *Johnson* | *Taylor** | *Mellor* | *McCulloch* | *Curran* | *Hornsby* |
| | | | | | | | | Ref: A Banks | The Owls sweep the Town aside after being fired-up by their manager, Jack Charlton, just before the match. Luton can only get into the game in the last 20 minutes, as Wednesday go off the boil, and gain a consolation when Ingram scores his sixth goal of the season in 12 appearances. | | | | | | | | | | | |
| 37 | H | QP RANGERS | | 5 | W | **3-0** | 1-0 | Ingram 20, Stein 54, Antic 56 | Findlay | Stephens | Donaghy | Grealish | Saxby | Price | Hill | Stein | Ingram | Antic | Moss | |
| | 11/4 | | 12,112 | *10* | 41 | | | | *Burridge* | *Shanks* | *Wicks* | *Roeder* | *Gillard** | *Currie* | *Francis* | *Silkman* | *Waddock* | *Flanagan* | *Sealy* | *Burke* |
| | | | | | | | | Ref: P Reeves | Ricky Hill turns in a five-star performance as the Hatters destroy their demoralised visitors and could have scored six had they not eased off in the final 20 minutes. 'You can't be despondent when you see your team beaten by a team like Luton,' reflects QPR manager, Terry Venables. | | | | | | | | | | | |
| 38 | H | BRISTOL ROV | | 5 | W | 1-0 | 1-0 | Moss 40p | Findlay | Stephens | Donaghy | Grealish | Saxby | Price | Hill | Stein | Ingram | Antic | Moss | |
| | 18/4 | | 9,009 | *22* | 43 | | | | *McAllister* | *Gillies* | *Hughes* | *Slatter* | *Mabbutt* | *McCaffery* | *Emmanuel* | *Williams G** | *Barrett* | *Randall* | *Lee* | *Williams D* |
| | | | | | | | | Ref: M Taylor | On a bumpy pitch, the Town have to rely on a dubious penalty decision, given when Stein falls over in the box, before condemning Rovers to Division 3 next season. McAllister is adjudged to have moved early when saving the first attempt from Moss, who welcomes a second chance. | | | | | | | | | | | |
| 39 | A | CHELSEA | | 3 | W | 2-0 | 1-0 | Moss 26, Hill 77 | Findlay | Stephens | Donaghy | Grealish | Saxby | Price | Hill | Stein | Ingram | Antic | Moss | |
| | 20/4 | | *12,868* | *9* | 45 | | | | *Borota* | *Pates* | *Nutton* | *Locke* | *Rofe* | *Bumstead* | *Chivers* | *Hutchings* | *Fillery* | *Lee* | *Mayes** | *Rh's-Brown* |
| | | | | | | | | Ref: A Robinson | The Town are making a late bid for promotion as Moss opens the scoring with a soft shot which goes past the eccentric Petar Borota. Hill hits the second from outside the area which gives the keeper no chance. 'I like to see good football rewarded,' praises Chelsea boss Geoff Hurst. | | | | | | | | | | | |
| 40 | H | OLDHAM | | 5 | L | 1-2 | 0-1 | Stein 55 | Findlay | Stephens | Donaghy | Grealish | Saxby | Price | Hill | Stein | Ingram | Antic* | Moss | West |
| | 25/4 | | 10,305 | *18* | 45 | | | *Wylde 10, 66* | *McDonnell* | *Sinclair* | *Clements* | *Futcher* | *Blair* | *Keegan* | *Heaton* | *Palmer* | *Atkinson* | *Wylde* | *Steel* | |
| | | | | | | | | Ref: A Gunn | Lowly Oldham take both points after a frustrating Luton performance. Rodger Wylde, scorer of both Latics'goals, is lucky to still be on the field after flattening Stephens with his elbow when in full view of the referee. The players are taken off for ten minutes during a pitch invasion. | | | | | | | | | | | |
| 41 | A | SWANSEA | | 5 | D | 2-2 | 1-2 | Hill 28, 50 | Findlay | Stephens | Donaghy | West | Saxby | Price | Hill | Stein | White | Antic | Moss | |
| | 27/4 | | *21,354* | *3* | 46 | | | *Craig 3, James L 22* | *Stewart* | *Evans* | *Stevens* | *Lewis* | *Hadziabdic* | *Robinson* | *Mahoney* | *Craig** | *Curtis* | *James R* | *James L* | *Charles* |
| | | | | | | | | Ref: B Newsome | Promotion hopes are finally dashed in front of the biggest Vetch Field crowd of the season. A 'goal' by Raddy Antic is disallowed for offside although the offender, David Moss, is running away from the goal as the ball screams into the net. Ricky Hill has another tremendous game. | | | | | | | | | | | |
| 42 | A | BOLTON | | 5 | W | **3-0** | 0-0 | Stein 55, White 65, Stephens 89 | Findlay | Stephens | Donaghy | Fuccillo | Saxby | Price | Hill | Stein | White | Antic | Moss | |
| | 2/5 | | *7,278* | *18* | 48 | | | | *Peacock* | *Nicholson* | *Jones* | *Walsh* | *Brennan* | *Cantello* | *Nikolic* | *Reid** | *Whatmore* | *Thomas* | *Gowling* | *Carter* |
| | | Home | Away | | | | | Ref: A Saunders | A meaningless end-of-season match sees the Town lucky to be level, going in to the half-time break but then change up a gear and baffle the Trotters with the speed of their counter-attacks. Stephens scores his first goal of the season with a thumping shot in the final minute of the game. | | | | | | | | | | | |
| Average | | 10,291 | 10,696 | | | | | | | | | | | | | | | | | |

| League Cup | | | F-A | H-T | Scorers, Times, and Referees | 1 | 2 | 3 | 4 | 5 | 6 | 7 | 8 | 9 | 10 | 11 | 12 sub used |
|---|---|---|---|---|---|---|---|---|---|---|---|---|---|---|---|---|---|
| 2:1 A READING | | W | 2-0 | 1-0 | Moss 1, Stein 65 | Findlay | Stephens | Donaghy | Grealish | Saxby | Price | Hill | Stein | Bunn* | Antic | Moss | White |
| 27/8 | *5,778* | | | | | *Death* | *Joslyn* | *White** | *Shipperley* | *Moreline* | *Bowman* | *Sanchez* | *Beavon* | *Earles* | *Heale* | *Dixon* | *Webb* |
| | | | | | Ref: D Lloyd | David Moss takes advantage of a pass from Frankie Bunn to open the scoring after just 59 seconds and a second follows when Brian Stein turns Dave Shipperley before hitting his shot into the corner of the net. Royals' manager Maurice Evans promises an all-out attack in the second leg. | | | | | | | | | | | |
| 2:2 H READING | 12 | D | 1-1 | 0-0 | Saxby 50 | Findlay | Stephens | Donaghy | Grealish | Saxby | Aizlewood | Hill | Stein | White | Antic | Heath* | Ingram |
| 2/9 | 5,707 *3:5* | | | | *Hetzke 63* | *Death* | *Joslyn* | *Cheetham* | *Hetzke* | *Hicks* | *Bowman* | *Wanklyn* | *Sanchez* | *Earles* | *Dixon* | *Beavon* | |
| | | | | | Ref: P Reeves (Hatters win 3-1 on aggregate) | The Hatters play plenty of pretty football but their finishing power is not strong enough for them to capitalise on their supremacy. Mike Saxby heads home a free-kick from Antic but Steve Hetzke equalises for Reading with a 25-yard free-kick, giving an unrealistic look to the final score. | | | | | | | | | | | |
| 3 H MANCHESTER C | 11 | L | 1-2 | 1-2 | Antic 25 | Findlay | Stephens | Donaghy | Grealish* | Saxby | Price | Hill | Stein | West | Antic | Moss | Smith |
| 23/9 | 10,030 *1:21* | | | | *Bennett 12, Henry 43* | *Corrigan* | *Ranson* | *Reid* | *Caton* | *Booth* | *Henry* | *Daley* | *Power* | *Palmer* | *Bennett* | *Reeves* | |
| | | | | | Ref: S Bates | First division City squeeze through against a Hatters side who battle hard. The visitors show the speed and inventiveness which is missing from the Town's repertoire and, although Antic equalises the Dave Bennett opener with a 20-yard free-kick, the Blues just about deserve their win. | | | | | | | | | | | |

| FA Cup | | | | | | | | | | | | | | | | | |
|---|---|---|---|---|---|---|---|---|---|---|---|---|---|---|---|---|---|
| 3 A ORIENT | 6 | W | 3-1 | 0-0 | Moss 51p, 60, Ingram 53 | Findlay | West | Donaghy | Grealish | Saxby | Price | Hill | Stein | Ingram | Aizlewood | Moss | |
| 3/1 | 9,891 *2:8* | | | | *Jennings 88* | *Day* | *Hughton* | *Taylor T* | *Gray* | *Roffey* | *Parsons* | *Bowles* | *Taylor P* | *Chiedozie* | *Moores* | *Jennings* | |
| | | | | | Ref: L Shapter | The Town move into the 4th Round of the Cup for the first time in three years with a three-goal burst in nine minutes at the start of the second half. Moss converts a penalty after Nigel Gray fouls Hill, Ingrams curls in a second and Moss chips keeper Mervyn Day from outside the area. | | | | | | | | | | | |
| 4 A NEWCASTLE | 8 | L | 1-2 | 0-1 | Ingram 64 | Findlay | Stephens | Donaghy | Grealish | West | Price | Hill | Stein | Ingram | Aizlewood | Moss | |
| 24/1 | 29,202 *2:13* | | | | *Clarke 6, Martin 60* | *Carr* | *Carney* | *Halliday* | *Boam* | *Johnson* | *Martin* | *Trewick* | *Wharton* | *Shinton* | *Clarke* | *Waddle* | |
| | | | | | Ref: T Morris | The Magpies put on their best display for years, according to the locals, and threaten to overrun the Town; however, it is the home supporters who beg for the final whistle after Ingram gets a goal back with a neat shot from the edge of the box and Hill hits a post with five minutes left. | | | | | | | | | | | |

| | Home | | | | | | Away | | | | | |
|---|---|---|---|---|---|---|---|---|---|---|---|---|
| | P | W | D | L | F | A | W | D | L | F | A | Pts |
| 1 West Ham | 42 | 19 | 1 | 1 | 53 | 12 | 9 | 9 | 3 | 26 | 17 | 66 |
| 2 Notts Co | 42 | 10 | 8 | 3 | 26 | 15 | 8 | 9 | 4 | 23 | 23 | 53 |
| 3 Swansea | 42 | 12 | 5 | 4 | 39 | 19 | 6 | 9 | 6 | 25 | 25 | 50 |
| 4 Blackburn | 42 | 12 | 8 | 1 | 28 | 7 | 4 | 10 | 7 | 14 | 22 | 50 |
| 5 LUTON TOWN | 42 | 10 | 6 | 5 | 35 | 23 | 8 | 6 | 7 | 26 | 23 | 48 |
| 6 Derby | 42 | 9 | 8 | 4 | 34 | 26 | 6 | 7 | 8 | 23 | 26 | 45 |
| 7 Grimsby | 42 | 10 | 8 | 3 | 21 | 10 | 5 | 7 | 9 | 23 | 32 | 45 |
| 8 QP Rangers | 42 | 11 | 7 | 3 | 36 | 12 | 4 | 6 | 11 | 20 | 34 | 43 |
| 9 Watford | 42 | 13 | 5 | 3 | 34 | 18 | 3 | 6 | 12 | 16 | 27 | 43 |
| 10 Sheffield Wed | 42 | 14 | 4 | 3 | 38 | 14 | 3 | 4 | 14 | 15 | 37 | 42 |
| 11 Newcastle | 42 | 11 | 7 | 3 | 22 | 13 | 3 | 7 | 11 | 8 | 32 | 42 |
| 12 Chelsea | 42 | 8 | 6 | 7 | 27 | 15 | 6 | 6 | 9 | 19 | 26 | 40 |
| 13 Cambridge | 42 | 13 | 1 | 7 | 36 | 23 | 4 | 5 | 12 | 17 | 42 | 40 |
| 14 Shrewsbury | 42 | 9 | 7 | 5 | 33 | 22 | 2 | 10 | 9 | 13 | 25 | 39 |
| 15 Oldham | 42 | 7 | 9 | 5 | 19 | 16 | 5 | 6 | 10 | 20 | 32 | 39 |
| 16 Wrexham | 42 | 5 | 8 | 8 | 22 | 24 | 7 | 6 | 8 | 21 | 21 | 38 |
| 17 Orient | 42 | 9 | 8 | 4 | 34 | 20 | 4 | 4 | 13 | 18 | 36 | 38 |
| 18 Bolton | 42 | 10 | 5 | 6 | 40 | 27 | 4 | 5 | 12 | 21 | 39 | 38 |
| 19 Cardiff | 42 | 7 | 7 | 7 | 23 | 24 | 5 | 5 | 11 | 21 | 36 | 36 |
| 20 Preston | 42 | 8 | 7 | 6 | 28 | 26 | 3 | 7 | 11 | 13 | 36 | 36 |
| 21 Bristol City | 42 | 6 | 10 | 5 | 19 | 15 | 1 | 6 | 14 | 10 | 36 | 30 |
| 22 Bristol Rov | 42 | 4 | 9 | 8 | 21 | 24 | 1 | 4 | 16 | 13 | 41 | 23 |
| | 924 | 217 | 144 | 101 | 668 | 405 | 101 | 144 | 217 | 405 | 668 | 924 |

Odds & ends

Double wins: (4) Bristol Rovers, Chelsea, Watford, West Ham.
Double losses: (1) Newcastle.

Won from behind: (4) Blackburn (h), Bristol City (h), Bristol Rovers (a), West Ham (a).
Lost from in front: (4) Bristol City (a), Derby (h), Newcastle (a), QPR (a).

High spots: A double win over Champions, West Ham.
Highest position in the league since 1974.
Another double over Watford!
Winning at Cambridge when down to 10 men, for the first win in seven.

Low spots: Failing to win promotion for the second successive season.
Three consecutive defeats in October which pushed the team down to 19th position.
Losing at home to Oldham at the end of the season.
The late disallowed goal at Swansea, which cost a vital promotion point.

Player of the Year: Ricky Hill.
Ever-presents: (3) Mal Donaghy, Ricky Hill, Brian Stein.
Hat-tricks: Brian Stein (1).
Leading scorer: David Moss and Brian Stein (19).

| | Appearances | | | | | | Goals | | | |
|---|---|---|---|---|---|---|---|---|---|---|
| | Lge | *Sub* | LC | *Sub* | FAC | *Sub* | Lge | LC | FAC | Tot |
| Aizlewood, Mark | **20** | *3* | 1 | | 2 | | | | | |
| Antic, Raddy | **18** | *6* | 3 | | | | **1** | 1 | | **2** |
| Bunn, Frank | **3** | | 1 | | | | **1** | | | **1** |
| Donaghy, Mal | **42** | | 3 | | 2 | | | | | |
| Findlay, Jake | **40** | | 3 | | 2 | | | | | |
| Fuccillo, Lil | **4** | *1* | | | | | **1** | | | **1** |
| Goodyear, Clive | **5** | | | | | | **1** | | | **1** |
| Grealish, Tony | **37** | | 3 | | 2 | | | | | |
| Harrow, Andy | **3** | *1* | | | | | | | | |
| Heath, Seamus | | | 1 | | | | | | | |
| Hill, Ricky | **42** | | 3 | | 2 | | **7** | | | **7** |
| Ingram, Godfrey | **15** | *2* | | *1* | 2 | | **5** | | 2 | **7** |
| Judge, Alan | **2** | | | | | | | | | |
| Moss, David | **41** | | 2 | | 2 | | **16** | 1 | 2 | **19** |
| Price, Paul | **41** | | 2 | | 2 | | **2** | | | **2** |
| Saxby, Mike | **31** | | 3 | | 1 | | **1** | 1 | | **2** |
| Smith Herbie | | | | *1* | | | | | | |
| Stein, Brian | **42** | | 3 | | 2 | | **18** | 1 | | **19** |
| Stephens, Kirk | **40** | | 3 | | 1 | | **1** | | | **1** |
| Turner, Wayne | **1** | | | | | | | | | |
| West, Alan | **16** | *9* | 1 | | 2 | | | | | |
| White, Steve | **19** | *2* | 1 | *1* | | | **7** | | | **7** |
| **22 players used** | **462** | ***24*** | **33** | ***3*** | **22** | | **61** | **4** | **4** | **69** |

| No | Date | Att | Pos | Pt | F-A | H-T | Scorers, Times, and Referees | 1 | 2 | 3 | 4 | 5 | 6 | 7 | 8 | 9 | 10 | 11 | 12 sub used |
|---|---|---|---|---|---|---|---|---|---|---|---|---|---|---|---|---|---|---|---|
| 1 | H CHARLTON | | | W | 3-0 | 2-0 | Donaghy 22, McAllister 31 (og), | Findlay | Stephens | Aizlewood | **Horton** | Saxby | Donaghy | Hill | Stein | White | Antic | Ingram | |
| | 29/8 | **8,776** | | 3 | | | [White 59] | *Phillips J* | *Naylor* | *McAllister* | *Phillips L* | *Harrison* | *Gritt* | *Walker* | *Lansdowne* | *Ferns* | *Walsh* | *Hales* | |
| | | | | | | | Ref: D Civil | Brian Horton marks his first Luton appearance with an impressive display against a newly-promoted Charlton side who had six players making their debuts. The Valiants are swamped after Donaghy dives to head the first goal from a Horton corner. Paul Walsh hits a post for the visitors. | | | | | | | | | | | |
| 2 | A QP RANGERS | | | W | 2-1 | 0-1 | Aizlewood 70, Hill 84 | Findlay | Stephens | Aizlewood | Horton | Saxby | Donaghy | Hill | Stein | White | Antic | Ingram | |
| | 1/9 | *18,703* | | 6 | | | *King 34* | *Burridge* | *Gregory* | *Hazell* | *Roeder* | *Fenwick* | *Waddock* | *Francis* | *King* | *Flanagan* | *Stainrod* | *Allen* | |
| | | | | | | | Ref: A Robinson | In the first league game on 'plastic', the Town are apprehensive at the start and allow ex-Hatter, Andy King, to head the home side into a half-time lead. Luton use their superior skills after the break and Hill thunders in a shot from the edge of the area which deserves to win any match. | | | | | | | | | | | |
| 3 | A BOLTON | | | W | 2-1 | 0-0 | Stein 70, Aizlewood 79 | Findlay | Stephens | Aizlewood | Horton | Saxby | Donaghy | Hill | Stein | White | Antic | Ingram* | **Small** |
| | 5/9 | *6,911* | | 9 | | | *Gowling 64* | *McDonagh* | *Nicholson* | *McElhinney* | *Jones* | *Bennett* | *Gowling* | *Cantello* | *Reid* | *Hoggan* | *Thomas* | *Kidd* | |
| | | | | | | | Ref: M Baker | 'We have played much better than that and lost,' said David Pleat after the Towns' third successive win. Bolton have plenty of possession and take the lead before Brian Stein equalises from close range. The Trotters lose their confidence and Aizlewood steals the points with a low shot. | | | | | | | | | | | |
| 4 | H SHEFFIELD WED | | 3 | L | **0-3** | 0-0 | | Findlay | Stephens | Aizlewood | Horton | Saxby | Donaghy | Hill | Stein | White | Antic | Turner* | Small |
| | 12/9 | 12,131 | *1* | 9 | | | *McCulloch 60, Megson 73, Bannister 83* | *Bolder* | *Sterland* | *Smith* | *Shirtliff* | *Williamson* | *Megson* | *Mirocevic* | *Taylor* | *Curran* | *Bannister* | *McCulloch* | |
| | | | | | | | Ref: D Vickers | The Town are steam-rollered by a young Sheffield Wednesday team who now move to the top of the league table. The Hatters are outclassed in every outfield department and only Jake Findlay earns his corn. BBC Television is pleased with its choice of game for Match of the Day. | | | | | | | | | | | |
| 5 | A LEICESTER | | 2 | W | 2-1 | 0-1 | White 46, 52 | Findlay | Stephens | Aizlewood | Horton | Saxby | Donaghy | Hill | Stein | White | Antic | Moss | |
| | 19/9 | *14,159* | *11* | 12 | | | *Lynex 39p* | *Wallington* | *Williams* | *May* | *O'Neill* | *Gibson* | *Peake* | *Wilson* | *Lynex* | *Robson* | *Melrose* | *Lineker* | |
| | | | | | | | Ref: D Shaw | The Town come from behind to win for the third time in an away game this season. Steve Lynex converts from the spot for the home side after Jake Findlay brings down Jim Melrose but the Hatters shift up a gear, after the break, and David Moss sets up two quick goals for Steve White. | | | | | | | | | | | |
| 6 | H CARDIFF | | 3 | L | 2-3 | 1-2 | Saxby 44, Antic 71 | Findlay | Stephens | Aizlewood* | Horton | Saxby | Donaghy | Hill | Stein | White | Antic | Moss | Fuccillo |
| | 22/9 | 9,015 | *17* | 12 | | | *Kitchen 8p, Sayer 31, Stevens 63* | *Healey* | *Jones* | *Pontin* | *Dwyer* | *Sullivan* | *Sayer* | *Lewis* | *Ronson* | *Kitchen* | *Stevens* | *Micallef* | |
| | | | | | | | Ref: R Lewis | Bogey-side Cardiff, who have won only one point so far this season, are gifted a two-goal lead by an over-generous defence. Peter Kitchen gets the chance to score from the spot after a handling offence by Aizlewood, after which the Hatters frantically attempt to pull the game back. | | | | | | | | | | | |
| 7 | H WATFORD | | 2 | W | 4-1 | 3-0 | Moss 33p, 37p, Stein 43, 52 | Findlay | Stephens | Aizlewood | Horton | Saxby | Donaghy | Hill | Stein | White | Fuccillo | Moss | |
| | 26/9 | 12,839 | *4* | 15 | | | *Bolton 66* | *Sherwood* | *Rice* | *Sims* | *Bolton* | *Jackett* | *Taylor* | *Callaghan* | *Blissett* | *Barnes* | *Jenkins** | *Armstrong* | *Poskett* |
| | | | | | | | Ref: B Stevens | Two penalties by Moss, the first after a foul by Gerry Armstrong on Moss and then by Ian Bolton on Stein, are followed by two strikes from Stein. The Hornets pull one back, with a deflected free-kick from Bolton, but the Hatters are able to enjoy their biggest derby win for 25 years. | | | | | | | | | | | |
| 8 | A ORIENT | | 1 | W | 3-0 | 2-0 | Aizlewood 20, Hill 25, White 74 | Findlay | Stephens | Aizlewood | Horton | Saxby | Donaghy | Hill | Stein | White | Fuccillo | Moss* | Antic |
| | 3/10 | *4,944* | *22* | 18 | | | | *Day* | *Hughton* | *Gray* | *Cunningham* | *Roffey* | *Taylor T* | *Margerrison* | *Taylor P* | *Godfrey* | *Moores** | *Jennings* | *Silkman* |
| | | | | | | | Ref: A Grey | The Hatters are in control for the whole match, the surprise being that only three goals are scored. Orient have not won since the opening day and show why they are bottom of the league by rarely threatening the Luton defence. The Town move two points clear at the top of the table. | | | | | | | | | | | |
| 9 | A OLDHAM | | 1 | D | 1-1 | 0-1 | White 84 | Findlay | Stephens | Aizlewood | Horton | Saxby* | Donaghy | Hill | Stein | White | Fuccillo | Moss | Antic |
| | 10/10 | *8,403* | *4* | 19 | | | *Wylde 37* | *McDonnell* | *Hoolickin* | *Clements* | *Futcher* | *Ryan* | *Sinclair* | *Heaton* | *Atkinson* | *Palmer* | *Wylde* | *Steel* | |
| | | | | | | | Ref: P Richardson | The 100% away record is lost as the Latics outplay the Town in the first period and then hold on as the Hatters fight back. Rodger Wylde taps in the rebound after Roger Palmer heads against the post. Steve White equalises, hitting a 20-yard shot which flies into the top corner of the net. | | | | | | | | | | | |
| 10 | H GRIMSBY | | 1 | W | **6-0** | 3-0 | Fuccillo 13, Moss 22p, | Findlay | Stephens | Aizlewood* | Horton | Saxby | Donaghy | Hill | Stein | White | Fuccillo | Moss | Bunn |
| | 17/10 | 9,090 | *15* | 22 | | | [White 34, 55, 60, 70] | *Batch* | *Moore D* | *Czuczman* | *Moore K* | *Crombie* | *Waters* | *Brolly* | *Mitchell* | *Ford** | *Whymark* | *Drinkell* | *Kilmore* |
| | | | | | | | Ref: B Daniels | Grimsby help to make this an open contest and are unlucky to catch the Town in such form as, on any normal day, they would have netted at least a couple of goals themselves. Moss converts the penalty after Stein is fouled by Dean Crombie and White scores four to silence his critics. | | | | | | | | | | | |

| No / Date | Venue | Opponent / Att | Pos | Res / Pts | F-A | H-T | Scorers, Times, and Referees | 1 | 2 | 3 | 4 | 5 | 6 | 7 | 8 | 9 | 10 | 11 | 12 sub used |
|---|---|---|---|---|---|---|---|---|---|---|---|---|---|---|---|---|---|---|---|
| 11 | A | WREXHAM | 1 | W | 2-0 | 2-0 | Donaghy 28, White 44 | Findlay | Stephens | Goodyear | Horton | Saxby | Donaghy | Hill | Stein | White | Fuccillo | Moss | |
| 24/10 | | ***4,059*** | 20 | 25 | | | | *Niedzwiecki* | *Jones* | *Dowman* | *Cegielski* | *Bater* | *Ronson* | *Carrodus* | *McNeil* | *Fox* | *Edwards* | *Vinter** | *Hunt* |
| | | | | | | | Ref: H King | On a saturated pitch Luton show more purpose, with David Moss hitting the bar before Mal Donaghy catches one right, firing his shot into the top corner of the net to open the scoring. Steve White splashes through for his tenth goal of the season to preserve the unbeaten away record. | | | | | | | | | | | |
| 12 | H | CRYS PALACE | 1 | W | 1-0 | 1-0 | Moss 29p | Findlay | Stephens | Goodyear | Horton | Saxby* | Donaghy | Hill | Stein | White | Fuccillo | Moss | Antic |
| 31/10 | | 11,712 | *14* | 28 | | | | *Barron* | *Bason* | *Cannon* | *Gilbert* | *Lovell* | *Galliers* | *Murphy* | *Smillie* | *Brooks** | *Mabbutt* | *Langley* | *Price* |
| | | | | | | | Ref: D Reeves | Steve White is tripped by Steve Lovell in the area and David Moss converts from the spot. Mike Saxby goes off with a knee injury after turning awkwardly, the resulting damage effectively ending his playing career. The Town have now gone nearly seven hours without conceding a goal. | | | | | | | | | | | |
| 13 | H | DERBY | 1 | W | 3-2 | 1-0 | Moss 37, Goodyear 65, Donaghy 76 | Findlay | Stephens | Goodyear | Horton | Aizlewood | Donaghy | Hill | Stein | White | Fuccillo | Moss | |
| 7/11 | | 10,784 | *17* | 31 | | | *Osgood 75, Clayton 88* | *Jones* | *Coop* | *Powell S* | *Sheridan* | *Buckley* | *Powell B* | *Reid** | *Hector* | *Wilson* | *Clayton* | *Emson* | *Osgood* |
| | | | | | | | Ref: T Bune | The Hatters go three points clear at the top, despite not being at their best against the Rams. It is only when Mal Donaghy heads the third goal that the match is made safe, although the final scoreline flatters the visitors. 'We will have to play better than this to stay at the top,' says Pleat. | | | | | | | | | | | |
| 14 | A | BLACKBURN | 1 | W | 1-0 | 0-0 | Moss 79p | Aleksic | Stephens | Goodyear | Horton | Aizlewood | Donaghy | Hill | Stein | White | Fuccillo | Moss | |
| 14/11 | | *9,862* | *8* | 34 | | | | *Gennoe* | *Branagan* | *Keeley** | *Fazackerley* | *Rathbone* | *Stonehouse* | *Miller* | *Burke* | *Lowey* | *Garner* | *Brotherston* | *Comstive* |
| | | | | | | | Ref: T Mills | White has a nightmare of a game and misses several good chances. David Moss scores the first Luton goal at Ewood Park since 1959 when he converts a penalty, awarded after Terry Gennoe upends Brian Stein. Milija Aleksic, on loan from Tottenham, is largely idle in the Hatters' goal. | | | | | | | | | | | |
| 15 | A | NEWCASTLE | 1 | L | 2-3 | 0-2 | Moss 83p, Donaghy 88 | Aleksic | Stephens | Aizlewood | Horton | Goodyear* | Donaghy | Hill | Stein | White | Fuccillo | Moss | Antic |
| 21/11 | | *21,084* | *8* | 34 | | | *Brown 1, 37, Varadi 89* | *Carr* | *Brownlie* | *Carney* | *Haddock* | *Saunders* | *Trewick* | *Wharton* | *Martin* | *Brown** | *Varadi* | *Waddle* | *Shoulder* |
| | | | | | | | Ref: T Fitzharris | Newcastle are two up and cruising when Stein is tripped by Wes Saunders, leaving Moss to score from the spot. The Town push forward but are unable to hold on as ex-Luton trialist, Imre Varadi, scores a spectacular winner in the final minute to end the Hatters' unbeaten away record. | | | | | | | | | | | |
| 16 | H | BOLTON | 1 | W | 2-0 | 0-0 | Stein 67, Moss 80 | Aleksic* | Stephens | Aizlewood | Horton | Goodyear | Donaghy | Hill | Stein | White | Fuccillo | Moss | Antic |
| 24/11 | | 8,889 | *21* | 37 | | | | *McDonagh* | *Whitworth* | *Jones* | *McElhinney* | *Bailey* | *Henry* | *Cantello* | *Hoggan* | *Chandler* | *Thompson** | *Carter* | *Foster* |
| | | | | | | | Ref: J Hunting | Battling against the drop, the Trotters defend in depth but cannot prevent Stein scoring his first goal in ten games to break the deadlock. Moss makes the points safe when scoring direct from a free-kick. Aleksic is injured in the final minute and Donaghy takes over between the sticks. | | | | | | | | | | | |
| 17 | H | ROTHERHAM | 1 | W | 3-1 | 0-0 | White 49, Donaghy 64, Stein 65 | Aleksic | Stephens | Aizlewood | Horton | Goodyear | Donaghy | Hill | Stein | White | Fuccillo | Moss | |
| 28/11 | | 11,061 | *18* | 40 | | | *Fern 57* | *Mountford* | *Forrest* | *Stancliffe* | *Green* | *Taylor* | *Rhodes* | *Gooding* | *Henson* | *Towner* | *Moore* | *Fern** | *Seasman* |
| | | | | | | | Ref: J Bray | Two goals in a minute are enough to finish off a fighting Rotherham side who had equalised through ex-Town forward, Rodney Fern. Millers' manager, Emlyn Hughes, reckons that the Hatters defend better than they attack. Luton are now ten points clear at the top of the league table. | | | | | | | | | | | |
| 18 | A | SHREWSBURY | 1 | D | 2-2 | 1-2 | White 15, Donaghy 76 | Judge | Stephens | Aizlewood | Horton | Goodyear | Donaghy | Hill* | Stein | White | Fuccillo | Moss | Antic |
| 5/12 | | *5,529* | *14* | 41 | | | *Dungworth 5, Atkins 32* | *Wardle* | *MacLaren* | *Griffin* | *Keay* | *Johnson* | *Cross* | *Tong* | *McNally* | *Bates* | *Dungworth* | *Atkins* | |
| | | | | | | | Ref: K Hackett | Treating the game like a cup-tie, the Shrews take a deserved interval lead through their effort and hard work. The Hatters are more determined in the second period and Donaghy equalises after a blind-side run. A scrambling save is required from Wardle to stop Luton from taking the lead. | | | | | | | | | | | |
| 19 | A | NORWICH | 1 | W | 3-1 | 3-1 | Antic 3, White 10, Stein 14 | Findlay | Stephens | Aizlewood | Horton | Goodyear | Donaghy | Antic | Stein | White | Fuccillo | Moss | |
| 28/12 | | *18,458* | *12* | 44 | | | *Deehan 43* | *Woods* | *Symonds* | *Walford* | *Watson* | *Downs* | *Barham* | *Muzinic** | *McGuire* | *Bennett* | *Deehan* | *Bertschin* | *Mendham* |
| | | | | | | | Ref: M Scott | The Town are unstoppable in the first 15 minutes but then sit back, allowing the Canaries to come back in to the game. Norwich pull a goal back, just before the interval, when John Deehan has a simple tap-in. Moss and Brian Horton both strike the bar in an end-to-end second-half. | | | | | | | | | | | |
| 20 | A | CHARLTON | 1 | D | 0-0 | 0-0 | | Findlay | Stephens | Aizlewood | Antic | Goodyear | Donaghy | Hill | Stein | White | Fuccillo | Moss | |
| 19/1 | | *7,013* | *9* | 45 | | | | *Johns* | *Naylor* | *Berry* | *Phillips* | *Ferns* | *Ambrose* | *Elliott* | *Gritt* | *Robinson* | *Hales* | *Walsh* | |
| | | | | | | | Ref: A Glasson | The first league game for over three weeks sees the Town having to battle on a pitch thick with mud. Both sides miss several opportunities but too often the attacks are bogged down. Ipswich manager Bobby Robson, who is on a spying mission ahead of the FA Cup-tie, learns little. | | | | | | | | | | | |
| 21 | H | LEICESTER | 1 | W | 2-1 | 1-0 | White 13, Donaghy 67 | Judge | Stephens | Aizlewood | Horton | Goodyear | Donaghy | Hill | Stein | White | Fuccillo* | Moss | Antic |
| 30/1 | | 11,810 | *14* | 48 | | | *Lineker 52* | *Wallington* | *Williams* | *May* | *O'Neill* | *Friar* | *Peake* | *Wilson* | *Ramsey** | *Lynex* | *Lineker* | *Young* | *Melrose* |
| | | | | | | | Ref: J Moules | The FA Cup defeat is swept aside when, in front of the TV cameras, Steve White heads the Town into a half-time lead. Some slack defending allows the visitors to equalise through Gary Lineker before a header from Donaghy, following a corner kick from David Moss, wins both points. | | | | | | | | | | | |

| No | Date | Att | Pos | Pt | F-A | H-T | Scorers, Times, and Referees | 1 | 2 | 3 | 4 | 5 | 6 | 7 | 8 | 9 | 10 | 11 | 12 sub used |
|---|---|---|---|---|---|---|---|---|---|---|---|---|---|---|---|---|---|---|---|
| 22 | A SHEFFIELD WED | | 1 | D | 3-3 | 1-1 | White 11, Moss 49p, Stein 89 | Judge | Stephens | Aizlewood | Horton | Goodyear | Donaghy | Hill | Stein | White | Fuccillo | Moss* | Antic |
| | 6/2 | *18,252* | *6* | 49 | | | *Pearson 25, 75, Bannister 82* | *Bolder* | *Sterland* | *Shirtliff Pete* | *Pickering* | *Williamson* | *Smith* | *Megson !* | *Shirtliff Paul* | *Mellor** | *Pearson* | *Bannister* | *Owen* |
| | | | | | | | Ref: J Lovatt | Aggressive Wednesday are made to pay for their intimidation when Gary Megson is sent off for a bad foul on Horton after 88 minutes, Luton equalising soon after. The Town had only three chances to score and took them all. Moss scores from the spot after a theatrical fall in the area. | | | | | | | | | | | |
| 23 | A WATFORD | | 1 | D | 1-1 | 1-1 | Stein 33 | Findlay | Stephens | Aizlewood | Horton | Goodyear | Donaghy | Hill | Stein | White | Fuccillo | Moss | |
| | 20/2 | ***22,798*** | *2* | 50 | | | *Rostron 8* | *Sherwood* | *Rice* | *Terry* | *Bolton* | *Rostron* | *Taylor* | *Blissett** | *Lohman* | *Callaghan* | *Jenkins* | *Barnes* | *Armstrong* |
| | | | | | | | Ref: K Hackett | The Town are a class above their arch-rivals, Watford, but allow the Hornets to gain Graham Taylor his first point against the Hatters in six meetings. Rostron fires into the top corner of the net from 25 yards before Stein turns Steve Terry inside-out and then equalises with a low shot. | | | | | | | | | | | |
| 24 | H OLDHAM | | 1 | W | 2-0 | 1-0 | Moss 8p, 55 | Findlay | Stephens | Aizlewood | Horton | Goodyear | Donaghy | Hill | Stein | White | Fuccillo | Moss | |
| | 27/2 | 11,506 | *3* | 53 | | | | *McDonnell* | *Edwards* | *Clements* | *Futcher* | *Ryan* | *Keegan* | *Heaton** | *McDonough !* | *Atkinson* | *Wylde* | *Palmer* | *Anderson* |
| | | | | | | | Ref: M Robinson | Third-placed Oldham are made to look second best against a Town side which strolls to victory. Ex-Hatter Paul Futcher pulls down Stein and David Moss scores his ninth penalty of the season. The Latics midfield player Darron McDonough is sent off after a late tackle on Lil Fuccillo. | | | | | | | | | | | |
| 25 | H CAMBRIDGE | | 1 | W | 1-0 | 0-0 | Horton 76 | Findlay | Stephens | Aizlewood | Horton | Goodyear | Donaghy | Hill | Stein | White | Fuccillo* | Moss | Antic |
| | 2/3 | 10,597 | *14* | 56 | | | | *Key* | *Donaldson* | *Smith* | *Fallon* | *Turner* | *Murray* | *O'Neill** | *Spriggs* | *Gibbins* | *Reilly* | *Mayo* | *Cartwright* |
| | | | | | | | Ref: D Letts | Cambridge come for a point and, playing with nine men at the back, very nearly achieve their objective. Brian Horton smacks in a shot from 30 yards midway through the second half, but the visitors are unable to break their defensive formation and the Hatters record another easy win. | | | | | | | | | | | |
| 26 | A GRIMSBY | | 1 | D | 0-0 | 0-0 | | Findlay | Stephens | Aizlewood | Horton | Goodyear | Donaghy | Hill | Stein | White | Antic | Moss | |
| | 6/3 | *7,734* | *21* | 57 | | | | *Batch* | *Moore D* | *Cooper* | *Moore K* | *Crombie* | *Waters* | *Brolly* | *Mitchell* | *Ford* | *Drinkell* | *Cumming* | |
| | | | | | | | Ref: R Nixon | The Mariners play their best football for months and succeed in keeping the Town at bay. The Hatters have the better chances in a game played in wet and windy conditions and David Moss believes that he should have been awarded a first-half penalty when he is fouled by Dean Crombie. | | | | | | | | | | | |
| 27 | H WREXHAM | | 1 | D | 0-0 | 0-0 | | Findlay | Stephens | Aizlewood* | Horton | Goodyear | Donaghy | Hill | Stein | White | Antic | Moss | Bunn |
| | 12/3 | 10,880 | *20* | 58 | | | | *Niedzwiecki* | *Hill* | *Dowman* | *Cegielski* | *Bater* | *Ronson* | *Leman* | *McNeil* | *Carrodus* | *Fox* | *Buxton* | |
| | | | | | | | Ref: A Gunn | The Hatters run of nine consecutive home wins comes to an end in a dreadful game where Wrexham seem to pass back to their goalkeeper at every opportunity. Mark Aizlewood is injured in the first half and the reshuffled formation never looks likely to break down the Welsh defence. | | | | | | | | | | | |
| 28 | A BARNSLEY | | 1 | L | 3-4 | 1-1 | Stein 10, 55, Law 80 (og) | Findlay | Stephens | Aizlewood | Horton | Goodyear | Donaghy | Hill | Stein | White | Fuccillo* | Moss | Antic |
| | 16/3 | *14,044* | *10* | 58 | | | *Walker 44, 53, Banks 67, Evans 75* | *Horn* | *Law* | *McCarthy* | *Evans* | *Chambers* | *Glavin* | *Banks* | *Mann* | *Walker* | *Aylott* | *Birch* | |
| | | | | | | | Ref: N Wilson | The Hatters have now gone three games without a win, suffering their first defeat since November. The Tykes are well worth their victory and only a late own-goal from Nicky Law gives the scoreline an unrealistic look. Colin Walker scores twice and has a goal disallowed for hand-ball. | | | | | | | | | | | |
| 29 | A CRYS PALACE | | 1 | D | 3-3 | 3-2 | Antic 12, Moss 14p, Stein 38 | Findlay | Stephens | Turner | Horton | Goodyear | Donaghy | Hill | Stein | White | Antic | Moss | |
| | 20/3 | *12,187* | *16* | 59 | | | *Smillie 8, 76, Mabbutt 13* | *Barron* | *Hinshelwood* | *Wicks* | *Gilbert* | *Boulter* | *Murphy* | *Giles* | *Smillie* | *Cannon* | *Langley** | *Mabbutt* | *Hilaire* |
| | | | | | | | Ref: C White | The Hatters are going through a bad patch but fight back to take the lead, after twice going behind, only to concede a late equaliser after Horton loses possession. The penalty from Moss is scored after Hinshelwood fouls Steve White. Watford are now level on points at the top of the table. | | | | | | | | | | | |
| 30 | A DERBY | | 2 | D | 0-0 | 0-0 | | Findlay | Stephens | **Money** | Horton | Goodyear | Donaghy | Hill | Stein | White | Turner | Moss | |
| | 27/3 | *15,836* | *15* | 60 | | | | *Banovic* | *Barton* | *Sheridan* | *McAlle* | *Buckley* | *Skivington* | *Attley* | *Emson* | *George* | *Wilson* | *Swindlehurst* | |
| | | | | | | | Ref: D Webb | Richard Money makes an impressive debut as the Hatters stroll through the game knowing that a point will be sufficient to keep their promotion hopes alive, bearing in mind the number of home games which are still to come. Brian Stein is the only Luton forward that looks likely to score. | | | | | | | | | | | |
| 31 | H ORIENT | | 1 | W | 2-0 | 0-0 | Moss 62p, Hill 71 | Findlay | Stephens | Money | Horton | Goodyear | Donaghy | Hill | Stein | White | Turner | Moss | |
| | 30/3 | 9,716 | *21* | 63 | | | | *Day* | *Banjo* | *Foster* | *Gray* | *Peach* | *Fisher* | *Godfrey* | *Silkman* | *Sussex* | *Houchen* | *Moores** | *Hughton* |
| | | | | | | | Ref: T Spencer | Dogged Orient, who are trying to avoid the drop, fight hard for a point but are undone when Mervyn Day brings down Stein in the area and the disputed penalty-kick is slotted home by Moss. Hill completes the scoring when taking a return pass from White. Town win 10-0 on corners. | | | | | | | | | | | |

| | | | | | | | | | | | | | | | | | | | | | |
|---|---|---|---|---|---|---|---|---|---|---|---|---|---|---|---|---|---|---|---|---|---|
| 32 | H | BLACKBURN | | 1 | W | | 2-0 | 1-0 | Stein 27, White 70 | Findlay | Stephens | Money | Horton | Goodyear | Donaghy | Hill* | Stein | White | Turner | Moss | **Jennings** |
| | | 3/4 | 10,721 | *6* | | 66 | | | | *Gennoe* | *Branagan* | *Keeley* | *Fazackerley* | *Rathbone* | *Miller* | *Speight* | *Stonehouse* | *Bell* | *Garner** | *Brotherston* | *Hamilton* |
| | | | | | | | | | Ref: A Grey | The Town end up as comfortable winners against the team with the best defensive record in the division. Stein opens the scoring when, after rounding Terry Gennoe, he fires in a shot from a narrow angle. Steve White makes sure of both points with a sharp shot struck on the turn. | | | | | | | | | | | |
| 33 | A | CAMBRIDGE | | 1 | D | | 1-1 | 0-0 | Turner 62 | Findlay | Stephens | Money | Horton | Goodyear | Donaghy | Antic | Stein | White | Turner* | Moss | Fuccillo |
| | | 10/4 | *8,815* | *15* | | 67 | | | *Reilly 63* | *Webster* | *Donaldson* | *Fallon* | *Smith* | *Murray* | *Cartwright* | *Finney* | *Gibbins* | *Street* | *Reilly* | *Christie* | |
| | | | | | | | | | Ref: M Baker | In front of a large, travelling Luton contingent, Wayne Turner scores his first ever league goal when taking advantage of a poor pass from Les Cartwright to hit his shot from the edge of the area. The U's equalise when a Reilly header bounces off several legs before going into the net. | | | | | | | | | | | |
| 34 | H | NORWICH | | 1 | W | | 2-0 | 0-0 | Stein 54, Jennings 57 | Findlay | Stephens | Money | Horton | Goodyear | Donaghy | Hill | Stein | White | Fuccillo | Moss* | Jennings |
| | | 12/4 | 15,061 | *9* | | 70 | | | | *Woods* | *Haylock** | *Walford* | *Watson* | *Downs* | *McGuire* | *O'Neill* | *Mendham* | *Deehan* | *Bertschin* | *Barham* | *Jack* |
| | | | | | | | | | Ref: B Martin | The Canaries are unlucky not to score at least twice before the interval as Dave Watson scoops the ball over the Luton goal and Greg Downs hits a post. Two quick goals, from Stein and Jennings, turn the game and the players now believe the championship to be there for the taking. | | | | | | | | | | | |
| 35 | H | NEWCASTLE | | 1 | W | | 3-2 | 0-1 | Stein 63, 81p, 85p | Findlay | Stephens | Money | Horton | Goodyear | Donaghy | Antic | Stein | White | Fuccillo | Turner | |
| | | 17/4 | 13,041 | *7* | | 73 | | | *Mills 23, Trewick 57p* | *Carr* | *Brownlie* | *Barton** | *Haddock* | *Saunders* | *Trewick* | *Martin* | *Cartwright* | *Mills* | *Varadi* | *Waddle* | *Wharton* |
| | | | | | | | | | Ref: A Seville | Missing both Moss and Hill through injury, the reshuffled Town side allows the Magpies to take a two-goal lead before fighting back with Stein scoring a memorable hat-trick. The two late penalties are both poorly struck but, on each occasion, Kevin Carr obligingly dives the wrong way. | | | | | | | | | | | |
| 36 | H | CHELSEA | | 1 | D | | 2-2 | 1-1 | Antic 44, Donaghy 76 | Findlay | Stephens | Money | Horton | Goodyear | Donaghy | Hill | Stein | White | Fuccillo | Antic | |
| | | 20/4 | 16,185 | *11* | | 74 | | | *Walker 34, Fillery 61* | *Francis* | *Locke* | *Nutton* | *Lee* | *Hutchings* | *Pates* | *Britton* | *Chivers* | *Fillery* | *Walker* | *Mayes* | |
| | | | | | | | | | Ref: A Hamil | Luton are limping closer towards the championship after allowing the Blues to steal a point in an end-to-end game. The Hatters fight back to equalise twice but Chelsea, who attack on the break, cause a few scares and may have won, even though the Town had the majority of the play. | | | | | | | | | | | |
| 37 | A | ROTHERHAM | | 1 | D | | 2-2 | 1-1 | Fuccillo 12, Money 65 | Judge | Stephens | Money | Horton | Goodyear | Donaghy | Hill* | Stein | White | Fuccillo | Moss | Antic |
| | | 24/4 | *11,290* | *7* | | 75 | | | *Moore 28, Seasman 64* | *Mountford* | *Hughes* | *Stancliffe* | *Green* | *Breckin* | *Rhodes** | *Gow* | *McEwan* | *Towner* | *Moore* | *Seasman* | *Alexander* |
| | | | | | | | | | Ref: D Scott | Alan Judge deputises in goal for the injured Findlay and saves an injury-time penalty from Gerry Gow, harshly awarded for a handball offence against Goodyear. The Millers are making a late bid for promotion and play above themselves but Luton are equal to all that is thrown at them. | | | | | | | | | | | |
| 38 | H | SHREWSBURY | | 1 | W | | 4-1 | 1-0 | Stein 14, Hill 78, White 80, Moss 88 | Findlay | Stephens | Money | Horton | Goodyear | Donaghy | Hill | Stein | White | Fuccillo* | Moss | Antic |
| | | 30/4 | 14,563 | *21* | | 78 | | | *Atkins 60* | *Wardle* | *MacLaren* | *Griffin* | *Keay* | *Johnson** | *Turner* | *McNally* | *Tong* | *Bates* | *Atkins* | *Cross* | *Petts* |
| | | | | | | | | | Ref: B Hill | Brian Stein lobs an early opening goal but Ian Atkins levels after the break. A superb volley from Ricky Hill opens the floodgates and the Town then go on to record a famous victory and clinch promotion to Division One. The happy supporters storm onto the pitch at the end of the game. | | | | | | | | | | | |
| 39 | A | CHELSEA | | 1 | W | | 2-1 | 1-1 | Antic 25, Stein 54 | Findlay | Stephens | Money | Horton | Goodyear | Donaghy | Antic | Stein | White | Fuccillo | Moss | |
| | | 8/5 | *15,044* | *11* | | 81 | | | *Walker 44* | *Francis* | *Locke* | *Lee* | *Droy* | *Hutchings* | *Pates* | *Chivers* | *Fillery* | *Rh's-Brown** | *Mayes* | *Walker* | *Canoville* |
| | | | | | | | | | Ref: M Taylor | The Chelsea players present champagne to the Hatters before the game, a gesture which does not stop the Town from winning a scrappy match. Antic scores with a 25-yard free-kick and, after Clive Walker equalises for the home side, Brian Stein strikes the winner from an acute angle. | | | | | | | | | | | |
| 40 | H | QP RANGERS | | 1 | W | | 3-2 | 1-0 | Hill 36, White 48, Moss 80p | Findlay | Stephens | Money | Horton | Goodyear | Donaghy | Hill | Stein | White | Antic | Moss | |
| | | 11/5 | **16,657** | *7* | | 84 | | | *Fenwick 69, Stainrod 85* | *Hucker* | *Neill* | *Wicks* | *Roeder !* | *Dawes* | *Waddock* | *Micklewhite* | *Flanagan* | *Fenwick* | *Allen* | *Stainrod* | |
| | | | | | | | | | Ref: K Baker | The FA Cup finalists are down to ten men when skipper Roeder is sent off after a second bookable offence on 32 minutes. Luton move into a two-goal lead before Rangers reduce the deficit with a diving header from Fenwick. Moss converts from the spot after he is tripped by Wicks. | | | | | | | | | | | |
| 41 | H | BARNSLEY | | 1 | D | | 1-1 | 0-0 | Stein 87 | Findlay | Stephens | Money | Horton | Goodyear | Donaghy | Hill | Stein | White | Fuccillo* | Moss | Antic |
| | | 15/5 | 14,483 | *6* | | 85 | | | *Birch 50p* | *Horn* | *Law* | *McCarthy* | *Evans* | *Chambers* | *Riley* | *Banks* | *McHale* | *Walker* | *Aylott* | *Birch* | |
| | | | | | | | | | Ref: J Martin | The championship trophy is presented before the kick-off but the game itself is an anti-climax. Barnsley take the lead when Alan Birch scores from the spot after he is pulled down by Findlay. Stein hits a late equaliser with a tremendous shot into the top corner from the edge of the area. | | | | | | | | | | | |
| 42 | A | CARDIFF | | 1 | W | | 3-2 | 1-0 | Stein 22, 81, Donaghy 72 | Findlay | Stephens | Money | Horton | Goodyear | Donaghy | Hill | Stein | White | Antic | Moss* | Small |
| | | 17/5 | *10,277* | *20* | | 88 | | | *Kitchen 83, Micallef 87* | *Healey* | *Jones* | *Pontin* | *Mullen* | *Henderson* | *Micallef* | *Grapes** | *Bennett G* | *Gilbert* | *Stevens* | *Bennett D* | *Kitchen* |
| | | Home | Away | | | | | | Ref: A Robinson | Cardiff are relegated as the Town end their season in style with a victory which was far more emphatic than the scoreline suggests. The Hatters cruise into a three-goal lead but then allow the Bluebirds back into the game during the last minutes. Luton finish the campaign with 88 points. | | | | | | | | | | | |
| Average | | 11,881 | 12,149 | | | | | | | | | | | | | | | | | | |

| League Cup | | F-A | H-T | Scorers, Times, and Referees | 1 | 2 | 3 | 4 | 5 | 6 | 7 | 8 | 9 | 10 | 11 | 12 sub used |
|---|---|---|---|---|---|---|---|---|---|---|---|---|---|---|---|---|
| 2:1 H WREXHAM | 1 L | 0-2 | 0-2 | | Findlay | Stephens | Antic | Horton | Saxby | Donaghy | Hill | Stein | White | Fuccillo | Moss | |
| 6/10 | 6,146 *2:19* | | | *Vinter 2, Hunt 23* | *Niedzwiecki* | *Jones* | *Dowman* | *Cegielski* | *Bater* | *Hunt* | *Fox* | *McNeil* | *Carrodus* | *Edwards* | *Vinter* | |
| | | | | Ref: V Callow | Wrexham by-pass the Luton midfield and attack on the break to good effect. After the Hatters concede two early goals they face a stiff, uphill battle which they are never likely to win. Moss hits the post from a free-kick, an effort which proves to be the closest the Town come to scoring. | | | | | | | | | | | |
| 2:2 A WREXHAM | 1 W | 1-0 | 0-0 | White 89 | Findlay | Stephens | Goodyear* | Horton | Saxby | Donaghy | Hill | Stein | White | Fuccillo | Moss | Ingram |
| 27/10 | *3,453 2:20* | | | | *Niedzwiecki* | *Jones** | *Dowman* | *Cegielski* | *Baker* | *Hunt* | *Hill* | *McNeil* | *Carrodus* | *Edwards* | *Vinter* | *Fox* |
| | | | | Ref: N Midgley (Hatters lose 1-2 on aggregate) | Three days after winning at the Racecourse Ground in the league, the Town are unable to overturn the two-goal deficit from the first leg. Moss is pushed in the area by Steve Dowman but his penalty is comfortably saved. White scores a consolation goal in the final minute after a solo run. | | | | | | | | | | | |

| FA Cup | | F-A | H-T | Scorers, Times, and Referees | 1 | 2 | 3 | 4 | 5 | 6 | 7 | 8 | 9 | 10 | 11 | 12 sub used |
|---|---|---|---|---|---|---|---|---|---|---|---|---|---|---|---|---|
| 3 H SWINDON | 1 W | 2-1 | 1-0 | Moss 19p, Horton 88 | Findlay | Stephens | Aizlewood | Horton | Goodyear | Donaghy | Hill | Stein | White | Fuccillo | Moss | |
| 2/1 | 9,488 *3:20* | | | *Emmanuel 75* | *Allen* | *Baddeley* | *Lewis* | *Stroud* | *Henry* | *Williams* | *Emmanuel* | *Carter* | *Pritchard* | *Rowland* | *Rideout* | |
| | | | | Ref: A Grey | Swindon level the tie with just 15 minutes remaining. Then Paul Rideout is flattened outside the area but recovers quickly to slot the ball into the net, but his effort is disallowed as the ref had already blown for the foul. The Hatters ride their luck and score the winner right at the end. | | | | | | | | | | | |
| 4 H IPSWICH | 1 L | 0-3 | 0-0 | | Findlay | Stephens | Aizlewood* | Horton | Goodyear | Donaghy | Hill | Stein | White | Fuccillo | Moss | Antic |
| 23/1 | 20,188 *1:1* | | | *Brazil 62, Gates 71, 87* | *Cooper* | *Burley* | *Osman* | *Butcher** | *McCall* | *Mills* | *Muhren* | *Wark* | *Gates* | *Brazil* | *Mariner* | *O'Callaghan* |
| | | | | Ref: C Thomas | The Town give as good as they get in the first period but are then sunk by a three-goal salvo from the 1st division leaders in the second period. 'Luton need not be frightened if they go into the first division; they will not meet teams like us every week,' says Paul Mariner, after the game. | | | | | | | | | | | |

| | | Home | | | | | Away | | | | | |
|---|---|---|---|---|---|---|---|---|---|---|---|---|
| | P | W | D | L | F | A | W | D | L | F | A | Pts |
| 1 LUTON TOWN | 42 | 16 | 3 | 2 | 48 | 19 | 9 | 10 | 2 | 38 | 27 | 88 |
| 2 Watford | 42 | 13 | 6 | 2 | 46 | 16 | 10 | 5 | 6 | 30 | 26 | 80 |
| 3 Norwich | 42 | 14 | 3 | 4 | 41 | 19 | 8 | 2 | 11 | 23 | 31 | 71 |
| 4 Sheffield Wed | 42 | 10 | 8 | 3 | 31 | 23 | 10 | 2 | 9 | 24 | 28 | 70 |
| 5 QP Rangers | 42 | 15 | 4 | 2 | 40 | 9 | 6 | 2 | 13 | 25 | 34 | 69 |
| 6 Barnsley | 42 | 13 | 4 | 4 | 33 | 14 | 6 | 6 | 9 | 26 | 27 | 67 |
| 7 Rotherham | 42 | 13 | 5 | 3 | 42 | 19 | 7 | 2 | 12 | 24 | 35 | 67 |
| 8 Leicester | 42 | 12 | 5 | 4 | 31 | 19 | 6 | 7 | 8 | 25 | 29 | 66 |
| 9 Newcastle | 42 | 14 | 4 | 3 | 30 | 14 | 4 | 4 | 13 | 22 | 36 | 62 |
| 10 Blackburn | 42 | 11 | 4 | 6 | 26 | 15 | 5 | 7 | 9 | 21 | 28 | 59 |
| 11 Oldham | 42 | 9 | 9 | 3 | 28 | 23 | 6 | 5 | 10 | 22 | 28 | 59 |
| 12 Chelsea | 42 | 10 | 5 | 6 | 37 | 30 | 5 | 7 | 9 | 23 | 30 | 57 |
| 13 Charlton | 42 | 11 | 5 | 5 | 33 | 22 | 2 | 7 | 12 | 17 | 43 | 51 |
| 14 Cambridge | 42 | 11 | 4 | 6 | 31 | 19 | 2 | 5 | 14 | 17 | 34 | 48 |
| 15 Crys Palace | 42 | 9 | 2 | 10 | 25 | 26 | 4 | 7 | 10 | 9 | 19 | 48 |
| 16 Derby | 42 | 9 | 8 | 4 | 32 | 23 | 3 | 4 | 14 | 21 | 45 | 48 |
| 17 Grimsby | 42 | 5 | 8 | 8 | 29 | 30 | 6 | 5 | 10 | 24 | 35 | 46 |
| 18 Shrewsbury | 42 | 10 | 6 | 5 | 26 | 19 | 1 | 7 | 13 | 11 | 38 | 46 |
| 19 Bolton | 42 | 10 | 4 | 7 | 28 | 24 | 3 | 3 | 15 | 11 | 37 | 46 |
| 20 Cardiff | 42 | 9 | 2 | 10 | 28 | 32 | 3 | 6 | 12 | 17 | 29 | 44 |
| 21 Wrexham | 42 | 9 | 4 | 8 | 22 | 22 | 2 | 7 | 12 | 18 | 34 | 44 |
| 22 Orient | 42 | 6 | 8 | 7 | 23 | 24 | 4 | 1 | 16 | 13 | 37 | 39 |
| | 924 | 239 | 111 | 112 | 710 | 461 | 112 | 111 | 239 | 461 | 710 | 1275 |

Odds & ends

Double wins: (6) Blackburn, Bolton, Leicester, Norwich, Orient, QPR.
Double losses: (0).

Won from behind: (4) Bolton (a), Leicester (a), Newcastle (h), QPR (a).
Lost from in front: (1) Barnsley (a).

High spots: The Division 2 championship, won by a mile in glorious style!
An unbeaten run of seven away games at the start of the season.
A 14-game unbeaten run at the end of the season.
A 4-1 home win over Watford.
The 6-0 home thrashing of Grimsby, with Steve White hitting four.

Low spots: A run of five games without a win in March.
The home defeat by Ipswich Town in the FA Cup.

Player of the Year: Ricky Hill.
Ever-presents: (4) Mal Donaghy, Brian Stein, Kirk Stephens, Steve White.
Hat-tricks: Brian Stein (1), Steve White (1).
Leading scorer: Brian Stein (21).

| | Appearances | | | | | | Goals | | | |
|---|---|---|---|---|---|---|---|---|---|---|
| | Lge | *Sub* | LC | *Sub* | FAC | *Sub* | Lge | LC | FAC | Tot |
| Aizlewood, Mark | **26** | | | | 2 | | **3** | | | **3** |
| Aleksic, Milija | **4** | | | | | | | | | |
| Antic, Raddy | **17** | *13* | 1 | | | *1* | **5** | | | **5** |
| Bunn, Frank | | *2* | | | | | | | | |
| Donaghy, Mal | **42** | | 2 | | 2 | | **9** | | | **9** |
| Findlay, Jake | **34** | | 2 | | 2 | | | | | |
| Fuccillo, Lil | **27** | *2* | 2 | | 2 | | **2** | | | **2** |
| Goodyear, Clive | **32** | | 1 | | 2 | | **1** | | | **1** |
| Hill, Ricky | **38** | | 2 | | 2 | | **5** | | | **5** |
| Horton, Brian | **41** | | 2 | | 2 | | **1** | | 1 | **2** |
| Ingram, Godfrey | **3** | | | *1* | | | | | | |
| Jennings, Billy | | *2* | | | | | **1** | | | **1** |
| Judge, Alan | **4** | | | | | | | | | |
| Money, Richard | **13** | | | | | | **1** | | | **1** |
| Moss, David | **36** | | 2 | | 2 | | **15** | | 1 | **16** |
| Saxby, Mike | **12** | | 2 | | | | **1** | | | **1** |
| Small, Mike | | *3* | | | | | | | | |
| Stein, Brian | **42** | | 2 | | 2 | | **21** | | | **21** |
| Stephens, Kirk | **42** | | 2 | | 2 | | | | | |
| Turner, Wayne | **7** | | | | | | **1** | | | **1** |
| White, Steve | **42** | | 2 | | 2 | | **18** | 1 | | **19** |
| (own-goals) | | | | | | | **2** | | | **2** |
| **21 players used** | **462** | *22* | **22** | *1* | **22** | *1* | **86** | **1** | **2** | **89** |

| No | Date | | Att | Pos | Pt | F-A | H-T | Scorers, Times, and Referees | 1 | 2 | 3 | 4 | 5 | 6 | 7 | 8 | 9 | 10 | 11 | 12 sub used |
|---|---|---|---|---|---|---|---|---|---|---|---|---|---|---|---|---|---|---|---|---|
| 1 | A | TOTTENHAM | | | D | 2-2 | 1-2 | Lacy 37 (og), Stein 53 | Findlay | Stephens | Money | Horton | Goodyear | Donaghy | Hill | Stein | **Walsh** | Antic | Moss | |
| | 28/8 | | *35,195* | | 1 | | | *Mabbutt 3, Hazard 19* | *Clemence* | *Hughton* | *Lacy* | *Miller* | *Perryman* | *Hazard* | *Hoddle* | *Galvin* | *Mabbutt* | *Archibald** | *Crooks* | *Brooke* |
| | | | | | | | | Ref: T Bune | The FA Cup holders open the scoring when new boy, Gary Mabbutt, heads home a Glenn Hoddle free-kick. Spurs then add a second through Hazard before the Town had settled. The Hatters then fight back and, after Stein nets the equaliser after the break, they finish the stronger side. | | | | | | | | | | | |
| 2 | H | WEST HAM | | | L | 0-2 | 0-0 | | Findlay | Stephens | Money | Horton | Goodyear | Donaghy | Hill | Stein | Walsh | Antic | Moss | |
| | 31/8 | | 13,403 | | 1 | | | *Goddard 50, Bonds 66* | *Parkes* | *Stewart* | *Martin* | *Bonds* | *Lampard* | *Devonshire* | *van der Elst* | *Clark* | *Neighbour** | *Goddard* | *Clark* | *Morgan* |
| | | | | | | | | Ref: A Seville | The Town have plenty of possession but poor marking allows the Hammers to take the points with Paul Goddard and Billy Bonds both scoring with headers. The players and the Kenilworth Road crowd witness at first hand the difference in the finishing skills between Divisions 1 and 2. | | | | | | | | | | | |
| 3 | H | NOTTS CO | | 11 | W | 5-3 | 2-2 | Walsh 16, 65, 67, Hill 42, Moss 50 | Findlay | Stephens | Money* | Horton | Goodyear | Donaghy | Hill | Stein | Walsh | Antic | Moss | Small |
| | 4/9 | | **9,071** | *18* | 4 | | | *Kilcline 24, Chiedozie 33, Goodwin 68* | *Avramovic* | *Benjamin* | *Kilcline* | *Richards* | *Worthington* | *Hunt* | *Goodwin** | *Mair* | *Chiedozie* | *Harkouk* | *Christie* | *McParland* |
| | | | | | | | | Ref: M Bodenham | Paul Walsh gets off the mark and notches a memorable hat-trick. The second strike, following a mazy run past several defenders, is an early contender for Goal of the Season. In a game which could have finished 7-7, the Hatters look brilliant going forward but are sloppy in defence. | | | | | | | | | | | |
| 4 | A | ASTON VILLA | | 15 | L | 1-4 | 0-3 | Moss 54p | Findlay | Stephens | Turner | Horton | Goodyear | Donaghy | Hill | Stein | Walsh | Antic* | Moss | **Kellock** |
| | 8/9 | | *18,823* | *19* | 4 | | | *Mortimer 8, Withe 21, Cowans 39p, 86p* | *Rimmer* | *Jones* | *Heard* | *Bremner* | *McNaught* | *Mortimer* | *Blair* | *Shaw** | *Withe* | *Cowans* | *Morley* | *Walters* |
| | | | | | | | | Ref: D Owen | The European Champions move off the bottom of the table as the Town defence again fails to come to terms with Division One attacking play. Gordon Cowans scores two from the spot, one for a foul by Horton on Tony Morley, and the other when Kellock climbs all over Peter Withe. | | | | | | | | | | | |
| 5 | A | LIVERPOOL | | 18 | D | 3-3 | 1-2 | Stein 27, 63, Moss 51 | Findlay* | Stephens | Money | Horton | Goodyear | Donaghy | Hill | Stein | Walsh | Turner | Moss | Antic |
| | 11/9 | | *33,694* | *4* | 5 | | | *Souness 32, Rush 42, Johnston 76* | *Grobbelaar* | *Neal* | *Thompson* | *Lawrenson* | *Kennedy* | *Whelan* | *Souness* | *Dalglish** | *Lee* | *Rush* | *Hodgson* | *Johnston* |
| | | | | | | | | Ref: M Heath | Liverpool score against three different Luton goalkeepers, the injured Jake Findlay and his replacements, Kirk Stephens and Mal Donaghy. The Hatters match the Reds in all respects in an end-to-end thriller. 'Luton play the way we usually do,' says Mark Lawrenson, after the game. | | | | | | | | | | | |
| 6 | H | BRIGHTON | | 11 | W | **5-0** | 1-0 | Stein 20, 77, 89, Turner 50, Moss 72 | Judge | Stephens | Money | Horton | Goodyear | Donaghy | Hill | Stein | Walsh | Turner | Moss | |
| | 18/9 | | 11,342 | *18* | 8 | | | | *Moseley* | *Shanks* | *Stevens* | *Gatting* | *Nelson* | *Case* | *Grealish* | *Stille* | *Smith* | *Ritchie** | *Ryan* | *Ring* |
| | | | | | | | | Ref: R Milford | The second goal, coming from an acrobatic overhead kick by Wayne Turner, eclipses the Brian Stein hat-trick. 'I really enjoyed that,' says ex-Brighton skipper, Brian Horton but Luton manager David Pleat reminds the players that matches will be much harder for the rest of the season. | | | | | | | | | | | |
| 7 | A | STOKE | | 12 | D | 4-4 | 2-2 | Walsh 20, Stein 43, 58, Donaghy 63 | Judge | Stephens | Money | Horton | Goodyear | Donaghy | Hill | Stein | Walsh* | Turner | Moss | Antic |
| | 25/9 | | *18,475* | *6* | 9 | | | *Berry 10, 22, Bracewell 50, O'Cal' 83* | *Fox !* | *Parkin* | *Watson* | *Berry* | *Hampton* | *Bracewell* | *Maguire* | *McIlroy* | *Chamberlain* | *O'Callaghan* | *Thomas** | *McAughtrie* |
| | | | | | | | | Ref: G Napthine | Stoke goalkeeper Peter Fox is ordered off for handling the ball outside the area, just before Paul Walsh nets. David Moss misses a penalty with two minutes to go after David McAughtrie trips Brian Stein. Town have now scored more goals than any other team in the Football League. | | | | | | | | | | | |
| 8 | H | MANCHESTER U | | 12 | D | 1-1 | 0-1 | Hill 59 | Findlay | Stephens | Money | Horton | Goodyear | Donaghy | Hill | Stein | Walsh | Turner* | Moss | Antic |
| | 2/10 | | 17,009 | *2* | 10 | | | *Grimes 13* | *Bailey* | *Duxbury* | *Moran* | *McQueen* | *Albiston* | *Wilkins* | *Robson* | *Moses* | *Grimes* | *Stapleton* | *Whiteside* | |
| | | | | | | | | Ref: B Stevens | Big spending United fail to impress. Out of respect for the free-scoring Hatters, they concentrate on defence. Ashley Grimes opens the scoring in a rare attack by the visitors, with a low shot from the edge of the area. Hill saves the day when heading a Horton free-kick past Gary Bailey. | | | | | | | | | | | |
| 9 | A | BIRMINGHAM | | 8 | W | 3-2 | 0-0 | Stein 60, Walsh 62, Moss 80 | Findlay | Stephens | Money | Horton | Goodyear | Donaghy | Hill | Stein | Walsh | Fuccillo | Moss | |
| | 9/10 | | *13,772* | *22* | 13 | | | *Langan 66p, Brazier 85* | *Blyth* | *Langan* | *Blake* | *Stevenson* | *v d Hauwe* | *Broadhurst* | *Dillon* | *Curbishley* | *Handysides* | *Bremner* | *Brazier* | |
| | | | | | | | | Ref: D Scott | The Blues have most of the game but it is the Town who score the goals. The referee awards a penalty when Donaghy blocks a cross from Alan Curbishley but Kevin Dillon sees his spot-kick saved. Jake Findlay is adjudged to have moved early and David Langan volunteers for the retake. | | | | | | | | | | | |
| 10 | H | IPSWICH | | 11 | D | 1-1 | 0-1 | Stein 59p | Findlay | Stephens | Money | Horton | Goodyear | Donaghy | Hill | Stein | Walsh | Fuccillo | Moss | |
| | 16/10 | | 13,378 | *20* | 14 | | | *Brazil 12* | *Cooper* | *Burley* | *Osman* | *Butcher* | *Gernon* | *Mills* | *Wark* | *McCall* | *Gates* | *Mariner* | *Brazil* | |
| | | | | | | | | Ref: D Lloyd | The arguments linger long into the night when an effort from Alan Brazil is allowed to stand, the referee having overruled the offside flag from his linesman. There is no dispute about the equaliser - Stein beating ace penalty stopper, Paul Cooper, after Paul Mariner fouls Kirk Stephens. | | | | | | | | | | | |

| | | | | | | | | | | | | | | | | | | | |
|---|---|---|---|---|---|---|---|---|---|---|---|---|---|---|---|---|---|---|---|
| 11 | A | WEST BROM | 13 | L | 0-1 | 0-1 | | Judge | Stephens | Money | Horton | Goodyear | Donaghy | Hill | Stein | Walsh | Fuccillo* | Moss | Turner |
| 23/10 | | *16,488* | *2* | 14 | | | *Whitehead 24* | *Godden* | *Batson* | *Bennett* | *Robertson* | *Statham* | *Zondervan* | *Jol* | *Owen* | *Brown* | *Regis* | *Whitehead* | |
| | | | | | | | Ref: M Scott | The Town are second best to a home side who show more invention in attack and look more solid in defence. The only goal comes when Luton full-back Kirk Stephens plays a totally unnecessary back-pass, which is intercepted by Clive Whitehead, who is able to score with ease. | | | | | | | | | | | |
| 12 | H | NOTT'M FOREST | 16 | L | 0-2 | 0-1 | | Findlay | Turner | Money | Horton | Goodyear | Donaghy | Hill | Stein | Walsh | Kellock* | Moss | Antic |
| 30/10 | | 12,648 | *7* | 14 | | | *Wallace 44, Gunn 63* | *v Breukelen* | *Swain* | *Young* | *Todd* | *Gunn* | *Proctor* | *Bowyer* | *Hodge* | *Birtles* | *Wallace* | *Robertson* | |
| | | | | | | | Ref: J Moules | Forest show their experience when pulling all of their players back when the Town attack and then quickly moving forward on the break. Ian Wallace nets after Ian Bowyer's shot hits the bar. Bryn Gunn then clinches the points after being set up by Gary Birtles and John Robertson. | | | | | | | | | | | |
| 13 | H | ARSENAL | 17 | D | 2-2 | 0-0 | Moss 63, Walsh 68 | Findlay | Turner* | Money | Horton | Goodyear | Donaghy | Hill | Stein | Walsh | Fuccillo | Moss | Antic |
| 6/11 | | 16,597 | *16* | 15 | | | *Rix 53, Talbot 55* | *Wood* | *O'Shea* | *O'Leary* | *Whyte* | *Sansom* | *Talbot* | *Woodcock* | *Davis* | *Rix* | *Sunderland* | *Robson* | |
| | | | | | | | Ref: E Read | Arsenal take a two-goal lead after focusing their attacks on Luton full-back Wayne Turner, but the Hatters then return the compliment when forcing inexperienced defender Danny O'Shea into two errors, both of which result in goals. Findlay makes some fine saves in the first half. | | | | | | | | | | | |
| 14 | A | SUNDERLAND | 18 | D | 1-1 | 0-0 | Moss 76 | Judge | Stephens | Money | Horton | Turner | Donaghy | Hill | Stein | Walsh | Kellock* | Moss | Bunn |
| 13/11 | | *14,238* | *20* | 16 | | | *Atkins 87* | *Turner* | *Munro* | *Atkins* | *Elliott* | *Venison* | *Nicholl* | *Cummins* | *Pickering* | *Rowell* | *McCoist* | *West* | |
| | | | | | | | Ref: D Allison | The Town are convinced that they are robbed when, defending a one-goal lead courtesy of Moss, the linesman flags for a corner though Hatters defender Turner insists that the ball was not out of play. Ian Atkins heads the equaliser from the corner-kick and Moss is booked for arguing. | | | | | | | | | | | |
| 15 | A | COVENTRY | 18 | L | 2-4 | 0-0 | Horton 64, Stein 79 | Findlay | Stephens | Money | Horton | Goodyear | Turner | Hill | Stein | Walsh | Antic | Moss | |
| 20/11 | | *9,670* | *11* | 16 | | | *Dyson 58, Whitton 63, 83, Thompson 84* | *Sealey* | *Thomas* | *Dyson* | *Gillespie* | *Roberts* | *Francis* | *Jacobs* | *Hunt* | *Whitton* | *Hateley* | *Thompson* | |
| | | | | | | | Ref: H King | After a goal-less first half, the Town gift Coventry two goals and then fight back to equalise, before two errors by Findlay hand all three points to the Sky Blues. Flu victim Donaghy is missing from the line-up after 155 consecutive league appearances and the defence looks all at sea. | | | | | | | | | | | |
| 16 | H | SOUTHAMPTON | 18 | D | 3-3 | 0-2 | Hill 63, Stein 69, Goodyear 87 | Findlay | Stephens | Money* | Horton | Goodyear | Donaghy | Hill | Stein | Walsh | Turner | Moss | Antic |
| 27/11 | | 11,196 | *19* | 17 | | | *Wallace 26, Cassells 40, Armstrong 84* | *Shilton* | *Agboola* | *Nicholl* | *Wright* | *Mills* | *Williams* | *Armstrong* | *Rofe* | *Moran* | *Cassells* | *Wallace* | |
| | | | | | | | Ref: K Barratt | Danny Wallace inspires the Saints to a two-goal interval lead but the Hatters fight back. Chris Nicholl uses his hand to block a cross from Hill and Moss smashes the penalty against the bar. Stephens follows up to net the rebound but his effort is disallowed as Moss is then given offside. | | | | | | | | | | | |
| 17 | A | SWANSEA | 19 | L | 0-2 | 0-0 | | Findlay | Stephens | Money | Horton | Goodyear | Donaghy | Hill | Stein | Walsh | Turner* | Moss | Antic |
| 4/12 | | *9,556* | *14* | 17 | | | *Curtis 51, Latchford 81* | *Davies* | *Stanley* | *Charles* | *Stevenson* | *Rajkovic* | *Hadziabdic* | *James R* | *Kennedy* | *Mahoney* | *Curtis** | *Latchford* | *James L* |
| | | | | | | | Ref: B Newsome | The Town go behind to an Alan Curtis header but then claw their way back into the game. Davies commits a 'professional foul' on Stein which prevents him from equalising. The resultant free-kick comes to nothing and, with the Hatters pushed upfield, Latchford makes the points safe. | | | | | | | | | | | |
| 18 | H | MANCHESTER C | 19 | W | 3-1 | 0-0 | Walsh 55, Stein 70, Hartford 86 (og) | Findlay | Stephens | Money | Horton | Goodyear | Donaghy | Hill | Stein | Walsh | Turner | Moss | |
| 11/12 | | 11,013 | *10* | 20 | | | *Cross 66* | *Corrigan* | *Ranson* | *Caton* | *Reid* | *McDonald* | *Power* | *Tueart* | *Hartford* | *Bond* | *Cross* | *Reeves* | |
| | | | | | | | Ref: D Axcell | City are a team in decline and it shows as the Town romp to their first home victory in three months. Walsh opens the scoring with a brilliant volley and, although City equalise, Stein makes the points safe by scoring one himself before forcing Asa Hartford to put through his own goal. | | | | | | | | | | | |
| 19 | A | EVERTON | 19 | L | **0-5** | 0-2 | *[Heath 73, 84]* | Findlay | Stephens | Money | Horton | Goodyear | Donaghy | Hill | Geddis | Walsh | Turner* | Moss | Fuccillo |
| 18/12 | | *14,986* | *12* | 20 | | | *Bailey 14, Sheedy 39, Curran 71,* | *Arnold* | *Stevens* | *Ratcliffe* | *Higgins* | *Bailey* | *McMahon* | *Richardson* | *Sheedy* | *Curran* | *Johnson** | *Heath* | *Sharp* |
| | | | | | | | Ref: M Peck | After the game last week against Manchester City, it was discovered that Brian Stein had broken a bone in his foot which will keep him out of the Luton side for some time. Terry Curran, on loan from Sheffield United, turns on a brilliant performance to mastermind this heavy defeat. | | | | | | | | | | | |
| 20 | H | WATFORD | 17 | W | 1-0 | 1-0 | Goodyear 37 | Findlay | Stephens | Money | Horton | Goodyear | Donaghy | Hill | Geddis | Walsh | Fuccillo | Moss | |
| 27/12 | | 21,145 | *5* | 23 | | | | *Sherwood* | *Rice* | *Sims* | *Bolton* | *Rostron* | *Taylor* | *Callaghan* | *Jackett* | *Barnes* | *Blissett* | *Jenkins* | |
| | | | | | | | Ref: B Daniels | In front of the first 'full house' of the season, the Town engage in a battling display against their high-flying local rivals. In a scrappy affair, the only goal is driven through a mass of legs by Goodyear. 'Luton seem to have the Indian sign over us,' moans Hornets' manager Graham Taylor. | | | | | | | | | | | |
| 21 | A | NORWICH | 17 | L | 0-1 | 0-1 | | Findlay | Stephens | Money | Horton | Goodyear | Turner | Hill | Geddis | Walsh | Fuccillo* | Moss | Antic |
| 28/12 | | *20,415* | *20* | 23 | | | *Channon 11* | *Woods* | *Haylock* | *Walford* | *Watson* | *Downs* | *Mendham* | *Barham* | *O'Neill* | *van Wijk* | *Channon* | *Bertschin* | |
| | | | | | | | Ref: T Mills | Fellow-strugglers Norwich exhibit more passion and just about deserve their narrow victory with a goal from veteran striker Mick Channon. The Canaries then shut up shop and, in the last ten minutes, pull everyone back behind the ball. Luton are already missing the services of Stein. | | | | | | | | | | | |

| No | Date | Att | Pos | Pt | F-A | H-T | Scorers, Times, and Referees | 1 | 2 | 3 | 4 | 5 | 6 | 7 | 8 | 9 | 10 | 11 | 12 sub used |
|---|---|---|---|---|---|---|---|---|---|---|---|---|---|---|---|---|---|---|---|
| 22 | H COVENTRY | | 18 | L | 1-2 | 0-2 | Donaghy 60 | Findlay | Stephens | Money | Horton | Goodyear | Donaghy | Hill | Geddis | Walsh | Fuccillo* | Moss | Antic |
| | 1/1 | 13,072 | *6* | 23 | | | *Whitton 10, Melrose 15* | *Sealey* | *Thomas* | *Dyson* | *Gillespie* | *Horm'tschuk* | *Francis* | *Butterworth* | *Whitton* | *Hunt* | *Hateley* | *Melrose* | |
| | | | | | | | Ref: D Vickers | The Sky Blues pulverise Luton in the first half and are well worth their interval lead. The Hatters fight back in the second half and force keeper Les Sealey to pull off two outstanding saves. His one error comes when he drops the ball, allowing Mal Donaghy to score a consolation goal. | | | | | | | | | | | |
| 23 | A WEST HAM | | 17 | W | 3-2 | 1-1 | Walsh 38, 73, 89 | Findlay | Stephens | **Thomas** | Horton | Goodyear | Donaghy | Hill | Bunn* | Walsh | Turner | Moss | Kellock |
| | 4/1 | *21,435* | *5* | 26 | | | *Cottee 19, Clark 65* | *Parkes* | *Allen* | *Gallagher* | *Martin** | *Stewart* | *Dickens* | *van der Elst* | *Pike* | *Devonshire* | *Cottee* | *Clark* | *Morgan* |
| | | | | | | | Ref: T Spencer | With a reshaped team, the Town reproduce their early season form and Paul Walsh nets a hat-trick in front of England manager Bobby Robson. His third goal comes in the final seconds when, taking advantage of a slip by Ray Stewart in the Hammers' defence, he runs through to score. | | | | | | | | | | | |
| 24 | H TOTTENHAM | | 17 | D | 1-1 | 1-0 | O'Reilly 35 (og) | Findlay | Stephens | Thomas | Horton | Goodyear | Donaghy | Hill | Bunn | Walsh | Turner | **Watts*** | Kellock |
| | 15/1 | **21,231** | *10* | 27 | | | *Hoddle 72* | *Clemence* | *Roberts* | *O'Reilly* | *Perryman* | *Hughton* | *Brooke* | *Ardiles* | *Villa* | *Mabbutt* | *Gibson** | *Archibald* | *Hoddle* |
| | | | | | | | Ref: M Heath | The biggest home gate of the season sees Ossie Ardiles for the first time since he left Britain at the outbreak of the Falklands War. Watts, making his debut, swings over a cross which O'Reilly heads past his own keeper before Glenn Hoddle equalises with a clever free-kick routine. | | | | | | | | | | | |
| 25 | A BRIGHTON | | 16 | W | 4-2 | 2-0 | Hill 5, 71, Stevens 24 (og), Case 74 (og) | Findlay | Stephens | Thomas | Horton | Goodyear | Donaghy | Hill | Bunn | Walsh | Turner* | Moss | Kellock |
| | 22/1 | *11,778* | *21* | 30 | | | *Ritchie 69, Grealish 73* | *Moseley* | *Ramsey* | *Pearce** | *Foster* | *Stevens* | *Case* | *Grealish* | *Smillie* | *Ward* | *Smith* | *Robinson* | *Ritchie* |
| | | | | | | | Ref: D Letts | The Town ease through against their fellow strugglers, who appear to commit suicide with two crazy own-goals. Gary Stevens heads past his own keeper from a short free-kick and then Jimmy Case does the same. The Seagulls try to fight back but their attacks show little invention. | | | | | | | | | | | |
| 26 | H LIVERPOOL | | 17 | L | 1-3 | 1-2 | Stein 31 | Findlay | Stephens | Money* | Horton | Goodyear | Donaghy | Hill | Stein | Walsh | Turner | Moss | Antic |
| | 5/2 | 18,434 | *1* | 30 | | | *Rush 32, Kennedy 43, Souness 79* | *Grobbelaar* | *Neal* | *Lawrenson* | *Hansen* | *Kennedy* | *Johnston** | *Dalglish* | *Lee* | *Souness* | *Rush* | *Hodgson* | *Whelan* |
| | | | | | | | Ref: B Hill | Stein returns to the side, his first appearance since before Christmas, and heads the Town into a shock lead. The league leaders equalise just 23 seconds later and go on to complete an easy victory with Graeme Souness scoring with a 25-yarder, shown many times on Match of the Day. | | | | | | | | | | | |
| 27 | A IPSWICH | | 18 | L | 0-3 | 0-1 | | Findlay | Stephens | Turner | Horton | Goodyear | Donaghy | Hill* | White | Walsh | Fuccillo | Moss | Kellock |
| | 26/2 | *18,632* | *11* | 30 | | | *Brazil 2, Wark 46, Putney 56* | *Cooper* | *Parkin* | *Osman* | *Butcher* | *Gernon* | *O'Callaghan* | *Putney* | *McCall* | *Wark* | *Mariner* | *Brazil* | |
| | | | | | | | Ref: M Bodenham | White, on loan from Charlton, gets his Division One chance at last but fails to make any impact in a poor team performance. Luton have only two shots on target in the whole match. Ipswich decide to indulge in some shooting practice but Findlay manages to keep the goal tally down. | | | | | | | | | | | |
| 28 | H WEST BROM | | 18 | D | 0-0 | 0-0 | | Findlay | Stephens | **Elliott** | Horton | Goodyear | Donaghy | Hill | White | Walsh | Turner | Moss | |
| | 5/3 | 10,852 | *11* | 31 | | | | *Barron* | *Bennett* | *Wile* | *Robertson* | *Statham* | *Zondervan* | *Jol* | *Owen* | *Eastoe* | *Cross* | *Thompson* | |
| | | | | | | | Ref: R Lewis | 18-year-old Paul Elliott, a £100,000 signing from Charlton, makes his debut but has little to do as West Brom do not show any attacking flair. In their fourth consecutive 0-0 draw, Albion blot out all of the attacks by the Town. This is the second clean-sheet for Jake Findlay this season. | | | | | | | | | | | |
| 29 | A NOTT'M FOREST | | 18 | W | 1-0 | 1-0 | Hill 13 | Findlay | Stephens | Elliott | Horton | Goodyear | Donaghy | Hill | White | Walsh | Turner | Moss | |
| | 12/3 | *14,387* | *4* | 34 | | | | *Sutton* | *Anderson* | *Young* | *Todd* | *Swain* | *Bowyer* | *Wilson* | *Hodge* | *Walsh** | *Wallace* | *Birtles* | *Davenport* |
| | | | | | | | Ref: N Ashley | Hill turns in a superb performance and scores the only goal when stealing the ball from Willie Young and running through to net with a well-placed shot. Forest have more of the play but their £1,000,000 strikers, Gary Birtles and Ian Wallace, are unable to force Findlay to make a save. | | | | | | | | | | | |
| 30 | A ARSENAL | | 19 | L | 1-4 | 0-3 | Moss 88 | Findlay | Stephens | Elliott | Horton | Goodyear | Donaghy | Hill | White | Walsh | Turner | Moss | |
| | 19/3 | *23,987* | *14* | 34 | | | *Woodcock 17, 24, 79, Davis 42* | *Jennings* | *O'Leary** | *Robson* | *Whyte* | *Sansom* | *Nicholas* | *Davis* | *Talbot* | *Rix* | *Sunderland* | *Woodcock* | *Meade* |
| | | | | | | | Ref: C Thomas | Arsenal storm into a three-goal lead and then sit back, knowing that they have done enough. The only consolation that Luton can gain from this match is that they played better in the second half and David Moss scores just as Pat Jennings is packing his bags and getting ready to go home. | | | | | | | | | | | |
| 31 | H SUNDERLAND | | 19 | L | 1-3 | 1-1 | Horton 26p | **Godden** | Stephens | Elliott | Horton | Goodyear | Donaghy | Hill | **Aylott** | Walsh | Turner* | Moss | **Daniel** |
| | 26/3 | 11,221 | *15* | 34 | | | *Pickering 3, 58, James 75* | *Turner* | *Nicholl* | *Atkins* | *Chisholm* | *Munro* | *Proctor* | *Venison* | *James* | *Pickering* | *Rowell* | *Worthington* | |
| | | | | | | | Ref: A Crickmore | The Town slump to their fifth home defeat of the season with defensive frailties rearing their head once again. Loan goalkeeper Tony Godden cannot be faulted for any of the Sunderland goals. Ian Munro fouls Moss in the area and Brian Horton scores the only Town goal from the spot. | | | | | | | | | | | |

| No | Date | Venue | Opponent | Att | Pos | Pts | Res | F-A | H-T | Scorers, Times, and Referees | 1 | 2 | 3 | 4 | 5 | 6 | 7 | 8 | 9 | 10 | 11 | 12 sub used |
|---|---|---|---|---|---|---|---|---|---|---|---|---|---|---|---|---|---|---|---|---|---|---|
| 32 | | H | NORWICH | | 21 | | L | 0-1 | 0-1 | | Godden | Stephens | Elliott | Horton | Goodyear | Thomas* | Hill | Aylott | Walsh | Donaghy | Moss | Daniel |
| | 2/4 | | | 11,211 | *19* | 34 | | | | *Bennett 26* | *Woods* | *Haylock* | *Walford* | *Watson* | *Downs* | *Mendham* | *O'Neill* | *Deehan* | *Bennett* | *Bertschin* | *Channon** | *Jack* |
| | | | | | | | | | | Ref: M James | Norwich appear to want to win more than the Town and Dave Bennett's volley is enough to settle the issue. The Canaries then erect a defensive barrier which the Hatters never look likely to break down until the final minute, when a wonder save by Woods keeps out an effort from Moss. | | | | | | | | | | | |
| 33 | | A | WATFORD | | 21 | | L | 2-5 | 2-2 | Aylott 16, Horton 29 *[Callaghan 78]* | Godden | Stephens | Money | Horton | Elliott | Donaghy | Hill | Aylott | Walsh | Antic ! | Moss | |
| | 4/4 | | | *20,120* | *2* | 34 | | | | *Blissett 6, 48p, Jobson 42, Barnes 49,* | *Sherwood* | *Rice* | *Terry* | *Jackett* | *Rostron* | *Taylor* | *Lohman* | *Jobson* | *Callaghan** | *Barnes* | *Blissett* | *Armstrong* |
| | | | | | | | | | | Ref: L Shapter | The Town match Watford in the first half but the ludicrous dismissal of Raddy Antic for an innocuous challenge kills the game and the Hornets run out the victors for the first time in eight attempts against the Hatters. Luton drop to the bottom of the table after Brighton draw at the Dell. | | | | | | | | | | | |
| 34 | | H | ASTON VILLA | | 19 | | W | 2-1 | 1-1 | Aylott 30, Moss 89 | Godden | Stephens | Money | Antic | Elliott | Donaghy | Hill | Aylott | Walsh | Turner | Moss | |
| | 9/4 | | | 10,924 | *4* | 37 | | | | *Shaw 41* | *Spink* | *Williams* | *Evans* | *McNaught* | *Gibson* | *Mortimer* | *Bremner* | *Cowans* | *Shaw* | *Withe* | *Walters* | |
| | | | | | | | | | | Ref: L Burden | Aylott opens the scoring on the half-hour but Gary Shaw equalises with a superb volley just before the break. The Hatters show plenty of fight and are rewarded when Moss instinctively sticks out a leg to steer the ball home in the final minute to end the run of four consecutive defeats. | | | | | | | | | | | |
| 35 | | H | BIRMINGHAM | | 19 | | W | 3-1 | 3-0 | Hill 4, 42, Horton 8p | Godden | Stephens | Money | Horton | Elliott | Donaghy | Hill | Aylott | Walsh | Antic | Moss* | Stein |
| | 12/4 | | | 12,868 | *22* | 40 | | | | *Hopkins 66* | *Coton* | *v d Hauwe* | *Stevenson* | *Blake* | *Hagan* | *Broadhurst** | *Gayle* | *Halsall* | *Hopkins* | *Ferguson* | *Harford* | *Phillips* |
| | | | | | | | | | | Ref: A Grey | Watched again by England manager Bobby Robson, Hill puts on a tremendous display as the Town dump the Blues to the bottom of the table. In a scintillating first-half performance, Hill scores with both a header and a shot and Horton scores from the spot after Jim Hagan trips Walsh. | | | | | | | | | | | |
| 36 | | A | NOTTS CO | | 19 | | D | 1-1 | 0-0 | Donaghy 89 | Godden | Stephens | Money | Horton | Elliott | Donaghy | Hill | Aylott | Walsh | Antic | Moss | |
| | 16/4 | | | ***8,897*** | *14* | 41 | | | | *Chiedozie 50* | *Avramovic* | *Benjamin* | *Kilcline* | *Richards* | *Hunt* | *Goodwin* | *Chiedozie* | *Lantinen** | *Worthington* | *Christie* | *McCulloch* | *Harkouk* |
| | | | | | | | | | | Ref: P Willis | The Town line up with Antic as a sweeper but a sloppy back-pass from Stephens allows John Chiedozie to intercept and score the opener. Antic takes a free-kick in the final minute which rebounds off the defensive wall and into the path of Donaghy, who strikes it home for the equaliser. | | | | | | | | | | | |
| 37 | | H | SWANSEA | | 18 | | W | 3-1 | 0-0 | Walsh 55, 74, 86 | Godden | Stephens | Money | Horton | Elliott | Donaghy | Hill | Aylott | Walsh | Turner | Moss | |
| | 23/4 | | | 11,561 | *22* | 44 | | | | *Latchford 85* | *Sander* | *Marustik* | *Charles* | *Lewis* | *Rajkovic* | *Richards* | *James* | *Robinson** | *Kennedy* | *Loveridge* | *Latchford* | *Pascoe* |
| | | | | | | | | | | Ref: A Hamil | Walsh scores for the first time in thirteen games and then goes on to show keen anticipation in completing a hat-trick, due to the supporting role played by Aylott in being able to hold the ball before laying it off. The visitors decide to defend in depth and then try to score on the break. | | | | | | | | | | | |
| 38 | | A | SOUTHAMPTON | | 17 | | D | 2-2 | 2-2 | Elliott 5, Antic 31 | Godden | Stephens | Money | Antic | Elliott | Donaghy | Hill | Aylott | Walsh* | Turner | Moss | Goodyear |
| | 30/4 | | | *18,367* | *8* | 45 | | | | *Wright 19, Armstrong 28* | *Shilton* | *Mills* | *Agboola* | *Nicholl* | *Wright* | *Williams* | *Holmes* | *Armstrong* | *Wallace* | *Baird** | *Moran* | *Puckett* |
| | | | | | | | | | | Ref: J Bray | All four goals are scored from set pieces in the first half, the final one from Antic, who hits a 30-yard free-kick which beats England goalkeeper Peter Shilton. Paul Walsh limps off with a thigh strain during the second period but the Hatters succeed in holding out for a share of the points. | | | | | | | | | | | |
| 39 | | H | STOKE | | 16 | | D | 0-0 | 0-0 | | Godden | Stephens | Money | Horton | Elliott | Donaghy | Hill | Turner | Aylott | Antic | Moss | |
| | 2/5 | | | 11,877 | *9* | 46 | | | | | *Fox* | *Bould* | *Hampton* | *O'Callaghan* | *McAughtrie* | *Bracewell* | *Thomas* | *McIlroy* | *Chamberlain* | *Painter* | *Maguire* | |
| | | | | | | | | | | Ref: A Gunn | The Town are forced to field a reshaped side, due to the injury to Walsh, and are frustrated by the successful offside game which is played by the visitors. Paul Elliott has a superb match and his performance is instrumental in ensuring that Luton are able to hold out for a valuable point. | | | | | | | | | | | |
| 40 | | H | EVERTON | | 21 | | L | 1-5 | 1-2 | Hill 5 *[Sheedy 63, 85]* | Godden | Stephens | Money | Horton | Goodyear | Donaghy | Hill | Aylott | Walsh | Turner | Moss* | Antic |
| | 7/5 | | | 12,447 | *6* | 46 | | | | *Johnson 40, Sharp 42p, 72,* | *Southall* | *Stevens* | *Ratcliffe* | *Higgins* | *Bailey* | *Richardson* | *McMahon* | *Heath* | *Sheedy* | *Johnson* | *Sharp* | |
| | | | | | | | | | | Ref: I Borrett | Needing all three points to be safe from relegation, Hill heads an early opening goal to ease the tension but, just before the interval, the Hatters fall apart and concede two quick goals. Everton go on the rampage after the break, scoring at will, to plunge Luton back into the bottom places. | | | | | | | | | | | |
| 41 | | A | MANCHESTER U | | 21 | | L | 0-3 | 0-2 | | Godden | Stephens | Money | Horton | Goodyear | Donaghy | Hill | Aylott | Walsh | **Parker*** | Daniel | Antic |
| | 9/5 | | | *34,213* | *3* | 46 | | | | *McGrath 35, 37, Stapleton 85* | *Bailey* | *Duxbury* | *Moran* | *McQueen* | *Grimes* | *McGrath* | *Robson* | *Muhren* | *Davies* | *Stapleton* | *Whiteside** | *McGarvey* |
| | | | | | | | | | | Ref: T Holbrook | Two teenagers, Gary Parker and Ray Daniel, make their full debuts against the team which boasts an unbeaten home record this season. Walsh hits the bar early on but the Town are rarely in the game and end up a well-beaten side after McGrath scores two tap-in goals to earn the points. | | | | | | | | | | | |
| 42 | | A | MANCHESTER C | | 18 | | W | 1-0 | 0-0 | Antic 85 | Godden | Stephens | Goodyear | Horton | Elliott | Donaghy | Hill | Aylott | Walsh | Turner* | Stein | Antic |
| | 14/5 | | | ***42,843*** | *20* | 49 | | | | | *Williams* | *Ranson* | *Reid* | *Caton* | *McDonald* | *Bond* | *Baker** | *Hartford* | *Power* | *Tueart* | *Reeves* | *Kinsey* |
| | Home | | Away | | | | | | | Ref: A Challinor | City need a point to stay up whilst Luton need all three, a factor which probably helps the Town as the home side battle deliberately for a draw. With just five minutes left, Alex Williams pushes out a ball which Antic seizes on and slams into the net. The Hatters hold on for a famous win. | | | | | | | | | | | |
| Average | 13,452 | | 19,998 | | | | | | | | | | | | | | | | | | | |

## Milk Cup

| Milk Cup | F-A | H-T | Scorers, Times, and Referees | 1 | 2 | 3 | 4 | 5 | 6 | 7 | 8 | 9 | 10 | 11 | 12 sub used |
|---|---|---|---|---|---|---|---|---|---|---|---|---|---|---|---|
| 2:1 H CHARLTON 12 W | 3-0 | 2-0 | Stein 23p, Fuccillo 44, 85 | Findlay | Stephens | Money | Horton | Goodyear | Donaghy | Hill | Stein | Walsh | Fuccillo | Moss | |
| 5/10 7,030 *2:17* | | | | *Johns* | *Curtis* | *Elliott* | *Berry* | *Lansdowne* | *Walker* | *Bullivant* | *Mehmet* | *Harris* | *White* | *Hales** | *Gritt* |
| | | | Ref: A Robinson | Stein opens the scoring from the penalty spot after he is tripped by Billy Lansdowne. Fuccillo, making his first appearance of the season, scores twice, with a volley and a fierce shot, to put the Town in total control. Ex-Hatters, Derek Hales and Steve White, both squander good chances. | | | | | | | | | | | |
| 2:2 A CHARLTON 13 L | 0-2 | 0-1 | | Findlay ! | Thomas | Money | Horton | Goodyear | Donaghy | Hill | Stein | Walsh | Turner | Moss | |
| 26/10 *5,973 2:17* | | | *Hales 3, 49p* | *Johns* | *Curtis* | *Elliott* | *Berry* | *Walker** | *Robinson* | *Bullivant* | *O'Sullivan* | *Harris* | *White* | *Hales* | *Ferns* |
| | | | Ref: L Shapter | Luton go two goals down and have to play with only ten men for most of the second half after Findlay is sent off for a handling offence outside the area. Carl Harris falls over a yard away from Donaghy but the referee, seeing a trip, awards a penalty which is converted by Derek Hales. | | | | | | | | | | | |
| 3 H BLACKPOOL 17 W | 4-2 | 1-1 | Kellock 40, 70, Bunn 55, Moss 68 | Judge | Stephens | Money | Horton | Goodyear* | Donaghy | Kellock | Stein | Walsh | Fuccillo | Moss | Bunn |
| 9/11 6,409 *4:8* | | | *Bamber 39, Pashley 78* | *Hesford* | *Simmonite* | *Hetzke* | *Serella* | *Hart* | *Deary* | *Hockaday* | *Pashley* | *Downes* | *Stewart* | *Bamber* | |
| | | | Ref: A Gunn | Close-season signing, Kellock, gets his chance as a replacement for the injured Hill and scores twice as the Hatters make hard work of beating a Blackpool side who play the long ball to good effect. The result flatters the Town as Dave Bamber often has the beating of the Luton defence. | | | | | | | | | | | |
| 4 A TOTTENHAM 18 L | 0-1 | 0-0 | | Findlay | Stephens | Money | Horton | Goodyear | Donaghy | Hill | Stein | Walsh | Turner* | Moss | Antic |
| 1/12 *27,461 1:10* | | | *Villa 64* | *Clemence* | *Hughton* | *Price* | *O'Reilly* | *Villa* | *Roberts* | *Mabbutt* | *Archibald* | *Galvin* | *Hoddle* | *Crooks* | |
| | | | Ref: J Martin | Both goalkeepers are on the top of their form and it takes a tremendous 30-yard strike from Argentinian Ricky Villa to settle the issue. Town enjoy as much of the game territorially as Spurs but the closest they come to scoring is with a header from Mal Donaghy which hits the post. | | | | | | | | | | | |

## FA Cup

| FA Cup | F-A | H-T | Scorers, Times, and Referees | 1 | 2 | 3 | 4 | 5 | 6 | 7 | 8 | 9 | 10 | 11 | 12 sub used |
|---|---|---|---|---|---|---|---|---|---|---|---|---|---|---|---|
| 3 H PETERBOROUGH 17 W | 3-0 | 2-0 | Horton 15p, Hill 44, Walsh 78 | Findlay | Stephens | Thomas | Horton | Goodyear | Donaghy | Hill | Bunn | Walsh | Turner | Watts | |
| 8/1 11,151 *4:12* | | | | *Seaman* | *Winters* | *Firm* | *Slack* | *Collins* | *Gynn* | *Rodaway* | *Benjamin* | *Quow* | *Cooke* | *Clarke* | |
| | | | Ref: J Martin | Posh have three chances in the opening ten minutes and only smart goalkeeping from Findlay keeps them out. The Hatters then take control of the game with a penalty from Horton, after Neil Firm fouls Walsh in the area, setting them on their way. Hill scores with a brilliant solo effort. | | | | | | | | | | | |
| 4 H MANCHESTER U 16 L | 0-2 | 0-0 | | Findlay | Stephens | Money | Horton | Goodyear | Donaghy | Hill | Stein | Walsh | Turner* | Moss | Kellock |
| 29/1 20,516 *1:2* | | | *Moses 46, Moran 89* | *Bailey* | *Duxbury* | *Moran* | *McQueen* | *Albiston* | *Moses* | *Coppell* | *Robson* | *Muhren* | *Stapleton* | *Whiteside* | |
| | | | Ref: R Lewis | United play it tight in the first half but then step up a gear in the second period with a 20-yard drive from Remi Moses putting them into the driving seat. Stein hits the post before Kevin Moran is first to react to a Frank Stapleton header blocked by Findlay to score in the final minute. | | | | | | | | | | | |

| | | Home | | | | | Away | | | | | |
|---|---|---|---|---|---|---|---|---|---|---|---|---|
| | P | W | D | L | F | A | W | D | L | F | A | Pts |
| 1 Liverpool | 42 | 16 | 4 | 1 | 55 | 16 | 8 | 6 | 7 | 32 | 21 | 82 |
| 2 Watford | 42 | 16 | 2 | 3 | 49 | 20 | 6 | 3 | 12 | 25 | 37 | 71 |
| 3 Manchester U | 42 | 14 | 7 | 0 | 39 | 10 | 5 | 6 | 10 | 17 | 28 | 70 |
| 4 Tottenham | 42 | 15 | 4 | 2 | 50 | 15 | 5 | 5 | 11 | 15 | 35 | 69 |
| 5 Nott'm Forest | 42 | 12 | 5 | 4 | 34 | 18 | 8 | 4 | 9 | 28 | 32 | 69 |
| 6 Aston Villa | 42 | 17 | 2 | 2 | 47 | 15 | 4 | 3 | 14 | 15 | 35 | 68 |
| 7 Everton | 42 | 13 | 6 | 2 | 43 | 19 | 5 | 4 | 12 | 23 | 29 | 64 |
| 8 West Ham | 42 | 13 | 3 | 5 | 41 | 23 | 7 | 1 | 13 | 27 | 39 | 64 |
| 9 Ipswich | 42 | 11 | 3 | 7 | 39 | 23 | 4 | 10 | 7 | 25 | 27 | 58 |
| 10 Arsenal | 42 | 11 | 6 | 4 | 36 | 19 | 5 | 4 | 12 | 22 | 37 | 58 |
| 11 West Brom | 42 | 11 | 5 | 5 | 35 | 20 | 4 | 7 | 10 | 16 | 29 | 57 |
| 12 Southampton | 42 | 11 | 5 | 5 | 36 | 22 | 4 | 7 | 10 | 18 | 36 | 57 |
| 13 Stoke | 42 | 13 | 4 | 4 | 34 | 21 | 3 | 5 | 13 | 19 | 43 | 57 |
| 14 Norwich | 42 | 10 | 6 | 5 | 30 | 18 | 4 | 6 | 11 | 22 | 40 | 54 |
| 15 Notts Co | 42 | 12 | 4 | 5 | 37 | 25 | 3 | 3 | 15 | 18 | 46 | 52 |
| 16 Sunderland | 42 | 7 | 10 | 4 | 30 | 22 | 5 | 4 | 12 | 18 | 39 | 50 |
| 17 Birmingham | 42 | 9 | 7 | 5 | 29 | 24 | 3 | 7 | 11 | 11 | 31 | 50 |
| 18 LUTON TOWN | 42 | 7 | 7 | 7 | 34 | 33 | 5 | 6 | 10 | 31 | 51 | 49 |
| 19 Coventry | 42 | 10 | 5 | 6 | 29 | 17 | 3 | 4 | 14 | 19 | 42 | 48 |
| 20 Manchester C | 42 | 9 | 5 | 7 | 26 | 23 | 4 | 3 | 14 | 21 | 47 | 47 |
| 21 Swansea | 42 | 10 | 4 | 7 | 32 | 29 | 0 | 7 | 14 | 19 | 40 | 41 |
| 22 Brighton | 42 | 8 | 7 | 6 | 25 | 22 | 1 | 6 | 14 | 13 | 46 | 40 |
| | 924 | 255 | 111 | 96 | 810 | 454 | 96 | 111 | 255 | 454 | 810 | 1275 |

Odds & ends

Double wins: (3) Birmingham, Brighton, Manchester City.
Double losses: (3) Coventry, Everton, Norwich.

Won from behind: (3) Notts County (h), West Ham (a), Blackpool (LC).
Lost from in front: (3) Everton (h), Liverpool (h), Watford (a).

High spots: The string of tremendous games at the beginning of the season.
The final 1-0 win at Manchester City.
Paul Walsh's hat-trick in the home game with Notts County.
The magnificent 3-3 draw at Anfield.

Low spots: The injury to Brian Stein.
The 1-5 home defeat by Everton, leaving it all to do.
Missing a last-minute penalty at Stoke, and dropping two points.

Player of the Year: Paul Walsh.
Ever-presents: (0).
Hat-tricks: Paul Walsh (3), Brian Stein (1).
Leading scorer: Brian Stein (15).

| | Appearances | | | | | | Goals | | | |
|---|---|---|---|---|---|---|---|---|---|---|
| | Lge | *Sub* | LC | *Sub* | FAC | *Sub* | Lge | LC | FAC | Tot |
| Antic,Raddy | **11** | *13* | | *1* | | | **2** | | | **2** |
| Aylott, Trevor | **12** | | | | | | **2** | | | **2** |
| Bunn, Frank | **3** | *1* | | *1* | 1 | | | 1 | | **1** |
| Daniel, Ray | **1** | *2* | | | | | | | | |
| Donaghy, Mal | **40** | | 4 | | 2 | | **3** | | | **3** |
| Elliott, Paul | **13** | | | | | | **1** | | | **1** |
| Findlay, Jake | **26** | | 3 | | 2 | | | | | |
| Fuccillo, Lil | **8** | *1* | 2 | | | | | 2 | | **2** |
| Geddis, David | **4** | | | | | | | | | |
| Godden, Tony | **12** | | | | | | | | | |
| Goodyear, Clive | **34** | *1* | 4 | | 2 | | **2** | | | **2** |
| Hill, Ricky | **42** | | 3 | | 2 | | **9** | | 1 | **10** |
| Horton, Brian | **40** | | 4 | | 2 | | **4** | | 1 | **5** |
| Judge, Alan | **4** | | 1 | | | | | | | |
| Kellock, Billy | **2** | *5* | 1 | | | *1* | | 2 | | **2** |
| Money, Richard | **31** | | 4 | | 1 | | | | | |
| Moss, David | **39** | | 4 | | 1 | | **9** | 1 | | **10** |
| Parker, Gary | **1** | | | | | | | | | |
| Small, Mike | | *1* | | | | | | | | |
| Stein, Brian | **20** | *1* | 4 | | 1 | | **14** | 1 | | **15** |
| Stephens, Kirk | **40** | | 3 | | 2 | | | | | |
| Thomas, Mitchell | **4** | | 1 | | 1 | | | | | |
| Turner, Wayne | **29** | *1* | 2 | | 2 | | **1** | | | **1** |
| Walsh, Paul | **41** | | 4 | | 2 | | **13** | | 1 | **14** |
| Watts, Mark | **1** | | | | 1 | | | | | |
| White, Steve | **4** | | | | | | | | | |
| (own-goals) | | | | | | | **5** | | | **5** |
| **26 players used** | **462** | *26* | **44** | *2* | **22** | *1* | **65** | **7** | **3** | **75** |

## CANON LEAGUE DIVISION 1    Manager: David Pleat    SEASON 1983-84

| No | Date | | Att | Pos | Pt | F-A | H-T | Scorers, Times, and Referees | 1 | 2 | 3 | 4 | 5 | 6 | 7 | 8 | 9 | 10 | 11 | 12 sub used |
|---|---|---|---|---|---|---|---|---|---|---|---|---|---|---|---|---|---|---|---|---|
| 1 | A | ARSENAL | | | L | 1-2 | 1-1 | Robson 39 (og) | **Sealey** | Stephens | Turner | Horton | Elliott | Donaghy | Hill | Stein B | Walsh | Bunn | Moss | |
| | 27/8 | | *39,347* | | - | | | *Woodcock 20, McDermott 49* | *Jennings* | *Robson* | *O'Leary* | *Hill* | *Sansom* | *Talbot* | *Davis* | *Rix* | *McDermott* | *Nicholas* | *Woodcock* | |
| | | | | | | | | Ref: J Martin | The Gunners give a debut to their new £750,000 signing Charlie Nicholas but it is Tony Woodcock who heads the home side into the lead. The Town level when Stewart Robson blasts the ball off the toes of Walsh for a spectacular own-goal, before Brian McDermott scores the winner. | | | | | | | | | | | |
| 2 | A | LEICESTER | | | W | 3-0 | 2-0 | Bunn 32, Moss 37, Hill 46 | Sealey | Stephens | Turner | Horton | Elliott | Donaghy | Hill | Stein B | Walsh | Bunn | Moss | |
| | 31/8 | | *12,629* | | 3 | | | | *Grew* | *Ramsey* | *Smith B* | *MacDonald* | *Banks* | *O'Neill* | *Lynex* | *Lineker* | *Smith A* | *Peake* | *Wilson* | |
| | | | | | | | | Ref: D Shaw | Bouncing back from the opening game defeat, Luton gain a convincing win against a promoted Leicester side who are still trying to find their feet at this level. Surging forward continuously, the Town tear into the Foxes' defence. All three goals are struck with venom and accuracy. | | | | | | | | | | | |
| 3 | H | SUNDERLAND | | 5 | W | 4-1 | 0-0 | Hill 46, Walsh 58, Munro 70 (og), | Sealey | Stephens | Turner | Horton | Elliott | Donaghy | Hill | Stein B | Walsh | Bunn | Moss | |
| | 3/9 | | 10,846 | *19* | 6 | | | *West 67* [Stein 76] | *Turner* | *Venison* | *Atkins* | *Chisholm* | *Munro* | *Elliott* | *Proctor* | *Pickering* | *Atkinson* | *Rowell* | *West* | |
| | | | | | | | | Ref: R Lewis | The bright early season form is continued as Sunderland are swept aside in the second half. David Moss puts over a stream of accurate crosses from which two of the goals are scored whilst goalkeeper Chris Turner is blamed for the others. Stein has a first-half penalty saved by Turner. | | | | | | | | | | | |
| 4 | H | NORWICH | | 6 | D | 2-2 | 0-2 | Elliott 58, Stein 89 | Sealey | Stephens | Turner | Horton | Elliott | Donaghy | Hill | Stein B | Walsh | Bunn* | Moss | Antic |
| | 6/9 | | 11,095 | *12* | 7 | | | *Channon 9, Mendham 19* | *Woods* | *Haylock* | *Young* | *Watson* | *Downs* | *Mendham* | *Barham* | *Deehan* | *van Wijk* | *Channon* | *Bertschin* | |
| | | | | | | | | Ref: A Gunn | The Canaries take a shock two-goal lead and, although the Town apply much pressure, Norwich always look dangerous on the break. Paul Elliott pulls a goal back after a corner from Moss is only partially cleared, and Brian Stein lets fly from 25 yards with only seconds remaining. | | | | | | | | | | | |
| 5 | A | MANCHESTER U | | 8 | L | 0-2 | 0-0 | | Sealey | Stephens | Turner | Horton | Elliott | Donaghy | Hill | Stein B | Walsh | Bunn* | Moss | Antic |
| | 10/9 | | ***41,013*** | *3* | 7 | | | *Muhren 49p, Albiston 72* | *Bailey* | *Gidman* | *McQueen* | *Moran* | *Albiston* | *Wilkins* | *Robson** | *Muhren* | *Stapleton* | *Whiteside* | *Graham* | *Moses* |
| | | | | | | | | Ref: F Roberts | Elliott handles the ball twice in the area. Arnold Muhren slots home the first but has his second shot saved by Sealey, although Arthur Albiston reacts quickly to the rebound. The Hatters are forced to defend for most of the game and they continue their sequence of defeats at Old Trafford. | | | | | | | | | | | |
| 6 | H | WOLVES | | 7 | W | **4-0** | 1-0 | Walsh 23, Stein 51, Moss 63, Horton 77 | Sealey | Stephens | Turner | Horton | Elliott | Donaghy | Hill | Stein B | Walsh | Bunn | Moss | |
| | 17/9 | | 10,975 | *21* | 10 | | | | *Burridge* | *Humphrey* | *Pender* | *Dodd* | *Palmer** | *Rudge* | *Cartwright* | *Towner* | *Livingstone* | *Gray* | *Eves* | *Hibbitt* |
| | | | | | | | | Ref: D Letts | Wolves are awful as the Hatters saunter to an easy victory. The Town should have scored a lot more goals, especially in the last twenty minutes when the visitors are thoroughly demoralised. The Wolves manager, Graham Hawkins, is grateful to go home without a seven-goal hammering. | | | | | | | | | | | |
| 7 | A | NOTT'M FOREST | | 13 | L | 0-1 | 0-0 | | Sealey | Stephens | Turner | Horton | Elliott | Donaghy | Hill | Stein B | Walsh | Bunn* | Moss | Antic |
| | 24/9 | | *16,296* | *7* | 10 | | | *Wallace 58* | *v Breukelen* | *Anderson* | *Todd* | *Hart* | *Swain* | *Bowyer* | *Hodge* | *Walsh* | *Wigley* | *Wallace* | *Birtles* | |
| | | | | | | | | Ref: J Worrall | Steve Wigley, a £2,000 signing from Ashton-under-Lyne, has a fifteen-minute spell in which he appears unstoppable and, during this period, he sets up Ian Wallace for the only goal of the game. Forest manager Brian Clough admits afterwards that the match could have swung either way. | | | | | | | | | | | |
| 8 | H | ASTON VILLA | | 9 | W | 1-0 | 0-0 | Moss 49p | Sealey | Stephens | Turner | Horton | Elliott | Donaghy | Hill | Stein B | Walsh | Bunn | Moss* | Antic |
| | 1/10 | | 12,747 | *11* | 13 | | | | *Spink* | *Williams* | *Evans* | *Ormsby* | *Gibson* | *Curbishley* | *Mortimer* | *Bremner* | *Walters* | *Withe* | *Morley** | *Shaw* |
| | | | | | | | | Ref: I Borrett | The England manager, Bobby Robson, is at Kenilworth Road to cast an eye over Stein, Elliott, Walsh and Hill. In a bad-tempered clash, it is no surprise that the only goal of the game comes from the penalty spot when Gary Williams brings down Bunn, leaving Moss to power in his kick. | | | | | | | | | | | |
| 9 | A | EVERTON | | 7 | W | 1-0 | 0-0 | Walsh 76 | Sealey | Stephens | Turner | Horton | Elliott | Donaghy | Hill | Stein B | Walsh | Bunn | Moss | |
| | 15/10 | | *14,327* | *15* | 16 | | | | *Southall* | *Harper* | *Ratcliffe* | *Higgins* | *Bailey* | *Reid* | *Steven* | *King* | *Heath* | *Sharp* | *Sheedy* | |
| | | | | | | | | Ref: J Hough | One flash of individual brilliance from Walsh settles the issue. The England international takes the ball down the middle, shrugs off Everton defender Mark Higgins, before beating Neville Southall low down. The Toffees have not won at home since the opening day of the season. | | | | | | | | | | | |
| 10 | H | SOUTHAMPTON | | 4 | W | 3-1 | 2-0 | Aylott 13, 33, Stein 64 | Sealey | Stephens | Turner | Horton | Elliott | Donaghy | Hill | Stein B | Aylott | Bunn* | Moss | Antic |
| | 22/10 | | 12,389 | *7* | 19 | | | *Armstrong D 68* | *Shilton* | *Baker* | *Armstrong K* | *Wright* | *Agboola* | *Williams* | *Holmes* | *Moran* | *Armstrong D* | *Baird* | *Wallace* | |
| | | | | | | | | Ref: V Callow | Aylott, playing as a replacement for the suspended Walsh, stakes his claim for a regular place in the team with two great strikes. However, the goal of the game is a volley from Stein after a lay-off from Aylott. Moss misses from the penalty spot after being tripped by Reuben Agboola. | | | | | | | | | | | |

| No / Date | H/A | Opponent / Att | Pos | Res / Pts | F-A | H-T | Scorers, Times, and Referees | 1 | 2 | 3 | 4 | 5 | 6 | 7 | 8 | 9 | 10 | 11 | subs used |
|---|---|---|---|---|---|---|---|---|---|---|---|---|---|---|---|---|---|---|---|
| 11 | A | LIVERPOOL | 7 | L | **0-6** | 0-4 | | Sealey | Stephens | Thomas | Horton | Elliott | Donaghy | Hill | Stein B | Walsh | Turner | Antic | |
| 29/10 | | *31,940* | *2* | 19 | | | *Rush 2, 5, 36, 54, 87, Dalglish 37* | *Grobbelaar* | *Neal* | *Lawrenson* | *Hansen* | *Kennedy* | *Lee* | *Souness* | *Dalglish* | *Nicol* | *Rush* | *Robinson* | |
| | | | | | | | Ref: J Key | Liverpool have one of those afternoons where everything comes off and the Town suffer their worst defeat for almost 20 years. In an awesome display of attacking football, Ian Rush hits five. The Hatters have three shots on target in the match and Walsh hits the bar in the final minute. | | | | | | | | | | | |
| 12 | A | QP RANGERS | 4 | W | 1-0 | 1-0 | Elliott 10 | Sealey | Stephens | Turner | Horton | Elliott | Donaghy | Hill | Stein B | Walsh | Aylott | Parker | |
| 5/11 | | *15,053* | *6* | 22 | | | | *Hucker* | *Neill* | *Wicks* | *Fenwick* | *Dawes* | *Waddock* | *Stewart* | *Gregory !* | *Micklewhite* | *Allen* | *Stainrod* | |
| | | | | | | | Ref: L Burden | Elliott heads in a right wing cross from Parker to score the only goal of the game and record a second win on the Loftus Road artificial surface. Rangers pile on the pressure but the Luton defence holds firm. John Gregory is sent off with 20 minutes to go for kicking Luton keeper Sealey. | | | | | | | | | | | |
| 13 | H | BIRMINGHAM | 5 | D | 1-1 | 1-1 | Stein 16 | Sealey | Stephens | Thomas | **Johnson** | Elliott | Donaghy | Hill | Stein B | Walsh | Turner | Parker* | Antic |
| 12/11 | | 11,111 | *14* | 23 | | | *Hopkins 8* | *Coton* | *Hagan* | *Blake* | *Wright* | *v d Hauwe* | *Stevenson* | *Phillips* | *Handysides* | *Hopkins* | *Gayle* | *Khul* | |
| | | | | | | | Ref: T Spencer | Five of the players are aged 21 or under, as the injury-hit Hatters battle for a draw against a tough Birmingham side. Robert Hopkins opens the scoring for the Blues, latching on to a rebound off centre-half Elliott, but Stein equalises in a similar fashion. Rob Johnson makes a solid debut. | | | | | | | | | | | |
| 14 | H | TOTTENHAM | 10 | L | 2-4 | 0-1 | Stein 63, Walsh 73 | Sealey | Stephens | Turner | Goodyear | Elliott | Donaghy | Hill | Stein B | Walsh | Aylott | Antic | |
| 19/11 | | **17,275** | *4* | 23 | | | *Cooke 32, Archibald 58, 71, Dick 87* | *Clemence* | *Hughton* | *Roberts* | *Stevens* | *Thomas* | *Cooke* | *Perryman* | *Hoddle* | *Archibald* | *Falco* | *Dick* | |
| | | | | | | | Ref: M Robinson | Due to injuries, the Town revert to the sweeper system and Goodyear is recalled to the defence. Ray Clemence upends Stephens in the area and then saves the penalty-kick from Stein. Glenn Hoddle also misses from the spot, his kick hitting a post. The final scoreline flatters Tottenham. | | | | | | | | | | | |
| 15 | A | WATFORD | 5 | W | 2-1 | 1-1 | Stein 2, Bunn 84 | Sealey | Stephens | Turner | Horton | Elliott | Donaghy | Hill | Stein B | Walsh | Aylott | Bunn | |
| 26/11 | | *17,791* | *20* | 26 | | | *Callaghan 31* | *Sherwood* | *Bardsley* | *Sims* | *Franklin* | *Price* | *Jobson* | *Rostron* | *Callaghan* | *Barnes* | *Reilly* | *Johnston* | |
| | | | | | | | Ref: D Hedges | Struggling Watford show honest toil but little else as the Town do not need to over-extend themselves. Stein turns in a cross from Walsh after just 74 seconds and the Hornets equalise against the run of play. Bunn scores a deserved winner with a low drive after some clever interplay. | | | | | | | | | | | |
| 16 | H | COVENTRY | 10 | L | 2-4 | 0-2 | Pearce 49 (og), Aylott 68 | Sealey | Stephens | Turner | Horton | Elliott | Donaghy | Hill | Stein B | Walsh | Aylott | Bunn* | Antic |
| 3/12 | | 10,698 | *5* | 26 | | | *Gibson 34, 36, Gynn 67, Bennett 73* | *Suckling* | *Roberts* | *Peake* | *Allardyce* | *Pearce* | *Bennett* | *Gynn* | *Hunt* | *Platnauer* | *Bamber* | *Gibson* | |
| | | | | | | | Ref: B Hill | In a repeat of the previous home game, the Town defence is full of holes and the Sky Blues counter-attack and make the most of their chances. Stuart Pearce heads past his own keeper, as though trying to help the Hatters back into the game, but the end result means they slip five places. | | | | | | | | | | | |
| 17 | A | STOKE | 8 | W | 4-2 | 2-1 | Walsh 19, 26, 88, Daniel 62 | Sealey | Stephens | Thomas | Horton | Elliott | Donaghy | Hill | Stein B | Walsh | Aylott | Daniel | |
| 10/12 | | *10,329* | *21* | 29 | | | *James 36p, 65* | *Fox* | *Bould* | *Berry* | *McAughtrie* | *Hampton* | *Maskery* | *McIlroy* | *Thomas* | *Chamberlain* | *Painter** | *James* | *Maguire* |
| | | | | | | | Ref: C Thomas | Walsh scores a hat-trick against the lowly Potters team who had sacked their manager, Richie Barker, the previous day. Robbie James converts from the spot after Ian Painter drives the ball at the hand of Mal Donaghy. The superb headed goal by Ray Daniel is his first for the Hatters. | | | | | | | | | | | |
| 18 | H | WEST BROM | 6 | W | 2-0 | 1-0 | Horton 41p, Aylott 64 | Sealey | Stephens | Thomas | Horton | Elliott | Donaghy | Hill | Stein B | Walsh | Aylott | Daniel | |
| 18/12 | | 11,566 | *13* | 32 | | | | *Barron* | *Zondervan* | *McNaught* | *Forsyth* | *Cowdrill* | *Luke* | *Jol !* | *Lewis* | *Morley* | *Regis* | *Cross* | |
| | | | | | | | Ref: M Taylor | Horton steps up to score, after Daniel is fouled in the area, to become the third Luton penalty-taker this season. Aylott curls a shot into the top left hand corner before Martin Jol is sent off for a second bookable offence. Nearly 400 spectators insist on free admission to this Sunday game. | | | | | | | | | | | |
| 19 | A | NOTTS CO | 3 | W | 3-0 | 1-0 | Aylott 18, 76, Daniel 71 | Sealey | Stephens | Thomas | Horton | Elliott | Donaghy | Hill | Stein B | Walsh | Aylott | Daniel | |
| 26/12 | | *9,789* | *20* | 35 | | | | *McDonagh* | *Goodwin* | *Richards* | *Hunt* | *Kilcline* | *Worthington* | *O'Neill* | *Christie* | *Chiedozie* | *Fashanu* | *McCulloch** | *Harkouk* |
| | | | | | | | Ref: T Mills | The Town briefly move up to third place in the table following three wins in a row. County have scored 11 goals in their last two home games and they attack on the break but goal-line clearances, together with some acrobatic saves from Sealey, prevent them from taking a first-half lead. | | | | | | | | | | | |
| 20 | H | WEST HAM | 5 | L | 0-1 | 0-0 | | Sealey | Stephens | Thomas | Horton | Elliott | Donaghy | Hill | Stein B | Walsh | Aylott* | Daniel | Turner |
| 27/12 | | 16,343 | *4* | 35 | | | *Cottee 79* | *Parkes* | *Stewart* | *Walford* | *Martin* | *Brush* | *Orr* | *Barnes* | *Brooking* | *Devonshire* | *Whitton* | *Cottee* | |
| | | | | | | | Ref: K Baker | Despite dominating the first half, the Hatters are unable to break the deadlock. The Hammers come more into the game in the second period and eventually steal the win when Tony Cottee nips in at the near post to turn in a cross from Steve Whitton. A draw would have been a fair result. | | | | | | | | | | | |
| 21 | A | SUNDERLAND | 6 | L | 0-2 | 0-0 | | Sealey | Johnson* | Turner | Horton | Elliott | Donaghy | Hill | Stein B | Walsh | Bunn | Daniel | Antic |
| 31/12 | | *19,482* | *12* | 35 | | | *Chisholm 53, Pickering 56* | *Turner* | *Venison* | *Atkins* | *Chisholm* | *Elliott* | *Bracewell* | *Proctor* | *Pickering* | *James** | *Chapman* | *West* | *Robson* |
| | | | | | | | Ref: A Robinson | Luton only have one shot on target all afternoon and are fortunate to concede just the two goals to a physical Sunderland side. Johnson is off the field and receiving treatment when Gordon Chisholm heads the first, whilst sloppy defensive play from Turner and Daniel gifts the second. | | | | | | | | | | | |

| No | Date | | Att | Pos | Pt | F-A | H-T | Scorers, Times, and Referees | 1 | 2 | 3 | 4 | 5 | 6 | 7 | 8 | 9 | 10 | 11 | 12 sub used |
|---|---|---|---|---|---|---|---|---|---|---|---|---|---|---|---|---|---|---|---|---|
| 22 | H | NOTT'M FOREST | | 9 | L | 2-3 | 1-3 | Walsh 9, Nwajiobi 63 | Sealey | Stephens | Thomas | Horton | Elliott | Donaghy | Hill | Stein B | Walsh | Bunn* | Nwajiobi | Antic |
| | 2/1 | | 12,126 | 4 | 35 | | | Birtles 37, Hodge 39, Davenport 43 | v Breukelen | Anderson | Hart | Fairclough | Swain | Wigley | Hodge | Bowyer | Walsh | Birtles | Davenport* | Wallace |
| | | | | | | | | Ref: D Axcell | After taking an early lead, the Town are caught by three goals in the space of six minutes, the first taking a wicked deflection which completely wrong-foots Sealey. Nwajiobi makes his debut after just three reserve games and leads the charge after the break to score the second Luton goal. | | | | | | | | | | | |
| 23 | H | ARSENAL | | 9 | L | 1-2 | 0-1 | Kay 56 (og) | Sealey | Stephens | Thomas | Horton | Elliott | Donaghy | Parker* | Stein B | Walsh | Aylott | Bunn | Nwajiobi |
| | 14/1 | | 16,320 | 11 | 35 | | | Sansom 37, Woodcock 67 | Jennings | Kay | O'Leary | Caton | Sansom | Talbot | Nicholas | Meade | Rix | Woodcock | Davis | |
| | | | | | | | | Ref: K Hackett | The Hatters slip further down the table after a match in which they hit the woodwork twice and outplay the Gunners at times, though they are often overrun in midfield where they are missing the injured Ricky Hill. John Kay turns the ball past his own keeper for the solitary Luton goal. | | | | | | | | | | | |
| 24 | A | WOLVES | | 7 | W | 2-1 | 1-1 | Parker 2, Walsh 86 | Sealey | Stephens | Thomas | Horton | Elliott | Donaghy* | Parker | Stein B | Walsh | Aylott | Bunn | Goodyear |
| | 21/1 | | 11,594 | 22 | 38 | | | Pender 34 | Burridge | Humphrey | Pender | Dodd | Palmer | Daniel | Troughton | Crainie | Towner | Clarke | Eves | |
| | | | | | | | | Ref: H King | Gary Parker scores from close range early on against a bottom of the table Wolves team who then seem to lose heart. Luton-born John Pender equalises with a header - scored against the run of play - before Paul Walsh scores with an instinctive overhead kick in the closing minutes. | | | | | | | | | | | |
| 25 | A | ASTON VILLA | | 7 | D | 0-0 | 0-0 | | Sealey | Stephens | Thomas | Horton | Elliott | Donaghy | Parker | Stein B | Walsh | Aylott | Bunn | |
| | 4/2 | | 18,656 | 9 | 39 | | | | Spink | Williams | Evans | Bremner | Gibson | Curbishley | Mortimer | McMahon | Walters | Rideout | Shaw | |
| | | | | | | | | Ref: R Dilkes | The Villa game plan is shot to pieces as they had expecting the Town to attack, so that they could counter on the break. Both teams put up a disappointing performance and, with neither goalkeeper being seriously tested, the match is destined to remain scoreless long before the end. | | | | | | | | | | | |
| 26 | H | MANCHESTER U | | 9 | L | 0-5 | 0-2 | [Stapleton 81] | Sealey | Stephens | Thomas* | Horton | Elliott | Donaghy | Hill | Stein B | Walsh | Aylott | Bunn | Antic |
| | 12/2 | | 11,265 | 3 | 39 | | | Robson 37, 79, Whiteside 40, 85, | Bailey | Duxbury | Moran | Hogg | Albiston | Moses | Wilkins | Robson* | Muhren | Stapleton | Whiteside | Graham |
| | | | | | | | | Ref: A Robinson | After a midweek game in Oman, the Town look forward to their first live televised fixture, but they are to be humiliated in front of an audience of millions. Bryan Robson and Ray Wilkins excel for the visitors and their manager, Ron Atkinson, admits his side is currently in top form. | | | | | | | | | | | |
| 27 | H | LIVERPOOL | | 8 | D | 0-0 | 0-0 | | Sealey | Stephens | Thomas | Horton | Elliott | Goodyear | Hill | Stein B | Walsh | Donaghy | Daniel | |
| | 18/2 | | 14,877 | 1 | 40 | | | | Grobbelaar | Neal | Lawrenson | Hansen | Kennedy | Lee | Whelan | Hodgson | Souness | Rush | Johnston | |
| | | | | | | | | Ref: J Bray | The Hatters win back their pride against the league leaders, following the debacle of last week. Liverpool are hassled and harried for the whole of the ninety minutes and are never allowed to settle. Goodyear makes a rare appearance and manages to keep the prolific Ian Rush subdued. | | | | | | | | | | | |
| 28 | A | SOUTHAMPTON | | 11 | L | 1-2 | 0-2 | Donaghy 89 | Sealey | Stephens | Thomas | Horton | Elliott | Donaghy | Hill | Stein B | Walsh | Daniel | Nwajiobi* | Goodyear |
| | 25/2 | | 17,947 | 5 | 40 | | | Wright 30, Armstrong 44 | Shilton | Agboola | Mills | Wright | Holmes | Dennis | Williams | Armstrong | Wallace | Moran | Worthington | |
| | | | | | | | | Ref: K Cooper | Saints miss a hatful of chances against a Luton side who tend to opt for safety first. A header from Donaghy brings the game within reach as the Southampton fans scream for the final whistle. Nwajiobi nets but his effort is disallowed as Stein is adjudged to have fouled Peter Shilton. | | | | | | | | | | | |
| 29 | H | QP RANGERS | | 10 | D | 0-0 | 0-0 | | Sealey | Stephens | Thomas | Horton | Elliott | Goodyear | Hill | Stein B | Walsh | Donaghy | Aylott | |
| | 3/3 | | 11,922 | 6 | 41 | | | | Hucker | Neill | Wicks | Fenwick | Dawes | Fillery | Waddock | Gregory | Stewart | Charles* | Stainrod | Allen |
| | | | | | | | | Ref: N Midgley | Terry Venables instructs his players to set out for a draw and they stifle the game as a spectacle. An early foul by Horton on Jeremy Charles turns the match into a ill-tempered affair. Paul Walsh and Stein both played for England in midweek but have little chance to shine in this game. | | | | | | | | | | | |
| 30 | H | IPSWICH | | 8 | W | 2-1 | 1-0 | Aylott 39p, 53 | Sealey | Stephens | Thomas | Antic | Elliott | Goodyear | Donaghy | Stein B | Walsh | Aylott | Bunn | |
| | 13/3 | | 8,776 | 19 | 44 | | | Putney 83 | Cooper | Burley | Osman | Butcher | Barnes | Putney | Wark | McCall | Gates | Turner* | Sunderland | Dozzell |
| | | | | | | | | Ref: H Taylor | On a cold, snowy night, Aylott warms the hearts of the supporters with a brace of goals, a wonderful chip and a penalty awarded after Russell Osman fouls Frank Bunn. Trevor Putney scores a consolation goal with a tap-in but it comes too late in the game to save struggling Ipswich. | | | | | | | | | | | |
| 31 | A | NORWICH | | 7 | D | 0-0 | 0-0 | | Sealey | Stephens | Thomas | Antic | Elliott | Goodyear | Donaghy | Stein B | Walsh | Aylott | Bunn | |
| | 17/3 | | 13,112 | 11 | 45 | | | | Woods | Haylock | Watson | Hareide | Downs | Mendham | Bennett | van Wijk | Channon | Deehan | Rigby | |
| | | | | | | | | Ref: M Scott | Mitchell Thomas does not allow veteran winger Mick Channon to have a kick of the ball and Walsh, unsettled after bids are reported to have been received from Liverpool, has a quiet game. In a surprisingly entertaining match, the Hatters shade the first half and Norwich the second. | | | | | | | | | | | |

| | | | | | | | | | | | | | | | | | | | | |
|---|---|---|---|---|---|---|---|---|---|---|---|---|---|---|---|---|---|---|---|---|
| 32 | A | BIRMINGHAM | | 8 | D | 1-1 | 1-0 | Stein 4 | Sealey | Stephens | Thomas | Antic | Elliott | Goodyear | Donaghy | Stein B | Walsh | Aylott | Bunn | |
| | 20/3 | | ***9,592*** | *15* | 46 | | | *Wright 81p* | *Coton* | *Roberts* | *Blake* | *Wright* | *Hagan* | *Broadhurst* | *v d Hauwe* | *Rees* | *Gayle* | *Harford* | *Hopkins* | |
| | | | | | | | | Ref: E Read | Stein opens the scoring with a quickly taken low shot to record his first goal in ten games. The Luton defence, although under pressure, appears to be holding out until Thomas handles a ball which is driven at him in the area. The referee awards a penalty from which Billy Wright scores. | | | | | | | | | | | |
| 33 | H | LEICESTER | | 10 | D | 0-0 | 0-0 | | Sealey | Stephens | Thomas | Horton | Elliott | Goodyear | Donaghy | Stein B | Walsh | Parker | Moss | |
| | 24/3 | | 10,509 | *15* | 47 | | | | *Wallington* | *Williams* | *Hazell* | *O'Neill* | *Smith B* | *Lynex* | *Wilson* | *Peake* | *MacDonald* | *Lineker* | *Smith A* | |
| | | | | | | | | Ref: A Crickmore | David Moss returns to the side after a five-month injury absence. On a mud-heap of a pitch, the Town cannot play their usual close-passing game and yet another goal-less draw is the consequence, this time against a robust Leicester team who, by playing the long-ball, take no prisoners. | | | | | | | | | | | |
| 34 | A | IPSWICH | | 11 | L | 0-3 | 0-0 | | Sealey | Stephens | Thomas | Horton | Antic | Goodyear | Donaghy | Stein B | Walsh | **Breacker** | Moss* | Bunn |
| | 31/3 | | *14,586* | *20* | 47 | | | *Gates 48, Putney 62, D'Avray 75* | *Cooper* | *Burley* | *Butcher* | *Osman* | *McCall* | *Zondervan** | *Brennan* | *Gates* | *Putney* | *D'Avray* | *Sunderland* | *Barnes* |
| | | | | | | | | Ref: R Lewis | The Hatters are swept away by a determined Ipswich side who are seeking their first home win for two months. Eric Gates opens the scoring with a simple goal after Sealey pushes out his penalty and it is one-way traffic after this. 19-year-old Breacker makes his debut for the Town. | | | | | | | | | | | |
| 35 | H | EVERTON | | 12 | L | 0-3 | 0-0 | | Sealey | Stephens | Thomas | Horton | Elliott | Donaghy ! | Breacker | Stein B | **Stein M*** | Aylott | Bunn | Goodyear |
| | 7/4 | | 9,224 | *11* | 47 | | | *Mountfield 63, Heath 77, 88p* | *Southall* | *Stevens* | *Mountfield* | *Harper* | *Bailey* | *Reid* | *Steven* | *Richardson* | *Curran* | *Heath* | *Sharp* | |
| | | | | | | | | Ref: J Ashworth | Donaghy is controversially dismissed for bringing down Adrian Heath, when he is in full flight, and the game ends as a contest from this point. Everton score three times as the match degenerates into a kicking contest. Mark Stein, the younger brother of Brian, comes in for his first game. | | | | | | | | | | | |
| 36 | A | TOTTENHAM | | 14 | L | 1-2 | 0-1 | Parker 88 | Sealey | Stephens | Thomas | Horton | Elliott | Donaghy | Parker | Stein B | Aylott* | Bunn | Moss | Antic |
| | 14/4 | | *25,390* | *7* | 47 | | | *Roberts 20, Falco 83* | *Parks* | *Thomas* | *Roberts* | *Miller* | *Hughton* | *Perryman* | *Hazard* | *Mabbutt* | *Archibald* | *Falco* | *Galvin** | *Stevens* |
| | | | | | | | | Ref: M Bodenham | Tottenham run the game, in spite of having played in a tough match in Europe during the week. They play an effective offside trap and stroll to a comfortable victory. The 20-yard drive from Gary Parker, towards the end, is an isolated moment of class on a day which is best forgotten. | | | | | | | | | | | |
| 37 | A | WEST HAM | | 14 | L | 1-3 | 0-2 | Walsh 64 | Sealey | Stephens | Thomas | Horton | Elliott | Donaghy | Parker | Stein B | Walsh | Bunn* | Moss | Goodyear |
| | 17/4 | | *15,430* | *6* | 47 | | | *Cottee 23, 80, Martin 37* | *Parkes* | *Stewart* | *Bonds* | *Martin* | *Walford* | *Barnes* | *Brooking* | *Allen* | *Pike* | *Cottee* | *Swindlehurst* | |
| | | | | | | | | Ref: D Reeves | Walsh scores from close range for his first goal in ten games and has a relatively simple chance to level the scores but wastes the opportunity. The Hammers break away and Tony Cottee thumps in the match-winning third goal. The Town attack has clearly lost its early season sparkle. | | | | | | | | | | | |
| 38 | H | NOTTS CO | | 10 | W | 3-2 | 0-0 | Moss 69, Horton 79p, Bunn 89 | Sealey | Stephens | Thomas | Horton | Elliott | Goodyear | Parker | Stein B | Walsh | Bunn | Moss* | Antic |
| | 21/4 | | **8,181** | *21* | 50 | | | *Christie 68, Chiedozie 85* | *Leonard* | *Hodson* | *Richards* | *Armstrong* | *Clarke* | *Hunt* | *O'Neill* | *Mair* | *McParland** | *Chiedozie* | *Christie* | *Harkouk* |
| | | | | | | | | Ref: J Martin | Trevor Christie scores after the break before Moss and Horton, from the spot, put the Town in front, only for John Chiedozie to equalise. The first victory in eight games is secured when Bunn scores in the final minute in front of the lowest Division One attendance at Kenilworth Road. | | | | | | | | | | | |
| 39 | H | WATFORD | | 12 | L | 1-2 | 0-2 | Walsh 84 | Sealey | Stephens | Thomas | Horton | Elliott ! | Goodyear | Parker | Stein B | Walsh | Bunn | Moss* | Antic |
| | 28/4 | | 12,594 | *10* | 50 | | | *Callaghan 18, Johnston 44* | *Sherwood* | *Bardsley* | *Terry* | *Sinnott* | *Price* | *Taylor* | *Atkinson* | *Rostron !* | *Callaghan* | *Barnes** | *Johnston* | *Sterling* |
| | | | | | | | | Ref: R Milford | The referee manages to antagonise both sides when he dismisses both Paul Elliott and Wilf Rostron for a 'handbags at ten paces' offence which means that the latter will now miss the FA Cup final. Watford win at Kenilworth Road for the first time since 1964, but it is a close run thing. | | | | | | | | | | | |
| 40 | A | COVENTRY | | 13 | D | 2-2 | 0-1 | Antic 61, Stein 74 | Sealey | Stephens | Thomas | Horton | Goodyear | Donaghy | Parker | Stein B | Walsh | Bunn | Antic | |
| | 5/5 | | *9,647* | *18* | 51 | | | *Platnauer 4, Gibson 78* | *Suckling* | *Butterworth* | *Allardyce* | *Jacobs* | *Pearce* | *Daly* | *Grimes** | *Platnauer* | *Bennett* | *Ferguson* | *Gibson* | *Gynn* |
| | | | | | | | | Ref: R Bridges | Antic curls in a free-kick to score what turns out to be his last goal for the club. Stein heads the Town into the lead and the points seem to be safe but a failure to properly clear a corner allows Terry Gibson to pick his spot to give the home side the point which they desperately need. | | | | | | | | | | | |
| 41 | H | STOKE | | 13 | L | 0-1 | 0-1 | | Sealey | Stephens | Thomas | Horton | Goodyear | Donaghy | Parker | Stein B | Walsh | Bunn* | Antic | Nwajiobi |
| | 7/5 | | 9,867 | *20* | 51 | | | *Painter 4* | *Fox* | *Bould* | *Berry* | *O'Callaghan* | *Hampton* | *James* | *McIlroy* | *Maguire* | *Painter* | *Russell** | *Chamberlain* | *Maskery* |
| | | | | | | | | Ref: M James | Stoke, battling for survival at the bottom of the table, are gifted an early goal when linesman David Elleray refuses to raise his flag to give Ian Painter offside. He continues unchallenged with his run and shoots past a statuesque Sealey. The stubborn Stoke defence hold on for the win. | | | | | | | | | | | |
| 42 | A | WEST BROM | | 16 | L | 0-3 | 0-0 | | Sealey | Donaghy | Turner* | Horton | Goodyear | **North** | Parker | Stein B | Walsh | Aylott | Bunn | Antic |
| | 12/5 | | *12,004* | *17* | 51 | | | *Morley 63, Regis 85, MacKenzie 89* | *Barron* | *Whitehead* | *McNaught* | *Bennett* | *Statham* | *Hunt* | *Grealish* | *Mackenzie* | *Cross* | *Regis* | *Morley* | |
| | Home | Away | | | | | | Ref: K Hackett | The season slides to a gentle close as Raddy Antic, Brian Horton, Trevor Aylott, Paul Walsh and Clive Goodyear all say goodbye to the Luton supporters. The Town look jaded and, having only picked up 16 points in the second half of the campaign, look to have been relegation fodder. | | | | | | | | | | | |
| Average | 11,938 | 17,902 | | | | | | | | | | | | | | | | | | |

## Milk Cup

| Milk Cup | | | F-A | H-T | Scorers, Times, and Referees | 1 | 2 | 3 | 4 | 5 | 6 | 7 | 8 | 9 | 10 | 11 | 12 sub used |
|---|---|---|---|---|---|---|---|---|---|---|---|---|---|---|---|---|---|
| 2:1 A ROTHERHAM | 9 | W | 3-2 | 2-0 | Walsh 3, Bunn 10, Aylott 89 | Sealey | Stephens | Turner | Elliott | Donaghy | Hill | Stein B | Walsh ! | Bunn | Aylott | Horton | |
| 4/10 | *4,305 3:14* | | | | *Gooding 66, Kilmore 88* | *Stevenson* | *Forrest* | *Johnson* | *Crosby* | *Friar* | *O'Dell* | *Gooding* | *Mitchell* | *Kilmore* | *Seasman* | *Raynes* | |
| | | | | | Ref: D Owen | | | | | | | | | | | | |

The Town are walking away with this tie as Walsh hits an early snap shot and then sets up Bunn in the first ten minutes, but his performance is spoilt when he is dismissed for swearing at the referee just before half-time. Rotherham level before Aylott hits the winner in the last seconds.

| Milk Cup | | | F-A | H-T | Scorers, Times, and Referees | 1 | 2 | 3 | 4 | 5 | 6 | 7 | 8 | 9 | 10 | 11 | 12 sub used |
|---|---|---|---|---|---|---|---|---|---|---|---|---|---|---|---|---|---|
| 2:2 H ROTHERHAM | 4 | L | 0-2 | 0-1 | | Sealey | Stephens | Turner | Horton | Elliott | Donaghy | Hill | Stein B | Aylott | Antic | Daniel | |
| 25/10 | 6,755 *3:14* | | *aet* | | *Walker 35, Kilmore 107* | *Stevenson* | *Forrest* | *Johnson* | *Stone* | *Crosby* | *McEwan* | *Gooding* | *Mitchell* | *Kilmore* | *Walker* | *Raynes** | *Rhodes* |
| | | | | | Ref: K Barratt | | | | | | | | | | | | |
| | | | | | (Hatters lose 3-4 on aggregate) | | | | | | | | | | | | |

The Millers deserve their overall victory as they seem to want to win the second leg more than Luton. Missing several key players, the Hatters are disjointed and the defence is all over the place when Walker scores a route-one goal. The winner from Kilmore in extra-time is no surprise.

## FA Cup

| FA Cup | | | F-A | H-T | Scorers, Times, and Referees | 1 | 2 | 3 | 4 | 5 | 6 | 7 | 8 | 9 | 10 | 11 | 12 sub used |
|---|---|---|---|---|---|---|---|---|---|---|---|---|---|---|---|---|---|
| 3 H WATFORD | 9 | D | 2-2 | 2-2 | Nwajiobi 18, Stein 27 | Sealey | Stephens | Thomas | Horton | Elliott | Donaghy | Hill | Stein B | Walsh | Bunn | Nwajiobi* | Antic |
| 7/1 | 15,007 *1:17* | | | | *Barnes 29, Johnston 38p* | *Sherwood* | *Bardsley* | *Sims* | *Franklin* | *Rostron* | *Taylor* | *Jackett* | *Callaghan* | *Barnes* | *Reilly* | *Johnston* | |
| | | | | | Ref: A Gunn | | | | | | | | | | | | |

Three deflected goals, several bad misses, a shot which hits the bar and frantic end-to-end football make this a classic cup-tie. The Hornets are lucky to hang on after their defence takes a pounding in the second half, but they nearly engineer the win when Nigel Callaghan hits the bar.

| FA Cup | | | F-A | H-T | Scorers, Times, and Referees | 1 | 2 | 3 | 4 | 5 | 6 | 7 | 8 | 9 | 10 | 11 | 12 sub used |
|---|---|---|---|---|---|---|---|---|---|---|---|---|---|---|---|---|---|
| 3R A WATFORD | 9 | L | 3-4 | 1-2 | Donaghy 44, Walsh 65,70 *[J'ston 108]* | Sealey | Stephens | Thomas | Horton | Elliott | Donaghy | Parker | Stein B | Walsh | Aylott | Bunn* | Nwajiobi |
| 10/1 | *20,586 1:17* | | *aet* | | *Callaghan 4, Reilly 28, Barnes 50,* | *Sherwood* | *Bardsley* | *Sims* | *Franklin* | *Rostron* | *Taylor* | *Jackett* | *Callaghan* | *Barnes* | *Reilly* | *Johnston* | |
| | | | | | Ref: A Gunn | | | | | | | | | | | | |

The Town go two goals down to the Hornets but, with Walsh in unstoppable form, they pull back to level in normal time. England manager Bobby Robson is watching Walsh, Stein and John Barnes, who all turn in towering performances. Mo Johnston hits the winner in extra-time.

| | | Home | | | | | Away | | | | | |
|---|---|---|---|---|---|---|---|---|---|---|---|---|
| | P | W | D | L | F | A | W | D | L | F | A | Pts |
| 1 Liverpool | 42 | 14 | 5 | 2 | 50 | 12 | 8 | 9 | 4 | 23 | 20 | 80 |
| 2 Southampton | 42 | 15 | 4 | 2 | 44 | 17 | 7 | 7 | 7 | 22 | 21 | 77 |
| 3 Nott'm Forest | 42 | 14 | 4 | 3 | 47 | 17 | 8 | 4 | 9 | 29 | 28 | 74 |
| 4 Manchester U | 42 | 14 | 3 | 4 | 43 | 18 | 6 | 11 | 4 | 28 | 23 | 74 |
| 5 QP Rangers | 42 | 14 | 4 | 3 | 37 | 12 | 8 | 3 | 10 | 30 | 25 | 73 |
| 6 Arsenal | 42 | 10 | 5 | 6 | 41 | 29 | 8 | 4 | 9 | 33 | 31 | 63 |
| 7 Everton | 42 | 9 | 9 | 3 | 21 | 12 | 7 | 5 | 9 | 23 | 30 | 62 |
| 8 Tottenham | 42 | 11 | 4 | 6 | 31 | 24 | 6 | 6 | 9 | 33 | 41 | 61 |
| 9 West Ham | 42 | 10 | 4 | 7 | 39 | 24 | 7 | 5 | 9 | 21 | 31 | 60 |
| 10 Aston Villa | 42 | 14 | 3 | 4 | 34 | 22 | 3 | 6 | 12 | 25 | 39 | 60 |
| 11 Watford | 42 | 9 | 7 | 5 | 36 | 31 | 7 | 2 | 12 | 32 | 46 | 57 |
| 12 Ipswich | 42 | 11 | 4 | 6 | 34 | 23 | 4 | 4 | 13 | 21 | 34 | 53 |
| 13 Sunderland | 42 | 8 | 9 | 4 | 26 | 18 | 5 | 4 | 12 | 16 | 35 | 52 |
| 14 Norwich | 42 | 9 | 8 | 4 | 34 | 20 | 3 | 7 | 11 | 14 | 29 | 51 |
| 15 Leicester | 42 | 11 | 5 | 5 | 40 | 30 | 2 | 7 | 12 | 25 | 38 | 51 |
| 16 LUTON TOWN | 42 | 7 | 5 | 9 | 30 | 33 | 7 | 4 | 10 | 23 | 33 | 51 |
| 17 West Brom | 42 | 10 | 4 | 7 | 30 | 25 | 4 | 5 | 12 | 18 | 37 | 51 |
| 18 Stoke | 42 | 11 | 4 | 6 | 30 | 23 | 2 | 7 | 12 | 14 | 40 | 50 |
| 19 Coventry | 42 | 8 | 5 | 8 | 33 | 33 | 5 | 6 | 10 | 24 | 44 | 50 |
| 20 Birmingham | 42 | 7 | 7 | 7 | 19 | 18 | 5 | 5 | 11 | 20 | 32 | 48 |
| 21 Notts Co | 42 | 6 | 7 | 8 | 31 | 36 | 4 | 4 | 13 | 19 | 36 | 41 |
| 22 Wolves | 42 | 4 | 8 | 9 | 15 | 28 | 2 | 3 | 16 | 12 | 52 | 29 |
| | 924 | 226 | 118 | 118 | 745 | 505 | 118 | 118 | 226 | 505 | 745 | 1268 |

Odds & ends

Double wins: (2) Notts County, Wolves.
Double losses: (5) Arsenal, Manchester United, Nott'm Forest, Tottenham, West Ham.

Won from behind: (1) Notts County (h).
Lost from in front: (1) Nott'm Forest (h).

High spots: The championship winning form before Christmas.
Touching top spot for a couple of hours on Boxing Day.

Low spots: The relegation form after Christmas.
The sale of Paul Walsh.
Losing to Rotherham in the League Cup.
Losing to Watford at Kenilworth Road for the first time since 1964.

Player of the Year: Kirk Stephens.
Ever-presents: (2) Les Sealey, Brian Stein.
Hat-tricks: Paul Walsh (1).
Leading scorer: Paul Walsh (14).

| | Appearances | | | | | | Goals | | | |
|---|---|---|---|---|---|---|---|---|---|---|
| | **Lge** | *Sub* | LC | *Sub* | FAC | *Sub* | **Lge** | LC | FAC | **Tot** |
| Antic, Raddy | **8** | *14* | 1 | | | *1* | **1** | | | **1** |
| Aylott, Trevor | **20** | | 2 | | 1 | | **8** | 1 | | **9** |
| Breacker, Tim | **2** | | | | | | | | | |
| Bunn, Frank | **29** | *1* | 1 | | 2 | | **3** | 1 | | **4** |
| Daniel, Ray | **7** | | 1 | | | | **2** | | | **2** |
| Donaghy, Mal | **40** | | 2 | | 2 | | **1** | | 1 | **2** |
| Elliott, Paul | **38** | | 2 | | 2 | | **2** | | | **2** |
| Goodyear, Clive | **13** | *4* | | | | | | | | |
| Hill, Ricky | **26** | | 2 | | 1 | | **2** | | | **2** |
| Horton, Brian | **37** | | 2 | | 2 | | **3** | | | **3** |
| Johnson, Rob | **2** | | | | | | | | | |
| Moss, David | **16** | | | | | | **4** | | | **4** |
| North, Stacey | **1** | | | | | | | | | |
| Nwajiobi, Emeka | **2** | *2* | | | 1 | *1* | **1** | | 1 | **2** |
| Parker, Gary | **13** | | | | 1 | | **2** | | | **2** |
| Sealey, Les | **42** | | 2 | | 2 | | | | | |
| Stein, Brian | **42** | | 2 | | 2 | | **9** | | 1 | **10** |
| Stein, Mark | **1** | | | | | | | | | |
| Stephens, Kirk | **40** | | 2 | | 2 | | | | | |
| Thomas, Mitchell | **26** | | | | 2 | | | | | |
| Turner, Wayne | **18** | *1* | 2 | | | | | | | |
| Walsh, Paul | **39** | | 1 | | 2 | | **11** | 1 | 2 | **14** |
| (own-goals) | | | | | | | **4** | | | **4** |
| **22 players used** | **462** | *22* | 22 | | 22 | *2* | **53** | 3 | 5 | **61** |

# CANON LEAGUE DIVISION 1 — Manager: David Pleat — SEASON 1984-85

| No | Date | Att | Pos | Pt | F-A | H-T | Scorers, Times, and Referees | 1 | 2 | 3 | 4 | 5 | 6 | 7 | 8 | 9 | 10 | 11 | 12 sub used |
|---|---|---|---|---|---|---|---|---|---|---|---|---|---|---|---|---|---|---|---|
| 1 | H STOKE | | | W | 2-0 | 1-0 | Elliott S 3, Bunn 65 | **Dibble** | Thomas | **Grimes** | Breacker | North | Donaghy | Hill | Stein | **Elliott S** | Bunn | Moss | |
| | 25/8 | 8,626 | | 3 | | | | *Fox* | *Bould* | *Dyson* | *O'Callaghan* | *Maskery* | *James* | *McIlroy* | *Hudson* | *Parkin* | *Heath* | *Painter* | |
| | | | | | | | Ref: T Bune | It is all so easy for the Town against a poor Stoke side who look as though they will be having a battle against relegation, even this early in the campaign. Steve Elliott scores a disputed goal, the Potters complaining about a foul on their keeper, and Bunn hits the second from 18 yards. | | | | | | | | | | | |
| 2 | A IPSWICH | | | D | 1-1 | 0-1 | Moss 80 | Dibble | Thomas | Grimes | Breacker | North | Donaghy | Hill | Stein | Elliott S | Bunn* | Moss | Nwajiobi |
| | 28/8 | *15,833* | | 4 | | | *Gates 2* | *Cooper* | *Burley* | *Osman* | *Butcher* | *McCall* | *Zondervan* | *Putney* | *Brennan* | *O'Callaghan* | *D'Avray* | *Gates* | |
| | | | | | | | Ref: M Bodenham | Ipswich pound away at the Luton defence for almost the whole game but the woodwork, and an inspired performance by keeper Dibble, means that they are unable to add to the early goal, scored by Eric Gates. Moss takes advantage of a long throw by North to hit an unlikely equaliser. | | | | | | | | | | | |
| 3 | A WEST BROM | | 11 | L | **0-4** | 0-2 | *[Thompson 71]* | Dibble | Thomas | Grimes | Breacker* | North | Donaghy | Hill | Stein | Elliott S | Bunn | Moss | Nwajiobi |
| | 1/9 | *11,653* | *3* | 4 | | | *Hunt 24, Regis 41, Cross 66,* | *Godden* | *Whitehead* | *Bennett* | *Robertson* | *Statham* | *MacKenzie* | *Grealish* | *Hunt* | *Thompson* | *Regis** | *Morley* | *Cross* |
| | | | | | | | Ref: R Bridges | In a below-par team performance, left-back Ashley Grimes, in particular, suffers a nightmare of a game with all four of the West Brom goals coming from right-wing crosses. Big centre-forwards, Cyrille Regis and Garry Thompson run riot, leaving the Luton defence to chase shadows. | | | | | | | | | | | |
| 4 | H LIVERPOOL | | 16 | L | 1-2 | 0-0 | Donaghy 63 | Dibble | Thomas | Grimes | Breacker | Elliott P | Donaghy | Hill | Stein | Elliott S* | Turner | Moss | Nwajiobi |
| | 4/9 | 14,127 | *2* | 4 | | | *Neal 47p, Dalglish 71* | *Grobbelaar* | *Neal* | *Lawrenson* | *Hansen* | *Kennedy* | *Lee* | *Whelan* | *Molby* | *Wark* | *Dalglish** | *Walsh* | *Robinson* |
| | | | | | | | Ref: D Letts | The Town very nearly match a Liverpool side who have to fight for their victory. Stein appears to be pushed onto the ball when he concedes a penalty, which is converted by Phil Neal. Donaghy equalises with a near-post header before Kenny Dalglish deceives Dibble to hit the winner. | | | | | | | | | | | |
| 5 | H SOUTHAMPTON | | 17 | D | 1-1 | 0-0 | Moss 53p | Dibble | Thomas | Grimes | Parker | Elliott P | Donaghy | Hill | Stein | Nwajiobi | Turner* | Moss | Bunn |
| | 8/9 | 8,657 | *22* | 5 | | | *Curtis 50* | *Shilton* | *Mills* | *Agboola* | *Wright* | *Dennis* | *Williams* | *Whitlock* | *Armstrong* | *Moran* | *Jordan* | *Curtis* | |
| | | | | | | | Ref: M Heath | Saints are determined not to lose this game and pull players back behind the ball at every opportunity. In a physical contest, Alan Curtis puts Southampton into the lead but the Town fight back. Moss equalises from the spot three minutes later after he is fouled by Reuben Agboola. | | | | | | | | | | | |
| 6 | A NOTT'M FOREST | | 19 | L | 1-3 | 0-0 | Moss 81 | Dibble | Thomas | Grimes | Turner* | Elliott P | Donaghy | Hill | Stein | Nwajiobi | Bunn | Moss | Parker |
| | 16/9 | *18,605* | *1* | 5 | | | *Hodge 58, 73, Davenport 71* | *Sutton* | *Gunn* | *Fairclough* | *Hart* | *Swain* | *Wigley* | *Bowyer* | *Metgod* | *Davenport* | *Christie** | *Hodge* | *Mills* |
| | | | | | | | Ref: K Redfern | The Town have much the better of the first half but their good approach play is let down by indifferent finishing. After Forest take the lead, the Hatters have nothing left to offer, apart from a Moss free-kick which arrives too late. Forest move to the top of the league with this victory. | | | | | | | | | | | |
| 7 | H CHELSEA | | 19 | D | 0-0 | 0-0 | | Dibble | Thomas | Grimes | Turner | Elliott P | Donaghy | Hill | Stein | Nwajiobi | Bunn | Moss | |
| | 22/9 | 16,066 | *11* | 6 | | | | *Niedzwiecki* | *Lee* | *Pates* | *McLaughlin* | *Rougvie* | *Bumstead* | *Spackman* | *Thomas* | *Nevin* | *Speedie* | *Dixon* | |
| | | | | | | | Ref: B Stevens | The match is played at a furious pace and both sides have the opportunity to win outright but the managers agree after the game that the draw is the fairest result. Luton-born Chelsea striker Kerry Dixon has not scored since the opening day of the season and is well held by Paul Elliott. | | | | | | | | | | | |
| 8 | A TOTTENHAM | | 19 | L | 2-4 | 2-2 | Moss 3, Bunn 27 *[Roberts 89p]* | Dibble | Thomas | Grimes | Turner | Elliott P | Donaghy | Hill | Stein | Bunn* | **Hilaire** | Moss | Parker |
| | 29/9 | *30,204* | *1* | 6 | | | *Hazard 21, Perryman 36, Falco 75,* | *Clemence* | *Stevens* | *Roberts* | *Miller* | *Hughton* | *Perryman* | *Hazard* | *Galvin* | *Chiedozie* | *Falco* | *Crooks* | |
| | | | | | | | Ref: A Gunn | The Town catch Spurs on the break in the first half with both Moss and Bunn beating a hesitant Ray Clemence. Donaghy misjudges a tackle on John Chiedozie in the area and Graham Roberts nets in the final minute to give the score an unrealistic look. Hilaire makes an impressive debut. | | | | | | | | | | | |
| 9 | A QP RANGERS | | 19 | W | 3-2 | 1-1 | Elliott S 17, Elliott P 77, Stein 82 | Dibble | Thomas | Grimes | Turner | Elliott P | Donaghy | Hill | Stein | Elliott S | Parker | Moss | |
| | 6/10 | *12,051* | *14* | 9 | | | *Fillery 26, Bannister 61* | *Hucker* | *Neill* | *Wicks* | *Fenwick* | *Dawes* | *Micklewhite* | *Fillery* | *Fereday* | *Gregory* | *Bannister* | *Stainrod* | |
| | | | | | | | Ref: H King | The Town win for the third successive time on the Loftus Road Omniturf surface, exploiting a weakness in the offside trap played by the home side which had been spotted by the Luton coaching staff. Playing a close-passing game, Stein scores the winner after he beats three defenders. | | | | | | | | | | | |
| 10 | H SHEFFIELD WED | | 19 | L | 1-2 | 0-1 | Bunn 81 | Dibble | Thomas | Turner | Bunn | Elliott P | Donaghy | Hill | Stein | Elliott S | Hilaire | Moss* | Parker |
| | 13/10 | 10,285 | *3* | 9 | | | *Chapman 35, Lyons 50* | *Hodge* | *Sterland* | *Oliver** | *Smith* | *Lyons* | *Ryan* | *Marwood* | *Blair* | *Chapman* | *Varadi* | *Shelton* | *Worthington* |
| | | | | | | | Ref: J Moules | The Hatters totally dominate the final 30 minutes of the game, after Parker replaces Moss and the formation changes to 4-3-3 from 4-2-4. Bunn hammers a shot into the roof of the net from 12 yards and then Vince Hilaire misses a sitter when blasting wide from six yards in the last minute. | | | | | | | | | | | |

| No | Venue | Opponent | Pos | Res | F-A | H-T | Scorers, Times, and Referees | 1 | 2 | 3 | 4 | 5 | 6 | 7 | 8 | 9 | 10 | 11 | 12 sub used |
|---|---|---|---|---|---|---|---|---|---|---|---|---|---|---|---|---|---|---|---|
| 11 | H | WATFORD | 16 | W | 3-2 | 2-2 | Bunn 21, 28, Elliott S 61 | Findlay | Thomas | Turner | Parker | Elliott P | Donaghy | Hill | Stein | Elliott S | Bunn | Hilaire | |
| 20/10 | | 12,192 | 21 | 12 | | | *Reilly 8, Blissett 27* | *Coton* | *Bardsley* | *Jobson* | *Sinnott* | *Rostron* | *Taylor** | *Callaghan* | *Jackett* | *Blissett* | *Reilly* | *Barnes* | *Gilligan* |
| | | | | | | | Ref: A Robinson | Watford have only one victory to show in eleven league meetings after this pulsating local derby where both sides suffer the jitters. The Hornets have the best of the first half but the Hatters equalise twice. After the break, Steve Elliott puts the Town in front with a cracking angled drive. | | | | | | | | | | | |
| 12 | A | SUNDERLAND | 19 | L | 0-3 | 0-1 | | Findlay | Thomas | Turner | Parker* | Elliott P | Donaghy | Hill | Stein | Elliott S | Bunn | Hilaire | Breacker |
| 27/10 | | *15,280* | *8* | 12 | | | *Chisholm 16, Wylde 53p, Pickering 75* | *Turner* | *Daniel* | *Chisholm* | *Elliott* | *Pickering* | *Proctor* | *Berry* | *Hodgson* | *Gayle** | *Wylde* | *Atkinson* | *West* |
| | | | | | | | Ref: J Hough | A penalty appeal is turned down by the referee after Brian Stein is upended by Sunderland goalkeeper Chris Turner in the area, but the trip by Mitchell Thomas on Howard Gayle is penalised and Rodger Wylde converts from the spot before Nick Pickering adds the decisive third goal. | | | | | | | | | | | |
| 13 | H | NEWCASTLE | 18 | D | 2-2 | 1-1 | Parker 26, Stein 87 | Dibble | Breacker | Turner | **Todd** | North | Donaghy | Hill | Stein | Elliott S | Parker | Daniel* | Hilaire |
| 3/11 | | 10,009 | *11* | 13 | | | *Beardsley 15, Heard 79* | *Carr* | *Brown* | *Anderson* | *Clarke* | *Saunders* | *McDonald* | *Heard* | *McCreery* | *Wharton* | *Waddle* | *Beardsley* | |
| | | | | | | | Ref: J Bray | Colin Todd brings all his years of experience to bear as he helps the Luton youngsters to earn a point against a very tough Newcastle side. Paul Elliott, Frank Bunn and David Moss are all absent through injury and the late tap-in goal from Brian Stein is no more than the Hatters deserve. | | | | | | | | | | | |
| 14 | A | NORWICH | 19 | L | 0-3 | 0-2 | | Dibble | Breacker | Turner | Todd | North | Donaghy | Hill | Stein | Bunn | Parker | Moss* | Nwajiobi |
| 10/11 | | *13,610* | *10* | 13 | | | *Mendham 18, Hartford 26, Gordon 46* | *Woods* | *Haylock* | *Bruce* | *Watson* | *Downs* | *Mendham** | *Hartford* | *Gordon* | *Channon* | *Deehan* | *Donowa* | *van Wijk* |
| | | | | | | | Ref: G Napthine | Norwich are made to look like world-beaters as the Town only start to play after they are three goals down. The experienced Mick Channon and Asa Hartford run the show whilst Brian Stein, who is going through a lean spell, has several very good opportunities to score but all go begging. | | | | | | | | | | | |
| 15 | A | MANCHESTER U | 21 | L | 0-2 | 0-0 | | Dibble* | Breacker | Turner | North | **Droy** | Donaghy | Hill | Stein | Elliott S | Bunn | Hilaire | Parker |
| 17/11 | | ***41,630*** | *2* | 13 | | | *Whiteside 56, 84* | *Bailey* | *Gidman* | *McQueen* | *Duxbury* | *Albiston* | *Moses* | *Robson** | *Strachan* | *Olsen* | *Hughes* | *Whiteside* | *Stapleton* |
| | | | | | | | Ref: G Courtney | New Chairman David Evans promises money to buy players as he concedes that the team is just not good enough. The Town drop into the relegation places as United, although not at their best, are still too good for the Hatters. Dibble is injured and Mal Donaghy deputises in goal. | | | | | | | | | | | |
| 16 | H | WEST HAM | 21 | D | 2-2 | 1-1 | Stein 36, Nwajiobi 47 | Findlay | Breacker | Donaghy | Turner | Droy* | North | Hill | Stein | Elliott S | Bunn | Nwajiobi | Parker |
| 24/11 | | 10,789 | *5* | 14 | | | *Whitton 9, Martin 84* | *McAlister* | *Stewart* | *Martin* | *Gale* | *Walford** | *Allen* | *Bonds* | *Whitton* | *Pike* | *Goddard* | *Cottee* | *Swindlehurst* |
| | | | | | | | Ref: K Barratt | The home debut of Droy lasts just 35 minutes as he is forced to go off with a hamstring injury. A sum of £500,000 has been made available to David Pleat to buy new players and he misses the match as he is away scouting. A late header from Alvin Martin steals a point for the Hammers. | | | | | | | | | | | |
| 17 | A | ARSENAL | 21 | L | 1-3 | 0-1 | Stein 74 | Sealey | Breacker | Thomas | Turner | **Foster** | Donaghy | Hill | Stein | Elliott S | Bunn* | Parker | Nwajiobi |
| 1/12 | | *26,336* | *3* | 14 | | | *Allinson 16, Woodcock 61, Anderson 67* | *Lukic* | *Anderson* | *Adams* | *Caton* | *Sansom* | *Talbot* | *Davis* | *Robson* | *Woodcock* | *Mariner* | *Allinson* | |
| | | | | | | | Ref: D Axcell | Pat Jennings is dropped for the first time in his 20-year league career but his replacement, John Lukic, has little to do apart from one acrobatic save. Ian Allinson is tripped in the area by Thomas but the spot-kick from Brian Talbot is saved by Sealey, replacing the injured Jake Findlay. | | | | | | | | | | | |
| 18 | H | ASTON VILLA | 20 | W | 1-0 | 1-0 | Preece 39 | Sealey | Breacker | Turner | Parker | Foster | Donaghy | Hill | Stein | Bunn | **Preece** | Moss | |
| 8/12 | | 7,696 | *18* | 17 | | | | *Spink* | *Williams* | *Evans* | *Ormsby* | *Gibson* | *McMahon** | *Curbishley* | *Cowans* | *Rideout* | *Withe* | *Walters* | *Dorigo* |
| | | | | | | | Ref: R Lewis | Only the Villa goalkeeper, Nigel Spink, prevents the Town from rattling up a much larger score as their new-look side runs away with the first half. Preece makes his debut and scores with a mis-hit shot near the end of the first half. Foster has a solid game and keeps out his old mates. | | | | | | | | | | | |
| 19 | A | LEICESTER | 21 | D | 2-2 | 1-0 | Stein 35, Harford 89 | Sealey | Breacker | Turner | Parker* | Foster | Donaghy | Hill | Stein | **Harford** | Preece | Moss | Thomas |
| 15/12 | | *10,476* | *15* | 18 | | | *Lynex 52, Smith A 56* | *Andrews* | *Feeley* | *Smith R* | *O'Neill* | *Wilson* | *Williams* | *Ramsey* | *Banks* | *Lynex* | *Eastoe* | *Smith A* | |
| | | | | | | | Ref: R Nixon | Stein opens the scoring when taking advantage of a through-pass from new signing Mick Harford. Steve Lynex then runs into Harford and the referee awards a penalty, but the kick is blasted wide. Alan Smith puts Leicester in front before Harford levels with a header in stoppage time. | | | | | | | | | | | |
| 20 | H | WEST BROM | 21 | L | 1-2 | 1-1 | Foster 15 | Sealey | Breacker | Turner | Parker | Foster | Donaghy | Thomas | Stein | Harford | Preece* | Moss | Nwajiobi |
| 18/12 | | **7,286** | *5* | 18 | | | *Thompson 40, Statham 54p* | *Godden* | *Nicholl* | *Bennett* | *Robertson* | *Statham* | *Valentine* | *Whitehead* | *MacKenzie* | *Grealish* | *Cross* | *Thompson* | |
| | | | | | | | Ref: E Read | It is back to square one against a fast and efficient West Brom side who gain a hotly contested penalty when Foster is adjudged to have fouled Nicky Cross with Derek Statham converting from the spot. Preece limps off injured on the hour and the chance of salvaging a point disappears. | | | | | | | | | | | |
| 21 | H | COVENTRY | 19 | W | 2-0 | 1-0 | Stein 14, Daniel 86 | Sealey | Breacker | Thomas | Turner | Foster | Donaghy | Hill | Stein | Harford | Daniel | Nwajiobi* | Bunn |
| 26/12 | | 9,237 | *21* | 21 | | | | *Ogrizovic* | *Stephens* | *Kilcline* | *Pearce* | *Adams* | *Jol** | *Bowman* | *Gynn* | *Gibson* | *Regis* | *Barnes* | *Bennett* |
| | | | | | | | Ref: M James | Stein scores with a 25-yard drive after an interchange of passes with Harford but, after two penalty appeals are turned down, a nervous end to the game is in prospect. Daniel takes advantage of some lax defending to score the all-important winner which lifts Luton out of the bottom three. | | | | | | | | | | | |

| No | Date | | Att | Pos | Pt | F-A | H-T | Scorers, Times, and Referees | 1 | 2 | 3 | 4 | 5 | 6 | 7 | 8 | 9 | 10 | 11 | 12 sub used |
|---|---|---|---|---|---|---|---|---|---|---|---|---|---|---|---|---|---|---|---|---|
| 22 | A | LIVERPOOL | | 19 | L | 0-1 | 0-1 | | Sealey | Breacker | Thomas | Turner | Foster | Donaghy | Hill | Stein | Harford | Daniel* | Bunn | Nwajiobi |
| | 29/12 | | *35,403* | *7* | 21 | | | *Wark 25* | *Grobbelaar* | *Neal* | *Hansen* | *Gillespie* | *Kennedy* | *Nicol* | *Whelan* | *MacDonald* | *Wark* | *Walsh* | *Dalglish* | |
| | | | | | | | | Ref: J Lovatt | In a game which was boring to watch, John Wark capitalises on a defensive error to head home a corner from Kenny Dalglish for the only goal of the game. The large Anfield crowd does not seem to appreciate the technical battle going on between the Luton defence and the home attack. | | | | | | | | | | | |
| 23 | A | EVERTON | | 21 | L | 1-2 | 0-1 | Harford 80 | Sealey | Breacker | Thomas* | Turner | Foster | Donaghy | Hill | Stein | Harford | Preece | Moss | Bunn |
| | 1/1 | | *31,641* | *2* | 21 | | | *Steven 10, 69* | *Southall* | *Bailey* | *Ratcliffe* | *Mountfield* | *v d Hauwe* | *Steven* | *Reid* | *Bracewell* | *Sheedy* | *Curran* | *Sharp* | |
| | | | | | | | | Ref: F Roberts | Everton create, and miss, a stack of chances as they give the Town the run-around. Trevor Steven scores twice, both from Kevin Sheedy passes, to put the home side in control. Harford heads past a committed Neville Southall with ten minutes to go and Moss misses in the final seconds. | | | | | | | | | | | |
| 24 | H | TOTTENHAM | | 21 | D | 2-2 | 0-0 | Stein 48, Nwajiobi 87 | Sealey | Breacker | Thomas | **Nicholas** | Foster | Donaghy | Hill | Stein | Harford | Nwajiobi | Preece* | Daniel |
| | 2/2 | | **17,511** | *2* | 22 | | | *Falco 84, Roberts 89* | *Clemence* | *Stevens* | *Roberts* | *Perryman* | *Hughton* | *Chiedozie** | *Hoddle* | *Mabbutt* | *Galvin* | *Crooks* | *Falco* | *Hazard* |
| | | | | | | | | Ref: N Midgley | The Town have now slipped to second from the bottom of Division 1 after a month without a league game. Spurs are lucky to escape with a point, courtesy of a last-minute equaliser from Graham Roberts, after new signing, Nicholas, had controlled the midfield for most of the match. | | | | | | | | | | | |
| 25 | A | NEWCASTLE | | 21 | L | 0-1 | 0-0 | | Sealey | Breacker | Thomas | Nicholas | Foster | Donaghy | Hill | Stein | Harford | Nwajiobi | Preece | |
| | 23/2 | | *24,515* | *14* | 22 | | | *Wharton 75* | *Thomas* | *Brown* | *Roeder* | *Clarke* | *Wharton* | *Megson* | *Heard* | *Beardsley* | *Cunningham* | *Reilly* | *Waddle* | |
| | | | | | | | | Ref: A Robinson | The Hatters are unable to find a way through the tough Newcastle defence and, just as Magpies' manager Jack Charlton prepares to introduce another defender, Kenny Wharton hits a shot from the edge of the area which screams past Sealey. Donaghy misses a sitter in the final minute. | | | | | | | | | | | |
| 26 | H | SUNDERLAND | | 21 | W | 2-1 | 2-0 | Harford 21, Hill 29 | Sealey | Breacker | Thomas | Nicholas | Foster | Donaghy | Hill | Stein | Harford | Nwajiobi | Preece | |
| | 2/3 | | 8,019 | *18* | 25 | | | *Bennett 51* | *Turner* | *Venison* | *Chisholm* | *Elliott* | *Agboola* | *Pickering* | *Bennett* | *Berry** | *Hodgson* | *Lemon* | *Walker* | *West* |
| | | | | | | | | Ref: M Robinson | The Hatters score twice in eight minutes when Harford heads home, followed by an overhead kick from Hill, and they appear to be cruising to their first victory since Boxing Day. The visitors step up a gear after the break with Gary Bennett latching onto a poor back-pass from Nicholas. | | | | | | | | | | | |
| 27 | A | SHEFFIELD WED | | 20 | D | 1-1 | 0-1 | Harford 54 | Sealey | Breacker | Thomas | Nicholas | Foster | Donaghy | Hill | Stein | Harford | Nwajiobi | Preece | |
| | 16/3 | | *18,856* | *6* | 26 | | | *Varadi 6* | *Hodge* | *Shirtliff* | *Smith* | *Lyons** | *Worthington* | *Blair* | *Jonsson* | *Shelton* | *Marwood* | *Chapman* | *Varadi* | *Morris* |
| | | | | | | | | Ref: J Worrall | Playing into a blizzard, Luton face a battering in the first half and ex-Town trialist, Imre Varadi, blasts home a cracking shot after six minutes. The Hatters are lucky to survive until the interval only one goal in arrears, after which, with the blizzard abating, Harford levels from close in. | | | | | | | | | | | |
| 28 | A | WATFORD | | 20 | L | 0-3 | 0-1 | | Sealey | Breacker | Thomas | Nicholas | Foster | Donaghy | Hill | Stein | Harford | Parker* | Preece | Nwajiobi |
| | 19/3 | | *14,185* | *17* | 26 | | | *Blissett 27p, 89, Callaghan 75* | *Coton* | *Bardsley* | *McClelland* | *Terry* | *Rostron* | *Callaghan* | *Taylor* | *Jackett* | *Barnes* | *Blissett* | *Gilligan* | |
| | | | | | | | | Ref: T Spence | The Hornets gain revenge for their FA Cup defeat but are flattered by the final score. The game turns on a penalty, when Luther Blissett scores from the spot after he is pushed in the box by Thomas. The Hatters commit everyone to the attack and Watford score twice more on the break. | | | | | | | | | | | |
| 29 | H | QP RANGERS | | 20 | W | 2-0 | 1-0 | Harford 19, 61 | Sealey | Breacker | Thomas | Nicholas | Foster | Donaghy | Hill | Stein | Harford | Nwajiobi | Preece | |
| | 23/3 | | 9,373 | *15* | 29 | | | | *Hucker* | *Chivers* | *McDonald* | *James* | *Gregory* | *Dawes* | *Waddock* | *Fillery* | *Fereday* | *Bannister* | *Byrne** | *Allen* |
| | | | | | | | | Ref: D Hedges | Mick Harford repays a large slice of his £250,000 transfer fee with two headed goals against a side who lack ambition. His first is from a cross from Nwajiobi and then a bullet of a header, following a corner from Preece. Stein wins a penalty but sees his spot-kick saved by Peter Hucker. | | | | | | | | | | | |
| 30 | H | IPSWICH | | 20 | W | 3-1 | 2-1 | Harford 30, 66, Nwajiobi 43 | Sealey | Breacker | Thomas | Nicholas | Foster | Donaghy | Hill | Stein | Harford | Nwajiobi* | Preece | Daniel |
| | 30/3 | | 12,640 | *21* | 32 | | | *Gates 18* | *Cooper* | *Burley* | *Osman* | *Butcher* | *Gernon* | *Zondervan* | *Brennan* | *Gates* | *Putney** | *D'Avray* | *Wilson* | *Dozzell* |
| | | | | | | | | Ref: D Letts | Ipswich miss a hatful of chances early on but take a deserved lead when Eric Gates scores from 20 yards. Harford is again leading the line and scores twice as he runs rings around England centre-half Terry Butcher. The Hatters win two consecutive games for the first time this season. | | | | | | | | | | | |
| 31 | A | SOUTHAMPTON | | 20 | L | 0-1 | 0-0 | | Sealey | Breacker | Thomas | Nicholas | Foster | Donaghy | Hill | Stein | Harford | Nwajiobi | Daniel | |
| | 2/4 | | *14,906* | *6* | 32 | | | *Wallace 74* | *Shilton* | *Mills** | *Wright* | *Bond* | *Holmes* | *Dennis* | *Case* | *Armstrong* | *Lawrence* | *Jordan* | *Wallace* | *Whitlock* |
| | | | | | | | | Ref: R Groves | A disputed goal from Danny Wallace, scored when the Luton defence expect him to be flagged offside, prevents the Town from moving out of the bottom three in the table. Breaker fires in a shot which flattens his colleague, Nwajiobi, but Peter Shilton is equal to all that is thrown at him. | | | | | | | | | | | |

| No | Venue | Opponent / Date | Att | Pos | Pts | F-A | H-T | Scorers, Times, and Referees | 1 | 2 | 3 | 4 | 5 | 6 | 7 | 8 | 9 | 10 | 11 | 12 |
|---|---|---|---|---|---|---|---|---|---|---|---|---|---|---|---|---|---|---|---|---|
| 32 | A | STOKE | | 18 | W | **4-0** | 1-0 | Harford 17, 47, Nwajiobi 68, Moss 64 | Sealey | Breacker | Thomas | Nicholas | Turner | Donaghy | Hill* | Stein | Harford | Nwajiobi | Preece | Moss |
| | | 8/4 | *7,108* | *22* | 35 | | | | *Siddall* | *Bould* | *Dodd* | *Dyson* | *Maskery* | *Painter* | *Hudson* | *McIlroy* | *Heath* | *Bertschin* | *Chamberlain* | |
| | | | | | | | | Ref: I Hendrick | The biggest away win for nine years is recorded against an awful Stoke side who are all but relegated. Moss comes on as a substitute for Hill to make his first appearance since January and scores with a typical goal. This is the best possible result before the upcoming FA Cup semi-final. | | | | | | | | | | | |
| 33 | H | NORWICH | | 20 | W | 3-1 | 0-1 | Nwajiobi 53, 89, Moss 77p | Sealey | Breacker | Thomas | Nicholas | Foster | Donaghy | Hill | Stein | Moss | Nwajiobi | Preece | |
| | | 16/4 | 8,794 | *15* | 38 | | | *Channon 14* | *Woods* | *Haylock* | *Bruce* | *Watson* | *van Wijk* | *Donowa* | *Devine* | *Rowell* | *Hartford* | *Channon* | *Deehan* | |
| | | | | | | | | Ref: M Cotton | After the disappointment of the FA Cup defeat, the Hatters fight back to beat a spirited Norwich side. Mick Channon opens the scoring from close range but Nwajiobi heads the teams level after the break. A penalty is awarded after Steve Bruce pushes Brian Stein which Moss converts. | | | | | | | | | | | |
| 34 | H | MANCHESTER U | | 17 | W | 2-1 | 0-0 | Harford 68p, 89 | Sealey | Breacker | Thomas | Nicholas | Foster | Donaghy | Hill | Stein | Harford | Nwajiobi | Preece | |
| | | 21/4 | 10,320 | *2* | 41 | | | *Whiteside 71* | *Bailey* | *Gidman* | *Hogg* | *McGrath* | *Albiston* | *Robson* | *Whiteside* | *Muhren* | *Olsen* | *Hughes* | *Stapleton* | |
| | | | | | | | | Ref: T Bune | Harford opens the scoring with a penalty after Stein is balked by the United keeper, Gary Bailey but within three minutes Norman Whiteside scrambles an equaliser. Harford then scores a last-minute goal when he is first to react to a free-kick from Steve Foster which had hit the bar. | | | | | | | | | | | |
| 35 | H | NOTT'M FOREST | | 18 | L | 1-2 | 1-1 | Moss 18p | Sealey | Breacker | Turner | Nicholas | Foster | Donaghy | Hill | Stein | Harford | Moss | Preece | |
| | | 24/4 | 10,156 | *7* | 41 | | | *Mills 3, Hodge 89* | *Segers* | *McInally* | *Fairclough** | *Hart* | *Swain* | *Mills* | *Bowyer* | *Metgod* | *Hodge* | *Davenport* | *Clough* | *Birtles* |
| | | | | | | | | Ref: B Hill | Gary Mills opens the scoring and then Moss equalises from the spot after Hill is fouled in the area by Chris Fairclough. A last-minute winner is scored, but this time it is against the Town as Steve Hodge, on the break, punishes the Luton defence and claims all three points for the visitors. | | | | | | | | | | | |
| 36 | A | WEST HAM | | 18 | D | 0-0 | 0-0 | | Sealey | Breacker | Thomas | Nicholas | Foster | Donaghy | Hill | Stein | Bunn* | Nwajiobi | Preece | Parker |
| | | 27/4 | *17,303* | *17* | 42 | | | | *Parkes* | *Stewart* | *Martin* | *Gale* | *Brush* | *Orr* | *Allen* | *Swindleh'rst** | *Dickens* | *Goddard* | *Cottee* | *Bonds* |
| | | | | | | | | Ref: A Gunn | West Ham have not won at home for five months but they force Les Sealey to pull off a couple of tremendous saves in the second half to ensure the points are divided. The Town are missing the services of Harford through suspension and the forwards rarely trouble goalkeeper Phil Parkes. | | | | | | | | | | | |
| 37 | H | ARSENAL | | 16 | W | 3-1 | 2-0 | Harford 2, 49p, Nwajiobi 14 | Sealey | Breacker | Thomas | Nicholas | Foster | Donaghy | Hill* | Stein | Harford | Nwajiobi | Preece | Parker |
| | | 4/5 | 12,051 | *7* | 45 | | | *Nicholas 52p* | *Lukic* | *Anderson* | *O'Leary* | *Caton** | *Sansom* | *Talbot* | *Robson* | *Allinson* | *Rix* | *Mariner* | *Nicholas* | *Davis* |
| | | | | | | | | Ref: N Ashley | A surprisingly easy win is achieved against a poor Arsenal side. Harford climbs above the defence to head the opener after 91 seconds and adds a second, from the spot, after Lukic pushes Stein. Ian Allinson is upended by Les Sealey and Charlie Nicholas pulls one back for the Gunners. | | | | | | | | | | | |
| 38 | A | ASTON VILLA | | 14 | W | 1-0 | 1-0 | Stein 21 | Sealey | Breacker | Thomas | Nicholas | Foster | Donaghy | Parker | Stein | Harford | Nwajiobi | Preece* | Turner |
| | | 6/5 | *14,130* | *10* | 48 | | | | *Poole* | *Williams* | *Evans* | *Glover* | *Dorigo* | *Gibson* | *McMahon* | *Birch* | *Cowans* | *With* | *Walters** | *Daley* |
| | | | | | | | | Ref: J McAulay | Gordon Cowans stumbles over the ball and, before he can regain his balance, Stein surges through to score the only goal of the match. Villa put the Hatters' defence under pressure but they hold firm, playing well as a unit. This result all but ends any fears of relegation for this campaign. | | | | | | | | | | | |
| 39 | A | CHELSEA | | 14 | L | 0-2 | 0-1 | | Sealey | Breacker | Thomas | Nicholas | Foster | Donaghy | Parker | Stein | Harford | Bunn* | Turner | Stein M |
| | | 8/5 | *13,789* | *7* | 48 | | | *Dixon 26, Nevin 79* | *Niedzwiecki* | *Jones* | *McLaughlin* | *Lee* | *Rougvie* | *Bumstead** | *Spackman* | *Thomas* | *Speedie* | *Nevin* | *Dixon* | *Canoville* |
| | | | | | | | | Ref: M James | The centre of the pitch is a bog after the ground staff had overdone the pre-match watering. A poor game results, the Blues just about deserving the win. Kerry Dixon, with a header, bags the first goal and Mal Donaghy slices the ball into his own net when under pressure from Pat Nevin. | | | | | | | | | | | |
| 40 | H | LEICESTER | | 14 | W | **4-0** | 2-0 | Nwajiobi 14, Preece 28, Stein 54, [Harford 86] | Sealey | Breacker | Thomas | Nicholas | Foster | Donaghy | Hill | Stein | Harford | Nwajiobi | Preece | |
| | | 11/5 | 11,802 | *15* | 51 | | | | *Andrews* | *Feeley** | *Williams* | *O'Neill* | *Wilson* | *Peake* | *Lynex* | *Ramsey* | *Banks* | *Lineker* | *Smith* | *Bright* |
| | | | | | | | | Ref: L Burden | The Hatters are in control from the start in a carnival performance and the threat of relegation now seems to be a distant memory. The reason for the turnaround in form is mainly due to the success of new boys Foster, Preece, Nicholas and Harford, all of whom have settled in quickly. | | | | | | | | | | | |
| 41 | A | COVENTRY | | 14 | L | 0-1 | 0-0 | | Sealey | Breacker | Thomas | Nicholas | Foster | Donaghy | Hill | Stein | Harford | Nwajiobi | Preece* | Daniel |
| | | 23/5 | *14,834* | *20* | 51 | | | *Kilcline 83* | *Ogrizovic* | *Butterworth* | *Kilcline* | *Peake* | *Pearce* | *Hibbitt** | *McGrath* | *Bennett* | *Adams* | *Regis* | *Gibson* | *Gynn* |
| | | | | | | | | Ref: B Stevens | The Sky Blues must win their last two games in order to stay up and to send Norwich down. In an entertaining game, which is played in a Cup final atmosphere, the only goal comes with just seven minutes left, when a 15-yard shot from Brian Kilcline sends the home fans in to raptures. | | | | | | | | | | | |
| 42 | H | EVERTON | | 13 | W | 2-0 | 2-0 | Nwajiobi 3, Hill 39 | Sealey | Breacker | Thomas | Nicholas | Foster | Donaghy | Hill | Stein* | Harford | Nwajiobi | Preece | Moss |
| | | 28/5 | 11,509 | *1* | 54 | | | | *Southall* | *Hughes* | *v d Hauwe* | *Harper* | *Bailey* | *Richardson* | *Morrisey* | *Danskin* | *Walsh* | *Wilkinson** | *Wakenshaw* | *Rimmer* |
| | | Home | Away | | | | | Ref: L Shapter | Everton field a makeshift team, due to international call-ups, with four teenagers making their first-team debuts. Headed goals from Nwajiobi and Hill end the game as a contest. The biggest cheer of the evening greets David Moss coming on as a substitute, his last game for the Town. | | | | | | | | | | | |
| Average | | 10,816 | 19,159 | | | | | | | | | | | | | | | | | |

# CANON DIVISION 1 (CUP-TIES)    Manager: David Pleat    SEASON 1984-85

| Milk Cup | | | | | F-A | H-T | Scorers, Times, and Referees | 1 | 2 | 3 | 4 | 5 | 6 | 7 | 8 | 9 | 10 | 11 | 12 sub used |
|---|---|---|---|---|---|---|---|---|---|---|---|---|---|---|---|---|---|---|---|
| 2:1 | A | ORIENT | 19 | W | 4-1 | 1-0 | Donaghy 18, Stein 48, 87, Parker 72 | Dibble | Thomas | Grimes | Turner | Elliott P | Donaghy | Hill | Stein | Bunn | Hilaire | Nwajiobi* | Parker |
| | 25/9 | | *3,080 3:23* | | | | *Cornwell 88* | *Wilmot* | *Hales* | *Foster* | *Banfield* | *Stride** | *Corbett* | *Silkman* | *Brooks* | *Godfrey* | *Sussex* | *Cadette* | *Cornwell* |
| | | | | | | | Ref: D Reeves | Orient have four consecutive wins behind them and play some attractive football but they are no match for the Hatters, who use the fixture as a confidence booster. Stein scores his first goals of the season whilst Hilaire, who gets his first start in place of Moss who is rested, is impressive. | | | | | | | | | | | |
| 2:2 | H | ORIENT | 19 | W | 3-1 | 1-0 | Bunn 26, Stein 53, Elliott S 62 | Dibble | Thomas | Grimes | Turner | Elliott P* | Donaghy | Hill | Stein | Elliott S | Bunn | Moss | Hilaire |
| | 9/10 | | 3,374 *3:19* | | | | *Silkman 76* | *Wilmot* | *Hales* | *Foster** | *Banfield* | *Corbett* | *Stride* | *Silkman* | *Brooks* | *Cornwell* | *Jones* | *Cadette* | *McNeil* |
| | | | | | | | Ref: T Holbrook (Hatters win 7-2 on aggregate) | The decision to charge normal admission prices is reflected in the poor attendance, the lowest at Kenilworth Road since 1965. The match is over when Bunn takes a pass from Grimes in his stride for a 5-1 aggregate. 'Our boys against their men,' summarises the O's manager, Frank Clark. | | | | | | | | | | | |
| 3 | H | LEICESTER | 19 | W | 3-1 | 0-0 | Moss 52, Williams 57 (og), Donaghy 67 | Dibble | Breacker | Turner | Todd | Elliott P* | Donaghy | Hill | Stein | Elliott S | Bunn | Moss | Parker |
| | 30/10 | | 8,015 *1:18* | | | | *Lineker 89* | *Andrews* | *Feeley* | *Williams* | *O'Neill* | *Wilson* | *MacDonald* | *Lynex* | *Ramsey* | *Jones** | *Lineker* | *Smith* | *Banks* |
| | | | | | | | Ref: J Martin | The victory, over a strong Leicester side, is overshadowed when Paul Elliott breaks his leg in a reckless tackle on Alan Smith. The Foxes miss three good chances in the opening minutes but gradually the Hatters get into the game. Moss hits the opener and sets up Donaghy for the third. | | | | | | | | | | | |
| 4 | A | SHEFFIELD WED | 21 | L | 2-4 | 0-2 | Elliott S 81, 85, | Findlay | Breacker | Turner* | North | Droy | Donaghy | Hill | Stein | Elliott S | Bunn | Hilaire | Parker |
| | 20/11 | | *18,313 1:7* | | | | *Blair 15p, 52p, 70p, Marwood 32* | *Hodge* | *Oliver* | *Smith* | *Lyons** | *Shirtliff* | *Worthington* | *Blair* | *Shelton* | *Marwood* | *Varadi* | *Chapman* | *Morris* |
| | | | | | | | Ref: T Fitzharris | A foul by Stein on Lee Chapman, a handball by Mal Donaghy and a trip by North on Gary Shelton set up Andy Blair for an amazing hat-trick of penalties. Wednesday put the Hatters under pressure until relaxing in the closing minutes, allowing Steve Elliott to score two opportunist goals. | | | | | | | | | | | |

| FA Cup | | | | | | | | | | | | | | | | | | | |
|---|---|---|---|---|---|---|---|---|---|---|---|---|---|---|---|---|---|---|---|
| 3 | H | STOKE | 21 | D | 1-1 | 0-0 | Foster 86 | Sealey | Breacker | Thomas | Turner | Foster | Donaghy | Hill | Stein | Harford | Daniel | Moss* | Nwajiobi |
| | 5/1 | | 7,270 *1:22* | | | | *Painter 78* | *Roberts* | *Bould* | *O'Callaghan** | *Dyson* | *Maskery* | *Parkin* | *McIlroy* | *Hudson* | *Painter* | *Chamberlain* | *Bertschin* | *Saunders* |
| | | | | | | | Ref: D Reeves | On an icy pitch, the Hatters put Stoke under pressure for almost the whole of the game but Ian Painter gives the visitors the shock lead when catching the Town on the break. Steve Foster leaves it late before scoring his second goal for the club, with a close-range shot, to earn a replay. | | | | | | | | | | | |
| 3R | A | STOKE | 21 | W | 3-2 | 2-0 | Hill 9, Harford 12, Donaghy 62 | Sealey | Breacker | Thomas | Turner | Foster | Donaghy | Hill | Stein | Harford | Daniel | Parker | |
| | 9/1 | | *9,917 1:22* | | | | *Painter 46, Chamberlain 66* | *Roberts* | *Bould* | *O'Callaghan* | *Dyson* | *Maskery* | *Parkin* | *McIlroy* | *Hudson** | *Painter* | *Chamberlain* | *Bertschin* | *Saunders* |
| | | | | | | | Ref: D Reeves | On a snow-covered pitch, Hill scores his first goal of the season and, when Harford nets the second after a lucky rebound, the game looks to be over. Stoke try to make a game of it and pull a goal back before Donaghy hits the third from close range; however, the Town manage to hang on. | | | | | | | | | | | |
| 4 | H | HUDDERSFIELD | 21 | W | 2-0 | 1-0 | Donaghy 34, Stein 56 | Sealey | Breacker | Thomas | Turner | Foster | Donaghy | Hill | Stein | Harford | Daniel | Parker* | Nwajiobi |
| | 26/1 | | 8,712 *2:7* | | | | | *Cox* | *Laws !* | *Stoutt* | *Allardyce* | *Burke* | *Cooper** | *Doyle* | *Wilson* | *Pugh* | *Lillis* | *Cowling* | *Winter* |
| | | | | | | | Ref: A Buksh | Huddersfield full-back Brian Laws is dismissed after two bookable offences in a minute. The free-kick awarded for the second misdemeanour is headed in by Donaghy and the Hatters then coast to an easy victory. Surprisingly, only one further goal is scored, a close-range shot from Stein. | | | | | | | | | | | |
| 5 | H | WATFORD | 21 | D | 0-0 | 0-0 | | Sealey | Breacker | Thomas | Turner | Foster | Donaghy | Hill | Stein | Harford | Nwajiobi | Daniel | |
| | 4/3 | | 18,506 *1:17* | | | | | *Sherwood* | *Sinnott* | *McClelland* | *Terry* | *Rostron* | *Taylor* | *Lohman* | *Callaghan* | *Gilligan* | *Blissett* | *Sterling* | |
| | | | | | | | Ref: B Hill | No quarter is given in this typical, local derby which is certainly not a match for the purists. The teams hammer each other to a standstill in a non-stop contest which is played at a fast and furious pace. Mick Harford hits a post at one end whilst Nigel Callaghan hits the bar at the other. | | | | | | | | | | | |
| 5R | A | WATFORD | 21 | D | 2-2 | 0-1 | Nwajiobi 76, Hill 80 | Sealey | Breacker | Thomas | Turner | Foster | Donaghy | Hill | Stein | Harford | Nwajiobi | Daniel* | Parker |
| | 6/3 | | *19,867 1:17* | | *aet* | | *Taylor 44, Terry 51* | *Sherwood* | *Sinnott* | *McClelland* | *Terry* | *Rostron* | *Taylor* | *Lohman* | *Callaghan* | *Gilligan* | *Blissett* | *Sterling** | *Bardsley* |
| | | | | | | | Ref: B Hill | Steve Terry creeps in at the far post to give the Hornets a two goal lead, shortly after half-time, and the game looks to be all over for the Town. Nwajiobi pulls a goal back from a seemingly offside position before Hill levels with a deflected shot. Extra-time fails to separate the two teams. | | | | | | | | | | | |
| 5R R | H | WATFORD | 21 | W | 1-0 | 0-0 | Turner 58 | Sealey | Breacker | Thomas | Turner | Foster | Donaghy | Hill | Stein | Harford | Nwajiobi | Parker | |
| | 9/3 | | 15,586 *1:17* | | | | | *Coton* | *Sinnott* | *McClelland* | *Terry* | *Rostron* | *Taylor* | *Jackett* | *Lohman* | *Callaghan* | *Barnes* | *Blissett* | |
| | | | | | | | Ref: J Bray | Wayne Turner celebrates his 24th birthday in style as he cracks in the only goal to settle this marathon tie. The Hornets have a justifiable claim for a penalty turned down after Thomas appears to handle the ball in the area. 'It is a shame that either side had to lose,' says Graham Taylor. | | | | | | | | | | | |

| | | | | | | | | | | | | | | | | | | |
|---|---|---|---|---|---|---|---|---|---|---|---|---|---|---|---|---|---|---|
| QF | H | MILLWALL | | 21 | W | 1-0 | 1-0 | Stein 31 | Sealey | Breacker | Thomas | Turner | Foster | Donaghy | Hill | Stein | Harford | Nwajiobi | Parker | |
| | 13/3 | | 17,470 | *3:2* | | | | | *Sansome* | *Stevens** | *Smith* | *Cusack* | *Hinshelwood* | *Lowndes* | *Briley* | *Chatterton* | *Lovell* | *Fashanu* | *Otulakowski* | *Bremner* |
| | | | | | | | | Ref: D Hutchinson | On a night of incredible brutality off the pitch, which will have far-reaching repercussions for years to come, the Town win through to their first FA Cup semi-final since 1959. In an unreal Kenilworth Road atmosphere, the hooliganism probably affects Millwall more than it does Luton. | | | | | | | | | | | |
| SF | N | EVERTON | | 18 | L | 1-2 | 1-0 | Hill 37 | Sealey | Breacker | Thomas | Turner | Foster | Donaghy | Hill | Stein | Harford* | Nwajiobi | Parker | Moss |
| | 13/4 | | *45,289* | *1:1* | | *aet* | | *Sheedy 86, Mountfield 115* | *Southall* | *Stevens* | *Mountfield* | *Ratcliffe* | *v d Hauwe* | *Steven* | *Reid* | *Bracewell* | *Sheedy* | *Sharp* | *Gray* | |
| | (at Villa Park) | | | | | | | Ref: J Martin | The Hatters put on a super performance against an Everton side who are on their way to a League & Cup-Winners' Cup double and control the game for 85 minutes. They only have a superb strike from Hill to show for it, however, and a cruel goal levels the tie. Everton win in extra-time. | | | | | | | | | | | |

| | | Home | | | | | | Away | | | | | |
|---|---|---|---|---|---|---|---|---|---|---|---|---|---|
| | P | W | D | L | F | A | W | D | L | F | A | Pts |
| 1 Everton | 42 | 16 | 3 | 2 | 58 | 17 | 12 | 3 | 6 | 30 | 26 | 90 |
| 2 Liverpool | 42 | 12 | 4 | 5 | 36 | 19 | 10 | 7 | 4 | 32 | 16 | 77 |
| 3 Tottenham | 42 | 11 | 3 | 7 | 46 | 31 | 12 | 5 | 4 | 32 | 20 | 77 |
| 4 Manchester U | 42 | 13 | 6 | 2 | 47 | 13 | 9 | 4 | 8 | 30 | 34 | 76 |
| 5 Southampton | 42 | 13 | 4 | 4 | 29 | 18 | 6 | 7 | 8 | 27 | 29 | 68 |
| 6 Chelsea | 42 | 13 | 3 | 5 | 38 | 20 | 5 | 9 | 7 | 25 | 28 | 66 |
| 7 Arsenal | 42 | 14 | 5 | 2 | 37 | 14 | 5 | 4 | 12 | 24 | 35 | 66 |
| 8 Sheffield Wed | 42 | 12 | 7 | 2 | 39 | 21 | 5 | 7 | 9 | 19 | 24 | 65 |
| 9 Nott'm Forest | 42 | 13 | 4 | 4 | 35 | 18 | 6 | 3 | 12 | 21 | 30 | 64 |
| 10 Aston Villa | 42 | 10 | 7 | 4 | 34 | 20 | 5 | 4 | 12 | 26 | 40 | 56 |
| 11 Watford | 42 | 10 | 5 | 6 | 48 | 30 | 4 | 8 | 9 | 33 | 41 | 55 |
| 12 West Brom | 42 | 11 | 4 | 6 | 36 | 23 | 5 | 3 | 13 | 22 | 39 | 55 |
| 13 LUTON TOWN | 42 | 12 | 5 | 4 | 40 | 22 | 3 | 4 | 14 | 17 | 39 | 54 |
| 14 Newcastle | 42 | 11 | 4 | 6 | 33 | 26 | 2 | 9 | 10 | 22 | 44 | 52 |
| 15 Leicester | 42 | 10 | 4 | 7 | 39 | 25 | 5 | 2 | 14 | 26 | 48 | 51 |
| 16 West Ham | 42 | 7 | 8 | 6 | 27 | 23 | 6 | 4 | 11 | 24 | 45 | 51 |
| 17 Ipswich | 42 | 8 | 7 | 6 | 27 | 20 | 5 | 4 | 12 | 19 | 37 | 50 |
| 18 Coventry | 42 | 11 | 3 | 7 | 29 | 22 | 4 | 2 | 15 | 18 | 42 | 50 |
| 19 QP Rangers | 42 | 11 | 6 | 4 | 41 | 30 | 2 | 5 | 14 | 12 | 42 | 50 |
| 20 Norwich | 42 | 9 | 6 | 6 | 28 | 24 | 4 | 4 | 13 | 18 | 40 | 49 |
| 21 Sunderland | 42 | 7 | 6 | 8 | 20 | 26 | 3 | 4 | 14 | 20 | 36 | 40 |
| 22 Stoke | 42 | 3 | 3 | 15 | 18 | 41 | 0 | 5 | 16 | 6 | 50 | 17 |
| | 924 | 237 | 107 | 118 | 785 | 503 | 118 | 107 | 237 | 503 | 785 | 1279 |

Odds & ends

Double wins: (3) Aston Villa, QPR, Stoke.
Double losses: (3) Liverpool, Nott'm Forest, West Brom.

Won from behind: (4) QPR (a), Watford (h), Ipswich (h), Norwich (h).
Lost from in front: (3) Tottenham (a), West Brom (h), Everton (FAC).

High spots: The signing of Steve Foster, David Preece, Mick Harford and Peter Nicholas to turn the season around.
Beating Leicester 4-0 at home to confirm safety from relegation.
Beating Manchester United at home for the first time since 1937.

Low spots: The FA Cup semi-final defeat by Everton.
The early season form, which left the team struggling from the start.

Player of the Year: Steve Foster.
Ever-presents: (2) Mal Donaghy, Brian Stein.
Hat-tricks: (0).
Leading scorer: Mick Harford (16).

| | Appearances | | | | | | Goals | | | |
|---|---|---|---|---|---|---|---|---|---|---|
| | Lge | *Sub* | LC | *Sub* | FAC | *Sub* | Lge | LC | FAC | Tot |
| Breacker, Tim | **34** | *1* | 2 | | 8 | | | | | |
| Bunn, Frank | **17** | *3* | 4 | | | | **5** | 1 | | **6** |
| Daniel, Ray | **4** | *3* | | | 5 | | **1** | | | **1** |
| Dibble, Andy | **13** | | 3 | | | | | | | |
| Donaghy, Mal | **42** | | 4 | | 8 | | **1** | 2 | 2 | **5** |
| Droy, Micky | **2** | | 1 | | | | | | | |
| Elliott, Paul | **9** | | 3 | | | | **1** | | | **1** |
| Elliott, Steve | **12** | | 3 | | | | **3** | 3 | | **6** |
| Findlay, Jake | **3** | | 1 | | | | | | | |
| Foster, Steve | **25** | | | | 8 | | **1** | | 1 | **2** |
| Grimes, Ashley | **9** | | 2 | | | | | | | |
| Harford, Mick | **22** | | | | 8 | | **15** | | 1 | **16** |
| Hilaire, Vince | **5** | *1* | 2 | *1* | | | | | | |
| Hill, Ricky | **39** | | 4 | | 8 | | **2** | | 3 | **5** |
| Moss, David | **17** | *2* | 2 | | 1 | *1* | **7** | 1 | | **8** |
| Nicholas, Peter | **19** | | | | | | | | | |
| North, Stacey | **7** | | 1 | | | | | | | |
| Nwajiobi, Emeka | **21** | *8* | 1 | | 5 | *2* | **9** | | 1 | **10** |
| Parker, Gary | **13** | *7* | | *3* | 5 | *1* | **1** | 1 | | **2** |
| Preece, David | **21** | | | | | | **2** | | | **2** |
| Sealey, Les | **26** | | | | 8 | | | | | |
| Stein, Brian | **42** | | 4 | | 8 | | **9** | 3 | 2 | **14** |
| Stein, Mark | | *1* | | | | | | | | |
| Thomas, Mitchell | **35** | *1* | 2 | | 8 | | | | | |
| Todd, Colin | **2** | | 1 | | | | | | | |
| Turner, Wayne | **23** | *1* | 4 | | 8 | | | | 1 | **1** |
| (own-goals) | | | | | | | | 1 | | **1** |
| **26 players used** | **463** | ***28*** | **44** | ***4*** | **88** | ***4*** | **57** | **12** | **11** | **80** |

| No | Date | Att | Pos | Pt | F-A | H-T | Scorers, Times, and Referees | 1 | 2 | 3 | 4 | 5 | 6 | 7 | 8 | 9 | 10 | 11 | 12 sub used |
|---|---|---|---|---|---|---|---|---|---|---|---|---|---|---|---|---|---|---|---|
| 1 | H NOTT'M FOREST | | | D | 1-1 | 1-0 | Stein B 20 | Dibble | Breacker | Thomas | Nicholas | Foster | Donaghy | Hill* | Stein B | Harford | Nwajiobi | Preece | Parker |
| | 17/8 | 11,318 | | 1 | | | *Webb 52* | *Segers* | *McInally* | *Butterworth* | *Walker* | *Pearce* | *Hodge* | *Mills* | *Webb* | *Davenport* | *Birtles* | *Robertson* | |
| | | | | | | | Ref: J Martin | Stein scores the first goal on the Towns' artificial surface with a delightful chip following an inch-perfect pass from Hill. Forest equalise against the run of play, when Neil Webb blasts home a harshly awarded 20-yard free-kick. Hill and Stein sign new contracts on the day before the game. | | | | | | | | | | | |
| 2 | A NEWCASTLE | | | D | 2-2 | 1-0 | Nwajiobi 32, Harford 48 | Dibble | Thomas | Grimes | Nicholas | Elliott | Donaghy | Parker | Stein B | Harford | Nwajiobi | Preece | |
| | 21/8 | *21,933* | | 2 | | | *Beardsley 72, Roeder 76* | *Thomas* | *Anderson* | *Clarke* | *Roeder* | *Wharton* | *Gascoigne* | *McDonald* | *Megson** | *Beardsley* | *Reilly* | *Stewart* | *McCreery* |
| | | | | | | | Ref: I Hendrick | Steve Foster, Tim Breacker and Ricky Hill are all injured but the reshaped side takes a comfortable two-goal lead. Gary Parker misses a penalty, which is awarded on 69 minutes after Stein is tripped in the area, and this inspires the Magpies, who draw level with two goals in four minutes. | | | | | | | | | | | |
| 3 | A WEST HAM | | 7 | W | 1-0 | 0-0 | Harford 48p | Dibble | Johnson | Thomas | Nicholas | Elliott | Donaghy | Parker | Stein B | Harford | Nwajiobi | Preece | |
| | 24/8 | *14,004* | *14* | 5 | | | | *Parkes* | *Stewart* | *Gale* | *Martin* | *Walford* | *Dickens* | *Orr* | *Devonshire* | *Ward* | *Cottee** | *McAvennie* | *Campbell* |
| | | | | | | | Ref: T Holbrook | Brian Stein is put through and is just about to score when he is brought down by Ray Stewart. Mick Harford takes over from Parker as penalty-taker and converts, with some ease, from the spot. Andy Dibble makes several late saves as the home side desperately attempt to earn a point. | | | | | | | | | | | |
| 4 | H ARSENAL | | 8 | D | 2-2 | 1-0 | Nwajiobi 2, Stein B 68 | Dibble | Breacker | Thomas | Nicholas | Parker | Donaghy | Hill | Stein B | Harford | Nwajiobi | Preece | |
| | 27/8 | 10,012 | *15* | 6 | | | *Donaghy 53 (og), Woodcock 71* | *Lukic* | *Anderson* | *O'Leary** | *Caton* | *Sansom* | *Robson* | *Davis* | *Allinson* | *Rix* | *Nicholas* | *Woodcock* | *Mariner* |
| | | | | | | | Ref: A Seville | Both sides are missing injured defenders which leads to an end-to-end encounter which neither team deserves to lose. The opening goal for the Town comes from a move started by Andy Dibble and, after four passes, the ball is in the back of the net without an Arsenal player touching it. | | | | | | | | | | | |
| 5 | A ASTON VILLA | | 11 | L | 1-3 | 0-3 | Stein B 53 | Dibble | Breacker | Thomas | Nicholas | Johnson* | Donaghy | Hill | Stein B | Harford | Nwajiobi | Preece | Parker |
| | 31/8 | *10,524* | *14* | 6 | | | *Walters 2, Hodge 16, Norton 34* | *Spink* | *Norton* | *Glover* | *Ormsby* | *Dorigo* | *Birch* | *Bradley* | *Hodge* | *Daley* | *Walker* | *Walters* | |
| | | | | | | | Ref: D Shaw | Villa have gone four games without a win and field six teenagers who, in front of the lowest league attendance at Villa Park since 1966, tear into the Town defence and take a deserved three-goal lead. The Hatters dominate the game after the break but are unable to pull the goals back. | | | | | | | | | | | |
| 6 | H CHELSEA | | 15 | D | 1-1 | 1-0 | Harford 35 | Dibble | Johnson | Thomas | Nicholas | Foster | Donaghy | Hill | Stein B | Harford | Nwajiobi | Preece* | Elliott |
| | 7/9 | 10,720 | *6* | 7 | | | *Dixon 47* | *Niedzwiecki* | *Lee* | *Pates* | *McLaughlin* | *Rougvie* | *Bumstead* | *Nevin* | *Spackman* | *Murphy* | *Dixon* | *Speedie* | |
| | | | | | | | Ref: K Barratt | Mick Harford takes advantage of a clever back-heel by Stein to smash the ball home from the edge of the area. Luton-born Kerry Dixon scores from close range as the Town fail to hang on to their advantage. Peter Nicholas is a limping passenger at the end with the substitute already on. | | | | | | | | | | | |
| 7 | A EVERTON | | 16 | L | 0-2 | 0-1 | | Dibble | Breacker | Thomas | Nicholas | Foster | Donaghy | Hill* | Stein B | Harford | Nwajiobi | Preece | Parker |
| | 14/9 | *25,487* | *2* | 7 | | | *Sheedy 44, Sharp 86* | *Southall* | *Stevens* | *Ratcliffe* | *Mountfield* | *v d Hauwe* | *Steven* | *Harper* | *Bracewell* | *Sheedy* | *Lineker* | *Heath** | *Sharp* |
| | | | | | | | Ref: P Tyldesley | The current league champions are well below par but the Hatters are unable to take advantage. Nwajiobi nets but the referee decides to call the play back and awards the Town a free-kick instead. Harford has very little service up front but Foster does a good marking job on Gary Lineker. | | | | | | | | | | | |
| 8 | H QP RANGERS | | 14 | W | 2-0 | 2-0 | Harford 21, Foster 28 | Sealey | Breacker | Thomas | Nicholas | Foster | Donaghy | Hill | Stein B | Harford ! | Stein M* | Preece | Nwajiobi |
| | 21/9 | 9,508 | *12* | 10 | | | | *Hucker* | *Chivers* | *McDonald* | *Fenwick* | *Dawes* | *Allen* | *Gregory !* | *Waddock* | *Fereday* | *Byrne* | *Bannister* | |
| | | | | | | | Ref: V Callow | Headers from Harford and Foster earn the Hatters their first home win of the season. Nwajiobi replaces Mark Stein in a bad-tempered clash which only calms down after Mick Harford and John Gregory are sent off for fighting. Rangers have not won at Kenilworth Road for 33 years. | | | | | | | | | | | |
| 9 | A SHEFFIELD WED | | 15 | L | 2-3 | 1-2 | Harford 44, 63 | Sealey | Breacker | Thomas | Nicholas* | Foster | Donaghy | Hill | Stein B | Harford | Nwajiobi | Preece | Elliott |
| | 28/9 | *17,877* | *7* | 10 | | | *Marwood 43, 61p, Chapman 45* | *Hodge* | *Sterland* | *Lyons* | *Shirtliff* | *Snodin* | *Marwood* | *Smith* | *Shelton* | *Blair* | *Thompson** | *Chapman* | *Chamberlain* |
| | | | | | | | Ref: A Banks | The team has gone off the boil, which is demonstrated by this poor performance against a predictable Owls side. Luton are always chasing the game after Foster handles a drive from Gary Thompson and Brian Marwood scores from the spot. The final result slightly flatters the Town. | | | | | | | | | | | |
| 10 | H IPSWICH | | 14 | W | 1-0 | 0-0 | Nwajiobi 61 | Sealey | Breacker | Thomas | Nicholas | Foster | Donaghy | Hill | Stein B | Harford | Nwajiobi | Preece | |
| | 1/10 | 8,553 | *21* | 13 | | | | *Cooper* | *Gernon* | *Steggles** | *Cranson* | *Zondervan* | *Yallop* | *Atkins* | *Putney* | *Wilson* | *Brennan* | *Sunderland* | *Dozzell* |
| | | | | | | | Ref: M Cotton | A welcome home win enables the Town to breathe a little more easily in their fight to move away from the bottom end of the table. Ipswich are unremarkable and concentrate on keeping out the Hatters, but Emeka Nwajiobi breaks the deadlock when latching onto a cross from Brian Stein. | | | | | | | | | | | |

| No | Venue | Opponent / Date | Att | Pos | Pts | FT | HT | Scorers, Times, and Referees | 1 | 2 | 3 | 4 | 5 | 6 | 7 | 8 | 9 | 10 | 11 | 12 sub used |
|---|---|---|---|---|---|---|---|---|---|---|---|---|---|---|---|---|---|---|---|---|
| 11 | H | MANCHESTER U | | 14 | D | 1-1 | 0-0 | Stein B 68 | Sealey | Breacker | Thomas | Nicholas | Foster | Donaghy | Hill | Stein B | **North M*** | Nwajiobi | Preece | Elliott |
| | | 5/10 | **17,454** | *1* | 14 | | | *Hughes 61* | *Bailey* | *Duxbury* | *McGrath* | *Moran* | *Albiston* | *Whiteside* | *Robson* | *Moses* | *Hughes* | *Stapleton* | *Barnes* | |
| | | | | | | | | Ref: K Baker | The attempt by Manchester United to equal the Tottenham record of 11 straight wins at the start of a season comes unstuck when Stein rockets in an equaliser from the edge of the box. A fine advertisement for football, although substitute Elliott hits a late chance wide of an empty net. | | | | | | | | | | | |
| 12 | A | OXFORD | | 14 | D | 1-1 | 1-0 | Stein B 23 | Sealey | Breacker | Thomas ! | Nicholas | Foster | Donaghy | Hill | Stein B | Harford | Nwajiobi | Preece | |
| | | 12/10 | *10,609* | *18* | 15 | | | *Hebberd 88* | *Hardwick* | *Langan* | *Briggs* | *Shotton* | *Slatter* | *Phillips* | *Houghton* | *Hebberd* | *R'des-Brown* | *Thomas** | *Aldridge !* | *Charles* |
| | | | | | | | | Ref: R Lewis | Thomas and John Aldridge are sent off, on the recommendation of the linesman, after tangling off the ball. The Town are already in the lead at this point through a Stein drive but United chase the game and score a late equaliser when unchallenged Trevor Hebberd heads in a long cross. | | | | | | | | | | | |
| 13 | H | SOUTHAMPTON | | 12 | W | **7-0** | 3-0 | Nwajiobi 5, Stein B 32, 55, 89p, Hill 35, [Preece 59, Daniel 88] | Sealey | Breacker | Thomas | Nicholas | Foster | Donaghy | Hill | Stein B | Harford | Nwajiobi | Preece* | Daniel |
| | | 19/10 | 8,876 | *18* | 18 | | | | *Shilton* | *Baker* | *Wright* | *Bond* | *Dennis* | *Case* | *Lawrence* | *Armstrong* | *Townsend* | *Cockerill* | *Moran* | |
| | | | | | | | | Ref: C Downey | The Hatters record their biggest ever win in Division 1 and, with every player on the top of his form, the score could easily have been ten, were it not for Peter Shilton in the Saints' goal. Stein hits a superb hat-trick and Glen Cockerill, who declined an offer to join Luton, makes his debut. | | | | | | | | | | | |
| 14 | A | LIVERPOOL | | 13 | L | 2-3 | 0-2 | Foster 46, Harford 75 | Sealey | Breacker | Johnson | Daniel | Foster | Donaghy | Hill | Stein B | Harford | Nwajiobi | Preece* | Grimes |
| | | 26/10 | *31,488* | *2* | 18 | | | *Walsh 30, 34, Molby 76* | *Grobbelaar* | *Nicol* | *Lawrenson* | *Hansen* | *Molby* | *Beglin* | *Johnston* | *Whelan* | *McMahon* | *Walsh* | *Dalglish* | |
| | | | | | | | | Ref: M Robinson | The Hatters are two goals down before they start to make a fight of it and then cause some anxious moments in the Anfield defence during the second half. Steve Foster pulls a goal back after a scramble in the penalty area, and Harford beats Bruce Grobbelaar with a shot from 25 yards. | | | | | | | | | | | |
| 15 | H | BIRMINGHAM | | 10 | W | 2-0 | 0-0 | Stein B 47, Harford 70 | Sealey | Breacker | Thomas | Nicholas | Foster | Donaghy | Hill | Stein B | Harford | Nwajiobi | Preece | |
| | | 2/11 | **8,550** | *17* | 21 | | | | *Seaman* | *Ranson* | *Hagan* | *Armstrong* | *Jones* | *Roberts* | *Bremner* | *Kuhl* | *Hopkins* | *Kennedy* | *Geddis* | |
| | | | | | | | | Ref: K Miller | The Blues defend in depth but are unable to control their old boy, Mick Harford, who enjoys his tussle with Ken Armstrong. Stein scores the first with a header and Harford beats David Seaman with a 25-yard drive. Sealey brings down Andy Kennedy but the referee refuses a penalty. | | | | | | | | | | | |
| 16 | A | TOTTENHAM | | 10 | W | 3-1 | 1-0 | Harford 19, Stein B 62, Hill 89 | Sealey | Breacker | Thomas | Nicholas | Foster | Donaghy | Hill | Stein B | Harford | Nwajiobi | Preece | |
| | | 9/11 | *19,163* | *13* | 24 | | | *Cooke 80* | *Clemence* | *Stevens* | *Roberts* | *Mabbutt* | *Hughton* | *Waddle* | *Crook** | *Perryman* | *Hoddle* | *Falco* | *Leworthy* | *Cooke* |
| | | | | | | | | Ref: L Shapter | The Town record their first win at White Hart Lane since 1948 against a poor Tottenham side. Several Luton players under-perform in a match where they should have scored six goals and the points are not made safe until the final minute, when Hill scores with a blockbuster of a shot. | | | | | | | | | | | |
| 17 | H | COVENTRY | | 11 | L | 0-1 | 0-1 | | Sealey | Breacker* | Thomas | Nicholas | Foster | Donaghy | Hill | Stein B | Harford | Nwajiobi | Preece | Parker |
| | | 16/11 | 9,607 | *15* | 24 | | | *Bowman 35* | *Ogrizovic* | *Borrows* | *Rodger* | *Peake* | *Adams* | *Bowman* | *Gynn** | *McGrath* | *Bennett* | *Evans* | *Gibson* | *Downs* |
| | | | | | | | | Ref: J Moules | The Hatters lose their first league game on a synthetic surface as the Sky Blues grab the win at Kenilworth Road. A shot from Dave Bowman takes a deflection and slips through the hand of Sealey to give Coventry a lucky lead. Steve Ogrizovic is equal to all of the Towns' best efforts. | | | | | | | | | | | |
| 18 | A | WATFORD | | 8 | W | 2-1 | 1-0 | Thomas 28, Terry 86 (og) | Sealey | Breacker | Thomas | Nicholas | Foster | Donaghy | Hill | Stein B | Harford | Nwajiobi | Preece | |
| | | 23/11 | *16,197* | *13* | 27 | | | *Talbot 82* | *Coton* | *Bardsley* | *Terry* | *Sinnott* | *Rostron* | *Talbot* | *Jackett* | *Sterling* | *Barnes* | *Allen* | *Porter** | *Smillie* |
| | | | | | | | | Ref: G Napthine | Watched by England manager Bobby Robson, Thomas opens the scoring with his first goal for the club. A late equaliser from Brian Talbot stirs the Hatters into action and, four minutes later, Steve Terry deflects a Stein cross past his own keeper to give the Town a deserved victory. | | | | | | | | | | | |
| 19 | H | MANCHESTER C | | 8 | W | 2-1 | 1-0 | Stein B 3, 64 | Sealey | Breacker | Thomas | Nicholas | Elliott | Donaghy | Hill | Stein B | Harford | Nwajiobi* | Preece | Daniel |
| | | 30/11 | 10,096 | *17* | 30 | | | *Lillis 83p* | *Nixon* | *Reid* | *McCarthy* | *Johnson* | *Power* | *May* | *Phillips* | *McNab* | *Wilson** | *Davies* | *Lillis* | *Baker* |
| | | | | | | | | Ref: D Axcell | Stein scores twice to help the Town win their fourth game out of the last five and only Eric Nixon in the Manchester City goal prevents a more convincing scoreline. Mark Lillis makes the match look closer than it is when he converts from the spot after Tim Breacker fouls Paul Power. | | | | | | | | | | | |
| 20 | H | NEWCASTLE | | 7 | W | 2-0 | 1-0 | Harford 6, North M 75 | Sealey | Breacker | Thomas | Nicholas | Foster | Donaghy | Hill | Stein B | Harford | King* | Preece | North M |
| | | 7/12 | 10,319 | *9* | 33 | | | | *Thomas* | *Davies* | *Clarke* | *Roeder* | *Bailey* | *McCreery* | *Anderson* | *Wharton* | *Beardsley* | *Whitehurst* | *Stewart* | |
| | | | | | | | | Ref: D Vickers | Andy King makes his second debut for the Club, after his transfer from Wolves, and has an easy time of it as the Hatters coast to victory over a poor Magpies side. Harford opens the scoring against his old team from inside the box and Marc North powers in a shot for his first league goal. | | | | | | | | | | | |
| 21 | A | NOTT'M FOREST | | 8 | L | 0-2 | 0-1 | | Sealey | Breacker | Thomas | Nicholas | Foster | Donaghy | Parker | Stein B | Harford | King* | Preece | North M |
| | | 14/12 | *12,078* | *10* | 33 | | | *Clough 30, Webb 78* | *Sutton* | *McInally* | *Walker* | *Butterworth* | *Pearce* | *Carr* | *Bowyer* | *Metgod** | *Robertson* | *Webb* | *Clough* | *Walsh* |
| | | | | | | | | Ref: J Bray | The Town put together several good attacks but ruin their approach work with some poor finishing. Nigel Clough scores for the home side with a disputed 20-yard free-kick and Neil Webb gets the winner when he is first to a ball pushed out by Sealey to end Forest's six-match losing run. | | | | | | | | | | | |

| No | Date | | Att | Pos | Pt | F-A | H-T | Scorers, Times, and Referees | 1 | 2 | 3 | 4 | 5 | 6 | 7 | 8 | 9 | 10 | 11 | 12 sub used |
|---|---|---|---|---|---|---|---|---|---|---|---|---|---|---|---|---|---|---|---|---|
| 22 | H | WEST HAM | | 8 | D | 0-0 | 0-0 | | Sealey | Breacker | Thomas | Nicholas | Foster | Donaghy | Hill | Stein B | Harford | North M | Preece | |
| | 21/12 | | 14,599 | *3* | 34 | | | | *Parkes* | *Stewart* | *Gale* | *Martin* | *Walford* | *Ward* | *Dickens* | *Orr* | *Devonshire* | *McAvennie* | *Cottee* | |
| | | | | | | | | Ref: D Hedges | After a run of nine straight wins, the Hammers are brought back down to earth. Although the Town are unlucky not to win, it is once again their poor finishing which is to blame. Frank McAvennie, who was a transfer target for the Hatters last summer, is well marshalled by Steve Foster. | | | | | | | | | | | |
| 23 | A | WEST BROM | | 8 | W | 2-1 | 2-1 | North M 4, Harford 44 | Sealey | Breacker | Thomas | Nicholas | Foster | Donaghy | Hill | Stein B | Harford | North M | Preece | |
| | 26/12 | | *12,508* | *22* | 37 | | | *Varadi 33* | *Godden* | *Nicholl* | *Bennett* | *Robertson* | *Statham* | *Mackenzie* | *Grealish** | *Hunt* | *Thomas* | *Varadi* | *Reilly* | *Dennison* |
| | | | | | | | | Ref: A Robinson | The Hatters have little trouble in disposing of the side which currently occupies bottom place in the table. Marc North turns in a rebound after a clever back-heel by Brian Stein hit the bar. Imre Varadi equalises with a near-post header before Mick Harford drives in the 20-yard winner. | | | | | | | | | | | |
| 24 | A | IPSWICH | | 8 | D | 1-1 | 0-1 | North M 82 | Sealey | Breacker | Thomas | Nicholas | North S | Donaghy | Hill | Stein B | Harford | North M | Preece | |
| | 28/12 | | *15,607* | *20* | 38 | | | *Gleghorn 10* | *Cooper* | *Yallop* | *Cranson** | *Butcher* | *McCall* | *Stockwell* | *Brennan* | *Dozzell* | *Wilson* | *D'Avray* | *Gleghorn* | *Sunderland* |
| | | | | | | | | Ref: A Gunn | Playing against another struggling side, the Town gift an opening goal when Nigel Gleghorn is left unmarked from a twice-taken free-kick. The move is identical to that of just seconds before, which is recalled as the kick is taken too quickly. Preece chips a perfect ball for North to stab in. | | | | | | | | | | | |
| 25 | H | LEICESTER | | 8 | W | 3-1 | 1-0 | Harford 27, 65, 75 | Sealey | Breacker | Thomas | Nicholas | Foster | Donaghy | Hill | Stein B | Harford | North M | Preece | |
| | 1/1 | | 10,917 | *16* | 41 | | | *Bright 70* | *Andrews* | *Feeley* | *Osman* | *O'Neill* | *Morgan* | *McAllister** | *Banks* | *Mauchlen* | *Smith R* | *Bright* | *Smith A* | *Lynex* |
| | | | | | | | | Ref: J Borrett | Harford notches a hat-trick in his last game before his suspension and sees another of his efforts hit the bar. The Foxes have their chances, with Ian Banks heading wide from three yards, before Mark Bright heads in. Luton are now just six points behind the club lying second in the table. | | | | | | | | | | | |
| 26 | A | CHELSEA | | 8 | L | 0-1 | 0-0 | | Sealey | Breacker | Thomas | Nicholas | Foster | Donaghy | Hill | Stein B | **Newell** | North M* | Preece | Daniel |
| | 11/1 | | *21,102* | *3* | 41 | | | *Speedie 55* | *Niedzwiecki* | *Lee* | *McLaughlin* | *Rougvie* | *Dublin* | *Bumstead* | *Spackman* | *Hazard* | *Nevin* | *Dixon* | *Speedie* | |
| | | | | | | | | Ref: J Martin | Chelsea hardly look like title challengers as the Hatters enjoy much the better of the first period, but again fail to take their chances. Route one football enables David Speedie to score the only goal of the game but Doug Rougvie is lucky to stay on the pitch after some physical challenges. | | | | | | | | | | | |
| 27 | H | ASTON VILLA | | 7 | W | 2-0 | 1-0 | Newell 16, Stein B 76 | Sealey | Breacker | Thomas | Nicholas | Foster | Donaghy | Hill | Stein B | Newell | North M | Grimes | |
| | 18/1 | | 10,217 | *18* | 44 | | | | *Spink* | *Norton* | *Evans* | *Elliott* | *Williams* | *Birch* | *Kerr* | *Glover* | *Walters* | *Stainrod** | *Gray* | *Shaw* |
| | | | | | | | | Ref: R Lewis | Mike Newell marks his home debut, scoring with a volley from a headed pass by Stein and then leads ex-Town centre-half Paul Elliott a merry dance. Foster heads against the bar as the Hatters fail to build on their lead, but Stein eventually makes the points safe with an instinctive shot. | | | | | | | | | | | |
| 28 | A | ARSENAL | | 9 | L | 1-2 | 1-1 | Harford 29 | Sealey | Breacker | Thomas | Nicholas | Foster | Donaghy | Hill | Stein B | Harford | Newell* | Preece | North M |
| | 1/2 | | *22,459* | *7* | 44 | | | *Allinson 4p, Rix 56* | *Lukic* | *Anderson* | *O'Leary* | *Keown* | *Sansom* | *Mariner* | *Rocastle* | *Allinson* | *Rix* | *Nicholas* | *Quinn* | |
| | | | | | | | | Ref: H Taylor | On a cold, wet day it is the referee who earns the headlines with four bookings and a dubious penalty decision, awarded when the ball hits Tim Breacker on the chest. The spot-kick is converted by Ian Allinson and, after Harford levels, Graham Rix hits a 25-yard winner from a free-kick. | | | | | | | | | | | |
| 29 | A | SOUTHAMPTON | | 6 | W | 2-1 | 1-0 | Newell 28, Stein B 88 | Sealey | Breacker | Thomas | Nicholas | Foster | Donaghy | Hill | Stein B | Harford | Newell | Preece | |
| | 8/2 | | *13,740* | *14* | 47 | | | *Armstrong 63* | *Shilton* | *Forrest* | *Wright* | *Bond* | *Holmes* | *Dennis* | *Case* | *Cockerill* | *Armstrong* | *Wallace* | *Moran* | |
| | | | | | | | | Ref: L Shapter | The referee orders the penalty spot to be remarked, after awarding a spot-kick for a foul by Thomas on Wallace. For a change, it is the Hatters who have the luck as David Armstrong sees his delayed kick saved by Sealey. Brian Stein then pinches a late winner against the run of play. | | | | | | | | | | | |
| 30 | A | QP RANGERS | | 6 | D | 1-1 | 0-1 | Newell 62 | Sealey | Johnson | Thomas | Nicholas | Foster | Donaghy | Hill | Newell | Harford | North M | Preece | |
| | 22/2 | | *13,252* | *16* | 48 | | | *Byrne 35* | *Barron* | *Neill* | *McDonald* | *Wicks* | *Dawes* | *Allen* | *Fenwick* | *Fillery* | *Fereday* | *Bannister* | *Byrne* | |
| | | | | | | | | Ref: J Ashworth | John Byrne hits the opening goal against the run of play as the Hatters fail to win on the Loftus Road Omniturf for the first time. Stein is missing through injury, so the Town opt to play with three big men up front. The plan does not work although Mike Newell does touch in the equaliser. | | | | | | | | | | | |
| 31 | H | SHEFFIELD WED | | 6 | W | 1-0 | 1-0 | Harford 16 | Sealey | Johnson | Thomas | Nicholas | Foster | Donaghy | Hill | Newell | Harford | North M | Preece | |
| | 1/3 | | 10,206 | *9* | 51 | | | | *Hodge* | *Morris* | *Hart* | *Shirtliff* | *Smith* | *Sterland* | *Megson* | *Shelton** | *Marwood* | *Thompson* | *Snodin* | *Shutt* |
| | | | | | | | | Ref: D Axcell | The Town are now technically clear of relegation with eleven games to play. Harford zigzags through a static Wednesday defence to head home a corner from Preece. The Owls do not show many attacking aspirations and their only serious effort is disallowed after a foul on Les Sealey. | | | | | | | | | | | |

| No Date | H/A | Opponent / Att | Pos | Res / Pts | F-A | H-T | Scorers, Times, and Referees | 1 | 2 | 3 | 4 | 5 | 6 | 7 | 8 | 9 | 10 | 11 | 12 sub used |
|---|---|---|---|---|---|---|---|---|---|---|---|---|---|---|---|---|---|---|---|
| 32 | H | OXFORD | 8 | L | 1-2 | 1-0 | Preece 15 | Sealey | Breacker | Thomas | Nicholas | Foster | Donaghy | Hill | Stein M* | Harford | Newell | Preece | North M |
| 15/3 | | 10,633 | *18* | 51 | | | *Aldridge 48p, Charles 62* | *Judge* | *Trewick* | *Briggs* | *Shotton* | *Slatter* | *Houghton* | *Phillips* | *Hebberd* | *Aldridge* | *Charles** | *R'des-Brown* | *Thomas* |
| | | | | | | | Ref: C Downey | Oxford are more desperate for the points and are therefore the more determined team. Preece curls in a 20-yard free-kick before a John Aldridge 'double-shuffle' penalty, awarded after he is fouled by Nicholas, levels the scores. Jeremy Charles finally puts the Hatters out of their misery. | | | | | | | | | | | |
| 33 | A | MANCHESTER U | 9 | L | 0-2 | 0-1 | | Sealey | Johnson | Thomas | Nicholas | North S | Donaghy | Hill | Stein M | Newell | Breacker | Daniel* | Preece |
| 19/3 | | ***33,668*** | *3* | 51 | | | *Hughes 37, McGrath 76* | *Turner* | *Duxbury* | *McGrath* | *Moran** | *Albiston* | *Gibson* | *Whiteside* | *Strachan* | *Olsen* | *Hughes* | *Davenport* | *Stapleton* |
| | | | | | | | Ref: G Napthine | A powerful Manchester United side are once again too strong for the Hatters, who are missing Harford up front and are pushed back into defence for most of the game. The Old Trafford crowd is beginning to get agitated until Paul McGrath hits a thunderous effort from the edge of the area. | | | | | | | | | | | |
| 34 | H | EVERTON | 8 | W | 2-1 | 0-0 | Foster 81, Newell 85 | Sealey | Johnson | Thomas | Nicholas | Foster | Donaghy | Hill | Newell | Harford | Breacker | Preece | |
| 22/3 | | 11,039 | *1* | 54 | | | *Richardson 46* | *Southall* | *Harper* | *v d Hauwe* | *Mountfield* | *Pointon* | *Steven* | *Richardson* | *Bracewell* | *Sheedy** | *Sharp* | *Lineker* | *Marshall* |
| | | | | | | | Ref: R Lewis | Everton appear to be well in control, despite their play-acting, after a shot from Kevin Richardson takes a deflection en route into the net. Luton fight back and win the points with two powerful headers from Foster, although Newell claims the second goal after adding the finishing touch. | | | | | | | | | | | |
| 35 | A | LEICESTER | 8 | D | 0-0 | 0-0 | | Sealey | Johnson | Thomas | Nicholas | Foster | Donaghy | King* | Newell | Harford | Breacker | Preece | Stein M |
| 29/3 | | *9,912* | *17* | 55 | | | | *Andrews* | *Feeley* | *Osman* | *O'Neill* | *Morgan* | *Lynex* | *McAllister* | *Mauchlen* | *Cunningham** | *Sealy* | *Smith* | *Banks* |
| | | | | | | | Ref: K Walmsley | A disappointing game, which is full of missed chances from both teams, leaves Leicester slightly the happier with the one point in their fight against relegation. Mitchell Thomas blasts the ball well over the bar from close range to squander the best chance the Hatters have of scoring. | | | | | | | | | | | |
| 36 | H | WEST BROM | 8 | W | 3-0 | 2-0 | Newell 14, Harford 15p, Hill 51 | Sealey | Johnson | Thomas | Nicholas | Foster | Donaghy | Hill | Newell | Harford | Breacker | Preece* | Stein M |
| 1/4 | | 9,226 | *22* | 58 | | | | *Naylor* | *Whitehead* | *Palmer* | *Dyson* | *Statham* | *Bradley* | *Dickinson* | *Mackenzie* | *Thompson* | *Varadi** | *Madden* | *Grealish* |
| | | | | | | | Ref: A Ward | West Brom are all but relegated and have no answer to the slick Luton approach play, which would have produced more goals except for the inspired performance of keeper Naylor. Martin Dickinson handles the ball, enabling Harford to score his 20th goal of the season from the spot. | | | | | | | | | | | |
| 37 | A | BIRMINGHAM | 6 | W | 2-0 | 0-0 | Harford 48, 89 | Sealey | Johnson | Thomas | Nicholas | Foster | Donaghy | Hill | Newell | Harford | Breacker | Preece | |
| 6/4 | | ***8,836*** | *21* | 61 | | | | *Seaman* | *Ranson* | *Garton* | *Wright* | *Dicks* | *Hopkins* | *Bremner* | *Kuhl* | *Handysides* | *Kennedy* | *Clarke* | |
| | | | | | | | Ref: K Breen | Languishing near the foot of the table, Birmingham are no match for the Town, although they do try to make a fight of it. Harford slots the ball home just after the break but Robert Hopkins nearly levels, Sealey being called on to make a wonder save. Harford hits the injury-time winner. | | | | | | | | | | | |
| 38 | H | TOTTENHAM | 6 | D | 1-1 | 0-1 | Newell 88 | Sealey | Johnson | Thomas | Nicholas | Foster | Donaghy | Hill | Stein B | Harford | Newell | Preece | |
| 12/4 | | 13,141 | *12* | 62 | | | *Allen C 18* | *Clemence* | *Allen P* | *Miller* | *Mabbutt* | *Hughton* | *Chiedozie* | *Waddle* | *Stevens* | *Galvin* | *Falco* | *Allen C* | |
| | | | | | | | Ref: R Hamer | Stein returns to the side, just six weeks after his knee operation, but he has a quiet game. Spurs open the scoring when Clive Allen hits home a 25-yarder, but the honours are taken by Newell, whose brilliant diving header late on gives the Town the point which is the least they deserve. | | | | | | | | | | | |
| 39 | H | LIVERPOOL | 7 | L | 0-1 | 0-1 | | Sealey | Johnson | Thomas | Nicholas | Foster | Donaghy | Hill | Stein B* | Harford | Newell | Preece | Breacker |
| 16/4 | | 15,503 | *1* | 62 | | | *Johnston 16* | *Grobbelaar* | *Nicol* | *Gillespie** | *Hansen* | *Beglin* | *MacDonald* | *Dalglish* | *Molby* | *Johnston* | *Rush* | *Whelan* | *Lee* |
| | | | | | | | Ref: P Vanes | Liverpool return to the top of the table after grinding out a narrow victory. Craig Johnston hits a low shot for the only goal and the visitors then funnel back into defence in order to deny the Town a scoring opportunity. The constant back-passing does not endear them to the home crowd. | | | | | | | | | | | |
| 40 | A | COVENTRY | 8 | L | 0-1 | 0-0 | | Sealey | Johnson* | Thomas | Nicholas | Foster | Donaghy | Hill | Breacker | Harford | Newell | Preece | Stein M |
| 19/4 | | *10,161* | *17* | 62 | | | *Pickering 46* | *Ogrizovic* | *Borrows* | *Kilcline* | *Peake* | *Downs* | *Bennett* | *McGrath* | *Pickering* | *Adams* | *Regis* | *Brazil* | |
| | | | | | | | Ref: D Phillips | The Town have no shots on target during the whole of the ninety minutes in their worst display of the season. The Coventry caretaker-manager, George Curtis, points out that his side shows a lot of effort and, except for some amazing misses by Alan Brazil, would have won comfortably. | | | | | | | | | | | |
| 41 | H | WATFORD | 7 | W | 3-2 | 2-0 | Harford 10, 30, 74 | Sealey | Breacker | Thomas | Nicholas | Foster | Donaghy | Hill | Stein B | Harford | Nwajiobi | Preece | |
| 26/4 | | 11,810 | *12* | 65 | | | *Jackett 59p, Sinnott 78* | *Coton* | *Gibbs* | *Terry* | *McClelland* | *Sinnott* | *Talbot* | *Barnes* | *Jackett* | *Sterling* | *Allen** | *West* | *Bardsley* |
| | | | | | | | Ref: D Hedges | The home campaign finishes with another hat-trick from Mick Harford in a game which is more comfortable than the final scoreline suggests. The Hornets are handed a lifeline when Thomas is adjudged to have handled a shot from McClelland and Kenny Jackett converts from the spot. | | | | | | | | | | | |
| 42 | A | MANCHESTER C | 9 | D | 1-1 | 0-1 | Nwajiobi 49 | Sealey | Johnson | Thomas | Nicholas | Foster | Donaghy | Hill | Stein B | Newell | Nwajiobi | Preece* | Breacker |
| 3/5 | | *20,361* | *15* | 66 | | | *Davies 22* | *Nixon* | *Barrett* | *Reid* | *McCarthy* | *May* | *McNab* | *McIlroy* | *Phillips** | *Wilson* | *Lillis* | *Davies* | *Simpson* |
| | Home | Away | | | | | Ref: A Saunders | In a gentle end-of-season game, the teams do not show much effort in front of a bored crowd. Emeka Nwajiobi is put clear by Ricky Hill to slot home to equalise the goal from Davies. City manager Billy McNeill thinks his side could have won, but neither side deserved the three points. | | | | | | | | | | | |
| Average | 11,062 | 17,188 | | | | | | | | | | | | | | | | | |

| Milk Cup | | | | | F-A | H-T | Scorers, Times, and Referees | 1 | 2 | 3 | 4 | 5 | 6 | 7 | 8 | 9 | 10 | 11 | 12 sub used |
|---|---|---|---|---|---|---|---|---|---|---|---|---|---|---|---|---|---|---|---|
| 2:1 | A | SHEFFIELD UTD | 14 | W | 2-1 | 0-1 | Stein B 78, Nwajiobi 89 | Sealey | Breacker | Thomas | Nicholas | Foster | Donaghy | Hill | Stein B | Harford | Nwajiobi | Preece | |
| | 24/9 | *8,943* | *2:9* | | | | *Foley 44* | *Burridge* | *Eckhardt* | *Thompson* | *McNaught* | *Bolton* | *Foley* | *Lewington* | *Cockerill* | *Morris* | *Withe* | *Edwards* | |
| | | | | | | | Ref: J Lovatt | The Hatters are always a class above their opponents, but Steve Foley heads the home side into a shock lead in first half injury-time. Pressure finally tells when Emeka Nwajiobi crosses for Stein to level before Nwajiobi hits the winner at the death, when he is left completely unmarked. | | | | | | | | | | | |
| 2:2 | H | SHEFFIELD UTD | 14 | W | 3-1 | 2-0 | Preece 13, North M 42, Hill 63 | Sealey | Breacker | Thomas | Nicholas | Foster | Donaghy | Hill | Stein B | North M | Nwajiobi | Preece | |
| | 8/10 | 5,660 | *2:11* | | | | *Edwards 51* | *Burridge* | *McGeeney* | *Thompson* | *Stancliffe* | *McNaught* | *Bolton* | *Lewington* | *Cockerill* | *Edwards* | *Morris* | *Withe* | |
| | | | | | | | Ref: B Stevens (Hatters win 5-2 on aggregate) | Blades keeper John Burridge hits his head against a post and, whilst he is off the field having his wound stitched, his stand-in, Glen Cockerill, sees a shot from Stein rebound off a post and Preece follows up to score. Ricky Hill bends in a curling, testimonial-type effort from 35 yards. | | | | | | | | | | | |
| 3 | H | NORWICH | 13 | L | 0-2 | 0-2 | | Sealey | Breacker | Johnson* | Daniel | Foster | Donaghy | Hill | Stein B | Harford | Nwajiobi | Parker | Grimes |
| | 29/10 | 8,203 | *2:5* | | | | *Mendham 28, Bruce 34* | *Woods* | *Culverhouse* | *Watson* | *Bruce* | *van Wijk* | *Barham* | *Mendham* | *Williams* | *Phelan* | *Drinkell* | *Rosario* | |
| | | | | | | | Ref: B Hill | In a disappointing display, the Town lose for the first time on their artificial surface to the Milk Cup holders, who show far more determination. Peter Mendham scores from close range and a fierce free-kick, six minutes later, from Steve Bruce finishes the cup aspirations of the Hatters. | | | | | | | | | | | |

| FA Cup | | | | | | | | 1 | 2 | 3 | 4 | 5 | 6 | 7 | 8 | 9 | 10 | 11 | 12 sub used |
|---|---|---|---|---|---|---|---|---|---|---|---|---|---|---|---|---|---|---|---|
| 3 | A | CRYS PALACE | 8 | W | 2-1 | 1-0 | Stein B 8, Preece 85 | Sealey | Breacker | Thomas | Nicholas | Foster | Donaghy | Hill | Stein B | Harford | North M | Preece | |
| | 6/1 | *9,886* | *2:9* | | | | *Taylor 86* | *Wood* | *Locke* | *Droy* | *Cannon* | *Hughton* | *Irvine* | *Taylor* | *Barber** | *Ketteridge* | *Wright* | *Gray* | *Higginbottom* |
| | | | | | | | Ref: B Stevens | An early header from Brian Stein is not capitalised on, but the proverbial banana skin is avoided when David Preece slots home with just five minutes left. The 25-yard shot from Kevin Taylor comes too late as the Town shut up shop. England manager Bobby Robson is again present. | | | | | | | | | | | |
| 4 | H | BRISTOL ROV | 7 | W | 4-0 | 2-0 | Harford 22, Hill 28, North M 63, | Sealey | Breacker | Thomas | Nicholas | Foster | Donaghy | Hill | Stein B | Harford | North M | Preece | |
| | 25/1 | 12,463 | *3:14* | | | | [Parkin 82 (og)] | *Green* | *Scales** | *Parkin* | *Spring* | *Tanner* | *Francis* | *Stevenson* | *O'Connor* | *Penrice* | *Morgan* | *White* | *Randall* |
| | | | | | | | Ref: J Moules | Third Division Rovers are no match for the Town in this form with the goals going in at regular intervals through the afternoon. Harford returns to the side only 18 days after his knee operation and runs the defence ragged. A deflection by Tim Parkin into his own net completes the misery. | | | | | | | | | | | |
| 5 | H | ARSENAL | 6 | D | 2-2 | 2-2 | Hill 8, Harford 39 | Sealey | Johnson | Thomas | Nicholas | Foster | Donaghy | Hill | Stein B* | Harford | North M | Preece | Parker |
| | 15/2 | 15,799 | *1:7* | | | | *Allinson 15, Rocastle 26* | *Lukic* | *Anderson* | *O'Leary* | *Keown* | *Sansom* | *Allinson* | *Williams* | *Rocastle* | *Rix* | *Woodcock* | *Nicholas** | *Mariner* |
| | | | | | | | Ref: A Gunn | In a physical, committed performance from both sides, England hopefuls Ricky Hill and Mick Harford catch the eye in a game which sees all the goals coming in the first half. The Gunners are fortunate to hold out for a replay and there are plenty of bruises in evidence on both sides. | | | | | | | | | | | |
| 5R | A | ARSENAL | 6 | D | 0-0 | 0-0 | | Sealey | Johnson | Thomas | Nicholas | Foster | Donaghy | Hill | King | Harford | North M | Preece | |
| | 3/3 | *26,547* | *1:8* | | *aet* | | | *Lukic* | *Anderson* | *O'Leary* | *Keown* | *Sansom* | *Allinson* | *Williams* | *Rocastle* | *Rix* | *Mariner* | *Nicholas* | |
| | | | | | | | Ref: A Gunn | This time it is the Town who are fortunate to hang on for a draw on a dangerous, icy pitch which is surprisingly passed playable. Luton have to defend for most of the two hours but Arsenal do not create many clear-cut chances. The Town win the toss for the venue of the second replay. | | | | | | | | | | | |
| 5R | H | ARSENAL | 6 | W | 3-0 | 1-0 | Foster 23, O'Leary 52 (og), Stein M 79 | Sealey | Johnson | Thomas | Nicholas | Foster | Donaghy | Hill | Stein M | Harford | King | Preece | |
| R | 5/3 | 13,251 | *1:8* | | | | | *Lukic* | *Anderson* | *O'Leary* | *Keown* | *Sansom* | *Williams* | *Rocastle* | *Allinson* | *Hayes** | *Nicholas* | *Mariner* | *Quinn* |
| | | | | | | | Ref: D Scott | Only 48 hours after the first replay, the players do battle again but this time the Town deservedly win through with their best team performance in years. The Gunners are swept aside with a half-volley from Foster, a clumsy own-goal from David O'Leary, and a close-in effort from Stein. | | | | | | | | | | | |
| QF | H | EVERTON | 6 | D | 2-2 | 1-0 | Harford 21, Stein M 63 | Sealey | Johnson | Thomas | Nicholas | Foster | Donaghy | Hill | Stein M | Harford | King* | Preece | North M |
| | 8/3 | 15,529 | *1:1* | | | | *Sharp 65, Heath 77* | *Southall* | *Stevens* | *Harper* | *v d Hauwe* | *Pointon** | *Steven* | *Reid* | *Bracewell* | *Sharp* | *Lineker* | *Richardson* | *Heath* |
| | | | | | | | Ref: K Hackett | Everton are made of strong stuff and show it by bouncing back from two goals down to level the tie and nearly pinch the victory when a free header from Gary Lineker is saved by Sealey. Luton are unable to exact revenge for last season's defeat as the Arsenal marathon takes its toll. | | | | | | | | | | | |
| QF | A | EVERTON | 6 | L | 0-1 | 0-1 | | Sealey | Johnson | Thomas | Nicholas | Foster | Donaghy | Hill | Stein M | Harford | Grimes* | Preece | Daniel |
| R | 12/3 | *44,264* | *1:1* | | | | *Lineker 16* | *Southall* | *Stevens* | *Harper* | *v d Hauwe* | *Pointon* | *Steven* | *Reid* | *Bracewell* | *Sharp* | *Lineker* | *Sheedy** | *Heath* |
| | | | | | | | Ref: K Hackett | Gary Lineker beats both Foster and Donaghy for speed to score an early goal and then misses a penalty after he is brought down by Les Sealey, seemingly outside the box. Luton come close to equalising when Ray Daniel hits the post, which prompts the crowd to yell for the final whistle. | | | | | | | | | | | |

| | | P | W | D | L | F | A | W | D | L | F | A | Pts |
|---|---|---|---|---|---|---|---|---|---|---|---|---|---|
| | | | Home | | | | | Away | | | | | |
| 1 | Liverpool | 42 | 16 | 4 | 1 | 58 | 14 | 10 | 6 | 5 | 31 | 23 | 88 |
| 2 | Everton | 42 | 16 | 3 | 2 | 54 | 18 | 10 | 5 | 6 | 33 | 23 | 86 |
| 3 | West Ham | 42 | 17 | 2 | 2 | 48 | 16 | 9 | 4 | 8 | 26 | 24 | 84 |
| 4 | Manchester U | 42 | 12 | 5 | 4 | 35 | 12 | 10 | 5 | 6 | 35 | 24 | 76 |
| 5 | Sheffield Wed | 42 | 13 | 6 | 2 | 36 | 23 | 8 | 4 | 9 | 27 | 31 | 73 |
| 6 | Chelsea | 42 | 12 | 4 | 5 | 32 | 27 | 8 | 7 | 6 | 25 | 29 | 71 |
| 7 | Arsenal | 42 | 13 | 5 | 3 | 29 | 15 | 7 | 4 | 10 | 20 | 32 | 69 |
| 8 | Nott'm Forest | 42 | 11 | 5 | 5 | 38 | 25 | 8 | 6 | 7 | 31 | 28 | 68 |
| 9 | LUTON TOWN | 42 | 12 | 6 | 3 | 37 | 15 | 6 | 6 | 9 | 24 | 29 | 66 |
| 10 | Tottenham | 42 | 12 | 2 | 7 | 47 | 25 | 7 | 6 | 8 | 27 | 27 | 65 |
| 11 | Newcastle | 42 | 12 | 5 | 4 | 46 | 31 | 5 | 7 | 9 | 21 | 41 | 63 |
| 12 | Watford | 42 | 11 | 6 | 4 | 40 | 22 | 5 | 5 | 11 | 29 | 40 | 59 |
| 13 | QP Rangers | 42 | 12 | 3 | 6 | 33 | 20 | 3 | 4 | 14 | 20 | 44 | 52 |
| 14 | Southampton | 42 | 10 | 6 | 5 | 32 | 18 | 2 | 4 | 15 | 19 | 44 | 46 |
| 15 | Manchester C | 42 | 7 | 7 | 7 | 25 | 26 | 4 | 5 | 12 | 18 | 31 | 45 |
| 16 | Aston Villa | 42 | 7 | 6 | 8 | 27 | 28 | 3 | 8 | 10 | 24 | 39 | 44 |
| 17 | Coventry | 42 | 6 | 5 | 10 | 31 | 35 | 5 | 5 | 11 | 17 | 36 | 43 |
| 18 | Oxford | 42 | 7 | 7 | 7 | 34 | 27 | 3 | 5 | 13 | 28 | 53 | 42 |
| 19 | Leicester | 42 | 7 | 8 | 6 | 35 | 35 | 3 | 4 | 14 | 19 | 41 | 42 |
| 20 | Ipswich | 42 | 8 | 5 | 8 | 20 | 24 | 3 | 3 | 15 | 12 | 31 | 41 |
| 21 | Birmingham | 42 | 5 | 2 | 14 | 13 | 25 | 3 | 3 | 15 | 17 | 48 | 29 |
| 22 | West Brom | 42 | 3 | 8 | 10 | 21 | 36 | 1 | 4 | 16 | 14 | 53 | 24 |
| | | 924 | 229 | 110 | 123 | 771 | 517 | 123 | 110 | 229 | 517 | 771 | 1276 |

Odds & ends

Double wins: (4) Birmingham, Southampton, Watford, West Brom.
Double losses: (2) Coventry, Liverpool.

Won from behind: (2) Everton (h), Sheff Utd (LC).
Lost from in front: (1) Oxford (h).

High spots: The highest league position since 1958.
The FA Cup win over Arsenal.
The 7-0 thrashing of Southampton at Kenilworth Road.
Mick Harford at his best.
Another double over Watford!
The first win at Tottenham since 1948.

Low spots: Losing to Everton in the FA Cup – again.
The first home defeat on the artificial surface, against Norwich in the Milk Cup.

Player of the Year: Mal Donaghy.
Ever-presents: (1) Mal Donaghy.
Hat-tricks: (3) Brian Stein (1), Mick Harford (2).
Leading scorer: (25) Mick Harford .

| | Appearances Lge | *Sub* | LC | *Sub* | FAC | *Sub* | Goals Lge | LC | FAC | Tot |
|---|---|---|---|---|---|---|---|---|---|---|
| Breacker, Tim | **34** | *2* | 3 | | 2 | | | | | |
| Daniel, Ray | **2** | *3* | 1 | | | *1* | **1** | | | **1** |
| Dibble, Andy | **7** | | | | | | | | | |
| Donaghy, Mal | **42** | | 3 | | 7 | | | | | |
| Elliott, Paul | **3** | *3* | | | | | | | | |
| Foster, Steve | **35** | | 3 | | 7 | | **3** | | 1 | **4** |
| Grimes, Ashley | **2** | *1* | | *1* | 1 | | | | | |
| Harford, Mick | **37** | | 2 | | 7 | | **22** | | 3 | **25** |
| Hill, Ricky | **38** | | 3 | | 7 | | **3** | 1 | 2 | **6** |
| Johnson, Rob | **15** | | 1 | | 5 | | | | | |
| King, Andy | **3** | | | | 3 | | | | | |
| Newell, Mike | **16** | | | | | | **6** | | | **6** |
| Nicholas, Peter | **41** | | 2 | | 7 | | | | | |
| North, Marc | **9** | *4* | 1 | | 4 | *1* | **3** | 1 | 1 | **5** |
| North, Stacey | **2** | | | | | | | | | |
| Nwajiobi, Emeka | **20** | *1* | 3 | | | | **5** | 1 | | **6** |
| Parker, Gary | **4** | *4* | 1 | | | *1* | | | | |
| Preece, David | **40** | *1* | 2 | | 7 | | **2** | 1 | 1 | **4** |
| Sealey, Les | **35** | | 3 | | 7 | | | | | |
| Stein, Brian | **33** | | 3 | | 3 | | **14** | 1 | 1 | **16** |
| Stein, Mark | **3** | *3* | | | 3 | | | | 2 | **2** |
| Thomas, Mitchell | **41** | | 2 | | 7 | | **1** | | | **1** |
| (own-goals) | | | | | | | **1** | | 2 | **3** |
| **22 players used** | **462** | *22* | **33** | *1* | **77** | *3* | **61** | **5** | **13** | **79** |

## TODAY LEAGUE DIVISION 1

## Manager: John Moore

## SEASON 1986-87



| No | Date | Att | Pos | Pt | F-A | H-T | Scorers, Times, and Referees | 1 | 2 | 3 | 4 | 5 | 6 | 7 | 8 | 9 | 10 | 11 | 12 sub used |
|---|---|---|---|---|---|---|---|---|---|---|---|---|---|---|---|---|---|---|---|
| 1 | A LEICESTER | | | D | 1-1 | 1-1 | Stein B 39, | Sealey | Breacker | Johnson | Nicholas | Foster | Donaghy | Hill | Stein B | Newell | **Wilson*** | Nwajiobi | North M |
| | 23/8 | *9,801* | | 1 | | | *Smith 16* | *Andrews* | *Ramsey* | *Osman* | *Walsh* | *Venus* | *Lynex* | *McAllister** | *Wilson* | *Banks* | *Bright* | *Smith* | *Sealy* |
| | | | | | | | Ref: D Scott | Alan Smith hits a shot home from close range for Leicester but the Hatters always look the more likely to win. Stein takes over the scoring responsibilities from the injured Harford and duly obliges when skipping past four defenders to hit a super solo goal. Wilson has a quiet debut. | | | | | | | | | | | |
| 2 | H SOUTHAMPTON | | | W | 2-1 | 1-0 | Wilson 3, Stein B 58 | Sealey | Breacker | Johnson | Nicholas | Foster | Donaghy | Hill | Stein B | Newell | Wilson | Nwajiobi | |
| | 26/8 | **8,777** | | 4 | | | *Clarke 72* | *Shilton* | *Forrest* | *Bond* | *Blake* | *Dennis* | *Lawrence* | *Cockerill* | *Case* | *Holmes** | *Wallace* | *Clarke* | *Baker* |
| | | | | | | | Ref: D Axcell | Richard Wilson heads in a cross from Rob Johnson in the opening minutes to set the Town up for a comfortable victory. Glen Cockerill upends Brian Stein but the spot-kick from Mike Newell is saved by Peter Shilton. Stein makes the points safe, shortly afterwards, with a clinical finish. | | | | | | | | | | | |
| 3 | H NEWCASTLE | | 8 | D | 0-0 | 0-0 | | Sealey | Breacker | Johnson | Nicholas | Foster | Donaghy | Hill | Stein B | Newell | Wilson | Nwajiobi | |
| | 30/8 | 9,254 | *18* | 5 | | | | *Thomas* | *Bailey* | *Anderson* | *Roeder* | *McDonald* | *Gascoigne* | *Bogie* | *McCreery* | *Wharton* | *Beardsley* | *Whitehurst* | |
| | | | | | | | Ref: R Lewis | An 'out of this world' display of goalkeeping from Martin Thomas saves the Magpies from a heavy defeat and thoroughly merits the standing ovation he receives from the crowd at the end of the match. Newcastle are swamped by the incisive passing and running of the Luton forwards. | | | | | | | | | | | |
| 4 | A ASTON VILLA | | 10 | L | 1-2 | 0-1 | Stein B 78 | Sealey | Breacker* | Johnson | Nicholas | Foster | Donaghy | Hill | Stein B | Newell | Wilson | Nwajiobi | North M |
| | 3/9 | *13,122* | *18* | 5 | | | *Kerr 44, 46* | *Poole* | *Keown* | *Evans* | *Elliott* | *Dorigo* | *Blair** | *Hunt* | *Hodge* | *Daley* | *Stainrod* | *Thompson* | *Kerr* |
| | | | | | | | Ref: K Breen | Villa take a two-goal lead, scoring either side of the interval, before North is carried off on the hour with an ankle injury. Reduced to ten men, Luton then play their best football of the game and Brian Stein pulls a goal back, but he's unable to prevent the first Luton defeat of the season. | | | | | | | | | | | |
| 5 | A CHELSEA | | 7 | W | 3-1 | 1-1 | Newell 45, 63, Stein B 85 | Sealey | Johnson | Grimes | Nicholas | Foster | Donaghy | Hill | Stein B | Newell | Wilson | Nwajiobi | |
| | 6/9 | *13,040* | *19* | 8 | | | *Dixon 30* | *Godden* | *Wood* | *McLaughlin* | *Pates* | *Millar* | *Bumstead** | *Nevin* | *Spackman* | *Dixon* | *Speedie* | *Murphy* | *Durie* |
| | | | | | | | Ref: R Milford | The Blues have most of the first-half play and a headed goal by Kerry Dixon gives them a deserved lead. Newell levels just before the interval and then puts the Town ahead when taking advantage of a long clearance. Pates goes off, reducing Chelsea to ten, before Stein fires the winner. | | | | | | | | | | | |
| 6 | H ARSENAL | | 8 | D | 0-0 | 0-0 | | Sealey | Johnson | Grimes | Nicholas | Foster | Donaghy | Hill | Stein B | Newell | Wilson | Nwajiobi* | Stein M |
| | 13/9 | 9,876 | *10* | 9 | | | | *Lukic* | *Anderson* | *O'Leary* | *Adams* | *Sansom* | *Williams* | *Rocastle* | *Davis* | *Rix* | *Nicholas* | *Quinn** | *Groves* |
| | | | | | | | Ref: M James | A one-minute silence is observed before the match as a mark of respect for the former Luton manager, Harry Haslam, who died last week. In a poor game, neither side looks likely to score. 'I am glad that I did not have to pay to watch,' says Town manager John Moore after the match. | | | | | | | | | | | |
| 7 | A WEST HAM | | 13 | L | 0-2 | 0-1 | | Sealey | Johnson | Grimes | Nicholas | Foster | Donaghy | Hill | Stein B ! | Newell* | Wilson | Preece | Stein M |
| | 20/9 | *19,133* | *4* | 9 | | | *Parris 41, Gale 57* | *Parkes* | *Stewart* | *Gale* | *Martin !* | *Walford* | *Keen* | *Dickens** | *Orr* | *Parris* | *McAvennie* | *Cottee* | *Pike* |
| | | | | | | | Ref: J Deakin | George Parris fires in a long shot and Tony Gale heads home from a corner-kick. But then Brian Stein and Alvin Martin are dismissed after they exchange blows, with Frank Bruno watching from the stand. The Town rarely threaten the West Ham defence in another poor performance. | | | | | | | | | | | |
| 8 | H MANCHESTER C | | 10 | W | 1-0 | 0-0 | Stein B 81 | Sealey | Johnson | Grimes | Nicholas | Foster | Donaghy | Hill | Stein B | Newell | Stein M | Preece | |
| | 27/9 | 9,371 | *17* | 12 | | | | *Suckling* | *May* | *Clements* | *McCarthy* | *Wilson* | *Hopkins* | *Redmond* | *McNab* | *Simpson* | *Christie** | *Beckford* | *White* |
| | | | | | | | Ref: J Borrett | Perry Suckling puts up an inspired performance to keep the Town at bay until Stein pops up in the 81st minute to break the deadlock. Moore is concerned that, with Stein about to start a two-match ban and Harford still on the injury list, there appears to be no one capable of scoring goals. | | | | | | | | | | | |
| 9 | A TOTTENHAM | | 10 | D | 0-0 | 0-0 | | Sealey | Johnson | Grimes | Nicholas | Foster | Donaghy | Hill | Stein M | Newell | North M | Preece | |
| | 4/10 | *22,738* | *7* | 13 | | | | *Clemence* | *Thomas D* | *Gough* | *Mabbutt* | *Thomas M* | *Roberts* | *Hoddle* | *Allen** | *Galvin* | *Howells* | *Waddle* | *Ardiles* |
| | | | | | | | Ref: A Seville | Ricky Hill is in his element and sprays the ball around the park all afternoon but his colleagues are unable to land a killer blow. Pleat, now with Tottenham, believes that his below-par side were lucky to escape with a point although Ray Clemence makes an unbelievable save from Newell. | | | | | | | | | | | |
| 10 | H NORWICH | | 11 | D | 0-0 | 0-0 | | Sealey | Johnson | Grimes | Nicholas | Foster | Donaghy | Hill | Stein M | Newell | North M* | Preece | **McDono'gh** |
| | 11/10 | 10,022 | *1* | 14 | | | | *Benstead* | *Culverhouse* | *Bruce* | *Butterworth* | *Spearing* | *Gordon* | *Williams** | *Phelan* | *Barham* | *Drinkell* | *Biggins* | *Crook* |
| | | | | | | | Ref: J Ashworth | The Town are unbeaten at home and Norwich have not lost away this season and therefore the scoreless draw is the predictable result. Chances are few in a match which is dominated by the defences. The closest Luton come to scoring is when a lob from Marc North bounces off the bar. | | | | | | | | | | | |

| No | Date | Opponent | Att | Pos | Pts | F-A | H-T | Scorers, Times, and Referees | 1 | 2 | 3 | 4 | 5 | 6 | 7 | 8 | 9 | 10 | 11 | 12 |
|---|---|---|---|---|---|---|---|---|---|---|---|---|---|---|---|---|---|---|---|---|
| 11 | A | MANCHESTER U | | 12 | L | 0-1 | 0-1 | | Sealey | Breacker | Grimes | Nicholas | Foster | Donaghy | Hill | Stein B | Newell | Stein M* | Preece | McDonough |
| | 18/10 | | *39,927* | *19* | 14 | | | *Stapleton 9* | *Turner* | *Sivebaek* | *McGrath* | *Hogg* | *Albiston* | *Whiteside* | *Robson* | *Strachan** | *Barnes* | *Stapleton* | *Davenport* | *Gibson* |
| | | | | | | | | Ref: D Hutchinson | Luton have never won at Old Trafford and have not scored a goal there since 1959. The record is maintained when a bad back-pass from Grimes lets in Frank Stapleton for an easy goal and, after Mark Stein is brought down by Paul McGrath, his brother Brian hits the penalty-kick wide. | | | | | | | | | | | |
| 12 | H | LIVERPOOL | | 12 | W | **4-1** | 3-0 | Newell 14, 37, 52, Hill 41 | Sealey | Johnson | Grimes* | Nicholas | Foster | Donaghy | Hill | Stein B | Newell | Stein M | Preece | Wilson |
| | 25/10 | | 13,140 | *5* | 17 | | | *Molby 81p* | *Grobbelaar* | *Venison** | *Lawrenson* | *Hansen* | *Molby* | *Beglin* | *Nicol* | *Whelan* | *McMahon* | *Walsh* | *Rush* | *Johnston* |
| | | | | | | | | Ref: M Bodenham | Liverpool fan Mike Newell silences the supporters who came to jeer by netting an unbelievable hat-trick against the team who are second best in every department. Newell looks the equal of the injured Harford. Les Sealey gets a hand to the late consolation penalty-kick by Jan Molby. | | | | | | | | | | | |
| 13 | H | QP RANGERS | | 6 | W | 1-0 | 0-0 | Neill 56 (og) | Sealey | Johnson | **Harvey** | Nicholas | Foster | Donaghy | Hill | Stein B | Newell | Stein M | Preece* | McDonough |
| | 1/11 | | 9,085 | *13* | 20 | | | | *Seaman* | *Neill* | *Chivers* | *Fenwick* | *Dawes* | *Channing* | *James* | *Allen* | *Fereday* | *Bannister** | *Byrne* | *Walker* |
| | | | | | | | | Ref: J Martin | In a miserable game, Warren Neill scores the only goal with a back-pass which beats his advancing goalkeeper, David Seaman. Ashley Grimes and Breacker both miss the match through injury, and this gives a perfect opportunity for 17-year-old Richard Harvey to make his Luton debut. | | | | | | | | | | | |
| 14 | A | WIMBLEDON | | 5 | W | 1-0 | 0-0 | Stein M 58 | Sealey | Breacker | Johnson | Nicholas | Foster | Donaghy | Hill | Stein B* | Newell | Stein M | McDonough | Wilson |
| | 8/11 | | *6,181* | *12* | 23 | | | | *Beasant* | *Kay* | *Thorn* | *Gayle* | *Winterburn* | *Downes* | *Galliers* | *Sanchez** | *Fairweather* | *Cork* | *Fashanu* | *Gage* |
| | | | | | | | | Ref: L Shapter | In their first ever visit to Plough Lane, the Hatters survive a bombardment from the Dons. Mark Stein scores his first league goal after Newell heads a long cross from Breacker into his path. The goal is against the run of play but the Town defence, under considerable pressure, hold out. | | | | | | | | | | | |
| 15 | H | NOTT'M FOREST | | 4 | W | 4-2 | 3-1 | Stein M 1, 10, Foster 16, Stein B 68 | Sealey | Breacker | Johnson | Nicholas | Foster | Donaghy | Wilson | Stein B | Newell | Stein M | Grimes* | McDonough |
| | 15/11 | | 11,097 | *3* | 26 | | | *Bowyer 24, Birtles 80* | *Segers* | *Butterworth* | *Walker* | *Metgod* | *Pearce* | *Bowyer* | *Webb* | *Mills* | *Carr* | *Clough* | *Birtles* | |
| | | | | | | | | Ref: A Buksh | Forest are stunned by the three goals scored against them in the first quarter, but they fight back and come within an ace of making the score 3-2 when Ian Bowyer heads against the bar. Stein makes the points safe with a curling shot, the final gesture from Gary Birtles coming far too late. | | | | | | | | | | | |
| 16 | A | SHEFFIELD WED | | 5 | L | 0-1 | 0-0 | | Sealey | Breacker | Johnson | Nicholas | Foster | Donaghy | McDonough | Stein B | Newell | Stein M | Grimes* | Wilson |
| | 22/11 | | *21,171* | *9* | 26 | | | *Megson 72* | *Hodge* | *Sterland* | *Hart* | *Madden* | *Worthington* | *Johnson* | *Megson* | *Shelton* | *Marwood* | *Hirst** | *Chapman* | *Snodin* |
| | | | | | | | | Ref: I Hendrick | The Luton defence is in superb form once again in this tough, physical confrontation, but failures at the other end result in a continual flow of one-way traffic and Gary Megson eventually manages to score from close range. The Town are now regarded as a most difficult team to beat. | | | | | | | | | | | |
| 17 | H | CHARLTON | | 5 | W | 1-0 | 1-0 | Stein M 20 | Sealey | Johnson | Grimes | Nicholas | Foster | Donaghy | Wilson | Stein B | Newell | Stein M | McDonough | |
| | 29/11 | | 9,273 | *19* | 29 | | | | *Johns* | *Humphrey* | *Thompson* | *Shirtliff* | *Reid* | *Peake** | *Shipley* | *Aizlewood* | *Stuart* | *Lee* | *Pearson* | *Walsh* |
| | | | | | | | | Ref: A Robinson | Mark Stein collects a pass from his brother and fires home the winner from the edge of the area, but ex-Hatter Mark Aizlewood is voted Man of the Match. Charlton manager Lennie Lawrence admits that 'we were so poor, even I could have played in goal for Luton in the second half'. | | | | | | | | | | | |
| 18 | A | OXFORD | | 7 | L | 2-4 | 0-1 | Stein B 70, Stein M 73 | Sealey | Johnson | Grimes | Nicholas | Foster | Donaghy | Breacker | Stein B | Newell | Stein M | McDono'gh* | North M |
| | 6/12 | | *8,800* | *13* | 29 | | | *Aldridge 40, 57, 89, Brock 63* | *Hardwick* | *Langan* | *Briggs* | *Dreyer* | *McDonald* | *Houghton* | *Trewick* | *Hebberd* | *Brock* | *Whitehurst* | *Aldridge* | |
| | | | | | | | | Ref: D Shaw | Oxford are made to look like world-beaters as the Town have a rare off-day. The home side coast into a 3-0 lead but the Hatters show some late fight with the Stein brothers each getting a goal. There is no grand finale, however, as John Aldridge gets his hat-trick goal in the final minute. | | | | | | | | | | | |
| 19 | H | EVERTON | | 4 | W | 1-0 | 0-0 | Newell 71 | Sealey | Breacker | Johnson | Nicholas | Foster | Donaghy | McDonough | Stein B | Newell | Stein M | Grimes | |
| | 13/12 | | 11,151 | *3* | 32 | | | | *Southall* | *Stevens* | *Ratcliffe* | *Watson* | *Pointon** | *Steven* | *Harper* | *Sheedy* | *Power* | *Sharp* | *Heath* | *Wilkinson* |
| | | | | | | | | Ref: D Reeves | The Town raise their game and take the lead through a header from Mike Newell. Everton feel that they should have had a penalty when Steve Foster handled in the area and Les Sealey, who is nursing a foot injury, has to react sharply as Everton pile on the pressure in the final minutes. | | | | | | | | | | | |
| 20 | A | ARSENAL | | 6 | L | **0-3** | 0-0 | | Sealey | Breacker | Johnson | Nicholas | North S | Donaghy | McDonough | Stein B | Newell | Stein M | Grimes | |
| | 20/12 | | *28,213* | *1* | 32 | | | *Quinn 70, Adams 81, Hayes 88* | *Lukic* | *Anderson* | *O'Leary* | *Adams* | *Sansom* | *Davis* | *Rocastle* | *Williams* | *Hayes* | *Groves** | *Quinn* | *Nicholas* |
| | | | | | | | | Ref: R Groves | The Town, who do not have a single shot on target in the whole of the game, decide to concentrate on defence. They almost succeed in earning a point until Niall Quinn heads home a cross from Perry Groves and the floodgates open. Stacey North deputises for flu victim Steve Foster. | | | | | | | | | | | |
| 21 | H | WATFORD | | 11 | L | 0-2 | 0-2 | | Sealey | Breacker | Johnson | Nicholas | North S | Donaghy | McDono'gh* | Stein B | Newell | Stein M | Grimes | **McEvoy** |
| | 26/12 | | 11,140 | *10* | 32 | | | *Porter 6, Richardson 17* | *Coton* | *Bardsley* | *Sims* | *McClelland* | *Rostron* | *Richardson* | *Jackett* | *Porter* | *Sterling* | *Falco* | *Barnes* | |
| | | | | | | | | Ref: C Downey | Mal Donaghy attempts to dribble the ball out of defence but is dispossessed by Kevin Richardson for the Hornets' second goal. Grimes is felled in the area by David Bardsley but Nicholas hammers the spot-kick wide. John Moore lays the blame for this derby defeat on his senior players. | | | | | | | | | | | |

# TODAY LEAGUE DIVISION 1 — Manager: John Moore — SEASON 1986-87



| No | Date | | Att | Pos | Pt | F-A | H-T | Scorers, Times, and Referees | 1 | 2 | 3 | 4 | 5 | 6 | 7 | 8 | 9 | 10 | 11 | 12 sub used |
|---|---|---|---|---|---|---|---|---|---|---|---|---|---|---|---|---|---|---|---|---|
| 22 | A | NOTT'M FOREST | | 8 | D | 2-2 | 1-0 | Stein B 10, Newell 85 | Sealey | Breacker | Johnson | Nicholas | Foster | Donaghy | Wilson* | Stein B | Newell | Harford | Grimes | Stein M |
| | 28/12 | | *20,273* | *5* | 33 | | | *Clough 73, Bowyer 89* | *Segers* | *Fleming* | *Walker* | *Fairclough* | *Pearce* | *Mills* | *Bowyer* | *Webb* | *Carr* | *Clough* | *Campbell* | |
| | | | | | | | | Ref: N Midgley | Harford makes a welcome return to the side and inspires the Hatters to a performance far removed from their Boxing Day debacle. Stein grabs the first and then Newell hits a superb effort with five minutes left. Forest net a second equaliser when Ian Bowyer scores with a deflected shot. | | | | | | | | | | | |
| 23 | A | COVENTRY | | 6 | W | 1-0 | 1-0 | Stein B 40 | Sealey | Breacker | Johnson | Nicholas | Foster | Donaghy | Wilson | Stein B | Newell | Harford | Grimes | |
| | 1/1 | | *16,667* | *11* | 36 | | | | *Ogrizovic* | *Borrows* | *Sedgley* | *Kilcline* | *Pickering* | *Bennett* | *Emerson* | *Gynn* | *Phillips* | *Regis* | *Houchen* | |
| | | | | | | | | Ref: F Roberts | Les Sealey returns to his old club and is barracked by the home supporters. Brian Stein converts one of only two chances which are created all afternoon by the Hatters, when he drives the ball into the far corner of the net to record the first Luton victory at Highfield Road since 1930. | | | | | | | | | | | |
| 24 | H | CHELSEA | | 5 | W | 1-0 | 0-0 | Newell 68 | Sealey | Breacker | Johnson | Nicholas | Foster | Donaghy | Wilson | Stein B | Newell | Harford | Grimes | |
| | 3/1 | | 10,556 | *18* | 39 | | | | *Niedzwiecki* | *Wood* | *Pates* | *McLaughlin* | *Dublin* | *McNaught* | *Spackman* | *Wegerle** | *Nevin* | *Dixon* | *Speedie* | *Durie* |
| | | | | | | | | Ref: J Bray | In a game dominated by the defences, Mike Newell takes advantage when Chelsea Eddy Niedzwiecki drops a shot from Harford to net the only goal. Blues chairman Ken Bates stays away as a personal protest against the ban on away fans and donates his tickets to Chelsea supporters. | | | | | | | | | | | |
| 25 | H | LEICESTER | | 4 | W | 1-0 | 0-0 | Newell 59 | Sealey | Breacker | Johnson | Nicholas | Foster | Donaghy | Hill | Stein B | Newell | Harford | Grimes | |
| | 24/1 | | 9,102 | *20* | 42 | | | | *Andrews* | *Feeley* | *O'Neill* | *Walsh* | *Morgan* | *Venus* | *Ramsey** | *McAllister* | *Mauchlen* | *Smith* | *Moran* | *Lynex* |
| | | | | | | | | Ref: P Don | Leicester have lost nine away games in a row and, with 14 goals conceded in their last three matches, opt for a defensive format which stifles the Town forward line. Their game plan is foiled when Newell knocks in Donaghy's cross. Ally Mauchlen has a shot well saved by Les Sealey. | | | | | | | | | | | |
| 26 | A | NEWCASTLE | | 5 | D | 2-2 | 1-2 | Grimes 12, Breacker 75 | Sealey | Breacker | Johnson | Nicholas | Foster | Donaghy | Wilson | Stein B | Newell | Harford | Grimes | |
| | 7/2 | | *22,447* | *22* | 43 | | | *Jackson P 22, Goddard 30* | *Thomas M* | *McDonald* | *Jackson P* | *Roeder* | *Wharton* | *McCreery** | *Craig* | *Thomas A* | *Beardsley* | *Cunningham* | *Goddard* | *Jackson D* |
| | | | | | | | | Ref: J Worrall | Ashley Grimes opens the scoring, direct from a free-kick, but bottom-placed Newcastle score twice to take the lead, helped in no small part by a vociferous St James' Park crowd. Tim Breacker slams his first ever league goal with 15 minutes left to earn the Hatters a share of the points. | | | | | | | | | | | |
| 27 | H | ASTON VILLA | | 5 | W | 2-1 | 2-0 | Foster 25, Harford 33p | Sealey | Breacker | Johnson | Nicholas | Foster | Donaghy | Wilson | Stein B | Newell | Harford | Grimes | |
| | 14/2 | | 9,174 | *21* | 46 | | | *Evans 76p* | *Spink* | *Williams* | *Evans* | *Keown* | *Elliott* | *Dorigo* | *Daley* | *Birch* | *Hunt* | *Thompson* | *Walters* | |
| | | | | | | | | Ref: B Stevens | The game opens in sparkling style when Steve Foster, seeing Villa goalkeeper Nigel Spink off his line, scores with a 25-yard volley. Harford converts from the spot after Dorigo handles in the area. Allan Evans pulls a goal back with a penalty for the visitors after Johnson trips Walters. | | | | | | | | | | | |
| 28 | A | MANCHESTER C | | 5 | D | 1-1 | 0-1 | Stein B 61 | Sealey | Johnson | Grimes | Nicholas | Foster | Donaghy | Hill | Stein B | Newell | Harford | Wilson | |
| | 21/2 | | *17,507* | *17* | 47 | | | *Lake 43* | *Suckling* | *Gidman* | *Clements* | *McCarthy* | *Wilson* | *Lake** | *Brightwell* | *Redmond* | *McNab* | *Varadi* | *Barnes* | *Moulden* |
| | | | | | | | | Ref: M Reed | An abject first half is drifting to a close when an under-hit back-pass from Johnson is intercepted by Paul Lake, who scores on his home debut. The Town fight back in the second period and Brian Stein scores direct from a free-kick to notch the seventh successive game without defeat. | | | | | | | | | | | |
| 29 | H | WEST HAM | | 4 | W | 2-1 | 1-1 | Nicholas 40, Grimes 70 | Sealey | Johnson | Grimes | Nicholas | Foster | Donaghy | Hill | Stein B | Newell | Harford | Wilson | |
| | 28/2 | | 11,101 | *13* | 50 | | | *Cottee 8* | *Parkes* | *Stewart* | *Gale* | *Bonds* | *Walford** | *Dickens* | *Pike* | *Robson* | *Ward* | *McAvennie* | *Cottee* | *Ince* |
| | | | | | | | | Ref: B Hill | Tony Cottee drives in the opening goal and Nicholas equalises, against the run of play, with a superb 25-yard shot just before the interval. After some strong half-time words from manager John Moore, the Town take control and a clever free-kick routine enables Grimes to hit the winner. | | | | | | | | | | | |
| 30 | A | LIVERPOOL | | 6 | L | 0-2 | 0-2 | | Sealey | Breacker | Johnson | Nicholas | Foster* | Donaghy | Hill | Stein B | Newell | Harford | Grimes | Wilson |
| | 7/3 | | *32,433* | *1* | 50 | | | *Molby 17p, Donaghy 40 (og)* | *Grobbelaar* | *Venison* | *Whelan* | *Hansen* | *Lawrenson* | *Johnston* | *Molby* | *McMahon* | *Spackman* | *Walsh* | *Rush* | |
| | | | | | | | | Ref: T Mills | On a snow-covered pitch and in a driving blizzard, Jan Molby scores from the spot after Foster handles and then Mal Donaghy deflects a cross from Ian Rush into his own net. Steve Foster limps off with ruptured knee ligaments which will keep him out for the remainder of the season. | | | | | | | | | | | |
| 31 | H | MANCHESTER U | | 4 | W | 2-1 | 2-0 | Harford 3, Stein B 40 | Sealey | Breacker | Johnson | Nicholas | North S | Donaghy | Hill | Stein B | Newell | Harford | Grimes | |
| | 14/3 | | 12,509 | *13* | 53 | | | *Robson 87* | *Bailey* | *Sivebaek* | *McGrath* | *Moran* | *Gibson C** | *Strachan* | *Robson* | *Duxbury* | *O'Brien* | *Whiteside* | *Gibson T* | *Davenport* |
| | | | | | | | | Ref: K Baker | Manchester United may not have lost a league game this year, but Alex Ferguson's side are well beaten by a Hatters team who are out to make amends for the poor performance at Liverpool the previous week. Stand-in skipper Harford knocks in an early goal and Stein adds the second. | | | | | | | | | | | |

| No / Date | H/A | Opponent / Att | Pos | Res / Pts | F-A | H-T | Scorers, Times, Referees | 1 | 2 | 3 | 4 | 5 | 6 | 7 | 8 | 9 | 10 | 11 | 12 |
|---|---|---|---|---|---|---|---|---|---|---|---|---|---|---|---|---|---|---|---|
| 32 | A | NORWICH | 4 | D | 0-0 | 0-0 | | Sealey | Breacker | Johnson | Nicholas | North S | Donaghy | Hill | Stein B | Newell | Harford | Grimes ! | |
| 21/3 | | *16,142* | *5* | 54 | | | | *Gunn* | *Brown* | *Bruce** | *Butterworth* | *Spearing* | *Phelan* | *Crook* | *Putney* | *Gordon* | *Drinkell* | *Rosario* | *Biggins* |
| | | | | | | | Ref: M James | The defences dominate in a match of few chances, the best of which are a header from Robert Rosario which hits the bar and a late effort from Newell. The game is enlivened by the dismissal of Grimes for spitting at his colleague, Johnson, an incident which doesn't please John Moore. | | | | | | | | | | | |
| 33 | A | SOUTHAMPTON | 4 | L | **0-3** | 0-2 | | Sealey | Breacker | Johnson* | Nicholas | North S | Donaghy | Hill | Stein B | Newell | Harford | Grimes | McDonough |
| 24/3 | | *12,117* | *16* | 54 | | | *Townsend 3, Lawrence 13, 75* | *Shilton* | *Forrest* | *Wright* | *Bond* | *Armstrong* | *Case* | *Cockerill* | *Townsend* | *Le Tissier* | *Lawrence* | *Wallace* | |
| | | | | | | | Ref: C Deakin | Sloppy defending enables the Saints to score two early goals and leave the Town with a mountain to climb. On a muddy surface which is made worse by the incessant rain, Southampton play a style of football more conducive to the conditions. Matt Le Tissier has a hand in all three goals. | | | | | | | | | | | |
| 34 | H | TOTTENHAM | 3 | W | 3-1 | 1-0 | Harford 5, Newell 54, McDonough 86 | Sealey | Breacker | Grimes | Nicholas | North S | Donaghy | Hill | Stein B | Newell | Harford | McDonough | |
| 28/3 | | **13,447** | *5* | 57 | | | *Waddle 62* | *Clemence* | *Stevens* | *Gough* | *Mabbutt* | *Thomas* | *Hodge** | *Waddle* | *Allen P* | *Hoddle* | *Claesen* | *Allen C* | *Ardiles* |
| | | | | | | | Ref: D Elleray | The biggest attendance of the season at Kenilworth Road sees the return of David Pleat and Mitchell Thomas, both of whom receive a less than warm welcome from the crowd and on the pitch. The Town turn on a five-star performance and Hill is at his very best, laying on all three goals. | | | | | | | | | | | |
| 35 | H | WIMBLEDON | 3 | D | 0-0 | 0-0 | | Sealey | Breacker | Harvey | Nicholas | North S | Donaghy | Hill | Stein B | Newell | Harford | McDonough | |
| 4/4 | | 9,729 | *8* | 58 | | | | *Beasant* | *Gage* | *Morris* | *Thorn* | *Winterburn* | *Hodges* | *Jones* | *Sanchez** | *Fairweather* | *Sayer* | *Cork* | *Joseph* |
| | | | | | | | Ref: J Key | After the euphoria of last week, it's now back to basics as Wimbledon bottle up the attacking moves of the Hatters, making it a tedious game to watch for the supporters. Dave Beasant is responsible for the highlight of the game when he saves a shot from Mick Harford with his legs. | | | | | | | | | | | |
| 36 | A | QP RANGERS | 4 | D | 2-2 | 1-0 | Stein M 21, Hill 87 | Sealey | Breacker | Harvey | Nicholas | North S | Donaghy | Hill | Stein B | Newell | Stein M | Preece | |
| 11/4 | | *9,450* | *10* | 59 | | | *Byrne 66, 77* | *Seaman* | *Neill* | *McDonald* | *Maguire* | *James* | *Lee* | *Byrne* | *Fillery* | *Fereday* | *Rosenior* | *Bannister* | |
| | | | | | | | Ref: A Gunn | The Hatters toy with Rangers in the first period and play some brilliant football. They have only a goal from Stein to show for their dominance, however, and the home side hit back to take an undeserved lead. Preece plays in Hill, who beats three defenders and side-foots the ball home. | | | | | | | | | | | |
| 37 | H | COVENTRY | 4 | W | 2-0 | 1-0 | Stein B 8, Newell 88 | Sealey | Breacker | Grimes* | Nicholas | North S | Donaghy | Hill | Stein B | Newell | Harford | Preece | McDonough |
| 18/4 | | 9,380 | *10* | 62 | | | | *Ogrizovic* | *Borrows* | *Kilcline* | *Peake* | *Downs** | *Gynn* | *Phillips* | *McGrath* | *Sedgley* | *Bennett* | *Houchen* | *Livingstone* |
| | | | | | | | Ref: H Taylor | The Sky Blues have their minds on their upcoming FA Cup final and the Town are able to enjoy a gentle afternoon in the sun. Brian Stein nets the first with a picture header from a centre by Tim Breacker, and the second goal comes with a perfectly executed volley from Mike Newell. | | | | | | | | | | | |
| 38 | A | WATFORD | 4 | L | 0-2 | 0-0 | | Dibble | Breacker | Grimes | Nicholas | North S | Donaghy | Hill | Stein B | Newell | Harford | Preece | |
| 21/4 | | *14,650* | *7* | 62 | | | *Sterling 48, Barnes 54* | *Sherwood* | *Gibbs* | *Bardsley* | *McClelland* | *Richardson* | *Porter* | *Rostron* | *Sterling* | *Blissett* | *Falco* | *Barnes* | |
| | | | | | | | Ref: A Buksh | The Hatters are second best and well-shackled by a Hornets outfit whose sheer pace and power deserves more than the two goals which they score - they even win the corner count 15-4. 'They won because they played better than us,' summarises the man of few words, John Moore. | | | | | | | | | | | |
| 39 | H | SHEFFIELD WED | 5 | D | 0-0 | 0-0 | | Sealey | Breacker | Grimes | Nicholas | North S | Donaghy | Hill | Stein B | Newell* | Harford | Preece | Stein M |
| 25/4 | | 9,278 | *16* | 63 | | | | *Hodge* | *Sterland* | *Morris* | *May* | *Madden* | *Smith* | *Megson* | *Marwood* | *Worthington* | *Chapman* | *Hirst** | *Snodin* |
| | | | | | | | Ref: J Martin | John Moore is unpopular when he introduces Mark Stein in place of Mike Newell, the only Luton player who appears capable of breaking the deadlock. Wednesday have no intention of entertaining the crowd but more of continuing the fight to get away from the foot of the league table. | | | | | | | | | | | |
| 40 | A | CHARLTON | 5 | W | 1-0 | 0-0 | Harford 86 | Sealey | Breacker* | Harvey | Nicholas | North S | Donaghy | Hill | **Cobb** | Newell | Harford | Preece | McDonough |
| 2/5 | | ***5,469*** | *20* | 66 | | | | *Bolder* | *Humphrey* | *Shirtliff* | *Miller* | *Reid* | *Milne* | *Peake* | *Walsh* | *Stuart* | *Crooks** | *Lee* | *Leaburn* |
| | | | | | | | Ref: J Borrett | The Valiants have most of the play and mount a barrage of non-stop attacks in their fight against relegation, but have only a Colin Walsh shot, which hits the bar, to show for it. After soaking up the pressure, the Town break away and debutant Cobb lays on the only goal for Harford. | | | | | | | | | | | |
| 41 | H | OXFORD | 6 | L | 2-3 | 0-2 | Newell 84, Stein M 88 | Sealey | Johnson | Harvey | Nicholas | North S* | Donaghy | Hill | Cobb | Newell | Stein M | Preece | McDonough |
| 5/5 | | 8,917 | *18* | 66 | | | *Saunders 5, 89, Hebberd 22* | *Hucker* | *Langan* | *Briggs* | *Caton* | *Slatter* | *Philips** | *Trewick* | *Brock* | *Rh'ds-Brown* | *Saunders* | *Hebberd* | *Dreyer* |
| | | | | | | | Ref: N Midgley | Oxford are two goals up and cruising towards a vital victory when a shot from Newell and a header from Stein bring the Hatters undeservedly level with just two minutes left. United find the energy to mount one last attack from which Dean Saunders heads in a cross from John Dreyer. | | | | | | | | | | | |
| 42 | A | EVERTON | 7 | L | 1-3 | 1-0 | Stein M 4 | Sealey | Johnson | McDonough | Nicholas ! | North S | Donaghy | Hill | Stein B | Newell | Stein M* | Preece | Wilson |
| 9/5 | | ***44,097*** | *1* | 66 | | | *Steven 51p, 54p, Sharp 60* | *Southall* | *Stevens* | *Ratcliffe* | *Watson* | *v d Hauwe* | *Steven* | *Harper* | *Reid* | *Snodin* | *Heath* | *Sharp* | |
| Home Average 10,256 | | Away 18,732 | | | | | Ref: G Tyson | Everton celebrate winning the championship in style, but they are made to fight for their win after Stein scores with a scorching 25-yard shot. The Toffees get back in the game with two controversial penalties, one for a supposed handball and the other when North pushed Trevor Steven. | | | | | | | | | | | |

| Littlewoods Cup | | | | | F-A | H-T | Scorers, Times, and Referees | 1 | 2 | 3 | 4 | 5 | 6 | 7 | 8 | 9 | 10 | 11 | subs used |
|---|---|---|---|---|---|---|---|---|---|---|---|---|---|---|---|---|---|---|---|
| Excluded from the competition by the Football League due to club's ban on away supporters | | | | | | | | | | | | | | | | | | | |

| FA Cup | | | | | | | | | | | | | | | | | | | |
|---|---|---|---|---|---|---|---|---|---|---|---|---|---|---|---|---|---|---|---|
| 3 | H | LIVERPOOL | 5 | D | 0-0 | 0-0 | | Sealey | Johnson | Grimes | Nicholas | Foster | Donaghy | Hill | Stein B | Newell | Harford | Preece | |
| | 11/1 | 11,085 | *3* | | | | | *Grobbelaar* | *Lawrenson* | *Hansen* | *Gillespie* | *Beglin* | *Johnston* | *Molby* | *Whelan* | *McMahon* | *Walsh* | *Rush* | |
| | | | | | | | Ref: A Gunn | Liverpool come to Kenilworth Road intent on forcing a replay, although this is denied by manager Kenny Dalglish. On a snow-covered pitch, in front of a live television audience, the Reds shut up shop, but Alan Hansen and Gary Gillespie are given a hard time by Newell and Harford. | | | | | | | | | | | |
| 3R | A | LIVERPOOL | 4 | D | 0-0 | 0-0 | | Sealey | Breacker | Johnson | Nicholas | Foster | Donaghy | Hill | Stein B | Newell | Harford | Grimes | |
| | 26/1 | *34,822* | *3* | | *aet* | | | *Grobbelaar* | *Venison* | *Gillespie* | *Hansen* | *Lawrenson* | *Whelan* | *Molby* | *Wark* | *Johnston* | *Walsh* | *Rush* | |
| | | | | | | | Ref: A Gunn | Liverpool have the greater number of chances and should have won but Donaghy and Foster are magnificent in the centre of the Luton defence. The FA Cup holders know that, when Ian Rush misses an open goal and a Jan Molby shot cannons off a post, it is not going to be their night. | | | | | | | | | | | |
| 3R | H | LIVERPOOL | 4 | W | 3-0 | 1-0 | Stein B 34, Harford 78p, Newell 81 | Sealey | Breacker | Johnson | Nicholas | Foster | Donaghy | Hill* | Stein B | Newell | Harford | Grimes | McDonough |
| R | 28/1 | 14,687 | *3* | | | | | *Grobbelaar* | *Venison* | *Gillespie* | *Hansen* | *Lawrenson* | *Whelan* | *Molby* | *Wark** | *Johnston* | *Walsh^* | *Rush* | *Irvine/Ablett* |
| | | | | | | | Ref: D Vickers | Back at Kenilworth Road, two days later, Stein curls in a 20-yard free-kick to open the scoring. Harford converts from the spot after Molby trips Stein and Newell makes it a memorable night, hitting the third. After the game, Dalglish tries to devalue the win with a myriad of excuses. | | | | | | | | | | | |
| 4 | H | QP RANGERS | 4 | D | 1-1 | 0-0 | Harford 88p | Sealey | Breacker | Johnson | Nicholas | Foster | Donaghy | Hill | Stein B | Newell | Harford | Grimes | |
| | 31/1 | 12,707 | *14* | | | | *Fenwick 83p* | *Seaman* | *Neill* | *McDonald* | *Fenwick* | *James* | *Fereday* | *Allen* | *Lee* | *Walker** | *Bannister* | *Byrne* | *Rosenior* |
| | | | | | | | Ref: A Seville | The first 80 minutes is poor entertainment value but Rangers then seem to have won the tie when Johnson fouls John Byrne in the area, Terry Fenwick netting the late penalty. Harford levels from the spot after Bannister trips Newell, and Stein almost gets the winner in the last seconds. | | | | | | | | | | | |
| 4R | A | QP RANGERS | 4 | L | 1-2 | 0-1 | Harford 55 | Sealey | Breacker | Johnson | Nicholas | Foster | Donaghy | Hill | Stein B | Newell | Harford | Grimes | |
| | 4/2 | *15,848* | *14* | | | | *Fenwick 35, Byrne 50* | *Seaman* | *Maguire* | *McDonald* | *Fenwick* | *James* | *Allen* | *Fillery* | *Fereday* | *Walker* | *Bannister** | *Byrne* | *Rosenior* |
| | | | | | | | Ref: A Seville | The cup dream is over for another season as the Town fail to perform on the night. Terry Fenwick hits Rangers into the lead after Steve Foster falls over . John Byrne adds another when he is put through on his own. Harford offers a lifeline when heading in a free-kick from Nicholas. | | | | | | | | | | | |

| | | Home | | | | | Away | | | | | |
|---|---|---|---|---|---|---|---|---|---|---|---|---|
| | P | W | D | L | F | A | W | D | L | F | A | Pts |
| 1 Everton | 42 | 16 | 4 | 1 | 49 | 11 | 10 | 4 | 7 | 27 | 20 | 86 |
| 2 Liverpool | 42 | 15 | 3 | 3 | 43 | 16 | 8 | 5 | 8 | 29 | 26 | 77 |
| 3 Tottenham | 42 | 14 | 3 | 4 | 40 | 14 | 7 | 5 | 9 | 28 | 29 | 71 |
| 4 Arsenal | 42 | 12 | 5 | 4 | 31 | 12 | 8 | 5 | 8 | 27 | 23 | 70 |
| 5 Norwich | 42 | 9 | 10 | 2 | 27 | 20 | 8 | 7 | 6 | 26 | 31 | 68 |
| 6 Wimbledon | 42 | 11 | 5 | 5 | 32 | 22 | 8 | 4 | 9 | 25 | 28 | 66 |
| 7 LUTON TOWN | 42 | 14 | 5 | 2 | 29 | 13 | 4 | 7 | 10 | 18 | 32 | 66 |
| 8 Nott'm Forest | 42 | 12 | 8 | 1 | 36 | 14 | 6 | 3 | 12 | 28 | 37 | 65 |
| 9 Watford | 42 | 12 | 5 | 4 | 38 | 20 | 6 | 4 | 11 | 29 | 34 | 63 |
| 10 Coventry | 42 | 14 | 4 | 3 | 35 | 17 | 3 | 8 | 10 | 15 | 28 | 63 |
| 11 Manchester U | 42 | 13 | 3 | 5 | 38 | 18 | 1 | 11 | 9 | 14 | 27 | 56 |
| 12 Southampton | 42 | 11 | 5 | 5 | 44 | 24 | 3 | 5 | 13 | 25 | 44 | 52 |
| 13 Sheffield Wed | 42 | 9 | 7 | 5 | 39 | 24 | 4 | 6 | 11 | 19 | 35 | 52 |
| 14 Chelsea | 42 | 8 | 6 | 7 | 30 | 30 | 5 | 7 | 9 | 23 | 34 | 52 |
| 15 West Ham | 42 | 10 | 4 | 7 | 33 | 28 | 4 | 6 | 11 | 19 | 39 | 52 |
| 16 QP Rangers | 42 | 9 | 7 | 5 | 31 | 27 | 4 | 4 | 13 | 17 | 37 | 50 |
| 17 Newcastle | 42 | 10 | 4 | 7 | 33 | 29 | 2 | 7 | 12 | 14 | 36 | 47 |
| 18 Oxford | 42 | 8 | 8 | 5 | 30 | 25 | 3 | 5 | 13 | 14 | 44 | 46 |
| 19 Charlton | 42 | 7 | 7 | 7 | 26 | 22 | 4 | 4 | 13 | 19 | 33 | 44 |
| 20 Leicester | 42 | 9 | 7 | 5 | 39 | 24 | 2 | 2 | 17 | 15 | 52 | 42 |
| 21 Manchester C | 42 | 8 | 6 | 7 | 28 | 24 | 0 | 9 | 12 | 8 | 33 | 39 |
| 22 Aston Villa | 42 | 7 | 7 | 7 | 25 | 25 | 1 | 5 | 15 | 20 | 54 | 36 |
| | 924 | 238 | 123 | 101 | 756 | 459 | 101 | 123 | 238 | 459 | 756 | 1263 |

Odds & ends

Double wins: (3) Charlton, Chelsea, Coventry.
Double losses: (2) Oxford, Watford.

Won from behind: (2) Chelsea (a), West Ham (h).
Lost from in front: (1) Everton (a).

High spots: The highest league position in the history of the club.
The two wins against Liverpool at Kenilworth Road.
Winning at Coventry for the first time since 1930.

Low spots: Exclusion from the Littlewoods Cup because of the stance on away supporters.
The defeat at home to Oxford, as a win would have given a final league position of fifth.
The defeat at QPR in the FA Cup, which closely followed the epic clashes against Liverpool.
Losing at Manchester United, with Brian Stein missing a penalty.
Watford achieving a rare double over the Hatters.
The resignation of John Moore as manager.

Player of the Year: Peter Nicholas.
Ever-presents: (3) Mal Donaghy, Mike Newell, Peter Nicholas.
Hat-tricks: (1) Mike Newell .
Leading scorer: (13) Brian Stein and Mike Newell.

| | Appearances | | | | | | Goals | | | |
|---|---|---|---|---|---|---|---|---|---|---|
| | Lge | *Sub* | LC | *Sub* | FAC | *Sub* | Lge | LC | FAC | Tot |
| Breacker, Tim | **29** | | | | 4 | | **1** | | | **1** |
| Cobb, Gary | **2** | | | | | | | | | |
| Dibble, Andy | **1** | | | | | | | | | |
| Donaghy, Mal | **42** | | | | 5 | | | | | |
| Foster, Steve | **28** | | | | 5 | | **2** | | | **2** |
| Grimes, Ashley | **31** | | | | 5 | | **2** | | | **2** |
| Harford, Mick | **18** | | | | 5 | | **4** | | 3 | **7** |
| Harvey, Richard | **5** | | | | | | | | | |
| Hill, Ricky | **30** | | | | 5 | | **2** | | | **2** |
| Johnson, Rob | **34** | | | | 5 | | | | | |
| McDonough, Darron | **10** | *8* | | | | *1* | **1** | | | **1** |
| McEvoy, Ricky | | *1* | | | | | | | | |
| Newell, Mike | **42** | | | | 5 | | **12** | | 1 | **13** |
| Nicholas, Peter | **42** | | | | 5 | | **1** | | | **1** |
| North, Mark | **2** | *3* | | | | | | | | |
| North, Stacey | **14** | | | | | | | | | |
| Nwajiobi, Emeka | **6** | | | | | | | | | |
| Preece, David | **14** | | | | 1 | | | | | |
| Sealey, Les | **41** | | | | 5 | | | | | |
| Stein, Brian | **38** | | | | 5 | | **12** | | 1 | **13** |
| Stein, Mark | **17** | *4* | | | | | **8** | | | **8** |
| Wilson, Robert | **16** | *5* | | | | | **1** | | | **1** |
| (own-goals) | | | | | | | **1** | | | **1** |
| **22 players used** | **462** | ***21*** | | | **55** | ***1*** | **47** | | **5** | **52** |

# BARCLAYS LEAGUE DIVISION 1    Manager: Ray Harford    SEASON 1987-88



| No | Date | | Att | Pos | Pt | F-A | H-T | Scorers, Times, and Referees | 1 | 2 | 3 | 4 | 5 | 6 | 7 | 8 | 9 | 10 | 11 | subs used |
|---|---|---|---|---|---|---|---|---|---|---|---|---|---|---|---|---|---|---|---|---|
| 1 | A | DERBY | | | L | 0-1 | 0-1 | | Sealey | Breacker | Grimes | Hill | Foster | Donaghy | **Wilson D** | Stein B | Harford ! | Wilson R* | Preece^ | Newell/McDonough |
| | 15/8 | | *17,204* | | - | | | *Gregory 16* | *Shilton* | *Sage* | *Hindmarch* | *MacLaren* | *Forsyth* | *Williams* | *Micklewhite* | *Gregory* | *Callaghan* | *Gee* | *Davison* | |
| | | | | | | | | Ref: G Courtney | Harford becomes the first recipient of a red card, reintroduced this season, after being ordered off for a late tackle in the fourth minute. Ten-men Town are all over the place for a while and John Gregory scores for newly promoted Derby with a shot after his header rebounds off Les Sealey. | | | | | | | | | | | |
| 2 | H | COVENTRY | | | L | 0-1 | 0-0 | | Sealey | Breacker | Grimes | Hill | Foster | McDonough | Wilson D | Newell | Harford | Wilson R* | Preece | Nwajiobi |
| | 18/8 | | 7,506 | | - | | | *Kilcline 66p* | *Ogrizovic* | *Borrows* | *Kilcline* | *Peake* | *Downs* | *Bennett* | *Gynn* | *McGrath* | *Pickering* | *Houchen* | *Speedie* | |
| | | | | | | | | Ref: D Hedges | A drab game is settled when Brian Kilcline scores from the spot for the Sky Blues after McDonough is harshly adjudged to have fouled David Speedie. The Hatters never look likely to break down the Coventry rearguard and resort to continually thumping long balls up to Mick Harford. | | | | | | | | | | | |
| 3 | H | WEST HAM | | 16 | D | 2-2 | 1-2 | Harford 5, 51 | Sealey | Breacker | Grimes | Hill | Foster | McDono'gh* | Wilson D | Cobb | Harford | Newell | Preece | North |
| | 22/8 | | 8,073 | *18* | 1 | | | *Brady 20, Stewart 30p* | *McAlister* | *Stewart* | *Strodder* | *Martin* | *Ince* | *McQueen* | *Robson* | *Ward* | *Brady* | *McAvennie* | *Cottee* | |
| | | | | | | | | Ref: J Martin | Mick Harford heads home a cross from Breacker but Liam Brady equalises with a shot that is deflected by McDonough. Ray Stewart converts from the spot, after Cottee is fouled, before Harford gets his second from close range. The end result is considered to be fair by both managers. | | | | | | | | | | | |
| 4 | A | CHELSEA | | 18 | L | 0-3 | 0-0 | | Sealey | Breacker | Grimes | Donaghy | Foster | Wilson R | Hill | Cobb | Newell | Nwajiobi | Preece | |
| | 29/8 | | *16,075* | *3* | 1 | | | *Coady 63, Nevin 70, Dixon 81* | *Niedzwiecki* | *Clarke* | *Wicks* | *McLaughlin* | *Dorigo* | *Nevin* | *Wood* | *Wilson* | *Coady* | *Dixon* | *Durie* | |
| | | | | | | | | Ref: V Callow | The Luton forward line looks lightweight, with Harford suspended and Stein still injured, and they never look like breaking through Chelsea's defence. The Blues huff and puff and, as frustration appears to be setting in, John Coady scores with a mis-hit shot which deceives everyone. | | | | | | | | | | | |
| 5 | H | ARSENAL | | 16 | D | 1-1 | 1-1 | Wilson 17p | Sealey | Breacker | Grimes | Hill | Foster | Donaghy | Wilson D | Stein B | Newell* | Nwajiobi | Preece | Stein M |
| | 31/8 | | 8,745 | *11* | 2 | | | *Davis 14* | *Lukic* | *Thomas* | *O'Leary* | *Adams* | *Sansom* | *Rocastle* | *Williams* | *Davis* | *Rix* | *Groves* | *Smith* | |
| | | | | | | | | Ref: R Lewis | An offside decision is expected, prior to the opening goal, but play is allowed to continue and Davis opens the scoring for the visitors. The Town level when the referee, alone, spots a push by David O'Leary on Mike Newell, and Danny Wilson gratefully blasts the ball home from the spot. | | | | | | | | | | | |
| 6 | A | OXFORD | | 14 | W | 5-2 | 2-1 | Stein B 33, Breacker 44, Nwajiobi 46, | Sealey | Breacker | Grimes | Hill | Foster | Donaghy | Wilson D | Stein B* | Harford | Nwajiobi | Preece^ | Stein M/Johnson R |
| | 5/9 | | *6,804* | *16* | 5 | | | *Slatter 41, Foyle 77* [Hill 70, Harford 74] | *Hucker* | *Langan* | *Slatter* | *Caton* | *Dreyer** | *Houghton* | *Reck^* | *Hebberd* | *Foyle* | *Whitehurst* | *Saunders* | *R'd-Brown/Mustoe* |
| | | | | | | | | Ref: J Deakin | A full squad is available for selection and, with a change of formation to 4-4-2, the poor early-season start by the Hatters is ended in style. Four players open their accounts for the season, Emeka Nwajiobi receiving applause from both sets of supporters when scoring with a diving header. | | | | | | | | | | | |
| 7 | H | EVERTON | | 12 | W | 2-1 | 1-1 | Stein B 18, Hill 51 | Sealey | Breacker | Grimes | Hill | Foster | Donaghy | Wilson D | Stein B | Harford | Nwajiobi* | Preece^ | Stein M/Johnson R |
| | 12/9 | | 8,124 | *9* | 8 | | | *Pointon 4* | *Southall* | *Harper* | *v d Hauwe* | *Ratcliffe* | *Watson* | *Reid* | *Steven* | *Heath* | *Adams** | *Snodin* | *Pointon^* | *Marshall/Mountfield* |
| | | | | | | | | Ref: A Gunn | Neil Pointon hits home an angled shot for the visitors before Brian Stein receives a knock-down from Mick Harford to level the scores. Ricky Hill capitalises on the same service and hits the winner, although Harford is fortunate to remain on the pitch after a flare-up with Dave Watson. | | | | | | | | | | | |
| 8 | A | CHARLTON | | 12 | L | 0-1 | 0-1 | | Sealey | Breacker | McDono'gh* | Hill | Foster | Donaghy | Wilson D | Stein B | Harford | Stein M | Preece^ | Johnson R/**Weir** |
| | 19/9 | | *5,002* | *20* | 8 | | | *Crooks 40* | *Johns* | *Humphrey* | *Shirtliff* | *Miller* | *Gritt* | *Stuart* | *Peake* | *Walsh* | *Mackenzie* | *Milne* | *Crooks* | |
| | | | | | | | | Ref: M Dimblebee | A volley from Garth Crooks earns Charlton their first win of the season as the Town turn in a poor performance. Keeper Les Sealey looks on in total disbelief as Crooks manages to miss an open goal. Micky Weir makes his Luton debut, as a substitute, but is unable to affect the result. | | | | | | | | | | | |
| 9 | A | QP RANGERS | | 15 | L | 0-2 | 0-0 | | Sealey | Breacker | Grimes | Hill | Foster | Donaghy | Wilson D | Stein B | Harford | Weir | **Black** | |
| | 26/9 | | *11,175* | *1* | 8 | | | *Coney 70, Fenwick 85p* | *Seaman* | *Fereday** | *Parker* | *McDonald* | *Dawes* | *Fenwick* | *Byrne* | *Brock* | *Bannister* | *Coney* | *Allen* | *Neill* |
| | | | | | | | | Ref: K Barrett | 19-year-old Kingsley Black makes his debut but the Town lose on the Loftus Road Omniturf for the first time in a league game. Rangers' system of sucking teams in and then catching them on the break seems to work, as they are currently top of the table, but it is boring for fans to watch. | | | | | | | | | | | |
| 10 | H | MANCHESTER U | | 14 | D | 1-1 | 1-0 | Harford 19 | Sealey | Breacker | Grimes | Hill | Foster | Donaghy | Wilson D | Stein B | Harford | Weir* | Black^ | McDon'gh/Stein M |
| | 3/10 | | 9,137 | *7* | 9 | | | *McClair 54* | *Walsh* | *Robson* | *Blackmore** | *Garton* | *McGrath* | *Gibson* | *Duxbury* | *Whiteside* | *Strachan* | *Olsen* | *McClair* | *O'Brien* |
| | | | | | | | | Ref: M Reed | Alex Ferguson pays Luton a compliment of playing Bryan Robson as a sweeper but Harford still manages to head the Hatters into the lead as they control the first period. United level after the interval, with a headed goal from Brian McClair, and the ultimate draw is the fairest result. | | | | | | | | | | | |

| No | H/A | Opponent | Pos | Res | F-A | H-T | Scorers, Times, Referees | 1 | 2 | 3 | 4 | 5 | 6 | 7 | 8 | 9 | 10 | 11 | 12 |
|---|---|---|---|---|---|---|---|---|---|---|---|---|---|---|---|---|---|---|---|
| 11 | A | PORTSMOUTH | 16 | L | 1-3 | 0-0 | Harford 89p | Sealey | Breacker | Grimes | Hill | Foster | Donaghy | Wilson D | Stein B | Harford | Johnson R* | Weir^ | McDono'gh/Nwajiobi |
| | 10/10 | *12,391* | *11* | 9 | | | *Dillon 55, 72p, Mariner 81* | *Knight* | *Swain* | *Shotton* | *Ball* | *Hardyman* | *Hilaire* | *Dillon* | *Horne* | *Kennedy* | *Baird** | *Quinn* | *Mariner* |
| | | | | | | | Ref: A Buksh | Chairman David Evans accuses some of the Town players of not trying after this poor performance. Kevin Dillon hits a 25-yard shot in off the post and then another from the spot after Hilaire is fouled by Sealey. Kevin Ball handles a shot from Hill, Harford hitting a consolation penalty. | | | | | | | | | | | |
| 12 | H | WIMBLEDON | 14 | W | 2-0 | 1-0 | Stein B 20, Wilson 59 | Sealey | Breacker | Grimes | McDonough | Foster | Donaghy | Wilson D | Stein B | Harford | Black* | Weir | **Allinson** |
| | 17/10 | 7,018 | *13* | 12 | | | | *Beasant* | *Ryan* | *Gayle* | *Thorn* | *Phelan* | *Jones* | *Gannon* | *Sanchez* | *Cork* | *Fashanu* | *Fairweath'r** | *Clement* |
| | | | | | | | Ref: B Hill | Stein opens the scoring from a pull-back by McDonough and then Wilson secures the points, to end the dismal run of four league games without a win, when he hits home at the end of a searching run. The Town do have some fortunate moments as the Dons hit the woodwork three times. | | | | | | | | | | | |
| 13 | H | LIVERPOOL | 17 | L | 0-1 | 0-0 | | Sealey | Breacker | Grimes | McDonough | Foster | Donaghy | Wilson D | Stein B | Harford | Allinson | Weir | |
| | 24/10 | **11,997** | *1* | 12 | | | *Gillespie 71* | *Grobbelaar* | *Gillespie* | *Whelan* | *Hansen* | *Venison* | *Nicol* | *McMahon* | *Houghton* | *Beardsley* | *Aldridge* | *Barnes* | |
| | | | | | | | Ref: A Seville | Liverpool are both unbeaten and top of the table but they have to work hard for the victory. Mick Harford hits the post early on and then hits the bar in the last minute. However, midway through the second half he fails to pick up Gary Gillespie, who heads the only goal from a corner-kick. | | | | | | | | | | | |
| 14 | H | NEWCASTLE | 14 | W | **4-0** | 1-0 | Stein M 2, 62, Nwajiobi 75, Stein B 88 | Sealey | Breacker | Grimes | McDonough | Foster | Donaghy | Wilson D | Stein B | Nwajiobi | Stein M | Allinson | |
| | 7/11 | 7,638 | *18* | 15 | | | | *Kelly* | *Anderson* | *Jackson P* | *Roeder* | *Tinnion** | *Wharton* | *McDonald* | *Gascoigne* | *Jackson D* | *Goddard* | *Mirandinha* | *O'Neill* |
| | | | | | | | Ref: M James | Mark Stein replaces flu victim Mick Harford, and grabs the opportunity to remind the manager of his abilities by blasting two goals. Nwajiobi also scores, giving Ray Harford a future team selection problem. Brian Stein hits the fourth to give the Town their best home win of the season. | | | | | | | | | | | |
| 15 | A | SHEFFIELD WED | 12 | W | 2-0 | 1-0 | Stein M 36, Allinson 80 | Sealey | Breacker | Grimes | McDonough | Foster | Donaghy | Wilson D | Stein B | Nwajiobi | Stein M | Allinson | |
| | 14/11 | *16,960* | *16* | 18 | | | | *Hodge* | *Jacobs* | *Pearson* | *Madden* | *Worthingt'n* | *Megson* | *Proctor* | *Galvin** | *Chamb'rlain* | *Chapman* | *West* | *Marwood* |
| | | | | | | | Ref: R Bridges | Mark Stein puts the Hatters into the lead with a cross which finds its way directly into the net. The points are made safe when Allinson scores a superb goal at the end of a sweeping move and the Town manage to record a win at Hillsborough for only the second time in the clubs' history. | | | | | | | | | | | |
| 16 | H | TOTTENHAM | 11 | W | 2-0 | 1-0 | Allinson 37, 63 | Sealey | Breacker | Grimes | McDonough | Foster | Donaghy | Johnson R | Stein B | Nwajiobi | Stein M ! | Allinson | |
| | 21/11 | 10,091 | *13* | 21 | | | | *Parks* | *Stevens** | *Fairclough* | *Mabbutt* | *Hughton* | *Allen P^* | *Ardiles* | *Samways* | *Hodge* | *Allen C* | *Howells* | *Thomas/Close* |
| | | | | | | | Ref: N Midgley | £10,000 signing Ian Allinson is outstanding as he beats the Tottenham offside trap to lob the first goal, and then hits a low shot from the edge of the box for the second after the break. Stein is dismissed with six minutes left for hitting Gary Stevens in retaliation for 'one foul too many'. | | | | | | | | | | | |
| 17 | H | NORWICH | 14 | L | 1-2 | 1-0 | Stein B 20 | Sealey | Breacker | Grimes | McDonough | Foster | Donaghy | Wilson D | Stein B | Nwajiobi* | Weir | Allinson | Hill |
| | 5/12 | 7,002 | *20* | 21 | | | *Gordon 61, Crook 88* | *Gunn* | *Culverhouse* | *Bruce* | *Butterw'rth* | *Elliott* | *Gordon** | *Phelan* | *Crook* | *Putney* | *Rosario* | *Drinkell* | *Fox* |
| | | | | | | | Ref: D Scott | The Hatters are lacklustre in all areas and seem to believe that the points are in the bag after Stein hits an interval lead. The Canaries fight back and, when Ian Crook lobs the winner, they record their first win in nine attempts and bring the Luton sequence of three straight wins to an end. | | | | | | | | | | | |
| 18 | A | WATFORD | 9 | W | 1-0 | 1-0 | Foster 30 | Sealey | Breacker | Grimes | McDonough | Foster | Donaghy | Wilson D | Stein B | Hill | Weir | Allinson | |
| | 12/12 | *12,152* | *19* | 24 | | | | *Coton* | *Chivers** | *Morris* | *McClelland* | *Rostron* | *Porter* | *Jackett* | *Hodges* | *Allen* | *Senior^* | *Blissett* | *Sterling/Holdsworth* |
| | | | | | | | Ref: P Tyldesley | When a shot from Allinson hits the bar and bounces down everyone, with the exception of the referee, believes it to be a goal. Trevor Senior is castigated by his manager and fellow players for allowing Foster to have a free header, following a free-kick, to score the only goal of the game. | | | | | | | | | | | |
| 19 | H | SOUTHAMPTON | 10 | D | 2-2 | 1-1 | McDonough 23, Harford 86 | Sealey | Breacker | Grimes | McDonough | Foster | Donaghy | Wilson D | Stein B | Hill | Stein M | Allinson* | Harford |
| | 18/12 | **6,618** | *11* | 25 | | | *Clarke 7p, 71* | *Burridge* | *Forrest* | *Moore* | *Bond* | *Statham* | *Cockerill* | *Case* | *Baker* | *Townsend* | *Wallace** | *Clarke* | *Le Tissier* |
| | | | | | | | Ref: R Milford | Danny Wallace runs the Town defence ragged in the first half and is brought down by Tim Breacker, enabling Colin Clarke to open the scoring from the spot before McDonough levels with a deflected shot. Wallace is unable to continue for the second half, suffering from a groin strain. | | | | | | | | | | | |
| 20 | A | EVERTON | 11 | L | 0-2 | 0-1 | | Sealey | Breacker | Grimes* | McDonough | Foster | Donaghy | Wilson D | Stein B | Harford ! | Hill^ | Allinson | Johnson R/Stein M |
| | 26/12 | ***32,128*** | *4* | 25 | | | *Heath 28, 57* | *Southall* | *Stevens* | *Ratcliffe* | *Watson* | *Pointon* | *Reid* | *Snodin* | *Wilson* | *Steven* | *Sharp* | *Heath* | |
| | | | | | | | Ref: G Alpin | Everton resort to rough tactics, though they do not need to, as they are clearly the better side. Hill is scythed down by Peter Reid and is carried off on a stretcher with a broken leg. Near the end, Kevin Ratcliffe punches Mick Harford, who then head-butts him in retaliation and is sent off. | | | | | | | | | | | |

| No | Date | | Att | Pos | Pt | F-A | H-T | Scorers, Times, and Referees | 1 | 2 | 3 | 4 | 5 | 6 | 7 | 8 | 9 | 10 | 11 | subs used |
|---|---|---|---|---|---|---|---|---|---|---|---|---|---|---|---|---|---|---|---|---|
| 21 | H | CHARLTON | | 9 | W | 1-0 | 1-0 | Wilson D 40 | Sealey | Breacker | Johnson R | McDonough | Foster | Donaghy | Wilson D | Stein B | Harford | Stein M | Allinson | |
| | 28/12 | | 7,243 | *20* | 28 | | | | *Bolder* | *Humphrey* | *Shirtliff* | *Thompson* | *Reid* | *Campbell* | *Mortimer* | *Stuart** | *Mackenzie* | *Williams^* | *Jones* | *Bennett/Lee* |
| | | | | | | | | Ref: I Borrett | The game is spoilt as a spectacle with over-anxiety exhibited by the Hatters. Charlton have little to offer up front and Wilson settles the issue when collecting a headed pass from Mick Harford. Lennie Lawrence admits that once Luton had scored there was only going to be one winner. | | | | | | | | | | | |
| 22 | H | CHELSEA | | 8 | W | 3-0 | 1-0 | Stein M 12, Stein B 50, Harford 64 | Sealey | Breacker | Johnson R | McDonough | Foster | Donaghy | Wilson D | Stein B | Harford | Stein M | Allinson | |
| | 1/1 | | 8,018 | *11* | 31 | | | | *Freestone* | *Wood* | *Clarke* | *McLaughlin* | *Dorigo* | *Bumstead* | *Hazard* | *Wilson* | *McAllister* | *Dixon* | *Durie* | |
| | | | | | | | | Ref: J Key | Chelsea have not won for eight games and are no contest for the Town, who stroll through the match. Mark Stein latches onto a poor back-pass from Clive Wilson. A lob from Brian Stein, together from a header from Mick Harford, finish off the job. Ken Bates again refuses to attend. | | | | | | | | | | | |
| 23 | A | WEST HAM | | 8 | D | 1-1 | 0-0 | Stein M 76 | Sealey | Breacker | Johnson R | McDonough | Foster | Donaghy | Wilson D | Stein B | Harford | Stein M | Allinson | |
| | 2/1 | | *16,716* | *14* | 32 | | | *Ince 60* | *McAlister* | *Potts* | *Gale* | *Strodder* | *Stewart* | *Ward* | *Robson* | *Parris** | *Bonds* | *Hilton* | *Cottee* | *Ince* |
| | | | | | | | | Ref: P Foakes | In wet and windy weather, the Town battle out their first away draw of the season. A goal for the Hammers from Paul Ince seems to kick-start the Hatters and, after a spell of concerted pressure, Brian Stein back-heels the ball to his brother, Mark, who makes no mistake from close range. | | | | | | | | | | | |
| 24 | H | DERBY | | 8 | W | 1-0 | 0-0 | McDonough 84 | Sealey | Breacker | Johnson R | McDonough | Foster | Donaghy | Wilson D | Stein B | Black | Stein M | Allinson | |
| | 16/1 | | 7,175 | *17* | 35 | | | | *Shilton* | *MacLaren* | *Wright* | *Blades* | *Forsyth* | *Williams* | *Gregory* | *McClaren* | *Callaghan* | *Gee* | *Garner* | |
| | | | | | | | | Ref: K Cooper | Derby are currently tumbling down the league table but Peter Shilton has one of those days where he stops almost everything, including making a world-class save from Allinson. McDonough scores with a rocket shot but Shilton manages to get a touch, splitting open a finger in the process. | | | | | | | | | | | |
| 25 | H | OXFORD | | 8 | W | 7-4 | 3-2 | Harford 6,71, Stein B 20, McDon 35, | Sealey | Breacker | Johnson R* | McDonough | Foster | Donaghy | Wilson D | Stein B | Harford | Stein M | Allinson | Grimes |
| | 6/2 | | 8,063 | *20* | 38 | | | *Hill 34p, 61, Foyle 41, Phillips 65* | *Hardwick* | *Hebberd* | *Bardsley* | *Briggs* | *Caton** | *R'ds-Brown* | *Shelton^* | *Hill* | *Phillips* | *Saunders* | *Foyle* | *Whitehurst/Mustoe* |
| | | | | | | | | Ref: N Butler [Stein M 51, 53, 62] | In a dress rehearsal for the up coming Littlewoods Cup semi-final, neither side gives any clues in an open game where both defences are all over the place. Mark Stein scores his first league hat-trick, but Mick Harford, with a diving header, hits the seventh and best goal of the game. | | | | | | | | | | | |
| 26 | A | ARSENAL | | 8 | L | 1-2 | 0-2 | Stein M 89 | Sealey | Breacker | Grimes | McDonough | Foster | Donaghy | Wilson D | Stein B | Harford | Stein M | Allinson | |
| | 13/2 | | *22,612* | *5* | 38 | | | *Thomas 20, Rocastle 26* | *Lukic* | *Dixon* | *O'Leary* | *Adams** | *Winterburn* | *Rocastle* | *Hayes* | *Thomas* | *Richardson* | *Smith* | *Groves* | *Caesar* |
| | | | | | | | | Ref: G Courtney | Harford, who has just been selected for the England team, gets in the way of Sealey, which enables the Gunners to score an easy goal. He then misses a sitter in the second half. A volley from Stein comes too late and the Town lose their unbeaten run which stretches back to Boxing Day. | | | | | | | | | | | |
| 27 | A | WIMBLEDON | | 9 | L | 0-2 | 0-1 | | Sealey | Breacker | Grimes | Johnson R | **Johnson M** | Donaghy | Wilson D | Stein B | Harford | Stein M | Allinson | |
| | 5/3 | | ***4,854*** | *7* | 38 | | | *Fashanu 11, Gibson 48* | *Beasant* | *Goodyear* | *Gayle* | *Thorn* | *Scales* | *Sanchez* | *Jones* | *Phelan* | *Gibson* | *Cork** | *Fashanu* | *Clement* |
| | | | | | | | | Ref: R Gifford | Nearly a month has passed since the Hatters last played a league game, having recently been involved in five cup-ties. Vinny Jones steals the ball from Johnson, who is making his Town debut, to lay on the first goal for Fashanu. Dave Beasant pulls off a decisive save from Harford. | | | | | | | | | | | |
| 28 | A | COVENTRY | | 14 | L | **0-4** | 0-2 | *[Regis 64]* | Sealey | Breacker | Grimes | McDonough | Foster | Donaghy | Wilson D | Johnson R* | Harford | Stein M | Allinson^ | Cobb/Black |
| | 15/3 | | *13,711* | *11* | 38 | | | *Sedgley 34, Bannister 38, Kilcline 60p,* | *Ogrizovic* | *Phillips* | *Kilcline** | *Peake* | *Downs* | *Emerson* | *Sedgley* | *Smith* | *Bannister* | *Speedie* | *Regis* | *Rodger* |
| | | | | | | | | Ref: D Allison | The Town are second best to a side which uses pace and power to good effect. The number of games played in recent weeks is starting to take its toll on the Luton players and only Harford has the strength to show his normal form. Kilcline converts from the spot after Emerson is fouled. | | | | | | | | | | | |
| 29 | H | PORTSMOUTH | | 12 | W | 4-1 | 1-0 | Wilson D 8, Stein M 53, Mariner 63 (og), | Sealey | Breacker | Grimes | McDonough | Foster | Donaghy | Wilson D | Stein B | Johnson R | Stein M | Allinson | |
| | 29/3 | | 6,740 | *9* | 41 | | | *Dillon 52* [Stein B 86] | *Knight* | *Swain* | *Blake* | *Gilbert* | *Sandford* | *Dillon* | *Horne* | *Fillery* | *Perry** | *Mariner* | *Hilaire* | *Kerr* |
| | | | | | | | | Ref: V Callow | After a poor performance against Reading in the Simod Cup, the Town players regain some pride when beating relegation-haunted Portsmouth out of sight. On a sad night for Pompey, Kevin Dillon crashes his penalty kick wide of a post and then Mariner heads a peach of an own-goal. | | | | | | | | | | | |
| 30 | A | NEWCASTLE | | 13 | L | **0-4** | 0-2 | | Sealey | Breacker | Grimes* | McDonough | Foster | Donaghy | Wilson D | Johnson R | Harford | Stein M^ | Black | Allinson/**Oldfield** |
| | 2/4 | | *20,752* | *10* | 41 | | | *O'Neill 16, 25, 81, Goddard 62* | *Kelly* | *McDonald* | *Anderson* | *Roeder* | *Tinnion* | *McCreery* | *Stephenson* | *Gascoigne* | *Wharton* | *Goddard* | *O'Neill* | |
| | | | | | | | | Ref: L Dilkes | The Town are heavily beaten in an away game for the fourth time in a row and are clearly second best right from the kick-off. So complete is the defeat that Magpies skipper Kenny Wharton has the time to arrogantly sit on the ball, much to the disgust of Luton manager Ray Harford. | | | | | | | | | | | |

| No Date | Venue | Opponent Att | Pos | Res Pts | FT | HT | Scorers, Times, and Referees | 1 | 2 | 3 | 4 | 5 | 6 | 7 | 8 | 9 | 10 | 11 | subs used |
|---|---|---|---|---|---|---|---|---|---|---|---|---|---|---|---|---|---|---|---|
| 31 | H | SHEFFIELD WED | 13 | D | 2-2 | 0-0 | McDonough 46, Stein B 55 | Sealey | Breacker | Grimes | McDono'gh* | Foster | Donaghy | Wilson D | Stein B | Harford | Stein M | Johnson R | Allinson |
| 5/4 | | 7,337 | *8* | 42 | | | *Chapman 50, Sterland 87* | *Pressman* | *Sterland* | *Cranson* | *May* | *Madden* | *Worthingt'n* | *Proctor** | *Megson* | *Jonsson* | *Chapman* | *Hirst^* | *Galvin/West* |
| | | | | | | | Ref: K Morton | Sealey is injured in a horrific mid-air clash with Lee Chapman and it is six minutes before he is able to resume. After the interval, McDonough blasts the opener but Chapman heads the Owls level. Stein appears to have won the game but Mel Sterland earns a point for the visitors late on. | | | | | | | | | | | |
| 32 | A | MANCHESTER U | 13 | L | 0-3 | 0-1 | | Dibble | Breacker | Johnson R | McDonough | Foster* | Donaghy | Wilson D | Stein B | Harford | Stein M | Allinson | Black |
| 12/4 | | *28,830* | *2* | 42 | | | *McClair 45, Robson 68, Davenport 70* | *Turner* | *Anderson* | *Bruce* | *McGrath* | *Blackmore* | *Duxbury* | *Robson* | *Gibson** | *Strachan* | *McClair* | *Davenport* | *Olsen* |
| | | | | | | | Ref: R Hart | Although heavily beaten, the Town show more effort than in recent away games. An efficient offside trap keeps United at bay until just before the interval when Brian McClair hits a cross-shot which completely eludes Andy Dibble. The crossbar saves the Hatters from a bigger defeat. | | | | | | | | | | | |
| 33 | H | QP RANGERS | 11 | W | 2-1 | 1-0 | Wilson D 16p, Foster 60 | Dibble | Breacker | Johnson R | McDonough | Foster | Johnson M | Wilson D | Stein B | Harford | Stein M | Preece | |
| 19/4 | | 6,735 | *4* | 45 | | | *Kerslake 59p* | *Seaman* | *Neill* | *Dawes* | *Parker* | *McDonald* | *Channing* | *Allen* | *Kerslake** | *Falco* | *Fereday* | *Francis^* | *Coney/Pizanti* |
| | | | | | | | Ref: K Miller | The Hatters warm up for the Littlewoods Cup final with a win which kills off any lingering fears of relegation. Preece makes a welcome return from injury after seven months and passes a perfect ball to Rob Johnson, whose cross is handled by McDonald. Wilson slots home the penalty. | | | | | | | | | | | |
| 34 | A | NORWICH | 12 | D | 2-2 | 0-0 | Stein M 87, Wilson D 89p | Dibble | Breacker | Johnson R | Hill | Foster | Donaghy* | Wilson D | Stein M | Allinson^ | Grimes | Black | Johnson M/Oldfield |
| 30/4 | | *13,171* | *13* | 46 | | | *Drinkell 51, Putney 63* | *Gunn* | *Culverhouse* | *Linighan* | *Butterw'rth* | *Spearing* | *Fox* | *Goss* | *Putney* | *Phelan* | *Drinkell** | *Fleck* | *Biggins* |
| | | | | | | | Ref: A Ward | A diving header from Kevin Drinkell and a poor back-pass which is intercepted by Trevor Putney see the Canaries cruising to what seems to be an easy win. Oldfield comes on and lays on a cross for Stein to pull one back. He is then felled by Bryan Gunn and Wilson levels from the spot. | | | | | | | | | | | |
| 35 | H | WATFORD | 11 | W | 2-1 | 2-1 | Oldfield 35, Wilson D 44p | Dibble | Breacker | Grimes | Johnson R | Foster | Johnson M | Wilson D | Allinson | Oldfield | Hill | Black | |
| 2/5 | | 10,409 | *20* | 49 | | | *Johnson M 31 (og)* | *Coton* | *Gibbs* | *Morris* | *McClelland* | *Rostron** | *Thomas^* | *Jackett* | *Porter* | *Holden* | *Rimmer* | *Roberts* | *Sherwood/Hodges* |
| | | | | | | | Ref: K Breen | 19-year-old David Oldfield keeps his place against a doomed Watford team. Marvin Johnson puts the visitors into the lead with an unfortunate own-goal when the ball cannons off him and into the net. Oldfield equalises with a left-foot shot before Wilson hits the winner from the spot. | | | | | | | | | | | |
| 36 | A | TOTTENHAM | 11 | L | 1-2 | 1-1 | Grimes 36 | Dibble | Breacker | Johnson R | Wilson D | Foster | Johnson M | Nwajiobi | Oldfield | Allinson | Grimes | Preece* | Cobb |
| 4/5 | | *15,437* | *13* | 49 | | | *Hodge 30, Mabbutt 52* | *Mimms* | *Statham* | *Fenwick** | *Fairclough* | *Thomas* | *Allen P* | *Hodge* | *Mabbutt* | *Waddle* | *Metgod* | *Allen C^* | *Samways/Gray* |
| | | | | | | | Ref: A Seville | Emeka Nwajiobi returns to the side after being out since just before Christmas. Grimes scores the goal of the game with a left-foot pile-driver, after a great pass from Oldfield, who then has the chance to level the scores but misses the net from two feet. Spurs are well worth their win. | | | | | | | | | | | |
| 37 | A | SOUTHAMPTON | 11 | D | 1-1 | 1-0 | Wilson D 29 | Dibble | Breacker | Grimes | Johnson R | Foster | Johnson M | Wilson D | Cobb* | Oldfield | Nwajiobi^ | Black | **James**/Allinson |
| 7/5 | | *12,722* | *12* | 50 | | | *Clarke 54* | *Burridge* | *Forrest* | *Moore* | *Bond* | *Statham* | *Case* | *Baker* | *Townsend** | *Wallace R* | *Clarke* | *Wallace D^* | *Cockerill/Le Tissier* |
| | | | | | | | Ref: D Hutchinson/W Phillips | Rod Wallace threatens to win the game on his own in the early stages with his phenomenal speed and ball control until Grimes gets his measure. The Saints have their problems in countering David Oldfield, who has pace to spare. Oldfield starts the move that allows Wilson to stab home. | | | | | | | | | | | |
| 38 | A | LIVERPOOL | 11 | D | 1-1 | 1-1 | Oldfield 28 | Dibble | Breacker | Johnson R* | Grimes | Foster | Johnson M | Wilson D | Allinson^ | Oldfield | Preece | Black | James/Cobb |
| 9/5 | | *30,374* | *1* | 51 | | | *Aldridge 16* | *Grobbelaar* | *Nicol* | *Gillespie* | *Spackman** | *Ablett* | *Johnston^* | *Whelan* | *McMahon* | *Barnes* | *Houghton* | *Aldridge* | *MacDonald/Dalglish* |
| | | | | | | | Ref: D Phillips | The Town put on a brilliant performance against the League champions. John Aldridge opens the scoring with an overhead kick but the Luton defence then plays as a unit, restricting Liverpool to long-range shots. Oldfield uses his speed before forcing a low shot past Bruce Grobbelaar. | | | | | | | | | | | |
| 39 | H | NOTT'M FOREST | 11 | D | 1-1 | 1-0 | Donaghy 5 | Dibble | Breacker | Grimes | Johnson R | Foster | Donaghy* | Wilson D | Oldfield | Harford | Preece | Black | Johnson M |
| 13/5 | | 9,108 | *3* | 52 | | | *Glover 46* | *Sutton* | *Fleming* | *Walker* | *Chettle* | *Williams** | *Carr* | *Wilson* | *Webb* | *Crosby* | *Clough* | *Glover* | *Foster* |
| | | | | | | | Ref: M Reed | Mal Donaghy blasts his first league goal for four years to give the Hatters an early lead but, with tiredness setting in, Lee Glover levels with a tap-in after a cross from Franz Carr is only parried by Dibble. The surprise announcement is made that Brian Stein is to receive a free transfer. | | | | | | | | | | | |
| 40 | A | NOTT'M FOREST | 9 | D | 1-1 | 1-0 | Oldfield 2 | Dibble | Breacker | Johnson R | Cobb* | Foster | Johnson M | Wilson D | Stein M | Oldfield | Preece^ | Allinson | James/Black |
| 15/5 | | *13,106* | *3* | 53 | | | *Webb 60* | *Sutton* | *Fleming* | *Walker* | *Foster* | *Chettle* | *Carr** | *Wilson* | *Webb* | *Rice* | *Clough* | *Glover* | *Crosby* |
| Average | Home 8,039 | Away 16,108 | | | | | Ref: B Stevens | The season draws to a close for the Hatters after having played 58 first-team games. Oldfield again shows his pace, beating the Forest defence to score after 88 seconds. Neil Webb levels on the hour with a shot into the corner of the net and Mark Stein hits the woodwork in a rare attack. | | | | | | | | | | | |

| Littlewoods Cup | | | | | F-A | H-T | Scorers, Times, and Referees | 1 | 2 | 3 | 4 | 5 | 6 | 7 | 8 | 9 | 10 | 11 | subs used |
|---|---|---|---|---|---|---|---|---|---|---|---|---|---|---|---|---|---|---|---|
| 2:1 | A | WIGAN | 12 | W | 1-0 | 1-0 | Weir 18 | Sealey | Breacker | Johnson R | Hill | Foster | Donaghy | Wilson D | Stein B | Harford | Weir | Preece* | Nwajiobi |
| | 22/9 | *5,018 3:1* | | | | | | *Adkins* | *Butler* | *Cribley* | *Beesley* | *Knowles* | *Hamilton* | *Hilditch* | *Cook** | *Storer* | *Campbell* | *Sewell* | *Griffiths* |
| | | | | | | | Ref: K Hackett | The Division 3 leaders put the Hatters defence under pressure for much of the game but they probably try too hard and their finishing is awful. They miss two good chances before Micky Weir, making his full Luton debut, hits a low shot into the corner of the net from the edge of the area. | | | | | | | | | | | |
| 2:2 | H | WIGAN | 14 | W | 4-2 | 3-0 | Harford 25, 35, 72, McDonough 38 | Sealey | Breacker | Grimes | McDonough | Foster | Donaghy | Wilson D | Stein B | Harford | Black | Weir | |
| | 6/10 | 4,240 *3:9* | | | | | *Hamilton 57, Foster 70 (og)* | *Redfern* | *Butler* | *Holden* | *Cribley* | *Beesley* | *Storer* | *Hilditch* | *Hamilton* | *Griffiths* | *Jewell* | *Campbell** | *Ainscow* |
| | | | | | | | Ref: R Groves (Hatters win 5-2 on aggregate) | Mick Harford is at his awesome best as he virtually beats Wigan on his own, scoring with two headers and a fierce shot. The Latics come back into the game after the break, albeit when 0-3 down, and David Hamilton heads home a corner-kick before Steve Foster fires into his own net. | | | | | | | | | | | |
| 3 | H | COVENTRY | 17 | W | 3-1 | 1-0 | Harford 28, 51, Weir 54 | Sealey | Breacker | Grimes | McDonough | Foster | Donaghy | Wilson D | Stein B | Harford | Johnson R | Weir | |
| | 27/10 | 11,448 *1:11* (at Leicester) | | | | | *Pickering 69* | *Ogrizovic* | *Borrows* | *Rodger* | *Sedgley* | *Downs* | *McGrath** | *Bennett* | *Gynn* | *Pickering* | *Houchen* | *Speedie* | *Cook* |
| | | | | | | | Ref: A Ward | In a home game played some 70 miles away, the Town turn on the style in atrocious conditions and hardly allow Coventry a kick. Mick Harford nearly scores his second hat-trick in this season's competition but Steve Ogrizovic saves his penalty, awarded when Stein is tripped by Sedgley. | | | | | | | | | | | |
| 4 | A | IPSWICH | 12 | W | 1-0 | 1-0 | Stein B 4 | Sealey | Breacker | Harvey | McDonough | Foster | Donaghy | Wilson D* | Stein B | Nwajiobi | Johnson R^ | Stein M | Black/Oldfield |
| | 17/11 | *15,643 2:6* | | | | | | *Hallworth* | *Stockwell* | *Cranson* | *Yallop* | *Harbey* | *Rimmer* | *Dozzell* | *Brennan* | *Zondervan* | *D'Avray** | *Lowe* | *Deehan* |
| | | | | | | | Ref: T Mills | The Town are missing seven of their first team regulars but silence the Portman Road crowd early on when Brian Stein scores a breathtaking goal. Taking a pass from his brother in his stride, he beats two defenders for speed and draws the keeper before netting with a clinical finish. | | | | | | | | | | | |
| QF | H | BRADFORD CITY | 8 | W | 2-0 | 0-0 | Foster 55, Harford 64 | Sealey | Breacker | Johnson R | McDonough | Foster | Donaghy | Wilson D | Stein B | Harford | Stein M | Black | |
| | 19/1 | 11,022 *2:6* | | | | | | *Tomlinson* | *Mitchell* | *Evans* | *Sinnott* | *Goddard** | *Abbott* | *Kennedy* | *Ellis* | *McCall* | *Hendrie* | *Futcher* | *Ormondroyd* |
| | | | | | | | Ref: J Martin | An error by Paul Tomlinson allows the breakthrough when he collects the ball, dribbles it out of his area and back in again before touching it for a second time. The indirect free-kick is played to Steve Foster who hammers the ball home. Mick Harford heads the second to clinch the tie. | | | | | | | | | | | |
| SF 1 | A | OXFORD | 8 | D | 1-1 | 1-0 | Stein B 40 | Sealey | Breacker | Johnson R | McDonough | Foster | Donaghy | Wilson D | Stein B | Harford | Stein M | Grimes | |
| | 10/2 | *12,943 1:20* | | | | | *Saunders 46p* | *Judge* | *Bardsley* | *Briggs* | *Caton* | *Dreyer* | *Shelton** | *Hebberd* | *Phillips* | *R'ds-Brown* | *Foyle* | *Saunders* | *Hill* |
| | | | | | | | Ref: K Hackett | On a soft, slushy pitch the Town enjoy a comfortable lead at the interval, courtesy of a precise shot from Brian Stein. After the break, Donaghy and Dean Saunders fall over in the area and Saunders nets the spot-kick. The same pair then clash again, but this time Sealey saves the penalty. | | | | | | | | | | | |
| SF 2 | H | OXFORD | 8 | W | 2-0 | 2-0 | Stein B 33, Grimes 42 | Sealey | Breacker | Grimes | McDonough | Foster | Donaghy | Wilson D | Stein B | Harford | Stein M | Johnson R | |
| | 28/2 | 13,010 *1:19* | | | | | | *Judge* | *Bardsley* | *Briggs* | *Caton* | *Dreyer* | *Hebberd* | *Hill** | *Phillips* | *R'ds-Brown^* | *Foyle* | *Saunders* | *Shelton/Leworthy* |
| | | | | | | | Ref: L Shapter (Hatters win 3-1 on aggregate) | This was always going to be the Hatters' day and the crowd go mad when Brian Stein heads in a Rob Johnson centre, and then Ashley Grimes scores direct from a free-kick. The Town control the second period, allowing Oxford only one chance, which is spurned by Dean Saunders. | | | | | | | | | | | |
| F | A | ARSENAL | 11 | W | 3-2 | 1-0 | Stein B 13, 89, Wilson D 83 | Dibble | Breacker | Johnson R | Hill | Foster | Donaghy | Wilson D | Stein B | Harford* | Preece^ | Black | Stein M/Grimes |
| | 24/4 | *95,732 1:6* (at Wembley) | | | | | *Hayes 71, Smith 74* | *Lukic* | *Winterburn* | *Caesar* | *Adams* | *Sansom* | *Rocastle* | *Thomas* | *Davis* | *Richardson* | *Groves** | *Smith* | *Hayes* |
| | | | | | | | Ref: J Worrall | After 103 years of trying, and in story-book fashion, Luton Town finally win a major trophy. The penalty save by Andy Dibble and the headed goal from Danny Wilson are climaxed by the winner in the final seconds from Brian Stein to remain forever in the memory of all Hatters' fans. | | | | | | | | | | | |
| **FA Cup** | | | | | | | | | | | | | | | | | | | |
| 3 | A | HARTLEPOOL | 8 | W | 2-1 | 0-0 | Weir 49, McDonough 73 | Sealey | Breacker | Johnson R | McDonough | Foster | Donaghy | Wilson D | Stein B | Weir | Stein M | Allinson | |
| | 9/1 | *6,187 4:11* | | | | | *Toman 88* | *Carr* | *Barratt* | *McKinnon* | *Nobbs* | *Smith* | *Haigh* | *Honour* | *Toman* | *Baker* | *Whellans* | *Gibb** | *Tinkler* |
| | | | | | | | Ref: K Breen | The Town have to fight hard to avoid a potential upset against their determined Fourth Division opponents. Micky Weir, who nets his third cup goal from close range, followed by a 20-yard strike from Darron McDonough, give the Hatters their first ever victory at the Victoria Ground. | | | | | | | | | | | |
| 4 | H | SOUTHAMPTON | 8 | W | 2-1 | 0-0 | Allinson 83, Stein B 85 | Sealey | Breacker | Johnson R* | McDonough | Foster | Donaghy | Wilson D | Stein B | Harford | Stein M | Allinson | Grimes |
| | 30/1 | 10,009 *1:11* | | | | | *Clarke 71* | *Burridge* | *Forrest* | *Moore* | *Blake* | *Statham* | *Hobson* | *Baker* | *Cockerill* | *Townsend* | *Clarke* | *Wallace* | |
| | | | | | | | Ref: D Vickers | Colin Clarke floats over a cross which beats Les Sealey and bounces in off the far post. Luckily the Saints then relax and the Hatters reply with a shot through a crowd of players from Allinson, which is deflected into the net, and Brian Stein scoring after taking a pass from his brother. | | | | | | | | | | | |

| Rd | Venue | Opponent | Pos | Res | Score | HT | Scorers, Times, and Referees | 1 | 2 | 3 | 4 | 5 | 6 | 7 | 8 | 9 | 10 | 11 | subs used |
|---|---|---|---|---|---|---|---|---|---|---|---|---|---|---|---|---|---|---|---|
| 5 | A | QP RANGERS | 8 | D | 1-1 | 0-0 | Harford 64 | Sealey | Breacker | Grimes | McDonough | Foster | Donaghy | Wilson D | Stein B | Harford | Stein M | Allinson | |
| 20/2 | | *15,856 1:6* | | | | | *Neill 58* | *Johns* | *Dawes* | *Neill* | *Parker* | *McDonald* | *Maguire* | *Allen* | *Falco* | *Bannister** | *Fereday* | *Brock* | *Byrne* |
| | | | | | | | Ref: A Gunn | The Omniturf surface is starting to show signs of wear and, with both sides slipping and sliding, the ball is in the air for much of the game. The unmarked Warren Neill volleys in a cross from Wayne Fereday before Mick Harford heads the equaliser from an Allinson free-kick soon after. | | | | | | | | | | | |
| 5R | H | QP RANGERS | 8 | W | 1-0 | 0-0 | Neill 60 (og) | Sealey | Breacker | Grimes | McDonough | Foster | Donaghy | Wilson D | Stein B | Harford | Stein M | Allinson | |
| 24/2 | | 10,854 *1:6* | | | | | | *Seaman* | *Dawes* | *Parker* | *McDonald* | *Maguire* | *Neill** | *Allen* | *Brock* | *Fereday* | *Falco* | *Byrne^* | *Kerslake/Coney* |
| | | | | | | | Ref: A Gunn | Warren Neill expertly lobs David Seaman to net an own-goal for the second successive season to give the Hatters the victory by the only goal. After this incident, the game livens up and Sealey saves superbly from John Byrne before Brian Stein hits a post from a Danny Wilson cross. | | | | | | | | | | | |
| QF | H | PORTSMOUTH | 9 | W | 3-1 | 2-1 | Wilson D 3, Stein M 22, Harford 88 | Sealey | Breacker | Grimes | McDonough | Foster | Donaghy | Wilson D | Johnson R | Harford | Stein M | Allinson | |
| 12/3 | | 12,857 *1:17* | | | | | *Quinn 33* | *Knight* | *Gilbert* | *Blake* | *Ball* | *Hardyman** | *Horne* | *Dillon* | *Fillery* | *Hilaire* | *Quinn !* | *Connor* | *Mariner* |
| | | | | | | | Ref: J Key | Wilson takes advantage of a Harford knock-down to score the opener and Mark Stein repeats the manoeuvre soon after. Mick Quinn bundles in a low cross from Terry Connor but is then sent off for a second bookable offence after tangling with Foster. Mick Harford seals the win late on. | | | | | | | | | | | |
| SF | A | WIMBLEDON | 13 | L | 1-2 | 0-0 | Harford 47 | Dibble | Breacker | Grimes* | McDonough | Foster | Donaghy | Wilson D | Stein B | Harford | Stein M | Johnson R | Black |
| 9/4 | | *25,963 1:7* | | | | | *Fashanu 54p, Wise 80* | *Beasant* | *Scales* | *Young* | *Thorn* | *Phelan* | *Sanchez* | *Jones* | *Wise* | *Cork* | *Gibson** | *Fashanu* | *Cunningham* |
| | | (at Tottenham) | | | | | Ref: K Hackett | Dibble deputises for the injured Sealey and has to make some important saves in the first half. Harford finds the space to power the Town into the lead after the break, but the Dons fight back and when Dibble fouls Gibson, Fashanu nets from the spot before Dennis Wise hits the winner. | | | | | | | | | | | |

| | | P | Home W | D | L | F | A | Away W | D | L | F | A | Pts |
|---|---|---|---|---|---|---|---|---|---|---|---|---|---|
| 1 | Liverpool | 40 | 15 | 5 | 0 | 49 | 9 | 11 | 7 | 2 | 38 | 15 | 90 |
| 2 | Manchester U | 40 | 14 | 5 | 1 | 41 | 17 | 9 | 7 | 4 | 30 | 21 | 81 |
| 3 | Nott'm Forest | 40 | 11 | 7 | 2 | 40 | 17 | 9 | 6 | 5 | 27 | 22 | 73 |
| 4 | Everton | 40 | 14 | 4 | 2 | 34 | 11 | 5 | 9 | 6 | 19 | 16 | 70 |
| 5 | QP Rangers | 40 | 12 | 4 | 4 | 30 | 14 | 7 | 6 | 7 | 18 | 24 | 67 |
| 6 | Arsenal | 40 | 11 | 4 | 5 | 35 | 16 | 7 | 8 | 5 | 23 | 23 | 66 |
| 7 | Wimbledon | 40 | 8 | 9 | 3 | 32 | 20 | 6 | 6 | 8 | 26 | 27 | 57 |
| 8 | Newcastle | 40 | 9 | 6 | 5 | 32 | 23 | 5 | 8 | 7 | 23 | 30 | 56 |
| 9 | LUTON TOWN | 40 | 11 | 6 | 3 | 40 | 21 | 3 | 5 | 12 | 17 | 37 | 53 |
| 10 | Coventry | 40 | 6 | 8 | 6 | 23 | 25 | 7 | 6 | 7 | 23 | 28 | 53 |
| 11 | Sheffield Wed | 40 | 10 | 2 | 8 | 27 | 30 | 5 | 6 | 9 | 25 | 36 | 53 |
| 12 | Southampton | 40 | 6 | 8 | 6 | 27 | 26 | 6 | 6 | 8 | 22 | 27 | 50 |
| 13 | Tottenham | 40 | 9 | 5 | 6 | 26 | 23 | 3 | 6 | 11 | 12 | 25 | 47 |
| 14 | Norwich | 40 | 7 | 5 | 8 | 26 | 26 | 5 | 4 | 11 | 14 | 26 | 45 |
| 15 | Derby | 40 | 6 | 7 | 7 | 18 | 17 | 4 | 6 | 10 | 17 | 28 | 43 |
| 16 | West Ham | 40 | 6 | 9 | 5 | 23 | 21 | 3 | 6 | 11 | 17 | 31 | 42 |
| 17 | Charlton | 40 | 7 | 7 | 6 | 23 | 21 | 2 | 8 | 10 | 15 | 31 | 42 |
| 18 | Chelsea | 40 | 7 | 11 | 2 | 24 | 17 | 2 | 4 | 14 | 26 | 51 | 42 |
| 19 | Portsmouth | 40 | 4 | 8 | 8 | 21 | 27 | 3 | 6 | 11 | 15 | 39 | 35 |
| 20 | Watford | 40 | 4 | 5 | 11 | 15 | 24 | 3 | 6 | 11 | 12 | 27 | 32 |
| 21 | Oxford | 40 | 5 | 7 | 8 | 24 | 34 | 1 | 6 | 13 | 20 | 46 | 31 |
| | | 840 | 182 | 132 | 106 | 610 | 439 | 106 | 132 | 182 | 439 | 610 | 1128 |

Odds & ends

Double wins: (2) Oxford, Watford.
Double losses: (1) Coventry.

Won from behind: (4) Everton (h), Watford (h), Arsenal (LC), . Southampton (FAC).
Lost from in front: (2) Norwich (h), Wimbledon (FAC).

High spots: Littlewoods Cup final win against Arsenal – and a trophy.
A creditable ninth place in the table after 58 competitive fixtures.
The crazy 12-6 aggregate score in the two league games with Oxford.
The late-season form of David Oldfield.

Low spots: Another FA Cup semi-final defeat.
The free transfer awarded to Brian Stein.
Consecutive 0-4 defeats at Coventry and Newcastle.

Player of the Year: Brian Stein.
Ever-presents: (1) Tim Breacker.
Hat-tricks: (2) Mark Stein (1), Mick Harford (1).
Leading scorer: Mick Harford (18).

| | Appearances Lge | *Sub* | LC | *Sub* | FAC | *Sub* | Goals Lge | LC | FAC | Tot |
|---|---|---|---|---|---|---|---|---|---|---|
| Allinson, Ian | **23** | *4* | | | 5 | | **3** | | 1 | **4** |
| Black, Kingsley | **10** | *3* | 3 | *1* | | *1* | | | | |
| Breacker, Tim | **40** | | 8 | | 6 | | **1** | | | **1** |
| Cobb, Gary | **4** | *3* | | | | | | | | |
| Dibble, Andy | **9** | | 1 | | 1 | | | | | |
| Donaghy, Mal | **32** | | 8 | | 6 | | **1** | | | **1** |
| Foster, Steve | **39** | | 8 | | 6 | | **2** | 1 | | **3** |
| Grimes, Ashley | **31** | *1* | 4 | *1* | 4 | *1* | **1** | 1 | | **2** |
| Harford, Mick | **24** | *1* | 7 | | 5 | | **9** | 6 | 3 | **18** |
| Harvey, Richard | | | 1 | | | | | | | |
| Hill, Ricky | **16** | *1* | 2 | | | | **2** | | | **2** |
| James, Julian | | *3* | | | | | | | | |
| Johnson, Marvin | **7** | *2* | | | | | | | | |
| Johnson, Rob | **21** | *4* | 7 | | 4 | | | | | |
| McDonough, Darron | **24** | *3* | 6 | | 6 | | **4** | 1 | 1 | **6** |
| Newell, Mike | **4** | *1* | | | | | | | | |
| North, Stacey | | *1* | | | | | | | | |
| Nwajiobi, Emeka | **10** | *2* | 1 | *1* | | | **2** | | | **2** |
| Oldfield, David | **6** | *2* | | *1* | | | **3** | | | **3** |
| Preece, David | **13** | | 2 | | | | | | | |
| Sealey, Les | **31** | | 7 | | 5 | | | | | |
| Stein, Brian | **28** | | 8 | | 5 | | **9** | 5 | 1 | **15** |
| Stein, Mark | **20** | *5* | 4 | *1* | 6 | | **11** | | 1 | **12** |
| Weir, Micky | **7** | *1* | 3 | | 1 | | | 2 | 1 | **3** |
| Wilson, Danny | **38** | | 8 | | 6 | | **8** | 1 | 1 | **10** |
| Wilson, Robert | **3** | | | | | | | | | |
| (own-goals) | | | | | | | **1** | | 1 | **2** |
| **26 players used** | **440** | ***37*** | **88** | ***5*** | **66** | ***2*** | **57** | **17** | **10** | **84** |

| No | Date | | Att | Pos | Pt | F-A | H-T | Scorers, Times, and Referees | 1 | 2 | 3 | 4 | 5 | 6 | 7 | 8 | 9 | 10 | 11 | subs used |
|---|---|---|---|---|---|---|---|---|---|---|---|---|---|---|---|---|---|---|---|---|
| 1 | A | SHEFFIELD WED | | | L | 0-1 | 0-0 | | Sealey | Breacker | **Dreyer** | **Williams** | Foster | Donaghy | Wilson | **Wegerle*** | Harford | Oldfield | Black | Allinson |
| | 27/8 | | *16,433* | | - | | | *Sterland 58* | *Pressman* | *Worthingt'n* | *Pearson* | *Madden* | *Proctor* | *Megson* | *Harper* | *Jonsson* | *Galvin** | *West* | *Sterland* | *Hirst* |
| | | | | | | | | Ref: G Tyson | After the pre-season hype, the Town defend well at Hillsborough and finish up losing by the single goal, although the corner count of 17-2 is in favour of the Owls. Mel Sterland nets with a near-post header, following a cross from Siggy Jonsson, but later sees his penalty saved by Sealey. | | | | | | | | | | | |
| 2 | H | WIMBLEDON | | | D | 2-2 | 1-1 | Ryan 44 (og), Black 56 | Sealey | Johnson R | Grimes | Williams | Foster | Donaghy | Wilson | Preece | Harford | Oldfield | Black | |
| | 3/9 | | 8,067 | | 1 | | | *Fashanu 42p, Fairweather 73* | *Green* | *Joseph* | *Young* | *Scales* | *Phelan* | *Ryan* | *Fairweather* | *Sanchez** | *Gibson^* | *Fashanu* | *Wise* | *Brooke/Turner* |
| | | | | | | | | Ref: B Stevens | John Fashanu scores from the spot after Foster trips Dennis Wise but Vaughan Ryan cancels it out with an own-goal. Black scores his first goal for the club, the result of a passing movement from one end of the pitch to the other, but Carlton Fairweather hits a soft equaliser for the draw. | | | | | | | | | | | |
| 3 | A | SOUTHAMPTON | | 16 | L | 1-2 | 0-1 | Foster 79 | Sealey | Johnson R | Grimes | Williams | Foster | Donaghy | Wilson | Oldfield | Harford | Preece* | Black | Wegerle |
| | 10/9 | | *13,214* | *1* | 1 | | | *Rideout 6, Wallace R 82* | *Burridge* | *Forrest* | *Moore* | *Osman* | *Statham* | *Cockerill* | *Case* | *Wallace R* | *Clarke* | *Rideout* | *Le Tissier** | *Wallace D* |
| | | | | | | | | Ref: P Don | The introduction of Wegerle as a second-half substitute boosts the Town as they fight to cancel out an early goal from Rideout. Foster equalises with a thumping header following a corner-kick by Williams. Sealey blocks a Colin Clarke shot but Rod Wallace follows up to grab the winner. | | | | | | | | | | | |
| 4 | H | MANCHESTER U | | 18 | L | 0-2 | 0-1 | | Sealey | Johnson R | Dreyer | Williams | Foster | Johnson M | Wilson | Oldfield* | Harford | Hill | Black | Wegerle |
| | 17/9 | | 11,010 | *8* | 1 | | | *Davenport 19, Robson 84* | *Leighton* | *Garton* | *Bruce* | *McGrath* | *Blackmore* | *Robson* | *Duxbury* | *Olsen* | *Davenport* | *Hughes* | *McClair* | |
| | | | | | | | | Ref: A Ward | After dominating for most of the match, the Town are caught out by two sucker punches. Marvin Johnson loses possession, just outside the box, to gift Peter Davenport the opener and then, with six minutes left and with Luton chasing the game, Bryan Robson cashes in on a quick break. | | | | | | | | | | | |
| 5 | A | EVERTON | | 15 | W | 2-0 | 0-0 | Oldfield 74, Black 83 | Sealey | Johnson R | Dreyer | Williams | Foster | Donaghy | Wilson | Oldfield* | Harford | Hill^ | Black | Allinson/Breacker |
| | 24/9 | | *26,002* | *8* | 4 | | | | *Southall* | *McDonald** | *Snodin* | *Watson* | *Wilson* | *Reid* | *Heath* | *McCall* | *Sheedy* | *Sharp* | *Cottee* | *Clarke* |
| | | | | | | | | Ref: M Peck | Oldfield follows up on a block by Neville Southall to open the scoring, midway through the second half. Black makes the points safe when he dribbles the ball around the keeper to net from an acute angle. Luton gain their first win of the season and the only away victory in ten months. | | | | | | | | | | | |
| 6 | A | NOTT'M FOREST | | 17 | D | 0-0 | 0-0 | | Sealey | Johnson R | Dreyer | Williams | Foster | Donaghy | Wilson | Oldfield | Harford* | Hill | Black | Allinson |
| | 1/10 | | *15,340* | *16* | 5 | | | | *Sutton* | *Chettle* | *Walker* | *Foster* | *Pearce* | *Crosby* | *Webb* | *Hodge* | *Rice* | *Clough* | *Gaynor** | *Carr* |
| | | | | | | | | Ref: K Redfern | Forest have most of the possession but are unable to find a way through the packed Luton rearguard. Manager Ray Harford denies after the game that the Hatters were playing for a point but that they were driven back by the home side. This is the fifth successive draw for Forest. | | | | | | | | | | | |
| 7 | H | LIVERPOOL | | 13 | W | 1-0 | 1-0 | Harford 3 | Sealey | Johnson R | Dreyer | Williams | Foster | Donaghy | Wilson | Oldfield* | Harford | Hill | Black | Wegerle |
| | 8/10 | | **12,117** | *4* | 8 | | | | *Hooper* | *Venison* | *Molby* | *Gillespie** | *Nicol* | *Whelan* | *Houghton* | *Beardsley* | *MacDonald* | *Rush* | *Barnes* | *Ablett* |
| | | | | | | | | Ref: J Martin | A home win comes at last when Mick Harford connects with an early header following a free-kick by Steve Williams. Liverpool spend the rest of the game trying to break through but some woeful finishing, by John Barnes in particular, leaves Reds' manager Kenny Dalglish fuming. | | | | | | | | | | | |
| 8 | A | MIDDLESBROUGH | | 16 | L | 1-2 | 0-2 | Wilson 86p | Sealey | Johnson R* | Dreyer | McDono'gh^ | Foster | Johnson M | Wilson | Oldfield | Harford | Hill | Black | Wegerle/Breacker |
| | 22/10 | | *17,792* | *8* | 8 | | | *Slaven 3, Cooper 42* | *Pears* | *Parkinson* | *Mowbray* | *Pallister* | *Cooper* | *Kerr* | *Hamilton* | *Brennan* | *Burke** | *Ripley* | *Slaven* | *Kernaghan* |
| | | | | | | | | Ref: A Fitzharris | Boro are all over the Town in the first 15 minutes and lead through a header from Bernie Slaven. A mis-hit shot by Colin Cooper just before the interval leaves the Town with a mountain to climb, although Wilson does pull back a goal from the spot, after Wegerle is fouled by Cooper. | | | | | | | | | | | |
| 9 | H | ARSENAL | | 16 | D | 1-1 | 0-1 | Black 56 | Sealey | Johnson R | Breacker | McDono'gh* | Foster | Johnson M | Wilson | Wegerle | Harford | Hill | Black | Oldfield |
| | 25/10 | | 10,548 | *3* | 9 | | | *Smith 13* | *Lukic* | *Dixon* | *Bould* | *Adams* | *Winterburn* | *Rocastle* | *Richardson* | *Thomas* | *Marwood* | *Merson* | *Smith* | |
| | | | | | | | | Ref: M Reed | A top-class volley from Alan Smith gives the Gunners a deserved half-time lead. Kingsley Black equalises with a 25-yard curled free-kick, after which the visitors are forced to defend in depth. 'I am quite pleased to come here and get a draw,' states the Arsenal manager, George Graham. | | | | | | | | | | | |
| 10 | H | QP RANGERS | | 16 | D | 0-0 | 0-0 | | Sealey | Johnson R | Dreyer | Williams | Foster | Johnson M | Wilson | Wegerle | Allinson* | Hill | Black | Oldfield |
| | 29/10 | | 8,453 | *14* | 10 | | | | *Seaman* | *Parker* | *McDonald* | *Maddix* | *Barker** | *Allen* | *Brock* | *Fereday* | *Falco* | *Stein* | *Francis^* | *Kerslake/Coney* |
| | | | | | | | | Ref: J Worrall | 'It was a poor game to watch. We started poorly and it was a non-event of a game,' admits manager Ray Harford. He then tries to explain away the performance by pointing out that the injury problems, and fielding players who are less than 100% fit, means getting one point is a success. | | | | | | | | | | | |

| No | Date | Venue | Opponent | Att | Pos | Pts | F-A | H-T | Scorers, Times, and Referees | 1 | 2 | 3 | 4 | 5 | 6 | 7 | 8 | 9 | 10 | 11 | 12 sub used |
|---|---|---|---|---|---|---|---|---|---|---|---|---|---|---|---|---|---|---|---|---|---|
| 11 | | A | MILLWALL | | 16 | L | 1-3 | 0-3 | Wilson 88 *[Dawes 24]* | Sealey | James* | Dreyer | Williams | Foster | Johnson M | Wilson | Oldfield | Wegerle | Hill | Black | Johnson R |
| | 5/11 | | | *12,511* | *2* | 10 | | | *Sheringham 17, O'Callaghan 21p,* | *Horne* | *Stevens* | *Thompson* | *McLeary* | *Dawes* | *Lawrence* | *Briley* | *Morgan* | *O'Callaghan* | *Sheringham* | *Cascarino* | |
| | | | | | | | | | Ref: K Barrett | School-boy defending gifts three first-half goals to the Lions as, firstly, Teddy Sheringham takes advantage of a slip by Marvin Johnson, and then O'Callaghan converts a spot kick, awarded when Oldfield knocks over Darren Morgan. Ian Dawes hits the third, direct from a free-kick. | | | | | | | | | | | |
| 12 | | A | COVENTRY | | 16 | L | 0-1 | 0-1 | | Sealey | Johnson R | Grimes | Williams* | Foster | Johnson M | Wilson | Wegerle | Harford | Hill | Black | Oldfield |
| | 12/11 | | | *12,625* | *6* | 10 | | | *Rodger 36* | *Ogrizovic* | *Borrows* | *Kilcline* | *Rodger* | *Downs* | *Clark* | *Speedie* | *Sedgley* | *Smith* | *Regis* | *Bannister* | |
| | | | | | | | | | Ref: K Burge | This is another game where the Town fail to impress in the first period and they concede a headed goal by Graham Rodger following a cross by David Smith. After the interval, Roy Wegerle is full of running and, with Mick Harford fit again, the Sky Blues survive some anxious moments. | | | | | | | | | | | |
| 13 | | H | WEST HAM | | 16 | W | 4-1 | 3-0 | Black 15, 38, Wegerle 19, Wilson 67 | Sealey | Johnson R | Grimes | Preece | Foster | Johnson M | Wilson | Wegerle | Harford | Oldfield | Black | |
| | 19/11 | | | 9,308 | *19* | 13 | | | *Martin 62* | *McKnight* | *Potts* | *Gale* | *Martin* | *Dicks* | *Ward* | *Brady* | *Dickens** | *Keen^* | *Ince* | *Rosenior* | *Parris/Hilton* |
| | | | | | | | | | Ref: V Callow | Manager Ray Harford reads the riot act and reshuffles the pack, leading to the best win of the season. Two quality left-foot shots from Kingsley Black, a Roy Wegerle goal, his first for the club and a Wilson right-foot thunderbolt completes the scoring, although the final score-line flatters. | | | | | | | | | | | |
| 14 | | A | NORWICH | | 15 | D | 2-2 | 1-1 | Wegerle 38, 57 | Sealey | Johnson R | Harvey | Preece | Foster | Johnson M | Wilson | Wegerle | Harford | Oldfield | Black | |
| | 26/11 | | | *13,541* | *1* | 14 | | | *Johnson R 3 (og), Gordon 62* | *Gunn* | *Culverhouse* | *Butterw'rth* | *Linighan* | *Bowen* | *Townsend* | *Phelan* | *Putney* | *Gordon* | *Allen** | *Fleck* | *Rosario* |
| | | | | | | | | | Ref: P Danson | The Hatters scrap their four-man midfield formation and revert to 4-3-3, with the result that the Carrow Road supporters are calling for full time, long before the whistle is due to be blown. Roy Wegerle scores two cracking goals, both instigated by probing passes from David Preece. | | | | | | | | | | | |
| 15 | | H | NEWCASTLE | | 15 | D | 0-0 | 0-0 | | Sealey | Johnson R | Harvey | Preece | Foster | Johnson M | Wilson | Wegerle | Oldfield* | Hill | Black | Allinson |
| | 3/12 | | | 8,338 | *20* | 15 | | | | *Beasant* | *Cornwell* | *Anderson* | *Thorn* | *Tinnion* | *McCreery* | *Hendrie* | *O'Brien* | *Jackson* | *Mirandinha** | *Payne* | *Gourlay* |
| | | | | | | | | | Ref: R Milford | 'Only one goal was needed to turn the game into a landslide,' was the view expressed by Town manager Ray Harford, but, missing the guile of the injured Harford, the Luton attack lacks the necessary thrust. Newcastle have little to offer and the game ends in frustration for the Hatters. | | | | | | | | | | | |
| 16 | | A | DERBY | | 15 | W | 1-0 | 1-0 | Harford 18 | Sealey | Johnson R | Harvey | Preece | Foster | Johnson M | Wilson | Wegerle* | Harford | Hill | Black | Oldfield |
| | 10/12 | | | *15,228* | *7* | 18 | | | | *Shilton* | *Patterson* | *Wright* | *Blades* | *Forsyth* | *Williams* | *Hebberd* | *Callaghan* | *McMinn* | *Goddard** | *Saunders* | *Gee* |
| | | | | | | | | | Ref: D Allison | The Rams win five corners in the first five minutes and their aggressive power play threatens to unsettle the Town but after regrouping they are able to turn on a cultured performance and outplay the home side. A right-foot shot from Mick Harford screams into the top corner of the net. | | | | | | | | | | | |
| 17 | | H | ASTON VILLA | | 16 | D | 1-1 | 1-0 | Wegerle 41 | Sealey | Johnson R | Harvey | Preece | Foster | Johnson M | Wilson | Wegerle | Harford | Hill | Black | |
| | 17/12 | | | 8,785 | *15* | 19 | | | *Johnson M 61 (og)* | *Spink* | *Price* | *Evans* | *Keown* | *Gray S* | *Gage* | *Gray A* | *Cowans* | *Daley** | *Platt* | *McInally* | *Birch* |
| | | | | | | | | | Ref: A Gunn | Marvin Johnson, who has taken the place of Mal Donaghy in the central defence, slices a clearance which balloons over the head of Les Sealey to gift Villa an undeserved share of the points. The game should have been made safe long before this incident, but good chances were wasted. | | | | | | | | | | | |
| 18 | | A | TOTTENHAM | | 16 | D | 0-0 | 0-0 | | Sealey | Johnson R | Harvey | Preece | Foster | Johnson M | Wilson | Wegerle | Harford | Hill | Oldfield | |
| | 26/12 | | | *27,337* | *11* | 20 | | | | *Mimms* | *Bergsson* | *Butters* | *Fenwick* | *Allen* | *Mabbutt* | *Waddle* | *Gascoigne** | *Thomas* | *Walsh^* | *Stewart* | *Samways/Moran* |
| | | | | | | | | | Ref: R Wiseman | Les Sealey saves a penalty from Terry Fenwick and then the follow-up shot from Paul Stewart, to give the Hatters the impetus to attack and almost grab a 1-0 win. Spurs enjoy a lot of the play but their chances of winning are diminished when Paul Gascoigne limps off at the interval. | | | | | | | | | | | |
| 19 | | A | WIMBLEDON | | 16 | L | 0-4 | 0-2 | *[Fashanu 84]* | Sealey | Johnson R | Harvey | Preece | Foster | Johnson M | Wilson | Wegerle* | Harford | Hill | Oldfield | Black |
| | 31/12 | | | ***4,899*** | *15* | 20 | | | *Jones 15, Gibson 29, Scales 46,* | *Segers* | *Curle* | *Young* | *Scales* | *Phelan* | *Jones* | *Sanchez* | *Fairweather* | *Wise* | *Fashanu* | *Gibson* | |
| | | | | | | | | | Ref: T Holbrook | The Wimbledon style of play has been strongly criticised but the Hatters are swept aside as Vinny Jones opens the scoring with a superb volley, after which it is one way traffic for the remainder of the game. 'It was just one of those days,' says shell-shocked Ray Harford after the match. | | | | | | | | | | | |
| 20 | | H | SOUTHAMPTON | | 15 | W | **6-1** | 2-0 | Harford 2,72, Black 7, Wegerle 53, 55, | Sealey | Johnson R | Harvey | Preece | Foster | Johnson M | Wilson | Wegerle | Harford | Hill | Black | |
| | 2/1 | | | 8,637 | *10* | 23 | | | *Wallace R 54* [Hill 68] | *Burridge* | *Forrest* | *Moore* | *Osman* | *Statham* | *Case* | *Baker* | *Maddison* | *Wallace R* | *Le Tissier* | *Wallace D* | |
| | | | | | | | | | Ref: D Vickers | Only two days after the thrashing by Wimbledon, the boot is on the other foot as the team rediscover their goal-scoring touch as Saints manager, Chris Nicholl condemns his back four for caving in. A towering header from Harford, his second and the Towns' sixth, is the pick of the bunch. | | | | | | | | | | | |

# BARCLAYS LEAGUE DIVISION 1

## Manager: Ray Harford

## SEASON 1988-89

| No | Date | | Att | Pos | Pt | F-A | H-T | Scorers, Times, and Referees | 1 | 2 | 3 | 4 | 5 | 6 | 7 | 8 | 9 | 10 | 11 | subs used |
|---|---|---|---|---|---|---|---|---|---|---|---|---|---|---|---|---|---|---|---|---|
| 21 | A | CHARLTON | | 16 | L | 0-3 | 0-3 | | Sealey | Johnson R | Harvey* | Preece | Foster | Johnson M | Wilson | Wegerle | Oldfield^ | Hill | Black | Breacker/Dowie |
| | 14/1 | | 5,212 | 18 | 23 | | | Mortimer 12, Crooks 22, Williams 33 | Bolder | Humphrey | Shirtliff | Pates | Mortimer | Mackenzie | Peake | Gritt* | Lee | Crooks^ | Williams | Minto/Leaburn |
| | | | | | | | | Ref: P Jones | Ray Harford locks his players in the dressing room for an hour, after a game in which the Valiants hardly have to break into a sweat in order to record an easy win. Andy Peake controls the play from the midfield and has a hand in all of the goals. 'What a load of rubbish,' chant the fans. | | | | | | | | | | | |
| 22 | H | EVERTON | | 13 | W | 1-0 | 1-0 | Wegerle 4 | Sealey | Breacker | Grimes | Preece | Foster | Dreyer | Wilson* | Wegerle | Harford | Hill | Black^ | Johnson R/Dowie |
| | 21/1 | | 9,013 | 9 | 26 | | | | Southall | Snodin | Ratcliffe | Watson | Pointon | Nevin* | Bracewell | McCall^ | Sheedy | Clarke | Cottee | Wilson/McDonald |
| | | | | | | | | Ref: R Lewis | Wegerle takes a pass from Preece, controls the ball on his chest and then turns and shoots in one movement to give Neville Southall no chance. The Town then have 86 minutes to defend their lead which they just manage to do. Everton have now lost all four games on the artificial surface. | | | | | | | | | | | |
| 23 | H | NOTT'M FOREST | | 14 | L | 2-3 | 2-2 | Harford 19, Black 44 | Sealey | Breacker | Grimes* | Preece | Foster | Dreyer | Wilson | Wegerle | Harford | Hill | Black | Oldfield |
| | 4/2 | | 10,465 | 4 | 26 | | | Parker 18, Clough 28p, 73 | Sutton | Laws | Chettle | Wilson | Pearce | Hodge | Webb | Parker | Carr | Chapman | Clough | |
| | | | | | | | | Ref: J Ashworth | Forest make it ten league and cup wins in a row as they prove that visiting sides can play good football on the Luton pitch. Although fortunate to be level at half-time, the Town reorganise and then appear to be more in control but Nigel Clough secures the points with a 25-yard free-kick. | | | | | | | | | | | |
| 24 | H | MIDDLESBROUGH | | 13 | W | 1-0 | 0-0 | Foster 55 | Sealey | Breacker | Grimes | Preece | Foster | **Beaumont** | Wilson | Wegerle | Harford | Hill | Black | |
| | 18/2 | | 8,187 | 12 | 29 | | | | Poole | Parkinson | Mowbray | Pallister | Cooper | Hamilton | Gill* | Slaven | Ripley | Brennan^ | Kerr | Burke/Kernaghan |
| | | | | | | | | Ref: B Hill | A single goal, headed in by skipper Steve Foster from a David Preece corner, flatters Bruce Rioch's Middlesbrough. Only heroics from Kevin Poole saves the visitors from a much heavier defeat. Dave Beaumont, a new signing from Dundee United, makes his home debut for the Hatters | | | | | | | | | | | |
| 25 | A | ARSENAL | | 14 | L | 0-2 | 0-0 | | Sealey | Breacker | Harvey | Preece* | Foster | Beaumont | Wilson | Wegerle | Harford | Hill | Black | Oldfield |
| | 25/2 | | 31,026 | 1 | 29 | | | Groves 62, Smith 89 | Lukic | O'Leary | Bould | Adams | Winterburn | Rocastle* | Richardson | Thomas | Marwood | Groves | Smith | Merson |
| | | | | | | | | Ref: J Deakin | A sound defensive performance against the league leaders is undone when Perry Groves scores with an overhead kick. The Town have to open up the game and come close to equalising before Alan Smith clinches the points with a header from a Brian Marwood cross in the final minute. | | | | | | | | | | | |
| 26 | H | MILLWALL | | 15 | L | 1-2 | 0-2 | Wilson 54p | Sealey | Breacker | Grimes | Preece* | McDonough | Beaumont | Wilson | Wegerle^ | Harford | Hill | Black | Dowie /Dreyer |
| | 11/3 | | 10,722 | 3 | 29 | | | Carter 24, 30 | Horne | McLeary | Sparham | Hurlock | Thompson | Wood | Carter | Briley | Sheringham | Cascarino | O'Callaghan | |
| | | | | | | | | Ref: J Worrall | McDonough makes his first full appearance for almost a year but is powerless to prevent Carter from scoring two goals. Manager Ray Harford changes things around at half-time and the Town are awarded a penalty, which Wilson converts, after David Preece is fouled by Terry Hurlock | | | | | | | | | | | |
| 27 | A | LIVERPOOL | | 15 | L | **0-5** | 0-2 | [McMahon 74] | Sealey | Breacker | Grimes | Preece* | Johnson M | Beaumont | Wilson | McDonough | Harford | Hill | Black | Dowie |
| | 14/3 | | 31,447 | 2 | 29 | | | Aldridge 34, 41, 72p, Beardsley 69, | Grobbelaar | Nicol | Gillespie* | Ablett | Staunton | Houghton | McMahon | Whelan | Barnes^ | Beardsley | Aldridge | Burrows/Watson |
| | | | | | | | | Ref: A Seville | Steve Foster is absent through suspension and is sorely missed as the Hatters are totally overwhelmed by a rampant Liverpool side, playing at the top of their form. Les Sealey has little to do, apart from picking the ball out of the net, as the Reds seem to make most of their efforts count. | | | | | | | | | | | |
| 28 | H | SHEFFIELD WED | | 16 | L | 0-1 | 0-0 | | Sealey | Breacker | Grimes* | Preece^ | Foster | Beaumont | Wilson | McDonough | Harford | Hill | Black | Harvey/Dowie |
| | 18/3 | | **7,776** | 17 | 29 | | | Hirst 49 | Turner | Harper | Pearson | Madden* | Rostron^ | Proctor | McCall | Palmer | Worthingt'n | Whitton | Hirst | Varadi/Galvin |
| | | | | | | | | Ref: D Reeves | In a battle between two sides who are both perilously close to the relegation places, a loose pass from Steve Foster lets in David Hirst to volley the ball with great power past a helpless Luton keeper, Les Sealey. The Town have again failed to turn their match dominance in to vital goals. | | | | | | | | | | | |
| 29 | A | QP RANGERS | | 15 | D | 1-1 | 0-0 | Hill 65 | Sealey | Breacker | Harvey | McDonough | Foster | Beaumont | Wilson | **Meade*** | Harford | Hill | Black | Dowie |
| | 21/3 | | 9,072 | 13 | 30 | | | Clarke 66 | Seaman | Parker | Fereday | McDonald | Maddix | Spackman | Reid | Allen | Stein | Clarke | Gray* | Barker |
| | | | | | | | | Ref: J Key | Rangers control the game in the first half but lack ideas in front of goal. Hatters then come to life and Hill shoots into the far corner with a low drive. The home side level within a minute, when Colin Clarke hammers in a 20-yard shot. Luton gain their first away point since Boxing Day. | | | | | | | | | | | |
| 30 | A | MANCHESTER U | | 16 | L | 0-2 | 0-2 | | Sealey | Breacker | Harvey | McDonough | Foster | Beaumont | Wilson* | Preece^ | Harford | Hill | Black | **Cooke**/Dowie |
| | 25/3 | | **36,335** | 8 | 30 | | | Milne 3, Blackmore 25 | Leighton | Martin | Blackmore | Bruce | McGrath | Donaghy | Robson | Beardsmore* | McClair | Hughes | Milne | Maiorana |
| | | | | | | | | Ref: R Nixon | It is now over 30 years since the Town last scored a goal at Old Trafford, a ground where they have never won. Preece attempts to clear but the ball goes to Milne for a simple goal and, after Blackmore runs onto a through ball from McClair to hit the second, United coast to an easy win. | | | | | | | | | | | |

| No | Venue | Opponent | Att | Pos | Res | Pts | FT | HT | Scorers, Times, and Referees | 1 | 2 | 3 | 4 | 5 | 6 | 7 | 8 | 9 | 10 | 11 | Subs used |
|---|---|---|---|---|---|---|---|---|---|---|---|---|---|---|---|---|---|---|---|---|---|
| 31 | H | TOTTENHAM | | 17 | L | | 1-3 | 1-0 | Foster 42 | Sealey | Breacker | Grimes | Preece | Foster | Beaumont | McDonough | Dowie* | Harford | Hill | Black | Cooke |
| | 28/3 | | 11,146 | *7* | | 30 | | | *Howells 55, Walsh 82, Gascoigne 89* | *Thorstvedt* | *Fenwick* | *Butters* | *Mabbutt* | *Hughton* | *Gascoigne* | *Howells* | *Allen* | *Walsh* | *Waddle* | *Stewart* | |
| | | | | | | | | | Ref: D Elleray | Steve Foster hits the Hatters into the lead but David Howells takes advantage of a lucky bounce to equalise. Paul Walsh follows up on a shot which rebounds off a post and Paul Gascoigne gets the third in the final minute. Luton have only gained one point from their last seven games. | | | | | | | | | | | |
| 32 | A | ASTON VILLA | | 18 | L | | 1-2 | 1-2 | Hill 26 | Sealey | Breacker | Grimes* | Wilson | Foster | Beaumont | McDono'gh^ | Wegerle | Harford | Hill | Black | Dreyer/Meade |
| | 1/4 | | *15,640* | *14* | | 30 | | | *Daley 2, Olney 35* | *Spink* | *Price* | *Keown* | *Sims* | *Evans* | *Callaghan* | *Gray* | *Cowans* | *Daley** | *Platt* | *McInally* | *Olney* |
| | | | | | | | | | Ref: S Lodge | A superb save from goalkeeper Nigel Spink, together with the woodwork, prevent the Town from achieving a comfortable victory. The winner for Villa comes from Luton-born Ian Olney. The Town will be playing in the Littlewoods Cup final but are now firmly in the relegation zone. | | | | | | | | | | | |
| 33 | H | COVENTRY | | 18 | D | | 2-2 | 0-0 | Dreyer 54, Wilson 75 | **Chamberl'n** | Breacker | Dreyer | Preece | Foster | Beaumont | Wilson | Wegerle | Meade* | Hill | Black | Cooke |
| | 15/4 | | 8,610 | *7* | | 31 | | | *Regis 70, Smith 80* | *Ogrizovic* | *Borrows* | *Rodger* | *Downs* | *Dobson* | *Phillips* | *Emerson** | *Sedgley* | *Smith* | *Speedie* | *Regis* | *Bannister* |
| | | | | | | | | | Ref: D Hedges | Dreyer heads his first goal for the club following a corner by Preece, but Cyrille Regis gets a lucky deflection off Foster to equalise. A penalty is awarded for handball which Wilson nets at the second attempt, only for David Smith to head the equaliser after a mix-up in the Town defence. | | | | | | | | | | | |
| 34 | A | NEWCASTLE | | 18 | D | | 0-0 | 0-0 | | Chamberlain | Breacker | Dreyer | Preece | Foster | Beaumont | Wilson | Wegerle* | Harford | Hill | Black^ | Meade/McDonough |
| | 22/4 | | *18,636* | *19* | | 32 | | | | *Kelly* | *Kristensen** | *Sansom* | *McCreery* | *Scott* | *Roeder* | *Hendrie* | *Sweeney* | *Thorn* | *O'Neill^* | *Brock* | *Whart'n/Mirandinha* |
| | | | | | | | | | Ref: M Peck | A relegation dog-fight at St James' Park ends all square, as the Town put on a committed performance against a disjointed home side but lack finishing power in front of goal. 'We need to win our final three home games,' summarises the Luton manager, Ray Harford, after the match. | | | | | | | | | | | |
| 35 | H | DERBY | | 18 | W | | 3-0 | 1-0 | Wilson 2p, Harford 63, Black 82 | Chamberlain | Breacker | Dreyer | Preece | Foster | Beaumont | Wilson* | Wegerle | Harford | Hill | Black | Cooke |
| | 29/4 | | 8,507 | *7* | | 35 | | | | *Shilton* | *Blades* | *Wright !* | *Hindmarch* | *Forsyth* | *Williams* | *McMinn* | *Hebberd** | *Micklewhite* | *Goddard^* | *Saunders* | *Cross/Gee* |
| | | | | | | | | | Ref: J Carter | Mick Harford puts on an inspired performance against two England defenders, Wright and Shilton. An early penalty is awarded when Shilton brings down Preece, which Wilson converts. Wright is sent off for disputing another penalty, awarded in the last minute, which is then saved. | | | | | | | | | | | |
| 36 | H | CHARLTON | | 17 | W | | 5-2 | 4-0 | Wilson 11, 42, Black 24, Harford 44, | Chamberlain | Breacker | Dreyer | Preece | Foster | Beaumont | Wilson | Wegerle | Harford | Hill | Black* | Cooke |
| | 2/5 | | 10,024 | *18* | | 38 | | | *Jones 70, 82* [Wegerle 77] | *Bolder* | *Humphrey* | *Caton** | *Shirtliff* | *Pates* | *Reid* | *Walsh* | *Mackenzie* | *Mortimer* | *Lee* | *Crooks^* | *Williams/Jones* |
| | | | | | | | | | Ref: T Holbrook | Lennie Lawrence, manager of fellow strugglers Charlton, tries three different players at centre-half against Mick Harford, who has a hand in all of the goals. The Town put on their best performance of the season and new coach Terry Mancini is praised for lifting the spirits of the team. | | | | | | | | | | | |
| 37 | A | WEST HAM | | 17 | L | | 0-1 | 0-1 | | Chamberlain | Breacker | Dreyer | Preece | Foster | Beaumont | Wilson | Wegerle | Harford | Hill | Black* | Cooke |
| | 6/5 | | *18,686* | *19* | | 38 | | | *Dickens 15* | *Parkes* | *Parris* | *Gale** | *Martin* | *Dicks* | *Dickens* | *Keen* | *Ince* | *Ward* | *Rosenior^* | *Slater* | *Potts/Kelly* |
| | | | | | | | | | Ref: L Shapter | The Hatters have the worst away record in Division 1 and let the Hammers take full advantage in another basement battle. Dickens opens the scoring when he runs through a square defence and onto a through pass from Keen. Apart from a late flurry, the Town are always second best. | | | | | | | | | | | |
| 38 | H | NORWICH | | 16 | W | | 1-0 | 0-0 | Wilson 62p | Chamberlain | Breacker | Dreyer | Preece | Foster | Beaumont | Wilson | Wegerle | Harford | Hill | Black | |
| | 13/5 | | 10,862 | *4* | | 41 | | | | *Gunn* | *Culverhouse* | *Butterw'rth* | *Phelan** | *Putney* | *Gordon^* | *Townsend* | *Crook* | *Cook* | *Fleck* | *Rosario* | *Coney/Allen* |
| Average | Home 9,504 | | Away 17,946 | | | | | | Ref: M Bailey | In a tense game, the Town have the advantage of an early penalty but Wilson blasts the spot-kick wide. Mick Harford sees a header hit the post before a second penalty is awarded for Rosario's push on Harford. Wilson makes no mistake this time and the Hatters are safe for another year. | | | | | | | | | | | |

# BARCLAYS DIVISION 1 (CUP-TIES) Manager: Ray Harford SEASON 1988-89



| Littlewoods Cup | F-A | H-T | Scorers, Times, and Referees | 1 | 2 | 3 | 4 | 5 | 6 | 7 | 8 | 9 | 10 | 11 | subs used |
|---|---|---|---|---|---|---|---|---|---|---|---|---|---|---|---|
| 2:1 H BURNLEY 15 | 1-1 | 1-1 | Johnson R 39 | Sealey | Johnson R* | Dreyer | Williams | Foster | Donaghy | Wilson | Oldfield | Harford | Hill | Black | Breacker |
| 27/9 6,282 *4:3* | | | *Comstive 42p* | *Pearce* | *Daniel* | *Davis* | *Gardner* | *Farrell* | *Britton* | *Rowell* | *Comstive* | *Atkinson* | *Oghani* | *O'Connell* | |
| | | | Ref: J Carter | Captain Steve Foster needs 11 stitches in a head wound but, covered in blood, stays on until the end of the game. In a frantic display by the Town, full-back Johnson opens the scoring with his first goal for the club but then spoils it by tripping Paul Comstive, who nets from the spot. | | | | | | | | | | | |
| 2:2 A BURNLEY 13 | 1-0 | 0-0 | Hill 53 | Sealey | Johnson R* | Dreyer | Williams | Foster | Donaghy | Wilson | Oldfield^ | Harford | Hill | Black | Breacker/Allinson |
| 11/10 *14,036* *4:1* | | | | *Pearce* | *Daniel* | *Zelem* | *Gardner* | *Farrell* | *Britton* | *Rowell* | *Comstive* | *Atkinson* | *O'Connell* | *Oghani* | |
| | | | Ref: P Wright (Hatters won 2-1 on aggregate) | Fired-up Burnley are boosted by a big crowd at Turf Moor and put the Town defence under a great deal of pressure. A simple goal from Ricky Hill, after a scramble in the area, is enough to settle the tie, however. Steve Foster has another six stitches inserted, this time in a gashed thigh. | | | | | | | | | | | |
| 3 A LEEDS 16 | 2-0 | 1-0 | Wilson 29, Oldfield 65 | Sealey | James ! | Dreyer | Williams | Foster | Johnson M | Wilson | Oldfield | Wegerle | Hill | Black | |
| 2/11 *19,450* *2:21* | | | | *Day* | *Aspin* | *Blake* | *Rennie* | *Snodin* | *Sheridan* | *Batty* | *Aizlewood* | *Hilaire* | *Davison* | *Baird* | |
| | | | Ref: N Midgley | Harford, Johnson and Breacker are all missing through injury as the Hatters score a classic breakaway goal, with Danny Wilson hitting a shot from 25 yards past Mervyn Day. David Oldfield hits the second, before 18-year-old Julian James is dismissed for bringing down Ian Baird. | | | | | | | | | | | |
| 4 H MANCHESTER C 15 | 3-1 | 2-1 | Oldfield 16, Wegerle 21, 86 | Sealey | Johnson R | Harvey | Preece | Foster | Johnson M | Wilson | Wegerle | Harford* | Oldfield | Black | Hill |
| 29/11 10,178 *2:3* | | | *White 8* | *Dibble* | *Seagraves* | *Gayle* | *Redmond* | *Gleghorn* | *Scott** | *McNab* | *White* | *Morley* | *Moulden* | *Biggins* | *Beckford* |
| | | | Ref: D Hedges | David White volleys City into an early lead but Roy Wegerle puts on an unstoppable display, scoring twice and seeing a third shot saved by Andy Dibble, only for David Oldfield to follow up to tap the ball in. It is not a happy return for goalkeeper Dibble, last year's Wembley hero. | | | | | | | | | | | |
| QF H SOUTHAMPTON 16 | 1-1 | 0-0 | Hill 70 | Sealey | Breacker | Grimes | Preece | Foster | Dreyer | Wilson | Wegerle | Dowie | Hill | Black | |
| 18/1 11,735 *1:13* | | | *Cockerill 79* | *Burridge* | *Wallace Ray* | *Blake* | *Moore* | *Cook* | *Rideout* | *Cockerill* | *Case* | *Baker* | *Wallace D* | *Wallace Rod* | |
| | | | Ref: A Gunn | In a drab game, played on a slippery surface, the Hatters cannot find the form which saw them put six past the Saints only three weeks ago. A flying header from Hill seems to have won the game but Glenn Cockerill fires in a spectacular long-range effort to take the tie back to the Dell. | | | | | | | | | | | |
| 5R A SOUTHAMPTON 13 | 2-1 | 0-0 | Harford 100, Hill 108 | Sealey | Breacker | Grimes | Preece | Foster | Dreyer | Wilson | Wegerle | Harford* | Hill | Black | Oldfield |
| 25/1 *18,872* *1:15* | *aet* | | *Wallace Rod 118* | *Burridge* | *Wallace Ray!* | *Moore* | *Osman* | *Cook* | *Baker* | *Case** | *Cockerill* | *Wallace D* | *Rideout^* | *Wallace Rod* | *Benali/Le Tissier* |
| | | | Ref: A Ward | The Saints exert a great deal of pressure but the Town defence holds firm. Harford breaks the deadlock in extra-time when he bravely heads the ball home and Hill then lashes a 20-yard shot past Burridge for the killer blow. Ray Wallace is sent off in the final minute for a foul on Black. | | | | | | | | | | | |
| SF 1 A WEST HAM 14 | 3-0 | 1-0 | Harford 44, Wegerle 55, Wilson 75p | Sealey | Breacker | Grimes | Preece | Foster | Beaumont | Wilson | Wegerle | Harford | Hill | Black | |
| 12/2 *24,602* *1:20* | | | | *McKnight* | *Potts* | *Gale* | *Martin* | *Dicks* | *Devonshire* | *Ince* | *Dickens* | *Brady** | *Ward* | *Rosenior* | *Kelly* |
| | | | Ref: G Courtney | Allen McKnight is blamed for the first two Luton goals but Mick Harford and Roy Wegerle are at the top of their form. Full-back Julian Dicks brings down Wegerle, leaving Danny Wilson to score from the spot to make the second leg a foregone conclusion. Beaumont makes his debut. | | | | | | | | | | | |
| SF 2 H WEST HAM 14 | 2-0 | 1-0 | Harford 43, Wegerle 55 | Sealey | Breacker | Grimes | Preece | Foster | Beaumont | Wilson | Wegerle | Harford | Hill | Black | |
| 1/3 12,020 *1:20* | | | | *Parkes* | *Potts* | *Gale* | *Martin* | *Dicks* | *Ward* | *Kelly* | *Parris* | *Slater* | *Brady* | *Ince* | |
| | | | Ref: D Axcell (Hatters won 5-0 on aggregate) | Veteran goalkeeper, Phil Parkes, takes over between the sticks for the visitors but strikes from Mick Harford and Roy Wegerle steer the Hatters to a comfortable victory. Thousands of fans pour on to the pitch at the end, but most of the celebrating had already been done after the first leg. | | | | | | | | | | | |
| F A NOTT'M FOREST 18 | 1-3 | 1-0 | Harford 35 | Sealey | Breacker | Grimes* | Preece | Foster | Beaumont | Wilson | Wegerle | Harford | Hill | Black | McDonough |
| 9/4 76,130 *1:4* | | | *Clough 53p, 76, Webb 68* | *Sutton* | *Laws* | *Walker* | *Wilson* | *Pearce* | *Gaynor* | *Webb* | *Hodge* | *Parker* | *Clough* | *Chapman* | |
| (at Wembley) | | | Ref: R Milford | A header from Mick Harford puts the Town in the driving seat but the game turns on a second-half penalty decision when Les Sealey needlessly brings down Steve Hodge and Nigel Clough levels from the spot. The goal lifts Forest who go on to win the game and lift the Littlewoods Cup. | | | | | | | | | | | |

| FA Cup | F-A | H-T | Scorers, Times, and Referees | 1 | 2 | 3 | 4 | 5 | 6 | 7 | 8 | 9 | 10 | 11 | subs used |
|---|---|---|---|---|---|---|---|---|---|---|---|---|---|---|---|
| 3 A MILLWALL 15 | 2-3 | 1-2 | Black 36, Wilson 49p | Sealey | Johnson R* | Harvey | Preece | Foster | Johnson M | Wilson | Wegerle | Harford | Hill | Black^ | James/Oldfield |
| 7/1 *12,504* *1:3* | | | *Cascarino 14, Carter 15, Sheringham 71* | *Horne* | *Stevens* | *Wood* | *McLeary* | *Salman* | *Morgan* | *Briley* | *O'Callaghan* | *Carter* | *Cascarino* | *Sheringham* | |
| | | | Ref: J Martin | After the home side score twice in a minute, Kingsley Black hits a tremendous drive in off the bar, and then Danny Wilson levels from the spot after he is brought down by Danis Salman. Teddy Sheringham puts the Lions back in front before a 28-minute stoppage for floodlight failure. | | | | | | | | | | | |

| | P | W | D | L | F | A | W | D | L | F | A | Pts |
|---|---|---|---|---|---|---|---|---|---|---|---|---|
| | | Home | | | | | Away | | | | | |
| 1 Arsenal | 38 | 10 | 6 | 3 | 35 | 19 | 12 | 4 | 3 | 38 | 17 | 76 |
| 2 Liverpool | 38 | 11 | 5 | 3 | 33 | 11 | 11 | 5 | 3 | 32 | 17 | 76 |
| 3 Nott'm Forest | 38 | 8 | 7 | 4 | 31 | 16 | 9 | 6 | 4 | 33 | 27 | 64 |
| 4 Norwich | 38 | 8 | 7 | 4 | 23 | 20 | 9 | 4 | 6 | 25 | 25 | 62 |
| 5 Derby | 38 | 9 | 3 | 7 | 23 | 18 | 8 | 4 | 7 | 17 | 20 | 58 |
| 6 Tottenham | 38 | 8 | 6 | 5 | 31 | 24 | 7 | 6 | 6 | 29 | 22 | 57 |
| 7 Coventry | 38 | 9 | 4 | 6 | 28 | 23 | 5 | 9 | 5 | 19 | 19 | 55 |
| 8 Everton | 38 | 10 | 7 | 2 | 33 | 18 | 4 | 5 | 10 | 17 | 27 | 54 |
| 9 QP Rangers | 38 | 9 | 5 | 5 | 23 | 16 | 5 | 6 | 8 | 20 | 21 | 53 |
| 10 Millwall | 38 | 10 | 3 | 6 | 27 | 21 | 4 | 8 | 7 | 20 | 31 | 53 |
| 11 Manchester U | 38 | 10 | 5 | 4 | 27 | 13 | 3 | 7 | 9 | 18 | 22 | 51 |
| 12 Wimbledon | 38 | 10 | 3 | 6 | 30 | 19 | 4 | 6 | 9 | 20 | 27 | 51 |
| 13 Southampton | 38 | 6 | 7 | 6 | 25 | 26 | 4 | 8 | 7 | 27 | 40 | 45 |
| 14 Charlton | 38 | 6 | 7 | 6 | 25 | 24 | 4 | 5 | 10 | 19 | 34 | 42 |
| 15 Sheffield Wed | 38 | 6 | 6 | 7 | 21 | 25 | 4 | 6 | 9 | 13 | 26 | 42 |
| 16 LUTON TOWN | 38 | 8 | 6 | 5 | 32 | 21 | 2 | 5 | 12 | 10 | 31 | 41 |
| 17 Aston Villa | 38 | 7 | 6 | 6 | 25 | 22 | 2 | 7 | 10 | 20 | 34 | 40 |
| 18 Middlesbro | 38 | 6 | 7 | 6 | 28 | 30 | 3 | 5 | 11 | 16 | 31 | 39 |
| 19 West Ham | 38 | 3 | 6 | 10 | 19 | 30 | 7 | 2 | 10 | 18 | 32 | 38 |
| 20 Newcastle | 38 | 3 | 6 | 10 | 19 | 28 | 4 | 4 | 11 | 13 | 35 | 31 |
| | 760 | 157 | 112 | 111 | 538 | 424 | 111 | 112 | 157 | 424 | 538 | 1028 |

Odds & ends

Double wins: (2) Derby, Everton.
Double losses: (3) Manchester United, Millwall, Sheffield Wednesday.

Won from behind: (1) Manchester City (LC).
Lost from in front: (1) Tottenham (h), Nottingham Forest (LC).

High spots: Winning the last three home games of the season to stay up.
Reaching the Littlewoods Cup final for the second year running.
The mid-season form of Roy Wegerle.
Beating Southampton 6-1 at Kenilworth Road.

Low spots: The poor away record.
Losing at Wembley to Nottingham Forest.
The sale of Mal Donaghy to Manchester United.
The departure of Ricky Hill.

Player of the Year: Mick Harford.
Ever-presents: (0).
Hat-tricks: (0).
Leading scorer: (12) Roy Wegerle and Danny Wilson.

| | Appearances | | | | | | Goals | | | |
|---|---|---|---|---|---|---|---|---|---|---|
| | Lge | *Sub* | LC | *Sub* | FAC | *Sub* | Lge | LC | FAC | Tot |
| Allinson, Ian | **1** | *4* | | *1* | | | | | | |
| Beaumont, David | **15** | | 3 | | | | | | | |
| Black, Kingsley | **36** | *1* | 9 | | 1 | | **9** | | 1 | **10** |
| Breacker, Tim | **19** | *3* | 5 | *2* | | | | | | |
| Chamberlain, Alec | **6** | | | | | | | | | |
| Cooke, Richard | | *6* | | | | | | | | |
| Donaghy, Mal | **6** | | 2 | | | | | | | |
| Dowie, Iain | **1** | *7* | 1 | | | | | | | |
| Dreyer, John | **16** | *2* | 5 | | | | **1** | | | **1** |
| Foster, Steve | **36** | | 9 | | 1 | | **3** | | | **3** |
| Grimes, Ashley | **12** | | 5 | | | | | | | |
| Harford, Mick | **33** | | 7 | | 1 | | **7** | 4 | | **11** |
| Harvey, Richard | **11** | *1* | 1 | | 1 | | | | | |
| Hill, Ricky | **33** | | 8 | *1* | 1 | | **3** | 3 | | **6** |
| James, Julian | **1** | | 1 | | | *1* | | | | |
| Johnson, Marvin | **16** | | 2 | | 1 | | | | | |
| Johnson, Rob | **19** | *2* | 3 | | 1 | | | 1 | | **1** |
| McDonough, Darron | **9** | *1* | | *1* | | | | | | |
| Meade, Rafael | **2** | *2* | | | | | | | | |
| Oldfield, David | **15** | *6* | 4 | *1* | | *1* | **1** | 2 | | **3** |
| Preece, David | **26** | | 6 | | 1 | | | | | |
| Sealey, Les | **32** | | 9 | | 1 | | | | | |
| Wegerle, Roy | **26** | *4* | 7 | | 1 | | **8** | 4 | | **12** |
| Williams, Steve | **10** | | 3 | | | | | | | |
| Wilson, Danny | **37** | | 9 | | 1 | | **9** | 2 | 1 | **12** |
| (own-goals) | | | | | | | **1** | | | **1** |
| **25 players used** | **418** | ***39*** | **99** | ***6*** | **11** | ***2*** | **42** | **16** | **2** | **60** |

| No | Date | | Att | Pos | Pt | F-A | H-T | Scorers, Times, and Referees | 1 | 2 | 3 | 4 | 5 | 6 | 7 | 8 | 9 | 10 | 11 | subs used |
|---|---|---|---|---|---|---|---|---|---|---|---|---|---|---|---|---|---|---|---|---|
| 1 | A | TOTTENHAM | | | L | 1-2 | 0-1 | Wegerle 46 | Chamberlain | Breacker | Dreyer | Williams* | McDonough | Beaumont | **Kennedy** | Wegerle | Wilson | Preece^ | Black | Harvey/Dowie |
| | 19/8 | | *17,668* | | | | | *Stewart 29, Allen 80* | *Thorstvedt* | *Bergsson* | *Fenwick* | *Mabbutt* | *Butters* | *Allen* | *Gascoigne** | *Howells* | *Samways^* | *Stewart* | *Lineker* | *Walsh/Sedgley* |
| | | | | | | | | Ref: T Holbrook | In front of a restricted crowd, due to ground redevelopment, Luton go a goal down when Stewart heads past Chamberlain from a Gascoigne free-kick. Roy Wegerle levels with a superb volley from a cross by Kennedy but, with the game heading for a draw, Paul Allen hits the winner. | | | | | | | | | | | |
| 2 | H | SHEFFIELD WED | | | W | 2-0 | 1-0 | Wilson 44p, Black 62 | Chamberlain | Breacker | Dreyer | Williams | McDonough | Beaumont | Kennedy | Wegerle | Wilson | Preece | Black* | **Farrell** |
| | 22/8 | | 9,503 | | 3 | | | | *Turner* | *Fee* | *Worthingt'n* | *Palmer* | *Pearson* | *Madden* | *Taylor* | *Harper** | *Atkinson* | *Hirst* | *Shak'speare* | *Bennett* |
| | | | | | | | | Ref: D Axcell | Roy Wegerle, who is currently going through a purple patch, is brought down in the box, leaving Danny Wilson to open the scoring from the penalty spot. He then collects a pass from Kennedy and races to the by-line before crossing to Black, who slots home his first right-footed goal. | | | | | | | | | | | |
| 3 | H | LIVERPOOL | | 10 | D | 0-0 | 0-0 | | Chamberlain | Breacker | Dreyer | Williams* | McDonough | Beaumont | Kennedy^ | Wegerle | Wilson | Preece | Black | **Elstrup**/Harvey |
| | 26/8 | | 11,124 | *5* | 4 | | | | *Grobbelaar* | *Gillespie* | *Hysen* | *Hansen* | *Burrows* | *Nicol* | *Whelan* | *McMahon* | *Barnes* | *Beardsley** | *Rush* | *Aldridge* |
| | | | | | | | | Ref: A Gunn | Liverpool have the better chances, although the Town play well as a unit with Chamberlain having a good game. Elstrup, a record signing for the Hatters, comes on as substitute but is not given long enough to make an impression on the game. Aldridge hits the post in the final minute. | | | | | | | | | | | |
| 4 | A | QP RANGERS | | 11 | D | 0-0 | 0-0 | | Chamberlain | Breacker | Dreyer | Williams | McDonough | Beaumont | Kennedy | Wegerle | Wilson | Preece | Black* | Elstrup |
| | 30/8 | | *10,565* | *8* | 5 | | | | *Seaman* | *Channing* | *Parker* | *McDonald* | *Sansom* | *Spackman* | *Reid** | *Sinton* | *Stein^* | *Clarke* | *Wright* | *Barker/Falco* |
| | | | | | | | | Ref: J Deakin | Rangers have the better chances but are let down by poor finishing, though Chamberlain is in top form, and makes two vital saves. The Hatters rarely threaten, but Danny Wilson blazes wide with a volley when well positioned. The only corner gained by the Town comes in injury-time. | | | | | | | | | | | |
| 5 | H | CHARLTON | | 7 | W | 1-0 | 0-0 | Wilson 59p | Chamberlain | Breacker | Dreyer | Wilson | McDonough | Beaumont | Kennedy | Wegerle | Elstrup | Preece | Black | |
| | 9/9 | | 8,859 | *10* | 8 | | | | *Bolder* | *Humphrey* | *McLaughlin* | *Pates* | *Reid* | *Lee* | *Peake* | *Walsh* | *Mortimer* | *Williams* | *Jones** | *Mackenzie* |
| | | | | | | | | Ref: R Nixon | Charlton's unbeaten start to the season is brought to an end in a fiercely competitive fixture in which neither side gains the upper hand. The game is settled by a Wilson penalty, awarded when Wegerle is shoved in the area by Reid, as the Town keep their fourth clean sheet in a row. | | | | | | | | | | | |
| 6 | A | COVENTRY | | 8 | L | 0-1 | 0-1 | | Chamberlain | Breacker | Dreyer | Wilson | McDon'ugh* | Beaumont | Kennedy | Wegerle | Elstrup | Preece^ | Black | Harvey/Cooke |
| | 16/9 | | *11,207* | *3* | 8 | | | *Bannister 17* | *Waugh* | *Borrows* | *Kilcline* | *Peake* | *Dobson* | *Gynn* | *Emerson* | *Speedie* | *McGuire** | *Regis^* | *Bannister* | *Macdonald/Liv'stone* |
| | | | | | | | | Ref: J Ashworth | The Sky Blues take the lead when Gary Bannister takes a pass from Micky Gynn in his stride and slots the ball home. The Town have the better of the second half and gain a penalty after a clumsy challenge by Trevor Peake on Roy Wegerle, but Danny Wilson blazes his spot-kick wide. | | | | | | | | | | | |
| 7 | H | WIMBLEDON | | 10 | D | 1-1 | 1-1 | Wegerle 34p | Chamberlain | Breacker | Dreyer | Wilson | McDon'ugh* | Beaumont | Kennedy ! | Wegerle | Elstrup^ | Preece | Black | Harvey/Cooke |
| | 23/9 | | 8,449 | *15* | 9 | | | *Kruszynski 28* | *Segers* | *Curle* | *Young* | *Scales* | *Phelan* | *Wise* | *Kruszynski** | *Ryan* | *Fairweather* | *Gibson* | *Fashanu^* | *Sanchez/Gayle* |
| | | | | | | | | Ref: K Hackett | In a bad-tempered clash, McDonough is carried off with a dislocated shoulder and Mick Kennedy is sent off after clashing with John Fashanu. Detzi Kruszynski nets with a simple strike before Wegerle equalises when a spot-kick is retaken, Danny Wilson having missed the first attempt. | | | | | | | | | | | |
| 8 | A | MANCHESTER C | | 13 | L | 1-3 | 1-2 | Black 43 | Chamberlain | Breacker | Dreyer | Wilson | Harvey | Beaumont | Kennedy* | Wegerle | Elstrup^ | Preece | Black | Johnson/Cooke |
| | 30/9 | | *23,863* | *10* | 9 | | | *Oldfield 11, Bishop 44, Brightwell 59* | *Cooper* | *Fleming* | *Redmond* | *Gayle* | *Hinchcliffe* | *White* | *Brightwell* | *Lake** | *Bishop* | *Morley* | *Oldfield* | *McNab* |
| | | | | | | | | Ref: R Milford | Fresh from the thrashing of their neighbours at United, City have a field day with David White unstoppable on the wing. He sets up all three of the goals, the first coming from David Oldfield with a flying header. Wegerle has his spot-kick saved by that ace penalty stopper, Paul Cooper. | | | | | | | | | | | |
| 9 | H | ASTON VILLA | | 16 | L | 0-1 | 0-1 | | Chamberlain | Breacker | Dreyer | Wilson | **Rodger*** | Beaumont | Williams | Wegerle^ | Elstrup | Preece | Black | Harvey/Cooke |
| | 14/10 | | 9,433 | *10* | 9 | | | *Mountfield 44* | *Spink* | *Price* | *Nielson* | *Mountfield* | *Gallacher** | *Blake* | *Cowans* | *Gray* | *Platt* | *Olney* | *Heath^* | *Daley/Birch* |
| | | | | | | | | Ref: P Don | Manager Ray Harford is booed from the pitch at the end of the game as the Town fail to trouble the Villa defence and tamely surrender their unbeaten home record. Roy Wegerle damages his ankle ligaments early on but limps on until half-time. Derek Mountfield taps in the only goal. | | | | | | | | | | | |
| 10 | H | NORWICH | | 12 | W | **4-1** | 1-0 | Black 4, Dreyer 54, Wilson 65, | Chamberlain | Breacker | Dreyer | Wilson | Rodger* | Beaumont | Williams | Wegerle | Elstrup | Preece | Black^ | Harvey/Dowie |
| | 21/10 | | 9,038 | *6* | 12 | | | *Allen 83p* [Williams 76] | *Gunn* | *Sherwood* | *Butterw'rth* | *Linighan* | *Bowen* | *Fox** | *Phillips* | *Crook* | *Gordon* | *Fleck^* | *Rosario* | *Goss/Allen* |
| | | | | | | | | Ref: B Stevens/J Coaten | The Town, firing on all cylinders, take the lead with a deflected shot from Black. Steve Williams completes the rout with his first goal for two years, hitting home a pass from the impressive Lars Elstrup. A push by Dreyer on Jeremy Goss gives Malcolm Allen a consolation from the spot. | | | | | | | | | | | |

| | | | | | | | | | | | | | | | | | | | |
|---|---|---|---|---|---|---|---|---|---|---|---|---|---|---|---|---|---|---|---|
| 11 | A | MILLWALL | 14 | D | 1-1 | 1-1 | Elstrup 42 | Chamberlain | Breacker | Dreyer | Wilson | McDon'ugh* | Beaumont | Williams | Wegerle^ | Elstrup | Kennedy | Black | Harvey/Dowie |
| | 28/10 | *11,140* | *10* | 13 | | | *Dawes 11* | *Horne* | *Stevens* | *Dawes* | *Hurlock* | *Wood** | *McLeary* | *Carter* | *Waddock* | *Sheringham* | *Cascarino* | *Anthrobus* | *Thompson* |
| | | | | | | | Ref: D Elleray | Wegerle limps off with another ankle injury which gives an opportunity to sub Iain Dowie, who is anxious for a run in the side after a loan spell at Fulham. He sets up Lars Elstrup for his first league goal for the club, which levels the opening goal scored by Ian Dawes for the Lions. | | | | | | | | | | | |
| 12 | H | DERBY | 11 | W | 1-0 | 0-0 | Dowie 48 | Chamberlain | Breacker | Dreyer | Wilson | Johnson | Beaumont | Williams | Dowie | Elstrup | Kennedy | Black* | Preece |
| | 4/11 | 8,919 | *17* | 16 | | | | *Shilton* | *Sage* | *Wright* | *Blades* | *Forsyth* | *Williams* | *Hebberd* | *Micklewhite* | *McMinn* | *Saunders* | *Goddard* | |
| | | | | | | | Ref: N Midgley | Ex-British Aerospace engineer Iain Dowie is the new Luton hero when he drives a centre from Kingsley Black past England goalkeeper Peter Shilton. Derby enjoy a lot of the play but the nearest they come to scoring is through a header from Mark Wright which smacks against the bar. | | | | | | | | | | | |
| 13 | A | CRYS PALACE | 10 | D | 1-1 | 0-1 | Wilson 57 | Chamberlain | Breacker | Dreyer | Wilson | Johnson | Beaumont* | Williams | Dowie | Elstrup^ | Kennedy | Black | Harvey/Wegerle |
| | 11/11 | *11,346* | *15* | 17 | | | *Bright 13* | *Parkin* | *Pemberton* | *Hopkins* | *Thomas* | *Dennis* | *McGoldrick* | *Pardew* | *Dyer* | *Gray* | *Bright* | *Wright* | |
| | | | | | | | Ref: G Courtney | Dreyer moves back into the central defence after Dave Beaumont twists his ankle. Palace open the scoring when Bright lobs Chamberlain. The Town gradually pull their way back into the match, and when Black crashes a volley against the bar Wilson is on hand to tap in the rebound. | | | | | | | | | | | |
| 14 | H | MANCHESTER U | 13 | L | 1-3 | 0-2 | Wilson 60 | Chamberlain | Breacker | Harvey | Wilson | Johnson | Dreyer | Williams* | Wegerle | Dowie | Kennedy | Black | Elstrup |
| | 18/11 | 11,414 | *9* | 17 | | | *Wallace 5, Blackmore 28, Hughes 74* | *Leighton* | *Ince* | *Bruce* | *Pallister* | *Martin* | *Robson* | *McClair* | *Phelan* | *Blackmore* | *Wallace* | *Hughes* | |
| | | | | | | | Ref: J Moules | Danny Wilson takes advantage of a slip by Jim Leighton to reduce the deficit and, although Mark Hughes scores a third from 30 yards, United are never comfortable. Dowie misses a hat-trick of chances in the closing minutes which would have rescued a point, at the least, for the Town. | | | | | | | | | | | |
| 15 | A | SOUTHAMPTON | 13 | L | **3-6** | 1-2 | Dreyer 24, Black 47, Elstrup 85 | Chamberlain | Breacker | Harvey | Wilson | Johnson* | Dreyer | Preece^ | Elstrup | Dowie | Kennedy | Black | James/Wegerle |
| | 25/11 | *14,014* | *5* | 17 | | | *Rideout 3, 84, Le T 41, Wallace 53,71,* | *Flowers* | *Dodd* | *Ruddock* | *Osman* | *Benali* | *Le Tissier* | *Cockerill* | *Case* | *Wallace* | *Shearer* | *Rideout* | |
| | | | | | | | Ref: R Groves *[Shearer 72]* | Marvin Johnson becomes the fourth Luton centre-half to limp off with an injury this season and his presence is missed as the Saints pile in the goals in the second half. The Town fight back to level twice but the policy of chasing the winner backfires, with the defence all over the place. | | | | | | | | | | | |
| 16 | H | TOTTENHAM | 15 | D | 0-0 | 0-0 | | Chamberlain | Breacker | Harvey | Wilson* | Johnson | Dreyer | Williams | Wegerle | Dowie | Kennedy | Black^ | Preece/Elstrup |
| | 2/12 | **12,620** | *11* | 18 | | | | *Thorstvedt* | *Bergsson* | *Mabbutt* | *Sedgley* | *Thomas* | *Allen* | *Howells* | *Gascoigne* | *Samways* | *Stewart* | *Lineker** | *Walsh* |
| | | | | | | | Ref: D Hedges | The supporters are calling for the head of the manager, Ray Harford, after the Town fail to beat a flu-ridden Spurs side. After the mauling of last week at Southampton, Alec Chamberlain answers his critics with a game-saving display, stopping ex-Hatter Paul Walsh in the final minute. | | | | | | | | | | | |
| 17 | A | SHEFFIELD WED | 15 | D | 1-1 | 0-1 | James 65 | Chamberlain | Breacker | Harvey | Wilson | Johnson* | Dreyer | Williams | James | Dowie | Elstrup | Preece | Cooke |
| | 9/12 | *16,339* | *18* | 19 | | | *Dreyer 16 (og)* | *Pressman* | *Nilsson* | *King* | *Palmer* | *Shirtliff* | *Pearson* | *Bennett** | *Sheridan* | *Hirst* | *Atkinson* | *Worthingt'n* | *Whitton* |
| | | | | | | | Ref: R Hart | James plays in his first game of the season and has a hand in both goals. He hammers a clearance against Dreyer which flies over the head of Chamberlain and then later heads a long cross from Williams past Kevin Pressman, to cancel out his error. Dowie misses in the final minute. | | | | | | | | | | | |
| 18 | A | ARSENAL | 18 | L | 2-3 | 1-2 | Elstrup 30, 51p | Chamberlain | Breacker | Harvey | Kennedy | Donaghy | Dreyer | Williams* | James | Dowie | Elstrup | Black^ | **Gray**/Cooke |
| | 16/12 | *28,760* | *1* | 19 | | | *Smith 19, Merson 33, Marwood 50* | *Lukic* | *Dixon* | *O'Leary* | *Adams* | *Winterburn* | *Rocastle* | *Thomas* | *Richardson* | *Marwood* | *Smith** | *Groves^* | *Merson/Jonsson* |
| | | | | | | | Ref: L Dilkes | Donaghy returns to the defence, on loan from Manchester United, due to the injury problems. Marwood nods down a free-kick from Dixon for Smith to fire in the first for the champions. Elstrup levels after a goalmouth scramble, but the match finishes in a glorious failure for the Town. | | | | | | | | | | | |
| 19 | H | NOTT'M FOREST | 17 | D | 1-1 | 0-1 | Cooke 82 | Chamberlain | Breacker | Dreyer | Kennedy | Donaghy | Johnson* | Williams | Cooke | Dowie | Elstrup^ | Black | Harvey/Harford |
| | 26/12 | 10,754 | *10* | 20 | | | *Hodge 35* | *Sutton* | *Laws* | *Walker* | *Chettle* | *Pearce* | *Crosby* | *Parker* | *Hodge* | *Orlygsson* | *Clough* | *Jemson* | |
| | | | | | | | Ref: D Vickers | Lars Elstrup limps off with a knee injury, which will require an operation, to be replaced by a partially fit Mick Harford, whose presence seems to inspire the Town. Richard Cooke, making his first full appearance since his signing from Bournemouth in March, slams home the equaliser. | | | | | | | | | | | |
| 20 | H | CHELSEA | 19 | L | 0-3 | 0-1 | | Chamberlain | Breacker | Harvey | Kennedy* | Donaghy | Dreyer | Cooke | Wilson | Dowie | Preece | Black | Harford |
| | 30/12 | 10,068 | *5* | 20 | | | *Wilson K 43, 68, Dixon 83* | *Beasant* | *Clarke* | *Roberts* | *Lee* | *Monkou* | *Dorigo* | *McAllister* | *Bumstead* | *Wilson C* | *Dixon* | *Wilson K* | |
| | | | | | | | Ref: H King | The Hatters end the decade with a disastrous performance as they enjoy 90% of the game but fail to capitalise on the possession. Kevin Wilson seizes on two opportunist headers and Kerry Dixon takes advantage of poor ball control by John Dreyer to run in the third goal for the Blues. | | | | | | | | | | | |

| No | Date | | Att | Pos | Pt | F-A | H-T | Scorers, Times, and Referees | 1 | 2 | 3 | 4 | 5 | 6 | 7 | 8 | 9 | 10 | 11 | subs used |
|---|---|---|---|---|---|---|---|---|---|---|---|---|---|---|---|---|---|---|---|---|
| 21 | A | EVERTON | | 19 | L | 1-2 | 0-2 | Wilson 68p | Chamberlain | Breacker | Harvey | Kennedy | Donaghy* | Dreyer | Wilson | James | Dowie | Preece | Gray^ | Harford/**Rees** |
| | 1/1 | | *21,755* | *8* | 20 | | | *Whiteside 2, Sharp 37* | *Southall* | *Snodin* | *Ratcliffe* | *Watson* | *McDonald* | *Nevin* | *Whiteside* | *McCall* | *Beagrie** | *Sharp* | *Newell* | *Atteveld* |
| | | | | | | | | Ref: M Peck | The Town failed to win a league game away from home during the whole of 1989 and this year starts by following the same trend. Two goals, conceded in the first half, are too much to recover from, despite a spirited performance after the interval, led by substitutes Harford and Rees. | | | | | | | | | | | |
| 22 | A | LIVERPOOL | | 19 | D | 2-2 | 0-1 | Black 70, Nogan 72 | Chamberlain | Breacker | Harvey | Kennedy | Donaghy | Dreyer | Wilson | **Nogan** | Harford | Preece | Black | |
| | 13/1 | | ***35,312*** | *1* | 21 | | | *Barnes 32, Nicol 75* | *Grobbelaar* | *Venison* | *Hysen* | *Hansen* | *Staunton** | *Nicol* | *Whelan* | *McMahon* | *Barnes* | *Beardsley* | *Rush* | *Burrows* |
| | | | | | | | | Ref: T Mills | It is all change at Kenilworth Road as Jim Ryan takes over in the hot seat from Ray Harford. Kurt Nogan makes his debut and silences the Kop when putting the Town ahead, slotting the ball past Grobbelaar from a cross by Black, but the day is spoilt when Steve Nicol powers in a header. | | | | | | | | | | | |
| 23 | H | QP RANGERS | | 19 | D | 1-1 | 1-1 | Preece 5 | Chamberlain | Breacker | Harvey | Kennedy | James | Dreyer | Wilson | Nogan | Dowie | Preece* | Black | Rees |
| | 20/1 | | 9,703 | *13* | 22 | | | *Falco 31* | *Seaman* | *Bardsley* | *Parker* | *McDonald* | *Maddix* | *Sansom* | *Wilkins* | *Barker* | *Sinton* | *Falco** | *Wegerle* | *Clarke* |
| | | | | | | | | Ref: T Simpson | Preece gets his first goal for the club for three years when following up on a block by Seaman. Falco levels when he volleys home after a slip by Dreyer. Nogan is tripped by Maddix but Wilson misses his third spot-kick of the season which leaves the Town without a win for 13 games. | | | | | | | | | | | |
| 24 | A | WIMBLEDON | | 18 | W | 2-1 | 0-0 | Nogan 51, Dowie 89 | Chamberlain | Breacker | Harvey | Kennedy | James | Dreyer | Wilson | Nogan | Dowie | Preece | Black* | Elstrup |
| | 14/2 | | ***3,618*** | *12* | 25 | | | *Wise 74* | *Segers* | *Curle* | *Young* | *Scales* | *Phelan* | *Bennett** | *Kruszynski* | *Sanchez* | *Cork* | *Gayle^* | *Wise* | *Ryan/McGee* |
| | | | | | | | | Ref: K Barratt | Nogan heads home a cross by Wilson but Dennis Wise is unmarked when he puts the Dons level. Dowie flings himself at a cross from Preece to give the Town their first away win in the league since December 1988. The game is played in front of the lowest post-war Division 1 crowd. | | | | | | | | | | | |
| 25 | A | CHARLTON | | 18 | L | 0-2 | 0-1 | | Chamberlain | Breacker | Harvey | Kennedy ! | James | Dreyer | Wilson | Nogan | Dowie* | Preece | Black^ | Elstrup/Johnson |
| | 19/2 | | *6,201* | *20* | 25 | | | *Jones 12, Walsh 77* | *Bolder* | *Humphrey* | *McLaughlin* | *Caton* | *Minto* | *Lee* | *Peake* | *Walsh** | *Williams* | *Jones* | *Mortimer* | *Mackenzie* |
| | | | | | | | | Ref: R Gifford | Andy Jones heads past Chamberlain to open the scoring for the Valiants but, after Mick Kennedy is dismissed for a high challenge on Andy Peake in the 64th minute, the game is as good as over. Charlton waste chances before Colin Walsh lobs Chamberlain from the edge of the box. | | | | | | | | | | | |
| 26 | H | SOUTHAMPTON | | 18 | D | 1-1 | 1-1 | Dowie 3 | Chamberlain | Breacker | Harvey | Kennedy* | James | Dreyer | Wilson | Nogan | Dowie | Preece | Black | Rees |
| | 24/2 | | 9,417 | *10* | 26 | | | *Shearer 44* | *Flowers* | *Case !* | *Dodd* | *Moore* | *Osman* | *Benali* | *Horne* | *Cockerill* | *Shearer* | *Rideout* | *Wallace** | *Maddison* |
| | | | | | | | | Ref: P Don | Iain Dowie puts the Town in front with a header but, when Jimmy Case is sent off for elbowing Mick Kennedy just before half-time, the away side appear to be stimulated by this loss and equalise through Alan Shearer. A fierce shot from Julian James in the second half hits the crossbar. | | | | | | | | | | | |
| 27 | A | MANCHESTER U | | 18 | L | 1-4 | 0-3 | Black 79 *[Robins 64]* | Chamberlain | Breacker | Harvey* | Rees | James | Dreyer | Wilson | Nogan | Dowie | Preece^ | Black | Johnson/Cooke |
| | 3/3 | | *35,237* | *16* | 26 | | | *McClair 23, Hughes 32, Wallace 44,* | *Leighton* | *Anderson* | *Bruce* | *Pallister* | *Martin* | *Robins* | *Phelan* | *Ince* | *McClair* | *Hughes* | *Wallace** | *Beardsmore* |
| | | | | | | | | Ref: K Redfern | United manage to put some daylight between themselves and the relegation zone as they storm into a four-goal lead. Injuries sustained by both Preece and Harvey do not help the Town's cause. Black drives home a consolation goal, the first Luton have scored at Old Trafford since 1959. | | | | | | | | | | | |
| 28 | H | COVENTRY | | 17 | W | 3-2 | 1-0 | Black 20, Gray 80, Dowie 86 | Chamberlain | Breacker | Harvey* | Rees | James | Dreyer | Wilson | Nogan | Dowie | Preece^ | Black | Johnson/Gray |
| | 7/3 | | **8,244** | *7* | 29 | | | *Drinkell 48, Regis 79* | *Ogrizovic* | *Borrows* | *Dobson** | *Peake* | *Downs* | *Gynn* | *Gallacher* | *Speedie* | *Smith* | *Regis* | *Drinkell* | *Billing* |
| | | | | | | | | Ref: K Cooper | An early effort from Kingsley Black is eclipsed by a chip from Kevin Drinkell and a full-blooded shot from Cyrille Regis. Paul Gray equalises following a cross by Tim Breacker and Iain Dowie hits a vital late winner which enables the Hatters to move away from the relegation places. | | | | | | | | | | | |
| 29 | A | ASTON VILLA | | 17 | L | 0-2 | 0-1 | | Chamberlain | Breacker | **Allpress** | Kennedy | James | Dreyer | Rees* | Nogan | Dowie | **Hughes^** | Black | **Poutch**/Gray |
| | 10/3 | | *22,505* | *1* | 29 | | | *Daley 29, Platt 49* | *Spink* | *Price* | *McGrath* | *Nielsen* | *Gage* | *Gray* | *Cowans* | *Williams* | *Daley* | *Platt* | *Olney* | |
| | | | | | | | | Ref: J Martin | Injury-hit Luton field one of the youngest sides in their history but are sunk by a brilliant goal from Tony Daley who sprints past two defenders in a 60-yard run. Villa do not look like potential champions and have to rely on a slip by Dreyer which enables Platt to nip in for the second. | | | | | | | | | | | |
| 30 | H | MANCHESTER C | | 17 | D | 1-1 | 0-0 | Wilson 72p | Chamberlain | Breacker | Harvey | Kennedy | James | Dreyer | Wilson | Nogan* | Dowie | Preece^ | Black | Gray/Rees |
| | 17/3 | | 9,765 | *18* | 30 | | | *Allen 79p* | *Dibble* | *Harper* | *Lake* | *Hendry* | *Redmond* | *Hinchcliffe** | *White* | *Ward* | *Megson^* | *Heath* | *Allen* | *Clarke/Brightwell* |
| | | | | | | | | Ref: B Hill | Danny Wilson steps up to blast the ball home from the spot after Paul Gray is hauled down by ex-Town keeper Andy Dibble. Richard Harvey's inexperience shows when he pulls back David White in the box, allowing Clive Allen to equalise with a penalty-kick in this relegation dog-fight. | | | | | | | | | | | |

| No | Venue | Opponent / Date | Att | Pos | Pts | Result | H-T | Scorers, Times, Referees | 1 | 2 | 3 | 4 | 5 | 6 | 7 | 8 | 9 | 10 | 11 | 12 sub used |
|---|---|---|---|---|---|---|---|---|---|---|---|---|---|---|---|---|---|---|---|---|
| 31 | H | MILLWALL | | 17 | W | 2-1 | 1-0 | McCarthy 42 (og), Black 76 | Chamberlain | Breacker | Harvey | Kennedy | James | Dreyer | Wilson | Gray* | Dowie | Preece | Black | Rees |
| | | 24/3 | 9,027 | *20* | 33 | | | *Briley 77* | *Branagan* | *Steven* | *McCarthy* | *Thompson* | *McLeary* | *Dawes* | *Hurlock* | *Reid** | *Stephenson^* | *Allen* | *Goddard* | *Briley/Sheringham* |
| | | | | | | | | Ref: K Hackett | Jim Ryan is offered a two-year extension to his contract after the Town see off fellow strugglers Millwall. Black, for whom a transfer bid by Nottingham Forest was turned down during the week, hits the second goal although Les Briley pulls one back for the Lions almost immediately. | | | | | | | | | | | |
| 32 | A | NORWICH | | 18 | L | 0-2 | 0-1 | | Chamberlain | Breacker | McDonough | Kennedy | James | Dreyer | Wilson | Nogan* | Dowie | Preece | Black | Rees |
| | | 31/3 | *14,451* | *8* | 33 | | | *Townsend 27p, Bowen 48* | *Gunn* | *Culverhouse* | *Tanner* | *Linighan* | *Bowen* | *Townsend* | *Sherwood* | *Crook* | *Phillips* | *Mortensen** | *Rosario^* | *Fox/Coney* |
| | | | | | | | | Ref: D Hedges | The worse performance since Jim Ryan took over as manager plunges the Town back into the relegation places. An appalling penalty decision is given after Henrik Mortensen throws himself theatrically to the ground after Chamberlain dives at his feet, Townsend netting from the spot. | | | | | | | | | | | |
| 33 | A | CHELSEA | | 18 | L | 0-1 | 0-0 | | Chamberlain | Breacker | McDonough | Kennedy* | James | Dreyer | Wilson | Cooke^ | Dowie | Preece | Black | Beaumont/Gray |
| | | 7/4 | *13,114* | *6* | 33 | | | *Durie 72* | *Beasant* | *Hall* | *Johnsen* | *Monkou* | *Dorigo* | *Bumstead** | *Nicholas* | *Wilson K^* | *McAllister* | *Durie* | *Dixon* | *Lee/Wilson C* |
| | | | | | | | | Ref:M Bodenham | Gordon Durie strikes the only goal of the game, when Chamberlain parries his header back to him, as Chelsea drive another nail in the Luton relegation coffin. The Town defence is rarely troubled and Beaumont, returning after a five-month absence through injury, has a quiet afternoon. | | | | | | | | | | | |
| 34 | H | EVERTON | | 18 | D | 2-2 | 2-0 | Dowie 2, 41 | Chamberlain | Breacker | McDonough | Kennedy* | James | Dreyer | Wilson | Rees^ | Dowie | Preece | Black | Beaumont/Cooke |
| | | 14/4 | **9,538** | *3* | 34 | | | *Cottee 66, Sharp 77* | *Southall* | *Atteveld* | *Watson* | *McDonald* | *Ebbrell* | *Nevin* | *McCall* | *Sheedy* | *Beagrie* | *Cottee* | *Sharp* | |
| | | | | | | | | Ref: V Callow | Luton are given a perfect start when Rees intercepts a back-pass and centres for Dowie to power his header home off a post. The Hatters move further ahead when Dowie side-foots a cross from Breacker past Neville Southall. Two sloppy goals after the interval gift the Toffees a point. | | | | | | | | | | | |
| 35 | A | NOTT'M FOREST | | 18 | L | 0-3 | 0-0 | | Chamberlain | Breacker | McDonough | Kennedy* | James | Dreyer | Wilson | Rees^ | Dowie | Preece | Black | Beaumont/Elstrup |
| | | 16/4 | *17,001* | *8* | 34 | | | *Carr 58, Parker 67, Clough 82* | *Crossley* | *Laws* | *Walker* | *Chettle* | *Pearce* | *Carr* | *Wilson* | *Hodge* | *Parker* | *Clough* | *Jemson* | |
| | | | | | | | | Ref: D Allison | A miserable Easter period is complete, with Forest dominating from the first kick, although it takes them nearly an hour before they are able to break through a stubborn defence, Carr driving in a superb 25-yard shot. A corner count of 17-1 in favour of Forest illustrates their superiority. | | | | | | | | | | | |
| 36 | H | ARSENAL | | 18 | W | 2-0 | 1-0 | Dowie 41, Black 58 | Chamberlain | Breacker | McDonough | Beaumont | James* | Dreyer | Wilson | Rees | Dowie | Preece | Black^ | Johnson/Elstrup |
| | | 21/4 | 11,595 | *5* | 37 | | | | *Lukic* | *Bould* | *Adams* | *O'Leary** | *Dixon* | *Thomas* | *Davis* | *Winterburn* | *Smith* | *Merson^* | *Campbell* | *Rocastle/Hayes* |
| | | | | | | | | Ref: A Gunn | The best display of the season has probably come too late to save the Town from relegation. Iain Dowie steals in to open the scoring before the break and then Tim Breacker tears down the wing, skips past Tony Adams and sends an accurate cross for Kingsley Black to double the lead. | | | | | | | | | | | |
| 37 | H | CRYS PALACE | | 18 | W | 1-0 | 0-0 | Dowie 89 | Chamberlain | Breacker | McDon'ugh* | Beaumont | James | Dreyer | Wilson | Rees | Dowie | Preece | Black^ | Kennedy/Elstrup |
| | | 28/4 | 10,369 | *16* | 40 | | | | *Martyn* | *Pemberton* | *O'Reilly* | *Hedman* | *Shaw* | *Gray* | *Thomas** | *Pardew* | *Barber* | *Bright* | *Thompson^* | *Madden/Salako* |
| | | | | | | | | Ref: P Foakes | Crystal Palace have one eye turned towards their forthcoming FA Cup final and are content to play for the single point. They almost succeed but, with just 30 seconds left and Division 2 football beckoning, Iain Dowie lunges at a cross from Rees and sends the ball past Nigel Martyn. | | | | | | | | | | | |
| 38 | A | DERBY | | 17 | W | 3-2 | 2-2 | Breacker 2, Black 18, 74 | Chamberlain | Breacker | McDonough | Beaumont | James* | Dreyer | Wilson | Rees^ | Dowie | Preece | Black | Kennedy/Elstrup |
| | | 5/5 | *17,044* | *16* | 43 | | | *Wright 29, Williams P 44* | *Shilton* | *Sage* | *Wright* | *Hindmarch* | *Forsyth* | *Williams G* | *Davison* | *Williams P* | *Ramage** | *Harford* | *Saunders* | *Hebberd* |
| | | Home | Away | | | | | Ref: B Stevens | A 30-yard cracker from Breacker and a low shot from Black give the Town a two-goal lead but they are pegged back by the interval. Black hits the vital winner in front of the 5,000 Luton travelling supporters, who see their team win for only the second time away from home this season. | | | | | | | | | | | |
| Average | | 9,886 | 17,428 | | | | | | | | | | | | | | | | | |

| Littlewoods Cup | F-A | H-T | Scorers, Times, and Referees | 1 | 2 | 3 | 4 | 5 | 6 | 7 | 8 | 9 | 10 | 11 | subs used |
|---|---|---|---|---|---|---|---|---|---|---|---|---|---|---|---|
| 2:1 A MANSFIELD 8 W | 4-3 | 2-3 | Wegerle 6, 81, Elstrup 26, 49 | Chamberlain | Breacker | Dreyer | Wilson | McDonough | Beaumont | Kennedy | Wegerle | Elstrup | Preece | Williams* | Black |
| 19/9 *5,361 3:15* | | | *Stringfellow 11, Christie 21, 29* | *Cox* | *McKernon* | *Foster* | *Coleman* | *Kearney* | *Lowery** | *Hunt* | *Charles* | *Hathaway* | *Stringfell'w* | *Christie* | *Prindiville* |
| | | | Ref: K Redfern | Lars Elstrup finally gets off the mark with two goals and his strike partner, Roy Wegerle, also weighs in with a brace. In an end-to-end game, Mansfield fight back to take a 3-2 half-time lead but, after a roasting from the manager, the Town pull through to win by the minimum margin. | | | | | | | | | | | |
| 2:2 H MANSFIELD 13 W | 7-2 | 3-1 | Weg 14,69, Preece 32, E'trup 44, 46,65, | Chamberlain | Breacker | Dreyer | Wilson | Rodger | Beaumont | Kennedy | Wegerle | Elstrup | Preece | Black | |
| 3/10 6,519 *3:20* | | | *Kearney 40, Wilkinson 58* [Dreyer 83] | *Beasley* | *Kearney* | *Hodges** | *Gray* | *Wilkinson* | *Prindiville* | *Lowery* | *Hunt* | *Charles* | *Stringfell'w* | *Christie* | *Hathaway* |
| | | | Ref: P Foakes (Hatters won 11-5 on aggregate) | Elstrup scores the first hat-trick of his career as the Hatters demolish plucky Mansfield. The Stags play with a sweeper but are totally overrun by a Luton side who also hit the woodwork three times. Graham Rodger makes his debut in defence for the Town but has little chance to shine. | | | | | | | | | | | |
| 3 A EVERTON 12 L | 0-3 | 0-0 | | Chamberlain | Breacker | Dreyer* | Wilson | McDonough | Beaumont | Harvey | Wegerle | Elstrup | Preece^ | Black | Johnson/Dowie |
| 24/10 *18,428 1:1* | | | *Newell 52, 58, Nevin 85* | *Southall* | *Ebbrell* | *Keown* | *Watson* | *McDonald* | *Nevin* | *McCall* | *Whiteside* | *Sheedy* | *Newell* | *Cottee** | *Sharp* |
| | | | Ref: R Milford | Hopes of a third consecutive Wembley appearance are ended abruptly as ex-Hatter Mike Newell heads the first goal. Having defended well to this point, Luton are now forced to chase the game and, as a result, the floodgates open. Preece hits the bar with the only chance of the game | | | | | | | | | | | |

| FA Cup | F-A | H-T | Scorers, Times, and Referees | 1 | 2 | 3 | 4 | 5 | 6 | 7 | 8 | 9 | 10 | 11 | subs used |
|---|---|---|---|---|---|---|---|---|---|---|---|---|---|---|---|
| 3 A BRIGHTON 19 L | 1-4 | 0-0 | Wilson 66 *[Curbishley 87]* | Chamberlain | Breacker | Harvey | James* | Johnson | Dreyer | Wilson | Kennedy | Harford | Preece | Black | Dowie |
| 6/1 *10,361 2:18* | | | *Dublin 60, Nelson 69, Codner 79,* | *Keeley* | *Chivers* | *Gatting* | *Dublin* | *Chapman* | *Curbishley* | *Nelson* | *Barham* | *Bremner* | *Codner* | *Wilkins* | |
| | | | Ref: D Axcell | Terry Mancini takes charge of the side as caretaker manager for the first and only time as the Hatters are bundled out of the Cup in a disastrous performance. Second division Brighton, who have gone three months without a home win, hit the Town with four goals in the last 30 minutes. | | | | | | | | | | | |

| | P | Home W | D | L | F | A | Away W | D | L | F | A | Pts |
|---|---|---|---|---|---|---|---|---|---|---|---|---|
| 1 Liverpool | 38 | 13 | 5 | 1 | 38 | 15 | 10 | 5 | 4 | 40 | 22 | 79 |
| 2 Aston Villa | 38 | 13 | 3 | 3 | 36 | 20 | 8 | 4 | 7 | 21 | 18 | 70 |
| 3 Tottenham | 38 | 12 | 1 | 6 | 35 | 24 | 7 | 5 | 7 | 24 | 23 | 63 |
| 4 Arsenal | 38 | 14 | 3 | 2 | 38 | 11 | 4 | 5 | 10 | 16 | 27 | 62 |
| 5 Chelsea | 38 | 8 | 7 | 4 | 31 | 24 | 8 | 5 | 6 | 27 | 26 | 60 |
| 6 Everton | 38 | 14 | 3 | 2 | 40 | 16 | 3 | 5 | 11 | 17 | 30 | 59 |
| 7 Southampton | 38 | 10 | 5 | 4 | 40 | 27 | 5 | 5 | 9 | 31 | 36 | 55 |
| 8 Wimbledon | 38 | 5 | 8 | 6 | 22 | 23 | 8 | 8 | 3 | 25 | 17 | 55 |
| 9 Nott'm Forest | 38 | 9 | 4 | 6 | 31 | 21 | 6 | 5 | 8 | 24 | 26 | 54 |
| 10 Norwich | 38 | 7 | 10 | 2 | 24 | 14 | 6 | 4 | 9 | 20 | 28 | 53 |
| 11 QP Rangers | 38 | 9 | 4 | 6 | 27 | 22 | 4 | 7 | 8 | 18 | 22 | 50 |
| 12 Coventry | 38 | 11 | 2 | 6 | 24 | 25 | 3 | 5 | 11 | 15 | 34 | 49 |
| 13 Manchester U | 38 | 8 | 6 | 5 | 26 | 14 | 5 | 3 | 11 | 20 | 33 | 48 |
| 14 Manchester C | 38 | 9 | 4 | 6 | 26 | 21 | 3 | 8 | 8 | 17 | 31 | 48 |
| 15 Crys Palace | 38 | 8 | 7 | 4 | 27 | 23 | 5 | 2 | 12 | 15 | 43 | 48 |
| 16 Derby | 38 | 9 | 1 | 9 | 29 | 21 | 4 | 6 | 9 | 14 | 19 | 46 |
| 17 LUTON TOWN | 38 | 8 | 8 | 3 | 24 | 18 | 2 | 5 | 12 | 19 | 39 | 43 |
| 18 Sheffield Wed | 38 | 8 | 6 | 5 | 21 | 17 | 3 | 4 | 12 | 14 | 34 | 43 |
| 19 Charlton | 38 | 4 | 6 | 9 | 18 | 25 | 3 | 3 | 13 | 13 | 32 | 30 |
| 20 Millwall | 38 | 4 | 6 | 9 | 23 | 25 | 1 | 5 | 13 | 16 | 40 | 26 |
| | 760 | 183 | 99 | 98 | 580 | 406 | 98 | 99 | 183 | 406 | 580 | 1041 |

Odds & ends

Double wins: (1) Derby.
Double losses: (3) Aston Villa, Chelsea, Manchester United.

Won from behind: (2) Coventry (h), Mansfield (LC).
Lost from in front: (0).

High spots: The final day win at Derby to stay up.
The 11-5 aggregate win over Mansfield in the Littlewoods Cup.
The goalscoring form of left-winger Kingsley Black.
Beating defending champions Arsenal at Kenilworth Road.

Low spots: The upheavals behind the scenes.
The injury problems depriving the team of several first choice players for large parts of the season.
The 0-3 defeat at Nott'm Forest, which seemed to signal relegation.
The FA Cup disaster at Brighton.
Lars Elstrup's inability through injury to repay in goals his record transfer fee.
The sale of Mick Harford.

Player of the Year: Tim Breacker.
Ever-presents: (3) Tim Breacker, Alec Chamberlain, John Dreyer.
Hat-tricks: (1) Lars Elstrup.
Leading scorer: (11) Kingsley Black.

| | Appearances Lge | *Sub* | LC | *Sub* | FAC | *Sub* | Goals Lge | LC | FAC | Tot |
|---|---|---|---|---|---|---|---|---|---|---|
| Allpress, Tim | **1** | | | | | | | | | |
| Beaumont, David | **16** | *3* | 3 | | | | | | | |
| Black, Kingsley | **36** | | 2 | *1* | 1 | | **11** | | | **11** |
| Breacker, Tim | **38** | | 3 | | 1 | | **1** | | | **1** |
| Chamberlain, Alec | **38** | | 3 | | 1 | | | | | |
| Cooke, Richard | **3** | *8* | | | | | **1** | | | **1** |
| Donaghy, Mal | **5** | | | | | | | | | |
| Dowie, Iain | **26** | *3* | | *1* | | *1* | **8** | | | **8** |
| Dreyer, John | **38** | | 3 | | 1 | | **2** | 1 | | **3** |
| Elstrup, Lars | **13** | *10* | 3 | | | | **4** | 5 | | **9** |
| Farrell, Sean | | *1* | | | | | | | | |
| Gray, Paul | **2** | *5* | | | | | **1** | | | **1** |
| Harford, Mick | **1** | *3* | | | 1 | | | | | |
| Harvey, Richard | **17** | *9* | 1 | | 1 | | | | | |
| Hughes, Ceri | **1** | | | | | | | | | |
| James, Julian | **19** | *1* | | | 1 | | **1** | | | **1** |
| Johnson, Marvin | **7** | *5* | | *1* | 1 | | | | | |
| Kennedy, Mick | **30** | *2* | 2 | | 1 | | | | | |
| McDonough, Darron | **15** | | 2 | | | | | | | |
| Nogan, Kurt | **10** | | | | | | **2** | | | **2** |
| Poutch, Neil | | *1* | | | | | | | | |
| Preece, David | **30** | *2* | 3 | | 1 | | **1** | 1 | | **2** |
| Rees, Jason | **8** | *6* | | | | | | | | |
| Rodger, Graham | **2** | | 1 | | | | | | | |
| Wegerle, Roy | **13** | *2* | 3 | | | | **2** | 4 | | **6** |
| Williams, Steve | **14** | | 1 | | | | **1** | | | **1** |
| Wilson, Danny | **35** | | 3 | | 1 | | **7** | | 1 | **8** |
| (own-goals) | | | | | | | **1** | | | **1** |
| **27 players used** | **418** | *61* | **33** | *3* | **11** | *1* | **43** | **11** | **1** | **55** |

# BARCLAYS LEAGUE DIVISION 1

## Manager: Jim Ryan

## SEASON 1990-91

| No | Date | Att | Pos | Pt | F-A | H-T | Scorers, Times, and Referees | 1 | 2 | 3 | 4 | 5 | 6 | 7 | 8 | 9 | 10 | 11 | subs used |
|---|---|---|---|---|---|---|---|---|---|---|---|---|---|---|---|---|---|---|---|
| 1 | H CRYS PALACE | | | D | 1-1 | 1-1 | Dowie 44 | Chamberlain | Breacker | James | McDonough | Beaumont | Dreyer | Elstrup | Preece | Dowie | Hughes* | Black | Rees |
| | 25/8 | 9,583 | | 1 | | | *Young 15* | *Martyn* | *Humphrey* | *Thorn* | *Young* | *Salako* | *Shaw* | *Hodges** | *Gray* | *Thomas* | *Barber* | *Wright* | *Dennis* |
| | | | | | | | Ref: A Gunn | A young Hatters side struggles in the heat after Eric Young heads Palace into the lead when he gets on the end of a free-kick by Glyn Hodges. Iain Dowie levels with a header and, as a result of Luton's raised tempo in the second half, Nigel Martyn is required to maintain the *status quo*. | | | | | | | | | | | |
| 2 | A ARSENAL | | | L | 1-2 | 1-1 | Elstrup 12 | Chamberlain | Breacker | James* | McDonough | Beaumont | Dreyer | Elstrup | Preece | Dowie | Hughes | Black^ | Harvey/Rees |
| | 29/8 | *32,723* | | 1 | | | *Merson 36, Thomas 65* | *Seaman* | *Dixon* | *Bould* | *Adams* | *Winterburn* | *Rocastle* | *Davis* | *Thomas* | *Merson* | *Smith* | *Limpar** | *Groves* |
| | | | | | | | Ref: B Hill | The Town make a bright and positive start against their multi-million pound rated opponents and Elstrup opens his account for the season with a near-post header from a cross by Preece. The Gunners then take the initiative with Michael Thomas netting the winner with a 20-yard shot. | | | | | | | | | | | |
| 3 | A SOUTHAMPTON | | 8 | W | 2-1 | 2-1 | Elstrup 18, 26 | Chamberlain | Breacker | James | McDon'ugh* | Beaumont | Dreyer | Elstrup | Preece | Dowie | Hughes | Rees^ | Harvey/Nogan |
| | 1/9 | *13,538* | *10* | 4 | | | *Rideout 31* | *Flowers* | *Cherednik* | *Moore* | *Osman* | *Adams* | *Horne* | *Case* | *Cockerill** | *Le Tissier* | *Rideout* | *Wallace^* | *Ruddock/Shearer* |
| | | | | | | | Ref: M Bodenham | Elstrup runs onto a through pass from Julian James and then steers home a cross with his head from Breacker as the Hatters race into a two-goal lead. The Saints pull a goal back but, although the Town have to reshuffle when McDonough picks up a rib injury, the defence holds firm. | | | | | | | | | | | |
| 4 | H MANCHESTER U | | 10 | L | 0-1 | 0-1 | | Chamberlain | Breacker | Harvey* | James^ | Beaumont | Dreyer | Elstrup | Preece | Dowie | Hughes | Black | Johnson/Rees |
| | 4/9 | 12,576 | *4* | 4 | | | *Robins 24* | *Sealey* | *Irwin* | *Blackmore* | *Bruce !* | *Phelan* | *Pallister* | *Webb* | *Ince* | *McClair* | *Robins** | *Beardsm're^* | *Donaghy/Hughes* |
| | | | | | | | Ref: R Lewis | After Mark Robins steals in to give United the lead, Dowie is through on goal and looks a certainty to score when he is hauled down by Steve Bruce, outside the area. The offender is dismissed for his troubles but the Town are unable to take advantage of the extra man in the second half. | | | | | | | | | | | |
| 5 | H LEEDS | | 8 | W | 1-0 | 1-0 | Black 5 | Chamberlain | Breacker | James | Rees | Beaumont | Dreyer | Elstrup | Preece* | Dowie | Hughes | Black^ | Johnson/Nogan |
| | 8/9 | 10,185 | *6* | 7 | | | | *Lukic* | *Sterland* | *Haddock* | *Whyte* | *Snodin** | *Strachan* | *Jones^* | *Batty* | *Whitlow* | *McAllister* | *Chapman* | *Speed/Varadi* |
| | | | | | | | Ref: P Foakes | Woeful finishing by newly-promoted Leeds, together with an amazing display of goalkeeping by Chamberlain, enable the Town to cling on to a Kingsley Black headed goal from a cross by Elstrup. Vinny Jones commits his first foul after just 40 seconds and is lucky to stay on the pitch. | | | | | | | | | | | |
| 6 | A QP RANGERS | | 11 | L | **1-6** | 0-1 | Hughes 57 *[Falco 65, Parker 85]* | Chamberlain | Breacker | James | Rees* | Beaumont | Dreyer | Elstrup | Preece | Dowie^ | Hughes | Black | McDonough/Nogan |
| | 15/9 | *10,196* | *7* | 7 | | | *Wegerle 6, 63, Sinton 48, Wilkins 55,* | *Roberts* | *Maddix* | *McDonald* | *Parker* | *Sansom* | *Bardsley* | *Wilkins* | *Wilson* | *Sinton* | *Wegerle* | *Falco** | *Ferdinand* |
| | | | | | | | Ref: K Morton | An incredible game sees the Hatters enjoy more of the play and create more scoring opportunities but Rangers attack on the break and make everything count. Roy Wegerle scores twice against his old team, the only reply coming from Ceri Hughes, who nets his first goal for the club. | | | | | | | | | | | |
| 7 | H COVENTRY | | 7 | W | 1-0 | 1-0 | Dowie 2 | Chamberlain | Breacker | Harvey | Rees | Beaumont | Dreyer | Elstrup* | Preece | Dowie | Hughes | Black | James |
| | 22/9 | 8,336 | *17* | 10 | | | | *Ogrizovic* | *Borrows* | *Kilcline* | *Peake* | *Edwards** | *Gallacher^* | *Gynn* | *MacDonald* | *Smith* | *Speedie* | *Drinkell* | *Titterton/Livingstone* |
| | | | | | | | Ref: J Rushton | The Hatters bounce back from their beating of last week in a game where the away side are flattered by their narrow defeat. Dowie scores with a faint touch to a corner-kick from Preece, but a mixture of poor finishing and stout goalkeeping by Steve Ogrizovic keeps the score-line down. | | | | | | | | | | | |
| 8 | A NORWICH | | 6 | W | **3-1** | 0-1 | Elstrup 48, 53, 62 | Chamberlain | Breacker | Harvey | Williams | Beaumont | Dreyer | Elstrup | Preece | Dowie | Hughes | Black | |
| | 29/9 | *12,794* | *17* | 13 | | | *Gordon 4* | *Gunn* | *Culverhouse* | *Butterw'rth* | *Blades** | *Bowen* | *Gordon^* | *Sherwood* | *Crook* | *Phillips* | *Fleck* | *Fox* | *Goss/Power* |
| | | | | | | | Ref: R Pawley | Two of the goals scored by Lars Elstrup come from free headers from almost identical free-kicks by a recalled Steve Williams, and the third is down to sheer pace and ball control. Norwich manager Dave Stringer complains that his men defended like schoolboys against the free-kicks. | | | | | | | | | | | |
| 9 | A SUNDERLAND | | 8 | L | 0-2 | 0-2 | | Chamberlain | Johnson | Harvey | Williams | Beaumont | Dreyer | Elstrup | Preece | Dowie | Hughes* | Black^ | McDonough/Rees |
| | 20/10 | *20,035* | *15* | 13 | | | *Gabbiadini 12, Davenport 30* | *Norman* | *Kay* | *Bennett* | *Ball* | *Smith* | *Bracewell* | *Owers* | *Armstrong* | *Davenport* | *Gabbiadini* | *Hardyman* | |
| | | | | | | | Ref: W Burns | Chamberlain is again in super form and is unfortunate to end up on the losing side. In an open game, the Town have just as many opportunities as the Rokermen but lack the finishing power that is shown by Marco Gabbiadini, who takes advantage of Dreyer's slip to crash the ball home. | | | | | | | | | | | |
| 10 | H EVERTON | | 7 | D | 1-1 | 1-0 | Elstrup 24 | Chamberlain | Johnson | Harvey | Williams | Beaumont | Dreyer | Elstrup* | Preece | Dowie | Hughes | Black | Rees |
| | 27/10 | 10,047 | *18* | 14 | | | *Nevin 50* | *Southall* | *Atteveld* | *Ratcliffe* | *Watson* | *Keown* | *Nevin* | *McDonald* | *McCall* | *Ebbrell* | *Cottee* | *Sharp* | |
| | | | | | | | Ref: S Bell | A draw against one of the big five, a position of seventh in the league table and an exhibition of exciting football does not satisfy Jim Ryan, who knows that his team should have won at a canter. Lars Elstrup nods in an accurate cross from Harvey before Nevin gets a lucky equaliser. | | | | | | | | | | | |

| | | | | | | | | | | | | | | | | | | | | |
|---|---|---|---|---|---|---|---|---|---|---|---|---|---|---|---|---|---|---|---|---|
| 11 | A | DERBY | | 8 | L | 1-2 | 0-1 | Black 48 | Chamberlain | Johnson | Harvey | Williams | Beaumont | Dreyer | Elstrup | Preece | Dowie* | Hughes^ | Black | Nogan/McDonough |
| | 3/11 | | *15,008* | *19* | 14 | | | *Saunders 31p, Callaghan 64* | *Shilton* | *Sage* | *Forsyth* | *Wright* | *Cross* | *Micklewhite* | *Williams* | *Ramage* | *Callaghan* | *Gee* | *Saunders* | |
| | | | | | | | | Ref: A Buksh | Preece concedes a penalty when he handles a shot from Michael Forsyth on the line and then has two good scoring opportunities but is thwarted by the Rams' 41-year-old goalkeeper Peter Shilton. Black levels with a neat shot but Nigel Callaghan fires a spectacular winner from 25 yards. | | | | | | | | | | | |
| 12 | A | LIVERPOOL | | 13 | L | 0-4 | 0-3 | | Chamberlain | Johnson | Harvey | Williams | Beaumont | Dreyer | Elstrup | Preece | Dowie | Hughes* | Black | Farrell |
| | 10/11 | | *35,207* | *1* | 14 | | | *Rush 5, 39, Molby 9p, Beardsley 71* | *Grobbelaar* | *Burrows* | *Gillespie* | *Hysen* | *Ablett* | *Nicol** | *Houghton* | *Molby* | *McMahon* | *Beardsley^* | *Rush* | *Staunton/Rosenthal* |
| | | | | | | | | Ref: G Ashby | Liverpool turn on their best display of the season, according to their manager, Kenny Dalglish. The Hatters are ripped apart in the first half by Ian Rush and Alec Chamberlain is sent the wrong way by Molby when he converts from the penalty spot after Harvey sends Steve Nicol flying. | | | | | | | | | | | |
| 13 | H | MANCHESTER C | | 12 | D | 2-2 | 0-2 | Dowie 77, Dreyer 89p | Chamberlain | Johnson | Harvey | Williams | Beaumont | Dreyer | Elstrup* | Preece | Dowie | Hughes^ | Black | McDonough/Farrell |
| | 17/11 | | 9,564 | *7* | 15 | | | *White 25, Redmond 41* | *Coton* | *Brightwell* | *Hendry* | *Redmond* | *Pointon* | *White** | *Megson* | *Harper* | *Ward* | *Heath* | *Quinn* | *Brennan* |
| | | | | | | | | Ref: K Burge | City appear to be cruising to victory when, with 20 minutes to go, Jim Ryan changes the Luton team in order to exploit some suspect defending. First, Dowie pulls a goal back with a header; then he is brought down by Colin Hendry in the final minute, Dreyer scoring off a short run-up. | | | | | | | | | | | |
| 14 | H | ASTON VILLA | | 9 | W | 2-0 | 1-0 | Black 44, Elstrup 85 | Chamberlain | Johnson | Harvey | Williams | McDonough | Dreyer | Elstrup | Preece | Dowie | Hughes | Black | |
| | 24/11 | | 10,071 | *13* | 18 | | | | *Spink* | *McGrath* | *Mountfield** | *Nielsen* | *Price* | *Platt* | *Cowans* | *Gray* | *Daley* | *Blake^* | *Cascarino* | *Yorke/Birch* |
| | | | | | | | | Ref: J Key | Villa come for a point but the Town are always in control and Black takes advantage of a ball which bounces around in the box to score before the break. Preece makes sure of the points when he dribbles along the by-line to set up Lars Elstrup who pokes in his eighth goal of the season. | | | | | | | | | | | |
| 15 | A | NOTT'M FOREST | | 10 | D | 2-2 | 1-1 | Elstrup 15, 46 | Chamberlain | Johnson | Harvey | Williams | McDonough | Dreyer | Elstrup | Preece | Dowie | Hughes* | Black | Beaumont |
| | 1/12 | | *16,498* | *11* | 19 | | | *Carr 6, Clough 75* | *Crossley* | *Laws* | *Walker* | *Chettle* | *Pearce* | *Keane* | *Parker* | *Crosby* | *Carr* | *Jemson** | *Clough* | *Starbuck* |
| | | | | | | | | Ref: R Dilkes | Forest take a shock lead through Carr, before Lars Elstrup beats England centre-half Des Walker for speed and crashes the ball home. Elstrup hits a second with a curling shot into the top corner of the net but, after Chamberlain makes a wonder save, Nigel Clough heads the equaliser. | | | | | | | | | | | |
| 16 | H | ARSENAL | | 11 | D | 1-1 | 0-1 | Dreyer 72p | Chamberlain | Johnson | Harvey | Williams | McDonough | Dreyer | Elstrup | Preece | Dowie | Rees* | Black | Farrell |
| | 8/12 | | 12,506 | *2* | 20 | | | *Smith 44* | *Seaman* | *O'Leary* | *Adams !* | *Bould* | *Winterburn* | *Dixon* | *Davis* | *Thomas* | *Limpar** | *Merson* | *Smith* | *Groves* |
| | | | | | | | | Ref: P Don | Alan Smith opens the scoring when he heads home a corner kick by Paul Davis but Luton fight back and Dowie hits the bar before he is sent tumbling in the area by Tony Adams, who is dismissed for the first time in his career. Dreyer levels from the spot, using his short run-up again. | | | | | | | | | | | |
| 17 | A | CRYS PALACE | | 11 | L | 0-1 | 0-1 | | Chamberlain | Johnson | Harvey | Williams | McDonough | Dreyer | Elstrup | Preece | Dowie | Beaumont* | Black^ | Farrell/Rees |
| | 16/12 | | *15,579* | *3* | 20 | | | *Bright 22* | *Martyn* | *Humphrey* | *Young* | *Thorn* | *Shaw* | *Gray* | *Thomas* | *McGoldrick* | *Wright* | *Bright* | *Salako* | |
| | | | | | | | | Ref: V Callow | High-flying Palace win the points with a headed goal from Mark Bright, who gets on the end of a cross from John Salako. The Town play with a sweeper, which does not work against the Eagles strike force of Wright and Bright, who both miss chances to make it a more emphatic win. | | | | | | | | | | | |
| 18 | A | TOTTENHAM | | 12 | L | 1-2 | 1-1 | Dowie 12 | Chamberlain | Johnson | Harvey | Williams | McDon'ugh* | Dreyer | Elstrup^ | Preece | Dowie | Hughes ! | Black | Beaumont/Farrell |
| | 22/12 | | *27,007* | *4* | 20 | | | *Stewart 34, 58* | *Thorstvedt* | *Thomas* | *Sedgley* | *Mabbutt* | *v d Hauwe !* | *Nayim !* | *Howells* | *Gascoigne* | *Walsh** | *Stewart* | *Lineker^* | *Allen/Samways* |
| | | | | | | | | Ref: D Elleray | Dowie gives the Town the lead when heading in a cross from Black. Nayim is sent off for swearing, followed by van den Hauwe for a high tackle on Dowie. Spurs take the lead with two headers by Stewart and, after Hughes is sent off for a late tackle on Lineker, they shut up shop. | | | | | | | | | | | |
| 19 | H | SHEFFIELD UTD | | 12 | L | 0-1 | 0-0 | | Chamberlain | Johnson | Harvey* | Williams | McDonough | Dreyer | Elstrup | Preece | Dowie | Hughes^ | Black | Beaumont/Farrell |
| | 26/12 | | 10,004 | *20* | 20 | | | *Deane 71* | *Tracey* | *Wilder* | *Hill* | *Beesley* | *Lucas* | *Bryson* | *Jones* | *Gannon* | *Hoyland* | *Bradshaw** | *Deane* | *Wood* |
| | | | | | | | | Ref: I Borrett | The season is over for Ceri Hughes when he sustains a serious knee injury. Brian Deane appears to be well offside when he races through for the winning goal but the Town deserve nothing from the game as they turn in an abysmal performance against the bottom placed club in the league. | | | | | | | | | | | |
| 20 | H | CHELSEA | | 12 | W | 2-0 | 0-0 | Cundy 56 (og), Black 83 | Chamberlain | Johnson* | Harvey | Williams | McDonough | Dreyer | Elstrup | Preece | Farrell | Rees | Black | James |
| | 29/12 | | 12,005 | *8* | 23 | | | | *Beasant* | *Hall* | *Cundy* | *Johnsen* | *Le Saux* | *Stuart* | *Bumstead** | *Lee^* | *Wise* | *Dixon* | *Wilson* | *Dickens/McAllister* |
| | | | | | | | | Ref: M Reed | Jason Cundy deflects a Preece free-kick into his own net and then Kingsley Black, with a half-volley, secures the victory as the Hatters record their first win for more than a month. Iain Dowie is dropped by manager Jim Ryan, due to his poor goal return, and Farrell is given his chance. | | | | | | | | | | | |

| No | Date | | Att | Pos | Pt | F-A | H-T | Scorers, Times, and Referees | 1 | 2 | 3 | 4 | 5 | 6 | 7 | 8 | 9 | 10 | 11 | subs used |
|---|---|---|---|---|---|---|---|---|---|---|---|---|---|---|---|---|---|---|---|---|
| 21 | A | WIMBLEDON | | 14 | L | 0-2 | 0-1 | | Chamberlain | Johnson* | Harvey | **Pembridge** | McDonough | Dreyer | Elstrup | Preece | Farrell | Rees^ | Black | James/Dowie |
| | 1/1 | | ***4,592*** | *9* | 23 | | | *Fashanu 44, Cork 84* | *Segers* | *Joseph* | *Blackwell* | *Curle* | *Phelan* | *Barton* | *Kruszynski* | *McGee* | *Scales* | *Fashanu** | *Gibson* | *Cork* |
| | | | | | | | | Ref: K Barratt | It is a year to the day since the Dons' manager, Ray Harford, left the Town but the Hatters fail to put one over on their old boss. John Fashanu is unmarked when he heads in a corner from Barton and the defensive frailty is underlined when Alan Cork fires the second to kill the game. | | | | | | | | | | | |
| 22 | H | SOUTHAMPTON | | 15 | L | 3-4 | 2-2 | Elstrup 24, James 26, Dreyer 78p | Chamberlain | James | Harvey | Pembridge* | McDonough | Dreyer | Elstrup | Preece | Farrell | Beaumont^ | Black | Williams/Dowie |
| | 12/1 | | 9,021 | *12* | 23 | | | *Wallace 9, 62, Le Tissier 28, 46* | *Flowers* | *Cherednik* | *Moore** | *Ruddock* | *Adams* | *Horne* | *Cockerill* | *McLoughlin* | *Shearer* | *Le Tissier* | *Wallace* | *Davis* |
| | | | | | | | | Ref: R Lewis | The Saints have trained on the artificial surface at Kenilworth Road before previous matches and, on each occasion, have been thumped. They did not bother this time and ultimately win a thrilling game, although a push by Steve Davis on Dreyer gives them a last few anxious minutes. | | | | | | | | | | | |
| 23 | A | LEEDS | | 16 | L | 1-2 | 0-1 | Elstrup 67 | Chamberlain | James | Harvey | Williams | McDonough | Dreyer | Elstrup | Rees* | Farrell | Pembridge | Black | Dowie |
| | 19/1 | | *27,010* | *4* | 23 | | | *Strachan 13p, Fairclough 59* | *Lukic* | *Sterland* | *Fairclough* | *Whyte* | *Snodin** | *Strachan* | *Batty* | *McAllister* | *Speed* | *Shutt* | *Chapman* | *Haddock* |
| | | | | | | | | Ref: C Trussell | Mr Trussell awards a penalty when both he, and a vociferous Elland Road crowd, decide that James has pulled back Gary McAllister. Gordon Strachan nets from the spot before Lee Chapman back-heels for Chris Fairclough to add the second. Lars Elstrup volleys in a cross from Black. | | | | | | | | | | | |
| 24 | H | QP RANGERS | | 16 | L | 1-2 | 1-0 | Black 16 | Chamberlain | Beaumont | Dreyer | Williams | McDonough | Rodger | Nogan | Preece | Dowie | Pembridge* | Black | **Holsgrove** |
| | 2/2 | | 8,479 | *18* | 23 | | | *Ferdinand 56, 89* | *Stejskal* | *Bardsley* | *Tillson* | *Peacock* | *Maddix* | *Sansom* | *Wilkins* | *Barker* | *Allen* | *Ferdinand* | *Sinton** | *Meaker* |
| | | | | | | | | Ref: M Bailey | Desperate for the three points, the Town pile everyone up for a corner in the final minute but when the ball is headed clear, Bradley Allen feeds Les Ferdinand who races 50 yards before slotting it past Chamberlain. The Town have now recorded seven defeats out of the last eight games. | | | | | | | | | | | |
| 25 | H | LIVERPOOL | | 15 | W | **3-1** | 0-1 | Black 47, Dowie 54, 80 | Chamberlain | Johnson | James* | Beaumont | Rodger | Dreyer | Elstrup | Preece | Dowie | Pembridge | Black | Rees |
| | 23/2 | | 12,032 | *2* | 26 | | | *Molby 16p* | *Hooper* | *Venison* | *Ablett* | *Hysen* | *Staunton** | *Nicol* | *Molby* | *Houghton* | *Barnes* | *Rush* | *Beardsley* | *Speedie* |
| | | | | | | | | Ref: J Ashworth | The shock departure of Liverpool manager Kenny Dalglish brings the press out in force to focus on the caretaker boss, Ronnie Moran. Molby converts a spot-kick after Steve Nicol hits a shot straight at James, who is adjudged to have handled, but Iain Dowie and Black settle the issue. | | | | | | | | | | | |
| 26 | H | NOTT'M FOREST | | 14 | W | 1-0 | 0-0 | Dowie 85 | Chamberlain | Johnson | McDonough | Beaumont | Rodger | Dreyer | Elstrup | Preece | Dowie | Pembridge | Black | |
| | 2/3 | | 9,577 | *12* | 29 | | | | *Crossley* | *Charles* | *Walker* | *Chettle* | *Pearce* | *Keane* | *Parker* | *Wilson* | *Woan* | *Clough* | *Jemson* | |
| | | | | | | | | Ref: B Hill | Forest are surprisingly negative and almost manage to hold out for a point but Iain Dowie, who was upset at being dropped for his poor goal-scoring record, is now on a roll and converts with a header following a David Preece free-kick. Cooke has joined Beaumont on the transfer list. | | | | | | | | | | | |
| 27 | A | MANCHESTER C | | 15 | L | 0-3 | 0-3 | | Chamberlain | Johnson | McDonough | Beaumont | Rodger | Dreyer | Elstrup | Preece | Dowie* | Pembridge | Black | Farrell |
| | 5/3 | | *20,404* | *6* | 29 | | | *Quinn 20, 41, Allen 31p* | *Coton* | *Brightwell** | *Hendry* | *Redmond* | *Pointon* | *White* | *Reid^* | *Megson* | *Allen* | *Quinn* | *Heath* | *Hill/Harper* |
| | | | | | | | | Ref: P Danson | Luton's defence has a nightmare of a game and only Chamberlain keeps the score down. McDonough slips at the vital moment allowing Niall Quinn to score both the first and third goals. A poor back-pass from Rodger puts Clive Allen through, but he then brings him down in the area. | | | | | | | | | | | |
| 28 | A | ASTON VILLA | | 13 | W | 2-1 | 2-0 | Mountfield 27 (og), Pembridge 44 | Chamberlain | Johnson | McDonough | Beaumont | Rodger | Dreyer | Elstrup | Preece | Dowie | Pembridge | Black | |
| | 9/3 | | *20,587* | *16* | 32 | | | *Cascarino 70* | *Spink* | *Price* | *Mountfield** | *Nielsen^* | *McGrath* | *Cowans* | *Gray* | *Platt* | *Yorke* | *Penrice* | *Cascarino* | *Olney/Gage* |
| | | | | | | | | Ref: L Dilkes | Derek Mountfield heads past his own keeper to put the Hatters into the lead and Mark Pembridge scores his first goal for the club with a brilliant volley. Tony Cascarino pulls a goal back with a header, but it is Luton who finish the stronger. Chamberlain saves a penalty from David Platt. | | | | | | | | | | | |
| 29 | A | COVENTRY | | 14 | L | 1-2 | 1-0 | Rodger 11 | Chamberlain | Johnson | McDonough | Beaumont* | Rodger | Dreyer | Elstrup | Preece | Dowie | Pembridge | Black | Farrell |
| | 13/3 | | *9,725* | *16* | 32 | | | *Borrows 60p, Pearce 83* | *Ogrizovic* | *McGrath* | *Pearce* | *Peake* | *Borrows* | *Emerson* | *Gynn* | *Woods* | *Gallacher* | *Regis* | *Smith* | |
| | | | | | | | | Ref: P Jones | Rodger touches in a volley from Dreyer to open the scoring against his old club. Chamberlain brings down Kevin Gallacher and Brian Borrows scores from the spot when the ball trickles over the line after being pushed against the post. Andy Pearce nods home a free-kick from Woods. | | | | | | | | | | | |
| 30 | H | NORWICH | | 14 | L | 0-1 | 0-1 | | Chamberlain | Johnson* | McDon'ugh^ | Beaumont | Rodger | Dreyer | Elstrup | Preece | Dowie | Pembridge | Black | Farrell/Harvey |
| | 16/3 | | 8,604 | *10* | 32 | | | *Sherwood 21* | *Gunn* | *Culverhouse* | *Blades* | *Polston* | *Bowen* | *Crook* | *Goss* | *Phillips* | *Gordon* | *Sherwood* | *Fleck* | |
| | | | | | | | | Ref: M Bodenham | The Canaries ride their luck and, but for some brilliant goalkeeping by Bryan Gunn, would probably have lost heavily. Luton spend most of the game camped out in their opponents' half, but a break down the left by David Phillips sets up Tim Sherwood for a shot into the far corner. | | | | | | | | | | | |

| No | Date | Opponent | Att | Pos | Pts | F-A | H-T | Scorers, Times, and Referees | 1 | 2 | 3 | 4 | 5 | 6 | 7 | 8 | 9 | 10 | 11 | subs used |
|---|---|---|---|---|---|---|---|---|---|---|---|---|---|---|---|---|---|---|---|---|
| 31 | A | MANCHESTER U | | 18 | L | 1-4 | 1-1 | Preece 34 | Chamberlain | Johnson | Harvey | Beaumont* | Rodger | Dreyer | Elstrup | Preece | Farrell | Pembridge | Black | Rees |
| | 23/3 | | ***41,752*** | *5* | 32 | | | *Bruce 7, 47, Robins 68, McClair 84* | *Sealey* | *Irwin* | *Bruce* | *Pallister* | *Blackmore* | *Robson* | *Phelan* | *Sharpe* | *Wallace** | *McClair* | *Hughes* | *Robins* |
| | | | | | | | | Ref: K Lupton | The shock sale of Dowie to West Ham further depletes the Luton forward line. Preece levels the score, at one point, with a fluke shot which hits a divot before flying over the head of Les Sealey. United are far more powerful, causing panic every time they attack, and finish worthy winners. | | | | | | | | | | | |
| 32 | A | SHEFFIELD UTD | | 18 | L | 1-2 | 1-0 | Elstrup 10 | Chamberlain | Johnson | Harvey | Beaumont* | Rodger | Dreyer | Elstrup | Preece | Farrell | Pembridge | Black^ | James/Nogan |
| | 30/3 | | *18,481* | *12* | 32 | | | *Bryson 55, Hodges 58* | *Tracey* | *Pemberton* | *Beesley* | *Hill* | *Barnes* | *Bradshaw* | *Jones* | *Hoyland* | *Hodges** | *Deane* | *Bryson* | *Marwood* |
| | | | | | | | | Ref: J Martin | Elstrup heads in a cross from Pembridge to give the Town an early lead but a mistake from Chamberlain, when caught in no-mans-land, leaves Ian Bryson with a simple task to equalise. Hodges powers in a header to win the points for the team who were bottom of the league in January. | | | | | | | | | | | |
| 33 | H | TOTTENHAM | | 18 | D | 0-0 | 0-0 | | Chamberlain | Johnson ! | Harvey | Rees* | Rodger | Dreyer | Elstrup^ | Preece | Farrell | Pembridge | Black | Beaumont/Nogan |
| | 1/4 | | 11,322 | *8* | 33 | | | | *Thorstvedt* | *Thomas* | *Tuttle* | *Mabbutt* | *v d Hauwe* | *Allen* | *Samways* | *Moncur* | *Nayim* | *Stewart* | *Walsh* | |
| | | | | | | | | Ref: R Wiseman | Pembridge is flattened by Mitchell Thomas in the area but Dreyer hits the bar with his spot-kick. Johnson is brought down by Erik Thorstvedt, which the referee fails to spot, but then later sends him off for a second bookable offence, an innocuous handball in the middle of the field. | | | | | | | | | | | |
| 34 | A | CHELSEA | | 18 | D | 3-3 | 3-1 | Elstrup 14, Farrell 17, Black 22 | Chamberlain | Johnson | Harvey | Beaumont | Rodger | Dreyer | Elstrup | Preece | Farrell* | Pembridge^ | Black | Nogan/James |
| | 6/4 | | *9,416* | *10* | 34 | | | *Le Saux 31, Stuart 54, Wise 66* | *Beasant* | *Hall* | *Cundy* | *Lee* | *Sinclair* | *Matthew** | *Townsend* | *Dickens* | *Wise* | *Stuart* | *Le Saux !* | *Myers* |
| | | | | | | | | Ref: T Holbrook | The Town grab a three-goal lead before allowing Chelsea to claw their way back. Le Saux gets their first before being dismissed for elbowing Rodger in the face. Dennis Wise hits a penalty-kick which Chamberlain saves, only for the ex-Wimbledon man to prod back into an empty net. | | | | | | | | | | | |
| 35 | H | WIMBLEDON | | 18 | L | 0-1 | 0-0 | | Chamberlain | Johnson | Harvey | Beaumont* | Rodger | Dreyer | Elstrup | Preece | Farrell | Pembridge | Black | Rees |
| | 13/4 | | **8,219** | *7* | 34 | | | *Fashanu 79* | *Segers* | *Joseph* | *Blackwell* | *Curle* | *Elkins* | *Barton* | *Scales* | *Sanchez* | *Clarke* | *Fashanu* | *Gibson** | *Newhouse* |
| | | | | | | | | Ref: J Moules | Luton show plenty of determination and effort but do not have the firepower to unsettle a tough Wimbledon side. John Fashanu, who is lucky to remain on the pitch after a terrible tackle on Beaumont, scores a simple goal towards the end to make it a day best forgotten for the Hatters. | | | | | | | | | | | |
| 36 | H | SUNDERLAND | | 18 | L | 1-2 | 1-1 | Rodger 34 | Chamberlain | James* | Harvey | Beaumont | Rodger | Dreyer | Elstrup | Preece | Farrell^ | Pembridge | Black | Rees/McDonough |
| | 20/4 | | 11,157 | *19* | 34 | | | *Armstrong 22, Pascoe 63* | *Norman* | *Kay** | *Bennett* | *Ball* | *Hardyman* | *Bracewell* | *Pascoe* | *Owers* | *Armstrong* | *Hauser* | *Mooney^* | *Brady/Gabbiadini* |
| | | | | | | | | Ref: K Barratt | Sunderland appear to have more passion and certainly show the will to win this relegation six-pointer as they open the scoring when Armstrong runs through unchallenged. Rodger side-foots in a cross from Black to level before Colin Pascoe strokes home the winner from a Gabbiadini pass. | | | | | | | | | | | |
| 37 | A | EVERTON | | 18 | L | 0-1 | 0-0 | | Chamberlain | Beaumont | Harvey | McDonough | Rodger* | Dreyer | Elstrup | Preece | Rees^ | Pembridge | Black | James/Telfer |
| | 4/5 | | *20,134* | *11* | 34 | | | *Cottee 49* | *Southall* | *Ebbrell* | *Ratcliffe* | *Watson* | *Hinchcliffe* | *Warzycha* | *McCall* | *Atteveld* | *Beagrie* | *Newell* | *Cottee* | |
| | | | | | | | | Ref: B Stevens | A sweeper system is employed by the Hatters in an attempt to snatch a point at Goodison Park, but the plan is wrecked when Sean Farrell, who is to be the delegated target man, is injured the day before the game. Cottee scores the only goal of the match as the Town continue to defend. | | | | | | | | | | | |
| 38 | H | DERBY | | 18 | W | 2-0 | 1-0 | Harford 41 (og), Elstrup 47 | Chamberlain | Beaumont | Harvey | Rees* | McDonough | Dreyer | Elstrup | Preece | Farrell^ | Pembridge | Black | James/Nogan |
| | 11/5 | | **12,889** | *20* | 37 | | | | *Shilton* | *Sage* | *Wright* | *Patterson* | *Forsyth* | *Micklewhite* | *Williams G* | *Williams P** | *McMinn^* | *Saunders* | *Harford* | *Hebberd/Cross* |
| | Home | | Away | | | | | Ref: G Courtney | The Town have to win well to be sure of staying up and sending Sunderland down. Derby, who are already relegated, are beaten by a fortunate own-goal from Mick Harford before the interval and a header from Elstrup. Sunderland lose at Manchester City and Luton survive once again. | | | | | | | | | | | |
| Average | 10,325 | | 19,509 | | | | | | | | | | | | | | | | | |

# BARCLAYS DIVISION 1 (CUP-TIES) Manager: Jim Ryan SEASON 1990-91



| Rumbelows Cup | | | | | F-A | H-T | Scorers, Times, and Referees | 1 | 2 | 3 | 4 | 5 | 6 | 7 | 8 | 9 | 10 | 11 | subs used |
|---|---|---|---|---|---|---|---|---|---|---|---|---|---|---|---|---|---|---|---|
| 2:1 | H | BRADFORD CITY | 7 | D | 1-1 | 1-0 | Harvey 2 | Chamberlain | Breacker | Harvey* | Rees | Beaumont | Dreyer | Elstrup^ | Preece | Dowie | Hughes | Black | James/Nogan |
| 25/9 | | 5,120 *3:12* | | | | | *James 55* | *Tomlinson* | *Mitchell* | *Oliver* | *Sinnott* | *Tinnion* | *Duxbury* | *James* | *Abbott* | *Stuart* | *McCarthy* | *Leonard* | |
| | | | | | | | Ref: A Ward | The Kenilworth Road crowd are expecting a goal avalanche after Harvey runs 40 yards with the ball before powering home with his right foot. City defend in depth, as a damage limitation exercise, before Robbie James seizes onto a loose ball and lashes in a shot from outside the area. | | | | | | | | | | | |
| 2:2 | A | BRADFORD CITY | 6 | D | 1-1 | 0-1 | Black 62 | Chamberlain | James* | Harvey | Williams | Beaumont | Dreyer | Nogan | Preece | Dowie | Hughes | Black^ | Johnson/Rees |
| 10/10 | | *6,180 3:16* | | | *aet* | | *James 36 (og)* | *Tomlinson* | *Mitchell* | *Oliver* | *Sinnott* | *Tinnion* | *James* | *Duxbury* | *Jewell* | *McCarthy* | *Leonard* | *Stuart* | |
| | | | | | | | Ref: M Peck (Hatters lost 4-5 on penalties) | City are a different side from the first leg and bombard the Luton goal from the kick-off. They take the lead when a clearance from Harvey hits James and flies into the net for a spectacular own-goal. Still under pressure, the Town break out and Black volleys in a cross from Williams. | | | | | | | | | | | |

| FA Cup | | | | | | | | | | | | | | | | | | | |
|---|---|---|---|---|---|---|---|---|---|---|---|---|---|---|---|---|---|---|---|
| 3 | A | SHEFFIELD UTD | 14 | W | 3-1 | 0-0 | Farrell 48, Elstrup 61, 75 | Chamberlain | James | Harvey | Pembridge | McDonough | Dreyer | Elstrup | Preece | Farrell | Beaumont | Black | |
| 5/1 | | *13,948 1:20* | | | | | *Bradshaw 79* | *Tracey* | *Wilder* | *Hill* | *Barnes* | *Lucas** | *Bryson* | *Jones* | *Gannon* | *Hoyland* | *Bradshaw* | *Deane* | *Marwood* |
| | | | | | | | Ref: J Worrall | Unable to capitalise upon a strong wind at their backs, the Hatters avenge their Boxing Day defeat by the Blades when playing into it in the second half. Two of the goals stem from a well-rehearsed corner routine by Preece and Black. They are converted by Farrell and Elstrup. | | | | | | | | | | | |
| 4 | H | WEST HAM | 16 | D | 1-1 | 0-1 | Black 70 | Chamberlain | James | Harvey | Williams | McDonough | Dreyer | Elstrup | Preece* | Farrell^ | Pembridge | Black | Rees/Dowie |
| 26/1 | | 12,087 *2:1* | | | | | *Parris 44* | *Miklosko* | *Breacker* | *Gale* | *Potts* | *Hughton* | *Keen** | *Bishop* | *Allen* | *Parris* | *Slater* | *Morley* | *McAvennie* |
| | | | | | | | Ref: R Groves | The Hammers take the lead just before half-time with their first attack of the game, when Chamberlain can only palm out a Stuart Slater shot, and George Parris makes no mistake from eight yards. Steve Williams flights the free-kick for Black to level at the far post to earn the replay. | | | | | | | | | | | |
| 4R | A | WEST HAM | 16 | L | 0-5 | 0-1 | *[Morley 68, 83]* | Chamberlain | James* | Harvey | Williams | McDonough | Dreyer | Elstrup^ | Preece | Dowie | Pembridge | Black | Johnson/Farrell |
| 30/1 | | *25,659 2:1* | | | | | *Parris 44, Bishop 53, McAvennie 55,* | *Miklosko* | *Breacker* | *Gale* | *Potts* | *Hughton* | *Keen* | *Bishop* | *Parris* | *Slater* | *McAvennie* | *Morley* | |
| | | | | | | | Ref: R Groves | Dowie is recalled to the side and twice goes close in an even first half, but is a spectator as the Division Two leaders destroy the Hatters with a second-half goal blitz where, but for Chamberlain, the humiliation could have been even worse. 'We got what we deserved,' reflects Jim Ryan. | | | | | | | | | | | |

| | | | Home | | | | | Away | | | | | |
|---|---|---|---|---|---|---|---|---|---|---|---|---|---|
| | P | W | D | L | F | A | W | D | L | F | A | Pts |
| 1 Arsenal | 38 | 15 | 4 | 0 | 51 | 10 | 9 | 9 | 1 | 23 | 8 | 83 |
| 2 Liverpool | 38 | 14 | 3 | 2 | 42 | 13 | 9 | 4 | 6 | 35 | 27 | 76 |
| 3 Crys Palace | 38 | 11 | 6 | 2 | 26 | 17 | 9 | 3 | 7 | 24 | 24 | 69 |
| 4 Leeds | 38 | 12 | 2 | 5 | 46 | 23 | 7 | 5 | 7 | 19 | 24 | 64 |
| 5 Manchester C | 38 | 12 | 3 | 4 | 35 | 25 | 5 | 8 | 6 | 29 | 28 | 62 |
| 6 Manchester U | 38 | 11 | 4 | 4 | 34 | 17 | 5 | 8 | 6 | 24 | 28 | 59 |
| 7 Wimbledon | 38 | 8 | 6 | 5 | 28 | 22 | 6 | 8 | 5 | 25 | 24 | 56 |
| 8 Nott'm Forest | 38 | 11 | 4 | 4 | 42 | 21 | 3 | 8 | 8 | 23 | 29 | 54 |
| 9 Everton | 38 | 9 | 5 | 5 | 26 | 15 | 4 | 7 | 8 | 24 | 31 | 51 |
| 10 Tottenham | 38 | 8 | 9 | 2 | 35 | 22 | 3 | 7 | 9 | 16 | 28 | 49 |
| 11 Chelsea | 38 | 10 | 6 | 3 | 33 | 25 | 3 | 4 | 12 | 25 | 44 | 49 |
| 12 QP Rangers | 38 | 8 | 5 | 6 | 27 | 22 | 4 | 5 | 10 | 17 | 31 | 46 |
| 13 Sheffield Utd | 38 | 9 | 3 | 7 | 23 | 23 | 4 | 4 | 11 | 13 | 32 | 46 |
| 14 Southampton | 38 | 9 | 6 | 4 | 33 | 22 | 3 | 3 | 13 | 25 | 47 | 45 |
| 15 Norwich | 38 | 9 | 3 | 7 | 27 | 32 | 4 | 3 | 12 | 14 | 32 | 45 |
| 16 Coventry | 38 | 10 | 6 | 3 | 30 | 16 | 1 | 5 | 13 | 12 | 33 | 44 |
| 17 Aston Villa | 38 | 7 | 9 | 3 | 29 | 25 | 2 | 5 | 12 | 17 | 33 | 41 |
| 18 LUTON TOWN | 38 | 7 | 5 | 7 | 22 | 18 | 3 | 2 | 14 | 20 | 43 | 37 |
| 19 Sunderland | 38 | 6 | 6 | 7 | 15 | 16 | 2 | 4 | 13 | 23 | 44 | 34 |
| 20 Derby | 38 | 3 | 8 | 8 | 25 | 36 | 2 | 1 | 16 | 12 | 39 | 24 |
| | 760 | 189 | 103 | 88 | 629 | 420 | 88 | 103 | 189 | 420 | 629 | 1034 |

Odds & ends

Double wins: (1) Aston Villa.
Double losses: (5) QP Rangers, Manchester U, Sheffield Utd, Sunderland, Wimbledon.

Won from behind: (2) Liverpool (h), Norwich (a).
Lost from in front: (6) Arsenal (a), Coventry (a), QPR (h), Sheffield United (a), Southampton (h), Tottenham (a).

High spots: Avoiding relegation again, albeit at the death.
The youngsters coming through the ranks.
Lars Elstrup's hat-trick in the 3-1 win at Norwich.
Mark Pembridge's volley in the 2-1 win at Aston Villa.

Low spots: The sale of Tim Breacker and Iain Dowie.
The home defeat by Sunderland which leaves Luton with it all to do.
Losing on penalties at Bradford City in the Rumbelows Cup, the first time a competitive Luton fixture has been determined this way.
The 0-5 drubbing at West Ham in the FA Cup.

Player of the Year: Alec Chamberlain.
Ever-presents: (2) Alec Chamberlain, John Dreyer.
Hat-tricks: (1) Lars Elstrup.
Leading scorer: (17) Lars Elstrup.

| | Appearances | | | | | | Goals | | | |
|---|---|---|---|---|---|---|---|---|---|---|
| | Lge | *Sub* | LC | *Sub* | FAC | *Sub* | Lge | LC | FAC | Tot |
| Beaumont, David | **29** | *4* | 2 | | 1 | | | | | |
| Black, Kingsley | **37** | | 2 | | 3 | | **7** | 1 | 1 | **9** |
| Breacker, Tim | **8** | | 1 | | | | | | | |
| Chamberlain, Alec | **38** | | 2 | | 3 | | | | | |
| Dowie, Iain | **26** | *3* | 2 | | 1 | *1* | **7** | | | **7** |
| Dreyer, John | **38** | | 2 | | 3 | | **3** | | | **3** |
| Elstrup, Lars | **37** | | 1 | | 3 | | **15** | | 2 | **17** |
| Farrell, Sean | **11** | *9* | | | 2 | *1* | **1** | | 1 | **2** |
| Harvey, Richard | **26** | *3* | 2 | | 3 | | | 1 | | **1** |
| Holsgrove, Paul | | *1* | | | | | | | | |
| Hughes, Ceri | **17** | | 2 | | | | **1** | | | **1** |
| James, Julian | **10** | *7* | 1 | *1* | 3 | | **1** | | | **1** |
| Johnson, Marvin | **24** | *2* | | *1* | | *1* | | | | |
| McDonough, Darron | **21** | *5* | | | 3 | | | | | |
| Nogan, Kurt | **1** | *8* | 1 | *1* | | | | | | |
| Pembridge, Mark | **18** | | | | 3 | | **1** | | | **1** |
| Preece, David | **37** | | 2 | | 3 | | **1** | | | **1** |
| Rees, Jason | **11** | *10* | 1 | *1* | | *1* | | | | |
| Rodger, Graham | **14** | | | | | | **2** | | | **2** |
| Telfer, Paul | | *1* | | | | | | | | |
| Williams, Steve | **15** | *1* | 1 | | 2 | | | | | |
| (own-goals) | | | | | | | **3** | | | **3** |
| **21 players used** | **418** | ***54*** | **22** | ***4*** | **33** | ***4*** | **42** | **2** | **4** | **48** |

| No | Date | Att | Pos | Pt | F-A | H-T | Scorers, Times, and Referees | 1 | 2 | 3 | 4 | 5 | 6 | 7 | 8 | 9 | 10 | 11 | subs used |
|---|---|---|---|---|---|---|---|---|---|---|---|---|---|---|---|---|---|---|---|
| 1 | A WEST HAM | | | D | 0-0 | 0-0 | | Chamberlain | Beaumont | Harvey | McDonough | Rodger | Dreyer | Farrell* | Preece | Stein | Pembridge | Black | **Gray** |
| | 17/8 | *25,079* | | 1 | | | | *Miklosko* | *Brown* | *Foster* | *Breacker* | *Thomas* | *Allen* | *Parris* | *Bishop** | *Slater* | *Small* | *Rosenior* | *Keen* |
| | | | | | | | Ref: M Bodenham | Newly promoted West Ham surprise the Town by playing a long-ball game in a physical match. Both sides have periods where they are on top but neither are able to find a way to break through their opponent's resolute defences. Brian Stein returns to the club after three years in France. | | | | | | | | | | | |
| 2 | A COVENTRY | | | L | **0-5** | 0-3 | *[Furlong 71]* | Chamberlain | Beaumont | Harvey | McDonough | Rodger | Dreyer | Farrell ! | Preece | Stein* | Pembridge | Black | Gray |
| | 21/8 | *9,848* | | 1 | | | *Gallacher 6, 38, Rosario 44, Smith 67,* | *Ogrizovic* | *Borrows* | *Pearce* | *Peake* | *McGrath* | *Woods* | *Robson* | *Gynn* | *Smith* | *Rosario* | *Gallacher** | *Furlong* |
| | | | | | | | Ref: M Bailey | The Sky Blues go one up after a catalogue of defensive errors sets up Kevin Gallacher. Sean Farrell is sent off after a clash with Trevor Peake as Coventry continue to pierce holes in a Luton defence which collectively suffers from a nightmare of a game, and run out the easy victors. | | | | | | | | | | | |
| 3 | H LIVERPOOL | | 19 | D | 0-0 | 0-0 | | Chamberlain | Beaumont | Harvey | McDonough | Rodger | Dreyer | Gray | Preece | Stein | Pembridge | Black | |
| | 24/8 | 11,132 | *11* | 2 | | | | *Grobbelaar* | *Tanner* | *Ablett* | *Nicol* | *Burrows* | *Houghton* | *McMahon !* | *Whelan** | *Walters^* | *Saunders* | *McManam'n* | *Marsh/Rosenthal* |
| | | | | | | | Ref: J Moules | After an even first half where both sides go close, Steve McMahon is dismissed for elbowing Phil Gray in the face. The Hatters are unable to make the extra man count and fail to pressurise the Reds' defence. Trevor Peake watches the game before signing for the Town for £100,000. | | | | | | | | | | | |
| 4 | A ARSENAL | | 21 | L | 0-2 | 0-1 | | Chamberlain | Beaumont* | Dreyer | McDon'ugh^ | Rodger | **Peake** | Gray | Preece | Stein | Pembridge | Black | **Jackson**/Farrell |
| | 27/8 | *25,898* | *15* | 2 | | | *Merson 18, Smith 49* | *Seaman* | *Dixon* | *Linighan* | *Adams* | *Winterburn* | *Rocastle* | *Davis* | *Thomas* | *Limpar !* | *Merson* | *Smith* | |
| | | | | | | | Ref: P Foakes | A pass from Lee Dixon is deflected into the path of Paul Merson for the first goal. Alan Smith turns Graham Rodger on the edge of the box and nets the second. Anders Limpar is then sent off for elbowing Pembridge. The Hatters have now gone four games without scoring a single goal. | | | | | | | | | | | |
| 5 | A CHELSEA | | 22 | L | 1-4 | 0-3 | Gray 47 *[Wise 59]* | Chamberlain | Beaumont* | Dreyer | McDonough | Rodger | Peake | Gray | Preece | Stein | Pembridge | Farrell^ | Jackson/Nogan |
| | 31/8 | *17,457* | *7* | 2 | | | *Le Saux 19, Townsend 32, Dixon 34,* | *Hitchcock* | *Clarke* | *Elliott* | *Monkou* | *Boyd* | *Wise* | *Jones* | *Townsend* | *Le Saux* | *Wilson** | *Dixon* | *Allon* |
| | | | | | | | Ref: M Pierce | The Town make it difficult for themselves by selling Black to Nottingham Forest before the game. Kerry Dixon and Dennis Wise cause havoc in the Luton defence, which is again shambolic. Gray pulls a goal back after an error by Kevin Hitchcock, but the end result is another disaster. | | | | | | | | | | | |
| 6 | H SOUTHAMPTON | | 18 | W | 2-1 | 2-1 | Gray 32, Harvey 40 | Chamberlain | Jackson* | Harvey | McDonough | Dreyer | Peake | Gray | Preece | **Glover^** | Pembridge | Stein | Beaumont/Nogan |
| | 4/9 | 8,055 | *19* | 5 | | | *Le Tissier 30p* | *Flowers* | *Dodd* | *Hall !* | *Ruddock* | *Adams* | *Lee** | *Cockerill* | *Horne* | *Le Tissier* | *Shearer* | *Dowie* | *Benali* |
| | | | | | | | Ref: A Smith | Le Tissier opens the scoring from the spot after Cockerill is tripped by Preece, but Phil Gray levels with a volley. Richard Hall is dismissed for pulling back Gray before Harvey lifts the Hatters off the foot of the table with a glorious strike from 25 yards to seal the first win of the season. | | | | | | | | | | | |
| 7 | A WIMBLEDON | | 20 | L | 0-3 | 0-1 | | Chamberlain | Jackson | Harvey* | McDonough | Dreyer | Peake | Gray | Preece | Nogan | Pembridge | Holsgrove^ | Rodger/Telfer |
| | 7/9 | ***3,231*** | *7* | 5 | | | *Clarke 32, Ryan 65, 77* | *Segers* | *Joseph* | *Scales* | *Fitzgerald* | *Elkins* | *Barton* | *Ryan* | *Phelan* | *Fairweath'r** | *Cork^* | *Clarke* | *McGee/Newhouse* |
| | | | | | | | Ref: A Bennett | The whole of the established Luton forward line is ruled out through injury and, in front of the lowest ever Division 1 crowd, the Dons prove to be too strong for the Hatters to cope with, the 0-15 corner count telling the story. Clarke and Vaughan Ryan seal the points for the home side. | | | | | | | | | | | |
| 8 | H OLDHAM | | 17 | W | 2-1 | 0-0 | Harford 85, 89 | Chamberlain | Jackson | Dreyer | McDon'ugh* | Rodger | Peake | Preece | Stein^ | Harford | Pembridge | **Thompson** | Telfer/Nogan |
| | 14/9 | 9,005 | *12* | 8 | | | *Marshall 52* | *Hallworth* | *Fleming* | *Barrett* | *Kilcline* | *Halle* | *Adams* | *Milligan* | *Henry* | *Holden* | *Sharp* | *Marshall** | *Ritchie* |
| | | | | | | | Ref: P Alcock | Ian Marshall heads the Latics into the lead and the game appears to be lost until, in true Roy of the Rovers fashion, Mick Harford - returning from Derby for £325,000 - taps in the equaliser and then scores the winner in the final minute with a right-foot volley over his left shoulder. | | | | | | | | | | | |
| 9 | H QP RANGERS | | 20 | L | 0-1 | 0-0 | | Chamberlain | Jackson | Dreyer | McDonough | Rodger | Peake | Preece | Stein* | Harford | Pembridge | Thompson^ | Nogan/Telfer |
| | 17/9 | 9,185 | *21* | 8 | | | *Barker 47* | *Stejskal* | *Bardsley* | *McDonald* | *Tillson* | *Maddix* | *Brevett** | *Barker* | *Wilson* | *Sinton* | *Walsh^* | *Thompson* | *Holloway/Bailey* |
| | | | | | | | Ref: P Durkin | Rangers notch their first win of the season when substitute Ian Holloway sets up Simon Barker to crash the ball home from the edge of the box. There is no fairy tale ending as the Luton players persist in hitting long balls into the Rangers box which are easily dealt with by Alan McDonald. | | | | | | | | | | | |
| 10 | A MANCHESTER U | | 21 | L | **0-5** | 0-1 | *[Hughes 86]* | Chamberlain | Jackson* | Dreyer | Telfer | Rodger | Peake | Preece | Stein^ | Harford | Pembridge | Thompson | Beaumont/Nogan |
| | 21/9 | ***46,491*** | *1* | 8 | | | *Ince 23, Bruce 63p, McClair 76, 80,* | *Schmeichel* | *Blackmore** | *Bruce* | *Pallister* | *Irwin* | *Phelan* | *Robson* | *Webb* | *Ince* | *Hughes* | *Giggs* | *McClair* |
| | | | | | | | Ref: A Gunn | After a fairly even first half, unbeaten United step up a gear in the second period and crush the Town with their power play. The linesman flags that the ball from a corner-kick has gone out of play, but he is ignored by the ref who awards a penalty instead after Mark Pembridge handles. | | | | | | | | | | | |

| | | | | | | | | | | | | | | | | | | | | |
|---|---|---|---|---|---|---|---|---|---|---|---|---|---|---|---|---|---|---|---|---|
| 11 | H | NOTTS CO | | 20 | D | 1-1 | 0-0 | Gray 68 | Chamberlain | Jackson | Dreyer | Telfer* | Rodger | Beaumont | Preece | Gray | Harford^ | Pembridge | Thompson | Hughes/Nogan |
| 28/9 | | | 7,629 | *11* | 9 | | | *Johnson 88p* | *Cherry* | *Short Ch's** | *Short Craig* | *Yates* | *Palmer* | *Paris* | *Harding* | *Thomas* | *Johnson* | *Rideout* | *Bartlett^* | *Draper/Turner* |
| | | | | | | | | Ref: J Rushton | A header from Phil Gray, when he connects with a perfect cross from Mark Pembridge, seems to have set the Town up for their third home win of the season. They are undone, however, when the referee awards a penalty for a seemingly legitimate tackle by Matt Jackson on Phil Turner. | | | | | | | | | | | |
| 12 | A | ASTON VILLA | | 21 | L | 0-4 | 0-1 | *[Mortimer 80]* | Chamberlain | Jackson | Dreyer | Thompson | Rodger* | Peake | Telfer | Gray | Nogan | Pembridge | Hughes^ | Beaumont/Stein |
| 5/10 | | | *18,722* | *14* | 9 | | | *Richardson 4, Regis 47, Yorke 59,* | *Spink* | *Kubicki* | *Teale* | *McGrath* | *Nielsen** | *Staunton* | *Richardson* | *Cowans* | *Yorke* | *Regis* | *Atkinson* | *Mortimer* |
| | | | | | | | | Ref: P Don | Shaun Teale handles a cross from Telfer but Gray blasts his spot-kick against the bar and the follow up, from Thompson, is tipped over by Nigel Spink. With the defence conceding four goals, the Town have now scored fewer and conceded more goals than any other team in the division. | | | | | | | | | | | |
| 13 | H | SHEFFIELD WED | | 21 | D | 2-2 | 1-1 | Harford 28, Nogan 80 | Chamberlain | James | Harvey* | Nogan | Dreyer | Peake | Telfer | Gray | Harford | Pembridge | Preece^ | Hughes/Stein |
| 19/10 | | | 9,401 | *5* | 10 | | | *Hirst 44, Sheridan 89* | *Woods* | *Nilsson* | *Anderson* | *Pearson* | *King* | *Wilson** | *Sheridan* | *Palmer* | *Worthingt'n^* | *Hirst* | *Williams* | *Hyde/Jemson* |
| | | | | | | | | Ref: D Elleray | Kurt Nogan misses three good chances before putting Luton into the lead with a rocket shot after Stein sends him clear. A free-kick in the last minute is rolled to John Sheridan, who tees the ball up for a spectacular equalising volley. Matt Jackson is sold as Barclays Bank gets tough. | | | | | | | | | | | |
| 14 | A | NORWICH | | 21 | L | 0-1 | 0-1 | | Chamberlain | Telfer | Dreyer | Hughes | Rodger* | Peake | Rees^ | James | Nogan | Pembridge | **Oakes** | **Linton**/Harvey |
| 26/10 | | | *10,514* | *11* | 10 | | | *Newman 41* | *Gunn* | *Phillips* | *Butterw'rth* | *Blades* | *Bowen* | *Gordon* | *Goss* | *Newman* | *Ullathorne** | *Fox* | *Fleck* | *Beckford* |
| | | | | | | | | Ref: K Hackett | Alec Chamberlain has conceded 24 goals in the last six games but plays a blinder as the Canaries threaten to run riot. He is unable to prevent Newman from slotting home a cross from Robert Fleck which wins the game. New boy Scott Oakes sees his free-kick hit the bar from 30 yards. | | | | | | | | | | | |
| 15 | H | EVERTON | | 21 | L | 0-1 | 0-0 | | Chamberlain | James* | Pembridge | **Kamara** | Dreyer | Peake | Telfer | Hughes | Harford | Gray^ | Oakes | Stein/Nogan |
| 2/11 | | | 8,002 | *12* | 10 | | | *Warzycha 67* | *Southall* | *Jackson** | *Watson* | *Keown* | *Hinchcliffe* | *Nevin^* | *Ebbrell* | *Atteveld* | *Beagrie* | *Beardsley* | *Newell* | *Cottee/Warzycha* |
| | | | | | | | | Ref: M Brandwood | In a drab game, Kamara makes a disappointing debut following his transfer from Leeds, and top scorer Phil Gray limps off with a knee injury. Everton play in Luton's away strip because of a colour clash but are little better than the Town. A shot from Warzycha is enough to gain the win. | | | | | | | | | | | |
| 16 | A | TOTTENHAM | | 21 | L | 1-4 | 1-0 | Harford 43 | Chamberlain | Linton* | Harvey | Kamara | Dreyer | Peake | Telfer | Stein | Harford | Pembridge | Oakes | Nogan |
| 16/11 | | | *27,543* | *11* | 10 | | | *Houghton 68, 75, Lineker 70, 83* | *Thorstvedt* | *v d Hauwe* | *Bergsson* | *Mabbutt* | *Edinburgh* | *Allen** | *Sedgley* | *Samways* | *Howells^* | *Walsh* | *Lineker* | *Houghton/Nayim* |
| | | | | | | | | Ref: D Frampton | Mick Harford gives the Town a deserved lead before half-time when tapping in a cross from Brian Stein, but a floodlight failure brings about a fifteen minute delay. Spurs bring on their substitutes and they steam-roller the Town into submission although the final score-line flatters them. | | | | | | | | | | | |
| 17 | H | MANCHESTER C | | 22 | D | 2-2 | 1-0 | Harford 17, Dreyer 56 | Chamberlain | Linton* | Harvey | Kamara | Dreyer | Peake | Telfer | Stein | Harford | Pembridge | Oakes | Preece |
| 23/11 | | | 10,031 | *3* | 11 | | | *Curle 46, Quinn 59* | *Margetson* | *Hill* | *Curle* | *Redmond !* | *Pointon* | *White** | *Megson* | *Brightwell* | *Hughes* | *Heath* | *Quinn* | *Sheron* |
| | | | | | | | | Ref: J Key | A blunder from Steve Redmond allows Mick Harford to give Luton the interval lead, but City fight back and a diving header from Keith Curle levels the scores. Dreyer restores the lead when his shot dribbles over the line before Niall Quinn heads in. Redmond is sent off for tripping Stein. | | | | | | | | | | | |
| 18 | A | SHEFFIELD UTD | | 22 | D | 1-1 | 0-0 | Telfer 79 | **Sutton** | James | Harvey | Kamara | Dreyer | Peake | Telfer | Stein | Harford* | Pembridge | **Campbell** | Preece |
| 30/11 | | | *21,804* | *20* | 12 | | | *Bryson 88* | *Tracey* | *Pemberton* | *Gayle* | *Beesley* | *Gage* | *Bradshaw** | *Gannon^* | *Hoyland* | *Whitehouse* | *Deane* | *Bryson* | *Lake/Hill* |
| | | | | | | | | Ref: M Reed | Telfer slams the ball into the roof of the net, after a tussle in the penalty area, which appears to have won the points but Richard Harvey gifts away a needless corner and Beesley's flick gives Ian Bryson a last gasp equaliser and extends the Town's run of games without a win to ten. | | | | | | | | | | | |
| 19 | H | LEEDS | | 22 | L | 0-2 | 0-0 | | Sutton | James* | Harvey | Kamara | Dreyer | Peake | Telfer | Stein^ | Harford | Pembridge | Oakes | Preece/Campbell |
| 7/12 | | | 11,550 | *1* | 12 | | | *Wallace 68, Speed 69* | *Lukic* | *Sterland* | *Fairclough* | *Whyte* | *Dorigo* | *Strachan* | *Batty* | *McAllister* | *Speed* | *Wallace* | *Chapman* | |
| | | | | | | | | Ref: P Vanes | The Hatters give as good as they get in an entertaining first half but, when Leeds step up a gear after the break, they are far too hot to handle. A throw from David Batty is flicked on by Lee Chapman and Rod Wallace hits an unstoppable volley past Steve Sutton, making his home debut. | | | | | | | | | | | |
| 20 | H | COVENTRY | | 22 | W | 1-0 | 0-0 | Harford 55 | Sutton | James | Harvey | Kamara | Dreyer | Peake | Telfer | Stein | Harford | Pembridge | Oakes* | Preece |
| 20/12 | | | **7,533** | *15* | 15 | | | | *Ogrizovic* | *Borrows* | *Atherton* | *Pearce* | *Hurst* | *Ndlovu** | *Emerson* | *McGrath* | *Smith* | *Furlong* | *Gallacher* | *Rosario* |
| | | | | | | | | Ref: K Cooper | An early Christmas present for the Hatters, although the result is far more important than the game, which is poor fare for the fans. A shot from Chris Kamara from outside the box is blocked and the ball runs to Mick Harford, who scores the only goal of the match with a right-foot drive. | | | | | | | | | | | |
| 21 | H | ARSENAL | | 22 | W | 1-0 | 0-0 | Harford 79 | Sutton | James | Harvey | Kamara | Dreyer | Peake | Telfer | Stein* | Harford | Pembridge | Preece | Oakes |
| 26/12 | | | 12,665 | *7* | 18 | | | | *Seaman* | *O'Leary* | *Bould* | *Adams* | *Winterburn* | *Limpar** | *Rocastle* | *Dixon* | *Merson* | *Wright* | *Smith* | *Campbell* |
| | | | | | | | | Ref: R Wiseman | The Gunners are never allowed to settle as Luton impose themselves on the game. Substitute Scott Oakes puts over a tempting diagonal pass which Harford volleys past David Seaman. Both Peake and Winterburn seem to handle the ball in the area but the referee sees neither incident. | | | | | | | | | | | |

# BARCLAYS LEAGUE DIVISION 1 Manager: David Pleat SEASON 1991-92

| No | Date | | Att | Pos | Pt | F-A | H-T | Scorers, Times, and Referees | 1 | 2 | 3 | 4 | 5 | 6 | 7 | 8 | 9 | 10 | 11 | subs used |
|---|---|---|---|---|---|---|---|---|---|---|---|---|---|---|---|---|---|---|---|---|
| 22 | H | CHELSEA | | 20 | W | 2-0 | 2-0 | Harvey 38, Dreyer 41p | Sutton | James | Harvey | Kamara | Dreyer | Peake | Telfer | Stein* | Harford | Pembridge | Preece^ | Campbell/Oakes |
| | 28/12 | | 10,738 | *12* | 21 | | | | *Beasant* | *Clarke** | *Elliott* | *Monkou* | *Boyd !* | *Wise* | *Jones^* | *Townsend* | *Le Saux* | *Dixon* | *Allen* | *Stuart/Dickens* |
| | | | | | | | | Ref: J Deakin | John Major watches as Harvey opens the scoring with a 25-yard rocket shot. Beasant pulls down Pembridge and Dreyer gets the second from the spot with one of his now-famous penalty kicks. Boyd is sent off for chopping down Telfer in the area, but Harford's spot-kick hits the bar. | | | | | | | | | | | |
| 23 | A | NOTT'M FOREST | | 19 | D | 1-1 | 1-0 | Pembridge 1 | Sutton | James | Harvey | Kamara | Dreyer | Peake | Telfer | Stein* | Harford | Pembridge | Preece^ | Oakes/Campbell |
| | 1/1 | | *23,809* | *11* | 22 | | | *Walker 89* | *Crossley* | *Charles* | *Walker* | *Tiler* | *Pearce* | *Crosby* | *Keane* | *Gemmill* | *Black* | *Clough* | *Sheringham* | |
| | | | | | | | | Ref: D Allinson | Pembridge scores the quickest goal of 1992 when, after just 33 seconds, his left-foot shot whistles past Mark Crossley. Luton play plenty of pretty football but it is Forest who apply the pressure in the last four minutes which results in Walker running through to net his first ever goal. | | | | | | | | | | | |
| 24 | A | LIVERPOOL | | 20 | L | 1-2 | 1-0 | Tanner 31 (og) | Sutton | James | Harvey | Kamara | Dreyer | Peake | Telfer | Stein | Nogan | Pembridge | Preece* | Oakes |
| | 11/1 | | *35,095* | *3* | 22 | | | *McManaman 85, Saunders 89* | *Grobbelaar* | *Jones* | *Wright* | *Tanner* | *Nicol* | *Houghton* | *Molby** | *Thomas* | *Barnes* | *McManaman* | *Saunders* | *Rosenthal* |
| | | | | | | | | Ref: W Burns | Tanner turns a Nogan cross into his own net and, just as the Hatters seem to have weathered Liverpool's storm, hesitancy in the Town defence allows McManaman to level. For the fifth time this season, the Hatters concede a late goal when Saunders knocks in a cross from John Barnes. | | | | | | | | | | | |
| 25 | H | WEST HAM | | 22 | L | 0-1 | 0-0 | | Sutton | James | Harvey | Kamara | Dreyer | Peake | Telfer* | Stein | Nogan^ | Pembridge | Preece | Oakes/Campbell |
| | 18/1 | | 11,088 | *20* | 22 | | | *Small 55* | *Miklosko* | *Breacker* | *Potts* | *Foster* | *Dicks* | *Brown* | *Thomas* | *Bishop* | *Slater** | *McAven'ie^* | *Morley* | *Keen/Small* |
| | | | | | | | | Ref: R Bigger | Mike Small, discarded by Luton ten years previously, scores the only goal with a shot that is deflected past Steve Sutton by Trevor Peake. The Hammers then pull everyone behind the ball and defend in depth as the Hatters try to find a way through. The Town are now bottom of the table. | | | | | | | | | | | |
| 26 | A | SHEFFIELD WED | | 22 | L | 2-3 | 2-1 | Preece 21, Oakes 35 | Sutton | James | Harvey | Kamara | Dreyer | Peake | Oakes | Stein* | Harford | Pembridge | Preece | Hughes |
| | 1/2 | | *22,291* | *5* | 22 | | | *Hirst 17, Williams 78, Harkes 85* | *Woods* | *Nilsson* | *Warhurst* | *Pearson* | *King* | *Harkes* | *Palmer* | *Hyde* | *Worthingt'n** | *Williams* | *Hirst* | *Francis* |
| | | | | | | | | Ref: P Harrison | On an icy pitch David Hirst scores from a cross by Paul Warhurst. The Hatters then open up the Owls' defence, firstly through Preece and then Oakes, who nets his first for the club. Paul Williams levels the scores before American John Harkes completes a miserable day for the Town. | | | | | | | | | | | |
| 27 | H | NORWICH | | 21 | W | 2-0 | 0-0 | Preece 67, Harford 88 | Sutton | James | Harvey | Kamara* | Dreyer | Peake | Oakes | Hughes | Harford | Pembridge | Preece | Stein |
| | 8/2 | | 8,554 | *16* | 25 | | | | *Walton* | *Culverhouse* | *Butterw'rth* | *Polston* | *Bowen* | *Fox* | *Goss* | *Crook* | *Phillips* | *Fleck* | *Beckford** | *Sutch* |
| | | | | | | | | Ref: P Jones | A lack of effort is shown in the first half against a poor Norwich side but after a half-time team talk Preece scores for the second game running, after Mark Bowen fails to control the ball. Mick Harford then makes the game safe with a simple tap-in following a cross from Pembridge. | | | | | | | | | | | |
| 28 | A | MANCHESTER C | | 21 | L | 0-4 | 0-1 | | Sutton | James* | Harvey | Kamara | Dreyer | Peake | Telfer^ | Stein | Harford | Pembridge | Preece | Hughes/Oakes |
| | 15/2 | | *22,137* | *3* | 25 | | | *White 13, 49, Hill 47, Heath 76* | *Coton* | *Hill* | *Curle* | *Redmond* | *Pointon* | *Brightwell* | *Reid** | *McMahon* | *Hughes^* | *White* | *Quinn* | *Heath/Sheron* |
| | | | | | | | | Ref: K Breen | The Hatters waste a total of 22 goalscoring chances in a game in which City take the lead when White appears to be well offside. The third goal is more bizarre - the Town stop playing for an offside but the referee waves play on, allowing White to shoot into an empty net from 45 yards. | | | | | | | | | | | |
| 29 | H | SHEFFIELD UTD | | 20 | W | 2-1 | 2-1 | Stein 6, Harford 23 | Sutton | James | Harvey | Kamara | Dreyer | Peake | Oakes | Stein* | Harford | Pembridge | Preece^ | Campbell/Hughes |
| | 22/2 | | 9,003 | *18* | 28 | | | *Bryson 10* | *Tracey* | *Gage* | *Gayle* | *Beesley** | *Barnes* | *Bradshaw* | *Rogers* | *Gannon* | *Hodges* | *Bryson^* | *Deane* | *Hoyl'nd/Whitehouse* |
| | | | | | | | | Ref: T Holbrook | Stein taps into an empty net, as Tracey misjudges a long through-pass by Pembridge, to score his first goal for the club since the Littlewoods Cup final in 1988. United level shortly after, but Harford heads the winner from a cross by Oakes. Tracey then saves a penalty from Dreyer. | | | | | | | | | | | |
| 30 | A | CRYS PALACE | | 20 | D | 1-1 | 0-1 | Pembridge 50p | Sutton | James | Harvey | Kamara | Dreyer | Peake | Oakes* | Stein^ | Harford | Pembridge | Preece | Hughes/Campbell |
| | 25/2 | | *12,109* | *9* | 29 | | | *Bright 19* | *Martyn* | *Humphrey* | *Young* | *Thorn* | *Sinnott** | *McGoldrick* | *Thomas* | *Osborn* | *Rodger* | *Bright* | *Whyte^* | *Colem'n/Southgate* |
| | | | | | | | | Ref: P Danson | Eddie McGoldrick sets up Mark Bright to scramble the Eagles into the lead, but the Hatters 'football' their way back into the match and James produces some deft footwork to take out three opponents and send Stein clear. He is brought down by Young and Pembridge nets from the spot. | | | | | | | | | | | |
| 31 | A | LEEDS | | 20 | L | 0-2 | 0-0 | | Sutton | James | Harvey | Kamara | Dreyer | Peake | Hughes* | Campbell^ | Harford | Pembridge | Preece | **Salton**/Stein |
| | 29/2 | | *28,227* | *2* | 29 | | | *Cantona 59, Chapman 85* | *Lukic* | *Sterland* | *Fairclough* | *Whyte* | *Dorigo** | *Strachan* | *Batty* | *McAllister* | *Speed* | *Wallace^* | *Chapman* | *Cantona/Agana* |
| | | | | | | | | Ref: A Flood | Kamara is given a warm welcome by the Elland Road crowd but it proves to be a miserable return for him. Luton have their chances but it is Leeds who win through. Cantona tucks the ball away from close in and then Chapman volleys a spectacular goal after a mistake from Dreyer. | | | | | | | | | | | |

| No | Ven | Opponent / Date | Att | Pos | Res | FT | HT | Scorers, Times, and Referees | 1 | 2 | 3 | 4 | 5 | 6 | 7 | 8 | 9 | 10 | 11 | subs used |
|---|---|---|---|---|---|---|---|---|---|---|---|---|---|---|---|---|---|---|---|---|
| 32 | H | CRYS PALACE | | 19 | D | 1-1 | 0-1 | Oakes 68 | **Day** | James | Harvey | Kamara | Dreyer | Peake | Oakes | Stein* | Campbell | Pembridge | Preece | Hughes |
| | | 7/3 | 8,591 | *11* | 30 | | | *McGoldrick 21* | *Martyn* | *Humphrey* | *Thorn* | *Young* | *Shaw** | *McGoldrick* | *Rodger* | *Southgate* | *Mortimer^* | *Coleman* | *Bright* | *Sinnott/Whyte* |
| | | | | | | | | Ref: D Elleray | Eddie McGoldrick opens the scoring with a header from a free-kick by Andy Thorn before Scott Oakes plays a one-two with Stein and blasts a right-foot volley past Nigel Martyn. Kamara has a late effort disallowed for offside, but the video replay shows that the linesman was wrong. | | | | | | | | | | | |
| 33 | H | TOTTENHAM | | 19 | D | 0-0 | 0-0 | | Day | James | Harvey | Kamara | Dreyer | Peake | Hughes | Stein | Campbell | Pembridge | Preece | |
| | | 11/3 | 11,494 | *17* | 31 | | | | *Thorstvedt* | *Fenwick* | *Sedgley* | *Mabbutt* | *Edinburgh* | *Allen* | *Howells* | *Stewart* | *Durie* | *Gray* | *Walsh** | *Bergsson* |
| | | | | | | | | Ref: R Hamer | Gordon Durie hits the bar and both Ceri Hughes and Brian Stein force Thorstvedt to come rushing out smartly to collect in an otherwise dismal game. The defences dominate and both managers are determined that their team doesn't lose. Spurs have now gone eight games without a win. | | | | | | | | | | | |
| 34 | A | EVERTON | | 19 | D | 1-1 | 1-0 | Stein 7 | Day | James | Harvey | Kamara | Dreyer | Peake | Rees* | Stein^ | Harford | Pembridge | Preece | Hughes/Campbell |
| | | 14/3 | *17,388* | *7* | 32 | | | *Johnston 51* | *Southall* | *Jackson** | *Watson* | *Keown* | *Ablett* | *Ward* | *Ebbrell* | *Harper* | *Beagrie* | *Beardsley* | *Johnston^* | *Hinchcliffe/Warzycha* |
| | | | | | | | | Ref: K Barratt | Pembridge hits a free-kick against the bar and, with Dave Watson failing to clear, Brian Stein nips in to score from close range. Everton then change their formation in the second half and get the equaliser when Mo Johnston glances in a header following a cross by Andy Hinchcliffe. | | | | | | | | | | | |
| 35 | A | SOUTHAMPTON | | 20 | L | 1-2 | 1-0 | Pembridge 1 | Day | James* | Harvey | Kamara | Dreyer | Peake | Rees | Stein^ | Harford | Pembridge | Preece | Hughes/**Williams** |
| | | 21/3 | *14,192* | *18* | 32 | | | *Shearer 68, Dowie 80* | *Flowers* | *Kenna* | *Moore* | *Ruddock* | *Benali* | *Cockerill* | *Hurlock* | *Horne** | *Gilkes* | *Dowie* | *Shearer* | *Powell* |
| | | | | | | | | Ref: C Wilkes | Mark Pembridge smacks a 20-yard free-kick which flies into the top corner of the net to give the Town the best possible start to the match after just 50 seconds. The Saints use brawn with which to fight back, and Shearer levels and then fouls Day, enabling Iain Dowie to lash the winner. | | | | | | | | | | | |
| 36 | H | WIMBLEDON | | 20 | W | 2-1 | 1-1 | Varadi 27, Preece 64 | Chamberlain | James | Harvey | Kamara | Dreyer | Peake | **Varadi** | Stein | Harford | Pembridge | Preece | |
| | | 4/4 | 7,753 | *14* | 35 | | | *Fashanu 6* | *Segers* | *Barton* | *Fitzgerald* | *Scales* | *Phelan* | *Ryan* | *Earle* | *Sanchez** | *Dobbs* | *Fashanu* | *Miller* | *Clarke* |
| | | | | | | | | Ref: B Hill | A physical Wimbledon side take the lead when John Fashanu thumps the ball home after the Luton defence fails to properly clear a cross from Terry Phelan. Loan player Imre Varadi bundles in a close-range effort for the equaliser before David Preece hits the winner with a left-foot shot. | | | | | | | | | | | |
| 37 | A | OLDHAM | | 20 | L | 1-5 | 1-2 | Harford 25 | Chamberlain | James | Harvey* | Kamara | Dreyer | Peake | Varadi | Stein | Harford | Pembridge | Preece^ | Rees/Hughes |
| | | 11/4 | *13,210* | *15* | 35 | | | *Sharp 10, 26, 80, 88, Milligan 82* | *Hallworth* | *Fleming* | *Marshall* | *Jobson* | *Barlow* | *Adams** | *Milligan* | *Henry* | *Holden* | *Sharp* | *Ritchie^* | *Bernard/Palmer* |
| | | | | | | | | Ref: R Hart | Andy King, commercial manager at Kenilworth Road, gives his old Everton colleague Graeme Sharp a lift to the game but regrets it afterwards as the tall Scot nets four goals to ensure Oldham pull clear of the relegation places. Mick Harford scores after a strike from Varadi hits the bar. | | | | | | | | | | | |
| 38 | H | NOTT'M FOREST | | 20 | W | 2-1 | 2-1 | Harford 12, James 24 | Chamberlain | James | Harvey | Kamara | Dreyer | Peake | Varadi* | Stein^ | Harford | Pembridge | Preece | Hughes/Gray |
| | | 14/4 | 8,014 | *10* | 38 | | | *Black 2* | *Crossley* | *Crosby* | *Walker** | *Clough* | *Williams* | *Orlygsson* | *Keane* | *Gemmill* | *Black* | *Glover* | *Sheringham* | *Kaminsky* |
| | | | | | | | | Ref: T Fitzharris | Ex-Hatter Kingsley Black has both the time and the space to score after the Luton defence, slipping and sliding on the wet pitch, fail to clear a cross from Toddy Orlygsson. Harford levels before James launches himself horizontally to powerfully head home a corner from David Preece. | | | | | | | | | | | |
| 39 | H | MANCHESTER U | | 20 | D | 1-1 | 0-1 | Harford 50 | Chamberlain | James | Harvey | Kamara | Dreyer | Peake | Varadi* | Oakes^ | Harford | Pembridge | Preece | Gray/Stein |
| | | 18/4 | 13,410 | *1* | 39 | | | *Sharpe 24* | *Schmeichel* | *Parker** | *Bruce* | *Pallister* | *Irwin* | *McClair* | *Phelan* | *Webb* | *Sharpe* | *Giggs* | *Hughes^* | *Blackmore/Kanch'kis* |
| | | | | | | | | Ref: M Bodenham | In front of the biggest crowd of the season, Lee Sharpe puts the visitors ahead, against the run of play, after getting on to the end of a long kick from Schmeichel, then beating Peake for pace. Harford heads a cross from Preece against the bar but is first to the rebound to level the scores. | | | | | | | | | | | |
| 40 | A | QP RANGERS | | 20 | L | 1-2 | 0-0 | Pembridge 64p | Chamberlain | James | Harvey* | Kamara | Dreyer | Peake | Varadi^ | Oakes | Harford | Pembridge | Preece | Hughes/Stein |
| | | 20/4 | *10,749* | *14* | 39 | | | *Ferdinand 80, 83* | *Stejskal* | *Bardsley* | *Peacock* | *McDonald* | *Wilson* | *Impey* | *Wilkins* | *Holloway* | *Sinton* | *Allen** | *Ferdinand* | *Penrice* |
| | | | | | | | | Ref: D Axcell | Mark Pembridge nets from the spot after Alan McDonald shoves Mick Harford in the area. Two goals in the last ten minutes from Les Ferdinand make for a heart-breaking finale for the large Luton following at Loftus Road. The Hatters have now gone 25 games without an away victory. | | | | | | | | | | | |
| 41 | H | ASTON VILLA | | 20 | W | **2-0** | 1-0 | Stein 10, Pembridge 48 | Chamberlain | James | Salton | Kamara | Dreyer | Peake | Oakes* | Stein | Harford | Pembridge | Preece | Varadi |
| | | 25/4 | 11,178 | *9* | 42 | | | | *Bosnich* | *Barrett* | *Teale* | *McGrath* | *Staunton* | *Cox* | *Richardson* | *Parker* | *Daley* | *Olney** | *Regis* | *Atkinson* |
| | | | | | | | | Ref: G Pooley | In a game that the Town must win to have any chance of avoiding relegation, they are helped by a below-par Aston Villa side. Stein opens the scoring when flicking home a cross by Pembridge and the provider turns scorer when beating Australian, Mark Bosnich, with a 25-yard shot. | | | | | | | | | | | |
| 42 | A | NOTTS CO | | 20 | L | 1-2 | 1-1 | James 18 | Chamberlain | James | Salton* | Kamara^ | Dreyer | Peake | Oakes | Stein | Harford | Pembridge | Preece | Gray/Rees |
| | | 2/5 | *11,380* | *21* | 42 | | | *Matthews 34, 71* | *Cherry* | *Palmer* | *Williams* | *Short Craig* | *Thomas* | *Short Chris* | *Draper* | *Harding* | *Wilson** | *Agana* | *Matthews* | *Devlin* |
| | | Home | Away | | | | | Ref: R Nixon | For the fourth season running, it is all down to the final day. James gives hope when he hits the opening goal but already relegated County fight back and Rob Matthews takes advantage of an error following a free-kick by Dean Thomas. His winner is a brilliant curling shot into the corner. | | | | | | | | | | | |
| | | Average 9,715 | 19,865 | | | | | | | | | | | | | | | | | |

# BARCLAYS DIVISION 1 (CUP-TIES) Manager: David Pleat SEASON 1991-92



| Rumbelows Cup | | | | | F-A | H-T | Scorers, Times, and Referees | 1 | 2 | 3 | 4 | 5 | 6 | 7 | 8 | 9 | 10 | 11 | subs used |
|---|---|---|---|---|---|---|---|---|---|---|---|---|---|---|---|---|---|---|---|
| 2:1 | H | BIRMINGHAM | 21 | D | 2-2 | 0-1 | Gray 48, Nogan 83 | Chamberlain | Jackson | Dreyer | Telfer | Rodger | Beaumont | Preece | Stein* | Gray^ | Pembridge | Thompson | Nogan/Salton |
| 25/9 | | 6,315 | *3:2* | | | | *Rogerson 3, Gleghorn 59* | *Thomas* | *Clarkson* | *Hicks* | *Mardon* | *Matthews'n* | *Rodgerson* | *Frain* | *Peer* | *Gleghorn* | *Donowa* | *Sturridge* | |
| | | | | | | | Ref: R Pawley | Ian Rodgerson opens the scoring with a free header but Phil Gray steers in a cross from Jackson to level. On the break, Rodgerson crosses for Gleghorn to head home before substitute Nogan heads in a cross from John Dreyer. The game is nicely poised for the second leg at St Andrews. | | | | | | | | | | | |
| 2:2 | A | BIRMINGHAM | 21 | L | 2-3 | 0-1 | Gray 61, 63 | Chamberlain | Jackson | Harvey | Thompson* | Beaumont | Peake | Telfer | Gray | Harford^ | Pembridge | Preece | Nogan/Stein |
| 8/10 | | *13,252* | *3:2* | | | | *Peer 28, Gleghorn 60, 89* | *Thomas* | *Clarkson* | *Hicks* | *Mardon* | *Matthews'n* | *Rodgerson* | *Peer* | *Frain* | *Gleghorn* | *Sturridge* | *Donowa* | |
| | | | | | | | Ref: K Burge (Hatters lost 4-5 on aggregate) | Louie Donowa crosses for Dean Peer to head the first goal. Nigel Gleghorn nets the second when receiving Ian Rodgerson's free-kick. Phil Gray pulls two goals back in the space of two minutes but Rodgerson crosses for Gleghorn to net the unlikely winner in the dying seconds. | | | | | | | | | | | |

| FA Cup | | | | | | | | 1 | 2 | 3 | 4 | 5 | 6 | 7 | 8 | 9 | 10 | 11 | subs used |
|---|---|---|---|---|---|---|---|---|---|---|---|---|---|---|---|---|---|---|---|
| 3 | A | SHEFFIELD UTD | 19 | L | 0-4 | 0-1 | *[Whitehouse 89]* | Chamberlain | James* | Harvey | Kamara | Dreyer | Peake | Telfer | Stein | Oakes | Pembridge | Preece | Campbell |
| 4/1 | | *12,201* | *1:20* | | | | *Hodges 44, Deane 64, Lake 86,* | *Tracey* | *Hill* | *Hoyland** | *Beesley* | *Cowan* | *Ward^* | *Gannon* | *Lake* | *Whitehouse* | *Deane* | *Hodges* | *Gage/Bryson* |
| | | | | | | | Ref: K Barratt | Alec Chamberlain has a nightmare of a game as the Blades power to victory. Glyn Hodges opens the scoring after Dreyer falls over and Brian Deane hits number two after a 40-yard run, with the Town pushing up looking to equalise. The last two goals only serve to flatter United. | | | | | | | | | | | |

| | Home | | | | | | Away | | | | | |
|---|---|---|---|---|---|---|---|---|---|---|---|---|
| | P | W | D | L | F | A | W | D | L | F | A | Pts |
| 1 Leeds | 42 | 13 | 8 | 0 | 38 | 13 | 9 | 8 | 4 | 36 | 24 | 82 |
| 2 Manchester U | 42 | 12 | 7 | 2 | 34 | 13 | 9 | 8 | 4 | 29 | 20 | 78 |
| 3 Sheffield Wed | 42 | 13 | 5 | 3 | 39 | 24 | 8 | 7 | 6 | 23 | 25 | 75 |
| 4 Arsenal | 42 | 12 | 7 | 2 | 51 | 22 | 7 | 8 | 6 | 30 | 24 | 72 |
| 5 Manchester C | 42 | 13 | 4 | 4 | 32 | 14 | 7 | 6 | 8 | 29 | 34 | 70 |
| 6 Liverpool | 42 | 13 | 5 | 3 | 34 | 17 | 3 | 11 | 7 | 13 | 23 | 64 |
| 7 Aston Villa | 42 | 13 | 3 | 5 | 31 | 16 | 4 | 6 | 11 | 17 | 28 | 60 |
| 8 Nott'm Forest | 42 | 10 | 7 | 4 | 36 | 27 | 6 | 4 | 11 | 24 | 31 | 59 |
| 9 Sheffield Utd | 42 | 9 | 6 | 6 | 29 | 23 | 7 | 3 | 11 | 36 | 40 | 57 |
| 10 Crys Palace | 42 | 7 | 8 | 6 | 24 | 25 | 7 | 7 | 7 | 29 | 36 | 57 |
| 11 QP Rangers | 42 | 6 | 10 | 5 | 25 | 21 | 6 | 8 | 7 | 23 | 26 | 54 |
| 12 Everton | 42 | 8 | 8 | 5 | 28 | 19 | 5 | 6 | 10 | 24 | 32 | 53 |
| 13 Wimbledon | 42 | 10 | 5 | 6 | 32 | 20 | 3 | 9 | 9 | 21 | 33 | 53 |
| 14 Chelsea | 42 | 7 | 8 | 6 | 31 | 30 | 6 | 6 | 9 | 19 | 30 | 53 |
| 15 Tottenham | 42 | 7 | 3 | 11 | 33 | 35 | 8 | 4 | 9 | 25 | 28 | 52 |
| 16 Southampton | 42 | 7 | 5 | 9 | 17 | 28 | 7 | 5 | 9 | 22 | 27 | 52 |
| 17 Oldham | 42 | 11 | 5 | 5 | 46 | 36 | 3 | 4 | 14 | 17 | 31 | 51 |
| 18 Norwich | 42 | 8 | 6 | 7 | 29 | 28 | 3 | 6 | 12 | 18 | 35 | 45 |
| 19 Coventry | 42 | 6 | 7 | 8 | 18 | 15 | 5 | 4 | 12 | 17 | 29 | 44 |
| 20 LUTON TOWN | 42 | 10 | 7 | 4 | 25 | 17 | 0 | 5 | 16 | 13 | 54 | 42 |
| 21 Notts Co | 42 | 7 | 5 | 9 | 24 | 29 | 3 | 5 | 13 | 16 | 33 | 40 |
| 22 West Ham | 42 | 6 | 6 | 9 | 22 | 24 | 3 | 5 | 13 | 15 | 35 | 38 |
| | 924 | 208 | 135 | 119 | 678 | 496 | 119 | 135 | 208 | 496 | 678 | 1251 |

Odds & ends

Double wins: (0).

Double losses: (2) Leeds, QPR.

Won from behind: (4) Nott'm Forest (h), Oldham (h), Southampton (h), Wimbledon (h).

Lost from in front: (6) Liverpool (a), Notts County (a), QPR (a), Sheffield Wednesday (a), Southampton (a), Tottenham (a).

High spots: The return of Mick Harford.

Three consecutive home wins over Christmas.

Only one home defeat after Christmas.

Low spots: The poor away record, especially the number of games lost through goals conceded in the final minutes.

Relegation from Division 1 after ten years in the top flight.

No goals scored in the opening four league games.

Losing 1-2 at Notts County in the final match, after taking the lead.

Player of the Year: David Preece.

Ever-presents: (2) Mark Pembridge, John Dreyer (league).

Hat-tricks: (0).

Leading scorer: (12) Mick Harford.

| | Appearances | | | | | | Goals | | | |
|---|---|---|---|---|---|---|---|---|---|---|
| | Lge | *Sub* | LC | *Sub* | FAC | *Sub* | Lge | LC | FAC | Tot |
| Beaumont, David | **6** | *3* | 2 | | | | | | | |
| Black, Kingsley | **4** | | | | | | | | | |
| Campbell, Jamie | **4** | *7* | | | | *1* | | | | |
| Chamberlain, Alec | **24** | | 2 | | 1 | | | | | |
| Day, Mervyn | **4** | | | | | | | | | |
| Dreyer, John | **42** | | 1 | | 1 | | **2** | | | **2** |
| Farrell, Sean | **3** | *1* | | | | | | | | |
| Glover, Lee | **1** | | | | | | | | | |
| Gray, Phil | **9** | *5* | 2 | | | | **3** | 3 | | **6** |
| Harford, Mick | **29** | | 1 | | | | **12** | | | **12** |
| Harvey, Richard | **31** | *1* | 1 | | 1 | | **2** | | | **2** |
| Holsgrove, Paul | **1** | | | | | | | | | |
| Hughes, Ceri | **6** | *12* | | | | | | | | |
| Jackson, Matthew | **7** | *2* | 2 | | | | | | | |
| James, Julian | **28** | | | | 1 | | **2** | | | **2** |
| Kamara, Chris | **28** | | | | 1 | | | | | |
| Linton, Des | **2** | *1* | | | | | | | | |
| McDonough, Darron | **9** | | | | | | | | | |
| Nogan, Kurt | **6** | *8* | | *2* | | | **1** | 1 | | **2** |
| Oakes, Scott | **15** | *6* | | | 1 | | **2** | | | **2** |
| Peake, Trevor | **38** | | 1 | | 1 | | | | | |
| Pembridge, Mark | **42** | | 2 | | 1 | | **5** | | | **5** |
| Preece, David | **34** | *4* | 2 | | 1 | | **3** | | | **3** |
| Rees, Jason | **3** | *2* | | | | | | | | |
| Rodger, Graham | **11** | *1* | 1 | | | | | | | |
| Salton, Darren | **2** | *1* | | *1* | | | | | | |
| Stein, Brian | **32** | *7* | 1 | *1* | 1 | | **3** | | | **3** |
| Sutton, Steve | **14** | | | | | | | | | |
| Telfer, Paul | **17** | *3* | 2 | | 1 | | **1** | | | **1** |
| Thompson, Steve | **5** | | 2 | | | | | | | |
| Varadi, Imre | **5** | *1* | | | | | **1** | | | **1** |
| Williams, Martin | | *1* | | | | | | | | |
| (own-goals) | | | | | | | **1** | | | **1** |
| **32 players used** | **462** | ***66*** | **22** | ***4*** | **11** | ***1*** | **38** | **4** | | **42** |

# BARCLAYS LEAGUE DIVISION 1 — Manager: David Pleat — SEASON 1992-93

| No | Date | Att | Pos | Pt | F-A | H-T | Scorers, Times, and Referees | 1 | 2 | 3 | 4 | 5 | 6 | 7 | 8 | 9 | 10 | 11 | subs used |
|---|---|---|---|---|---|---|---|---|---|---|---|---|---|---|---|---|---|---|---|
| 1 | A LEICESTER | | | L | 1-2 | 1-1 | Campbell 38 | **Petterson** | Linton | James | Kamara | Peake | Dreyer | Oakes* | Hughes | Gray | Preece | Campbell | **Claridge** |
| | 15/8 | *17,424* | | - | | | *Walsh 43, Whitlow 89* | *Muggleton* | *Mills* | *Smith* | *Walsh* | *Hill* | *Whitlow* | *Oldfield* | *Thompson* | *Davison* | *Ormondr'yd** | *Gee* | *Gordon* |
| | | | | | | | Ref: R Hamer | Jamie Campbell opens his account for the Town with a scrambled goal but Steve Walsh levels before the interval when he heads home a corner from ex-Hatter Steve Thompson. Mike Whitlow fires in the winner in injury-time to ensure that Luton continue in the same style as last season. | | | | | | | | | | | |
| 2 | H BRISTOL CITY | | 22 | L | 0-3 | 0-1 | | Petterson | Linton | James* | Kamara | Peake | Dreyer | Claridge | Hughes | Gray | Preece | Campbell^ | Johnson/Oakes |
| | 22/8 | 7,926 | 7 | - | | | *Mellon 12, Dreyer 51 (og), Cole 75* | *Welch* | *Mitchell* | *Osman* | *Thompson* | *Bryant* | *Scott* | *Mellon* | *Shelton** | *Dziekan'wski^* | *Cole* | *Rosenior* | *Edwards/Harrison* |
| | | | | | | | Ref: R Bigger | Andy Cole destroys the Hatters with a performance of both pace and power and he has a hand in all three of the City goals. The sweeper system played by the Robins, with Russell Osman outstanding, stifles the Town forwards, who do not muster a serious shot on target all afternoon. | | | | | | | | | | | |
| 3 | A CHARLTON | | 21 | D | 0-0 | 0-0 | | Petterson | Linton | James | Salton | Peake | Dreyer | Claridge | Hughes | Gray* | Preece | Rees | Oakes |
| | 29/8 | *6,291* | *1* | 1 | | | | *Bolder* | *Balmer* | *Webster* | *Gatting* | *Barness* | *Lee* | *Pardew* | *Bumstead* | *Walsh* | *Dyer** | *Nelson* | *Grant* |
| | | | | | | | Ref: D Elleray | Charlton are playing their 'home' games at West Ham's Upton Park this season and, after winning their first four matches of the campaign, seem lethargic as the Town keep their first away clean sheet in a year. The Hatters only have hard work to offer in a contest which is devoid of thrills. | | | | | | | | | | | |
| 4 | A NEWCASTLE | | 22 | L | 0-2 | 0-2 | | Petterson | Linton | James | Salton | Peake | Dreyer | Claridge | Oakes | Gray | Preece | Rees* | Campbell |
| | 2/9 | ***27,082*** | *2* | 1 | | | *Clark 36, Kelly 44* | *Wright* | *Venison* | *Scott* | *Howey* | *Ranson* | *Carr* | *Clark* | *O'Brien* | *Sheedy* | *Peacock* | *Kelly* | |
| | | | | | | | Ref: J Kirkby | The injury crisis worsens as Jason Rees is added to the sick list after being carried off on a stretcher with a twisted knee. The Town play some attractive football in the first half, but are undone when Lee Clark fires into an empty net. David Kelly then side-foots the second goal. | | | | | | | | | | | |
| 5 | H TRANMERE | | 23 | D | 3-3 | 2-3 | Claridge 21, Linton 34, Oakes 69 | Petterson | Linton | James | Salton | Peake | Dreyer | Claridge | Oakes | Gray* | Preece | Rees | Campbell |
| | 5/9 | 6,801 | *9* | 2 | | | *Aldridge 27, Muir 29, Nevin 39* | *Nixon* | *Brannon* | *Vickers* | *Garnett* | *Nolan* | *Morrissey* | *McNab* | *Irons* | *Nevin* | *Aldridge* | *Muir* | |
| | | | | | | | Ref: P Foakes | Steve Claridge scores his first goal for the club after an opening period where the Town go close on eight occasions in the best spell of football for months. Aldridge steals the equaliser against the run of play, but the defence then falls to pieces. Oakes salvages the draw with a fierce shot. | | | | | | | | | | | |
| 6 | A BRENTFORD | | 21 | W | 2-1 | 0-0 | James 57, Gray 79 | Petterson | Linton | James | Salton | Peake | Johnson | Claridge | Kamara | Gray | Preece | Rees | |
| | 13/9 | *7,413* | *17* | 5 | | | *Blissett 50* | *Bayes* | *Statham* | *Millen* | *Bates* | *Hughton* | *Bennett* | *Ratcliffe* | *Manuel* | *Gayle* | *Blissett* | *Jones** | *Luscombe* |
| | | | | | | | Ref: R Groves | Gary Blissett shoots the Bees into the lead but the Town keep playing their football and a fortuitous cross from Julian James finds its way into the top corner of the net. Chris Kamara sends in a pinpoint cross for Phil Gray to head the second and record the first away win for 18 months. | | | | | | | | | | | |
| 7 | H BIRMINGHAM | | 21 | D | 1-1 | 0-0 | Claridge 89p | Petterson | Linton | James | Salton | Peake | Johnson | Claridge | Kamara* | Gray | Preece^ | Rees | Campbell/Oakes |
| | 19/9 | 8,481 | *4* | 6 | | | *Rowbotham 49* | *Gosney* | *Clarkson* | *Hicks* | *Matthewson* | *Rogers* | *Frain* | *Tait** | *Gleghorn^* | *Rowbotham* | *Donowa* | *Sale* | *Cooper/Sturridge* |
| | | | | | | | Ref: P Jones | Darren Rowbotham puts the Blues ahead with a flying header from a cross by John Frain. A corner count of 12-1 in favour of the Town serves to illustrate their superiority in the match and justice is done when Claridge keeps his head to level from the spot after Mark Cooper handles. | | | | | | | | | | | |
| 8 | A NOTTS CO | | 21 | D | 0-0 | 0-0 | | Petterson | Linton | James | Salton | **Matthew** | Dreyer | Claridge | Kamara | Gray | Preece* | Rees^ | Oakes/Campbell |
| | 26/9 | *5,992* | *17* | 7 | | | | *Cherry* | *Short* | *Johnson* | *O'Riordan* | *Thomas* | *Draper* | *Palmer* | *Turner* | *Smith* | *Slawson** | *Lund* | *Devlin* |
| | | | | | | | Ref: L Dilkes | Employing long ball and muscle, Notts County try to get a 0-6 thrashing at Millwall out of their system by bombarding an injury-hit Hatters defence, which stays solid. The Town have a shout for a penalty turned down when it seems that Charlie Palmer handled the ball in the area. | | | | | | | | | | | |
| 9 | H PORTSMOUTH | | 22 | L | 1-4 | 1-3 | Dreyer 18 | Petterson | Linton | James | Salton | Oakes | Dreyer | Claridge | Kamara | Gray | Preece* | Rees^ | Campbell/Matthew |
| | 3/10 | 7,954 | *11* | 7 | | | *Whittingham 27, 39, 75, Clarke 37* | *Knight* | *Neill* | *Awford* | *Maguire* | *Symons* | *Daniel* | *Aspinall* | *McLoughlin** | *Clarke* | *Whittingham* | *Walsh^* | *Burns/Chamberlain* |
| | | | | | | | Ref: B Hill | Mr Hill is criticised for passing the water-logged surface fit for play, but John Dreyer gives the Town an early lead. Strength and experience are the key factors on the heavy surface as Guy Whittingham goes on to notch a hat-trick. Luton now drop into the bottom three in the league. | | | | | | | | | | | |
| 10 | A BARNSLEY | | 23 | L | 0-3 | 0-3 | | Petterson | Linton* | James | Salton | Johnson | Dreyer | Claridge | Kamara | Gray | Preece | Rees^ | Oakes/Matthew |
| | 10/10 | *5,261* | *22* | 7 | | | *Biggins 3, 32, Pearson 27* | *Butler* | *Robinson M* | *Bishop* | *Fleming* | *Robinson J* | *Rammell** | *Bullimore* | *Archdeacon* | *Redfearn^* | *Pearson* | *Biggins* | *O'Connell/Godfrey* |
| | | | | | | | Ref: K Lupton | Bottom club Barnsley sweep aside a defence which is missing the injured Peake. Biggins makes his home debut for the Tykes and scores with a left-foot drive and then with a back-heel. Pearson adds to the woe with a header but the Town hit the woodwork three times after the break. | | | | | | | | | | | |
| 11 | H DERBY | | 23 | L | 1-3 | 0-1 | Johnson 53 | Petterson | Linton | James | Salton | Johnson | Matthew | Claridge | Kamara | Gray | Preece | Oakes* | Campbell |
| | 17/10 | 8,848 | *15* | 7 | | | *Kitson 39, 57, Johnson 61* | *Sutton* | *Comyn* | *Short* | *Wassall* | *Forsyth* | *Simpson** | *Kuhl* | *Johnson* | *Pembridge* | *Gabbiadini* | *Kitson* | *McMinn* |
| | | | | | | | Ref: P Alcock | Derby have spent £10 million on their squad and they deserve their win, although they are slightly flattered by the final score. Marvin Johnson scores the first league goal of his career, which levels the scores at one stage, when he nets the rebound after a Darren Salton header is parried. | | | | | | | | | | | |

| No Date | H/A | Opponent / Att | | | F-A | H-T | Scorers, Times, and Referees | 1 | 2 | 3 | 4 | 5 | 6 | 7 | 8 | 9 | 10 | 11 | subs used |
|---|---|---|---|---|---|---|---|---|---|---|---|---|---|---|---|---|---|---|---|
| 12 | A | PETERBOROUGH | 22 | W | 3-2 | 3-1 | Gray 10, 40, Telfer 38 | Petterson | Linton | James | Salton | Johnson | Matthew | Claridge | Kamara | Preece* | Gray | Telfer | Oakes |
| 24/10 | | 7,125 | 13 | 10 | | | Cooper 26, Adcock 70 | Bennett | Luke | Howarth | Welsh | Robinson | Barnes* | Cooper | Halsall | Sterling | Adcock | Philliskirk | Iorfa |
| | | | | | | | Ref: P Danson | Telfer returns to the side after being out for nine months with a broken foot. He scores a goal to add to the pair from Phil Gray, which gives the Town a decisive lead at the break. Posh are irate when Petterson brings down Philliskirk for a blatant penalty which the referee overrules. | | | | | | | | | | | |
| 13 | H | SOUTHEND | 22 | D | 2-2 | 2-0 | James 9, Gray 31 | Petterson | Linton | James | Salton | Johnson | Peake | Claridge | Kamara | Preece | Gray | Telfer* | Oakes |
| 31/10 | | 7,256 | 23 | 11 | | | Powell 60, O'Callaghan 85 | Sansome | Parkinson | Edwards | Prior | Powell | Locke | Cornwell | Martin | Tilson* | Ansah^ | Benjamin | Scully/O'Callaghan |
| | | | | | | | Ref: T Holbrook | Julian James opens the scoring with a shot to climax a surging run, and Phil Gray adds a second with a 20-yard dipping effort. Southend make up for their first-half misses when they equalise, leaving the Town as the only team in the Football League without a home win this season. | | | | | | | | | | | |
| 14 | A | CAMBRIDGE | 22 | D | 3-3 | 1-0 | Oakes 21, Gray 48, 54 | Petterson | Linton | James | Salton | Johnson | Peake | Claridge | Kamara | Preece | Gray | Oakes | |
| 3/11 | | 5,716 | 17 | 12 | | | Philpott 73, Francis 77, 87 | Sheffield | Fensome | Heathcote | O'Shea | Kimble | Rowett* | Raynor | Clayton^ | Philpott | Norbury | White | Francis/Ainsworth |
| | | | | | | | Ref: V Callow | Playing sharp, accurate football, the Town are a class above the home side and with 17 minutes to go are 3-0 up and cruising. A drive from Lee Philpott appears to be just a consolation goal for Cambridge but, as the Luton defence collapses, John Francis scores twice to level the game. | | | | | | | | | | | |
| 15 | H | GRIMSBY | 22 | L | 1-4 | 0-3 | Gray 70 | Chamberlain | Linton* | James | Salton | Johnson | Peake | Claridge^ | Kamara | Rees | Gray | Oakes | Telfer/Campbell |
| 7/11 | | 6,928 | 12 | 12 | | | Groves 18, 27, 82, Rees 23 | Beasant | McDermott | Futcher | Lever* | Croft | Watson | Dobbin^ | Groves | Gilbert | Rees | Mendonca | Rodger/Smith |
| | | | | | | | Ref: J Martin | The players are jeered off the pitch as the Mariners find it all too easy in seizing a three-goal lead against abject defending. The second half is little better, although Phil Gray pulls a goal back with a far-post header from Jason Rees' cross. Paul Groves hits the fourth for his hat-trick. | | | | | | | | | | | |
| 16 | A | OXFORD | 22 | L | **0-4** | 0-2 | | Chamberlain | Linton | James | Salton | Johnson | Peake | Claridge | Telfer | Rees* | Gray | Preece | Oakes |
| 14/11 | | 5,759 | 13 | 12 | | | Durnin 23, 30, 74, 80 | Reece | Smart | Evans | Melville | Ford | Beauchamp | Magilton | Lewis | Allen | Penney* | Durnin | Cusack |
| | | | | | | | Ref: P Don | The Oxford management duo of Brian Horton and David Moss praise the Town for continuing to try and play football, but it's goals, rather than platitudes that are required to win games. The final score flatters the home side as the last two goals come when the Hatters are pushing up. | | | | | | | | | | | |
| 17 | H | MILLWALL | 23 | D | 1-1 | 1-0 | Gray 27 | Chamberlain | Dreyer | James | Salton | Hughes* | Peake | Telfer^ | **Benjamin** | Rees | Gray | Preece | Johnson/Oakes |
| 21/11 | | 8,371 | 5 | 13 | | | Byrne 59 | Keller | Cunningham | Cooper | Stevens | Dawes | Rae* | May | Allen | Barber | Byrne | Moralee | Roberts |
| | | | | | | | Ref: D Gallagher | Well-travelled striker Ian Benjamin makes his Luton debut as the Town take the lead through Phil Gray, who glances in a header from a cross by Julian James. The woodwork, and a brilliant display from Kasey Keller, keeps the score down before John Byrne gets a fortunate equaliser. | | | | | | | | | | | |
| 18 | H | WATFORD | 22 | W | 2-0 | 0-0 | Benjamin 71, Oakes 74 | Chamberlain | Dreyer | James | Johnson | Hughes | Peake | Oakes* | Benjamin | Rees | Gray | Preece | Williams |
| 29/11 | | 8,341 | 14 | 16 | | | | Suckling | Lavin* | Dublin | Holdsworth | Ashby | Drysdale | Hessenthaler | Porter | Putney | Charlery | Willis | Bazeley |
| | | | | | | | Ref: D Frampton | The game is overshadowed by the road accident which leaves Darren Salton critically injured. On a muddy pitch, the Hornets are hardly in the game and Ian Benjamin dives in to head home a cross from John Dreyer, closely followed by a drive from Scott Oakes to round off a solo run. | | | | | | | | | | | |
| 19 | A | BRISTOL ROV | 22 | L | 0-2 | 0-2 | | Chamberlain | Dreyer | James | Johnson | Hughes* | Peake | Oakes | Benjamin^ | Rees | Gray | Preece | Linton/Williams |
| 5/12 | | 6,240 | 21 | 16 | | | Saunders 21, Channing 24 | Parkin | Alexander | Tillson | Yates | Jones | Channing | Waddock | Stewart | Hardyman | Saunders | Taylor | |
| | | | | | | | Ref: K Barratt | On the first visit to Twerton Park, the Hatters fail to build on their recent good form and defensive errors allow Rovers to steal a two-goal lead. Luton have the majority of the play and Gray hits the bar with a header but they are unable to hurt their opponents in this relegation six-pointer. | | | | | | | | | | | |
| 20 | A | WOLVES | 19 | W | 2-1 | 1-1 | Gray 21, 85 | Chamberlain | Dreyer | James | Johnson | Hughes | Peake | Oakes* | Telfer | Rees^ | Gray | Preece | Linton/Benjamin |
| 12/12 | | 13,932 | 6 | 19 | | | Blades 17 | Jones | Ashley | Mountfield | Blades | Edwards* | Burke | Birch | Cook | Downing | Bull | Roberts | Madden |
| | | | | | | | Ref: S Lodge | Blades fires Wolves into the lead after Rees heads a corner off the line, but the Town fight back. Both goals from Gray have a touch of luck about them, with the ball sitting up for him by way of deflections. It is a victory on a large, well-grassed pitch that suits the Luton style of play. | | | | | | | | | | | |
| 21 | H | SUNDERLAND | 20 | D | 0-0 | 0-0 | | Chamberlain | Dreyer | James | Johnson | Hughes* | Peake | Telfer | Rees^ | Benjamin | Gray | Preece | Oakes/Linton |
| 19/12 | | 8,286 | 18 | 20 | | | | Norman | Kay | Butcher | Ball | Ord | Mooney | Armstrong | Cunnington | Gray | Davenport* | Rush | Hawke |
| | | | | | | | Ref: K Hackett | The club have called in experts to sort out the problems with the drainage of the pitch as this game is played in the proverbial paddy field. Both sides do well in their efforts to play positive football but the game is drifting towards a 0-0 draw long before the referee blows the final whistle. | | | | | | | | | | | |
| 22 | A | WEST HAM | 20 | D | 2-2 | 0-0 | Hughes 67, Dreyer 70 | Chamberlain | Dreyer | James | Johnson | Hughes | Peake | Williams* | Telfer | Rees^ | Gray | Preece | Benjamin/Oakes |
| 28/12 | | 18,786 | 3 | 21 | | | Dicks 51p, Breacker 66 | Miklosko | Breacker | Potts | Martin | Dicks | Robson | Butler | Allen M | Keen | Morley | Allen C | |
| | | | | | | | Ref: M Pierce | A nudge by Hughes on Mark Robson allows Julian Dicks to blast home from the spot and then Tim Breacker hits a 25-yard screamer. Straight from the restart, Hughes runs at the West Ham defence and lashes in a 30-yarder, and then takes a corner-kick which is headed home by Dreyer. | | | | | | | | | | | |
| 23 | A | BIRMINGHAM | 22 | L | 1-2 | 1-1 | Hughes 29 | Chamberlain | Dreyer | James | Johnson | Hughes | Peake | Oakes* | Telfer | Rees | Gray | Preece | Williams |
| 9/1 | | 9,601 | 19 | 21 | | | Frain 13p, Gayle 86 | Gosney | Clarkson | Hicks | Matthewson | Potter | Tait | Fitzpatrick* | Frain | Peschisolido | Speedie^ | Gayle | Rennie/Sturridge |
| | | | | | | | Ref: K Cooper | Marvin Johnson fouls John Gayle in the area, allowing John Frain to score from the spot. The Hatters equalise when Ceri Hughes scores direct from a corner-kick and appear to be hanging on for a point until Gayle swoops late, hammering a 25-yard shot into the top corner of the net. | | | | | | | | | | | |

| No | Date | | Att | Pos | Pt | F-A | H-T | Scorers, Times, and Referees | 1 | 2 | 3 | 4 | 5 | 6 | 7 | 8 | 9 | 10 | 11 | subs used |
|---|---|---|---|---|---|---|---|---|---|---|---|---|---|---|---|---|---|---|---|---|
| 24 | H | NOTTS CO | | 22 | D | 0-0 | 0-0 | | Chamberlain | Dreyer | James* | Johnson | Hughes | Peake | Telfer | Benjamin^ | Rees | Gray | Preece | Oakes/Williams |
| | 16/1 | | 6,729 | 24 | 22 | | | | Cherry | Williams | Palmer | Johnson | Dryden | Devlin | Draper | Thomas | Smith | Agana | Wilson* | Matthews |
| | | | | | | | | Ref: V Callow | Another two home points are lost when managerless Notts County force a stalemate, in front of the lowest crowd of the season. The Town have the better chances, with Phil Gray hitting the wood twice in the opening minutes and Scott Oakes heading tamely over the bar in injury time. | | | | | | | | | | | |
| 25 | H | NEWCASTLE | | 24 | D | 0-0 | 0-0 | | Chamberlain | Dreyer | James | Johnson | Hughes | Peake | Telfer | Williams* | Rees^ | Gray | Preece | Benjamin/Oakes |
| | 27/1 | | 10,237 | 1 | 23 | | | | Srnicek | Venison | Scott | Howey | Beresford | Bracewell | O'Brien | Clark | Peacock | Kelly | Lee | |
| | | | | | | | | Ref: A Buksh | The league leaders are unable to break down the resolute Town defence in an end-to-end contest which makes a nonsense of the current lowly position occupied by the Hatters. A good display from keepers Alec Chamberlain and Pavel Srnicek ensures that the game remains scoreless. | | | | | | | | | | | |
| 26 | A | BRISTOL CITY | | 24 | D | 0-0 | 0-0 | | Chamberlain | Dreyer | James | Johnson | Hughes | Peake | Telfer | Williams* | Rees^ | Gray | Preece | Benjamin/Oakes |
| | 30/1 | | 8,877 | 19 | 24 | | | | Welch | Llewellyn | Osman* | Bryant | Aizlewood | Scott | Shelton^ | Harrison | Dziekan'wski | Cole | Rosenior | Allison/Mellon |
| | | | | | | | | Ref: J Carter | The single point from the third scoreless game in succession is not enough to lift the Town off the bottom of the table. City play with five at the back until, with 20 minutes remaining, they decide to pursue the win. Gray has the best chance to score, his shot being saved by Keith Welch. | | | | | | | | | | | |
| 27 | H | LEICESTER | | 21 | W | 2-0 | 1-0 | Johnson 40, Gray 61 | Chamberlain | Dreyer | James | Johnson | Hughes | Peake | Telfer | Williams* | Oakes^ | Gray | Preece | Benjamin/Rees |
| | 6/2 | | 9,140 | 8 | 27 | | | | Hoult | Smith | Walsh | Hill | Whitlow* | Mills | Thompson | Oldfield | Joachim^ | Lowe | Philpott | Gibson !/Ormondr'yd |
| | | | | | | | | Ref: J Martin | Johnson heads home a cross from Oakes just before the interval and Gray makes the points safe when he hits home a low shot after collecting a through-ball from Preece. Leicester have little to offer and have Colin Gibson sent off four minutes from time for a second bookable offence. | | | | | | | | | | | |
| 28 | H | BRENTFORD | | 20 | D | 0-0 | 0-0 | | Chamberlain | Dreyer | James | Johnson | Hughes | Peake | Telfer | Williams | Oakes | Gray | Preece | |
| | 9/2 | | 7,248 | 14 | 28 | | | | Benstead | Bennett | Millen | Bates | Mortimer | Buckle* | Statham | Manuel | Luscombe | Allon | Blissett | Godfrey |
| | | | | | | | | Ref: J Rushton | The suspect Brentford defence puts up the shutters but Gary Blissett, attacking on the break, has two gilt-edged chances to put the Bees ahead but spurns them both. Luton do not look like improving their goalscoring record but have not conceded a home goal since the end of November. | | | | | | | | | | | |
| 29 | A | TRANMERE | | 19 | W | 2-0 | 1-0 | Gray 17, Johnson 65 | Chamberlain | Dreyer | James | Johnson | Hughes | Peake | Telfer | Rees | Oakes* | Gray | Preece | Williams |
| | 13/2 | | 8,723 | 5 | 31 | | | | Nixon | Mungall | Higgins | Vickers | Nolan | Morrissey | Irons | McNab* | Nevin | Aldridge | Malkin^ | Martindale/Muir |
| | | | | | | | | Ref: K Redfern | Playing against a team who have yet to lose at home this season, the Town put on their best team performance. They take the lead when Preece feeds Gray, who scores with a low drive. Steve Mungall is hustled by Ceri Hughes and the loose ball is fired into the net by Marvin Johnson. | | | | | | | | | | | |
| 30 | H | CHARLTON | | 19 | W | 1-0 | 0-0 | Gray 46 | Chamberlain | Dreyer | James | Johnson | Hughes | Peake | Telfer | **Dixon** | Oakes | Gray | Preece | |
| | 20/2 | | 8,443 | 10 | 34 | | | | Salmon | Balmer | Webster | Gatting | Minto | Warden* | Pardew | Pitcher | Walsh | Leaburn | Nelson^ | Bacon/Gorman |
| | | | | | | | | Ref: I Borrett | 15 years after being discarded by his home town club, Dixon makes his debut. In a dull game, Gray notches his 14th goal of the season when he fires into the corner following a long ball from David Preece. The seventh consecutive clean sheet by the Hatters equals their record of 1923. | | | | | | | | | | | |
| 31 | H | BARNSLEY | | 19 | D | 2-2 | 1-0 | Dixon 10, Gray 82p | Chamberlain | Dreyer | James | Johnson | Hughes* | Peake | Telfer | Dixon | Oakes | Gray | Preece | Williams |
| | 27/2 | | 7,595 | 14 | 35 | | | O'Connell 49, Currie 75 | Watson | Robinson | Fleming | Davis | Taggart | Archdeacon | O'Connell | Redfearn | Currie | Biggins | Rammell | |
| | | | | | | | | Ref: A Gunn | Kerry Dixon opens his Luton account with a header after ten minutes. After a half-time roasting by Mel Machin, Barnsley storm into the lead with headers by Brendan O'Connell and David Currie. Gray saves the day when he nets from the spot after Neil Redfearn handles in the box. | | | | | | | | | | | |
| 32 | A | PORTSMOUTH | | 20 | L | 1-2 | 1-1 | Gray 14 | Chamberlain | Dreyer | James | Johnson | Rees* | Peake | Telfer | Dixon | Oakes | Gray | Preece | Hughes^/Williams |
| | 6/3 | | 10,457 | 4 | 35 | | | Whittingham 16, Aspinall 51p | Knight | Price | Symons | Awford | Daniel* | Aspinall | McLoughlin | Burns^ | Powell | Walsh | Whittingham | Chamberlain/Russell |
| | | | | | | | | Ref: S Dunn | Gray scores with a header from a corner by Oakes but Whittingham beats the Town defence to fire home. Peake is penalised for fouling Walsh and Aspinall scores the winner from the spot. Ceri Hughes becomes the first Luton player to come on as a substitute and then be substituted. | | | | | | | | | | | |
| 33 | H | OXFORD | | 18 | W | **3-1** | 1-1 | Preece 16, Gray 77, Oakes 87 | Chamberlain | Dreyer | James | Johnson | Williams* | Peake | Telfer | Dixon | Oakes | Gray | Preece | Rees |
| | 9/3 | | **6,687** | 16 | 38 | | | Cusack 44 | Reece | Smart | Evans | Melville | Ford | Robinson | Magilton | Lewis | Beauchamp | Cusack | Penney | |
| | | | | | | | | Ref: D Elleray | Brian Horton's Oxford make little contribution as David Preece heads the Town into the lead when Paul Reece fails to cut out a cross from Williams. Nick Cusack heads the equaliser before Phil Gray thumps in a tremendous drive and Oakes crashes in the third for a flattering win. | | | | | | | | | | | |
| 34 | A | GRIMSBY | | 18 | L | 1-3 | 0-1 | Gray 88 | Chamberlain | Dreyer | James ! | Johnson | Hughes* | **Greene^** | Telfer | Dixon | Oakes | Gray | Preece | Williams/Rees |
| | 13/3 | | **5,193** | 8 | 38 | | | Ford 24, 73, Mendonca 87 | Wilmot | McDermott | Futcher | Lever | Croft | Ford | Jobling | Groves | Gilbert | Mendonca | Rees | |
| | | | | | | | | Ref: J Winter | David Greene makes his Luton debut, in place of flu victim Trevor Peake. Greene is unable to contain Clive Mendonca, who has a hand in all three of the Grimsby goals as the Mariners play the game the Luton way. James is sent off in the 75th minute for a second yellow card offence. | | | | | | | | | | | |

| No | H/A | Opponent | Att | Pos | Res | F-A | H-T | Scorers, Times, Referees | 1 | 2 | 3 | 4 | 5 | 6 | 7 | 8 | 9 | 10 | 11 | 12 subs used |
|---|---|---|---|---|---|---|---|---|---|---|---|---|---|---|---|---|---|---|---|---|
| 35 | H | SWINDON | | 17 | D | 0-0 | 0-0 | | Chamberlain | Dreyer | James* | Johnson | Rees^ | Peake | Telfer | Dixon | Oakes | Gray | Preece | Hughes/Williams |
| 17/3 | | | 8,902 | 3 | 39 | | | | Digby | Summerbee | Viveash | Calderwood | Taylor | Bodin | MacLaren | Ling | Hunt* | Mitchell | White | Marwood |
| | | | | | | | | Ref: R Wiseman | Swindon disappoint by swamping the midfield with five men and close the game down. Fraser Digby saves well to deny Paul Telfer, whilst a downward header from Kerry Dixon bounces just over the bar. The first shot that Swindon have on target comes seven minutes from the end. | | | | | | | | | | | |
| 36 | H | BRISTOL ROV | | 17 | D | 1-1 | 0-0 | Maddison 58 (og) | Chamberlain | Dreyer | James* | Johnson | Rees | Peake | Telfer | Dixon | Oakes | Gray | Preece | Hughes |
| 20/3 | | | 7,717 | 24 | 40 | | | Taylor 72 | Parkin | Alexander* | Tillson | Yates | Maddison | Mehew | Browning | Waddock | Pounder | Stewart^ | Saunders | Clark/Taylor |
| | | | | | | | | Ref: A Ward | Bottom of the table Rovers come to defend in depth but it is the Hatters who take a fortunate lead, when Lee Madison volleys a cross from Marvin Johnson into his own net. John Taylor heads the equaliser, although Town goalkeeper Alec Chamberlain complains that he was fouled. | | | | | | | | | | | |
| 37 | A | MILLWALL | | 18 | L | 0-1 | 0-1 | | Chamberlain | Dreyer | Linton* | Johnson | Rees | Peake | Telfer | Hughes | Oakes^ | Gray | Harvey | Dixon/Williams |
| 24/3 | | | 8,287 | 5 | 40 | | | Moralee 25 | Keller | Cunningham | Cooper | Stevens | Dawes | Rae | Roberts | Bogie* | Barber | Moralee | Allen | Kerr |
| | | | | | | | | Ref: P Durkin | Injuries and illness deplete the Town side on their final visit to the Den. The Hatters play with a five-man midfield who are intent on stifling the game but a clever move down the wing sets up Alex Rae who gets to the by-line before crossing to the onrushing Jamie Moralee to crash in. | | | | | | | | | | | |
| 38 | H | CAMBRIDGE | | 17 | W | 2-0 | 1-0 | Dixon 20, Oakes 50 | Chamberlain | Dreyer | Telfer | Johnson | Rees | Peake | Hughes | Dixon | Oakes | Kamara | Williams | |
| 27/3 | | | 8,077 | 21 | 43 | | | | Vaughan | Clayton | Heathcote | Chapple | Kimble | Rush* | Raynor | O'Shea | Leadbitter | Claridge | Butler^ | Bartlett/Lyne |
| | | | | | | | | Ref: R Milford | The game is settled by two quality strikes which rise above the desperate football being played by two teams who are trying to pull away from the foot of the table. Kerry Dixon hits a volley on the turn from the edge of the area and Oakes dives in to head home a cross from Williams. | | | | | | | | | | | |
| 39 | A | WATFORD | | 17 | D | 0-0 | 0-0 | | Chamberlain | Dreyer | Telfer | Johnson | Rees | Peake | Hughes* | Kamara | Dixon | Gray | Preece | Oakes |
| 3/4 | | | 10,656 | 14 | 44 | | | | Waugh | Soloman | Holdsworth | Ashby | Dublin | Willis | Hessenthaler | Porter | Lavin* | Furlong | Nogan | Bazeley |
| | | | | | | | | Ref: K Barratt | In the worst local derby for years, a combination of tension, the wind, a bumpy pitch and a poor referee make it a game best forgotten for the 4,000 Luton supporters, as neither side looks likely to end the deadlock. Gray admits that a recent abortive move to Chelsea has unsettled him. | | | | | | | | | | | |
| 40 | H | WOLVES | | 18 | D | 1-1 | 0-0 | Gray 50 | Chamberlain | Dreyer | James | Johnson | Rees* | Peake | Kamara | Oakes | Dixon | Gray | Preece^ | Telfer/Williams |
| 7/4 | | | 7,948 | 9 | 45 | | | Bull 81 | Stowell | Simkin | Mountfield | Blades | Venus | Rankine | Downing | Cook | Dennison | Mutch | Bull* | Thompson |
| | | | | | | | | Ref: K Morton | Wolves still have an outside chance of reaching the play-offs and seem to be content to hold on for the draw, although they are rescued on several occasions by keeper Mike Stowell. The Town get the breakthrough when Kamara sets up Gray but Steve Bull equalises after a solo run. | | | | | | | | | | | |
| 41 | A | SWINDON | | 21 | L | 0-1 | 0-0 | | Chamberlain | Dreyer | Telfer | Johnson | James | Peake | Hughes* | Kamara | Dixon | Gray | Preece | Oakes |
| 10/4 | | | 11,004 | 4 | 45 | | | Bodin 83 | Digby | Summerbee | Hoddle | Calderwood | Taylor | Bodin | Marwood* | MacLaren^ | Ling | Maskell | Close | Hazard/Hamon |
| | | | | | | | | Ref: P Vanes | The Town fail to turn their promising attacking play into goals and, after holding the championship chasers for most of the game, concede a late goal when full-back Paul Bodin shoots past Chamberlain and into the top corner of the net. Luton are now back in the drop zone again. | | | | | | | | | | | |
| 42 | H | WEST HAM | | 18 | W | 2-0 | 0-0 | Gray 84p, Williams 88 | Chamberlain | Dreyer | Telfer* | Johnson | James | Peake | Hughes^ | Kamara | Dixon | Gray | Preece | Williams/Oakes |
| 13/4 | | | **10,959** | 3 | 48 | | | | Miklosko | Breacker | Potts | Gale | Dicks | Keen | Butler | Bishop | Allen* | Morley | Speedie | Holmes |
| | | | | | | | | Ref: G Singh | In an end-to-end game of 33 goal attempts and 19 corners, the highest crowd of the season see Luton end the stalemate six minutes from time. Dicks handles a Dixon shot on the line and Gray hammers the spot-kick home. Williams is played through by Gray to score his first goal. | | | | | | | | | | | |
| 43 | A | SUNDERLAND | | 16 | D | 2-2 | 0-1 | Preece 49, Telfer 89 | Chamberlain | Dreyer | Telfer | Johnson* | James | Peake | Rees | Kamara | Dixon | Gray^ | Preece | Oakes/Williams |
| 17/4 | | | 16,493 | 18 | 49 | | | Goodman 31, 86 | Norman | Kay | Butcher | Ball | Gray | Owers | Armstrong | Cunnington | Atkinson | Goodman | Harford* | Davenport |
| | | | | | | | | Ref: S Bell | Sunderland bombard the Hatters' defence and take the lead when Don Goodman curls a drive into the top corner. Preece levels when cleverly flighting a wind-assisted free-kick over Tony Norman. Goodman pops up to head home just before the end with Telfer equalising in injury-time. | | | | | | | | | | | |
| 44 | A | DERBY | | 17 | D | 1-1 | 1-0 | Preece 35 | Chamberlain | Dreyer | James | Johnson | Hughes | Peake | Telfer | Kamara | Dixon | Gray | Preece | |
| 24/4 | | | 13,741 | 9 | 50 | | | Short 89 | Taylor | Patterson | Short | Forsyth | Nicholson | Sturridge | Kuhl* | Pembridge | Simpson | Kitson | Gabbiadini | Coleman^/Stallard |
| | | | | | | | | Ref: I Cruickshanks | Derby, despite all their spending, have not had a particularly good season and their lacklustre, unimaginative play shows why. Preece beats the offside trap with a carefully timed run to score from a threaded pass by Peake. Mark Pembridge crosses for Craig Short to head the late leveller. | | | | | | | | | | | |
| 45 | H | PETERBOROUGH | | 17 | D | 0-0 | 0-0 | | Chamberlain | Dreyer | James | Johnson | Oakes | Peake | Telfer | Kamara* | Dixon | Gray | Preece | Williams |
| 1/5 | | | 10,011 | 10 | 51 | | | | Bennett | Retallick* | Welsh | Howarth | Spearing | Sterling | Ebdon | Bradshaw | Cooper | Adcock | Philliskirk | Greenham |
| | | | | | | | | Ref: P Foakes | The Town are hoping for a win to sweep away any lingering fears of relegation but must now wait for the final day, after a dull draw against defensively-minded Posh, who ride their luck. 'We were not sharp enough and did not have the guile to get through,' admits manager Pleat. | | | | | | | | | | | |
| 46 | A | SOUTHEND | | 20 | L | 1-2 | 1-2 | Dixon 43 | Chamberlain | Dreyer | James | Johnson | Hughes | Peake | Telfer* | Kamara^ | Dixon | Gray | Preece | Williams/Oakes |
| 8/5 | | | 11,913 | 18 | 51 | | | Sussex 21, Angell 39 | Sansome | Edwards | Scully | Prior | Powell | Hall | Sussex | Jones | Tilson | Collymore | Angell | |
| | | Home | Away | | | | | Ref: J Carter | Luton are guilty of defending far too deep, out of respect for Stan Collymore, as Andy Sussex cracks a first-time shot to open the scoring. Brett Angell heads home a free-kick from Steve Tilson for the second before Kerry Dixon scores with a close-range shot, against the run of play. | | | | | | | | | | | |
| Average | | 8,212 | 10,520 | | | | | | | | | | | | | | | | | |

# BARCLAYS DIVISION 1 (CUP-TIES) — Manager: David Pleat — SEASON 1992-93

| Coca Cola Cup | | | | F-A | H-T | Scorers, Times, and Referees | 1 | 2 | 3 | 4 | 5 | 6 | 7 | 8 | 9 | 10 | 11 | subs used |
|---|---|---|---|---|---|---|---|---|---|---|---|---|---|---|---|---|---|---|
| 2:1 H PLYMOUTH | | 21 | D | 2-2 | 1-0 | Claridge 10, 80 | Petterson | Linton | James | Salton | Peake* | Johnson^ | Claridge | Kamara | Gray | Preece | Oakes | Rees/Campbell |
| 23/9 | 3,702 *2:18* | | | | | *Regis 49, 75* | *Shilton* | *Poole* | *Hill* | *Morrison* | *Morgan* | *Skinner* | *Joyce* | *Edworthy* | *McCall* | *Nugent* | *Regis* | |
| | | | | | | Ref: A Gunn | Johnson and Peake are out through injury as Claridge hits home a low drive. Dave Regis uses his pace to reach a through-ball from Warren Joyce to fire home, and then nets a second when converting a Nugent cross. Claridge heads the equaliser from a Des Linton cross near the end. | | | | | | | | | | | |
| 2:2 A PLYMOUTH | | 22 | L | 2-3 | 0-1 | Claridge 61, Preece 68 | Petterson | Linton | James* | Salton | Peake^ | Johnson | Claridge | Kamara | Gray | Preece | Rees | Oakes/Dreyer |
| 6/10 | *8,946 2:10* | | | | | *Nugent 3, Poole 50, Regis 54* | *Shilton* | *Edworthy* | *Morrison* | *Hill* | *Spearing* | *Skinner* | *Joyce* | *Garner* | *Poole* | *Nugent** | *Regis* | *Adcock* |
| | | | | | | Ref: M Bodenham (Hatters lose 4-5 on aggregate) | The Pilgrims seem to have settled the tie when they go three goals up, but the introduction of Oakes as a substitute puts a different complexion on the game. His 25-yard shot is fumbled by Shilton, Claridge knocking in the rebound. A pile-driver is later deflected into the net by Preece. | | | | | | | | | | | |

| FA Cup | | | | F-A | H-T | Scorers, Times, and Referees | 1 | 2 | 3 | 4 | 5 | 6 | 7 | 8 | 9 | 10 | 11 | subs used |
|---|---|---|---|---|---|---|---|---|---|---|---|---|---|---|---|---|---|---|
| 3 H BRISTOL CITY | | 22 | W | 2-0 | 1-0 | Gray 30, Hughes 81 | Chamberlain | Dreyer | James | Johnson* | Hughes | Peake | Telfer | Benjamin^ | Rees | Gray | Preece | Harvey/Oakes |
| 19/1 | 6,092 *1:18* | | | | | | *Welch* | *Llewellyn* | *Osman* | *Bryant* | *Scott !* | *Mellon** | *Shelton* | *Harrison* | *Gavin^* | *Allison* | *Cole* | *Rosenior/Aizlewood* |
| | | | | | | Ref: G Willard | Gray shoots the opener when taking advantage of a left-wing cross from Preece. Hughes hits the second when hammering the ball into the roof of the net. Martin Scott is sent off for retaliating against a nasty tackle by Gray. City manager Denis Smith is sacked 48 hours after the game. | | | | | | | | | | | |
| 4 H DERBY | | 22 | L | 1-5 | 1-3 | Telfer 24 *[Gabbiadini 81]* | Chamberlain | Dreyer | James | Johnson | Hughes | Peake | Telfer | Benjamin* | Rees^ | Gray | Preece | Harvey/Oakes |
| 23/1 | 9,170 *1:9* | | | | | *Short 29, Pembridge 42, 44, 55,* | *Sutton* | *Kavanagh* | *Short* | *Wassall* | *Forsyth* | *Goulooze** | *Kuhl* | *Pembridge* | *Kitson* | *Gabbiadini* | *Johnson* | *Micklewhite* |
| | | | | | | Ref: P Harrison | Mark Pembridge returns to Kenilworth Road and nets a hat-trick against his old club after Paul Telfer opened the scoring, connecting with a free-kick from Jason Rees. The Hatters play some pretty football but it is ineffective against a side who attack on the break with amazing pace. | | | | | | | | | | | |

| | Home | | | | | | Away | | | | | |
|---|---|---|---|---|---|---|---|---|---|---|---|---|
| | P | W | D | L | F | A | W | D | L | F | A | Pts |
| 1 Newcastle | 46 | 16 | 6 | 1 | 58 | 15 | 13 | 3 | 7 | 34 | 23 | 96 |
| 2 West Ham | 46 | 16 | 5 | 2 | 50 | 17 | 10 | 5 | 8 | 31 | 24 | 88 |
| 3 Portsmouth | 46 | 19 | 2 | 2 | 48 | 9 | 7 | 8 | 8 | 32 | 37 | 88 |
| 4 Tranmere | 46 | 15 | 4 | 4 | 48 | 24 | 8 | 6 | 9 | 24 | 32 | 79 |
| 5 Swindon * | 46 | 15 | 5 | 3 | 41 | 23 | 6 | 8 | 9 | 33 | 36 | 76 |
| 6 Leicester | 46 | 14 | 5 | 4 | 43 | 24 | 8 | 5 | 10 | 28 | 40 | 76 |
| 7 Millwall | 46 | 14 | 6 | 3 | 46 | 21 | 4 | 10 | 9 | 19 | 32 | 70 |
| 8 Derby | 46 | 11 | 2 | 10 | 40 | 33 | 8 | 7 | 8 | 28 | 24 | 66 |
| 9 Grimsby | 46 | 12 | 6 | 5 | 33 | 25 | 7 | 1 | 15 | 25 | 32 | 64 |
| 10 Peterborough | 46 | 7 | 11 | 5 | 30 | 26 | 9 | 3 | 11 | 25 | 37 | 62 |
| 11 Wolves | 46 | 11 | 6 | 6 | 37 | 26 | 5 | 7 | 11 | 20 | 30 | 61 |
| 12 Charlton | 46 | 10 | 8 | 5 | 28 | 19 | 6 | 5 | 12 | 21 | 27 | 61 |
| 13 Barnsley | 46 | 12 | 4 | 7 | 29 | 19 | 5 | 5 | 13 | 27 | 41 | 60 |
| 14 Oxford | 46 | 8 | 7 | 8 | 29 | 21 | 6 | 7 | 10 | 24 | 35 | 56 |
| 15 Bristol City | 46 | 10 | 7 | 6 | 29 | 25 | 4 | 7 | 12 | 20 | 42 | 56 |
| 16 Watford | 46 | 8 | 7 | 8 | 27 | 30 | 6 | 6 | 11 | 30 | 41 | 55 |
| 17 Notts Co | 46 | 10 | 7 | 6 | 33 | 21 | 2 | 9 | 12 | 22 | 49 | 52 |
| 18 Southend | 46 | 9 | 8 | 6 | 33 | 22 | 4 | 5 | 14 | 21 | 42 | 52 |
| 19 Birmingham | 46 | 10 | 4 | 9 | 30 | 32 | 3 | 8 | 12 | 20 | 40 | 51 |
| 20 LUTON TOWN | 46 | 6 | 13 | 4 | 26 | 26 | 4 | 8 | 11 | 22 | 36 | 51 |
| 21 Sunderland | 46 | 9 | 6 | 8 | 34 | 28 | 4 | 5 | 14 | 16 | 36 | 50 |
| 22 Brentford | 46 | 7 | 6 | 10 | 28 | 30 | 6 | 4 | 13 | 24 | 41 | 49 |
| 23 Cambridge | 46 | 8 | 6 | 9 | 29 | 32 | 3 | 10 | 10 | 19 | 37 | 49 |
| 24 Bristol Rov | 46 | 6 | 6 | 11 | 30 | 42 | 4 | 5 | 14 | 25 | 45 | 41 |
| | 1104 | 263 | 147 | 142 | 859 | 590 | 142 | 147 | 263 | 590 | 859 | 1509 |

* promoted after play-offs

Odds & ends

Double wins: (0).
Double losses: (2) Portsmouth, Grimsby.

Won from behind: (2) Brentford (a), Wolves (a).
Lost from in front: (4) Leicester (a), Portsmouth (h) & (a), Derby (FAC).

High spots: 7 consecutive clean sheets and 683 minutes without conceding a league goal in January-February – the same defence of Chamberlain, Dreyer, James, Johnson and Peake played in every game.
On 13 September, Hatters recorded their first league away win for 554 days – the previous victory being at Villa Park, 9 April 1991.
Phil Gray scores in six consecutive games between 13 February and 13 March.

Low spots: Losing 1-5 to Derby in the FA Cup after scoring first.
Bottom of the table in late January.
The injuries to Darren Salton which ended his career.
The early season home form.
Drawing 3-3 at Cambridge after leading 3-0.

Player of the Year: John Dreyer.
Ever-presents: (0).
Hat-tricks: (0).
Leading Scorer: (20) Phil Gray.

| | Appearances | | | | | | Goals | | | |
|---|---|---|---|---|---|---|---|---|---|---|
| | Lge | *Sub* | LC | *Sub* | FAC | *Sub* | Lge | LC | FAC | Tot |
| Benjamin, Ian | **5** | *5* | | | 2 | | **1** | | | **1** |
| Campbell, Jamie | **2** | *7* | | *1* | | | **1** | | | **1** |
| Chamberlain, Alec | **32** | | | | 2 | | | | | |
| Claridge, Steve | **15** | *1* | 2 | | | | **2** | 3 | | **5** |
| Dixon, Kerry | **16** | *1* | | | | | **3** | | | **3** |
| Dreyer, John | **38** | | | *1* | 2 | | **2** | | | **2** |
| Gray, Phil | **45** | | 2 | | 2 | | **19** | | 1 | **20** |
| Greene, David | **1** | | | | | | | | | |
| Harvey, Richard | **1** | | | | | *2* | | | | |
| Hughes, Ceri | **26** | *3* | | | 2 | | **2** | | 1 | **3** |
| James, Julian | **43** | | 2 | | 2 | | **2** | | | **2** |
| Johnson, Marvin | **38** | *2* | 2 | | 2 | | **3** | | | **3** |
| Kamara, Chris | **21** | | 2 | | | | | | | |
| Linton, Des | **17** | *3* | 2 | | | | **1** | | | **1** |
| Matthew, Damian | **3** | *2* | | | | | | | | |
| Oakes, Scott | **25** | *19* | 1 | *1* | | *2* | **5** | | | **5** |
| Peake, Trevor | **40** | | 2 | | 2 | | | | | |
| Petterson, Andy | **14** | | 2 | | | | | | | |
| Preece, David | **43** | | 2 | | 2 | | **3** | 1 | | **4** |
| Rees, Jason | **29** | *3* | 1 | *1* | 2 | | | | | |
| Salton, Darren | **15** | | 2 | | | | | | | |
| Telfer, Paul | **30** | *2* | | | 2 | | **2** | | 1 | **3** |
| Williams, Martin | **7** | *15* | | | | | **1** | | | **1** |
| (own-goals) | | | | | | | **1** | | | **1** |
| **23 players used** | **506** | *63* | **22** | *4* | **22** | *4* | **48** | **4** | **3** | **55** |

## ENDSLEIGH LEAGUE DIVISION 1     Manager: David Pleat     SEASON 1993-94



| No | Date | | Att | Pos | Pt | F-A | H-T | Scorers, Times, and Referees | 1 | 2 | 3 | 4 | 5 | 6 | 7 | 8 | 9 | 10 | 11 | subs used |
|---|---|---|---|---|---|---|---|---|---|---|---|---|---|---|---|---|---|---|---|---|
| 1 | H | WATFORD | | | W | 2-1 | 0-0 | Telfer 51, Dixon 82 | **Sommer*** | Johnson | James | Williams | Peake | Dreyer | Telfer | Oakes | Dixon | Rees^ | Preece | Petterson/**Houghton** |
| | 14/8 | | 9,149 | | 3 | | | *Furlong 87* | *Sheppard* | *Lavin* | *Ashby !* | *Holdsworth* | *Drysdale !* | *Bazeley** | *Johnson^* | *Soloman* | *Porter* | *Furlong* | *Charlery* | *Nogan/Dublin* |
| | | | | | | | | Ref: P Alcock | Barry Ashby is dismissed after a foul on Preece, followed by Jason Drysdale for a similar offence on Rees. The Town struggle against the nine men until Telfer side-foots home. Dixon hits the winner with an expert strike to record the first Luton win on the opening day for nine seasons. | | | | | | | | | | | |
| 2 | A | PORTSMOUTH | | 16 | L | 0-1 | 0-1 | | Sommer | Johnson | James | Williams* | Peake | Dreyer | Telfer | Oakes^ | Dixon | Hughes | Preece | Houghton/Benjamin |
| | 21/8 | | *12,248* | *10* | 3 | | | *Hall 40* | *Knight* | *Neill* | *Symons* | *Awford* | *Stimson* | *Hall* | *McLoughlin** | *Blake* | *Burns* | *Chapman* | *Walsh^* | *Aspinall/Horne* |
| | | | | | | | | Ref: G Poll | Paul Hall makes his full debut for Pompey and gives Johnson a hard time. He scores the only goal of the game when Kerry Dixon loses the ball on the edge of the area. The Town come back in to the game during the second period and Scott Houghton misses a good chance at the end. | | | | | | | | | | | |
| 3 | H | NOTT'M FOREST | | 22 | L | 1-2 | 1-1 | Hartson 22 | Sommer | Johnson | James | Telfer* | Peake | Dreyer | **Hartson** | Hughes^ | Dixon | Houghton | Preece | Williams/Rees |
| | 28/8 | | 9,788 | *3* | 3 | | | *Black 27, Woan 85* | *Crossley* | *Lyttle* | *Warner* | *Chettle* | *Pearce* | *Black** | *Stone* | *Webb* | *Woan* | *Rosario* | *Glover* | *Phillips* |
| | | | | | | | | Ref: G Willard | Hartson begins his footballing career by heading the first goal for the Town, midway through the first half. Ex-Hatter, Kingsley Black, levels after a shot from Stone is parried by Sommer. Ian Woan hits the winner for the visitors to register the first Luton home defeat in ten months. | | | | | | | | | | | |
| 4 | H | BOLTON | | 24 | L | 0-2 | 0-1 | | Sommer | Johnson | James* | Telfer | Peake | Dreyer | Hartson^ | Hughes | Dixon | Houghton | Preece | Oakes/Williams |
| | 11/9 | | 7,199 | *11* | 3 | | | *McGinlay 37, 67* | *Branagan* | *Brown* | *Darby* | *Stubbs* | *Phillips* | *Lee* | *McAteer** | *Kelly* | *Patterson^* | *Coyle* | *McGinlay* | *Thompson/Seagraves* |
| | | | | | | | | Ref: K Cooper | Bruce Rioch's newly promoted Bolton play with a spirit and self-belief that is too much for the Hatters. David Lee robs Marvin Johnson to set up John McGinlay for the first, and a through-pass from Tony Kelly enables McGinlay to notch the second with the Luton defence stretched. | | | | | | | | | | | |
| 5 | A | TRANMERE | | 24 | L | **1-4** | 0-1 | Benjamin 73 *[Aldridge 89]* | Sommer | **Harper** | Johnson | Telfer | Peake | Dreyer | Benjamin | Hughes | Oakes | Rees* | Preece | Williams |
| | 14/9 | | *5,871* | *3* | 3 | | | *Muir 34, Thomas 55, Brannan 71,* | *Nixon* | *Thomas* | *Garnett** | *Higgins* | *Mungall* | *Nevin* | *Brannan* | *Martindale* | *Irons* | *Aldridge* | *Muir^* | *Hughes/Kenworthy* |
| | | | | | | | | Ref: S Lodge | The Town show as much enterprise as Tranmere but finish up as heavy losers. Juergen Sommer is at fault with two of the goals and appears to be nervous all evening. Alan Harper, a new signing from Everton, is bewildered by it all. 'A Mickey Mouse result,' is David Pleat's verdict. | | | | | | | | | | | |
| 6 | A | MIDDLESBROUGH | | 23 | D | 0-0 | 0-0 | | Sommer | Harper | Johnson | Telfer | Peake | Dreyer | Benjamin* | Oakes | Rees^ | Hughes | Preece | Hartson/James |
| | 18/9 | | *12,487* | *4* | 4 | | | | *Pears* | *Morris** | *Mohan* | *Whyte* | *Liburd* | *Hignett^* | *Pollock* | *Mustoe* | *Moore* | *Hendrie* | *Wilkinson* | *Fleming/Kavanagh* |
| | | | | | | | | Ref: M Peck | Juergen Sommer compensates for his poor display at Tranmere in midweek by making a string of tremendous saves. He keeps his team in the match and helps to earn them their first clean sheet of the season. The point earned lifts the Hatters off the bottom of the league table. | | | | | | | | | | | |
| 7 | A | BIRMINGHAM | | 23 | D | 1-1 | 0-1 | Telfer 77 | Sommer | Johnson | James | Telfer | Peake | Dreyer | Harper | Oakes | Rees* | Hughes | Hartson | Williams |
| | 25/9 | | *11,801* | *12* | 5 | | | *Shutt 31* | *Miller* | *Hiley* | *Whyte* | *Dryden* | *Frain* | *Donowa* | *Smith* | *Tait** | *McMinn^* | *Shutt* | *Saville* | *Mardon/Peschisolido* |
| | | | | | | | | Ref: T Lunt | Blues control most of the game and take a deserved lead when Carl Shutt is unmarked after Trevor Peake inadvertently flicks a corner across goal. The Hatters come on stronger in the last 20 minutes and Telfer equalises after a goalmouth scramble. Ceri Hughes misses a sitter late on. | | | | | | | | | | | |
| 8 | H | BARNSLEY | | 21 | W | **5-0** | 2-0 | Hartson 28, Oakes 40,88, James 60, [Houghton 84] | Sommer | Johnson | James | Williams* | Peake | Dreyer | Telfer | Oakes | Hartson | Hughes^ | Harper | Houghton/Linton |
| | 2/10 | | 6,201 | *18* | 8 | | | | *Watson* | *Fleming* | *Anderson* | *Taggart !* | *Bishop* | *Redfearn* | *Wilson* | *O'Connell** | *Archdeacon* | *Rammell* | *Bryson^* | *Eaden/Liddell* |
| | | | | | | | | Ref: A Smith | Barnsley are reduced to ten men after just three minutes when Gerry Taggart is sent off for an awful tackle on James. For once, the Town make the extra man count and, using space, notch up their biggest win for four years. A scorcher, hit by James from the edge of the box, is the pick. | | | | | | | | | | | |
| 9 | H | BRISTOL CITY | | 22 | L | 0-2 | 0-0 | | Sommer | Johnson | James | Williams | Peake | Dreyer | Telfer | Oakes* | Hartson | Hughes | Harper | Houghton |
| | 5/10 | | **5,956** | *10* | 8 | | | *Tinnion 53p, Baird 56* | *Welch* | *Borrows* | *Shail* | *Bryant* | *Munro* | *Gavin* | *Martin* | *Tinnion** | *Scott* | *Baird* | *Robinson* | *Edwards* |
| | | | | | | | | Ref: K Morton | The Town play the same team that won well against Barnsley, but they are a shambles as City win with ease. Mark Gavin is brought down by Johnson and Brian Tinnion nets from the penalty spot. Gavin then skips down the right before crossing for Baird to tuck home at the near post. | | | | | | | | | | | |
| 10 | A | DERBY | | 23 | L | 1-2 | 0-1 | Williams 89 | Sommer | Linton | Johnson | Harper* | Peake | Dreyer | Telfer | Oakes^ | Hartson | Hughes | **Dickov** | Campbell/Williams |
| | 9/10 | | *15,885* | *6* | 8 | | | *Kitson 17, Johnson 72* | *Taylor* | *Kavanagh* | *Short* | *Wassall* | *Forsyth* | *Johnson* | *Harkes* | *Pembridge* | *Simpson* | *Kitson* | *Gabbiadini* | |
| | | | | | | | | Ref: J Kirkby | Sommer drops a cross from Simpson, leaving Paul Kitson with an easy header for the opener. The Rams are the physically stronger side and Tommy Johnson is unmarked when he fires the second. The Town fight back and Martin Williams scores a goal, albeit too late, with his head. | | | | | | | | | | | |
| 11 | H | NOTTS CO | | 21 | W | 1-0 | 1-0 | Dickov 13 | Sommer | Linton | Johnson | Harper | Peake | Dreyer | Telfer | Oakes | Hartson* | Hughes | Dickov^ | Williams/Campbell |
| | 16/10 | | 6,366 | *16* | 11 | | | | *Cherry* | *Gallagher* | *Walker* | *Palmer* | *Johnson** | *Devlin* | *Draper* | *Simpson* | *Legg^* | *McSwegan* | *Lund* | *Cox/Wilson* |
| | | | | | | | | Ref: J Brandwood | Loan player, Paul Dickov, heads in a cross from Scott Oakes as Notts County chalk up the unwanted record of going 25 away games without a win. They hardly look like breaking their duck and it is only their goalkeeper, Steve Cherry, and the woodwork, which keeps the score down. | | | | | | | | | | | |

| No | Venue | Opponent | Pos | Res | F-A | H-T | Scorers, Times, Referees | 1 | 2 | 3 | 4 | 5 | 6 | 7 | 8 | 9 | 10 | 11 | Subs used |
|---|---|---|---|---|---|---|---|---|---|---|---|---|---|---|---|---|---|---|---|
| 12 | A | SUNDERLAND | 21 | L | 0-2 | 0-2 | | Sommer | Linton | Johnson | Hughes | Peake | Dreyer | Telfer | Oakes | Hartson* | Rees | Dickov^ | Williams/Campbell |
| 20/10 | | *13,645* | *15* | 11 | | | *Goodman 12, Smith 20* | *Chamberlain* | *Owers* | *Ball* | *Melville* | *Gray* | *Lawrence** | *Ferguson^* | *Atkinson* | *Smith* | *Goodman* | *Howey* | *Russell/Sampson* |
| | | | | | | | Ref: K Lynch | Don Goodman shoots home from the edge of the box and Martin Smith, making his Sunderland debut, fires in a second, direct from a free-kick, as the Wearsiders have the game won by half-time. They also hit the bar twice and dominate a Town side who are lightweight by comparison. | | | | | | | | | | | |
| 13 | A | OXFORD | 19 | W | 1-0 | 1-0 | Hughes 20 | Sommer | Linton | Johnson* | Harper | Peake | Dreyer | Telfer | Hughes | Dixon^ | Houghton | Dickov | Oakes/Campbell |
| 23/10 | | ***5,161*** | *24* | 14 | | | | *Whitehead* | *Robinson* | *Collins* | *Ford* | *Rogan* | *Beauchamp* | *Lewis* | *Magilton* | *Allen* | *Penney** | *Dyer^* | *Keeble/Wanless* |
| | | | | | | | Ref: G Pooley | Hughes scores for the first time in ten months, his 25-yard shot arriving against the run of play, as the Town record their first away win of the season and lift themselves clear of the relegation zone. Oxford suffer the fate, seen in the past with the Hatters, of failing to take their chances. | | | | | | | | | | | |
| 14 | H | LEICESTER | 21 | L | 0-2 | 0-1 | | Sommer | Linton | Johnson* | Harper^ | Peake | Dreyer | Telfer | Oakes | Hartson | Hughes | Dickov | Dixon/Houghton |
| 30/10 | | 8,813 | *2* | 14 | | | *Thompson 38p, Speedie 46* | *Ward* | *Grayson* | *Carey* | *Hill** | *Whitlow* | *Mills* | *Thompson* | *Agnew* | *Ormondroyd* | *Speedie* | *Joachim* | *Smith* |
| | | | | | | | Ref: J Lloyd | Telfer handles a header from Simon Grayson in the box and ex-Hatter Steve Thompson scores from the penalty spot. David Speedie fires in the second from close range, shortly after the restart, as Leicester play the game tight, remembering their defeat of last season at Kenilworth Road. | | | | | | | | | | | |
| 15 | A | CRYS PALACE | 21 | L | 2-3 | 2-3 | Aunger 2, Hughes 15 | Sommer | Linton* | Johnson | Harper | Peake | Dreyer | Telfer | Oakes^ | Dixon | Hughes | **Aunger** | Campbell/Dickov |
| 2/11 | | *10,925* | *2* | 14 | | | *Young 11, Shaw 26, Whyte 35* | *Martyn* | *Humphrey* | *Young* | *Thorn** | *Coleman* | *Southgate* | *Shaw* | *Rodger* | *Gordon* | *Armstrong* | *Whyte* | *Salako* |
| | | | | | | | Ref: I Borrett | Geoff Aunger scores the opening goal with his first touch in league football. Young equalises before Ceri Hughes beats four defenders and hits the second. That restores the Hatters' lead, but they are unable to withstand the aerial bombardment from Palace and finish up losing 2-3. | | | | | | | | | | | |
| 16 | H | CHARLTON | 18 | W | 1-0 | 1-0 | Telfer 22 | Sommer | Linton | Johnson | Harper | Peake | Dreyer | Telfer | Oakes* | Dixon | Hughes | Aunger^ | Williams/Dickov |
| 7/11 | | 6,327 | *1* | 17 | | | | *Salmon* | *Balmer* | *McLeary* | *Chapple* | *Minto* | *Newton** | *Walsh* | *Pitcher* | *Robinson^* | *Leaburn* | *Nelson* | *Bailey/Grant* |
| | | | | | | | Ref: M Bailey | Charlton have not lost an away game since August. Although the match is not brilliant entertainment for the live television audience, armchair fans see a great header from Paul Telfer, who takes advantage of Marvin Johnson's accurate cross to earn the Hatters three valuable points. | | | | | | | | | | | |
| 17 | A | SOUTHEND | 18 | L | 1-2 | 0-1 | Dixon 46 | Sommer | Linton | Thomas | Harper* | Peake | Dreyer | Telfer | Houghton | Dixon | Hughes^ | Aunger | Campbell/Dickov |
| 13/11 | | *5,567* | *4* | 17 | | | *Otto 2, Hunt 58* | *Sansome* | *Poole* | *Bressington* | *Edwards* | *Powell* | *Hunt* | *Jones* | *Payne* | *Otto* | *Jones* | *Angell* | |
| | | | | | | | Ref: G Poll | Ricky Otto heads an early goal for the Shrimpers before Juergen Sommer is called upon to make three crucial saves to keep the Hatters in the game. Kerry Dixon levels after the break with a stunning 20-yard drive but a shot from Jon Hunt is deflected into his own net by Trevor Peake. | | | | | | | | | | | |
| 18 | H | STOKE | 15 | W | 6-2 | 3-2 | Dixon 21, 71, 79, Hughes 35, Oakes 37, [Hartson 89] | Sommer | Linton | Thomas | Harper | Peake | Campbell | Hughes | Oakes | Dixon | Rees* | Dickov^ | **Thorpe**/Hartson |
| 27/11 | | 7,384 | *10* | 20 | | | *Regis 2, Linton 19 (og)* | *Marshall* | *Butler* | *Overson* | *Sandford* | *Cowan* | *Orlygsson* | *Foley* | *Ware* | *Gleghorn* | *Carruthers** | *Regis* | *Bannister* |
| | | | | | | | Ref: B Hill | The Potters take an early two-goal lead and appear to be well on top until Kerry Dixon pounces. His first goal is a quality strike, and he goes on to complete his hat-trick, the first to be scored by a Luton player in the league at Kenilworth Road since Mark Stein's in February 1988. | | | | | | | | | | | |
| 19 | A | CHARLTON | 17 | L | 0-1 | 0-0 | | Sommer | Linton | Thomas | Harper | Peake | Campbell | Rees* | Oakes | Dixon | Hughes | Dickov^ | Telfer/Hartson |
| 4/12 | | *7,570* | *1* | 20 | | | *Chapple 59* | *Salmon* | *Balmer* | *Chapple* | *McLeary* | *Minto* | *Robinson** | *Pitcher* | *Garland* | *Walsh^* | *Leaburn* | *Nelson* | *Newton/Robson* |
| | | | | | | | Ref: P Jones | Juergen Sommer is again the hero of the hour and keeps Charlton at bay until defender Phil Chapple heads in the flick-on from a corner kick from close range. The Town are unable to trouble the Valiants who, in avenging their defeat of last month, move back to the top of the league. | | | | | | | | | | | |
| 20 | H | TRANMERE | 19 | L | 0-1 | 0-0 | | Sommer | Linton | Thomas | Harper | Peake | Campbell | Telfer | Hughes* | Dixon | Preece | Dickov^ | Oakes/Hartson |
| 11/12 | | 7,075 | *1* | 20 | | | *Aldridge 63* | *Nixon* | *Thomas* | *Garnett* | *Higgins* | *Nolan* | *Morrissey* | *Brannan* | *Proctor* | *Nevin* | *Aldridge* | *Malkin* | |
| | | | | | | | Ref: D Frampton | The Town enjoy the majority of the possession and, on the balance of the play, deserve the win. However, they are unable to create any scoring chances and it is left to the 35-year-old veteran, John Aldridge, to take his one opportunity, controlling and volleying the ball in one movement. | | | | | | | | | | | |
| 21 | A | WATFORD | 19 | D | 2-2 | 0-2 | Preece 47, Dreyer 85p | Sommer | Linton | Thomas | Harper | Peake | Dreyer | Telfer* | Oakes^ | Dixon | Hughes | Preece | Dickov/Houghton |
| 19/12 | | *7,567* | *22* | 21 | | | *Dyer 9, 27* | *Digweed* | *Lavin* | *Holdsworth* | *Watson* | *McCarthy* | *Hessenthaler* | *Nogan* | *Porter* | *Johnson* | *Furlong* | *Dyer* | |
| | | | | | | | Ref: V Callow | The pace of Bruce Dyer in the first half threatens to totally destroy the Town as the Hornets race into a deserved two-goal lead. Preece pulls a goal back after the break and a precious point is salvaged after McCarthy handles a cross from Houghton with Dreyer converting from the spot. | | | | | | | | | | | |
| 22 | A | PETERBOROUGH | 20 | D | 0-0 | 0-0 | | Sommer | Linton* | Thomas | Harper | Peake | Dreyer | Telfer | Hughes | Dixon | Houghton^ | Preece | James/Dickov |
| 27/12 | | *9,522* | *24* | 22 | | | | *Barber* | *McDonald* | *Bradshaw* | *Howarth* | *Welsh* | *Spearing** | *Adcock* | *Ebdon* | *Fulton* | *Charlery* | *Furnell^* | *Barnes/Philliskirk* |
| | | | | | | | Ref: D Elleray | The Town are always in full control but again fail to convert their dominance into goals against a Posh side which is fighting for its life. Kerry Dixon hits the post during a spell in which he may well have had a hat-trick and John Dreyer has his effort ruled out by the referee for pushing. | | | | | | | | | | | |
| 23 | H | GRIMSBY | 18 | W | 2-1 | 0-1 | Harper 71, Hughes 82 | Sommer | Linton | Thomas | Harper | Peake | Dreyer | Telfer | Oakes* | Dixon | Hughes | Hartson^ | James/Dickov |
| 29/12 | | 7,234 | *21* | 25 | | | *Groves 38* | *Crichton* | *McDermott** | *Futcher* | *Handyside* | *Croft* | *Ford* | *Dobbin* | *Gilbert^* | *Groves* | *Mendonca* | *Livingstone* | *Shakespeare/Rees* |
| | | | | | | | Ref: D Gallagher | Grimsby are in control for most of the game and take the lead before the break through Groves. Their dominance gains no rewards, however, as the Town equalise through a 25-yard shot from Alan Harper, and win all three points with a Ceri Hughes special from a similar distance. | | | | | | | | | | | |

| No | Date | | Att | Pos | Pt | F-A | H-T | Scorers, Times, and Referees | 1 | 2 | 3 | 4 | 5 | 6 | 7 | 8 | 9 | 10 | 11 | subs used |
|---|---|---|---|---|---|---|---|---|---|---|---|---|---|---|---|---|---|---|---|---|
| 24 | A | WEST BROM | | 18 | D | 1-1 | 1-0 | Preece 36 | Sommer | Linton | Thomas | Harper | Peake | Dreyer | Telfer | Hughes* | Dixon | Houghton^ | Preece | James/Dickov |
| | 1/1 | | *16,138* | *20* | 26 | | | *Mellon 68* | *Lange* | *Burgess* | *Mardon* | *Raven* | *Lilwall* | *Ashcroft** | *Mellon* | *Coldicott* | *Hamilton* | *Garner* | *Taylor* | *Fereday* |
| | | | | | | | | Ref: K Breen | The Town are unable to get their passing game going, due to the state of the heavy pitch, but take the lead when Preece scores with a low drive after being put through with a flick, expertly executed by Dixon. Albion battle back and level through a thundering drive from Micky Mellon. | | | | | | | | | | | |
| 25 | A | NOTTS CO | | 17 | W | 2-1 | 0-0 | Dixon 81, 88 | Sommer | Linton | James | Harper | Peake | Dreyer | Telfer | Oakes* | Dixon | Hughes | Preece^ | Hartson/Campbell |
| | 15/1 | | *6,589* | *14* | 29 | | | *Agana 70* | *Cherry* | *Gannon* | *Johnson* | *Foster* | *Dijkstra* | *Legg** | *Turner* | *Draper* | *Agana* | *Devlin* | *Lund* | *McSwegan* |
| | | | | | | | | Ref: W Burns | Both sides play well between the penalty areas but are unable to find the finishing touch. A close-range effort from Tony Agana seems to have won the points for County until Dixon heads home a corner to level the match. Dixon, late on, strikes from 20 yards for the unlikely winner. | | | | | | | | | | | |
| 26 | H | DERBY | | 17 | W | 2-1 | 1-0 | Telfer 44, Oakes 74 | Sommer | Linton | James | Harper | Peake | Dreyer | Telfer | Oakes | Dixon* | Hughes ! | Campbell | Hartson |
| | 22/1 | | 9,371 | *7* | 32 | | | *Forsyth 51* | *Taylor* | *Charles* | *Forsyth* | *Ratcliffe** | *Wassall* | *Nicholson^* | *Kuhl* | *Pembridge* | *Johnson* | *Kitson* | *Gabbiadini* | *Kavanagh/Simpson* |
| | | | | | | | | Ref: M Reed | Scott Oakes scores a wonder goal which will be talked about for years when, with the Hatters reduced to ten men after the dismissal of Hughes for two bookable offences, he collects the ball inside his own half and beats seven men before slamming a dipping shot past Martin Taylor. | | | | | | | | | | | |
| 27 | H | OXFORD | | 16 | W | 3-0 | 2-0 | Oakes 42, Thomas 44, Thorpe 77 | Sommer | Linton* | James | Harper | Peake | Dreyer | Telfer | Oakes^ | Hartson | Preece | Thomas | Thorpe/Houghton |
| | 5/2 | | 7,366 | *23* | 35 | | | | *Whitehead* | *Robinson* | *Ford* | *Elliott* | *Rogan* | *Beauchamp* | *Lewis** | *Magilton* | *Dyer* | *Cusack^* | *Byrne* | *Allen/Penney* |
| | | | | | | | | Ref: G Ashby | A 25-yard drive from Scott Oakes and a diving header from Mitchell Thomas, just before the break, set the Hatters up to record their seventh game without defeat. Thorpe nets the third with a clever shot to put the Town in readiness for the upcoming FA Cup replay against Newcastle. | | | | | | | | | | | |
| 28 | A | LEICESTER | | 17 | L | 1-2 | 0-1 | James 66 | Sommer | Linton* | James | Harper | Peake | Dreyer | Telfer | Oakes | Hartson | Hughes | Preece^ | Houghton/Campbell |
| | 12/2 | | *16,194* | *4* | 35 | | | *Coatsworth 7, Roberts 65* | *Ward* | *Grayson* | *Carey* | *Whitlow* | *Lewis* | *Mills* | *Thompson* | *Coatsworth* | *Ormondroyd* | *Speedie* | *Roberts* | |
| | | | | | | | | Ref: P Harrison | The Town are below par after their Cup exploits against Newcastle. The opening goal from 30 yards by Coatsworth could have gone anywhere but there was no doubting the second, scored from close range by Roberts. A low shot from James keeps the game alive until the final whistle. | | | | | | | | | | | |
| 29 | H | PORTSMOUTH | | 15 | W | 4-1 | 2-0 | Telfer 5, Preece 28, Hughes 50, Oakes 51 | Sommer | Linton | James | Harper | Peake | Dreyer | Telfer | Oakes* | Dixon^ | Hughes | Preece | Thorpe/Hartson |
| | 22/2 | | 6,533 | *14* | 38 | | | *Symons 54* | *Knight* | *Neill** | *Gittens* | *Symons* | *Daniel^* | *Kristensen* | *Blake* | *Dobson* | *Powell* | *Hall* | *Creaney* | *Wood/Durnin* |
| | | | | | | | | Ref: G Singh | The Town adapt more readily to the blizzard-like conditions and, after Telfer opens the scoring with a far-post header, it is all one-way traffic. Preece hammers in the second with a left-foot shot but the goal of game comes from Oakes who chips over the defenders' heads from 30 yards. | | | | | | | | | | | |
| 30 | H | SUNDERLAND | | 14 | W | 2-1 | 2-0 | Hughes 4, Oakes 34 | Sommer | Linton | James | Harper | Peake | Dreyer | Telfer | Oakes* | Dixon | Hughes | Preece^ | Thorpe/Hartson |
| | 26/2 | | 9,367 | *17* | 41 | | | *Howey 87* | *Chamberlain* | *Owers** | *Bennett* | *Melville* | *Gray M ^* | *Atkinson* | *Ferguson* | *Ball* | *Russell* | *Gray P* | *Howey* | *Ord/Smith* |
| | | | | | | | | Ref: K Morton | Ceri Hughes is credited with the opener, after a goalmouth scramble, but there are no doubts about the second, when Scott Oakes fires in a free-kick. Lee Howey pulls back a late goal for the visitors but the confident Hatters hold out and record their seventh consecutive home win. | | | | | | | | | | | |
| 31 | A | NOTT'M FOREST | | 16 | L | 0-2 | 0-0 | | Sommer ! | Linton | James | Harper | Johnson* | Dreyer | Telfer | Hughes | Dixon | Thorpe^ | Preece | Petterson/**Burke** |
| | 5/3 | | *22,249* | *3* | 41 | | | *Cooper 59, Pearce 81p* | *Crossley* | *Lyttle* | *Cooper* | *Chettle* | *Pearce* | *Stone* | *Phillips* | *Gemmill* | *Bohinen** | *Black* | *Lee* | *Webb* |
| | | | | | | | | Ref: R Dilkes | The Town are but a shadow of the side of late with both Scott Oakes and Trevor Peake absent through injury. Forest take a long time to open the scoring but the points are made safe when Sommer is dismissed for bringing down Stone in the area, Pearce scoring from the penalty spot. | | | | | | | | | | | |
| 32 | H | MIDDLESBROUGH | | 16 | D | 1-1 | 0-0 | Dreyer 84p | Sommer | Linton* | James | Harper | Greene | Dreyer | Telfer | Hughes | Dixon | Preece | Burke^ | Williams/Hartson |
| | 8/3 | | 6,741 | *14* | 42 | | | *Mustoe 46* | *Pears* | *Fleming* | *Vickers* | *Whyte* | *Mohan* | *Mustoe* | *Peake* | *Pollock* | *Moore* | *Hendrie* | *Wilkinson* | |
| | | | | | | | | Ref: M Pierce | Robbie Mustoe toe-pokes Boro into the lead from close range before Dixon, having one of those games where nothing goes right, misses three good chances to equalise. Andy Peake handles a cross from Hughes and Dreyer levels from the spot but the winning home run comes to an end. | | | | | | | | | | | |
| 33 | H | BIRMINGHAM | | 18 | D | 1-1 | 1-0 | Telfer 41 | Petterson | Linton | James | Harper | Greene | Dreyer | Telfer | Oakes | Hartson* | Burke^ | Preece | Williams/Thorpe |
| | 19/3 | | 7,690 | *24* | 43 | | | *Claridge 49* | *Bennett* | *Scott* | *Daish* | *Whyte* | *Frain* | *Willis* | *Cooper** | *Harding* | *Dominguez^* | *Claridge* | *Saville* | *Moulden/Shutt* |
| | | | | | | | | Ref: P Durkin | Paul Telfer hits a close-range shot to put the Town into an interval lead but, with the FA Cup run beginning to take its toll, the Blues fight back after the break. A right-foot curling strike from ex-Hatter Steve Claridge earns a share of the points for the bottom-placed club in the league. | | | | | | | | | | | |
| 34 | A | BARNSLEY | | 18 | L | 0-1 | 0-0 | | Sommer | Williams | James | Harper | Peake | Dreyer | Telfer | Oakes | Dixon* | Hughes | Preece^ | Hartson/Thomas |
| | 26/3 | | *6,289* | *19* | 43 | | | *Payton 68* | *Butler* | *Eaden* | *Fleming* | *Taggart* | *Bishop* | *Archdeacon* | *Liddell* | *Wilson* | *Redfearn* | *Rammell* | *Payton* | |
| | | | | | | | | Ref: K Wolstenholme | Sommer again keeps the Hatters in the game, but is unable to stop Andy Payton from scoring with a fierce, close-range shot. The Tykes show the greater power and determination as the Town, who have reached the semi-finals of the FA Cup, slip to their third consecutive away defeat. | | | | | | | | | | | |

| No | | Opponent | Att | Pos | Res | Pts | FT | HT | Scorers, Times, and Referees | 1 | 2 | 3 | 4 | 5 | 6 | 7 | 8 | 9 | 10 | 11 | Subs used |
|---|---|---|---|---|---|---|---|---|---|---|---|---|---|---|---|---|---|---|---|---|---|
| 35 | A | MILLWALL | | 18 | D | | 2-2 | 1-1 | Dreyer 44, Hartson 61 | Sommer | Thomas | James | Harper | Peake | Dreyer | Telfer | Oakes | Hartson* | Hughes | Preece | Campbell |
| | 30/3 | | *9,235* | *4* | | 44 | | | *Moralee 10, Berry 48* | *Keller* | *Huxford* | *Stevens* | *Cunningham* | *Dawes* | *Verveer* | *Allen* | *Roberts* | *Berry* | *Moralee* | *Mitchell* | |
| | | | | | | | | | Ref: A Gunn | The Town pay their first visit to the New Den and, in a match which is littered with errors, Juergen Sommer allows a clearance from Keller to bounce over his head, leaving Moralee with the easiest of chances. The Lions then give the ball away in front of their goal and Hartson levels. | | | | | | | | | | | |
| 36 | H | PETERBOROUGH | | 17 | W | | 2-0 | 1-0 | Dixon 29, 77 | Sommer | Thomas | James | Harper | Peake | Dreyer | Telfer | Oakes | Dixon | Hartson* | Preece^ | Rees/Campbell |
| | 2/4 | | 8,398 | *24* | | 47 | | | | *Barber* | *Greenman* | *Bradshaw* | *Welsh* | *Spearing* | *Iorfa* | *McGlashan* | *Williams** | *Hackett^* | *Adcock* | *Charlery* | *McGorry/McGee* |
| | | | | | | | | | Ref: P Jones | A header from Hartson hits a post and Kerry Dixon follows up to score with a tap-in. Struggling Peterborough fight back but a rocket shot on the volley from Dixon midway through the second half settles the issue and the Hatters are able to record their first league win in over a month. | | | | | | | | | | | |
| 37 | A | GRIMSBY | | 18 | L | | 0-2 | 0-1 | | Sommer | Linton | Thomas | James | Greene | Dreyer | Telfer | Hughes | Hartson* | Rees^ | Aunger | Campbell/Harper |
| | 4/4 | | *5,542* | *11* | | 47 | | | *Gilbert 17, 51* | *Crichton* | *Ford* | *Handyside* | *Rodger* | *Agnew* | *Childs** | *Shakespeare* | *Groves* | *Gilbert* | *Mendonca^* | *Livingstone* | *Croft/Woods* |
| | | | | | | | | | Ref: T Lunt | Five players are rested in advance of the forthcoming FA Cup semi-final but the replacements fail to shine as the Mariners coast to victory. Dave Gilbert is allowed to pick his spot for the first goal and is on hand to put away the rebound after Steve Livingstone's shot hits the bar. | | | | | | | | | | | |
| 38 | H | WOLVES | | 19 | L | | 0-2 | 0-1 | | Sommer | Linton | James | Harper | Greene | Dreyer | Telfer | Oakes | Dixon* | Hughes^ | Preece | Thomas/Hartson |
| | 12/4 | | 8,545 | *9* | | 47 | | | *Burke 23, Whittingham 47* | *Stowell* | *Thompson* | *Blades** | *Shirtliff* | *Venus^* | *Birch* | *Burke* | *Bennett* | *Cook* | *Whittingham* | *Mills* | *Mountfield/Ferguson* |
| | | | | | | | | | Ref: P Foakes | Mark Burke, who was nondescript during his loan spell with the Town, opens the scoring at the second attempt, against the run of play. But the visitors always look the more likely winners. Having again failed to make possession count, the Town are finally eclipsed by Whittingham. | | | | | | | | | | | |
| 39 | H | CRYS PALACE | | 20 | L | | 0-1 | 0-1 | | Sommer | Linton | Thomas | Harper | Greene | James | Telfer | Oakes* | Hartson^ | Hughes | Preece | Thorpe/Dixon |
| | 16/4 | | 9,880 | *1* | | 47 | | | *Coleman 2* | *Martyn* | *Humphrey* | *Young* | *Coleman* | *Gordon* | *Matthew* | *Rodger* | *Southgate* | *Salako* | *Armstrong* | *Stewart* | |
| | | | | | | | | | Ref: M Bailey | Palace are walking away with the league title and score after just 70 seconds, when Chris Coleman hooks in a shot after the Hatters fail to clear a corner. The Town attack at will but are unable to seriously trouble Nigel Martyn and his strong defence, and are now slipping down the table. | | | | | | | | | | | |
| 40 | A | BRISTOL CITY | | 20 | L | | 0-1 | 0-1 | | Sommer | Linton* | James | Harper | Greene | Dreyer | Telfer | Hughes | Dixon | Aunger^ | Preece | Hartson/Thorpe |
| | 19/4 | | *5,350* | *13* | | 47 | | | *Edwards 20* | *Welch* | *Harriott* | *Munro* | *Edwards* | *Scott* | *Wyatt* | *Martin* | *Robinson* | *Hewlett* | *Barclay** | *Partridge* | *Bent* |
| | | | | | | | | | Ref: M Reed | In another lacklustre display, against a City team who have nothing to play for, a poor back-pass by John Dreyer produces a corner-kick which is consequently dropped by Sommer, leaving Rob Edwards with a simple chance to score. This is the Robins' 24th clean sheet this season. | | | | | | | | | | | |
| 41 | A | WOLVES | | 20 | L | | 0-1 | 0-1 | | Sommer | Linton | Thomas | Harper | Greene | James | Telfer | Hughes* | Dixon | Thorpe | Preece | Houghton |
| | 23/4 | | ***25,479*** | *8* | | 47 | | | *Whittingham 42* | *Stowell* | *Rankine* | *Blades* | *Shirtliff* | *Thompson* | *Birch* | *Burke* | *Bennett* | *Cook* | *Whittingham* | *Bull* | |
| | | | | | | | | | Ref: I Cruikshanks | The Town fall to their fifth defeat in a row, despite having just as much of the play as the promotion-chasing Wolves. James is bundled over by Steve Bull and, with the ball running loose, Guy Whittingham nets with the type of finish that seems to be beyond the Luton forwards at present. | | | | | | | | | | | |
| 42 | H | MILLWALL | | 20 | D | | 1-1 | 0-0 | Preece 66 | Sommer | James | Thomas | Harper | Greene | Dreyer | Telfer | Hughes | Dixon | Thorpe* | Preece | Hartson |
| | 26/4 | | 8,257 | *5* | | 48 | | | *Kerr 72* | *Keller* | *Cunningham* | *Emblen* | *Stevens* | *Thatcher** | *Roberts* | *Hurlock* | *Kerr* | *Rae* | *Moralee* | *Allen* | *Berry* |
| | | | | | | | | | Ref: M Bodenham | David Preece steers the ball home after it runs loose, following a tackle by Thorpe on Kasey Keller, but John Kerr equalises from a cross by Cunningham. The Hatters, scoring for the first time in six games, hit the wood twice and would be worthy winners, but have to settle for a point. | | | | | | | | | | | |
| 43 | H | SOUTHEND | | 20 | D | | 1-1 | 0-0 | Hartson 80 | Sommer | Linton* | James | Harper | Greene | Dreyer | Telfer | Oakes^ | Hartson | Hughes | Preece | Thomas/Thorpe |
| | 30/4 | | 7,504 | *16* | | 49 | | | *Otto 58* | *Sansome* | *Poole* | *Edwards* | *Bodley* | *Powell* | *Ansah* | *Gridelet* | *Tilson* | *Hunt* | *Sussex* | *Otto* | |
| | | | | | | | | | Ref: T Holbrook | Ricky Otto gives the Shrimpers the lead when running onto a through ball from Andy Sussex. The Hatters are far too frantic in their attempts to grab the equaliser although, when it does eventually come, the Southend defence claim that the header from Hartson did not cross the line. | | | | | | | | | | | |
| 44 | H | WEST BROM | | 20 | W | | 3-2 | 1-0 | Preece 35, James 69, Hartson 76 | Sommer* | James | Thomas ! | Harper | Peake | Dreyer | Telfer | Oakes^ | Hartson | Hughes | Preece | Petterson/Thorpe |
| | 3/5 | | **10,053** | *21* | | 52 | | | *Taylor 51, Ashcroft 78* | *Naylor** | *Parsley* | *Strodder !* | *Burgess^* | *Darton* | *McNally* | *Donovan* | *Hamilton* | *Smith* | *Ashcroft* | *Taylor* | *Lange/Mellon* |
| | | | | | | | | | Ref: P Danson | A classic game on an over-watered pitch settles the fate of the Town for another season. Five goals scored, four goalkeepers used, three players hospitalised, two players, Thomas and Strodder, sent off for fighting and finally one goal in it, makes for a dramatic countdown to the evening. | | | | | | | | | | | |
| 45 | A | BOLTON | | 20 | L | | 1-2 | 1-0 | Hughes 44 | Petterson | Linton* | James | Harper | Peake | Dreyer | Telfer | Oakes | Hartson ! | Hughes^ | Thomas | Preece/Thorpe |
| | 5/5 | | *7,102* | *14* | | 52 | | | *McGinlay 82, Thompson 86* | *Davison* | *Spooner* | *Seagraves* | *Stubbs* | *Phillips* | *Lee* | *McAteer* | *Fulton* | *Whittaker* | *McGinlay* | *Thompson* | |
| | | | | | | | | | Ref: J Kirkby | The dismissal of Hartson after 29 minutes, for the use of an elbow on Alan Stubbs, seems to spur the Hatters and they open the scoring through a sweet strike by Hughes. Bolton pile on the pressure after the break and eventually pull one back. The winner comes from a goalkeeping error. | | | | | | | | | | | |
| 46 | A | STOKE | | 20 | D | | 2-2 | 0-2 | Oakes 46, Telfer 80p | **Davis** | Linton | James | Harper* | Peake | Greene | Telfer | Oakes^ | Hartson | Hughes | Thorpe | **McLaren**/Campbell |
| | 8/5 | | *15,893* | *10* | | 53 | | | *Biggins 16, Regis 32* | *Prudhoe* | *Butler* | *Cranson !* | *Overson* | *Sandford* | *Walters* | *Gleghorn* | *Gynn** | *Adams* | *Biggins* | *Regis* | *Orlygsson* |
| | | Home | Away | | | | | | Ref: J Key | Kelvin Davis makes his debut in goal but is powerless to prevent Stoke from taking a two-goal interval lead. The Potters relax and a volley by Oakes, seconds after the restart, is followed by a penalty conceded by Ian Cranson when he handles a header from Tony Thorpe and is sent off. | | | | | | | | | | | |
| Average | | 7,878 | 11,056 | | | | | | | | | | | | | | | | | | |

| Coca-Cola Cup | | | | | F-A | H-T | Scorers, Times, and Referees | 1 | 2 | 3 | 4 | 5 | 6 | 7 | 8 | 9 | 10 | 11 | subs used |
|---|---|---|---|---|---|---|---|---|---|---|---|---|---|---|---|---|---|---|---|
| 1:1 | A | CAMBRIDGE | | L | 0-1 | 0-1 | | Sommer | James | Johnson | Oakes | Peake | Dreyer | Rees* | Preece | Telfer | Hughes | Benjamin | Houghton |
| | 17/8 | *4,065 D2* | | | | | *Claridge 17* | *Filan* | *Jeffrey* | *Heathcote* | *Daish* | *Barrick* | *Middleton* | *O'Shea* | *Clayton* | *Danzey* | *Butler* | *Claridge* | |
| | | | | | | | Ref: R Wiseman | The Town show no apparent signs of urgency in the first period and allow old boy, Steve Claridge, to open the scoring with a header following a corner-kick. The Hatters are livelier in the second half but the nearest they come to equalising is when a strike from Jason Rees hits the bar. | | | | | | | | | | | |
| 1:2 | H | CAMBRIDGE | 16 | L | 0-1 | 0-0 | | Sommer | Williams* | Johnson | James | Peake | Dreyer | Benjamin | Hughes | Campbell^ | Houghton | Preece | Oakes/Hartson |
| | 24/8 | 3,861 *2:11* | | | | | *Claridge 80* | *Filan* | *Jeffrey* | *Heathcote* | *Daish* | *O'Shea* | *Barrick* | *Fowler* | *Clayton* | *Danzey* | *Butler* | *Claridge* | |
| | | | | | | | Ref: B Hill (Hatters lost 0-2 on aggregate) | Cambridge come to defend their first-leg lead but soon realise that the game is there for the taking. Keeper John Filan has just one save to make all evening whilst, at the other end, Steve Claridge makes no mistake when Town goalkeeper Juergen Sommer palms the ball out to him. | | | | | | | | | | | |

| FA Cup | | | | | | | | | | | | | | | | | | | |
|---|---|---|---|---|---|---|---|---|---|---|---|---|---|---|---|---|---|---|---|
| 3 | H | SOUTHEND | 17 | W | 1-0 | 0-0 | Telfer 50 | Sommer | Linton | James | Harper | Peake | Dreyer | Telfer | Oakes | Dixon* | Hughes | Preece^ | Hartson/Campbell |
| | 18/1 | 7,953 *1:9* | | | | | | *Royce* | *Poole* | *Edwards* | *Bodley* | *Powell* | *Hunt** | *Jones K* | *Payne* | *Otto* | *Jones G* | *Lee* | *Sussex* |
| | | | | | | | Ref: M Bailey | The Shrimpers pulverise the Luton defence in the first period and squander three good chances. Paul Telfer shows them how to do it, shortly after the break, when he hits a cross from Ceri Hughes on the run and into the top of the net. The Southend boss, Peter Taylor, has no excuses. | | | | | | | | | | | |
| 4 | A | NEWCASTLE | 17 | D | 1-1 | 1-0 | Thorpe 35 | Sommer | Linton | James | Harper | Peake | Dreyer | Telfer | Oakes | Dixon | Thorpe* | Preece | Campbell |
| | 29/1 | *32,216 P:4* | | | | | *Beardsley 65p* | *Hooper* | *Watson* | *Venison* | *Howey* | *Beresford* | *Lee* | *Bracewell* | *Clark* | *Sellars* | *Beardsley* | *Cole* | |
| | | | | | | | Ref: J Parker | 19-year-old Tony Thorpe makes his debut for the Town and smashes a 25-yard shot past Mike Hooper in the Newcastle goal. For half an hour they believe that they can hold on for the win until Beardsley tumbles theatrically in the area. He recovers to convert an undeserved equaliser. | | | | | | | | | | | |
| 4R | H | NEWCASTLE | 16 | W | 2-0 | 1-0 | Hartson 16, Oakes 79 | Sommer | Linton | James | Harper | Peake | Dreyer | Telfer | Oakes* | Hartson | Campbell^ | Preece | Houghton/Thorpe |
| | 9/2 | 12,503 *P:4* | | | | | | *Hooper* | *Watson* | *Venison* | *Howey* | *Beresford* | *Lee* | *Clark* | *Elliott* | *Sellars* | *Cole* | *Beardsley* | |
| | | | | | | | Ref: J Parker | John Hartson puts the Town ahead after he rounds Mike Hooper and places the ball into the empty net. Scott Oakes seals the tie with a shot from a measured pass from Des Linton. This famous Hatters' victory is sportingly acknowledged by the Magpies manager, Kevin Keegan. | | | | | | | | | | | |
| 5 | A | CARDIFF | 17 | W | 2-1 | 1-0 | Oakes 38, Preece 70 | Sommer | Linton | James | Harper | Peake | Dreyer | Telfer | Oakes | Hartson* | Hughes | Preece | Dixon |
| | 20/2 | *17,296 2:20* | | | | | *Stant 65* | *Grew** | *Brazil* | *Baddeley* | *Perry* | *Searle* | *Bird* | *Millar* | *Richardson* | *Griffith* | *Dale^* | *Thompson* | *Kite/Stant* |
| | | | | | | | Ref: L Dilkes | In the intimidating atmosphere of Ninian Park, the Town deservedly take the lead when Scott Oakes rifles home the first goal. Phil Stant gets a shock equaliser for a side that showed plenty of passion but little else before David Preece runs through with the ball and calmly slots it home. | | | | | | | | | | | |
| QF | A | WEST HAM | 16 | D | 0-0 | 0-0 | | Sommer | Linton | James | Harper | Greene | Dreyer | Telfer | Oakes* | Dixon^ | Hughes | Preece | Burke/Hartson |
| | 14/3 | *27,331 P:13* | | | | | | *Miklosko* | *Breacker* | *Potts* | *Martin* | *Burrows* | *Marsh* | *Bishop* | *Allen M* | *Holmes* | *Chapman** | *Morley* | *Allen C* |
| | | | | | | | Ref: B Hill | The Town set out to stifle the Hammers at Upton Park with a five-man midfield, and rely on attacking on the break. The plan works well and Sommer only has one real save to make with dangerman Lee Chapman well held by Greene, making only his third first team appearance. | | | | | | | | | | | |
| QF R | H | WEST HAM | 18 | W | 3-2 | 1-1 | Oakes 35, 47, 74 | Sommer | Linton | James | Harper | Peake | Dreyer | Telfer | Oakes | Dixon | Hughes | Preece | |
| | 23/3 | 13,166 *P:14* | | | | | *Allen M 30, Bishop 56* | *Miklosko* | *Breacker* | *Potts* | *Martin* | *Burrows* | *Marsh** | *Allen M* | *Bishop* | *Morley* | *Butler* | *Chapman* | *Jones* |
| | | | | | | | Ref: B Hill | A magnificent game see-saws first one way and then the other but the match winner is undoubtedly Scott Oakes who appears to be unstoppable on the night. The third goal of his hat-trick, when he robbed Steve Potts and ran through before unleashing a hard drive, brings the house down. | | | | | | | | | | | |
| SF | A | CHELSEA | 18 | L | 0-2 | 0-1 | | Sommer | Linton* | James | Harper | Peake | Dreyer | Telfer | Oakes | Dixon | Hughes | Preece | Hartson |
| | 9/4 | *59,989 P:14* | | | | | *Peacock 13, 47* | *Kharine* | *Clarke* | *Johnsen* | *Kjeldbjerg* | *Sinclair* | *Burley** | *Newton* | *Peacock* | *Wise* | *Spencer* | *Cascarino* | *Barnard* |
| | | (at Wembley) | | | | | Ref: R Dilkes | A complete anti-climax as the Town fail to make any impression on the game and present the Blues with a straightforward victory. The Luton defence is never able to come to terms with the heading ability of Tony Cascarino, whose efforts are instrumental in both strikes from Peacock. | | | | | | | | | | | |

| | | Home | | | | | Away | | | | | |
|---|---|---|---|---|---|---|---|---|---|---|---|---|
| | P | W | D | L | F | A | W | D | L | F | A | Pts |
| 1 Crys Palace | 46 | 16 | 4 | 3 | 39 | 18 | 11 | 5 | 7 | 34 | 28 | 90 |
| 2 Nott'm Forest | 46 | 12 | 9 | 2 | 38 | 22 | 11 | 5 | 7 | 36 | 27 | 83 |
| 3 Millwall | 46 | 14 | 8 | 1 | 36 | 17 | 5 | 9 | 9 | 22 | 32 | 74 |
| 4 Leicester * | 46 | 11 | 9 | 3 | 45 | 30 | 8 | 7 | 8 | 27 | 29 | 73 |
| 5 Tranmere | 46 | 15 | 3 | 5 | 48 | 23 | 6 | 6 | 11 | 21 | 30 | 72 |
| 6 Derby | 46 | 15 | 3 | 5 | 44 | 25 | 5 | 8 | 10 | 29 | 43 | 71 |
| 7 Notts Co | 46 | 16 | 3 | 4 | 43 | 26 | 4 | 5 | 14 | 22 | 43 | 68 |
| 8 Wolves | 46 | 10 | 10 | 3 | 34 | 19 | 7 | 7 | 9 | 26 | 28 | 68 |
| 9 Middlesbro | 46 | 12 | 6 | 5 | 40 | 19 | 6 | 7 | 10 | 26 | 35 | 67 |
| 10 Stoke | 46 | 14 | 4 | 5 | 35 | 19 | 4 | 9 | 10 | 22 | 40 | 67 |
| 11 Charlton | 46 | 14 | 3 | 6 | 39 | 22 | 5 | 5 | 13 | 22 | 36 | 65 |
| 12 Sunderland | 46 | 14 | 2 | 7 | 35 | 22 | 5 | 6 | 12 | 19 | 35 | 65 |
| 13 Bristol City | 46 | 11 | 7 | 5 | 27 | 18 | 5 | 9 | 9 | 20 | 32 | 64 |
| 14 Bolton | 46 | 10 | 8 | 5 | 40 | 31 | 5 | 6 | 12 | 23 | 33 | 59 |
| 15 Southend | 46 | 10 | 5 | 8 | 34 | 28 | 7 | 3 | 13 | 29 | 39 | 59 |
| 16 Grimsby | 46 | 7 | 14 | 2 | 26 | 16 | 6 | 6 | 11 | 26 | 31 | 59 |
| 17 Portsmouth | 46 | 10 | 6 | 7 | 29 | 22 | 5 | 7 | 11 | 23 | 36 | 58 |
| 18 Barnsley | 46 | 9 | 3 | 11 | 25 | 26 | 7 | 4 | 12 | 30 | 41 | 55 |
| 19 Watford | 46 | 10 | 5 | 8 | 39 | 35 | 5 | 4 | 14 | 27 | 45 | 54 |
| 20 LUTON TOWN | 46 | 12 | 4 | 7 | 38 | 25 | 2 | 7 | 14 | 18 | 35 | 53 |
| 21 West Brom | 46 | 9 | 7 | 7 | 38 | 31 | 4 | 5 | 14 | 22 | 38 | 51 |
| 22 Birmingham | 46 | 9 | 7 | 7 | 28 | 29 | 4 | 5 | 14 | 24 | 40 | 51 |
| 23 Oxford | 46 | 10 | 5 | 8 | 33 | 33 | 3 | 5 | 15 | 21 | 42 | 49 |
| 24 Peterborough | 46 | 6 | 9 | 8 | 31 | 30 | 2 | 4 | 17 | 17 | 46 | 37 |
| | 1104 | 276 | 144 | 132 | 864 | 586 | 132 | 144 | 276 | 586 | 864 | 1512 |

* promoted after play-offs

Odds & ends

Double wins: (2) Oxford, Notts Co.
Double losses: (6) Bolton, Bristol City, Crystal Palace, Leicester, Nott'm Forest, Tranmere.

Won from behind: (4) Grimsby (h), Notts Co (a), Stoke (h), W Ham (FAC).
Lost from in front: (3) Bolton (a), Crystal Palace (a), Nott'm Forest (h).

High spots: The brilliant FA Cup run, culminating in a third semi-final appearance in nine years.
A run of seven games without a defeat in the New Year.
Scott Oakes' winning goal against Derby at Kenilworth Road.
The 6-2 home win over Stoke, after trailing 0-2.
The 3-2 home victory over West Brom in a game that had everything!
The signing of Kerry Dixon.

Low spots: The FA Cup semi-final defeat by Chelsea.
A run of five games without a goal in April.
The early season home form.
Losing to Cambridge in the Coca-Cola Cup.

Player of the Year: David Preece.
Ever-presents: (0).
Hat-tricks: (2) Kerry Dixon (1), Scott Oakes (1).
Leading scorer: (13) Scott Oakes.

| | Appearances | | | | | | Goals | | | |
|---|---|---|---|---|---|---|---|---|---|---|
| | Lge | *Sub* | LC | *Sub* | FAC | *Sub* | Lge | LC | FAC | Tot |
| Aunger, Geoff | **5** | | | | | | **1** | | | **1** |
| Benjamin, Ian | **2** | *1* | 2 | | | | **1** | | | **1** |
| Burke, Mark | **2** | *1* | | | | *1* | | | | |
| Campbell, Jamie | **4** | *12* | 1 | | 1 | *2* | | | | |
| Davis, Kelvin | **1** | | | | | | | | | |
| Dickov, Paul | **8** | *7* | | | | | **1** | | | **1** |
| Dixon, Kerry | **27** | *2* | | | 5 | *1* | **9** | | | **9** |
| Dreyer, John | **40** | | 2 | | 7 | | **3** | | | **3** |
| Greene, David | **10** | | | | 1 | | | | | |
| Harper, Alan | **40** | *1* | | | 7 | | **1** | | | **1** |
| Hartson, John | **21** | *13* | | *1* | 2 | *3* | **6** | | 1 | **7** |
| Houghton, Scott | **6** | *9* | 1 | *1* | | *1* | **1** | | | **1** |
| Hughes, Ceri | **42** | | 2 | | 5 | | **7** | | | **7** |
| James, Julian | **29** | *4* | 2 | | 7 | | **3** | | | **3** |
| Johnson, Marvin | **17** | | 2 | | | | | | | |
| Linton, Des | **32** | *1* | | | 7 | | | | | |
| McLaren, Paul | | *1* | | | | | | | | |
| Oakes, Scott | **33** | *3* | 1 | *1* | 7 | | **8** | | 5 | **13** |
| Peake, Trevor | **36** | | 2 | | 6 | | | | | |
| Petterson, Andy | **2** | *3* | | | | | | | | |
| Preece, David | **28** | *1* | 2 | | 7 | | **5** | | 1 | **6** |
| Rees, Jason | **8** | *2* | 1 | | | | | | | |
| Sommer, Juergen | **43** | | 2 | | 7 | | | | | |
| Telfer, Paul | **44** | *1* | 1 | | 7 | | **7** | | 1 | **8** |
| Thomas, Mitchell | **17** | *3* | | | | | **1** | | | **1** |
| Thorpe, Tony | **4** | *10* | | | 1 | *1* | **1** | | 1 | **2** |
| Williams, Martin | **5** | *10* | 1 | | | | **1** | | | **1** |
| **27 players used** | **506** | *85* | 22 | *3* | 77 | *9* | **56** | | 9 | **65** |

| No | Date | | Att | Pos | Pt | F-A | H-T | Scorers, Times, and Referees | 1 | 2 | 3 | 4 | 5 | 6 | 7 | 8 | 9 | 10 | 11 | subs used |
|---|---|---|---|---|---|---|---|---|---|---|---|---|---|---|---|---|---|---|---|---|
| 1 | H | WEST BROM | | | D | 1-1 | 0-1 | Oakes 49 | Sommer | James | Johnson M | **Skelton*** | Greene | Peake | Telfer | Oakes | Dixon | Preece | Houghton^ | Linton/**Marshall** |
| | 13/8 | | 8,640 | | 1 | | | *Taylor 4* | *Naylor* | *Parsley* | *Burgess* | *Herbert* | *Edwards* | *Ashcroft** | *McNally* | *Phelan* | *Hamilton* | *Taylor* | *Heggs* | *Donovan* |
| | | | | | | | | Ref: G Pooley | The Town kick off the campaign with a lacklustre first-half display during which Bob Taylor opens the scoring for Albion, running on to score from a seemingly offside position. The tactics are changed after the break, when Oakes uses his free role to sneak in and head in Telfer's cross. | | | | | | | | | | | |
| 2 | A | DERBY | | 14 | D | 0-0 | 0-0 | | Sommer | James | Johnson M | Linton | Greene | Peake | Telfer | Marshall | Dixon | Preece | Hughes | |
| | 20/8 | | *13,060* | *19* | 2 | | | | *Taylor* | *Charles* | *Short* | *Wassall* | *Forsyth* | *Hayward* | *Cowans* | *Pembridge* | *Simpson* | *Johnson** | *Kitson* | *Gabbiadini* |
| | | | | | | | | Ref: K Breen | Sommer is given only one difficult shot to save by the team which cost over £13 million to assemble whilst, at the other end, Dwight Marshall causes the Rams' defence huge problems as both he, and Johnson, have shots cleared off the line. Derby are booed off the pitch at the end. | | | | | | | | | | | |
| 3 | H | SOUTHEND | | 17 | D | 2-2 | 1-0 | Hartson 44, Hughes 70 | Sommer | James* | Johnson M | Oakes | Greene | Peake | Telfer | Marshall^ | Hartson | Preece | Hughes | Dixon/Thomas |
| | 27/8 | | 5,918 | *20* | 3 | | | *Dublin 51, Otto 75* | *Sansome* | *Poole* | *Edwards* | *Dublin* | *Powell* | *Jones* | *Hone* | *Sussex* | *Otto* | *Thomson** | *Iorfa^* | *Hunt/Martin* |
| | | | | | | | | Ref: J Brandwood | The first half is brightened by an effort from Hartson, who turns his marker after collecting Telfer's pass just before the break. Schoolboy errors let in Keith Dublin for the Shrimpers but, after Hughes strikes when the ball is deflected into his path, the volley from Otto is a corker. | | | | | | | | | | | |
| 4 | A | TRANMERE | | 18 | L | 2-4 | 0-0 | Hughes 54, Hartson 87 | Sommer | James | Johnson M | Skelton* | Greene | Peake | Telfer | Oakes | Hartson | Preece | Hughes | Marshall |
| | 30/8 | | *5,480* | *10* | 3 | | | *Aldridge 52, 58, 67p, Malkin 83* | *Coyne* | *Thomas* | *Higgins* | *McGreal* | *Brannan* | *Morrissey* | *O'Brien* | *Irons* | *Nevin* | *Aldridge* | *Malkin* | |
| | | | | | | | | Ref: R Poulain | The Town hold Rovers during the first period and have a couple of chances to open the scoring with Hartson and James both going close. The game turns when ace goal-poacher John Aldridge hits a second-half hat-trick, the third goal coming from the spot after Sommer up-ends Nevin. | | | | | | | | | | | |
| 5 | A | PORT VALE | | 15 | W | 1-0 | 0-0 | Marshall 69 | Sommer | James* | Johnson M | Skelton | Greene | Peake | Telfer | Marshall | Dixon | Preece^ | Oakes | Thomas/**Woodsford** |
| | 3/9 | | *8,541* | *12* | 6 | | | | *Musselwhite* | *Sandeman* | *Griffiths* | *Glover D* | *Tankard* | *Porter** | *van der Laan* | *Kent* | *Glover L* | *Foyle* | *Naylor^* | *Walker/Burke* |
| | | | | | | | | Ref: J Winter | Luck evens itself out, or so they say and, after the defeat at Tranmere, the Town bounce back with a smash-and-grab raid at Vale Park, Dwight Marshall heading in an accurate cross from Preece. Vale have not lost at home for a year and they attack at will, hitting the woodwork twice. | | | | | | | | | | | |
| 6 | H | BURNLEY | | 18 | L | 0-1 | 0-1 | | Sommer | James | Johnson M | **Waddock*** | Greene^ | Peake | Telfer | Marshall | Hartson | Preece | Oakes | Dixon/Thomas |
| | 10/9 | | 6,911 | *21* | 6 | | | *Robinson 43* | *Russell* | *Parkinson* | *Davis* | *Winstanley* | *Vinnicombe* | *Harrison* | *Randall* | *Harper* | *McMinn* | *Heath* | *Robinson* | |
| | | | | | | | | Ref: S Dunn | Against a team who have not won this season, the Town put on a poor performance and throw away the points. Juergen Sommer drops the ball, which allows Adrian Heath to centre for Liam Robinson to tap in. Steve Davis, the Burnley skipper, heads his own sliced clearance off the line. | | | | | | | | | | | |
| 7 | H | BOLTON | | 18 | L | 0-3 | 0-0 | | Sommer | James | Johnson M | Waddock | Thomas* | Peake | Telfer | Oakes | Dixon | Preece | Hartson^ | Linton/Marshall |
| | 13/9 | | **5,764** | *10* | 6 | | | *McGinlay 51, 71, Sneekes 69* | *Brannagan* | *Lydiate* | *Phillips* | *McAteer* | *Kernaghan* | *Stubbs* | *Fisher* | *Sneekes* | *Paatelainen* | *McGinlay* | *Kelly* | |
| | | | | | | | | Ref: K Leach | All the first half opportunities fall to a luckless Mitchell Thomas, who sees a shot headed off the line and others just whistle over the bar. He is shackled after the break as Bolton show the Hatters how to score. A brace from McGinlay and a 25-yard shot from Sneekes wins the points. | | | | | | | | | | | |
| 8 | A | WATFORD | | 16 | W | 4-2 | 3-2 | Oakes 28, Dixon 31, Telfer 41, 54 | Sommer | James | Johnson M | Waddock | Thomas | Peake | Telfer | Oakes | Dixon | Preece | Marshall | |
| | 17/9 | | *8,880* | *19* | 9 | | | *Moralee 20, Mooney 43* | *Digweed* | *Bazeley* | *Holdsworth* | *Fitzgerald** | *Johnson* | *Hessenthaler* | *Payne* | *Porter* | *Ramage* | *Moralee* | *Mooney* | *Soloman* |
| | | | | | | | | Ref: M Bailey | Mistakes from skipper Andy Hessenthaler allow Oakes to score from 25 yards and Dixon from the edge of the box to set up a famous victory over the old enemy. The Hatters are totally dominant and in the last quarter of the game play 'keep ball', reminiscent of Leeds in the 1970's. | | | | | | | | | | | |
| 9 | A | MILLWALL | | 16 | D | 0-0 | 0-0 | | Sommer | James | Johnson M | Waddock | Thomas | Peake | Telfer | Oakes | Dixon* | Preece | Marshall | Hartson |
| | 24/9 | | *7,150* | *15* | 10 | | | | *Keller* | *Cunningham* | *v d Hauwe* | *McCarthy* | *Thatcher* | *Savage* | *Rae* | *Roberts* | *Kennedy* | *Mitchell** | *Goodman^* | *van Blerk/Kerr* |
| | | | | | | | | Ref: D Orr | The Lions' manager, Mick McCarthy, writes off the Hatters in his programme notes but his players are booed off at the end, after they fail to break down the Luton rearguard. The Town forwards often slice through the Millwall defence but are let down by some wayward finishing. | | | | | | | | | | | |
| 10 | H | BRISTOL CITY | | 20 | L | 0-1 | 0-0 | | Sommer | James | Johnson M | Waddock | Thomas* | Peake | Telfer | Oakes | Dixon^ | Preece | Marshall | Hughes/Hartson |
| | 1/10 | | 6,633 | *17* | 10 | | | *Baird 56* | *Welch* | *Harriott* | *Shail* | *Munro* | *Scott* | *Bent** | *Simpson* | *Edwards* | *Tinnion* | *Bryant* | *Baird* | *Partridge* |
| | | | | | | | | Ref: P Foakes | The first and only worthwhile strike from City produces the solitary goal of the game when Sommer fails to hold an effort from Junior Bent, leaving Ian Baird with a simple chance. The Town's style of passing football cannot be faulted, but this is now the third home defeat in a row. | | | | | | | | | | | |
| 11 | A | STOKE | | 18 | W | 2-1 | 1-0 | Marshall 22, Preece 81 | Sommer | James | Johnson M | Waddock | Thomas | Peake | Telfer | Hughes | Hartson | Preece* | Marshall | Oakes |
| | 9/10 | | *11,682* | *7* | 13 | | | *Carruthers 80* | *Muggleton* | *Butler* | *Cranson* | *Dreyer !* | *Sandford* | *Wallace** | *Orlygsson* | *Downing* | *Gleghorn* | *Peschis'lido^* | *Carruthers* | *Beckford/Overson* |
| | | | | | | | | Ref: T Heilbron | Ex-Hatter John Dreyer suffers a nightmare, slipping to allow Marshall through to score the first, handling the ball to concede a penalty which is missed by Preece and then being sent off for wrestling Marshall to the floor. Stoke then equalise after a scramble before Preece gets the winner. | | | | | | | | | | | |

| No | Venue | Opponent / Date | Att | Pos | Res / Pts | Score | HT | Scorers, Times, and Referees | 1 | 2 | 3 | 4 | 5 | 6 | 7 | 8 | 9 | 10 | 11 | 12 subs used |
|---|---|---|---|---|---|---|---|---|---|---|---|---|---|---|---|---|---|---|---|---|
| 12 | H | MIDDLESBROUGH | | 11 | W | **5-1** | 3-0 | Wilkinson 21 (og), Marshall 35, 58, | Sommer | James | Johnson M | Waddock | Thomas | Peake | Telfer | Hughes | Hartson | Preece* | Marshall | Oakes |
| | | 15/10 | 8,412 | *4* | 16 | | | *Whyte 83* [Preece 40, Hartson 63] | *Pears* | *Cox* | *Vickers* | *Whyte* | *Fleming* | *Hignett* | *Pollock* | *Blackmore* | *Wright** | *Wilkinson* | *Hendrie* | *Kavanagh* |
| | | | | | | | | Ref: K Cooper | The Hatters turn on a brilliant performance as they attack Bryan Robson's Boro from the start and the contest is effectively over by the interval. Paul Wilkinson heads a cross from Ceri Hughes into his own net to start the rout and a scorching angled drive from John Hartson finishes it. | | | | | | | | | | | |
| 13 | A | SHEFFIELD UTD | | 7 | W | 3-1 | 1-1 | Gayle 33 (og), James 71, Dixon 78 | Sommer | James | Johnson M | Waddock | Thomas | Peake | Telfer | Hughes | Dixon | Preece* | Marshall | Oakes |
| | | 22/10 | *13,317* | *17* | 19 | | | *Blake 17* | *Kelly* | *Gage* | *Gayle* | *Marshall* | *Scott* | *Reed* | *Rogers** | *Gannon* | *Whitehouse* | *Blake* | *Flo^* | *Littlejohn/Hodgson* |
| | | | | | | | | Ref: E Parker | The Town survive an opening blitz and then reorganise when Jostein Flo goes off injured. They fall one behind when Nathan Blake heads in a cross from Kevin Gage but then take control of the midfield for the rest of the game. Brian Gayle heads an own-goal to set them on their way. | | | | | | | | | | | |
| 14 | H | BARNSLEY | | 10 | L | 0-1 | 0-0 | | Sommer | James | Johnson M | Waddock* | Thomas | Peake | Telfer | Hughes | Hartson | Preece | Marshall^ | Dixon/Oakes |
| | | 29/10 | 7,212 | *9* | 19 | | | *Rammell 72* | *Watson* | *Davis* | *Fleming* | *Taggart* | *Eaden* | *O'Connell* | *Wilson* | *Redfearn* | *Sheridan* | *Rammell* | *Payton* | |
| | | | | | | | | Ref: M Pierce | The Town are woeful and are never allowed to play their football by a formidable Barnsley side. Their player-manager and ex-Hatter, Danny Wilson, is superb, setting up the only goal when crossing for Andy Rammell to control the ball and shoot strongly past keeper Juergen Sommer. | | | | | | | | | | | |
| 15 | H | GRIMSBY | | 12 | L | 1-2 | 0-0 | Oakes 82 | Sommer | James | Johnson M | Waddock | Thomas | Peake | Telfer | Hughes* | Hartson | Preece | Marshall | Oakes |
| | | 1/11 | 5,839 | *8* | 19 | | | *Gilbert 70, 89* | *Crichton* | *Croft** | *Handyside* | *Lever* | *Jobling* | *Watson* | *Dobbin* | *Groves* | *Gilbert* | *Livingstone* | *Woods* | *Agnew* |
| | | | | | | | | Ref: P Alcock | The Hatters fail to take their chances again as they suffer their fifth home defeat of the season. After Oakes rifles in a late goal, a point seems safe, but Dave Gilbert nets his second, direct from a free-kick in added time. Hughes suffers an injury which will keep him out for the season. | | | | | | | | | | | |
| 16 | A | WOLVES | | 8 | W | 3-2 | 1-0 | Preece 38, Marshall 46, Dixon 54 | Sommer | James | Johnson M | Waddock | Thomas | Peake | Telfer | Oakes | Dixon* | Preece | Marshall | Hartson |
| | | 5/11 | ***26,749*** | *1* | 22 | | | *Stewart 80, Johnson 84 (og)* | *Stowell* | *Smith* | *Blades* | *Venus* | *Thompson* | *Walters** | *Ferguson* | *Thomas* | *Froggatt* | *Bull^* | *Kelly* | *Stewart/Emblen* |
| | | | | | | | | Ref: E Wolstenholme | The Hatters cruise into a three-goal lead, easily combating the Wolves long-ball game. The home side pull back two late goals, against the run of play, and aided by the unwitting Marvin Johnson. Press talk of David Pleat returning to Tottenham detracts from a splendid performance. | | | | | | | | | | | |
| 17 | A | OLDHAM | | 8 | D | 0-0 | 0-0 | | Sommer | James | Johnson M | Waddock | Thomas | Peake | Telfer | Oakes | Dixon | Preece | Marshall* | Hartson |
| | | 12/11 | *7,907* | *15* | 23 | | | | *Gerrard* | *Makin* | *Jobson* | *Redmond* | *Pointon* | *Halle !* | *Graham* | *Henry* | *Holden* | *Banger** | *Ritchie* | *Beckford* |
| | | | | | | | | Ref: K Lynch | On a wet pitch, the Hatters are unable to adopt their preferred tactics of attacking on the break and are forced to defend in depth. Gunnar Halle is sent off in the last minute for kicking Julian James, but post-match video evidence shows it was Richard Graham who committed the offence. | | | | | | | | | | | |
| 18 | H | PORTSMOUTH | | 8 | W | 2-0 | 1-0 | Dixon 2, Preece 55 | Sommer | James | Johnson M | Waddock | Thomas | Peake | Telfer | Oakes | Dixon | Preece | Marshall* | Thorpe |
| | | 19/11 | 8,214 | *21* | 26 | | | | *Knight* | *Kristensen* | *Gittens* | *Russell* | *Dobson* | *Preki** | *McLoughlin* | *Powell* | *Pethick* | *Creaney* | *Burton^* | *Rees/Totten* |
| | | | | | | | | Ref: J Kirkby | Pompey are hit by an early goal when Dixon heads home a left-wing cross from Preece and the Town never look back from that point onwards. James hits the post from close range but Preece in on hand to convert the rebound. A shot by Robbie Pethick hits both posts before it is cleared. | | | | | | | | | | | |
| 19 | A | SWINDON | | 5 | W | 2-1 | 1-1 | Dixon 43, Oakes 60 | Sommer | James | Johnson M | Waddock | Thomas | Peake | Telfer | Oakes | Dixon* | Preece | Linton | Hartson |
| | | 26/11 | *9,228* | *19* | 29 | | | *Scott 10* | *Digby* | *Robinson* | *Thomson* | *Kilcline* | *Bodin* | *MacLaren** | *O'Sullivan^* | *Horlock* | *Mutch* | *Fjortoft* | *Scott* | *Beauchamp/Hamon* |
| | | | | | | | | Ref: R Wilkes | A poor back-pass from Peake gives Keith Scott the opener but Luton fight back against a side who have just dispensed with their manager, John Gorman. A header from Kerry Dixon, followed by a powerful low drive from Scott Oakes, secures the sixth away victory of the season. | | | | | | | | | | | |
| 20 | H | SHEFFIELD UTD | | 8 | L | 3-6 | 0-2 | Hartson 67, Gayle 71 (og), Johnson 74p | Sommer | James | Johnson M | Waddock ! | Thomas | Peake | Telfer | Oakes | Dixon | Preece* | Linton^ | Marshall/Hartson |
| | | 3/12 | 8,516 | *6* | 29 | | | *Gage 12, 24, Veart 52, 88, Hodges 69,* | *Kelly* | *Gage* | *Gayle* | *Beesley* | *Nilsen* | *Rogers* | *Starbuck** | *Hartfield* | *Hodges* | *Veart* | *Scott^* | *Ward/Flo* |
| | | | | | | | | Ref: P Foakes *[Scott 82]* | The Town have a disastrous first half, with Preece limping off with an ankle injury and Waddock dismissed for bringing down the goal-bound Andy Scott. Luton pull back from 1-4 to 3-4, a great save by Alan Kelly from Dixon preventing the equaliser, before they run out of steam. | | | | | | | | | | | |
| 21 | H | DERBY | | 10 | D | 0-0 | 0-0 | | Sommer | James | Johnson M | Waddock | Thomas | Peake | Telfer | Oakes | Dixon* | Preece | **Allen^** | Marshall/Hartson |
| | | 11/12 | 6,400 | *14* | 30 | | | | *Sutton* | *Harkes* | *Short* | *Williams* | *Kavanagh* | *Sturridge* | *Carsley* | *Kuhl* | *Simpson* | *Johnson* | *Stallard* | |
| | | | | | | | | Ref: K Cooper | A game which Luton dominate. They are unable to find a way past Steve Sutton, previously on loan at Kenilworth Road. The match is poor entertainment for the live television audience and Paul Allen, on loan from Southampton, fails to shine. Juan Andrades comes to Luton on trial. | | | | | | | | | | | |
| 22 | A | WEST BROM | | 12 | L | 0-1 | 0-1 | | Sommer | James* | Johnson M | Allen | Thomas | Peake | Telfer | Oakes | Dixon | Preece | Marshall | Hartson |
| | | 18/12 | *14,392* | *21* | 30 | | | *Donovan 35* | *Naylor* | *O'Regan* | *Mardon* | *Raven* | *Lilwall* | *Donovan* | *Bradley* | *Hamilton* | *Ashcroft* | *Hunt* | *Taylor** | *Heggs^/Parsley* |
| | | | | | | | | Ref: J Brandwood | West Brom play like the away team and defend in depth in the first period but score against the run of play. Kevin Donovan hits a low drive through a crowded penalty area after a corner had been headed to him by Johnson. Luton attack after the break and John Hartson goes close. | | | | | | | | | | | |
| 23 | A | READING | | 12 | D | 0-0 | 0-0 | | Sommer | James | Johnson M | Waddock | Thomas | Peake | Telfer | Allen* | Dixon^ | Preece | Marshall | Oakes/Hartson |
| | | 26/12 | *11,623* | *6* | 31 | | | | *Hislop* | *Jones* | *Wdowczyk* | *Bernal* | *Gooding* | *Taylor** | *Parkinson* | *Osborn* | *Gilkes* | *Quinn* | *Lovell* | *Lambert* |
| | | | | | | | | Ref: G Singh | The midfields dominate as the sides cancel each other out, although the introduction of Scott Oakes as substitute for Paul Allen gives the Town more running power. Shaka Hislop is forced to tip over a thundering 20-yard drive from Oakes, and Stuart Lovell hits the post near the end. | | | | | | | | | | | |

| No | Date | | Att | Pos | Pt | F-A | H-T | Scorers, Times, and Referees | 1 | 2 | 3 | 4 | 5 | 6 | 7 | 8 | 9 | 10 | 11 | subs used |
|---|---|---|---|---|---|---|---|---|---|---|---|---|---|---|---|---|---|---|---|---|
| 24 | H | SUNDERLAND | | 9 | W | 3-0 | 2-0 | Oakes 22, 26, Hartson 49 | Sommer | James | Johnson M | Waddock | Thomas | Peake | Telfer | Oakes | Hartson | Preece* | Marshall^ | Skelton/Williams |
| | 27/12 | | 8,953 | _17_ | 34 | | | | _Chamberlain_ | _Kubicki_ | _Ball_ | _Melville_ | _Scott_ | _Atkinson_ | _Gray M_ | _Cunnington*_ | _Smith_ | _Gray P_ | _Russell_ | _Howey_ |
| | | | | | | | | Ref: J Holbrook | Sunderland manager Mick Buxton feels the game should not have been played due to the pouring rain and water-logged surface. The conditions suit the Town style of play and two fierce shots from Oakes gives them a comfortable lead. Hartson heads in a cross from Thomas for the third. | | | | | | | | | | | |
| 25 | A | NOTTS CO | | 8 | W | 1-0 | 0-0 | Telfer 71 | Sommer | James | Johnson M | Waddock | Thomas | Peake | Telfer | Oakes | Hartson | Preece | Marshall* | **Adcock** |
| | 31/12 | | _6,249_ | _24_ | 37 | | | | _Cherry_ | _Mills_ | _Murphy_ | _Johnson_ | _Legg*_ | _Butler_ | _Marsden_ | _Turner_ | _McSwegan_ | _White^_ | _Devlin_ | _Matthews/Jemson_ |
| | | | | | | | | Ref: R Harris | A 20-yard shot from Telfer seals another away victory against the bottom-placed club who are suffering their third successive 0-1 home defeat. The poor state of the pitch is blamed by Pleat for the number of passes which go astray in a game where the result surpasses the performance. | | | | | | | | | | | |
| 26 | H | CHARLTON | | 8 | L | 0-1 | 0-1 | | Sommer | James* | Johnson M | Waddock | Thomas | Peake | Telfer | Oakes | Hartson | Allen | Marshall | Adcock |
| | 2/1 | | 7,642 | _15_ | 37 | | | _Whyte 19_ | _Salmon_ | _Bennett_ | _Chapple_ | _McLeary_ | _Mortimer_ | _Robinson_ | _Pardew_ | _Brown_ | _Robson*_ | _Leaburn_ | _Whyte_ | _Nelson_ |
| | | | | | | | | Ref: P Alcock | The Valiants adapt better to the icy pitch and defend and attack as a unit against a Town side which, collectively, has an off-day. Charlton grab the points, to belie their lowly league position with a far-post header from David Whyte. Carl Leaburn hits a post when it looks easier to score. | | | | | | | | | | | |
| 27 | A | BARNSLEY | | 11 | L | 1-3 | 0-0 | Dixon 47 | Sommer | James | Johnson M | Waddock | Thomas | Peake | Telfer | Oakes | Dixon | Harvey* | Marshall | Skelton |
| | 14/1 | | _4,808_ | _6_ | 37 | | | _Redfearn 66, Liddell 71, 79_ | _Watson_ | _Eaden_ | _Davis_ | _Fleming_ | _Moses_ | _O'Connell_ | _Redfearn_ | _Wilson_ | _Sheridan_ | _Rammell_ | _Liddell_ | |
| | | | | | | | | Ref: N Barry | After an even first half, Kerry Dixon shocks Barnsley with a superb 30-yard chip after seeing keeper David Watson off his line. Stunned by this goal, the Tykes power their way back and end up far too strong for Luton. The Hatters have not won at Oakwell since the 1952-53 season. | | | | | | | | | | | |
| 28 | H | OLDHAM | | 10 | W | 2-1 | 1-0 | Marshall 1, 80 | Sommer | James | Johnson M | Waddock | Thomas | Peake | Telfer | Oakes | Dixon* | **Biggins** | Marshall | Thorpe |
| | 4/2 | | 6,903 | _13_ | 40 | | | _Holden 75_ | _Gerrard_ | _Snodin_ | _Graham_ | _Redmond_ | _Pointon_ | _Halle_ | _Henry*_ | _Richardson_ | _Brennan_ | _Ritchie^_ | _Banger_ | _Holden/McCarthy_ |
| | | | | | | | | Ref: P Vanes | Oldham have most of the play but it is the Town who hang on for victory. Loan signing Wayne Biggins threads the ball through for Marshall to fire the opening goal after only 32 seconds and, after Rick Holden hits the deserved equaliser, Marshall is again on hand to secure the points. | | | | | | | | | | | |
| 29 | A | GRIMSBY | | 10 | L | **0-5** | 0-2 | _[Watson 75, 86]_ | Sommer | James | Johnson M | Waddock | Thomas | Peake | Preece | Oakes | Dixon* | Biggins^ | Marshall | Woodsford/Telfer |
| | 11/2 | | _4,615_ | _8_ | 40 | | | _Dobbin 8, Gilbert 27, Woods 73,_ | _Crichton_ | _McDermott_ | _Handyside_ | _Lever*_ | _Jobling_ | _Watson_ | _Dobbin_ | _Groves_ | _Gilbert^_ | _Woods_ | _Mendonca_ | _Laws/Childs_ |
| | | | | | | | | Ref: R Furnandiz | After the midweek thrashing at Southampton in the FA Cup, the Town suffer another mauling, this time against a Grimsby side who adapt far better to the conditions. On a glue-pot of a pitch, the Mariners play direct football combined with pace, rattling in five goals in a game to forget. | | | | | | | | | | | |
| 30 | H | SWINDON | | 9 | W | 3-0 | 1-0 | Horlock 19 (og), Marshall 50, 63 | Sommer | James | Johnson M | Waddock | Thomas | Peake | Telfer | Oakes | Biggins* | Preece | Marshall^ | Dixon/Woodsford |
| | 18/2 | | 6,595 | _22_ | 43 | | | | _Hammond_ | _O'Sullivan_ | _Horlock_ | _Robinson_ | _Murray_ | _Beauchamp_ | _McMahon_ | _Ling_ | _Gooden*_ | _Fjortoft_ | _Thorne_ | _Mutch_ |
| | | | | | | | | Ref: J Kirkby | The Town record an easy victory against a team whose thoughts are more on the upcoming Coca-Cola Cup semi-final. Kevin Horlock runs into the ball, conceding an own-goal and Marshall nets twice after being given a rough ride by Swindon's defence. Oakes hits a post from the spot. | | | | | | | | | | | |
| 31 | A | PORTSMOUTH | | 9 | L | 2-3 | 1-0 | Telfer 1, James 73 | Sommer | James | Johnson M | Waddock* | Thomas | Peake | Telfer | Oakes^ | Dixon | Preece | Marshall | Woodsford/Harvey |
| | 21/2 | | _7,373_ | _15_ | 43 | | | _McLoughlin 49, Preki 75, Creaney 79p_ | _Knight_ | _Pethick_ | _Symons_ | _Butters_ | _Daniel_ | _Preki_ | _McLoughlin_ | _McGrath_ | _Rees*_ | _Creaney_ | _Hall_ | _Doling_ |
| | | | | | | | | Ref: K Leach | James hammers a 25-yard shot to put the Town 2-1 up but Johnson is dispossessed shortly after by Preki who runs on to level with a solo effort. Preki appears to collide with his team-mate as he tumbles in the area but the referee awards a penalty, which is converted by Gerry Creaney. | | | | | | | | | | | |
| 32 | A | BRISTOL CITY | | 10 | D | 2-2 | 1-0 | Oakes 28, 53 | Sommer | James | Johnson M | Waddock | Thomas | Peake | Telfer | Oakes | Dixon | Preece* | Marshall | Williams |
| | 25/2 | | _7,939_ | _21_ | 44 | | | _Owers 65, Bent 85_ | _Welch_ | _Hansen_ | _Dryden_ | _Bryant_ | _Munro_ | _Bent_ | _Owers_ | _Kuhl_ | _Tinnion_ | _Allison_ | _Fleck_ | |
| | | | | | | | | Ref: A Flood | Two long-range efforts from Oakes set the Town up and, when Brian Tinnion sees his penalty-kick saved by Sommer, the Hatters appear to be cruising against their relegation-threatened opponents. Owers pulls one back from a seemingly offside position before Junior Bent levels late on. | | | | | | | | | | | |
| 33 | H | MILLWALL | | 10 | D | 1-1 | 1-0 | Marshall 33 | Sommer | James | Johnson M | Waddock* | Thomas | Peake | Telfer | Oakes | Biggins^ | Preece | Marshall | **Matthews**/Dixon |
| | 4/3 | | 6,864 | _11_ | 45 | | | _Mitchell 57_ | _Keller_ | _Joseph_ | _Witter_ | _Webber_ | _Thatcher_ | _Savage*_ | _Rae_ | _May_ | _van Blerk_ | _Oldfield_ | _Mitchell_ | _Beckford_ |
| | | | | | | | | Ref: J Lloyd | The blistering pace of Dwight Marshall allows him to get clear of the Millwall defence as he fires the Hatters into a deserved half-time lead. The Lions, who are ably led by the midfield power of Alex Rae, eventually equalise when Dave Mitchell bundles the ball in from close range. | | | | | | | | | | | |
| 34 | H | PORT VALE | | 9 | W | 2-1 | 0-0 | Telfer 50, Dixon 82 | Sommer | James | Johnson M | Waddock* | Thomas | Peake | Telfer | Oakes | Biggins^ | Preece | Marshall | Matthews/Dixon |
| | 7/3 | | 5,947 | _17_ | 48 | | | _Porter 84_ | _Musselwhite_ | _Sandeman_ | _Aspin_ | _Scott_ | _Tankard_ | _Porter_ | _v der Laan*_ | _Walker_ | _Guppy_ | _Foyle_ | _Naylor^_ | _Glover/Allon_ |
| | | | | | | | | Ref: P Foakes | Port Vale come to Kenilworth Road intent on saving a point in their bid to escape relegation. Telfer beats two defenders and nets the opening goal. Vale then proceed to miss two good chances. Rob Matthews hits a superb shot which Musselwhite parries, leaving Dixon to tap in. | | | | | | | | | | | |

| No Date | H/A | Opponent | Att | Pos | Res/Pts | F-A | H-T | Scorers, Times, and Referees | 1 | 2 | 3 | 4 | 5 | 6 | 7 | 8 | 9 | 10 | 11 | 12 sub used |
|---|---|---|---|---|---|---|---|---|---|---|---|---|---|---|---|---|---|---|---|---|
| 35 | A | SOUTHEND | | 11 | L | 0-3 | 0-1 | | Sommer | James | Johnson M | Waddock | Thomas | Peake | Telfer | Oakes | Dixon* | Matthews | Marshall | Biggins |
| 11/3 | | | **4,558** | *16* | 48 | | | *Jones 28, Thomson 76, Dublin 89* | *Royce* | *Hone* | *Bodley* | *Edwards* | *Powell* | *Sussex* | *Whelan* | *Tilson** | *Jones^* | *Thomson* | *Dublin* | *Perkins/Hails* |
| | | | | | | | | Ref: J Holbrook | A run of four consecutive home defeats is ended by the Shrimpers when they play like the away side and catch the Town on the break. Juergen Sommer is at fault for the first two goals, each time failing to collect the ball and leaving the Southend forwards with easy scoring opportunities. | | | | | | | | | | | |
| 36 | H | TRANMERE | | 10 | W | 2-0 | 1-0 | James 14, Biggins 68 | Sommer | James | Johnson M | Waddock | Thomas | Peake | Telfer | Oakes | Biggins* | Preece | Marshall | Matthews |
| 18/3 | | | 6,660 | *1* | 51 | | | | *Nixon* | *Stevens* | *McGreal* | *Garnett* | *Thomas* | *O'Brien* | *Brannan** | *Irons* | *Nevin* | *Aldridge* | *Malkin^* | *Kenworthy/Jones* |
| | | | | | | | | Ref: G Pooley | The Town are well worth their win and prove once again that they always seem to play better against the top clubs. Julian James hammers in a shot from outside the box to open the scoring and Wayne Biggins signs off from his loan period with the Hatters by netting from close range. | | | | | | | | | | | |
| 37 | A | BURNLEY | | 11 | L | 1-2 | 0-0 | Marshall 60 | Sommer | James | Johnson M | Waddock | Thomas* | Peake | Telfer | Matthews | Dixon | Preece^ | Marshall | Harvey/Woodsford |
| 21/3 | | | *9,551* | *24* | 51 | | | *Mullin 73, Harrison 83* | *Russell* | *Harrison* | *Davis* | *Pender** | *Winstanley* | *Vinnicombe* | *Thompson* | *Randall* | *Eyres* | *Nogan* | *Robinson* | *Mullin* |
| | | | | | | | | Ref: R Poulain | Bottom club Burnley earn the points after the Town appear to be coasting to their first away win of 1995, courtesy of a Dwight Marshall goal on the hour. Sommer seems to be impeded before John Mullin hits the equaliser but has no chance with the fierce winner from Gerry Harrison. | | | | | | | | | | | |
| 38 | H | WATFORD | | 11 | D | 1-1 | 1-0 | Telfer 4 | Davis | James | Johnson M | Waddock | Harvey | Peake | Telfer | Matthews* | **Taylor** | Preece | Marshall | Thorpe |
| 26/3 | | | 7,984 | *9* | 52 | | | *Phillips 63* | *Miller* | *Lavin* | *Millen* | *Foster* | *Porter* | *Hessenthaler* | *Ramage* | *Johnson* | *Payne* | *Quinn** | *Phillips* | *Beadle* |
| | | | | | | | | Ref: K Breen | The Town score first when Telfer volleys home a cross from Richard Harvey, who later forces Kevin Miller to make a finger-tip save. Kevin Phillips springs the offside trap to level. Kelvin Davis brings down Peter Beadle, but then atones by saving the penalty-kick from Gary Porter. | | | | | | | | | | | |
| 39 | H | WOLVES | | 11 | D | 3-3 | 2-0 | Telfer 6, 11, Taylor 51 | Davis | James | Johnson M | Waddock | Harvey | Peake | Telfer | Oakes | Taylor | Preece | Marshall* | Woodsford |
| 4/4 | | | **9,651** | *3* | 53 | | | *Kelly 48, 59, Emblen 89* | *Stowell* | *Blades* | *Law* | *Richards* | *Masters** | *Birch^* | *Cowans* | *Emblen* | *Venus* | *Bull* | *Goodman* | *Dennison/Kelly* |
| | | | | | | | | Ref: G Pooley | On a well-watered pitch, Luton outplay Wolves in the first half with Telfer scoring twice. David Kelly reduces the deficit before Taylor gets his first goal for the club when deflecting a shot from Johnson. Kelly nets again before Neil Emblen and Oakes tangle, the ball ending up the net. | | | | | | | | | | | |
| 40 | H | NOTTS CO | | 12 | W | 2-0 | 1-0 | Telfer 3, Oakes 68p | Davis | James* | Johnson M | Waddock | Harvey | Peake | Telfer | Oakes | Taylor | Preece | Marshall^ | Linton/Matthews |
| 8/4 | | | 6,428 | *24* | 56 | | | | *Cherry* | *Murphy* | *Hoyle* | *Johnson* | *Short** | *Turner* | *Simpson* | *Nicol* | *Mills* | *White^* | *Russell* | *Galloway/Devlin* |
| | | | | | | | | Ref: M Pierce | The Town have most of the play but, after Telfer side-foots home a cross from Harvey, they make hard work of it. Marshall is sent flying in the area by Colin Hoyle and Scott Oakes converts the resultant penalty. Steve Cherry plays a blinder, preventing Oakes from claiming a hat-trick. | | | | | | | | | | | |
| 41 | A | BOLTON | | 12 | D | 0-0 | 0-0 | | Davis | James* | Johnson M | Waddock | Harvey | Peake | Telfer | Oakes | Taylor | Preece | Matthews^ | Linton/Marshall |
| 11/4 | | | *13,619* | *3* | 57 | | | | *Branagan* | *Green* | *Seagraves* | *Stubbs* | *Phillips* | *McAteer* | *Sneekes* | *Bergsson* | *Thompson* | *Paatelainen* | *De Freitas** | *McGinlay* |
| | | | | | | | | Ref: U Rennie | Keith Branagan is the man-of-the-match with a string of fine saves against a Town side who play most of the football. Only in the last minutes do Bolton look like promotion contenders, when they throw everyone forward. Thompson's header hits the post and Peake clears off the line. | | | | | | | | | | | |
| 42 | A | SUNDERLAND | | 11 | D | 1-1 | 1-0 | Taylor 9 | Davis | Linton* | Johnson M | Waddock | Harvey | Peake | Telfer | Oakes | Taylor | Preece | Matthews^ | Greene/Marshall |
| 15/4 | | | *17,292* | *19* | 58 | | | *Gray P 58* | *Norman* | *Kubicki* | *Ord* | *Bennett** | *Scott* | *Atkinson* | *Gray Martin* | *Ball* | *Smith* | *Angell^* | *Gray P* | *Gray Michael/Russell* |
| | | | | | | | | Ref: P Richards | The Town play possession football in the first half but have only a goal from John Taylor, following a cross from Rob Matthews, to show for it. Backed by a partisan Roker Park crowd, the Wearsiders attack with vengeance and ex-Hatter Phil Gray heads his first goal of the year to level. | | | | | | | | | | | |
| 43 | H | READING | | 11 | L | 0-1 | 0-1 | | Davis | James* | Johnson M | Waddock^ | Harvey | Peake | Telfer | Oakes | Taylor | Preece | Marshall | Linton/Matthews |
| 17/4 | | | 8,717 | *5* | 58 | | | *Taylor 43 (og)* | *Hislop* | *Bernal* | *Wdowczyk* | *McPherson* | *Williams* | *Taylor* | *Gooding* | *Osborn* | *Kerr* | *Nogan* | *Lovell** | *Gilkes* |
| | | | | | | | | Ref: J Kirkby | Oakes shoots wide when one-on-one with the goalkeeper, and then fails to control the ball when in a similar situation. Reading take the lead, against the run of play, when Adrian Williams and John Taylor both go for the ball, following a free-kick, which ends up in the back of the net. | | | | | | | | | | | |
| 44 | A | CHARLTON | | 12 | L | 0-1 | 0-0 | | Davis | Greene | Johnson M | Waddock | Thomas* | Peake | Telfer | Oakes | Taylor | Preece | Matthews^ | Marshall/Harvey |
| 22/4 | | | *10,918* | *13* | 58 | | | *Whyte 71* | *Ammann* | *Brown !* | *Rufus* | *Balmer* | *Stuart* | *Robson* | *Jones* | *Walsh* | *Mortimer* | *Leaburn** | *Whyte* | *McGleish* |
| | | | | | | | | Ref: P Alcock | The Town look to be odds on to record the win after Steve Brown is sent off for a second bookable offence on 31 minutes. Charlton raise their game and, as the Hatters fail to get a shot on target in the second half, it is David Whyte who scores the winner when set up by Mark Robson. | | | | | | | | | | | |
| 45 | A | MIDDLESBROUGH | | 16 | L | 1-2 | 0-1 | Taylor 62 | Davis | Linton | Johnson M | Waddock | Harvey | Peake | Telfer | Oakes* | Taylor | Preece | Marshall | Thorpe |
| 30/4 | | | *23,903* | *1* | 58 | | | *Hendrie 44, 71* | *Miller* | *Cox* | *Vickers* | *Pearson* | *Whyte* | *Blackmore* | *Robson* | *Pollock* | *Moore* | *Fjortoft* | *Hendrie* | |
| | | | | | | | | Ref: P Vanes | John Taylor hits an equaliser, following a quick free-kick, and Davis saves a penalty from Neil Cox, awarded when Linton handles in the area, but Boro are too strong for Luton and John Hendrie fires home the winner for the champions in the last game ever played at Ayresome Park. | | | | | | | | | | | |
| 46 | H | STOKE | | 16 | L | 2-3 | 1-0 | Harvey 43, Waddock 83 | Davis | Johnson M | Harvey | Waddock | Thomas | Peake | Telfer | Oakes | Taylor | Preece | Woodsford* | Marshall |
| 7/5 | | | 8,252 | *11* | 58 | | | *Orlygsson 52, Peschisolido 79, Scott 87* | *Sinclair* | *Butler* | *Overson* | *Sigurdsson* | *Sandford* | *Keen* | *Wallace* | *Orlygsson* | *Gleghorn* | *Scott* | *Peschisolido** | *Clarkson* |
| Home | | Away | | | | | | Ref: G Pooley | The story of the season is repeated as the Town again play pretty football but fail to add to a cracking 20-yard shot from Richard Harvey. Stoke up the tempo in the second half and take the lead before Waddock scores his first goal for over a year. Keith Scott's header seals the points. | | | | | | | | | | | |
| Average 7,350 | | 10,818 | | | | | | | | | | | | | | | | | | |

| Coca-Cola Cup | | | | | F-A | H-T | Scorers, Times, and Referees | 1 | 2 | 3 | 4 | 5 | 6 | 7 | 8 | 9 | 10 | 11 | subs used |
|---|---|---|---|---|---|---|---|---|---|---|---|---|---|---|---|---|---|---|---|
| 1:1 | H | FULHAM | | D | 1-1 | 0-0 | Oakes 81 | Sommer | James | Johnson M | Hughes* | Greene | Peake | Telfer | Oakes | Dixon | Preece | Houghton^ | Marshall/Linton |
| 16/8 | | 3,287 | *D3* | | | | *Moore 89* | *Stannard* | *Jupp* | *Moore* | *Thomas* | *Herrera* | *Marshall* | *Mison* | *Morgan* | *Brazil* | *Cork* | *Haworth* | |
| | | | | | | | Ref: R Bigger | Luton are unable to break down a strong Fulham rearguard and a spectacular 25-yard shot from Scott Oakes is out of character with all that has gone before. The game is thrown away when a flick on by Alan Cork, following a corner, is headed home by Kevin Moore in the last minute. | | | | | | | | | | | |
| 1:2 | A | FULHAM | 14 | D | 1-1 | 0-1 | Marshall 73 | Sommer | James | Johnson M | Linton* | Greene^ | Peake | Telfer | Marshall | Dixon | Preece | Hughes ! | Skelton/Oakes |
| 23/8 | | *5,134* | *3:6* | | *aet* | | *Haworth 15* | *Stannard* | *Jupp* | *Moore* | *Thomas* | *Herrera* | *Marshall ** | *Mison* | *Morgan* | *Brazil* | *Cork* | *Haworth ^* | *Hailes/Hurlock* |
| | | | | | | | Ref: M Pierce (Hatters lost 3-4 on penalties) | Fulham take an early lead with a header from Haworth before Hughes is dismissed for retaliation after a foul by Mison. Preece thumps the ball forward from a free-kick for Marshall to level and Brazil blasts an extra-time penalty over the bar. Marshall misses his kick in the shoot-out. | | | | | | | | | | | |

| FA Cup | | | | | | | | 1 | 2 | 3 | 4 | 5 | 6 | 7 | 8 | 9 | 10 | 11 | subs used |
|---|---|---|---|---|---|---|---|---|---|---|---|---|---|---|---|---|---|---|---|
| 3 | H | BRISTOL ROV | 8 | D | 1-1 | 1-1 | Hartson 37 | Sommer | James | Johnson M | Waddock | Thomas | Peake | Telfer | Oakes | Hartson | Preece | Marshall* | Adcock |
| 7/1 | | 7,571 | *2:8* | | | | *Stewart 20* | *Parkin* | *Channing* | *Tillson* | *Clark* | *Gurney* | *Sterling* | *Hardyman* | *Skinner* | *Archer* | *Miller** | *Stewart* | *Taylor* |
| | | | | | | | Ref: P Rejer | Marvin Johnson has his penalty saved by Brian Parkin, after Waddock is tripped by Billy Clark. Marcus Stewart is then put through by Paul Hardyman to score against the run of play but, with half-time approaching, Hartson thunders a 12-yard shot into the roof of the net to equalise. | | | | | | | | | | | |
| 3R | A | BRISTOL ROV | 11 | W | 1-0 | 0-0 | Marshall 62 | Sommer | Chenery | Johnson M | Waddock | Thomas | Peake | Telfer | Oakes | Dixon | Preece | Marshall | |
| 18/1 | | *8,213* | *2:8* | | | | | *Parkin* | *Pritchard** | *Clark* | *Tillson* | *Gurney* | *Sterling* | *Browning* | *Channing* | *Archer* | *Miller* | *Taylor* | *Hardyman* |
| | | | | | | | Ref: P Rejer | Rovers chase the game early on and put the Town under immense pressure. A far-post cross from Preece is headed home by Dwight Marshall for the only goal of the game. It is a baptism of fire for 17-year-old Ben Chenery, who makes his debut in place of the suspended Julian James. | | | | | | | | | | | |
| 4 | H | SOUTHAMPTON | 11 | D | 1-1 | 0-0 | Biggins 81 | Sommer | Oakes | Johnson M | Waddock | Thomas | Peake | Telfer | Biggins | Dixon* | Preece | Marshall | Williams |
| 28/1 | | 9,938 | *P:14* | | | | *Shipperley 54* | *Grobbelaar* | *Kenna* | *Hall* | *Benali* | *Charlton* | *Magilton* | *Widdrington* | *Maddison* | *Heaney* | *Le Tissier* | *Shipperley* | |
| | | | | | | | Ref: G Ashby | Saints manager Alan Ball is furious with his players at the interval as the Town have all the play. Neil Shipperley then opens the scoring but Luton are offered a life-line when Benali handles in the area. Telfer misses the spot-kick and it is left to Biggins to hit the deserved equaliser. | | | | | | | | | | | |
| 4R | A | SOUTHAMPTON | 10 | L | 0-6 | 0-4 | *[Monkou 50, Hughes 67]* | Sommer | James* | Johnson M | Waddock | Thomas | Peake | Telfer | Oakes | Biggins^ | Preece | Marshall | Thorpe/Dixon |
| 8/2 | | *15,075* | *P:15* | | | | *Le Tissier 6,36p, Magilton 32, Heaney 40,* | *Grobbelaar* | *Dodd* | *Monkou* | *Hall* | *Kenna* | *Widdrington* | *Maddison** | *Magilton* | *Heaney* | *Le Tissier^* | *Shipperley* | *Tisdale/Hughes* |
| | | | | | | | Ref: G Ashby | Thomas handles a cross in the area and Matt Le Tissier steps up to hammer home the spot-kick to make the score 3-0. He is in awesome form, even though he is supposed to be suffering from flu and by the time he is substituted on the hour the Saints are leading 5-0 with the game won. | | | | | | | | | | | |

| | P | Home W | D | L | F | A | Away W | D | L | F | A | Pts |
|---|---|---|---|---|---|---|---|---|---|---|---|---|
| 1 Middlesbro | 46 | 15 | 4 | 4 | 41 | 19 | 8 | 9 | 6 | 26 | 21 | 82 |
| 2 Reading | 46 | 12 | 7 | 4 | 34 | 21 | 11 | 3 | 9 | 24 | 23 | 79 |
| 3 Bolton * | 46 | 16 | 6 | 1 | 43 | 13 | 5 | 8 | 10 | 24 | 32 | 77 |
| 4 Wolves | 46 | 15 | 5 | 3 | 39 | 18 | 6 | 8 | 9 | 38 | 43 | 76 |
| 5 Tranmere | 46 | 17 | 4 | 2 | 51 | 23 | 5 | 6 | 12 | 16 | 35 | 76 |
| 6 Barnsley | 46 | 15 | 6 | 2 | 42 | 19 | 5 | 6 | 12 | 21 | 33 | 72 |
| 7 Watford | 46 | 14 | 6 | 3 | 33 | 17 | 5 | 7 | 11 | 19 | 29 | 70 |
| 8 Sheffield Utd | 46 | 12 | 9 | 2 | 41 | 21 | 5 | 8 | 10 | 33 | 34 | 68 |
| 9 Derby | 46 | 12 | 6 | 5 | 44 | 23 | 6 | 6 | 11 | 22 | 28 | 66 |
| 10 Grimsby | 46 | 12 | 7 | 4 | 36 | 19 | 5 | 7 | 11 | 26 | 37 | 65 |
| 11 Stoke | 46 | 10 | 7 | 6 | 31 | 21 | 6 | 8 | 9 | 19 | 32 | 63 |
| 12 Millwall | 46 | 11 | 8 | 4 | 36 | 22 | 5 | 6 | 12 | 24 | 38 | 62 |
| 13 Southend | 46 | 13 | 2 | 8 | 33 | 25 | 5 | 6 | 12 | 21 | 48 | 62 |
| 14 Oldham | 46 | 12 | 7 | 4 | 34 | 21 | 4 | 6 | 13 | 26 | 39 | 61 |
| 15 Charlton | 46 | 11 | 6 | 6 | 33 | 25 | 5 | 5 | 13 | 25 | 41 | 59 |
| 16 LUTON TOWN | 46 | 8 | 6 | 9 | 35 | 30 | 7 | 7 | 9 | 26 | 34 | 58 |
| 17 Port Vale | 46 | 11 | 5 | 7 | 30 | 24 | 4 | 8 | 11 | 28 | 40 | 58 |
| 18 Portsmouth | 46 | 9 | 8 | 6 | 31 | 28 | 6 | 5 | 12 | 22 | 35 | 58 |
| 19 West Brom | 46 | 13 | 3 | 7 | 33 | 24 | 3 | 7 | 13 | 18 | 33 | 58 |
| 20 Sunderland | 46 | 5 | 12 | 6 | 22 | 22 | 7 | 6 | 10 | 19 | 23 | 54 |
| 21 Swindon | 46 | 9 | 6 | 8 | 28 | 27 | 3 | 6 | 14 | 26 | 46 | 48 |
| 22 Burnley | 46 | 8 | 7 | 8 | 36 | 33 | 3 | 6 | 14 | 13 | 41 | 46 |
| 23 Bristol City | 46 | 8 | 8 | 7 | 26 | 28 | 3 | 4 | 16 | 16 | 35 | 45 |
| 24 Notts Co | 46 | 7 | 8 | 8 | 26 | 28 | 2 | 5 | 16 | 19 | 38 | 40 |
| | 1104 | 275 | 153 | 124 | 838 | 551 | 124 | 153 | 275 | 551 | 838 | 1503 |

* promoted after play-offs

Odds & ends

Double wins: (3) Notts County, Port Vale, Swindon.
Double losses: (4) Barnsley, Burnley, Charlton, Grimsby.

Won from behind: (3) Sheffield Utd (a), Swindon (a), Watford (a).
Lost from in front: (4) Barnsley (a), Burnley (a), Portsmouth (a), Stoke (h).

High spots: The away form before Christmas.
The blossoming talents of John Hartson.
Being safe from relegation with six games to go.
Magnificent 5-1 home win over champions-to-be Middlesbrough.
Taking part in Middlesbrough's last ever game at Ayresome Park.

Low spots: The home form before Christmas.
Losing 0-6 to Southampton in the FA Cup.
Losing the last four games of the season.
Losing to Fulham on penalties in the Coca-Cola Cup.
Losing 3-6 at home to Sheffield United.
Being thrashed 0-5 at Grimsby.

Player of the Year: Trevor Peake.
Ever-presents: (2) Marvin Johnson, Trevor Peake.
Hat-tricks: (0).
Leading scorer: (13) Dwight Marshall.

| | Appearances Lge | *Sub* | LC | *Sub* | FAC | *Sub* | Goals Lge | LC | FAC | Tot |
|---|---|---|---|---|---|---|---|---|---|---|
| Adcock, Tony | | *2* | | | | *1* | | | | |
| Allen, Paul | **4** | | | | | | | | | |
| Biggins, Wayne | **6** | *1* | | | 2 | | **1** | | 1 | **2** |
| Chenery, Ben | | | | | 1 | | | | | |
| Davis, Kelvin | **9** | | | | | | | | | |
| Dixon, Kerry | **23** | *6* | 2 | | 2 | *1* | **7** | | | **7** |
| Greene, David | **7** | *1* | 2 | | | | | | | |
| Hartson, John | **11** | *9* | | | 1 | | **5** | | 1 | **6** |
| Harvey, Richard | **9** | *3* | | | | | **1** | | | **1** |
| Houghton, Scott | **1** | | 1 | | | | | | | |
| Hughes, Ceri | **8** | *1* | 2 | | | | **2** | | | **2** |
| James, Julian | **42** | | 2 | | 2 | | **3** | | | **3** |
| Johnson, Marvin | **46** | | 2 | | 4 | | **1** | | | **1** |
| Linton, Des | **5** | *5* | 1 | *1* | | | | | | |
| Marshall, Dwight | **36** | *9* | 1 | *1* | 4 | | **11** | 1 | 1 | **13** |
| Matthews, Rob | **6** | *5* | | | | | | | | |
| Oakes, Scott | **37** | *6* | 1 | *1* | 4 | | **9** | 1 | | **10** |
| Peake, Trevor | **46** | | 2 | | 4 | | | | | |
| Preece, David | **42** | | 2 | | 4 | | **4** | | | **4** |
| Skelton, Aaron | **3** | *2* | | *1* | | | | | | |
| Sommer, Juergen | **37** | | 2 | | 4 | | | | | |
| Taylor, John | **9** | | | | | | **3** | | | **3** |
| Telfer, Paul | **45** | *1* | 2 | | 4 | | **9** | | | **9** |
| Thomas, Mitchell | **33** | *3* | | | 4 | | | | | |
| Thorpe, Tony | | *4* | | | | *1* | | | | |
| Waddock, Gary | **40** | | | | 4 | | **1** | | | **1** |
| Williams, Martin | | *2* | | | | *1* | | | | |
| Woodsford, Jamie | **1** | *6* | | | | | | | | |
| (own-goals) | | | | | | | **4** | | | **4** |
| **28 players used** | **506** | ***66*** | **22** | ***4*** | **44** | ***4*** | **61** | **2** | **3** | **66** |

# ENDSLEIGH LEAGUE DIVISION 1 — Manager: Westley ⇨ Lawrence — SEASON 1995-96

| No | Date | | Att | Pos | Pt | F-A | H-T | Scorers, Times, and Referees | 1 | 2 | 3 | 4 | 5 | 6 | 7 | 8 | 9 | 10 | 11 | subs used |
|---|---|---|---|---|---|---|---|---|---|---|---|---|---|---|---|---|---|---|---|---|
| 1 | H | NORWICH | | | L | 1-3 | 0-1 | Guentchev 53p | Davis K | Thomas | Johnson M | Waddock | Hughes | Peake | **Alexander** | Oldfield | Thorpe | **Guentch'v*** | Harvey | Taylor |
| | 13/8 | | 7,848 | | - | | | *Newsome 14, 55, Adams 69* | *Gunn* | *Mills* | *Newsome* | *Prior* | *Bowen* | *Adams* | *Milligan** | *Johnson^* | *Eadie* | *Akinbiyi* | *Ward* | *Sutch"/Ullathorne/Polston* |
| | | | | | | | | Ref: M Pierce | A new manager and some new players but the same old pretty football with no bite. Norwich, who were relegated last season, take a two-goal lead through Jon Newsome. Guentchev pulls one back from the spot after Danny Mills fouled Alexander, but Neil Adams fires in from 25 yards. | | | | | | | | | | | |
| 2 | A | SOUTHEND | | 17 | W | 1-0 | 0-0 | Thorpe 76 | Sommer | James | Johnson M | **Davis S** | Hughes ! | Oldfield | Alexander* | Marshall^ | Taylor | Guentchev" | Harvey | Thomas/Thorpe/Waddock |
| | 19/8 | | *4,630* | *23* | 3 | | | | *Royce* | *Dublin** | *Bodley* | *Lapper* | *Powell* | *Gridelet* | *Hone^* | *Tilson* | *Jones"* | *Regis* | *Thomson* | *Hails/Iorfa/Ansah* |
| | | | | | | | | Ref: G Pooley | The early dismissal of Ceri Hughes for retaliation against a bad tackle by Phil Gridelet seems to spur on Luton. In sweltering heat, the Town defence contains the Shrimpers' attacks and an opportunist effort from Tony Thorpe clinches an unlikely win, the first at Roots Hall since 1964. | | | | | | | | | | | |
| 3 | H | LEICESTER | | 16 | D | 1-1 | 1-0 | Hughes 20 | Sommer | James* | Johnson M | Davis S | Hughes | Oldfield^ | Linton | Marshall^ | Taylor" | **Johnson G** | Harvey | Peake/Guentchev/Thorpe |
| | 26/8 | | 7,612 | *10* | 4 | | | *Parker 64* | *Poole* | *Hill* | *Willis* | *Walsh* | *Whitlow* | *Joachim* | *Taylor* | *Parker* | *Corica* | *Robins** | *Roberts* | *Lowe* |
| | | | | | | | | Ref: M Bailey | The Town dominate the game but again fail to convert their superiority into goals. Hughes scores with a strike from 20 yards, midway through the first half and ex-Hatter Gary Parker equalises with a free-kick which takes a deflection off Tony Thorpe to wrong-foot Juergen Sommer. | | | | | | | | | | | |
| 4 | A | GRIMSBY | | 16 | D | 0-0 | 0-0 | | Davis K | James | Johnson M | Davis S | Alexander | Oldfield* | Linton^ | Marshall" | Guentchev | Johnson G | Harvey | Woodsford/Peake/Taylor |
| | 29/8 | | ***4,289*** | *12* | 5 | | | | *Crichton* | *Laws* | *Handyside* | *Lever* | *Croft* | *Dobbin** | *Groves* | *Shak'speare* | *Southall* | *Woods* | *Livingstone* | *Fickling* |
| | | | | | | | | Ref: W Burns | The Town set out to keep the point they start with and, after a few scares, manage to hang on. Paul Groves misses the best chance of the game for the Mariners when he is through on goal with only Davis to beat. After the 0-5 thrashing at Blundell Park last season, this is a useful result. | | | | | | | | | | | |
| 5 | H | DERBY | | 17 | L | 1-2 | 1-1 | Marshall 1 | Davis K | James | Johnson M | Davis S | Alexander* | Oldfield^ | Marshall | Guentchev" | Taylor | Johnson G | Harvey | Peake/Thorpe/Woodsford |
| | 2/9 | | 6,427 | *16* | 5 | | | *Sturridge 15, 63* | *Hoult* | *Webster* | *van der Laan* | *Powell** | *Kavanagh* | *Carsley* | *Preece* | *Nicholson* | *Harkes* | *Sturridge* | *Flynn^* | *Wassell/Simpson* |
| | | | | | | | | Ref: J Brandwood | Dwight Marshall gives the Town a perfect start when he converts a pass from Guentchev after just 31 seconds. Bontcho Guentchev then misses an open goal soon afterwards as the Hatters fall in a heap. Dean Sturridge runs riot, scoring twice and having the chances to score three more. | | | | | | | | | | | |
| 6 | A | READING | | 20 | L | 1-3 | 1-1 | Marshall 5 | Davis K | James | Johnson M | Davis S | Waddock | Alexander | Linton* | Marshall | Oldfield | Johnson G | Harvey | Guentchev |
| | 9/9 | | *8,550* | *11* | 5 | | | *Nogan 17, 69, Lovell 60p* | *Sheppard* | *Bernal* | *Williams A* | *Wdowczyk** | *Gilkes* | *Williams M* | *Parkinson* | *Gooding^* | *Meaker* | *Nogan* | *Lovell* | *Jones/Quinn* |
| | | | | | | | | Ref: K Leach | The Town are gifted a goal when Simon Sheppard collides with Dariusz Wdowczyk, leaving Dwight Marshall to walk the ball into an empty net. The Royals equalise and then take the lead with Lovell scoring from the spot after Des Linton is harshly adjudged to have fouled Gooding. | | | | | | | | | | | |
| 7 | A | MILLWALL | | 22 | L | 0-1 | 0-0 | | **Feuer** | Peake | Johnson M* | Davis S | Waddock | **Vilstrup** | Linton | Marshall | Oldfield | Guentchev | Harvey | James |
| | 13/9 | | *7,354* | *2* | 5 | | | *Malkin 89* | *Keller* | *Newman* | *Witter* | *Stevens* | *Thatcher* | *Savage** | *Doyle* | *Bowry* | *van Blerk^* | *Fuchs"* | *Dixon* | *Forbes/McRobert/Malkin* |
| | | | | | | | | Ref: R Gifford | Ian Feuer, on loan from West Ham, makes his Luton debut. He makes a brilliant save from Keith Stevens, as the Hatters defend in depth, and frustrate the Lions. Steve Davis makes a mistake just seconds from the end which allows Chris Malkin to run through unchallenged and score. | | | | | | | | | | | |
| 8 | H | SUNDERLAND | | 23 | L | 0-2 | 0-0 | | Feuer | Peake | James | Davis S | Waddock* | Vilstrup | Linton^ | Marshall | Oldfield | Hughes | Harvey | Taylor/Guentchev |
| | 16/9 | | 6,955 | *9* | 5 | | | *Mullin 51, Gray P 81* | *Chamberlain* | *Kubicki* | *Melville* | *Ord* | *Scott* | *Russell** | *Ball* | *Bracewell* | *Gray M* | *Mullin^* | *Gray P* | *Smith/Howey* |
| | | | | | | | | Ref: R Poulain | John Mullin latches onto a through ball from Kevin Ball to open the scoring and Phil Gray chips Ian Feuer to earn Sunderland a comfortable victory. With one win from the first eight games and no recognisable pattern to the play, the knives are now out for manager Terry Westley. | | | | | | | | | | | |
| 9 | A | WOLVES | | 24 | D | 0-0 | 0-0 | | Feuer | Peake | Johnson M | Davis S | Hughes | Vilstrup* | Alexander | Marshall | Taylor^ | Guentchev | Harvey | Waddock/Oldfield |
| | 23/9 | | ***23,659*** | *19* | 6 | | | | *Stowell* | *Rankine* | *Young* | *Richards* | *Thompson* | *Daley* | *Atkins** | *Ferguson* | *Wright^* | *Goodman* | *Bull* | *Cowans/Williams* |
| | | | | | | | | Ref: N Barry | The Town put up a committed and determined rearguard display against high-spending Wolves. Don Goodman and Steve Bull are continually flagged for offside as the Luton defence dominates, whilst at the other end John Taylor hits the bar for the Hatters' best chance of the game. | | | | | | | | | | | |
| 10 | H | PORTSMOUTH | | 23 | W | **3-1** | 2-1 | Marshall 7, Davis S 23, Guentchev 59p | Feuer | Peake | Johnson M | Davis S | Hughes | Vilstrup* | Alexander^ | Marshall | Taylor | Guentchev | Harvey | Waddock/James |
| | 30/9 | | 7,795 | *22* | 9 | | | *Walsh 43* | *Knight* | *Pethick** | *Butters* | *Gittens !* | *Russell* | *Hall* | *McLo'ghlin^* | *Simpson* | *Rees"* | *Walsh* | *Bradbury* | *Wood/Igoe/Durnin* |
| | | | | | | | | Ref: P Rejer | Strikes from both Marshall and Davis set the Town up for the win against a poor Portsmouth side. Walsh pulls a goal back before Gittens fouls Marshall in the area and Guentchev scores from the spot. Gittens is sent off for flattening Taylor after 61 minutes, his second bookable offence. | | | | | | | | | | | |
| 11 | A | TRANMERE | | 24 | L | 0-1 | 0-1 | | Feuer | Peake | Johnson M | Davis S | Waddock | McLaren | Alexander | Marshall | Oakes | Guentchev* | Harvey | Oldfield |
| | 7/10 | | *6,680* | *7* | 9 | | | *Aldridge 4* | *Coyne* | *Thomas* | *McGreal* | *Teale* | *Stevens* | *Nevin* | *Jones* | *Irons* | *Brannan* | *Bennett** | *Aldridge* | *Moore* |
| | | | | | | | | Ref: P Richards | John Aldridge is unmarked when he puts the home side into an early lead. Bontcho Guentchev misses several good opportunities as the Hatters continue to play attractive football but still lack the killer blow in front of goal. Town manager Terry Westley is searching for a target man. | | | | | | | | | | | |

| No | Ven | Opponent | Att | Pos | Pts | F-A | H-T | Scorers, Times, and Referees | 1 | 2 | 3 | 4 | 5 | 6 | 7 | 8 | 9 | 10 | 11 | Subs used |
|---|---|---|---|---|---|---|---|---|---|---|---|---|---|---|---|---|---|---|---|---|
| 12 | H | WEST BROM | | 24 | L | 1-2 | 1-0 | Harvey 19 | Feuer | Peake* | Johnson M | Davis S | Waddock | Hughes | Alexander | Marshall | Oldfield | Woodsford | Harvey | James |
| | | 14/10 | 8,042 | *3* | 9 | | | *Ashcroft 74, Hunt 83* | *Naylor* | *Burgess* | *Mardon* | *Raven* | *Agnew** | *Ashcroft* | *Coldicott* | *Cunnington* | *Donovan* | *Gilbert^* | *Taylor* | *Smith/Hunt* |
| | | | | | | | | Ref: G Barber | Harvey gets Luton off to a good start as they dominate the first half. Baggies substitute Andy Hunt comes on and transforms the game, being involved in Ashcroft's headed equaliser and then scrambling home the winner. Davis sees his penalty saved after Mardon brings down Marshall. | | | | | | | | | | | |
| 13 | A | IPSWICH | | 21 | W | 1-0 | 1-0 | Oldfield 24 | Feuer | Peake | Johnson M | Davis S | Hughes | Vilstrup* | Alexander | Oakes | Oldfield | Marshall^ | Harvey" | Waddock/J'son G/Guentchev |
| | | 22/10 | *9,157* | *14* | 12 | | | | *Forrest* | *Stockwell* | *Linighan* | *Mowbray* | *Taricco* | *Uhlenbeek* | *Sedgley** | *Williams* | *Slater* | *Mathie^* | *Marshall* | *Tanner/Gregory* |
| | | | | | | | | Ref: T West | In an awful game, the Town pull themselves off the bottom with a strike from Oldfield, his first since returning to the club. After the goal, the Town frustrate a poor Ipswich side who have now suffered four home defeats in a row. Terry Westley dances a jig on the pitch after the game. | | | | | | | | | | | |
| 14 | H | CHARLTON | | 22 | L | 0-1 | 0-1 | | Feuer | Peake | Johnson M | Davis S | Hughes* | Waddock^ | Alexander" | Oakes | Oldfield | Marshall | Harvey | **Riseth**/Guentchev/Linton |
| | | 29/10 | 6,270 | *8* | 12 | | | *Nelson 16* | *Salmon* | *Humphrey* | *Chapple* | *Rufus* | *Stuart* | *Newton* | *Walsh* | *Bowyer* | *Robinson* | *Nelson** | *Leaburn* | *Grant* |
| | | | | | | | | Ref: J Kirkby | Charlton catch the Hatters on the break and Gary Nelson rounds a hesitant Feuer before slotting the ball into the empty net. Oakes side-foots a shot against the bar which is the nearest Luton come to scoring. Charlton manager Alan Curbishley admits his side are lucky to take the points. | | | | | | | | | | | |
| 15 | A | STOKE | | 24 | L | **0-5** | 0-1 | *[Gleghorn 89]* | Feuer | Peake | Johnson G | Davis S | Hughes | Vilstrup* | Alexander | Oakes | Riseth | Marshall | Harvey | Oldfield |
| | | 4/11 | *9,349* | *15* | 12 | | | *Peschisolido 14, Sturridge 73, 87, Gayle 75,* | *Prudhoe* | *Clarkson** | *Sigurdsson* | *Overson* | *Sandford* | *Keen* | *Wallace* | *Gleghorn* | *Potter* | *Peschisolido^* | *Carruthers"* | *Cranson/Gayle/Sturridge* |
| | | | | | | | | Ref: J Lloyd | Paul Peschisolido takes advantage of some slack defending to open the scoring but the Town fight back and make a fist of it until Steve Davis misses a through-ball which leaves Simon Sturridge to net with ease. The Town defence then falls apart and Stoke might well have scored ten. | | | | | | | | | | | |
| 16 | H | OLDHAM | | 23 | D | 1-1 | 1-0 | Douglas 40 | Feuer | Peake | Johnson M | Davis S | Hughes | McLaren* | Alexander | Oakes^ | Riseth | **Douglas** | Harvey | **Patterson**/Oldfield |
| | | 11/11 | 6,047 | *11* | 13 | | | *Halle 65* | *Gerrard* | *Snodin* | *Fleming* | *Redmond* | *Makin* | *Halle* | *Rickers* | *Richardson* | *Brennan* | *Wilkinson** | *McCarthy* | *Beresford* |
| | | | | | | | | Ref: A D'Urso | 17-year-old YTS striker, Stuart Douglas, makes a dream debut when he hammers the ball into the roof of the net after Patterson heads down a cross from Oakes. Oldham bring Beresford on for the second half and he transforms the game. His fierce shot is parried to Halle who taps in. | | | | | | | | | | | |
| 17 | H | BIRMINGHAM | | 23 | D | 0-0 | 0-0 | | Feuer | Peake | Johnson M | James | Hughes | McLaren* | Alexander | Oakes | Riseth | Marshall^ | Harvey | Douglas/Thorpe |
| | | 18/11 | 7,920 | *3* | 14 | | | | *Bennett* | *Hiley* | *Edwards* | *Johnson* | *Cooper* | *Hunt* | *Tait** | *Ward* | *Otto^* | *Charlery"* | *Claridge* | *Finnan/Martin/Rushveldt* |
| | | | | | | | | Ref: J Rushworth | Birmingham extend their unbeaten run to 15 games in a disjointed match which is poor entertainment for the fans. The Town create few chances and a 25-yard shot from Ceri Hughes is the closest they come to a goal. Jae Martin sees Ian Feuer stretch to push his shot onto the bar late on. | | | | | | | | | | | |
| 18 | A | WATFORD | | 23 | D | 1-1 | 1-0 | Davis S 25 | Feuer | Peake | Johnson M | Davis S* | Hughes | McLaren | James^ | Oakes | Riseth | Marshall" | Harvey | Patterson/Thorpe/Douglas |
| | | 21/11 | *10,042* | *21* | 15 | | | *Phillips 84* | *Miller* | *Lavin* | *Millen* | *Holdsworth* | *Mooney* | *Hessenthaler* | *Ramage* | *Palmer* | *Caskey* | *Penrice** | *Phillips* | *Moralee* |
| | | | | | | | | Ref: M Pierce | Steve Davis returns after a bout of flu and, playing in midfield, rises to head in a corner from Richard Harvey. Hughes is harshly adjudged to have pulled down Hessenthaler but the spot-kick from Ramage is saved by Feuer. A casual back-pass from Peake allows Phillips to net late on. | | | | | | | | | | | |
| 19 | A | BARNSLEY | | 23 | L | 0-1 | 0-0 | | Feuer | Peake | Johnson M | Patterson | Hughes | McLaren* | James | Oakes | Riseth^ | Marshall" | Harvey | Alexander/Douglas/Thorpe |
| | | 25/11 | *6,437* | *11* | 15 | | | *Redfearn 68* | *Watson* | *Shirtliff* | *Davis* | *De Zeeuw* | *Eaden* | *Bullock* | *Redfearn* | *Archdeacon* | *Liddell** | *Payton* | *Sheridan* | *Rammell* |
| | | | | | | | | Ref: A Leake | The Hatters miss three good opportunities in the first period with Marshall spurning the best of them when he hits a post. Barnsley step up a gear in the second half and a fierce effort by Neil Redfearn is enough to win the game although they nearly get a second as the Town try to equalise. | | | | | | | | | | | |
| 20 | H | TRANMERE | | 23 | W | 3-2 | 1-1 | Marshall 6, 60, McLaren 71 | Feuer | Alexander | Johnson M | Waddock | Hughes | McLaren | James | Oakes | Thorpe | Marshall | Harvey | |
| | | 2/12 | 6,025 | *9* | 18 | | | *Bennett 2, Jones 52* | *Coyne* | *Thomas* | *Teale* | *Garnett** | *Rogers* | *Jones* | *Brannan* | *Nevin* | *Aldridge* | *Bennett^* | *Moore* | *O'Brien/Branch* |
| | | | | | | | | Ref: K Leach | The Town put on their best performance of the season with every player on the top of his form. Dwight Marshall ends his nine-week lean spell with two expert strikes before McLaren gets the winner, his first league goal. The fans chanting for the head of Westley are silenced - for now. | | | | | | | | | | | |
| 21 | H | WOLVES | | 24 | L | 2-3 | 1-3 | Oakes 31, Marshall 50 | Davis K | Patterson | Johnson M | Waddock | Hughes* | McLaren^ | Davis S | Oakes | Thorpe | Marshall | Harvey | Guentchev/Taylor |
| | | 10/12 | 6,997 | *20* | 18 | | | *Richards 7, Goodman 18, Bull 41* | *Stowell* | *Law* | *Richards* | *Venus* | *Rankine* | *Atkins* | *Emblen* | *Ferguson* | *Thompson* | *Goodman* | *Bull* | |
| | | | | | | | | Ref: K Lynch | Wolves go in at half-time with a 3-1 lead but the Town then stage a fight back. Thorpe makes a solo run past two defenders before setting up Marshall to shoot into an empty net. Scott Oakes and Paul McLaren both go close and it is the visitors who are pleased to hear the final whistle. | | | | | | | | | | | |
| 22 | A | PORTSMOUTH | | 24 | L | 0-4 | 0-3 | | Feuer | Patterson | Johnson M | Davis S | Waddock | McLaren | Alexander* | Oakes | Taylor | Marshall | Harvey^ | Thomas/Thorpe |
| | | 16/12 | *7,012* | *17* | 18 | | | *Hall 3, 40, Walsh 44, Carter 46* | *Knight* | *Pethick* | *Butters* | *Whitbread* | *Stimson* | *Durnin* | *McLoughlin* | *Carter* | *Simpson* | *Hall* | *Walsh* | |
| | | | | | | | | Ref: E Lomas | Portsmouth play like the away side and attack on the break with incredible ease. Paul Hall runs riot down the wing and scores twice before half-time. Terry Westley reaches the end of the managerial road and, on the day after this humiliating defeat, he leaves the club by mutual consent. | | | | | | | | | | | |
| 23 | H | HUDDERSFIELD | | 24 | D | 2-2 | 1-0 | Marshall 35, Oldfield 79 | Feuer | Patterson | Thomas | Waddock | Davis S ! | Johnson M | McLaren * | Oakes | Taylor^ | Marshall | Thorpe" | Oldfield/Guentchev/Harvey |
| | | 23/12 | 7,076 | *5* | 19 | | | *Booth 56, Makel 64* | *Francis* | *Jenkins* | *Sinnott* | *Gray* | *Cowan** | *Dalton* | *Bullock* | *Makel* | *Turner* | *Booth* | *Jepson* | *Collins* |
| | | | | | | | | Ref: D Allison | Lennie Lawrence takes charge as the Town salvage a point against the odds. Marshall opens the scoring but, after Steve Davis is dismissed for an alleged professional foul on Booth, the Terriers take the lead. A flying header from Oldfield, following Marshall's cross, gains the draw. | | | | | | | | | | | |

| No | Date | | Att | Pos | Pt | F-A | H-T | Scorers, Times, and Referees | 1 | 2 | 3 | 4 | 5 | 6 | 7 | 8 | 9 | 10 | 11 | subs used |
|---|---|---|---|---|---|---|---|---|---|---|---|---|---|---|---|---|---|---|---|---|
| 24 | H | SOUTHEND | | 24 | W | **3-1** | 1-0 | Guentchev 44, Oakes 54, 71 | Feuer | James | Thomas | Waddock | Davis S | Johnson M | Guentchev | Oakes* | Taylor^ | Alexander | Thorpe | Harvey/Oldfield |
| | 13/1 | | 6,566 | *9* | 22 | | | *Byrne 80* | *Royce* | *Dublin** | *McNally* | *Bodley* | *Powell* | *Byrne* | *Gridelet^* | *Marsh* | *Hails* | *Regis* | *Thomson"* | *Hone/Tilson/Charlery* |
| | | | | | | | | Ref: A Wiley | The players show a lot more effort and determination following the debacle in the FA Cup at Grimsby. Guentchev knocks in a cross from Tony Thorpe, just before the interval, but a 25-yard drive from Oakes steals the headlines. This is the first defeat suffered by Southend in nine games. | | | | | | | | | | | |
| 25 | A | NORWICH | | 23 | W | 1-0 | 1-0 | Guentchev 33p | Feuer | James | Thomas | Waddock | Davis S | Johnson M | Guentchev | Oakes* | Taylor | Alexander | Harvey | Oldfield |
| | 20/1 | | *12,474* | *9* | 25 | | | | *Gunn* | *Bradshaw** | *Polston* | *Prior* | *Bowen^* | *Eadie"* | *Molby* | *Adams* | *O'Neill* | *Ward* | *Fleck* | *Newman/Scott/Goss* |
| | | | | | | | | Ref: C Wilkes | The Hatters defend in depth in order to stop the Canaries from using their fast, raiding wingmen. Guentchev runs from his own half to collect a through-ball from Harvey but, after rounding Bryan Gunn, he is upended by Polston. He recovers to net the only goal of the game from the spot. | | | | | | | | | | | |
| 26 | H | SHEFFIELD UTD | | 21 | W | 1-0 | 1-0 | Guentchev 39 | Feuer | Patterson | Thomas | Waddock | Davis S | Johnson M* | Guentchev | Oakes^ | Taylor | Alexander | Thorpe" | Hughes/Oldfield/Harvey |
| | 31/1 | | 6,995 | *24* | 28 | | | | *Kelly* | *Nilson* | *Vonk* | *Tuttle* | *Ward* | *Patterson* | *Cowans** | *Hutchison* | *Whitehouse* | *White^* | *Angell* | *Heath/Veart* |
| | | | | | | | | Ref: D Orr | The Blades resort to pumping long balls into the Luton area as the Hatters defend in depth. Thorpe is tripped by David Tuttle, just outside the area, and Guentchev bends his free-kick around the wall and into the far corner of the net. Three wins in a row lifts the Town off the bottom. | | | | | | | | | | | |
| 27 | A | LEICESTER | | 21 | D | 1-1 | 0-0 | Thorpe 55 | Feuer | Patterson | Thomas | Waddock | Davis S | Oldfield* | Thorpe | Hughes^ | Taylor" | Alexander | Harvey | Marshall/Linton/Riseth |
| | 3/2 | | *15,687* | *7* | 29 | | | *Roberts 60* | *Poole* | *Rolling* | *Hill* | *Walsh* | *Grayson* | *Lowe* | *Parker* | *Corica** | *Lewis^* | *Heskey* | *Roberts* | *Robins/Philpott* |
| | | | | | | | | Ref: G Barber | A disciplined performance sees the Town take advantage of the recent loss of form by Leicester. Thorpe shows cool finishing after rounding the keeper to slot the ball home but Iwan Roberts levels after escaping from Davis for the only time in the match. Linton misses a late chance. | | | | | | | | | | | |
| 28 | H | GRIMSBY | | 20 | W | 3-2 | 1-1 | Alexander 7, Guentchev 68, Marshall 74 | Feuer | James | Thomas | Waddock | Davis S | Patterson | Guentchev | Hughes | Taylor* | Alexander | Thorpe^ | Oldfield/Marshall |
| | 10/2 | | 7,158 | *14* | 32 | | | *Forrester 17, 58* | *Crichton* | *Laws* | *Lever* | *Warner* | *Croft* | *Childs** | *Groves* | *Butler* | *Bonetti* | *Woods* | *Forrester^* | *Southall/Lester* |
| | | | | | | | | Ref: B Knight | The Hatters are 1-2 down and struggling when Lennie Lawrence changes the formation. Guentchev, who is back in favour, neatly shoots in the equaliser before the two substitutes combine to allow Dwight Marshall to run through, outpacing two defenders before slotting home the winner. | | | | | | | | | | | |
| 29 | H | MILLWALL | | 19 | W | 1-0 | 0-0 | Thorpe 84p | Feuer | James | Thomas | Waddock | Davis S | Patterson | Guentchev* | Hughes ! | Taylor^ | Alexander" | Thorpe | Harvey/Marshall/Oldfield |
| | 17/2 | | 7,308 | *9* | 35 | | | | *Keller* | *Lavin* | *Stevens* | *Witter* | *Thatcher* | *Neil* | *Savage* | *Bowry* | *van Blerk* | *Taylor** | *Malkin* | *Dolby* |
| | | | | | | | | Ref: J Rushton | Ceri Hughes is sent off again, this time for a second bookable offence, making it the fifth dismissal he has received in his Luton career. Marshall is brought down by Witter outside the area. The referee awards a penalty which is gratefully converted by Thorpe for the only goal of the game. | | | | | | | | | | | |
| 30 | A | DERBY | | 19 | D | 1-1 | 0-0 | Marshall 56 | Feuer | James | Thomas | Waddock | Davis S | Patterson | Marshall* | Hughes | Oldfield | Alexander | Thorpe^ | Riseth/Guentchev |
| | 21/2 | | *14,825* | *1* | 36 | | | *Powell D 50* | *Hoult* | *Rowett* | *Yates* | *Stimac* | *Carsley** | *v der Laan^* | *Powell D* | *Powell C* | *Simpson"* | *Sturridge* | *Willems* | *Gabbiadini/Hodges/Flynn* |
| | | | | | | | | Ref: M Riley | The Town have plenty of possession but are forced to shoot from long range. Feuer is powerless to stop Darryl Powell from taking advantage of a slip by Alexander to open the scoring but Marshall anticipates a poor pass from Carsley, across his own area, to level shortly afterwards. | | | | | | | | | | | |
| 31 | A | SUNDERLAND | | 19 | L | 0-1 | 0-1 | | Feuer | James | Thomas | Waddock | Oldfield | Johnson M | Guentchev | Hughes* | Marshall^ | Alexander | Harvey" | Thorpe/Riseth/Taylor |
| | 24/2 | | *16,693* | *3* | 36 | | | *James 38 (og)* | *Given* | *Kubicki* | *Melville* | *Ord* | *Scott* | *Cooke* | *Bracewell* | *Ball* | *Gray* | *Russell* | *Howey** | *Bridges* |
| | | | | | | | | Ref: A Butler | Julian James heads an unfortunate own-goal but the match is overshadowed by an injury to Dwight Marshall, who breaks an ankle after falling awkwardly in the 64th minute. 19-year-old goalkeeper Shay Given pulls off some tremendous late saves as Luton go in search of the equaliser. | | | | | | | | | | | |
| 32 | H | READING | | 20 | L | 1-2 | 1-1 | Guentchev 5p | Feuer | James | Thomas | Waddock* | Peake | Linton | Guentchev | Oldfield | Taylor^ | Alexander | Thorpe" | Vilstrup/Riseth/Oakes |
| | 27/2 | | 6,683 | *19* | 36 | | | *Booty 44, Lovell 78* | *Mihailov* | *Wdowczyk** | *Williams* | *Hopkins* | *Bernal* | *Meaker* | *Parkinson* | *Holsgrove* | *Booty* | *Nogan^* | *Lovell* | *Gilkes/Quinn* |
| | | | | | | | | Ref: P Rejer | Trevor Peake becomes the oldest player ever to turn out for the Hatters as he takes the place of the suspended Steve Davis. Guentchev opens the scoring from the spot after he is pulled back by Jeff Hopkins. Martin Booty levels with a free header and Stuart Lovell hits the late winner. | | | | | | | | | | | |
| 33 | H | CRYS PALACE | | 20 | D | 0-0 | 0-0 | | Feuer | James | Thomas | Waddock | Davis S | Johnson M | Guentchev* | Oakes | Riseth^ | Alexander | Thorpe" | Oldfield/Taylor/Harvey |
| | 2/3 | | 8,478 | *9* | 37 | | | | *Martyn* | *Gordon* | *Davies* | *Roberts* | *Edworthy* | *Hopkin* | *Houghton* | *Vincent** | *Freedman* | *Ndah* | *Dyer^* | *Andersen/Taylor* |
| | | | | | | | | Ref: J Kirkby/T Howes | The Town are missing the pace of Marshall and show little up front as Palace pummel the Luton defence. Only some smart saves from Feuer, and the woodwork, enable the Hatters to keep a clean sheet. Lawrence is looking for a new striker as the transfer deadline day fast approaches. | | | | | | | | | | | |
| 34 | A | HUDDERSFIELD | | 20 | L | 0-1 | 0-0 | | Feuer | James | Thomas | Waddock* | Davis S | Patterson | Guentchev | Oakes | Taylor | Oldfield^ | Thorpe | McLaren/Linton |
| | 9/3 | | *11,950* | *6* | 37 | | | *Edwards 75* | *Francis* | *Jenkins* | *Sinnott* | *Gray* | *Cowan* | *Bullock* | *Makel* | *Thornley* | *Edwards* | *Booth* | *Jepson* | |
| | | | | | | | | Ref: E Wolstenholme | Luton fail to seriously trouble goalkeeper, Steve Francis, the few chances that are created all seeming to fall to Guentchev. The defence is solid and Feuer makes several top-class saves. The winner is a superb effort from Rob Edwards, who fires an unstoppable bullet into the top corner. | | | | | | | | | | | |

| | | | | | | | | | | | | | | | | | | | | |
|---|---|---|---|---|---|---|---|---|---|---|---|---|---|---|---|---|---|---|---|---|
| 35 | A | CRYS PALACE | | 22 | L | 0-2 | 0-0 | | Feuer | James | Thomas | Waddock | Davis S | Patterson | Guentchev* | Oakes | Taylor^ | Oldfield | Thorpe | Hughes/Linton |
| | 19/3 | | *14,703* | *3* | 37 | | | *Dyer 83, 88* | *Martyn* | *Edworthy* | *Andersen** | *Tuttle* | *Pitcher* | *Roberts* | *Hopkin* | *Houghton* | *Vincent* | *Freedman^* | *Ndah* | *Dyer/Veart* |
| | | | | | | | | Ref: P Taylor | The Hatters seem to be holding out for a point but Palace then introduce Bruce Dyer as a late substitute. He takes advantage of hesitancy in the defence and, following a long throw from David Hopkin, hammers the ball home. The second goal comes when the Hatters are all pushing up. | | | | | | | | | | | |
| 36 | A | SHEFFIELD UTD | | 23 | L | 0-1 | 0-0 | | Feuer | James | Thomas | Waddock | Davis S | Patterson | Oldfield* | Oakes | Taylor | Alexander^ | Harvey" | **Tomlins'n**/McLaren/Thorpe |
| | 23/3 | | *14,935* | *20* | 37 | | | *Hutchison 77* | *Tracey* | *Short** | *Hodgson* | *Ablett* | *Nilsen* | *Ward* | *Hutchison* | *Patterson* | *Whiteho'se^* | *Taylor"* | *Walker* | *Starbuck/Cowans/White* |
| | | | | | | | | Ref: T West | The referee decides that a cross by Roger Nilsen, which is hammered against the thigh of Mitchell Thomas before deflecting into the hands of Feuer, is a back-pass. From seven yards out the free-kick is driven home by Don Hutchison, eluding all of the eleven Luton players on the line. | | | | | | | | | | | |
| 37 | H | IPSWICH | | 23 | L | 1-2 | 0-1 | Grant 49 | Feuer | James | Thomas | Waddock* | Davis S | Patterson | Oldfield^ | Oakes" | **Wilkinson** | **Grant** | Thorpe | Alex'der/Guentchev/Tomlinson |
| | 30/3 | | 9,151 | *5* | 37 | | | *Milton 5, 51* | *Wright* | *Uhlenbeek* | *Sedgley* | *Thomson* | *Taricco* | *Stockwell* | *Scowcroft* | *Williams* | *Milton** | *Marshall* | *Mathie* | *Slater* |
| | | | | | | | | Ref: G Singh | Simon Milton gives the Blues an early lead with a volley which could have gone anywhere. Kim Grant, making his debut, fires in a spectacular equaliser after the break but James, in attempting to kick a ball out of the hands of Feuer, only succeeds in presenting Milton with the winner. | | | | | | | | | | | |
| 38 | A | WEST BROM | | 23 | W | 2-0 | 1-0 | Guentchev 22, Grant 84 | Feuer | Alexander | Thomas | Oldfield* | Davis S | Patterson | Guentchev | Thorpe^ | Wilkinson | Grant | Harvey | Oakes/Johnson M |
| | 2/4 | | *15,130* | *19* | 40 | | | | *Naylor* | *Burgess* | *Raven** | *Mardon* | *Butler* | *Darby^* | *Hamilton"* | *Sneekes* | *Nicholson* | *Taylor* | *Hunt* | *Gilbert/Angell/Donovan* |
| | | | | | | | | Ref: J Lloyd | Albion are forced back into the relegation zone after the Town put in a spirited performance, scoring twice in an away game for the first time in over a year. Guentchev heads in the first, following a cross by Thorpe, and Kim Grant seals the points when beating two defenders on the break. | | | | | | | | | | | |
| 39 | A | CHARLTON | | 22 | D | 1-1 | 1-0 | Thorpe 22 | Feuer | Alexander | Thomas | Waddock | Davis S | Patterson | Guentchev | Harvey* | Wilkinson | Grant^ | Thorpe" | Johnson M/Oakes/Tomlinson |
| | 5/4 | | *14,515* | *4* | 41 | | | *Allen 70p* | *Petterson* | *Brown* | *Rufus* | *Whyte C* | *Stuart** | *Robson* | *Bowyer^* | *Jones* | *Robinson* | *Leaburn* | *Allen* | *Linger/Whyte D* |
| | | | | | | | | Ref: W Burns | Thorpe opens the scoring with a cross shot which takes a deflection before Grant misses a sitter against his old side. Davis is harshly adjudged to have handled the ball in the area, leaving Bradley Allen to fire home from the spot. A late shot from the substitute, Paul Linger, hits the post. | | | | | | | | | | | |
| 40 | H | STOKE | | 22 | L | 1-2 | 1-0 | Grant 44 | Feuer | Alexander | Thomas | Waddock | Johnson M | Patterson | Guentchev | Thorpe* | Oldfield^ | Grant | Oakes | Tomlinson/Taylor |
| | 9/4 | | 7,689 | *6* | 41 | | | *Sturridge 86, Sheron 89* | *Prudhoe* | *Clarkson* | *Sandford* | *Sigurdsson* | *Whittle* | *Dreyer** | *Beeston^* | *Wallace* | *Gleghorn* | *Sheron"* | *Sturridge* | *Potter/Carruthers/Keen* |
| | | | | | | | | Ref: U Rennie | Grant scrambles a cross from Guentchev over the line, but bold goalkeeping from Mark Prudhoe prevents the Hatters from adding to their lead. Simon Sturridge uses his pace to take him clear for the equaliser and Mike Sheron is completely unmarked when he heads the winner at the end. | | | | | | | | | | | |
| 41 | A | BIRMINGHAM | | 23 | L | 0-4 | 0-1 | | Feuer | Alexander | Thomas | Waddock* | Johnson M | Patterson | Guentchev^ | Thorpe | Oldfield" | Grant | Oakes | Harvey/Taylor/Tomlinson |
| | 13/4 | | *15,426* | *9* | 41 | | | *Devlin 1, Francis 76, Barnes 77, 89* | *Griemink* | *Poole* | *Breen* | *Edwards* | *Grainger* | *Tait** | *Cornforth^* | *Devlin* | *Hunt"* | *Barnes* | *Peschisolido* | *Legg/Francis/Johnson* |
| | | | | | | | | Ref: R Gifford | On the 60th anniversary of the ten-goal performance by Joe Payne against Bristol Rovers, the Town concede the first goal after just 18 seconds. From then on, they never look likely to pull the game back and are forced to play with ten men for the last 20 minutes as Grant goes off injured. | | | | | | | | | | | |
| 42 | H | WATFORD | | 24 | D | 0-0 | 0-0 | | Feuer | Alexander ! | Thomas | Johnson M | Davis S | Patterson | Guentchev | Thorpe* | Oldfield^ | Grant | Oakes | Harvey/Tomlinson |
| | 20/4 | | **9,454** | *23* | 42 | | | | *Miller* | *Bazeley* | *Ward* | *Palmer* | *Ludden* | *Ramage* | *Hessenthaler* | *Porter** | *Mooney* | *White* | *Connolly^* | *Payne/Moralee* |
| | | | | | | | | Ref: G Cain | In the poorest local derby for years, the teams cut each other's throats and, with a result that does neither team any favours, both now look odds on for relegation. A total of eleven players are booked, and Graham Alexander is dismissed in the final minute for his second bookable offence. | | | | | | | | | | | |
| 43 | A | PORT VALE | | 24 | L | 0-1 | 0-1 | | Feuer | James | Thomas | Waddock | Davis S | Johnson M | Alexander | Tomlinson* | Douglas | Grant | Oakes | Thorpe |
| | 23/4 | | *6,054* | *10* | 42 | | | *Mills 34* | *van Heusden* | *Hill* | *Griffiths* | *Aspin* | *Stokes* | *Porter* | *Corden** | *Lawton^* | *Guppy* | *Mills* | *Naylor* | *Talbot/Glover* |
| | | | | | | | | Ref: R Furnandiz | Lee Mills opens the scoring for the home side with a deflected shot before Graeme Tomlinson, on loan from Manchester Utd and making his full debut for the Town, breaks his leg. Luton fail to trouble the Vale keeper and, as the game peters out, relegation now looks to be inevitable. | | | | | | | | | | | |
| 44 | H | BARNSLEY | | 24 | L | 1-3 | 0-2 | Thorpe 52 | Feuer | Patterson | Thomas | Waddock | Davis S | Johnson M | Guentchev | Alexander* | Thorpe | Grant^ | Oakes" | Harvey/Taylor/Douglas |
| | 27/4 | | 6,194 | *13* | 42 | | | *Redfearn 30, 72, O'Connell 41* | *Watson* | *Eaden* | *Moses* | *De Zeeuw* | *Archdeacon* | *Bullock* | *O'Connell* | *Sheridan* | *Redfearn* | *Regis** | *Liddell* | *Ten-Heuvel* |
| | | | | | | | | Ref: J Brandwood | The outfield players are jeered off at the break, following a poor first-half performance in which Barnsley, who have nothing to play for, ease into a two-goal lead. A 25-yard chip from Thorpe raises hopes of a comeback but the Tykes make the game safe when Redfearn nets the third. | | | | | | | | | | | |
| 45 | H | PORT VALE | | 24 | W | 3-2 | 1-1 | Thorpe 22, 82, Guentchev 78 | Davis K | **Chenery** | Thomas | Waddock | Patterson | Johnson M | Douglas* | Alexander | Thorpe | Grant^ | **Evers"** | Guentchev/Taylor/McLaren |
| | 30/4 | | **5,443** | *12* | 45 | | | *Porter 7, Mills 87* | *Mus'elwhite* | *Hill* | *Glover D* | *Aspin* | *Stokes* | *McCarthy* | *Porter* | *Bogie** | *Guppy* | *Mills^* | *Naylor* | *Walker/Glover L* |
| | | | | | | | | Ref: N Barry | Ben Chenery and Sean Evers make their league debuts whilst Kelvin Davis and Stuart Douglas are recalled to the side for a game that matters little as the Town are already relegated. Thorpe takes advantage of a bad back-pass by Andy Hill to score the third goal, making the game safe. | | | | | | | | | | | |
| 46 | A | OLDHAM | | 24 | L | 0-1 | 0-0 | | Feuer | Chenery* | Thomas | Waddock | Patterson | Johnson M | Guentchev | Taylor | Thorpe | Grant^ | Oakes | James/Douglas |
| | 5/5 | | *6,623* | *18* | 45 | | | *Barlow 84* | *Hallworth* | *Fleming* | *Redmond* | *Graham* | *Halle* | *Rickers* | *Richardson* | *Orlygsson** | *Serrant* | *Beckford^* | *Creaney"* | *Snodin/Barlow/McCarthy* |
| | | Home | Away | | | | | Ref: M Riley | The season drifts to a close, with the Town playing plenty of neat football but not forcing Jon Hallworth in the Oldham goal to make a single save. The nearest Luton come to scoring is when Oakes hits the bar with the ball rebounding into the keeper's arms. Barlow flicks in the winner. | | | | | | | | | | | |
| Average | | 7,223 | 11,138 | | | | | | | | | | | | | | | | | |

| Coca-Cola Cup | | | | | F-A | H-T | Scorers, Times, and Referees | 1 | 2 | 3 | 4 | 5 | 6 | 7 | 8 | 9 | 10 | 11 | subs used |
|---|---|---|---|---|---|---|---|---|---|---|---|---|---|---|---|---|---|---|---|
| 1:1 | H | BOURNEMOUTH | | D | 1-1 | 0-1 | Marshall 70 | Sommer | Thomas | Johnson M | Davis S | Hughes | Oldfield | Alexander | Marshall* | Taylor | Guentchev | Harvey | Thorpe |
| | 15/8 | | *2,728 D2* | | | | *Jones 16* | *Andrews* | *Beardsmore* | *Murray* | *Mean* | *Morris* | *Young* | *Holland* | *Robinson** | *Brissett* | *Jones* | *Fletcher^* | *McElhatton/Bailey* |
| | | | | | | | Ref: G Singh | Steve Jones, with time and space, blasts a shot over the bar but, one minute later, he is on target after he outruns Johnson and cracks a shot past Sommer. Steve Davis makes his debut for the Town and hits a long-range drive which Ian Andrews fumbles and Marshall follows up to score. | | | | | | | | | | | |
| 1:2 | A | BOURNEMOUTH | 17 | L | 1-2 | 1-1 | Johnson M 43 | Sommer | James | Johnson M | Davis S | Waddock | Oldfield* | Alexander | Marshall | Taylor^ | Guentchev | Harvey" | Matthews/Thorpe/Thomas |
| | 22/8 | | *4,884 2:10* | | *aet* | | *Jones 12, Morris 97* | *Andrews* | *Beardsmore* | *Murray* | *Mean* | *Morris* | *Young* | *Holland* | *Pennock** | *Brissett^* | *Jones* | *Bailey* | *Victory/Town"/Rawlinson* |
| | | | | | | | Ref: D Orr (Hatters lose 2-3 on aggregate) | Steve Jones gets in behind the Hatters' defence when he converts a cross by Neil Young for the opening goal. Marvin Johnson dives to head a shock equaliser which takes the game into extra-time. Mark Morris heads the deserved winner, when connecting with a cross from Scott Mean. | | | | | | | | | | | |

| FA Cup | | | | | | | | | | | | | | | | | | | |
|---|---|---|---|---|---|---|---|---|---|---|---|---|---|---|---|---|---|---|---|
| 3 | A | GRIMSBY | 24 | L | 1-7 | 1-4 | Marshall 38 *[Southall 80, Woods 84]* | Feuer | Patterson | Thomas | Waddock | James | Johnson M | Guentchev* | Oakes | Oldfield | McLaren^ | Marshall | Thorpe/Alexander |
| | 6/1 | | *5,387 1:8* | | | | *Forrester 15, 31, L'stone 22,72, Bonetti 44,* | *Crichton* | *Laws* | *Rodger* | *Groves* | *Croft* | *Childs** | *Handyside* | *Dobbin^* | *Bonetti* | *Livingstone"* | *Forrester* | *Southall/Shakespeare/Woods* |
| | | | | | | | Ref: P Richards | The Town are unable to contain the strike force of Jamie Forrester and Steve Livingstone and each bag a brace of goals. Mariners' boss Brian Laws brings on his three substitutes, with twelve minutes left, to give them a run-out and two of them score to compound the embarrassment. | | | | | | | | | | | |

| | | Home | | | | | Away | | | | | |
|---|---|---|---|---|---|---|---|---|---|---|---|---|
| | P | W | D | L | F | A | W | D | L | F | A | Pts |
| 1 Sunderland | 46 | 13 | 8 | 2 | 32 | 10 | 9 | 9 | 5 | 27 | 23 | 83 |
| 2 Derby | 46 | 14 | 8 | 1 | 48 | 22 | 7 | 8 | 8 | 23 | 29 | 79 |
| 3 Crys Palace | 46 | 9 | 9 | 5 | 34 | 22 | 11 | 6 | 6 | 33 | 26 | 75 |
| 4 Stoke | 46 | 13 | 6 | 4 | 32 | 15 | 7 | 7 | 9 | 28 | 34 | 73 |
| 5 Leicester * | 46 | 9 | 7 | 7 | 32 | 29 | 10 | 7 | 6 | 34 | 31 | 71 |
| 6 Charlton | 46 | 8 | 11 | 4 | 28 | 23 | 9 | 9 | 5 | 29 | 22 | 71 |
| 7 Ipswich | 46 | 13 | 5 | 5 | 45 | 30 | 6 | 7 | 10 | 34 | 39 | 69 |
| 8 Huddersfield | 46 | 14 | 4 | 5 | 42 | 23 | 3 | 8 | 12 | 19 | 35 | 63 |
| 9 Sheffield Utd | 46 | 9 | 7 | 7 | 29 | 25 | 7 | 7 | 9 | 28 | 29 | 62 |
| 10 Barnsley | 46 | 9 | 10 | 4 | 34 | 28 | 5 | 8 | 10 | 26 | 38 | 60 |
| 11 West Brom | 46 | 11 | 5 | 7 | 34 | 29 | 5 | 7 | 11 | 26 | 39 | 60 |
| 12 Port Vale | 46 | 10 | 5 | 8 | 30 | 29 | 5 | 10 | 8 | 29 | 37 | 60 |
| 13 Tranmere | 46 | 9 | 9 | 5 | 42 | 29 | 5 | 8 | 10 | 22 | 31 | 59 |
| 14 Southend | 46 | 11 | 8 | 4 | 30 | 22 | 4 | 6 | 13 | 22 | 39 | 59 |
| 15 Birmingham | 46 | 11 | 7 | 5 | 37 | 23 | 4 | 6 | 13 | 24 | 41 | 58 |
| 16 Norwich | 46 | 7 | 9 | 7 | 26 | 24 | 7 | 6 | 10 | 33 | 31 | 57 |
| 17 Grimsby | 46 | 8 | 10 | 5 | 27 | 25 | 6 | 4 | 13 | 28 | 44 | 56 |
| 18 Oldham | 46 | 10 | 7 | 6 | 33 | 20 | 4 | 7 | 12 | 21 | 30 | 56 |
| 19 Reading | 46 | 8 | 7 | 8 | 28 | 30 | 5 | 10 | 8 | 26 | 33 | 56 |
| 20 Wolves | 46 | 8 | 9 | 6 | 34 | 28 | 5 | 7 | 11 | 22 | 34 | 55 |
| 21 Portsmouth | 46 | 8 | 6 | 9 | 34 | 32 | 5 | 7 | 11 | 27 | 37 | 52 |
| 22 Millwall | 46 | 7 | 6 | 10 | 23 | 28 | 6 | 7 | 10 | 20 | 35 | 52 |
| 23 Watford | 46 | 7 | 8 | 8 | 40 | 33 | 3 | 10 | 10 | 22 | 37 | 48 |
| 24 LUTON TOWN | 46 | 7 | 6 | 10 | 30 | 34 | 4 | 6 | 13 | 10 | 30 | 45 |
| | 1104 | 233 | 177 | 142 | 804 | 613 | 142 | 177 | 233 | 613 | 804 | 1479 |

* promoted after play-offs

Odds & ends

Double wins: (1) Southend.
Double losses: (4) Barnsley, Reading, Stoke, Sunderland.

Won from behind: (2) Grimsby (h), Port Vale (h), Tranmere (h).
Lost from in front: (5) Derby (h), Reading (h & a), Stoke (h), West Brom (h).

High spots: The eight-game unbeaten run following the appointment of Lennie Lawrence as manager.
The 2-0 victory at West Brom, a beacon in a sea of gloom.
Winning 1-0 at East Anglian outposts Norwich and Ipswich.

Low spots: Winning just two of the last 17 games, which resulted in relegation.
The 1-7 humiliation at Grimsby in the FA Cup.
Going out at the first hurdle of the Coca-Cola Cup for the sixth season running.
Dwight Marshall's broken ankle at Sunderland.

Player of the Year: Ian Feuer.
Ever-presents: (0).
Hat-tricks: (0).
Leading scorer: Dwight Marshall (11).

| | Appearances | | | | | | Goals | | | |
|---|---|---|---|---|---|---|---|---|---|---|
| | **Lge** | *Sub* | LC | *Sub* | FAC | *Sub* | **Lge** | LC | FAC | **Tot** |
| Alexander, Graham | **35** | *2* | 2 | | | *1* | **1** | | | **1** |
| Chenery, Ben | **2** | | | | | | | | | |
| Davis, Kelvin | **6** | | | | | | | | | |
| Davis, Steve | **36** | | 2 | | | | **2** | | | **2** |
| Douglas, Stuart | **3** | *5* | | | | | **1** | | | **1** |
| Evers, Sean | **1** | | | | | | | | | |
| Feuer, Ian | **38** | | | | 1 | | | | | |
| Grant, Kim | **10** | | | | | | **3** | | | **3** |
| Guentchev, Bontcho | **25** | *10* | 2 | | 1 | | **9** | | | **9** |
| Harvey, Richard | **28** | *8* | 2 | | | | **1** | | | **1** |
| Hughes, Ceri | **21** | *2* | 1 | | | | **1** | | | **1** |
| James, Julian | **23** | *4* | 1 | | 1 | | | | | |
| Johnson, Gavin | **5** | *1* | | | | | | | | |
| Johnson, Marvin | **33** | *2* | 2 | | 1 | | | 1 | | **1** |
| Linton, Des | **6** | *4* | | | | | | | | |
| Marshall, Dwight | **23** | *3* | 2 | | 1 | | **9** | 1 | 1 | **11** |
| Matthews, Rob | | | | *1* | | | | | | |
| McLaren, Paul | **9** | *3* | | | 1 | | **1** | | | **1** |
| Oakes, Scott | **26** | *3* | | | 1 | | **3** | | | **3** |
| Oldfield, David | **23** | *11* | 2 | | 1 | | **2** | | | **2** |
| Patterson, Darren | **21** | *2* | | | 1 | | | | | |
| Peake, Trevor | **15** | *3* | | | | | | | | |
| Riseth, Vidar | **6** | *5* | | | | | | | | |
| Sommer, Juergen | **2** | | 2 | | | | | | | |
| Taylor, John | **18** | *10* | 2 | | | | | | | |
| Thomas, Mitchell | **25** | *2* | 1 | *1* | 1 | | | | | |
| Thorpe, Tony | **23** | *10* | | *2* | | *1* | **7** | | | **7** |
| Tomlinson, Graeme | **1** | *6* | | | | | | | | |
| Vilstrup, Johnny | **6** | *1* | | | | | | | | |
| Waddock, Gary | **32** | *4* | 1 | | 1 | | | | | |
| Wilkinson, Paul | **3** | | | | | | | | | |
| Woodsford, Jamie | **1** | *2* | | | | | | | | |
| **32 players used** | **506** | ***103*** | **22** | ***4*** | **11** | ***2*** | **40** | **2** | **1** | **43** |

| No | Date | | Att | Pos | Pt | F-A | H-T | Scorers, Times, and Referees | 1 | 2 | 3 | 4 | 5 | 6 | 7 | 8 | 9 | 10 | 11 | subs used |
|---|---|---|---|---|---|---|---|---|---|---|---|---|---|---|---|---|---|---|---|---|
| 1 | H | BURNLEY | | | L | 1-2 | 1-2 | Thorpe 36 | Feuer | James | Thomas | Waddock | Patterson* | Johnson | Guentchev | Alexander | Oldfield^ | Grant" | Thorpe | Davis/**Fotiadis**/Linton |
| | 17/8 | | 7,064 | | - | | | Thompson 23, Nogan 31 | Beresford | Parkinson | Hoyland | Harrison | Winstanley | Eyres | Matthew | Thompson | Gleghorn | Nogan | Cooke* | Robinson |
| | | | | | | | | Ref: P Rejer | Steve Thompson and Kurt Nogan take advantage of some wayward defending to put the Clarets into a commanding lead. The Town fight back and Thorpe turns David Eyres before netting with a tremendous shot. Guentchev is fouled by Eyres but Marlon Beresford saves his spot kick. | | | | | | | | | | | |
| 2 | A | BRENTFORD | | 22 | L | 2-3 | 1-0 | Thorpe 43p, Hughes 68 | Feuer | James | Thomas | Waddock | Davis | Patterson | Hughes | Alexander | Oldfield | Grant* | Thorpe | Guentchev |
| | 24/8 | | 5,409 | 3 | - | | | Asaba 65, Bates 80, Taylor 88 | Dearden | Hurdle | Ashby | Bates | Anderson | Abrahams* | Smith^ | McGee | Bent | Asaba | Taylor | Hutchings/Harvey |
| | | | | | | | | Ref: S Baines | Thorpe scores from the spot, after Oldfield is fouled, and then Hughes puts the Town 2-1 up with a deflected shot. The defence fails to clear a cross from Lee Harvey, allowing Jamie Bates to head the equaliser and Bob Taylor glances in a cross from Hurdle, two minutes from time. | | | | | | | | | | | |
| 3 | A | BRISTOL CITY | | 22 | L | **0-5** | 0-2 | [Cundy 63] | Feuer | James | Thomas | Waddock | Davis | Patterson | **Showler*** | Hughes | Oldfield^ | Grant" | Thorpe ! | Alexand'r/Guentch'v/Fotiadis |
| | 27/8 | | 7,028 | 12 | - | | | Goodridge 12, 50, Nugent 41, Goater 46, | Welch | Carey | Cundy | Shail | Barnard | Goodridge* | Owers | Kuhl | Tinnion | Nugent | Goater^ | Partridge/McLeary |
| | | | | | | | | Ref: S Bennett | The Luton defence appears to be incapable of being able to deal with any ball which is played into the area and the debacle is compounded when Thorpe is dismissed for retaliation after a foul by Darren Barnard. The Hatters only manage to get one shot on target during the entire match. | | | | | | | | | | | |
| 4 | H | ROTHERHAM | | 19 | W | 1-0 | 0-0 | Thomas 58 | Feuer | James* | Thomas | Waddock | Davis | Johnson | Hughes | Alexander | Oldfield^ | Grant" | Showler | **Upson**/Thorpe/Guentchev |
| | 31/8 | | 5,112 | 23 | 3 | | | | Cherry | Sandeman* | Monington | Richardson | Breckin | Smith | Goodwin | Garner | Berry^ | Hayward | Glover" | Hurst/Dobbin/Slawson |
| | | | | | | | | Ref: M Bailey | In a dismal game between two poor sides, the Town manage to pick up their first win of the season when full-back Mitchell Thomas powers in a header, following a free-kick from Alexander. The Millers spurn a good chance to level when Steve Slawson lobs over the bar at the end. | | | | | | | | | | | |
| 5 | A | WYCOMBE | | 15 | W | 1-0 | 0-0 | Oldfield 52 | Feuer | James | Thomas | Waddock | Davis | Johnson | Hughes | Alexander | Oldfield | Fotiadis* | Guentchev | Thorpe |
| | 7/9 | | 6,471 | 21 | 6 | | | | Parkin | Cousins | McCarthy | Evans | Bell | Carroll | Lawrence | Wilkins | Farrell | Williams* | DeSouza | Mahoney-Johnson |
| | | | | | | | | Ref: E Lomas | The Hatters open up and play all the football against a basic Wycombe side which powers the ball forward at every opportunity. The only goal comes when Fotiadis heads a cross from Thomas to Oldfield, who bundles the ball into the net. Paul McCarthy hits the bar with a shot late on. | | | | | | | | | | | |
| 6 | H | GILLINGHAM | | 14 | W | 2-1 | 1-0 | Guentchev 13, Oldfield 52 | Feuer | James | Thomas | Waddock | Davis | Johnson | Hughes | Alexander | Oldfield | Fotiadis* | Guentchev | Grant |
| | 10/9 | | 5,171 | 15 | 9 | | | Chapman 81 | Stannard | Humphrey* | Harris | Bryant | Chapman | Smith | Ratcliffe | Hessenthaler | Piper | Fort'-West | Butler^ | Onoura/Bailey |
| | | | | | | | | Ref: C Wilkes | Guentchev flicks in a cross from Davis and then Oldfield is the first to react when a fierce shot from Hughes rebounds off keeper Jim Stannard to put the Town into a two goal lead against a physical Gillingham side. Ian Chapman pulls a goal back to create an anxious last few minutes. | | | | | | | | | | | |
| 7 | H | CHESTERFIELD | | 12 | L | 0-1 | 0-1 | | Feuer | James | Thomas | Waddock | Davis | Johnson | Hughes | Alexander | Oldfield* | Fotiadis^ | Guentchev | Showler/Grant |
| | 14/9 | | 5,292 | 3 | 9 | | | Curtis 26p | Mercer | Hewitt | Williams | Dyche | Rogers | Gaughan | Curtis | Holland | Jules | Davies | Morris* | Lormor |
| | | | | | | | | Ref: R Furnandiz | Marvin Johnson needlessly handles a cross shot from Tom Curtis who then nets the resultant spot kick to give the visitors the lead. Chesterfield have won their last two away games by the same score and, well organised, they defend in depth all afternoon to frustrate the Town forwards. | | | | | | | | | | | |
| 8 | A | BURY | | 15 | D | 0-0 | 0-0 | | Feuer | James | Thomas | Waddock | Davis | Johnson | Hughes | Alexander | Oldfield | Fotiadis* | Guentchev | Douglas |
| | 21/9 | | 3,588 | 5 | 10 | | | | Kiely | West | Armstrong | Daws | Butler | Jackson | Johnson* | Hughes | Jepson | Johnrose | Carter^ | Matthews/Stant |
| | | | | | | | | Ref: I Cruikshanks/G Edgley | The Town become the first side to visit Gigg Lane and keep a clean sheet this season. In a battling performance, which makes for a dour game, the chances are few but Johnson is required to clear a header from Mark Carter off the line. The game reaches a stalemate long before the end. | | | | | | | | | | | |
| 9 | H | BLACKPOOL | | 12 | W | 1-0 | 1-0 | Grant 16 | Feuer | James | Thomas | Waddock | Davis | Johnson | Thorpe | Alexander | Oldfield* | Grant^ | Guentchev | Douglas/Fotiadis |
| | 28/9 | | 5,785 | 13 | 13 | | | | Banks | Bryan* | Dixon | Lydiate | Linighan | Brabin | Bonner | Mellon | Quinn^ | Ellis | Onwere" | Butler/Barlow/Preece |
| | | | | | | | | Ref: M Fletcher | The Town put up a battling performance in the first half as Thorpe hits the post and Banks makes several good saves. Linighan loses possession of the ball to Oldfield in the area. His shot is parried but Grant hits home the rebound. Grant then heads against the bar in the second period. | | | | | | | | | | | |
| 10 | H | WALSALL | | 11 | W | 3-1 | 1-0 | Thorpe 44, Showler 60, Fotiadis 69 | Feuer | James | Thomas | Waddock | Davis | Johnson | Thorpe | Alexander | Fotiadis* | Hughes^ | Guentchev" | Douglas/McLaren/Showler |
| | 5/10 | | 5,456 | 18 | 16 | | | Lightbourne 70 | Wood | Ntamark | Marsh | Viveash | Butler* | Mountfield | Blake | Keister | Lightbourne | Wilson | Hodge^ | Bradley/Daniel"/Watson |
| | | | | | | | | Ref: B Knight | An astute pass from Hughes allows Thorpe to open the scoring against the run of play. After the break, Showler dives full length to head the second and Andrew Fotiadis gets the third when he lobs Trevor Wood from 25 yards. A 20-yard response from Carl Lightbourne is admirable. | | | | | | | | | | | |
| 11 | A | SHREWSBURY | | 8 | W | 3-0 | 1-0 | Showler 3, Thomas 58, Grant 88 | Feuer | James* | Thomas | Waddock | Davis | Johnson | Hughes | Alexander | Thorpe^ | Grant | Showler | McLar'n/Douglas"/Guentch'v |
| | 12/10 | | 3,357 | 14 | 19 | | | | Gall | Seabury | Nielsen | Currie* | Spink | Scott | Rowbotham | Stevens | Anthrobus | Walton | Dempsey | Berkley^/Taylor |
| | | | | | | | | Ref: R Poulain | Feuer makes a brilliant diving save before Showler touches in a shot by Alexander and, after Thomas heads home a corner by Alexander, it is one-way traffic. Substitute Douglas is clattered, as he heads on the ball for Kim Grant to score in the closing minutes, and suffers concussion. | | | | | | | | | | | |

| No | H/A | Opponent / Date | Att | Pos | Res / Pts | FT | HT | Scorers, Times, Referees | 1 | 2 | 3 | 4 | 5 | 6 | 7 | 8 | 9 | 10 | 11 | subs used |
|---|---|---|---|---|---|---|---|---|---|---|---|---|---|---|---|---|---|---|---|---|
| 12 | A | STOCKPORT | | 8 | D | 1-1 | 1-0 | Davis 26 | Feuer | James | Thomas | Waddock | Davis | Johnson | Hughes | Alexander | Thorpe* | Grant | Showler | Oldfield |
| | | 15/10 | *5,352* | *11* | 20 | | | *Angell 57* | *Jones* | *Connelly* | *Flynn* | *Gannon* | *Todd* | *Durkan** | *Bennett* | *Marsden* | *Jeffers* | *Angell* | *Mutch* | *Cavaco* |
| | | | | | | | | Ref: D Laws | The Town find the home side a much tougher proposition than Shrewsbury but take the lead when Davis heads home a corner from Alexander, midway through the first period. After the interval, Stockport batter the Luton defence and, after four quick corners, Brett Angell equalises. | | | | | | | | | | | |
| 13 | H | PETERBOROUGH | | 7 | W | 3-0 | 2-0 | Davis 10, Showler 24, 54 | Feuer | James | Thomas | Waddock | Davis | Johnson | Hughes* | Alexander | Oldfield^ | Thorpe" | Showler | McLaren/Fotiadis/Guentchev |
| | | 19/10 | 6,387 | *19* | 23 | | | | *Sheffield* | *Huxford* | *Drury* | *O'Connor* | *Heald* | *Clark* | *Ebdon* | *Payne** | *Rowe^* | *Charlery"* | *Houghton* | *Willis/Griffith/Regis* |
| | | | | | | | | Ref: R Pearson | The Posh defence is all over the place as the Town score two almost identical goals from corner kicks. Paul Showler hits his second goal of the game after a shot from Tony Thorpe is blocked. Ian Feuer has little to do but does have to react quickly to stop a drive from Richard Huxford. | | | | | | | | | | | |
| 14 | H | BOURNEMOUTH | | 5 | W | 2-0 | 0-0 | Thorpe 58p, 60 | Feuer | James | Thomas | Waddock | Johnson | Skelton | Thorpe | Alexander* | Oldfield^ | Hughes | Showler" | McLaren/Douglas/Guentchev |
| | | 26/10 | 6,086 | *19* | 26 | | | | *Marshall* | *Young* | *Beardsmore* | *Coll** | *Cox* | *Bailey^* | *Holland* | *Robinson* | *Fletcher* | *Omoyimni* | *Dean"* | *Howe/O'Neill/Watson* |
| | | | | | | | | Ref: C Finch | Ian Feuer makes two tremendous saves, firstly from Matt Holland and then Steve Robinson. Tony Thorpe scores from the spot after he is rashly challenged in the area by Owen Coll and then, two minutes later, seizes on a weak back-pass by Ian Cox to extend the unbeaten run to seven. | | | | | | | | | | | |
| 15 | A | WATFORD | | 5 | D | 1-1 | 0-0 | Showler 76 | Feuer | James | Thomas | Waddock | Davis | Johnson | Hughes | Alexander | Oldfield* | Thorpe | Showler | Douglas |
| | | 29/10 | *14,109* | *6* | 27 | | | *Bazeley 92* | *Miller* | *Gibbs* | *Millen* | *Page* | *Ludden** | *Bazeley* | *Johnson* | *Palmer* | *Mooney* | *Andrews^* | *White"* | *Robinson/Penrice/Williams* |
| | | | | | | | | Ref: T West | After a poor first half, the game springs to life and an expert right-foot drive into the roof of the net from Paul Showler opens the scoring. The Town hit the woodwork three times as they dominate but the referee inexplicably plays injury time and Bazeley gets an undeserved equaliser. | | | | | | | | | | | |
| 16 | A | PLYMOUTH | | 8 | D | 3-3 | 1-1 | Thorpe 9, 64, 86 | Feuer | James | Thomas ! | Waddock | Davis | Johnson | Hughes | Alexander | Douglas* | Thorpe | Showler^ | Grant/Guentchev |
| | | 2/11 | *7,134* | *14* | 28 | | | *Mauge 32, Evans 71p, 74* | *Grobbelaar* | *Billy** | *Williams* | *Mauge^* | *Heathcote* | *James* | *Simpson* | *Curran* | *Illman"* | *Evans* | *Barlow* | *Rowbotham/Leadbitter/Phillips* |
| | | | | | | | | Ref: A Wiley | At a wet and windswept Home Park, the Town move in to a 2-1 lead before Mitchell Thomas is dismissed when he handles the ball on the line. Mike Evans levels from the spot and then puts Argyle into the lead, shortly afterwards. Thorpe completes his hat-trick from a cross by Grant. | | | | | | | | | | | |
| 17 | H | NOTTS CO | | 5 | W | 2-0 | 2-0 | Thorpe 21, Hughes 22 | Feuer | James | Thomas | Waddock | Davis | Johnson | Hughes | Alexander | Grant | Thorpe* | Guentchev | Douglas |
| | | 9/11 | 6,134 | *21* | 31 | | | | *Ward* | *Wilder* | *Walker* | *Hogg* | *Strodder* | *Derry* | *Kennedy* | *Robinson* | *Farrell* | *Jones* | *Agana* | |
| | | | | | | | | Ref: M Bailey | The Hatters score twice in a minute, midway through the first half, firstly when Thorpe takes a pass from Grant and shoots on the turn and then a 40-yard free-kick from Hughes, which confuses everyone and ends up in the back of the net. The Magpies hardly trouble the Luton defence. | | | | | | | | | | | |
| 18 | A | PRESTON | | 6 | L | 2-3 | 1-2 | Davis 44, 89 | Feuer | James | Thomas | Waddock* | Davis | Johnson | Hughes | Alexander | Douglas^ | Guentchev" | Showler | McLaren/Marshall/Skelton |
| | | 19/11 | *7,004* | *20* | 31 | | | *Moyes 35, 40, Ashcroft 88* | *Mimms* | *Sparrow* | *Wilcox* | *Moyes* | *Kidd* | *Ashcroft* | *Rankine* | *McDonald* | *Kilbane* | *Reeves* | *Wilkinson** | *Holt* |
| | | | | | | | | Ref: D Laws | David Moyes heads two goals, both from corner kicks, to put the home side into a comfortable lead. Steve Davis pulls one back, just before the interval but Lee Ashcroft adds a third near the end. Davis scores a late consolation as the Hatters suffer their first defeat for over two months. | | | | | | | | | | | |
| 19 | H | BRISTOL ROV | | 4 | W | 2-1 | 1-0 | Marshall 29, Thorpe 89p | Feuer | James | Thomas | McLaren | Davis | Johnson | Hughes | Alexander | Marshall* | Thorpe | Showler^ | Grant/Guentchev |
| | | 23/11 | 5,791 | *14* | 34 | | | *Harris 80* | *Collett* | *Pritchard* | *Power* | *Clark* | *Lockwood* | *Gurney* | *Browning* | *Hayfield* | *Archer* | *Beadle* | *Cureton** | *Harris* |
| | | | | | | | | Ref: G Pooley | Marshall returns to the team, after breaking his ankle in February, and converts a clever pass from Thorpe. The Town are not at their best and an equaliser by Jason Harris appears to have saved a point for Rovers. Marcus Browning handles in the last minute and Thorpe nets the penalty. | | | | | | | | | | | |
| 20 | A | BOURNEMOUTH | | 6 | L | 2-3 | 2-1 | James 23, Marshall 44 | Feuer | James | Thomas | Skelton* | Davis | Johnson | Hughes | Alexander | Showler^ | Thorpe" | Marshall | Linton/Guentchev/Grant |
| | | 30/11 | *4,322* | *17* | 34 | | | *Robinson 16, 80, Cox 77* | *Glass* | *Young* | *Ferdinand* | *Cox* | *Vincent* | *Gordon** | *Dean^* | *Holland* | *O'Neill"* | *Robinson* | *Brissett* | *Murray/Rawlinson/Christie* |
| | | | | | | | | Ref: J Brandwood | The Hatters recover from a one goal deficit to take an interval lead through a 25-yard strike from James and a brilliant near-post header from Marshall. The defence then seems to collapse, under pressure from a long ball assault, which brings about the unlikely victory for the Cherries. | | | | | | | | | | | |
| 21 | H | YORK | | 4 | W | 2-0 | 0-0 | Marshall 47, Thorpe 69 | Feuer | James | Thomas | McLaren | Davis | Johnson | Hughes | Alexander | Showler | Thorpe | Marshall* | Grant |
| | | 3/12 | **4,987** | *14* | 37 | | | | *Clarke* | *McMillan* | *Tutill* | *Barras* | *Murty* | *Stephenson* | *Pepper* | *Pouton** | *Himsworth^* | *Tolson"* | *Bull* | *Randall/Atkinson/Cresswell* |
| | | | | | | | | Ref: D Orr | The Town are kept at bay in the first half by a competent York defence who have kept a clean sheet in each of their four previous games. After the break, a header from Thorpe is parried by Clarke, Marshall hitting in the rebound. A swift passing movement leaves Thorpe clear to score. | | | | | | | | | | | |
| 22 | H | CREWE | | 3 | W | **6-0** | 3-0 | Alexander 2, Thorpe 20, 29p, 60, [Showler 64, Oldfield 89] | Feuer | James | Thomas | Waddock | Davis | Johnson | McLaren | Alexander | Showler | Thorpe* | Marshall^ | Oldfield/Grant |
| | | 14/12 | 5,977 | *11* | 40 | | | | *Kearton* | *Barr** | *Westwood !* | *Macauley* | *Smith !* | *Garvey^* | *Charnock* | *Murphy* | *Launders* | *Adebola* | *Moralee"* | *Unsworth/Little/Billing* |
| | | | | | | | | Ref: S Bennett | Shaun Smith is dismissed after bringing down Dwight Marshall in the box with Tony Thorpe converting the penalty for the third goal. Ashley Westwood is sent off after 75 minutes for a second yellow card offence when he fouls Thorpe. The Town are now leading scorers in the league. | | | | | | | | | | | |
| 23 | A | MILLWALL | | 1 | W | 1-0 | 0-0 | Hughes 89 | Feuer | James | Thomas | Waddock | Davis | Johnson | Hughes | Alexander | Marshall* | Thorpe | Guentchev | Oldfield |
| | | 18/12 | *7,077* | *2* | 43 | | | | *Carter* | *Sinclair* | *Lavin* | *Rogan* | *van Blerk* | *Hartley** | *Newman* | *Neill^* | *Dair"* | *Bright* | *Crawford* | *Savage/Dolby/Harle* |
| | | | | | | | | Ref: G Singh | The defence keeps the game tight and pushes well up the field. Thorpe misses three good chances before, in the final few seconds, Ceri Hughes dispossesses David Sinclair and fires in a shot from the edge of the area which squeezes into the far corner. Luton are now top of the league. | | | | | | | | | | | |

| No | Date | Opponent | Att | Pos | Pt | F-A | H-T | Scorers, Times, and Referees | 1 | 2 | 3 | 4 | 5 | 6 | 7 | 8 | 9 | 10 | 11 | subs used |
|---|---|---|---|---|---|---|---|---|---|---|---|---|---|---|---|---|---|---|---|---|
| 24 | A 26/12 | GILLINGHAM | 8,491 | 2 21 | W 46 | 2-1 | 1-1 | Thorpe 23, 51 | Feuer | James | Thomas | Waddock | Davis | Johnson | Hughes | Alexander | Guentchev | Thorpe | Marshall* | Oldfield |
| | | | | | | | | Onoura 25 | Stannard | Bryant | Green | Butters | Smith | Hessenthaler | Pennock | Ratcliffe* | O'Connor^ | Onoura | Butler | Manuel/Piper |
| | | | | | | | | Ref: P Rejer | Thorpe intercepts a poor back-pass by Steve Butler to put the Town into the lead but Iffy Onoura hammers the equaliser. Thorpe nets with an angled drive and, in injury time, a raised arm by Guentchev gives Hessenthaler the chance to fall over in the area but Feuer saves the spot kick. | | | | | | | | | | | |
| 25 | H 18/1 | WREXHAM | 6,167 | 2 10 | D 47 | 0-0 | 0-0 | | Feuer | James | Thomas | McLaren* | Davis | Johnson | Hughes | Alexander | Showler^ | Thorpe | Marshall" | Linton/Guentchev/Oldfield |
| | | | | | | | | | Marriott | McGregor | Humes | Carey | Hardy | Chalk | Hughes | Ward | Owen | Connolly | Watkin | |
| | | | | | | | | Ref: R Styles | This is the first league game for the Town for over three weeks, due to the recent bad weather. Wrexham appear to have done their homework and defend in depth, preventing the Hatters from playing and creating a couple of scoring opportunities. Luton are now second in the league. | | | | | | | | | | | |
| 26 | H 27/1 | WATFORD | 7,977 | 2 11 | D 48 | 0-0 | 0-0 | | Feuer | James | Thomas | Linton | Davis | Johnson | Hughes | Alexander | Showler | Thorpe | Marshall* | Oldfield |
| | | | | | | | | | Miller | Bazeley | Ward | Page | Gibbs | Slater | Palmer | Johnson | Armstrong | Connolly* | White | Andrews |
| | | | | | | | | Ref: M Pierce | This is a typical local derby, with plenty of activity but little good football to please the live television audience. Watford have gone 21 games without defeat with most of these being drawn and this is reflected by the way in which they pack their defence and keep two men on Thorpe. | | | | | | | | | | | |
| 27 | A 1/2 | NOTTS CO | 4,866 | 2 23 | W 51 | 2-1 | 0-0 | Hughes 65, Alexander 87 | Feuer | James | Thomas | Linton* | Davis | Johnson | Hughes | Alexander | Oldfield | Thorpe^ | Guentchev | Marshall/Grant |
| | | | | | | | | Richardson 61 | Ward | Redmile | Hogg* | Strodder | Wilder | Robinson | Derry | Richardson^ | Baraclough | Battersby | Jones" | Finnan/Martindale/Ridgeway |
| | | | | | | | | Ref: T West | The Hatters amble around against lowly County but a careless clearance by Hughes is intercepted by Phil Robinson who sets up Richardson for an easy finish. Hughes makes reparation with a 30-yard drive that should have been saved by Ward and Alexander hits the winner near the end. | | | | | | | | | | | |
| 28 | H 8/2 | PLYMOUTH | 6,827 | 2 19 | D 52 | 2-2 | 0-0 | Thorpe 56, 61 | Feuer | James | Thomas | Evers* | Davis | Johnson | Guentchev | Alexander | Oldfield | Thorpe | Marshall^ | Linton/Fotiadis |
| | | | | | | | | Littlejohn 58, Evans 68 | Grobbelaar | Logan | James | Heathcote | Billy | Corazzin | Barlow | Saunders | Williams* | Littlejohn | Evans | Mauge |
| | | | | | | | | Ref: T Lunt | The Town seem to be heavily reliant on the goalscoring abilities of Thorpe as they seem to be unable to reproduce their pre-Christmas form. Mick Evans, shortly to go to Southampton, is lively although his spot kick, awarded after Evers grabs the shirt of Saunders, is saved by Feuer. | | | | | | | | | | | |
| 29 | A 15/2 | BRISTOL ROV | 5,612 | 2 18 | L 52 | 2-3 | 1-1 | Thorpe 9p, Waddock 63 | Feuer | James | Thomas* | McLaren | Davis | Johnson | Guentchev ! | Alexander | Oldfield^ | Thorpe | Linton" | Marshall/Fotiadis/Waddock |
| | | | | | | | | Miller 22, Tillson 46, Holloway 53 | Collett | Pritchard | White | Tillson | Lockwood | Miller* | Holloway | Skinner | Archer | Beadle^ | Cureton | Hayfield/Alsop |
| | | | | | | | | Ref: F Stretton | Thorpe is brought down by Tom White in the area and he nets from the spot before slack defending allows Rovers to level. Guentchev is sent off for using his elbow on Dave Pritchard but the ten-men appear to be holding out until more defensive errors gives the Pirates the advantage. | | | | | | | | | | | |
| 30 | H 22/2 | PRESTON | 6,896 | 2 18 | W 55 | 5-1 | 4-0 | Oldfield 23, 33, 38, Waddock 44, [Thomas 72] | Feuer | James | Thomas | Waddock | Davis | Johnson | Hughes* | Alexander | Oldfield^ | Thorpe" | Showler | McLaren/Marshall/Grant |
| | | | | | | | | Reeves 46 | O'Hanlon | Moyes* | Teale | Gregan | Rankine | McDonald^ | McKenna | Davey | Bryson | Reeves | Stallard | Barrick/Kilbane |
| | | | | | | | | Ref: C Wilkes | The team is back to full strength for the first time since Christmas and a hat-trick in fifteen minutes from David Oldfield settles the game before the interval. He opens the scoring with a header and then strikes with both a left and right foot shot as the Town bounce back to their best form. | | | | | | | | | | | |
| 31 | A 1/3 | YORK | 3,788 | 2 20 | D 56 | 1-1 | 1-0 | Davis 11 | Feuer | James | Thomas* | Waddock | Davis | Johnson | Hughes | Alexander | Oldfield^ | Thorpe | Showler | McLaren/Marshall |
| | | | | | | | | Tolson 48 | Warrington | McMillan | Barras | Sharples | Himsworth | Jordan | Bushell | Pouton | Tolson | Rowe | Bull | |
| | | | | | | | | Ref: T Heilbron | A thumping header from Steve Davis following a cross by Hughes opens the scoring for a confident Hatters side who seem to be well in control until Thomas goes off with a broken nose. The defence and mid-field are reorganised, leading to Neil Tolson hitting a powerful drive to level. | | | | | | | | | | | |
| 32 | A 4/3 | CHESTERFIELD | 3,731 | 2 12 | D 57 | 1-1 | 1-1 | Thorpe 40p | Feuer | James | Patterson | Waddock | Davis | Johnson | Hughes | Alexander | Oldfield* | Thorpe | Showler | Grant |
| | | | | | | | | Davies 15 | Mercer | Jules | Williams | Carr | Perkins | Dunn | Patterson | Hewitt | Beaumont | Gaughan* | Davies | Howard |
| | | | | | | | | Ref: P Richards | At a very foggy Saltergate, Kevin Davies is unmarked when he heads in a cross from Chris Beaumont. Tony Thorpe falls over after a tussle with Chris Perkins and then slams home the resultant penalty. The half-time interval is extended to 30 minutes to allow the visibility to improve. | | | | | | | | | | | |
| 33 | H 8/3 | MILLWALL | 9,109 | 2 3 | L 57 | 0-2 | 0-0 | | Feuer | James ! | Patterson | Waddock* | Davis | Johnson | Hughes^ | Alexander | Oldfield" | Thorpe | Showler | McLaren/Marshall/Grant |
| | | | | | | | | Dolby 78, Hartley 88 | Carter | Neill | McLeary | Witter | Berry | Hartley | Savage | Doyle | Roche* | Dolby | Crawford | Sadlier |
| | | | | | | | | Ref: G Frankland | Julian James is dismissed on 25 minutes for a second bookable offence but the players raise their game and hit the woodwork four times in a scintillating performance. The ball will not go into the net for Luton but Dolby hits home a 20-yard free-kick and Hartley nets another late on. | | | | | | | | | | | |
| 34 | A 12/3 | WREXHAM | 3,392 | 2 11 | L 57 | 1-2 | 1-1 | Davis 22 | Feuer | James | Patterson | Waddock* | Davis | Johnson | Hughes | Alexander | Oldfield^ | Thorpe" | Showler | McLaren/Grant/Marshall |
| | | | | | | | | Bennett 23p, 56 | Marriott | McGregor | Humes | Carey | Brace* | Chalk | Owen | Phillips | Russell | Watkin | Bennett | Jones |
| | | | | | | | | Ref: E Lomas | A header from Steve Davis gets the Town off to a perfect start but Marvin Johnson brings down Martyn Chalk, shortly afterwards, which leaves Gary Bennett to equalise from the penalty spot. Bennett scores the winner at the third attempt, after his first two efforts are both blocked. | | | | | | | | | | | |

| No | Venue | Opponent | Att | Pos | Res | F-A | H-T | Scorers, Times, Referees | 1 | 2 | 3 | 4 | 5 | 6 | 7 | 8 | 9 | 10 | 11 | Subs used |
|---|---|---|---|---|---|---|---|---|---|---|---|---|---|---|---|---|---|---|---|---|
| 35 | A | CREWE | | 2 | D | 0-0 | 0-0 | | Feuer | James | Patterson | Waddock | Davis | Johnson | Hughes | Alexander | Oldfield | Thorpe | McLaren | |
| | 15/3 | | *4,474* | *5* | 58 | | | | *Kearton* | *Unsworth* | *Lightfoot* | *Westwood* | *Smith S* | *Barr** | *Savage* | *Murphy* | *Whalley* | *Garvey* | *Rivers^* | *Smith P/Tierney* |
| | | | | | | | | Ref: B Coddington | The two defences cancel each other out in a game in which both sides are determined not to lose. The Hatters show grit and determination and carve out the best chance of the match but David Oldfield hits the bar. Both of the managers seem to be pleased with the share of the points. | | | | | | | | | | | |
| 36 | H | BRENTFORD | | 1 | W | 1-0 | 1-0 | Thorpe 65 | Feuer | James | Thomas | Waddock | Davis | Johnson | Hughes | Alexander | Oldfield | Thorpe* | Showler^ | Grant/McLaren |
| | 21/3 | | 8,680 | *2* | 61 | | | | *Dearden* | *Hutchings* | *Ashby* | *Bates* | *Anderson* | *Bent** | *Smith* | *McGhee* | *Asaba* | *Taylor* | *Omigie* | *Dennis* |
| | | | | | | | | Ref: P Taylor | Brentford demonstrate why they have the best away record in the division as they put the Hatters under enormous pressure for the first quarter of an hour. After the break, Thorpe takes a short pass from Showler, turns defender Jamie Bates and rifles home a shot into the bottom corner. | | | | | | | | | | | |
| 37 | A | BURNLEY | | 2 | W | 2-0 | 2-0 | Thorpe 13, 38 | Feuer | **McGowan*** | Thomas | Waddock | Davis | Johnson | McLaren | Alexander | Oldfield | Thorpe | **Kiwomya^** | Guentchev/Marshall |
| | 29/3 | | ***15,490*** | *6* | 64 | | | | *Beresford* | *Winstanley* | *Brass* | *Hoyland** | *Parkinson* | *Weller* | *Thompson^* | *Matthew* | *Smith* | *Barnes* | *Cooke* | *Little/Guinan* |
| | | | | | | | | Ref: T Jones | Thorpe fires a shot into the far corner of the net, after the ball is deflected into his path, and is again on target when he receives a flick-on from Mitchell Thomas, following a corner from Alexander. Burnley hit back in the second half but good goalkeeping from Feuer keeps them at bay. | | | | | | | | | | | |
| 38 | H | BRISTOL CITY | | 2 | D | 2-2 | 1-2 | Davis 44, Thorpe 73 | Feuer | McGowan* | Thomas | Waddock | Davis | Johnson | Hughes | Alexander | Oldfield^ | Thorpe | Guentchev" | McLaren/Grant/Marshall |
| | 1/4 | | 7,550 | *9* | 65 | | | *Goater 4, Agostino 40* | *Welch* | *Carey* | *Shail* | *Paterson* | *Owers* | *Brennan* | *Allen* | *Kuhl* | *Hewlett* | *Agostino** | *Goater^* | *Bent/Nugent* |
| | | | | | | | | Ref: G Singh | Agostino is fouled by Johnson, in the area, and Shaun Goater scores from a rebound after his spot kick is blocked by Ian Feuer. Agostino again catches the Town on the break but Davis pulls one back, just before the interval. Thorpe heads in a Hughes corner but Oldfield misses late on. | | | | | | | | | | | |
| 39 | A | ROTHERHAM | | 2 | W | 3-0 | 2-0 | Thorpe 5, 41, 79 | Feuer | James | Thomas | Waddock | Davis | Johnson* | Hughes | Alexander | Oldfield | Thorpe^ | McLaren" | Patterson/Marshall/Grant |
| | 5/4 | | ***2,609*** | *23* | 68 | | | | *Pilkington* | *Breckin* | *Bain* | *Dillon** | *Bowman* | *Haywood* | *Garner* | *McGlashan* | *Roscoe^* | *Landon"* | *McDougald* | *Hurst/McKenzie/Judejean* |
| | | | | | | | | Ref: I Cruikshanks | Tony Thorpe becomes the first Luton player to hit 30 goals in a season since the days of Malcolm MacDonald when he nets a hat-trick against a poor Rotherham side. Alexander and James provide the crosses for two headed goals and a 30-yard chip over the keeper completes the rout. | | | | | | | | | | | |
| 40 | H | WYCOMBE | | 3 | D | 0-0 | 0-0 | | Feuer | James | Thomas | Waddock | Davis | Johnson | Hughes | Alexander | Oldfield* | Thorpe | McLaren^ | Marshall/Grant |
| | 8/4 | | 8,117 | *21* | 69 | | | | *Taylor* | *Cousins* | *Forsyth* | *McCarthy* | *Kavanagh* | *Bell* | *Carroll* | *Brown* | *McGavin* | *Stallard** | *Scott* | *Read* |
| | | | | | | | | Ref: R Furnandiz | Wycombe opt for a back five and make no pretence that they have come to Kenilworth Road for anything other than a single point in their fight to avoid relegation. Thorpe has two efforts disallowed and Davis goes close with a header but the Town run out of ideas as the game is stifled. | | | | | | | | | | | |
| 41 | A | WALSALL | | 3 | L | 2-3 | 0-1 | Kiwomya 53, Davis 55 | Feuer | James | Thomas | Waddock* | Davis | Johnson^ | McLaren | Alexander | Oldfield" | Thorpe | Kiwomya | Guentch'v/Patterson/Fotiadis |
| | 12/4 | | *5,415* | *7* | 69 | | | *Lightbourne 18, 60, Hodge 76* | *Walker* | *Evans* | *Mountfield* | *Viveash* | *Blake* | *Hodge** | *Watson* | *Keister* | *Butler* | *Wilson^* | *Lightbourne* | *Ntamark/Beckford* |
| | | | | | | | | Ref: A Leake | Lightbourne gives the home side the lead when he heads past Feuer at the second attempt. Loan signing, Kiwomya curls in a 25-yard free-kick which is quickly followed by a Davis header but Lightbourne and Hodge score as the Town throw away the lead for the tenth time this season. | | | | | | | | | | | |
| 42 | A | BLACKPOOL | | 3 | D | 0-0 | 0-0 | | Feuer | James | Thomas | Waddock | Davis | Johnson | McLaren | Fotiadis | Oldfield | Thorpe | Kiwomya* | Marshall |
| | 15/4 | | *4,382* | *12* | 70 | | | | *Banks* | *Bryan* | *Brabin* | *Linighan* | *Barlow* | *Lydiate* | *Mellon* | *Bonner** | *Clarkson* | *Preece^* | *Ellis* | *Ormerod/Philpott* |
| | | | | | | | | Ref: A Bates | The Hatters show more discipline than they did at Walsall but neither side looks likely to win in a game which is dominated by the respective defences. Goal-mouth excitement is rare although Thorpe misses an early opportunity and Tony Ellis spurns a similar chance for the Seasiders. | | | | | | | | | | | |
| 43 | H | SHREWSBURY | | 3 | W | 2-0 | 1-0 | Thorpe 44p, Marshall 74 | Feuer | James | Thomas | Waddock | Davis | Johnson | McLaren* | Alexander | Oldfield | Thorpe | Fotiadis^ | Marshall/Harvey |
| | 19/4 | | 7,501 | *21* | 73 | | | | *Edwards* | *Blamey* | *Walton** | *Taylor L* | *Dempsey* | *Taylor M* | *Evans* | *Seabury* | *Currie* | *Spink* | *Stevens* | *Brown* |
| | | | | | | | | Ref: C Foy | The Hatters are less than convincing against lowly Shrewsbury and have a let off when Thomas tries to pull down Ian Stevens in the area. The referee waves play on but the forward sees his shot saved by Feuer. Lee Taylor trips Fotiadis and Thorpe notches his eighth penalty this season. | | | | | | | | | | | |
| 44 | H | BURY | | 3 | D | 0-0 | 0-0 | | Feuer | James | Thomas | Waddock | Davis | Johnson | Hughes | Alexander* | Fotiadis | Thorpe | Kiwomya^ | Marshall/Oldfield |
| | 22/4 | | 8,281 | *1* | 74 | | | | *Kiely* | *West* | *Lucketti* | *Armstrong* | *Butler* | *Reid** | *Daws* | *Hughes* | *Johnrose* | *Battersby^* | *Jepson* | *Johnson/Carter* |
| | | | | | | | | Ref: A D'Urso | The last hopes of automatic promotion seem to die in the depths of an eight-man Bury defence which kills the game and enables the visitors to go home with the single point that they wanted. Bury are the only club to keep a clean sheet in both league games against the Town this season. | | | | | | | | | | | |
| 45 | A | PETERBOROUGH | | 3 | W | 1-0 | 0-0 | Fotiadis 53 | Feuer | James | Thomas | Waddock | Davis | Johnson | Hughes | Alexander | Oldfield | Thorpe | Kiwomya* | Fotiadis |
| | 26/4 | | *9,499* | *22* | 77 | | | | *Griemink* | *Neal* | *Bodley* | *Edwards* | *Clark* | *Donowa** | *Bullimore* | *Linton* | *Otto^* | *Willis* | *DeSouza"* | *Rowe/Carter/Heald* |
| | | | | | | | | Ref: B Knight | On a mud-bath of a pitch, Posh miss many first half chances as they desperately attempt to avoid the drop. Only good saves from Feuer, a goal-line clearance from James and poor shooting keeps the game goalless at half-time. Fotiadis scores the games only goal from an Oldfield cross. | | | | | | | | | | | |
| 46 | H | STOCKPORT | | 3 | D | 1-1 | 1-1 | Fotiadis 38 | Feuer | James | Thomas | Waddock | Patterson | Johnson | McLaren | Alexander | Oldfield | Fotiadis* | Harvey^ | Marshall/Grant |
| | 3/5 | | **9,623** | *2* | 78 | | | *Cooper 7p* | *Jones* | *Connelly* | *Flynn* | *Gannon* | *Todd* | *Durkan** | *Bennett* | *Marsden* | *Cooper* | *Angell^* | *Armstrong* | *Mutch/Charlery* |
| | Home | | Away | | | | | Ref: D Orr | Stockport are already promoted and the Hatters are in the play-offs which provides for a carnival end to the season. Feuer upends Armstrong allowing Cooper to convert the spot kick but Fotiadis equalises when running on to a clearance from Johnson and lobbing the advancing keeper. | | | | | | | | | | | |
| Average | 6,781 | | 6,200 | | | | | | | | | | | | | | | | | |

| Play-offs | | | | F-A | H-T | Scorers, Times, and Referees | 1 | 2 | 3 | 4 | 5 | 6 | 7 | 8 | 9 | 10 | 11 | subs used |
|---|---|---|---|---|---|---|---|---|---|---|---|---|---|---|---|---|---|---|
| SF: A | CREWE | | L | 1-2 | 1-0 | Oldfield 3 | Feuer | James ! | Thomas | Waddock* | Davis | Patterson | McLaren | Alexander | Oldfield | Thorpe | Fotiadis^ | Marshall/Grant |
| 1 11/5 | | *5,467* | | | | *Rivers 52, Little 67* | *Kearton* | *Unsworth* | *Westwood* | *Macauley* | *Smith* | *Murphy* | *Charnock* | *Whalley* | *Little** | *Adebola* | *Rivers^* | *Johnson/Tierney* |
| | | | | | | Ref: T Heilbron | Oldfield puts the Hatters into an early lead but, with Hughes and Johnson both missing the match through injury and Waddock going off after eight minutes with a gashed leg it is all uphill. Rivers levels before James is sent off for a second bookable offence and then Little gains the win. | | | | | | | | | | | |
| SF: H | CREWE | | D | 2-2 | 2-1 | Oldfield 19, 30 | Feuer | Patterson | Thomas | Waddock* | Davis | Johnson | McLaren | Alexander | Oldfield | Thorpe | Showler^ | Fotiadis/Marshall |
| 2 14/5 | | 8,168 | | | | *Little 32, Smith 62* | *Kearton* | *Unsworth** | *Smith* | *Westwood* | *Macauley* | *Charnock* | *Whalley* | *Little* | *Rivers^* | *Murphy"* | *Adebola* | *Johnson/Garvey/Lightfoot* |
| | | | | | | Ref: R Pearson (Hatters lost 3-4 on aggregate) | After some early pressure from Crewe, Oldfield fires home a cross from Showler and then scores again after a clever back-heel from Thorpe. Little reduces the deficit and Smith equalises soon after half-time as the Wembley dream dies against an admittedly superior footballing side. | | | | | | | | | | | |

| Coca-Cola Cup | | | | | | | | | | | | | | | | | | |
|---|---|---|---|---|---|---|---|---|---|---|---|---|---|---|---|---|---|---|
| 1:1 H | BRISTOL ROV | | W | 3-0 | 1-0 | Thorpe 44p, Grant 55, Oldfield 56 | Feuer | James* | Thomas | Waddock ! | Davis | Johnson^ | Hughes | Alexander | Oldfield | Grant | Thorpe" | Guentchev/Patterson/Showler |
| 20/8 | | 2,643 | | | | | *Collett* | *Martin* | *Clark* | *Tillson* | *Lockwood* | *Gurney** | *Browning* | *Holloway* | *Archer* | *Miller^* | *Beadle* | *Low/Parmenter* |
| | | | | | | Ref: P Taylor | Billy Clark upends Grant in the area and Thorpe opens the scoring from the spot. Grant is left with an open goal after Clark and Collett collide and then, a minute later, Oldfield dives full length to power home a header. Waddock is sent off near the end for a second yellow card offence. | | | | | | | | | | | |
| 1:2 A | BRISTOL ROV | 19 | L | 1-2 | 0-2 | Oldfield 63 | Feuer | James | Thomas | Hughes | Davis | Johnson | Linton | Alexander | Oldfield | Guentchev | Showler* | Fotiadis |
| 4/9 | | *2,320 2:12* | | | | *Gurney 6, Archer 18* | *Collett* | *Martin* | *Clark* | *Tillson* | *Lockwood* | *Gurney** | *Holloway* | *Browning* | *Archer* | *Parmenter^* | *Miller* | *French/Low* |
| | | | | | | Ref: A D'Urso (Hatters won 4-2 on aggregate) | Andy Gurney taps in a cross from Lee Archer who then scores with a cracking drive into the far corner as the Hatters appear to be on the wrong end of a hiding. After the break, Oldfield is sent clear by Fotiadis and, after dribbling round the keeper, shoots into the empty net to kill the tie. | | | | | | | | | | | |
| 2:1 H | DERBY | 12 | W | 1-0 | 1-0 | James 25 | Feuer | James | Thomas | Waddock | Davis | Johnson | Hughes | Alexander | Oldfield | Grant* | Guentchev | Fotiadis |
| 17/9 | | 4,459 *P:9* | | | | | *Hoult* | *Rowett* | *Stimac* | *Parker* | *Laursen* | *vander Laan** | *Asanovic* | *Dailly* | *Powell* | *Simpson^* | *Ward* | *Carsley/Cooper* |
| | | | | | | Ref: G Poll | The Hatters outplay their Premiership opponents in the first half but have only the one goal to show for their superiority as Alexander sets up James for a shot which beats Hoult all ends up. Davis then hits the bar with a tremendous strike and Hughes sees his free-kick just tipped over. | | | | | | | | | | | |
| 2:2 A | DERBY | 15 | D | 2-2 | 1-2 | Grant 11, Thorpe 68 | Feuer | James | Thomas | Waddock | Davis | Johnson | Hughes* | Alexander | Oldfield | Grant | Guentchev | Thorpe |
| 25/9 | | *13,569 P:9* | | | | *Sturridge 39, Simpson 43* | *Hoult* | *Parker** | *Rowett* | *Carbon* | *Laursen^* | *Carsley* | *Powell* | *Dailly* | *Simpson* | *Gabbiadini"* | *Sturridge* | *Cooper/van der Laan/Ward* |
| | | | | | | Ref: J Brandwood (Hatters won 3-2 on aggregate) | Grant opens the scoring when he converts a cross from Oldfield but Derby level when Dean Sturridge is given both time and space. A rocket shot by Paul Simpson levels the tie on aggregate but Thorpe then nets the overall winner when hitting home after some clever build up play. | | | | | | | | | | | |
| 3 A | WIMBLEDON | 7 | D | 1-1 | 1-1 | Hughes 41 | Feuer | James | Thomas | Waddock | Davis | Johnson | Thorpe | Alexander | Oldfield | Hughes | Showler | |
| 22/10 | | *5,043 P:3* | | | | *Holdsworth 24* | *Sullivan* | *Cunningham* | *Blackwell* | *Perry* | *Kimble* | *Fear* | *Earle* | *Jones* | *Leonhards'n* | *Holdsworth** | *Gayle* | *Clarke* |
| | | | | | | Ref: M Pierce | The Dons have won seven consecutive league games and, when Dean Holdsworth scores with an angled drive, it seems they are on their way to another victory. Hughes cracks the equaliser and Oldfield hits a volley straight at Sullivan before putting in a cross which just eludes Showler. | | | | | | | | | | | |
| 3R H | WIMBLEDON | 5 | L | 1-2 | 1-0 | Blackwell 27 (og) | Feuer | James | Thomas | Waddock | Davis | Johnson | Hughes | Alexander | Grant* | Thorpe^ | Showler" | McLaren/Douglas/Guentchev |
| 12/11 | | 8,076 *P:3* | | *aet* | | *Castledine 89, Fear 98* | *Sullivan* | *Blackwell* | *Holdsworth** | *Perry* | *Cunningham* | *Ardley* | *Castledine* | *Fear* | *Kimble* | *Gayle^* | *Ekoku"* | *Harford/Clarke/Reeves* |
| | | | | | | Ref: M Riley | The Town are the better side in the first half and take the lead when Dean Blackwell heads a free-kick into his own net. Castledine gets the late equaliser from a corner, for which all eleven Wimbledon players are in the Luton box, and Fear hits the winner after eight minutes of extra-time. | | | | | | | | | | | |

**FA Cup**

| No | H/A | Opponent | Att / Pos | Res | F-A | H-T | Scorers, Times, and Referees | 1 | 2 | 3 | 4 | 5 | 6 | 7 | 8 | 9 | 10 | 11 | subs used |
|---|---|---|---|---|---|---|---|---|---|---|---|---|---|---|---|---|---|---|---|
| 1 | A | TORQUAY | 5 | W | 1-0 | 1-0 | Hughes 41 | Feuer | James* | Skelton | Waddock | Davis | Johnson | Hughes | Alexander | Douglas^ | Guentchev | Showler | Patterson/Marshall |
| 16/11 | | | *3,450 3:6* | | | | | *Wilmot* | *Gittens* | *Watson* | *Barrow* | *Hancox** | *Winter^* | *Hawthorne* | *Oatway* | *Stamps* | *Laight"* | *Nelson* | *Hathaway/Mitchell/Ndah* |
| | | | | | | | Ref: J Brandwood | | | | | | | | | | | | |
| 2 | H | BOREHAMWOOD | 4 | W | 2-1 | 0-0 | Marshall 66, 83 | Feuer | James | Skelton* | Waddock | Davis | Patterson | Hughes | Alexander^ | Showler | Thorpe | Marshall | Grant/Guentchev |
| 7/12 | | | 5,332 *IS:P* | | | | *Robbins 59* | *Sheppard* | *Howard* | *Harrigan* | *Nisbet* | *Daly* | *Joyce** | *Heffer* | *Prutton* | *Shaw* | *Robbins* | *Samuels A^* | *Hollingdale/Samuels D* |
| | | | | | | | Ref: B Knight | | | | | | | | | | | | |
| 3 | H | BOLTON | 2 | D | 1-1 | 0-1 | Johnson 89 | Feuer | James | Thomas | Linton | Davis | Johnson | Hughes | Alexander | Showler | Thorpe | Marshall* | Grant |
| 21/1 | | | 7,414 *1:1* | | | | *Pollock 26* | *Ward* | *Bergsson* | *Fairclough* | *Coleman* | *Small* | *Lee* | *Pollock* | *Sheridan* | *Sellars* | *Blake* | *Green** | *Frandsen* |
| | | | | | | | Ref: C Finch | | | | | | | | | | | | |
| 3R | A | BOLTON | 2 | L | 2-6 | 2-1 | Thorpe 30, M'shall 35 *[Pollock 83, Green 90]* | Feuer | James | Thomas | Linton | Davis | Johnson | Hughes | Alexander | Showler* | Thorpe | Marshall^ | Guentchev/Fotiadis |
| 25/1 | | | *9,713 1:1* | | | | *McGinlay 8, Blake 52, 66, Thompson 64,* | *Ward* | *Bergsson* | *Taggart* | *Fairclough* | *Small* | *Frandsen* | *Pollock* | *Sheridan** | *Sellars^* | *McGinlay"* | *Blake* | *Thompson/Johansen/Green* |
| | | | | | | | Ref: C Finch | | | | | | | | | | | | |

Round 1: Feuer is required to make three early saves as the Gulls open up with a blitz on the Luton goal. Hughes blasts the only goal, from the edge of the box, after Torquay fail to deal with a corner from Alexander. The second half is a total non-event with neither side looking like scoring.

Round 2: The Town are lucky to go through to the next round after making very heavy weather of beating their ICIS league opponents who play with five men at the back and rely on attacking on the break, a ploy which succeeds when Tony Samuels sets up Terry Robbins for the opening goal.

Round 3: The Hatters are outplayed in the first half but Nathan Blake is well offside as he sets up Jamie Pollock to give the Trotters the lead. The Town fight back after the break but when Steve Davis hits a post late on, the tie seems to be over. Johnson lashes home the equaliser after a scramble.

Round 3R: John McGinlay expertly shoots into the far corner early on but the Hatters fight back and a flick from Thorpe and a volley from Marshall gives them the interval lead. The Division One leaders turn on the power in the second half and crush the Town as they push up, chasing the game.

| | | Home | | | | | | Away | | | | | |
|---|---|---|---|---|---|---|---|---|---|---|---|---|---|
| | P | W | D | L | F | A | W | D | L | F | A | Pts |
| 1 Bury | 46 | 18 | 5 | 0 | 39 | 7 | 6 | 7 | 10 | 23 | 31 | 84 |
| 2 Stockport | 46 | 15 | 5 | 3 | 31 | 14 | 8 | 8 | 7 | 28 | 27 | 82 |
| 3 LUTON TOWN | 46 | 13 | 7 | 3 | 38 | 14 | 8 | 8 | 7 | 33 | 31 | 78 |
| 4 Brentford | 46 | 8 | 11 | 4 | 26 | 22 | 12 | 3 | 8 | 30 | 21 | 74 |
| 5 Bristol City | 46 | 14 | 4 | 5 | 43 | 18 | 7 | 6 | 10 | 26 | 33 | 73 |
| 6 Crewe * | 46 | 15 | 4 | 4 | 38 | 15 | 7 | 3 | 13 | 18 | 32 | 73 |
| 7 Blackpool | 46 | 13 | 7 | 3 | 41 | 21 | 5 | 8 | 10 | 19 | 26 | 69 |
| 8 Wrexham | 46 | 11 | 9 | 3 | 37 | 28 | 6 | 9 | 8 | 17 | 22 | 69 |
| 9 Burnley | 46 | 14 | 3 | 6 | 48 | 27 | 5 | 8 | 10 | 23 | 28 | 68 |
| 10 Chesterfield | 46 | 10 | 9 | 4 | 25 | 18 | 8 | 5 | 10 | 17 | 21 | 68 |
| 11 Gillingham | 46 | 13 | 3 | 7 | 37 | 25 | 6 | 7 | 10 | 23 | 34 | 67 |
| 12 Walsall | 46 | 12 | 8 | 3 | 35 | 21 | 7 | 2 | 14 | 19 | 32 | 67 |
| 13 Watford | 46 | 10 | 8 | 5 | 24 | 14 | 6 | 11 | 6 | 21 | 24 | 67 |
| 14 Millwall | 46 | 12 | 4 | 7 | 27 | 22 | 4 | 9 | 10 | 23 | 33 | 61 |
| 15 Preston | 46 | 14 | 5 | 4 | 33 | 19 | 4 | 2 | 17 | 16 | 36 | 61 |
| 16 Bournemouth | 46 | 8 | 9 | 6 | 24 | 20 | 7 | 6 | 10 | 19 | 25 | 60 |
| 17 Bristol Rov | 46 | 13 | 4 | 6 | 34 | 22 | 2 | 7 | 14 | 13 | 28 | 56 |
| 18 Wycombe | 46 | 13 | 4 | 6 | 31 | 14 | 2 | 6 | 15 | 20 | 42 | 55 |
| 19 Plymouth | 46 | 7 | 11 | 5 | 19 | 18 | 5 | 7 | 11 | 28 | 40 | 54 |
| 20 York | 46 | 8 | 6 | 9 | 27 | 31 | 5 | 7 | 11 | 20 | 37 | 52 |
| 21 Peterborough | 46 | 7 | 7 | 9 | 38 | 34 | 4 | 7 | 12 | 17 | 39 | 47 |
| 22 Shrewsbury | 46 | 8 | 6 | 9 | 27 | 32 | 3 | 7 | 13 | 22 | 42 | 46 |
| 23 Rotherham | 46 | 4 | 7 | 12 | 17 | 29 | 3 | 7 | 13 | 22 | 41 | 35 |
| 24 Notts Co | 46 | 4 | 9 | 10 | 20 | 25 | 3 | 5 | 15 | 13 | 34 | 35 |
| | 1104 | 264 | 155 | 133 | 759 | 510 | 133 | 155 | 264 | 510 | 759 | 1501 |

* promoted after play-offs

**Odds & ends**

Double wins: (5) Gillingham, Peterborough, Notts County, Rotherham, Shrewsbury.
Double losses: (0).

Won from behind: (2) Notts County (a), Bournemouth (FAC).
Lost from in front: (8) Bournemouth (a), Brentford (a), Bristol Rov (a), Walsall (a), Wrexham (a), Wimbledon (LC), Bolton (FAC), Crewe (play-off).

High spots: Looking at the top of the league table, rather than the bottom, for the first time since 1988.
The unbeaten runs of ten games and twelve games during the season.
The goal-scoring form of Tony Thorpe.
The 6-0 home thumping of Crewe.
David Oldfield's hat-trick in the 5-1 home victory over Preston.

Low spots: Failing to win promotion via the play-offs.
The dropping of too many home points in the second half of the season.
The defeat at Walsall which effectively ruled out an automatic promotion place.
Losing the first three games at the start of the season.
The extra-time defeat by Wimbledon in the Coca-Cola Cup.

Player of the Year: Ian Feuer.
Ever-presents: Ian Feuer.
Hat-tricks: Tony Thorpe (3), David Oldfield (1).
Leading scorer: Tony Thorpe (31).

| | Appearances | | | | | | Goals | | | |
|---|---|---|---|---|---|---|---|---|---|---|
| | Lge | *Sub* | LC | *Sub* | FAC | *Sub* | Lge | LC | FAC | Tot |
| Alexander, Graham | 44 | *1* | 6 | | 4 | | 2 | | | 2 |
| Davis, Steve | 43 | *1* | 6 | | 4 | | 8 | | | 8 |
| Douglas, Stuart | 2 | *7* | | *1* | 1 | | | | | |
| Evers, Sean | 1 | | | | | | | | | |
| Feuer, Ian | 46 | | 6 | | 4 | | | | | |
| Fotiadis, Andrew | 9 | *8* | | *2* | | *1* | 3 | | | 3 |
| Grant, Kim | 8 | *17* | 4 | | | *2* | 2 | 2 | | 4 |
| Guentchev, Bontcho | 15 | *12* | 3 | *2* | 1 | *2* | 1 | | | 1 |
| Harvey, Richard | 1 | *1* | | | | | | | | |
| Hughes, Ceri | 36 | | 6 | | 4 | | 4 | 1 | 1 | 6 |
| James, Julian | 44 | | 6 | | 4 | | 1 | 1 | | 2 |
| Johnson, Marvin | 44 | | 6 | | 3 | | | | 1 | 1 |
| Kiwomya, Andy | 5 | | | | | | 1 | | | 1 |
| Linton, Des | 3 | *4* | 1 | | 2 | | | | | |
| Marshall, Dwight | 9 | *15* | | | 3 | *1* | 4 | | 3 | 7 |
| McGowan, Gavin | 2 | | | | | | | | | |
| McLaren, Paul | 13 | *11* | | *1* | | | | | | |
| Oldfield, David | 31 | *7* | 5 | | | | 6 | 2 | | 8 |
| Patterson, Darren | 8 | *2* | | *1* | 1 | *1* | | | | |
| Showler, Paul | 21 | *2* | 3 | *1* | 4 | | 6 | | | 6 |
| Skelton, Aaron | 2 | *1* | | | 2 | | | | | |
| Thomas, Mitchell | 42 | | 6 | | 2 | | 3 | | | 3 |
| Thorpe, Tony | 39 | *2* | 3 | *1* | 3 | | 28 | 2 | 1 | 31 |
| Upson, Matthew | | *1* | | | | | | | | |
| Waddock, Gary | 38 | *1* | 5 | | 2 | | 2 | | | 2 |
| (own-goals) | | | | | | | | 1 | | 1 |
| **25 players used** | **506** | ***93*** | **66** | ***9*** | **44** | ***7*** | **71** | **9** | **6** | **86** |

| No | Date | | Att | Pos | Pt | F-A | H-T | Scorers, Times, and Referees | 1 | 2 | 3 | 4 | 5 | 6 | 7 | 8 | 9 | 10 | 11 | subs used |
|---|---|---|---|---|---|---|---|---|---|---|---|---|---|---|---|---|---|---|---|---|
| 1 | A | BLACKPOOL | | - | L | 0-1 | 0-1 | | Feuer | McGowan | Thomas | Waddock | Davis S | Johnson | McLaren | Alexander | Oldfield | Thorpe | **Davies*** | Douglas |
| | 9/8 | | 6,547 | - | | | | Lydiate 11 | Banks | Bryan | Bradshaw | Butler | Lydiate | Brabin | Bonner | Clarkson | Quinn | Phillpott | Preece | |
| | | | | | | | | Ref: S Mathieson | The Hatters control the game for the last 70 minutes, at a sunny Bloomfield Road, but create only one chance which is missed by Tony Thorpe. The Seasiders take the lead when a corner from Lee Philpott is flicked on at the near post, Jason Lydiate managing to scramble the ball home. | | | | | | | | | | | |
| 2 | H | SOUTHEND | | 12 | W | 1-0 | 0-0 | Douglas 76 | Feuer | James | Thomas | Waddock | Davis S | Johnson | Davies | Alexander | Fotiadis* | Thorpe^ | Marshall | Douglas/McLaren |
| | 18/8 | | 5,140 | 19 | 3 | | | | Royce | Harris | Jones | Marsh | Roget | Dublin | Byrne | Beeston | Boere* | Thompson | Clarke | Rammell |
| | | | | | | | | Ref: C Foy | Ian Feuer rips his shoulder muscles in the first half but plays on and is so well protected that he does not have a save to make. Substitute Stuart Douglas scores the only goal, in front of the live television cameras, when he is first to react after Simon Royce deflects a shot from Thorpe. | | | | | | | | | | | |
| 3 | A | FULHAM | | 15 | D | 0-0 | 0-0 | | Davis K | James | Thomas | Waddock | Davis S | Johnson | Davies* | Alexander^ | Oldfield | Douglas" | Marshall | Harvey/McLaren/McGowan |
| | 23/8 | | 8,142 | 6 | 4 | | | | Walton | Lawrence | Herrera | Cullip | Smith | Brooker | Newhouse | Hayward | Conroy* | Morgan^ | Carpenter" | Scott/McAree/Cockerill |
| | | | | | | | | Ref: M Pierce | Kelvin Davis is recalled from his loan spell at Hartlepool to replace Feuer and gives an assured performance against a newly-promoted Fulham side who only threaten occasionally. The injury crisis continues, with Graham Alexander limping off with a torn hamstring after ten minutes. | | | | | | | | | | | |
| 4 | H | OLDHAM | | 12 | D | 1-1 | 0-0 | Thorpe 60 | Davis K | James* | Thomas | Waddock | Davis S | Johnson | Davies^ | McLaren | Oldfield | Thorpe | Marshall" | McGowan/Douglas/Showler |
| | 30/8 | | 5,404 | 7 | 5 | | | Barlow 53 | Pollitt | Redmond* | Serrant | Sinnott | Hodgson | Garnett ! | McNiven | Duxbury | Graham^ | Barlow | Reid | Wright/Ormondroyd |
| | | | | | | | | Ref: A Butler | Shaun Garnett is dismissed in the 49th minute after committing a professional foul on Gary Waddock but instead of motivating Luton, it has the opposite effect and Stuart Barlow gives the Latics the lead four minutes later. Tony Thorpe heads the equaliser to earn a share of the points. | | | | | | | | | | | |
| 5 | H | MILLWALL | | 15 | L | 0-2 | 0-0 | | Davis K | James* | McGowan | Waddock | Davis S | Johnson | McLaren | Alexander^ | Oldfield | Thorpe | Marshall" | Evers/**Doherty**/Douglas |
| | 2/9 | | 5,781 | 13 | 5 | | | Law 67, Hockton 71 | Carter | Brown | Sturgess | Bowry | Law | McLeary | Allen | Newman | Hockton | Grant* | Savage | Doyle |
| | | | | | | | | Ref: R Furnandiz | The injury problems continue with Thomas straining his groin in the pre-match warm-up and James twisting his ankle after only ten minutes. Millwall take full advantage and Brian Law soars to head home a corner from Paul Allen, quickly followed by a strike from Danny Hockton. | | | | | | | | | | | |
| 6 | A | NORTHAMPTON | | 18 | L | 0-1 | 0-1 | | Davis K | McGowan ! | **Small** | Waddock | Davis S | Johnson | McLaren | Evers* | Oldfield | Douglas | Marshall^ | Doherty/Davies |
| | 9/9 | | 7,246 | 3 | 5 | | | Parrish 1 | Woodman | Clarkson | Frain | Sampson | Warburton | Brightwell | Parrish | Peer | Seal* | Gayle | Hunter | Wilson |
| | | | | | | | | Ref: R Harris | The Hatters get off to the worst possible start when conceding a goal after just 22 seconds as the ball is hustled through to Sean Parrish who makes no mistake. The situation is made worse when Gavin McGowan is dismissed for his second yellow card offence, just before the interval. | | | | | | | | | | | |
| 7 | A | BOURNEMOUTH | | 21 | D | 1-1 | 1-0 | Marshall 43 | Davis K | McGowan | Small | Waddock | Davis S | Johnson | Davies* | McLaren | Oldfield | Douglas^ | Marshall | Evers/Doherty |
| | 13/9 | | 4,561 | 6 | 6 | | | O'Neill 83 | Glass | Young | Vincent | Rolling* | Cox | Bailey | Beardsmore | Robinson | Tomlinson^ | Fletcher | O'Neill | Howe/Harrington |
| | | | | | | | | Ref: C Wilkes | The Town create more chances in the first half than they have done all season but only have the one goal from Dwight Marshall to show for it. The defence is put under enormous pressure after the break and the Cherries earn the draw when John O'Neill shoots into the bottom corner. | | | | | | | | | | | |
| 8 | H | WREXHAM | | 23 | L | 2-5 | 1-2 | Davis 41, Gray 50 [Skinner 62p] | Dibble | McGowan | Harvey* | Waddock^ | Davis S | Small | Gray | McLaren | Oldfield | Douglas | Marshall" | Peake/Thorpe/Evers |
| | 20/9 | | 5,241 | 12 | 6 | | | Brammer 10, Connolly 26, 63, 73, | Marriott | McGregor | Hardy | Phillips | Jones | Carey | Skinner | Owen | Connolly* | Spink | Brammer | Watkin |
| | | | | | | | | Ref: P Rejer | The makeshift defence allows the visitors to ease into a two goal lead but a header from Davis and tap-in from Phil Gray, making his second debut for the Town, restores some pride. Small pulls back Craig Skinner who converts from the spot before Connolly completes his hat-trick.. | | | | | | | | | | | |
| 9 | A | BRISTOL CITY | | 23 | L | 0-3 | 0-3 | | Davis K | Evers | Harvey | Waddock* | Small | **White** | Davies | McLaren | Oldfield | Thorpe | **George^** | **Kean/Spring** |
| | 27/9 | | 8,509 | 15 | 6 | | | Bell 5p, Torpey 27, 31 | Welch | Locke | Bell | Dyche | Taylor | Edwards | Goodridge* | Owers | Torpey | Cramb^ | Tinnion | Doherty/Barclay |
| | | | | | | | | Ref: E Lomas | Four teenagers make their debuts as the manager, Lennie Lawrence picks the only team available due to the injury problems. Alan White, a new signing from Middlesbrough, fouls Colin Cramb in the area and Micky Bell converts from the spot. Steve Torpey gets two goals before the break. | | | | | | | | | | | |
| 10 | H | WATFORD | | 23 | L | **0-4** | 0-4 | | Davis K | McGowan* | Harvey | Waddock | Small | White | Gray | McLaren | Oldfield | Thorpe | Davies^ | James/Douglas |
| | 4/10 | | **9,041** | 1 | 6 | | | Johnson 5, Thomas 19, Kennedy 27, 29 | Chamberlain | Gibbs | Kennedy | Page | Millen | Mooney | Slater | Palmer | Thomas | Johnson | Rosenthal* | Noel-Williams |
| | | | | | | | | Ref: T Heilbron | In a highly-charged atmosphere for this local derby, the Hornets secure their first win against the Town for ten years as the injury-ridden Luton team collapses against the league leaders. Julian James is introduced at the interval to help shore up the defence but by then the damage is done. | | | | | | | | | | | |
| 11 | H | PLYMOUTH | | 23 | W | **3-0** | 1-0 | Thorpe 36, 58, Davies 82 | Davis K | Alexander | Small | Waddock | James | White | Spring ! | McLaren | Oldfield | Thorpe* | Doherty^ | Evers/Davies |
| | 11/10 | | 4,931 | 22 | 9 | | | | Sheffield | Collins | Williams | Mauge | Heathcote | Wotton | Barlow | Saunders | Littlejohn | Billy | Wilson* | Jean |
| | | | | | | | | Ref: D Crick | The Town get the breaks against their fellow strugglers and Thorpe opens the scoring when he gets on the end of a route one clearance and then nets after Waddock dispossesses Paul Wotton on the edge of the area. Matthew Spring, on his full debut, is dismissed for a two-footed challenge. | | | | | | | | | | | |

| No | Venue | Opponent / Date | Att | Pos | Res / Pts | F-A | H-T | Scorers, Times, and Referees | 1 | 2 | 3 | 4 | 5 | 6 | 7 | 8 | 9 | 10 | 11 | Subs used |
|---|---|---|---|---|---|---|---|---|---|---|---|---|---|---|---|---|---|---|---|---|
| 12 | A | WIGAN | | 22 | D | 1-1 | 0-0 | Oldfield 68 | Davis K | James | Small | Spring* | Davis S | White | Gray^ | McLaren | Oldfield | Thorpe | Alexander | Davies/Marshall |
| | | 18/10 | 4,466 | 8 | 10 | | | Jones 72p | Butler | Bradshaw | Sharp | Greenall | Bishop | Martinez | Lee* | O'Connell | Jones | Smeets^ | Lowe" | Johnson/McGibbon/Warne |
| | | | | | | | | Ref: D Messias | The Town are in control for most of the game but lack the finishing power to make the game safe. Oldfield scores with a curling, side-foot shot but Roberto Martinez tumbles dramatically to the ground, after he is tackled by Steve Davis in the box, and Graeme Jones levels from the spot. | | | | | | | | | | | |
| 13 | A | CARLISLE | | 21 | W | 1-0 | 0-0 | White 87 | Davis K | James | Small | Spring* | Davis S | White | Gray^ | McLaren | Oldfield | Thorpe | Alexander | Waddock/Marshall |
| | | 21/10 | 4,341 | 22 | 13 | | | | Caig | Bowman | Archdeacon | Harrison | Varty | Pounew'tchy | Barr | Couzens | Dobie* | Jansen | Aspinall^ | Stevens/McAlinden |
| | | | | | | | | Ref: G Cain | Alan White has an eventful evening when firstly he is lucky to stay on the pitch after chopping down Scott Dobie from behind when he is clean through on goal, heads a shot from Ian Stevens off the line and then, with three minutes left, heads in a corner from Alexander to win the points. | | | | | | | | | | | |
| 14 | H | BRENTFORD | | 18 | W | 2-0 | 1-0 | Alexander 20, Thorpe 59 | Davis K | James* | Small | Waddock | Davis S | White | Gray | McLaren | Oldfield | Thorpe^ | Alexander | Johnson/Marshall |
| | | 25/10 | 5,972 | 20 | 16 | | | | Colgan | McGhee | Anderson | Hutchings | Bates | Hall | Denys | Oatway | Bent* | Rapley | Taylor | Canham |
| | | | | | | | | Ref: J Kirkby | A header from Phil Gray falls in to the path of Alexander who lobs the ball over the advancing Nick Colgan to open the scoring. Tony Thorpe converts with a point blank header after Oldfield flicks on a corner kick from Alexander. This victory lifts the Town out of the relegation area. | | | | | | | | | | | |
| 15 | A | WYCOMBE | | 18 | D | 2-2 | 1-1 | Oldfield 44, Thorpe 74 | Davis K | James | Small | Waddock | Davis S | Johnson | Gray | McLaren | Oldfield | Thorpe | Alexander | |
| | | 1/11 | 6,219 | 11 | 17 | | | Stallard 12, McGavin 62 | Taylor | Cousins | Kavanagh | Ryan | Mohan | Forsyth | Carroll | Scott | Stallard | McGavin | Brown* | Harkin |
| | | | | | | | | Ref: J Brandwood | The Town twice fall behind after enjoying 90% of the possession. Steve McGavin crosses for Mark Stallard to open the scoring but Oldfield fires home through a crowd of players, just before the interval. McGavin restores the lead before Thorpe loops a header over Martin Taylor. | | | | | | | | | | | |
| 16 | H | BURNLEY | | 19 | L | 2-3 | 2-1 | Alexander 32, 35 | Davis K | James | Small | Waddock* | Davis S | Johnson | Gray | McLaren | Oldfield | Thorpe | Alexander | Fotiadis |
| | | 4/11 | 5,315 | 18 | 17 | | | Williams 25, Creaney 61, Barnes 64 | Beresford | Brass | Vinnicombe | Cowans* | Howey | Moore | Waddle^ | Williams | Creaney" | Barnes | Weller | Blatherwick/Smith/Cooke |
| | | | | | | | | Ref: B Knight | The Clarets take the lead with a soft goal but Graham Alexander hits a 25-yard shot to level and then puts the Town into a half-time lead, three minutes later. The second-half is a disaster with the Luton defence gifting two goals to the visitors to end the run of five games without defeat. | | | | | | | | | | | |
| 17 | H | PRESTON | | 22 | L | 1-3 | 1-2 | Thorpe 25 | Davis K | James | Small* | Waddock^ | White | Johnson | Gray" | McLaren | Oldfield | Thorpe | Alexander | Davies/Marshall/Fotiadis |
| | | 8/11 | 5,767 | 12 | 17 | | | Lormor 15, Eyres 44, Ashcroft 89 | Moilanen | Parkinson | Barrick | Kidd | Jackson | Gregan | Appleton | Ashcroft* | Lormor | Rankine | Eyres | Macken |
| | | | | | | | | Ref: C Wilkes | Thorpe gets a lucky equaliser but, with the confidence of the Luton team at a low ebb, the good fortune is not capitalised on. David Eyres is allowed to steal in, unmarked, to convert a cross from Tony Lormor and Lee Ashcroft completes the misery when he rolls the ball into the net. | | | | | | | | | | | |
| 18 | H | WALSALL | | 23 | L | 0-1 | 0-0 | | Feuer | James | Small | Waddock* | White | Davies^ | Fotiadis | McLaren | Oldfield | Thorpe | Alexander | Spring/Douglas |
| | | 22/11 | 4,726 | 18 | 17 | | | Hodge 59 | Walker | Evans | Marsh | Viveash | Mountfield | Peron | Boli* | Porter | Keates | Watson | Hodge | Ricketts |
| | | | | | | | | Ref: M Halsey | Wayne Turner is relieved of his first-team coaching duties but the Town still suffer their fourth consecutive home defeat as they again have the majority of the possession but fail to carve out any goal-scoring chances. Gary Porter crosses for John Hodge to hit the winner with a volley. | | | | | | | | | | | |
| 19 | A | YORK | | 20 | W | 2-1 | 1-0 | Alexander 13, Thorpe 72 | Feuer | James | Small | Waddock | Davis S | White | **Allen C** | McLaren | Oldfield | Thorpe | Alexander | |
| | | 29/11 | 3,636 | 7 | 20 | | | Cresswell 87 | Warrington | Murty | Atkinson | Bushell | Reed | Barras | Pouton | Tinkler | Bull* | Rowe | Stephenson | Cresswell |
| | | | | | | | | Ref: D Pugh | Loan signing, Chris Allen, makes his debut for the Town and gives width on the left as the Hatters put on a better performance against a team who have won their last six home games. Alexander opens the scoring with a shot into the bottom corner and Thorpe coolly hits the winner. | | | | | | | | | | | |
| 20 | H | GILLINGHAM | | 21 | D | 2-2 | 1-1 | Davis 27, Thorpe 77 | Feuer | James | Small | Waddock* | Davis S | White^ | Allen C | McLaren | Oldfield | Thorpe | Alexander | Fotiadis/Thomas |
| | | 2/12 | 4,408 | 15 | 21 | | | Akinbiyi 28, 56 | Stannard | Statham | Masters | Smith | Ashby | Bryant ! | Hessenthaler | Ratcliffe | Onuera | Akinbiyi | Galloway* | Green |
| | | | | | | | | Ref: P Taylor | In a fast and furious contest, a careful header from Steve Davis breaks the deadlock. Akinbiyi nets twice in a performance of aggressive power and the equaliser from Tony Thorpe goes through the legs of Jim Stannard. Matt Bryant is sent off in the final minute for a foul on Ian Feuer. | | | | | | | | | | | |
| 21 | A | CHESTERFIELD | | 22 | D | 0-0 | 0-0 | | Feuer | James* | Thomas | Waddock | Davis S | White | Allen C | McLaren | Oldfield | Thorpe | Alexander | Douglas |
| | | 13/12 | 4,358 | 4 | 22 | | | | Mercer | Hewitt | Jules | Beaumont | Williams | Breckin | Willis | Holland | Wilkinson | Ebdon | Perkins | |
| | | | | | | | | Ref: J Robinson | The Town pick up another away point in a dour display at Saltergate. In a game of few chances, Tony Thorpe has an effort cleared off the line by Chris Perkins and this is the nearest that either team comes to scoring. Bryan Small has now returned to Bolton after his loan spell at Luton. | | | | | | | | | | | |
| 22 | H | BRISTOL ROV | | 22 | L | 2-4 | 2-4 | Allen 8, Oldfield 25 | Feuer | Patterson | Thomas | Douglas* | Davis S | White | Allen C | McLaren^ | Oldfield | Thorpe | Alexander | Fotiadis/Davies |
| | | 20/12 | 5,296 | 12 | 22 | | | Cureton 12, Hayles 21, 37, Beadle 30 | Collett | Hayfield | Lockwood | Penrice | White | Foster | Holloway | Ramasut* | Beadle | Cureton | Hayles | Bashford |
| | | | | | | | | Ref: D Orr | Rovers are without four of their regular players, due to suspensions, but are still able to hand out a football lesson to the Hatters. Allen fires the Town into an early lead but Rovers take advantage of hesitancy to seemingly score at will with ex-Stevenage striker, Barry Hayles, running riot. | | | | | | | | | | | |
| 23 | H | NORTHAMPTON | | 21 | D | 2-2 | 0-2 | Oldfield 68, Thorpe 86 | Feuer | Patterson | Thomas | Waddock | Davis S | White | Allen C | McLaren | Oldfield | Thorpe | Alexander* | Fotiadis |
| | | 26/12 | 8,035 | 3 | 23 | | | Dozzell 8p, White 12 (og) | Woodman | Clarkson | Frain | Hill | Gibb | Brightwell | Peer | Heggs | Freestone* | Dozzell^ | Hunt | Tait/Warner |
| | | | | | | | | Ref: C Wilkes | Jason Dozzell nets from the spot, after he collapses in the box when challenged by Thomas, and a mix-up in defence leads to White heading past Feuer as the high-flying Cobblers take a two goal lead. David Oldfield reduces the deficit and then sets up Tony Thorpe for the late equaliser. | | | | | | | | | | | |

| No | Date | | Att | Pos | Pt | F-A | H-T | Scorers, Times, and Referees | 1 | 2 | 3 | 4 | 5 | 6 | 7 | 8 | 9 | 10 | 11 | subs used |
|---|---|---|---|---|---|---|---|---|---|---|---|---|---|---|---|---|---|---|---|---|
| 24 | A | MILLWALL | | 20 | W | 2-0 | 0-0 | Davis 89, Thorpe 90 | Feuer | Patterson | Thomas | Waddock | Davis S | White | Allen C | McLaren | Oldfield | Thorpe | Alexander | |
| | 28/12 | | *7,461* | *10* | 26 | | | | *Spink* | *Brown* | *Sturgess* | *Bowry* | *Law* | *Fitzgerald* | *Newman* | *Grant* | *Veart** | *Shaw* | *Stevens* | *Allen* |
| | | | | | | | | Ref: A Bates | The game seems to be drifting to another scoreless draw when Davis squeezes a header past Nigel Spink in the final minute. From the restart, Bobby Bowry is dispossessed by Thorpe who scampers through to add a second. The Town have now not lost an away game for three months. | | | | | | | | | | | |
| 25 | A | SOUTHEND | | 19 | W | 2-1 | 1-1 | Alexander 2, 62 | Feuer | Patterson | Thomas | Waddock | Davis S | White | Allen C | McLaren | Oldfield | Thorpe | Alexander | |
| | 3/1 | | *5,056* | *20* | 29 | | | *Thomson 20* | *Southall* | *Hails* | *Stimson* | *Coulbault* | *Harris* | *Dublin* | *Jones* | *Gridelet* | *Thomson* | *N'Diaye** | *Clarke* | *Fitzpatrick* |
| | | | | | | | | Ref: B Knight | At a wet and windy Roots Hall, Alexander bursts through to fire past Neville Southall in the opening minutes. Keith Dublin heads down for Andy Thomson to head the equaliser and herald the start of an onslaught but, with the storm weathered, Alexander side-foots home the winner. | | | | | | | | | | | |
| 26 | H | BLACKPOOL | | 18 | W | **3-0** | 1-0 | Thorpe 33, 74, 76 | Feuer | Patterson | Thomas | Waddock | Davis S | White | Allen C | McLaren | Oldfield | Thorpe | Alexander | |
| | 10/1 | | 5,574 | *14* | 32 | | | | *Banks* | *Bryan* | *Lydiate* | *Butler* | *Linighan** | *Hughes^* | *Bonner* | *Clarkson* | *Ormerod* | *Philpott* | *Preece* | *Carlisle/Bent* |
| | | | | | | | | Ref: R Styles | A clever lob, a left-foot strike and a volley make up the brilliant hat-trick for Tony Thorpe which earns the first home win for the Hatters in seven games. It might have been a different story as Feuer handles the ball outside of his area but only receives a yellow card for the offence. | | | | | | | | | | | |
| 27 | A | OLDHAM | | 18 | L | 1-2 | 0-0 | Alexander 78 | Feuer | Patterson | Thomas | Waddock* | Davis S | White | Allen C | Spring^ | Oldfield | Thorpe | Alexander | Marshall/Davies |
| | 17/1 | | *6,057* | *7* | 32 | | | *Graham 55, 65* | *Kelly* | *Rickers* | *Thompson* | *Garnett* | *Graham* | *Redmond* | *Rush** | *Duxbury* | *Jepson* | *Barlow^* | *Reid* | *McNiven/McCarthy* |
| | | | | | | | | Ref: T Heilbron | The unbeaten away record, stretching back to last September, comes to an end when Feuer carries the blame for failing to impose his presence as two identical in-swinging corners are headed home by Richard Graham. Alexander pulls a goal back, off the post, from a Thorpe lay-back. | | | | | | | | | | | |
| 28 | H | FULHAM | | 19 | L | 1-4 | 1-2 | Thorpe 44 | Feuer | Patterson | Thomas | Waddock | Davis S | White* | Allen C | McLaren | Oldfield | Thorpe | Alexander | Davies |
| | 24/1 | | 8,366 | *3* | 32 | | | *Moody 1, 37, 56p, Hayward 61* | *Taylor* | *Smith* | *Lawrence* | *Trollope* | *Coleman* | *Neilson* | *Moody* | *Bracewell* | *Lightbo'rne** | *Peschisolido^* | *Hayward* | *Freeman/Collins* |
| | | | | | | | | Ref: S Matthieson | Big Fulham striker, Paul Moody, takes just 43 seconds to hit his first goal. He then clashes with White, who leaves the field, and the reshuffled Town side is no match for the big spending Cottagers. A poor clearance from Feuer leads to a handball by Davis and Moody gets his hat-trick. | | | | | | | | | | | |
| 29 | H | BOURNEMOUTH | | 19 | L | 1-2 | 0-1 | Johnson 72 | Davis K | Patterson | Harvey | Waddock* | Davis S | Johnson | Allen C^ | McLaren" | Oldfield | Thorpe | Alexander | Davies/Evers/Marshall |
| | 31/1 | | 5,466 | *9* | 32 | | | *Brissett 11, Fletcher 59* | *Glass* | *Young* | *Vincent* | *Howe* | *Cox* | *Bailey* | *O'Neill* | *Robinson* | *Warren* | *Fletcher* | *Brissett** | *Teather* |
| | | | | | | | | Ref: R Furnandiz | The Hatters go down to their ninth home defeat of the season in a poor performance. Jason Brissett heads in from close range but the killer goal comes when Harvey back-heads into the path of Steve Fletcher who makes no mistake. Marvin Johnson heads home a corner from Alexander. | | | | | | | | | | | |
| 30 | A | WREXHAM | | 20 | L | 1-2 | 0-0 | Davis 89 | Davis K | Patterson | Harvey | Waddock* | Davis S | Johnson | Allen C | McLaren | Oldfield | Thorpe | Alexander | Marshall |
| | 7/2 | | ***3,527*** | *11* | 32 | | | *Brammer 67, Roberts 88* | *Marriott* | *McGregor* | *Hardy* | *Brammer* | *Ridler* | *Carey* | *Skinner** | *Owen* | *Spink^* | *Roberts* | *Ward* | *Wainwright/Basham* |
| | | | | | | | | Ref: T Jones | After a poor first half, the game bursts into life when substitute Neil Wainwright sets up Dave Brammer for the opener. A poor pass from David Oldfield enables Steve Basham to power down the wing and cross for Neil Roberts to shoot home. The effort from Steve Davis comes too late. | | | | | | | | | | | |
| 31 | A | WATFORD | | 20 | D | 1-1 | 0-0 | Johnson 81 | Davis K | Patterson | Thomas | Waddock* | White | Johnson^ | Allen C" | McLaren | Oldfield | Thorpe | Alexander | Evers/Davies/Marshall |
| | 14/2 | | ***15,182*** | *1* | 33 | | | *Robinson 52* | *Chamberlain* | *Gibbs* | *Palmer* | *Page* | *Millen* | *Mooney* | *Slater** | *Hyde* | *Lee* | *Johnson* | *Robinson* | *Noel-Williams* |
| | | | | | | | | Ref: J Kirkby | After a string of poor results, the Town bounce back and just shade this local derby. Paul Robinson opens the scoring when a ricochet breaks to him and he lifts the ball over the keeper. Marvin Johnson is the unlikely hero when he diverts a shot from McLaren past ex-Hatter Chamberlain. | | | | | | | | | | | |
| 32 | H | BRISTOL CITY | | 21 | D | 0-0 | 0-0 | | Davis K | Patterson | Thomas | Evers* | Davis S | White | Allen C^ | McLaren | Oldfield | Gray | Alexander | Marshall/Fotiadis |
| | 21/2 | | 6,405 | *2* | 34 | | | | *Welch* | *Locke* | *Bell* | *Goodridge** | *Taylor* | *Carey* | *Edwards* | *Hewlett* | *Goater* | *Johansen^* | *Tinnion* | *Murray/Cramb* |
| | | | | | | | | Ref: K Leach | Chances are missed at both ends in an entertaining contest which sees Kelvin Davis make good saves from each of the City forwards. Luton are denied two blatant penalty appeals but, as they await their first spot kick of the season, the return of Phil Gray to the side is a welcome boost. | | | | | | | | | | | |
| 33 | H | WIGAN | | 20 | D | 1-1 | 1-1 | Oldfield 29 | Davis K | Patterson | Thomas | Evers | Davis S | White | Marshall* | McLaren | Oldfield | Gray | Alexander | Fotiadis |
| | 24/2 | | **4,403** | *17* | 35 | | | *Jones 16* | *Carroll* | *Green* | *Sharp* | *Greenall* | *McGibson* | *Bradshaw* | *Lee** | *Morgan* | *Jones^* | *Kilford* | *Lowe* | *Rogers/Warne* |
| | | | | | | | | Ref: S Bennett | Leading scorer, Graeme Jones, flicks in a corner from David Lee, with the Town defence static, to open the scoring. David Oldfield makes a determined run at the Wigan defence and, after exchanging passes with Dwight Marshall, fires an unstoppable shot past keeper, Roy Carroll | | | | | | | | | | | |
| 34 | A | PLYMOUTH | | 19 | W | 2-0 | 0-0 | Fotiadis 79, Evers 88 | Davis K | Alexander | Thomas | Waddock | Davis S | Patterson | Evers | McLaren | Oldfield | Gray | Marshall* | Fotiadis^/Doherty |
| | 28/2 | | *4,846* | *21* | 38 | | | | *Sheffield* | *Collins* | *Williams* | *Saunders* | *Heathcote* | *Rowboth'm** | *Barlow* | *Conlon* | *Littlejohn* | *Corazzin* | *Billy* | *Wotton* |
| | | | | | | | | Ref: A D'Urso | At a windy Home Park, heroics from Kelvin Davis eventually sets up the deserved win. Jason Rowbotham sells his keeper short with a poor back-header and Fotiadis steals in to head home. In a thrilling finale, Fotiadis misses a good chance before Gray sets up Evers for the second. | | | | | | | | | | | |

| No | Venue | Opponent / Date | Att | Pos | Res / Pts | F-A | H-T | Scorers, Times, and Referees | 1 | 2 | 3 | 4 | 5 | 6 | 7 | 8 | 9 | 10 | 11 | Subs used |
|---|---|---|---|---|---|---|---|---|---|---|---|---|---|---|---|---|---|---|---|---|
| 35 | A | PRESTON | | 20 | L | 0-1 | 0-0 | | Davis K | Alexander | Thomas | Waddock* | Davis S | Patterson | Evers^ | McLaren | Oldfield | Gray | Marshall" | Davies/Spring/Fotiadis |
| | | 3/3 | *6,992* | *17* | 38 | | | *Kidd 67* | *Moilanen* | *Parkinson* | *Kidd* | *Murdock* | *Jackson* | *Gregan* | *Appleton* | *Davey* | *Ashcroft* | *Sissoko** | *Eyres* | *Mullin* |
| | | | | | | | | Ref: B Coddington | In a game between two poor sides, the mid-field is unable to cope and all three players are changed during the course of the match. Ryan Kidd scores the only goal after Kelvin Davis punches a corner to him which he returns into the top corner. Gray has a shot saved in the final minute. | | | | | | | | | | |
| 36 | H | WYCOMBE | | 21 | D | 0-0 | 0-0 | | Davis K | Alexander | Thomas | Spring* | Davis S | Patterson | Evers | McLaren | Oldfield | Gray | Marshall^ | Davies/Fotiadis |
| | | 7/3 | 6,114 | *14* | 39 | | | | *Taylor* | *Kerslake* | *Kavanagh* | *Ryan* | *Cousins* | *Mohan* | *Carroll* | *Scott* | *Stallard** | *McGavin* | *Brown* | *Harkin* |
| | | | | | | | | Ref: M Pierce | Relegation is now staring the Hatters in the face after the third game in a row where they are unable to break down a strong defence. Wycombe have only one shot on target during the game and Marshall drags the Towns best opportunity wide. Trevor Peake has now moved to Coventry. | | | | | | | | | | |
| 37 | A | BURNLEY | | 21 | D | 1-1 | 0-0 | Thomas 80 | Davis K | James | Thomas | Waddock* | Davis S | Patterson | Evers | McLaren | Oldfield | Gray | Fotiadis^ | Davies/Marshall |
| | | 14/3 | *9,656* | *23* | 40 | | | *Payton 61* | *Woods* | *Brass* | *Winstanley* | *Harrison** | *Moore* | *Weller* | *Vinnic'mbe^* | *Ford* | *Cooke* | *Payton* | *Robertson* | *Howey/Smith* |
| | | | | | | | | Ref: M Dean | The loss of Tony Thorpe to Fulham is now evident as the Town squander several late opportunities to win the game. Andy Payton beats the offside trap to race through and open the scoring, against the run of play. Mitchell Thomas stoops to head home a rare goal following a corner. | | | | | | | | | | |
| 38 | H | GRIMSBY | | 23 | D | 2-2 | 0-0 | Evers 66, Davis 85 | Davis K | James | Thomas | Evers | Davis S | Patterson | Fotiadis* | McLaren | Oldfield | Marshall | Alexander | Douglas |
| | | 21/3 | 5,722 | *4* | 41 | | | *Gallimore 54, Donovan 64* | *Davison* | *McDermott* | *Gallimore* | *Handyside* | *Lever* | *Burnett* | *Donovan* | *Smith* | *Nogan** | *Lester* | *Groves* | *Livingstone* |
| | | | | | | | | Ref: A Hall | In a pulsating game, the powerful Mariners steam into a two-goal lead before Evers thumps a beautiful shot into the top corner. In a do or die effort, Steve Davis pushes up and heads the equaliser and in a frantic finale, Oldfield misses a sitter which would have secured an unlikely win. | | | | | | | | | | |
| 39 | A | WALSALL | | 21 | W | 3-2 | 1-0 | Oldfield 35, Allen 58, Marshall 73 | Davis K | James | Thomas | Waddock | Davis S | White | Marshall | McLaren* | Oldfield^ | **Allen R** | Alexander | Evers/Doherty |
| | | 28/3 | *3,922* | *17* | 44 | | | *Viveash 53, Tholot 74* | *Walker* | *Evans* | *Marsh* | *Viveash* | *Roper* | *Peron* | *Boli* | *Keates** | *Platt^* | *Porter* | *Tholot* | *Eydelie/Ricketts* |
| | | | | | | | | Ref: W Burns | Loan signing from Tottenham, Rory Allen, chases a lost cause and pulls the ball back for Oldfield to open the scoring. Adrian Viveash powers in a header before Oldfield breaks, with his shot against a post being steered home by Allen. Marshall side-foots the third from a narrow angle. | | | | | | | | | | |
| 40 | H | YORK | | 19 | W | **3-0** | 2-0 | Alexander 35p, Oldfield 44, Gray 85 | Davis K | James | Thomas | Evers | Davis S* | Patterson | Marshall^ | McLaren | Oldfield | Allen R | Alexander | White/Gray |
| | | 4/4 | 5,541 | *15* | 47 | | | | *Warrington* | *McMillan* | *Thompson* | *Jordan* | *Jones* | *Rennison !* | *Pouton* | *Tinkler !* | *Rowe** | *Cresswell^* | *Bushell* | *Tolson/Gabbiadini* |
| | | | | | | | | Ref: D Crick | Alexander converts the first penalty of the season for the Hatters after debutant, Graham Rennison, is dismissed for handling the ball on the line. David Oldfield side-foots into the top corner and then Phil Gray hits the third before Mark Tinkler is sent off, late on, for a second yellow card. | | | | | | | | | | |
| 41 | A | GRIMSBY | | 17 | W | 1-0 | 0-0 | Allen 54 | Davis K | James | Thomas | Waddock | Patterson | White | Marshall* | McLaren | Oldfield^ | Allen R" | Alexander | Evers/Gray/Doherty |
| | | 7/4 | *4,455* | *3* | 50 | | | | *Davison* | *Butterfield* | *Gallimore* | *Handyside* | *Lever** | *Burnett* | *Donovan* | *Smith^* | *Clare* | *Lester"* | *Groves* | *Dobbin/Black/Woods* |
| | | | | | | | | Ref: R Pearson | Luton put in a fine all-round team performance with Kelvin Davis pulling off amazing saves from Paul Groves and Kingsley Black. Oldfield hits the post but Allen follows up to net the only goal of the game. In a frantic final minute, Neil Woods shoots wide and Doherty hits the post. | | | | | | | | | | |
| 42 | A | GILLINGHAM | | 19 | L | 1-2 | 1-1 | Allen 44 | Davis K | James* | Thomas | Waddock^ | Patterson ! | White | Marshall" | McLaren | Oldfield | Allen R | Alexander | Evers/Doherty/Gray |
| | | 11/4 | *6,846* | *6* | 50 | | | *Akinbiyi 28, 49* | *Bartram* | *Patterson* | *Pennock* | *Smith* | *Ashby* | *Bryant* | *Hessenthaler* | *Galloway* | *Butler** | *Akinbiyi^* | *Southall"* | *Thom's/Fortune-West/Corb'tt* |
| | | | | | | | | Ref: F Stretton | Steve Butler crosses for Ade Akinbiyi to score with a simple effort but Allen levels after taking advantage of a poor back-pass by Hessenthaler. Akinbiyi hits the winner before Patterson is sent off in the 81st minute for tripping the goalscorer but the Town are a well-beaten side by then. | | | | | | | | | | |
| 43 | H | CHESTERFIELD | | 17 | W | **3-0** | 1-0 | Williams 24 (og), Allen 48, Oldfield 65 | Davis K | James | Thomas | Evers | Davis S | Patterson | Marshall | Spring* | Oldfield | Allen R^ | Alexander | Waddock/Douglas |
| | | 14/4 | 5,884 | *9* | 53 | | | | *Mercer* | *Hewitt* | *Jules** | *Curtis* | *Williams* | *Carr* | *Willis* | *Howard* | *Reeves* | *Breckin* | *Perkins* | *Beaumont* |
| | | | | | | | | Ref: M Bailey | Rory Allen is proving to be the best loan signing of all time. He sets up Marshall for a shot which takes a deflection to open the scoring and then slides in a knock-down from Thomas for the second, shortly after the break. Evers rolls a pass to Oldfield who side-foots home the third. | | | | | | | | | | |
| 44 | A | BRISTOL ROV | | 19 | L | 1-2 | 0-2 | Oldfield 75 | Davis K | James* | Thomas | Waddock^ | Davis S | Patterson | Marshall" | Evers | Oldfield | Allen R | Alexander | White/Spring/Douglas |
| | | 18/4 | *8,038* | *5* | 53 | | | *Beadle 4, Tillson 32* | *Jones* | *Pritchard* | *Lockwood* | *Holloway* | *Foster* | *Tillson* | *Zabek* | *Ramasut* | *Beadle* | *Cureton* | *Hayles* | |
| | | | | | | | | Ref: A Leake | The Town go a goal down when a long range effort from Peter Beadle is fumbled by Kelvin Davis but the game is marred when Julian James breaks his leg following a clash with Barry Hayles. Andy Tillson has a free header to extend the lead before David Oldfield reduces the deficit. | | | | | | | | | | |
| 45 | A | BRENTFORD | | 18 | D | 2-2 | 1-1 | Marshall 13, Allen 59 | Davis K | Alexander | Thomas | Waddock | Davis S | White | Evers | McLaren* | Oldfield | Allen R | Marshall^ | Spring/Douglas"/Doherty |
| | | 25/4 | *6,598* | *20* | 54 | | | *Scott 22, Hutchings 80* | *Dearden* | *Hutchings* | *Watson* | *Cullip* | *Bates* | *Hogg* | *Blaney* | *Cockerill** | *Scott* | *Aspinall^* | *Thompson"* | *Dennis/Oatway/Rapley* |
| | | | | | | | | Ref: M Halsey | Marshall puts the Town into the lead but a long throw from Jamie Bates finds an unmarked Andy Scott who nods home a soft equaliser. Allen shows superb skill in holding off three players before netting but Carl Hutchings heads the Bees level again to set up an anxious end to the game. | | | | | | | | | | |
| 46 | H | CARLISLE | | 17 | W | 3-2 | 1-0 | Evers 26, Oldfield 84, Allen 89 | Davis K | Patterson | **Fraser** | Evers | Davis S | White* | Fotiadis^ | McLaren" | Oldfield | Allen R | Alexander | Doherty/Douglas/Spring |
| | | 2/5 | 6,729 | *23* | 57 | | | *Anthony 53, Wright 82* | *Caig* | *Liburd* | *Sandwith* | *Prokas* | *Varty* | *Foster* | *Anthony* | *Dobie* | *Stevens* | *Smart* | *Wright* | |
| | | Home | Away | | | | | Ref: M Fletcher | Sean Evers fires the Hatters in to the lead but the already relegated Cumbrians fight back strongly with Anthony and Wright setting them up for the win. Rory Allen signs off from his loan spell with a goal in the last minute which goes in off the bar, winning all three points for the Town. | | | | | | | | | | |
| Average | | 5,880 | 6,376 | | | | | | | | | | | | | | | | | |

| Coca-Cola Cup | | | | F-A | H-T | Scorers, Times, and Referees | 1 | 2 | 3 | 4 | 5 | 6 | 7 | 8 | 9 | 10 | 11 | subs used |
|---|---|---|---|---|---|---|---|---|---|---|---|---|---|---|---|---|---|---|
| 1:1 A COLCHESTER | | | W | 1-0 | 0-0 | Thorpe 87 | Feuer | Douglas | Thomas | Waddock | Davis S | Johnson | McLaren | Alexander | Oldfield* | Thorpe | Davies | Harvey |
| 12/8 | 2,840 | D3 | | | | | *Emberson* | *Gregory* | *Stamps* | *Skelton** | *Greene* | *Cawley* | *Wilkins* | *Buckle* | *Sale^* | *Abrahams"* | *Hathaway* | *Forbes/Lock/Adcock* |
| | | | | | | Ref: S Bennett | In a game dominated by the defences, few chances are created as the Town lose control of the mid-field in the last twenty minutes. Ex-Hatter, David Greene, gives the ball away in his own area. Thorpe seizes on it and hammers in into the top corner of the net for the unlikely winner. | | | | | | | | | | | |
| 1:2 H COLCHESTER | | 15 | D | 1-1 | 1-0 | Thorpe 34 | Abbey | James | Thomas | Waddock | Davis S | Johnson | Davies* | McLaren | Oldfield | Thorpe | Marshall | Douglas |
| 26/8 | 2,816 | 3:8 | | | | *Hathaway 51* | *Emberson* | *Gregory* | *Stamps* | *Forbes* | *Greene* | *Cawley* | *Wilkins* | *Buckle* | *Sale* | *Abrahams** | *Hathaway^* | *Adcock/Lock* |
| | | | | | | Ref: D Orr (Hatters win 2-1 on aggregate) | Good combination play, which carves an opening in the Colchester defence, allows Thorpe to score, giving the Town a 2-0 aggregate lead. What was turning into a stroll is changed when a volley from Hathaway flies into the top corner of the net and, for a time, the visitors look dangerous. | | | | | | | | | | | |
| 2:1 H WEST BROM | | 21 | D | 1-1 | 1-1 | Douglas 24 | Dibble | Alexander | Harvey | Waddock | Davis S | Johnson* | Evers^ | McLaren | Oldfield | Douglas | Marshall | Davies/George |
| 16/9 | 3,437 | 1:3 | | | | *Taylor 34* | *Miller* | *Holmes* | *Smith* | *Sneekes* | *Burgess* | *Raven* | *Coldicott* | *Hamilton* | *Taylor* | *Hunt* | *Kilbane* | |
| | | | | | | Ref: E Wolstenholme | Early pressure from the Town leads to Douglas netting, only for the effort to be ruled out for a foul. He opens the scoring when he hits a shot, on the turn, which flies into the bottom corner of the net. Albion level when Bob Taylor heads in a cross from close range from David Smith. | | | | | | | | | | | |
| 2:2 A WEST BROM | | 23 | L | 2-4 | 1-1 | Davis 38, Thorpe 73 | Dibble | Evers | Harvey | Waddock | Davis S | White | Gray | McLaren | Oldfield | Douglas* | Davies^ | Thorpe/George |
| 23/9 | 7,227 | 1:3 | | | | *Rav'n 41, McDerm't 51, Pesch'ldo 66, 88* | *Miller* | *McDermott* | *Smith* | *Sneekes* | *Burgess* | *Raven* | *Flynn* | *Hamilton* | *Taylor** | *Hunt* | *Kilbane* | *Peschisolido* |
| | | | | | | Ref: P Richards (Hatters lose 3-5 on aggregate) | Dibble, who is supported by a make-shift back four, has a shaky night in the Luton goal. Steve Davis rockets in a 25-yard free-kick but Paul Raven levels soon after when the defence fails to clear a cross. Tony Thorpe reduces the arrears before Paul Peschisolido makes the game safe. | | | | | | | | | | | |

| FA Cup | | | | | | | | | | | | | | | | | | |
|---|---|---|---|---|---|---|---|---|---|---|---|---|---|---|---|---|---|---|
| 1 H TORQUAY | | 22 | L | 0-1 | 0-0 | | Feuer | James | Harvey* | Waddock^ | White | Spring" | Fotiadis | McLaren | Oldfield | Thorpe | Alexander | Doherty/Patterson/Davies |
| 15/11 | 3,446 | 3:13 | | | | *Gibbs 74p* | *Gregg* | *Gurney* | *Gibbs* | *Robinson* | *Gittens* | *Watson* | *Clayton* | *Hill* | *Jack* | *Bedau* | *Hapgood* | |
| | | | | | | Ref: P Durkin | The Town fail to get beyond the first round for the first time since 1929 in a dismal performance. The Torquay defence soaks up the pressure and they twice go close to scoring before Tony Bedau is fouled by Alexander in the area. Paul Gibbs confidently shoots home from the spot. | | | | | | | | | | | |

| | | Home | | | | | Away | | | | | |
|---|---|---|---|---|---|---|---|---|---|---|---|---|
| | P | W | D | L | F | A | W | D | L | F | A | Pts |
| 1 Watford | 46 | 13 | 7 | 3 | 36 | 22 | 11 | 9 | 3 | 31 | 19 | 88 |
| 2 Bristol City | 46 | 16 | 5 | 2 | 41 | 17 | 9 | 5 | 9 | 28 | 22 | 85 |
| 3 Grimsby * | 46 | 11 | 7 | 5 | 30 | 14 | 8 | 8 | 7 | 25 | 23 | 72 |
| 4 Northampton | 46 | 14 | 5 | 4 | 33 | 17 | 4 | 12 | 7 | 19 | 20 | 71 |
| 5 Bristol Rov | 46 | 13 | 2 | 8 | 43 | 33 | 7 | 8 | 8 | 27 | 31 | 70 |
| 6 Fulham | 46 | 12 | 7 | 4 | 31 | 14 | 8 | 3 | 12 | 29 | 29 | 70 |
| 7 Wrexham | 46 | 10 | 10 | 3 | 31 | 23 | 8 | 6 | 9 | 24 | 28 | 70 |
| 8 Gillingham | 46 | 13 | 7 | 3 | 30 | 18 | 6 | 6 | 11 | 22 | 29 | 70 |
| 9 Bournemouth | 46 | 11 | 8 | 4 | 28 | 15 | 7 | 4 | 12 | 29 | 37 | 66 |
| 10 Chesterfield | 46 | 13 | 7 | 3 | 31 | 19 | 3 | 10 | 10 | 15 | 25 | 65 |
| 11 Wigan | 46 | 12 | 5 | 6 | 41 | 31 | 5 | 6 | 12 | 23 | 35 | 62 |
| 12 Blackpool | 46 | 13 | 6 | 4 | 35 | 24 | 4 | 5 | 14 | 24 | 43 | 62 |
| 13 Oldham | 46 | 13 | 7 | 3 | 43 | 23 | 2 | 9 | 12 | 19 | 31 | 61 |
| 14 Wycombe | 46 | 10 | 10 | 3 | 32 | 20 | 4 | 8 | 11 | 19 | 33 | 60 |
| 15 Preston | 46 | 10 | 6 | 7 | 29 | 26 | 5 | 8 | 10 | 27 | 30 | 59 |
| 16 York | 46 | 9 | 7 | 7 | 26 | 21 | 5 | 10 | 8 | 26 | 37 | 59 |
| 17 LUTON TOWN | 46 | 7 | 7 | 9 | 35 | 38 | 7 | 8 | 8 | 25 | 26 | 57 |
| 18 Millwall | 46 | 7 | 8 | 8 | 23 | 23 | 7 | 5 | 11 | 20 | 31 | 55 |
| 19 Walsall | 46 | 10 | 8 | 5 | 26 | 16 | 4 | 4 | 15 | 17 | 36 | 54 |
| 20 Burnley | 46 | 10 | 9 | 4 | 34 | 23 | 3 | 4 | 16 | 21 | 42 | 52 |
| 21 Brentford | 46 | 9 | 7 | 7 | 33 | 29 | 2 | 10 | 11 | 17 | 42 | 50 |
| 22 Plymouth | 46 | 10 | 5 | 8 | 36 | 30 | 2 | 8 | 13 | 19 | 40 | 49 |
| 23 Carlisle | 46 | 8 | 5 | 10 | 27 | 28 | 4 | 3 | 16 | 30 | 45 | 44 |
| 24 Southend | 46 | 8 | 7 | 8 | 29 | 30 | 3 | 3 | 17 | 18 | 49 | 43 |
| | 1104 | 262 | 162 | 128 | 783 | 554 | 128 | 162 | 262 | 554 | 783 | 1494 |

* promoted after play-offs

Odds & ends

Double wins: (4) Carlisle, Plymouth, Southend, York.
Double losses: (3) Bristol Rovers, Preston, Wrexham.

Won from behind: (1) Carlisle (h).
Lost from in front: (3) Bristol Rovers (h), Burnley (h), West Brom (LC).

High spots: The form of the younger players towards the end of the season.
The signing of Rory Allen, on loan from Tottenham.
Three consecutive wins just before Easter, raising hopes of survival.
Beating Chesterfield 3-0 at Kenilworth Road, to virtually ensure safety.

Low spots: The dismal home record before Christmas.
The chronic injury situation.
Only one penalty awarded over the whole season.
The sale of Tony Thorpe.
The 0-4 home humiliation by Watford.
Exiting the FA Cup in Round 1 for the first time since 1929.

Player of the Year: David Oldfield.
Ever-presents: (0).
Hat-tricks: Tony Thorpe (1).
Leading scorer: Tony Thorpe (17).

| | Appearances | | | | | | Goals | | | |
|---|---|---|---|---|---|---|---|---|---|---|
| | Lge | *Sub* | LC | *Sub* | FAC | *Sub* | Lge | LC | FAC | Tot |
| Abbey, Nathan | | | 1 | | | | | | | |
| Alexander, Graham | **39** | | 2 | | 1 | | **8** | | | **8** |
| Allen, Chris | **14** | | | | | | **1** | | | **1** |
| Allen, Rory | **8** | | | | | | **6** | | | **6** |
| Davies, Simon | **8** | *12* | 3 | *1* | | *1* | **1** | | | **1** |
| Davis, Kelvin | **32** | | | | | | | | | |
| Davis, Steve | **38** | | 4 | | | | **5** | 1 | | **6** |
| Dibble, Andy | **1** | | 2 | | | | | | | |
| Doherty, Gary | **1** | *9* | | | | *1* | | | | |
| Douglas, Stuart | **5** | *12* | 3 | *1* | | | **1** | 1 | | **2** |
| Evers, Sean | **14** | *9* | 2 | | | | **3** | | | **3** |
| Feuer, Ian | **13** | | 1 | | 1 | | | | | |
| Fotiadis, Andrew | **5** | *10* | | | 1 | | **1** | | | **1** |
| Fraser, Stuart | **1** | | | | | | | | | |
| George, Liam | **1** | | | *2* | | | | | | |
| Gray, Phil | **14** | *3* | 1 | | | | **2** | | | **2** |
| Harvey, Richard | **5** | *1* | 2 | *1* | 1 | | | | | |
| James, Julian | **23** | *1* | 1 | | 1 | | | | | |
| Johnson, Marvin | **13** | *1* | 3 | | | | **2** | | | **2** |
| Kean, Robert | | *1* | | | | | | | | |
| Marshall, Dwight | **19** | *10* | 2 | | | | **3** | | | **3** |
| McGowan, Gavin | **6** | *2* | | | | | | | | |
| McLaren, Paul | **41** | *2* | 4 | | 1 | | | | | |
| Oldfield, David | **45** | | 4 | | 1 | | **10** | | | **10** |
| Patterson, Darren | **23** | | | | | *1* | | | | |
| Peake, Trevor | | *1* | | | | | | | | |
| Showler, Paul | | *1* | | | | | | | | |
| Small, Bryan | **15** | | | | | | | | | |
| Spring, Matthew | **6** | *6* | | | 1 | | | | | |
| Thomas, Mitchell | **27** | *1* | 2 | | | | **1** | | | **1** |
| Thorpe, Tony | **27** | *1* | 2 | *1* | 1 | | **14** | 3 | | **17** |
| Waddock, Gary | **36** | *2* | 4 | | 1 | | | | | |
| White, Alan | **26** | *2* | 1 | | 1 | | **1** | | | **1** |
| (own-goals) | | | | | | | **1** | | | **1** |
| **33 players used** | **506** | ***87*** | **44** | ***6*** | **11** | ***3*** | **60** | **5** | | **65** |

| No | Date | | Att | Pos | Pt | F-A | H-T | Scorers, Times, and Referees | 1 | 2 | 3 | 4 | 5 | 6 | 7 | 8 | 9 | 10 | 11 | subs used |
|---|---|---|---|---|---|---|---|---|---|---|---|---|---|---|---|---|---|---|---|---|
| 1 | A | WYCOMBE | | | W | 1-0 | 1-0 | Davis S 35 | Davis K | Alexander | Thomas | Spring | Davis S | Johnson | McKinnon | Evers | Bacque* | Gray | Marshall^ | George/McGowan |
| | 8/8 | | 5,252 | | 3 | | | | Taylor | Kavanagh* | Vinnicombe | Ryan | Cousins | McCarthy | Carroll | Stallard | Harkin^ | Scott | Brown | Cornforth/Read |
| | | | | | | | | Ref: A Bates | On a scorching hot day, a 25-yard rocket free-kick from skipper Steve Davis is good enough to win any game. Town have the majority of the play; however, Keith Scott hits the post when it looks easier to score. Bacque says 'It was much hotter than any game I have played in France.' | | | | | | | | | | | |
| 2 | H | PRESTON | | 7 | D | 1-1 | 0-1 | Marshall 54 | Davis K | Alexander | McGowan* | Spring | Davis S | Johnson | McKinnon^ | Evers | Bacque" | Gray | Marshall | White/McLaren/George |
| | 15/8 | | 5,392 | 6 | 4 | | | Macken 41 | Moilanen | Parkinson | Ludden | Murdock | Jackson | Gregan | Appleton ! | Rankine | Nogan* | Macken^ | Eyres | Holt/Cartwright |
| | | | | | | | | Ref: S Bennett | 'A game of two halves' says Lawrence using the classic cliché. Preston take a deserved interval lead but the Hatters fight back resolutely in the second period and could have secured all three points after Appleton is dismissed with 15 minutes left for a nasty lunge on Dwight Marshall. | | | | | | | | | | | |
| 3 | A | READING | | 12 | L | 0-3 | 0-1 | | Davis K | Alexander | McGowan | Spring | Davis S | White | McLaren* | Evers | Douglas^ | Gray | Marshall" | George/Thomas/McKinnon |
| | 22/8 | | 18,108 | 15 | 4 | | | Brebner 10, McIntyre 51, Fleck 84 | v der Kwaak | Bernal* | Gray | Brebner | Primus | Kromher | Houghton | Caskey | McIntyre^ | Reilly | Saar" | Booty/Fleck/Williams |
| | | | | | | | | Ref: R Styles | The Hatters fail to spoil the party on the opening day of the Madejski Stadium, although the final score-line flatters the home side. Lawrence bemoans the fact that two players have to limp off in the first 15 minutes, but also praises Mass Saar who runs rings around the Luton defence. | | | | | | | | | | | |
| 4 | H | COLCHESTER | | 9 | W | 2-0 | 0-0 | Douglas 62, Davis S 82 | Davis K | Alexander | McGowan | Spring | Davis S | Johnson ! | McKinnon | Evers | Douglas* | Gray^ | George" | Fotiadis/Thomas/Bacque |
| | 29/8 | | 5,005 | 11 | 7 | | | | Emberson | Dunne* | Stamps^ | Williams | Greene | Buckle | Wilkins | Gregory D | Sale | Gregory N" | Abrahams | Forbes/Haydon/Duguid |
| | | | | | | | | Ref: R Furnandiz | A red card for Marvin Johnson, after he pulled down a clear-on-goal Neil Gregory, angers the Luton players and spurs them on to a deserved first home win of the season, much to the relief of Lawrence. Colchester show very little in attack, even after the Town go down to ten men. | | | | | | | | | | | |
| 5 | A | WIGAN | | 5 | W | 3-1 | 1-0 | Davis S 42, Evers 78, Gray 80 | Davis K | Alexander | McGowan | Spring | Davis S | Johnson | McKinnon | Evers | Douglas* | Gray | George^ | Bacque/McIndoe |
| | 31/8 | | 3,778 | 18 | 10 | | | Barlow 62 | Carroll | Green | Bradshaw | Griffiths | McGibbon | Rogers | Lee | Martinez* | Warne^ | Kilford | Barlow | Sharp/Lowe |
| | | | | | | | | Ref: W Burns | After being booed in his previous game, Phil Gray answers his critics by turning in a match-winning performance. The only black spot to the game is the foul by Scott Green on Liam George, when through on goal, which leaves the forward with a broken foot and out for six months. | | | | | | | | | | | |
| 6 | H | BURNLEY | | 2 | W | 1-0 | 0-0 | Douglas 47 | Davis K | Alexander | McGowan | Spring | Davis S | Johnson | McKinnon | Evers | Douglas* | Gray | McIndoe^ | Fotiadis/Thomas |
| | 5/9 | | 5,554 | 19 | 13 | | | | Ward | Robertson | Armstrong | Reid | Swan | Brass | Little | Jepson | Cooke | Payton | Smith | |
| | | | | | | | | Ref: K Leach | Another inconsistent refereeing decision, with Burnley's Brian Reid escaping punishment for a bear-hug on Stuart Douglas after he had got behind the defence; however, he is the quickest to react to a Davis header and scores the winning goal which puts the Town up to second spot. | | | | | | | | | | | |
| 7 | A | WREXHAM | | 3 | D | 1-1 | 1-1 | McKinnon 35 | Davis K | Alexander | McGowan | Spring | Davis S | Johnson | McKinnon | Evers | Douglas* | Gray | McIndoe | Bacque |
| | 8/9 | | 2,951 | 6 | 14 | | | Skinner 42 | Cartwright | McGregor | Brace | Brammer | Ridler | Humes | Skinner* | Owen | Spink | Roberts^ | Russell | Connolly/Rishworth |
| | | | | | | | | Ref: A Hall | Wrexham is a bogey ground for the Town and a point is therefore most acceptable. Ray McKinnon nets his first goal for the club but an error from Kelvin Davis when the ball slips out of his hands gives the home side a simple leveller. Wrexham have a late penalty appeal turned down. | | | | | | | | | | | |
| 8 | H | BRISTOL ROV | | 3 | W | 2-0 | 2-0 | Davis S 7, Alexander 9 | Davis K | Alexander | McGowan | Spring | Davis S | White | McKinnon* | Evers | Douglas^ | Gray | McIndoe | Thomas/Fotiadis |
| | 12/9 | | 5,558 | 13 | 17 | | | | Collett | Leoni | Basford | Trees | Foster | Tillson | Holloway* | Meaker | Roberts | Cureton | Hayles | Shore |
| | | | | | | | | Ref: B Coddington | Lawrence is immensely proud of his young side as they overcome a highly-rated Pirates outfit. Steve Davis helps to keep the much-vaunted Rovers forward line at bay and also manages to slot home his fourth goal of the season to make him the leading scorer by a very wide margin. | | | | | | | | | | | |
| 9 | A | BLACKPOOL | | 5 | L | 0-1 | 0-0 | | Davis K | Alexander | McGowan | Spring | Davis S | Johnson | Cox | Evers | Douglas* | Gray^ | McIndoe" | Marshall/Bacque/Thomas |
| | 19/9 | | 5,695 | 4 | 17 | | | Nowland 88 | Banks | Bryan | Shuttlew'rth | Bardsley | Carlisle | Ormerod* | Thompson | Clarkson | Aldridge^ | Bushell | Malkin" | Nowland/Bent/Hughes |
| | | | | | | | | Ref: G Cain | Casual Town are made to pay when the 17-year-old substitute Adam Nowland nets the only goal in the 88th minute. Manager Lawrence keeps the players behind in a locked changing room to read them the Riot Act, with the only player to escape criticism being debutant Jimmy Cox. | | | | | | | | | | | |
| 10 | H | WALSALL | | 7 | L | 0-1 | 0-0 | | Davis K | Alexander | McGowan ! | Spring* | Davis S | Johnson | McKinnon | Evers | Douglas^ | Fotiadis | Cox" | White/Gray/McIndoe |
| | 26/9 | | 5,530 | 5 | 17 | | | Rammell 87 | Walker | Marsh | Pointon | Keates | Green | Viveash | Wrack | Brissett* | Rammell | Larusson | Simpson | Watson |
| | | | | | | | | Ref: P Richards | It is a game too far for the Luton youngsters after their midweek exertions in defeating Ipswich Town, and they put on a tired performance. The strong Saddlers side miss several chances before netting a late winner. McGowan is sent off in the last minute for a second bookable offence. | | | | | | | | | | | |
| 11 | A | FULHAM | | 7 | W | 3-1 | 1-0 | Gray 5, Douglas 48, Davis S 65 | Davis K | Alexander | Thomas | Spring | Davis S | Johnson | McKinnon | Evers | Douglas* | Gray | McGowan^ | Fotiadis/Cox |
| | 3/10 | | 11,856 | 4 | 20 | | | Neilson 86 | Taylor | Collins | Brevett | Neilson | Coleman | Symons | Beardsley | Bracewell* | Scott^ | Lehmann" | Hayward | Davis/Uhlenbeek/Cornwall |
| | | | | | | | | Ref: J Kirkby | The Town bounce back from the previous poor performance to completely overwhelm Fulham in all departments. Manager Kevin Keegan admits that Luton put on the best display against his side since his arrival at Craven Cottage and that the Hatters could have scored more goals. | | | | | | | | | | | |

| No | Venue | Opponent / Date | Att | Pos | Res | F-A | H-T | Scorers, Times, and Referees | 1 | 2 | 3 | 4 | 5 | 6 | 7 | 8 | 9 | 10 | 11 | Subs used |
|---|---|---|---|---|---|---|---|---|---|---|---|---|---|---|---|---|---|---|---|---|
| 12 | A | YORK | | 4 | D | 3-3 | 2-2 | Douglas 22, Evers 43, Gray 55 | Davis K | Alexander | Thomas | Spring | Davis S | Johnson | McKinnon* | Evers | Douglas^ | Gray | McIndoe | White/Cox |
| | | 10/10 | *3,780* | *8* | 21 | | | *Connolly 1, Cresswell 10,64* | *Mimms* | *McMillan* | *Thompson* | *Jordan** | *Tinkler* | *Barras* | *Connelly* | *Garratt^* | *Cresswell* | *Tolson"* | *Agnew* | *Jones/Hall/Rowe* |
| | | | | | | | | Ref: T Jones | The Town are awful in the opening 20 minutes, but after they find their stride, they attack with a will, although both sides are poor defensively. Heroics from the injured Kelvin Davis keeps York at bay in the closing minutes and Phil Gray is now starting to justify his £400,000 price tag. | | | | | | | | | | | |
| 13 | H | OLDHAM | | 4 | W | 2-0 | 0-0 | Gray 82, Scarlett 90 | Davis K | Alexander | Thomas | Spring | Davis S | Johnson | McKinnon* | Evers | Douglas^ | Gray | McIndoe" | White/Fotiadis/**Scarlett** |
| | | 17/10 | 5,447 | *21* | 24 | | | | *Kelly* | *McNiven S ! McLean** | *Garnett* | *Thom* | *Sinnott* | *Rickers* | *Orlygsson* | *Littlejohn^* | *Allott* | *Reid* | *Holt/McNiven D* | |
| | | | | | | | | Ref: R Olivier | The Latics come for a point but the game opens up when Scott McNiven is harshly red-carded for clattering pint-sized debutant Andre Scarlett. Phil Gray finally breaks the deadlock with a trademark header and Scarlett slams home the second in stoppage time to ensure all three points. | | | | | | | | | | | |
| 14 | H | NORTHAMPTON | | 3 | W | 1-0 | 1-0 | Alexander 19 | Davis K | Alexander | Thomas | Spring* | Davis S | Johnson | McKinnon | Evers | Douglas^ | Gray | McIndoe | White/Fotiadis |
| | | 20/10 | 6,087 | *19* | 27 | | | | *Woodman* | *Gibb* | *Frain* | *Sampson* | *Hodgson** | *Parrish* | *Hunt* | *Wilkinson* | *Corazzin* | *Savage^* | *Hill* | *Freestone/Heggs* |
| | | | | | | | | Ref: M Fletcher | The score-line flatters Northampton, who rarely troubled the Luton defence, as the Hatters move up to third behind Stoke and Preston after a Graham Alexander 25-yard deflected goal. The Cobblers preferred to thump the ball up to the tall Paul Wilkinson all evening without success. | | | | | | | | | | | |
| 15 | A | GILLINGHAM | | 4 | L | 0-1 | 0-0 | | Davis K | Alexander | Thomas | Spring | Davis S | Johnson | McKinnon* | Evers | Douglas | Gray | McGowan^ | White/Fotiadis |
| | | 24/10 | *5,602* | *12* | 27 | | | *Asaba 61* | *Bartram* | *Pennock* | *Patterson* | *Smith* | *Ashby* | *Bryant* | *Hodge** | *Elliott* | *Asaba* | *Southall* | *Taylor* | *Saunders* |
| | | | | | | | | Ref: M Brandwood | In a game of few chances, played on a waterlogged pitch, the team making the fewest errors was always likely to be the winner. Kelvin Davis charged 40 yards out of his goal in an attempt to stop Asaba but missed the ball, leaving the forward with a difficult but successful conversion. | | | | | | | | | | | |
| 16 | A | STOKE | | 6 | L | 1-3 | 0-2 | Douglas 81 | Davis K | Alexander ! | Thomas* | Spring^ | Davis S | Johnson | McKinnon | Evers | Douglas | Gray | McGowan | McLaren/Doherty |
| | | 7/11 | *12,964* | *1* | 27 | | | *Oldfield 5, Forsyth 37, Lightbourne 90* | *Muggleton* | *Short** | *Small^* | *Sigurdsson* | *Robinson* | *Woods* | *Keen* | *Forsyth* | *Thorne"* | *Lightbourne* | *Oldfield* | *Mackenzie/Whittle/Wallace* |
| | | | | | | | | Ref: M Jones | In a bad-tempered game which included nine bookings and a sending-off for Graham Alexander, the Hatters were unable to cope with the trickery and pace of ex-Town duo Bryan Small and David Oldfield. The header from Douglas, nine minutes from time, is too little too late. | | | | | | | | | | | |
| 17 | A | LINCOLN | | 6 | D | 2-2 | 1-1 | Gray 43, Doherty 76 | Davis K | McGowan | Thomas | Spring* | White | Johnson | McKinnon | Evers | Douglas | Gray | Davies^ | McLaren/Doherty |
| | | 21/11 | *4,893* | *24* | 28 | | | *Smith 40, McGowan 61 (og)* | *Richardson* | *Holmes* | *Bimson* | *Fleming* | *Brown* | *Austin* | *Smith* | *Finnigan* | *Battersby** | *Thorpe* | *Gordon^* | *Miller/Alcide* |
| | | | | | | | | Ref: M Cowburn | Basement battlers Lincoln, with chairman John Reames taking over as manager, give the Town the fright of their lives. Lawrence admits that City are difficult to play against and, after coming from behind twice, is grateful for a point, but the travelling supporters expect much better. | | | | | | | | | | | |
| 18 | H | MANCHESTER C | | 7 | D | 1-1 | 0-1 | Doherty 76 | Davis K | Alexander | McGowan* | Spring | Davis S | Johnson | McKinnon | Evers | Douglas^ | Gray | Davies" | McLaren/Doherty/White |
| | | 28/11 | **9,070** | *8* | 29 | | | *Morrison 29* | *Weaver* | *Edghill* | *Vaughan* | *Morrison** | *Wiekens* | *Crooks* | *Mason* | *Bishop^* | *Goater* | *Taylor* | *Russell* | *Tiatto/Brown* |
| | | | | | | | | Ref: A Bates | Super-sub Gary Doherty scores an identical goal and at an identical time to the one which saved a point at Lincoln the previous week. Physical City have adapted well to the rigours of Division Two but, after winning the first half, are forced back and, in the end, are lucky to earn a point. | | | | | | | | | | | |
| 19 | A | MACCLESFIELD | | 8 | D | 2-2 | 1-1 | Douglas 3, Gray 90 | Davis K | Alexander | Thomas | Spring* | Davis S | Johnson | McLaren | Evers | Douglas^ | Gray | McIndoe" | Doherty/Showler/White |
| | | 12/12 | ***2,902*** | *21* | 30 | | | *Sorvel 36, Tomlinson 46* | *Price* | *Hitchen* | *Ingram* | *Howarth* | *McDonald* | *Sodje* | *Askey* | *Sorvel* | *Tomlinson* | *Wood* | *Whittaker** | *Sedgmore* |
| | | | | | | | | Ref: M Warren | The Town fail to build on a bright start and it is Macclesfield who take up the running until forgotten man, Paul Showler, comes on for his first appearance in more than 15 months. He puts some spark back into the Town, although the last-minute lob from Gray is more than they deserve. | | | | | | | | | | | |
| 20 | H | MILLWALL | | 11 | L | 1-2 | 0-1 | Davis S 69 | Davis K | McGowan | Fraser | Spring | Davis S | Johnson | Scarlett | McLaren | Douglas | Gray* | Showler^ | White/Fotiadis |
| | | 19/12 | 5,939 | *8* | 30 | | | *Harris 45, Neill 82* | *Spink* | *Lavin* | *Ryan* | *Cahill* | *Stuart* | *Fitzgerald* | *Reid** | *Newman^* | *Harris* | *Shaw* | *Neill* | *Hockton/Stevens* |
| | | | | | | | | Ref: E Lomas | The Hatters have lost their way after six games without a win and, after a barn-storming opening period when Paul Showler squandered three opportunities, the confidence drops. A rare mistake from Steve Davis, nodding the ball into the path of Neil Harris, sets the Lions on their way. | | | | | | | | | | | |
| 21 | A | BOURNEMOUTH | | 14 | L | 0-1 | 0-0 | | Davis K | White | Thomas | Spring | Davis S | Johnson | Evers | **Harrison*** | Fotiadis | Gray | Showler^ | Bacque/Scarlett |
| | | 28/12 | *8,863* | *5* | 30 | | | *Cox 53* | *Ovendale* | *Young* | *Howe* | *Cox* | *Vincent* | *Bailey* | *Robinson* | *Hughes* | *Warren* | *Stein* | *Fletcher* | |
| | | | | | | | | Ref: D Crick | Although playing nice football in midfield, the Hatters lack a cutting edge and only have two shots on target all afternoon. Steve Davis has difficulties in making sorties up the field as he has problems coping with the big Steve Fletcher. The Fulham win now seems light years away. | | | | | | | | | | | |
| 22 | A | COLCHESTER | | 14 | D | 2-2 | 1-1 | Alexander 7p, White 72 | Davis K | Alexander | Thomas | Spring | White | Johnson | McLaren | Harrison | Douglas* | Gray | Evers | Doherty |
| | | 2/1 | *4,694* | *16* | 31 | | | *Gregory D 21p, Abrahams 84* | *Fernandes* | *Dunne* | *Betts* | *Williams** | *Greene* | *Buckle* | *Wilkins* | *Gregory D* | *Sale ^* | *Abrahams* | *Duguid"* | *Haydon/Gregory N/Lock* |
| | | | | | | | | Ref: B Knight | Steve Davis has departed to his spiritual home of Burnley for £800,000 and the loss is greatly felt as the Town struggle against a very ordinary Colchester. Replacement Alan White seems to have won the game with his header, but slackness at the back allows the U's to salvage a point. | | | | | | | | | | | |
| 23 | H | WYCOMBE | | 13 | W | **3-1** | 1-0 | Spring 16, Evers 69, Douglas 75 | Davis K | Harrison | White | Spring | **Dyche** | Johnson | Evers | McLaren | Douglas* | Gray ! | **Zah'na-Oni^** | Scarlett/Doherty |
| | | 9/1 | 5,063 | *22* | 34 | | | *Carroll 89p* | *Westhead* | *Lawrence* | *Kavanagh* | *Ryan !* | *Cousins* | *McCarthy !* | *Simpson* | *Emblen* | *McSporran* | *Scott* | *Carroll* | |
| | | | | | | | | Ref: M Messias | At last a win in a game which is spoilt by referee Matt Messias who sends off three and books another six. Amazingly, Kelvin Davis is lucky to stay on the field after clattering McSporran with the most blatant foul of the match. Wycombe manager Neil Smillie is sacked after the game. | | | | | | | | | | | |

| No | Date | | Att | Pos | Pt | F-A | H-T | Scorers, Times, and Referees | 1 | 2 | 3 | 4 | 5 | 6 | 7 | 8 | 9 | 10 | 11 | subs used |
|---|---|---|---|---|---|---|---|---|---|---|---|---|---|---|---|---|---|---|---|---|
| 24 | A | PRESTON | | 12 | L | 1-2 | 1-0 | Fotiadis 15 | Davis K | Harrison | White | Spring | Dyche | Johnson | Evers | McLaren | Douglas* | Fotiadis | McGowan^ | Doherty/Fraser |
| | 16/1 | | *11,034* | *3* | 34 | | | *Nogan 56, Harris 90* | *Lucas* | *Parkinson* | *Harrison* | *Murdock* | *Jackson* | *Gregan* | *McKenna* | *Rankine* | *Nogan** | *Macken^* | *Eyres"* | *Darby/Harris/Appleton* |
| | | | | | | | | Ref: F Stretton | The Hatters take a surprise lead at Deepdale, despite missing five senior players, and the back four succeeds in frustrating the home side until the 96th minute. Lennie Lawrence is proud of his men but bemoans Luton's quality of play on the break as several opportunities went begging. | | | | | | | | | | | |
| 25 | H | WIGAN | | 13 | L | **0-4** | 0-2 | *[Haworth 77]* | Davis K ! | Harrison | White | Spring | Dyche | Johnson | McGowan | Evers | Douglas | Fotiadis* | Zahana-Oni^ | Doherty/McIndoe |
| | 23/1 | | 4,934 | *11* | 34 | | | *McGibbon 15, Liddell 29, Jones 64,* | *Carroll* | *Green* | *Sharp* | *McGibbon* | *Balmer** | *Rogers* | *Liddell* | *Greenall* | *Jones^* | *O'Neill* | *Barlow"* | *Kilford/Lee/Haworth* |
| | | | | | | | | Ref: G Singh | 'If you've got six players missing, your best player is sold and the goalkeeper is sent off we are going to get bashed now and again,' moans Lennie Lawrence. Kelvin Davis is sent off for handling the ball outside the area and is replaced by Gerry Harrison. Wigan take full advantage. | | | | | | | | | | | |
| 26 | H | BOURNEMOUTH | | 14 | D | 2-2 | 1-0 | McKinnon 6, Doherty 53 | Davis K | Harrison* | McGowan | Spring | Dyche | Johnson | Evers | McLaren | Douglas^ | Doherty | McKinnon | White/Zahana-Oni |
| | 30/1 | | 5,426 | *5* | 35 | | | *Robinson 62, Vincent 69* | *Ovendale* | *Young* | *Vincent* | *Howe* | *O'Neill* | *Bailey* | *Cox* | *Robinson* | *Stein* | *Fletcher* | *Hughes* | |
| | | | | | | | | Ref: K Lynch | After the previous week's battering, Hatters play with passion for two thirds of the game, making the form team in the division look ordinary. McKinnon returns after seven weeks on the sidelines and slams home a beauty but, after Doherty scores the second, the Cherries fight back. | | | | | | | | | | | |
| 27 | A | BURNLEY | | 12 | W | 2-1 | 1-1 | Fotiadis 34, Doherty 87 | **Abbey** | Harrison | McGowan* | Spring | Dyche | Johnson | Evers | McLaren | Douglas^ | Fotiadis | McKinnon" | White/Doherty/Alexander |
| | 6/2 | | *10,285* | *16* | 38 | | | *Mellon 29* | *Crichton* | *Moore !* | *Morgan* | *Mellon* | *Davis* | *Reid* | *Little** | *Armstrong* | *Cooke* | *Payton^* | *Branch"* | *Swan/Robertson/Maylett* |
| | | | | | | | | Ref: P Walton | Hatters play some great football but then lose their way after the Clarets are reduced to ten men. Debutant keeper Nathan Abbey plays a blinder and the day is complete when Doherty hits an unstoppable shot just before the end. 'That's as good as we've played all season,' says Lawrence. | | | | | | | | | | | |
| 28 | H | WREXHAM | | 13 | L | 1-2 | 0-0 | Doherty 47 | Davis K | Harrison* | Alexander | Spring | Dyche | Johnson | Evers | McLaren | Doherty | Fotiadis^ | McKinnon" | White/Gray/Cox |
| | 13/2 | | 4,759 | *17* | 38 | | | *Edwards 57, Griffiths 67* | *Cartwright* | *McGregor* | *Hardy* | *Brammer* | *Spink* | *Carey* | *Chalk* | *Russell* | *Edwards* | *Griffiths** | *Whitley* | *Roberts* |
| | | | | | | | | Ref: A Wiley | A dull game picks up early in the second half when Doherty fires in from an acute angle but the Luton players then seem to wave the white flag after Wrexham equalise. Graham Alexander is booed for refusing to sign his new contract and the 'Lawrence out' chants are heard once again. | | | | | | | | | | | |
| 29 | A | BRISTOL ROV | | 13 | L | 0-1 | 0-1 | | Davis K | Alexander | White | McIndoe* | Dyche | Johnson | Scarlett^ | McLaren | Douglas | Doherty | McKinnon | **Kandol**/Zahana-Oni |
| | 20/2 | | *6,361* | *14* | 38 | | | *Tillson 26* | *Jones* | *Pethick* | *Challis* | *Trees* | *Thomson* | *Tillson* | *Shore* | *Low** | *Holloway* | *Cureton* | *Roberts* | *Penrice* |
| | | | | | | | | Ref: G Cain | Chairman David Kohler has resigned, the new stadium has been turned down, seven Luton first-team players are out and Bristol Rovers record their first home win since last October. The young Town side tries hard enough but does not have the quality to break down the home defence. | | | | | | | | | | | |
| 30 | H | NOTTS CO | | 13 | L | 0-1 | 0-0 | | Davis K | Alexander | McGowan | Spring | Dyche | Johnson* | Cox^ | McLaren | Douglas" | Doherty | McKinnon | White/Scarlett/Gray |
| | 23/2 | | **4,021** | *23* | 38 | | | *Rapley 72* | *Ward* | *Hendon* | *Pearce* | *Liburd* | *Warren* | *Richardson* | *Owers* | *Bowland* | *Rapley* | *Beadle* | *Tierney* | |
| | | | | | | | | Ref: R Styles | Another three points dropped, this time to relegation-threatened Notts County. The introduction of Gray livens up the Luton attack, but his shot rattles off both posts before falling to Scarlett, who is flagged for offside. Skipper Johnson is the latest of the senior players to limp off injured. | | | | | | | | | | | |
| 31 | H | BLACKPOOL | | 12 | W | 1-0 | 0-0 | Douglas 54 | Davis K | Alexander | Thomas | Spring* | **Willmott** | White | Harrison^ | McKinnon | Douglas | Gray | George" | McGowan/McLaren/Cox |
| | 27/2 | | 4,646 | *13* | 41 | | | | *Banks* | *Bryan* | *Hills* | *Carlisle* | *Hughes* | *Bardsley** | *Conroy* | *Clarkson* | *Aldridge^* | *Bushell* | *Ormerod* | *Thompson"/Bent/Nowland* |
| | | | | | | | | Ref: R Furnandiz | Town keep their first clean sheet for 13 games, with Chris Willmott forming a solid central defensive partnership with Alan White. Douglas nets with perhaps his hardest chance of the afternoon, but the good work is nearly undone as Blackpool attack with venom in the final minutes. | | | | | | | | | | | |
| 32 | A | WALSALL | | 13 | L | 0-1 | 0-0 | | Davis K | Alexander | Thomas | Spring | White | Johnson | Harrison* | McKinnon | Douglas | Gray | George^ | McLaren/McGowan |
| | 6/3 | | *4,508* | *3* | 41 | | | *Wrack 69* | *Walker* | *Marsh* | *Pointon** | *Keates* | *Viveash* | *Roper* | *Wrack* | *Cramb* | *Rammell* | *Larusson^* | *Mavrak"* | *Evans/Thomas/Brissett* |
| | | | | | | | | Ref: M Cowburn | On a wet, windy and miserable afternoon, shot-shy Luton manage just one feeble effort on target all game. Dean Keates runs the midfield and sets up Darren Wrack for the only goal. Sean Dyche has returned to Bristol City as Luton cannot sign anyone due to the off-field situation. | | | | | | | | | | | |
| 33 | H | FULHAM | | 13 | L | **0-4** | 0-1 | | Davis K | Alexander | Thomas* | Spring | White ! | Johnson | Harrison | McKinnon | Douglas^ | Gray | George" | McGowan/McLaren/Cox |
| | 9/3 | | 7,424 | *1* | 41 | | | *Horsfield 34,73, Trollope 64, Hayles 85* | *Taylor* | *Finnan* | *Brevett* | *Morgan* | *Coleman* | *Symons* | *Hayward* | *Smith** | *Horsfield^* | *Trollope* | *Hayles"* | *McAnespie/Betsy/Lehmann* |
| | | | | | | | | Ref: M Dean | The dismissal of Alan White after 32 minutes for a professional foul on Barry Hayles effectively ends the game as Fulham gain full revenge for their hammering by the Town five months earlier. This fifth defeat in six games could have been worse, as Davis saved a penalty from Finnan. | | | | | | | | | | | |
| 34 | H | STOKE | | 14 | L | 1-2 | 0-2 | Alexander 47p | Davis K | Alexander | Thomas | Spring | White* | Johnson | Harrison^ | McKinnon | Douglas | Gray | George" | Willmott/McLaren/Doherty |
| | 13/3 | | 5,221 | *7* | 41 | | | *Kavanagh G 10p, 17* | *Ward* | *Kavanagh J* | *Woods* | *Sigurdsson* | *Mohan* | *Short* | *Robinson* | *Kavanagh G* | *Forsyth** | *Crowe^* | *Oldfield* | *Wallace/Keen* |
| | | | | | | | | Ref: A D'Urso | Town have scored just one goal from open play in 583 minutes and have kept only one clean sheet in 22 matches as they sink further down the league. Stoke, who came into the game in poor form, are gifted two goals by Mitchell Thomas. Goalkeeper Gavin Ward has an easy afternoon. | | | | | | | | | | | |

| No | Date | Opponent | Att | Pos | Pt | F-A | H-T | Scorers, Times, and Referees | | | | | | | | | | | | |
|---|---|---|---|---|---|---|---|---|---|---|---|---|---|---|---|---|---|---|---|---|
| 35 | A | CHESTERFIELD | | 14 | L | 1-3 | 0-0 | Gray 82 | Davis K | Alexander | Thomas | Spring | Willmott | Johnson | Harrison* | McKinnon^ | Douglas" | Gray | McGowan | Doherty/McLaren/George |
| | 20/3 | | *3,921* | *10* | 41 | | | *Wilkinson 52, 56, Reeves 66* | *Mercer* | *Hewitt* | *Nicholson* | *Curtis* | *Williams* | *Blatherwick* | *Howard** | *Holland* | *Reeves* | *Beaumont* | *Wilkinson* | *Lee* |
| | | | | | | | | Ref: R Pearson | Lawrence pleads for two or three experienced players before the transfer deadline next Thursday as the Hatters slump to their fourth defeat on the trot and edge ever nearer to the relegation places. The Town are truly awful again, allowing an average Spireites team to stroll to victory. | | | | | | | | | | | |
| 36 | H | READING | | 14 | D | 1-1 | 1-0 | Spring 12 | Davis K | Alexander | McGowan | Spring | Willmott | Johnson | Harrison* | McLaren ! | Douglas^ | Gray | Doherty" | McIndoe/Zah'na-Oni/Thomas |
| | 23/3 | | 5,527 | *7* | 42 | | | *Barras 84* | *Howie* | *Bernal* | *Gray* | *Parkinson* | *Barras* | *Casper* | *Murty** | *Caskey* | *McIntyre* | *Houghton* | *McKeever* | *Brebner* |
| | | | | | | | | Ref: L Cable | News that the Town are in receivership seems to galvanise the players who turn in their best performance for weeks. Alexander misses an early penalty after Doherty is hauled down but Spring soon opens the scoring. The Hatters miss a hatful of chances before conceding a late goal. | | | | | | | | | | | |
| 37 | H | GILLINGHAM | | 13 | W | 1-0 | 1-0 | Dyche 42 | Davis K | Willmott | Thomas | Spring | Dyche | Johnson | Gray | McLaren | Douglas | Thorpe* | McGowan | White |
| | 27/3 | | 6,705 | *6* | 45 | | | | *Bartram* | *Southall* | *Carr** | *Smith* | *Butters* | *Pennock* | *Patterson* | *Hessenth'ler* | *Asaba^* | *Saunders"* | *Taylor* | *Galloway/Browning/Hodge* |
| | | | | | | | | Ref: S Baines | Alexander and Evers leave the club before the transfer deadline, with Dyche and Thorpe coming to Kenilworth Road on loan. Thorpe looks a bit rusty but appears to be a class above the other players on the pitch. Dyche both shores up the defence and scores the only goal of the game. | | | | | | | | | | | |
| 38 | A | OLDHAM | | 13 | D | 1-1 | 1-0 | Gray 4 | Davis K | Willmott | Thomas | Spring | Dyche | Johnson | Gray | McLaren* | Douglas^ | Thorpe" | McGowan ! | McIndoe/White/Fotiadis |
| | 2/4 | | *4,948* | *20* | 46 | | | *Garnett 62* | *Kelly* | *Mardon* | *Holt* | *Garnett* | *Rickers* | *Duxbury* | *Gray** | *Sheridan* | *Tipton^* | *Allott* | *Reid* | *Innes/Whitehall* |
| | | | | | | | | Ref: P Danson | The Town take an early lead before both McLaren and Thorpe limp off with seemingly long-term injuries. Relegation-threatened Oldham fight back to gain a point in a game that Hatters would have lost a few weeks ago before McGowan is sent off, seconds from the end, for retaliation. | | | | | | | | | | | |
| 39 | H | YORK | | 12 | W | 2-1 | 0-1 | Spring 51, Douglas 90 | Davis K | Willmott | Thomas | Spring | Dyche | Johnson | Gray | Fotiadis* | Douglas | McIndoe | McGowan | Kandol |
| | 6/4 | | 4,667 | *19* | 49 | | | *Thompson 29* | *Mimms* | *Hocking* | *Thompson* | *Jordan* | *Jones* | *Fairclough* | *Pouton* | *Garratt* | *Williams* | *Rowe** | *Dawson* | *Tolson* |
| | | | | | | | | Ref: C Foy | Stuart Douglas earns all three points with a late scrambled goal, shortly after missing a sitter, virtually assuring the Hatters of safety from the drop. City caretaker boss Neil Thompson threatens to spoil things with a 25-yard rocket but Spring equalises with a lob from a similar distance. | | | | | | | | | | | |
| 40 | A | NORTHAMPTON | | 12 | L | 0-1 | 0-1 | | Davis K | Willmott | Thomas | Spring | Dyche | White | Kandol* | Fotiadis | Douglas | McIndoe | McGowan | Zahana-Oni |
| | 10/4 | | *6,856* | *21* | 49 | | | *Corazzin 35* | *Turley* | *Hendon* | *Frain* | *Sampson* | *Howey* | *Hope* | *Peer* | *Wilson** | *Corazzin* | *Howard^* | *Hunt* | *Savage/Lee* |
| | | | | | | | | Ref: T Jones | A terrible game between two poor sides is settled by Corazzin's left-foot cross which somehow finds its way into the corner of the net. Town's first-choice forwards are injured, the Luton attack is shot-shy and Zahana-Oni misses an open goal in the final minute which annoys Lawrence. | | | | | | | | | | | |
| 41 | A | MANCHESTER C | | 12 | L | 0-2 | 0-2 | | Davis K | Willmott | Thomas | Spring | Dyche | Johnson | Kandol* | Zahana-Oni^ | Douglas | McIndoe | McGowan | Thorpe/Fraser |
| | 14/4 | | ***26,130*** | *4* | 49 | | | *Dickov 4, Vaughan 10* | *Weaver* | *Crooks* | *Edghill** | *Vaughan* | *Morrison* | *Horlock* | *Brown* | *Bishop* | *Dickov* | *Goater^* | *Cooke* | *Mason/Taylor* |
| | | | | | | | | Ref: W Richards | The game is over as a contest after ten minutes, with City two up and cruising against an injury-hit young Luton side. Matthew Spring is the only Town player to force a save out of Nicky Weaver as high-flying City are content to soak up what little pressure there is from the Hatters. | | | | | | | | | | | |
| 42 | H | LINCOLN | | 14 | L | 0-1 | 0-0 | | Davis K | Willmott | Thomas | Spring | Dyche | Johnson | Thorpe | Zahana-Oni* | Douglas | McIndoe | **Boyce^** | Doherty/Fraser |
| | 17/4 | | 5,122 | *23* | 49 | | | *Thorpe 61* | *Vaughan* | *Barnett* | *Phillips* | *Fleming* | *Holmes* | *Austin* | *Thorpe* | *Finnigan** | *Battersby^* | *Gordon* | *Miller* | *Philpott/Brown* |
| | | | | | | | | Ref: P Dowd | Tony Thorpe is back but it is his namesake who scores the only goal after Battersby, from an offside position, steams down the left and puts in a cross. Veteran Mitchell Thomas plays the last quarter up front but Luton, with no goals in three games, slump to their third defeat in a row. | | | | | | | | | | | |
| 43 | A | NOTTS CO | | 12 | W | 2-1 | 1-0 | Thorpe 32, 65 | Davis K | Willmott | Thomas | Spring | White | Johnson | Thorpe* | McKinnon | Douglas^ | McIndoe | Fraser | Doherty/Fotiadis |
| | 24/4 | | *5,583* | *17* | 52 | | | *Redmile 55* | *Ward* | *Owers* | *Pearce** | *Hughes^* | *Redmile* | *Warren* | *Creaney* | *Richardson* | *Stallard* | *Beadle* | *Murray"* | *Tierney/Liburd/Rapley* |
| | | | | | | | | Ref: D Laws | Hatters ease to safety, courtesy of now fully fit Tony Thorpe. His second goal, where he takes one touch when others may have taken two or three, has Lawrence purring. Supporters Club Player of the Year, Kelvin Davis, makes several important saves as County apply late pressure. | | | | | | | | | | | |
| 44 | H | CHESTERFIELD | | 12 | W | 1-0 | 0-0 | Thorpe 63 | Davis K | Willmott | Thomas | Spring | White | Johnson | Thorpe | McKinnon | Douglas* | McIndoe | Fraser | Fotiadis |
| | 27/4 | | 4,287 | *9* | 55 | | | | *Mercer* | *Hewitt* | *Jules** | *Beaumont* | *Blatherwick* | *Breckin* | *Howard* | *Holland* | *Lenagh^* | *Ebdon* | *Carss* | *Perkins/Willis* |
| | | | | | | | | Ref: M Messias | Lawrence wants to keep Tony Thorpe and take him on loan next season after he scores his third goal in two games. The visitors, whose hopes of a play-off place have now disappeared, have their moments but skipper Johnson and find of the season Chris Willmott keep them at bay. | | | | | | | | | | | |
| 45 | H | MACCLESFIELD | | 12 | L | 1-2 | 0-2 | Doherty 88 | Davis K | Willmott | Thomas | Spring | White | Johnson | Thorpe | McKinnon* | Douglas^ | McIndoe | Fraser" | Doherty/Fotiadis/George |
| | 1/5 | | 5,738 | *24* | 55 | | | *Sorvel 26, Davies 36* | *Price* | *Tinson* | *Hitchen** | *Payne* | *Sedgmore* | *Sodje* | *Askey^* | *Sorvel* | *Tomlinson"* | *Matias* | *Durkan* | *Davies/Landon/Soley* |
| | | | | | | | | Ref: A Butler | Macclesfield create a shock against a lack-lustre Luton with Hatters reject Simon Davies, as will always happen, scoring against his old club. Town spring to life in the last ten minutes and nearly force a draw. The surviving members of the 1959 Cup final side take a bow at half-time. | | | | | | | | | | | |
| 46 | A | MILLWALL | | 12 | W | 1-0 | 1-0 | Thorpe 13 | Abbey | Willmott | Thomas | Spring | White | Johnson | Thorpe* | Gray^ | Douglas" | McIndoe | Fraser | Fotiadis/Doherty/George |
| | 8/5 | | *8,494* | *10* | 58 | | | | *Roberts* | *Neill* | *Stuart* | *Bircham* | *Nethercott* | *Fitzgerald* | *Ifill** | *Newman* | *Harris* | *Sadlier* | *Reid^* | *Bubb/Grant* |
| | | Home | Away | | | | | Ref: P Robinson | The Town, and Tony Thorpe, sign off the season in style. An early strike from Thorpe, when he gets on the end of a clever free-kick from Spring, is enough to win the game and manager Lennie Lawrence appreciates that without his goals, the Hatters may well have been relegated. | | | | | | | | | | | |
| Average | | 5,527 | 7,802 | | | | | | | | | | | | | | | | | |

| Worthington Cup | Att | | F-A | H-T | Scorers, Times, and Referees | 1 | 2 | 3 | 4 | 5 | 6 | 7 | 8 | 9 | 10 | 11 | subs used |
|---|---|---|---|---|---|---|---|---|---|---|---|---|---|---|---|---|---|
| 1:1 H OXFORD | | L | 2-3 | 0-2 | Alexander 60p, 63p | Davis K | Alexander | Thomas* | Spring | Davis S | Johnson | McGowan | Evers | Bacque | Gray^ | Marshall" | McLaren/McIndoe/George |
| 11/8 | 3,165 | | | | *Murphy 43, 45, Weatherstone 88* | *Whitehead* | *Robinson* | *Marsh* | *Gray* | *Wilsterman* | *Gilchrist* | *Banger** | *Windass^* | *Rose"* | *Murphy* | *Beauchamp* | *Weatherstone/Smith/Powell* |
| | | | | | Ref: B Knight | The Hatters are feeling sorry for themselves by the interval, having lost Mitchell Thomas to concussion and conceding two soft goals. The half-time verbal volley from Lawrence has the desired effect and the scores are soon level after two penalty strikes. The Oxford winner is sickening. | | | | | | | | | | | |
| 1:2 A OXFORD | 7 | W | 3-1 | 1-1 | Gray 37, Evers 47, McLaren 70 | Davis K | Alexander | McGowan | Spring | Davis S | Johnson | McLaren | Evers | Douglas* | Gray | Marshall^ | George/McKinnon |
| 18/8 | *5,099 1:19* | | | | *Whelan 25* | *Whitehead* | *Robinson* | *Marsh* | *Smith* | *Whelan* | *Gilchrist* | *Banger** | *Windass* | *Thomson^* | *Murphy"* | *Beauchamp* | *Hill/Cook/Weatherstone* |
| | | | | | Ref: C Wilkes (Hatters win 5-4 on aggregate) | Oxford are in the driving seat after an early goal but the Hatters complete a memorable cup fight-back. Evers worries the home side all evening with his forward runs and has a hand in all three Luton goals. McLaren, who smashes home the winner, failed to score in 50 games last season. | | | | | | | | | | | |
| 2:1 A IPSWICH | 3 | L | 1-2 | 0-0 | Douglas 60 | Davis K | Alexander | McGowan | Spring | Davis S | Johnson | Cox* | Evers | Douglas^ | Gray | McIndoe | Bacque/Fotiadis |
| 15/9 | *9,032 1:11* | | | | *Scowcroft 48, Thetis 79* | *Wright* | *Stockwell* | *Taricco* | *Clapham* | *Thetis* | *Venus** | *Dyer* | *Holland* | *Johnson* | *Scowcroft* | *Petta* | *Tanner* |
| | | | | | Ref: A D'Urso | The young Luton side, with an average age of just 22, acquit themselves well and are unlucky to concede a late scrambled effort from Thetis which gives the home side a first-leg lead. Town's 20-year-old veteran, Stuart Douglas, equalises and nearly nets another but is flagged offside. | | | | | | | | | | | |
| 2:2 H IPSWICH | 5 | W | 4-2 | 0-1 | Fotiadis 52, Douglas 84, Davis S 98, | Davis K | Alexander | McGowan | Spring | Davis S | Johnson | McKinnon* | Evers | Douglas | Fotiadis^ | Marshall" | White/Bacque/Cox |
| 22/9 | 5,665 *1:10* | | *aet* | | *J'son 35, Davis 118(og)* [Johnson 119] | *Wright* | *Stockwell** | *Taricco^* | *Tanner* | *Thetis* | *Venus* | *Dyer* | *Holland* | *Johnson* | *Scowcroft* | *Petta* | *Mathie/Sonner* |
| | | | | | Ref: P Taylor (Hatters win 5-4 on aggregate) | On a night of high drama, the game swings firstly one way and then the other, Steve Davis fires in a tremendous own-goal with only seconds remaining to seemingly gift a lucky Ipswich the game but, straight from the restart, marvellous Marvin Johnson lifts the roof with a rare goal. | | | | | | | | | | | |
| 3 H COVENTRY | 4 | W | 2-0 | 0-0 | Gray 50, Davis S 78 | Davis K | Alexander | Thomas | Spring | Davis S | Johnson | McKinnon | Evers | Douglas* | Gray | McGowan | Fotiadis |
| 27/10 | 9,051 *P:18* | | | | | *Hedman* | *Brightwell* | *Hall M* | *Breen* | *Shaw* | *Boateng* | *Telfer* | *Whelan* | *Huckersby* | *McAllister* | *Hall P** | *Soltvedt* |
| | | | | | Ref: C Wilkes | A giant-killing night at Kenilworth Road with Premiership Coventry lucky to escape with only a two-goal beating. The Sky Blues do not look interested and manager Gordon Strachan spits feathers afterwards. The last time Luton beat Coventry in this competition they lifted the trophy. | | | | | | | | | | | |
| 4 H BARNSLEY | 6 | W | 1-0 | 0-0 | Gray 81 | Davis K | Alexander | McGowan | Spring | Davis S | Johnson | McKinnon* | Evers | Douglas^ | Gray | McIndoe" | McLaren/White/Nyamah |
| 10/11 | 8,453 *1:18* | | | | | *Bullock T* | *Morgan* | *De Zeeuw* | *Jones* | *Tinkler** | *Appleby* | *Bullock M^* | *Sheridan* | *Ward* | *Fjortoft* | *Barnard* | *McClare/Hendrie* |
| | | | | | Ref: S Bennett | Another higher division scalp, but Barnsley make the Town work hard this time for their narrow victory. The visitors have the better of the first half but, as the game wears on, the Hatters come to the fore and Phil Gray eases the tension with a clever strike with nine minutes remaining. | | | | | | | | | | | |
| QF A SUNDERLAND | 7 | L | 0-3 | 0-1 | | Davis K | Alexander | Thomas ! | Spring | Davis S | Johnson | McKinnon* | Evers | Douglas^ | Gray | McGowan" | McLaren/Doherty/White |
| 1/12 | *35,742 1:1* | | | | *Johnson 40 (og), Bridges 89, Quinn 90* | *Sorensen* | *Makin* | *Scott* | *Ball* | *Melville* | *Butler* | *Summerbee* | *Clark* | *Quinn* | *Bridges* | *Johnston* | |
| | | | | | Ref: E Lomas | The game is as good as over after Mitchell Thomas is controversially sent off on 35 minutes with even the Sunderland players amazed by the decision. A deflected own-goal from Marvin Johnson and then two very late strikes from the home side give the score-line a flattering look. | | | | | | | | | | | |

| FA Cup | | | | | | | | | | | | | | | | | |
|---|---|---|---|---|---|---|---|---|---|---|---|---|---|---|---|---|---|
| 1 A BOREHAMWOOD | 6 | W | 3-2 | 1-0 | Gray 33, 53 Davis S 76 | Davis K | Alexander | McGowan | McLaren | Davis S | Johnson | McKinnon* | Evers | Douglas^ | Gray | Nyamah" | Spring/Doherty/McIndoe |
| 15/11 | *1,772 RP* | | | | *Nisbet 54, Xavier 81* | *Taylor* | *Sanders* | *McCarthy* | *Shaw* | *Nisbet* | *Brown** | *Grime* | *Heffer* | *Dixon* | *Samuels^* | *Brady"* | *Daly/Xavier/Ireland* |
| | | | | | Ref: P Alcock | Phil Gray celebrates his recall to the Northern Ireland side with two goals against a stubborn Borehamwood. The Hatters are never in any real danger but after Mark Xavier narrows the score towards the end, several scrambles in the Luton penalty box could have ended in an equaliser. | | | | | | | | | | | |
| 2 H HULL | 7 | L | 1-2 | 1-1 | Davis S 36 | Davis K | Alexander | McGowan | Spring | Davis S | White | McKinnon* | Evers | Doherty^ | Gray | McLaren" | McIndoe/Douglas/Scarlett |
| 5/12 | 5.021 *3:24* | | | | *Morley 29, Dewhurst 63* | *Wilson* | *Greaves* | *Edwards* | *Hocking* | *Whittle* | *Dewhurst* | *French* | *D'Auria* | *Brown** | *Morley* | *McGinty* | *Ellington* |
| | | | | | Ref: C Foy | The Tigers are without ten first-team regulars and are currently propping up Division Three. A 17-year-old YTS debutant and a reserve centre-half score the goals that knock Luton out of the Cup, the only bright spot being the Steve Davis equaliser when he ran from the halfway line. | | | | | | | | | | | |

| | | P | W | D | L | F | A | W | D | L | F | A | Pts |
|---|---|---|---|---|---|---|---|---|---|---|---|---|---|
| | | | Home | | | | | Away | | | | | |
| 1 | Fulham | 46 | 19 | 3 | 1 | 50 | 12 | 12 | 5 | 6 | 29 | 20 | 101 |
| 2 | Walsall | 46 | 13 | 7 | 3 | 37 | 23 | 13 | 2 | 8 | 26 | 24 | 87 |
| 3 | Manchest C* | 46 | 13 | 6 | 4 | 38 | 14 | 9 | 10 | 4 | 31 | 19 | 82 |
| 4 | Gillingham | 46 | 15 | 5 | 3 | 45 | 17 | 7 | 9 | 7 | 30 | 27 | 80 |
| 5 | Preston | 46 | 12 | 6 | 5 | 46 | 23 | 10 | 7 | 6 | 32 | 27 | 79 |
| 6 | Wigan | 46 | 14 | 5 | 4 | 44 | 17 | 8 | 5 | 10 | 31 | 31 | 76 |
| 7 | Bournemouth | 46 | 14 | 7 | 2 | 37 | 11 | 7 | 6 | 10 | 26 | 30 | 76 |
| 8 | Stoke | 46 | 10 | 4 | 9 | 32 | 32 | 11 | 2 | 10 | 27 | 31 | 69 |
| 9 | Chesterfield | 46 | 14 | 5 | 4 | 34 | 16 | 3 | 8 | 12 | 12 | 28 | 64 |
| 10 | Millwall | 46 | 9 | 8 | 6 | 33 | 24 | 8 | 3 | 12 | 19 | 35 | 62 |
| 11 | Reading | 46 | 10 | 6 | 7 | 29 | 26 | 6 | 7 | 10 | 25 | 37 | 61 |
| 12 | LUTON TOWN | 46 | 10 | 4 | 9 | 25 | 26 | 6 | 6 | 11 | 26 | 34 | 58 |
| 13 | Bristol Rov | 46 | 8 | 9 | 6 | 35 | 28 | 5 | 8 | 10 | 30 | 28 | 56 |
| 14 | Blackpool | 46 | 7 | 8 | 8 | 24 | 24 | 7 | 6 | 10 | 20 | 30 | 56 |
| 15 | Burnley | 46 | 8 | 7 | 8 | 23 | 33 | 5 | 9 | 9 | 31 | 40 | 55 |
| 16 | Notts Co | 46 | 8 | 6 | 9 | 29 | 27 | 6 | 6 | 11 | 23 | 34 | 54 |
| 17 | Wrexham | 46 | 8 | 6 | 9 | 21 | 28 | 5 | 8 | 10 | 22 | 34 | 53 |
| 18 | Colchester | 46 | 9 | 7 | 7 | 25 | 30 | 3 | 9 | 11 | 27 | 40 | 52 |
| 19 | Wycombe | 46 | 8 | 5 | 10 | 31 | 26 | 5 | 7 | 11 | 21 | 32 | 51 |
| 20 | Oldham | 46 | 8 | 4 | 11 | 26 | 31 | 6 | 5 | 12 | 22 | 35 | 51 |
| 21 | York | 46 | 6 | 8 | 9 | 28 | 33 | 7 | 3 | 13 | 28 | 47 | 50 |
| 22 | Northampton | 46 | 4 | 12 | 7 | 26 | 31 | 6 | 6 | 11 | 17 | 26 | 48 |
| 23 | Lincoln | 46 | 9 | 4 | 10 | 27 | 27 | 4 | 3 | 16 | 15 | 47 | 46 |
| 24 | Macclesfield | 46 | 7 | 4 | 12 | 24 | 30 | 4 | 6 | 13 | 19 | 33 | 43 |
| | | 1104 | 243 | 146 | 163 | 769 | 589 | 163 | 146 | 243 | 589 | 769 | 1510 |

* promoted after play-offs

Odds & ends

Double wins: (2) Wycombe, Burnley.
Double losses: (2) Walsall, Stoke.

Won from behind: (1) York (h).
Lost from in front: (2) Preston (a), Wrexham (h).

High spots: The early season form which culminated in the 3-1 win at Fulham.
The best run in the Worthington Cup since 1989, which included the win over Premiership Coventry.
The late-season form of Sean Dyche and Tony Thorpe.

Low spots: The miserable form after Christmas.
Losing at home to the Division 3 bottom club Hull City in the FA Cup.
Mitchell Thomas being cruelly sent of at Sunderland in the Worthington Cup, which effectively killed the game.

Player of the Year: Kelvin Davis.
Ever presents: (0).
Hat-tricks: (0).
Leading scorer: Phil Gray (13).

| | Appearances | | | | | | Goals | | | |
|---|---|---|---|---|---|---|---|---|---|---|
| | Lge | *Sub* | LC | *Sub* | FAC | *Sub* | Lge | LC | FAC | Tot |
| Abbey, Nathan | **2** | | | | | | | | | |
| Alexander, Graham | **28** | *1* | 7 | | 2 | | **4** | 2 | | **6** |
| Bacque, Herve | **2** | *5* | 1 | *2* | | | | | | |
| Boyce, Emmerson | **1** | | | | | | | | | |
| Cox, Jimmy | **3** | *5* | 1 | *1* | | | | | | |
| Davies, Simon | **2** | | | | | | | | | |
| Davis, Kelvin | **44** | | 7 | | 2 | | | | | |
| Davis, Steve | **20** | | 7 | | 2 | | **6** | 2 | 2 | **10** |
| Doherty, Gary | **5** | *15* | | *1* | 1 | *1* | **6** | | | **6** |
| Douglas, Stuart | **42** | | 6 | | 1 | *1* | **9** | 2 | | **11** |
| Dyche, Sean | **14** | | | | | | **1** | | | **1** |
| Evers, Sean | **27** | | 7 | | 2 | | **3** | 1 | | **4** |
| Fotiadis, Andrew | **8** | *13* | 1 | *2* | | | **2** | 1 | | **3** |
| Fraser, Stuart | **5** | *3* | | | | | | | | |
| George, Liam | **6** | *6* | | *2* | | | | | | |
| Gray, Phil | **32** | *3* | 6 | | 2 | | **8** | 3 | 2 | **13** |
| Harrison, Gerry | **14** | | | | | | | | | |
| Johnson, Marvin | **42** | | 7 | | 1 | | | 1 | | **1** |
| Kandol, Tresor | **2** | *2* | | | | | | | | |
| Marshall, Dwight | **3** | *1* | 3 | | | | **1** | | | **1** |
| McGowan, Gavin | **27** | *4* | 7 | | 2 | | | | | |
| McIndoe, Michael | **17** | *5* | 2 | *1* | | *2* | | | | |
| McKinnon, Ray | **29** | *1* | 4 | *1* | 2 | | **2** | | | **2** |
| McLaren, Paul | **14** | *9* | 1 | *3* | 2 | | | 1 | | **1** |
| Nyamah, Kofi | | | | *1* | 1 | | | | | |
| Scarlett, Andre | **2** | *4* | | | | *1* | **1** | | | **1** |
| Showler, Paul | **2** | *1* | | | | | | | | |
| Spring, Matthew | **45** | | 7 | | 1 | *1* | **3** | | | **3** |
| Thomas, Mitchell | **26** | *6* | 3 | | | | | | | |
| Thorpe, Tony | **7** | *1* | | | | | **4** | | | **4** |
| White, Alan | **18** | *15* | | *3* | 1 | | **1** | | | **1** |
| Willmott, Chris | **13** | *1* | | | | | | | | |
| Zahana-Oni, L'Andry | **4** | *4* | | | | | | | | |
| **33 players used** | **506** | ***105*** | **77** | ***17*** | **22** | ***6*** | **51** | **13** | **4** | **68** |

# NATIONWIDE LEAGUE DIVISION 2

## Manager: Lennie Lawrence

## SEASON 1999-2000

| No | Date | | Att | Pos | Pt | F-A | H-T | Scorers, Times, and Referees | 1 | 2 | 3 | 4 | 5 | 6 | 7 | 8 | 9 | 10 | 11 | subs used |
|---|---|---|---|---|---|---|---|---|---|---|---|---|---|---|---|---|---|---|---|---|
| 1 | A | NOTTS CO | | | D | 0-0 | 0-0 | | Abbey | Fraser | **Taylor*** | **Watts** | White | Johnson | Gray | McLaren | Douglas | Spring | McIndoe | Boyce |
| | 7/8 | | *6,141* | | 1 | | | | *Ward* | *Holmes* | *Blackmore* | *Ramage* | *Warren* | *Redmile** | *Liburd^* | *Richardson* | *Beadle* | *Stallard"* | *Murray* | *Bolland/Robson/Darby* |
| | | | | | | | | Ref: A Leake | After an eleventh-hour agreement, the Football League gives the go-ahead for the Hatters to kick off the new season after a turbulent summer. The average age of the playing squad now remaining is just 22, a new record. The game is a score-bore but the supporters do not care one jot. | | | | | | | | | | | |
| 2 | H | BLACKPOOL | | | W | 3-2 | 1-0 | George 21,74, Spring 82 | Abbey | Fraser | Taylor | Watts | Doherty | Johnson | George | McLaren* | Douglas^ | Spring | Fotiadis" | McIndoe/Zah'na-Oni/McKin'n |
| | 14/8 | | 5,176 | | 4 | | | *Ormerod 80, Nowland 86* | *Barnes* | *Couzens* | *Hills* | *Bardsley* | *Carlisle* | *Hughes* | *Clarkson* | *Ormerod* | *Thompson* | *Bryan** | *Murphy* | *Nowland* |
| | | | | | | | | Ref: R Olivier | The formation, using Liam George just behind the front two, bamboozles Blackpool but, after cruising into a 2-0 lead, the Hatters are hanging on at the end after errors by goalkeeper Nathan Abbey. Luton manager Lennie Lawrence states afterwards that he will stick by his goalkeeper. | | | | | | | | | | | |
| 3 | A | READING | | 3 | W | 2-1 | 0-0 | Fotiadis 54, George 86 | Abbey | Fraser | Taylor | Spring | Watts | Johnson | Doherty | McLaren | Gray | Fotiadis* | George | McIndoe |
| | 21/8 | | *8,741* | *19* | 7 | | | *Williams 56* | *Howie* | *Gray* | *Hunter* | *Casper* | *Caskey* | *McIntyre** | *Grant* | *Scott* | *Williams* | *Gurney* | *Smith* | *Forster* |
| | | | | | | | | Ref: S Bennett | Still smarting from the defeat the previous season at Reading, the Hatters outplay the home side with the late winner from Liam George fully deserved. The introduction of McIndoe for the tiring Fotiadis is seen as a masterstroke by Lennie Lawrence, as that player sets up the winner. | | | | | | | | | | | |
| 4 | H | CARDIFF | | 2 | W | 1-0 | 0-0 | Gray 81 | Abbey | Fraser | Taylor | Spring | Doherty | Watts | Johnson | Gray | McLaren* | Fotiadis^ | George" | McIndoe/Douglas/McKinnon |
| | 28/8 | | 5,374 | *13* | 10 | | | | *Hallworth* | *Faerber** | *Legg* | *Young* | *Ford* | *Bowen* | *Nugent* | *Brazier* | *Fowler^* | *Eckhardt* | *Cornforth"* | *Phillips/Middleton/Carpenter* |
| | | | | | | | | Ref: R Furnandiz | Hatters win the battle of the undefeated sides and move up to second in the table. In a closely fought contest, the goal-line clearance by Fraser leads moments later to the same player making the telling pass for Gray to score the winner. Lawrence hopes to extend the loan spell of Watts. | | | | | | | | | | | |
| 5 | A | BOURNEMOUTH | | 3 | L | 0-1 | 0-0 | | Abbey | Fraser | Taylor | Spring | Watts | Johnson | Doherty | McLaren* | Gray | Fotiadis^ | George | McIndoe/Douglas |
| | 31/8 | | *4,797* | *7* | 10 | | | *Fletcher 72* | *Ovendale* | *Young* | *Warren* | *Howe* | *Cox* | *Huck* | *Mean* | *Robinson* | *Stein** | *Fletcher* | *Hughes* | *Watson* |
| | | | | | | | | Ref: A Bates | The record is over after a tight game at Dean Court which could have gone either way. The Hatters hit the woodwork twice through Andrew Fotiadis and Spring, but it is big Steve Fletcher who nets the only goal with a firm header just as the game seems to be petering out for a draw. | | | | | | | | | | | |
| 6 | H | BURY | | 5 | D | 1-1 | 0-0 | Fotiadis 53 | Abbey | Fraser | Watts | Doherty | Johnson | George* | McLaren | Gray | Spring | Fotiadis^ | Taylor | McIndoe/Douglas |
| | 4/9 | | **4,633** | *7* | 11 | | | *Richardson 69* | *Kenny* | *Collins* | *Swailes* | *Billy* | *Daws* | *Richardson** | *Reid* | *Redmond* | *Littlejohn* | *Lawson* | *James^* | *Bullock/Preece* |
| | | | | | | | | Ref: D Crick | Both sides play a wing-back system and, with George man-marked, the Town rarely look threatening on a hot afternoon. A fierce opener from Fotiadis is cancelled out by a soft equaliser and with the visitors finishing the stronger side, manager Lennie Lawrence is happy with a draw. | | | | | | | | | | | |
| 7 | H | WREXHAM | | 3 | W | 3-1 | 3-1 | Taylor 6, Spring 15, George 37 | Abbey | Fraser | Watts | Doherty | Johnson* | George | McLaren^ | Douglas | Spring | Fotiadis" | Taylor | **Sodje**/McKinnon/Kandol |
| | 11/9 | | 5,121 | *9* | 14 | | | *Stevens 19* | *Dearden* | *McGregor* | *Hardy !* | *Owen* | *Carey** | *Spink* | *Lowe^* | *Barrett* | *Williams* | *Stevens* | *Faulc'nbridge* | *Brace/Connolly* |
| | | | | | | | | Ref: M Fletcher | Luton's young forwards are far too quick for the ageing back line of Wrexham, and three tremendous strikes finish the game by the half-time break. 17-year-old Matthew Taylor scores his first goal for the club with an unstoppable shot which rockets into the top corner from 25 yards. | | | | | | | | | | | |
| 8 | A | BRENTFORD | | 5 | L | 0-2 | 0-0 | | Abbey | Doherty | Watts | Johnson | Fraser | Spring | **Locke** | Taylor | George | Douglas | Kandol* | Sodje |
| | 18/9 | | *7,039* | *8* | 14 | | | *Powell 55, Partridge 72* | *Woodman* | *Anderson* | *Quinn* | *Powell* | *Hreidarsson* | *Evans* | *Mahon** | *Owusu^* | *Partridge* | *Scott* | *Rowlands* | *Folan/Bryan* |
| | | | | | | | | Ref: P Taylor | Although Fotiadis is now on the injured list, it is still surprising to see the Town attack so shot-shy after the performance of last week. Luton only manage three shots on target as the Bees make it 22 league games without defeat and score the winning goal after Doherty is sent up front. | | | | | | | | | | | |
| 9 | H | OXFORD | | 3 | W | 4-2 | 3-0 | George 13, 45, Fraser 22, Locke 89 | Abbey | Fraser | Watts | Doherty | Johnson | George | Locke | Douglas | Spring | **Midgley*** | Taylor | McIndoe |
| | 25/9 | | 6,102 | *19* | 17 | | | *Powell 59, Lilley 65* | *Arendse* | *Robinson* | *Powell* | *Fear* | *Beauchamp* | *Davis* | *Lewis** | *Murphy* | *Tait^* | *Anthrobus* | *Folland"* | *Watson/Lilley/Cook* |
| | | | | | | | | Ref: S Baines | Town put on a master-class display of attacking football in the first half with Liam George unstoppable but then gift Oxford two goals after the break to set the nerves jangling. A last-minute winner from Locke is netted from 40 yards after a skewed clearance by Arendse lands at his feet. | | | | | | | | | | | |
| 10 | A | WIGAN | | 8 | L | 0-1 | 0-0 | | Abbey | Fraser | Taylor | Spring | Doherty | Watts | Johnson | Locke* | McLaren^ | Douglas | George | Midgley/McIndoe |
| | 2/10 | | *6,866* | *2* | 17 | | | *Barlow 75* | *Carroll* | *Bradshaw* | *Sharp** | *Balmer* | *de Zeeuw* | *Kilford* | *O'Neill* | *Sheridan* | *Haworth* | *Liddell* | *Barlow* | *Martinez* |
| | | | | | | | | Ref: M Pike | A tale of two headers as Doherty firstly sees a perfectly good effort disallowed and then produces a poor clearance which sets up the winner from Barlow. Despite the gulf in both financial clout and Football League experience, the Luton side are deserving of a draw at the very least. | | | | | | | | | | | |
| 11 | A | OLDHAM | | 10 | L | 1-2 | 0-0 | Midgley 86 | Abbey | Fraser | Taylor | Spring | Sodje | Watts | Johnson | Gray* | McLaren^ | Douglas" | Locke | Kandol/McIndoe/Midgley |
| | 9/10 | | *4,532* | *21* | 17 | | | *McNiven D 66, Allott 90* | *Kelly* | *McNiven S* | *Holt* | *Thom** | *Duxbury* | *Rickers* | *Sheridan* | *Allott* | *McNiven D* | *Adams* | *Graham* | *Hotte* |
| | | | | | | | | Ref: M Cowburn | Despite a second-half barrage, Town appear to have salvaged a point when Midgley rounds the keeper just before the end; however, a reckless challenge from Fraser in the final minute of the game leads to the Latics winner, a perfectly-flighted Sheridan free-kick which is nodded home. | | | | | | | | | | | |

| | | | | | | | | | | | | | | | | | | | | |
|---|---|---|---|---|---|---|---|---|---|---|---|---|---|---|---|---|---|---|---|---|
| 12 | H | GILLINGHAM | | 7 | W | 3-1 | 0-1 | George 52p, 74, Douglas 65 | Abbey | Fraser | Watts | Doherty | Johnson | George | McLaren* | Douglas | Spring | Midgley^ | Taylor | McIndoe/Locke |
| 16/10 | | | 6,394 | *12* | 20 | | | *Lewis 16* | *Bartram* | *Smith** | *Ashby* | *Butters^* | *Hessenthal'r* | *Omoyinmi* | *Saunders* | *Pennock* | *Lewis* | *Thomson* | *McGlinchey* | *Hodge/Nosworthy* |
| | | | | | | | | Ref: E Wolstenholme | The first game since coming out of receivership is against the Gills who were the first opponents back in March when the receiver was called in. George, back from international duty, wins and converts a penalty after a clumsy challenge by Hessenthaler and rounds off with the winner. | | | | | | | | | | | |
| 13 | H | WYCOMBE | | 7 | D | 1-1 | 0-1 | Douglas 48 | Abbey | Doherty | Watts | Johnson | Fraser | Spring | McLaren | Taylor | George | Douglas | Midgley* | McIndoe |
| 19/10 | | | 5,820 | *10* | 21 | | | *Cousins 24* | *Taylor* | *Lawrence* | *Vinnicombe* | *Cousins* | *Bates* | *Brown* | *Ryan* | *Devine* | *Emblen** | *McSporran^* | *Simpson* | *Beeton/Senda* |
| | | | | | | | | Ref: S Mathieson | On a frustrating evening, a physical Wycombe side hold on to a point despite conceding the majority of the possession. Cousins out-jumps Fraser to head home a free-kick from Steve Brown, but the Luton defender then provides the cross which is brilliantly headed in by Douglas. | | | | | | | | | | | |
| 14 | A | OXFORD | | 7 | W | 1-0 | 1-0 | George 3 | Abbey | Fraser | Taylor | Spring | Watts | Johnson | Doherty | McLaren | Douglas* | Midgley^ | George | Locke/McIndoe |
| 23/10 | | | *5,866* | *21* | 24 | | | | *Arendse* | *Robinson* | *Powell** | *Fear* | *Watson* | *Davis* | *Murphy^* | *Tait* | *Lilley"* | *Lewis* | *Beauchamp* | *McGow'n/Anthr'bus/Lambert* |
| | | | | | | | | Ref: G Cain | A brilliant early move allows Midgley to cross leaving George with a simple tap-in. The Hatters then soak up the pressure with ease and have chances to extend their lead before the end. Oxford have now lost five games on the trot and have not scored in over seven hours of football. | | | | | | | | | | | |
| 15 | A | MILLWALL | | 8 | L | 0-1 | 0-0 | | Abbey | Boyce | Taylor | Spring | Watts | Johnson | Doherty | McLaren | Douglas | Midgley* | George | McIndoe |
| 2/11 | | | *6,181* | *11* | 24 | | | *Cahill 74* | *Warner* | *Fitzgerald* | *Neill* | *Ryan* | *Nethercott* | *Ifill* | *Reid* | *Cahill* | *Bircham* | *Sadlier* | *Shaw** | *Harris* |
| | | | | | | | | Ref: K Leach | The Town fail to make it four consecutive wins at the New Den when a scrambled effort by Tim Cahill gains all three points. Luton do not show much in attack and Stuart Douglas squanders the best opportunity when, one-on-one with Warner, he shoots straight at the goalkeeper. | | | | | | | | | | | |
| 16 | H | BURNLEY | | 8 | W | 2-1 | 0-0 | Midgley 50, 70 | Abbey | Boyce | Watts | Doherty | Johnson | George | McLaren* | Douglas^ | Spring | Midgley" | Taylor | Locke/McIndoe/Kandol |
| 6/11 | | | **7,205** | *4* | 27 | | | *Cooke 50* | *Crichton* | *Brass** | *Thomas* | *Mellon* | *Davis* | *Armstrong^* | *Little* | *Cook* | *Cooke* | *Payton"* | *Mullin* | *Jepson/Lee/Branch* |
| | | | | | | | | Ref: F Stretton | After an ineffective display at Millwall, loan player Neil Midgley responds with a two-goal blast. Manager Lawrence agrees that the Clarets are the biggest scalp claimed so far this season after an absorbing encounter of youth and exuberance against the visitors' strength and experience. | | | | | | | | | | | |
| 17 | A | CAMBRIDGE | | 9 | L | 1-3 | 0-2 | George 90 | Abbey | Boyce* | Taylor | Spring | Watts | Johnson | Doherty | McLaren^ | Douglas | Midgley" | George | Sodje/McIndoe/Locke |
| 12/11 | | | *6,211* | *21* | 27 | | | *Butler 39, Benjamin 44, Kyd 59* | *Marshall* | *Ashbee* | *Joseph* | *Mustoe* | *Wanless* | *Butler* | *Benjamin* | *Kyd** | *Wilson* | *McKenzie* | *McNeil* | *Taylor* |
| | | | | | | | | Ref: T Heilbron | Over two thousand Town supporters see the away-day nightmare continue against struggling Cambridge. Matthew Taylor hits the woodwork with a 30-yard free-kick before the late consolation goal from Liam George, which comes as most Luton fans are streaming out of the ground. | | | | | | | | | | | |
| 18 | H | PRESTON | | 10 | L | 0-2 | 0-2 | | Abbey | Doherty | Watts | Sodje | Fraser* | Spring | McLaren^ | Taylor | George | Douglas | Midgley" | Boyce/McIndoe/White |
| 23/11 | | | 5,124 | *3* | 27 | | | *Eyres 32, 45* | *Moilanen* | *Alexander* | *Kidd* | *Edwards* | *Jackson* | *Gregan* | *Cartwright* | *Rankine* | *Macken* | *Nogan* | *Eyres* | |
| | | | | | | | | Ref: R Styles | The Hatters surrender their unbeaten home record with barely a whimper against high-flying Preston. Defensive blunders from both Abbey and Fraser lead to the gift of a two-goal half-time lead for the away side. Only when Doherty is sent up front do the Town test keeper Moilanen. | | | | | | | | | | | |
| 19 | A | BRISTOL ROV | | 10 | L | 0-3 | 0-2 | | Abbey | Doherty* | Watts^ | Johnson | Fraser | McLaren | Spring | Locke | Sodje | McIndoe | George | Thorpe/Boyce |
| 27/11 | | | *7,805* | *4* | 27 | | | *Thomson 12, Walters 19, Cureton 48* | *Jones* | *Pethick** | *Thomson* | *Tillson* | *Foster* | *Walters^* | *Hillier* | *Mauge* | *Pritchard* | *Cureton* | *Roberts* | *Bennett/Challis* |
| | | | | | | | | Ref: P Dowd | Four league visits to the Memorial Ground and all have resulted in defeat. Luton never look like breaking their duck and take 52 minutes to get a shot on target. The first two goals are both scored from set-pieces which gives cause for concern. Thorpe returns on loan from Bristol City. | | | | | | | | | | | |
| 20 | H | NOTTS CO | | 11 | D | 2-2 | 2-0 | Doherty 38, Thorpe 41 | Abbey | Fraser* | Watts | Thorpe | Johnson | George | Locke | Douglas^ | Spring | Doherty | Taylor | Boyce/Sodje |
| 4/12 | | | 5,195 | *7* | 28 | | | *Richardson 54, Owers 73* | *Ward* | *Holmes** | *Pearce* | *Warren* | *Redmile* | *Richardson* | *Stallard* | *Fenton* | *Hughes* | *Owers* | *Ramage^* | *Tierney/Rapley* |
| | | | | | | | | Ref: S Tomlin | 'A two-goal lead never seems to be enough for us,' laments Lawrence as defensive errors leave Luton content to hang on to a point by the end. Thorpe, who makes a goal and scores one, is negotiating through his agent, ex-Hatter Paul Walsh, to turn his loan deal into a permanent move. | | | | | | | | | | | |
| 21 | A | COLCHESTER | | 11 | L | 0-3 | 0-0 | | Abbey | Fraser | Taylor | Spring | Watts | Johnson | Sodje ! | Locke | Thorpe | Doherty | George* | McLaren |
| 17/12 | | | *3,049* | *18* | 28 | | | *McGavin 48, 54, Dozzell 74* | *Brown* | *Dunne* | *Richard* | *Greene* | *Skelton* | *Keith* | *Johnson* | *Gregory* | *Dozzell* | *McGavin* | *Lualua* | |
| | | | | | | | | Ref: L Cable | Central defender Sodje receives a red card for a disputed handling offence in the area but justice appears to be done when former Hatter, David Greene, hits the bar from the penalty spot. Previously, only the bottom club Chesterfield have failed to score against Colchester this season. | | | | | | | | | | | |
| 22 | H | CHESTERFIELD | | 13 | D | 1-1 | 1-0 | Locke 38 | Abbey | Boyce | Watts | Doherty | Johnson | George | Locke | Douglas | Spring* | Thorpe^ | Taylor | McLaren/Gray |
| 26/12 | | | 5,870 | *24* | 29 | | | *Reeves 74* | *Muggleton* | *Hewitt* | *Breckin* | *Blatherwick* | *Beaumont* | *Galloway* | *Curtis* | *Williams* | *Howard** | *Reeves* | *D'Auria^* | *Willis/Wilkinson* |
| | | | | | | | | Ref: P Joslin | The Town head downhill after an exquisite right-footed curler from Locke. The Spireites are unlucky not to break their run after a second-half performance which belies their lowly league position. Coincidently, Chesterfield were also the visitors to Luton 100 years ago to the day. | | | | | | | | | | | |
| 23 | A | BRISTOL CITY | | 12 | D | 0-0 | 0-0 | | Abbey | Boyce | Taylor | Spring | Watts | Johnson | Gray | Locke | White | Douglas* | Doherty | Fotiadis |
| 28/12 | | | *11,832* | *14* | 30 | | | | *Mercer* | *Bell* | *Taylor* | *Tinnion* | *Mortimer* | *Hutchings** | *Torpey^* | *Beadle* | *Lavin"* | *Millen* | *Black* | *Tistimetanu/Thorpe/Murray* |
| | | | | | | | | Ref: M Ryan | Gray returns to the side after injury and inspires the team to gain their first away point since October. Hatters have most of the play and efforts from Gray, Taylor and Fotiadis either flash narrowly wide or are saved by Mercer. Thorpe is shown playing for both sides in the programme! | | | | | | | | | | | |

| No | Date | | Att | Pos | Pt | F-A | H-T | Scorers, Times, and Referees | 1 | 2 | 3 | 4 | 5 | 6 | 7 | 8 | 9 | 10 | 11 | subs used |
|---|---|---|---|---|---|---|---|---|---|---|---|---|---|---|---|---|---|---|---|---|
| 24 | H | SCUNTHORPE | | 11 | W | **4-1** | 3-0 | Douglas 34, Gray 36, Spring 40,79 | Abbey | Boyce | Watts | Doherty | Johnson | George | Locke | Douglas | Spring | Gray* | Taylor | Fotiadis |
| | 3/1 | | 5,574 | *17* | 33 | | | *Hodges 78* | *Evans* | *Harsley* | *Dawson** | *Logan* | *Fickling* | *Graves* | *Walker^* | *Hodges* | *Ipoua* | *Omoyinmi* | *Stanton"* | *Wilcox/Sparrow/Housham* |
| | | | | | | | | Ref: C Wilkes | Three goals in six minutes make it a bright start to the millennium. In an open game, in which shots rain in from all angles and at both ends of the pitch, Spring scores twice with 30-yard scorchers. Manager Lennie Lawrence is now talking of making a late run for the play-off positions. | | | | | | | | | | | |
| 25 | A | STOKE | | 12 | L | 1-2 | 0-1 | Spring 59p | Abbey | Boyce | Taylor ! | Doherty | Watts | Johnson | Spring | Locke | White* | Douglas^ | Gray | George/Fotiadis |
| | 8/1 | | *10,016* | *5* | 33 | | | *Connor 24, Lightbourne 87* | *Ward* | *Mohan* | *Kavanagh* | *Thorne** | *Hansson* | *Connor* | *O'Connor* | *Petty^* | *Clarke"* | *Jacobsen* | *Kippe* | *Lightb'ne/Gun'son/Dan'son* |
| | | | | | | | | Ref: C Foy | Bizarre refereeing decisions allow Stoke to go ahead with a dubious penalty, Taylor to be sent off for an innocuous challenge, and the Hatters awarded a spot-kick for a push which only the official saw. Lightbourne scores his customary goal against the Town after an error by Abbey. | | | | | | | | | | | |
| 26 | A | BLACKPOOL | | 13 | D | 3-3 | 1-1 | Locke 27, Gray 82, Taylor 90 | Abbey | Boyce | Taylor | Watts | Johnson | Doherty | Spring | Locke | Douglas | Gray | George* | Fotiadis |
| | 15/1 | | *5,262* | *22* | 34 | | | *Ablett 8, Clarkson 47, Bushell 56* | *Caig* | *Bardsley* | *Beesley* | *Carlisle* | *Ablett* | *Bushell* | *Clarkson* | *Richardson* | *Bent* | *Matthews* | *Murphy** | *Coid* |
| | | | | | | | | Ref: T Parkes | The Town could easily have been three goals up after ten minutes before they gift three goals to the lowly Seasiders. A late header from Phil Gray appears to be all too little too late, but a speculative 30-yard volley from Matt Taylor in the final seconds brings about an unlikely point. | | | | | | | | | | | |
| 27 | H | READING | | 10 | W | 3-1 | 1-0 | Watts 18, George 70,90 | Abbey | Boyce | Watts | Doherty | Johnson | George | Locke | McGowan | Gray | Douglas* | Scarlett | Fotiadis |
| | 22/1 | | 6,044 | *22* | 37 | | | *Caskey 60* | *Howie* | *Primus* | *Bernal** | *Polston* | *Gurney* | *Parkinson* | *Caskey* | *Gray^* | *Scott* | *Forster* | *Smith"* | *Williams/Nicholls/Evers* |
| | | | | | | | | Ref: R Beeby | The only Luton player to have cost any money is Phil Gray, which is in stark contrast to the 'Bank of England' side from Reading. Scarlett and McGowan each make their seasonal debut but it is two-goal George who steals the show against a side who have gone 13 games without a win. | | | | | | | | | | | |
| 28 | A | CARDIFF | | 10 | W | 3-1 | 2-0 | Watts 22, Spring 45, George 57 | Abbey | Boyce | McGowan | Spring | Watts | Doherty | Fraser | Gray | Douglas* | Scarlett | George | Fotiadis |
| | 30/1 | | *6,185* | *18* | 40 | | | *Bowen 89* | *Hallworth* | *Legg* | *Perrett* | *Ford* | *Boland** | *Bonner* | *Nugent* | *Eckhardt^* | *Carpenter* | *Humphreys* | *Low* | *Bowden/Faerber* |
| | | | | | | | | Ref: C Foy | The first away win since October is achieved despite the absence of seven regular first-team players who are missing through either injury or suspension. Watts and Spring score before the interval, after which, with Gray withdrawn to protect the lead, George manages to grab a third. | | | | | | | | | | | |
| 29 | H | BOURNEMOUTH | | 10 | L | 1-2 | 0-1 | Boyce 59 | Abbey | Doherty | Watts | Johnson | Boyce | Spring | Locke | McGowan* | George | Gray | Douglas^ | Scarlett/Fotiadis |
| | 5/2 | | 5,961 | *12* | 40 | | | *Mean 34, Watts 46 (og)* | *Ovendale* | *Young* | *O'Shea* | *Howe* | *Warren* | *Mean* | *Robinson* | *Hughes* | *Hayter* | *O'Neill** | *Stein* | *Jorgensen* |
| | | | | | | | | Ref: M Jones | A first senior goal by Emmerson Boyce is not enough to save the Hatters. Julian Watts scores for the third week running, but this time into his own goal when he flicks a cross from Mean past Abbey. 'We were never at the races,' says Luton manager Lennie Lawrence after the match. | | | | | | | | | | | |
| 30 | H | STOKE | | 9 | W | 2-1 | 0-1 | Gray 63, 79 | Abbey | Boyce* | Watts | Doherty | Johnson | George^ | Locke | Spring | Taylor | Gray | Douglas | McGowan/Fotiadis |
| | 8/2 | | 5,396 | *6* | 43 | | | *O'Connor 32* | *Ward* | *Hansson* | *Clarke* | *Mohan** | *Jacobsen* | *Kippe* | *O'Connor* | *Gunnarsson* | *Kavanagh* | *Oldfield^* | *Connor"* | *Petty/Lightbourne/Thorne* |
| | | | | | | | | Ref: W Burns | Town are back on track after a thrilling contest which sees a second-half brace from Gray cancel out a first-half strike from O'Connor. Kippe and Lightbourne both hit the Luton bar in the second period. Boyce has now agreed new terms, keeping him at Kenilworth Road until 2002. | | | | | | | | | | | |
| 31 | A | BURY | | 10 | L | 0-1 | 0-0 | | Abbey | Doherty | Watts | Johnson | McGowan* | Locke | White^ | Spring | Taylor | Gray | Douglas" | Boyce/George/Fotiadis |
| | 12/2 | | *3,760* | *14* | 43 | | | *Littlejohn 61* | *Kenny* | *Williams* | *Daws* | *Bullock* | *James** | *Redmond* | *Preece* | *Lawson^* | *Littlejohn* | *Swailes* | *Barrass* | *Avdlu/Billy* |
| | | | | | | | | Ref: S Robinson | A misplaced lay-off by Douglas leads to the Bury goal but the Town still have enough chances to sew up the game. Paddy Kenny is made to look like a world-beater as the Luton forwards shoot straight at him. Williams deliberately handles in the area and is seen by all bar the referee. | | | | | | | | | | | |
| 32 | H | BRISTOL ROV | | 10 | L | **1-4** | 1-2 | Gray 13 | Abbey | Boyce | Watts | Doherty | Johnson | George* | Locke | Spring^ | Gray | Douglas | Taylor | Fotiadis/White |
| | 19/2 | | 6,520 | *2* | 43 | | | *Roberts 27, 90, Cureton 38,58* | *Jones* | *Pethick* | *Thomson* | *Tillson* | *Foster* | *Walters* | *Challis* | *Hillier* | *Astafjevs* | *Cureton* | *Roberts* | |
| | | | | | | | | Ref: M Fletcher | The Hatters take the game to Rovers and the early goal from Gray, after the pace from Douglas exposes a shaky defence, is no more than they deserve. Two amazing errors from Nathan Abbey turn the game in favour of the visitors. Lawrence is now anxious to get a loan goalkeeper. | | | | | | | | | | | |
| 33 | H | BRENTFORD | | 12 | L | 1-2 | 1-1 | Gray 9 | **Roberts** | Boyce* | Watts ! | Doherty | Johnson | George^ | Locke | Spring | Gray | Douglas" | Taylor | McGowan/Fotiadis/White |
| | 26/2 | | 6,029 | *9* | 43 | | | *Owusu 45, Evans 62* | *Woodman* | *Boxall** | *Anderson* | *Quinn* | *Powell* | *Evans* | *Mahon* | *Owusu* | *Ingimarsson* | *Jones^* | *Rowlands* | *Scott/Partridge* |
| | | | | | | | | Ref: K Lynch | New on-loan keeper, Ben Roberts, blames lack of match fitness for the errors which gifts the game to the Bees. He races 35 yards off his line but misses his tackle, leaving his unguarded net to the mercy of Owusu. He then allows a 30-yard volley from Evans to slip through his fingers. | | | | | | | | | | | |
| 34 | A | WREXHAM | | 12 | L | 0-1 | 0-0 | | Roberts | McGowan* | Fraser^ | Doherty | Watts | Johnson | Locke | Spring | Douglas | Gray | Fotiadis" | Taylor/Boyce/George |
| | 4/3 | | *2,703* | *17* | 43 | | | *Allsopp 55* | *Dearden* | *McGregor* | *Hardy* | *Carey* | *Ridler* | *Owen* | *Russell* | *Ferguson* | *Gibson* | *Connolly* | *Allsopp* | |
| | | | | | | | | Ref: D Laws | It is now four defeats in a row against a side who only have one league win to their name since September. Lawrence is worried about the lack of spark and blames Roberts for the Wrexham goal where the ball is shot between his legs. Hatters only have three shots on target all afternoon. | | | | | | | | | | | |

| No | Venue | Opponent | Att | Pos | Pts | F-A | H-T | Scorers, Times, and Referees | 1 | 2 | 3 | 4 | 5 | 6 | 7 | 8 | 9 | 10 | 11 | subs used |
|---|---|---|---|---|---|---|---|---|---|---|---|---|---|---|---|---|---|---|---|---|
| 35 | A | BURNLEY | | 11 | W | 2-0 | 1-0 | White 25, Gray 55 | Roberts | Boyce | McGowan | Watts | Doherty | Johnson | Gray | Spring | Douglas* | Locke | White | Fotiadis |
| | 7/3 | | *12,080* | *5* | 46 | | | | *Crichton* | *Branch** | *Cook^* | *Davis* | *Johnrose* | *Little* | *Mullin"* | *Thomas* | *Wright* | *Cooke* | *Cox* | *Smith/Payton/Mellon* |
| | | | | | | | | Ref: P Danson | The Town turn the form book upside down at a wet and windy Turf Moor against the high-flying Clarets. Ex-Hatters Steve Davis and Mitchell Thomas can only watch as Alan White fires in from the edge of the area. Gray capitalises on a slip by Ian Cox for the second after the break. | | | | | | | | | | | |
| 36 | H | MILLWALL | | 11 | L | 0-2 | 0-2 | | Roberts | Boyce | White | Doherty | Johnson | Sodje* | Locke | Spring | Gray | Douglas^ | McGowan" | George/Fotiadis/Taylor |
| | 11/3 | | 6,341 | *3* | 46 | | | *Cahill 18, 38* | *Warner* | *Dyche* | *Tuttle* | *Ryan* | *Neill* | *Ifill* | *Bull* | *Gilkes* | *Cahill* | *Sadlier* | *Harris** | *Moody* |
| | | | | | | | | Ref: M Dean | Millwall win at Luton for the fourth consecutive time as the inconsistent Hatters throw away the points. Town are extremely poor in the first half, their worst defensive display of the season, but fight back in the second period. Four goal attempts, all within the six-yard box, are missed. | | | | | | | | | | | |
| 37 | A | PRESTON | | 13 | L | 0-1 | 0-1 | | Roberts | Boyce | Taylor | Spring | Doherty | Watts | Johnson | Locke* | White^ | Gray | Douglas" | George/McLaren/Fotiadis |
| | 18/3 | | ***13,731*** | *1* | 46 | | | *Anderson 8* | *Moilanen* | *Alexander* | *Kidd* | *Jackson* | *Murdock* | *Anderson** | *Gregan* | *Rankine* | *Macken^* | *Angell* | *Eyres"* | *Cartwright/Basham/Edwards* |
| | | | | | | | | Ref: P Reijer | The Town enjoy the majority of the possession but still go down narrowly to the top-of-the-table North End. Moilanen is not unduly troubled until three minutes from time, when Andrew Fotiadis is upended by Michael Jackson, leading to a penalty which is shot wide by Liam George. | | | | | | | | | | | |
| 38 | H | CAMBRIDGE | | 12 | D | 2-2 | 1-1 | Doherty 19, McLaren 90 | Roberts | Boyce | Watts | Doherty | Johnson | George | Locke | Spring* | Fotiadis^ | White | Taylor | McLaren/Douglas |
| | 21/3 | | 5,379 | *19* | 47 | | | *Benjamin 26, Ashbee 56* | *Marshall** | *Kavanagh* | *Joseph* | *Eustace* | *McNeill* | *Youngs^* | *Wanless* | *Taylor* | *Mackenzie"* | *Benjamin* | *Ashbee* | *v Heusden/Chenery/Hansen* |
| | | | | | | | | Ref: R Pearson | An acrobatic volley from Paul McLaren in injury-time earns the Town a point in a pulsating end-to-end game. Gary Doherty picks up a loose clearance by Kavanagh and fires past Marshall who is then injured in a collision with Tom Youngs. Doherty heads against the bar near the end. | | | | | | | | | | | |
| 39 | A | CHESTERFIELD | | 11 | W | 3-1 | 3-0 | Doherty 1, Watts 17, George 42 | Roberts | White | Watts | Johnson | Boyce | McLaren | Locke* | Taylor | George | Doherty | Douglas^ | Spring/Fotiadis |
| | 25/3 | | ***2,597*** | *24* | 50 | | | *Howard 76* | *Gayle* | *Hewitt* | *Perkins* | *Beaumont* | *Blatherwick* | *Williams* | *Carss* | *Howard* | *Payne* | *Wilkinson* | *Willis* | |
| | | | | | | | | Ref: R Beeby | The Hatters take the lead after just 48 seconds against all-but-relegated Chesterfield. A brilliant centre by Taylor is headed home by Doherty, followed by a header from Watts and a fierce shot from Liam George. Standards drop in the second half but Town are rarely 3 up at the break. | | | | | | | | | | | |
| 40 | H | COLCHESTER | | 10 | W | 3-2 | 1-0 | Watts 10, Doherty 76, Taylor 82 | Roberts | White | Watts | Johnson | Boyce | McLaren | Spring | Taylor | George | Doherty | Gray | |
| | 1/4 | | 5,125 | *18* | 53 | | | *McGavin 52, Lock 59* | *Brown* | *Keith* | *Johnson R* | *Dozzell* | *Gregory** | *Duguid* | *Lock* | *Skelton* | *McGavin* | *Johnson G^* | *Sodje"* | *Dunne/Arnott/Lualua* |
| | | | | | | | | Ref: G Barber | The Hatters squander first-half opportunities before the visitors steal a lead through poor defending. Doherty slides in to convert a cross from Matthew Spring, setting up a grandstand finish which goes the way of Luton when Taylor beats the offside trap to fire in an unstoppable shot. | | | | | | | | | | | |
| 41 | A | SCUNTHORPE | | 10 | W | 2-1 | 2-0 | Gray 17, Doherty 45 | Roberts | Boyce* | Watts | Johnson | White | McLaren | Spring | Taylor | George* | Doherty | Gray | Locke |
| | 8/4 | | *3,811* | *23* | 56 | | | *Dawson 71* | *Evans* | *Harsley* | *Dawson* | *Logan* | *Hope* | *Walker* | *Hodges* | *Torpey* | *Stanton* | *Sheldon** | *Ipoua* | *Graves* |
| | | | | | | | | Ref: P Joslin | The Hatters overcome a struggling Scunthorpe to record a third successive victory for the first time in 19 months. The visitors rarely threaten although Guy Ipoua, a Town trialist last summer, wins his side a penalty after being tripped by Emmerson Boyce but then misses the spot-kick. | | | | | | | | | | | |
| 42 | H | BRISTOL CITY | | 10 | L | 1-2 | 0-1 | Doherty 78 | Roberts | Boyce* | Watts | White | Johnson | George | McLaren^ | Spring | Gray" | Doherty | Taylor | McGowan/Locke/Douglas |
| | 18/4 | | 4,771 | *9* | 56 | | | *Murray 29, Bell 77* | *Mercer* | *Bell* | *Carey* | *Jordan* | *Millen* | *Tinnion* | *Murray** | *Holland* | *Spencer^* | *Beadle* | *Thorpe"* | *Burnell/Hill/Burns* |
| | | | | | | | | Ref: A Leake | The winning run for the Town ends against bogey-side Bristol City. Hatters are always chasing the game after Murray chips Roberts from 25 yards. Chances are both made and missed by each side in the final quarter but it is City who takes all three points. Doherty is wanted by Spurs. | | | | | | | | | | | |
| 43 | A | GILLINGHAM | | 13 | L | 0-2 | 0-1 | | Roberts | Boyce | Taylor | Spring | White | Watts | Johnson | Gray | McLaren* | Douglas | George | Locke |
| | 22/4 | | *8,667* | *4* | 56 | | | *Hessenthaler 9, Southall 60* | *Bartram* | *Pennock* | *Lewis* | *Ashby* | *Butters* | *Southall* | *Smith* | *Hes'enthal'r** | *Gooden* | *Butler* | *Asaba^* | *Nosworthy/Matthews* |
| | | | | | | | | Ref: A Wiley | Gary Doherty has now gone to Tottenham for £1 million. Hessenthaler fires the home side into an early lead before a text-book volley from Southall gets a second on the hour. The Gills manager, Peter Taylor, is then able to afford the luxury of substituting some of his key players. | | | | | | | | | | | |
| 44 | H | WIGAN | | 13 | D | 1-1 | 0-1 | Gray 57 | Roberts | White | Watts | Johnson | McGowan | McLaren | Spring | Locke | Taylor | Gray | Douglas* | George |
| | 24/4 | | 5,010 | *3* | 57 | | | *Redfearn 35p* | *Stillie* | *Cooke** | *McGibbon* | *de Zeeuw* | *Balmer* | *Bradshaw* | *Nicholls^* | *Redfearn* | *Liddell* | *Peron* | *Haworth* | *McLoughlin/Martinez* |
| | | | | | | | | Ref: A Kaye | Town have the better of the first half but find themselves one down after Haworth tumbled dramatically over the outstretched Ben Roberts with Redfearn netting from the spot. Phil Gray heads Hatters level but Wigan enjoy the better of the chances, a drawn game being the fairest result. | | | | | | | | | | | |
| 45 | A | WYCOMBE | | 10 | W | 1-0 | 0-0 | Taylor 87 | Roberts | McGowan | Taylor | Spring | White | Watts | Johnson | Locke | McLaren | Gray | Douglas* | George |
| | 29/4 | | *5,379* | *14* | 60 | | | | *Taylor* | *Vinnicombe* | *McCarthy** | *Bates* | *Devine* | *McSporran* | *Rogers* | *Bulman* | *Lee^* | *Simpson* | *Senda"* | *Cousins/Harkin/Baird* |
| | | | | | | | | Ref: D Crick | Wycombe are made to rue missed chances after Matt Taylor drills a low shot into their net with just three minutes to go. Wycombe manager Lawrie Sanchez is so upset that he refuses to attend the post-match press conference. Town have won 60 points and hit 60 goals for the season. | | | | | | | | | | | |
| 46 | H | OLDHAM | | 13 | D | 1-1 | 1-0 | Gray 10 | Roberts* | McGowan^ | Watts | White | Johnson | McLaren | Locke | Spring | George | Gray | Taylor | Abbey/Boyce |
| | 6/5 | | 5,963 | *14* | 61 | | | *Tipton 90p* | *Kelly* | *McNiven* | *Holt* | *Garnett* | *Thom** | *Duxbury* | *Innes* | *Dudley^* | *Hotte* | *Jones* | *Boshell* | *Sugden/Tipton* |
| | | Home | Away | | | | | Ref: G Frankland | In the 89th minute, Hatters were tenth in the league but finished thirteenth after conceding a penalty in the last minute. Earlier, Phil Gray had headed the Town into the lead and the home side seemed to be cruising to victory until Alan White handled a McNiven cross unnecessarily. | | | | | | | | | | | |
| Average | | 5,657 | 6,663 | | | | | | | | | | | | | | | | | |

# NATIONWIDE DIVISION 2 (CUP-TIES) Manager: Lennie Lawrence SEASON 1999-2000

| Worthington Cup | Att | F-A | H-T | Scorers, Times, and Referees | 1 | 2 | 3 | 4 | 5 | 6 | 7 | 8 | 9 | 10 | 11 | subs used |
|---|---|---|---|---|---|---|---|---|---|---|---|---|---|---|---|---|
| 1:1 H BRISTOL ROV |  | 0-2 | 0-1 |  | Abbey | Fraser | Taylor | Watts | White* | Boyce | Gray | McLaren | Douglas^ | Spring | McIndoe" | Doherty/George/Fotiadis |
| 10/8 | 2,984 *D2* |  |  | *Roberts 39, 60* | *Jones* | *Pritchard* | *Challis* | *Foster* | *Thomson* | *Tillson* | *Mauge** | *Hillier* | *Cureton* | *Roberts* | *Pethick* | *Trees* |
|  |  |  |  | Ref: P Jones | Early season injury problems leave the Town as no match for a powerful Rovers outfit, with Jason Roberts a problem for the home defence all evening. Hatters have chances, the best of which is wasted by Douglas who shoots over the bar. Johnson is injured in the pre-match warm-up. |  |  |  |  |  |  |  |  |  |  |  |
| 1:2 A BRISTOL ROV | 3 | 2-2 | 0-0 | Kandol 47, Doherty 80 | Abbey | Locke | Sodje | Boyce | White | Watts | Gray | McKinnon | Douglas* | McIndoe | Kandol^ | Doherty/Fotiadis |
| 25/8 | *4,414 2:6* |  |  | *Roberts 60, Cureton 72* | *Jones* | *Pritchard* | *Challis* | *Foster* | *Thomson* | *Tillson* | *Mauge** | *Hillier* | *Cureton* | *Roberts* | *Pethick* | *Bryant* |
|  |  |  |  | Ref: B Knight<br>(Hatters lose 2-4 on aggregate) | Hatters rest eight players from the side which beat Reading the previous Saturday, while Rovers are at full strength. Town take the lead through Kandol, who has now scored for the juniors, reserves and first team this season. Gary Doherty earns the draw with a header into an empty net. |  |  |  |  |  |  |  |  |  |  |  |

| FA Cup | Att | F-A | H-T | Scorers, Times, and Referees | 1 | 2 | 3 | 4 | 5 | 6 | 7 | 8 | 9 | 10 | 11 | subs used |
|---|---|---|---|---|---|---|---|---|---|---|---|---|---|---|---|---|
| 1 H KINGSTONIAN | 7 | 4-2 | 1-1 | Gray 12, George 67, Spring 77, | Abbey | Fraser | Watts* | Doherty | Johnson | George | McLaren | Douglas | Spring | Gray^ | Taylor | Boyce/McIndoe |
| 30/10 | 4,682 *C:2* |  |  | *Crossley 35, Leworthy 47* [Taylor 80] | *Farrelly* | *Mustafa* | *Luckett* | *Crossley* | *Harris* | *Allan* | *Smith** | *Pitcher* | *Marshall* | *Leworthy* | *Wingfield* | *Kadi* |
|  |  |  |  | Ref: P Joslin | Town are made to sweat after the high-flying Conference side, aided by ex-Hatter Dwight Marshall, move into a 2-1 lead. George levels and then Spring fires in the 'goal-of-the-season' from 30 yards which would have graced any match. Marshall praises his former boot-boy, George. |  |  |  |  |  |  |  |  |  |  |  |
| 2 H LINCOLN | 10 | 2-2 | 0-1 | Doherty 64, 84 | Abbey | Fraser | Watts | Doherty | Johnson | George | McLaren* | Douglas | Spring | Locke^ | Taylor | McIndoe/Sodje |
| 19/11 | 4,291 *3:12* |  |  | *Gordon 14, Barnett 81* | *Richardson* | *Fleming* | *Barnett* | *Henry* | *Bimson* | *Smith** | *Finnigan* | *Miller* | *Gain* | *Gordon^* | *Thorpe* | *Phillips/Stant* |
|  |  |  |  | Ref: S Lodge | The Sky TV cameras are hoping for an upset and, with the Imps ahead at the interval, it looks like they get their wish. Gary Doherty is pushed up front and levels as he puts the ball into an empty net. Barnett adds a second for Lincoln only for Doherty to tap the ball home to level again. |  |  |  |  |  |  |  |  |  |  |  |
| 2R A LINCOLN | 10 | 1-0 | 0-0 | Douglas 85 | Abbey | Fraser | Taylor | Spring | Sodje | Watts | Johnson | Doherty | McLaren* | Douglas | George | Locke |
| 30/11 | *3,822 3:14* |  |  |  | *Richardson* | *Fleming* | *Barnett* | *Henry* | *Bimson* | *Smith** | *Finnigan* | *Miller* | *Gain^* | *Gordon* | *Thorpe* | *Stant/Philpott* |
|  |  |  |  | Ref: S Lodge | Sky will not give up in their quest for an upset but they are to be disappointed once again as Stuart Douglas nets the only goal. The game is ruined by a strong wind, which sees the ball playing tricks but an excellent pass from Taylor finds Douglas who sprints past the static defence. |  |  |  |  |  |  |  |  |  |  |  |
| 3 A FULHAM | 10 | 2-2 | 1-2 | George 6, Spring 83 | Abbey | Fraser | Taylor | Spring | Watts | Johnson | Sodje | Locke | Douglas | Doherty | George |  |
| 11/12 | *8,251 1:6* |  |  | *Horsfield 11, Davis 14* | *Taylor* | *Finnan* | *Brevett* | *Melville* | *Coleman* | *Symons* | *Davis** | *Clark* | *Horsfield* | *Hayles* | *Hayward^* | *Collins/Trollope* |
|  |  |  |  | Ref: G Frankland | This Town side cost nothing in transfer fees, whereas the home side boasted £14 million worth of talent. The Hatters take an early lead when George taps in but, after Fulham hit back twice, it is left to Spring to score a stunning goal near the end to earn a deserved draw and replay. |  |  |  |  |  |  |  |  |  |  |  |
| 3R H FULHAM | 11 | 0-3 | 0-0 |  | Abbey | Fraser* | Watts | Doherty | Johnson | George | Locke | Douglas | Spring | McLaren | Taylor | Boyce |
| 21/12 | 8,170 *1:7* |  |  | *Hayles 57, 60, Hayward 63* | *Taylor* | *Finnan* | *Brevett* | *Melville** | *Morgan* | *Symons* | *Collins* | *Clark* | *Horsfield* | *Hayles* | *Hayward* | *Trollope* |
|  |  |  |  | Ref: G Frankland | The dream of a 4th round clash with Premiership Wimbledon dies in six mad minutes in which Fulham knock in three goals. Fraser is at fault for the first and is immediately substituted. Hayles gets a second before Doherty trips Hayward, the free-kick sealing the game for the visitors. |  |  |  |  |  |  |  |  |  |  |  |

| | | Home | | | | | Away | | | | | |
|---|---|---|---|---|---|---|---|---|---|---|---|---|
| | P | W | D | L | F | A | W | D | L | F | A | Pts |
| 1 Preston | 46 | 15 | 4 | 4 | 37 | 23 | 13 | 7 | 3 | 37 | 14 | 95 |
| 2 Burnley | 46 | 16 | 3 | 4 | 42 | 23 | 9 | 10 | 4 | 27 | 24 | 88 |
| 3 Gillingham* | 46 | 16 | 3 | 4 | 46 | 21 | 9 | 7 | 7 | 33 | 27 | 85 |
| 4 Wigan | 46 | 15 | 3 | 5 | 37 | 14 | 7 | 14 | 2 | 35 | 24 | 83 |
| 5 Millwall | 46 | 14 | 7 | 2 | 41 | 18 | 9 | 6 | 8 | 35 | 32 | 82 |
| 6 Stoke | 46 | 13 | 7 | 3 | 37 | 18 | 10 | 6 | 7 | 31 | 24 | 82 |
| 7 Bristol Rov | 46 | 13 | 7 | 3 | 34 | 19 | 10 | 4 | 9 | 35 | 26 | 80 |
| 8 Notts Co | 46 | 9 | 6 | 8 | 32 | 27 | 9 | 5 | 9 | 29 | 28 | 65 |
| 9 Bristol City | 46 | 7 | 14 | 2 | 31 | 18 | 8 | 5 | 10 | 28 | 39 | 64 |
| 10 Reading | 46 | 10 | 9 | 4 | 28 | 18 | 6 | 5 | 12 | 29 | 45 | 62 |
| 11 Wrexham | 46 | 9 | 6 | 8 | 23 | 24 | 8 | 5 | 10 | 29 | 37 | 62 |
| 12 Wycombe | 46 | 11 | 4 | 8 | 32 | 24 | 5 | 9 | 9 | 24 | 29 | 61 |
| 13 LUTON TOWN | 46 | 10 | 7 | 6 | 41 | 35 | 7 | 3 | 13 | 20 | 30 | 61 |
| 14 Oldham | 46 | 8 | 5 | 10 | 27 | 28 | 8 | 7 | 8 | 23 | 27 | 60 |
| 15 Bury | 46 | 8 | 10 | 5 | 38 | 33 | 5 | 8 | 10 | 23 | 31 | 57 |
| 16 Bournemouth | 46 | 11 | 6 | 6 | 37 | 19 | 5 | 3 | 15 | 22 | 43 | 57 |
| 17 Brentford | 46 | 8 | 6 | 9 | 27 | 31 | 5 | 7 | 11 | 20 | 30 | 52 |
| 18 Colchester | 46 | 9 | 4 | 10 | 36 | 40 | 5 | 6 | 12 | 23 | 42 | 52 |
| 19 Cambridge | 46 | 8 | 6 | 9 | 38 | 33 | 4 | 6 | 13 | 26 | 32 | 48 |
| 20 Oxford | 46 | 6 | 5 | 12 | 24 | 38 | 6 | 4 | 13 | 19 | 35 | 45 |
| 21 Cardiff | 46 | 5 | 10 | 8 | 23 | 34 | 4 | 7 | 12 | 22 | 33 | 44 |
| 22 Blackpool | 46 | 4 | 10 | 9 | 26 | 37 | 4 | 7 | 12 | 23 | 40 | 41 |
| 23 Scunthorpe | 46 | 4 | 6 | 13 | 16 | 34 | 5 | 6 | 12 | 24 | 40 | 39 |
| 24 Chesterfield | 46 | 5 | 7 | 11 | 17 | 25 | 2 | 8 | 13 | 17 | 38 | 36 |
| | 1104 | 234 | 155 | 163 | 770 | 634 | 163 | 155 | 234 | 634 | 770 | 1501 |

* promoted after play-offs

Odds & ends

Double wins: (5) Reading, Cardiff, Oxford, Burnley, Scunthorpe.
Double losses: (5) Bournemouth, Brentford, Millwall, Preston, Bristol Rovers.

Won from behind: (2) Gillingham (h), Stoke (h).
Lost from in front: (2) Bristol Rovers (h), Brentford (h).

High spots: Moving out of administration.
The form, particularly at home, at the start of the season.
The draw at Fulham in the FA Cup.
Matt Taylor is the latest addition from the Luton conveyor belt and is nearly ever-present.

Low spots: The 1-4 home defeat by Bristol Rovers.
The last-minute penalty conceded at home to Oldham on the final day, which meant a drop of three league places.
The sale of Gary Doherty.

Player of the Year: Gary Doherty.
Ever presents: (0).
Hat-tricks: (0).
Leading scorer: Liam George (16).

| | Appearances | | | | | | Goals | | | |
|---|---|---|---|---|---|---|---|---|---|---|
| | **Lge** | *Sub* | LC | *Sub* | FAC | *Sub* | **Lge** | LC | FAC | **Tot** |
| Abbey, Nathan | **32** | *1* | 2 | | 5 | | | | | |
| Boyce, Emmerson | **23** | *7* | 2 | | | *2* | **1** | | | **1** |
| Doherty, Gary | **40** | | | *2* | 5 | | **6** | 1 | 2 | **9** |
| Douglas, Stuart | **35** | *5* | 2 | | 5 | | **3** | | 1 | **4** |
| Fotiadis, Andrew | **8** | *15* | | *2* | | | **2** | | | **2** |
| Fraser, Stuart | **20** | | 1 | | 5 | | **1** | | | **1** |
| George, Liam | **35** | *7* | | *1* | 5 | | **14** | | 2 | **16** |
| Gray, Phil | **28** | *1* | 2 | | 1 | | **11** | | 1 | **12** |
| Johnson, Marvin | **44** | | | | 5 | | | | | |
| Kandol, Tresor | **1** | *3* | 1 | | | | | 1 | | **1** |
| Locke, Adam | **27** | *7* | 1 | | 3 | *1* | **3** | | | **3** |
| McGowan, Gavin | **10** | *3* | | | | | | | | |
| McIndoe, Michael | **2** | *15* | 2 | | | *2* | | | | |
| Mc Kinnon, Ray | | *3* | 1 | | | | | | | |
| McLaren, Paul | **25** | *4* | 1 | | 4 | | **1** | | | **1** |
| Midgley, Neil | **8** | *2* | | | | | **3** | | | **3** |
| Roberts, Ben | **14** | | | | | | | | | |
| Scarlett, Andre | **2** | *1* | | | | | | | | |
| Sodje, Efetobore | **5** | *4* | 1 | | 2 | *1* | | | | |
| Spring, Matthew | **44** | *1* | 1 | | 5 | | **6** | | 2 | **8** |
| Taylor, Matthew | **39** | *2* | 1 | | 5 | | **4** | | 1 | **5** |
| Thorpe, Tony | **3** | *1* | | | | | **1** | | | **1** |
| Watts, Julian | **45** | | 2 | | 5 | | **4** | | | **4** |
| White, Alan | **16** | *3* | 2 | | | | **1** | | | **1** |
| Zahana-Oni, L'Andry | | *1* | | | | | | | | |
| **25 players used** | **506** | ***86*** | **22** | ***5*** | **55** | ***6*** | **61** | **2** | **9** | **72** |

| No | Date | | Att | Pos | Pt | F-A | H-T | Scorers, Times, and Referees | 1 | 2 | 3 | 4 | 5 | 6 | 7 | 8 | 9 | 10 | 11 | subs used |
|---|---|---|---|---|---|---|---|---|---|---|---|---|---|---|---|---|---|---|---|---|
| 1 | H | NOTTS CO | | 20 | L | 0-1 | 0-1 | | **Ovendale** | Boyce | Watts* | McLaren | Johnson | Taylor | Spring | Locke^ | George | Stein | Fotiadis | Fraser/**Holmes** |
| | 12/8 | | 7,059 | *6* | 0 | | | *Stallard 24* | *Ward* | *Warren* | *Redmile* | *McDermott* | *Hughes* | *Ramage* | *Stallard* | *Joseph* | *Dyer* | *Owers* | *Liburd** | *Holmes* |
| | | | | | | | | Ref: A D'Urso | The Ricky Hill era starts at Kenilworth Road but the game ends as a massive disappointment after a poor display. The Magpies are comfortable in defence after the goal from Stallard, and restrict the Town to snap shots. Hill felt that the players had stage fright and lacked in confidence. | | | | | | | | | | | |
| 2 | A | WIGAN | | 23 | L | 1-2 | 0-1 | Watts 53 | Ovendale | Boyce | Johnson* | Watts | Taylor | Holmes^ | McLaren | Locke" | George | Fotiadis | Stein | Fraser/**Brennan**/Scarlett |
| | 19/8 | | *6,518* | *5* | 0 | | | *McGibbon 10, Liddell 79* | *Carroll* | *Green** | *McGibbon* | *de Zeeuw* | *Griffiths* | *Bradshaw* | *Nicholls^* | *Sheridan* | *Redfearn* | *Haworth* | *Liddell* | *Ashcroft/Martinez* |
| | | | | | | | | Ref: J Winter | The Town are undone by two set-pieces with the winner from Liddell following an intricate free-kick routine which is good enough to win any game. Watts heads the Luton goal from an in-swinging corner from Taylor. Ex-Hatter Bruce Rioch is introduced as the new Latics manager. | | | | | | | | | | | |
| 3 | H | BOURNEMOUTH | | 19 | W | 1-0 | 0-0 | Spring 75p | Ovendale | Fraser | Boyce | Watts | Taylor | Holmes* | McLaren | Spring | George^ | Fotiadis | Stein | Locke/Brennan |
| | 26/8 | | 5,221 | *20* | 3 | | | | *Menetrier* | *Young* | *Purches* | *Tindall* | *Fenton* | *Hughes* | *Jorgensen* | *Grant** | *Fletcher C^* | *Fletcher S* | *Eribenne"* | *Huck/Angus/Hayter* |
| | | | | | | | | Ref: D Crick | The first home goal of the season is scored from the spot after the experienced Mark Stein falls spectacularly in the area after a tackle from Richard Hughes. Both Ovendale and Stein are playing against their old club and the former makes a tremendous reflex save from Jorgensen. | | | | | | | | | | | |
| 4 | A | WYCOMBE | | 17 | D | 1-1 | 0-1 | Kandol 80 | Ovendale | Fraser | Boyce | Watts | Taylor | Scarlett | McLaren | Spring | George* | Fotiadis^ | Stein | Brennan/Kandol |
| | 28/8 | | *6,001* | *3* | 4 | | | *Brown 17* | *Taylor* | *Rogers* | *Vinnicombe* | *Bates* | *McCarthy* | *Brown* | *Bulman** | *Simpson* | *Jones* | *Baird* | *McSporran^* | *Castledine/Senda* |
| | | | | | | | | Ref: F Stretton | Andrew Baird falls over the leg of Boyce as he flicks the ball past Ovendale but the referee has already pointed to the spot. The spot-kick from Brown is palmed onto the post but he nets the rebound. The Town dominate in the second period and substitute Kandol heads the late leveller. | | | | | | | | | | | |
| 5 | A | ROTHERHAM | | 17 | D | 1-1 | 1-0 | Fotiadis 6 | Ovendale | Locke | Watts | Boyce | Taylor | Holmes* | Scarlett | Spring | McLaren | Fotiadis^ | Stein" | Brennan/Kandol/George |
| | 2/9 | | *4.061* | *9* | 5 | | | *Robins 65* | *Gray* | *Hurst* | *Watson* | *Bryan* | *F'tune-W'st* | *Branston* | *Robins* | *Wilsterman* | *Talbot* | *Garner** | *Warne^* | *Monkhouse/Berry* |
| | | | | | | | | Ref: C Foy | Town hit the woodwork twice through Stein and Kandol but do not deserve any more than the one point as Rotherham enjoy the lion's share of the play. Fotiadis looks lively but the striker limps off injured at half-time. Robins' goal is the first to be conceded from open play this season. | | | | | | | | | | | |
| 6 | H | NORTHAMPTON | | 19 | L | 0-2 | 0-1 | | Abbey | Fraser | Watts | Boyce | Taylor | Scarlett | Spring* | McLaren | Brennan^ | Stein | George | Holmes/Kandol |
| | 9/9 | | 6,712 | *13* | 5 | | | *Forrester 38, Howard 60* | *Welch* | *Henson* | *Frain* | *Sampson* | *Dryden* | *Hunt* | *Howard* | *Hodge** | *Hargreaves* | *Forrester^* | *Green* | *Savage/Gabbiadini* |
| | | | | | | | | Ref: R Furnandiz | The Hatters fail to compete anywhere on the pitch with the only Town player to gain any credit being Nathan Abbey, who is called into the side as a late replacement for Mark Ovendale, who is forced to miss the game after suffering a neck spasm just one hour before the kick-off. | | | | | | | | | | | |
| 7 | H | WALSALL | | 19 | D | 0-0 | 0-0 | | Abbey | Locke | Boyce | Watts | Taylor | Scarlett* | Spring | McLaren | Brennan^ | **Thomson**" | Stein | Holmes/George/Kandol |
| | 12/9 | | **4,362** | *1* | 6 | | | | *Walker* | *Brightwell* | *Bennett* | *Tillson* | *Byfield* | *Keates* | *Wrack** | *Leitao^* | *Matias* | *Aranalde* | *Barras"* | *Hall/Angell/Roper* |
| | | | | | | | | Ref: D Elleray | The Hatters go 87 minutes before forcing Walsall keeper James Walker to make his first save of the game. New striker Peter Thomson, signed for £100,000 from NAC Breda, fails to impress in a dismal game. Walsall manage to hit the woodwork but are dragged down to Luton's level. | | | | | | | | | | | |
| 8 | A | SWANSEA | | 19 | L | **0-4** | 0-2 | *[Roberts 89]* | Ovendale | Boyce | Watts | **Stirling** ! | Locke | Holmes | Spring | McLaren | Taylor | Kandol | Stein* | George |
| | 16/9 | | *6,011* | *10* | 6 | | | *Bound 22p, Boyd 45, Cusack 70* | *Freestone* | *Howard* | *Cusack* | *Bound* | *Thomas* | *Coates** | *O'Leary* | *Price* | *Phillips* | *Jenkins* | *Boyd^* | *Roberts/Morgan* |
| | | | | | | | | Ref: D Pugh | A shot from Nick Cusack hits Town debutant Jude Stirling, who is standing on the line, and the referee deems it to be deliberate handball. A penalty is awarded, Stirling dismissed and the Hatters all but capitulate. Luton have now gone 354 minutes since scoring their last league goal. | | | | | | | | | | | |
| 9 | H | SWINDON | | 21 | L | 2-3 | 2-2 | Stein 13, George 43 | Ovendale | Fraser | Watts | Boyce | Taylor | Spring* | Holmes | Scarlett | George | Kandol^ | Stein | Locke/Thomson |
| | 23/9 | | 4,933 | *20* | 6 | | | *Duke 29, Williams 41, 67* | *Griemink* | *Cobian** | *Reeves* | *Davis* | *Tuomela* | *Duke^* | *O'Halloran* | *Hewlett* | *Williams* | *Alexander* | *Robertson"* | *Robinson/Invincible/Young* |
| | | | | | | | | Ref: P Reijer | The pack is shuffled once more, with the formation reverting to 4-3-3. George, playing in his best position just behind the strikers, sets up Stein for his first league goal since returning to the club and then scores the second, but the Town still drop into the bottom four in place of Swindon. | | | | | | | | | | | |
| 10 | A | BRISTOL ROV | | 22 | D | 3-3 | 1-2 | Kandol 45, 72, George 83 | Ovendale | Watts | McLaren | Boyce | Fraser* | Spring^ | Locke | Taylor | George | Thomson" | Kandol | McGowan/Holmes/Stein |
| | 30/9 | | *7,901* | *9* | 7 | | | *Foster 14, Ellington 31,61* | *Culkin* | *Bignot* | *Jones* | *Walters** | *Foster* | *Wilson* | *Bryant* | *Hogg* | *Astafjevs* | *Ellis^* | *Ellington"* | *Dagnogo/Challis/Plummer* |
| | | | | | | | | Ref: G Cain | Liam George secures a point for the Hatters with a 25-yard volley in a game where both defences are woeful. Kandol proves a handful for the visitors, scoring twice and setting up Thomson for a chance that looks impossible to miss. Thomson is subbed at the interval, along with Fraser. | | | | | | | | | | | |
| 11 | H | MILLWALL | | 22 | L | 0-1 | 0-0 | | Ovendale | McLaren | Watts | Boyce | McGowan | Spring | Locke | Taylor | George | Stein | Kandol | |
| | 8/10 | | 5,345 | *5* | 7 | | | *McGowan 83 (og)* | *Warner* | *Lawrence* | *Nethercott* | *Dyche* | *Ryan* | *Neill* | *Cahill** | *Livermore* | *Kinet* | *Harris* | *Parkin* | *Odunsi* |
| | | | | | | | | Ref: A Wiley | The Town look good for a point after a poor first-half performance until McGowan, who is making his first start of the season, smashes the ball into the roof of his own net when attempting to clear a header from Neil Harris. Manager Hill is desperate to bring in experienced loan players. | | | | | | | | | | | |

| No | Venue | Opponent | Att | | Res | | FT | HT | Scorers | 1 | 2 | 3 | 4 | 5 | 6 | 7 | 8 | 9 | 10 | 11 | Subs |
|---|---|---|---|---|---|---|---|---|---|---|---|---|---|---|---|---|---|---|---|---|---|
| 12 | A | CAMBRIDGE | | 23 | L | | 1-2 | 1-0 | Stein 16 | Ovendale | McLaren | Watts | Boyce | McGowan* | Spring ! | Locke | Taylor | George | Stein | Kandol^ | Brennan/Holmes |
| | 13/10 | | *6,191* | *6* | 7 | | | | *Youngs 54, Abbey 79* | *Perez* | *McAnespie* | *Cowan* | *Duncan* | *Dreyer* | *Youngs* | *Wanless* | *Ashbee* | *Axeldal** | *Abbey^* | *Russell* | *Mustoe/Taylor* |
| | | | | | | | | | Ref: J Brandwood | Mark Stein hooks the Hatters in to an early lead but Matthew Spring is sent off shortly afterwards for a second bookable offence and it is all downhill thereafter. With only one league win in the first twelve games, this is now officially the worst start Luton have made to any season. | | | | | | | | | | | |
| 13 | A | OXFORD | | 23 | D | | 0-0 | 0-0 | | Abbey | Fraser | Watts | McGowan* | Boyce | Taylor | Holmes | Spring | George | Stein | Kandol^ | **Breitenfelder**/Brennan |
| | 17/10 | | *4,537* | *24* | 8 | | | | | *Knight* | *Ricketts* | *McGowan* | *Jarman* | *Linighan* | *Richardson* | *Whitehead* | *Tait** | *Beauchamp* | *Lilley* | *Cook^* | *Robertson/Omoyinmi* |
| | | | | | | | | | Ref: R Styles | Abbey is recalled to the side but it his counterpart, Richard Knight, who prevents the Town from achieving only their second league win of the season with brilliant saves from George, Kandol and Taylor. Boyce heads wide from two yards out with just three minutes left on the clock. | | | | | | | | | | | |
| 14 | H | BRENTFORD | | 23 | W | | 3-1 | 3-0 | Douglas 17, 29, Spring 35p | Abbey | McLaren | Watts | Boyce | Locke* | Spring | Holmes | Taylor | George^ | Stein | Douglas" | B'felder/Brennan/Thomson |
| | 21/10 | | 5,382 | *14* | 11 | | | | *Scott 73* | *Gottskalksson* | *Crowe** | *Marshall* | *Ingimarsson* | *Evans^* | *Mahon* | *Quinn* | *Partridge"* | *Scott* | *Rowlands* | *Gibbs* | *Folan/Williams/Pinamonte* |
| | | | | | | | | | Ref: S Dunn | Douglas makes his first appearance of the campaign after picking up a pre-season hamstring injury. He scores twice before Spring adds a third from the spot after Stein tumbles in the box. Douglas leaves the pitch to a standing ovation. Assistant manager Chris Ramsey has left the club. | | | | | | | | | | | |
| 15 | H | WREXHAM | | 23 | L | | 3-4 | 2-0 | Stein 38, Watts 44, George 55 | Abbey | Boyce | Watts | Johnson | Breitenfelder | McLaren* | Holmes | Taylor | George | Stein | Fotiadis^ | Fraser/Thomson |
| | 28/10 | | 5,341 | *11* | 11 | | | | *F'bridge 59, Kill'n 63, Chalk 83, F'son 87* | *Dearden* | *McGregor* | *Ridler** | *Chalk* | *Faulconbridge* | *Ferguson* | *Barrett^* | *Edwards* | *Roche* | *Killen* | *Bouanane* | *Mardon/Owen* |
| | | | | | | | | | Ref: M Cowburn | The Town are flattered by their three-goal lead and have Nathan Abbey to thank for pulling off a string of brilliant saves. After midfielder Paul McLaren is forced to limp off with an injury, the floodgates open and the late winner from Darren Ferguson has an air of inevitability about it. | | | | | | | | | | | |
| 16 | A | BURY | | 23 | D | | 1-1 | 0-0 | Helin 56 | Abbey | **Karlsen** | Watts | Boyce | **Helin** | Spring | McLaren | Taylor | George* | Douglas^ | Stein | Holmes/**Baptiste** |
| | 4/11 | | ***2,861*** | *10* | 12 | | | | *Littlejohn 47* | *Kenny* | *Barrick** | *Daws* | *Collins* | *Swailes* | *Billy* | *Littlejohn* | *Reid* | *Redmond* | *Preece* | *Unsworth^* | *Bhutia/James* |
| | | | | | | | | | Ref: J Robinson | Petri Helin was in the Finland team which held England to a draw in the World Cup only a few weeks ago. He now finds himself at Gigg Lane where he scores on his Luton debut. Hill is upbeat after the game and feels that his new signings will soon send the team shooting up the table. | | | | | | | | | | | |
| 17 | H | BRISTOL CITY | | 23 | L | | 0-3 | 0-0 | | Abbey | McLaren | Karlsen | Boyce | McGowan | Spring | Helin | Taylor | George | Douglas* | Stein^ | Fotiadis/Baptiste |
| | 11/11 | | 6,595 | *8* | 12 | | | | *Murray 56, Peacock 64, Bell 67* | *Philips* | *Millen* | *Carey* | *Hill* | *Murray* | *Bell* | *Tinnion** | *Clist* | *Brown^* | *Thorpe"* | *Peacock* | *Tistimetanu/Burnell/Beadle* |
| | | | | | | | | | Ref: M Cooper | Ricky Hill is given the dreaded vote of confidence by his chairman before the game. Eight new signings have been made since he took charge of the club but the team have only managed two wins in 21 games. It is therefore no surprise when he is dismissed on the following Thursday. | | | | | | | | | | | |
| 18 | A | PORT VALE | | 23 | L | | 0-3 | 0-1 | | Abbey | **Whitbread** | Watts | Karlsen | Boyce | Spring | McLaren | Helin* | Taylor | George | **Nogan^** | Fraser/Fotiadis |
| | 25/11 | | *4,194* | *18* | 12 | | | | *Walsh 34, Naylor 64, Minton 70* | *Goodlad* | *Carragher* | *Tankard** | *Brammer^* | *Walsh* | *Cummins* | *Naylor"* | *Widdrington* | *Brdge-Wilk'n* | *Minton* | *Smith* | *Burton/O'Callaghan/Eyre* |
| | | | | | | | | | Ref: A Kaye | The first game in charge for new manager Lil Fuccillo is marked by the worst display of the season. Only on-loan Adrian Whitbread can take any satisfaction from the match. Vale conceded four goals to Canvey Island in the FA Cup last week but carve open the Town defence at will. | | | | | | | | | | | |
| 19 | A | STOKE | | 23 | W | | 3-1 | 1-1 | McLaren 15, Thomson 51, 62 | Abbey | Whitbread | Watts | Johnson | Helin | Locke | Spring | McLaren | Taylor | George* | Thomson^ | Karlsen/Fotiadis |
| | 2/12 | | ***12,389*** | 7 | 15 | | | | *Mohan 35* | *Muggleton* | *Hansson* | *Clarke* | *Mohan* | *Gunnarsson** | *Kavanagh* | *Thorne* | *Dorigo^* | *O'Connor* | *Kippe* | *Cooke"* | *Risom/Thordarson/Dadason* |
| | | | | | | | | | Ref: B Curson | The second trip to the Potteries in a week and the Town are a changed side. They take advantage of a Stoke outfit that was beaten by Nuneaton in the FA Cup and 0-8 by Liverpool in the Worthington. A 30-yarder from McLaren is unstoppable and a brace from Thomson seals the points. | | | | | | | | | | | |
| 20 | H | COLCHESTER | | 23 | L | | 0-3 | 0-1 | | Abbey | Whitbread | Watts | Johnson | Helin | Spring | Locke* | McLaren | Taylor | George | Nogan | Fotiadis |
| | 16/12 | | 4,791 | *12* | 15 | | | | *Conlon 28, Gregory 48, Pinault 76* | *Woodman* | *Johnson* | *Fitzgerald* | *Skelton* | *Dunne** | *Stockwell^* | *Keeble* | *Gregory* | *Dozzell"* | *Conlon* | *Duguid* | *Clark/Pinault/McGavin* |
| | | | | | | | | | Ref: M Pike | The Town create a total of 19 scoring opportunities against the lowest goal-scoring side in the division but, apart from hitting the woodwork, have nothing to show for their efforts. The final result flatters the visitors, whose busiest player by far is their goalkeeper, Andy Woodman. | | | | | | | | | | | |
| 21 | A | READING | | 23 | L | | 1-4 | 0-2 | Nogan 70 | Abbey | Boyce | Whitbread | Johnson* | Helin | Spring | McLaren^ | Taylor | George" | Fotiadis | Nogan | Fraser/Locke/Baptiste |
| | 23/12 | | *10,771* | *5* | 15 | | | | *Hunter 22, Cureton 35, 80, 89* | *Whitehead* | *Robinson* | *Viveash* | *Hunter* | *Caskey* | *Butler* | *Hodges** | *Cureton^* | *Parkinson* | *Smith* | *Newman* | *Igoe/Rougier* |
| | | | | | | | | | Ref: S Tomlin | Fuccillo dismisses half of his players as 'dead wood' after watching the Hatters collapse to another dismal defeat. The Town start brightly with Fotiadis, George and Taylor all going close, but Reading take the lead in their first attack through Hunter before Jamie Cureton nets a hat-trick. | | | | | | | | | | | |
| 22 | H | PETERBOROUGH | | 23 | W | | 3-2 | 2-1 | Spring 4, Holmes 13, Boyce 49 | Abbey | Boyce | Whitbread | Fraser | Helin | Locke | Spring | Holmes* | Taylor | Fotiadis | Nogan^ | Scarlett/Kandol |
| | 26/12 | | 7,374 | *14* | 18 | | | | *Farrell 41, McKenzie 69p* | *Tyler* | *Hooper** | *Drury* | *Edwards* | *McKenzie* | *Farrell* | *Forsyth* | *Shields* | *Gill* | *Rogers^* | *Clarke"* | *Green/Jelleyman/Forinton* |
| | | | | | | | | | Ref: B Knight | Spring is given the captain's armband in the absence of both Johnson and McLaren and he responds by opening the scoring with a 20-yard effort. Holmes and Boyce both put their names on the scoresheet before Forinton falls over the arm of Abbey in the area to set up a tight finish. | | | | | | | | | | | |
| 23 | H | WIGAN | | 23 | L | | 0-2 | 0-1 | | Ovendale | Whitbread | Watts | Fraser | Helin | Spring | Locke | Holmes* | Taylor | Fotiadis | Nogan^ | Thomson/Stein |
| | 30/12 | | 5,322 | *3* | 18 | | | | *Haworth 11, Bidstrup 54* | *Stillie* | *Balmer* | *Sharp* | *McGibbon* | *de Zeeuw* | *Sheridan* | *Bidstrup* | *Green* | *Ashcroft** | *Liddell* | *Haworth* | *Roberts* |
| | | | | | | | | | Ref: G Laws | 50 volunteers help to clear snow off the pitch but, after the game, probably wished they had not bothered. Wigan have the meanest defence in the division and keep the Town at arm's length all afternoon. The Latics only have two shots on target during the game but score from both. | | | | | | | | | | | |

# NATIONWIDE LEAGUE DIVISION 2 — Manager: Hill / Fuccillo / Kinnear — SEASON 2000-01

| No | | Date | | Att | Pos | Pt | F-A | H-T | Scorers, Times, and Referees | 1 | 2 | 3 | 4 | 5 | 6 | 7 | 8 | 9 | 10 | 11 | subs used |
|---|---|---|---|---|---|---|---|---|---|---|---|---|---|---|---|---|---|---|---|---|---|
| 24 | A | | BOURNEMOUTH | | 23 | L | 2-3 | 2-1 | Fotiadis 45, Locke 45 | Ovendale | Whitbread | Watts* | Fraser^ | Helin | Locke | Spring | Holmes | Taylor ! | Fotiadis" | Nogan | Stirling/Br'felder/Scarlett |
| | | 1/1 | | *5,411* | *13* | 18 | | | *Fletcher 39, Hughes 83p, Defoe 86* | *Stewart* | *Purches** | *Howe* | *Fletcher* | *Elliott* | *Tindall* | *Defoe* | *Broadhurst* | *Grant^* | *Hughes* | *Jorgensen* | *O'Connor/Hayter* |
| | | | | | | | | | Ref: P Alcock | The Cherries open the scoring when the Town are down to ten men, Watts having limped off and substitute Stirling having left his shirt in the dressing-room! In an amazing spell, the Hatters score twice in a minute, but Matt Taylor is sent off in stoppage time for swearing at the referee. | | | | | | | | | | | |
| 25 | H | | WYCOMBE | | 23 | L | 1-2 | 1-0 | Locke 20 | Ovendale | Boyce* | Whitbread | Fraser | Briet'nfelder^ | Locke | Spring | Taylor | George | Thomson" | Douglas | Stirling/Scarlett/Kandol |
| | | 12/1 | | 4,551 | *9* | 18 | | | *Rammell 50, 64* | *Taylor* | *Vinnicombe* | *Cousins* | *McCarthy* | *Brady** | *Bulman* | *Simpson* | *Brown^* | *Senda* | *Baird"* | *Rammell* | *Lee/Rogers/Parkin* |
| | | | | | | | | | Ref: T Parkes | The Hatters take the lead when a volley from Locke hits the post and then bounces off the shoulder of the Wycombe keeper and into the net. Wycombe make 3 substitutions at the interval, after which there is only one team in the game, with Rammell scoring twice to secure the points. | | | | | | | | | | | |
| 26 | A | | OLDHAM | | 23 | L | 0-2 | 0-1 | | Ovendale | Boyce | Holmes* | **Mansell** | Karlsen | Nogan^ | Whitbread | Spring | McGowan | Fotiadis" | Douglas | George/Thomson/Stein |
| | | 23/1 | | *3,011* | *16* | 18 | | | *Rickers 30, Sheridan 67* | *Kelly* | *McNiven* | *Garnett** | *Duxbury* | *Rickers* | *Sheridan^* | *Tipton"* | *Corazzin* | *Hotte* | *Eyres* | *Carss* | *Innes/Boshell/Dudley* |
| | | | | | | | | | Ref: C Webster | Four defeats in a row are recorded as the Town manage only one shot on target all night. A Duxbury cross is headed against the bar by Eyres and Rickers diverts the rebound over the line. Karlsen tugs the shirt of Corazzin on the edge of the area and Sheridan scores from the free kick. | | | | | | | | | | | |
| 27 | A | | NORTHAMPTON | | 23 | W | 1-0 | 1-0 | Douglas 4 | Ovendale | Stirling | Boyce | **Dryden** | Helin | Mansell | Spring | **Rowland** | Taylor | George | Douglas* | Fotiadis |
| | | 10/2 | | *6,633* | *9* | 21 | | | | *Welch* | *Canoville** | *Frain* | *Sampson* | *Savage* | *Hunt* | *Gabbiadini* | *Hodge^* | *Hope* | *Forrester* | *Hargreaves"* | *Green/Howard/Nicholson* |
| | | | | | | | | | Ref: M Fletcher | It is all change once again with Joe Kinnear taking over the managerial reins. Douglas is unmarked when he heads a right wing cross from Helin into the roof of the net and the Hatters hold onto their lead until the end, despite Spring missing a penalty after George is brought down. | | | | | | | | | | | |
| 28 | A | | NOTTS CO | | 23 | W | 3-1 | 1-1 | Boyce 22, George 55, Fotiadis 82 | Ovendale | Stirling | Boyce | Dryden | Helin | Mansell | Spring | Rowland | Taylor | George | Douglas* | Kandol^/Fotiadis |
| | | 13/2 | | *4,333* | *8* | 24 | | | *Stallard 44* | *Ward* | *McDermott* | *Stallard* | *Liburd* | *Brough** | *Pearce^* | *Hamilton* | *Fenton* | *Allsopp"* | *Newton* | *Jacobsen* | *Murray/Joseph/Farrell* |
| | | | | | | | | | Ref: M Warren | The Hatters gain consecutive victories as Kinnear weaves his magic spell. Boyce heads in a cross from Taylor before Stallard levels. George gets the second as the Town play with a spring in their step. Substitute Fotiadis makes the points safe with a fierce shot into the roof of the net. | | | | | | | | | | | |
| 29 | H | | SWANSEA | | 22 | W | **5-3** | 2-1 | Mansell 3, 51, Douglas 9, Rowland 70 | Ovendale | Stirling | Boyce | Dryden | Helin | Mansell | Spring | Rowland* | Taylor | George | Douglas^ | Locke/Fotiadis |
| | | 17/2 | | 7,085 | *23* | 27 | | | *Savarese 18, 65, 80* *[George 83]* | *Freestone* | *Bound* | *Savarese* | *O'Leary* | *Lacey** | *Roberts* | *Price^* | *Jenkins"* | *de Vulgt* | *Romo* | *Verschave* | *Watkin/Cusack/Fabiano* |
| | | | | | | | | | Ref: | The Town hit five goals for the first time since 1997 as the terrific start by Kinnear continues. The win sees the Hatters leapfrog Swansea in an entertaining game of defensive errors. Venezuelan striker Savarese, thrown out after a Luton trial by ex-manager Ricky Hill, grabs a hat-trick. | | | | | | | | | | | |
| 30 | A | | WALSALL | | 22 | L | 1-3 | 0-2 | Spring 55 | Ovendale | Stirling | Boyce | Dryden | Helin | Mansell* | Spring | Rowland | Taylor | George^ | Douglas" | Locke/Thomson/Fotiadis |
| | | 20/2 | | *4,816* | *2* | 27 | | | *Leitao 13, Bennett 36, Byfield 67* | *Walker* | *Aranalde* | *Roper* | *Barras* | *Brightwell* | *Bennett** | *Keates* | *Hall^* | *Matias* | *Angell* | *Leitao"* | *Ekelund/Wrack/Byfield* |
| | | | | | | | | | Ref: N Barry | The honeymoon is over as a physical Walsall side deny the visitors any time on the ball and expose weaknesses in the Luton defence. The pitch is awful and home skipper Bennett sees his weak 25-yard effort finish up in the net after hitting a divot. Byfield races clear to clinch the points. | | | | | | | | | | | |
| 31 | A | | SWINDON | | 22 | W | 3-1 | 1-1 | Rowland 42, Boyce 70, Mansell 90 | Ovendale | Boyce | McLaren | Dryden | Helin | Locke* | Spring | Rowland | Taylor | Fotiadis^ | George | Mansell/Stein"/Thomson |
| | | 24/2 | | *7,160* | *20* | 30 | | | *Alexander 39* | *Mildenhall* | *van d' Linden* | *O'Halloran* | *Hewlett** | *Reddy* | *Alexander* | *Heywood* | *Reeves* | *Robinson* | *Williams^* | *Duke* | *Grazioli/Invincible* |
| | | | | | | | | | Ref: M Cowburn | McLaren returns to the defence for his first game since Christmas and his presence brings assurance to a back line, which has conceded three goals in each of the previous two fixtures. Rowland and Boyce make headed goals for each other and Mansell provides the icing on the cake. | | | | | | | | | | | |
| 32 | H | | BRISTOL ROV | | 22 | D | 0-0 | 0-0 | | Abbey | Boyce | Watts | Dryden | Helin | Locke | McLaren* | Rowland | Stein^ | George | Taylor | Stirling/Douglas |
| | | 3/3 | | **7,405** | *20* | 31 | | | | *Culkin* | *Wilson* | *Foster* | *Jones* | *Challis* | *Bignot* | *Plummer* | *Bryant** | *McKeever* | *Ellington* | *Owusu^* | *Asafjevs/Ellis* |
| | | | | | | | | | Ref: P Danson | A tense relegation dog-fight with both sides grateful to escape with a point at the end. The referee disallows a header from Scott Jones after 69 minutes for offside and Watts has a free header which he cannot keep on target but, apart from that, it is a midfield battle with little excitement. | | | | | | | | | | | |
| 33 | H | | CAMBRIDGE | | 22 | W | 1-0 | 0-0 | Taylor 86 | Abbey | Boyce | McLaren | Dryden | Helin | Mansell | Spring | Rowland* | Taylor | Douglas^ | George | Watts/Fotiadis"/Stein |
| | | 6/3 | | 6,370 | *20* | 34 | | | | *Perez* | *Cowan* | *Joseph* | *Mustoe* | *Duncan* | *Riza* | *Dreyer* | *Oakes** | *Wanless* | *Ashbee* | *Humphreys^* | *Russell/Taylor* |
| | | | | | | | | | Ref: R Olivier | A hard-fought struggle is heading for a scoreless draw when substitute Stein chases a hopeful long ball up-field which Perez appears to have cleared as he races off his line. The ball is returned brilliantly from nearly 40 yards by Taylor, into an unguarded net, to earn a priceless win. | | | | | | | | | | | |
| 34 | A | | MILLWALL | | 22 | L | 0-1 | 0-1 | | Abbey | Boyce | McLaren | Dryden* | Helin | Mansell^ | Spring | Rowland | Taylor | Douglas" | George | Watts/Stein/Fotiadis |
| | | 10/3 | | *11,691* | *1* | 34 | | | *Nethercott 41* | *Gueret* | *Lawrence* | *Ryan* | *Tuttle* | *Nethercott* | *Neill** | *Cahill^* | *Livermore* | *Harris* | *Moody"* | *Kinet* | *Reid/Bircham/Sadlier* |
| | | | | | | | | | Ref: R Beeby | Kinnear is searching for a big target man to play up front. He calls on his side to be more ruthless as three clear chances are missed. At the other end, Abbey has little to do, the only goal coming when Nethercott charges into the area to meet a Neill corner with a powerful header. | | | | | | | | | | | |

| No | Date | Opponent | Att | Pos | Pt | F-A | H-T | Scorers, Times, and Referees | 1 | 2 | 3 | 4 | 5 | 6 | 7 | 8 | 9 | 10 | 11 | subs used |
|---|---|---|---|---|---|---|---|---|---|---|---|---|---|---|---|---|---|---|---|---|
| 35 | A | PETERBOROUGH | | 22 | D | 1-1 | 0-0 | Mansell 79 | Abbey | Taylor | Dryden | Boyce | Spring | McLaren | Helin | Mansell | Rowland | **Howard** | George* | Stein |
| | 27/3 | | *5,425* | *18* | 35 | | | *Clarke 75* | *Tyler* | *Hooper* | *Morrow* | *Rea* | *Edwards* | *Farrell* | *Clarke* | *Williams** | *McKenzie* | *Shields* | *Forsyth* | *Lee* |
| | | | | | | | | Ref: D Laws | The pitch surprisingly survives a late inspection, despite large pools of surface water, which makes the game a lottery. Steve Howard, signed from Northampton for £50,000, is the big target man who the fans have been asking for. He soon shows his worth with several early headers. | | | | | | | | | | | |
| 36 | A | COLCHESTER | | 22 | L | 1-3 | 0-3 | Howard 83p | Abbey | Boyce | McLaren | Dryden | Helin | Mansell | Spring | Rowland* | Taylor | Howard | George | Douglas |
| | 31/3 | | *4,271* | *14* | 35 | | | *Stockwell 17, 37,Skelton 43p* | *Woodman* | *Keith** | *Johnson* | *Fitzgerald* | *Clark* | *White* | *Stockwell^* | *Skelton* | *Duguid* | *Scott"* | *McGleish* | *Izzet/McGavin/Conlon* |
| | | | | | | | | Ref: M Warren | Kinnear is furious after his pre-match warning of midfield players running unopposed into the penalty box is apparently ignored. The first two shots on target by the home side result in goals and both come from the predicted source. Howard opens his Luton goal-account from the spot. | | | | | | | | | | | |
| 37 | H | READING | | 22 | D | 1-1 | 1-1 | Harper 9 (og) | Abbey | Boyce | Dryden | Helin | Taylor | Spring | McLaren | Mansell | Rowland* | Howard | Stein^ | George/Douglas |
| | 3/4 | | 6,132 | *3* | 36 | | | *Butler 4* | *Whitehead* | *Robinson* | *Caskey** | *Viveash* | *Whitbread* | *Murty* | *Parkinson* | *Harper* | *McIntyre^* | *Cureton"* | *Butler* | *Newman/Rougier/Forster* |
| | | | | | | | | Ref: G Poll | The Royals take the lead with their first attack when Butler lobs from 25 yards over Abbey after he slips on the edge on his area. The equaliser follows five minutes later. James Harper leaves his goalkeeper helpless as he heads an in-swinging free-kick from Spring into his own net. | | | | | | | | | | | |
| 38 | H | STOKE | | 22 | L | 1-2 | 1-2 | Mansell 4 | Abbey | Boyce | McLaren | Dryden | Helin | Mansell | Spring | Rowland* | Taylor | Howard | Stein^ | Douglas/George |
| | 7/4 | | 6,456 | *5* | 36 | | | *Kavanagh 30, 40* | *Ward* | *Hansson* | *Clarke* | *Thomas* | *Gunnarsson* | *Gudjonsson** | *Kavanagh* | *O'Connor* | *Cooke^* | *Thorne* | *Mohan* | *Lightbourne/Risom* |
| | | | | | | | | Ref: W Burns | The persistence of Mansell enables him to score early on, before Kavanagh takes advantage of an unlucky ricochet off Spring to fire a shot into the roof of the net. The same player then unleashes a full-blooded volley into the top corner to take the game and the points from the Hatters. | | | | | | | | | | | |
| 39 | H | OXFORD | | 22 | D | 1-1 | 1-0 | Watts 18 | Abbey | Boyce | Dryden | Helin* | Taylor | Spring^ | McLaren | Mansell | Watts | Howard | George | Stein/Stirling |
| | 10/4 | | 6,010 | *24* | 37 | | | *Scott 78* | *Knight* | *Robertson* | *Powell** | *Richardson* | *Hatswell* | *Patterson* | *Ricketts* | *Murphy* | *Tait^* | *Scott* | *Gray* | *Beauchamp/Fear* |
| | | | | | | | | Ref: D Pugh | Watts gets the faintest of touches to a corner by Taylor to open the scoring and it seems likely that this will be sufficient to win the game until an overhead kick from ex-Hatter Gray is nudged home by Andy Scott. Oxford are already relegated and the Town now look like joining them. | | | | | | | | | | | |
| 40 | H | OLDHAM | | 22 | D | 0-0 | 0-0 | | Ovendale | Boyce | Watts | Dryden | **Shepherd** | Mansell | McLaren | Taylor | George | Howard | Douglas | |
| | 14/4 | | 4,886 | *11* | 38 | | | | *Kelly* | *McNiven* | *Garnett* | *Hotte** | *Prendeville* | *Salt^* | *Duxbury* | *Corazzin* | *Carss* | *Tipton"* | *Eyres* | *Futcher/Sheridan/Parkin* |
| | | | | | | | | Ref: P Richards | Kinnear will make a 20-goal per season man a priority this summer after seeing his side miss nine clear-cut chances. Former Leeds full-back Paul Shepherd catches the eye although the defence is rarely troubled. Sadly, it is reported that ex-Town manager Alec Stock has died aged 84. | | | | | | | | | | | |
| 41 | A | WREXHAM | | 22 | L | 1-3 | 1-1 | Watts 27 | Ovendale | Boyce | Watts | Dryden | Shepherd | Mansell | McLaren* | Taylor | George | Howard | Douglas | Locke |
| | 16/4 | | *3,329* | *9* | 38 | | | *McGregor 18, Carey 83, Ferguson 85* | *Walsh* | *McGregor* | *Hardy* | *Carey* | *Russell* | *Faulconbridge* | *Ferguson* | *Gibson** | *Williams* | *Roche* | *Thomas^* | *Edwards/Blackwood* |
| | | | | | | | | Ref: H Webb | Julian Watts levels the scores when he heads in a corner from Taylor but two late goals from an experimental Wrexham side carve open the Luton defence. Darren Ferguson both makes one and scores one in front of his proud father which finally condemns the Hatters to relegation. | | | | | | | | | | | |
| 42 | H | BURY | | 22 | L | 1-2 | 1-1 | George 6 | Ovendale | Boyce | Watts | Dryden | Shepherd | Mansell* | Spring | McLaren | Taylor | Howard | George | Douglas |
| | 21/4 | | 4,902 | *13* | 38 | | | *Swailes C 9, Cramb 90* | *Kenny* | *Billy* | *Swailes C* | *Hill* | *Swailes D !* | *Daws* | *Reid* | *Armstrong* | *Jarrett* | *Newby* | *Cramb** | *Forrest* |
| | | | | | | | | Ref: S Tomlin | George side-foots his effort against the post before bundling in the rebound to open the scoring. Bury level with their first goal attempt before Danny Swailes is dismissed for wrestling George to the ground on the edge of the area. Cramb breaks clear to slot home in the final minute. | | | | | | | | | | | |
| 43 | H | ROTHERHAM | | 22 | L | 0-1 | 0-0 | | Ovendale | Boyce | Johnson | Dryden | Shepherd | Spring | McLaren | Taylor | George* | Douglas | Howard | Stein |
| | 24/4 | | 4,854 | *2* | 38 | | | *Sedgwick 76* | *Pettinger* | *Artell* | *Scott* | *Bryan* | *Robins** | *Barker* | *Sedgwick* | *Talbot^* | *Watson* | *Hurst* | *Branston* | *Monkhouse/Minton* |
| | | | | | | | | Ref: P Armstrong | Town show fight and character, which has been lacking in recent matches against a promotion-chasing Rotherham. Few chances are created by either side but Mark Robins is blatantly offside when he breaks down the left wing before crossing to Chris Sedgwick who nets the only goal. | | | | | | | | | | | |
| 44 | A | BRISTOL CITY | | 22 | L | 1-3 | 0-1 | George 59 | Ovendale | Shepherd | Taylor | Helin* | Boyce | Dryden | George^ | McLaren | Howard" | Johnson | Spring | Locke/Stein/Douglas |
| | 28/4 | | *9,161* | *8* | 38 | | | *Brown 34, 65, Thorpe 78* | *Phillips* | *Carey* | *Bell* | *Murray* | *Tinnion* | *Peacock* | *da Silva** | *Brown* | *Burnell^* | *Hill* | *Clist"* | *Thorpe/Amankwaah/Maddison* |
| | | | | | | | | Ref: P Walton | Kinnear begins his summer clear-out by releasing five players, including Nathan Abbey. The season can not end quickly enough and, although George gathers a clever through ball from Spring before side-footing a goal of class, the home side have the upper hand and score three times. | | | | | | | | | | | |
| 45 | A | BRENTFORD | | 22 | D | 2-2 | 1-0 | Howard 26, McLaren 51 | Ovendale ! | Shepherd* | Boyce | Dryden | Johnson | Mansell^ | Spring | McLaren | Taylor | Howard | George | **Ward**/Locke |
| | 3/5 | | *3,287* | *14* | 39 | | | *Partridge 55, Williams 66* | *Gottskalksson* | *Ingimarsson* | *Theobald* | *Folan* | *Smith* | *Hutchinson* | *Lovett* | *Somner** | *Tabb^* | *Owusu* | *Partridge* | *Williams/Graham* |
| | | | | | | | | Ref: M Jones | This meaningless end-of-season game has everything – Ovendale is sent off after 76 seconds after hauling down Partridge, which leads to Scott Ward saving the spot-kick from Owusu. Howard opens the scoring with a 50-yarder into an unguarded goal, but the match finishes all square. | | | | | | | | | | | |
| 46 | H | PORT VALE | | 22 | D | 1-1 | 1-1 | Howard 15 | Ovendale | Shepherd* | Dryden | Boyce | Mansell | Douglas^ | Spring | McLaren | Taylor | Howard | George | Karlsen/Stein |
| | 5/5 | | 5,260 | *11* | 40 | | | *Tankard 16* | *Goodlad* | *Carragher* | *Tankard* | *Naylor* | *Widdrington* | *Burton* | *Brdge-Wilk'n* | *Smith* | *Cummins** | *Brooker* | *Dodd* | *Burns* |
| | | Home | Away | | | | | Ref: M Pike | The Hatters finish the season without a single victory in the last 13 games, the longest sequence since 1964. Steve Howard scores with a fierce header from a Taylor cross but the lead is cancelled out straight away by Tankard. Basement football now beckons for the first time since 1968. | | | | | | | | | | | |
| Average | | 5,754 | 6,085 | | | | | | | | | | | | | | | | | |

# NATIONWIDE DIVISION 2 (CUP-TIES) Manager: Hill / Fuccillo/ Kinnear SEASON 2000-01

| Worthington Cup | Att | F-A | H-T | Scorers, Times, and Referees | 1 | 2 | 3 | 4 | 5 | 6 | 7 | 8 | 9 | 10 | 11 | subs used |
|---|---|---|---|---|---|---|---|---|---|---|---|---|---|---|---|---|
| 1:1 H PETERBOROUGH | 23 | 0-0 | 0-0 | | Ovendale | Boyce | Watts | McLaren | Fraser | Taylor | Spring | Holmes | George | Stein | Fotiadis* | Brennan |
| 22/8 | 3,175 *3* | | | | *Tyler* | *Drury* | *Hooper* | *Rea* | *Edwards* | *Oldfield** | *Forinton* | *Forsyth* | *Green* | *Hanlon^* | *Shields"* | *Cullen/Farrell/Scott* |
| | | | | Ref: R Beeby | The Town have a dozen attempts on the visitors' goal and dominate for long periods, but only manage to get one shot on target all evening. A tremendous save by Mark Ovendale from the speedy striker Francis Green, seven minutes from the end, prevents this first leg from being lost. | | | | | | | | | | | |
| 1:2 A PETERBOROUGH | 17 | 2-2 | 1-1 | Stein 31, Scarlett 52 | Ovendale | Fraser | Watts | Boyce | Taylor | Scarlett | Spring* | McLaren | Brennan^ | Stein" | George | Locke/Holmes/Kandol |
| 5/9 | *4,286* *6* | *aet* | | *Farrell 34, Clarke 69* | *Tyler* | *Hooper** | *Drury* | *Rea* | *Edwards* | *Farrell^* | *Oldfield* | *Clarke* | *Forsyth* | *Whittingham* | *Green"* | *Scott/Hanlon/Shields* |
| | | | | Ref: U Rennie (Hatters won on away-goals rule) | The Town take the lead twice but are pegged back on each occasion. Ovendale performs miracles in the Luton goal as he is bombarded by the Posh forwards during the last 20 minutes of normal time. The game goes in to extra-time, the Hatters finally winning it on the away-goals rule. | | | | | | | | | | | |
| 2:1 A SUNDERLAND | 20 | 0-3 | 0-0 | | Ovendale | Fraser | Watts | McLaren | Boyce | Spring | Taylor | Holmes | Scarlett | Stein* | Kandol^ | George/Thomson |
| 19/9 | *24,668* *P:14* | | | *Oster 51, Phillips 61, Thirlwell 87* | *Sorensen* | *Maley** | *Holloway^* | *Roy* | *Williams* | *Butler* | *Peeters* | *Thirlwell* | *Oster* | *Phillips* | *Wainwright* | *Fredgaard/McCartney* |
| | | | | Ref: M Cowburn | Premiership Sunderland rest eight players from the side which played last Saturday but they are still far too good for the Hatters. Paul McLaren misses the target from three yards out before striker Kevin Phillips leads the Luton defence a merry dance and is involved in all three goals. | | | | | | | | | | | |
| 2:2 H SUNDERLAND | 21 | 1-2 | 0-2 | Kandol 90 | Ovendale | Boyce | Watts | McLaren | Fraser | Taylor | Spring | Locke | Kandol | George | Thomson* | Brennan |
| 26/9 | 5,262 *P:14* | | | *Reddy 31, Butler P 39* | *Macho* | *McCartney* | *Clark* | *Roy** | *Williams^* | *Butler P* | *Rae* | *Thirlwell"* | *Oster* | *Reddy* | *Dichio* | *Butler T/McGill/Nunez* |
| | | | | Ref: R Harris (Hatters lost 1-5 on aggregate) | This time Sunderland make ten changes to their team which results in the game being a more even contest than at the Stadium of Light. Despite having little of the play, the visitors are allowed to steal the lead with their first serious attempt and then go two up when Roy shows his class. | | | | | | | | | | | |

| FA Cup | Att | F-A | H-T | Scorers, Times, and Referees | 1 | 2 | 3 | 4 | 5 | 6 | 7 | 8 | 9 | 10 | 11 | subs used |
|---|---|---|---|---|---|---|---|---|---|---|---|---|---|---|---|---|
| 1 H RUSHDEN | 23 | 1-0 | 0-0 | George 56 | Abbey | Karlsen | Watts | Fraser | Boyce | Spring | McLaren | Helin | Taylor | George | Stein* | Thomson |
| 17/11 | 5,771 *C:1* | | | | *Turley* | *Mustafa* | *Underwood* | *Mills** | *Rodwell* | *Warburton* | *Peters^* | *Brady* | *Jackson* | *Sigere* | *Burgess* | *Wormull/Setchell* |
| | | | | Ref: D Laws | Lil Fuccillo manages his first match for the Hatters as the Sky TV cameras descend on Kenilworth Road in the hope of an upset. They almost get one as Rushden have most of the play but it is Luton who score the all-important goal when George beats the offside trap to side-foot home. | | | | | | | | | | | |
| 2 A DARLINGTON | 23 | 0-0 | 0-0 | | Abbey | Whitbread | Watts | Johnson | Fraser | McLaren | Locke | Spring | Taylor | Thomson | George | |
| 9/12 | *3,641* *3:14* | | | | *Collett* | *Liddle* | *Reed* | *Aspin* | *Himsworth* | *Gray** | *Atkinson* | *Kyle* | *Naylor* | *Hodgson^* | *Butler"* | *Walklate/Brumwell/Elliott* |
| | | | | Ref: J Brandwood | Abbey impresses with a string of brilliant saves, with one in particular, a 30-yard pile-driver from Gary Himsworth, worthy of the Save of the Month award. Peter Thomson heads over an unguarded goal from five yards – 'he must have closed his eyes'– slams the unimpressed manager. | | | | | | | | | | | |
| 2R H DARLINGTON | 23 | 2-0 | 0-0 | Nogan 60, McLaren 78 | Abbey | Whitbread | Watts* | Johnson | Helin | Spring^ | McLaren | Taylor | George | Fotiadis | Nogan | Boyce/Locke |
| 19/12 | 3,563 *3:17* | | | | *Collett* | *Heckingbott'm* | *Liddle** | *Reed* | *Aspin* | *Himsworth^* | *Gray* | *Atkinson* | *Kyle"* | *Elliott* | *Naylor* | *Brumwell/Hodgson/Hjorth* |
| | | | | Ref: J Brandwood | The game is evenly balanced until Nogan, with his first goal for the Hatters and against his old club, breaks the deadlock. Fotiadis is the victim of rough treatment all night but he wins a free-kick which is floated to the far post. Whitbread heads the ball back for Nogan to power home. | | | | | | | | | | | |
| 3 H QP RANGERS | 23 | 3-3 | 2-0 | Fotiadis 27, George 36, Douglas 77 | Ovendale | Boyce | Whitbread | Fraser | Helin* | Locke | Spring | Taylor | George | Fotiadis^ | Nogan | Stirling/Douglas |
| 6/1 | 8,677 *1:23* | | | *Crouch 48,53, Peacock 90p* | *Miklosko* | *Carlisle* | *Morrow** | *Plummer* | *Darlington* | *Langley* | *Kulcsar^* | *Baraclough* | *Connolly* | *Crouch* | *Koejoe* | *Wardley/Peacock* |
| | | | | Ref: R Furnandiz | The Town are two up and looking comfortable but a change of tactics in the second half sees the visitors draw level. Douglas nets a third and a home tie against Arsenal beckons, until Nogan needlessly handles the ball in the final minute which gives Rangers both a penalty and a replay. | | | | | | | | | | | |
| 3R A QP RANGERS | 23 | 1-2 | 1-0 | Mansell 1 | Ovendale | Fraser* | McGowan | Holmes | Whitbread | Karlsen | Nogan | Mansell | Douglas^ | Fotiadis" | Spring | Stirling/Stein/Scarlett |
| 17/1 | *14,395* *1:23* | *aet* | | *Kiwomya 90,112* | *Miklosko* | *Darlington* | *Baraclough* | *Plummer** | *Carlisle* | *Perry* | *Rose* | *Connolly^* | *Langley* | *Koejoe"* | *Crouch* | *Kiwomya/Ngonge/Wardley* |
| | | | | Ref: R Furnandiz | Lee Mansell scores after 58 seconds on his debut but it all goes downhill thereafter for the Hatters. Stuart Fraser breaks his leg but Luton hold on to their advantage until deep into stoppage time. Kiwomya levels to take the game into extra-time and then scores an undeserved winner. | | | | | | | | | | | |

| | | P | W | D | L | F | A | W | D | L | F | A | Pts |
|---|---|---|---|---|---|---|---|---|---|---|---|---|---|
| | | | Home | | | | | Away | | | | | |
| 1 | Millwall | 46 | 17 | 2 | 4 | 49 | 11 | 11 | 7 | 5 | 40 | 27 | 93 |
| 2 | Rotherham | 46 | 16 | 4 | 3 | 50 | 26 | 11 | 6 | 6 | 29 | 29 | 91 |
| 3 | Reading | 46 | 15 | 5 | 3 | 58 | 26 | 10 | 6 | 7 | 28 | 26 | 86 |
| 4 | Walsall* | 46 | 15 | 5 | 3 | 51 | 23 | 8 | 7 | 8 | 28 | 27 | 81 |
| 5 | Stoke | 46 | 12 | 6 | 5 | 39 | 21 | 9 | 8 | 6 | 35 | 28 | 77 |
| 6 | Wigan | 46 | 12 | 9 | 2 | 29 | 18 | 7 | 9 | 7 | 24 | 24 | 75 |
| 7 | Bournemouth | 46 | 11 | 6 | 6 | 37 | 23 | 9 | 7 | 7 | 42 | 32 | 73 |
| 8 | Notts Co | 46 | 10 | 6 | 7 | 37 | 33 | 9 | 6 | 8 | 25 | 33 | 69 |
| 9 | Bristol City | 46 | 11 | 6 | 6 | 47 | 29 | 7 | 8 | 8 | 23 | 27 | 68 |
| 10 | Wrexham | 46 | 10 | 6 | 7 | 33 | 28 | 7 | 6 | 10 | 32 | 43 | 63 |
| 11 | Port Vale | 46 | 9 | 8 | 6 | 35 | 22 | 7 | 6 | 10 | 20 | 27 | 62 |
| 12 | Peterborough | 46 | 12 | 6 | 5 | 38 | 27 | 3 | 8 | 12 | 23 | 39 | 59 |
| 13 | Wycombe | 46 | 8 | 7 | 8 | 24 | 23 | 7 | 7 | 9 | 22 | 30 | 59 |
| 14 | Brentford | 46 | 9 | 10 | 4 | 34 | 30 | 5 | 7 | 11 | 22 | 40 | 59 |
| 15 | Oldham | 46 | 11 | 5 | 7 | 35 | 26 | 4 | 8 | 11 | 18 | 39 | 58 |
| 16 | Bury | 46 | 10 | 6 | 7 | 25 | 22 | 6 | 4 | 13 | 20 | 37 | 58 |
| 17 | Colchester | 46 | 10 | 5 | 8 | 32 | 23 | 5 | 7 | 11 | 23 | 36 | 57 |
| 18 | Northampton | 46 | 9 | 6 | 8 | 26 | 28 | 6 | 6 | 11 | 20 | 31 | 57 |
| 19 | Cambridge | 46 | 8 | 6 | 9 | 32 | 31 | 6 | 5 | 12 | 29 | 46 | 53 |
| 20 | Swindon | 46 | 6 | 8 | 9 | 30 | 35 | 7 | 5 | 11 | 17 | 30 | 52 |
| 21 | Bristol Rov | 46 | 6 | 10 | 7 | 28 | 26 | 6 | 5 | 12 | 25 | 31 | 51 |
| 22 | LUTON TOWN | 46 | 5 | 6 | 12 | 24 | 35 | 4 | 7 | 12 | 28 | 45 | 40 |
| 23 | Swansea | 46 | 5 | 9 | 9 | 26 | 24 | 3 | 4 | 16 | 21 | 49 | 37 |
| 24 | Oxford | 46 | 5 | 4 | 14 | 23 | 34 | 2 | 2 | 19 | 30 | 66 | 27 |
| | | | 242 | 151 | 159 | 842 | 624 | 159 | 151 | 242 | 624 | 842 | 1505 |

* promoted after play-offs

**Odds & ends**

Double wins: (0).
Double losses:(5) Wigan, Millwall, Wrexham, Bristol City, Colchester.

Won from behind: (1) Swindon (a).
Lost from in front: (8) Swindon (h), Cambridge (a), Wrexham (h), Bournemouth (a), Wycombe (h), Stoke (h), Bury (h), QPR (a, FAC).

High spots: The winning run after Joe Kinnear is appointed as manager.

Low spots: Relegation with the worst squad of players since the 1966-67 season.
Losing 3-4 at home to Wrexham after being 3-0 up.
A miserable run of thirteen games without a win at the end of the season.

Player of the Year: Matthew Taylor.
Ever-presents: (0).
Hat-tricks: (0).
Leading scorer: (9) Liam George.

| | Appearances | | | | | | Goals | | | |
|---|---|---|---|---|---|---|---|---|---|---|
| | Lge | *Sub* | LC | *Sub* | FAC | *Sub* | Lge | LC | FAC | Tot |
| Abbey, Nathan | 20 | | | | 3 | | | | | |
| Baptiste, Rocky | | *3* | | | | | | | | |
| Boyce, Emmerson | 42 | | 4 | | 2 | *1* | 3 | | | 3 |
| Breitenfelder, Friedrich | 2 | *3* | | | | | | | | |
| Brennan, Dean | 2 | *7* | 1 | *2* | | | | | | |
| Douglas, Stuart | 15 | *6* | | | 1 | *1* | 4 | | 1 | 5 |
| Dryden, Richard | 20 | | | | | | | | | |
| Fotiadis, Andrew | 12 | *10* | 1 | | 3 | | 3 | | 1 | 4 |
| Fraser, Stuart | 10 | *5* | 4 | | 4 | | | | | |
| George, Liam | 37 | *6* | 3 | *1* | 4 | | 7 | | 2 | 9 |
| Helin, Petri | 23 | | | | 3 | | 1 | | | 1 |
| Holmes, Peter | 12 | *6* | 2 | *1* | 1 | | 1 | | | 1 |
| Howard, Steve | 12 | | | | | | 3 | | | 3 |
| Johnson, Marvin | 9 | | | | 2 | | | | | |
| Kandol, Tresor | 6 | *7* | 2 | *1* | | | 3 | 1 | | 4 |
| Karlsen, Kent | 4 | *2* | | | 2 | | | | | |
| Locke, Adam | 17 | *8* | 1 | *1* | 2 | *1* | 2 | | | 2 |
| Mansell, Lee | 17 | *1* | | | 1 | | 5 | | 1 | 6 |
| McGowan, Gavin | 5 | *1* | | | 1 | | | | | |
| McLaren, Paul | 35 | | 4 | | 3 | | 2 | | 1 | 3 |
| Nogan, Lee | 7 | | | | 3 | | 1 | | 1 | 2 |
| Ovendale, Mark | 26 | | 4 | | 2 | | | | | |
| Rowland, Keith | 12 | | | | | | 2 | | | 2 |
| Scarlett, Andre | 5 | *4* | 2 | | | *1* | | 1 | | 1 |
| Shepherd, Paul | 7 | | | | | | | | | |
| Spring, Matthew | 41 | | 4 | | 5 | | 4 | | | 4 |
| Stein, Mark | 19 | *11* | 3 | | 1 | *1* | 3 | 1 | | 4 |
| Stirling, Jude | 5 | *4* | | | | *2* | | | | |
| Taylor, Matthew | 45 | | 4 | | 4 | | 1 | | | 1 |
| Thomson, Peter | 4 | *7* | 1 | *1* | 1 | *1* | 2 | | | 2 |
| Ward, Scott | | *1* | | | | | | | | |
| Watts, Julian | 26 | *2* | 4 | | 3 | | 4 | | | 4 |
| Whitbread, Adrian | 9 | | | | 4 | | | | | |
| (own-goals) | | | | | | | 1 | | | 1 |
| **33 players used** | **506** | ***94*** | **44** | ***7*** | **55** | ***8*** | **52** | **3** | **7** | **62** |

| No | Date | | Att | Pos | Pt | F-A | H-T | Scorers, Times, and Referees | 1 | 2 | 3 | 4 | 5 | 6 | 7 | 8 | 9 | 10 | 11 | subs used |
|---|---|---|---|---|---|---|---|---|---|---|---|---|---|---|---|---|---|---|---|---|
| 1 | A | CARLISLE | | | W | 2-0 | 0-0 | Hughes 46, Griffiths 57 | **Emberson** | Boyce | **Perrett** | Skelton | Johnson* | Mansell^ | **Nicholls** | **Hughes** | Taylor | Howard | **Griffiths"** | Locke/Douglas/Fotiadis |
| | 11/8 | | *4,432* | | 3 | | | | *Weaver* | *Andrews* | *Horley* | *Thurstan** | *Winstanley* | *Maddison* | *Halliday* | *Whitehead^* | *Hopper* | *Soley* | *Allan"* | *Willis/Murphy/Stevens* |
| | | | | | | | | Ref: M Clattenburg | Five players make their debut for the Town against a home side which struggled to find 11 professionals. Two clever pieces of play after the break are enough to break the resolve of Carlisle. Kinnear can see that Division 3 will be physical and has brought in the players to compete. | | | | | | | | | | | |
| 2 | H | CHELTENHAM | | 1 | W | 2-1 | 2-0 | Hughes 30, Griffiths 37 | Emberson | **Hillier** | Boyce | Perrett | Taylor | **Forbes*** | Nicholls ! | Hughes | Mansell | Howard^ | Griffiths" | George/Fotiadis/Locke |
| | 18/8 | | 6,177 | *16* | 6 | | | *Howarth 71* | *Muggleton* | *Jones** | *Banks* | *Walker* | *Victory* | *Duff* | *Yates* | *Milton* | *McAuley^* | *Devaney* | *Alsop"* | *Howarth/Grayson/Naylor* |
| | | | | | | | | Ref: G Hegley | Paul Hughes side-foots a shot from the edge of the box and Carl Griffiths poaches the second to put the Hatters in a comfortable position by the interval. Cheltenham strike back in the second half and Duff hits the post in the final minute. Nicholls is sent off for a second bookable offence. | | | | | | | | | | | |
| 3 | A | BRISTOL ROV | | 5 | L | 2-3 | 1-1 | Taylor 42, Mansell 81 | Emberson | Boyce | Johnson | Stirling | Hillier* | Locke | Nicholls | Hughes^ | Taylor | Howard | Griffiths" | Douglas/Mansell/Forbes |
| | 25/8 | | *9,057* | *1* | 6 | | | *Ellington 30, Hillier 64, Gall 75* | *Howie* | *Wilson* | *Thomson* | *Foster* | *Trought* | *Jones* | *Gall* | *Mauge* | *Hillier* | *Cameron** | *Ellington* | *Gilroy* |
| | | | | | | | | Ref: C Penton | The Hatters have six players out through injury and Rovers take full advantage to leap-frog back to the top of the table. The makeshift defence is led a merry dance by Ellington who creates enough chances for his team-mates to have won three matches. The final score flatters the Town. | | | | | | | | | | | |
| 4 | H | SOUTHEND | | 2 | W | 2-0 | 0-0 | Griffiths 80, Fotiadis 83 | Emberson | Hillier | Boyce | Dryden | Johnson | Mansell | Nicholls | Hughes* | Taylor | Howard^ | Griffiths | Douglas/Fotiadis |
| | 27/8 | | 6,496 | *7* | 9 | | | | *Flahavan* | *Hutchings* | *Whelan* | *Cort* | *Johnson* | *Bramble** | *Thurgood* | *Maher* | *Rawle !* | *Webb^* | *Richards* | *McSweeney/Holness* |
| | | | | | | | | Ref: J Ross | The Town bounce back with a deserved victory against a tough Southend side. Rawle is sent off for a crude challenge on Ian Hillier, his third dismissal in 15 games. Emberson trips Bramble on the edge of the box and is lucky to stay on the pitch. He then saves the penalty from Maher. | | | | | | | | | | | |
| 5 | A | EXETER | | 2 | D | 2-2 | 1-1 | Taylor 35, 53 | Emberson | Boyce | Dryden | Perrett | Johnson | Mansell | Spring | Hughes ! | Taylor | Douglas* | Griffiths^ | Fotiadis"/Holmes/George |
| | 1/9 | | *3.088* | *24* | 10 | | | *Flack 29, Mansell 68 (og)* | *van Heusden* | *McConnell* | *Watson* | *Campbell* | *Power* | *Barlow* | *Zabek* | *Cronin** | *Roberts^* | *Flack* | *Breslan"* | *Roscoe/Moor/Birch* |
| | | | | | | | | Ref: B Curson | Perrett allows a through-ball to go past him and Flack seizes on it to shoot the bottom side in the League in to the lead. Taylor levels before Hughes is sent off for a second bookable offence. A second goal from Taylor is cancelled out when a clearance by Boyce bounces off Mansell. | | | | | | | | | | | |
| 6 | H | OXFORD | | 5 | D | 1-1 | 1-1 | Nicholls 9 | Emberson | Skelton | Perrett | Boyce | Johnson | Forbes* | Spring | Nicholls | Taylor | Howard | Griffiths^ | Hillier/Douglas |
| | 8/9 | | 6,736 | *12* | 11 | | | *Scott 5* | *McCaldon* | *Guyett* | *Bolland* | *Hatswell* | *Stockley* | *Thomas* | *Savage* | *Whitehead* | *Ricketts* | *Gray* | *Scott* | |
| | | | | | | | | Ref: C Penton | Town enjoy most of the possession but Oxford have the better scoring opportunities in an otherwise evenly-matched encounter. A twice-taken 20-yard free-kick from Scott takes the lead before a header from Nicholls levels the game when a long throw from Skelton bounces in the box. | | | | | | | | | | | |
| 7 | A | YORK | | 3 | W | 2-1 | 1-1 | Griffiths 42, Hillier 74 | Emberson | Boyce | Perrett | Skelton | Johnson | Forbes* | Spring | Nicholls | George | Howard^ | Griffiths" | Mansell/Hillier/Douglas |
| | 15/9 | | *3,247* | *11* | 14 | | | *Nogan 32* | *Fettis* | *Edmondson* | *Basham* | *Fielding* | *Potter* | *Evans** | *Brass* | *Bullock* | *Richardson^* | *Nogan* | *Proctor* | *Salvati/Fox* |
| | | | | | | | | Ref: G Salisbury | Douglas is pushed in the box and, although Skelton is the nominated penalty taker, Howard grabs the ball. His kick is saved by Fettis but the referee orders it to be retaken. Howard insists on taking it but again it is saved. He is replaced by Hillier who thunders in an unstoppable shot. | | | | | | | | | | | |
| 8 | H | LINCOLN | | 3 | D | 1-1 | 1-0 | Skelton 9 | Emberson | Boyce | **Coyne** | Perrett | Hillier | Skelton* | Spring | Nicholls | George^ | Douglas | Griffiths" | Hughes/Forbes/Mansell |
| | 18/9 | | **5,066** | *19* | 15 | | | *Coyne 86 (og)* | *Marriott* | *Barnett** | *Holmes* | *Morgan* | *Gain* | *Black* | *Finnigan* | *Sedgmore^* | *Buckley* | *Battersby"* | *Thorpe* | *Brown/Walker/Cameron* |
| | | | | | | | | Ref: S Baines | On a cold and wet night, the Town fail to win at home once again although Lincoln are fortunate to escape with a share of the spoils. A header by Skelton from a George left-wing cross seems to be enough to win the game but debutant Chris Coyne deflects a shot-cross into his own net. | | | | | | | | | | | |
| 9 | H | TORQUAY | | 3 | W | 5-1 | 3-1 | Howard 18, Griffiths 31, 45, 79 | Ovendale | Boyce | Perrett | Coyne | Taylor | Hughes* | Spring | Nicholls | **Valois^** | Howard | Griffiths | Hillier"/Forbes/Douglas |
| | 22/9 | | 6,392 | *21* | 18 | | | *Nicholls 41 (og)* [Valois 61] | *Dearden* | *McNeil** | *Woozley* | *Douglin* | *Tully^* | *Rees* | *Nicholls"* | *Hill* | *Russell* | *Richardson* | *Graham* | *Holmes/Bedeau/Williams* |
| | | | | | | | | Ref: L Cable | Jean-Louis Valois takes the headlines on his debut with a virtuoso performance which is capped with a 35-yard strike. The display of skill from the Frenchman overshadows the hat-trick of headers from Carl Griffiths. Steve Howard is now forgiven for his indiscretions in the York match. | | | | | | | | | | | |
| 10 | A | LEYTON ORIENT | | 3 | W | 3-1 | 1-0 | Taylor 30, Valois 53, Howard 66 | Ovendale | Boyce | Perrett | Coyne | Taylor | Holmes* | Spring | Nicholls | Valois | Howard | Griffiths^ | Mansell/Forbes |
| | 25/9 | | *6,540* | *9* | 21 | | | *Houghton 85p* | *Bayes* | *Joseph* | *Smith* | *Downer* | *Harris* | *McGhee* | *Minton* | *Oakes** | *Martin^* | *Constantine"* | *Ibehre* | *Gough/Houghton/Fletcher* |
| | | | | | | | | Ref: P Rejer | A powerful performance from the Town shatters the home record of the Orient. It starts with a header from Taylor, includes another superb strike from Valois into the top corner of the net, and ends with a header from Howard. Ex-Hatter Scott Houghton gets one back from the spot. | | | | | | | | | | | |
| 11 | A | PLYMOUTH | | 3 | L | 1-2 | 1-2 | Crowe 15 | Ovendale | Boyce | Coyne | Perrett | Taylor | Holmes* | Spring^ | Nicholls | Valois" | Howard | **Crowe** | Mansell/Douglas/Forbes |
| | 29/9 | | *5,782* | *4* | 21 | | | *Phillips 22, Friio 45* | *Larrieu* | *Worrell* | *Coughlan* | *Wotton* | *McGlinchey* | *Bent** | *Adams* | *Friio* | *Phillips^* | *Evans !* | *Stonebridge* | *Banger/Hodges* |
| | | | | | | | | Ref: A Hall | Loan player Dean Crowe, a replacement for the injured Carl Griffiths, scores from close range on his debut. The dismissal of Evans for the use of an elbow seems to work against Luton as ten-man Plymouth fight with passion and score twice before Valois hits the bar with a free-kick. | | | | | | | | | | | |

| No | Venue | Opponent / Date | Att | Pos | Pts | Res | HT | Scorers, Times, Referee | 1 | 2 | 3 | 4 | 5 | 6 | 7 | 8 | 9 | 10 | 11 | Subs used |
|---|---|---|---|---|---|---|---|---|---|---|---|---|---|---|---|---|---|---|---|---|
| 12 | H | DARLINGTON | | 2 | W | 5-2 | 1-1 | Spring 35, Howard 48, Crowe 67, Nicholls 73p | Emberson | Boyce | Perrett | Coyne | Taylor | Mansell* | Spring | Nicholls^ | Valois | Howard | Crowe | Hillier/Forbes |
| | | 5/10 | 7,219 | *6* | 24 | | | *Mellanby 25, Wainwright 50* [Valois 83] | *Collett* | *Betts* | *Liddle* | *Jeannin* | *Heckingbott'm* | *Wainwright* | *Atkinson* | *Brumwell* | *Hodgson** | *Mellanby* | *Conlon* | *Jackson* |
| | | | | | | | | Ref: J Brandwood | After an even first half, the second period bursts into life with five goals, which includes another special from Valois, and frantic action. Also, two penalties are missed, the first when Emberson saves from Conlon, then Collett foils Spring after Valois is fouled at the end of a mazy run. | | | | | | | | | | | |
| 13 | A | SCUNTHORPE | | 1 | W | 2-0 | 0-0 | Forbes 65, Perrett 72 | Emberson | Boyce* | Coyne | Perrett | Taylor | Mansell^ | Spring | Nicholls | Valois" | Howard | Crowe | Hillier/**Brkovic**/Forbes |
| | | 13/10 | *3,939* | *11* | 27 | | | | *Evans* | *Stanton* | *Jackson* | *Cotterill* | *Dawson** | *Hodges* | *Bradshaw* | *Kell^* | *Beagrie* | *Quailey"* | *Carruthers* | *Sheldon/C'-Garcia/Torpey* |
| | | | | | | | | Ref: H Webb | A clever through ball from Nicholls sets Forbes free to score the first. Then Perrett shoots home from the first Luton corner of the game for the second to send the Hatters back to the top of the league table. Valois is out of sorts having moved his furniture from France during the week. | | | | | | | | | | | |
| 14 | H | ROCHDALE | | 3 | L | 0-1 | 0-1 | | Emberson | Hillier | Perrett* | Coyne | Taylor | Brkovic^ | Spring | Nicholls | Valois | Howard | Crowe | Boyce"/Fotiadis/Forbes |
| | | 20/10 | 7,696 | *1* | 27 | | | *Wheatcroft 39* | *Hahnemann* | *Evans* | *Jobson* | *Griffiths* | *McAuley* | *Ford** | *Jones* | *Oliver* | *Doughty* | *Platt* | *Wheatcr'ft^* | *Flitcroft/Townson* |
| | | | | | | | | Ref: S Tomlin | The visitors score from one of just three shots on target all afternoon. The Hatters pound the Rochdale goal in the second half but Jobson twice clears off the line and Hahnemann makes two excellent saves. Crowe has a 'goal' ruled out after Howard was penalised for fouling the keeper. | | | | | | | | | | | |
| 15 | A | HALIFAX | | 2 | W | 4-2 | 2-1 | Crowe 31, 45, Nicholls 86, Forbes 88 | Emberson | Hillier | Coyne | Perrett | Taylor | Brkovic | Spring | Nicholls | Valois* | Howard | Crowe | Forbes |
| | | 23/10 | ***2,140*** | *22* | 30 | | | *Harsley 6, Fitzpatrick 78* | *Butler* | *Harsley* | *Mitchell* | *Stoneman* | *Clarke* | *Jules* | *Middleton* | *Swales** | *Smith* | *Kerrigan^* | *Fitzpatrick* | *Wood/Jones* |
| | | | | | | | | Ref: M Pike | Halifax take an early lead but are then clearly second best as the Town step up a gear. The game is all square at 2-2 with just five minutes to go before the Hatters pile on the pressure and score twice in two minutes. 'We came alive after they scored,' says a slightly disappointed Kinnear. | | | | | | | | | | | |
| 16 | H | SWANSEA | | 2 | W | 3-0 | 1-0 | Crowe 23, Perrett 55, Forbes 61 | Emberson | Skelton | Perrett | Coyne | Hillier | Brkovic | Spring | Nicholls | Valois | Howard* | Crowe^ | Fotiadis/Forbes |
| | | 27/10 | 6,705 | *20* | 33 | | | | *Freestone* | *Phillips* | *Sharp** | *Bound* | *Todd* | *Howard* | *Casey^* | *Cusack* | *Coates"* | *Williams* | *Tyson* | *Smith/Watkin/Lacey* |
| | | | | | | | | Ref: P Durkin | When Russell Perrett heads the second from a Valois cross it is carnival time and, long before the end, a demoralised Swansea are on a damage limitation exercise. 'Luton are a magnificent team, without doubt the best we have played this season,' says Swans manager Colin Addison. | | | | | | | | | | | |
| 17 | A | MANSFIELD | | 4 | L | **1-4** | 0-1 | Crowe 86 *[Bradley 80]* | Emberson | Skelton | Coyne ! | Perrett | Taylor | Brkovic* | Spring | Nicholls | Valois^ | Howard | Crowe | Forbes/Hillier |
| | | 3/11 | *5,973* | *5* | 33 | | | *Greenacre 21, 56, Pemberton 63* | *Pilkington* | *Hassell* | *Barrett* | *Robinson* | *Pemberton !* | *Lawrence** | *Williamson* | *Disley* | *Corden* | *Greenacre^* | *Bradley !* | *Jervis/White* |
| | | | | | | | | Ref: D Pugh | Eight bookings and three dismissals may indicate that this was bad-tempered game but it was nothing of the sort. Although a good many of the decisions by the referee are puzzling, the Town are out of sorts and are two goals down before Coyne is sent off for a second bookable offence. | | | | | | | | | | | |
| 18 | H | SHREWSBURY | | 4 | W | 1-0 | 0-0 | Spring 72 | Emberson | Skelton* | Coyne | Perrett | Taylor | Brkovic | Spring | Nicholls | Valois | Howard | Crowe | Hillier |
| | | 9/11 | 6,809 | *7* | 36 | | | | *Dunbavin* | *Drysdale* | *Redmile* | *Tretton* | *Rioch* | *Moss** | *Atkins* | *Murray* | *Jagielka* | *Rodgers* | *Jemson* | *Lowe* |
| | | | | | | | | Ref: F Stretton | Kinnear is unhappy with the first-half performance and threatens mass substitutions if no improvement is made after the break. The words hit home as improve they do, with Spring surging into the box, playing a 1-2 with Dean Crowe, and smashing the ball over the advancing keeper. | | | | | | | | | | | |
| 19 | H | HULL | | 4 | L | 0-1 | 0-0 | | Emberson | Hillier | Perrett* | Coyne | Taylor | Brkovic^ | Nicholls | Spring | Valois | Howard | Crowe" | Boyce/Forbes/**Street** |
| | | 20/11 | 7,214 | *3* | 36 | | | *Matthews 51* | *Glennon* | *Edwards* | *Petty* | *Whittle* | *Goodison* | *Williams* | *Whitmore* | *Johnsson* | *Matthews* | *Dudfield* | *Alexander* | |
| | | | | | | | | Ref: D Elleray | Hull are one of the better sides to be seen at Kenilworth Road this season but are fortunate to leave with all three points. Former Hatter Rob Matthews pokes home the winner after the Town fail to deal with a long throw. The Tigers then pack their midfield and defence and hang on. | | | | | | | | | | | |
| 20 | A | MACCLESFIELD | | 5 | L | **1-4** | 1-1 | Howard 33 | Emberson | Boyce | Skelton* | Coyne | Taylor | Street^ | Spring | Nicholls | Valois" | Forbes | Howard | Hillier/Fotiadis/Crowe |
| | | 24/11 | *2,250* | *22* | 36 | | | *Lambert 10, 63, 90, Byrne 53* | *Wilson* | *Hitchen* | *Tinson* | *Ridler* | *Adams* | *Keen* | *Priest* | *Byrne* | *Smith* | *McAvoy** | *Lambert* | *Tracey* |
| | | | | | | | | Ref: R Pearson | Lowly Macclesfield record their second home win in ten attempts and Ricky Lambert notches their first ever hat-trick in the Football League. Truly an afternoon to forget with Joe Kinnear offering an apology to the travelling supporters after the shambolic and inept display by his team. | | | | | | | | | | | |
| 21 | A | HARTLEPOOL | | 4 | W | 2-1 | 2-0 | Crowe 30, Taylor 45 | Ovendale | Boyce | Coyne | **Bayliss** | Hillier ! | Brkovic | Spring | Nicholls | Taylor | Howard | Crowe* | Forbes |
| | | 8/12 | 3,585 | *14* | 39 | | | *Humphreys 64* | *Williams* | *Bass** | *Barron* | *Simms^* | *Westwood* | *Clarke* | *Tinkler* | *Widdrington* | *Smith* | *Humphreys* | *Lormor"* | *Arnison/Robinson/Boyd* |
| | | | | | | | | Ref: A Leake | A greatly improved performance from that of last week finds the Town two up and cruising by the interval. With five players booked, Kinnear warns his players to stay on their feet but Hillier is dismissed for a lunge. Hartlepool then apply the pressure and the last few minutes are tense. | | | | | | | | | | | |
| 22 | H | RUSHDEN | | 2 | W | 1-0 | 1-0 | Crowe 34 | Ovendale | Boyce | Coyne* | Bayliss | Taylor | Brkovic | Spring^ | Nicholls | Valois" | Howard | Crowe | Perrett/Holmes/Hillier |
| | | 15/12 | 7,495 | *9* | 42 | | | | *Turley* | *Sambrook* | *Peters* | *Hunter* | *Underwood* | *Hall* | *Hanlon** | *Butterworth* | *Burgess* | *Lowe* | *Darby^* | *McElhatton/Partridge* |
| | | | | | | | | Ref: P Danson | The visitors enjoy as much possession as the Town but are undone by the predatory sharpness of Crowe. Underwood slices his clearance off a post and the ball runs loose to Brkovic who passes inside for Crowe to poach the only goal. Influential players Coyne and Spring both limp off. | | | | | | | | | | | |
| 23 | H | HARTLEPOOL | | 2 | D | 2-2 | 1-1 | Howard 35, Johnson 84 | Ovendale | Boyce | Perrett | Bayliss | Taylor | Brkovic* | Spring | Nicholls | Valois^ | Howard | Crowe" | Forbes/Fotiadis/Johnson |
| | | 22/12 | 6,739 | *12* | 43 | | | *Clarke 45, 59* | *Williams* | *Barron* | *Westwood* | *Lee* | *Robinson* | *Clarke* | *Widdrington* | *Tinkler* | *Smith* | *Humphreys* | *Watson** | *Boyd* |
| | | | | | | | | Ref: G Cain | Howard puts the Town ahead against his old club and then forces a point-blank save out of the keeper. Hartlepool take the lead, forcing Luton to push four up-field which leads to Marvin Johnson saving the day with an expertly-placed shot after the ball was laid back to him in the area. | | | | | | | | | | | |

# NATIONWIDE LEAGUE DIVISION 3

## Manager: Joe Kinnear

## SEASON 2001-02

| No | Date | | Att | Pos | Pt | F-A | H-T | Scorers, Times, and Referees | 1 | 2 | 3 | 4 | 5 | 6 | 7 | 8 | 9 | 10 | 11 | subs used |
|---|---|---|---|---|---|---|---|---|---|---|---|---|---|---|---|---|---|---|---|---|
| 24 | A | OXFORD | | 2 | W | 2-1 | 1-1 | Crowe 39, Spring 46 | Ovendale | Boyce | Perrett | Bayliss | Taylor | Forbes* | Spring | Nicholls | Valois^ | Howard | Crowe | Brkovic/Hillier |
| | 26/12 | | *11,121* | *18* | 46 | | | *Scott 20* | *McCaldon* | *Richardson* | *Bound* | *Crosby* | *Hatswell** | *Stockley* | *Quinn^* | *Savage* | *Powell* | *Gray"* | *Scott* | *Omoyinmi/Whitehead/Moody* |
| | | | | | | | | Ref: M Warren | On their first visit to the Kassam Stadium, and in front of the largest crowd to date, a misplaced pass by Nicholls gifts Oxford with the opener. A carefully placed drive from Crowe is followed by a cracking shot from Spring which enables the Town to run out the comfortable winners. | | | | | | | | | | | |
| 25 | A | SOUTHEND | | 2 | W | 2-1 | 0-0 | Crowe 68, Taylor 83 | Ovendale | Boyce | Bayliss | Perrett | Taylor | Forbes* | Nicholls | Spring | Valois^ | Howard | Crowe | Brkovic/Hillier |
| | 29/12 | | *5.973* | *13* | 49 | | | *Hutchings 53* | *Gay* | *Broad** | *Cort* | *Whelan* | *Searle* | *Clark* | *Maher* | *Hutchings* | *Thurgood"* | *Bramble* | *Belgrave* | *McSweeney^/Rawle/Forbes* |
| | | | | | | | | Ref: M Ryan | Steven Clark sets up Hutchings for the opener but the Town force Southend back when Crowe levels. Taylor then smashes his sixth goal of the campaign which gives Luton their third successive victory on their travels and the best away form in the whole of the English Football League. | | | | | | | | | | | |
| 26 | A | KIDDERMINSTER | | 2 | W | 4-1 | 0-0 | Taylor 53, Spring 55, 70, Howard 58 | Ovendale | Boyce | Perrett | Bayliss | Taylor | Brkovic* | Spring | Nicholls | Valois^ | Howard" | Crowe | Hughes/Hillier/Forbes |
| | 8/1 | | *4,147* | *9* | 52 | | | *Williams 50* | *Brock* | *Clarkson* | *Ayres* | *Hinton* | *Stamps** | *Appleby^* | *Blake* | *Williams* | *Bennett* | *Broughton* | *Henriksen* | *Joy/Foster* |
| | | | | | | | | Ref: J Ross | Stuart Brock, the Kidderminster keeper, has a nightmare of a game and is responsible for three of the Luton goals. The Harriers take the lead from a free-kick which rebounded off both defenders and the woodwork before crossing the line. Matt Taylor has a field-day on the left wing. | | | | | | | | | | | |
| 27 | A | CHELTENHAM | | 2 | D | 1-1 | 0-1 | Howard 73 | Ovendale | Boyce | Perrett | Bayliss | Hillier* | Brkovic^ | Spring | Nicholls | Taylor | Howard | Crowe" | Valois/Forbes/Hughes |
| | 12/1 | | *5,026* | *8* | 53 | | | *Naylor 22* | *Book* | *Griffin* | *Duff* | *Banks* | *Victory* | *Williams* | *Howells* | *Yates* | *Milton* | *Grayson* | *Naylor* | |
| | | | | | | | | Ref: S Baines | A tremendous 25-yard strike from Tony Naylor is against the run of play in the first half, which sees Taylor hit the bar and Howard having his effort cleared off the line. The Town are clearly on top during the final half-hour, the persistence of Howard saving the day with the equaliser. | | | | | | | | | | | |
| 28 | H | CARLISLE | | 2 | D | 1-1 | 0-0 | Perrett 68 | Ovendale | Boyce | Perrett | Bayliss | Taylor | Brkovic* | Spring | Nicholls | Valois | Howard | Crowe^ | Forbes/Johnson |
| | 19/1 | | 6,647 | *22* | 54 | | | *Soley 52* | *Keen* | *Andrews* | *Winstanley* | *Rogers* | *Birch** | *Soley* | *Whitehead* | *Green* | *Murphy* | *Foran* | *Stevens^* | *Hopper/Halliday* |
| | | | | | | | | Ref: P Alcock | Carlisle are a totally changed side from the one the Town faced on the opening day of the season. They take the lead when Soley heads in from a corner but the Hatters level it up when a Taylor free-kick is headed back across goal by Howard and Perrett launches himself to head home. | | | | | | | | | | | |
| 29 | A | DARLINGTON | | 2 | L | 2-3 | 1-1 | Howard 13, Valois 60 | Ovendale | Hillier | Boyce | Perrett* | Taylor | Brkovic | Spring | Nicholls | Valois^ | Howard | Crowe" | Dryden/Hughes/Forbes |
| | 26/1 | | *3,560* | *15* | 54 | | | *Pearson 29, Sheeran 81, 85* | *Collett* | *Brumwell* | *Liddle* | *Pearson* | *Heckingbott'm* | *Atkinson* | *Ford* | *Maddison** | *Wainwright^* | *Conlon"* | *Clark* | *Hodgson/Harper/Sheeran* |
| | | | | | | | | Ref: E Wolstenholme | A firm header from Howard and a Valois special put the Town firmly in the driving seat but the eight-game unbeaten run ends when two late goals are conceded. The energetic Mark Sheeran, a 19-year-old YTS substitute picks up a rebound to equalise and then heads home the winner. | | | | | | | | | | | |
| 30 | H | PLYMOUTH | | 2 | W | 2-0 | 0-0 | Nicholls 80p, Howard 87 | Emberson | Boyce | Perrett | Bayliss | Taylor | Forbes | Spring | Nicholls | Valois | Howard | Crowe* | Brkovic |
| | 2/2 | | **9.585** | *1* | 57 | | | | *Larrieu* | *Worrell* | *Coughlan* | *Wotton* | *Besw'therick* | *Phillips** | *Adams* | *Friio* | *Stonebridge^* | *Hodges* | *Keith"* | *Evers/Heaney/Evans* |
| | | | | | | | | Ref: P Joslin | The first full house for eight years sees Plymouth playing for a point with a 4-5-1 formation and nearly managing to hold out. Taylor is brought down in the box and Nicholls opening the scoring from the spot. A late header from Howard, following a corner-kick, is the icing on the cake. | | | | | | | | | | | |
| 31 | A | ROCHDALE | | 2 | L | 0-1 | 0-1 | | Emberson | Boyce | Perrett | Bayliss ! | Taylor | Forbes | Spring | Nicholls | Valois* | Howard | Crowe^ | Coyne/Hughes |
| | 9/2 | | *4,306* | *3* | 57 | | | *McCourt 12* | *Banks* | *Evans* | *Jobson* | *Griffiths* | *Doughty* | *Flitcroft* | *Oliver* | *McCourt* | *Jones** | *McEvilly^* | *Townson* | *McLaughlin/Durkin* |
| | | | | | | | | Ref: M Messias | The game is played on a cow-pasture of a pitch and a strike by McCourt from the edge of the box takes a deflection which leaves Emberson stranded. Bayliss is dismissed for supposedly going in over the top; his cause is not helped by his ex-team-mates who protest long and loud. | | | | | | | | | | | |
| 32 | H | SCUNTHORPE | | 3 | L | 2-3 | 1-2 | Howard 36. Taylor 78 | Emberson | Coyne | Perrett | Bayliss | Taylor | Forbes* | Spring | Nicholls | Valois | Howard | **McSweg'n^** | Crowe/Boyce |
| | 16/2 | | 6,371 | *6* | 57 | | | *Beagrie 9, Graves 45, Sparrow 90* | *Evans* | *Stanton* | *Jackson* | *McGibbon* | *Dawson* | *Sparrow* | *Calvo-Garcia* | *Graves** | *Beagrie* | *Quailey* | *Torpey* | *Hodges* |
| | | | | | | | | Ref: R Olivier | A furious Joe Kinnear keeps the players behind for an hour after the Town are outfought by a Scunthorpe side in which veteran Peter Beagrie is outstanding. He scores one and sets up two as Luton, who include on-loan Gary McSwegan of Hearts, collectively fail to get their act together. | | | | | | | | | | | |
| 33 | H | BRISTOL ROV | | 2 | W | 3-0 | 0-0 | Howard 47, Coyne 65, Nicholls 77p | Emberson | Boyce | Perrett | Bayliss | Taylor | Brkovic | Spring | Nicholls | Valois* | Howard | Crowe^ | Coyne/Forbes |
| | 19/2 | | 5,651 | *18* | 60 | | | | *Howie* | *Smith* | *Foran** | *Thomson* | *Foster !* | *Jones* | *Hogg^* | *Wilson* | *Plummer* | *Ellington* | *Ommel* | *Walters/McKeever* |
| | | | | | | | | Ref: P Walton | The strong words issued after the last match seem to have had the desired effect as the Town pound Rovers from the start. The Pirates hold out until just after the interval but cannot keep out a close-range shot from Howard. Steve Foster is dismissed for a professional foul on Howard. | | | | | | | | | | | |
| 34 | H | YORK | | 2 | W | 2-1 | 1-1 | Howard 19, 50 | Emberson | Boyce | **Neilson** | Coyne | Taylor | Brkovic | Spring | Skelton* | Valois^ | Howard | Forbes | Hughes/Johnson |
| | 23/2 | | 6,188 | *21* | 63 | | | *Proctor 17* | *Fettis* | *Basham** | *Hobson* | *Parkin* | *Edmondson* | *Brass* | *Bullock* | *Potter* | *Duffield^* | *Nogan* | *Proctor* | *Wise/Mathie* |
| | | | | | | | | Ref: R Harris | The Hatters have three key players suspended and again have to fight back, after going behind, to earn all three points. Steve Howard hits two more goals, taking his tally to seven in nine games since the turn of the year. His second goal goes in off his knee, wrong-footing the keeper. | | | | | | | | | | | |

| No | V | Opponent / Date | Att | Pos | Pts | Res | F-A | H-T | Scorers, Times, and Referees | 1 | 2 | 3 | 4 | 5 | 6 | 7 | 8 | 9 | 10 | 11 | Subs used |
|---|---|---|---|---|---|---|---|---|---|---|---|---|---|---|---|---|---|---|---|---|---|
| 35 | A | LINCOLN | | 2 | W | | 1-0 | 1-0 | Taylor 42 | Emberson | Neilson | Coyne | Perrett | Johnson | Brkovic | Spring | Hughes | Taylor | Howard | Forbes | |
| | | 26/2 | *2,921* | *20* | 66 | | | | | *Marriott* | *Bailey* | *Morgan* | *Brown* | *Bimson* | *Smith** | *Hamilton^* | *Walker* | *Gain"* | *Thorpe* | *Cameron* | *Battersby/Buckley/Sedgemore* |
| | | | | | | | | | Ref: A Bates | The final score-line flatters the Imps, who have just one shot on target all evening. The Hatters, and in particular Matthew Taylor, spurn several good chances and the only goal is a fluke when keeper Marriott stands like a statue as a 30-yard cross-shot from Taylor rolls gently past him. | | | | | | | | | | | |
| 36 | A | TORQUAY | | 2 | W | | 1-0 | 1-0 | Brkovic 20 | Emberson | Neilson | Perrett | Coyne | Johnson* | Brkovic^ | Spring | Nicholls | Taylor | McSwegan" | Crowe | Boyce/Hughes/Valois |
| | | 2/3 | *3,280* | *23* | 69 | | | | | *Dearden* | *Holmes* | *Hazell* | *Hankin* | *Russell L* | *Hill* | *Goodridge** | *Rees^* | *Russell A* | *Brandon* | *Logan"* | *Graham/Benefield/Richardson* |
| | | | | | | | | | Ref: D Crick | Brkovic sets up the record-breaking eleventh away win of the season when he runs on to a through-ball from Nicholls before rounding Luton-born goalkeeper, Kevin Dearden. The Town should have scored more than just once against a team who are second best in every department. | | | | | | | | | | | |
| 37 | H | LEYTON ORIENT | | 2 | W | | 3-0 | 1-0 | Coyne 36, Crowe 49, Forbes 66 | Emberson | Neilson | Perrett | Coyne | Taylor | Hughes | Nicholls* | Spring | Valois^ | Crowe" | Forbes | Bayliss/Johnson/McSwegan |
| | | 5/3 | 6,683 | *22* | 72 | | | | | *Barrett* | *Hutchings* | *Smith* | *McGhee* | *Lockwood* | *Canham* | *Harris* | *Martin** | *Brazier* | *Nugent^* | *Christie"* | *Gough/Watts/McLean* |
| | | | | | | | | | Ref: C Penton | Orient have the better of the opening half-hour and could have been four goals to the good had they taken their chances. Once Coyne is left to shoot the Town into the lead, the visitors capitulate and it is one-way traffic thereafter. Crowe and Forbes both score to ensure all three points. | | | | | | | | | | | |
| 38 | A | RUSHDEN | | 2 | W | | 2-1 | 0-0 | Crowe 58, Howard 82 | Emberson | Neilson | Perrett | Coyne | Johnson* | Forbes^ | Nicholls | Spring | Taylor | Howard | Crowe | Bayliss/Hughes |
| | | 9/3 | *5,876* | *9* | 75 | | | | *Hall 49* | *Turley* | *Mustafa* | *Peters* | *Tillson* | *Underwood* | *Hall* | *Hanlon* | *Wardley* | *Burgess* | *Partridge** | *Lowe* | *Darby* |
| | | | | | | | | | Ref: M Fletcher | A strong wind threatens to ruin the first League meeting of these sides at Nene Park and Kinnear is relieved when the Town are still level at the break, having played against the gale. With the wind dropping, Hall puts the home side ahead but Luton net twice for the sixth win on the trot. | | | | | | | | | | | |
| 39 | H | EXETER | | 2 | W | | 3-0 | 1-0 | Howard 27, 65, Taylor 79 | Emberson | Neilson | Perrett | Coyne | Taylor | Forbes* | Nicholls | Spring | Valois^ | Howard | Crowe | Hughes/Bayliss |
| | | 12/3 | 6,327 | *14* | 78 | | | | | *van Heusden* | *Buckle* | *Watson* | *Curran* | *Power* | *McConnell* | *Barlow* | *Richardson* | *Roscoe** | *Read^* | *Roberts* | *Breslan/Flack* |
| | | | | | | | | | Ref: S Tomlin | After a few early scares, the Town take control with Steve Howard heading in at the far post following a Nicholls free-kick. A looping header by Matthew Taylor impresses the scouts and it now seems inevitable that the 20-year-old will leave Kenilworth Road at the end of this season. | | | | | | | | | | | |
| 40 | H | KIDDERMINSTER | | 2 | W | | 1-0 | 1-0 | Hughes 16 | Ovendale | Bayliss | Perrett | Coyne | Neilson* | Hughes ! | Nicholls | Spring | Taylor | Howard | Crowe^ | Boyce/Forbes |
| | | 16/3 | 6,488 | *10* | 81 | | | | | *Brock !* | *Clarkson** | *Hinton* | *Sall* | *Joy* | *Bird* | *Smith* | *Williams* | *Henriksen* | *Foster^* | *Broughton* | *Danby/Larkin* |
| | | | | | | | | | Ref: G Hegley | Hughes cracks in a low shot against a side with seemingly limited ambition before keeper Brock, who had a terrible game at Aggborough, adds to his Luton phobia when he is sent off for handling the ball outside of his area. Ovendale only has two shots to deal with on his reintroduction. | | | | | | | | | | | |
| 41 | H | HALIFAX | | 2 | W | | **5-0** | 2-0 | Spring 21, Coyne 32, Howard 49 [Crowe 75, Valois 87] | Emberson | Bayliss | Perrett | Coyne | Taylor | Hughes | Nicholls | Spring | Valois | Howard | Crowe* | Forbes |
| | | 23/3 | 6,830 | *24* | 84 | | | | | *Richardson* | *Jules* | *Mitchell* | *Woodward* | *Clarke** | *Harsley* | *Redfearn* | *Bushell* | *Midgley^* | *Farrell* | *Fitzpatrick"* | *Swales/Middleton/Jones !* |
| | | | | | | | | | Ref: P Prosser | The difference between the top and bottom of Division 3 is ruthlessly illustrated as the Hatters cruise to the record-equalling ninth consecutive victory. The Town have 20 attempts on goal in a brilliant display which just about confirms promotion. Jones is dismissed for use of an elbow. | | | | | | | | | | | |
| 42 | A | SWANSEA | | 2 | W | | 3-1 | 1-0 | Taylor 31, Holmes 58, Howard 78 | Emberson | Bayliss* | Perrett | Coyne | Johnson | Valois^ | Nicholls | Spring | Taylor" | Howard | Crowe | Boyce/Forbes/Holmes |
| | | 30/3 | *5,436* | *15* | 87 | | | | *Mumford 90* | *Freestone* | *de Vulgt* | *Todd* | *O'Leary* | *Howard* | *Brodie* | *Mumford* | *Case** | *Coates* | *Williams^* | *Watkin* | *Romo/Sidibe* |
| | | | | | | | | | Ref: R Beeby | The Town clinch promotion against a Swansea side who are always second best. Taylor opens the scoring and a rare strike from Peter Holmes follows. Steve Howard completes the misery for the visitors and signals the start of the celebrations which continue long after the final whistle. | | | | | | | | | | | |
| 43 | H | MANSFIELD | | 2 | W | | 5-3 | 4-2 | Valois 11, Crowe 22, Nicholls 30p, [Howard 35,50] | Emberson | Boyce | Coyne | Johnson | Taylor | Holmes | Nicholls | Spring | Valois* | Howard | Crowe^ | Forbes/**Kabba** |
| | | 1/4 | 8,231 | *4* | 90 | | | | *Murray 12, Sellars 4* [*Greenacre 90*] | *Pilkington* | *Hassell* | *Robinson** | *Barrett* | *Clarke* | *Murray* | *Williamson* | *Disley* | *Sellars* | *White* | *Corden^* | *Reddington/Greenacre* |
| | | | | | | | | | Ref: J Brandwood | The Hatters exact full revenge for their hammering at Field Mill in November and are 4-1 up after 35 minutes in an open game which also sees chances missed at both ends. The game is played in a carnival atmosphere but the final result puts a dent in the promotion hopes of Mansfield. | | | | | | | | | | | |
| 44 | A | HULL | | 1 | W | | 4-0 | 2-0 | Howard 23, 79, 89, Crowe 38 | Emberson | Boyce | Perrett | Coyne | Taylor | Holmes* | Nicholls | Spring | Valois^ | Howard | Crowe" | Hughes/Johnson/Forbes |
| | | 6/4 | *9,379* | *11* | 93 | | | | | *Musselwhite* | *Edwards* | *Greaves* | *Mohan* | *van Blerk* | *Williams** | *Sneekes* | *Petty* | *Lightbo'rne^* | *Alexander* | *Bradshaw"* | *Whitmore/Norris/Holt* |
| | | | | | | | | | Ref: P Dowd | The Hatters complete their 12th consecutive win against a Hull side who have missed out on the play-offs after looking so good earlier in the campaign. Taylor shows his Premiership credentials when setting up three of the goals. Steve Howard notches his first hat-trick at senior level. | | | | | | | | | | | |
| 45 | H | MACCLESFIELD | | 2 | D | | 0-0 | 0-0 | | Emberson | Boyce | Perrett | Coyne | Taylor | Hughes* | Nicholls | Spring | Valois^ | Howard | Crowe" | Johnson/Forbes/Kabba |
| | | 13/4 | 7,873 | *13* | 94 | | | | | *Wilson* | *Hitchen* | *Adams* | *Tinson* | *Ridler* | *Glover* | *Lambert** | *Whitaker* | *Munroe* | *Welch* | *Tipton* | *Askey* |
| | | | | | | | | | Ref: M Ryan | It is unlucky thirteen for the Hatters as David Moss's side get ten players behind the ball all afternoon. The Town have thirteen attempts on target against a goalkeeper who wears the number thirteen shirt and is the first visiting goalkeeper to keep a clean sheet in thirteen matches. | | | | | | | | | | | |
| 46 | A | SHREWSBURY | | 2 | W | | 2-0 | 1-0 | Rioch 36(og), Howard 90 | Emberson | Neilson | Perrett | Coyne | Taylor | Forbes* | Hughes | Spring | Valois^ | Howard | Crowe" | Boyce/Johnson/Kabba |
| | | 20/4 | *7,858* | *9* | 97 | | | | | *Dunbavin* | *Thompson* | *Rioch** | *Tolley* | *Redmile* | *Heathcote* | *Lowe* | *Atkins^* | *Rodgers* | *Guinan"* | *Woan* | *Moss/Murray/Aiston* |
| | | Home / Away | | | | | | | Ref: M Cooper | A win for Shrewsbury would put them into the play-offs but the Hatters are in no mood to roll over. Ex-Hatter Greg Rioch turns the ball into his own net before Howard finishes the season as the leading marksman in Division 3 when he slides in to score number 24 in the final minute. | | | | | | | | | | | |
| Average | | 6,853 / 5,170 | | | | | | | | | | | | | | | | | | | |

| Worthington Cup | | | Att | | F-A | H-T | Scorers, Times, and Referees | 1 | 2 | 3 | 4 | 5 | 6 | 7 | 8 | 9 | 10 | 11 | subs used |
|---|---|---|---|---|---|---|---|---|---|---|---|---|---|---|---|---|---|---|---|
| 1 | A | READING | | 1 | 0-4 | 0-2 | *[Smith 51]* | Emberson | Boyce | Perrett* | Johnson | Taylor | Forbes | Nicholls | Hughes | Mansell^ | Howard | Griffiths" | Dryden/Holmes/Douglas |
| | 21/8 | | *5,115* | *2:3* | | | *Henderson 38, 90, Parkinson 45* | *Whitehead* | *Murty* | *Shorey* | *Whitbread* | *Williams* | *Parkinson** | *Igoe* | *Harper* | *Forster^* | *Henderson* | *Smith"* | *Gamble/Rougier/Tyson* |
| | | | | | | | Ref: D Crick | Reading are far too slick for the Hatters and are the winners all over the pitch. Henderson heads in a Smith cross with the first for the Royals and Parkinson doubles their advantage on the stroke of half-time. Kinnear withdraws three players and it is then a case of limiting the damage. | | | | | | | | | | | |

| FA Cup | | | | | | | | | | | | | | | | | | | |
|---|---|---|---|---|---|---|---|---|---|---|---|---|---|---|---|---|---|---|---|
| 1 | A | SOUTHEND | | 4 | 2-3 | 1-1 | Forbes 34, Brkovic 75 | Emberson | Skelton | Hillier | Dryden | Taylor | Brkovic | Holmes* | Spring | Brennan^ | Forbes | Crowe | Fotiadis/George |
| | 17/11 | | *6,526* | *14* | | | *Rawle 45, Bramble 56, 85* | *Flahavan* | *McSweeney* | *Searle* | *Johnson* | *Cort* | *Whelan* | *Thurgood* | *Maher* | *Rawle* | *Belgrave* | *Bramble* | |
| | | | | | | | Ref: B Knight | A depleted Luton side, missing 12 senior players through injury, crash out of the FA Cup. The makeshift defence is told by Kinnear not to give away unnecessary free-kicks on the edge of the area but they are out-powered by a physical Southend side who treat the game like a cup-final. | | | | | | | | | | | |

| | | Home | | | | | Away | | | | | |
|---|---|---|---|---|---|---|---|---|---|---|---|---|
| | P | W | D | L | F | A | W | D | L | F | A | Pts |
| 1 Plymouth | 46 | 19 | 2 | 2 | 41 | 11 | 12 | 7 | 4 | 30 | 17 | 102 |
| 2 LUTON TOWN | 46 | 15 | 5 | 3 | 50 | 18 | 15 | 2 | 6 | 46 | 30 | 97 |
| 3 Mansfield | 46 | 17 | 3 | 3 | 49 | 24 | 7 | 4 | 12 | 23 | 36 | 79 |
| 4 Cheltenham* | 46 | 11 | 11 | 1 | 40 | 20 | 10 | 4 | 9 | 26 | 29 | 78 |
| 5 Rochdale | 46 | 13 | 8 | 2 | 41 | 22 | 8 | 7 | 8 | 24 | 30 | 78 |
| 6 Rushden | 46 | 14 | 5 | 4 | 40 | 20 | 6 | 8 | 9 | 29 | 33 | 73 |
| 7 Hartlepool | 46 | 12 | 6 | 5 | 53 | 23 | 8 | 5 | 10 | 21 | 25 | 71 |
| 8 Scunthorpe | 46 | 14 | 5 | 4 | 43 | 22 | 5 | 9 | 9 | 31 | 34 | 71 |
| 9 Shrewsbury | 46 | 13 | 4 | 6 | 36 | 19 | 7 | 6 | 10 | 28 | 34 | 70 |
| 10 Kidderminster | 46 | 13 | 6 | 4 | 35 | 17 | 6 | 3 | 14 | 21 | 30 | 66 |
| 11 Hull | 46 | 12 | 6 | 5 | 38 | 18 | 4 | 7 | 12 | 19 | 33 | 61 |
| 12 Southend | 46 | 12 | 5 | 6 | 36 | 22 | 3 | 8 | 12 | 15 | 32 | 58 |
| 13 Macclesfield | 46 | 7 | 7 | 9 | 23 | 25 | 8 | 6 | 9 | 18 | 27 | 58 |
| 14 York | 46 | 11 | 5 | 7 | 26 | 20 | 5 | 4 | 14 | 28 | 47 | 57 |
| 15 Darlington | 46 | 11 | 6 | 6 | 37 | 25 | 4 | 5 | 14 | 23 | 46 | 56 |
| 16 Exeter | 46 | 7 | 9 | 7 | 25 | 32 | 7 | 4 | 12 | 23 | 41 | 55 |
| 17 Carlisle | 46 | 11 | 5 | 7 | 31 | 21 | 1 | 11 | 11 | 18 | 35 | 52 |
| 18 Leyton Orient | 46 | 10 | 7 | 6 | 37 | 25 | 3 | 6 | 14 | 18 | 46 | 52 |
| 19 Torquay | 46 | 8 | 6 | 9 | 27 | 31 | 4 | 9 | 10 | 19 | 32 | 51 |
| 20 Swansea | 46 | 7 | 8 | 8 | 26 | 26 | 6 | 4 | 13 | 27 | 51 | 51 |
| 21 Oxford | 46 | 8 | 7 | 8 | 34 | 28 | 3 | 7 | 13 | 19 | 34 | 47 |
| 22 Lincoln | 46 | 8 | 4 | 11 | 25 | 27 | 2 | 12 | 9 | 19 | 35 | 46 |
| 23 Bristol Rov | 46 | 8 | 7 | 8 | 28 | 28 | 3 | 5 | 15 | 12 | 32 | 45 |
| 24 Halifax | 46 | 5 | 9 | 9 | 24 | 28 | 3 | 3 | 17 | 15 | 56 | 36 |
| | 1104 | 266 | 146 | 140 | 845 | 552 | 140 | 146 | 266 | 552 | 845 | 1510 |

* promoted after play-offs

Odds & ends

Double wins: (9) Southend, York, Torquay, Leyton Orient, Halifax, Swansea, Shrewsbury, Rushden, Kidderminster.
Double losses: (1) Rochdale.

Won from behind: (8) York (a), Darlington (h), Halifax (a), Oxford (a), Southend (a), Kidderminster (a), York (h), Rushden (a).
Lost from in front: (3) Plymouth (a), Darlington (a), Southend (FAC).

High spots: Promotion won at a canter in a record breaking season. The following records were broken: Total wins 30, away wins 15, away goals 46, points 97, consecutive wins 12.

Low spots: A run of three successive defeats in November which culminated in an awful 1-4 reversal at Macclesfield.
Early exits in both the Worthington and FA Cup competitions.

Player of the Year: Steve Howard.
Ever-presents: (0).
Hat-tricks: (2) Griffiths (1), Howard (1).
Leading Scorer: (24) Steve Howard.

| | Appearances | | | | | | Goals | | | |
|---|---|---|---|---|---|---|---|---|---|---|
| | Lge | *Sub* | LC | *Sub* | FAC | *Sub* | Lge | LC | FAC | Tot |
| Bayliss, David | **15** | *3* | | | | | | | | |
| Boyce, Emmerson | **30** | *7* | 1 | | | | | | | |
| Brennan, Dean | | | | | 1 | | | | | |
| Brkovic, Ahmet | **17** | *4* | | | 1 | | **1** | | 1 | **2** |
| Coyne, Chris | **29** | *2* | | | | | **3** | | | **3** |
| Crowe, Dean | **32** | *2* | | | 1 | | **15** | | | **15** |
| Douglas, Stuart | **2** | *7* | | *1* | | | | | | |
| Dryden, Richard | **2** | *1* | | *1* | 1 | | | | | |
| Emberson, Carl | **33** | | 1 | | 1 | | | | | |
| Forbes, Adrian | **15** | *25* | 1 | | 1 | | **4** | | 1 | **5** |
| Fotiadis, Andrew | | *8* | | | | *1* | **1** | | | **1** |
| George, Liam | **2** | *2* | | | | *1* | | | | |
| Griffiths, Carl | **10** | | 1 | | | | **7** | | | **7** |
| Hillier, Ian | **11** | *12* | | | 1 | | **1** | | | **1** |
| Holmes, Peter | **4** | *3* | | *1* | 1 | | **1** | | | **1** |
| Howard, Steve | **42** | | 1 | | | | **24** | | | **24** |
| Hughes, Paul | **12** | *10* | 1 | | | | **3** | | | **3** |
| Johnson, Marvin | **11** | *7* | 1 | | | | **1** | | | **1** |
| Kabba, Steve | | *3* | | | | | | | | |
| Locke, Adam | **1** | *2* | | | | | | | | |
| Mansell, Lee | **6** | *5* | 1 | | | | **1** | | | **1** |
| McSwegan, Gary | **2** | *1* | | | | | | | | |
| Neilson, Alan | **8** | | | | | | | | | |
| Nicholls, Kevin | **42** | | 1 | | | | **6** | | | **6** |
| Ovendale, Mark | **13** | | | | | | | | | |
| Perrett, Russell | **39** | *1* | 1 | | | | **3** | | | **3** |
| Skelton, Aaron | **9** | | | | 1 | | **1** | | | **1** |
| Spring, Matthew | **42** | | | | 1 | | **6** | | | **6** |
| Stirling, Jude | **1** | | | | | | | | | |
| Street, Kevin | **1** | *1* | | | | | | | | |
| Taylor, Matthew | **43** | | 1 | | 1 | | **11** | | | **11** |
| Valois, Jean-Louis | **32** | *2* | | | | | **6** | | | **6** |
| (own-goals) | | | | | | | **1** | | | **1** |
| **32 players used** | **506** | ***108*** | **11** | ***3*** | **11** | ***2*** | **96** | | **2** | **98** |

| No | Date | | Att | Pos | Pt | F-A | H-T | Scorers, Times, and Referees | 1 | 2 | 3 | 4 | 5 | 6 | 7 | 8 | 9 | 10 | 11 | subs used |
|---|---|---|---|---|---|---|---|---|---|---|---|---|---|---|---|---|---|---|---|---|
| 1 | H | PETERBOROUGH | | | L | 2-3 | 0-2 | Crowe 45, Brkovic 82 | Emberson | Neilson | Perrett | Coyne | **Kimble** | **Robinson*** | Spring | Nicholls | **Winters^** | Howard | Thorpe" | Brkovic/Crowe/Fotiadis |
| | 10/8 | | 7,860 | | 0 | | | _Green 2, Newton 30, Clarke 68_ | _Tyler_ | _Gill*_ | _Joseph_ | _Rea_ | _Pearce^_ | _Danielsson_ | _Forsyth_ | _Bullard"_ | _Newton_ | _Clarke_ | _Green_ | _Lee/MacDonald/Shields_ |
| | | | | | | | | Ref: B Curson | Outplayed in midfield, virtually non-existent as an attacking force and struggling against pace in defence, the Town lose for the first time since February. Things are marginally better in the second half but by then it is too late as the damage is already done. Welcome back to Division 2. | | | | | | | | | | | |
| 2 | A | BLACKPOOL | | | L | 2-5 | 1-2 | Howard 6, Thorpe 71 _[Dalglish 79]_ | Emberson | Neilson* | Bayliss | Coyne | Kimble | Brkovic | Spring^ | Nicholls | Holmes" | Howard | Thorpe | Boyce/Fotiadis/Crowe |
| | 13/8 | | _6,377_ | | 0 | | | _Clarke 19p, 24, Taylor 65, 90_ | _Barnes_ | _Grayson_ | _Clarke P_ | _Clarke C_ | _Jaszczun_ | _Bullock_ | _Southern_ | _Wellens_ | _Hills_ | _Walker*_ | _Dalglish_ | _Taylor_ |
| | | | | | | | | Ref: M Clattenberg | A Howard header from a Nicholls corner gives the Town a perfect start but the defence is found wanting once more with the pacey Seasiders attacking down the flanks. Tony Thorpe heads a beauty to make it 2-3 but, as they chase the game, the Town are undone by two late goals. | | | | | | | | | | | |
| 3 | A | PLYMOUTH | | 23 | L | 1-2 | 0-0 | Howard 67 | Emberson | Boyce | Perrett | Coyne ! | **Davis** | Robinson | Spring* | Nicholls^ | Brkovic | Howard | Thorpe" | Crowe/Neilson/Bayliss |
| | 17/8 | | _10,973_ | _6_ | 0 | | | _McGlinchey 57, Wotton 82_ | _Larrieu_ | _Worrell_ | _Wotton_ | _Malcolm_ | _McGlinchey_ | _Bent_ | _Adams_ | _Friio_ | _Phillips*_ | _Lowndes^_ | _Evans"_ | _Hodges/Keith/Sturrock_ |
| | | | | | | | | Ref: T Parkes | Coyne is sent off for pulling back Evans after ten minutes and it is then an uphill struggle, even though the Town play their best football of the campaign. Howard's thumping drive levels McGlinchey's 25-yard strike but Wotton's long-range effort somehow eludes Emberson's grasp. | | | | | | | | | | | |
| 4 | H | BARNSLEY | | 23 | L | 2-3 | 1-2 | Nicholls 43p, Spring 61 | Roberts | Boyce | Perrett | Coyne | Davis | Robinson | Spring | Nicholls* | Brkovic^ | Howard | Thorpe | Fotiadis/Crowe |
| | 24/8 | | 6,230 | _10_ | 0 | | | _Perrett 20 (og), Sheron 43, Dyer 58_ | _Marriott_ | _Austin_ | _Curle_ | _Morgan_ | _Holt !_ | _Betsy_ | _Gorre_ | _Lumsdon*_ | _Gibbs_ | _Dyer^_ | _Sheron"_ | _Crooks/Mulligan/Rankin_ |
| | | | | | | | | Ref: R Beeby | Andy Holt is dismissed for fouling Robinson in the area and, with Nicholls equalising from the spot, the Town's poor start looks likely to come to an end. Barnsley, though, go ahead straight from the restart and then defend in numbers. Kinnear is now considering a major reshuffle. | | | | | | | | | | | |
| 5 | A | CARDIFF | | 24 | D | 0-0 | 0-0 | | Roberts | Boyce | Perrett | Coyne | Davis | Brkovic | Spring | Nicholls | Hughes* | Howard | Crowe | Robinson |
| | 26/8 | | _13,564_ | _5_ | 1 | | | | _Alexander_ | _Weston_ | _Prior_ | _Gabbidon_ | _Croft_ | _Kavanagh*_ | _Whalley_ | _Thorne_ | _Legg_ | _Campbell^_ | _Fort'-West"_ | _Maxwell/Earnshaw/Boland_ |
| | | | | | | | | Ref: P Danson | The previous Saturday's dressing-down seems to work, with a solid professional display against the bookies' promotion favourites. In the last minute Steve Robinson is clear one on one with the Cardiff goalkeeper but spurns the opportunity. Lennie Lawrence feels the result is fair. | | | | | | | | | | | |
| 6 | H | CHESTERFIELD | | 21 | W | 3-0 | 1-0 | Perrett 36, Howard 69, Crowe 84 | Roberts | Boyce* | Perrett | Bayliss | Davis | Brkovic | Spring | Nicholls | Hughes^ | Howard | Crowe | Neilson/Robinson |
| | 31/8 | | 6,060 | _12_ | 4 | | | | _Muggleton_ | _Payne_ | _Dawson_ | _Howson_ | _Davies*_ | _Booty_ | _Brandon^_ | _Hudson_ | _Innes"_ | _Hurst_ | _Reeves_ | _Howard/Allott/Rushbury_ |
| | | | | | | | | Ref: P Taylor | The speed of Crowe unsettles the left hand side of the Chesterfield defence all afternoon, although the first two Town goals are from set pieces. Crowe drives in the third to confirm an emphatic victory, the first of the season. The players are now finding their feet after the miserable start. | | | | | | | | | | | |
| 7 | A | BRENTFORD | | 21 | D | 0-0 | 0-0 | | Roberts | Boyce | Perrett | Bayliss | Davis | Brkovic* | Spring | Nicholls | Hughes^ | Howard | Crowe | Robinson/Neilson |
| | 7/9 | | _7,145_ | _2_ | 5 | | | | _Smith P_ | _Dobson_ | _Sonko_ | _Somner_ | _Anderson_ | _O'Connor*_ | _Smith J^_ | _Hutchinson_ | _Hunt"_ | _McCammon_ | _Vine_ | _Williams/Fullarton/Hughes_ |
| | | | | | | | | Ref: D Pugh | The Town pass this major test against the league leaders who play a physical long-ball game. Bayliss and Perrett reign supreme at the heart of the Luton defence, while at the other end Steve Howard is closest to breaking the deadlock with a header that cannons back off the crossbar. | | | | | | | | | | | |
| 8 | H | NOTTS CO | | 21 | D | 2-2 | 0-2 | Perrett 78, Howard 86 | Roberts* | Neilson^ | Perrett | Bayliss | Davis | Brkovic | Nicholls | Spring | Hughes" | Howard | Crowe | Emberson/Coyne/Fotiadis |
| | 14/9 | | 6,456 | _19_ | 6 | | | _Bolland 26, Allsopp 45_ | _Garden_ | _Ramsden_ | _Fenton_ | _Ireland_ | _Nicholson_ | _Liburd_ | _Bolland_ | _Caskey_ | _Baraclough*_ | _Allsopp_ | _Heffernan^_ | _Brough/Stallard_ |
| | | | | | | | | Ref: A Kaye | Notts are gifted two goals after defensive errors. Roberts is suffering from flu and fails to appear in the second half, by which time Kinnear has rallied the troops for an all-out assault. Headers from Perrett and Howard level the score but Fotiadis misses an easy chance in injury-time. | | | | | | | | | | | |
| 9 | H | MANSFIELD | | 22 | L | 2-3 | 0-2 | Howard 85, Nicholls 87 | Emberson | Boyce | Perrett | Bayliss* | Davis | Brkovic^ | Nicholls | Spring | Hughes" | Howard | Crowe | Fotiadis/Robinson/Coyne |
| | 17/9 | | 6,004 | _23_ | 6 | | | _Lawrence 9, Sellars 23, Christie 50_ | _Pilkington_ | _Clarke_ | _Moore_ | _Lever*_ | _Delaney_ | _Lawrence_ | _Disley_ | _Williamson_ | _Mackenzie_ | _Sellars^_ | _Christie_ | _Reddington/White_ |
| | | | | | | | | Ref: B Knight | Again the Town are generous in defence and gift their fellow strugglers three goals before a late fight-back. Mansfield had lost five games on the trot before this clash, which an angry Kinnear says is the worst performance since he joined the club. The players are jeered off at the end. | | | | | | | | | | | |
| 10 | A | HUDDERSFIELD | | 19 | W | 1-0 | 0-0 | Howard 90 | Emberson | Boyce | Perrett | Coyne | Davis* | Robinson^ | Spring | Nicholls | Hughes | Howard | Crowe" | Hillier/Holmes/Fotiadis |
| | 21/9 | | _9,249_ | _21_ | 9 | | | | _Bevan_ | _Jenkins_ | _Dyson_ | _Brown_ | _Sharp_ | _Thorringt'n*_ | _Irons_ | _Holland_ | _Schofield_ | _Gallacher^_ | _Booth_ | _Macari/Stead_ |
| | | | | | | | | Ref: F Stretton | The Town are much better defensively in a tight game which sees Irons hit a 25-yard free-kick against the bar and Hughes smashing a drive against a post. A draw seems a fair result but Howard scrambles in his seventh of the season in added time after being set up by sub Fotiadis. | | | | | | | | | | | |
| 11 | H | SWINDON | | 15 | W | 3-0 | 1-0 | Howard 14, Fotiadis 47, Robinson 87p | Emberson | Boyce | Perrett | Coyne | Davis | Robinson | Spring | Nicholls* | Hughes | Howard | Fotiadis^ | Holmes/Crowe |
| | 28/9 | | 6,393 | _21_ | 12 | | | | _Griemink_ | _Gurney_ | _Heywood_ | _Willis_ | _Duke_ | _Robinson*_ | _Hewlett_ | _Jackson_ | _Invincible^_ | _Parkin_ | _Sabin_ | _Edds/Young_ |
| | | | | | | | | Ref: P Joslin | Andrew Fotiadis, making his first start for over a year, wins the Man-of-the-Match award on an afternoon when he might have scored four. Due to his misses, the win is only made safe when Crowe is fouled by Gurney, leaving Robinson to net his first goal for the club from the spot. | | | | | | | | | | | |

| No | Venue | Opponent / Date | Att | Pos | Pts | F-A | H-T | Scorers, Times, and Referees | 1 | 2 | 3 | 4 | 5 | 6 | 7 | 8 | 9 | 10 | 11 | subs used |
|---|---|---|---|---|---|---|---|---|---|---|---|---|---|---|---|---|---|---|---|---|
| 12 | A | STOCKPORT | | 14 | W | 3-2 | 1-2 | Spring 14, 71, Fotiadis 74 | **Berthelin** | Boyce | Hillier | Coyne | Davis | Robinson | Spring | Neilson | Hughes | Howard | Fotiadis* | Crowe |
| | | 5/10 | *5,932* | *17* | 15 | | | *Beckett 19, Daly 45* | *Jones* | *Goodwin* | *Palmer* | *Challinor* | *Gibb* | *Briggs* | *Lescott* | *Hardiker** | *Tonkin* | *Beckett* | *Daly* | *Ellison* |
| | | | | | | | | Ref: M Cowburn | A mistake from Berthelin gifts Stockport an interval lead, but a stung Town are dominant in the second period and the final score flatters the home side. Fotiadis sets up Spring's first, scores himself and then watches as Jones and Palmer tangle, leaving Spring to pounce for the winner. | | | | | | | | | | | |
| 13 | H | CHELTENHAM | | 10 | W | 2-1 | 0-1 | Coyne 54, Fotiadis 70 | Berthelin | Boyce | Neilson* | Coyne | Davis | Robinson | Spring | Skelton | Hughes^ | Howard | Fotiadis" | Crowe/Holmes/Brkovic |
| | | 12/10 | 6,447 | *24* | 18 | | | *Milton 12* | *Book* | *Howarth* | *Duff* | *Walker* | *Victory** | *Williams^* | *Finnigan* | *Forsyth* | *Milton* | *Alsop* | *Naylor"* | *Brough/Spencer/Brayson* |
| | | | | | | | | Ref: C Penton | Injury-hit Hatters allow Milton to take advantage of sloppy defending to give Cheltenham an interval lead. A 25-yard cracker from Coyne breaks the ice and there is only one winner after that, with Fotiadis spurning an easy opportunity and then netting from a more difficult chance. | | | | | | | | | | | |
| 14 | A | OLDHAM | | 10 | W | 2-1 | 1-1 | Fotiadis 33, Thorpe 58 | Berthelin | Boyce | Perrett | Coyne | Davis | Robinson | Spring | Skelton* | Holmes^ | Fotiadis | Crowe" | Brkovic/Hillier/Thorpe |
| | | 19/10 | *6,916* | *4* | 21 | | | *Holden 4* | *Pogliacomi* | *Hall* | *Duxbury** | *Armstrong* | *Eyre* | *Holden^* | *Sheridan* | *Carss* | *Eyres* | *Corazzin"* | *Killen* | *Haining/Lavrenco/Andrews* |
| | | | | | | | | Ref: C Boyeson | A bogey ground, two more players injured, leading scorer Howard suspended, deputy Crowe limping off and Oldham taking the lead with a soft early goal is not the recipe for success. The Hatters, however, buckle down and the returning Thorpe scores the Town's deserved winner. | | | | | | | | | | | |
| 15 | H | WIGAN | | 10 | D | 1-1 | 1-0 | Skelton 24 | Berthelin | Boyce | Perrett | Coyne | Davis | Robinson | Spring | Skelton | Holmes | Howard | Fotiadis | |
| | | 26/10 | 7,364 | *1* | 22 | | | *de Vos 88* | *Filan* | *Eaden* | *Jackson !* | *de Vos* | *McMillan* | *Teale** | *Dinning* | *Jarrett* | *McCulloch* | *Roberts* | *Ellington* | *Liddell* |
| | | | | | | | | Ref: S Tomlin | The Town open better against the big spending league leaders with Skelton sliding in to net from close range. They are, though, pinned back in the second period until ex-Hatter Matt Jackson is dismissed for a second yellow, but an unmarked de Vos cruelly heads in a very late leveller. | | | | | | | | | | | |
| 16 | A | CREWE | | 9 | W | 1-0 | 0-0 | Howard 85 | Berthelin | Boyce | Hillier | Coyne | Davis | Robinson | Spring | Skelton | Brkovic | Howard | Fotiadis* | Thorpe |
| | | 29/10 | *6,030* | *5* | 25 | | | | *Ince* | *Sodje* | *Walker* | *Foster* | *Wright* | *Sorvel** | *Lunt* | *Brammer* | *Jones^* | *Hulse* | *Jack* | *Rix/Ashton* |
| | | | | | | | | Ref: A Bates | A brilliant team performance, with the Town holding the promotion challengers at bay and then scoring on the break at the death. Crewe are given little chance to shine but the game seems destined to be scoreless until Davis hurdles a couple of weak tackles before setting up Howard. | | | | | | | | | | | |
| 17 | A | NORTHAMPTON | | 10 | L | 0-3 | 0-2 | | Berthelin | Boyce | Hillier | Coyne | Davis | Robinson* | Spring | Skelton^ | Brkovic" | Howard | Thorpe | Nicholls/Neilson/Holmes |
| | | 2/11 | *5,750* | *16* | 25 | | | *Forrester 9, 19, Gabbiadini 50* | *Harper* | *Gill* | *Sampson* | *Burgess* | *Frain** | *Asamoah^* | *Harsley* | *Trollope* | *Hargreaves* | *Forrester* | *Gabbiadini"* | *Carruthers/Rickers/Hope* |
| | | | | | | | | Ref: P Durkin | The formbook counts for nothing as the Town's unbeaten run ends against a team that has just suffered four defeats in a row. After woeful errors by the defence, Thorpe misses a simple opportunity to claw the game back. Gabbiadini's clever chip after the break kills the contest. | | | | | | | | | | | |
| 18 | H | PORT VALE | | 10 | D | 0-0 | 0-0 | | Berthelin | Boyce | Perrett | Coyne | Davis | Robinson | Nicholls | Neilson | Holmes* | Howard | Thorpe | Hughes |
| | | 9/11 | 6,112 | *13* | 26 | | | | *Goodlad* | *Carragher* | *Burns* | *Brightwell* | *Collins* | *Rowland* | *Durnin* | *Br'-Wilkins'n* | *Cummins* | *McPhee* | *Paynter** | *Brooker* |
| | | | | | | | | Ref: P Robinson | The Valiants become the first visitors to go home from Kenilworth Road with a clean sheet this season. Berthelin has only one serious save to make, while at the other end a siege develops with Vale riding their luck as the Town hit woodwork twice and see efforts cleared off the line. | | | | | | | | | | | |
| 19 | H | QP RANGERS | | 8 | D | 0-0 | 0-0 | | Berthelin | Boyce | Neilson | Coyne | Davis | Robinson | Nicholls ! | Spring | Brkovic | Howard ! | Thorpe* | Fotiadis^/Hillier |
| | | 23/11 | **9,477** | *6* | 27 | | | | *Royce* | *Forbes* | *Shittu* | *Carlisle* | *Williams* | *Burgess* | *Bircham* | *Palmer* | *Willock* | *Angell** | *Thomson^* | *Gallen"/Furlong/Oli* |
| | | | | | | | | Ref: E Wolstenholme | The Hatters are down to ten men after 14 minutes and nine after 50. Howard is red-carded for a late challenge and Nicholls for two yellows. They make up for their manpower deficiency with a controlled passing performance and even miss late chances. Rangers are lucky to escape. | | | | | | | | | | | |
| 20 | A | TRANMERE | | 7 | W | 3-1 | 0-1 | Spring 70, Brkovic 79, Howard 89 | Berthelin | Boyce | Neilson | Coyne | Davis* | Robinson | Nicholls | Spring | Brkovic^ | Howard | Thorpe" | Kimble/Hughes/Fotiadis |
| | | 30/11 | *8,273* | *11* | 30 | | | *Roberts 24* | *Achterberg* | *Allen* | *Edwards* | *Gray* | *Roberts* | *Taylor* | *Jones* | *Harrison** | *Nicholson* | *Robinson* | *Barlow^* | *Olsen/Hume* |
| | | | | | | | | Ref: A Penn | Tranmere win a debatable penalty when Nicholls is pushed onto the ball. Barlow's kick is saved by Berthelin who keeps out a follow-up effort before Roberts makes it third time lucky. The Town get their act together in the second half, dominating proceedings and winning at a canter. | | | | | | | | | | | |
| 21 | H | COLCHESTER | | 7 | L | 1-2 | 1-1 | Fotiadis 35 | Ovendale | Boyce | Neilson | Coyne | Kimble | Robinson | Nicholls | Spring* | Brkovic | Crowe | Fotiadis | Hughes |
| | | 14/12 | **5,890** | *15* | 30 | | | *Duguid 45, Morgan 58* | *Brown* | *Warren** | *Fitzgerald* | *White* | *Duguid* | *Bowry* | *Izett* | *Stockley* | *Stockwell* | *Morgan* | *Rapley^* | *Baldwin/Pinault* |
| | | | | | | | | Ref: M Cowburn | Fotiadis crashes in an 18-yarder and the Town seem set fair before Duguid nets a superb free-kick in first half added time. Town do not seem able to get over this blow and Morgan's headed winner seems inevitable. The opportunity to move into the play-off positions has been wasted. | | | | | | | | | | | |
| 22 | A | BRISTOL CITY | | 8 | D | 1-1 | 0-0 | Howard 53 | Emberson | Boyce | Neilson* | Coyne | Davis ! | Crowe | Robinson | Hughes | Brkovic | Howard | Thorpe^ | Hillier/Kimble |
| | | 21/12 | *14,057* | *3* | 31 | | | *Beadle 90* | *Phillips* | *Coles* | *Carey* | *Hill* | *Bell* | *Murray* | *Tinnion** | *Doherty* | *Burnell^* | *Roberts"* | *Peacock* | *Beadle/Brown/Rosenior* |
| | | | | | | | | Ref: M Cooper | After the previous week's capitulation the Town play as a determined, solid unit. City pound away after Howard's blind side-effort without creating much until Davis is sent off on 91 minutes and the game is bizarrely allowed to continue until Beadle equalises five minutes later. | | | | | | | | | | | |
| 23 | H | CARDIFF | | 6 | W | 2-0 | 0-0 | Thorpe 80, Howard 90 | Emberson | Boyce | Hillier | Coyne | Kimble | Robinson | Hughes | Brkovic | Crowe | Howard | Thorpe | |
| | | 26/12 | 7,805 | *3* | 34 | | | | *Alexander* | *Weston* | *Prior* | *Zhiyi* | *Barker* | *Boland* | *Kavanagh* | *Legg** | *Campbell^* | *Earnshaw* | *Thorne* | *Bowen/Fortune-West* |
| | | | | | | | | Ref: P Armstrong | The Hatters are on top from first whistle to last in a tremendous attacking display against the promotion favourites. The goals come late on, though, with Thorpe netting ten minutes from the end and then an absolute belter from Howard into the top corner sealing things at the death. | | | | | | | | | | | |

| No | Date | | Att | Pos | Pt | F-A | H-T | Scorers, Times, and Referees | 1 | 2 | 3 | 4 | 5 | 6 | 7 | 8 | 9 | 10 | 11 | subs used |
|---|---|---|---|---|---|---|---|---|---|---|---|---|---|---|---|---|---|---|---|---|
| 24 | A | WYCOMBE | | 6 | W | 2-1 | 2-0 | Howard 21, 34 | Emberson | Boyce | Hillier | Coyne | Davis | Crowe* | Robinson | Hughes | Brkovic^ | Howard | Thorpe" | Mansell/Kimble/Fotiadis |
| | 28/12 | | *7,740* | *13* | 37 | | | *Dixon 65* | *Talia* | *Senda* | *McCarthy* | *Rogers* | *Anderson* | *Roberts** | *Simpson* | *Bulman* | *Brown* | *Dixon* | *Rammell^* | *Cook/Faulconbridge* |
| | | | | | | | | Ref: P Walton | Steve Howard nets with a right-foot shot and a header to give the Town a comfortable interval lead, but in the second period they surprisingly tire allowing Wycombe back into the game. An error from Emberson leads to the Chairboys pulling a goal back and the final minutes are tense. | | | | | | | | | | | |
| 25 | A | CHESTERFIELD | | 6 | L | 1-2 | 1-0 | Brkovic 8 | Emberson | Boyce | Hillier | Coyne | Davis | Robinson | Hughes | Brkovic | Fotiadis* | Howard | Thorpe | Bayliss |
| | 1/1 | | *4,638* | *9* | 37 | | | *Hurst 55, Reeves 59* | *Williams* | *Davies* | *Blatherwick* | *O'Hare* | *Howson* | *Brandon* | *Ebdon* | *Booty* | *Edwards* | *Hurst* | *Reeves** | *Bradley* |
| | | | | | | | | Ref: M Ryan | Three points are thrown away after the Town are in full control but allow the opposition back into the match. Brkovic scores direct from a corner and sees his colleagues spurn several good chances in the first half, but poor defending gifts the home side two goals in four minutes. | | | | | | | | | | | |
| 26 | A | BARNSLEY | | 7 | W | 3-2 | 1-1 | Spring 45, Thorpe 50, 64 | Emberson ! | Hillier* | Neilson | Coyne | Kimble | Robinson^ | Spring | Nicholls | Hughes | Howard | Thorpe" | Bayliss/Ovendale/Crowe |
| | 18/1 | | *9,079* | *22* | 40 | | | *Betsy 1, Dyer 76p* | *Marriott* | *Austin* | *Morgan* | *O'Callagh'n** | *Williams* | *Donovan^* | *Hayward* | *Jones* | *Neil"* | *Betsy* | *Dyer* | *Crooks/Bar'clough/Fallon* |
| | | | | | | | | Ref: S Mathieson | Hesitation between Coyne and his goalkeeper allows Barnsley to score in the first minute, with Emberson sent off soon after for handling outside the area. Ten-man Town score three against an equally generous defence before hanging on after Neilson fouls Jones for a late penalty. | | | | | | | | | | | |
| 27 | H | WYCOMBE | | 7 | W | 1-0 | 0-0 | Spring 57 | Emberson | Boyce | Neilson | Coyne | Kimble | Robinson* | Spring | Nicholls | Hughes | Howard | Thorpe | Brkovic |
| | 25/1 | | 7,351 | *14* | 43 | | | | *Talia* | *Senda* | *Rogers* | *Thomson** | *Johnson* | *Ryan^* | *Bulman* | *Simpson* | *Brown"* | *Harris* | *Faulconbr'e* | *Currie/Cook/Roberts* |
| | | | | | | | | Ref: C Wilkes | Wycombe come for a point but after the Town break the deadlock they are unable to change their style. Hughes crosses to Thorpe who knocks the ball on to Spring to hammer in a shot from a narrow angle. Wycombe's Lawrie Sanchez amazingly feels his side were deserving winners. | | | | | | | | | | | |
| 28 | A | PETERBOROUGH | | 8 | D | 1-1 | 1-1 | Howard 12 | Ovendale | Neilson | Coyne* | Kimble | Robinson^ | Spring | Hughes | Brkovic | Boyce | Howard | Thorpe | Willmott/Crowe |
| | 1/2 | | *6,760* | *15* | 44 | | | *Fenn 39* | *Harrison* | *Burton* | *Rea* | *Arber* | *Scott* | *Gill** | *Shields* | *Danielsson* | *Jelleyman^* | *Clarke* | *Fenn* | *Semple/Farrell* |
| | | | | | | | | Ref: P Joslin | The Hatters are cruising after Howard nets but seem to ease off too much and slack defending costs an equaliser. The Posh goalkeeper prevents Thorpe, who is on fire, from bagging a hat-trick. Howard collects yet another booking and will be suspended for the third time this campaign. | | | | | | | | | | | |
| 29 | A | PORT VALE | | 7 | W | 2-1 | 0-0 | Thorpe 49, Nicholls 76p | Ovendale | Boyce | Willmott | Coyne | Neilson | Hughes* | Nicholls | Spring | Brkovic | Howard | Thorpe | Crowe |
| | 8/2 | | *4,714* | *19* | 47 | | | *Boyd 87* | *Goodlad* | *Rowland** | *Collins* | *Brightwell* | *Byrne* | *McPhee* | *Br'-Wilkins'n* | *Boyd* | *Armstrong* | *Paynter* | *Brooker* | *Carragher* |
| | | | | | | | | Ref: L Mason | Thorpe is left with a free header from a corner, is booked for throwing a snowball at the Luton supporters, and is then fouled by Brightwell on the edge of the area with Nicholls hammering in the resultant spot-kick. Vale put on a spirited late rally but Coyne and Willmott stand firm. | | | | | | | | | | | |
| 30 | H | BLACKPOOL | | 8 | L | 1-3 | 0-1 | Thorpe 48 | Ovendale | Boyce | Willmott | Coyne | Neilson | Crowe | Nicholls | Spring | Brkovic* | Howard | Thorpe | Hillier |
| | 11/2 | | 6,563 | *9* | 47 | | | *Murphy 10, 52, 74* | *Barnes* | *Grayson* | *Flynn* | *Hendry** | *Richardson* | *Bullock* | *Evans* | *Southern* | *Coid* | *Murphy* | *Taylor* | *Clarke* |
| | | | | | | | | Ref: G Hegley | This is the Martin Bullock show as the Seasiders' tricky winger tears the Luton defence to shreds in a virtuoso performance. John Murphy benefits from Bullock's wing play and gratefully hits home a superb hat-trick on a night when the Hatters are second best in most departments. | | | | | | | | | | | |
| 31 | H | NORTHAMPTON | | 8 | W | 3-2 | 1-1 | Hughes 26, 84, Nicholls 58 | Emberson | Boyce* | Willmott | Coyne | Neilson | Brkovic | Nicholls | Spring | Hughes | Crowe | Thorpe | Hillier |
| | 15/2 | | 7,048 | *22* | 50 | | | *Burgess 23, Johnson 71p* | *Thompson* | *Gill* | *Burgess* | *Reid* | *Carruthers* | *Asamoah* | *McGregor** | *Trollope* | *Johnson* | *Rahim* | *Stamp* | *Harsley* |
| | | | | | | | | Ref: K Hill | The Town leave it late before overcoming the Cobblers, with Paul Hughes' acrobatic effort finally sealing the points. Earlier, the Town wasted opportunities to put the game beyond the visitors but Nicholls' 22-yard free-kick which hits the top corner like a rocket brings the house down. | | | | | | | | | | | |
| 32 | H | BRENTFORD | | 9 | L | 0-1 | 0-0 | | Emberson | Neilson | Coyne | Willmott | Davis | Brkovic | Spring* | Nicholls | Hughes | Crowe^ | Thorpe | Hillier/Robinson |
| | 22/2 | | 6,940 | *13* | 50 | | | *Vine 50* | *Smith P* | *Dobson* | *Somner* | *Frampton* | *Fieldwick* | *O'Connor* | *Smith J* | *Fullarton** | *Hunt* | *McCammon* | *Vine* | *Hutchinson* |
| | | | | | | | | Ref: A Hall | The Bees have a makeshift back four but are still able to hold the Hatters' forward line at bay. Crowe opts to set up Thorpe rather than take on the keeper and overhits the pass. Vine shows Luton how its done when he takes a long ball in his stride and lashes a 25-yard drive into the net. | | | | | | | | | | | |
| 33 | H | PLYMOUTH | | 8 | W | 1-0 | 0-0 | Thorpe 50 | **Hirschfeld** | Hillier | Willmott | Coyne | Davis | Crowe | Nicholls | Spring* | Hughes | Howard | Thorpe | Brkovic |
| | 25/2 | | 7,589 | *10* | 53 | | | | *Larrieu* | *Worrell** | *Coughlan* | *Wotton* | *Hodges* | *Bent* | *Norris* | *Friio* | *McGlinch'y^* | *Evans* | *Stonebridge* | *Lowndes/Keith* |
| | | | | | | | | Ref: A Bates | The battle with Plymouth continues from the previous season with again the Town running out the winners in a pulsating contest. The margin of victory might have been greater but Thorpe's alertness enables him to turn in the winner when he reacts quickest to Hillier's long throw. | | | | | | | | | | | |
| 34 | A | NOTTS CO | | 9 | L | 1-2 | 0-0 | Thorpe 88 | Hirschfeld | Hillier | Willmott | Coyne | Davis | Crowe* | Nicholls | Spring | Hughes^ | Howard | Thorpe | Brkovic/**Jupp** |
| | 1/3 | | *6,778* | *15* | 53 | | | *Heffernan 79, 84* | *Mildenhall* | *Bolland* | *Richardson* | *Ireland* | *Nicholson* | *Francis** | *Caskey* | *Baraclough* | *Liburd^* | *Heffernan* | *Stallard* | *Ramsden/Riley* |
| | | | | | | | | Ref: M Messias | The Town show their inconsistency with a below-par performance against a struggling side. Defenders stand off as Heffernan thumps in two efforts with Thorpe's reply too little too late. Joe Kinnear is baffled by the topsy-turvy form but still feels that the Town are worth a point. | | | | | | | | | | | |

| No | Venue | Opponent / Date | Att | Pos | Res | Pts | F-A | H-T | Scorers, Times, and Referees | 1 | 2 | 3 | 4 | 5 | 6 | 7 | 8 | 9 | 10 | 11 | subs used |
|---|---|---|---|---|---|---|---|---|---|---|---|---|---|---|---|---|---|---|---|---|---|
| 35 | A | MANSFIELD | | 9 | L | | 2-3 | 1-2 | Thorpe 13, 82 | Hirschfeld | Jupp | Willmott | Coyne | Davis | Brkovic | Nicholls | Spring | Hughes* | Crowe^ | Thorpe | Holmes/Perrett |
| | | 4/3 | *4,829* | *22* | | 53 | | | *Day 9, Christie 29, Corden 79* | *Welch* | *Hassell** | *Day* | *Curle* | *Eaton* | *Mendes* | *Curtis* | *Williamson* | *Corden^* | *Christie* | *Mitchell"* | *Gadsby/Lawrence/White* |
| | | | | | | | | | Ref: C Wilkes | Tony Thorpe is on top form but the rest of the side let him down in a tired and jaded display. Relegation-threatened Mansfield look fresher and are up for it but are helped by a generous Luton defence. Thorpe's second goal sets the nerves jangling but the damage had already been done. | | | | | | | | | | | |
| 36 | H | HUDDERSFIELD | | 8 | W | | 3-0 | 0-0 | Thorpe 50, Holmes 71, Howard 89 | Emberson | Jupp* | Perrett | Coyne | Davis | Brkovic^ | Nicholls | Spring | Hughes" | Howard | Thorpe | Hillier/Robinson/Holmes |
| | | 8/3 | 6,122 | *21* | | 56 | | | | *Senior* | *Heary** | *Moses* | *Brown* | *Sharp* | *Mattis* | *Irons !* | *Holland^* | *Smith"* | *Booth* | *Baldry* | *Worthingt'n/Scott/Stead* |
| | | | | | | | | | Ref: I Williamson | Basement battlers Huddersfield play for a point but are undone when Thorpe, from a suspiciously offside position, opens the scoring. Irons is booked for protesting and is then dismissed for a terrible tackle on Davis. For once the Town are ruthless against ten men and are easy victors. | | | | | | | | | | | |
| 37 | A | WIGAN | | 8 | D | | 1-1 | 0-0 | Howard 57 | Hirschfeld | Bayliss | Perrett | Coyne | Hillier* | Robinson | Nicholls | Spring | Brkovic | Howard | Thorpe | Jupp |
| | | 15/3 | *7,087* | *1* | | 57 | | | *Roberts 75* | *Filan* | *Eaden* | *de Vos* | *Jackson* | *McMillan* | *Teale** | *Bullard* | *Mitchell^* | *McCulloch* | *Ellington* | *Liddell* | *Roberts/Jarrett* |
| | | | | | | | | | Ref: S Mathieson | A determined Town side battle out a well-deserved draw against the runaway leaders. Howard is impeded whilst tracking back to mark de Vos, leaving the big stopper to set up the Latics equaliser. Earlier Howard heads in his 17th of the season to send the big away support into raptures. | | | | | | | | | | | |
| 38 | H | OLDHAM | | 8 | D | | 0-0 | 0-0 | | Hirschfeld* | Hillier | Perrett | Coyne | Davis | Hughes^ | Nicholls | Spring | Brkovic | Howard | Thorpe | Emberson/Holmes |
| | | 18/3 | 6,142 | *4* | | 58 | | | | *Pogliacomi* | *Murray* | *Haining* | *Duxbury* | *Beharall* | *Armstrong* | *Eyre* | *Sheridan* | *Carss* | *Wijnhard* | *Andrews* | |
| | | | | | | | | | Ref: R Styles | Oldham boss Iain Dowie plays for a point and deploys defenders to man-mark Howard and Thorpe. Howard is denied when his superb volley is expertly saved, while Thorpe sets up Spring for an effort that flies narrowly wide. The tense game sees a lot of long ball and little excitement. | | | | | | | | | | | |
| 39 | H | CREWE | | 8 | L | | **0-4** | 0-2 | | Emberson | Hillier | Perrett | Coyne | Davis* | Forbes^ | Nicholls | Spring | Brkovic" | Howard | Thorpe | Bayliss/ Hughes/Holmes |
| | | 22/3 | 6,607 | *2* | | 58 | | | *Ashton 7, 21, Vaughan 50, Jack 78* | *Ince* | *McCready* | *Walker* | *Walton* | *Tierney* | *Lunt* | *Sorvell* | *Brammer* | *Vaughan* | *Ashton** | *Jack^* | *Oakes/Little* |
| | | | | | | | | | Ref: S Baines | Hopes of creeping into the play-offs take a huge knock as the Hatters are completely outplayed by a stupendous Crewe outfit. Using quick, accurate, passing football Crewe tear through the Luton defence, and in Dean Ashton they have a striker who proves unplayable on the day. | | | | | | | | | | | |
| 40 | H | TRANMERE | | 8 | D | | 0-0 | 0-0 | | Emberson | Boyce* | Perrett | Coyne | Davis | **Igoe** | Nicholls | Spring | Brkovic^ | Howard | Thorpe" | Hillier/Hughes/Forbes ! |
| | | 5/4 | 6,326 | *7* | | 59 | | | | *Howarth* | *Connelly* | *Allen* | *Sharps* | *Roberts* | *Anderson* | *Jones** | *Loran* | *Nicholson^* | *Haworth* | *Hume* | *Mellon/Hay* |
| | | | | | | | | | Ref: A D'Urso | The play-off dream is now over as ten-man Town, despite having the majority of the play, cannot find a way past Rovers' debutant goalkeeper. Thorpe limps off and his replacement is dismissed for violent conduct. Tranmere, who also need promotion points, are surprisingly lack-lustre. | | | | | | | | | | | |
| 41 | A | CHELTENHAM | | 8 | D | | 2-2 | 2-1 | Hughes 12, Forbes 38 | Emberson | Willmott | Perrett* | Coyne | Davis | Igoe | Nicholls | Spring | Hughes | Howard | Forbes^ | Hillier"/Holmes/Jupp |
| | | 8/4 | ***3,762*** | *21* | | 60 | | | *McCann 27p, Alsop 81* | *Higgs* | *Bird** | *Duff M* | *Duff S* | *Victory* | *Devaney* | *Yates* | *Finnigan* | *McCann* | *Brough* | *Brown^* | *Alsop/Naylor* |
| | | | | | | | | | Ref: T Parkes | Loanee Igoe is Man-of-the-Match against desperate opponents and has a hand in both goals, a brilliant angled drive from Hughes and a Thorpe tap-in. Cheltenham net from the spot after Nicholls fouls Finnigan and then score a second late on when the tall Alsop is allowed a free header. | | | | | | | | | | | |
| 42 | A | QP RANGERS | | 8 | L | | 0-2 | 0-1 | | Ovendale | Boyce | Willmott | Coyne | Davis | Holmes | Spring | Nicholls | Hughes* | Howard | Forbes | Neilson |
| | | 12/4 | ***15,786*** | *6* | | 60 | | | *McLeod 39, 83* | *Day* | *Kelly* | *Carlisle* | *Shittu* | *Padula* | *Langley* | *Bircham* | *Palmer* | *McLeod* | *Furlong* | *Gallen* | |
| | | | | | | | | | Ref: J Ross | Decimated by injuries, the Town are a pale shadow of their normal selves. A large Luton following sees Rangers dominate and McLeod is unmarked and unchallenged to score with a header, and then fires in a 25-yard shot into the top corner after a free-kick was touched onto him. | | | | | | | | | | | |
| 43 | H | BRISTOL CITY | | 9 | D | | 2-2 | 1-0 | Howard 2, 82 | **Beckwith** | Boyce | Neilson | Willmott | Davis | Holmes* | Nicholls | Spring | Hughes^ | Howard | Griffiths | **Foley**/Kimble |
| | | 19/4 | 6,381 | *5* | | 61 | | | *Tinnion 66p, Peacock 75* | *Phillips* | *Carey* | *Doherty** | *Butler* | *Hill* | *Murray* | *Burnell* | *Peacock* | *Tinnion^* | *Roberts"* | *Coles* | *Brown/Lita/Beadle* |
| | | | | | | | | | Ref: G Salisbury | Ovendale is injured in the warm-up and 18-year old rookie Robert Beckwith is handed an unexpected debut in goal. He is not at fault with the two defensive errors which allow City to take the lead. Howard nods in early and adds his second, the leveller, with a towering far-post header. | | | | | | | | | | | |
| 44 | A | COLCHESTER | | 8 | W | | **5-0** | 4-0 | Howard 14, 45, 90, Griffiths 21, [Nicholls 43p] | Beckwith | Boyce* | Neilson | Willmott | Davis | Hughes | Nicholls | Spring^ | Holmes | Howard | Griffiths" | Bayliss/Skelton/**Judge** |
| | | 21/4 | *3,967* | *10* | | 64 | | | | *McKinney* | *Halford** | *White* | *Fitzgerald* | *Edwards* | *Duguid* | *Izzet* | *Canham^* | *Morgan* | *May* | *McGleish* | *Baldwin/Pinault* |
| | | | | | | | | | Ref: C Penton | Steve Howard scores the second hat-trick of his career as the Town steam-roller a side that is unbeaten in eight games. The Colchester keeper has a nightmare after bringing down Griffiths for a penalty, which is despatched by Nicholls, and then allowing the big Howard to bully him. | | | | | | | | | | | |
| 45 | H | STOCKPORT | | 8 | D | | 1-1 | 0-0 | Howard 61 | Beckwith | Boyce | Willmott* | Neilson | Davis | Hughes^ | Nicholls | Spring | Holmes | Howard | Griffiths" | Bayliss/Brkovic/Skelton |
| | | 26/4 | 6,010 | *14* | | 65 | | | *Challinor 83* | *Tidman* | *Goodwin* | *Challinor* | *Greer* | *Clark* | *Lescott* | *McLachlan** | *Gibb* | *Welsh^* | *Daly* | *Wilbraham* | *Clare/Lambert* |
| | | | | | | | | | Ref: M Thorpe | The patchy home form continues with young Beckwith the more active goalkeeper. Howard's opener is followed by Challinor being gifted a free header from a corner. The normally reliable and fit again Griffiths misses a simple chance but both managers agree that a draw is fair. | | | | | | | | | | | |
| 46 | A | SWINDON | | 9 | L | | 1-2 | 1-2 | Thorpe 31 | Beckwith | Boyce* | Bayliss | Neilson | Kimble | Hughes | Brkovic^ | Nicholls | Spring" | Howard | Thorpe | Foley/Forbes/Skelton |
| | | 3/5 | *6,455* | *10* | | 65 | | | *Miglioranzi 41, Parkin 43* | *Griemink* | *Hewlett* | *Heywood* | *Gurney* | *Invincible** | *Lewis* | *Robinson* | *Sabin^* | *Duke* | *Miglioranzi"* | *Parkin* | *Bampton/Herring/Taylor* |
| | | Home | Away | | | | | | Ref: A Penn | The Town stumble over the finishing line with a limp display which allows arch-rivals Plymouth to overtake them on goal-difference. Thorpe squeezes in a goal against the run of play but the Town defenders are unable to cope with Sam Parkin who is a thorn in their sides all afternoon. | | | | | | | | | | | |
| Average | | 6,746 | 7,646 | | | | | | | | | | | | | | | | | | |

| Worthington Cup | Att | F-A | H-T | Scorers, Times, and Referees | 1 | 2 | 3 | 4 | 5 | 6 | 7 | 8 | 9 | 10 | 11 | subs used |
|---|---|---|---|---|---|---|---|---|---|---|---|---|---|---|---|---|
| 1 A WATFORD 10/9 | 21 14,171 1:11 | 2-1 | 2-0 | Spring 31, Howard 41<br>*Foley 75*<br>Ref: P Walton | Emberson<br>*Chamberlain* | Boyce<br>*Ardley* | Davis<br>*Robinson* | Spring<br>*Doyley* | Perrett<br>*Dyche* | Bayliss<br>*Cox* | Nicholls<br>*Hyde* | Brkovic*<br>*Hand** | Howard<br>*Foley* | Crowe<br>*Smith* | Hughes^<br>*Glass^* | Robinson/Neilson<br>*Norville/McNamee* |
| | | | | | On a highly charged evening, the Hatters are well worth the victory over their bitter adversaries. A hammer strike from Spring into the top corner is the goal of this or any other season, and after Howard cleverly knocks in number two the Town are able to keep their rivals at bay. | | | | | | | | | | | |
| 2 A ASTON VILLA 2/10 | 15 20,833 P:12 | 0-3 | 0-2 | *de la Cruz 9, Dublin 25, 48*<br>Ref: C Webster | Emberson<br>*Enckelman* | Boyce<br>*de la Cruz* | Perrett*<br>*Samuel* | Coyne<br>*Mellberg* | Davis<br>*Johnsen* | Robinson<br>*Staunton** | Spring<br>*Kinsella* | Holmes^<br>*Hendrie* | Hughes<br>*Dublin^* | Howard<br>*Vassell"* | Fotiadis"<br>*Barry* | Hillier/Neilson/Crowe<br>*Leonhardsen/Allback/Moore* |
| | | | | | Villa's international class proves too much for the Hatters in a one-sided cup-tie. Veteran striker Dion Dublin nets twice as the Town rarely threaten despite the encouragement of 5,000 supporters. There is only one likely winner after de la Cruz stabs in early past a static defence. | | | | | | | | | | | |

| FA Cup | Att | F-A | H-T | Scorers, Times, and Referees | 1 | 2 | 3 | 4 | 5 | 6 | 7 | 8 | 9 | 10 | 11 | subs used |
|---|---|---|---|---|---|---|---|---|---|---|---|---|---|---|---|---|
| 1 H GUISELEY 16/11 | 10 5,248 *NL* | 4-0 | 3-0 | Spring 3, Thorpe 44, Brkovic 45, 65<br>Ref: J Ross | Emberson<br>*Hill* | Boyce*<br>*Atkinson* | Perrett^<br>*Shaw* | Coyne<br>*Henry* | Davis<br>*Freeman* | Robinson<br>*Trevitt* | Nicholls<br>*Nettleton** | Spring<br>*Sumner* | Brkovic<br>*Senior^* | Howard<br>*Cooke* | Thorpe<br>*Stuart"* | Holmes/Neilson<br>*Reilly/Newhouse/Chattoe* |
| | | | | | Any hopes of a giant-killing are extinguished early on, when a long-range effort from Spring flies past the Unibond League side's goalkeeper. It is one-way traffic after that with players queuing up to try to beat Chris Hill in the Guiseley goal. Hill makes a string of impressive saves. | | | | | | | | | | | |
| 2 A WIGAN 7/12 | 7 4,544 *1* | 0-3 | 0-1 | *Ellington 37, 64, Flynn 86*<br>Ref: H Webb | Emberson<br>*Filan* | Boyce<br>*Eaden* | Neilson<br>*Baines* | Coyne<br>*Dinning* | Kimble<br>*Breckin* | Robinson<br>*Jackson* | Hughes<br>*Green** | Spring<br>*Jarrett* | Holmes*<br>*Ellington* | Brkovic<br>*Roberts^* | Fotiadis^<br>*Kennedy"* | Hillier/Judge<br>*Mitchell/Flynn/Teale* |
| | | | | | Injury and suspension cost the Town 12 players and not surprisingly, despite a sluggish start, the Division 2 table-toppers run out comfortable winners. Wigan's record signing, Nathan Ellington, costs nine times the whole of Kinnear's side but he shows his pedigree when netting twice. | | | | | | | | | | | |

| | | Home | | | | | Away | | | | | |
|---|---|---|---|---|---|---|---|---|---|---|---|---|
| | P | W | D | L | F | A | W | D | L | F | A | Pts |
| 1 Wigan | 46 | 14 | 7 | 2 | 37 | 16 | 15 | 6 | 2 | 31 | 9 | 100 |
| 2 Crewe | 46 | 11 | 5 | 7 | 29 | 19 | 14 | 6 | 3 | 47 | 21 | 86 |
| 3 Bristol City | 46 | 15 | 5 | 3 | 43 | 15 | 9 | 6 | 8 | 36 | 33 | 83 |
| 4 QP Rangesr | 46 | 14 | 4 | 5 | 38 | 19 | 10 | 7 | 6 | 31 | 26 | 83 |
| 5 Oldham | 46 | 11 | 6 | 6 | 39 | 18 | 11 | 10 | 2 | 29 | 20 | 82 |
| 6 Cardiff * | 46 | 12 | 6 | 5 | 33 | 20 | 11 | 6 | 6 | 35 | 23 | 81 |
| 7 Tranmere | 46 | 14 | 5 | 4 | 38 | 23 | 9 | 6 | 8 | 28 | 34 | 80 |
| 8 Plymouth | 46 | 11 | 6 | 6 | 39 | 24 | 6 | 8 | 9 | 24 | 28 | 65 |
| 9 LUTON TOWN | 46 | 8 | 8 | 7 | 32 | 28 | 9 | 6 | 8 | 35 | 34 | 65 |
| 10 Swindon | 46 | 10 | 5 | 8 | 34 | 27 | 6 | 7 | 10 | 25 | 36 | 60 |
| 11 Peterborough | 46 | 8 | 7 | 8 | 25 | 20 | 6 | 9 | 8 | 26 | 34 | 58 |
| 12 Colchester | 46 | 8 | 7 | 8 | 24 | 24 | 6 | 9 | 8 | 28 | 32 | 58 |
| 13 Blackpool | 46 | 10 | 8 | 5 | 35 | 25 | 5 | 5 | 13 | 21 | 39 | 58 |
| 14 Stockport | 46 | 8 | 8 | 7 | 39 | 38 | 7 | 2 | 14 | 26 | 32 | 55 |
| 15 Notts Co | 46 | 10 | 7 | 6 | 37 | 32 | 3 | 9 | 11 | 25 | 38 | 55 |
| 16 Brentford | 46 | 8 | 8 | 7 | 28 | 21 | 6 | 4 | 13 | 19 | 35 | 54 |
| 17 Port Vale | 46 | 9 | 5 | 9 | 34 | 31 | 5 | 6 | 12 | 20 | 39 | 53 |
| 18 Wycombe | 46 | 8 | 7 | 8 | 39 | 38 | 5 | 6 | 12 | 20 | 28 | 52 |
| 19 Barnsley | 46 | 7 | 8 | 8 | 27 | 31 | 6 | 5 | 12 | 24 | 33 | 52 |
| 20 Chesterfield | 46 | 11 | 4 | 8 | 29 | 28 | 3 | 4 | 16 | 14 | 45 | 50 |
| 21 Cheltenham | 46 | 6 | 9 | 8 | 26 | 31 | 4 | 9 | 10 | 27 | 37 | 48 |
| 22 Huddersfield | 46 | 7 | 9 | 7 | 27 | 24 | 4 | 3 | 16 | 12 | 37 | 45 |
| 23 Mansfield | 46 | 9 | 2 | 12 | 38 | 45 | 3 | 6 | 14 | 28 | 52 | 44 |
| 24 Northampton | 46 | 7 | 4 | 12 | 23 | 31 | 3 | 5 | 15 | 17 | 48 | 39 |
| | 1104 | 236 | 150 | 166 | 793 | 628 | 166 | 150 | 236 | 628 | 793 | 1506 |

* promoted
after play-offs

Odds & ends

Double wins: (2) Huddersfield, Wycombe.
Double losses: (2) Blackpool, Mansfield.

Won from behind: (6) Stockport (a), Cheltenham (h), Oldham (a), Tranmere (a), Barnsley (a), Northampton (h).
Lost from in front: (4) Blackpool (a), Colchester (h), Chesterfield (a), Swindon (a).

High spots: First ever league wins at Crewe and Stockport as well as the first league win at Barnsley since 1952.
The team is always within a shout of the play-offs until the season draws to a close.
The 5-0 thrashing of Colchester at Layer Road.

Low spots: The disappointment of failing to reach the play-offs.
The poor home form.
The terrible start to the season with the first four games lost.

Player of the Year: Chris Coyne.
Ever-presents: (0)..
Hat-tricks: Howard (1).
Leading scorer: Steve Howard (23).

| | Appearances | | | | | | Goals | | | |
|---|---|---|---|---|---|---|---|---|---|---|
| | Lge | *Sub* | LC | *Sub* | FAC | *Sub* | Lge | LC | FAC | Tot |
| Bayliss, David | **7** | *6* | 1 | | | | | | | |
| Beckwith, Rob | **4** | | | | | | | | | |
| Berthelin, Cedric | **9** | | | | | | | | | |
| Boyce, Emmerson | **33** | *1* | 2 | | 2 | | | | | |
| Brkovic, Ahmet | **29** | *7* | 1 | | 2 | | **3** | | 2 | **5** |
| Coyne, Chris | **38** | *2* | 1 | | 2 | | **1** | | | **1** |
| Crowe, Dean | **17** | *10* | 1 | *1* | | | **2** | | | **2** |
| Davis, Sol | **34** | | 2 | | 1 | | | | | |
| Emberson, Carl | **18** | *2* | 2 | | 2 | | | | | |
| Foley, Kevin | | *2* | | | | | | | | |
| Forbes, Adrian | **3** | *2* | | | | | **1** | | | **1** |
| Fotiadis, Andrew | **8** | *9* | 1 | | 1 | | **5** | | | **5** |
| Griffiths, Carl | **3** | | | | | | **1** | | | **1** |
| Hillier, Ian | **12** | *10* | | *1* | | *1* | | | | |
| Hirschfeld, Lars | **5** | | | | | | | | | |
| Holmes, Peter | **8** | *9* | 1 | | 1 | *1* | **1** | | | **1** |
| Howard, Steve | **41** | | 2 | | 1 | | **22** | 1 | | **23** |
| Hughes, Paul | **30** | *5* | 2 | | 1 | | **3** | | | **3** |
| Igoe, Sammy | **2** | | | | | | | | | |
| Judge, Matthew | | *1* | | | | *1* | | | | |
| Jupp. Duncan | **2** | *3* | | | | | | | | |
| Kimble, Alan | **8** | *4* | | | 1 | | | | | |
| Mansell, Lee | | *1* | | | | | | | | |
| Neilson, Alan | **21** | *5* | | *2* | 1 | *1* | | | | |
| Nicholls, Kevin | **35** | *1* | 1 | | 1 | | **5** | | | **5** |
| Ovendale, Mark | **5** | *1* | | | | | | | | |
| Perrett, Russell | **19** | *1* | 2 | | 1 | | **2** | | | **2** |
| Roberts, Ben | **5** | | | | | | | | | |
| Robinson, Steve | **23** | *6* | 1 | *1* | 2 | | **1** | | | **1** |
| Skelton, Aaron | **5** | *3* | | | | | **1** | | | **1** |
| Spring, Matthew | **41** | | 2 | | 2 | | **6** | 1 | 1 | **8** |
| Thorpe, Tony | **28** | *2* | | | 1 | | **13** | | 1 | **14** |
| Willmott, Chris | **12** | *1* | | | | | | | | |
| Winters, Robbie | **1** | | | | | | | | | |
| **34 players used** | **506** | ***94*** | **22** | ***5*** | **22** | ***4*** | **67** | **2** | **4** | **73** |

| No | Date | | Att | Pos | Pt | F-A | H-T | Scorers, Times, and Referees | 1 | 2 | 3 | 4 | 5 | 6 | 7 | 8 | 9 | 10 | 11 | subs used |
|---|---|---|---|---|---|---|---|---|---|---|---|---|---|---|---|---|---|---|---|---|
| 1 | H | RUSHDEN | | | W | 3-1 | 0-1 | Thorpe 50, 59, Spring 90 | Beckwith | Spring | **Pitt*** | Neilson | Boyce | Coyne | Nicholls | Hughes | Howard | Thorpe | Foley | Brkovic |
| | 9/8 | | 6,878 | | 3 | | | *Lowe 37* | *Turley* | *Bignot* | *Underwood* | *Bell* | *Hunter* | *Edwards* | *Hall* | *Gray** | *Darby^* | *Lowe* | *Burgess* | *Jack/Mills* |
| | | | | | | | | Ref: I Williamson | It is a winning start for Mike Newell despite his side going in one down at the interval. On a blazingly hot day Thorpe takes advantage of Pitt's pass to level and then nods in a quick Howard corner with the keeper caught in no-man's land. Springs's late header is the icing on the cake. | | | | | | | | | | | |
| 2 | A | STOCKPORT | | 1 | W | 2-1 | 1-0 | Neilson 32, Howard 56 | Beckwith | Foley | Coyne | Boyce | Neilson | Hillier* | Nicholls | Hughes | Pitt | Howard | Thorpe | Brkovic |
| | 16/8 | | *4,566* | *21* | 6 | | | *Jones 72* | *Colgan* | *Goodwin* | *Clarke* | *Jones* | *Hardiker* | *Morrison* | *Lambert* | *McLachlan** | *Ellison^* | *Barlow* | *Wilbraham"* | *Collins/Welsh/Daly* |
| | | | | | | | | Ref: P Joslin | Alan Neilson gets a touch to Nicholls' whipped in free-kick for his first Town goal while Howard looks to be well offside before being allowed to take on the goalkeeper and slot home. Although Jones gives the home side a glimmer of hope, it is the Town who miss further opportunities. | | | | | | | | | | | |
| 3 | H | GRIMSBY | | 7 | L | 1-2 | 0-1 | Nicholls 85p | Beckwith | Foley | Coyne | Boyce | Neilson | Nicholls | Hughes | Spring* | Pitt | Howard | **McSheffr'y^** | /Brkovic/Crowe |
| | 23/8 | | 5,827 | *16* | 6 | | | *Anderson 34, Boulding 77* | *Davison* | *Crowe* | *Crane* | *Ford* | *Barnard* | *Cas** | *Campbell* | *Hamilton* | *Anderson^* | *Boulding* | *Tenheuvel"* | *Groves/Mansaran/Rowan* |
| | | | | | | | | Ref: G Cain | Gary McSheffrey is brought in on loan to replace Thorpe and looks bewildered as the Town come back to earth after their good start. Grimsby have just two on-target attempts and score from both. At the other end, Crowe is fouled by Ford with Nicholls slamming home from the spot. | | | | | | | | | | | |
| 4 | A | BRIGHTON | | 12 | L | 0-2 | 0-1 | | Beckwith | Foley | Coyne | Bayliss | Davis | Nicholls | Spring | Hughes | Pitt | Howard ! | McSheffr'y* | Crowe |
| | 25/8 | | *6,604* | *3* | 6 | | | *Coyne 16 (og), Oatway 85* | *Roberts* | *Hinshelwood* | *Butters* | *Pethick* | *Mayo* | *Hart* | *Carpenter* | *Oatway* | *Jones* | *Knight** | *Henderson^* | *Piercy/McPhee* |
| | | | | | | | | Ref: P Crossley | Howard is dismissed for something he says to the linesman and Newell for stepping out of his technical area. Earlier, Chris Coyne gets the final touch to a Henderson shot and, although the ten men step up a gear, Oatway's long-range effort finds its way through Beckwith's hands. | | | | | | | | | | | |
| 5 | H | HARTLEPOOL | | 6 | W | 3-2 | 3-1 | Howard 6, 23, McSheffrey 14 | Beckwith | Boyce | Coyne | Bayliss | Neilson* | Foley | Hughes | Spring | Pitt^ | Howard | McSheff'y" | Davis/Brkovic/Crowe |
| | 30/8 | | 5,515 | *9* | 9 | | | *Clarke 40, Robinson 71p* | *Provett* | *Barron* | *Nelson* | *Westwood* | *Robson* | *Clarke* | *Tinkler** | *Strachan* | *Humphreys* | *Robinson^* | *Gabbiadini"* | *Istead/Boyd/Henderson* |
| | | | | | | | | Ref: B Curson | The Hatters regain their self-respect and are unstoppable for the first half-hour. McSheffrey sets up Howard and then receives a perfect pass from Pitt to enable him to chip the advancing goalkeeper. Howard heads in number three before Pool wake up and have the Town sweating. | | | | | | | | | | | |
| 6 | A | NOTTS CO | | 8 | D | 1-1 | 1-0 | Coyne 43 | Beckwith | Boyce | Coyne | Bayliss | Neilson* | Foley | Spring | Hughes ! | Brkovic^ | Howard | McSheffrey | Davis/Crowe |
| | 6/9 | | *7,505* | *24* | 10 | | | *Barras 61* | *Mildenhall* | *Bolland* | *Livesey* | *Barras* | *Richardson* | *Baldry* | *Caskey* | *McFaul** | *Baraclough* | *Heffernan* | *Platt* | *Stallard* |
| | | | | | | | | Ref: L Webster | The fans turn out in force to help save County, who are only 48 hours from oblivion. McSheffrey floats in a free-kick for Coyne to head the opener but Barras levels against the run of play with a speculative 30-yard shot. The game ends with Hughes dismissed for a second yellow. | | | | | | | | | | | |
| 7 | A | PLYMOUTH | | 12 | L | 1-2 | 0-0 | McSheffrey 58 | Beckwith | Boyce | Coyne | Bayliss* | Davis | Foley | Hughes | Spring | Brkovic | **Showunmi^** | McSheffrey | Hillier/Crowe |
| | 13/9 | | *9,894* | *7* | 10 | | | *Evans 82, Friio 90* | *McCormick* | *Worrell* | *Wotton* | *Coughlan* | *Gilbert** | *Norris* | *Adams^* | *Friio* | *Hodges* | *Evans* | *Stonebridge"* | *Sturrock/Bent/Keith* |
| | | | | | | | | Ref: A Bates | With only 16 fit players, Showunmi is given a debut but is subbed for his own good after earning the referee's wrath. This leaves the tiny Crowe and McSheffrey up front and while they lead Plymouth a merry dance the home side bludgeon their way to an undeserved victory. | | | | | | | | | | | |
| 8 | H | PORT VALE | | 8 | W | 2-0 | 1-0 | McSheffrey 31, Foley 71 | Beckwith | Boyce | Coyne | Bayliss | Davis | Foley | Hughes | Spring | Brkovic | Forbes* | McSheffrey | Showunmi |
| | 16/9 | | 5,079 | *1* | 13 | | | | *Delaney* | *Pilkington* | *Collins* | *Burns** | *Brown^* | *McPhee* | *Boyd* | *Lipa* | *Littlejohn"* | *Brooker* | *Paynter* | *Briscoe/Rowland/Armstrong* |
| | | | | | | | | Ref: J Ross | A hugely entertaining game with the Town having the measure of the league leaders and crowning the night with two well-taken goals. Foley's pass to McSheffrey gives Luton the lead but it is surprising that the supporters have to wait so long before Foley carefully places the second. | | | | | | | | | | | |
| 9 | H | QP RANGERS | | 9 | D | 1-1 | 0-0 | Howard 60 | Beckwith | Boyce | Coyne | Bayliss | Davis | Foley | **Leary** | Spring | Brkovic | McSheffr'y* | Howard | Pitt |
| | 20/9 | | 8,339 | *3* | 14 | | | *Furlong 90* | *Day* | *Edghill* | *Gnohere* | *Shittu* | *Padula* | *Rowlands** | *Palmer^* | *Bean* | *McLeod"* | *Gallen* | *Furlong* | *Thorpe/Bircham/Ainsworth* |
| | | | | | | | | Ref: U Rennie | The Town welcome(!) back Tony Thorpe on a highly-charged afternoon. The breakthrough finally comes on the hour with Howard's shot deflected into the net. In a last desperate fling Rangers push men forward and Furlong muscles his way past Coyne to slot in the late equaliser. | | | | | | | | | | | |
| 10 | A | OLDHAM | | 14 | L | 0-3 | 0-2 | | Beckwith ! | Hillier* | Boyce | Coyne | Davis | Brkovic^ | Leary | Hughes | Pitt" | McSheffrey | Howard | Mansell/**Brill**/Perrett |
| | 27/9 | | *6,077* | *16* | 14 | | | *Sheridan J 30p, Zola 45, Holden 47* | *Pogliacomi* | *Clegg* | *Hall* | *Hudson* | *Holden* | *Eyre** | *Sheridan J^* | *Murray* | *Eyres* | *Zola* | *Vernon"* | *Cooksey/Sheridan D/Killen* |
| | | | | | | | | Ref: M Pike | After the marathon cup-tie in midweek, three more players are out injured. 39-year-old John Sheridan converts from the spot after Leary is accused of shirt tugging, Excellent efforts put the Latics firmly in the driving seat before Beckwith is dismissed for handling outside the area. | | | | | | | | | | | |
| 11 | A | SWINDON | | 13 | D | 2-2 | 0-1 | McSheffrey 65p, Forbes 67 | Beckwith | Boyce | Coyne | Perrett | Davis ! | Foley | Robinson | Hughes | Pitt | McSheffrey | Forbes* | Leary |
| | 1/10 | | *7,573* | *3* | 15 | | | *Milner 8, Howard 89* | *Evans* | *Ifil* | *Heywood* | *Viveash* | *Miglioranzi* | *Gurney* | *Igoe** | *Hewlett^* | *Duke"* | *Mooney* | *Milner* | *Howard/Robinson/Reeves* |
| | | | | | | | | Ref: P Danson | The referee takes centre stage in a dramatic match which sees nine yellows, two reds and Mike Newell banished from the dug-out for swearing. Igoe sets up Milner's first but a twice-taken McSheffrey penalty levels. Forbes' excellent strike is followed by a last-gasp Swindon equaliser. | | | | | | | | | | | |

| No | Venue | Opponent / Date | Att | Pos | Pts | Res | HT | Scorers / Ref | 1 | 2 | 3 | 4 | 5 | 6 | 7 | 8 | 9 | 10 | 11 | Subs |
|---|---|---|---|---|---|---|---|---|---|---|---|---|---|---|---|---|---|---|---|---|
| 12 | H | TRANMERE | | 9 | W | 3-1 | 1-0 | Perrett 45, McSheffrey 64, Forbes 72 | Beckwith | Boyce | Coyne | Perrett | Davis | Foley* | Spring | Hughes | Pitt | McSheffrey | Forbes | Robinson |
| | | 6/10 | **5,002** | *20* | 18 | | | *Dagnall 54* | *Achterberg* | *Taylor** | *Loran* | *Connolly* | *Roberts* | *Hume* | *Mellon* | *Harrison* | *Nicholson^* | *Dagnall* | *Haworth* | *Allen/Hay* |
| | | | | | | | | Ref: G Hegley | Tranmere put nine men behind the ball but are undone when a Spring free-kick is headed home by Perrett just before the interval. Rovers start the second period by forcing the Hatters back and produce a tap-in goal for Dagnall before Gary McSheffrey and Forbes secure the Luton win. | | | | | | | | | | | |
| 13 | H | WYCOMBE | | 8 | W | 3-1 | 0-0 | McSheffrey 76, 89, Perrett 85 | Brill | Boyce | Coyne | Perrett | Davis | Robinson* | Hughes | Spring | Pitt | McSheffrey | Forbes^ | Mansell/Showunmi |
| | | 11/10 | 5,695 | *23* | 21 | | | *Brown 49p* | *Talia* | *Senda* | *Thomson* | *Branston* | *Vinnicombe* | *Bulman* | *Simpson* | *Brown* | *Currie* | *Holligan** | *Ryan^* | *Harris/Bell* |
| | | | | | | | | Ref: R Beeby | Pitt fouls Senda in the area which leads to a penalty conversion by Brown before the Hatters net three goals in the last 24 minutes. McSheffrey levels and Perrett heads the second before the former, showing predatory instincts, anticipates a Thomson clearance and curls in the clincher. | | | | | | | | | | | |
| 14 | A | BRENTFORD | | 10 | L | 2-4 | 0-1 | Forbes 48, 88 | Brill | Boyce | Coyne | Perrett | Hillier | Foley | Spring | Hughes | Pitt* | McSheffrey | Forbes | Judge |
| | | 18/10 | *5,579* | *18* | 21 | | | *Hunt 12, Tabb 58, 65, May 87* | *Smith P* | *Dobson* | *Roget** | *Kitamirike* | *Somner* | *Rougier* | *Evans^* | *O'Connor* | *Hunt* | *May* | *Wright"* | *Sonko/Smith J/Tabb* |
| | | | | | | | | Ref: C Penton | The performance from the Town is below par, even allowing for the fact that some players are not 100% match fit. Forbes gives the Town the hope of a point before Brentford raise their game and the match is over well before Forbes nets his second just minutes before the end of play. | | | | | | | | | | | |
| 15 | A | BOURNEMOUTH | | 12 | L | **3-6** | 2-4 | Purches 10(og), Hughes 25, Forbes 60 | Beckwith | Boyce | Coyne | Perrett | Hillier | Foley* | Spring | Hughes^ | Pitt | McSheffrey | Forbes | Mansell/Robinson |
| | | 21/10 | *6,388* | *5* | 21 | | | *Fl'r S 7, 45, Stock 34, 62, O'Conn'r 42* | *Moss* | *Purches* | *Broadhurst* | *Fletcher C* | *Cummings* | *Elliott** | *Hayter* | *Browning^* | *O'Connor"* | *Feeney* | *Fletcher S* | *Thomas/Stock/Tindall* |
| | | | | | | | | Ref: A Marriner *[Elliott 67]* | In a bizarre incident-packed game both sides show defensive frailties. The Hatters lead midway through the first half but then go on to concede six goals for the first time in nine seasons. 'Every time Bournemouth went forward we looked likely to concede,' bemoans Newell afterwards. | | | | | | | | | | | |
| 16 | H | PETERBOROUGH | | 12 | D | 1-1 | 1-0 | Forbes 29 | **Beresford** | Foley | Boyce | Coyne | Hillier ! | Mansell* | Robinson | Spring | Brkovic | McSheffrey | Forbes | Neilson |
| | | 25/10 | 6,067 | *21* | 22 | | | *McKenzie 64* | *Tyler* | *Gill** | *Arber* | *Burton* | *Jelleyman* | *Willock* | *Woodhouse* | *Thomson* | *Clarke^* | *Logan"* | *McKenzie* | *Newton/Farrell/Fotiadis* |
| | | | | | | | | Ref: D Crick | A grounded Forbes swings his boot to record his sixth goal in as many games but then the match turns sour as Hillier is dismissed for a second yellow card. McKenzie heads the equaliser as the Posh drive forward but the Town hold firm and almost win the game when Spring hits a post. | | | | | | | | | | | |
| 17 | A | BRISTOL CITY | | 14 | D | 1-1 | 1-1 | McSheffrey 18 | Beresford | Neilson* | Boyce | Coyne | Davis | Mansell | Robinson | Spring | Brkovic | McSheffrey | Forbes^ | Hillier/Showunmi |
| | | 1/11 | *9,735* | *9* | 23 | | | *Burnell 2* | *Phillips* | *Coles* | *Butler* | *Hill* | *Amankwa'h** | *Wilkshire* | *Burnell* | *Tinnion* | *Woodman* | *Roberts* | *Peacock* | *Lita^/Miller* |
| | | | | | | | | Ref: A Peake | Burnell, the City skipper, scores his first ever goal after just 90 seconds but the Town net a classic equaliser as Boyce surges out of defence and lays the ball off to Spring. He makes an inch-perfect pass to McSheffrey who outpaces his marker, draws the keeper and slides the ball home. | | | | | | | | | | | |
| 18 | H | WREXHAM | | 12 | W | 3-2 | 1-2 | Forbes 45, Robinson 52, Mansell 58 | Beresford | Foley | Boyce | Coyne | Davis | Mansell | Robinson | Spring | Brkovic | McSheffrey | Forbes | |
| | | 15/11 | 5,505 | *11* | 26 | | | *Sam 19, Boyce 43 (og)* | *Dibble* | *Pejic* | *Carey* | *Lawrence* | *Thomas** | *Barrett* | *Ferguson !* | *Crowell* | *Edwards* | *Sam* | *Llewllyn^* | *Jones/Armstrong* |
| | | | | | | | | Ref: T Kettle | The Town are second best for most of the first half but manage to pull a goal back straight after Wrexham score their second. Robinson fires in to level from the edge of the box before Mansell hits the winner from an unlikely angle. Ferguson is sent off near the end for thumping Forbes. | | | | | | | | | | | |
| 19 | A | SHEFFIELD WED | | 13 | D | 0-0 | 0-0 | | Beresford | Boyce | Howard | Hillier | Mansell | Robinson | Spring | Brkovic | Holmes* | McSheffrey | Forbes | Leary |
| | | 22/11 | ***21,027*** | *17* | 27 | | | | *Pressman* | *Lee* | *Bromby* | *Smith* | *Geary* | *Reddy* | *Mustoe* | *Haslam* | *B'y-Murphy** | *Owusu* | *Proudlock* | *Antoine-Curier* |
| | | | | | | | | Ref: P Robinson | Due to an injury crisis, the only two defenders available are Boyce and Hillier so Howard steps in as a centre-half in a back three. Although the Town rarely look like winning, their determination and teamwork make it a day to remember on the first visit to Hillsborough for eleven years. | | | | | | | | | | | |
| 20 | H | CHESTERFIELD | | 10 | W | 1-0 | 1-0 | Howard 3 | Beresford | Hillier | Boyce | Coyne | Davis | Forbes | Robinson | Spring | Brkovic* | McSheffrey | Howard | Holmes |
| | | 29/11 | 5,453 | *23* | 30 | | | | *Muggleton* | *Dawson* | *Blatherwick* | *Evatt* | *O'Hare* | *Uhlenbeek* | *Allott* | *Howson* | *Innes** | *Reeves^* | *Brandon* | *Rushbury/Robinson* |
| | | | | | | | | Ref: R Olivier | Steve Howard heads home an early goal but the Hatters are then unable to beat Spireites goalkeeper, Carl Muggleton, who is on top form. On a couple of occasions he denies Gary McSheffrey, who is hoping to score a final goal before his loan period ends, as Luton grind out the result. | | | | | | | | | | | |
| 21 | A | BLACKPOOL | | 6 | W | 1-0 | 1-0 | Robinson 35 | Beresford | Foley | Boyce | Coyne | Davis | Mansell | Robinson | Spring | Brkovic* | Forbes | Howard | Leary |
| | | 13/12 | *5,739* | *12* | 33 | | | | *Jones* | *Grayson^* | *Flynn* | *Elliott* | *Evans* | *Bullock^* | *Coid* | *Wellens* | *Johnson* | *Sheron"* | *Taylor* | *Burns/McMahon/Davis* |
| | | | | | | | | Ref: M Warren | Robinson hits a cracking 25-yard shot to open the scoring but the Hatters are forced back after the break. The defence, with help from Howard, who drops back as a central defender, holds firm and the Town notch a first win at Blackpool since 1971 and move up to the play-off positions. | | | | | | | | | | | |
| 22 | H | BARNSLEY | | 7 | L | 0-1 | 0-0 | | Beresford | Foley | Boyce | Coyne | Davis | Mansell | Robinson | Spring | Brkovic | Forbes | Howard | |
| | | 20/12 | 6,162 | *3* | 33 | | | *Kay 90* | *Ilic* | *O'Callaghan** | *Ireland* | *Monk* | *Austin* | *Burns* | *Hayward* | *Kay* | *Carson^* | *Betsy* | *Walters"* | *Warhurst/Neil/Rankin* |
| | | | | | | | | Ref: P Armstrong | Robinson hits the bar from a free-kick but it is the Tykes who both create and spurn several better chances. Luton are on the back foot towards the end and have to deal with several corners, one of which is bundled over the line for the late winner and moves the visitors up to third spot. | | | | | | | | | | | |
| 23 | A | COLCHESTER | | 9 | D | 1-1 | 1-1 | Mansell 28 | Beresford | Foley | Boyce | Coyne | Davis | Mansell* | Robinson | Spring | Brkovic | Forbes | Howard | Holmes |
| | | 26/12 | *5,083* | *6* | 34 | | | *McGleish 12* | *Brown* | *Stockley* | *Chilvers* | *White* | *Myers* | *Fagan* | *Pinault* | *Izzet* | *Vine* | *Andrews* | *McGleish** | *Cade* |
| | | | | | | | | Ref: J Ross | The Town have plenty of possession but some poor finishing lets them down. Scott McGleish throws himself at the ball to score a spectacular opener before Spring sees his shot from outside the box deflected into the path of Mansell whose drive thunders in to grab a share of the spoils. | | | | | | | | | | | |

# NATIONWIDE LEAGUE DIVISION 2 — Manager: Mike Newell — SEASON 2003-04

| No | Date | | Att | Pos | Pt | F-A | H-T | Scorers, Times, and Referees | 1 | 2 | 3 | 4 | 5 | 6 | 7 | 8 | 9 | 10 | 11 | subs used |
|---|---|---|---|---|---|---|---|---|---|---|---|---|---|---|---|---|---|---|---|---|
| 24 | H | NOTTS CO | | 7 | W | 2-0 | 1-0 | Forbes 4, Boyce 79 | Beresford | Foley | Boyce | Coyne | Davis | Mansell | Robinson | Spring* | Brkovic^ | Forbes" | Howard | Hillier/Holmes/Showunmi |
| | 28/12 | | 7,181 | 23 | 37 | | | | Mildenhall | Jenkins | Barras | Richardson | Nicholson | Baldry | Bolland* | Baraclough | Riley^ | Platt | Heffernan" | Hackworth/Caskey/Stallard |
| | | | | | | | | Ref: L Probert | Forbes beats the offside trap and the Hatters take an early lead; however, although well on top, they cannot add to their tally by the break. The visitors start the second half strongly but spurn several opportunities before Coyne sets up Emmerson Boyce for a thumping right-foot volley. | | | | | | | | | | | |
| 25 | A | RUSHDEN | | 8 | D | 2-2 | 2-1 | Forbes 6, Holmes 39 | Beresford | Foley | Boyce | Coyne | Hillier* | Mansell | Robinson | Holmes | Brkovic | Forbes | Howard | Leary |
| | 10/1 | | 5,823 | 11 | 38 | | | Kitson 17, Hunter 65 | Ashdown | Sambrook | Hunter | Quinn | Bignot | Hall | Hanlon | Burgess | Jack | Kitson | Lowe | |
| | | | | | | | | Ref: S Tanner | Rushden are played off the park during the first half and could easily have found themselves more than one goal adrift by half-time. They raise their game in the second period and Beresford saves a penalty from Hanlon before a terrible miss from Lowe ensures the Hatters gain a point. | | | | | | | | | | | |
| 26 | H | STOCKPORT | | 9 | D | 2-2 | 1-1 | Griffin 32 (og), Howard 85 | Beresford | Foley | **Davies** | Coyne | Davis | Mansell* | Robinson | Holmes | Brkovic | Forbes ! | Howard | Showunmi |
| | 17/1 | | 5,920 | 21 | 39 | | | Lynch 18, McLachlan 72 | Spencer | Hardiker | Clare | Griffin | Jackman | Gibb* | Lambert | McLachlan | Welsh | Barlow | Lynch^ | Morrison/Wilbraham |
| | | | | | | | | Ref: A Butler | Forbes is dismissed for alleged violent conduct after he competes for a high ball. The ten men have the better of the chances but have to wait until the end before securing the equaliser via a deflected indirect free-kick which is awarded after Clare plays a back-pass to his goalkeeper. | | | | | | | | | | | |
| 27 | H | COLCHESTER | | 10 | W | 1-0 | 0-0 | Showunmi 52 | **Hyldgaard** | Foley | Boyce | Coyne | Davis | Nicholls | Robinson | Spring | Holmes | Showunmi* | Howard | Crowe |
| | 7/2 | | 5,662 | 14 | 42 | | | | Brown | Stockley* | White | Chilvers | Tierney | Duguid | Izzet^ | Pinault" | Keith | Fagan | Vine | McGleish/Cade/Andrews |
| | | | | | | | | Ref: E Ilderton | 21-year-old Enoch Showunmi, who had never played at any level higher than Saturday parks football before joining Luton, steals the show when having spurned easier chances, he receives a pass from Holmes, turns and shoots in one movement to send the ball whipping into the net. | | | | | | | | | | | |
| 28 | H | BRIGHTON | | 9 | W | 2-0 | 1-0 | Holmes 27, Nicholls 77p | Hyldgaard | Foley | Boyce | Coyne | Davis | Nicholls* | Robinson | Spring | Holmes^ | Showunmi" | Howard | Leary/Brkovic/Crowe |
| | 10/2 | | 6,846 | 6 | 45 | | | | Jones S | Virgo | Cullip | Butters | Mayo | Oatway | Hart* | Carpenter | Watson^ | Knight ! | Benjamin | Robinson/Jones N/McPhee |
| | | | | | | | | Ref: T Parkes | The Hatters settle an old score after recalling their poor performance at Withdean in August. Holmes sweeps in the opener from a Showunmi cross and, after Leon Knight is dismissed for a second yellow card, Cullip trips Showunmi in the box leaving Nicholls to convert from the spot. | | | | | | | | | | | |
| 29 | A | WYCOMBE | | 9 | D | 0-0 | 0-0 | | Hyldgaard | **Keane** | Boyce | Coyne | Davis | Nicholls | Robinson | Spring | Holmes* | Showunmi | Howard | Brkovic |
| | 14/2 | | 6,407 | 24 | 46 | | | | Bevan | Senda | Johnson | Nethercott | Vinnicombe | Currie | Simpson | Bulman | Brown | McSporran | Tyson | |
| | | | | | | | | Ref: S Bennett/L Cable | The Town are expected to win against the bottom club but it is Wycombe who are left to rue their missed chances. 17-year old Keith Keane makes his debut and the pace of McSporran threatens to embarrass him but he rides through the ordeal. Luton have only one effort on target. | | | | | | | | | | | |
| 30 | H | BRENTFORD | | 6 | W | **4-1** | 1-0 | Boyce 10, Showunmi 49, 66, 80 | Hyldgaard | Keane* | Davis | Leary^ | Boyce | Coyne | Nicholls | Robinson" | Showunmi | Howard | Holmes | Neilson/Hughes/**O'Leary** |
| | 21/2 | | 6,273 | 18 | 49 | | | Wright 63 | Julian | Dobson | Sonko | Kitimarike | Bull* | O'Connor | Talbot | Hutchinson | Rougier^ | May" | Wright | Somner/Tabb/Evans |
| | | | | | | | | Ref: P Taylor | Brentford are a poor side and after Boyce heads in an early corner from Robinson there is only going to be one winner. The new darling of the terraces, Enoch Showunmi, grabs the match ball after he nets a memorable hat-trick with two powerful left-foot strikes and one with his right. | | | | | | | | | | | |
| 31 | A | GRIMSBY | | 6 | L | 2-3 | 1-0 | Howard 19, 80 | Hyldgaard | Keane | Boyce | Coyne | Davis | Nicholls* | Leary | Robinson | Holmes^ | Showunmi | Howard | Hughes/Brkovic |
| | 24/2 | | **3,143** | 20 | 49 | | | Jevons 55, 69p, Ford 90 | Davison | Ford | Crane | Armstrong | Barnard | Campbell | Daws | Coldicott* | Anderson^ | Mansaram | Rankin | Soames/Jevons |
| | | | | | | | | Ref: C Boyeson | Howard ends his long-goal drought but the Town end up losing to a cruel last-minute effort. Newell fumes about the penalty which changes the game after Rankin tumbles over with Davis nowhere near. Even Grimsby caretaker boss, Graham Rodger, admits that the decision was harsh. | | | | | | | | | | | |
| 32 | A | PETERBOROUGH | | 5 | W | 2-1 | 1-0 | Howard 26, Brkovic 77 | Hyldgaard | Keane* | Boyce | Coyne | Davis | Nicholls | Robinson | Hughes | Brkovic | Showunmi | Howard | Neilson |
| | 28/2 | | 6,628 | 22 | 52 | | | Willock 79 | Tyler | Burton | Branston | Arber | Newton | Woodhouse | Legg | Thomson* | Williams^ | Willock | Clarke" | Kanu/Farrell/Logan |
| | | | | | | | | Ref: P Crossley | Posh fire in many crosses but lack the players to convert chances, whereas Luton have Howard. He fires the first into the top corner before Brkovic steals in to convert a Robinson cross. The Town do not play well against a side with a poor home record and are grateful for the win. | | | | | | | | | | | |
| 33 | A | BARNSLEY | | 7 | D | 0-0 | 0-0 | | Hyldgaard | Keane | Boyce | Coyne | Davis | Nicholls | Robinson | Hughes | Brkovic* | Showunmi | Howard | Holmes |
| | 6/3 | | 8,656 | 11 | 53 | | | | Beresford | Austin | Handyside | Kay | Williams* | Betsy | Hayward | Neil^ | Boulding | Stallard | Nardiello | Atkinson/Davies |
| | | | | | | | | Ref: A Marriner | Barnsley are a team on the slide with injury problems and a new manager. Town boss Mike Newell believes that the opposition are there for the taking but many chances are missed. In the final minute Howard chips Beresford, only for the home side skipper to hack clear off the line. | | | | | | | | | | | |
| 34 | H | BLACKPOOL | | 6 | W | 3-2 | 1-0 | Boyce 25, Holmes 66, Showunmi 74 | Hyldgaard | Keane | Boyce | Coyne | Davis | Nicholls | Robinson | Hughes | Holmes | Showunmi | Howard | |
| | 13/3 | | 6,343 | 15 | 56 | | | Dinning 69p, Blinkhorn 79 | Barnes | Grayson | Davis | Hessey | Elliott | Evans* | Wellens | Dinning | McMahon^ | Sheron" | Walker | Jaszczun/Bullock/Blinkhorn |
| | | | | | | | | Ref: S Tomlin | Blackpool up their game after the Town take a two-goal lead and when Boyce is penalised for a foul on Walker it produces their first shot on target, from the spot. Showunmi curls in a clever free-kick to restore the advantage but the defence is caught napping by the lively Blinkhorn. | | | | | | | | | | | |

| No | Venue | Opponent / Date | Att | Pos | Res / Pts | FT | HT | Scorers, Times, and Referees | 1 | 2 | 3 | 4 | 5 | 6 | 7 | 8 | 9 | 10 | 11 | subs used |
|---|---|---|---|---|---|---|---|---|---|---|---|---|---|---|---|---|---|---|---|---|
| 35 | A | PORT VALE | | 6 | L | 0-1 | 0-0 | | Hyldgaard | Keane | Boyce | Coyne | Davis | Nicholls | Robinson | Hughes* | Holmes | Showunmi | Howard | Brkovic |
| | | 16/3 | 5,048 | 9 | 56 | | | Cummins 84 | Brain | Pilkington | Walsh | Collins | Rowland | Paynter | Cummins | Br-Wilkinson | Brisco* | Brooker | McPhee | Armstrong |
| | | | | | | | | Ref: G Cain | A close contest between two of the play-off contenders sees Showunmi outpacing Collins before hitting a post, Hyldgaard making two excellent saves and Hughes clearing an effort off the line. Luton seem to have earned a draw but a routine high cross is headed in by Cummins. | | | | | | | | | | | |
| 36 | H | PLYMOUTH | | 7 | D | 1-1 | 1-0 | Coyne 42 | Hyldgaard | Keane | Boyce | Coyne* | Neilson | Nicholls ! | Robinson | Hughes | Holmes | Showunmi^ | Howard | Davies/Crowe |
| | | 20/3 | **8,499** | 1 | 57 | | | Adams 90 | McCormick | Connolly | Wotton | Coughlan | Gilbert | Norris | Friio | Adams | Capaldi* | Evans^ | Lowndes" | Phillips/Sturrock/Keith |
| | | | | | | | | Ref: G Salisbury | On a windy day, Luton are more than a match for the table-toppers and deserve their lead when Coyne heads home at the far post. Nicholls is dismissed after tangling with Lowndes, who collapses in a heap, but the ten men hold out until the 93rd minute when Adams hits the equaliser. | | | | | | | | | | | |
| 37 | A | QP RANGERS | | 8 | D | 1-1 | 0-1 | Showunmi 76 | Hyldgaard | Keane | Boyce | Davies | Neilson | Nicholls | Hughes* | Robinson | **Underw'd**^ | Brkovic | Showunmi | Forbes/Holmes"/Foley |
| | | 27/3 | 17,695 | 2 | 58 | | | Furlong 45 | Camp | Bignot | Gnohere | Carlisle | Edghill | Rowlands | Bean* | Johnson | Gallen | Furlong | Thorpe^ | Cureton/McLeod |
| | | | | | | | | Ref: A D'Urso | Three midfielders are lost in the first 20 minutes, including new man Underwood, but the Hatters still manage to hold on for a point. Furlong heads in a cross in first-half stoppage time but the unpredictable Showunmi, who gives Carlisle nightmares, holds off his markers to slot home. | | | | | | | | | | | |
| 38 | H | OLDHAM | | 8 | D | 1-1 | 1-1 | Showunmi 34 | Hyldgaard | Keane | Boyce | Coyne | Davis | Foley* | Neilson^ | Robinson | Brkovic | Howard | Showunmi | Forbes/O'Leary |
| | | 3/4 | 5,966 | 17 | 59 | | | Crowe 33 | Pogliacomi | Holden | Owen | Haining | Griffin | Eyre | Murray | Sheridan | Cooksey | Wilkinson* | Crowe | Johnson |
| | | | | | | | | Ref: R Beeby | Crowe makes his debut for Oldham, just ten days after being released by the Town, and opens the scoring with a cross which sails into the net. Showunmi levels but chances are spurned which could have proved expensive as Crowe shoots wide when clear through in the final minute. | | | | | | | | | | | |
| 39 | A | HARTLEPOOL | | 8 | L | 3-4 | 2-1 | Howard 3, Leary 31, 59 | Hyldgaard | Keane* | Davies | Coyne | Davis | Foley | Robinson | Leary | Brkovic | Howard | Showunmi | Forbes |
| | | 6/4 | 4,434 | 9 | 59 | | | Sweeney 14, Boyd 53, 90p, R'tson 55 | Provett | Craddock | Westwood | Tinkler | Robertson | Clarke* | Sweeney | Strachan | Humphries | Porter^ | Boyd | Istead/Williams |
| | | | | | | | | Ref: F Stretton | The game ebbs and flows with the Town twice in the lead. Davies trips Williams at the end which leads to a penalty which is not disputed but the Luton bench believe the attacker was offside. There is still time for Showunmi to have a header ruled out so another late goal proves costly. | | | | | | | | | | | |
| 40 | A | TRANMERE | | 9 | L | 0-1 | 0-1 | | Hyldgaard | Foley | Boyce | Coyne | Davis | Mansell | Leary | Robinson | Brkovic* | Howard | Showunmi | Forbes |
| | | 10/4 | 7,937 | 11 | 59 | | | Jones 30 | Achterberg | Loran | Allen | Sharps | Goodison | Hall* | Mellon | Harrison | Roberts | Jones | Dadi^ | Beresford/Hume |
| | | | | | | | | Ref: M Cooper | An acrobatic volley from Jones goes in off the far post, while Achterberg has to be at his best to keep out Mansell and Boyce. Loran shoves Howard in the area but the spot-kick from Robinson is too close to the keeper. It is home supporters who are delighted to hear the final whistle. | | | | | | | | | | | |
| 41 | H | SWINDON | | 9 | L | 0-3 | 0-3 | | Hyldgaard | Foley | Boyce | Coyne | Davis | Mansell* | Leary^ | Robinson | Nicholls | Howard | Showunmi | Keane/Forbes |
| | | 12/4 | 7,008 | 4 | 59 | | | Fallon 3, 21, Hewlett 44 | Evans | Gurney | O'Hanlon | Heywood | Nicholas | Igoe | Hewlett | Miglioranzi | Duke | Fallon | Parkin* | Mooney |
| | | | | | | | | Ref: M Jones | The game is effectively over by the interval as the Swindon plan of quick counter-attacking makes them look like world-beaters. Headed goals from Fallon and a shot from Hewlett leave the visitors sitting pretty and they are happy to allow the Town plenty of the ball in the second half. | | | | | | | | | | | |
| 42 | H | BRISTOL CITY | | 8 | W | 3-2 | 1-0 | Howard 26, Boyce 56, Keane 90 | Hyldgaard | Keane | Boyce | Coyne | Davis | Foley | Robinson | Nicholls | Brkovic | Howard | Forbes* | Showunmi |
| | | 17/4 | 6,944 | 3 | 62 | | | Roberts 59, Coles 89 | Phillips | Carey | Butler | Coles | Hill | Rougier | Doherty | Wilkshire* | Bell^ | Peacock | Roberts" | Tinnion/Miller/Goodfellow |
| | | | | | | | | Ref: M Atkinson | City waste several good opportunities before Howard heads in a Robinson free-kick. Boyce heads a controversial second and the dramatic last-minute effort from Keane brings the house down as Luton finally manage to beat Bristol City at Kenilworth Road for the first time since 1981. | | | | | | | | | | | |
| 43 | H | BOURNEMOUTH | | 8 | D | 1-1 | 1-0 | Howard 15 | Hyldgaard | Keane | Boyce* | Coyne | Davis | Foley | Robinson | Nicholls | Brkovic^ | Howard | Forbes" | Davies/Leary/Showunmi |
| | | 20/4 | 6,485 | 9 | 63 | | | Feeney 75 | Moss | Buxton | Broadhurst | Fletcher C | Cummings | Hayter | Browning | Purches* | Jorgensen | Feeney | Holmes | Tindall |
| | | | | | | | | Ref: D Pugh | Robinson provides the free-kick for Howard to head the Town into the lead before making a blunder in his own half which gives the ball to Feeney who makes no mistake. A point is of no use to either side and with both going for a win an entertaining end-to-end contest ensues. | | | | | | | | | | | |
| 44 | A | WREXHAM | | 10 | L | 1-2 | 0-1 | Howard 63 | Hyldgaard | Foley | Davies | Coyne | Davis | Keane* | Nicholls^ | Leary | O'Leary | Howard | Showunmi | Forbes/Mansell |
| | | 24/4 | 3,239 | 14 | 63 | | | Sam 35, 62 | Ingham | Roberts | Lawrence | Spender | Barrett | Crowell* | Ferguson | Thomas | Edwards | Sam | Llewllyn | Jones |
| | | | | | | | | Ref: K Friend | Injuries, suspensions and the inability to bring players in finally catches up with the Town. Although they play nice football it is no use without an end product and Sam shows them how to do it with a header and a toe poke and sees his hat-trick goal denied when Davis clears off the line. | | | | | | | | | | | |
| 45 | H | SHEFFIELD WED | | 9 | W | 3-2 | 0-2 | Howard 54, 90, O'Leary 78 | Brill | Coyne | Davis | Foley | Boyce | Neilson | Robinson | Nicholls | O'Leary | Forbes* | Howard | Showunmi |
| | | 1/5 | 7,157 | 16 | 66 | | | Shaw J 23, Cooke 33 | Pressman | B'y-Murphy | Wood | Smith D | Geary* | McLaren | Brunt | McMahon | Cooke^ | Shaw | Robins" | Carr/Chambers/Olsen |
| | | | | | | | | Ref: D Gallagher | The Town are two down at the interval after defensive lapses and could easily have thrown in the towel with nothing left to play for. That they do not is a big plus, and goals from Howard and O'Leary set up an entertaining finale with Howard sliding in the last-minute unlikely winner. | | | | | | | | | | | |
| 46 | A | CHESTERFIELD | | 10 | L | 0-1 | 0-0 | | Brill | Coyne | Davis | Foley | Neilson | Boyce | Robinson | Nicholls | O'Leary | Forbes | Showunmi | |
| | | 8/5 | 6,285 | 20 | 66 | | | Hurst 88 | Muggleton | O'Hare | Dawson* | Blatherwick | Brandon | Evatt | Niven | Hudson | Allott^ | Hurst | Reeves" | de Bolla/Davies/Robinson |
| | | Home | Away | | | | | Ref: E Evans | Chesterfield need a win to avoid relegation but the Town are in no mood to roll over. With Howard suspended, they show little in attack but seem to have weathered the frantic attacking threat of the Spireites until Hurst latches on to Sol Davis' back-header and slots the ball past Brill. | | | | | | | | | | | |
| Average | | 6,339 | 7,437 | | | | | | | | | | | | | | | | | |

## Carling Cup

| Rd | | Opponent | Att | F-A | H-T | Scorers, Times, and Referees | 1 | 2 | 3 | 4 | 5 | 6 | 7 | 8 | 9 | 10 | 11 | subs used |
|---|---|---|---|---|---|---|---|---|---|---|---|---|---|---|---|---|---|---|
| 1 | H | YEOVIL | | 4-1 | 1-0 | Foley 25, Thorpe 56, Pitt 64, | Beckwith | Foley | Coyne | Boyce | Neilson* | Nicholls | Hughes | Spring | Pitt | Howard | Thorpe^ | Davis/Crowe"/Okai |
| | 12/8 | | 4,337 *3:* | | | *Boyce 47 (og)* [Howard 68] | *Weale* | *Lockwood* | *Crittenden** | *Gosling^* | *O'Brien* | *Rodrigues"* | *Williams* | *Way* | *Jackson* | *Gall* | *Johnson* | *El Kholti/Reed/Lindegaard* |
| | | | | | | Ref: L Cable | Conference Champions Yeovil enter the cup for the first time and are soon taught the harsh lessons of taking your chances and having mistakes punished. Foley nets a glorious first and although Boyce heads into his own net normal service is soon resumed with Thorpe's clever toe-poke. | | | | | | | | | | | |
| 2 | A | CHARLTON | 9 | 4-4 | 2-1 | Foley 30, Bayl's 32, McSh' 78, Coyne 110 | Beckwith | Boyce | Coyne | Bayliss* | Davis | Foley^ | Hughes | Spring | Brkovic" | McSheffrey | Howard | Hillier/Leary/Pitt |
| | 23/9 | | *10,905 P:14* | *aet* | | *Park'r 41, Lisb' 58, di Can' 90, Jens' 95* | *Kiely* | *Young* | *Powell** | *Holland* | *Fortune* | *Fish* | *Stuart^* | *Jensen* | *Lisbie^* | *di Canio* | *Parker* | *Euell/Johansson/C'll-Ryce* |
| | | | | | | Ref: P Armstrong (Hatters lose 7-8 on penalties) | The Town make a mockery of the difference in league standing between the two teams on a night of high entertainment. The home side are fortunate twice, in being allowed enough stoppage time to snatch a 92nd-minute equaliser, and then to win the lottery of the penalty shoot-out. | | | | | | | | | | | |

## FA Cup

| Rd | | Opponent | Att | F-A | H-T | Scorers, Times, and Referees | 1 | 2 | 3 | 4 | 5 | 6 | 7 | 8 | 9 | 10 | 11 | subs used |
|---|---|---|---|---|---|---|---|---|---|---|---|---|---|---|---|---|---|---|
| 1 | A | THURROCK | 14 | 1-1 | 1-0 | Boyce 39 | Beresford | Hillier | Boyce | Coyne | Davis | Mansell* | Spring | Robinson | Brkovic | Forbes^ | Showunmi | Leary/Crowe |
| | 7/11 | | *1,551 NL* | | | *Bowes 80* | *Gothard* | *Collis* | *Goodfellow* | *Heffer* | *Purdie* | *McFarlane* | *Akurang** | *Lee D* | *Lee K^* | *Kandol* | *Bowes* | *Allen/Linger* |
| | | | | | | Ref: M Thorpe | The Sky cameras are again hoping for a cup upset and they nearly get it when Thurrock stage a grandstand finish following their late equaliser. Ex-Hatters Kandol and Akurang have a point to prove and the former misses a glorious opportunity when put clear through down the middle. | | | | | | | | | | | |
| 1R | H | THURROCK | 12 | 3-1 | 1-0 | Forbes 39, 76, 87p | Beresford | Foley* | Boyce | Coyne | Barnett^ | Mansell" | Spring | Robinson | Brkovic | Forbes | Howard | Hillier/Crowe/Okai |
| | 18/11 | | 3,667 *NL* | | | *Akurang 49* | *Gothard* | *Collis* | *Goodfellow* | *Heffer* | *Purdie* | *McFarlane* | *Akurang* | *Linger* | *Howard** | *Kandol* | *Bowes* | *Lee K* |
| | | | | | | Ref: M Thorpe | Until superior fitness tells towards the end, Forbes is the only difference between the sides. He deservedly wins the Man-of-the-Match award with a hat-trick to sink the plucky non-leaguers. Earlier a tremendous save from Beresford prevents Kandol from pulling the score back to 2-2. | | | | | | | | | | | |
| 2 | A | ROCHDALE | 10 | 2-0 | 1-0 | Robinson 20p, Mansell 77 | Beresford | Hillier | Boyce | Coyne | Davis | Mansell | Robinson | Holmes | Brkovic | Forbes | Howard | |
| | 6/12 | | *2,807 3:19* | | | | *Edwards* | *Evans* | *Simpkins* | *Beech** | *Burgess* | *Grand* | *McCourt* | *Jones* | *Connor^* | *Bishop"* | *Doughty* | *Patterson/McEvilly/Townson* |
| | | | | | | Ref: A Hall | The Town win their way through to the third round for the first time in three years, and at the same time exact revenge for the league double imposed during the promotion season. Forbes is brought down twice in the area but Robinson only manages to put away one of the spot-kicks. | | | | | | | | | | | |
| 3 | A | BRADFORD C | 7 | 2-1 | 1-0 | Forbes 20, 48 | Beresford | Foley | Boyce | Coyne | Davis | Mansell | Robinson | Spring* | Brkovic | Forbes | Howard | Holmes |
| | 3/1 | | *8,222 1:23* | | | *Gray 83p* | *Combe* | *Atherton* | *Heckingb'm* | *Kearney** | *Wetherall^* | *Bower* | *Evans* | *Windass* | *Armstrong* | *Gray"* | *Farrelly* | *Muirhead/Gavin/Branch* |
| | | | | | | Ref: M Clattenburg | Luton win at Valley Parade for the first time with goals from Forbes putting the away side in the driving seat. Windass is supposedly fouled leaving Gray to hit home a late penalty but Forbes is given a chance for his hat-trick after Howard is brought down. His spot-kick was saved. | | | | | | | | | | | |
| 4 | H | TRANMERE | 9 | 0-1 | 0-0 | | Beresford | Foley | Boyce | Coyne | Davis | Mansell* | Nicholls^ | Leary | Holmes | Brkovic | Showunmi | Keane/Crowe |
| | 24/1 | | 8,767 *17* | | | *Mellon 81* | *Achterberg* | *Taylor* | *Roberts* | *Sharps* | *Allen* | *Jones* | *Harrison* | *Mellon* | *Dadi** | *Hume* | *Beresford* | *Hay* |
| | | | | | | Ref: M Messias | The fourth round is reached as a lower league side for the first time since 1933 but injuries and suspensions finally catch up when least needed. The Town are denied a penalty when Keane is fouled but when Mellon scores at the end of a surging run the supporters know the game is over. | | | | | | | | | | | |

| | | Home | | | | | Away | | | | | |
|---|---|---|---|---|---|---|---|---|---|---|---|---|
| | P | W | D | L | F | A | W | D | L | F | A | Pts |
| 1 Plymouth | 46 | 17 | 5 | 1 | 52 | 13 | 9 | 7 | 7 | 33 | 28 | 90 |
| 2 QP Rangers | 46 | 16 | 7 | 0 | 47 | 12 | 6 | 10 | 7 | 33 | 33 | 83 |
| 3 Bristol City | 46 | 15 | 6 | 2 | 34 | 12 | 8 | 7 | 8 | 24 | 25 | 82 |
| 4 Brighton* | 46 | 17 | 4 | 2 | 39 | 11 | 5 | 7 | 11 | 25 | 32 | 77 |
| 5 Swindon | 46 | 12 | 7 | 4 | 41 | 23 | 8 | 6 | 9 | 35 | 35 | 73 |
| 6 Hartlepool | 46 | 10 | 8 | 5 | 39 | 24 | 10 | 5 | 8 | 37 | 37 | 73 |
| 7 Port Vale | 46 | 15 | 6 | 2 | 45 | 28 | 6 | 4 | 13 | 28 | 35 | 73 |
| 8 Tranmere | 46 | 13 | 7 | 3 | 36 | 18 | 4 | 9 | 10 | 23 | 38 | 67 |
| 9 Bournemouth | 46 | 11 | 8 | 4 | 35 | 25 | 6 | 7 | 10 | 21 | 26 | 66 |
| 10 LUTON TOWN | 46 | 14 | 6 | 3 | 44 | 27 | 3 | 9 | 11 | 25 | 39 | 66 |
| 11 Colchester | 46 | 11 | 8 | 4 | 33 | 23 | 6 | 5 | 12 | 19 | 33 | 64 |
| 12 Barnsley | 46 | 7 | 12 | 4 | 25 | 19 | 8 | 5 | 10 | 29 | 39 | 62 |
| 13 Wrexham | 46 | 9 | 6 | 8 | 27 | 21 | 8 | 3 | 12 | 23 | 39 | 60 |
| 14 Blackpool | 46 | 9 | 5 | 9 | 31 | 28 | 7 | 6 | 10 | 27 | 37 | 59 |
| 15 Oldham | 46 | 9 | 8 | 6 | 37 | 25 | 3 | 13 | 7 | 29 | 35 | 57 |
| 16 Sheffield Wed | 46 | 7 | 9 | 7 | 25 | 26 | 6 | 5 | 12 | 23 | 38 | 53 |
| 17 Brentford | 46 | 9 | 5 | 9 | 34 | 38 | 5 | 6 | 12 | 18 | 31 | 53 |
| 18 Peterborough | 46 | 5 | 8 | 10 | 36 | 33 | 7 | 8 | 8 | 22 | 25 | 52 |
| 19 Stockport | 46 | 6 | 8 | 9 | 31 | 36 | 5 | 11 | 7 | 31 | 34 | 52 |
| 20 Chesterfield | 46 | 9 | 7 | 7 | 34 | 31 | 3 | 8 | 12 | 15 | 40 | 51 |
| 21 Grimsby | 46 | 10 | 5 | 8 | 36 | 26 | 3 | 6 | 14 | 19 | 55 | 50 |
| 22 Rushden | 46 | 9 | 5 | 9 | 37 | 34 | 4 | 4 | 15 | 23 | 40 | 48 |
| 23 Notts Co | 46 | 6 | 9 | 8 | 32 | 27 | 4 | 3 | 16 | 18 | 51 | 42 |
| 24 Wycombe | 46 | 5 | 7 | 11 | 31 | 39 | 1 | 12 | 10 | 19 | 36 | 37 |
| | 1104 | 251 | 166 | 135 | 861 | 599 | 135 | 166 | 251 | 599 | 861 | 1490 |

* promoted after play-offs

**Odds & ends**

Double wins: (1) Blackpool
Double losses: (1) Grimsby

Won from behind: (4) Rushden (h), Wycombe (h), Wrexham (h) Sheffield Wed (h)
Lost from in front: (5) Plymouth (a), Bournemouth (a), Grimsby (a), Hartlepool (a), Charlton (a - CC)

High spots: Managing to stay in the play-off hunt right until the end of the season despite being in administrative receivership.
Reaching the fourth round of the FA Cup after entering at the first round stage, for the first time since 1933.
The wonderful performance at Charlton in the Carling Cup.
The introduction of promising youngsters to the side, because of the Club's financial position, and who did not disappoint.

Low spots: The inability to strengthen the squad during the season.
Losing to Tranmere in the FA Cup with a severely depleted side.
The cruel defeat at Charlton in the Carling Cup on penalties.
Too many games lost after conceding in the final minutes.

Player of the Year: Emmerson Boyce.
Ever-presents: (0).
Hat-tricks: Forbes (1).
Leading scorer: Steve Howard (16).

| | Appearances | | | | | | Goals | | | |
|---|---|---|---|---|---|---|---|---|---|---|
| | Lge | Sub | LC | Sub | FAC | Sub | Lge | LC | FAC | Tot |
| Barnett, Leon | | | | | 1 | | | | | |
| Bayliss, David | 6 | | 1 | | | | | 1 | | 1 |
| Beckwith, Rob | 13 | | 2 | | | | | | | |
| Beresford, Marlon | 11 | | | | 5 | | | | | |
| Boyce, Emmerson | 42 | | 2 | | 5 | | 4 | | 1 | 5 |
| Brill, Dean | 4 | 1 | | | | | | | | |
| Brkovic, Ahmet | 24 | 8 | 1 | | 5 | | 1 | | | 1 |
| Coyne, Chris | 44 | | 2 | | 5 | | 2 | 1 | | 3 |
| Crowe, Dean | | 8 | | 1 | | 3 | | | | |
| Davies, Curtis | 4 | 2 | | | | | | | | |
| Davis, Sol | 34 | 2 | 1 | 1 | 4 | | | | | |
| Foley, Kevin | 32 | 1 | 2 | | 3 | | 1 | 2 | | 3 |
| Forbes, Adrian | 21 | 6 | | | 4 | | 9 | | 5 | 14 |
| Hillier, Ian | 8 | 3 | | 1 | 2 | 1 | | | | |
| Holmes, Peter | 11 | 5 | | | 2 | 1 | 3 | | | 3 |
| Howard, Steve | 34 | | 2 | | 3 | | 15 | 1 | | 16 |
| Hughes, Paul | 20 | 2 | 2 | | | | 1 | | | 1 |
| Hyldgaard, Morten | 18 | | | | | | | | | |
| Judge, Matthew | | 1 | | | | | | | | |
| Keane, Keith | 14 | 1 | | | | 1 | 1 | | | 1 |
| Leary, Michael | 8 | 6 | | 1 | 1 | 1 | 2 | | | 2 |
| Mansell, Lee | 12 | 4 | | | 5 | | 2 | | 1 | 3 |
| McSheffrey, Gary | 18 | | 1 | | | | 8 | 1 | | 9 |
| Neilson, Alan | 11 | 3 | 1 | | | | 1 | | | 1 |
| Nicholls, Kevin | 21 | | 1 | | 1 | | 2 | | | 2 |
| Okai, Parys | | | | 1 | | 1 | | | | |
| O'Leary, Stephen | 3 | 2 | | | | | 1 | | | 1 |
| Perrett, Russell | 5 | 1 | | | | | 2 | | | 2 |
| Pitt, Courtney | 11 | 1 | 1 | 1 | | | | 1 | | 1 |
| Robinson, Steve | 32 | 2 | | | 4 | | 2 | | 1 | 3 |
| Showunmi, Enoch | 18 | 8 | | | 2 | | 7 | | | 7 |
| Spring, Matthew | 24 | | 2 | | 3 | | 1 | | | 1 |
| Thorpe, Tony | 2 | | 1 | | | | 2 | 1 | | 3 |
| Underwood, Paul | 1 | | | | | | | | | |
| (own-goals) | | | | | | | 2 | | | 2 |
| **34 players used** | **506** | *67* | **22** | *6* | **55** | *8* | **69** | **8** | **8** | **85** |

| Subscriber | Scorer of Best Goal | Opponents | Season | Competition |
|---|---|---|---|---|
| *Andrew Ackrill* | Matthew Spring | Watford | 2002-03 | Worthington Cup |
| *Alan Adair* | Graham French | Mansfield Town | 1968-69 | League |
| *John Arnold* | Matthew Spring | Watford | 2002-03 | Worthington Cup |
| *Gary Barker* | Brian Stein | Arsenal (2nd goal) | 1987-88 | Littlewoods Cup final |
| *Emily Bassill* | Brian Stein | Arsenal (2nd goal) | 1987-88 | Littlewoods Cup final |
| *Phil Bassill* | Graham French | Mansfield Town | 1968-69 | League |
| *Frank Batt* | Graham French | Mansfield Town | 1968-69 | League |
| *Chris Beard* | Scott Oakes | Derby Co | 1993-94 | League |
| *Paul K Billson* | Matthew Spring | Watford | 2002-03 | Worthington Cup |
| *Mike Bowley* | Tim Breacker | Derby Co | 1989-90 | League |
| *Steven Bracken* | Brian Stein | Arsenal (2nd goal) | 1987-88 | Littlewoods Cup final |
| *Mike Broadbent* | Graham French | Mansfield Town | 1968-69 | League |
| *Sam Brooks* | Jean-Louis Valois | Torquay United | 2001-02 | League |
| *Keith Brooksbank* | Matthew Spring | Watford | 2002-03 | Worthington Cup |
| *Anthony Brown* | Brian Stein | Arsenal (2nd goal) | 1987-88 | Littlewoods Cup final |
| *David Brown* | Graham French | Mansfield Town | 1968-69 | League |
| *Jonathan Brown* | Tim Breacker | Derby Co | 1989-90 | League |
| *Paul Brown* | Matthew Spring | Watford | 2002-03 | Worthington Cup |
| *J Browning* | Graham French | Mansfield Town | 1968-69 | League |
| *Warwick Browning* | Brian Stein | Arsenal (2nd goal) | 1987-88 | Littlewoods Cup final |
| *David Burgoine* | Brian Stein | Arsenal (2nd goal) | 1987-88 | Littlewoods Cup final |
| *Jim Callaghan* | Brian Stein | Arsenal (2nd goal) | 1987-88 | Littlewoods Cup final |
| *David Cannon* | Raddy Antic | Manchester City | 1982-83 | League |
| *Paul Carey* | Brian Stein | Arsenal (2nd goal) | 1987-88 | Littlewoods Cup final |
| *Daniel Chapman* | Matthew Spring | Watford | 2002-03 | Worthington Cup |
| *T R J Clarke* | Brian Stein | Arsenal (2nd goal) | 1987-88 | Littlewoods Cup final |
| *Dermot Collon* | Brian Stein | Arsenal (2nd goal) | 1987-88 | Littlewoods Cup final |
| *Ian Corkett* | Brian Stein | Arsenal (2nd goal) | 1987-88 | Littlewoods Cup final |
| *M R Dack* | | | | |
| *Andy Davis* | Graham French | Mansfield Town | 1968-69 | League |
| *Robert Day* | Scott Oakes | West Ham | 1993-94 | FA Cup |
| *Paul Deason* | David Moss | QPR | 1980-81 | League |
| *Keiran Fitzpatrick* | Kingsley Black | Derby Co | 1989-90 | League |
| *David & Matthew Fleckney* | Jean-Louis Valois | Torquay United | 2001-02 | League |
| *Anthony Folbigg* | Graham French | Mansfield Town | 1968-69 | League |
| *Lyn Folland* | | | | |
| *David Foxen* | Matthew Spring | Watford | 2002-03 | Worthington Cup |
| *Joan Glenister* | Brian Stein | Arsenal (2nd goal) | 1987-88 | Littlewoods Cup final |
| *Clive Goodall* | Graham French | Mansfield Town | 1968-69 | League |
| *Michael Grange* | Matthew Spring | Watford | 2002-03 | Worthington Cup |
| *Richard Gray* | Scott Oakes | Derby Co | 1993-94 | League |
| *Andrew Green* | Brian Stein | Arsenal (2nd goal) | 1987-88 | Littlewoods Cup final |
| *Kevin Griffin* | Brian Stein | Arsenal (2nd goal) | 1987-88 | Littlewoods Cup final |
| *Colin Guy* | Scott Oakes | West Ham | 1993-94 | FA Cup |
| *Rob Hadgraft* | Paul Walsh | Notts Co | 1982-83 | League |
| *Paul Hale* | Brian Stein | Arsenal (2nd goal) | 1987-88 | Littlewoods Cup final |
| *Finn Harkin* | Brian Stein | Arsenal (2nd goal) | 1987-88 | Littlewoods Cup final |
| *Barry Hart* | Brian Stein | Arsenal (2nd goal) | 1987-88 | Littlewoods Cup final |
| *Peter Hird* | Jean-Louis Valois | Torquay United | 2001-02 | League |
| *David & Shirley Hobbs* | Graham French | Mansfield Town | 1968-69 | League |
| *Nigel Holland* | Brian Stein | Arsenal (2nd goal) | 1987-88 | Littlewoods Cup final |
| *Richard Holland* | Raddy Antic | Manchester City | 1982-83 | League |

| Subscriber | Scorer of Best Goal | Opponents | Season | Competition |
|---|---|---|---|---|
| *Andrew Holmes* | Brian Stein | Arsenal (2nd goal) | 1987-88 | Littlewoods Cup final |
| *Kevin Horne* | Raddy Antic | Manchester City | 1982-83 | League |
| *Peter Houghton* | Raddy Antic | Manchester City | 1982-83 | League |
| *Bob Hughes* | Jean-Louis Valois | Torquay United | 2001-02 | League |
| *Tom Hunt* | Graham French | Mansfield Town | 1968-69 | League |
| *John Jackson* | Matthew Spring | Watford | 2002-03 | Worthington Cup |
| *Jim Jardine* | Freddie Jardine | Oldham Athletic | 1968-69 | League |
| *David Jellis* | Ricky Hill | Bristol Rovers | 1975-76 | League |
| *Paul Jinks* | Paul Walsh | Notts Co | 1982-83 | League |
| *Graeme Jones* | Brian Stein | Arsenal (2nd goal) | 1987-88 | Littlewoods Cup final |
| *Dave Jordan* | Graham French | Mansfield Town | 1968-69 | League |
| *Nick Josling* | Raddy Antic | Manchester City | 1982-83 | League |
| *Roland Joy* | Brian Stein | Arsenal (2nd goal) | 1987-88 | Littlewoods Cup final |
| *Ian Kelly* | Jean-Louis Valois | Torquay United | 2001-02 | League |
| *Darren Kerins* | Scott Oakes | West Ham | 1993-94 | FA Cup |
| *Andrew King* | Graham French | Mansfield Town | 1968-69 | League |
| *Trevor King* | Brian Stein | Arsenal (2nd goal) | 1987-88 | Littlewoods Cup final |
| *Roger Lambert* | Graham French | Mansfield Town | 1968-69 | League |
| *Steve Lindsay* | Scott Oakes | Derby Co | 1993-94 | League |
| *Mick Lowrie* | Graham French | Mansfield Town | 1968-69 | League |
| *B T Lynch* | | | | |
| *Niall Mackinnon* | | | | |
| *Steve Marks* | Tim Breacker | Derby Co | 1989-90 | League |
| *S Mayne* | Matthew Spring | Watford | 2002-03 | Worthington Cup |
| *Aidan McClung* | Raddy Antic | Manchester City | 1982-83 | League |
| *Michael McConkey* | Graham French | Mansfield Town | 1968-69 | League |
| *Robin Meadows* | Graham French | Mansfield Town | 1968-69 | League |
| *Ann Mercel* | Paul Walsh | Notts Co | 1982-83 | League |
| *Jonathan Miller* | Scott Oakes | West Ham | 1993-94 | FA Cup |
| *Les Miller* | Graham French | Mansfield Town | 1968-69 | League |
| *Kevin Morris* | Brian Stein | Arsenal (2nd goal) | 1987-88 | Littlewoods Cup final |
| *Brian Mugridge* | Scott Oakes | West Ham | 1993-94 | FA Cup |
| *John Murphy* | Scott Oakes | Derby Co | 1993-94 | League |
| *Mick Murphy* | Brian Stein | Spurs | 1985-86 | League |
| *Daniel Musson* | Mick Harford | Oldham Athletic | 1991-92 | League |
| *Phil Norton* | Tim Breacker | Derby Co | 1989-90 | League |
| *Nicholas O'Leary* | Brian Stein | Oxford | 1987-88 | Littlewoods Cup |
| *Phill Oliver* | Matthew Spring | Watford | 2002-03 | Worthington Cup |
| *John M Patmore* | Graham French | Orient | 1969-70 | League |
| *Rob Piggott* | Ricky Hill | Everton | 1984-85 | FA Cup |
| *Dave Planson* | | | | |
| *Daniela Poulton* | | | | |
| *Steve Prior* | Matthew Spring | Watford | 2002-03 | Worthington Cup |
| *Darren Pullen* | Matthew Spring | Watford | 2002-03 | Worthington Cup |
| *Phil Putman* | Matthew Spring | Watford | 2002-03 | Worthington Cup |
| *John Pyper* | Scott Oakes | West Ham | 1993-94 | FA Cup |
| *Adrian Quarry* | Scott Oakes | West Ham | 1993-94 | FA Cup |
| *Dave Quinnell* | Paul Walsh | Notts Co | 1982-83 | League |
| *Keith Raeburn* | Scott Oakes | Derby Co | 1993-94 | League |
| *Clive Ramsay* | Bruce Rioch | Rotherham | 1968-69 | League |
| *Tony 'Tub' Reynolds* | Graham French | Mansfield Town | 1968-69 | League |
| *David Robertson* | Brian Stein | Arsenal (2nd goal) | 1987-88 | Littlewoods Cup final |
| *Alan Robinson* | Brian Horton | Cambridge Utd | 1981-82 | League |

| Subscriber | Scorer of Best Goal | Opponents | Season | Competition |
|---|---|---|---|---|
| *Paul Rodell* | Raddy Antic | Manchester City | 1982-83 | League |
| *Michael Rogan* | Brian Stein | Arsenal (2nd goal) | 1987-88 | Littlewoods Cup final |
| *Danilo 'Dan' Ronzani* | Brian Stein | Arsenal (2nd goal) | 1987-88 | Littlewoods Cup final |
| *Lucy Russell* | | | | |
| *Andrew Sarkar* | Paul Walsh | Notts Co | 1982-83 | League |
| *Ross Scott* | Graham French | Mansfield Town | 1968-69 | League |
| *Don Scrace* | Raddy Antic | Manchester City | 1982-83 | League |
| *A J Sendall* | | | | |
| *Kevin Shepherd* | Scott Oakes | Derby Co | 1993-94 | League |
| *Graham Sheridan* | Scott Oakes | Derby Co | 1993-94 | League |
| *William Sherwood* | Jean-Louis Valois | Torquay United | 2001-02 | League |
| *Stephen Sims* | Jean-Louis Valois | Torquay United | 2001-02 | League |
| *Neil Slater* | Graham French | Mansfield Town | 1968-69 | League |
| *Ian Smith* | Brian Stein | Nottingham Forest | 1986-87 | League |
| *Ian Smith* | Scott Oakes | Derby Co | 1993-94 | League |
| *Mark Smith* | Ashley Grimes | Oxford Utd | 1987-88 | Littlewoods Cup |
| *Stewart Smith* | Matthew Spring | Watford | 2002-03 | Worthington Cup |
| *David Snoxell* | Graham French | Mansfield Town | 1968-69 | League |
| *Kevin Snoxell* | Scott Oakes | Derby Co | 1993-94 | League |
| *Tim Sprague* | Jean-Louis Valois | Torquay United | 2001-02 | League |
| *Robert Stein* | Matthew Spring | Watford | 2002-03 | Worthington Cup |
| *Richard Stocken* | | | | |
| *Gary Stratford* | Scott Oakes | Derby Co | 1993-94 | League |
| *Andrew Swann* | Ricky Hill | Everton | 1984-85 | FA Cup |
| *Mike Symons* | Raddy Antic | Manchester City | 1982-83 | League |
| *Robert Taylor* | Jean-Louis Valois | Torquay United | 2001-02 | League |
| *Richard Tilley* | Scott Oakes | Derby Co | 1993-94 | League |
| *Matthew Turk* | | | | |
| *Steve Turner* | | | | |
| *James Usher* | Enoch Showunmi | Brentford | 2003-04 | League |
| *Andrew Wallace* | Scott Oakes | Derby Co | 1993-94 | League |
| *R E Wasem* | | | | |
| *David Watkins* | Raddy Antic | Manchester City | 1982-83 | League |
| *Alan G Wheatley* | Brian Stein | Arsenal (2nd goal) | 1987-88 | Littlewoods Cup final |
| *Jo Wheeler* | Matthew Spring | Watford | 2002-03 | Worthington Cup |
| *John Wheeler* | Matthew Spring | Watford | 2002-03 | Worthington Cup |
| *Steven Whitehead* | Graham French | Mansfield Town | 1968-69 | League |
| *Paul Williams* | Graham French | Mansfield Town | 1968-69 | League |
| *Ray Williams* | Kirk Stephens | Watford | 1979-80 | League |
| *G Winterbone* | | | | |
| *Terence M Worrell* | Graham French | Mansfield Town | 1968-69 | League |
| *Steve Wurst* | Graham French | Mansfield Town | 1968-69 | League |
| *Richard Yallop* | Billy Bingham | Norwich City | 1958-59 | FA Cup |
| *A J Yates* | Brian Stein | Arsenal (2nd goal) | 1987-88 | Littlewoods Cup final |
| *Chris Young* | Raddy Antic | Manchester City | 1982-83 | League |

*25 different goals were chosen*

| | | | | |
|---|---|---|---|---|
| *1st* | Brian Stein | Arsenal (2nd goal) | 1987-88 | Littlewoods Cup final |
| *2nd* | Graham French | Mansfield Town | 1968-69 | League |
| *3rd* | Matthew Spring | Watford | 2002-03 | Worthington Cup |
| *4th* | Scott Oakes | Derby Co | 1993-94 | League |
| *5th* | Raddy Antic | Manchester City | 1982-83 | League |